Popular Mechanics

ENCYCLOPEDIA OF TOOLS AND TECHNIQUES

Popular Mechanics

ENCYCLOPEDIA OF TOOLS AND TECHNIQUES

EDITED BY STEVEN WILLSON
FOREWORD BY JOE OLDHAM

HEARST BOOKS • NEW YORK

Library of Congress Cataloging-in Publication Data
Popular mechanics: encyclopedia of tools and techniques.
p. cm.
ISBN: 1-58816-019-X (paperback)
0-688-12460-7 (out-of-print hardcover)

1. Woodworking tools. 2. Power tools. 3. Workshops-Equipment and supplies.
I. Popular mechanics (Chicago, Ill.: 1959) II. Title: Encyclopedia of tools & techniques.
III. Title: Encyclopedia of tools and techniques.
TT186.P66 1994
684'.08—dc2O 94-5953
CIP

Produced by St. Remy Press

Cover design: Howard R. Roberts

First Paperback Edition 2001
1 2 3 4 5 6 7 8 9 10
Printed in China

FOREWORD

For the past century, readers have faithfully turned to *Popular Mechanics* for information on tools and techniques. Their needs and concerns are as diverse as their workshop experience. Some seek guidance on the tools they should buy. Some are looking to get the most out of the tools they already own. Some want to learn new ways of doing things. Some are struggling with how to begin a project.

The editors at *Popular Mechanics* sit down every year to reflect on the magazine —specifically, to discuss what has and hasn't worked. A large part of our evaluation centers on readers' response to the articles and features that have appeared. Our readers are quick to tell us when we hit the mark, and judging from the letters that arrive from every corner of the country, we've stayed consistently on target through the years for a great number of people. Thus was born the idea of compiling an encyclopedia of tools and techniques, a collection of *Popular Mechanics* Home and Shop Journal "greatest hits." What you hold in your hands is the outcome.

Whether you're a new homeowner seeking the right tool to use for a job or a seasoned woodworker keen on expanding your horizons—or you qualify somewhere in between—you'll find this book an indispensable reference on tools and techniques, packed with easy-to-follow instructions, tips, and advice.

Joe Oldham,
Editor-in-Chief
Popular Mechanics

CONTENTS

TOP—
PINE
3 1/2"
(4 REQD.)
SECTION
10 9/16"
• Work only with double
or properly grounded power
• Keep tool safety guards in
at all times, or make your own
specific needs. Turn off and unplug
tool, then let it cool before changing
adjusting parts. Keep work surfaces
stationary tools clean and uncluttered.
• Concentrate on the job at hand;
rush or take short cuts. Never
you are tired, stressed or have
alcohol or using med-
induces drowsiness.
users away from
the shop.
a smoke
fire extin-
Best of all, this

SHOP
SETUP

SHOP SETUP

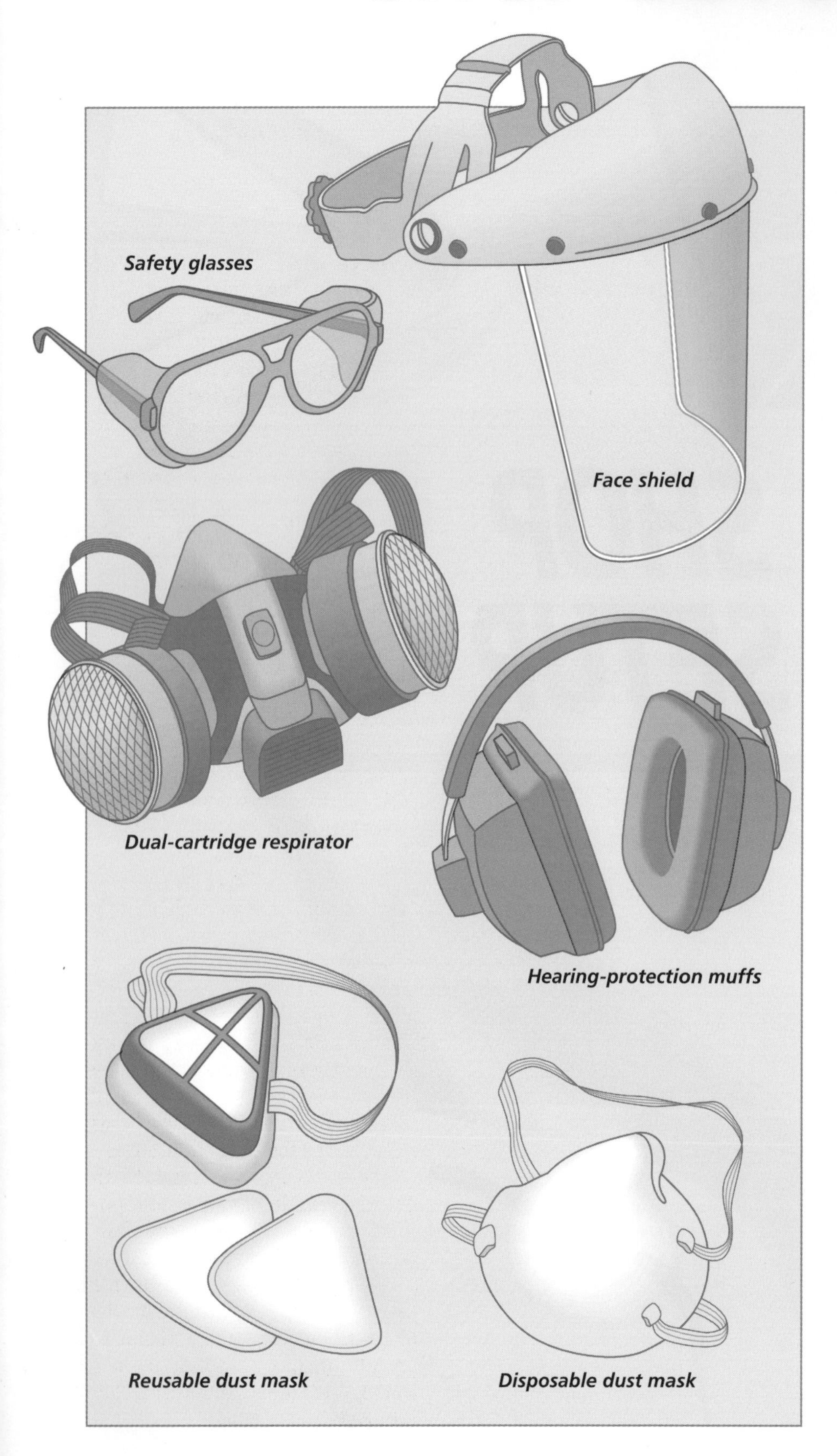

The old adage that a tool is only as good as the person using it has a corollary that applies to workshop safety: A tool is only as safe as the person using it. Observe the following general safety rules:

• Organize and maintain your shop. Keep work areas clean, uncluttered and as dust-free as possible.

• Familiarize yourself with all your tools. Read the owner's manual supplied by a tool's manufacturer. Always choose the right tool for the job.

• Wear clothes suitable for work in the shop. Take off loose-fitting items and roll up long sleeves, remove jewelry, and tie back long hair. Wear rubber-soled shoes or boots, preferably with toe protection.

• Use safety gear appropriate to the job: eye, breathing and hearing protection. Keep your fingers as far away as possible from a tool's action.

• Keep all your cutting tools sharp. Remember that when least effort is required, control is greatest.

• Work only with double-insulated or properly grounded power tools.

• Keep tool safety guards in place at all times, or make your own to suit specific needs. Turn off and unplug a tool, then let it cool before changing or adjusting parts. Keep work surfaces of stationary tools clean and uncluttered.

• Concentrate on the job at hand; don't rush or take short cuts. Never work if you are tired, stressed or have been drinking alcohol or using medication that induces drowsiness.

• Keep unqualified users away from your tools and out of the shop.

• Equip your shop with a smoke detector and a properly rated fire extinguisher. Keep a well stocked first-aid kit on hand.

• Post emergency telephone numbers of your local fire department, hospital emergency room and physician near the telephone.

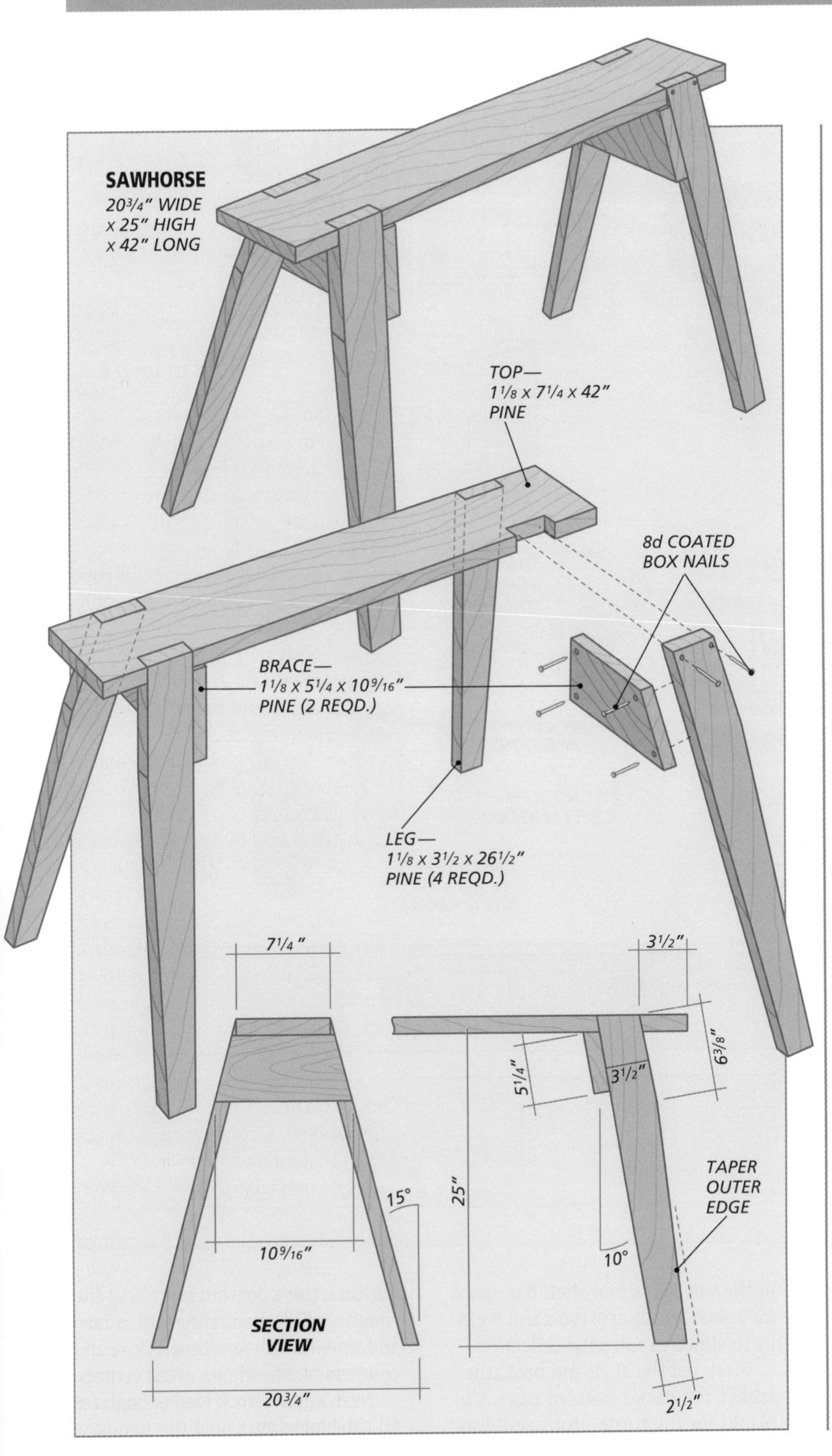

SAWHORSES

Even the most elementary repair or woodworking project requires a surface on which to work. And while you might use the kitchen table or a few dining room chairs, these options certainly won't increase your popularity with the rest of the family. The simple solution is to build yourself a pair of sawhorses, the universally accepted tools for getting a project off the ground—where you can work on it.

While sawhorses can be built from construction lumber or plywood and kits are available to make the assembly easier, the design that's shown here has several distinct advantages. First, its splayed legs offer excellent stability and strength without the need for standard leg braces. This means that the units can be stacked and set over objects on the floor or ground. The 5/4 pine that is recommended makes for a lightweight, easily portable sawhorse. Best of all, this design features a broad, flat top board that turns each sawhorse into a small portable bench.

Begin construction of the sawhorses by cutting blanks for the legs 1 or 2 in. longer than the finished dimensions out of 5/4 x 4 stock, then cut the tapers on the edges and make the compound angle cuts at the ends. Next, cut the tops to length out of 5/4 x 8 stock and carefully make the notches for the legs. Cut blanks for the braces out of 5/4 x 6 stock, then cut the angled ends and bevel the top and bottom edges.

The sawhorses are assembled with glue and nails. If they will be used primarily for work indoors, ordinary carpenter's glue will do; otherwise, choose a waterproof type of glue. Fasten the legs to the tops first, then secure the braces to the legs. Allow the glue to dry fully, then smooth sharp corners and edges of the assemblies using 120-grit sandpaper.

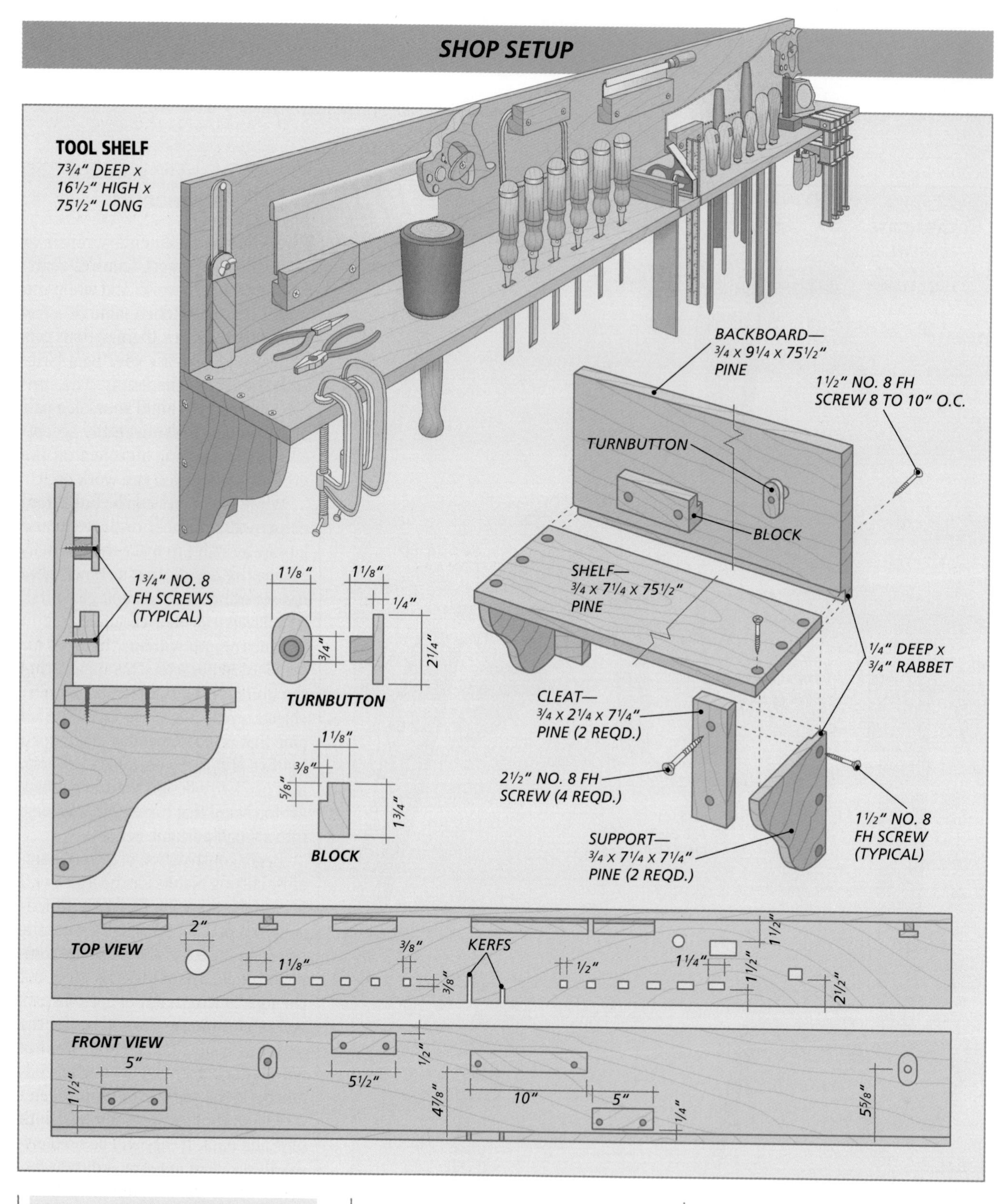

TOOL SHELF

Besides keeping your hand tools sharp and ready for work, you'll need a place to put them—a place where they're always accessible, yet safely stored out of the way. This tool shelf has space for a good selection of tools and is easily modified to suit your collection.

First, cut the shelf and back, then rabbet the back's bottom edge. Cut blanks for the turnbuttons and draw outlines. Use a dovetail saw to cut the rough shapes, then refine with a rasp and smooth with sandpaper. Bore and countersink screwholes in the centres.

Next, cut 5/4 stock long enough for all the blocks that hold the handsaw

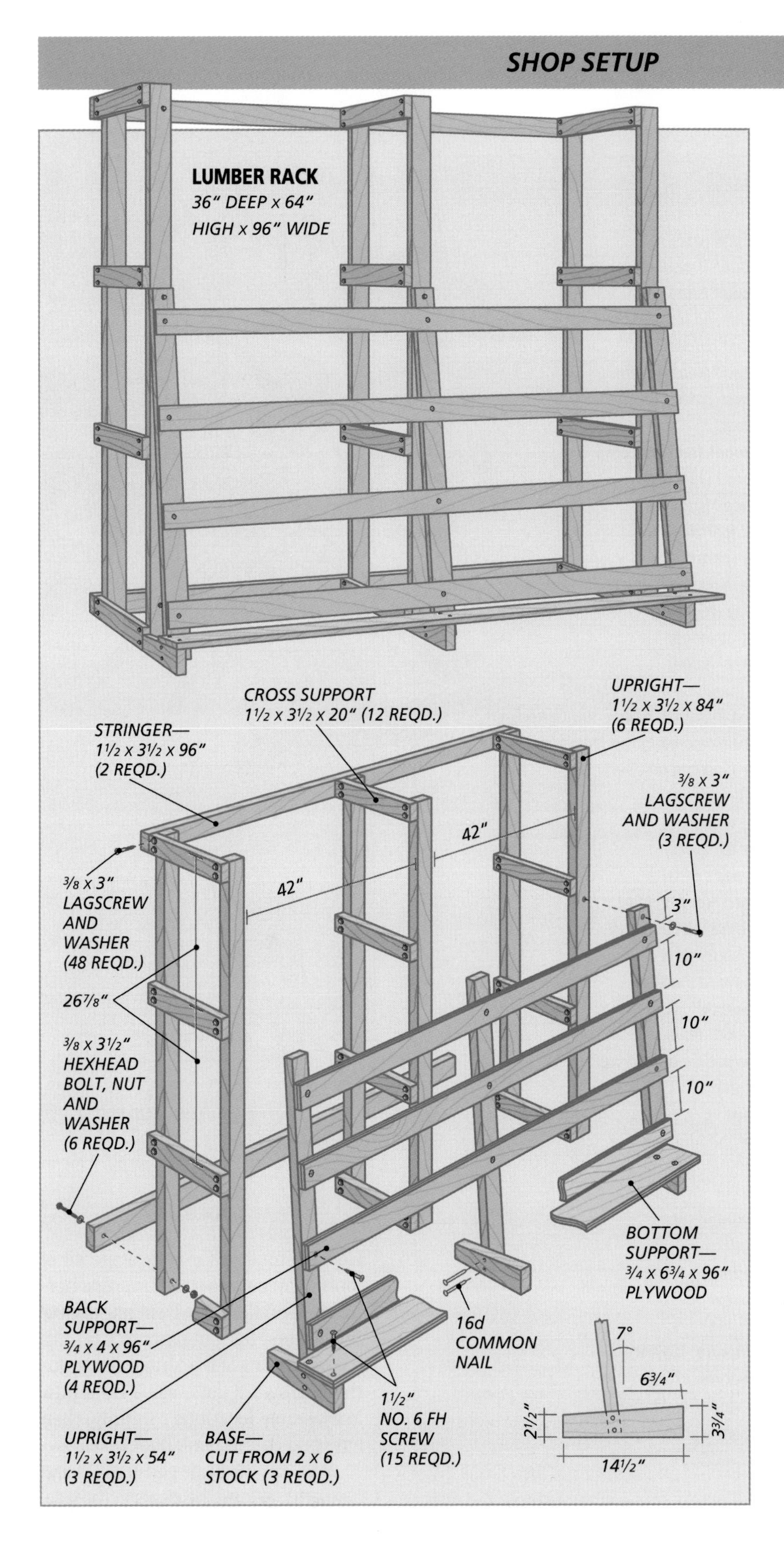

blades and coping and dovetail saws. Rabbet the entire length of the stock, then cut the shorter lengths needed.

Lay the back on a worktable and position your tools, then mount the blocks and turnbuttons. Next, lay out each tool on the shelf. For large round holes, use a Forstner bit in a drill press. To form rectangular openings, bore holes inside the layout lines, then trim to finished shape with a chisel.

Next, use a table saw to cut slots in the shelf edge to hold try and combination squares. Use a router with an edge guide and straight bit to cut elongated holes for chisels and files.

Clamp the shelf and back together, bore countersunk pilot holes along the back edge and attach the pieces with glue and screws. Lay out the support brackets on 1 x 8 stock, and rabbet the back edges. Cut the bracket curves on a band saw and smooth edges with a file. Then, cut the mounting cleats and secure them to the brackets. Finally, screw the brackets to the shelf.

LUMBER RACK

Once your shop is set up, it's time to place the actual center of attention—the wood. This lumber rack holds solid and plywood stock, and is built with construction lumber and plywood.

Begin by cutting all 2 x 4 parts to length and boring holes in the cross supports for fastening to the uprights. Lay out the cross supports as a group to ensure alignment and clamp them to the uprights, then bore pilot holes for the lagscrews and assemble.

Lay the upright sections down and clamp the back stringers in place. Bore holes for bolts and attach the stringers. Cut the bases for the plywood rack and join them to the short uprights. Then, bore a hole at the top of each upright.

Position each plywood rack section up against a main upright and attach it. Finally, rip strips of plywood for the plywood rack base and back supports, then screw them in place.

MATERIALS LIST

KEY	NO.	SIZE AND DESCRIPTION (USE)
A	2	1/2 x 14 x 22" plywood* (front/back)
B	2	1/2 x 14 x 15" plywood* (side)
C	2	1/2 x 2 x 22" plywood* (lid front/back)
D	2	1/2 x 2 x 15" plywood* (lid side)
E	2	1/2 x 15 x 21" plywood* (top/bottom)
F	1	1/4 x 5 x 8 1/2" plywood (blade partition)
G	2	1/2 x 1/2 x 5" pine (cleat)
H	1	1/2 x 4 1/2 x 11" plywood* (saw platform)
I	1	1/2 x 3 x 4 1/2" plywood* (support)
J	1	1/2 x 3 x 7 1/4" plywood* (support)
K	1	1/2 x 1 1/4 x 3 3/4" pine (partition)
L	1	1/2 x 1 1/2 x 3 3/4" pine (partition)
M	2	7/8 x 1 1/8 x 1 1/2" pine (hacksaw hanger)
N	2	1/2 x 1/2 x 8" pine (tray ledge)
O	2	1/2 x 1/2 x 13" pine (tray ledge)
P	2	1/2 x 1/2 x 14" pine (tray ledge)
Q	1	3/4 x 7/8 x 3 3/4" pine (handsaw blade retainer)
R	1	1 1/8 x 1 1/4 x 2 3/8" pine (handsaw handle turnbutton)
S	1	1 1/8 x 1 1/2 x 2 1/2" pine (combination square retainer)
T	1	3/4 x 1 1/2 x 3 1/2" pine (Surform retainer)
U1	1	3/4 x 3 1/2" leather (Surform strap)
U2	2	snap
V	1	3/4 x 1 1/4 x 6 1/2" pine (bit block)
W	2	1/2 x 2 x 14 3/4" plywood* (side)
X	3	1/2 x 2 x 6 3/4" plywood* (end/divider)
Y	1	3/4 x 1 x 6 3/4" pine (chisel blade guard)
Z	1	3/4 x 3/4 x 6 3/4" pine (chisel rack)
AA	1	1/4 x 7 3/4 x 14 3/4" plywood (bottom)
BB	2	1/2 x 3 1/2 x 14 3/4" plywood* (side)
CC	2	1/2 x 3 1/2 x 12" plywood* (end)
DD	1	1/4 x 13 x 14 3/4" plywood (bottom)
EE	1	12"-long, 3/8" brass chain
FF	1	22" brass piano hinge
GG	3	1 1/2" No. 8 fh screw
HH	2	1 3/4" No. 8 fh screw
II	2	1 1/4" No. 8 fh screw
JJ	73	1" No. 6 fh screw
KK	18	3/4" No. 6 fh screw
LL	14	1/2" No. 4 fh brass screw
MM	12	1/2" No. 7 fh brass screw
NN	24	3/8" No. 4 rh screw
OO	2	handle, Brainerd stock No. 1257PB
PP	8	corner, Brainerd stock No. 476PB
QQ	1	drawbolt, Brainerd stock No. 0867PB

Misc.: glue; 4d finishing nails; 5/8" brads; polyurethane varnish.

* Baltic birch plywood.

TOOLBOX
16" HIGH x 16" DEEP x 22" LONG

DETAIL 5

TOOLBOX

Here's a toolbox for an average kit of tools. Plan cuts so the grain runs horizontally on the sides, front and back of the box and lid. Cut parts to size with a circular saw and a straightedge; for the narrow lid cuts, use a rip guide. Mark screw locations carefully, then bore and countersink pilot holes.

Next, cut the blade partition (F) and cleats (G). Secure the cleats to the side,

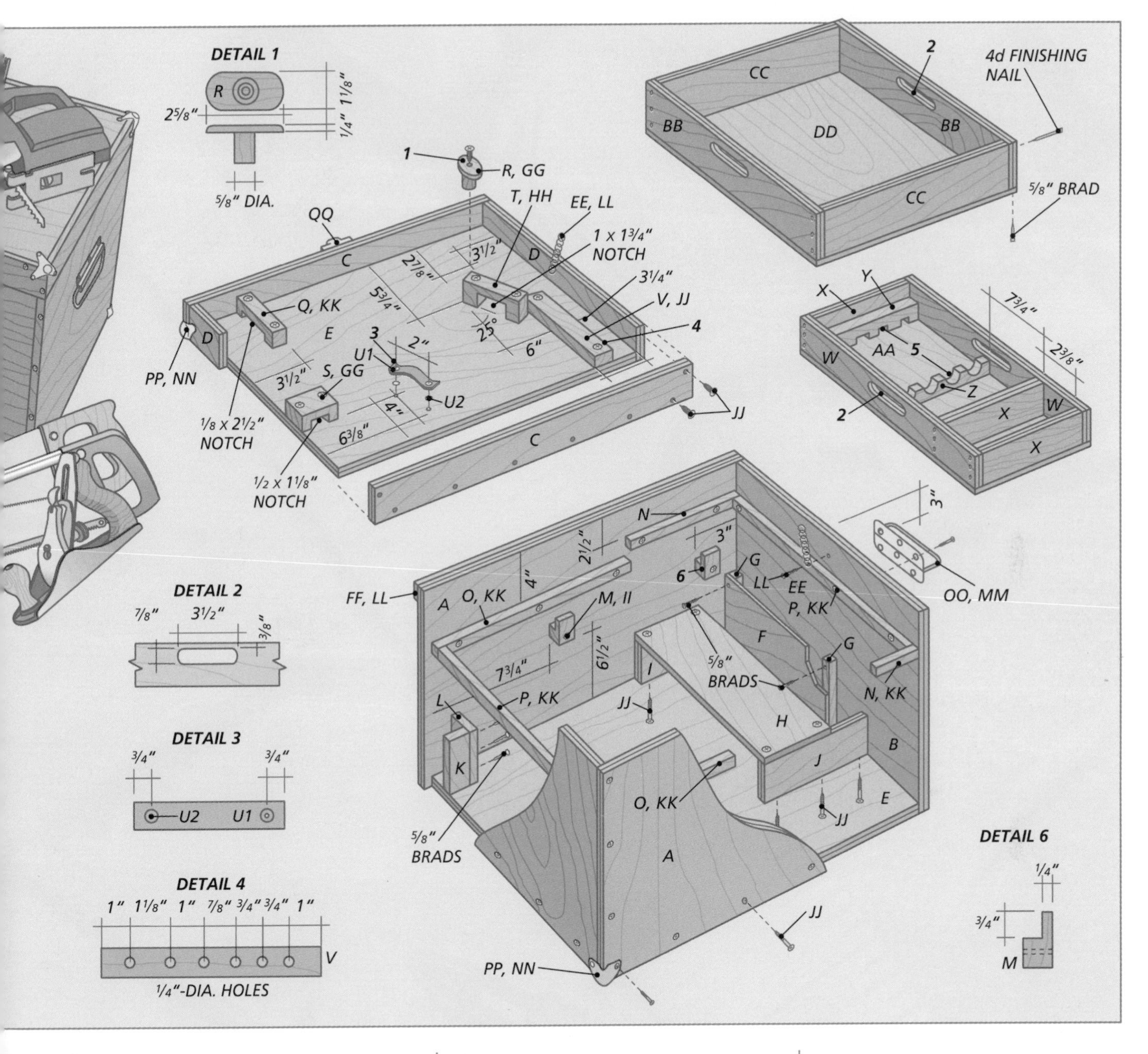

then attach the partition. Before making the saw platform (H) and supports (I, J), check that the dimensions work for your saw. Glue, clamp and screw the supports to the box bottom, then attach the platform.

Fasten the right box side to the bottom, then the left box side to the back. Build the partitions (L, K), then glue them to the back and left side. Fasten the left side and back to the right side and bottom, then add the front panel.

To assemble the lid, join the sides and top, then the front and back.

Cut and install the hacksaw hangers (M), then secure the tray ledges (N, O, P). Construct the retainers (Q, S, T), then shape the saw turnbutton (R) and make the bit block (V), checking that your tools will fit. Rivet the top snap halves (U2) to the leather (U1) and screw the bottom halves to the lid.

Cut the piano hinge to length with a hacksaw and install it, then attach the brass chain to act as a lid restraint. Cut the parts for the trays, make the cutouts by boring holes and using a sabre saw, and assemble the trays. To make the chisel rack (Z), bore holes in wide stock, then rip the piece along the row centerline. Cut the notches for the blade guard (Y) with a handsaw and chisel, then glue both pieces to the tray. Finish with three coats of polyurethane varnish, then install the brass box corners, handles and latch.

HAND TOOLS

MEASURING TOOLS

Of the many tools employed during a typical do-it-yourself project, none is more vital to its successful completion than the various measuring and marking tools used. All craftsmen, regardless of their skill level, must rely heavily on these tools for accuracy throughout each step of the building process.

The diverse collection of measuring and marking tools shown here includes traditional, time-honored tools as well as recent, state-of-the-art devices. Note that some of the tools are designed for precision shopwork while others are used primarily by the building trades. Many of the tools, however, overlap and can be used for nearly all types of do-it-yourself work.

SHOP REQUIREMENTS

The variety of measuring and marking tools that you need depends mostly on the type of work and materials you're involved with. A typical home workshop, though, should be equipped with a 16-ft. tape measure, 6-ft. folding rule, marking gauge, scratch awl, steel straightedge rules of various lengths, and several squares, including a combination, try, framing and sliding bevel square. Add tools to this basic starter group as you require them.

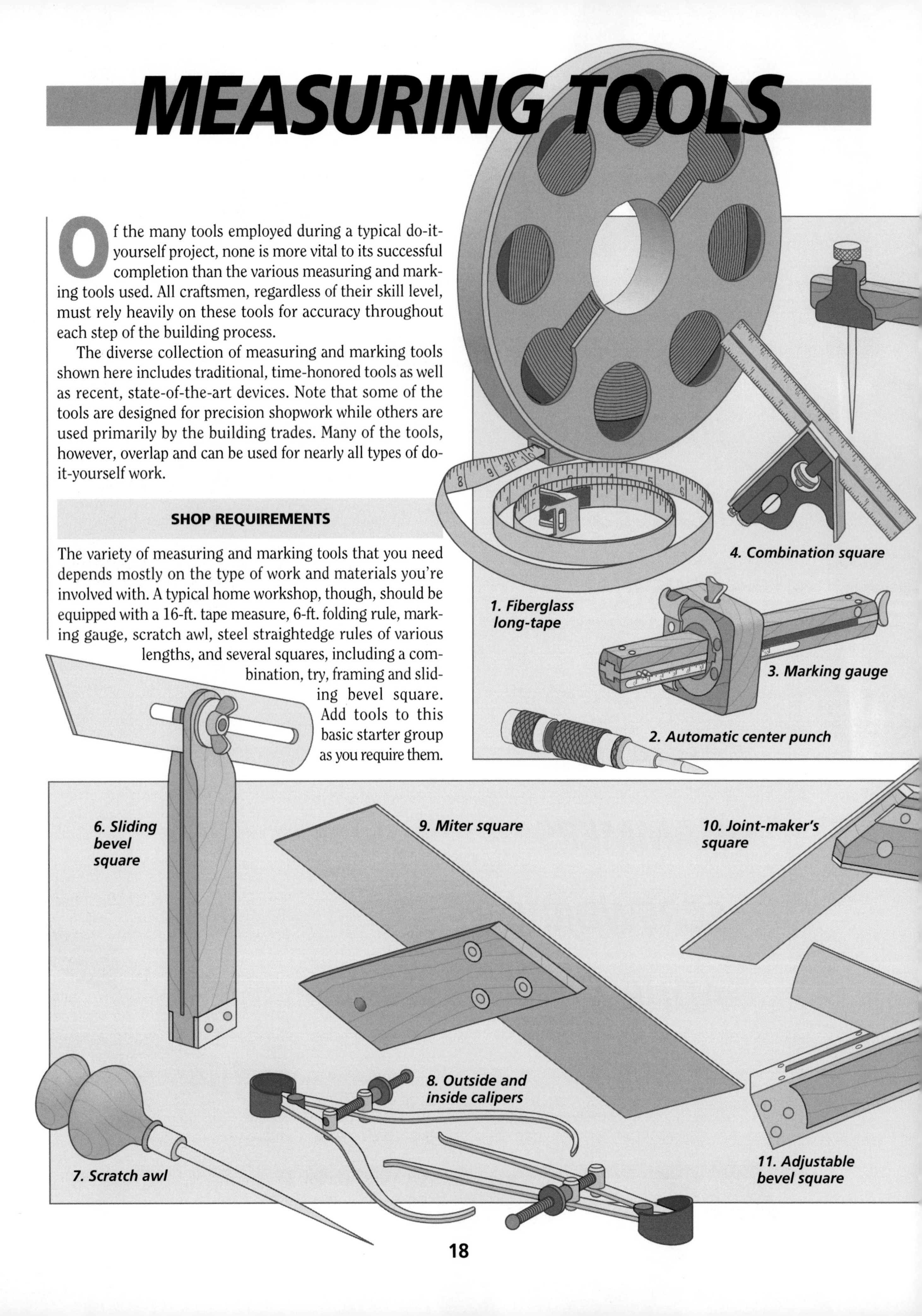

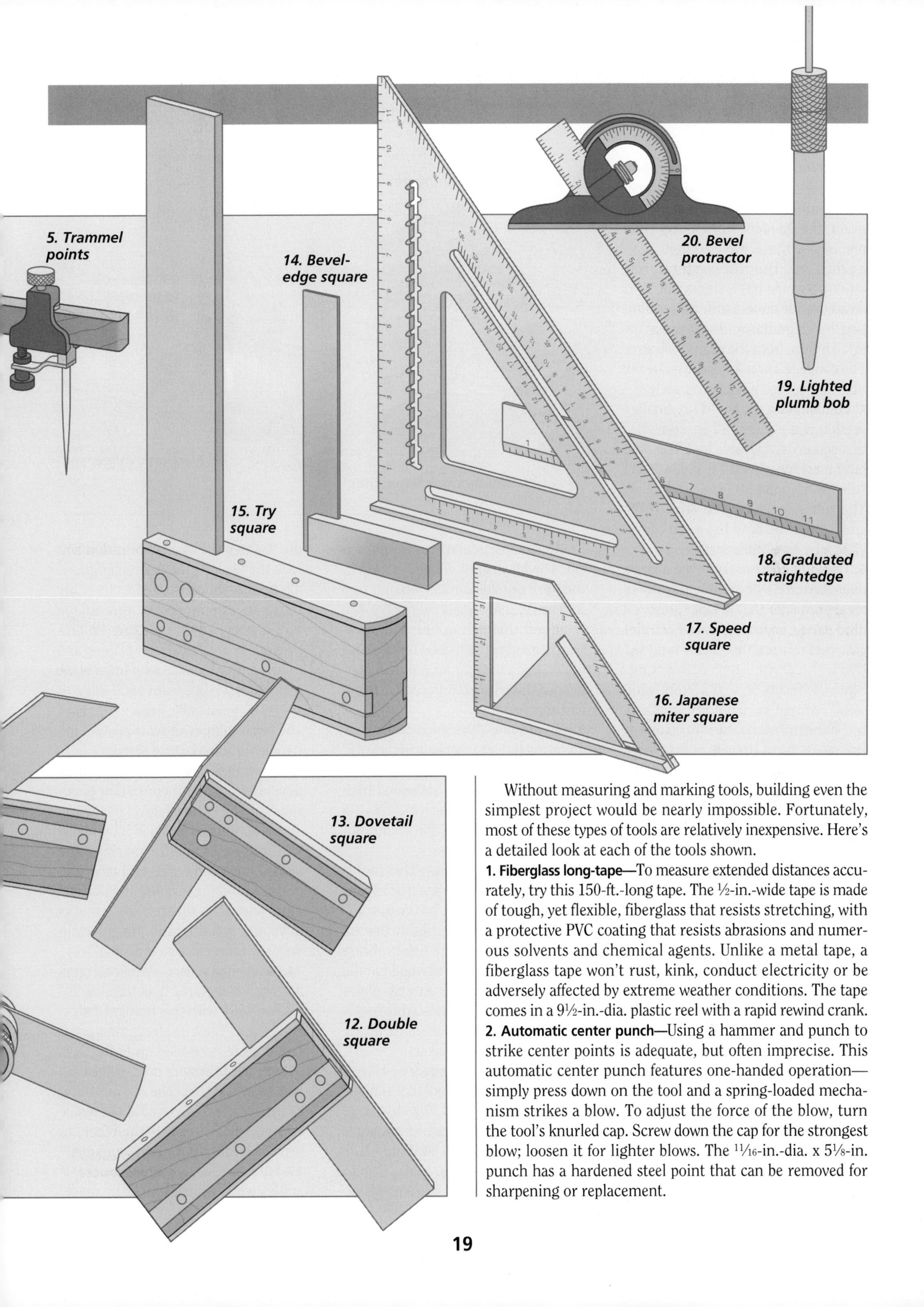

Without measuring and marking tools, building even the simplest project would be nearly impossible. Fortunately, most of these types of tools are relatively inexpensive. Here's a detailed look at each of the tools shown.

1. Fiberglass long-tape—To measure extended distances accurately, try this 150-ft.-long tape. The ½-in.-wide tape is made of tough, yet flexible, fiberglass that resists stretching, with a protective PVC coating that resists abrasions and numerous solvents and chemical agents. Unlike a metal tape, a fiberglass tape won't rust, kink, conduct electricity or be adversely affected by extreme weather conditions. The tape comes in a 9½-in.-dia. plastic reel with a rapid rewind crank.

2. Automatic center punch—Using a hammer and punch to strike center points is adequate, but often imprecise. This automatic center punch features one-handed operation—simply press down on the tool and a spring-loaded mechanism strikes a blow. To adjust the force of the blow, turn the tool's knurled cap. Screw down the cap for the strongest blow; loosen it for lighter blows. The 11⁄16-in.-dia. x 5⅛-in. punch has a hardened steel point that can be removed for sharpening or replacement.

3. Marking gauge—To lay out wood joint lines-of-cut, use a marking gauge. Designed for marking *with* the wood grain, the gauge scribes a very fine, precise line that is more accurate than a pencil line. This rosewood and brass marking gauge has a single spur and an adjustable double spur for scribing two lines simultaneously. It can mark up to 5¾ in. from the edge of a board. The gauge features a unique guide for marking curved pieces accurately.

4. Combination square—This smaller version of a standard 12-in. combination square is a valuable tool. The steel head is equipped with a 6-in.-long steel rule for marking 90° and 45° angles. The rule is graduated in 8ths, 16ths and 32nds. The head has a spirit level vial and a removable scriber.

5. Trammel points—To scribe a large diameter circle or arc, or to transfer measurements that are too great for dividers, use trammel points. Each die-cast metal head has a 3-in.-long leg that is fitted with a replaceable point. Slide the heads on a ⅜ x ¾-in.-wide wood beam of virtually any length. A fine-adjustment mechanism on one of the heads gives precise point placement. The trammel points come with a pencil holder that replaces one leg and a dozen extra points.

6. Sliding bevel square—Use this essential tool to lay out various odd angles and dovetail joints. Simply adjust the 9⅞-in.-long steel blade to the desired angle and tighten the wingnut. The 7⅛-in.-long rosewood handle is reinforced with brass end plates.

7. Scratch awl—A quality awl is necessary for all types of precision layout work and general scribing. This fine-crafted tool has a 4½-in.-long hardened tool-steel blade that is fitted into an attractive, hand-turned rosewood handle. The blade tip is ground to a very fine, sharp point.

8. Outside and inside calipers—These two tools are designed for accurately transferring and measuring outside and inside dimensions. Calipers are invaluable, particularly to woodturners. The bowlegged caliper is used to measure outside dimensions up to 6 in. The straight-legged caliper has two small feet that flair outward for measuring inside dimensions up to about 6½ in. Each tool has forged steel legs, tempered steel bow spring and a quick-adjust screw.

9. Miter square—Designed exclusively for laying out and marking precise 45° angles, this handsome tool features a blue-steel blade and a rosewood handle. The oversized blade measures 2¼ x 10 in. long, suitable for accommodating large workpieces.

10. Joint-maker's square—This tool is slightly smaller than most standard miter squares. Use it to lay out 45° miters on small-scale, highly precise work. The 1-in.-wide x 6½-in. brass blade is riveted to a rosewood handle that is accented with brass wear plates and inlay brass rivet seats. This tool is an especially helpful one for furniture builders and model-makers.

11. Adjustable bevel square—Here's another scaled-down tool that is made of brass and rosewood. Use this bevel square to lay out and transfer any angle accurately. The ⅞ x 5-in.-long blade rotates 360°. Brass wear plates help to protect a 3½-in.-long rosewood handle. Tighten the knurled brass knob to lock the blade at the desired angle.

12. Double square—Sized to fit easily into a work apron pocket, this unique tool is designed for checking squareness of a board's edge after planing and jointing. The 1 x 5-in.-long brass blade protrudes 1⅞ in. from each edge of the rosewood handle. Brass wear plates and brass inlay rivet seats protect the handle for long-lasting accuracy.

13. Dovetail square—Lay out and mark dovetail joints with consistent accuracy using this novel dovetail square. The 5-in.-long brass blade is equipped with a tapered end for marking the angled lines of the pins and tails, and a square end for scribing the vertical joint lines. The square shown marks dovetails at a 6:1 ratio. An 8:1 ratio dovetail square is also available.

14. Bevel-edge square—When extreme accuracy is required to determine 90° angles, work with this hardened-steel try square. The 6-in.-long, non-graduated blade is beveled on both edges of each side to provide precise line contact with the tool. The 4$\frac{5}{16}$-in.-long beam (handle) is grooved at the inside corner, where it meets the blade, to provide clearance for burrs and dirt.

15. Try square—Lay out and mark 90° angles with this exceptionally made,

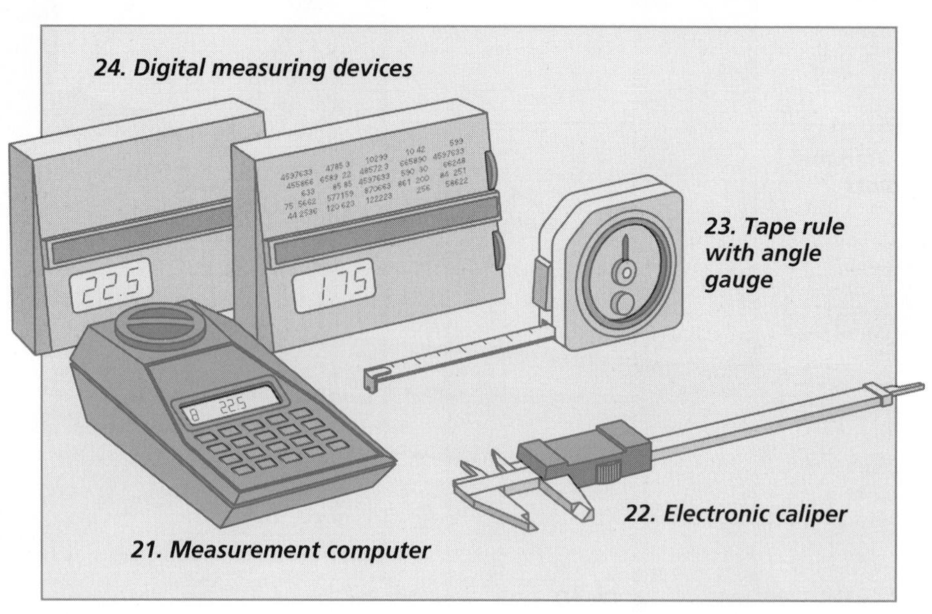

super-precise try square. Featuring a 1/8-in.-thick x 1 1/2 x 8-in.-long brass blade and rosewood handle, the square is guaranteed accurate to within .002 in. of 90°. The handle's edges are faced with brass wear plates and the sides have brass inlay rivet seats.

16. Japanese miter square—Designed unlike any Western square, this versatile Japanese tool can mark 90° and 45° angles. The lightweight, all-steel tool measures 4 x 6 3/4 in. It has a 9/16-in.-wide base and a handy inch scale that measures the depth of a miter, not the length along the 45° line.

17. Speed square—This simple square is arguably one of the most versatile carpenter's layout tools available, combining the best features of a framing, try and miter square with the angle-finding capability of a protractor. Use the 12 x 12-in. aluminum-alloy square for all framing layout work including wall and roof construction and stairway building. The tool comes with a comprehensive 40-page instruction booklet and a bolt-on layout bar that adjusts to fit out-of-square corners.

18. Graduated straightedge—A quality steel straightedge is indispensable for scribing perfectly straight lines and checking the flatness of a surface. This precision-ground 1 13/32-in.-wide x 12-in.-long tool is graduated in 32nds of an inch and beveled along one edge. Graduated straightedges are available up to 48 in. long. Non-graduated and non-beveled models come in lengths up to 72 in.

19. Lighted plumb bob—Here's a fine example of how a simple, yet clever, idea can vastly improve the accuracy of one of the world's oldest tools—the plumb bob. The Laser plumb bob emits a 1/16-in.-dia. spot of light that indicates exactly where to mark—there is no guesswork involved. This tool is especially useful in low-light areas. The 7/8-in.-dia. x 7 3/4-in. bob operates on two AA-size batteries.

20. Bevel protractor—Read, transfer and mark angles quickly and accurately with this bevel protractor. The tool features a rotating head that has a double 180° scale, spirit level and knurled lock bolts. The head is fitted with a 12-in.-long steel rule calibrated in 8ths, 16ths, 32nds and 64ths. Eighteen- and 24-in.-long rules are also available.

21. Measurement computer—To measure distances from 1 to 50 ft. instantly, try using the DMC-100 hand-held computer. Simply push a button and the unit emits inaudible sound waves that bounce off the facing surface and return as echoes. The unit receives the echoes, calculates the distance and displays it in feet and inches, yards or meters. Use the DMC-100 to calculate volume and area as well as to perform various arithmetic functions. It even gives ambient temperature readings in Fahrenheit or Celsius degrees. The 1 3/4 x 3 1/4 x 6-in. unit weighs 7 1/2 oz. and comes with a 6-volt battery.

22. Electronic caliper—Work with this Swiss-made digital caliper to obtain super-precise measurements. Made of hardened stainless steel, the tool utilizes a microprocessor chip to display English and metric measurements up to 6 in. Use the device for making accurate inside and outside measurements to 1/1000 in. The caliper comes with two 1.5-volt batteries and a molded plastic case.

23. Tape rule with angle gauge—This versatile tool serves as a tape measure, level, plumb and angle finder. The tape rule combines a 1/2-in. x 10-ft. steel tape that is graduated in inches and millimeters with an adjustable angle gauge. Rotate the double-graduated scale to read and transfer angles from 0° to 120°. The high-impact plastic case is equipped with a tape lock switch and a belt clip.

24. Digital measuring devices—These two Blade Finders are instant digital readout measuring devices for a table saw. The Blade Height model measures blade elevation up to 3 in. and to within 1/100 in. The Blade Angle device reads the angle of the saw blade from 0° to 65° and to within 1/10 of a degree. Each 2 x 3 1/2 x 5-in. unit uses a standard 9-volt battery. Follow the step-by-step instruction booklet and install one or both devices on your saw. They can also be installed on a radial-arm saw, planer, drill press and jointer.

TYPES OF LEVELS

No homeowner's toolbox is complete without at least one level. For do-it-yourself home improvement projects, a level is needed to determine level (horizontal) and plumb (vertical) alignment. The level, thought of first as a carpenter's tool, is also essential to masons, plumbers, electricians, engineers and millwrights.

One of the original levels, a wood A-frame with a weighted line hanging from its vertex, was used by ancient Egyptian pyramid builders. The spirit, or bubble, level was invented around 1660 and used on telescopes. However, it wasn't until the mid-19th century that the sealed glass tube containing alcohol and an air bubble was set in a wood or iron rail for use by craftsmen.

Today, many different types of levels are available. Some are general-

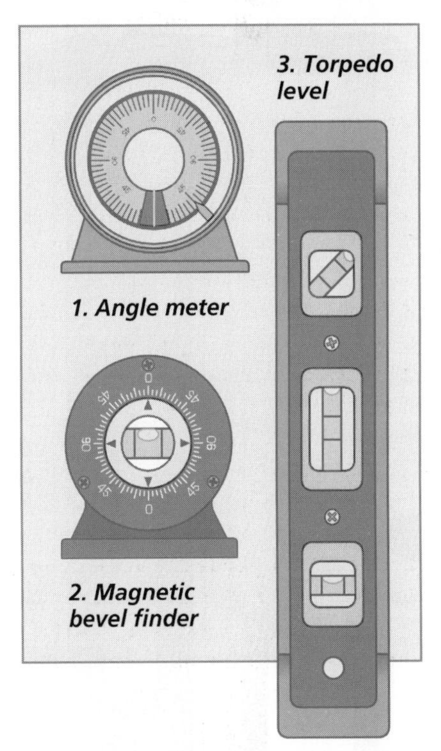

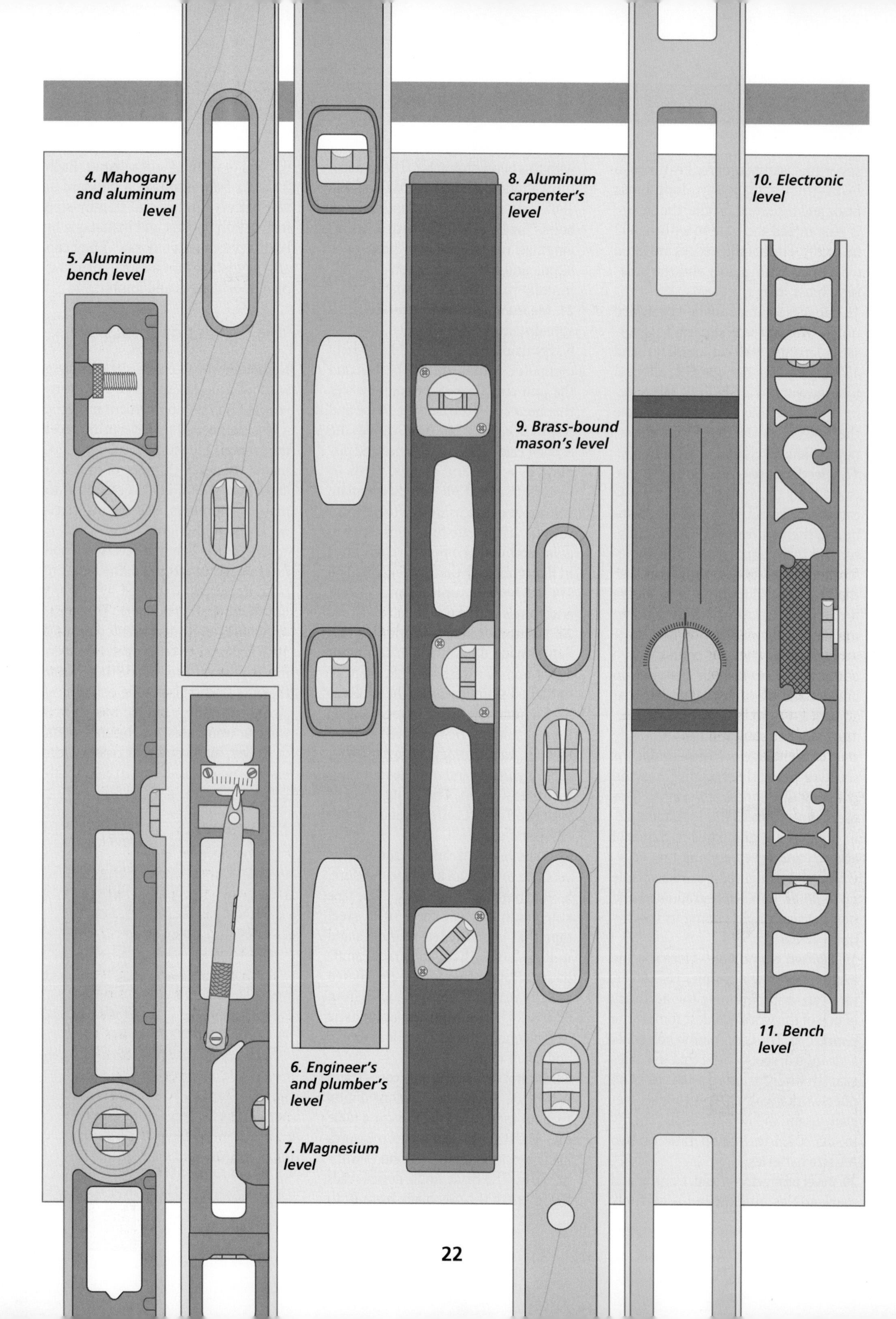
4. Mahogany and aluminum level
5. Aluminum bench level
6. Engineer's and plumber's level
7. Magnesium level
8. Aluminum carpenter's level
9. Brass-bound mason's level
10. Electronic level
11. Bench level

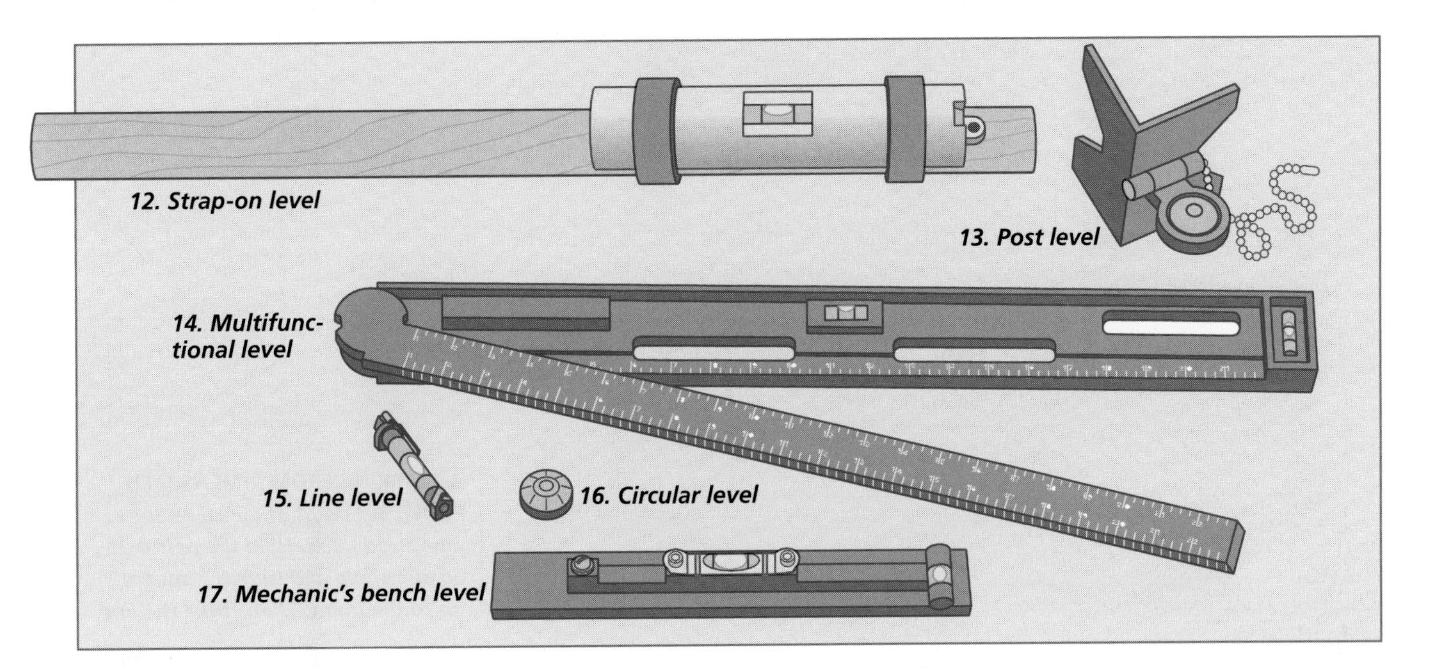

purpose levels while others are specially designed for a particular type of work. Levels are made of various materials including wood, aluminum, magnesium, cast iron and plastic. They range in size from about 2 in. to 10 ft. An active do-it-yourselfer should own at least four levels: a line level, a 9-in. torpedo level, and 2-ft. and 4-ft. carpenter's levels.

Level vials are made of glass or plastic and are often protected behind a window. Most levels have vials that can be replaced if broken—a highly recommended feature. Note that some levels have two vials behind each window. This original design provides one vial for each tool edge. A more recent design makes use of a single vial per window. A single-vial level will work 360° on both edges or when laid flat. And not all of today's levels make use of liquid-filled vials. The battery-operated electronic level offers the latest in level design and technology. Let's take a look at the 17 different types of levels shown here.

1. Angle meter—Use this versatile tool to measure any angle easily, including level (0°) and plumb (90°). The easy-to-

TIP

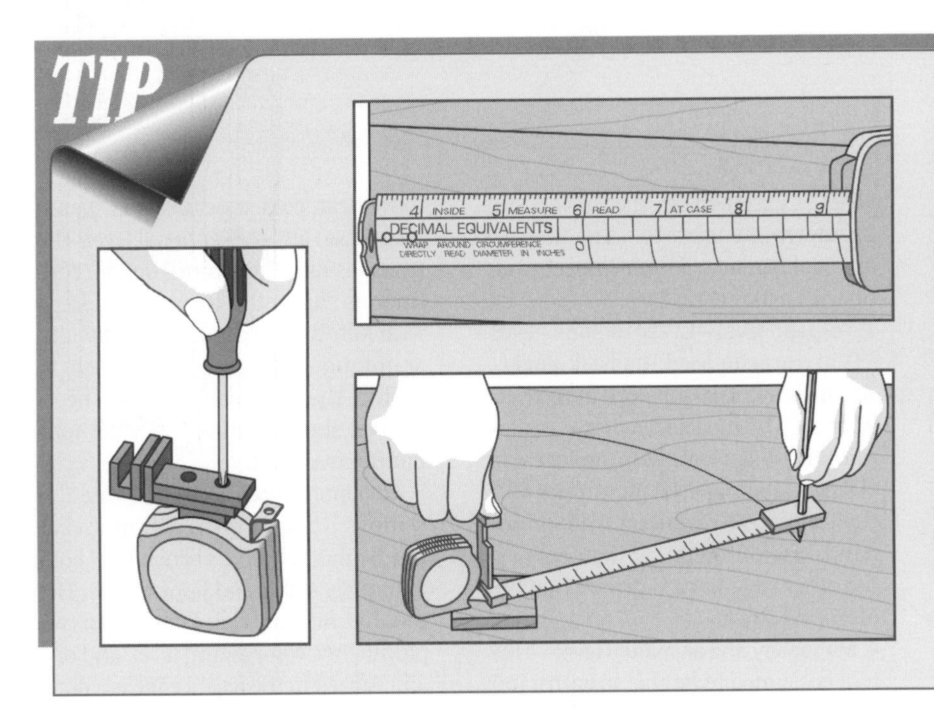

EASY READER / WRITER

A measuring tape with inside measurements on the reverse side is a valuable asset. It eliminates the need to add the tape's case width to a measurement *(near left, top).*

A circle scriber lets you mark arcs or circles of a radius from 2 in. to a tape's length. Screw the main body over the rule's locking button *(far left)* and fit the pencil holder on the tape's tip. Pull the tape to the desired measurement, then press down on the pivot and scribe clockwise *(near left, bottom).*

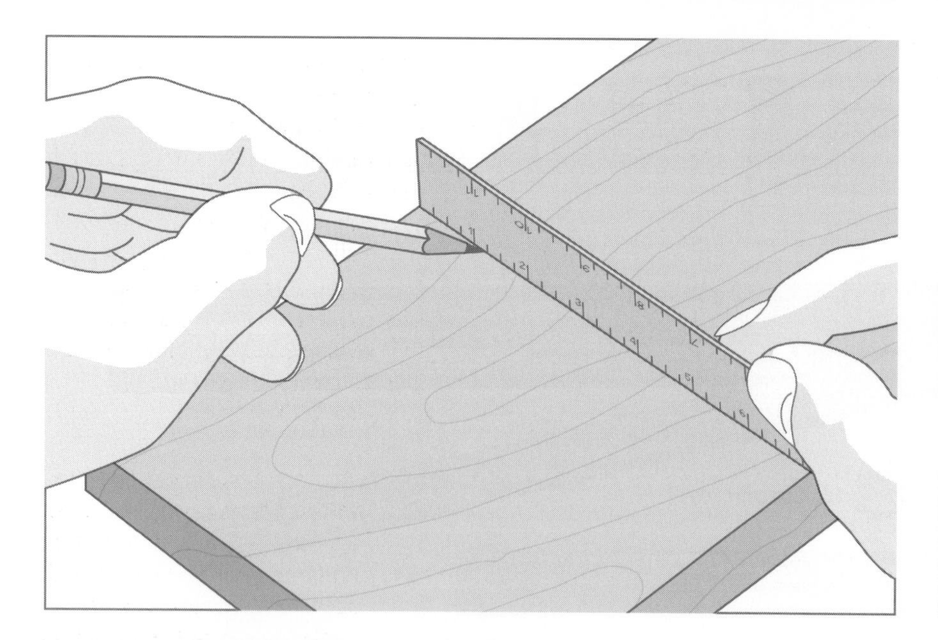

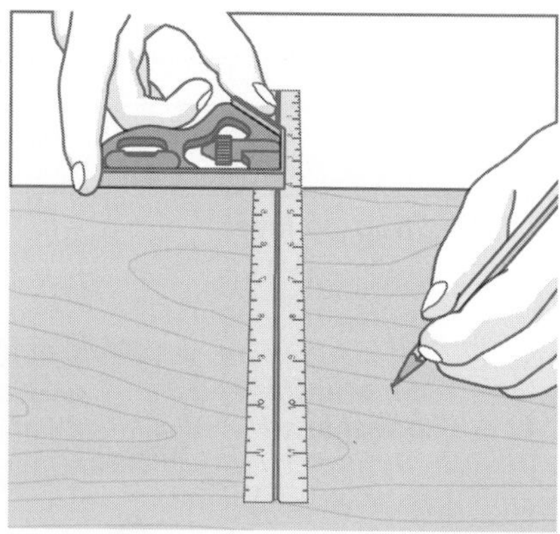

▲ **MARKING FROM A MEASURED POINT.** ***Set point of pencil on the measured mark. Hold the pencil at an 80° angle and slide the square up to the point. Then strike the line.***

▲ **STRIKING OFF.** ***Hold a thick rule on edge to strike off a measurement for greatest accuracy—distortion from viewing angle is minimized. Always use a hard-lead pencil and keep the point sharp.***

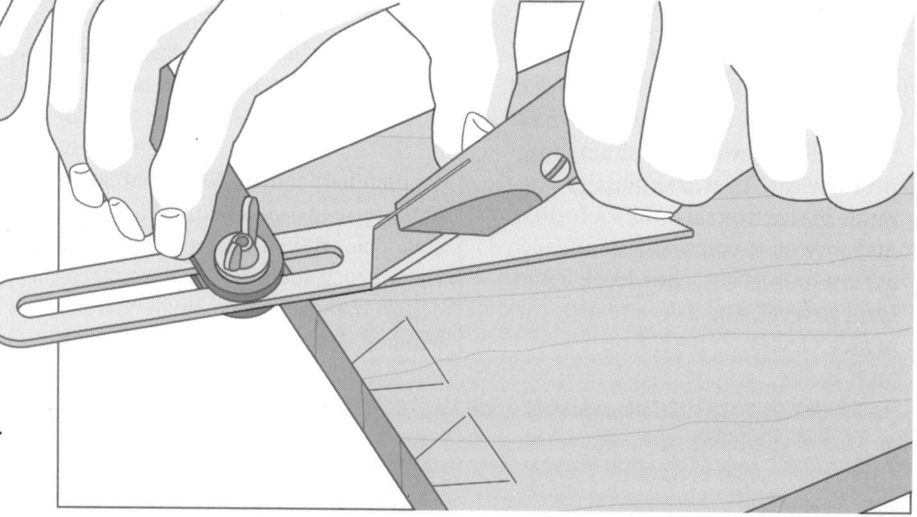

► **SCORING.** ***To mark dovetails, for example, a utility knife gives greater accuracy than a pencil. Score also aids in beginning cutting work.***

read 4¼-in.-dia. plastic dial is marked 0° to 90° in each quadrant. Magnetic strips on the tool's base and back hold fast to metal work. Use the movable pointer to repeat and transfer angles. On the back of the meter is a calculator for finding rise, run, pitch angle and rafter-to-run ratio.

2. Magnetic bevel finder—Here's proof that good things can come in small packages. This pocket-size tool is really four tools in one: a level, protractor, square and pitch gauge. A single vial is enclosed in a dial that can be adjusted 360°. Set the dial to 0° to read level. To find plumb, turn the dial to 90°. It's excellent for measuring and transferring angles, too. The 2⅝-in.-dia. tool is made of high-impact plastic with a magnetic base.

3. Torpedo level—Every toolbox needs a 9-in. torpedo level. Its back-pocket size makes it ideal for work in restricted areas. The model shown has an aluminum I-beam rail with replaceable vials for reading level, plumb and 45°. One edge has a magnetic strip for no-hands use on metal workpieces and the other edge has a V-groove that fits on round stock.

4. Mahogany and aluminum level—This tool is claimed to be able to withstand more heat, cold, moisture and overall abuse than any conventional level. The reason is its unique construction: continuous aluminum I-beam reinforced with kiln-dried mahogany. Full-width aluminum edges and end caps help to protect the tool against wear. The 4-ft. level shown features six vials: four plumb, two level.

5. Aluminum bench level—Die-cast aluminum I-beam construction makes this 24-in. mechanic's bench level both extremely stable and lightweight. The tool has four durable Pyrex vials: two plumb, one top-reading level, and one 45°. Affixed to the level's edge is a dual-

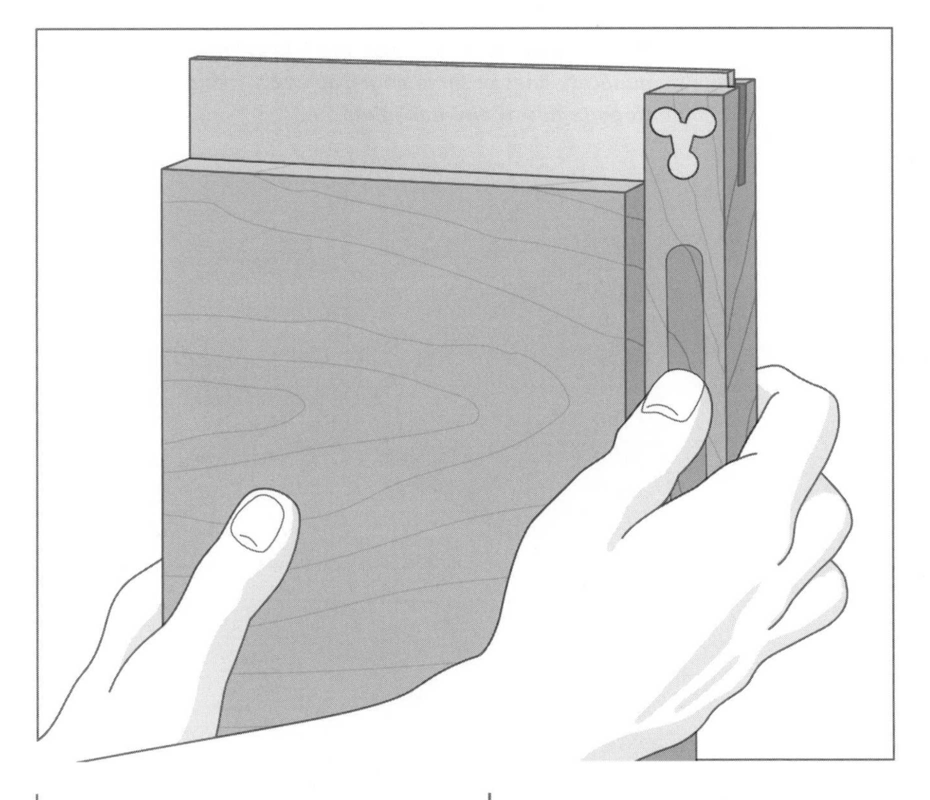

▲ **CHECKING SQUARENESS, 1.** ***Use a try or combination square to check for squareness after making a cross-cut. If the cut is out of square, trim using block plane.***

function steel rule that is marked with 1⁄16-in. graduations on one edge and a 1⁄8-in. centering rule on the other. An 18-in. model is also available.

6. Engineer's and plumber's level—This is a unique three-function tool made specifically for engineers, plumbers and other mechanical-trade types. It features a fixed-level vial, a plumb vial and an adjustable-level vial that reads degree of incline. Incline is given by the pointer at the end of the adjustable tube and read off a steel plate that has 1⁄16-in.-per-ft. graduations. The level reads up to 2 in. per ft. of incline. An involute groove in one edge fits onto round work. The 15-in. tool is made of high-grade cast iron.

7. Magnesium level—Lighter in weight and more durable than aluminum levels, magnesium levels are the choice of many professional carpenters. The 4-ft. level shown features a heavy-duty extruded magnesium I-beam rail with three replaceable single vials for reading level and plumb. The tool is available in sizes ranging from 2 ft. to 10 ft.

8. Aluminum carpenter's level—Here's a good all-purpose level: a 24-in. aluminum level with three replaceable vials; two plumb, one top-reading level. The vials are tinted yellow for easy reading and the aluminum rail has a black enamel finish. A 4-ft. model is also available.

9. Brass-bound mason's level—Designed especially for masons, this handsome level features a solid mahogany rail that is reinforced with wear-resistant brass edges and end caps. Take readings from the six clear-glass vials: two double plumb and one double level.

10. Electronic level—This tool makes use of blinking lights and a beeping signal to indicate level, plumb, pre-

▼ **CHECKING SQUARENESS, 2.** ***Edges on boards that are to be edge-joined must be absolutely square. Check them carefully using a try or combination square.***

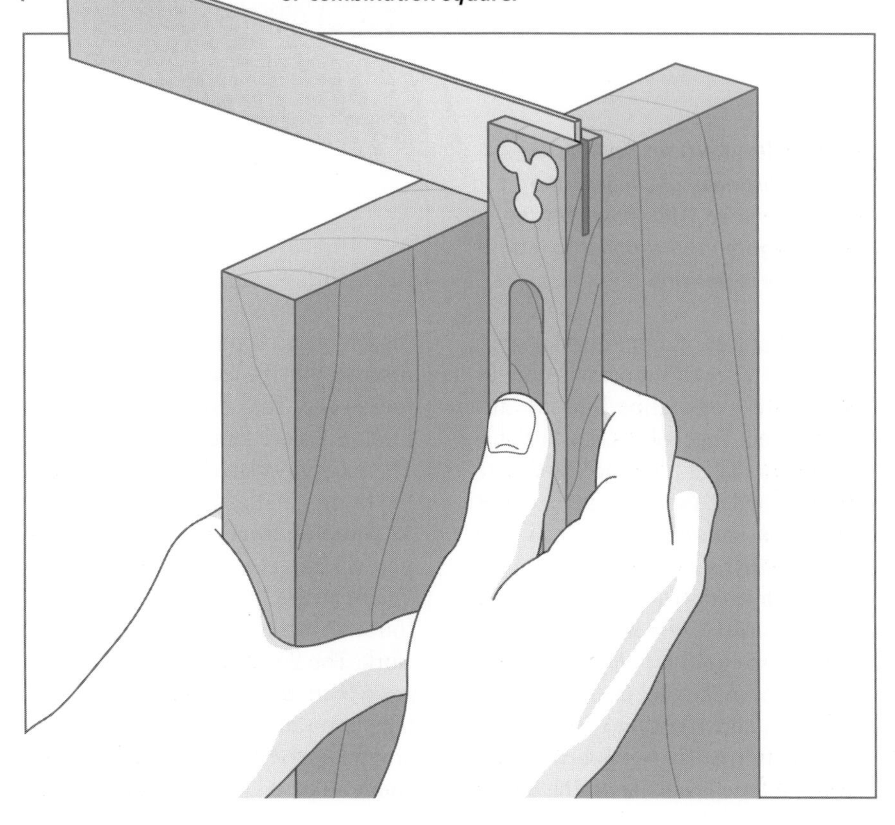

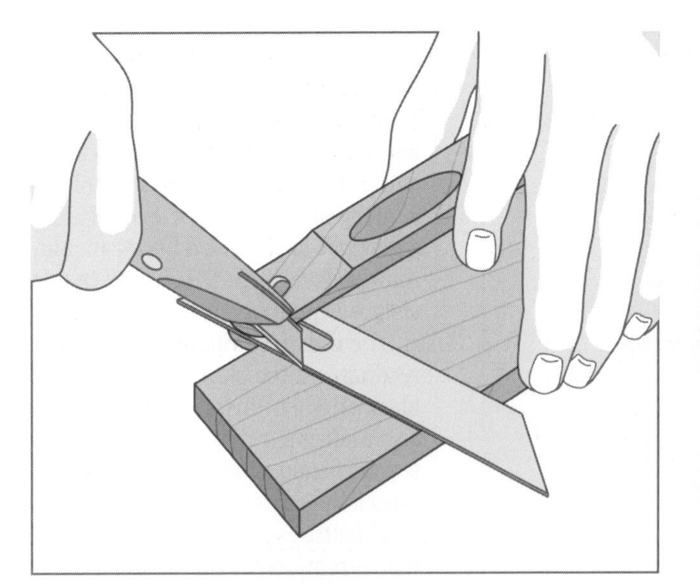

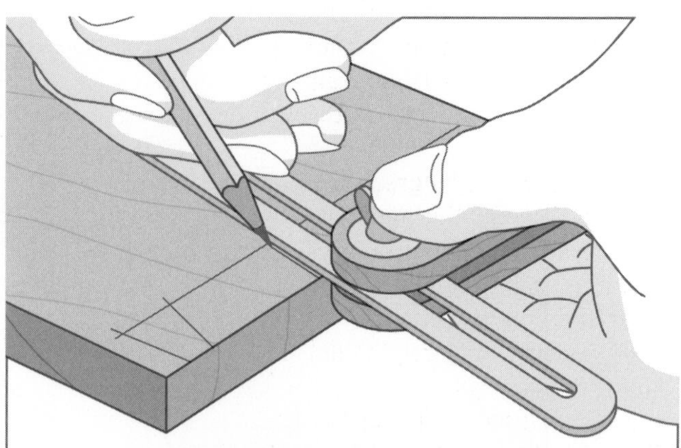

▼ **MARKING ANGLES, 2.** ***Use the T-bevel to lay off duplicate lines at same angle, as when laying out sloped sides of dovetail joints.***

▲ **MARKING ANGLES, 1.** ***Set the T-bevel to the desired angle with the aid of a protractor. Hold the T-bevel firmly against the workpiece with fingers out of the way, then mark the angle using a utility knife.***

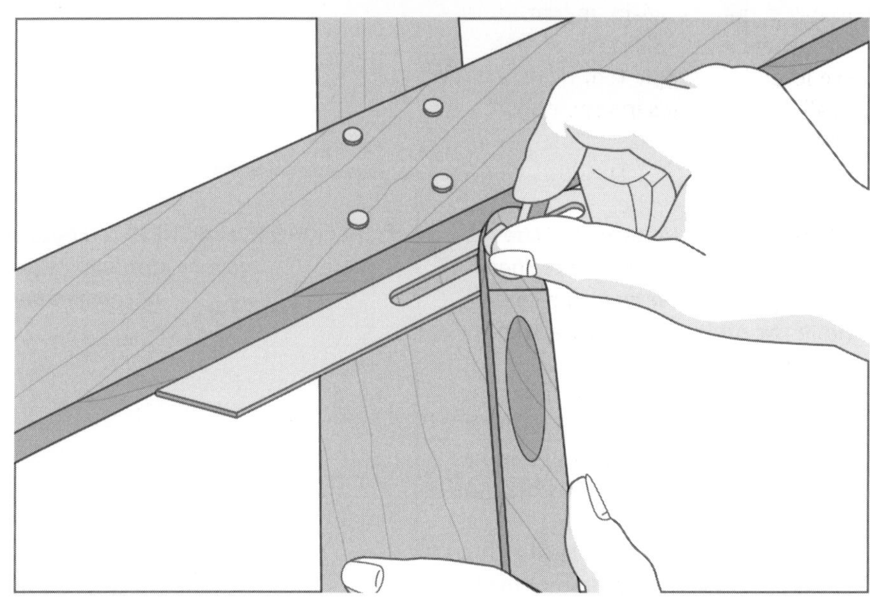

► **TRANSFERRING ANGLES.** ***To transfer an existing angle, loosen the blade and slide T-bevel against the angle. Tighten the wingnut to lock the blade in position.***

selected angles and unknown angles. The electronic unit operates on a 9-volt battery and clips into an aluminum rail. The tool has an adjustable protractor dial, durable polycarbonate housing and it's effective in low-light situations. Rails come in 2-, 3-, 4- and 6-ft. lengths.

11. Bench level—Designed primarily for machinists, this highly accurate level can be used for all types of precision work. The tool features ornate cast-iron construction with a black wrinkle finish. There are two plumb vials and one level vial on the 18-in. model shown. Top-reading feature permits viewing the level vial through the tool's edge. The opposite edge has an involute groove for use on round work. The tool is available in six sizes ranging from 4 in. to 24 in.

12. Strap-on level—Keep both hands free with this clever strap-on level. Two Velcro straps hold the level securely to round, square and irregular-shape work. The 2 x 10-in. polystyrene tool has a 5⁄8-in.-dia. circular level for reading plumb and a level vial. It will wrap around up to 8 in. dia. Use it to plumb and level pipes, poles, rails and posts.

13. Post level—Here's another hands-free level, one that is designed specifically for determining plumb. Made of high-impact plastic, the tool has an easy-to-read 1 1⁄8-in.-dia. circular level and a length of bead chain that will accommodate work up to about 5 1⁄2 in. dia. Additional chain can be added for use on virtually any size object. Use it to plumb posts for mailboxes, signs, fences, decks and antennas.

14. Multifunctional level—Read level and plumb with this versatile 24-in. level that unfolds to become a 48-in. level. The tool will also read and transfer angles up to 180°. A locking lever secures the tool at the desired angle. Made of tough ABS plastic, the level is marked with inch graduations along its edges. A 12-in. model (that opens to 24 in.) is also available; magnetic-edge types are available in both 12-in. and 24-in. sizes.

15. Line level—Level great distances across walls using this mini-level. Clip the level's two hooks onto a taut string. Adjust the string until the bubble reads level, then mark the wall. Use a line level to install chair-rail molding and suspended ceilings. The model shown can also be used on flat surfaces and the vial is graduated to read up to ½-in.-per-ft. pitch in ⅛-in. increments.

16. Circular level—Also called a bull's-eye level, this simple tool reads level in all directions. It's indispensable for leveling machines, appliances, turntables and pool tables. The 1⅜-in.-dia. level is made of acrylic.

17. Mechanic's bench level—This type of bench level is used mostly by machinists and millwrights to set up sophisticated machinery. Made of heavy-duty cast iron, this supersensitive 12-in. tool features three vials: level, plumb and cross-test that reads perpendicular to the level vial. The level vial is graduated to read .005-in.-per-ft. pitch and it's protected by a rotating metal tube.

GOOD CRAFTSMANSHIP

Good craftsmanship begins with proper measuring and marking. It doesn't matter how carefully and consistently you cut "right on the line." If the line itself is off, you make a bad cut.

Accuracy in measuring and marking is primarily a matter of using the right tool in the correct manner. When using any measuring or marking tool, be conscious of your angle of view, or you may err because of the parallax effect. This is the apparent displacement of two points (the desired point on a tool and the corresponding point you want to make on a piece) that is caused by different angles of view.

For this reason, some rules have graduation marks on a bevel that tapers down as close to the

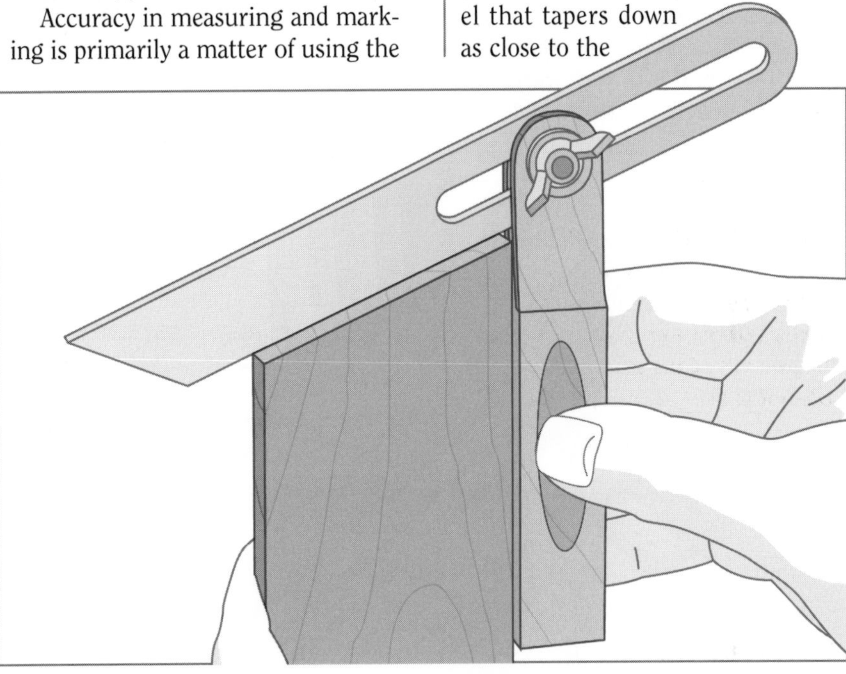

▲ CHECKING MITER CUTS. *Holding the T-bevel's handle firmly against the workpiece edge, check the angle of a miter cut. Tighten wingnut to hold blade securely in position.*

◄ CHECKING CHAMFERS. *The T-bevel is a useful tool for checking chamfers and bevels. Here, the tool is adjusted to a 45° angle to check a chamfer.*

work surface as possible. Most sturdy metal rules don't have bevels, so turn these types of rules on edge to bring their graduation marks closer to the work surface.

MAKING YOUR MARK

For general marking tasks, use a pencil with a medium-hard lead such as 2H. This produces a thin line that is much easier to work with than a bold, irregular line. Keep the point of the pencil sharp. If you work with a dull, soft-lead pencil, the thick, wide lines you strike are sure to produce inaccuracies—avoidable errors that are time-consuming and difficult to correct.

The way you hold most tools is also very important. Hold a pencil at about 80° to the work surface so the point rides in the corner formed by the rule edge and the work. When marking a line with a square or T-bevel, place the pencil point on the measured mark and slide the other tool up to it.

Some jobs require greater accuracy than is possible with a pencil. Laying out cutting lines for good-fitting joints, for example, requires the greater accuracy that you get with a utility knife

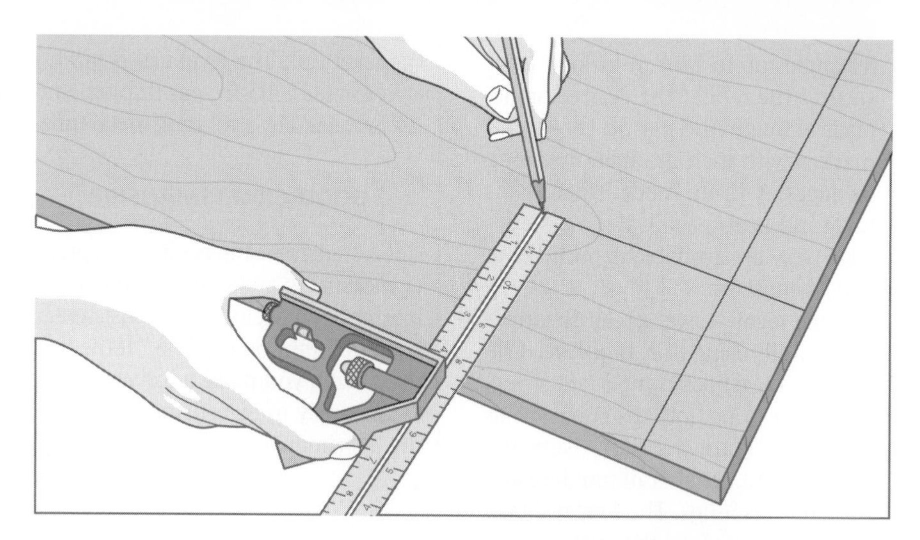

▲ **MARKING PARALLEL TO EDGES.** ***Use a combination square to mark a line parallel to a board's edge. Hold a sharp pencil against the blade end and slide the square along the board.***

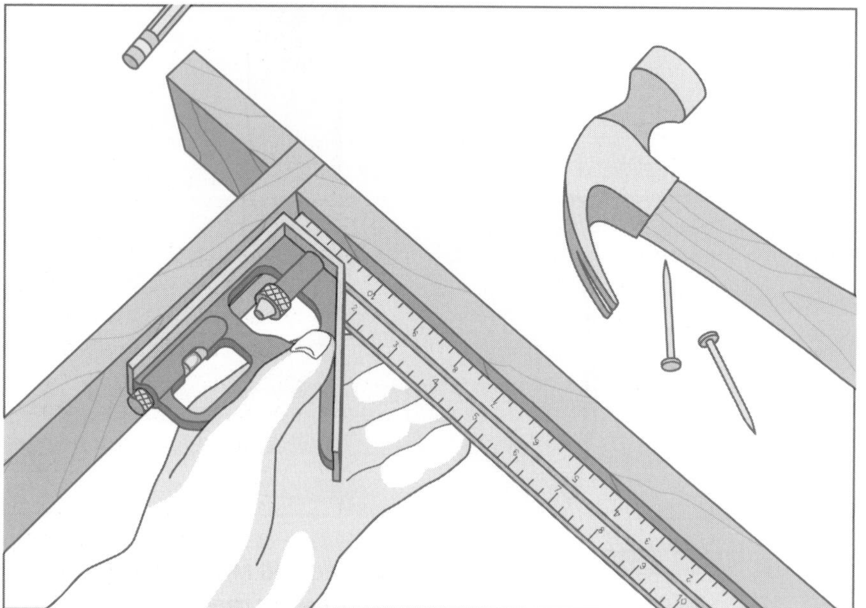

◀ **CHECKING INSIDE CORNERS.** ***Check for square inside corners with combination square. Lock the blade so its end is flush with edge of handle.***

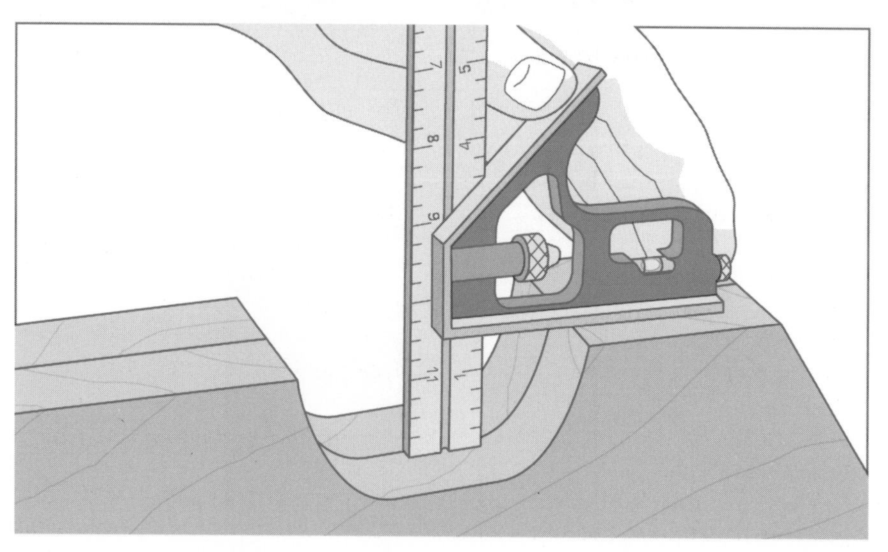

▼ **TAKING DEPTH READINGS.** ***Adjustable blade of combination square allows tool to be used as a depth gauge. Slide the blade down, tighten the locknut and take the blade's reading.***

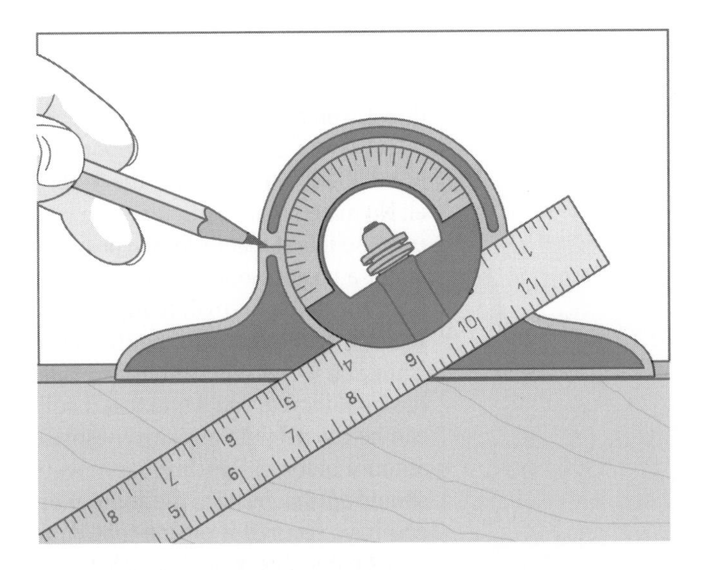

◀ **MEASURING AND MARKING ANGLES.** ***Adjustable protractor head of versatile combination square has double-graduated, direct-reading scale for measuring and marking angles from 0° to 180°.***

▶ **MARKING ROUND STOCK CENTERS.** ***Center-finder head of combination square set allows the center of round stock to be marked quickly and easily. Secure the head to the rule by tightening the knurled lock bolt.***

or artist's blade. Blades produce very fine lines that also help in starting the cutting tool and avoiding ragged edges. An awl performs the same kind of job when you have to mark off points.

Work with a compass or trammel points to mark out circles or curved lines. Measure diameters with a caliper rule—its stepped jaw projections on inside measuring. Use a protractor for angles. For any small-scale work, use miniature tools—such as the sliding T-bevel known as a universal miter.

WORKING WITH SQUARES

One of the first things the neophyte woodworker learns is that *all* pieces of wood in a project must be smoothed flat and square (unless, of course, some other shape is called for). If you start a project by first making certain boards are square and true, you will have fewer problems down the line (as you lay out the pieces). Professionals always start a project by checking the stock to be used—it's a good habit for you to acquire as well.

The angle used most often in carpentry is the basic right angle—90°. To help you make perfect right angles there are three types of squares—the try, combination and steel, or framing. The task at hand determines the tool you should turn to. For transferring unusual angles, there's the T-bevel square.

USING A TRY SQUARE

The try square features a hefty wooden or metal handle that is designed to serve as a right-angle fence. The blade is graduated into inches and fractions of an inch. Generally, the try square is used for three main tasks: (1) to test a surface or edge for identical thickness throughout its length; (2) to test an edge or surface for squareness with its adjoining surface or edge; and (3) to serve as the guide for marking a line at a right angle to an edge or surface. Be sure that you hold the handle of the square flush against the edge or surface being used as reference.

USING A COMBINATION SQUARE

The combination square is the tool that combines the best features of the other squares. This requisite tool is most often used for marking and checking square (90°) and 45° angles. However, the square also serves as a marking gauge, depth gauge, level and straightedge rule. Many squares also feature a miniature scratch awl, called a scriber, housed in the handle. Use the scriber as a fine-line marker and to pinpoint exact positions. A small level vial, used to determine level and plumb, is also often housed in the handle.

A typical combination square consists of a handle, or head, and a 12-in.-long steel blade, or rule. The handle slides along the blade and is locked securely into position by tightening the locknut. The handle features two working edges—90° and 45°—that are used in conjunction with the blade for marking or checking the corresponding angle. On most squares, the blade can be removed from the handle and used as a ruler or straightedge.

Another common technique is to use the combination square as a marking gauge. Lock the handle into place at the desired distance from the end of the blade. Then, slide the handle

▶ **RULE PLUMBING.** ***Multipurpose tool's 18-in.-long rule folds for use as a straightedge and for easy storage. Here, the tool's level is being used to determine plumb.***

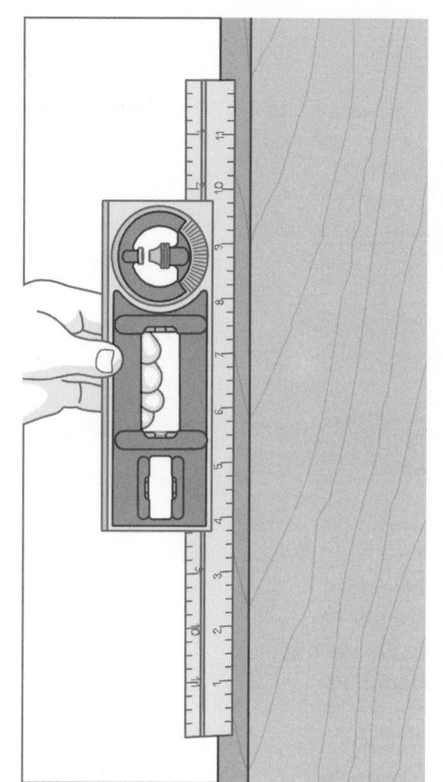

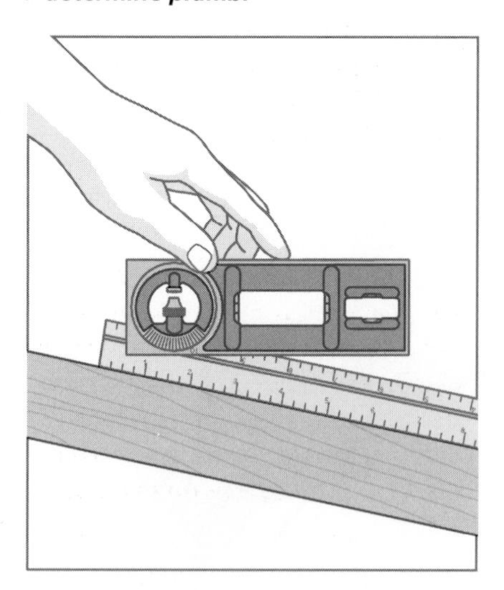

▲ **TAKING PITCH READINGS.** ***Reverse side of turret on multipurpose tool has 1/2-in. pitch graduations. Adjust the stock until it reads level, then read the pitch directly off the turret.***

▶ **MARKING DOVETAILS.** ***Solid brass marking gauge permits accurate layout of dovetail joints. The double-angled plate offers two different dovetail angles—one for hardwoods, one for softwoods.***

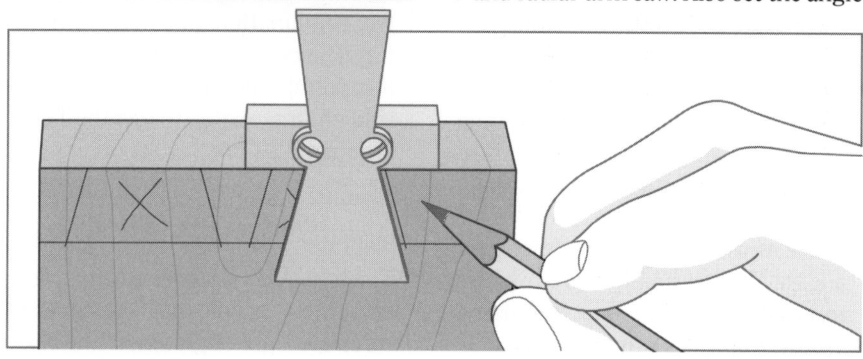

smoothly along the edge of the board while holding a sharpened pencil point against the end of the blade.

USING A BEVEL SQUARE

The sliding bevel square, or T-bevel, is indispensable for marking, transferring and checking angles. This simple tool features a steel blade from 6 to 12-in. long, with a 45° bevel point at one end. The other end of the blade is fitted into a slotted wooden or metal handle that has a wingnut for locking the blade where desired—anywhere from 0° to 180°. The T-bevel is helpful when you're marking odd angles and dovetail joints, and is especially useful when you must cut a board to fit an existing angle.

Use a protractor to set the T-bevel to a desired angle. Hold the tool's handle against the base of the protractor, align the blade's edge with the protractor centerline and adjust the blade to the desired angle. Lock the blade by tightening the wingnut.

Using the T-bevel to copy and transfer an existing angle is an even easier task. Simply adjust the blade to match the angle that you desire and then lock it securely in position. You can now transfer the copied angle to a workpiece or read the degrees of the angle directly off a protractor.

However, there is one important point about working with the T-bevel: No matter what particular type you use, you'll find that its locked position is not a positive one. Thus, once you have the angle desired, hold the tool securely without disturbing the blade while you lock it. Even after the blade has been locked, you'll find that it still can be moved with a relatively small amount of force. For this reason, you should *always* recheck the angle after you have secured it on the tool. And check it once again on the angle being copied *after* you have transferred it to the new piece to be cut.

Another useful application for a T-bevel is to check stationary tools when doing angular work. This includes setting exact blade angles on a table saw and radial-arm saw. Also set the angle of the worktable on drill presses, band saws and jointer fences. Although these tools have angle indicators, the scales often are inaccurate. Use the T-bevel to check and reset the indicators.

USING A STEEL SQUARE

The steel, or framing, square is large and flat, shaped in a right angle, and has many calculations on it. You can lay out any angle on a board using the square simply by measuring the graduations on the body (long arm) and the tongue (short arm) as they cross parallel lines.

◀ **MARKING STAIR STRINGERS.** ***Multipurpose layout tool accepts removable angle gauges that bolt to the edges of the guide. Align the gauges on the appropriate scales to mark the desired angle-cut, then hold the guide with the gauges against the board's edge and mark the angled line of cut.***

▼ **MARKING STUD LOCATIONS.** ***Partition layout tool aids in laying out wall studs (both middle partition and corners), squaring windows and doors, and scribing angles, rafters and seat notches. Here, tool is used to mark stud locations on sole plate.***

TYPICAL CARPENTRY ANGLES

ANGLE	TONGUE	BODY
30°	*12 in.*	*20 7/8 in.*
45°	*12 in.*	*12 in.*
60°	*12 in.*	*6 15/16 in.*
70°	*12 in.*	*4 3/8 in.*
75°	*12 in.*	*3 7/32 in.*
80°	*12 in.*	*2 1/8 in.*

Create an angle with a steel square by measuring the graduations on the body and tongue as they cross parallel lines. Above are the typical angles used in carpentry with the tongue and body graduations to achieve them.

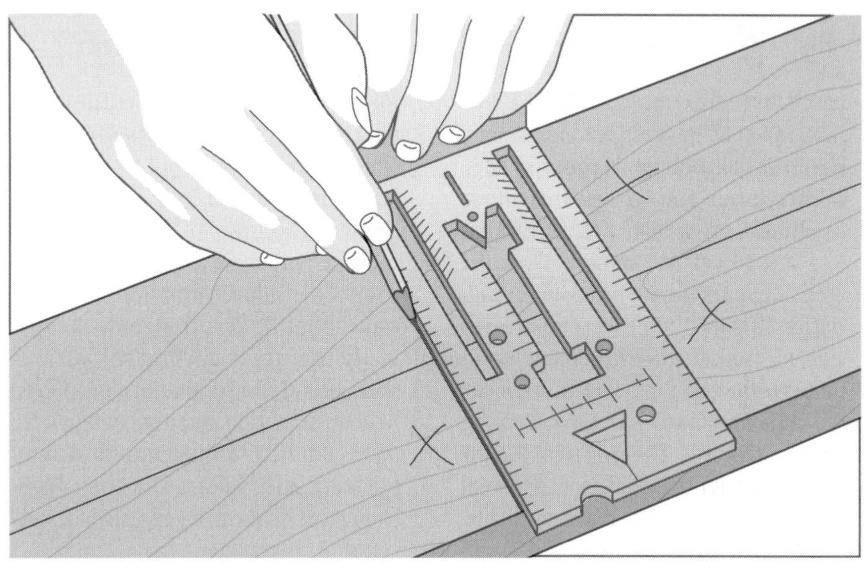

Most framing squares feature graduations of measurements on both sides of the tool—one in 16ths of an inch, the other in 10ths, 12ths, 16ths and 20ths. When you are using the square, grasp the body in your left hand and the tongue in your right hand. The face of the square is the side that is directed toward you when the blade is held in your left hand, with the heel pointed away from you. While you're working with the square, make sure the tongue is kept sitting flat across the face of your work.

VERSATILE COMBINATIONS

There are many types of multipurpose measuring and marking tools available on the market. One top-quality combination square set consists of a 12-in.-long tempered steel rule that is fitted with three different heads: a combination square, bevel protractor and center finder.

The precision-ground square head has a 90° face and a 45° miter face. The protractor head rotates on a revolving turret to read and mark angles from 0° to 180°. It has a double-graduated protractor scale and a spirit level vial. The Y-shaped center head finds centers quickly and accurately.

Use this tool as a try square, miter gauge, level, height gauge, plumb, center finder, scriber, straightedge rule or bevel protractor. Eighteen- and 24-in.-long rules are also available.

MULTIPURPOSE BUILDER'S TOOL

One precision builder's tool combines the functions of seven tools—a rule,

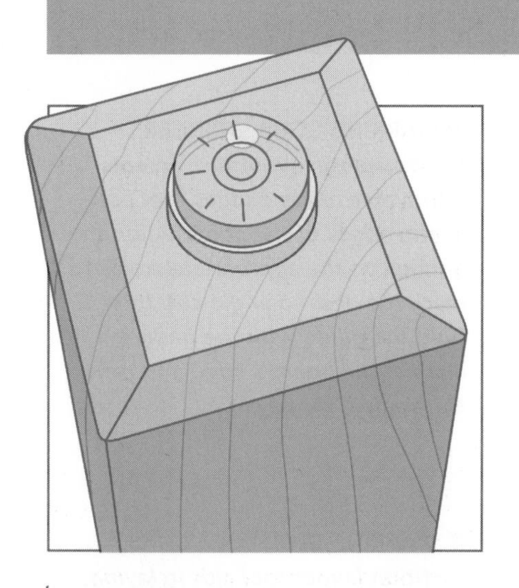

▲ PLUMBING POSTS. *A bull's-eye level set on top of a post shows plumb in both directions at once—as long as the post's top is perfectly square to the post's sides.*

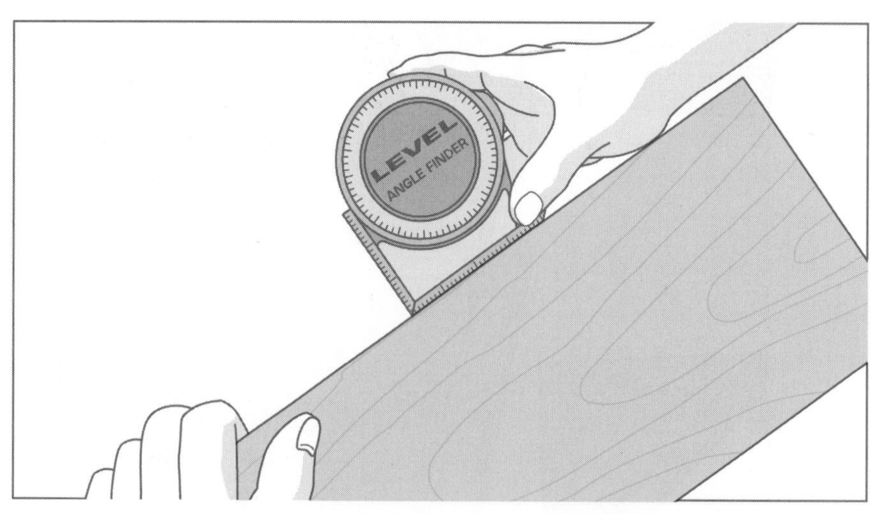

▲ CHECKING ANGLES. *An inclinometer (level and angle finder) gives needle readings from 0° to 90° in any quadrant. On the back of the tool, there is an angle and grade chart.*

square, level, protractor, bevel, plumb and pitch-to-ft. indicator. The handy, versatile tool is equipped with a 1½-in.-wide x 18-in.-long tempered steel rule that has inch graduations in 8ths, 16ths, 32nds and 64ths. The rule is mounted onto a revolving turret that lets you adjust the angle of the rule. One side of the turret has double graduations from 0° to 90°. The reverse side is graduated in ½-in. pitch increments. Also, the 9-in.-long stock is fitted with four level vials to determine level and plumb. The rule folds flat for use as a straightedge and for easy storage. A 24-in.-long rule is also available.

CARPENTER'S FRIEND

Measuring, marking and cutting take up a major part of a carpenter's day. One multipurpose layout tool is specifically designed to help increase the speed and accuracy of these three common carpentry functions.

Made of aluminum and weighing only about 32 oz., the guide is especially useful for cutting the various short wood blocks that are needed in new construction and remodeling jobs, such as solid bridging and short cripple studs and nailers. The guide has a sliding bar that can be adjusted for cutting blocks from 2 to 14½ in. long. Simply hold the guide against the end of the board and make the cut—no measuring or marking is necessary. But block-cutting is only part of what this time-saving tool can handle.

Use the guide to lay out and cut hip, valley and common rafters, ridge cuts, seat cuts and plumb cuts. A chart that is printed on the guide provides information on the allowable spans for ceiling and floor joists. The tool accepts two removable angle gauges that bolt to the edges of the guide. Align the gauges on the appropriate scales to mark the desired angle-cut. Then, hold

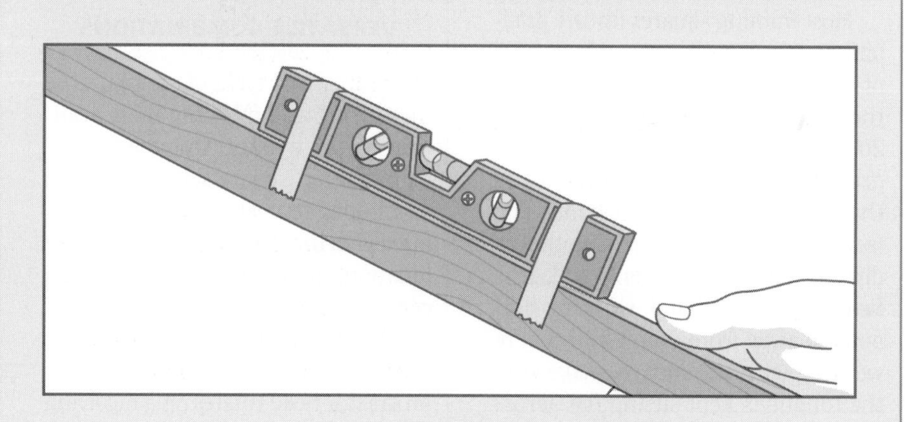

KEEPING ON THE LEVEL
As a substitute for a long level, tape a short level securely to the center of a long board. The board must be straight *and* have a uniform width.

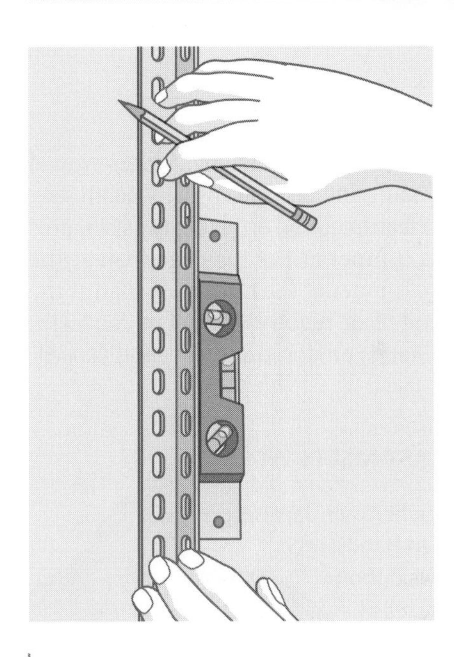

◀ **FREE-HANDS PLUMBING.** ***A torpedo level with magnetic edge holds tool on steel or iron workpieces, freeing hands to hold the project and mark its proper position.***

▼ **LEVELING OVER LONG SPANS.** ***Run a taut line between the endpoints of a long span and hook on a line level. Made of aluminum, the line level weighs under 1 oz. and does not sag the line. Flat bottom allows for tool's use as a surface level.***

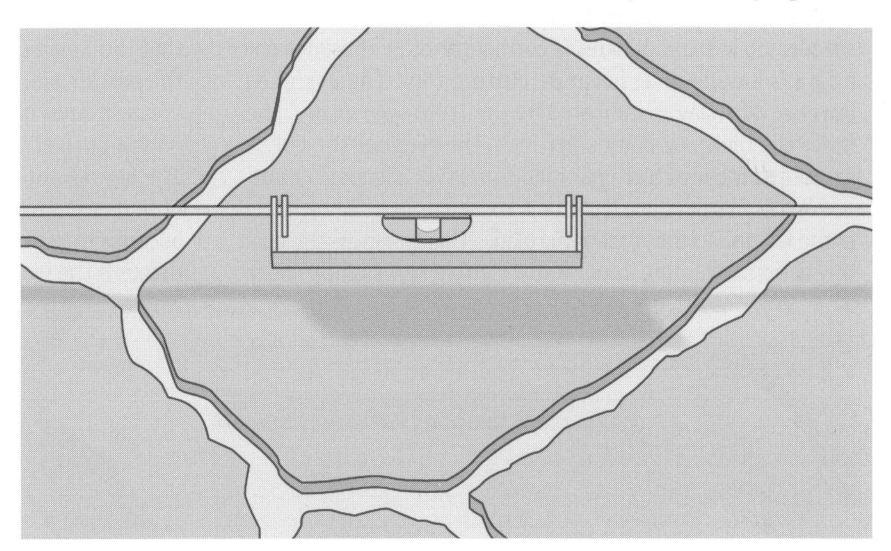

the guide with the two gauges against the board's edge and mark the angled line of cut. (Angle gauges are available at hardware stores and lumberyards.)

The guide is helpful for laying out and cutting stair stringers, too. Simply position the angle gauges for marking the desired size tread and riser.

The guide can also be used to mark rip cuts. Position the adjustable bar to the desired width cut and then slide the guide along the board's edge while marking the line of cut with a pencil.

Other timesaving features of the guide include a scale for speed-cutting any angle from 1° to 180° and a convenient ¼-in. equals 1-ft. scale used to estimate blueprint dimensions. The ¼-in. scale will measure up to 38 ft. The edge of the guide serves as a 13-in. straightedge ruler.

LAYOUT TIME-SAVER

Whether you're a professional carpenter or a do-it-yourself remodeler, a specialty wall partition layout tool may replace the steel square as your most helpful tool. It's a simple tool that is designed to aid in laying out wall studs (both middle partitions and corners), squaring windows and doors, and scribing angles, rafters and seat notches. Two pivot points show layouts for 2 x 4, 2 x 6 and 2 x 8 walls.

Made of a lightweight, noncorrosive aluminum alloy, this versatile tool can provide a helping hand to hold a chalkline or tape measure. It can also be used as a saw guide to make square cuts with a circular saw.

DOVETAIL GAUGE

When you're cutting dovetails by hand, marking the angles of the pins and tails accurately is vital in order to achieve tight-fitting joints. A simple dovetail gauge that provides two angles—one for hardwoods, one for softwoods—is a helpful aid. Position the gauge on the workpiece and then scribe along the edges of the template to mark the pin or tail. The guide's double-angled plate is pinned firmly to a ⅜ x ⅜ x 1½-in. base to permit marking angles up to 1-in. long.

WORKING WITH LEVELS

Using a level requires no special skill. Just make sure that both the base of the level and your work surface are absolutely free of debris before you position the tool.

Remember that a level is a precision tool that you'll be relying on for accuracy. Try to reduce the inevitable banging about that a tool suffers by never leaving the level where it may be knocked over, dropped, kicked or otherwise abused.

ACCURACY-TESTING LEVELS

Before purchasing a level, test it for accuracy. Place the level on a flat, even surface and note the position of the bubble. Then, reverse the tool end for end, keeping the same edge down. Now check the bubble's position a second time and compare it to the first reading. If the level is accurate, the bubble should come to rest in the same position for both readings. This is a good way to test old levels, too.

HANDSAWS

Whether you're a fine furniture builder, a house carpenter or an active do-it-yourselfer, the handsaw is an essential tool. Although the portable power saw is the choice for many cutting jobs, handsaws are far from obsolete. In fact, there has been a renewed interest in handsaws due partially to the advent of Japanese tools.

Presented here are 25 saws, each designed to handle a specific cutting task. The diverse collection includes standard Western and Japanese saws in various styles and sizes. Note that the tools shown, which represent a sampling of the wide range of saws available, will cut everything from logs to veneer and from steel to bricks.

Choosing a handsaw, as with any tool, depends on the specific job at hand. When the correct handsaw is used properly, it's an effective, accurate cutting tool. The designed purpose of a saw is indicated by the teeth. Generally, the fewer the teeth, or points, per inch, the rougher the cut. A greater number of teeth per inch (tpi) gives a smoother cut.

Nearly all saws have teeth that are set, or bent, alternately to the left and to the right of the blade. This enhances the cutting action and, more importantly, forms a kerf slightly wider than the blade's thickness to prevent binding. A taper-ground blade also prevents binding and helps to ensure smooth sawing. Taper grinding, a feature found on all quality saws, produces a blade that is thinner at the top edge than at the toothed edge. It's also thinner at the blade's toe than at the handle. A taper-ground blade requires less set on the teeth; therefore, a narrower kerf is produced and less effort is needed to make the cut.

EAST MEETS WEST

The biggest difference between Japanese handsaws and Western handsaws is that the Japanese saws cut on the pull stroke. Most Western saws cut on the push stroke. The key advantage of Japanese saws is that because they are pulled through the wood, the blades

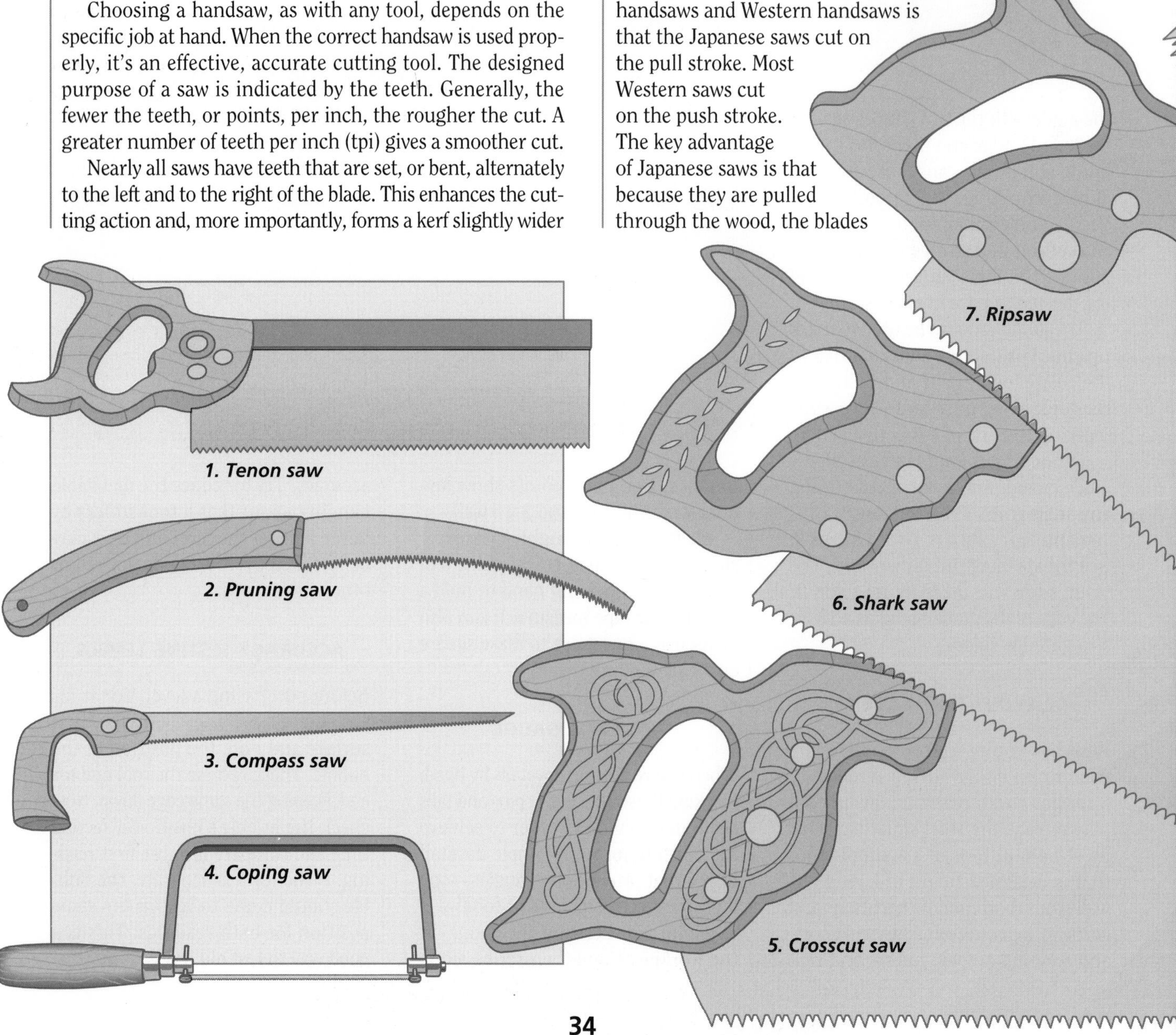

1. Tenon saw

2. Pruning saw

3. Compass saw

4. Coping saw

5. Crosscut saw

6. Shark saw

7. Ripsaw

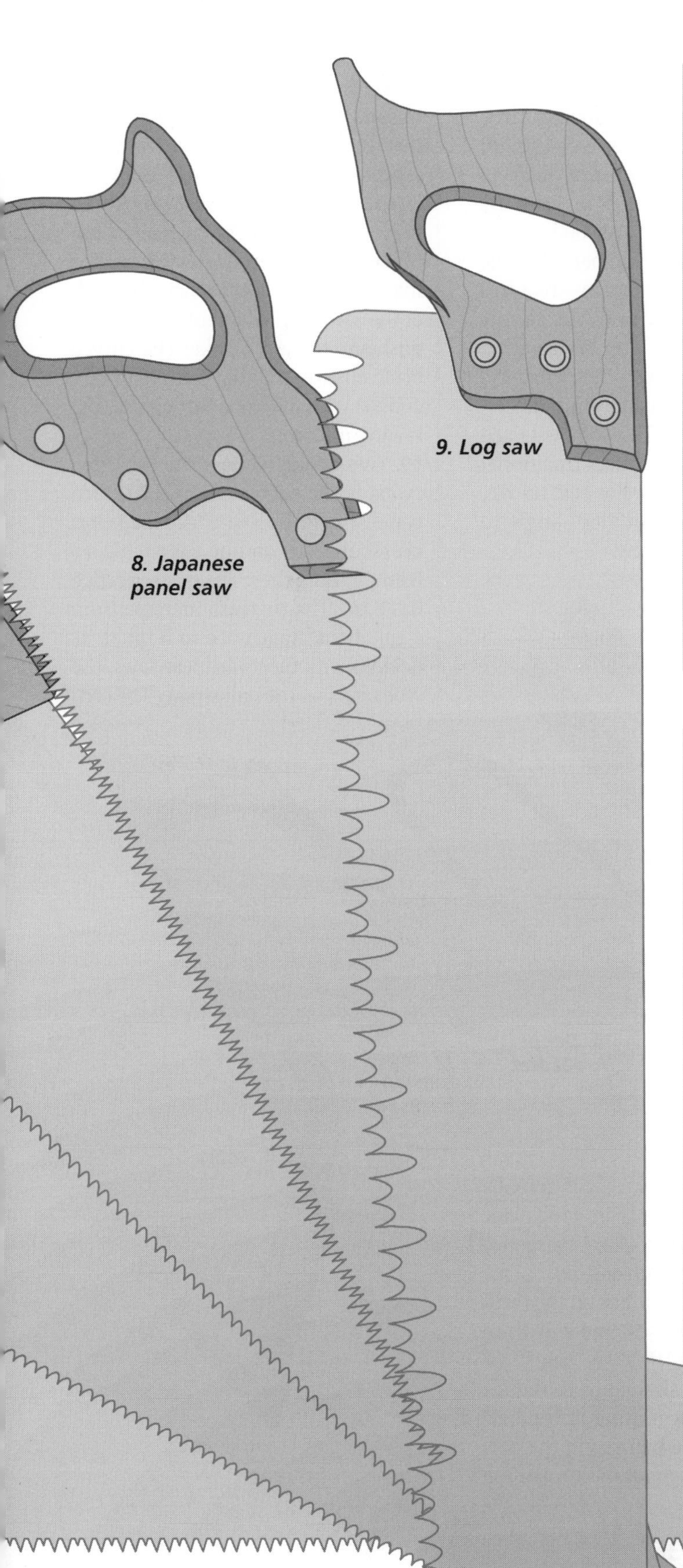

can be made virtually paper thin—a must when cutting precise, intricate joints. Western saw blades are made of heavy-gauge steel to prevent buckling when the saw is pushed. Learning how to use Japanese saws takes no special skills—only a little patience and practice.

You may already own some of the saws shown. Others you may want to add to your tool collection. A basic starter group of saws should include a ripsaw, crosscut saw, backsaw, compass saw and hacksaw. Then, simply add other saws as you need them. Let's look at each of the 25 saws shown.

1. Tenon saw—As its name suggests, this fine-toothed handsaw is used to cut tenons and other wood joints accurately. The tenon saw is similar to the backsaw except that it's shorter to offer greater control. The tenon saw shown has a 12-in.-long nickel-chrome alloy blade with 14 tpi. The saw blade is stiffened with a heavy spine of solid brass to prevent flexing. The red beech handle is attached to the blade with three brass screws.

2. Pruning saw—Here's an excellent saw for trimming trees and bushes. And since the curved blade folds back into the handle, the tool is convenient to take along on camping and

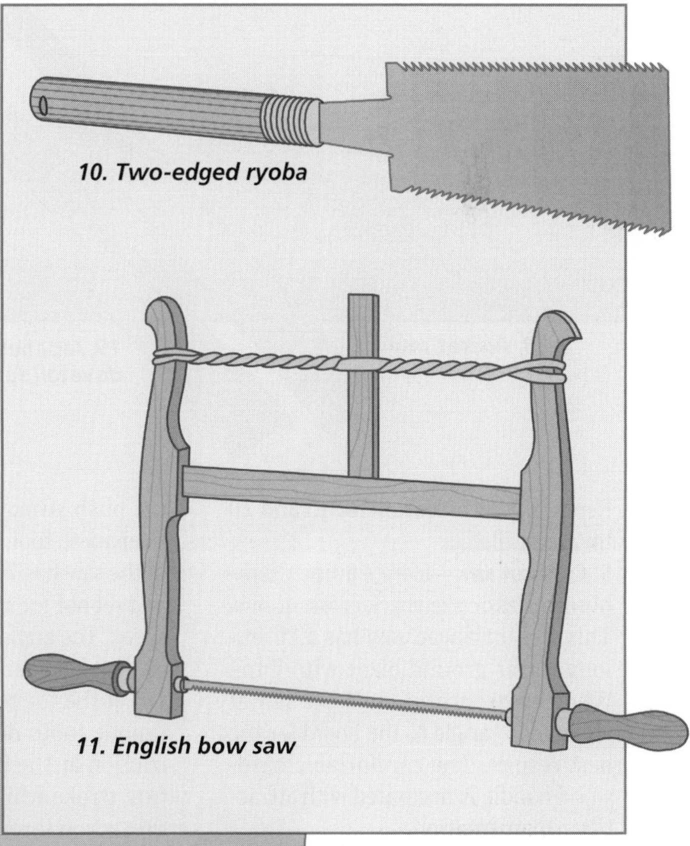

backpacking trips, too. The 10-in.-long blade has 5 tpi and it cuts on the pull stroke. It comes with a curved, lacquered hardwood handle.

3. Compass saw—Use this versatile saw for rough-cutting a variety of materials, including plywood, plasterboard, hardboard and most types of paneling. It's especially helpful for cutting access holes when installing pipes and electrical boxes. The saw's pointed, 14-in.-long blade is bolted to a hardwood, pistol-grip handle. Replacement blades are available.

4. Coping saw—For intricate curves and scroll work, this small-frame coping saw is the best choice. The coping saw makes a finer cut than the compass saw, and its removable blade permits shallow internal cutouts up to the depth of the tool's throat—which is 4½ in. This is accomplished by fitting the blade through an entry hole bored in the waste area, then attaching the blade to the frame to make the cut. Replacement blades of 10, 15 and 20 tpi are available.

5. Crosscut saw—Here's a fine example of a classic skewback crosscut saw. This well-balanced saw has a 26-in.-long, taper-ground blade with 7 tpi. When crosscutting, hold the saw at about a 45° angle to the board for the best results. The comfortable hardwood handle is decorated with attractive ornamentation.

6. Shark saw—This Western style handsaw features a razor-sharp Japanese blade with 7 tpi. The saw can crosscut and rip virtually all wood and wood composite materials, including particleboard, plywood and oriented strand board. The high-carbon-steel blade of this fast-cutting saw is 22 in. long; the handle is enameled hardwood.

7. Ripsaw—Ripping lumber—that is, sawing parallel to the grain—requires a large, heavy-duty saw. The ripsaw shown has a 26-in.-long blade with 5 tpi. The heavy-gauge, taper-ground blade is made from a chrome-nickel-molybdenum alloy. The walnut-stained hardwood handle features traditional wheat-grain carvings. For best results, keep a ripsaw held at a 60° angle to the board when sawing.

8. Japanese panel saw—Although it looks like a standard Western handsaw (and it even cuts on the push stroke), this saw is actually a Japanese tool. The 22-in.-long blade of the saw has 7 tpi that are sharpened and set not for smooth cutting, but for speed. The angle of attack on the teeth of the blade decreases gradually from 16° at the toe to 10° at the heel. This unique tooth design helps to reduce friction at the beginning of the cutting stroke while increasing the cutting action throughout the stroke. The saw is designed for crosscutting, but it can be used for ripping, too.

9. Log saw—Designed specifically for crosscutting logs and large timbers, this saw comes with a 28-in.-long blade that features 15 sets of three teeth. The sets of teeth are separated by deep gullets that remove sawdust quickly to prevent clogging. The toe end of the blade has smaller starter teeth. For maximum cutting efficiency, the teeth of the saw are filed to cut on both the push and the pull stroke. The curved blade ensures that the teeth maintain contact with the wood throughout the sawing motion.

10. Two-edged ryoba—The Japanese ryoba is the equivalent of a Western panel saw. Its double-edged blade has crosscut teeth on one edge with rip teeth on the other. The crosscut edge has 9 tpi. The rip teeth increase from 4 tpi at the blade's toe to 5 tpi at its heel. As with most Japanese saws, the ryoba cuts on the pull stroke. The cen-

12. All-angle saw

13. Pocket saw

14. Dozuki saw

15. Japanese dovetail saw

16. Deep-throat fret saw

17. High-tension hacksaw

ter of the blade is thinner than at the cutting edges to prevent binding.

11. English bow saw—Gentle curves and straight lines can be cut accurately with this handsome white beech bow saw. The narrow, 12-in.-long blade has 9 tpi. Tension of the blade is maintained by a twisted cord and toggle stick. By releasing the tension, you can rotate the blade 360° to the most convenient working position.

12. All-angle saw—Have you ever had difficulty cutting a workpiece because it was in an awkward position? The all-angle saw was designed to tackle such frustrating cutting chores. The saw features an adjustable handle that can be secured anywhere along the tool's bow, or frame. This allows the handle to be locked at the most convenient working position. The saw accepts a 6-in.-long blade and it comes with one woodworking blade (14 tpi) and one metal-cutting blade (32 tpi).

13. Pocket saw—This folding pocket saw accepts standard saber saw blades and reciprocating saw blades to handle a wide variety of cutting jobs. The saw folds like a jackknife to conceal the cutting edge. The 8-in.-long plastic handle has a spare-blade storage compartment and a positive blade lock that secures the saw in the open position. The saw comes with one all-purpose blade of 10 tpi.

14. Dozuki saw—The dozuki saw is the Japanese equivalent to the Western backsaw. The model shown features a 9 7/16-in.-long replaceable blade. The saw is equipped with a steel back support that adds rigidity to the blade. The 13 tpi, pull-cut stroke blade fits into a 10 3/4-in.-long, bamboo-wrapped wood handle. Use the dozuki to cut tenons and precise joints.

15. Japanese dovetail saw—Like the dozuki saw, this Japanese saw features a replaceable blade. But the dovetail saw comes with a shorter, stiffer blade to provide greater control when cutting dovetails and other tight-fitting joints. The very fine-cutting, 7-in.-long blade has 25 tpi. Maximum depth of cut is 1 3/4 in.

16. Deep-throat fret saw—The fret saw is designed to make intricate cuts in veneer and other delicate, thin-sheet materials. The saw frame holds a 5- or 6-in.-long blank-end jeweler's blade. Attach the blade so that the teeth are pointing down toward the handle. The saw's deep throat allows you to cut up to 12 in. from the edge of the work.

17. High-tension hacksaw—To cut metal quickly and smoothly, try this high tension hacksaw. The tool features a cranking handle and a tension indicator that allows you to apply just the right amount of tension on the blade. The proper amount of tension prevents the blade from flexing during the cut, which in turn helps the blade to last longer and cut easier. The blade can be installed at a 90° position or at a 45° angle for flush-cutting. The saw's comfortable, closed, die-cast aluminum handle gives excellent knuckle protection. The saw frame accepts 12-in.-long hacksaw blades.

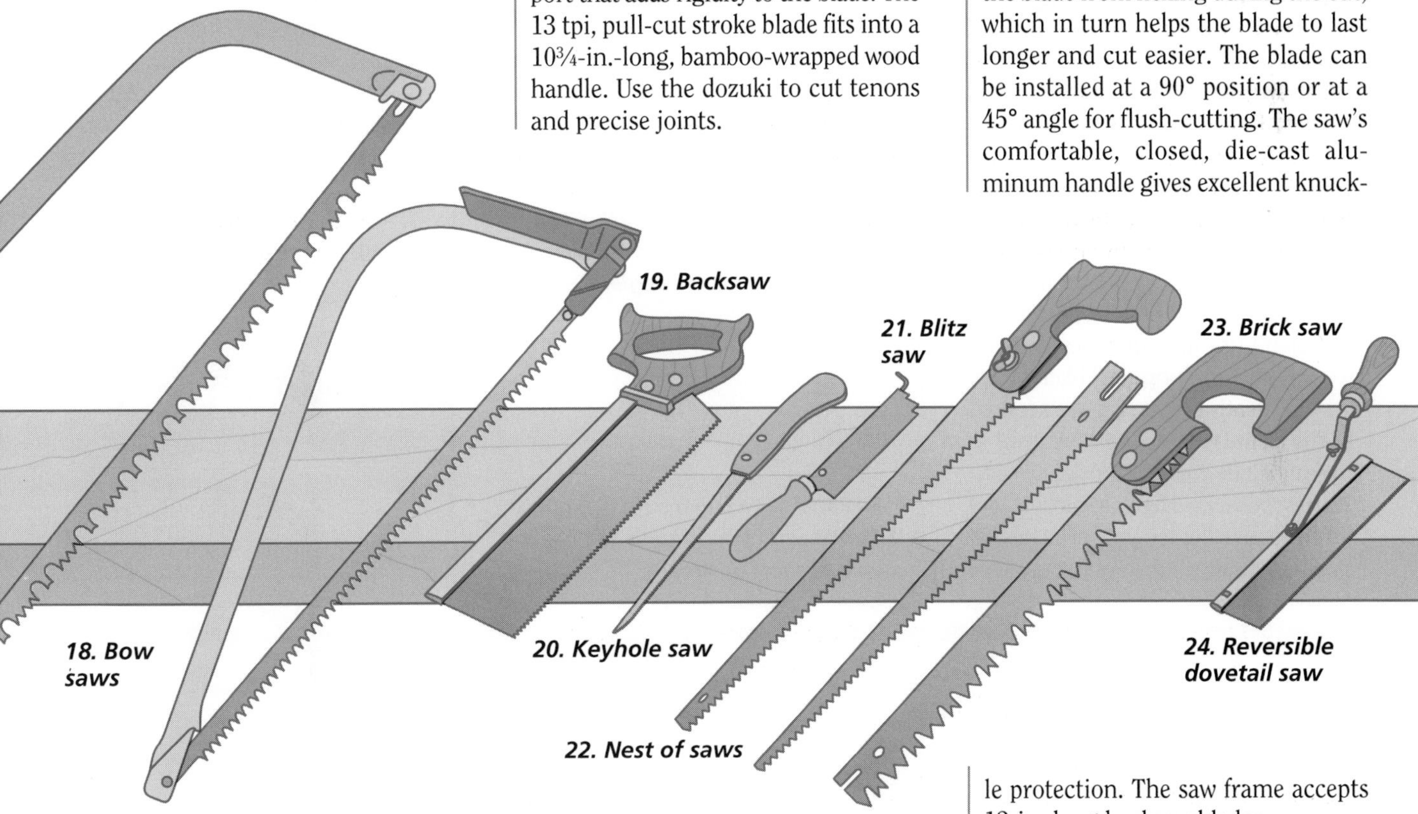

18. Bow saws—Here are two saws that make pruning and landscaping work easy. Each saw features a tubular steel frame with a quick-action blade-tensioning lever that snaps closed to form a handle. The 36-in. bow saw *(18, left)* is designed to tackle large pruning jobs and for sawing firewood. Use the 21-in. bow saw *(18, right)* for light pruning chores. Replacement blades are available for both saws.

19. Backsaw—Use this traditional backsaw to cut precise tenons and joints. Also use it in a miter box to crosscut stock to length. The saw has a 14-in.-long blade with 13 tpi. The teeth are bevel ground to ensure smooth cuts. A heavy steel spine is added to the blade to provide stiffness, making precision cutting easy. Two brass screws secure the hardwood handle to the blade.

20. Keyhole saw—Unlike its Western counterpart, this Japanese keyhole saw has a short, narrow blade that cuts on the pull stroke. The 15½-in.-long saw has an 8-in.-long blade with 12 tpi. Use this agile saw to cut small keyholes, curves and slots.

21. Blitz saw—This versatile German-made saw comes with three interchangeable blades for cutting wood, metal and plastic. Use the saw for delicate slotting and to cut small dovetails. A curved tip on the frame's end serves as a second handle, permitting two-hand use during super-delicate work. The 5-in.-long steel blades have a ¾-in. depth of cut and are secured to the frame with a single wingnut—making blade changes quick and easy.

22. Nest of saws—Here's a valuable tool for the active homeowner. The nest of saws is actually four saws in one. This

▲ CROSSCUTTING. *Use a thumb knuckle as a guide to start crosscut saw precisely on waste side of cutting line. Draw the blade back a few times to gain entry, then push the blade forward at a 45° angle.*

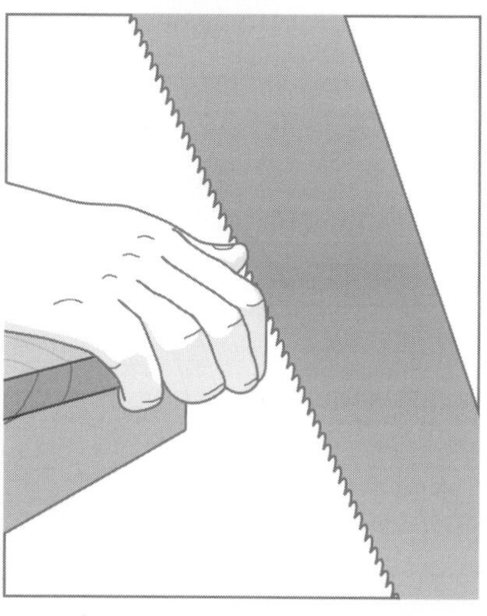

► RIPPING, 1. *To begin a rip cut, guide the blade with your thumb and use a couple of short upstrokes.*

TIP

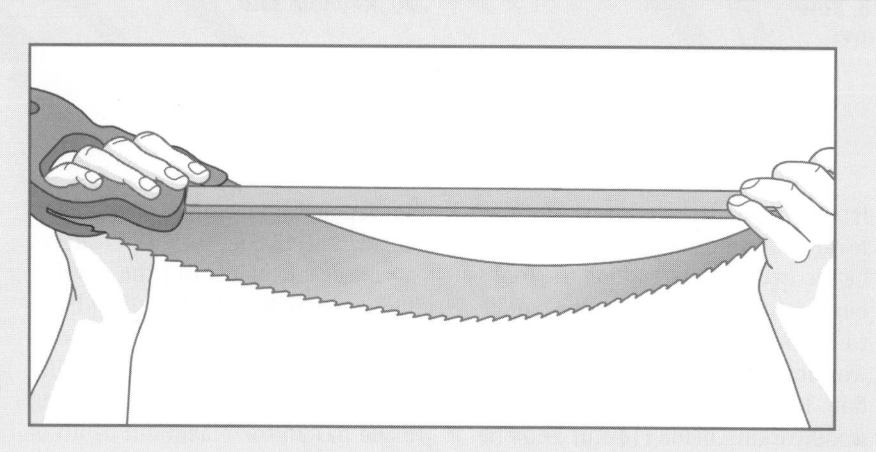

CHECKING TENSION OF A RIPSAW
To check the tension of a ripsaw, flex it slightly and place a straightedge across the blade. The blade should form a perfect arc—an indication of a well-balanced saw.

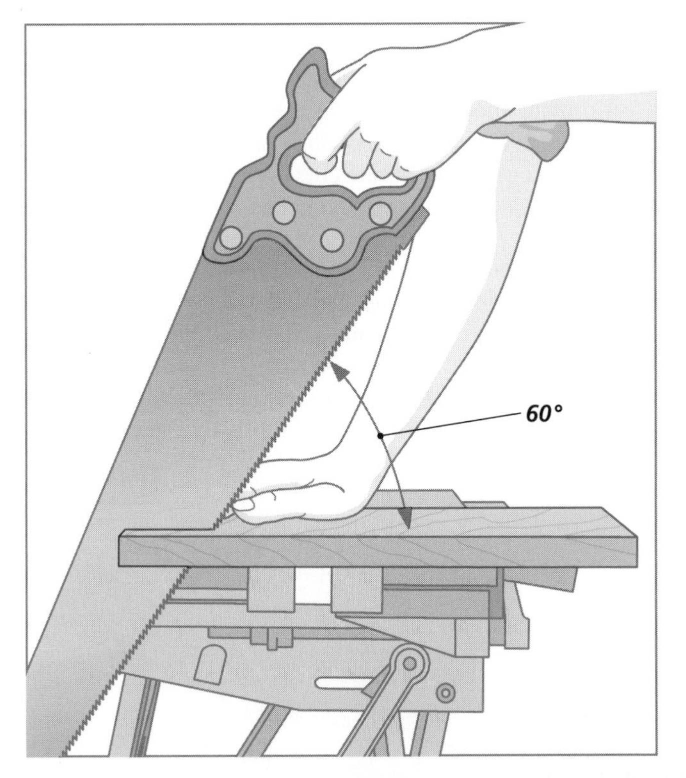

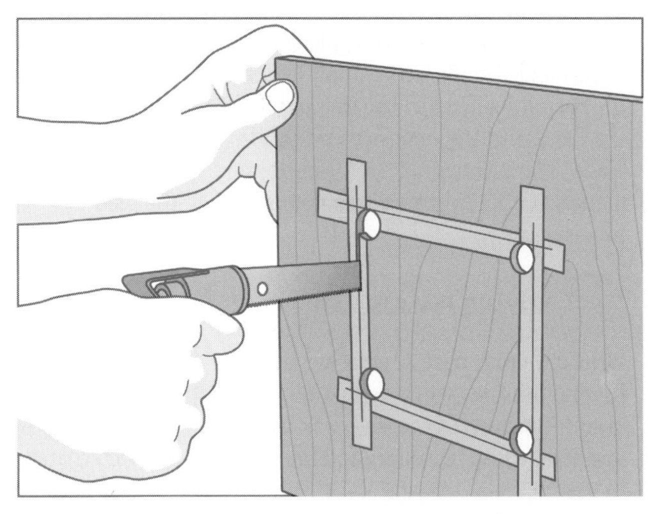

▲ **MAKING INTERNAL CUTS.** ***Use a compass saw to make internal cuts. Bore a blade entry hole at each corner, then cut out waste between holes. Cut lines drawn on masking tape aid visibility.***

◀ **RIPPING, 2.** ***Once the kerf is started, make smooth, full downstrokes. Hold the saw at 60° angle to work surface.***

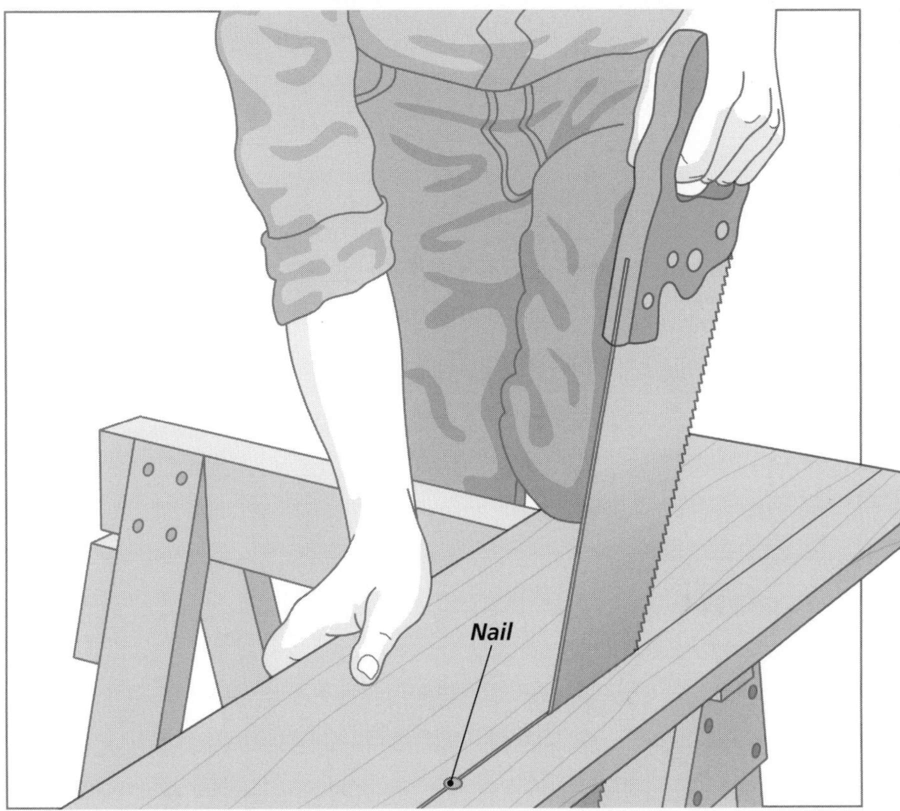

▲ **RIPPING, 3.** ***On long rip cuts, the kerf may close and bind the blade. To prevent binding, insert a nail or wedge to spread the kerf open.***

versatile tool comes with three interchangeable blades (one blade has two cutting edges) to handle many cutting jobs around the home and yard. The hardwood pistol-grip handle is shown holding a 16-in.-long double-edged blade that has fast-cutting pruning teeth on one edge opposite a crosscut edge with 7 tpi. The tool also comes with a 14-in.-long compass blade (7 tpi) and a square-ended 10-in.-long finishing blade (9 tpi). A quick-change wingnut and bolt hold the steel blades securely to the handle.

23. Brick saw—You may not have to saw bricks very often, but when you do, this is the saw to use. This specialized tool is designed to cut magnesia bricks and most furnace-lining insulating bricks. The coarse-cutting 15-in.-long blade of the tool cuts on both the push and the pull stroke.

24. Reversible dovetail saw—Cut tight-fitting dovetail joints with this lightweight, versatile saw. The tool's offset handle permits you to cut flush to the work's surface. And the handle can be positioned on either end of the saw blade to accommodate both left- and right-handed craftsmen. Simply loosen the spring-loaded locking nut and flip the handle to the opposite end of the blade. The saw has a 1⅞ x 10-in.-long blade with 13 tpi to ensure smooth, precise cuts.

BUYING HANDSAWS

When you purchase a handsaw, make it your practice to go with a quality brand. Because of the way it is used, saw steel must be tough and hard in order to hold a cutting edge. An accurately tempered saw will ensure a long-lasting cutting edge, yet provide the resilience to withstand buckling. The steel must permit filing and setting of the teeth.

Today, most types of handsaws are taper ground; that is, the entire blade is tapered from teeth to back (spine). Without this fine, wedge-like shape, the blade would bind or buckle—an all too common problem with many inexpensive saws. Saw teeth are also set—alternately bent outward—to create a kerf slightly wider than the body of the blade. Hold out the saw at arm's length to check its teeth for uniform set. A poorly set saw will cause inaccurate cuts every time it is used.

When choosing a saw, make sure you pick it up and heft it about. The handle must feel comfortable in *your* hand; you're the one who will be using it. And the handle should be designed to ensure that your sawing energy—your cut stroke—is directed straight to the cutting teeth and not simply against the back of the saw. A well-

▲ **USING A MITER BOX, 1.** ***A miter box guides a fine-tooth backsaw for cutting accurate 45° miter and 90° square cuts. Hold the workpiece securely to keep it from shifting.***

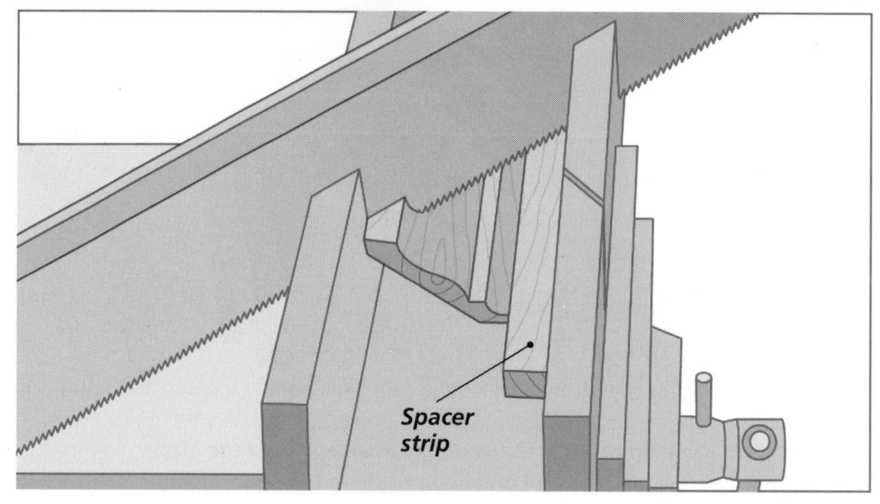

► **USING A MITER BOX, 2.** ***When cutting crown molding, insert a spacer strip to prop it up at the correct angle. Make a 45° cut to produce a compound-angle cut.***

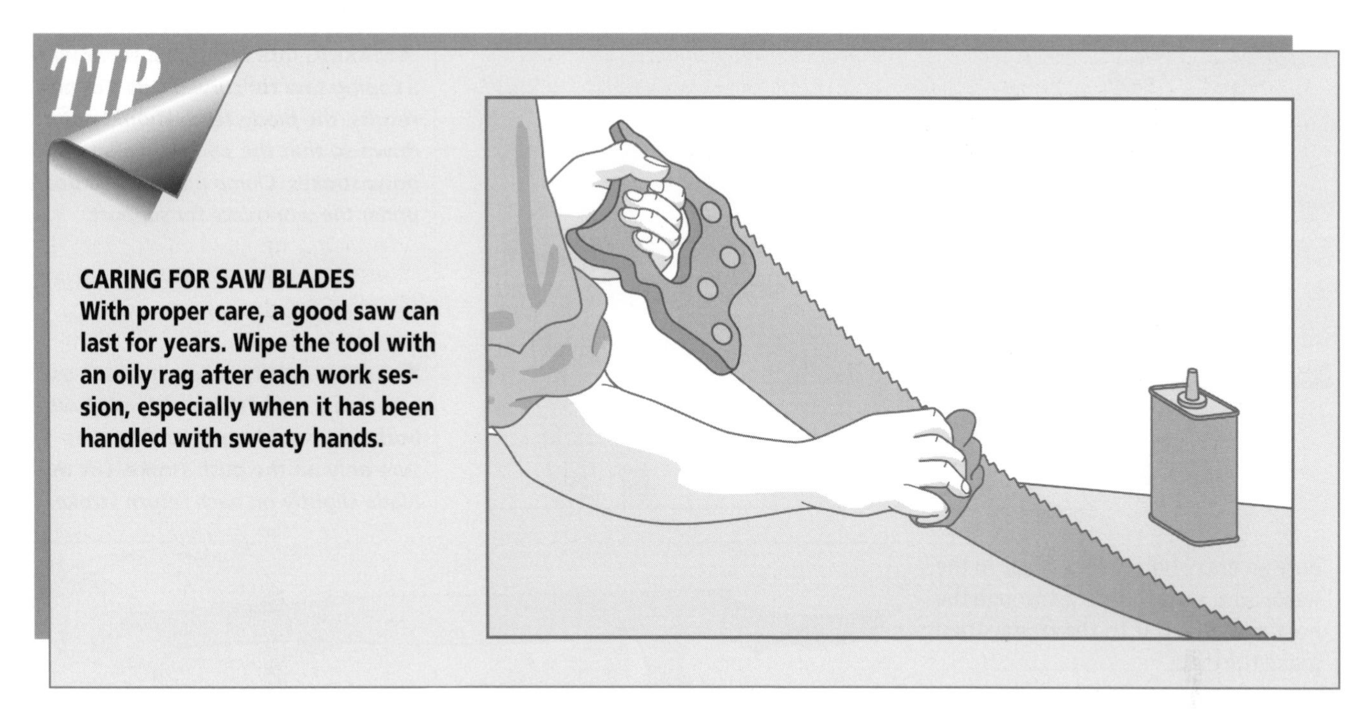

CARING FOR SAW BLADES
With proper care, a good saw can last for years. Wipe the tool with an oily rag after each work session, especially when it has been handled with sweaty hands.

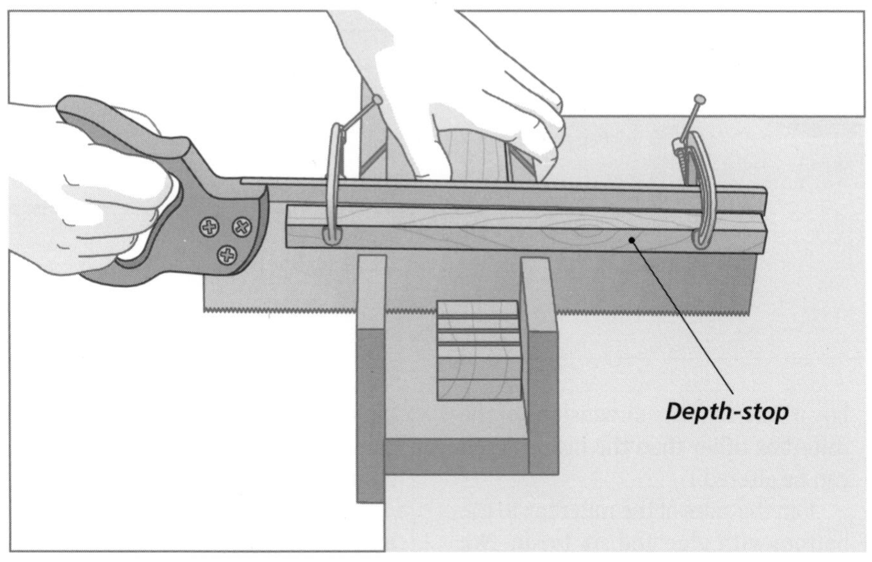

▲ USING A MITER BOX, 3. *Clamp a wood strip to the saw blade to act as a depth-stop—used here to cut halfway through a board to produce a half-lap joint.*

designed and properly located handle means that cutting with the saw will be easy on your wrist.

RIPSAW VERSUS CROSSCUT SAW

Ripsaws and crosscut saws may seen similar in appearance, but a close look at their teeth reveals quite a difference. Because a ripsaw cuts with the grain, the tool meets less resistance than a crosscut saw. Therefore, the ripsaw has larger and fewer teeth than the crosscut saw.

The ripsaw, used to cut lengthwise in the direction of the grain, has teeth that are filed straight across to form chisel-like points. These teeth cut by chipping away the wood. The crosscut saw, used for cutting across the grain, has teeth that are beveled on both sides like knife edges. The blade cuts by slicing through the wood fibers.

Both types of saws (and the others shown) are classified by the number of teeth per inch. This factor determines whether the saw will cut fast but rough—lower teeth per inch—or slow and smooth—higher teeth per inch. Ripsaws, for example, are commonly 5 or 6 tpi while crosscut saws are usually 7 or 8 tpi. If you intend to use the saw most often on thick stock, buy one with coarse teeth. Conversely, for thin stock, you should pick a saw with finer teeth.

COMPASS VERSUS COPING SAW

The compass saw is used for making cuts where the ripsaw or crosscut saw won't fit, and for cutting curves and internal cutouts. For intricate curves and scroll work, however, the coping saw is the better choice. It makes a finer cut and its removable blade allows for shallow internal cutouts up to the depth of the tool throat. To do this,

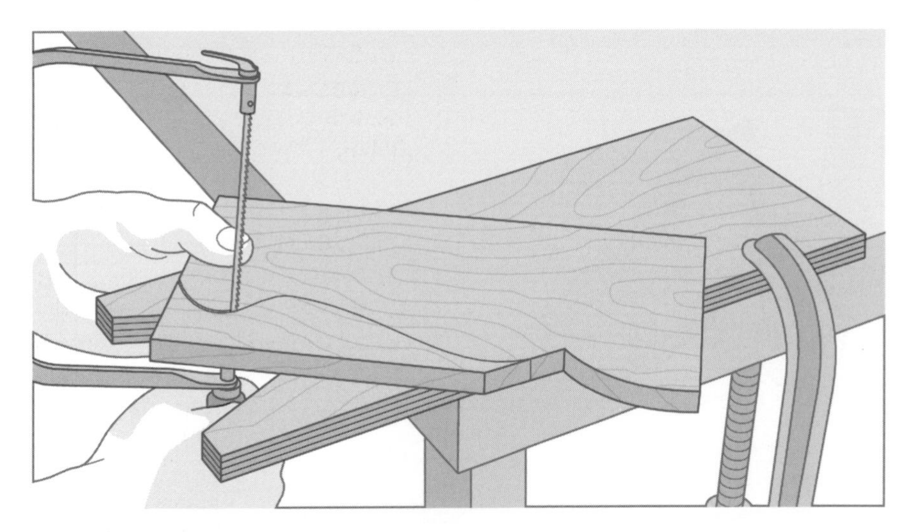

◀ **MAKING CURVED CUTS.** ***Work with a coping saw for curved cuts. For best results, the blade teeth should point down so that the saw works on pulled downstrokes. Clamp a V-notched board under the workpiece for support.***

▼ **CUTTING METAL.** ***To cut metal, use a hacksaw. Hold the tool firmly with both hands and apply cutting pressure only on the push stroke. Lift the blade slightly on each return stroke.***

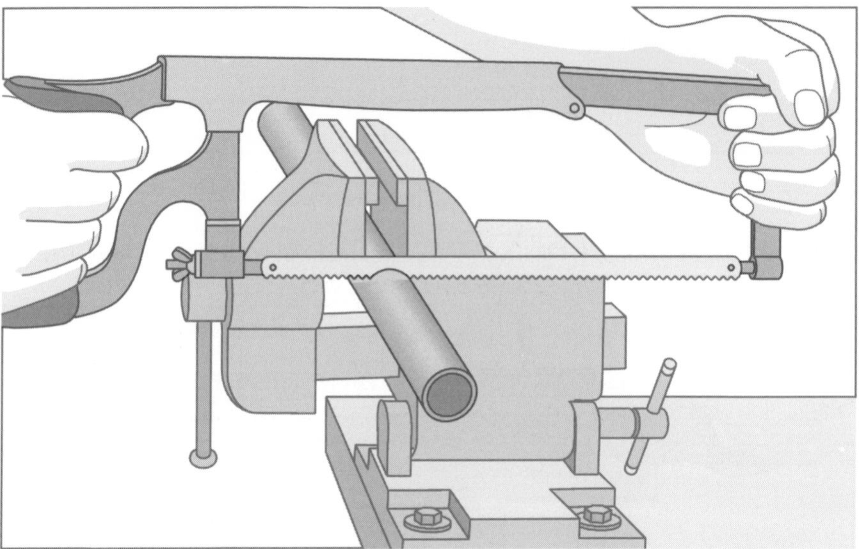

bore an entry hole for the blade in the waste area, slide the blade through the hole and attach it to the frame, then make the cut.

DOVETAIL VERSUS BACKSAW

The dovetail and backsaws also resemble each other. Both have a thin blade with fine teeth and a stiff spine across the top to keep the blade rigid. And both excel at making precise, clean cuts. The dovetail saw is ideal for dovetail depth cuts and for trimming off installed dowel plugs flush with the surface. For cutting tenons and dovetail joints too deep for the dovetail saw, use a backsaw.

BACKSAW AND MITERBOX

Use the backsaw in a miterbox for making accurate 90° square and 45° miter cuts—essential for finishing trim, picture frames and other small-dimension work. You can make a miterbox with three 18-in.-long pieces of maple, birch or beech. Make the bottom with 4-in. x 1½-in. stock and use ¾-in. stock for the sides.

The inside depth of the miterbox must be ⅛ in. less than the height of the saw blade—as measured from the teeth to the bottom edge of the spine. Allow for an overhang of 2 in. on the bottom edge of one side of the miterbox. (Note that the dimensions of the miterbox other than the inside depth can be altered.)

Join the sides of the miterbox to the bottom with glue and six 1½-in. No. 8 screws. The miterbox described is of a size that permits you to make a 90° slot and two 45° angle slots—one to the left, one to the right—starting 4 in. from one end. If desired, you can make additional slots for other angles such as 22½° and 30°.

The accuracy of your miterbox will depend entirely on how accurately you cut the slots. Don't try to cut the slots freehand. Instead, clamp wood blocks to the interior sides of the miterbox to guide the saw and ensure perpendicular slots. While cutting the slots, the spine of the saw should be supported securely in position by the blocks.

When using the miterbox, clamp its overhanging bottom edge in a vise. Hold the work firmly in the miterbox to keep it from shifting and start cutting by making a few light backstrokes to establish a starting kerf for the saw. Continue the cut applying only light pressure on the saw, allowing the slots of the miterbox to guide the blade.

CUTTING DOVETAIL JOINTS

The classic dovetail joint features interlocking dovetails and pins. It is frequently used for drawer construction

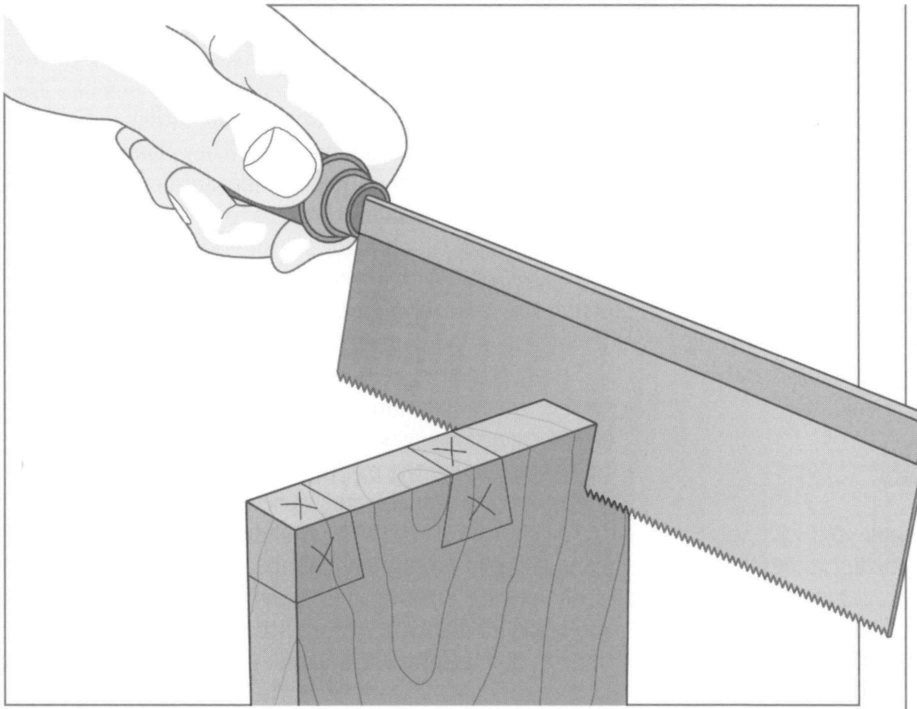

▲ **CUTTING DOVETAILS, 1.** ***Clearly mark waste, then make dovetail depth cuts first. Use fine-tooth dovetail saw and be sure to cut on waste side of line.***

▼ **CUTTING DOVETAILS, 2.** ***Make crosscuts between dovetails using coping saw. Make sure that the blade follows the line on both sides of the board.***

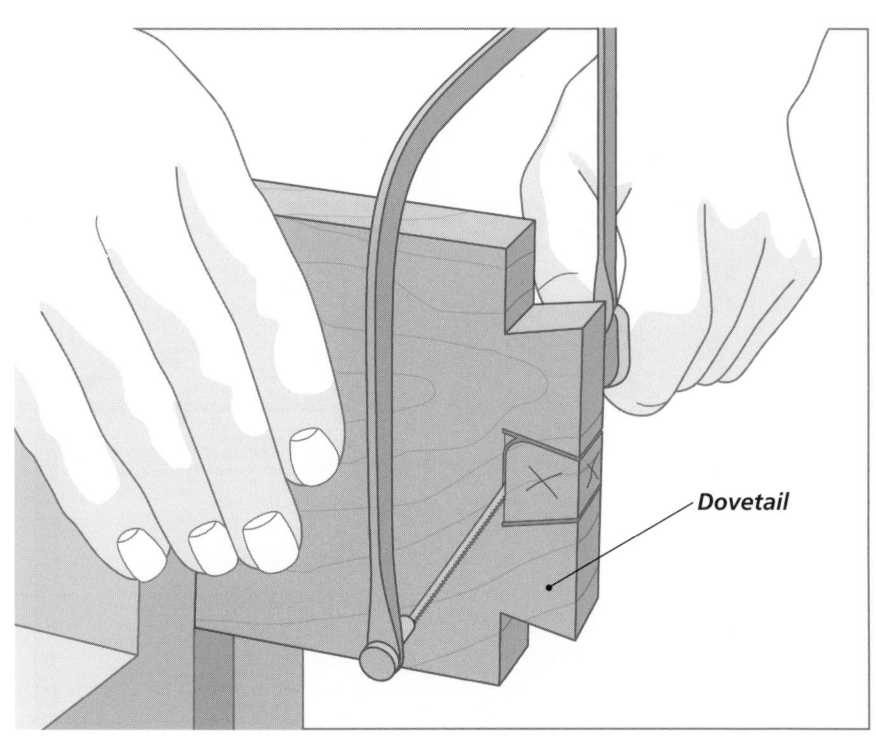

and other assemblies in high-quality furniture. With a precise fit, the joint is as strong as it is eye-catching—and will hold even if the glue fails.

There are numerous ways to cut the dovetail joint with power tools. But hand cutting the joint will help you to develop your hand-tool skills and at the same time provide you with the real sense of satisfaction associated with traditional building methods.

Begin by laying out and cutting the dovetail member first, then use this board as a template for the pins of the mating board. The angle of the dovetails relative to the edge of the board should be about 80°. However, the size and spacing of the dovetails and pins are a matter of personal preference. Just make sure that the half pins at the top and bottom of the joint are as wide as they are deep to avoid having them break off.

Work with a sharp pencil to lay out the dovetail joint precisely on the first board. Use a combination square to mark the edges and a T-bevel square to mark the surfaces. Clearly mark the waste to be cut on both the edges and the surfaces.

Cut out the bulk of the waste with a dovetail saw and a coping saw. Be sure that you cut on the waste side of the lines and make sure that the blade follows the lines on both sides of the board. Trim the edges of the sawcuts with a sharp chisel. Use a knife to clean out corners that cannot be reached with the chisel.

When the dovetail cuts are complete, use the first board as a template to establish the position of the mating pins on the other board. Use a utility knife to mark the pins with precision. Cut the pins the same way as you did the dovetails. Trim the sides of the pins square with the chisel before cleaning the crosscuts.

Test-fit the joint frequently to check your progress. Mark any high spot with a soft pencil, then use the chisel to carefully shave it to fit.

PLANES

More than any other tool, the hand plane evokes strong images of handcrafted woodworking. In fact, the plane—unlike many other tools found in the workshop—is strictly a *wood*working tool. It's the one tool that provides today's woodworkers with the strongest link to Old World craftsmen.

The hand plane is one of the world's original woodworking tools, dating back more than 2,000 years. The tool's original design and principle, however, have remained relatively unchanged until today.

TYPES OF PLANES

As shown here, hand planes are available in a wide variety of sizes, shapes and configurations, featuring bodies that are either of wood or of steel. Nonetheless, despite their many apparent differences, planes are tools that actually can be divided into two principal categories: bench planes and specialty planes.

Generally, bench planes are used to flatten and smooth large wood surfaces and long edges. They characteristically have large, flat soles and straight, square blades. Bench planes are commonly available in lengths from 8½ to 24 in.

When using bench planes to smooth the rough surface of a board, start with a jack plane followed by a smoothing plane. Use a larger plane, such as a trying plane, for the smoothing of long, uneven edges.

Specialty planes are designed for making specific cuts, such as shaping various molding profiles and cutting rabbets, tongues, grooves, dadoes and other joints. Some specialty planes, like the multiplane, feature interchangeable blades that are available in a variety of shapes and sizes.

The choice between a wood-bodied plane and an all-steel plane is based largely on personal preference, since both types perform equally well. Many woodworkers find that wood-bodied planes are more attractive and easier to use since they are lighter than steel planes. Also, their wood soles won't mar the workpiece. The two greatest advantages

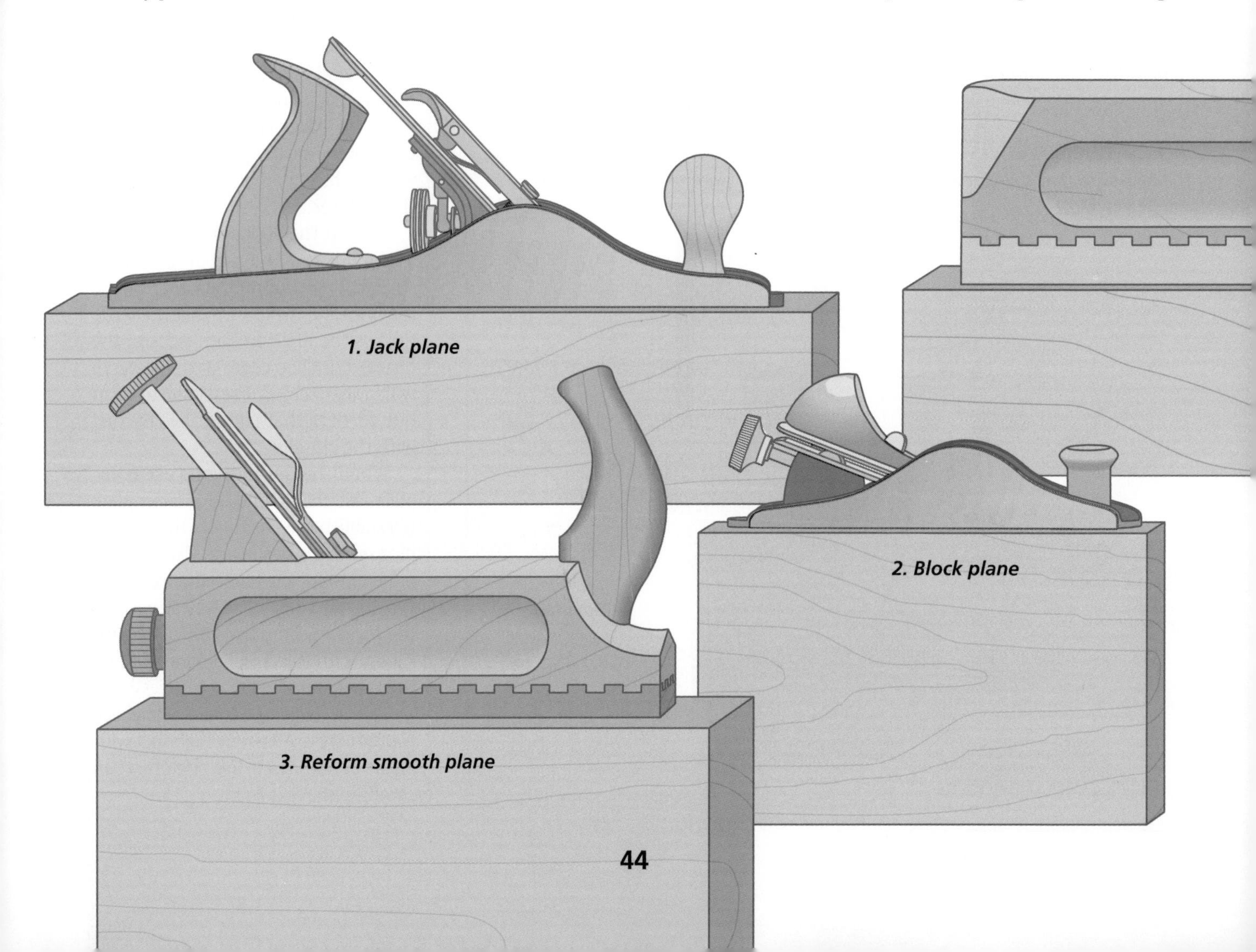

of steel-bodied planes are that they're available in a much greater variety than wooden planes and they offer more precise control and adjustment of the blade, known as the iron. Many wooden planes use a wood wedge arrangement to secure the iron. Some planes combine the best features of both tools—a wood body with a precise steel adjustment mechanism. Now, let's take a close look at the planes shown.

1. Jack plane—The all-purpose jack plane is considered the most useful of all bench planes. Use it to smooth rough boards and flatten uneven surfaces. This top-quality jack plane has long grooves machined in its sole that are designed to help make the tool slide easier—especially on resinous woods—by breaking the suction between the sole and the workpiece. The plane has a 2½ x 14-in.-long sole and two hardwood handles. It comes with a 2-in.-wide tungsten vanadium steel plane iron.

2. Block plane—The block plane is a tool that is designed for trimming end grain. Also use it for smoothing small wood pieces and for edge-planing plywood, particleboard and even plastic laminate. The block plane's major differences from a bench plane are that the iron is held at a low angle—21° on this particular model—and it's installed with the bevel facing *up*. The block plane features a 2 x 7-in.-long sole with a 1⅝-in.-wide iron.

3. Reform smooth plane—Feature for feature, this is clearly one of the finest planes you can work with. This smooth plane features a special, patented blade adjustment mechanism that provides you with supersensitive control of the

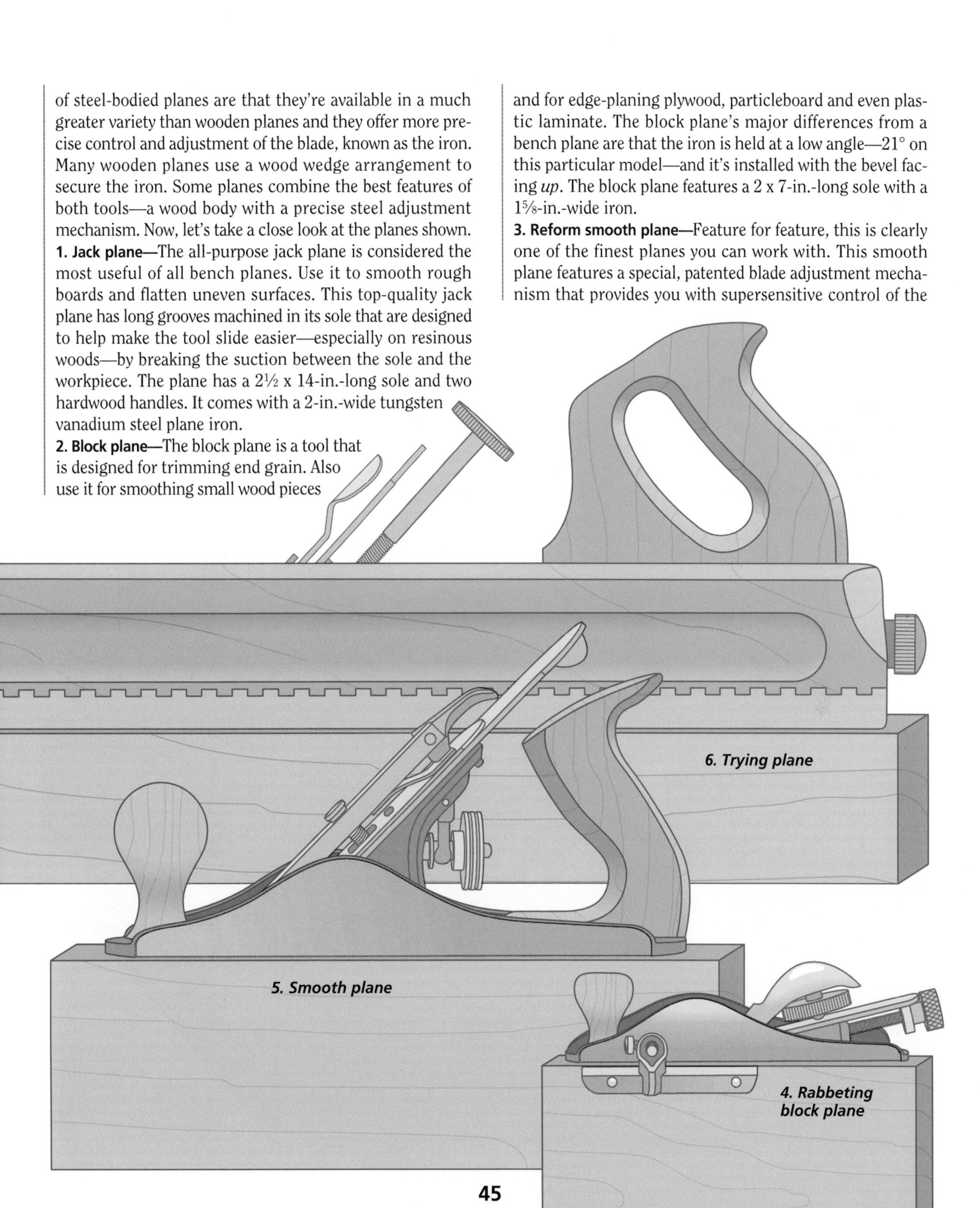

plane iron. A spring-tensioned rod that pulls the iron back tightly against the body helps to eliminate chatter, which in turn promotes smooth planing. This handsome tool features a lacquered pearwood body with a sole of lignum vitae—a super-hard, self-lubricating wood that secretes natural oils to make planing easier. The plane also comes with an adjustable shoe cut into the sole that allows you to narrow or widen the space in front of the protruding iron. Generally, the harder the wood, the narrower the mouth setting. The 2½ x 8½-in.-long plane comes with a 1⅞-in.-wide iron.

4. Rabbeting block plane—This tool is a replica of a famous skew-blade rabbeting block plane that was discontinued in the 1930s. As compared to a standard block plane, this tool cuts much easier and cleaner—thanks to the plane iron's super-low 12° skewed angle. The plane's right side is removable for use as a rabbeting plane. It comes with an adjustable fence and a 1½-in.-wide iron. The 1⅞ x 6⅞-in.-long professional-quality plane is made of cast manganese bronze.

5. Smooth plane—Designed for general-purpose planing, the smooth plane is often used after the jack plane for final finishing. This popular, easy-to-handle plane features a 2½ x 9¾-in. cast-iron body that has an adjustable mouth opening.

6. Trying plane—The great length of this plane—nearly 24 in.—makes it ideal for planing long, straight edges and for leveling broad, uneven surfaces. The tool is equipped with the same patented blade adjustment mech-

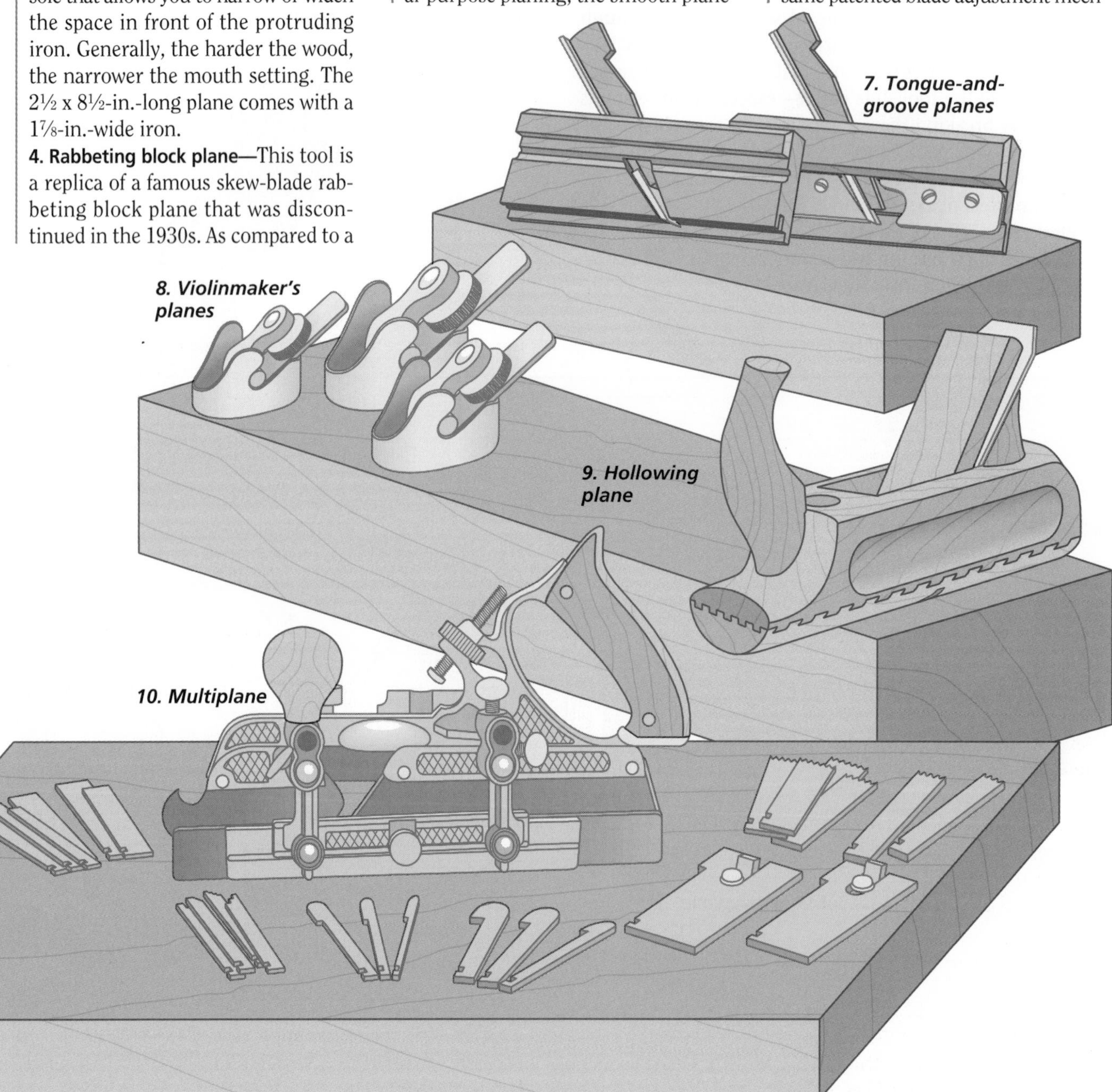

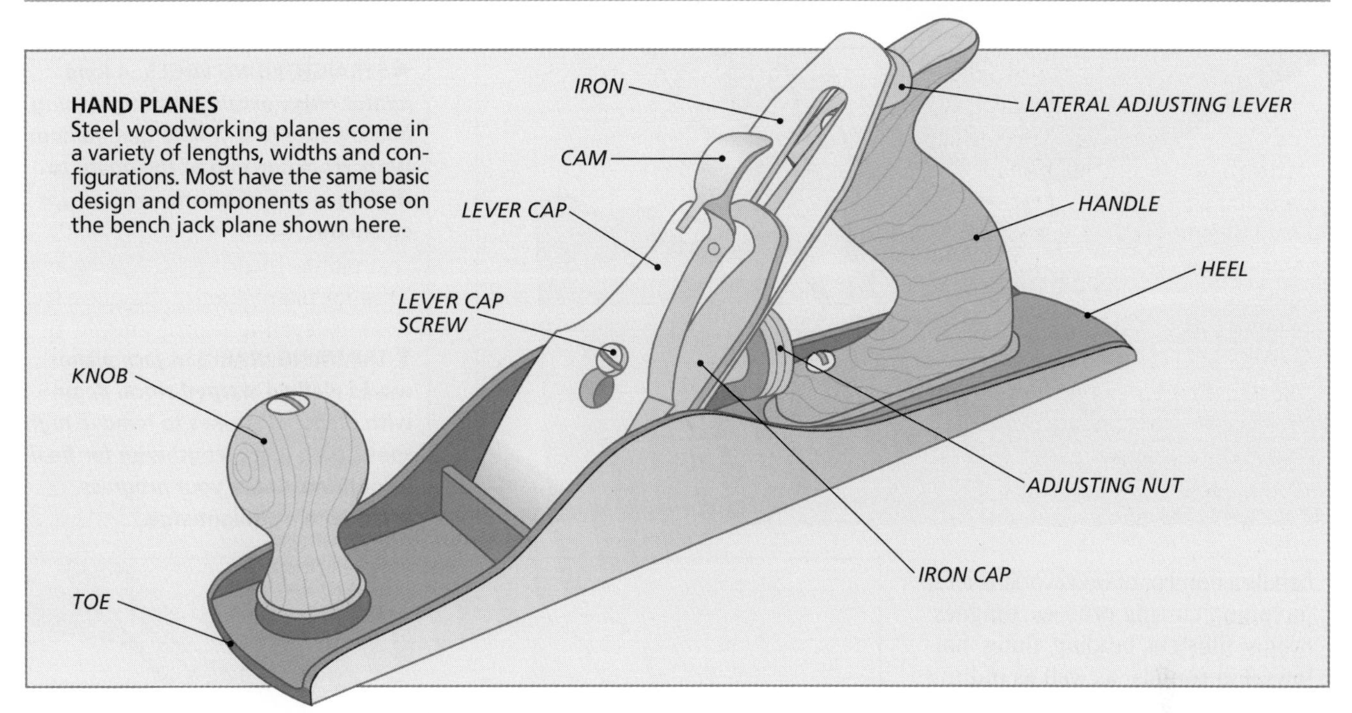

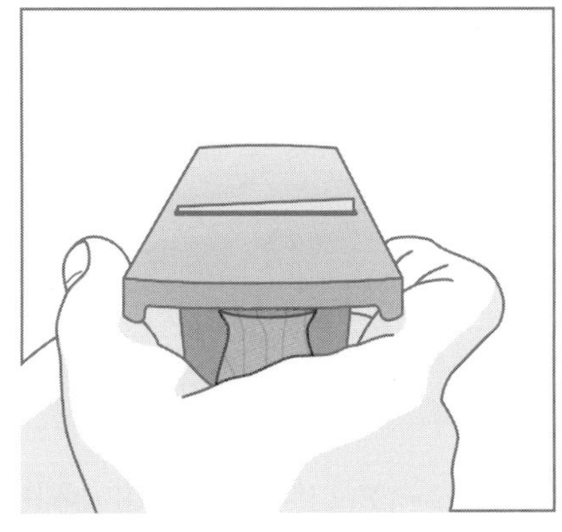

▲ **ADJUSTING IRONS.** ***Depth and evenness of cut are determined by the amount of iron projection below the plane's base and the side-to-side angle of projection. Adjust both while sighting down the base.***

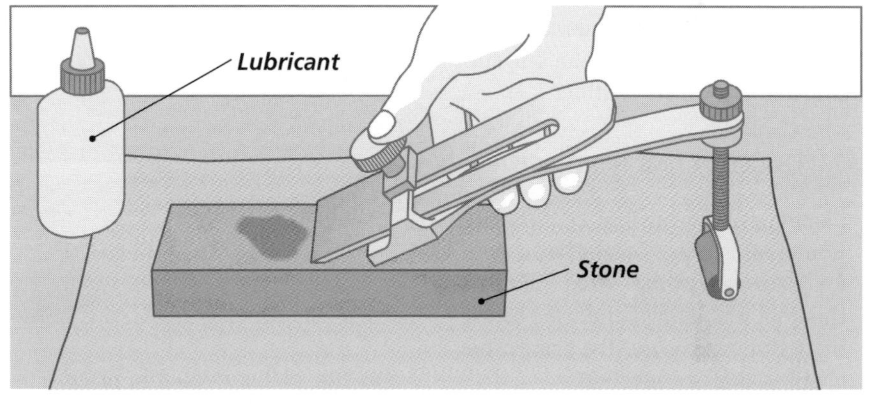

▲ **SHARPENING IRONS.** ***For a plane to work well, its iron (blade) must be sharp. While this can be done by hand, a more precise bevel angle is achieved using a sharpening guide—even an old-style one.***

anism described for the reform smooth plane. The 3-in.-wide red beech body has a white beech sole. It comes with a 2⅜-in.-wide chrome vanadium steel plane iron.

7. Tongue-and-groove planes—Here's a matching pair of hand planes that are designed specifically for milling tight-fitting tongue-and-groove joints onto the edges of ¾-in.-thick boards. The 1⅜ x 9⅜-in.-long red beech planes use wood wedges to secure the plane irons. Matching pairs of tongue-and-groove planes are available for ⅝-, 13/16- and ⅞-in.-thick boards.

8. Violinmaker's planes—Don't allow yourself to be fooled by the Lilliputian dimensions of these planes. They are superbly designed and highly precise. Cast from silicon-bronze, the planes are used for ultra-fine finishing work. The set of three includes a ¾ x 1⅜-in. plane with a ½-in.-wide iron, a ⅝ x 1⅛-in. plane with a ⅜-in.-wide iron and a ½ x 1-in. plane fitted with a 5/16-in.-wide iron.

9. Hollowing plane—The unique, convex-shaped sole of this tool identifies it as a hollowing, or rounding, plane. The 9½-in.-long tool has a red beech body with a hornbeam sole. The 1⅞-in.-wide iron is rounded to match the convex sole. Use this plane for cutting hollows with or across the grain.

10. Multiplane—Here's a fine example of a classic hand tool. Offered as a successor to now-discontinued models, this super-versatile plane comes with 24 cutters. An optional 16-cutter set is also available. Use the multiplane to

◀ **STRAIGHTENING EDGES.** ***A long jointer plane excels for straightening board edges that will be glue-joined. Work from one end of the board to the other using smooth, uninterrupted strokes.***

▼ **TRIMMING WARPS.** ***A jack plane works well on warped stock. Begin with diagonal strokes to remove high spots, then work lengthwise for final smoothing. Check your progress often with a straightedge.***

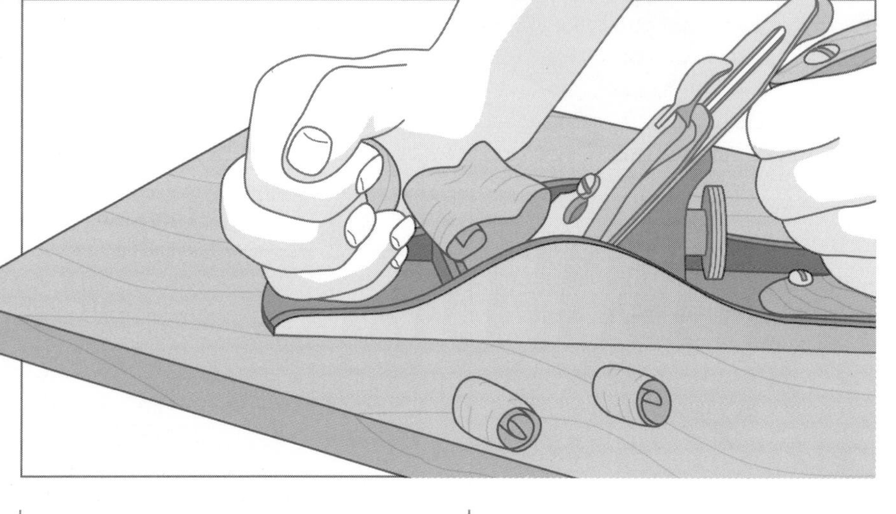

handle a number of woodworking jobs, including cutting grooves, tongues, ovolos, fillisters, beading, flutes, hollows and rounds, as well as milling sash work. The 24 standard cutters include 13 plough and dado, five beading, two tongue, two ovolo, one slitting and one fillister cutter.

HAND PLANE HERITAGE

Planes survive from first-century A.D. Rome. And earlier Greeks had a word for plane—*rhykane*—that indicates this tool was known and used before then. But exactly *how* the plane came about is another question.

Some have suggested that the plane evolved from the adze, a wood-surfacing tool with a separate cutter held by a wedge. By adding wood in front of and behind the cutting edge, something resembling a plane appeared—the blocks acting as a kind of jig that limited and controlled the depth of cut.

But another tool common to the period, the scratch stock, was used to cut moldings. It had a narrow, profiled cutter secured to a block of wood or stock that acted as a handle. Since the earliest surviving planes had narrow cutters and almost all were molding planes, it seems possible that the first planes evolved from the scratch stock.

The early Roman planes had bodies of wood, or wood with an iron sole and side plates riveted in place. The cutter was held by a wedge that pressed on a pin across the opening. This cutter-securing system is still used today and remains a popular design for shop-built planes.

One of the oldest surviving planes after the Roman examples is a wooden smoothing plane with a horn-shaped handle mounted on a slightly lowered front section. This plane also had a single cutter held by a wedge, but featured tapered notches on both sides of the blade opening that increased the wearing surface on the wedge. This became the standard cutter-securing system for North American wooden bench planes.

During the next 200 years, woodworking underwent an extraordinary evolution. But it wasn't until about 1760 that a truly important change in the engineering of the plane occurred. Before then, the cutter was a single metal component tapered thicker at the cutting edge to increase rigidity. Now, a second piece of metal—called the cap or back iron—was secured to the face of the cutter. This not only stabilized the cutting edge, but caused each shaving to break in short, connected segments, reducing tear out. It also meant the blade could be stamped out of thinner sheet steel, making its production easier and cheaper.

The invention of the metal plane was an extended process that began on this side of the Atlantic around the mid-1800s. It started with the development of a metal blade-securing and

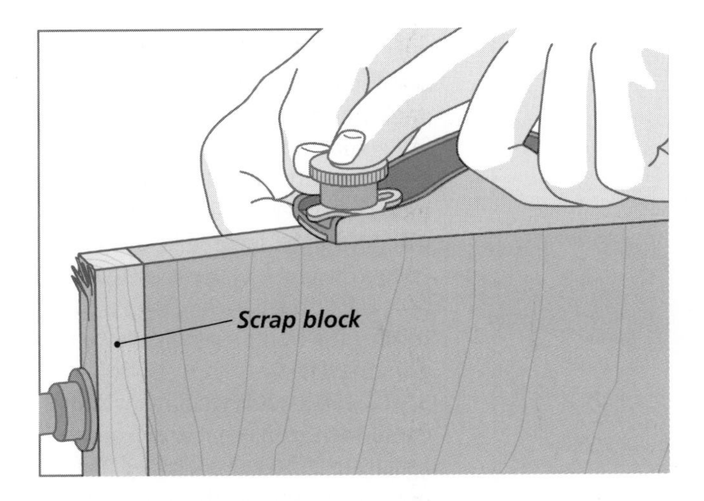

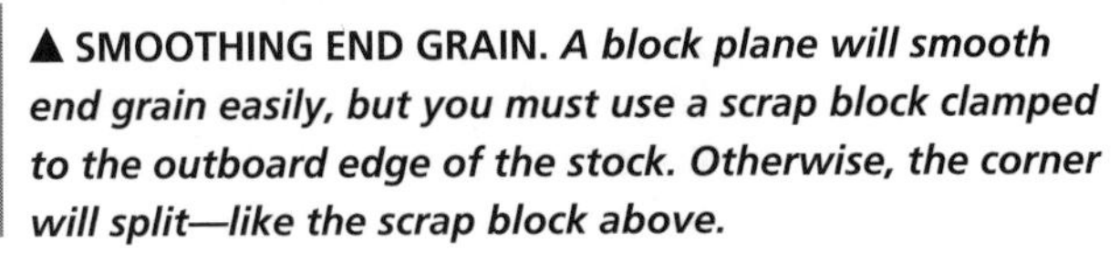

▲ SMOOTHING END GRAIN. *A block plane will smooth end grain easily, but you must use a scrap block clamped to the outboard edge of the stock. Otherwise, the corner will split—like the scrap block above.*

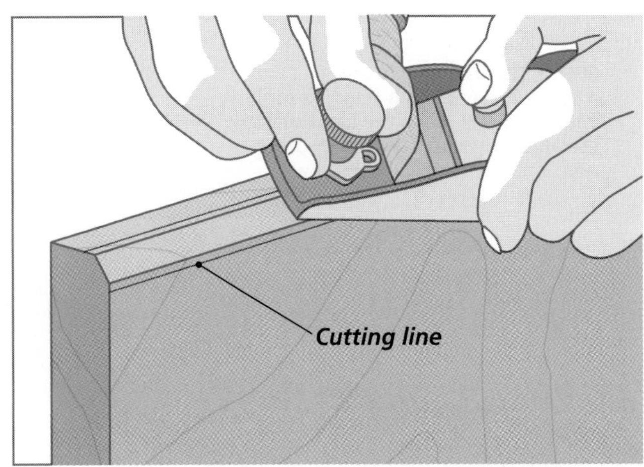

▲ CHAMFERING EDGES. *To chamfer or round edges with a plane, mark the depth of cut limits in pencil, then make repeated continuous passes until the lines are reached. The plane cuts best when held at a slight angle.*

adjustment mechanism that was simply fixed to the top of wooden plane bodies. In principle, this design is the same as that of the modern plane. A lever cap locked the cutter in place on a cast-iron bed—called the frog—and an adjustment wheel controlled the depth of cut. Transitional wood/metal planes led quickly to the development of today's cast-iron body.

TYPICAL SHOP PLANES

In this day and age of specialized power equipment, it's refreshing to know that a human-powered tool like the bench plane is still virtually indispensable. When properly sharpened, the plane excels at smoothing rough surfaces, trimming stock to size and cutting rounds and chamfers.

Although these hand tools are available in a wide variety of sizes and configurations, the most common types are the block, smoothing, jack, fore and jointer planes. These measure 6, 9, 14, 18 and 22 in. long, respectively. The function of each of these planes overlaps its neighbors considerably, so you certainly don't need all of them in the average shop. Smoothing, block and jointer planes are good general-purpose ones to start off with for most do-it-yourselfers.

SHARPENING PLANE IRONS

Unless its iron, or blade, is properly sharpened, a plane will not perform well. Sharpening the iron involves two basic steps: honing a bevel on the cutting edge and another bevel on part of the first one, and removing, or lapping, the burr that results from the honing process. Although the proce-

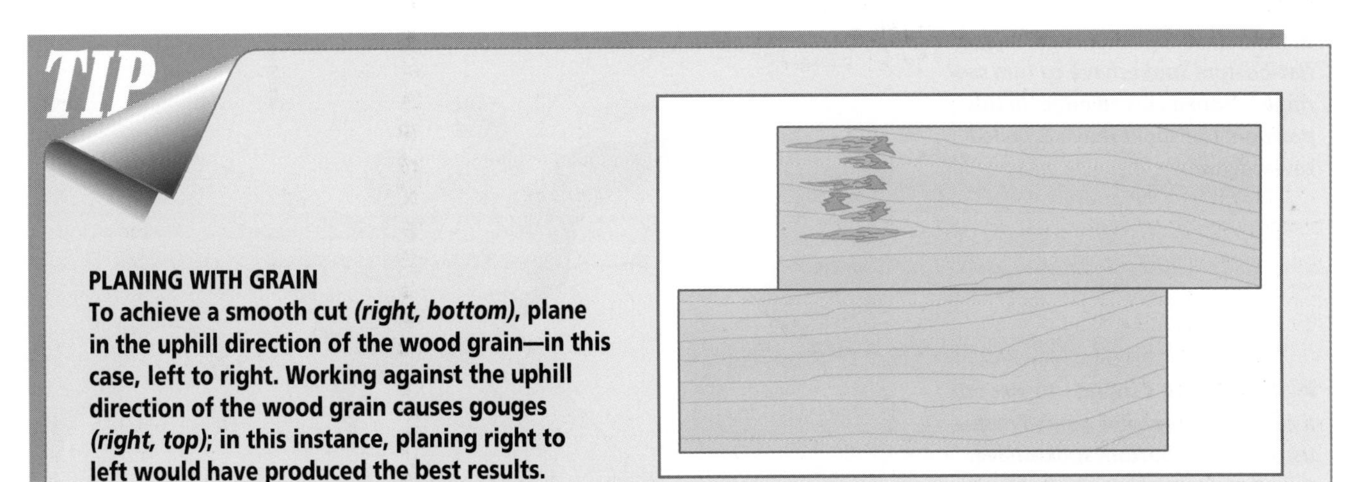

PLANING WITH GRAIN

To achieve a smooth cut *(right, bottom)*, plane in the uphill direction of the wood grain—in this case, left to right. Working against the uphill direction of the wood grain causes gouges *(right, top)*; in this instance, planing right to left would have produced the best results.

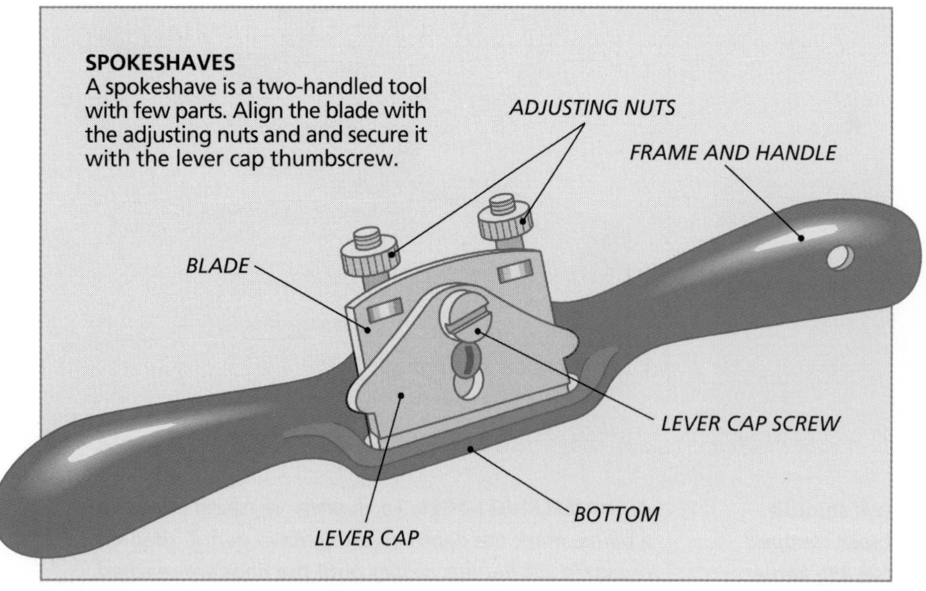

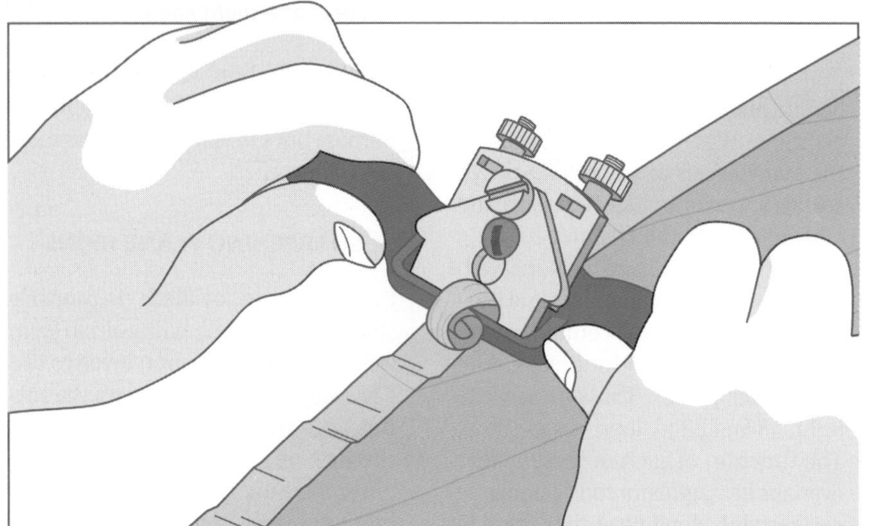

▲ **TRIMMING RIPPLES.** ***Work with a flat-bottom spokeshave to trim saw ripples from a curved edge. In this position, the spokeshave is pulled toward you.***

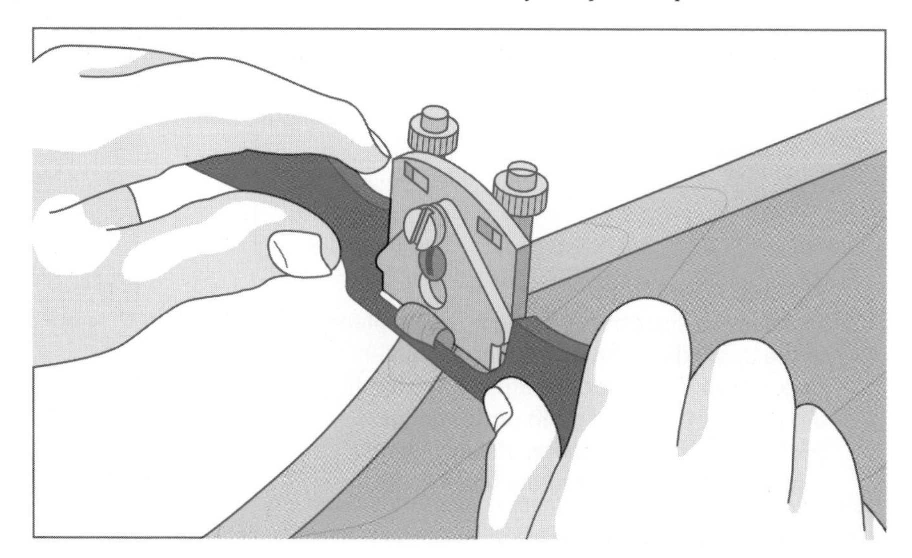

▶ **SMOOTHING CURVES.** ***To smooth a concave curve with a small radius, use a convex-bottom spokeshave. For all strokes, always pull or push in the direction of the wood grain.***

dure can be done by hand, you are best assured of achieving a precise bevel angle on the iron by using a sharpening guide.

If the cutting edge of the iron is nicked or otherwise damaged, the end will need to be squared before sharpening. The best tool to use for this purpose is a grinder—along with a guide to keep the iron perpendicular to the grinding wheel.

It's worth noting that many planes come with irons that are ground—usually to 25°—but not honed. Before use, you must hone the iron's edge to 30° on a flat, oiled stone until a burr is formed. Then, lay the iron flat on the stone, with its beveled edge facing up, and make a few light passes to remove the burr.

Note that the grinding and honing procedure for your plane may differ. Check with the plane's manufacturer for specific instructions.

ADJUSTING PLANE IRONS

The plane's depth and evenness of cut are determined by the amount of blade projecting from the base as well as by the side-to-side angle of the blade's projection. Sight down the base of the plane to adjust the iron for both.

It does take some practice to properly sharpen the plane's iron—which

◀ **CUTTING CHAMFERS.** ***Use pencil guidelines to cut a chamfer. Position a lamp directly over this kind of work to see your results clearly.***

▼ **SHAPING EDGES.** ***Contour an arm for a chair by first chamfering, then adding guidelines as shaping progresses. Use long, smooth strokes.***

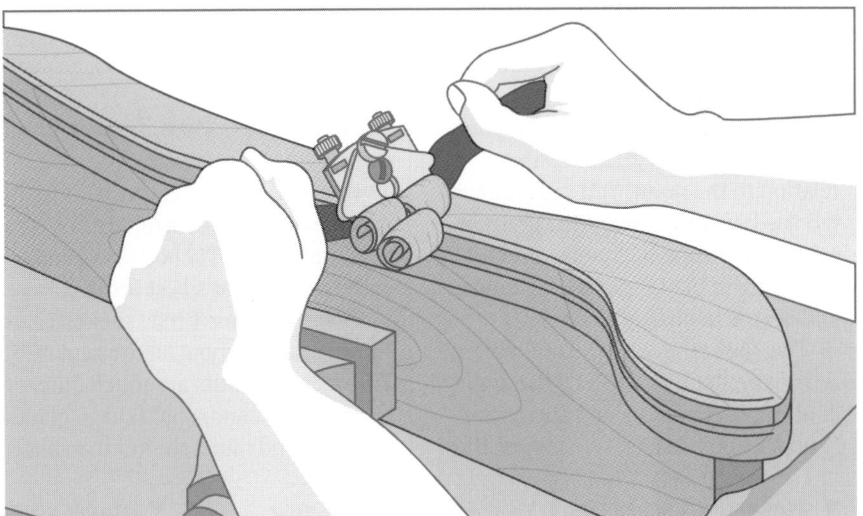

is essential—and to adjust the blade projection and angle for the best cut. For these reasons, you should adopt the habit of testing the plane on a piece of scrap before starting to work with it on a specific project.

USING PLANES

The basic operating techniques are the same for all bench planes. Begin by resting the toe of the tool flat at one end of the board. Then, apply slightly more pressure to the knob than to the handle and begin the stroke. When you reach the other end of the board, relax the knob pressure slightly and continue the pass with a smooth motion directed from the rear handle. Do not stop or start in the middle of a board, and always work in the uphill direction of the wood grain.

CARING FOR PLANES

Careful handling and occasional maintenance are all that's required to keep your planes in great condition for generations to come. The following tips will ensure years of smooth planing. Keep the plane's mouth clear of wood chips during use. Remove buildups of resin on the plane's base with a solvent such as paint thinner. Rub a little wax on the base to speed the planing motion. Retract the iron after using the plane, and store the tool upright to keep the sole from being damaged.

Keep unplated and unpainted plane parts lightly oiled to prevent rusting. Protect wooden planes from excessive humidity to prevent warping. If slight warping does occur, it usually can be corrected by making a few light passes over a jointer. If a wooden plane's varnish finish wears off, apply an occasional coat of linseed oil to prevent the wood from drying out and cracking. You should completely disassemble a plane at least once every year to clean each part thoroughly. Apply a light coat of oil to all metal parts of the plane before reassembly.

TYPES OF SPOKESHAVES

The spokeshave is a special double-handled plane used for shaping and smoothing irregular or curved surfaces. The tool has a wide blade and a short base, which allows it to follow curves easily. Spokeshaves are indispensable for smoothing out ripples and bumps on edges cut by hand, sabre or band saws. They are particularly useful for rounding compound curves.

There are two major types of spokeshaves: flat bottom and convex bottom. The flat-bottomed one is most widely used because it handles both convex curves and moderate- to long-sweep concave curves equally well. The curved-bottom one is meant for use on concave curves with as small as a 5-in. ra.

ADJUSTING SPOKESHAVES

Blade projection is the only adjustment made on a spokeshave. This is done by turning two adjustment nuts while sighting across the bottom. The blade should project evenly and just far enough to make a fine shaving.

USING SPOKESHAVES

You can master the spokeshave easily if you keep the blade very sharp and always make strokes with the grain. Cutting against the grain results in lumps and gouging that may ruin your work. Change the direction of your strokes as the curvature changes in relation to the grain. You can't always tell the true direction of the grain by eye, but the time to change direction is when the blade meets resistance, and begins to chatter and skip.

The spokeshave tool itself makes only flat cuts. By changing the angle continuously and making successively finer cuts, you can form almost the entire contour. Then, final sanding completes the curves.

While spokeshaves can be pushed or pulled, greater control results from a pulling stroke. Try both ways and go with the way that's best for you.

Two final tips: First, spokeshaves come with or without adjustment nuts. The ones with nuts are much quicker to adjust. Second, spokeshave blades are wider and much shorter than plane

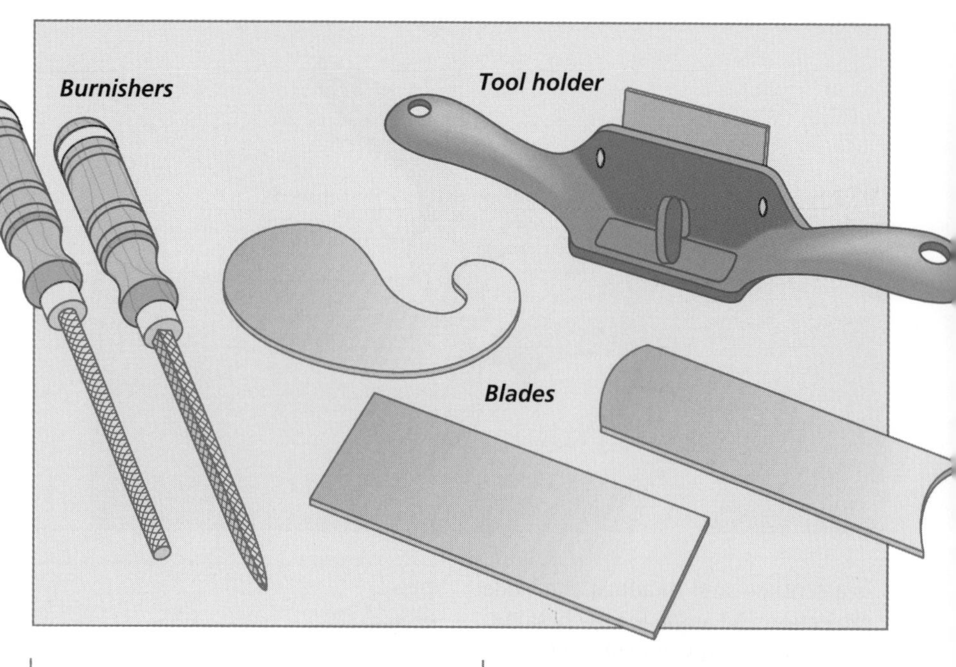

▲ **CABINET SCRAPERS.** *Cabinet scraper blades come in three basic shapes: rectangular; straight with concave and convex ends; and gooseneck. Your choice of the one to use depends on the shape of the workpiece. For heavy-duty jobs, there's also a tool holder that accommodates a rectangular blade. Sharpening burnishers come with either round or triangular blades.*

▼ **SHARPENING SCRAPERS, 1.** *To sharpen a scraper, first clamp the blade securely in a vise. Using full, firm strokes, file the edges of the blade flat with a single-cut fine mill file. To remove file marks from the edges, hone the blade on an oilstone.*

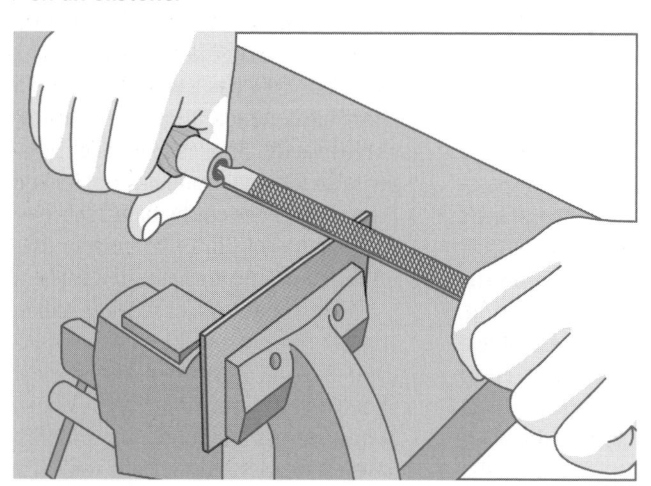

▼ **SHARPENING SCRAPERS, 2.** *While honing, keep the blade perpendicular and avoid rocking it. After honing the edges, lay the blade flat and hone both faces. Then, clamp the blade back in the vise, apply a little oil and draw a burnisher across each side of the edges several times.*

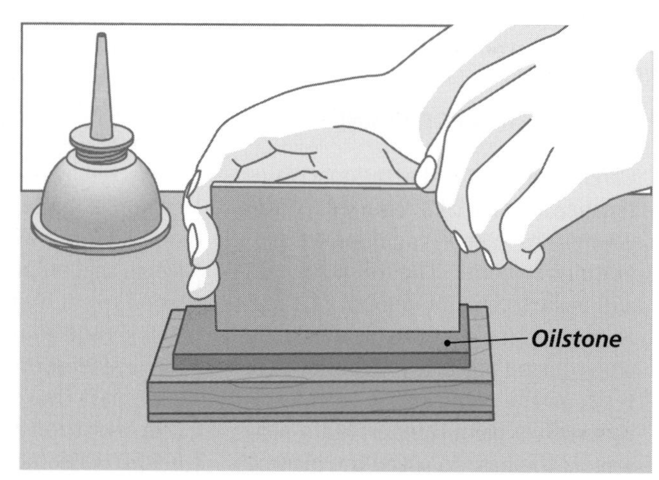

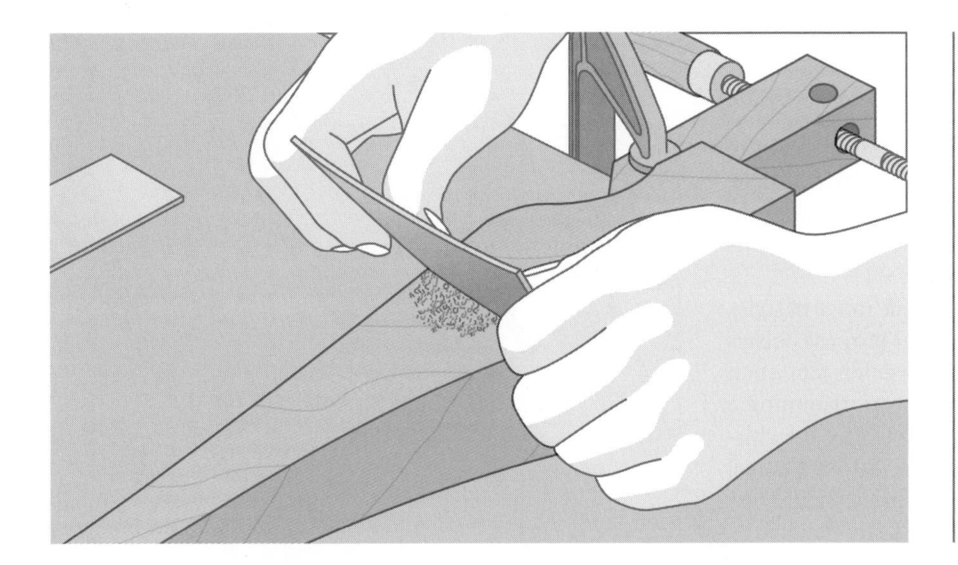

◀ **SMOOTHING FLAT SURFACES.** ***For work on flat surfaces, hold the cabinet scraper tightly in both hands. Bow the blade slightly with your thumbs and tilt it in the direction of the cut, then push the blade firmly across the surface.***

▼ **SMOOTHING CURVED SURFACES.** ***To smooth curved surfaces like those on a cabriole leg, use a straight blade with concave and convex ends or a gooseneck scraper. Work with both hands, bowing the blade slightly and tilting it in the direction of the cut.***

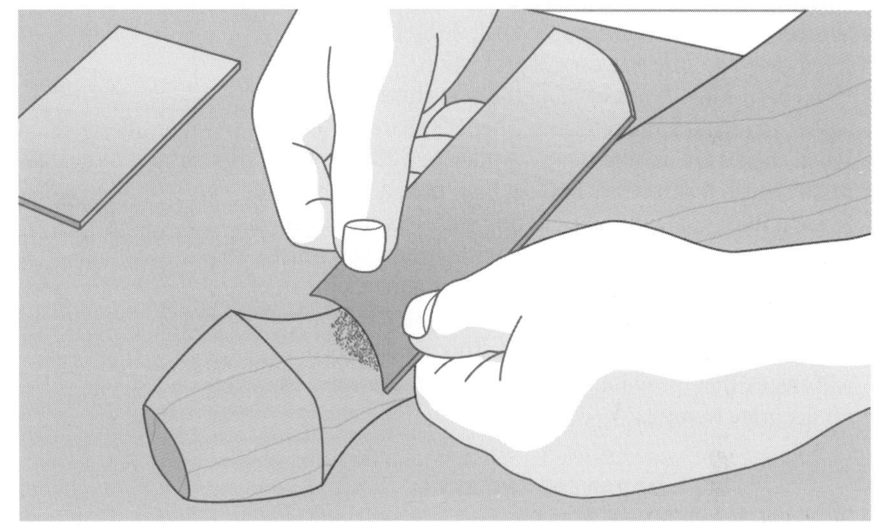

irons. A honing guide can be used if your sharpening stone is wide enough. Otherwise, sharpen the blade by hand, holding it slightly askew so the whole blade fits on the stone.

TYPES OF SCRAPERS

It's a good bet that many home workshoppers are unfamiliar with cabinet scrapers. If you're one of them, you've been missing out on something good. These simple tools excel at smoothing wood and, when properly sharpened, they can yield a ready-to-finish surface without the need for a lot of tedious—and expensive—sanding preparation.

Cabinet scrapers are available in three basic blade shapes: rectangular, straight with concave and convex ends, and gooseneck. There's also a frame-mounted type of scraper with a rectangular blade that looks much like a spokeshave. For normal use, the hand-held blades will do the job well. But for heavy-duty work, the type with a handle is a better idea. Unfortunately, many hardware stores do not stock these tools; they are, however, listed in most woodworker supply catalogs.

USING SCRAPERS

Used with moderate to heavy pressure, cabinet scrapers can eliminate tool burns, saw marks and milling defects such as planer ripples in virtually any kind of wood stock. The scraper can remove ridge marks left by a smoothing plane and can also flatten wavy-grained stock that doesn't respond well to routine planing.

A scraper is actually nothing more than a flat piece of tough, but malleable steel that is about 1⁄32 in. thick. The steel lends itself to burnishing, or "turning over," the edge, which forms a slightly hooked flare of steel. When the blade is held at an angle of about 70° to the workpiece and pushed or pulled over the surface, this hook cuts the stock, producing very fine shavings. Despite its name, the only time the tool actually scrapes is when the edge is dull and produces dusty particles, not shavings.

Although using the scraper is easy, sharpening the blade is a bit tricky. When an edge just begins to dull, it can be revived with a few burnishing strokes. This will work several times before filing and honing have to be repeated. To burnish properly, make four or five progressive passes over each edge until you obtain a flare of about 10° relative to the blade edge.

To sharpen the gooseneck scraper and the blades with concave and convex ends, use the same method, but different tools: a round file, slip stone and round blade burnisher.

CHISELS

To call a chisel a simple tool is an understatement of colossal proportions. Even though its design *is* simple, it's essential for most types of do-it-yourself work. In fact, no toolbox or workshop is complete without an assortment of chisels.

The chisels collected here represent a wide range of styles and sizes to suit all work. Some are general-purpose chisels while others are specially designed for specific jobs such as cleaning out the bottom of a deep mortise, trimming a dovetail joint or shearing off a bolthead. Note that the chisels have either a wood or plastic handle, or feature all-steel construction. Generally, wood-handled chisels should be struck only with a wood or plastic mallet. Plastic-handled chisels can be hit with a mallet or hammer. Strike an all-steel chisel with a ball-peen or small sledge hammer. In *all* cases, be sure to wear eye protection.

As with most types of hand tools, a chisel is easiest to use and most effective when it's sharp. Wood chisels are usually factory-ground to a 25° to 30° bevel. A secondary bevel is then honed on the blade to form the actual cutting edge. Some chisels come honed and ready to use. Others are ground only and you must hone them before use. Keep your chisels honed with a hard Arkansas sharpening stone or a Japanese waterstone. Also invest in a honing guide. This simple tool will ensure that the chisel is held at the correct angle for accurate honing.

JAPANESE CHISELS

Traditional Japanese wood chisels have two unique features. First, the chisel's blade is made of laminated steel. Very hard high-carbon steel forms the bottom layer and cutting edge of the chisel. The rest of the blade is made of softer steel that provides strength and resiliency. Laminated construction saves valuable hard steel and makes sharpening easier since only the cutting edge is hard steel.

Another unique feature is that the blade's back surface is hollow ground. Some Japanese chisels have a single, full-width hollow that is similar to a very shallow spoon. Other chisels have a multiple-groove back with two, three or four shallow hollow-ground grooves. The number of grooves depends on the width of the chisel blade. One touted advantage of hollow-ground chisels is that grinding the back surface perfectly flat is easy. Since there's less back surface for you to grind, you end up saving both time and wear on the sharpening stone.

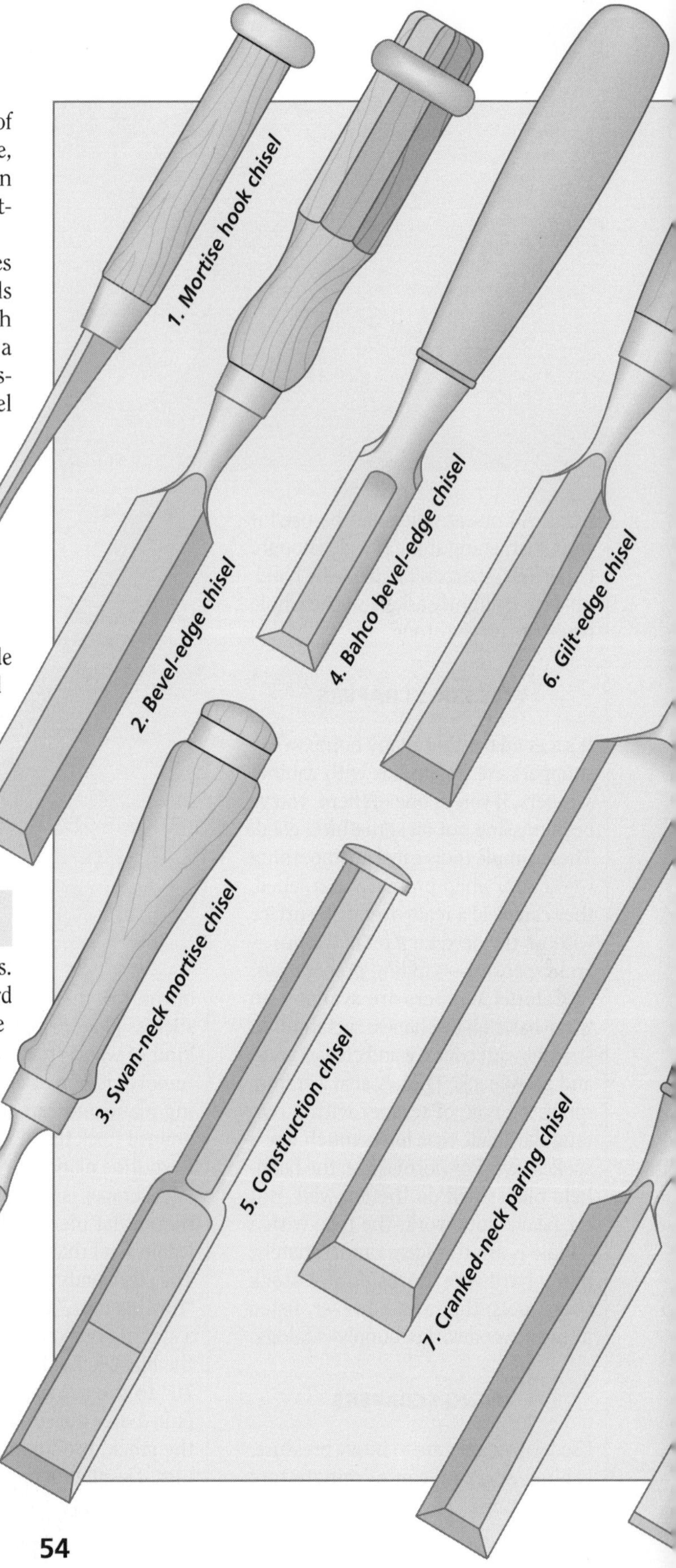

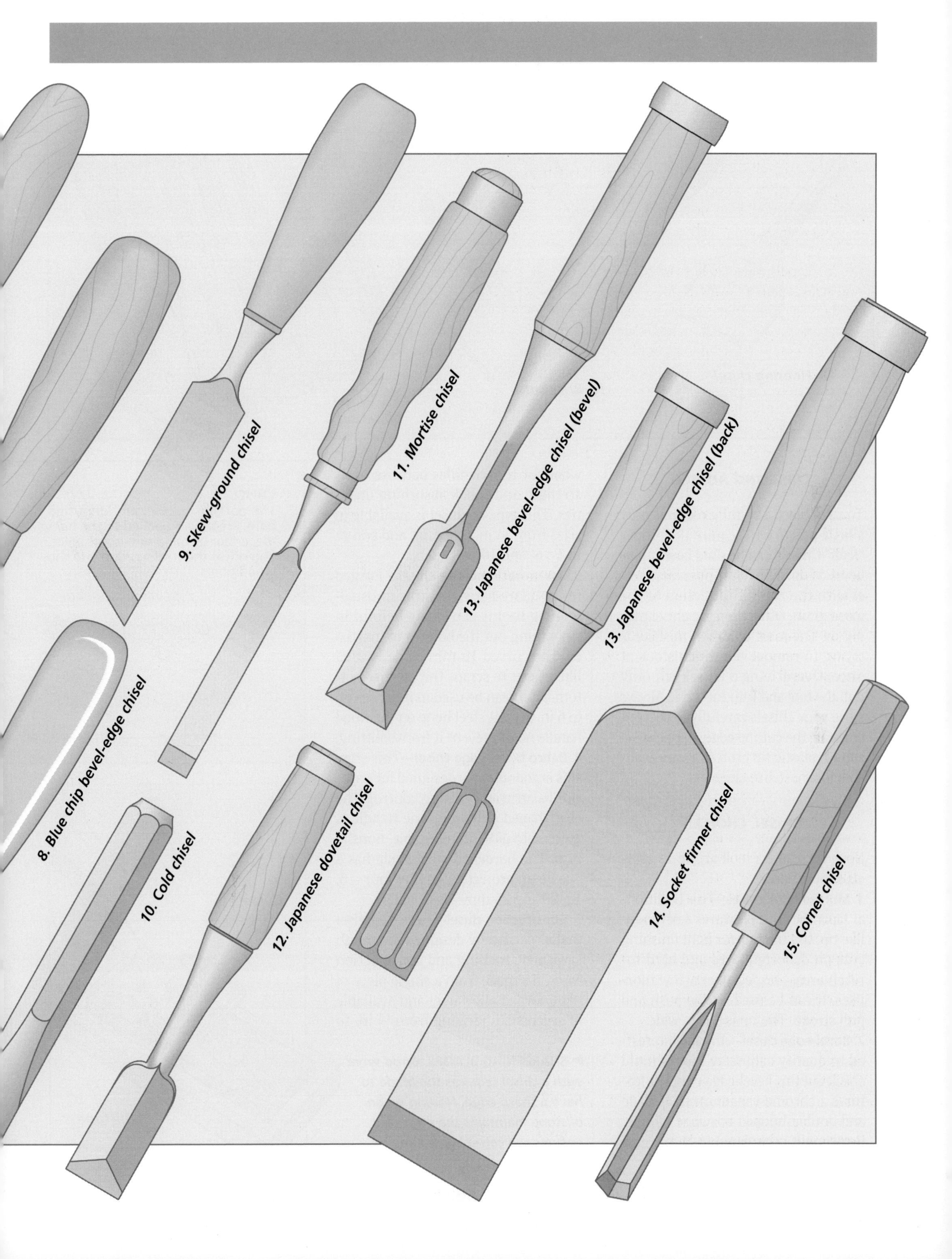
8. Blue chip bevel-edge chisel
9. Skew-ground chisel
10. Cold chisel
11. Mortise chisel
12. Japanese dovetail chisel
13. Japanese bevel-edge chisel (bevel)
13. Japanese bevel-edge chisel (back)
14. Socket firmer chisel
15. Corner chisel

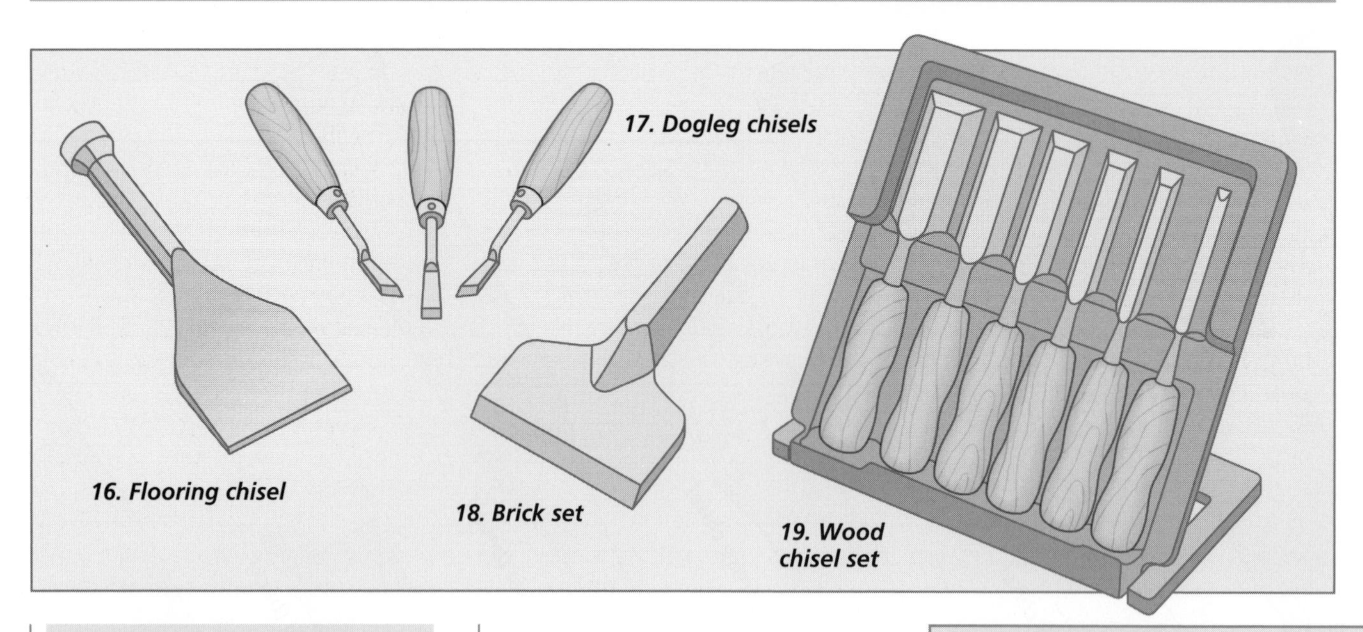

CHISELING ADVICE

To use chisels skillfully requires only a little practice to acquire the proper "feel." Chisels can be used bevel up or bevel down. Whenever possible, chisel with the "uphill" direction of the wood grain. Otherwise, the chisel may dig in. The most common mistake is trying to remove too much stock at once. Overdriving a chisel will only dull the tool and ruin the work. Always store your chisels carefully to prevent chipping the cutting edge. Inexpensive, slip-on plastic tip protectors are available for most size chisels.

CHISEL CHOICES

Now, let's take a look at the 19 chisels shown here.

1. Mortise hook chisel—This traditional Japanese chisel features a harpoon-like tip. Use the tool for light finishing cuts on delicate pieces and hard-to-reach areas—especially narrow mortises. It can be used on the push and pull stroke. The tip is 3/16 in. wide.

2. Bevel-edge chisel—Anyone interested in quality cabinetry tools should check out this bevel-edge chisel. It features a chrome-vanadium steel blade and double-hooped boxwood handle. Boxwood is considered to be the best wood for tool handles because of its strength and shock absorbing qualities. This type of chisel is available in sizes from 1/4 in. to 1 1/2 in. and comes in 4-, 6- and 10-piece sets.

3. Swan-neck mortise chisel—Forged from square bar stock, this unusual-looking tool is extremely helpful in smoothing out the bottom of mortises. The curved 10-mm blade is used like a lever to scrape the mortise bottom flat. It can be used in mortises up to 6 in. deep. A steel hoop on the wood handle helps prevent it from splitting.

4. Bahco bevel-edge chisel—This chisel is ergonomically designed for superior balance and cutting control. The oval-shaped polypropylene handle is grooved to give a comfortable, nonslip grip. The hardened-steel blade has a plastic tip protector. A set of four—6, 12, 20 and 25 mm—is available.

5. Construction chisel—Here's a chisel that's specifically designed for rough carpentry, framing and construction work. It's made from a single piece of hand-forged alloy steel and available in seven sizes ranging from 1/4 in. to

CHISEL
The parts of a chisel are identified here. Pressure is applied to the handle, either by hand or with a mallet. This drives the cutting edge into the wood fibers.

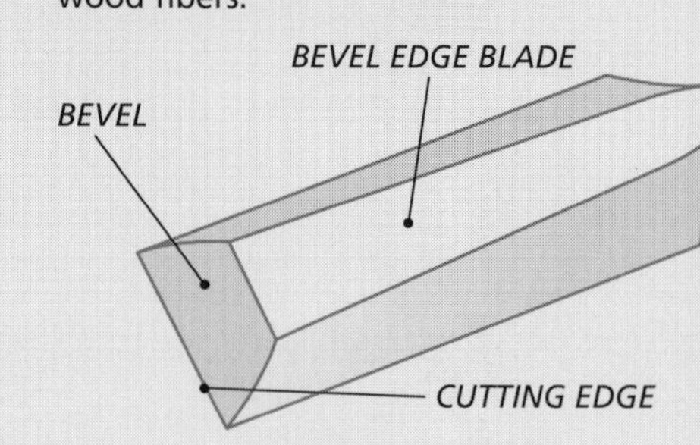

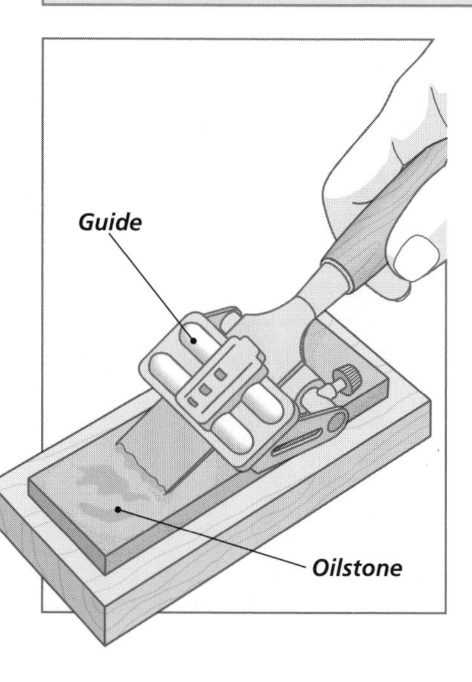

► **SHARPENING BLADES.** ***Good work with a chisel requires the blade to have a sharp edge. Honing on an oilstone maintains the edge and ensures the correct bevel angle.***

2¾ in. A set of four includes ¼-, ½-, ¾- and 1-in. chisels.

6. Gilt-edge chisel—The features of this craftsman-quality chisel include a rosewood handle, a brass bolster and a diamond-honed steel blade. A set of five chisels—¼, ⅜, ½, ¾ and 1 in.—with plastic tip protectors is available.

7. Cranked-neck paring chisel—Looking somewhat like a narrow trowel, this tool features a 1¼-in.-wide x 8-in.-long blade and an offset handle. This design allows you to make light, finishing cuts with the blade flat on the stock—even when working in the middle of a wide board. It's available in five sizes ranging from ¼ in. to 1¼ in.

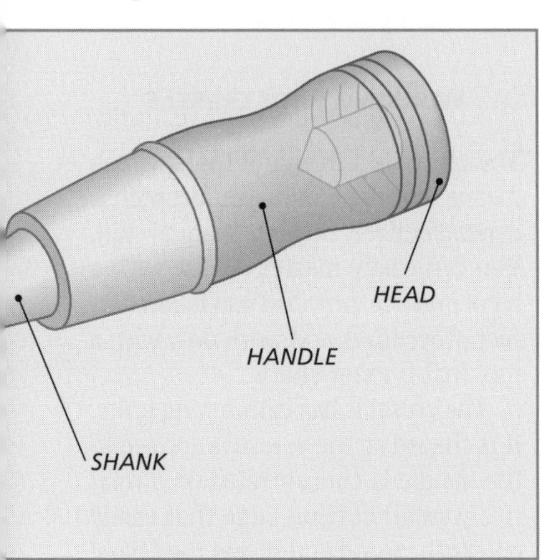

8. Blue chip bevel-edge chisel—This is an excellent general-use chisel. It has a virtually indestructible polypropylene handle and quality forged tool-steel blade. The tool's no-roll handle is square with rounded corners for a comfortable grip. A set of five is available: ¼, ⅜, ½, ¾ and 1 in.

9. Skew-ground chisel—Designed for light finishing cuts, this unique chisel is ground to a 60° angle. Use it to clean up sliding dovetails and other hard-to-reach joints. The thick steel blade is fitted with a tough cellulose acetate handle. The tool is sold in pairs with a right-hand and left-hand skew.

10. Cold chisel—This all-steel chisel is used to cut through metals that are softer than its hardened cutting edge. Made of double heat-treated chrome-vanadium steel, this ⅞ x 7½-in.-long tough tool will shear through bolts, nails, screws and sheet metal. Strike cold chisels with a ball-peen hammer and *always* wear eye goggles. A three-piece set of cold chisels comes in sizes of ¼, ⅜ and ½ in.

11. Mortise chisel—Unlike a standard chisel, this tool's blade has straight, non-beveled edges—identifying it as a mortise chisel. It's designed to take heavy pounding and prying. Features of this ½-in. chisel include a thick, hardened-steel blade and an ash handle with a steel hoop at each end to help deter splitting. A leather washer between the blade and handle acts as a shock absorber.

12. Japanese dovetail chisel—Like most traditional Japanese chisels, this one is made of laminated steel with a hollow-ground back. However, the blade's triangular cross section is designed for shaping sliding dovetail joints. It's also helpful for cleaning out long, narrow grooves and tight, inside corners.

13. Japanese bevel-edge chisel—This is one of the finest chisels ever made. Its features include a laminated steel blade and hooped boxwood handle. The 7-in.-long blade provides superior control. Note that both the beveled and

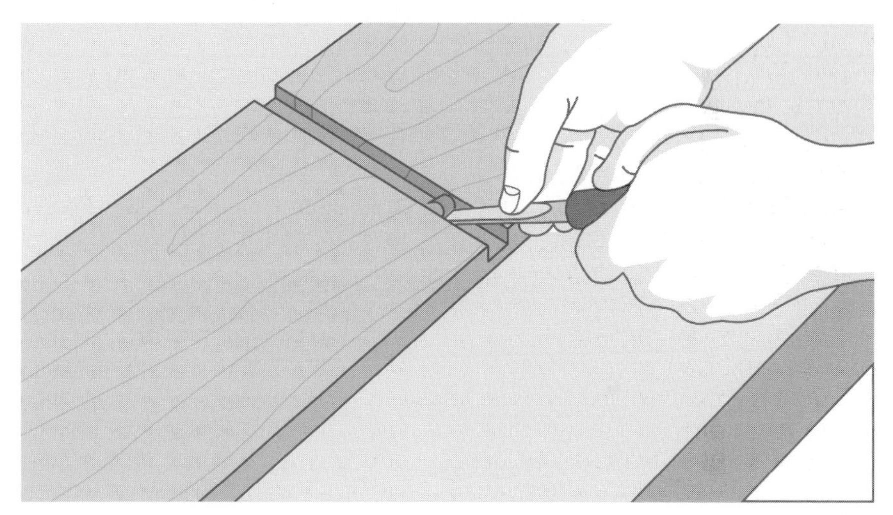

▲ **MAKING DADOS.** ***First, cut the sides of the dado with a back saw. Then, chisel the waste to depth with the bevel down—this gives hand clearance. Work toward the center to prevent splintering of the wood.***

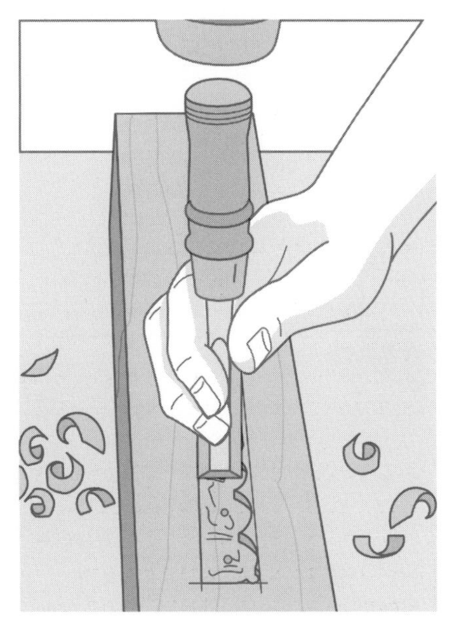

◀ **CUTTING MORTISES.** ***To cut a mortise, bore overlapping holes to depth and trim off webs between holes with a chisel. Bore tiny holes in the corners to simplify squaring them.***

back surfaces of a 30-mm chisel are shown to reveal the multiple-groove, hollow-ground back. It's available in eight sizes from 3 mm to 36 mm.

14. Socket firmer chisel—Firmer chisels are designed for heavy-duty work such as timber framing. The tool shown features a 2-in.-wide x 8-in.-long blade that tapers from 7/16 in. thick at the shoulder to 3/16 in. thick at the bevel. A hooped ash handle fits into the blade's socket. A four-piece set—¾, 1, 1½ and 2 in.—is available.

15. Corner chisel—Use this tool for cutting clean, sharp inside corners. The hand-forged alloy steel blade forms a 90° angle and measures ½ x ½ in. The tool's blade is fitted into an octagonal hornbeam handle. This type of chisel is reserved for the serious woodworker and enthusiastic tool collector.

16. Flooring chisel—Also called an electrician's chisel, this all-steel tool has a double-beveled 2¾-in.-wide blade. It's used primarily for ripping up old wood strip flooring. Electricians work with this style of chisel to notch house framing when installing cable and electrical boxes.

17. Dogleg chisels—Basically woodcarvers' tools, these small-scale chisels are ideal for fine cabinet work such as mortising locks and hinges. The 5/16-in.-wide x 1¼-in.-long blades of the chisels are offset to permit proper tool clearance. The three-piece set includes a straight-blade, right-hand skew and left-hand skew chisels.

18. Brick set—Use this all-steel chisel to score, cut and trim bricks and concrete blocks. This type of chisel should be struck only with a small sledge or ball-peen hammer—*not* a bricklayer's or nail hammer. It features a 3½-in.-wide blade.

19. Wood chisel set—Shown here is a good, basic set of chisels for general woodworking and light carpentry. The set includes six wood chisels—¼, ½, ¾, 1, 1¼ and 1½ in.—in a convenient plastic storage tray and stand. Each chisel is equipped with an impact-resistant plastic handle with a steel cap and high-quality steel blade.

WORKING WITH CHISELS

The chisel is a freehand tool—which means that the results you get with it depend entirely on your manual skill. You can easily master its use with a bit of practice, provided you follow correct procedures and work only with a tool that is razor-sharp.

The chisel is basically a long knife. It is shaped so the pressure applied to the handle is concentrated on a relatively small cutting edge that easily enters the wood and severs the fibers.

▲ **SETTING HINGES.** ***Outline the hinge with a knife, then work with a mallet to chisel vertical cuts along the lines, bevel toward the waste. Make slant cuts along the lines with the bevel down. Using the mallet, make score cuts and cut waste with the bevel up.***

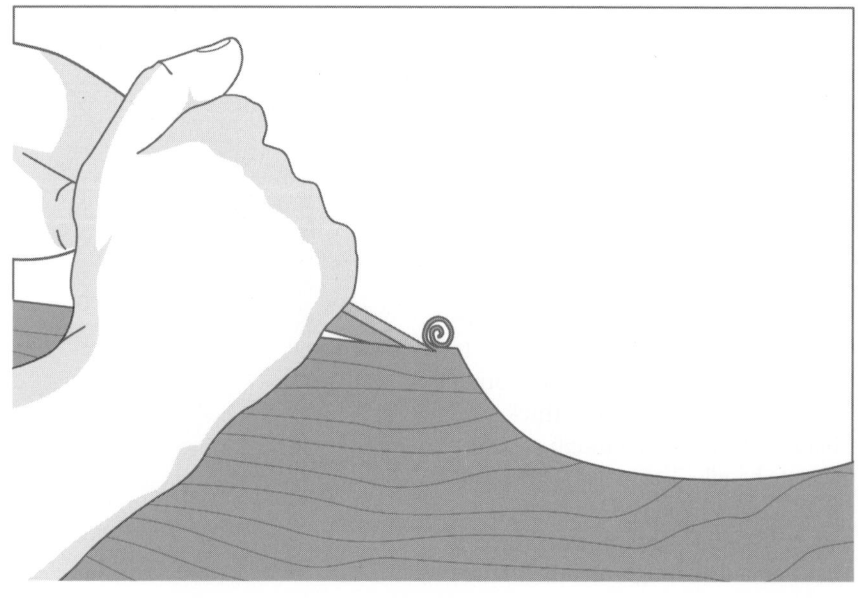

► **CUTTING CURVES.** ***Hold the bevel side of the chisel against the workpiece to cut a concave curve. Push the handle down while pressing the blade forward, working from the edge toward the end grain.***

Unless you are applying the driving force with a mallet, both hands are always kept in contact with the chisel. One hand grips the blade and controls movement of the cutting edge, while the other hand applies pressure on the handle. The grip may be varied depending upon the nature of the cut and personal preference. A comfortable grip aids good blade control.

The blade is flat on one side and beveled on the other. In general, use the chisel with the bevel up for finish (paring) cuts and with the bevel down for roughing cuts.

In some situations, however, you must make the finish cut with the bevel down. For example, when cleaning out a long groove the bevel must be down so that the handle will be elevated and will clear the workpiece. This also applies when working in confined areas, such as when cutting a mortise. Concave cuts are also easily made with the bevel down; these would be quite difficult with the bevel up.

Whenever possible, work with the chisel held at a slight side angle in relation to the direction of travel rather than following a straight path. In this position, the chisel presents a smaller leading edge to the wood, resulting in smoother shavings.

Unless you have no choice, always cut *with* the grain. Otherwise, the chisel edge will act much like a wedge and split the wood ahead of it.

Although the chisel can do aggressive cutting when necessary. there's no need to overwork it. Use other tools such as saws and drills when feasible to remove the bulk of the waste before working with a chisel.

WOODCARVING

If your carving experience is limited to things like shaping the legs of furniture or adding simple carved details to a chair back, or if you haven't tried carving yet, then you're missing out on one of the most enjoyable, relaxing and rewarding areas of woodworking.

The three types of carving presented here are chip carving, relief carving and carving in the round. A duck motif was chosen to illustrate the techniques because its graceful contours and simple details are not too difficult to reproduce.

CARVING TOOLS

Carving tools are available in a wide variety of shapes and sizes, but you'll only need a few basic tools for the projects described here: straight and bent

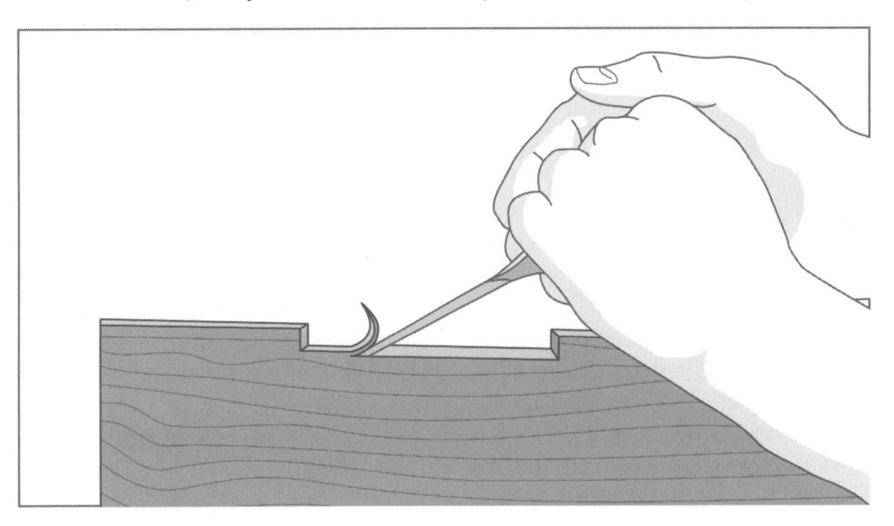

▲ **WORKING TIGHT SPOTS.** ***Direct the bevel down to cut in confined areas. Here, the left hand is positioned far from the blade for clarity; it should be close to the cutting edge.***

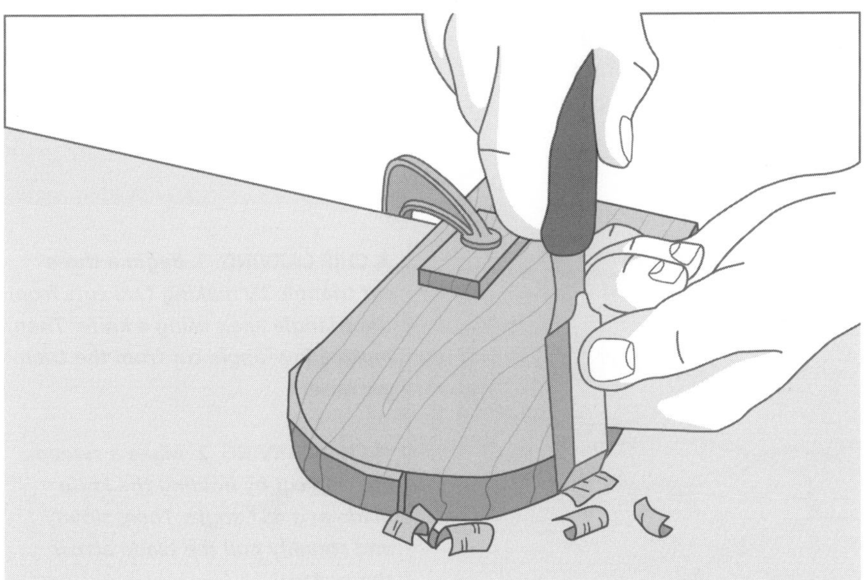

◀ **SHAPING EDGES.** ***Chisel vertical paring cuts after rough-sawing the shape. Make shallow cuts with a side-to-side paring action, keeping the flat side tangent to the curve.***

CHISELS

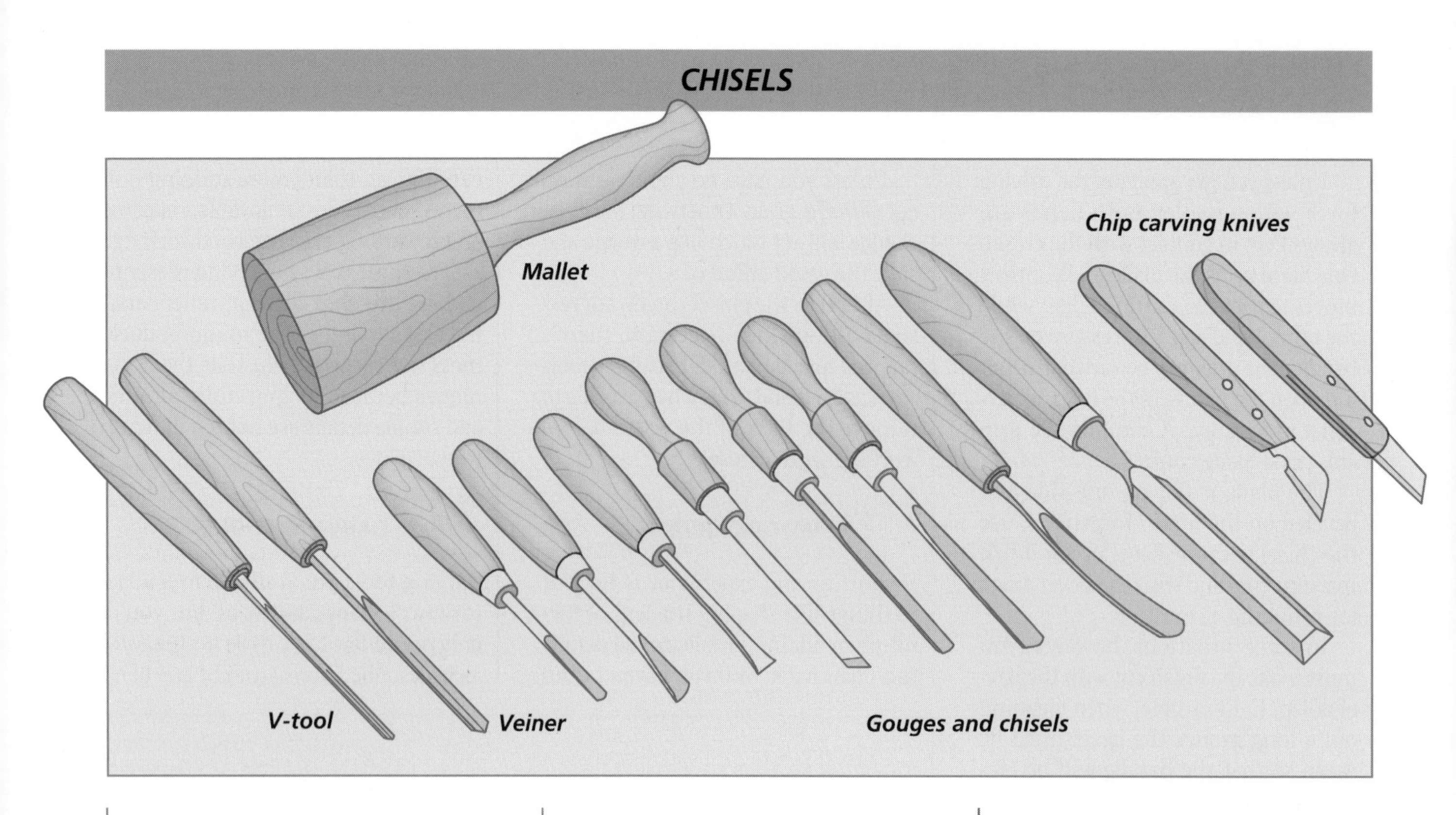

gouges, straight and skew chisels, a veiner, a V-tool, chip carving knives and a mallet. A standard carpenter's chisel is also handy and can be used in place of the straight carving chisel, if necessary.

The most important requisite for carving is a razor-sharp cutting edge. If a tool bevel needs reshaping, do this on a coarse bench stone. Then, shift to a medium stone to smooth the bevel until a wire edge, or burr, is formed. Remove the wire edge on a fine stone. Use a fine slipstone of the proper shape to hone the inside of a gouge or V-tool. Polish the bevel on an extra-fine stone and then strop on a strip of leather charged with jeweler's rouge.

There are many woods that are suitable for carving. Basswood is one of the easiest to work with and it has a tight, straight-grained structure that holds detail well. White or sugar pine will also work for these projects.

CHIP CARVING

In chip carving, small knives are used to make shallow incisions on the surface of the wood. The designs produced are traditionally decorative patterns made up of repetitive geometric ele-

▲ **CARVING TOOLS.** ***A basic kit of carving tools includes straight and bent gouges, straight and skew chisels, a veiner, a V-tool and a mallet. Chip carving knifes are used for decorative surface carving.***

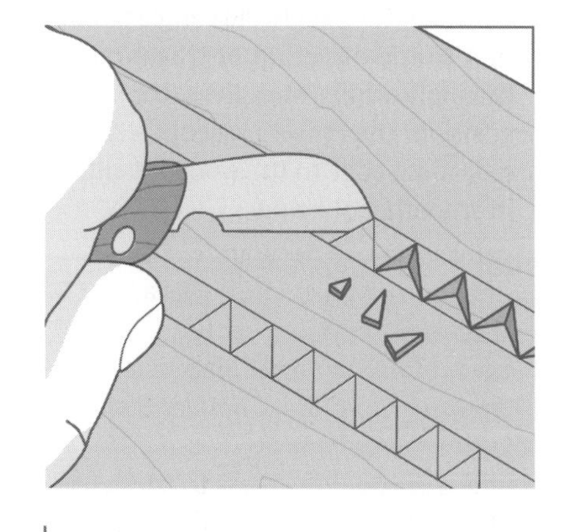

▲ **CHIP CARVING, 1.** ***Begin a three-cut triangle by making two cuts from the triangle apex using a knife. Then, make a low-angle cut from the triangle base.***

◀ **CHIP CARVING, 2.** ***Make a sweeping chip cut by holding the knife blade at a 45° angle. Then, slowly and steadily pull the blade across the surface.***

◀ **RELIEF CARVING, 1.** ***Begin relief carving by using the V-tool to outline profile. Keep the cut in the waste area, about 1/8 in. from the line.***

▼ **RELIEF CARVING, 2.** ***After making vertical cuts around outline, remove waste with a gouge. As work progresses, alternate between grounding cuts made with a bent gouge and cuts that follow outline.***

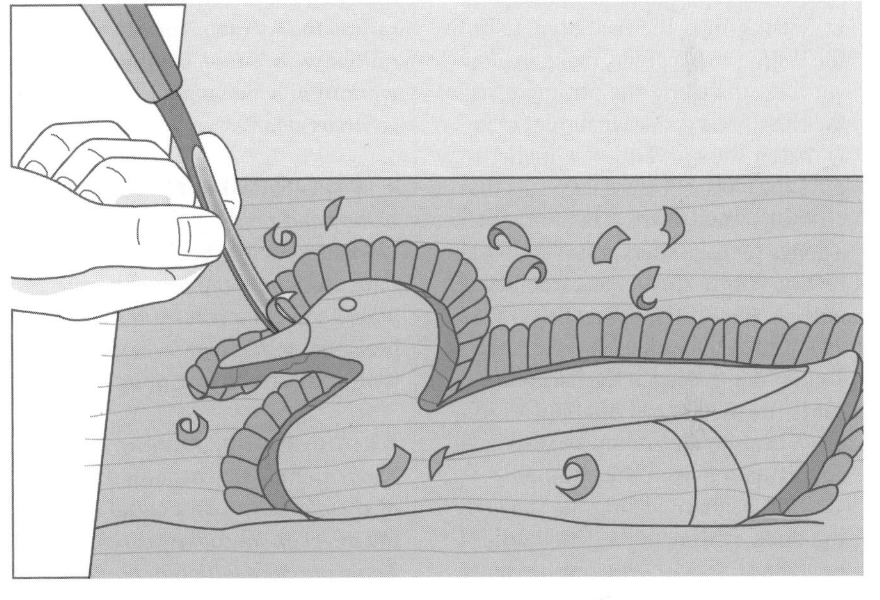

ments. Basic chip carving cuts include three-cut and six-cut triangles and the sweeping curved cut.

To chip carve a three-cut triangle motif, first lay out a row of triangles along the grain. Then, make stop cuts on the two sides of each triangle that go across the grain. These cuts meet at the triangle apex, where they should be about 1/8 in. deep. They taper to zero depth at the triangle baseline. Then, remove the chip by holding the knife at a low angle and cutting in at the baseline to meet the stop cuts.

To make the six-cut triangle—basically an inverted-pyramid shape—lay out another row of triangles and draw three lines from the center to the corners of each triangle. Make three vertical stop cuts along these centerlines, inclining each cut so that it's deepest at the center and tapers to zero depth at the corners. Then, make a slanting cut from each triangle side to remove the three chips.

To make a sweeping cut, draw the outline on the wood and make a vertical stop cut along the center of the line. Then, hold the knife at 45° to the surface at the far end of the line and draw the knife toward you while making a slicing cut. Make a similar cut on the other side of the line to complete the V-cut.

When you feel comfortable using the chip carving knife, tackle the duck panel. Begin by making a paper pattern of the shape and transferring the outline to the stock. To emphasize the outline, create deeper shadow areas and increase contrast, use a cut that isn't a true V, but has one slanted side while the other is vertical.

Make a vertical stop cut along the entire outline. Using a French curve, draw a parallel line about 1/8 in. outside the original outline; at the beak, the spacing should be only about 1/16 in. Also add parallel lines on the lower side of the wings and a water line at the bottom of the duck. Vertical stop cuts must be made where lines intersect to prevent the wood from splitting beyond that point.

To form the grooves, hold the knife at a 45° angle and make slow slicing cuts on the secondary lines. Cut with the grain. Where the grain direction changes in the middle of a cut, it may be necessary to stop the cut and finish it from the opposite direction. To finish the panel, lightly sand with 220-grit sandpaper. Then, bore a hole for a glass eye and attach it with glue.

RELIEF CARVING

A relief carving is a carved design that projects from a recessed background. The background might be level and smooth or trench-carved, as in this example. To begin, select a block of wood at least 1 in. thick and transfer the duck outline from a pattern. Screw a 2 x 4 block to the back of the work so that it can be held securely in a vise. Position the screws under the thickest part of the carving.

Use a small V-tool to make an outlining cut around the figure. Keep the cut about ⅛ in. outside the line and change the direction of the cut when needed to keep working with the grain.

Setting-in is the next step. Using the V-groove as a guide, make shallow vertical cuts along the outline using the chisels and gouges that most closely match the curves. Use a mallet to drive the tools, but avoid deep cuts that crush the wood fibers. Next, work with a gouge to make short passes up to the vertical cuts to create walls around the outline. Repeat the process to gradually deepen the walls.

In order to deepen the background to its finished depth of about ⅝ in., use a bent gouge and make scalloped cuts radiating from the outline.

Next, begin modeling the shape of the duck by drawing a pencil guideline about a ½ in. in from the body perimeter. Use gouges to roughly contour the body, taking off small chips around the head and chest areas. Use wide chisels to make the long sweeping cuts that define the wing and tail sections. Shape the wing indents with the V-tool and then make paring cuts to fine trim the contours.

Bore a 5⁄16-in. eye socket before final rounding of the head. Pare down the beak with a shallow gouge and use the V-tool to incise the lower jaw. Use a razor knife to form the nostril. Smooth the beak details with rifflers, sand all but the background with 220 paper and glue in the eye.

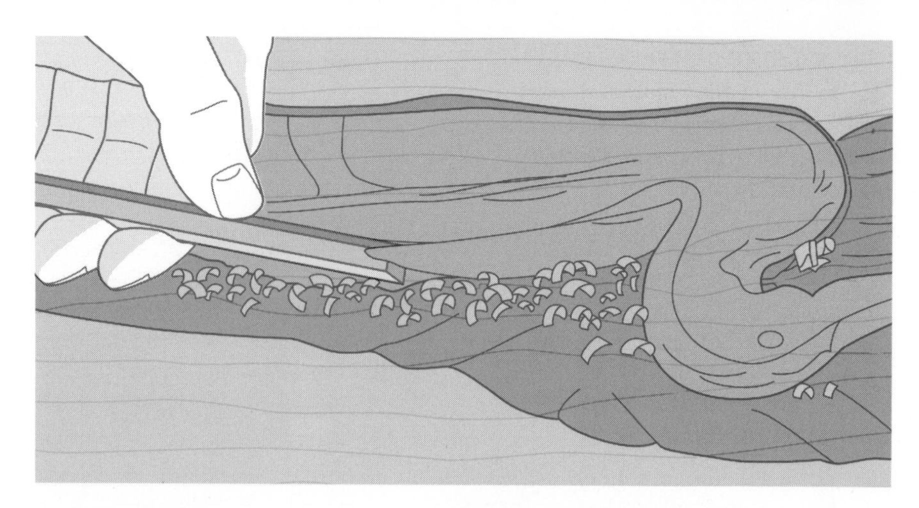

▲ **RELIEF CARVING, 3.** ***Shape convex curves with a straight chisel, changing cut direction as necessary to follow grain. Incise separations with V-tool. Light your work from a low angle to see contours clearly.***

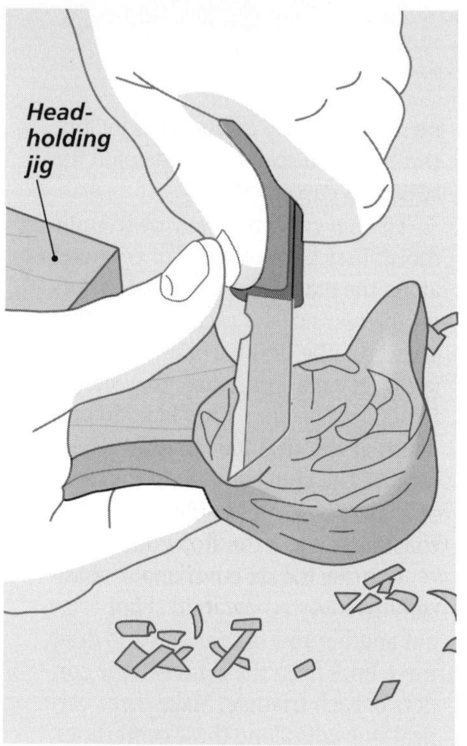

▶ **IN-THE-ROUND CARVING, 1.** ***Using head-holding jig to secure workpiece, shape head by whittling. Note how the thumbs are placed to help control cut. After preliminary shaping, form details with skew chisels and gouges.***

▼ **IN-THE-ROUND CARVING, 2.** ***Begin rounding by making a series of chamfer cuts. Use a chisel with the bevel up on convex curves. Apply pressure with hand on the handle and control cut with hand on the blade.***

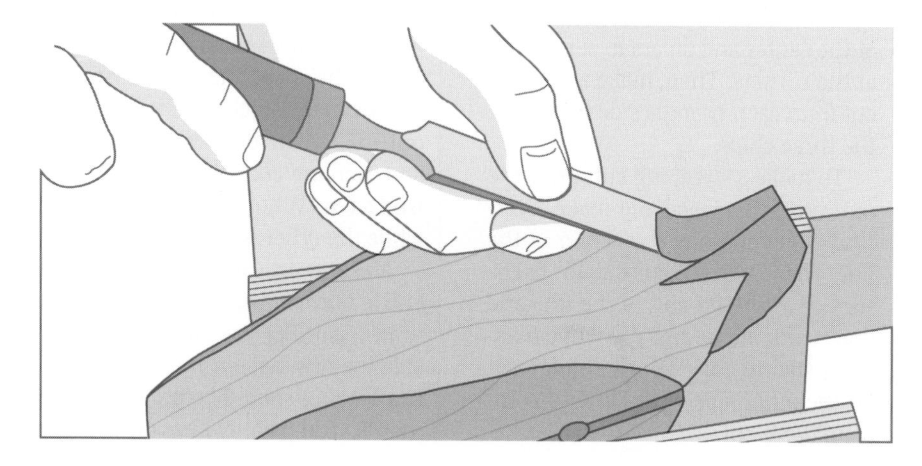

▼ IN-THE-ROUND CARVING, 3. ***Use a gouge in a pivoting motion to form concave curvatures. Always be sure to follow the wood grain direction of the workpiece.***

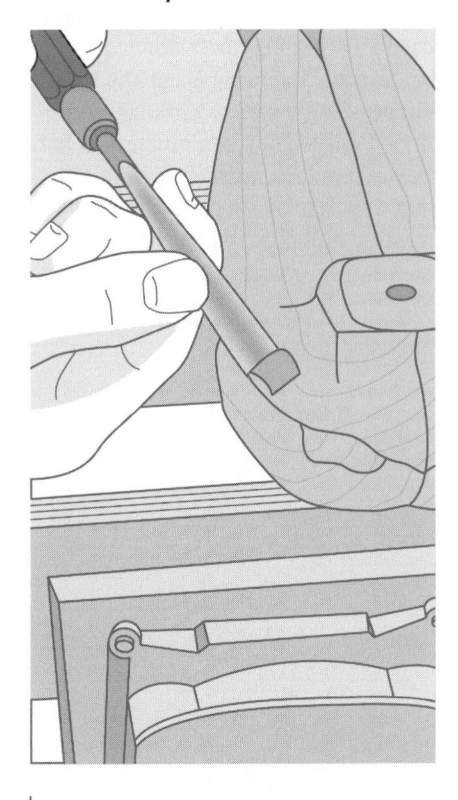

▼ IN-THE-ROUND CARVING, 4. ***Work with a skew chisel to clean out tight areas. Screw a 2 x 4 wood block to workpiece and secure it in a vise.***

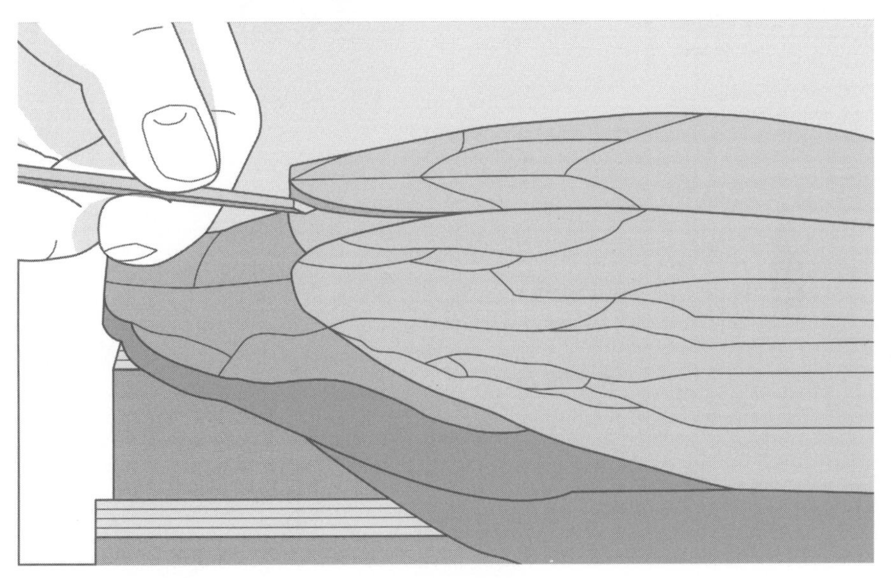

CARVING IN THE ROUND

Carving a decoy duck in three dimensions is a little more challenging than the relief-carved version. Not only is there much more carving involved, but the work must be symmetrical and sensitively done in order to appear realistic. The tools and techniques are similar to those used in relief carving.

If you cannot find a large enough block of wood for your project, you can make one by gluing together smaller pieces. Two pieces of 1¾ x 5¼ x 12-in. basswood were used here. Be sure to orient the grain direction of the pieces in the same way to avoid grain reversal problems when carving across glue joints. The head is carved from a separate block for ease of handling and better control.

Use paper patterns to transfer the top and side profiles of the body to the block. Band saw the side profile and tack the waste back onto the block to replace the top profile outline. Then, band saw the top profile. Before sawing the head roughly to shape, bore a 1/16-in.-dia. hole through the head at the eye location. This will serve as a pilot for the final eye socket hole to be bored later. Then, cut the side and top profiles of the head in the same way as was done for the body.

Bore and counterbore holes for a lagscrew to hold the head to the body. Make a head-holding jig and secure the head blank to it with a lagscrew. Use four brads with the heads nipped off to keep the head from rotating on the holding jig.

Begin shaping the head by whittling with a knife. For more careful shaping and detailing, secure the holding jig in a vise. Use a knife, V-tool and skew chisel to finish detailing the bill; use a fine razor knife to form the nostrils. After the head is roughed out, use a gouge to shape the characteristic eye trough on each side of the head.

Remove the head from the holding jig and temporarily secure it to the body to check the mating surfaces for a good fit. Trace the neck outline on the body block and remove the head. Then, screw a 2 x 4 block to the bottom of the body blank for holding the blank in a vise.

Begin carving the body of the duck to rough shape with a large straight chisel and gouge. Drive the tools using a mallet for initial heavy stock removal and resort to hand power only for final shaping. Generally, use the hand that you have on the tool handle to apply cutting power and allow the hand on the blade to guide the cut. For sweeping, modeling cuts, allow both hands to guide and power the tool.

Attach the head permanently with glue and the lagscrew after the body is carved. Then, blend the neck to the body with a gouge. Use a combination of rasps and files to remove the carving marks and smooth the work. Some ducks, such as the mallard that this carving is modeled after, have primary feathers that project well out of the body. Because they're difficult to carve out of the solid block, they're carved separately and inserted into slots cut below the large feathers carved at the rear. Sand the entire carving, finishing off with 220-grit sandpaper. Use a 5/16-in. drill bit to bore the eye sockets. Secure the glass eyes with glue.

FILES

Most homeowners have at least one file lying in the bottom of the toolbox or in the back of a drawer. And when the time comes to sharpen the lawnmower blade or clean up the rough edges after cutting a bolt to length, it's this simple hand tool that comes to the rescue.

While the basic idea of a file may be simple—a bar of hardened steel with rows of finely spaced cutting teeth—the variations on this theme are practically endless. For every smoothing, trimming and sharpening job that you can imagine, there's a specially designed file for the job.

CLASSIFICATIONS OF FILES

Since there are so many types, knowing which file suits your needs isn't always easy. And the problem is compounded by nomenclature for these tools that isn't quite as informative as you might like. Knowing you need a small file for smoothing steel, for instance, is no help when you're asked if you'd prefer a 6-in. mill bastard or an 8-in. second-cut hand file.

1. Detailing file

2. Spiral-cut chain saw file

3. Needle rasps

Fortunately, many files are designated by the job that they perform, such as a chain saw file or a warding file. However, the best way to know what you're looking for is to understand the standard way that files are classified.

Files are classified in terms of their shape, cut and length. The cross-sectional shape of a file can be circular, rectangular, triangular, diamond-shaped or a combination of flats and rounds. Many types are available with either straight or tapered sides. Choosing a particular shape simply involves finding a file to fit the work. Mill files and flat files are suit-

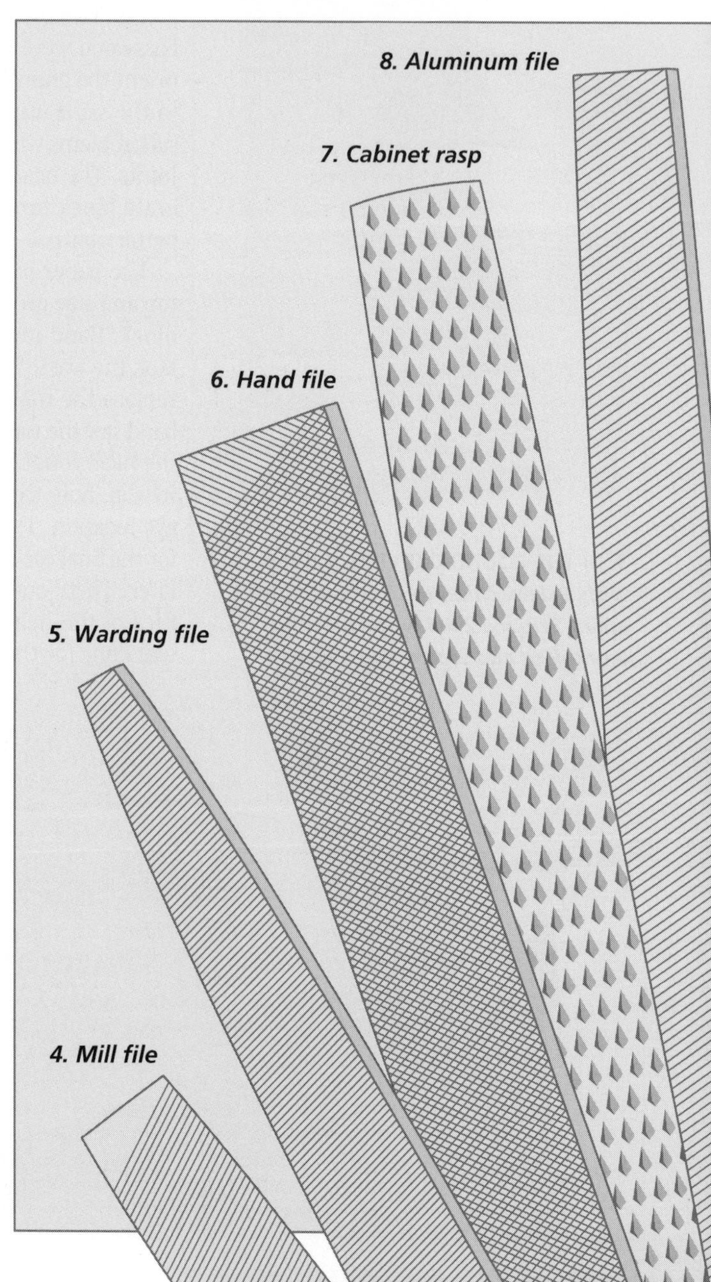

able for flat edges or surfaces, but a triangular saw file is best suited for fitting between the teeth of your handsaw.

The cut of a file refers to both the tooth configuration and to the space between the teeth, or coarseness. A single-cut file, such as a mill file, has a series of parallel, diagonal teeth and is the choice for sharpening and smoothing surfaces, and when only a small amount of material must be removed. For faster cutting and when a rougher finish is acceptable, a double-cut file is used. Here, a second, opposing row of diagonal teeth are cut over the first. The first row of teeth is called the overcut, and the second, opposing row is called the upcut.

While the faces of a typical rectangular-section file do most of the work, the edges are often cut for working in slots or cleaning out corners. However, some files have "safe," or uncut, edges for filing in corners without marring the adjoining surface.

Both single- and double-cut files are commonly available in three grades of coarseness: smooth cut, second cut and bastard cut. However, the actual space between the teeth is also related to the length of the file body—as the length increases, the file gets coarser. In general, a 6-in. bastard-cut file (short, but coarse) will produce results similar to a 10-in. second-cut file or a 14-in. smooth-cut file.

Rasps differ from single- and double-cut files in that the teeth are individual points rather than lines. This reduces clogging and makes for a fast, but rough finished surface. Although rasps are generally used on wood, they can be used to trim virtually any material, including metals. Use a pat-

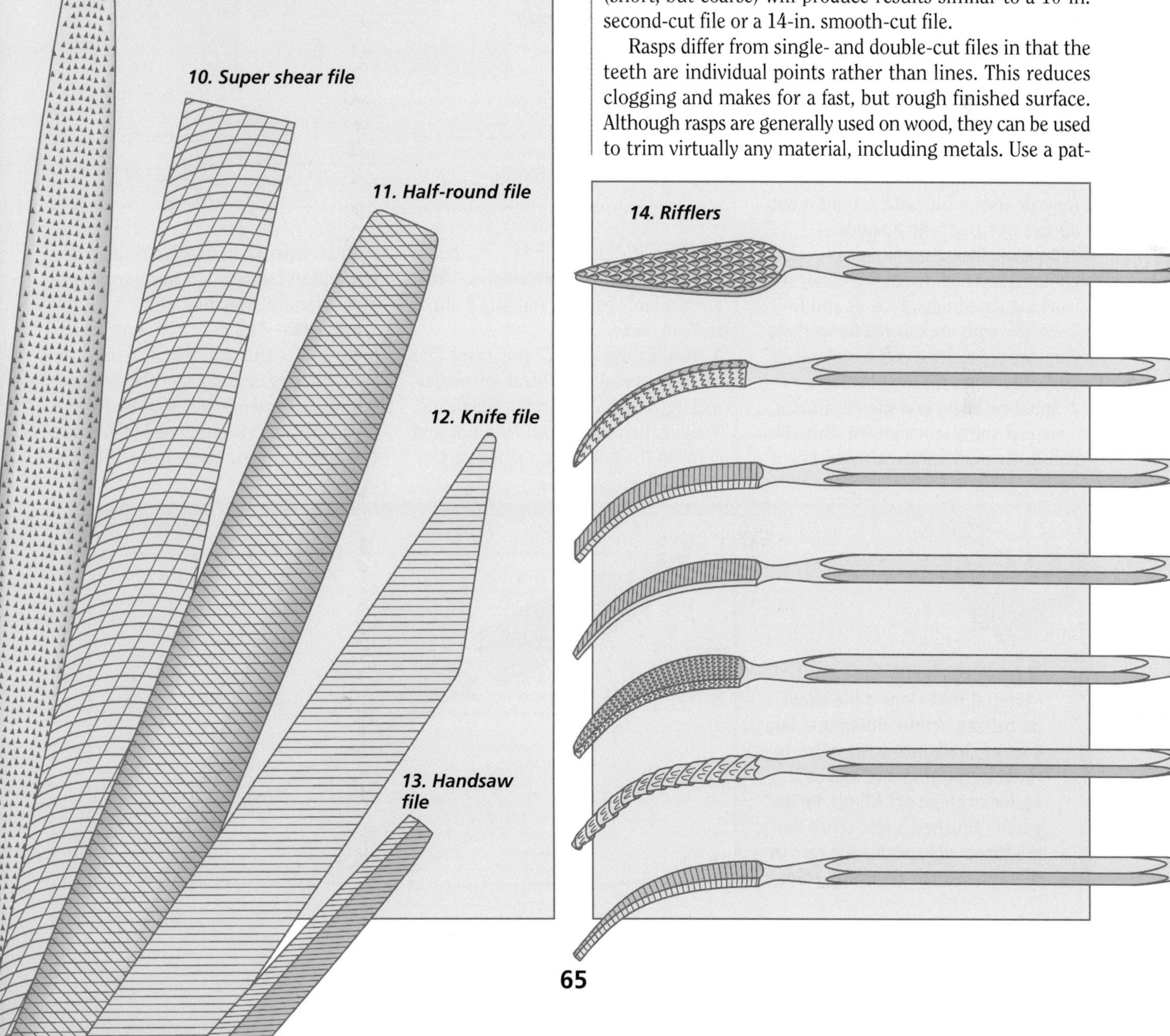

ternmaker's rasp for fine work, a cabinetmaker's rasp for quicker cutting and, finally, a wood rasp for the fastest stock removal.

In addition to single, double and rasp cuts, you'll find files with curved teeth and specialty files designed for more efficient cutting in specific materials. Keep in mind that files are not abrasives. They cut the wood in one direction only. Rubbing a file back and forth over a surface won't get the job done any faster, and you're likely to wear out the file sooner. Always have a file card on hand for cleaning out clogged material and store the files so they won't become dulled by striking other metal tools.

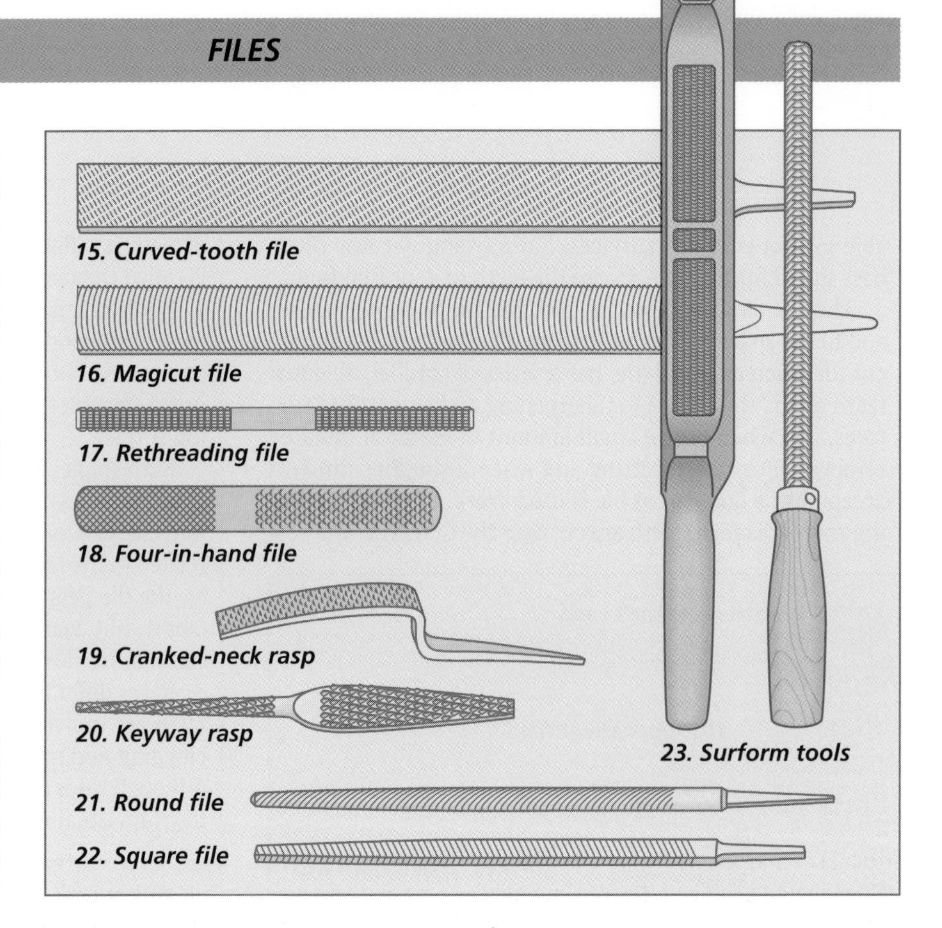

INVENTORY OF FILES

The following is just a small sampling of the many files available. Note that for safe use, a file with a tang must *always* be fitted with a handle.

1. Detailing file—Basically a half-round combination file, this tool is handy for working small flats, rounds and hollows. The ends are tapered for work in confined spaces; one end is bastard cut while the other is second cut.

2. Spiral-cut chain saw file—Featuring a special spiral-cut pattern, this file cuts faster than standard, round chain saw files. It's offered in 5/32, 3/16 and 7/32 in. dia. Regular, smooth chain saw files are available in sizes ranging from 1/8 to 3/8-in. dia.

3. Needle rasps—These tiny rasps (5 1/2 in. long overall) are ideal for model-making or detailed carving and fitting. They feature a smooth rasp cut and come in the following shapes: rectangular, tapered, triangular, round, half-round and square. For metalwork, needle files are available.

4. Mill file—The most common single-cut file is the mill file. It's used for sharpening circular saw blades, draw-filing, lathe work and anywhere else a smooth finish is required. Mill files are available in lengths from 4 to 16 in.

TIP

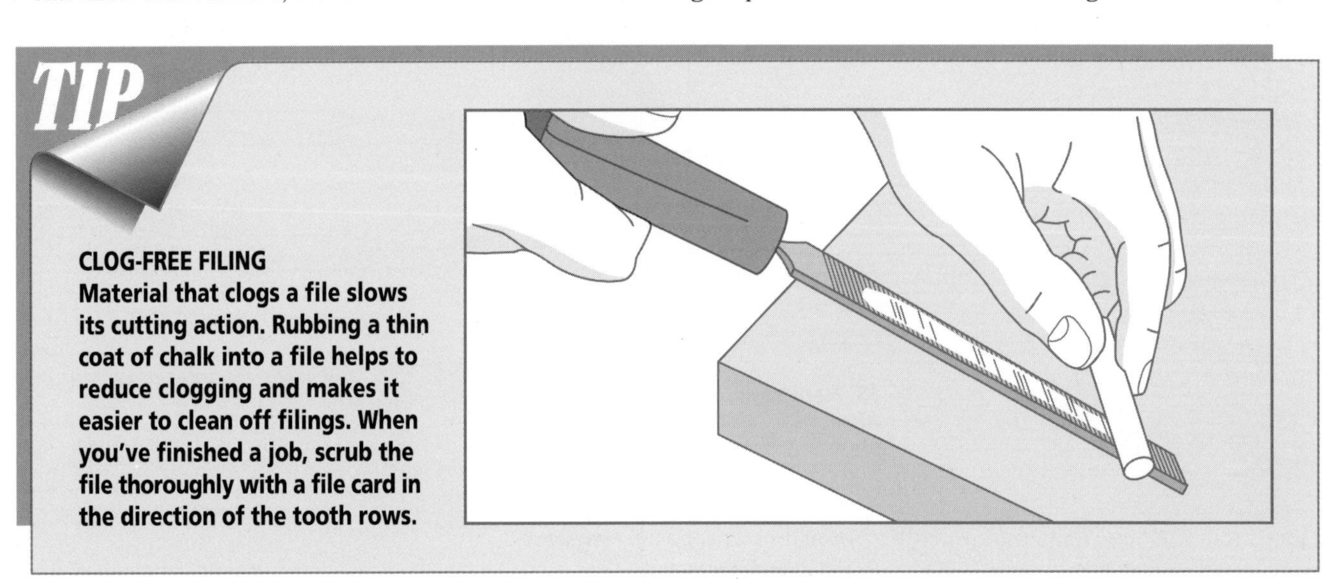

CLOG-FREE FILING

Material that clogs a file slows its cutting action. Rubbing a thin coat of chalk into a file helps to reduce clogging and makes it easier to clean off filings. When you've finished a job, scrub the file thoroughly with a file card in the direction of the tooth rows.

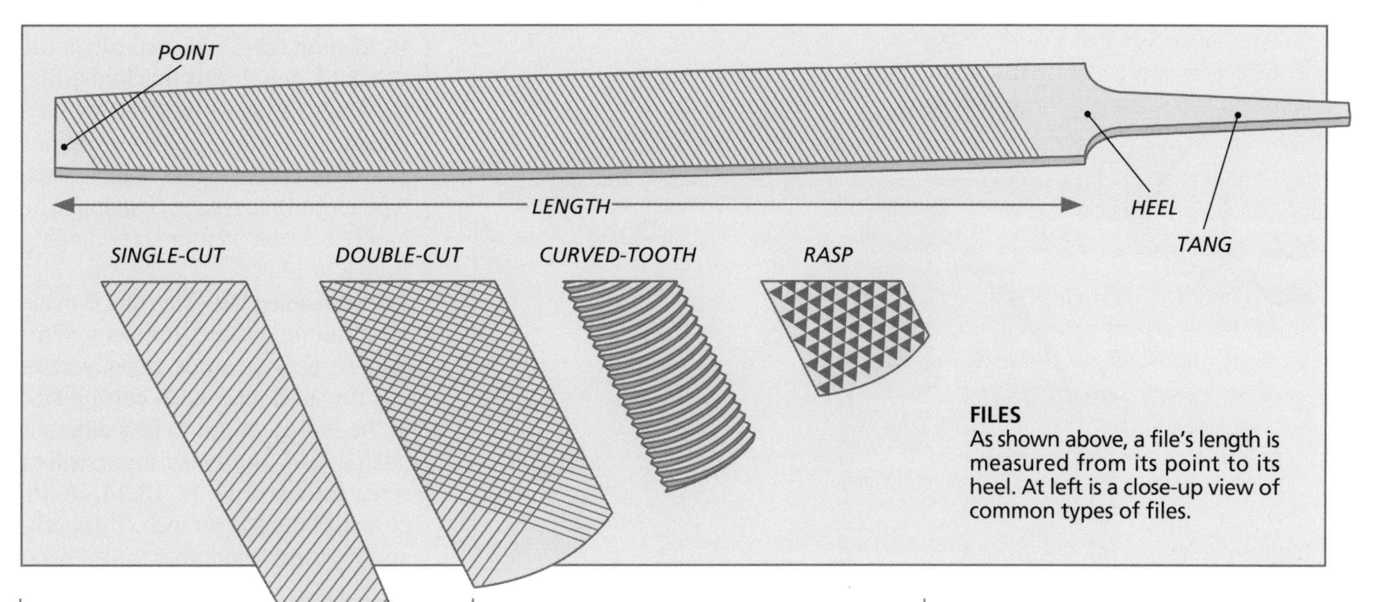

FILES
As shown above, a file's length is measured from its point to its heel. At left is a close-up view of common types of files.

5. Warding file—This file is designed for shaping and trimming notches in locks and keys. It's double cut on the faces and single cut on the edges. The tapered profile of the warding file is useful in situations where an ordinary file won't fit. Produced in bastard, second and smooth cut, it's available in lengths from 4 to 10 in.

6. Hand file—Double-cut files of a variety of shapes are generally classified as machinist files. And while they're all used by hand, the term "hand file" usually refers to a flat file with straight, uncut (safe) edges. This particular 8-in. model is actually half hand file, half mill file. The other side is single cut for smooth work.

7. Cabinet rasp—While coarse files that are designed for use on metal *can* be useful in woodworking, the quickest way to remove stock is with a rasp. This typical model is 8 in. long, and has a round and flat face.

8. Aluminum file—Ordinary files tend to clog when they're used on soft aluminum. This file addresses the problem with a unique double-cut pattern that resists clogging. The initial deep overcut is followed by a light upcut on the opposite diagonal. This gives a scalloped-tooth pattern that cuts cleanly and leaves a fine finish.

9. Patternmaker's rasp—Like regular rasps, these tools have individual teeth for fast cutting. However, the teeth are staggered and smaller to give a finer finished surface in wood. Available in second and smooth cut, patternmaker's rasps also have cut edges for working in corners.

10. Super shear file—Designed for work on softer metals, iron, annealed steel, plastic and hardwood, this file has an offset circular tooth that cuts both fast and smooth. A light upcut, almost parallel to the plane, breaks each circular cutting edge for clog-free filing.

11. Half-round file—This bastard-cut file is double cut for fast stock removal and one face is round for working concave shapes. Although it's classified as a machinist file, the tool is useful for fine trimming in wood. Half-round files are available in smooth and second cut, and some of the finer varieties are single cut on the round side.

12. Knife file—The single-cut edge of this file is about 1/16 in. thick; its double-cut faces are at about a 10° angle to each other. The wide top edge is uncut. Used by tool and die makers, this file is excellent for tight, acute angles.

► **SETTING HANDLES.** ***Set a file into its handle by tapping. Never use a file with a bare tang.***

13. Handsaw file—Single-cut triangular saw files are available in a range of sizes to suit the size of the saw teeth being filed. This 6-in. slim taper file is best for 7- or 8-tpi saws. Other sizes include heavy, regular, extra slim and double extra slim. Double-cut triangular files are called three-square files and are used for trimming internal angles in metalwork.

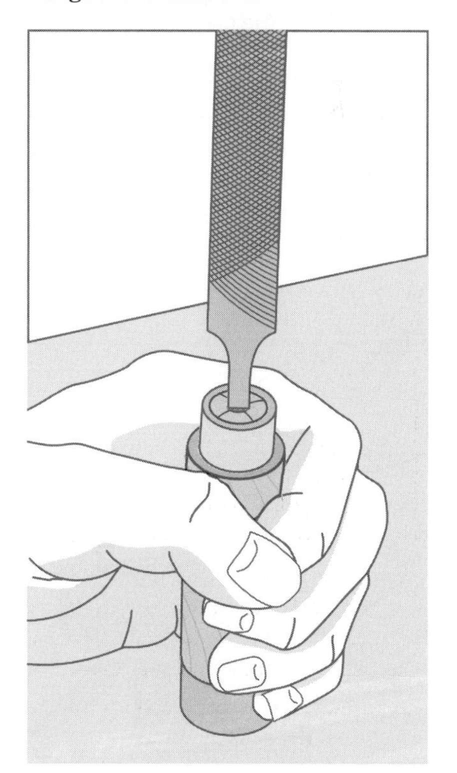

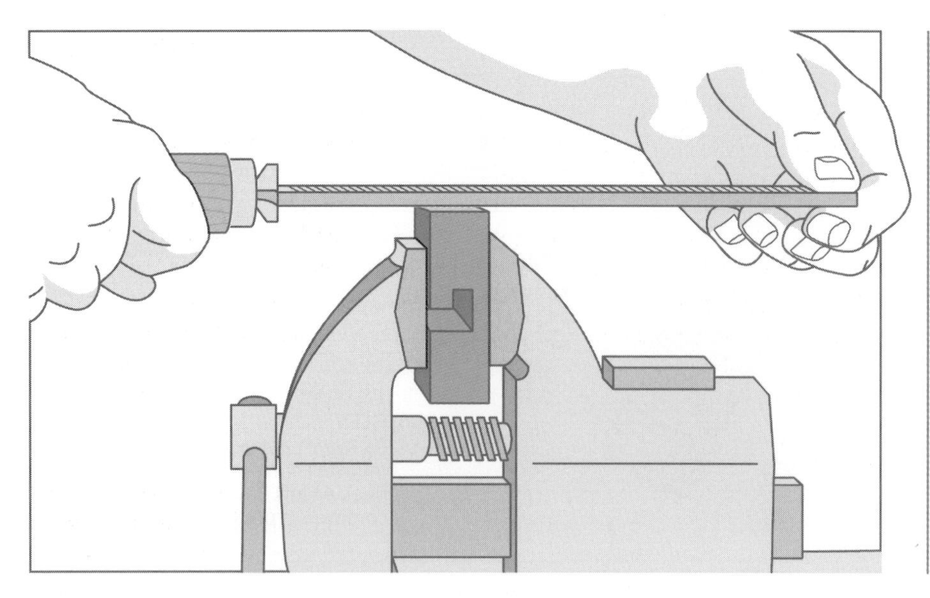

16. **Magicut file**—A close cousin of the standard, double-cut machinist file, the Magicut file is designed for fast, yet smooth cutting. Angled serrations across the teeth create a chipbreaker-type tooth that resists clogging. The tool is available in four sizes ranging from 8 to 14 in.

17. **Rethreading file**—This tool is made for cleaning out and restoring damaged threads on studs, bolts, screws and threaded pipe. Each cutting face of the tool is shaped to fit a different pitch thread. The model shown will fit screw threads of 11, 12, 13, 14, 16, 18, 20 and 24 threads per inch. Three others are available for other thread sizes.

▲ **HOLDING FILES.** ***Stroke a file by applying only arm pressure; don't lean on the tool. A heavy grip and upper body movement produce an uneven, rocky motion instead of smooth, even strokes.***

► **STRAIGHT FILING.** ***In straight or cross filing, hold the file level and diagonal to the workpiece. Begin the stroke at the file's point.***

▼ **DRAW FILING.** ***Draw file with a single-cut bastard file. Holding the file level and perpendicular to the surface, push and pull it along smoothly.***

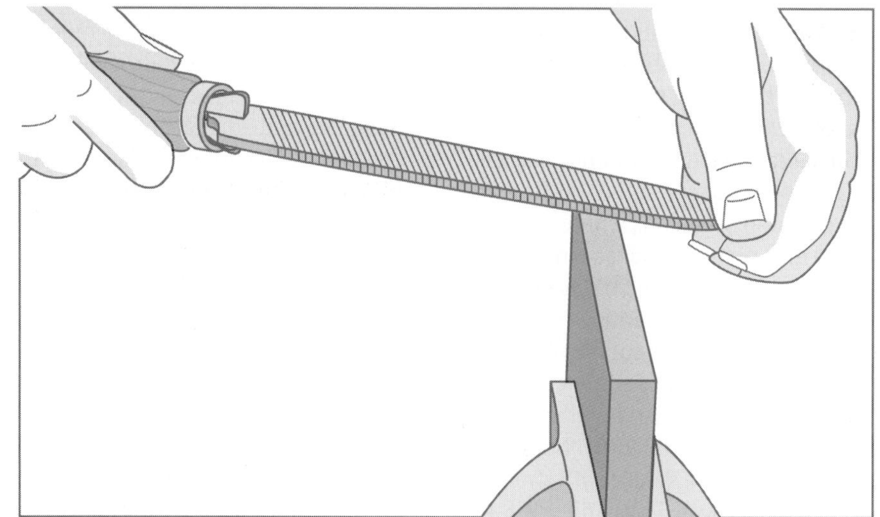

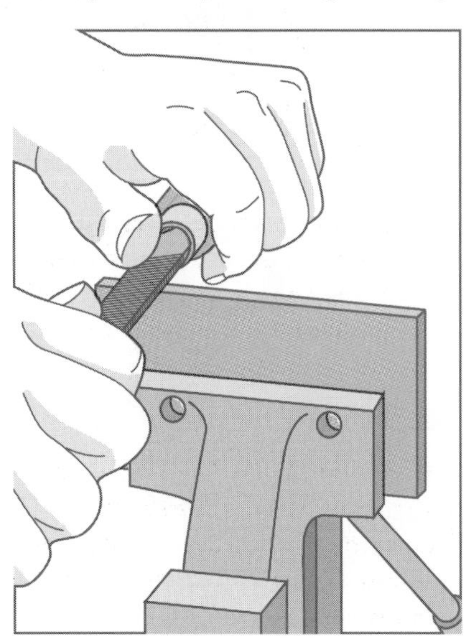

14. **Rifflers**—These tools are for shaping and smoothing details that other files can't handle. One end of each uniquely shaped rasp-cut riffler is fine; the other end is coarse. For an extra fine finish, fine cut types are available.

15. **Curved-tooth file**—This 14-in.-long file features deeply cut, curved teeth for fast cutting and reduced clogging in soft material. Widely used in autobody work and on aluminum and sheet steel, it's also available in 8-, 10- and 12-in. lengths. And there's a flexible type that fits in a special holder with handles similar to a plane. The holder can be adjusted to bend the blade for working convex and concave surfaces.

18. **Four-in-hand file**—If you're going to own only one file, then this combination tool might be what you need. The 8-in.-long file has both round and flat surfaces, and each side of the file has a double-cut and rasp-cut end.

19. **Cranked-neck rasp**—Curved rasps come in a wide variety of shapes and sizes, each making a particular shaping operation easier. This 3/4 x 2½-in. rasp is ideal for carefully shaping flat or slightly concave surfaces and is especially useful in woodcarving.

20. **Keyway rasp**—This is a combination rasp for shaping wood. One end is flat and tapered with cut edges. The other end is a tapered round rasp.

21. Round file—This is the standard file for cleaning up or enlarging holes and shaping tight internal curves. It works on metal or wood. It's available in single- or double-cut and smooth-, second-cut or bastard grades.
22. Square file—Whenever you need to make a round hole square, this is the file to reach for. Its long, tapered profile also makes it useful for cleaning up right-angle shapes such as slots and keyways. Available in widths from 5/32 to 5/8 in. and lengths from 4 to 14 in.
23. Surform tools—Versatility and speed make these tools the good choice for shaping wood, body filler, fiberglass, aluminum and other soft materials. The Surform file *(23, left)* accepts three different hardened steel replacement blades and two grades of abrasive cutters. The round Surform *(23, right)* is ideal for roughing out tight curves and shaping holes.

USING FILES

Filing looks easy, but it does require some practice to become skilled at it. Knowing the different classifications of files and which is right for the job also will help in their use.

In general, your workpiece should be held at elbow level. However, there are exceptions. For heavy filing, the work is held lower than elbow level. Conversely, fine, delicate filing requires that you sit at the bench and keep the work at eye level. When filing long, thin edges that can't be clamped close to the vise jaws, sandwich the workpiece between two pieces of scrap to keep the file from chattering as it cuts.

To straight or cross file, hold the file diagonal to the workpiece. Starting with the file's point, advance the tool forward and laterally across the surface, finishing the stroke at the file's heel. This technique requires a file that is about one-third longer than the area being worked.

Draw filing is slower than straight filing, but results in a smoother surface. Use a single-cut bastard file, gripping it at the point and handle while holding it perpendicular to the work. Push and pull the file over the workpiece with even pressure.

Lathe filing is often used for fine fitting of a turned piece. You can buy a lathe file with rows of teeth at an oblique angle to its length, but a single-cut bastard file will do. Work with a moderate- to high-rpm spindle speed.

CARING FOR FILES

Files, unlike other tools, cannot be resharpened. Although hard use will dull a file, improper use will dull it just as fast. Apply ample pressure to the file to make it cut; simply sliding it over the work will rapidly dull it.

To keep the file from sliding, avoid touching the work or the face of the file with oily fingers and make sure the work surface is free of oil. Scale—a black, hard crust often found on cast iron—should be removed before filing because it dulls the tool. Avoid filing over a vise's jaws; they're made out of extra-hard steel and rapidly dull a file.

Files are so hard that they are actually brittle. Avoid striking or dropping them. Never store or carry files in a way that they hit or rub against each other. Hang files separately or store them in a drawer with partitions.

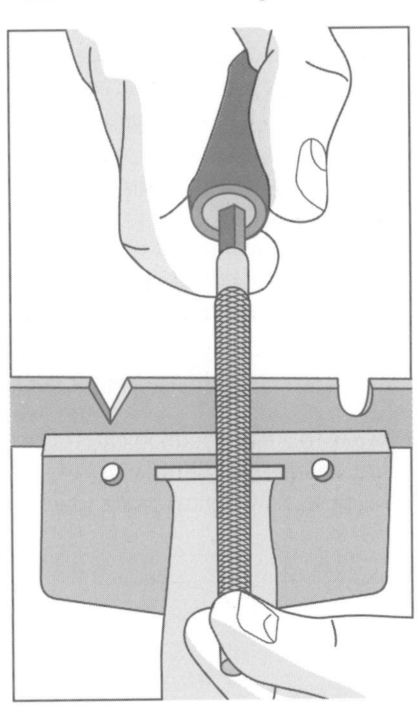

▲ **ROUNDING SLOTS.** ***To form a rounded slot, use a hacksaw to cut a V-shaped notch, then use a round file to shape the slot. For a large curve, use a half-round file.***

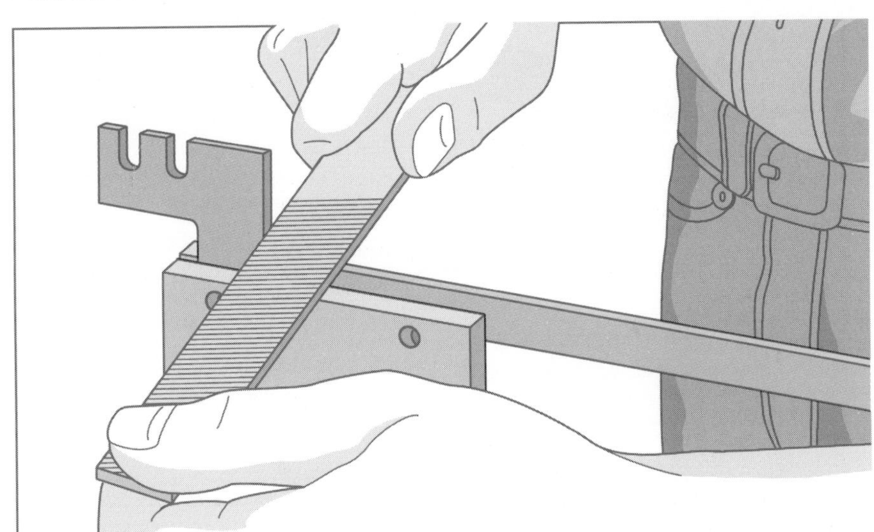

◀ **SQUARING CORNERS.** ***Here, a safe-edge (uncut) file is used to square up an inside corner. Note that the work surface is secured as close as possible to the vise jaws.***

ABRASIVES

Sanding is one of the most common construction and repair tasks performed around the home and shop. As the final stage in smoothing a workpiece, sanding is also indispensable in eliminating any blemishes and imperfections left by other tools. Even fine-cutting tools such as planes and scrapers will sometimes leave marks and ridges on wood surfaces. They also tend to compress the fibers of the wood and close the pores, inhibiting the wood's ability to properly accept a finish. However, sanding, as the final step in preparing the surfaces of a workpiece, opens up closed wood pores, allowing for the uniform application and adhesion of the finish.

COATED ABRASIVES

Although sanding is one of the easiest-to-do jobs in the workshop, unless you select the correct type of abrasive and use it properly, you'll have a hard time achieving good results. To begin with, sandpaper, or "coated abrasive" as it is technically known, is identified by three things: the type of abrasive particles on its surface, the grit (or coarseness) of the particles and the actual amount of abrasive on an individual sheet. Your choice of the sandpaper to use depends on the type of work that you're doing.

SANDPAPER COATINGS

Two of the most common types of coating for sandpaper are flint and garnet. Flint is less expensive than garnet and, therefore, is the logical choice when you're sanding surfaces that clog the paper quickly and spoil it, such as soft, gummy woods, or when you're removing coats of paint or other finishes. Garnet, reddish in color, is tougher and longer lasting, and generally works better for sanding all types of hardwoods.

The closest thing to an all-purpose abrasive is aluminum-oxide paper. It can be used on wood, metal, plastics and fiberglass. Its abrasive coating, colored light gray to brown, is a tough synthetic that is the same material used in grinding wheels, so it's very durable and holds up especially well when used in power sanders.

Silicon carbide is the hardest abrasive generally available for home and shop use. Its particles are almost as hard as a diamond, making it an ideal choice for sanding materials such as nonferrous metals, composition boards and most types of plastics—as well as wood. It can also be used with water or mineral oil for rubbing down finishes of varnish, polyurethane or lacquer.

GRITS AND BACKINGS

The grit of an individual sheet of sandpaper is identified by the number printed on its backing. These numbers range from a very coarse No. 12 up to a super fine No. 600, with 22 increments between; the ones most commonly available are presented in the chart here.

The finer-grit sandpapers frequently are available with cloth backings, as well as with the standard paper backing. You'll find that the cloth-backed abrasives are more flexible, and tend to perform better when you're sanding curved

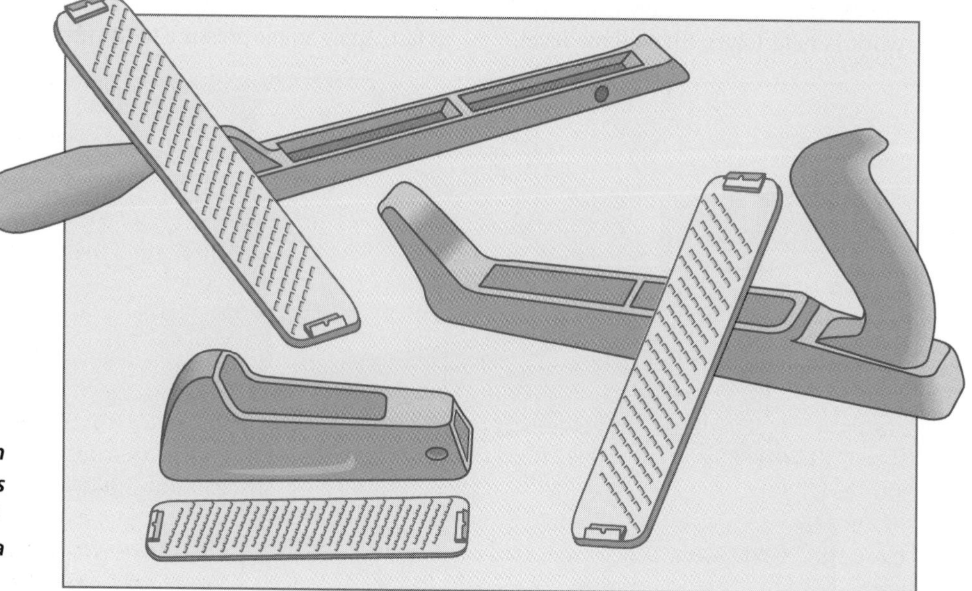

► **SURFORM TOOLS.** ***Surform tools of 5½- and 10-in. lengths come in different styles for trimming wood and other materials. Carbide grit sanding blades available for surform tools are long-wearing abrasive plates that work well on wood, plastic and metal; they are easily cleaned with a solvent or wire brush.***

WORKSHOP ABRASIVES

SANDPAPER	GRIT	GRADE	USES
Very coarse	20	3½	Fast, heavy removing of material or many thick layers of finish
	30	2½	
	36	2	
	40	1½	
	50	1	
Coarse	60	½	Moderate to light removing of material or thick layers of finish
	80	1/0(0)	
Medium	100	2/0	Light removing of material or thick layer of finish
	120	3/0	
Fine	150	4/0	Final smoothing before applying paint
	180	5/0	
Very fine	220	6/0	Final smoothing before applying clear finish
	240	7/0	
Extra fine	280	8/0	Fine sanding or abrading to remove blemishes between coats of clear finish
	320	9/0	
Super fine	400	10/0	Fine sanding or abrading to remove blemishes before last coat of lacquer Deglossing finish

STEEL WOOL	GRADE	USES
Very coarse	3	Fast, heavy removing of material or many thick layers of finish Rough trimming or shaping
Coarse	2	Moderate to light removing of material or thick layers of finish Preliminary smoothing; leveling of deep depressions or scratches
Medium	1	Light removing of material or thick layer of finish Intermediate smoothing; leveling of shallow depressions or scratches Preliminary wiping of residue off wood stripped with chemical stripper
Medium fine or fine	1/0 (0)	Final smoothing before applying paint Light abrading between coats of paint Heavy cleaning; removing deep stains or scuff marks
Very fine	2/0 (00)	General smoothing or abrading Final cleaning of residue off wood stripped with chemical stripper Deglossing finish Light cleaning; removing surface stains or scuff marks
Extra fine	3/0 (000)	Final smoothing before applying clear finish Light abrading between coats of clear finish Deglossing finish; with lubricant to spot-repair clear finish Removing paint spots; general polishing of metal
Super fine	4/0 (0000)	Applying stain, wax or oil Fine abrading of finish to reduce gloss or sheen Fine polishing of metal

and irregular shapes. The weight of backing material ranges from A (lightest) to E (sturdiest) for paper; for cloth, X is sturdier than J.

On many abrasives, you'll also have a choice between closed and open coats, which indicate how many particles are on the surface of an individual sheet. Closed coat means

▲ **CHOOSING ABRASIVES.** ***Sandpaper is usually identified by its coarseness, expressed as either grit or grade; its backing, which may or may not be of paper, lists the type and size of the grit as well as the weight of the backing. Steel wool comes in pads typically ranging from grade No. 3 to No. 4/0 (0000).***

coverage over the entire sheet, which provides for fast cutting. Open coat indicates 50 to 70 percent coverage; this type cuts more slowly, but it won't clog as quickly.

STEEL WOOL

Steel wool is an abrasive that comes in pads, usually ranging from a very coarse No. 3 to a super fine No. 4/0 (0000). The grade descriptors for steel wool are roughly comparable to those for sandpaper—grades 2/0 and 4/0, for instance, being respectively equivalent to very fine and super fine sandpaper.

Avoid relying on steel wool for the initial smoothing of wood surfaces; use sandpaper instead. Steel wool tends to have a polishing effect and may close the wood's pores.

However, steel wool works especially well for intermediate and final smoothing of irregular-shaped wood surfaces, where the pad can be molded to match the contours. And to polish a fine wood finish, use a 4/0 pad lubricated with furniture oil.

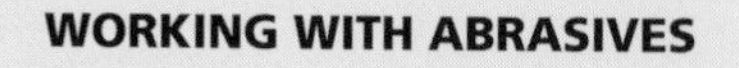

WORKING WITH ABRASIVES

For most types of work with abrasives, you should wear a dust mask to avoid inhaling any harmful particles. Wear gloves, if necessary, to protect your hands. Goggles also should be worn whenever there is a risk of particles getting in your eyes.

When using abrasives on wood surfaces, always work *with* the grain—that is, in the direction parallel to it. Working against, or across, the grain yields deep scratches in the wood and can ruin the surface. Progress from coarser to finer grades of abrasives, stopping often to clear particles off the surface with a soft-bristle brush.

Replace the abrasive you're using as soon it becomes clogged, worn or torn. Check your work at a low angle under a good light source; as well as your eyes, inspect with your fingers.

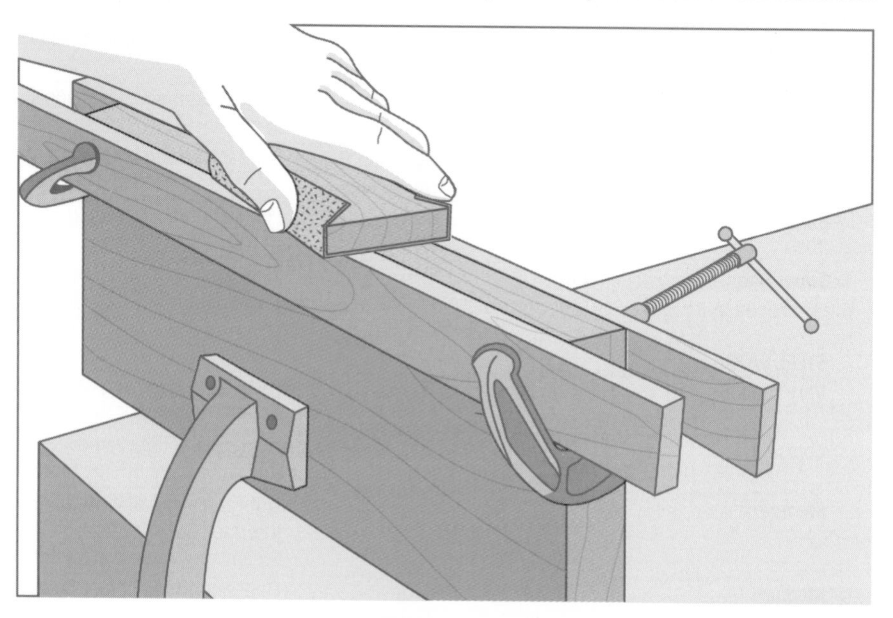

▶ SANDING FLAT SURFACES. ***Sandpaper on an unpadded block can be used to achieve a true flat edge with the aid of two straightedged boards clamped to the workpiece.***

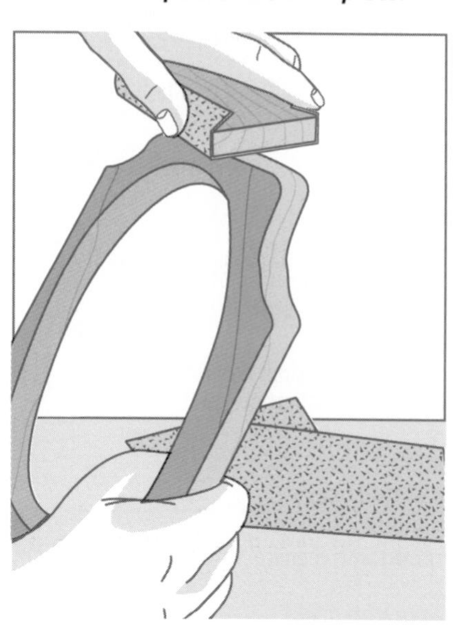

▲ SANDING IRREGULAR SURFACES, 1. ***When sanding rounded corners and contours, abrasive works best if it's backed with a resilient block. Padding allows the paper to conform to workpiece's shape.***

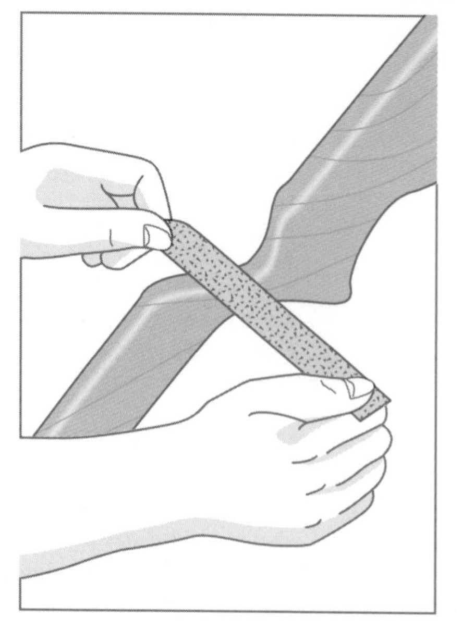

▶ SANDING IRREGULAR SURFACES, 2. ***To sand sculptural shapes, cut cloth-backed abrasive into narrow strips and use like a shoeshine rag. Paper-backed abrasive will work if you apply masking tape to back.***

SANDING BLOCKS

When sanding flat or convex-shaped surfaces, use a sanding block. Sanding blocks of varying styles are available at most hardware stores, but it's not that difficult to make your own. As an alternative to simply wrapping sandpaper around a wood block and holding it securely, here's a sanding block that's easy to make and gives you more than one face to work with at a time.

Use a backsaw to cut a 1 x 4 wood block about 3 in. long, then saw a slot ⅛ in. deep along the center of one edge and sand off any sharp corners. To pad the block, glue a thick piece of felt onto each of its faces. Use a piece of short-nap carpeting to pad a block you're using for polishing a finish.

To fit the block with sandpaper, use scissors or a utility knife to cut a sheet that is large enough to wrap all the way around it, plus ¼ in. Insert one edge of the sandpaper into the block's slot, wrap the sheet around the block and tuck the other end into the slot. Staple or tack the ends of the sandpaper to hold it tight.

Make short, straight passes with the sanding block, using moderate, even pressure; ease up if the sandpaper cuts too deeply. Lift the sanding block to reposition it rather than sand across the grain. If the sandpaper's leading edge catches, turn the sanding block 90° to sand with a secured edge.

To prevent the rounding of edges, keep the sanding block flat; don't overhang an edge by more than half the width and length of the sanding block. For a true flat edge, clamp straight-edged boards to the side surfaces as a guide and use an unpadded sanding block. A padded sanding block works best for rounded corners and contours, helping the sandpaper to conform to the surface's shape.

SANDING STICKS

For sanding concave-shaped surfaces, trim a sheet of sandpaper to fit snugly around a wood dowel with a bit of overlap. Wrap the sandpaper around the dowel, then secure the edges using masking tape. Press the sanding stick against the contour and twist it slowly and evenly.

TAPES AND CORDS

Abrasives in the form of flat tapes and round cords let you smooth otherwise inaccessible spots. The cords typically come in diameters from 0.150 to 0.012 in., the tapes in widths from 1⁄16 to ¼ in. Both cords and tapes are available in aluminum oxide, crocus and silicon carbide. Oil cords are also made.

As a substitute for tape, however, you can use narrow strips of cloth-backed abrasive cut from the length

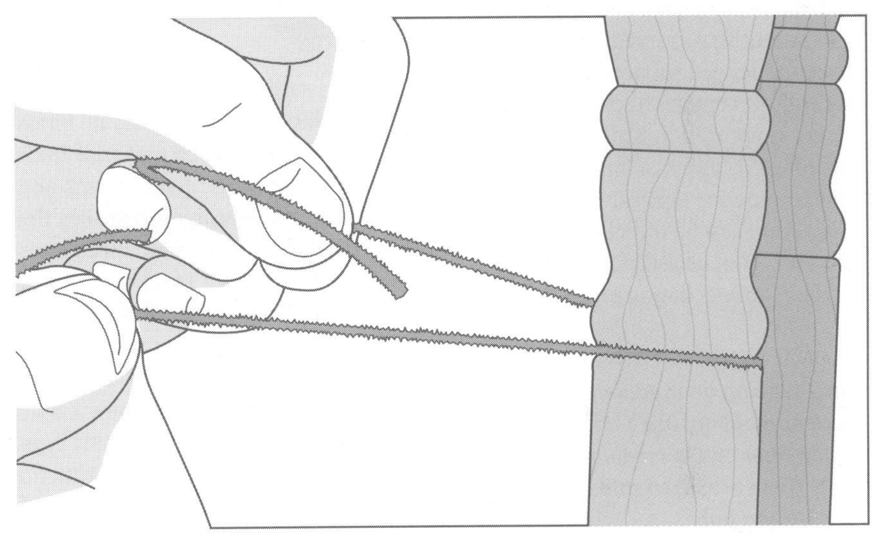

▲ **SANDING TIGHT SPOTS.** ***Round abrasive cords quickly smooth areas like the fine grooves in spindles.***

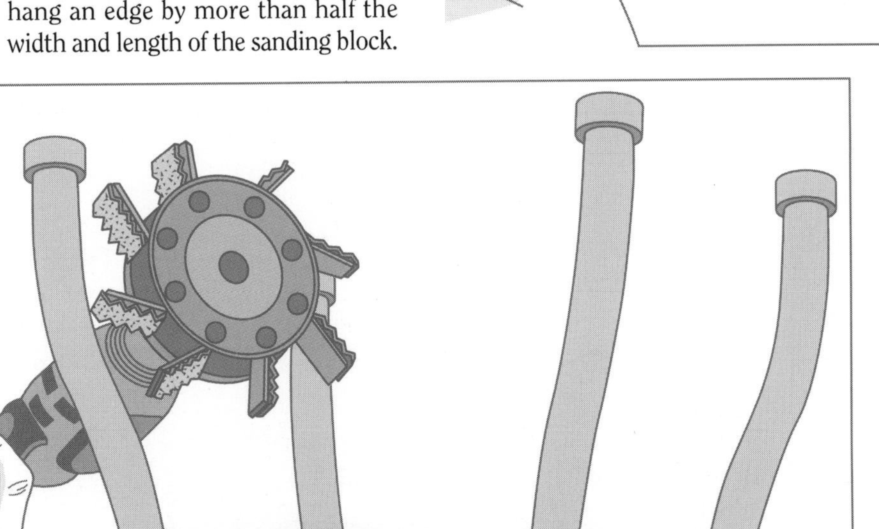

◀ **FLAP SANDING.** ***Flexing action of abrasive strips and support brushes on flap sander make the sanding of irregular surfaces a snap.***

of sheets. Paper-backed abrasive will work just as well if you reinforce the back with masking tape. Wrap the strip snugly around the turning of a chair back, for example, then grip it at each end and draw it smoothly back and forth shoeshine-style.

For the fine grooves in spindles and other crevices, braid your own cord out of a pad of steel wool. Twist together enough strands from the pad to fit tightly into the detail without touching adjacent surfaces and apply the same shoeshine-style technique.

FLAP SANDER

For smoothing curved or otherwise irregular-shaped surfaces, a flap sander is handy. It contains a series of abrasive strips supported by stiff brushes and fits into the chuck of an electric drill. But because the direction of the abrading action can be difficult to control, the tool is not advised for use on wood surfaces unless they are to be painted.

▼ **FINAL SANDING CONTOURS.** ***For final sanding on irregular shapes such as molding, use a non-woven nylon fiber pad in medium or fine grit. These are often sold for cleaning kitchen pots.***

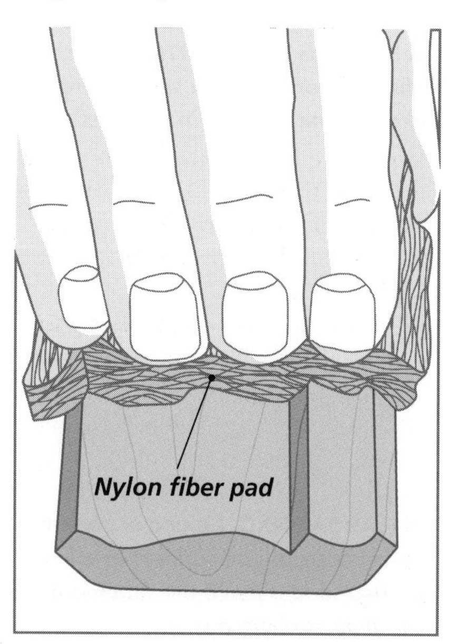

WET ABRASIVES

While standard sandpaper is indispensable for smoothing wood surfaces, to smooth and polish a wood's finish—specifically lacquer, varnish or shellac—there are special wet abrasives available. These are used with water or oil (mineral or paraffin), which acts as a lubricant to help get rid of abraded material and reduce friction. Water is usually favored because it's cheap and easy to clean up. However, *do not* use water on shellac. Work only with oil on this type of finish.

Waterproof abrasive paper, coated with silicone carbide, is typically available in 9 x 11-in. sheets ranging from 220 grit (very fine) to 600 grit (very fine). Use wet abrasive paper with water or oil to sand between coats of finish to remove drips, brush marks and other

TIP

ABRASIVE ERASERS
Abrasive erasers are quite effective in removing all kinds of embedded material from sanding belts, discs, drums and sheets, thereby increasing the life of all abrasives. Three sizes of abrasive erasers are most common. A small pocket-size eraser is 1 in. square x 6 in. long, while the workshop size *(right)* is 1½ in. square x 8 in. long. The bench-mount type *(below)* is 3 in. square and 1½ in. thick; it frees up both of your hands for cleaning.

◀ **WET SANDING, 1.** ***Sand between finish coats to remove drips and other imperfections using waterproof abrasive paper with water or oil. Wrap the paper around a rubber sanding block.***

▼ **WET SANDING, 2.** ***Keep the work surface well lubricated and rinse the abrasive paper frequently. When sanding has been completed, polish the surface with pumice stone, followed by rottenstone.***

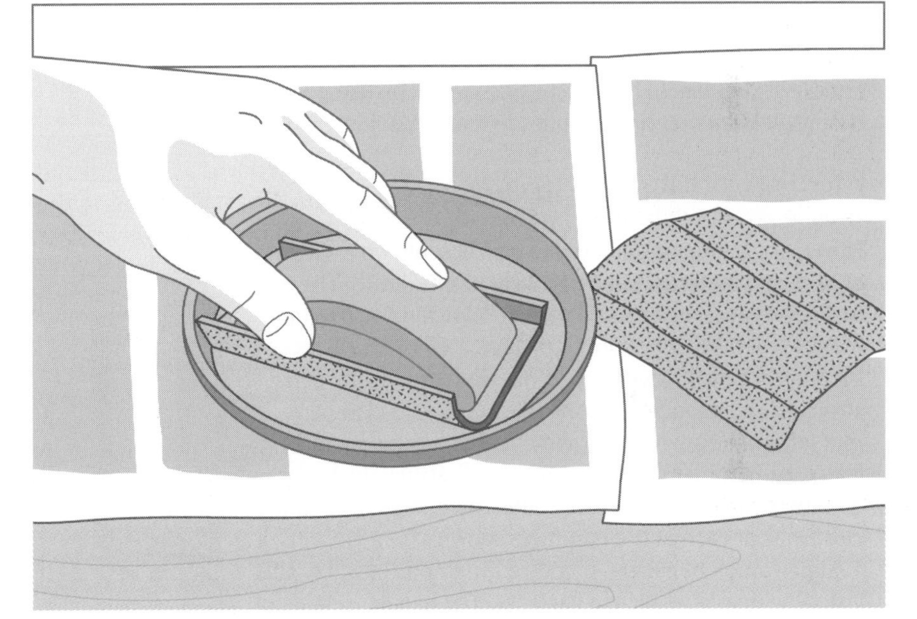

imperfections. Wrap the paper around a rubber sanding block or a wood block covered with felt. Keep the work surface well lubricated and rinse the abrasive paper frequently.

After you've finished sanding with 600-grit wet paper, polish the surface with pumice stone, followed by rottenstone. Use water or oil once again as a lubricant. Pumice stone, which comes from lava rock, is available in four grades from coarse (1F) to very fine (4F). Super-fine rottenstone is made of decomposed limestone.

REUSABLE SANDING SHEETS

A relatively new type of sanding sheet is available that's made of cloth-backed aluminum-oxide grit bonded to a foam backing. These 9 x 10-in. sheets are washable and come in three grits: 60 (coarse), 100 (medium) and 150 (fine). They can be used either wet or dry on wood and metal.

Although the foam-backed sheets are often only a little more durable than standard sandpaper when working on flat wood surfaces, they are an advantage in sanding curved surfaces. When sanding a convex wood surface, the grits are quickly sheared off the face of regular sandpaper, but on the foam-backed paper, they are pushed into the backing so they are less prone to being sheared off. This flexibility is particularly useful when sanding work that's turning on a lathe.

TACK CLOTHS

Thorough cleaning of all surfaces—especially ones of wood—is imperative before a finish is applied. Brush off particles and then vacuum, always working as much as possible in the direction of the grain to avoid leaving scratches in the wood. Follow up by wiping off each surface carefully with a tack cloth.

While tack cloths can be purchased at hardware stores, they're also easy to make. All that's required is a piece of cheesecloth, some turpentine and a little varnish.

Dip the cheesecloth in warm water and wring it out, then saturate it with turpentine and shake it out. Drip varnish evenly over the cheesecloth, folding it up and kneading it as you go until it becomes uniformly sticky.

Use a clean fold of your tack cloth with each wiping pass. To keep it from drying out between uses, store it in a sealed glass container.

HAMMERS

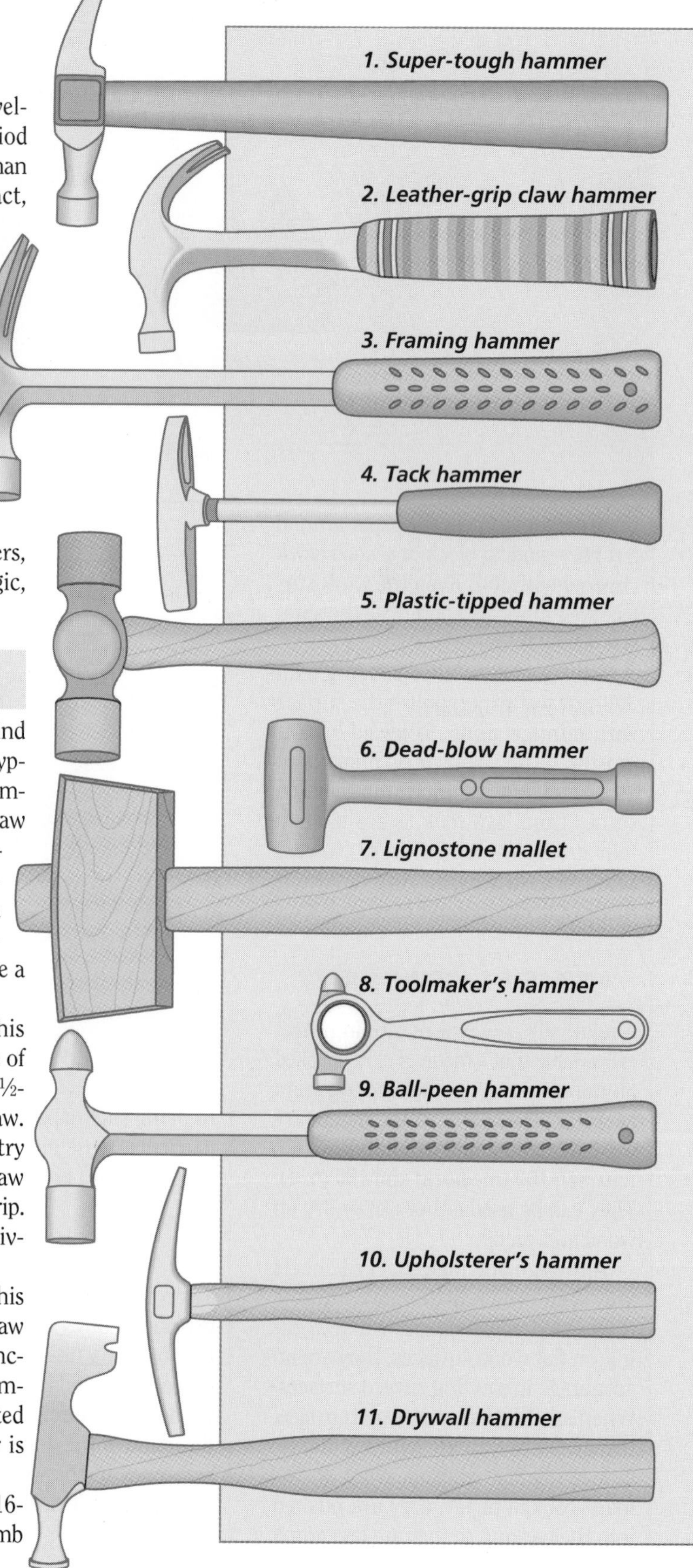

The tool we now know as the hammer was first developed around 7000 B.C. during the Neolithic period (the New Stone Age). It was during this time that man first lashed a branch to a sharpened stone. With this act, known as hafting—fitting a handle to a tool otherwise held in the hand—the hammer was born.

Today, the hammer has evolved into a large family of specialized striking tools. As a sample of the various tools that are available, 21 hammers are gathered together here; each is designed for a specific purpose. Note that the tools are made from a variety of materials including steel, wood, brass, fiberglass, leather, rubber and plastic. Despite the variety of hammers available, it's surprising to find that many homeowners own only one or two models. It's common to have several different sizes and styles of screwdrivers, handsaws or pliers to handle specific tasks. This same logic, though seldom practiced, applies to hammers, too.

TYPES OF HAMMERS

How many hammers you need to own depends on what kind of work and materials you're actively involved with. The typical do-it-yourselfer should own at least four or five hammers. Generally, they should include a 16-oz. curved-claw hammer for nail driving, a 22-oz. rip hammer for construction and remodeling work, a 12-oz. curved-claw hammer for finish carpentry, a cabinetmaker's hammer and a ball-peen hammer for metalworking. Fortunately, high-quality hammers are relatively affordable. Now, let's take a close look at each of the hammers shown.

1. Super-tough hammer—If you're tough on tools, try this virtually indestructible rip hammer. The handle is made of a super-resilient, shock-absorbent copolymer resin. The 14½-oz. hammer is available with a rip (straight) or curved claw.

2. Leather-grip claw hammer—Designed for finish carpentry and other light-duty nailing jobs, this 12-oz. curved-claw hammer features an attractive, comfortable, leather handgrip. The grip is a lamination of leather washers pressed and riveted to the solid steel handle.

3. Framing hammer—Designed for use by house framers, this 28-oz. hammer features an extra-long handle, a ripping claw and a milled, checkerboard-pattern face that reduces glancing blows and flying nails. The nearly indestructible hammer is forged from a single piece of solid steel and is fitted with a long-lasting nylon/vinyl handgrip. The hammer is also available with a smooth, polished face.

4. Tack hammer—Driving small brads and tacks with a 16-oz. claw hammer can be a real pain—especially in the thumb

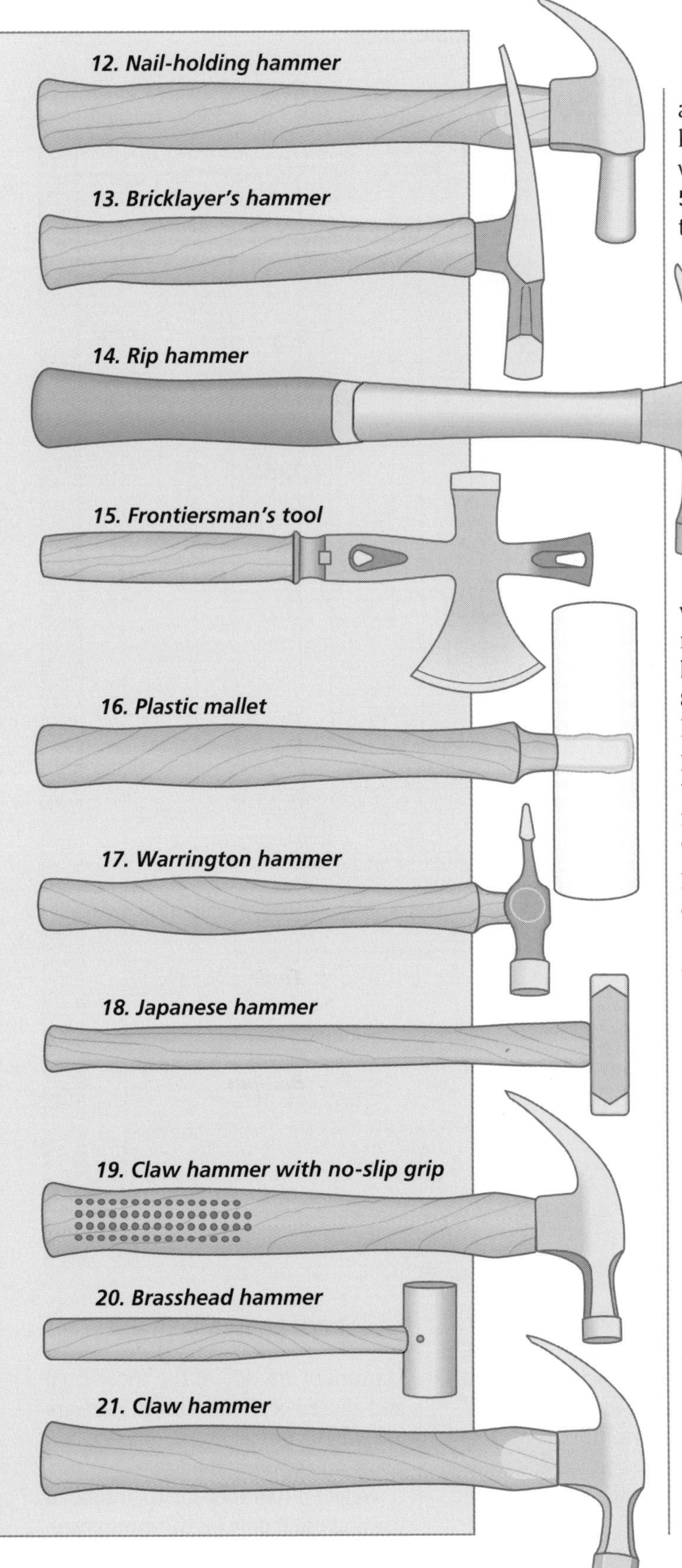

and forefinger. This 7-oz. tack hammer has a magnetized head that holds a tack for one-hand starting. Drive the tack with the opposite, non-magnetic face.

5. Plastic-tipped hammer—This 12-oz. steel-core hammer features two replaceable plastic faces. One side has a hard plastic face, the opposite side has a soft face. Use the hammer for striking, without marring, various materials including wood, metals, plastic and stone.

6. Dead-blow hammer—Use a dead-blow hammer to strike blows without damaging the work's surface. The tool's hollow head is partially filled with small metal shot, which reduces rebounding. Durable urethane completely encloses a solid steel handle that's welded to a cylindrical steel head. Dead-blow hammers are available in five styles in sizes from 8 oz. to 14 lb.

7. Lignostone mallet—Use a wooden mallet to strike wood- and plastic-handled chisels and gouges, to install wood dowel pins and to assemble wood parts. This 25-oz. mallet is made of laminated beech veneers that is claimed to be five times harder than solid beech and twice as elastic.

8. Toolmaker's hammer—Here's an excellent example of just how specialized a hammer can be. This 4-oz. miniature ball-peen hammer has a magnifying lens built into its head. Use the lens to check centerline and intersection punch marks for accuracy.

9. Ball-peen hammer—Featuring a hardened head, the ball-peen hammer is used for striking cold chisels and punches and for general metalwork. The ball-shaped peen was originally used to mushroom rivet heads. They are commonly available in sizes ranging from 8 to 32 oz.

10. Upholsterer's hammer—The magnetic face of this 7-oz. hammer makes it easy to start upholstery tacks and small nails. Use the non-magnetic face to continue driving the tack. The curved, narrow head fits in restricted spaces.

11. Drywall hammer—Designed for installing drywall, this 12-oz. hammer has a milled striking face opposite a hatchet blade. Use the hatchet blade to score the drywall to permit snapping it along the scored line of cut.

12. Nail-holding hammer—Driving a nail in a tight corner while in an awkward position, say, upside down, is almost impossible when using two hands. However, this 20-oz. hammer allows you to accomplish such a feat easily while using just one hand. A magnet set into the head grips an iron or steel nail. One sharp strike starts the nail. The hammer has a hickory handle and will hold a 2- to 4½-in.-long nail.

13. Bricklayer's hammer—An indispensable masonry tool, this hammer is designed exclusively for setting and splitting bricks, masonry tile and concrete block. The tool features a 16-oz. forged-steel head with a square striking face opposite a flat, sharp cutting edge. Never strike metal using a bricklayer's hammer, including a brickset or stone chisel.

14. Rip hammer—Great for rough carpentry work, this 22-oz. hammer has a straight ripping claw, a fiberglass handle and a rubber handgrip. Many workers prefer fiberglass-handled tools because they are virtually unbreakable and are more shock absorbent than steel-handled tools.

15. Frontiersman's tool—This rugged 24-oz. tool is more than just a hammer; it's also a crowbar, nail puller and hatchet. You'll find this tool particularly useful on camping trips and for opening wooden crates.

16. Plastic mallet—Use a plastic mallet to strike blows without damaging the work's surface. The 1⅞-in.-dia. x 6-in. head of plastic weighs 16 oz. and is pinned to a 13-in.-long wood handle. The mallet is useful for assembling and disassembling furniture parts and for setting wood dowel pins.

17. Warrington hammer—Considered the ultimate cabinetmaker's hammer, this perfectly balanced tool is equipped with a tapered cross-peen that allows you to start small nails and brads without striking your fingers. The forged steel head is attached to an ash handle. Warrington hammers are available in weights from 3½ to 16 oz.

18. Japanese hammer—The square steel head of this hammer has one flat striking face opposite a slightly crowned face. Use this 8-oz. tool for both woodworking and metalworking.

19. Claw hammer with no-slip grip—The ash handle of this 16-oz. hammer features a dimpled, anti-slip surface. The striking face and curved claw are hardened individually to ensure both strength and durability. It's also available in a 20-oz. model.

20. Brasshead hammer—Use this 16-oz. solid brass, wood-handled hammer during metalworking to avoid marring the work's surface. The tool has a 1-in.-dia. x 2 ½-in. head and is about 10 in. long.

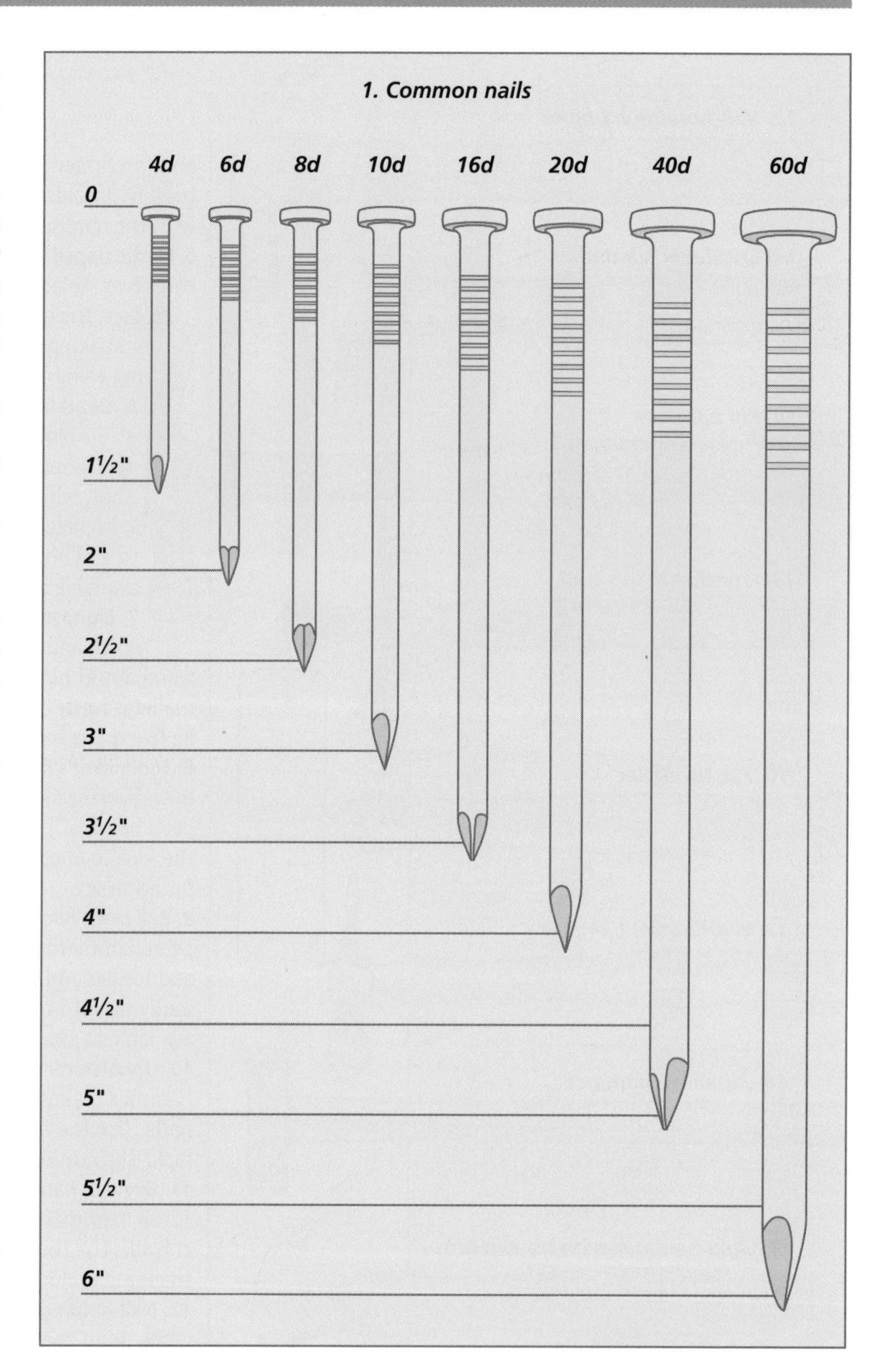

21. Claw hammer—Here's a fine example of a standard carpenter's nailing hammer. This 16-oz., hickory-handled hammer is designed for most general types of nailing work. Its curved claw features two sharp, beveled edges for the gripping and drawing out of stubborn nails.

PROPER HAMMER USE

Hammers are one of the most used and abused of all hand tools. Here are a few basic guidelines to follow when using any striking tool.

Select a hammer for its intended use and use it only for those purposes.

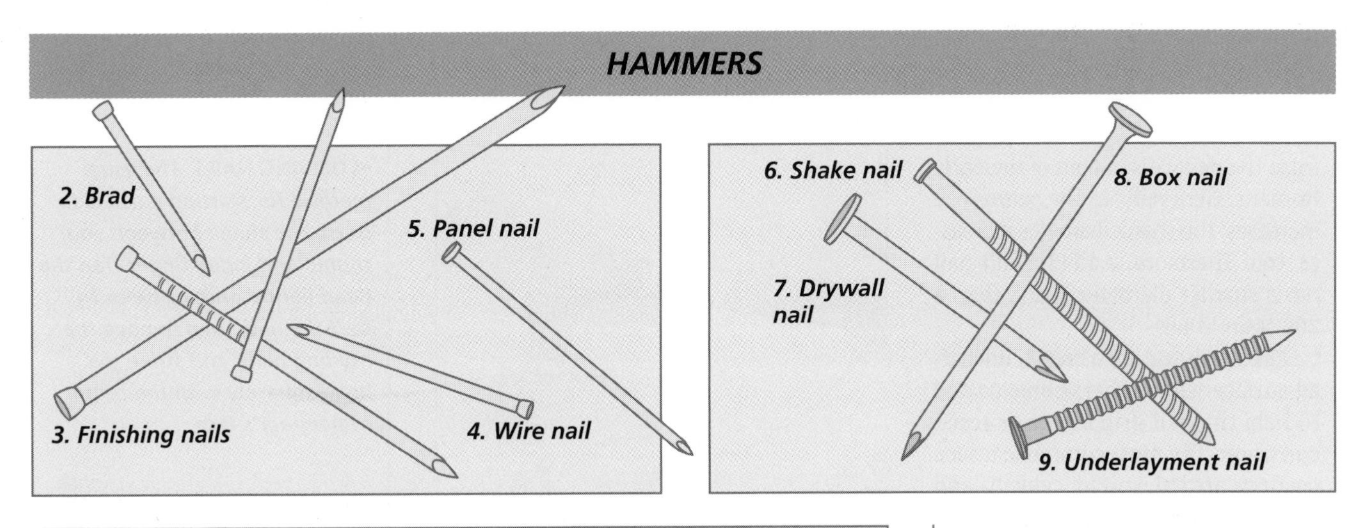

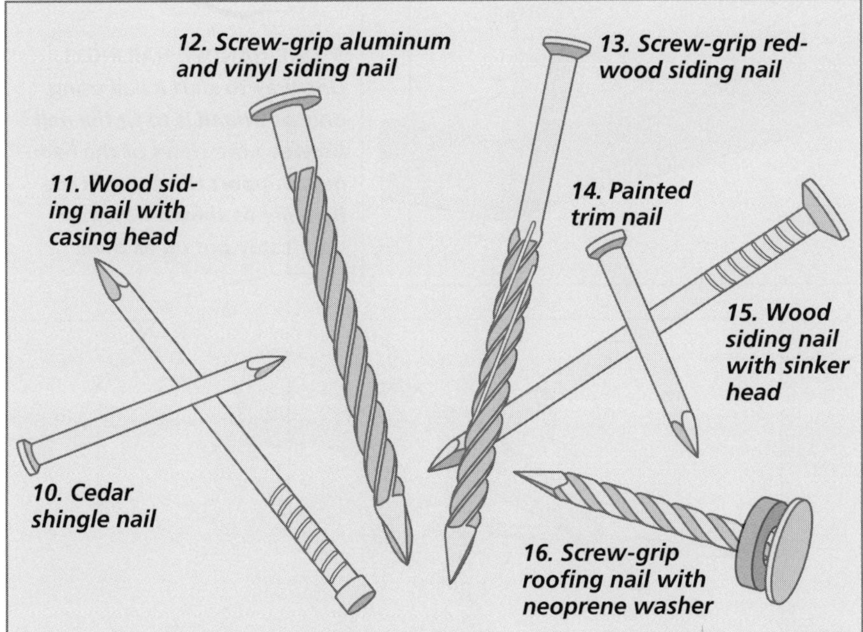

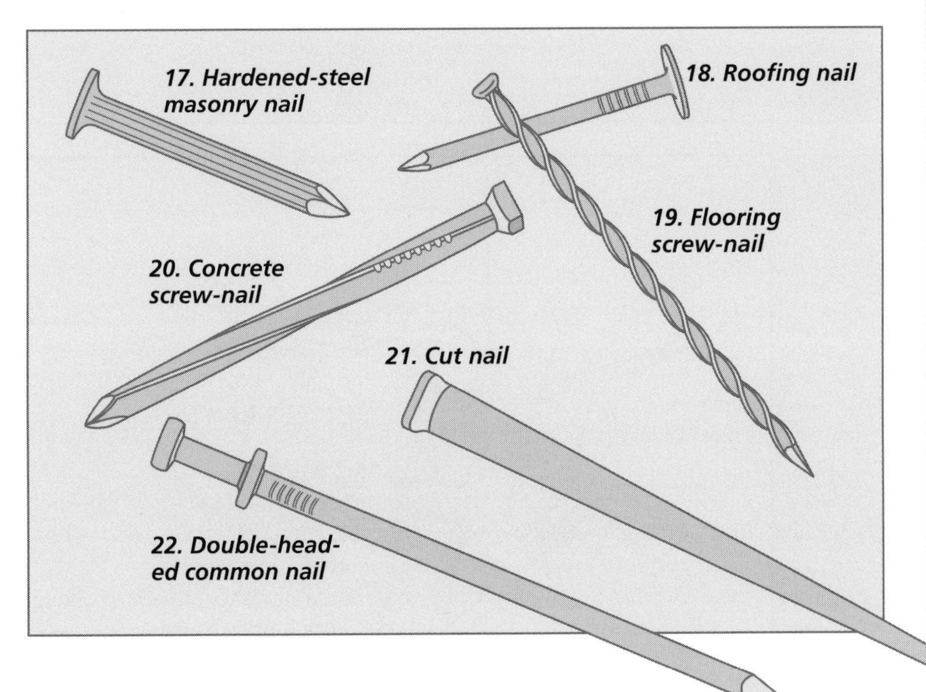

Always wear safety goggles to protect your eyes and never use a hammer that has a loose or damaged handle. Replace a damaged handle immediately with a new handle. Never strike one hammer with another. Discard a tool if its striking face is chipped, dented or mushroomed. Don't strike with the cheek, or side, of the hammer's head.

NAILING SPECIFICS

The simple task of driving a nail with a hammer is the most frequently practiced do-it-yourselfer act. Typically, it is also the very first do-it-yourselfer accomplishment experienced by most people. However, using the right nail for the job is as important as driving it correctly. If the nails are too small, the joint won't hold; too big and the wood will split. Nails are available in hundreds of different styles, shapes and sizes, and each is designed for a particular application. Shown here are 22 types of nails that every do-it-yourselfer should know about.

There are several factors to consider when buying nails, including the material that the nails are made of, length, gauge (diameter of shank), surface finish, and the type of head, shank and point. Most nails are made of mild steel, but aluminum, stainless steel, copper and bronze are also used. Nail length is designated by "penny" size—a term that originally indicated the price per hundred nails. Now, the penny symbol, a lowercase "d," refers only to the nail length. The letter "d" derives from the denarius, a coin of the early Romans. Generally, as the penny size increases, the shank diameter increases, too. Therefore, a 4d (1½-in.) nail has a smaller diameter shank than a 20d (4-in.) nail.

Most nails feature a bright, uncoated surface while others come coated to help the nail grip better or resist corrosion. The most common surface coatings are galvanized, cement- and resin-coated. The designed purpose of a nail is often indicated by its head. Large, flat-headed nails distribute pressure over a wider area; therefore, they hold best. Finishing and casing nails and brads have small, round heads for setting below the wood's surface.

For extra holding power, select nails with shanks that feature spiral grooves, flutes, annular rings or barbs. These nails are particularly effective when installing flooring, shingles and siding. Most nails have diamond points. Needle, chisel and blunt points, however, are also popular.

INVENTORY OF NAILS

Common nails **(1)**, just as their name implies, are the type most widely used. Shown are eight of the most readily available common nails from 4d (1½ in.) to 60d (6 in.). Use common nails for general construction and carpentry. Thick shanks and large heads allow the nails to hold fast. Typically, the nails have a bright finish; for exterior use, they're available with a galvanized finish to resist rust and corrosion.

The next most popular nails include brads **(2)** and finishing nails **(3)**. The two types are similar except that brads are smaller. Brads are designated by length in inches and gauge number.

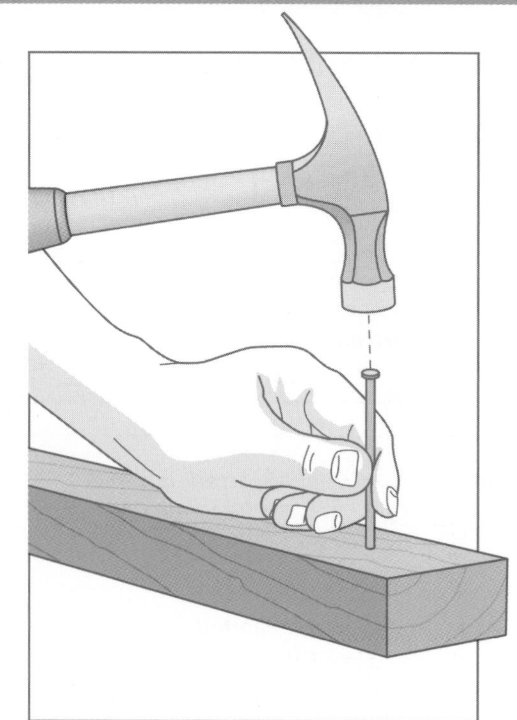

◀ **DRIVING NAILS.** ***The usual method for starting a nail is to grasp the shank between your thumb and index finger. Tap the head lightly once or twice to seat the nail, then remove the holding hand and strike the head squarely with the center of hammer's face.***

▼ **ONE-HANDED NAILING, 1.** ***One way to start a nail using only one hand is to fit the nail between the claws of the hammer. Support the nail and the hammer as shown—the nail won't stay put on its own.***

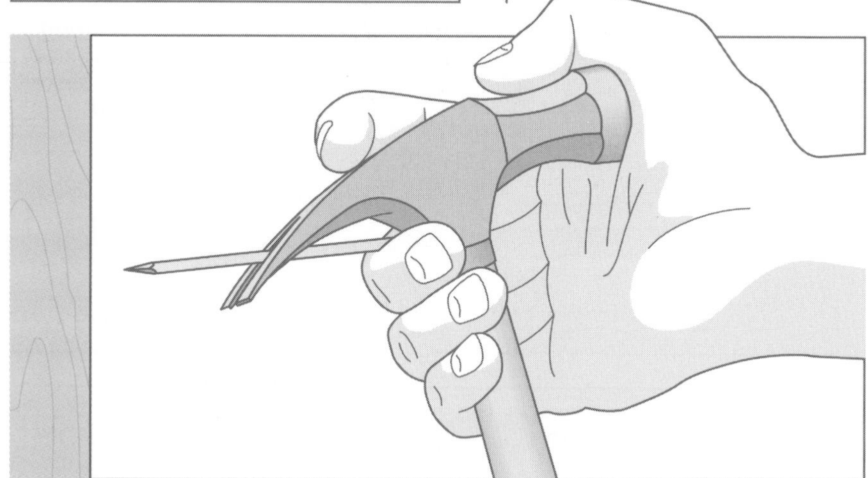

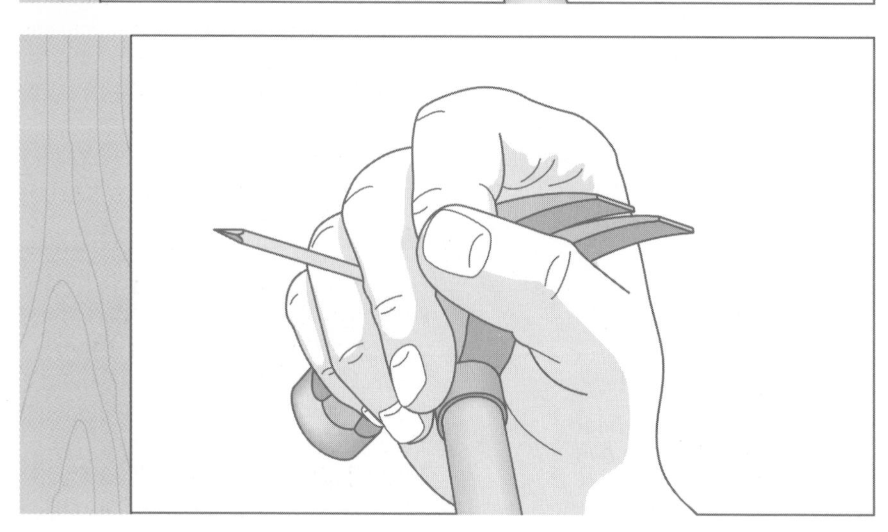

▶ **ONE-HANDED NAILING, 2.** ***Another one-handed method for hard-to-reach spots is to place the head of the nail against the cheek of the hammer. Using the grip shown, the nail is then "punched" to start it.***

TIP

PULLING OUT NAILS

The "cat's paw" is a tool named for its shape. It's a nail puller that is useful on carpentry projects—*not* for removing nails from cabinetry and the like. Position the work end of the cat's paw so that its claws will dig into the wood under the nailhead and straddle the nail's shank, then strike the tool sharply with a hammer *(inset)*. Once the claws are firmly embedded beneath the nailhead, use the cat's paw alone to raise the nail enough for a conventional hammer to fit under the nailhead *(right)*. This method usually damages only the surface of the stock so in most instances the lumber can be reused. However, don't drive new nails through holes left by old nails. Reposition the board and drive new nails into solid wood.

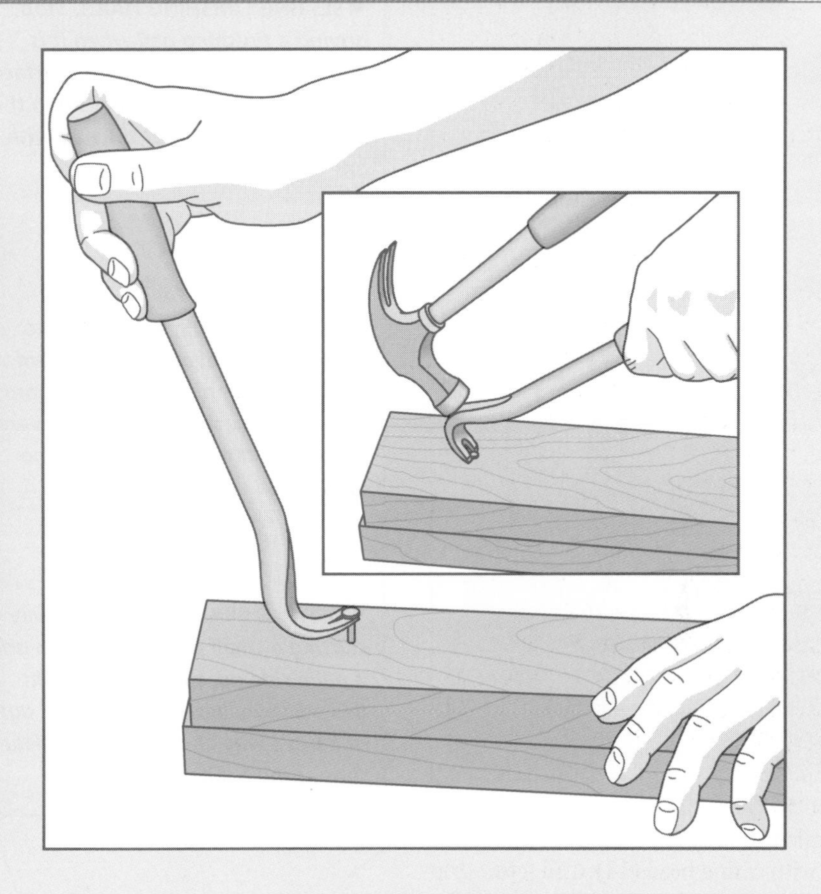

The highest number represents the smallest diameter shank. Shown is a 1-in., 16-ga. brad. Finishing nails are usually available from 2d (1 in.) to 10d (3 in.). Use these nails to install door and window trim, moldings, and for lightweight construction. Shown are 4d, 6d and 10d nails. Finishing nails also come galvanized.

Other entries in the lightweight category are wire nails **(4)** and panel nails **(5)**. Wire nails, like brads, are listed by length in inches and gauge number. Shown is a 1¼-in., 18-ga. wire nail. These super-thin, flat-headed nails are indispensable for fastening thin materials that other nails would split or that small-headed brads couldn't hold. Panel nails, identified by small, flat heads and annular-ringed shanks, are designed specifically for installing wall paneling. They range in size from 1 to about 2 in. and come in various colors to match the finished paneling.

Next comes a group of specialty-type nails made for specific applications. Shake nails **(6)** are for installing wood shingles and hand-split shakes. The 6d galvanized nail shown features a small, flat head, blunt diamond point that reduces splitting, and a slender, annular-ringed shank.

The following two nails are similar in appearance and manufacture, but not in purpose: a 1½-in. drywall nail **(7)** used to install gypsum wallboard; and a 2⅜-in. box nail **(8)** used to build crates and boxes. Both nails feature long diamond points, small-diameter shanks and a resin coating to increase their holding power. However, drywall nails have large, flat heads that prevent pull-through to hold the wallboard tightly to the house framing.

Next is a 1½-in. underlayment nail **(9)**. These nails, commonly available in lengths from 1 to 2½ in., are used for nailing plywood subflooring and other underlayment sheet material such as structural particleboard and oriented strand board. They have mid-sized flat heads, long diamond points and annular-ringed shanks.

The next group is made up of aluminum nails, which have a couple of advantages over steel nails—including being rust *and* stain resistant, and lightweight. Aluminum nails are particularly effective where exposure to weather is a concern. And, since nails are sold by the pound, you get more nails per pound. You can expect about 105 No. 8 common steel nails in one pound. A pound of No. 8 common aluminum nails yields about 230 nails. The nails shown are: a 3d cedar shin-

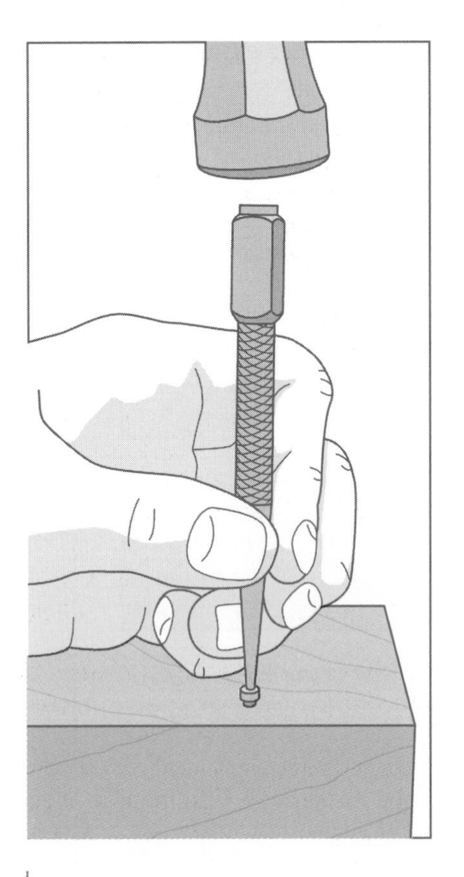

◀ **SETTING FINISHING NAILS.** ***Stop driving a finishing nail when it is about 1/8 in. above the wood surface. Then, position a 1/32-in. nailset in the head's dimple and set the nail with one or two sharp hammer raps.***

▶ **DRIVING BRADS, 1.** ***One way to start a small nail or brad is to hold it with a V-cut made in a cardboard scrap. This method works for several nails, then the notch becomes too big to hold up a nail.***

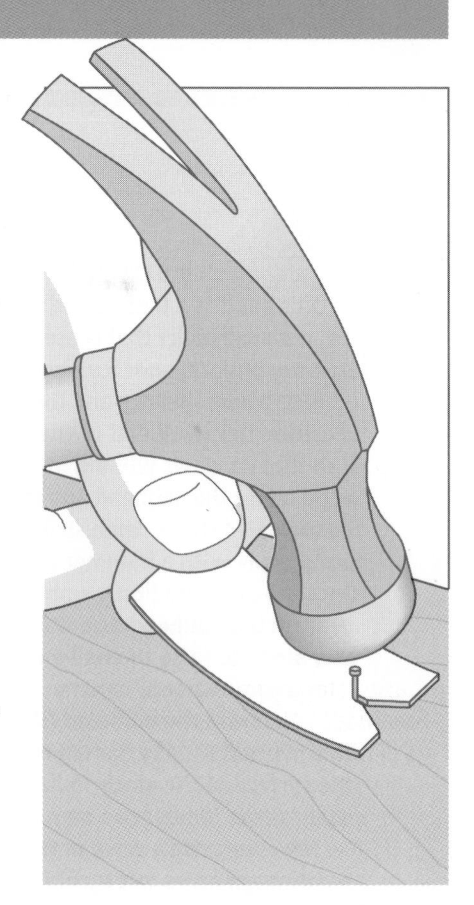

▼ **DRIVING BRADS, 2.** ***Another way of starting a small nail or brad is to grip it palm side up, as shown here. In this position, hefty knuckles are out of harm's way and you have a clear shot at the nailhead.***

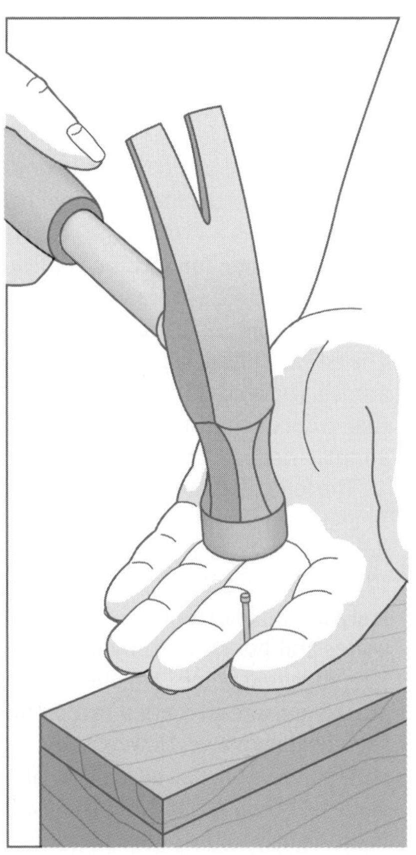

gle nail **(10)**; a 1⅞-in. wood siding nail with casing head **(11)**; a 6d screw-grip aluminum and vinyl siding nail **(12)**; a 2⅜-in. screw-grip redwood siding nail **(13)**; a 2d (1-in.) painted trim nail **(14)** for installing hardwood molding; a 2⅛-in. wood siding nail with sinker head **(15)**; and a 3d (1¼-in.) screw-grip roofing nail with neoprene washer **(16)** for use on aluminum roofs.

Leading off the last group of specialty-type nails is a 1½-in. hardened-steel masonry nail **(17)**. Flutes in the shank help it to grip tightly. This type of nail has a larger head than most masonry nails, which makes it excellent for attaching furring strips onto block walls. It's available in lengths from ⅝ to 4 in.

Apply asphalt roof shingles and roll roofing with—that's right—roofing nails **(18)**. Very large, flat heads deter pull-throughs when blustery winds lift shingles. The 1½-in. nail shown is electrogalvanized to resist rusting. Roofing nails come in lengths of ¾ to 3 in.

To penetrate cured concrete, use a concrete screw-nail **(19)**. Made from square tempered-steel stock, the nail is twisted so it turns as it's hammered. Concrete screw-nails come in lengths ranging from ¾ to 3 in.

Another sure-hold type of nail that features a twisted shank is a flooring screw-nail **(20)**. This 8d square-headed nail provides an alternative to cut nails when attaching hardwood strip flooring. The nails turn into the wood as they're hammered to give excellent holding power.

The rectangular cross section and tapering shank identifies the next nail as a cut nail **(21)**. Use cut nails for attaching wood to concrete blocks and fastening hardwood strip flooring to the subfloor. They're available in sizes ranging from 3d to 20d. Shown is a 10d cut nail. *Caution:* Cut nails are extremely brittle. Protect your eyes with goggles.

The final nail shown is a 10d double-headed common nail **(22)**, which

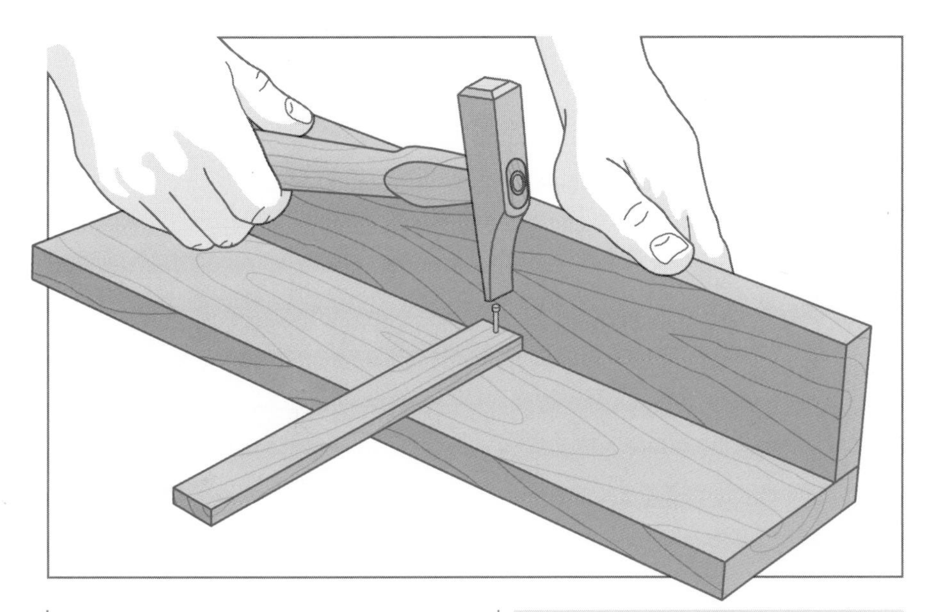

◀ **DRIVING BRADS, 3.** ***A French joiner's hammer is handy for driving small nails or brads. Use the cross-peen end of the hammer to start the nail as shown, then rotate the hammer head and finish the driving with the broad, square face.***

is also called a scaffold nail or duplex head nail. This "removable" nail can be driven in tightly and then yanked out by pulling on the protruding upper head. These nails are designed for use in temporary construction projects such as wood scaffolding and concrete forms. They're available in sizes ranging from 6d to 20d.

NAILING DOWN BASICS

Driving a nail seems to be a natural act for human beings to perform. To help develop motor skills, one of the first toys many people give their children is a mallet, various-shaped pegs and a board with holes to match. Yet, there are guidelines and techniques to be learned to use a hammer correctly and safely.

Always wear eye protection when hammering nails. Many home carpenters hold nails in their mouths to expedite the task of a multi-nail job. Don't start this habit if you're a beginner, and try to break it if you already do it. Many nails today are coated, and the galvanizing, resin or other coatings can cause a toxic reaction.

Whenever possible, nail through the thinner piece and into the thicker piece. As a general rule, two thirds of the nail's length should be driven into the thicker wood. To increase their holding power, drive nails at angles. When nailing into hardwoods or near the

GUN-POWERED FASTENING

Lightweight, yet powerful staple guns are available for driving different sizes of staples and nailpins (headless nails). The tool shown here drives 1/4 and 9/16-in.-long staples and 9/16-in.-long nailpins. It has a tough plastic housing and weighs only 11 oz. To drive two nailpins simultaneously, simply load a nailpin strip in each side of the staple channel. Other features include dual power settings, a safety lock-off, and a rehammering setting for driving the staples of nailpins again until they're flush.

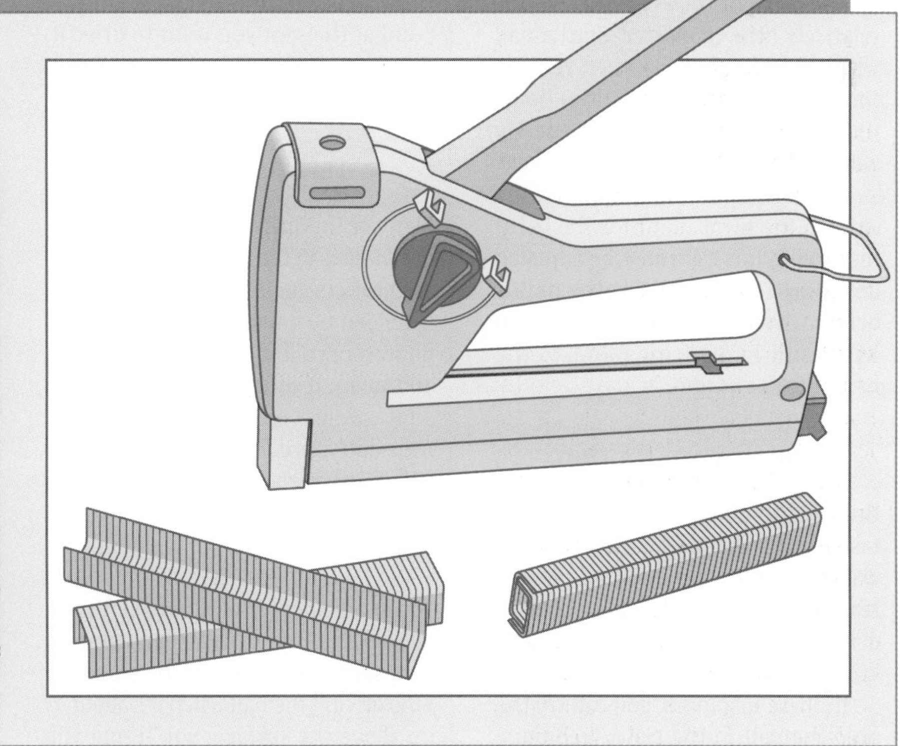

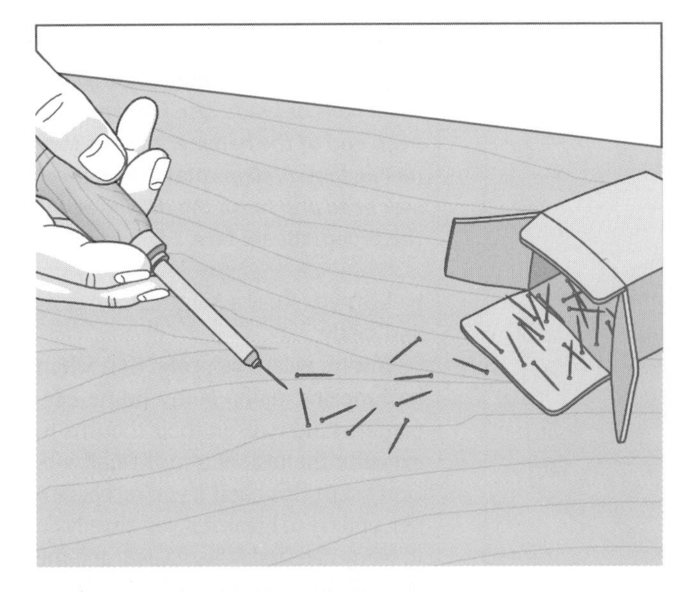

▲ **USING A BRAD PUSHER, 1.** ***To pick up a small nail or brad, retract the sleeve and touch the magnetized tip to the nailhead. Gently release the sleeve to grip the nail.***

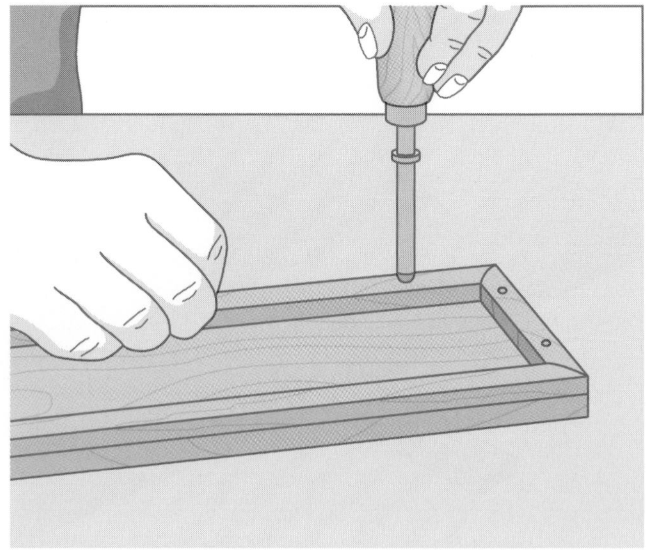

▲ **USING A BRAD PUSHER, 2.** ***Position the nail and push down on the handle of the brad pusher to drive the nail. In one operation, the tool drives and sets the nailhead.***

end or edge of a board, bore pilot holes first to prevent splitting. Clinch nailing gives the strongest joint, but it's also the most unattractive. It involves driving long nails through both boards, then bending over protruding ends.

For conventional nailing there is relatively little to master: Start a nail with several light taps, then remove the nail-holding hand and drive home the nail by striking its head squarely with the center of the hammer's face.

Carpenters know that because the wrist is the pivot point for the hammer swing (arc), it must be adjusted downward continually as the nail is being driven home. Failure to do so will result in glancing blows to the nail's head.

ONE-HANDED NAILING

But what about more complex nailing tasks? For example, when framing a wall from a ladder you often have to reach out with your hammer hand to drive a nail while you hold onto the ladder with your other hand.

In these instances, you can try the hold-the-nail-in-the-claws technique to start the nail, a popular do-it-yourselfer trick. However, most carpenters prefer to use the nail-against-the-cheek method. Simply place the head of the nail against the hammer cheek and flank it with your fingers grasping the hammer's head, then "punch" the nail point at the spot you want to drive it. Done correctly, one punch will seat the nail in the wood.

TELL-ALL NAILING

Many of the little tasks that a homeowner does in the course of do-it-yourself projects go unnoticed. Subflooring is hidden by finish flooring or carpet, plasterboard joints are papered over, and so on. If your work happens to be a bit careless on such jobs, it makes little difference. But this isn't the case with finish carpentry. Here, everybody gets to see exactly what kind of craftsman you really are.

So take time to master the basics. Grasp a finishing nail between your thumb and index finger, and start it with several light taps of the hammer. Stop driving the nail when it's about 1/8 in. above the surface; you'll mar the wood with the head of the hammer if you try to drive it home. Place a 1/32-in. nailset in the dimple of the nailhead and hold it firmly so that it won't "dance" out and punch the wood, then set the nail below the surface with one or two sharp raps of hammer.

FINISHING POINTERS

The finish carpentry that you are most likely to encounter as a homeowner will involve "trimming out" a room. This includes the installation of moldings and trim that are intended to conceal joints and framing details, and give the room a finished appearance. It also includes the application of baseboards, door and window casings, outside corner guards, ceiling moldings, chair rails and the like. Sloppy work is a sure sign of a careless carpenter. For example, there's no excuse for an opened joint in a baseboard or in the casings around a door or window.

The wrong way to install a long run of baseboard is with square-cut ends simply butted together. Instead, make miter joints, using a miterbox for accurate cuts. Install the strip with the open

CORDLESS FINISH NAILER

To drive nails quickly with the least amount of effort, house framers and production woodworkers often use electric or pneumatic nailers. Here's an innovative tool that combines the cordless freedom of a hand-held hammer with the effortless speed of power nailing—designed for finish carpentry and cabinetwork.

The nailer weighs about 6 lb. It uses a replaceable cell of liquid hydrocarbon fuel *(right, top left)* to power an internal-combustion driving mechanism. A rechargeable battery powers the ignition system and handles about 8,000 nails between charges. The tool drives 16-gauge chisel-point coated finish nails in sizes ranging from 3/4 to 2½ in. They come in 50-nail strips and can be loaded two at a time into the magazine *(right, top right)*.

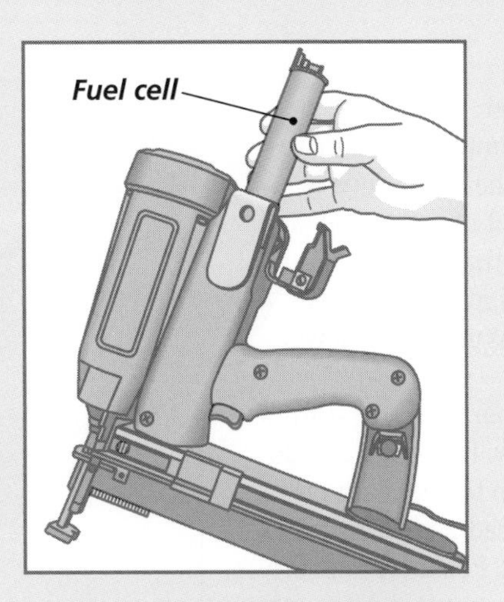

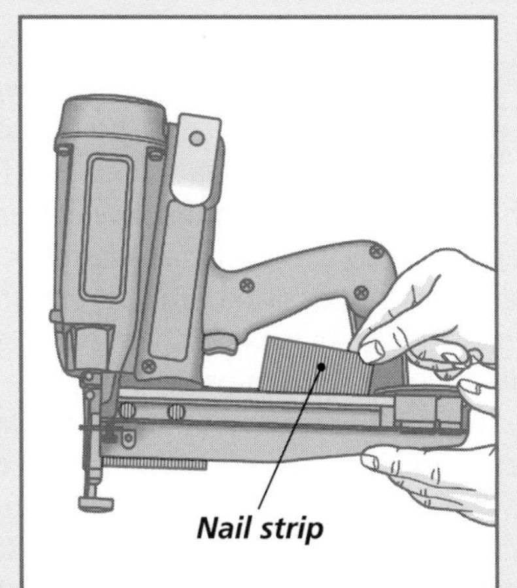

The tool is capable of driving between two and three nails per second with no kickback and only a low, muffled pop as each nail is driven. The plastic tip of the drive mechanism prevents marring of the work surface and controls the the nail depth *(right, bottom)*; unless the tip contacts the work surface, the tool doesn't function. Different tips are available for nailing flush and for setting nails below the surface.

miter, then apply a little glue to the joint surfaces and install the second mitered piece. Secure the joint with a couple of 3d (1¼-in.) finishing nails, driving them in at a slight angle. Close the joint tightly and it will stay that way, without ever opening up.

Door casing should be set back a uniform distance from the jamb edge; ¼ in. is the usual reveal. Mark the setback in several places on the side and header jambs. Cut the miter at one end of the casing, then mark the casing length from the inside corner—including the reveal. Install the casing with 4d finishing nails through the thin edge into the jamb and 6d finishing nails through the thick edge into the stud behind. Space the nails about 10 to 12 in. apart. To guarantee that your miter joints will stay closed, cut the header casing to suit the span between the horizontal casings. Apply glue sparingly to the mating surfaces and join them, then bore slightly undersize lead holes through the joint from opposite casing edges and secure the joint with two 6d finishing nails.

WORKING WITH BRADS

One of the paradoxes of woodworking, it seems, is that most workshoppers have good-sized hands. Consequently, a relatively easy task—such as starting 5/8 to 1¼-in. brads—is often a nuisance job. But it won't be if you work with the right tools.

One aid is a French joiner's hammer, an ideal tool for work with small nails and in close quarters. The striking head and the body are both square-shaped and the underside is flat, as well. The result is a hammer with a full striking surface, even when working in a tight corner. To start a brad, use the cross-peen end; usually, you can finish driving with the square end.

For very small brads—any under a length of 7/8 in.—turn to a magnetized brad pusher. When driving brads, you can simply dump a small batch on the worktable and pick them up individually with the tool's magnetized tip. The sleeve is returned to full extension for the driving. You then push the handle down to drive and set the brad.

SCREWDRIVERS

The standard flat-blade screwdriver, or turnscrew as it was first called, began as a simple tool to drive and remove slotted screws. But, the limitations of the slotted screw led to the development of many "better" screw designs—that is, a fastener that can be driven quicker, easier and with less tool slippage, which is known as cam-out. As each new screw was produced, however, another driver was needed.

Today, the two most popular fasteners are the slotted screw and the cross-point Phillips screw. However, as a do-it-yourselfer you must also be tooled-up to deal with other screws, such as Torx, square-recess, Reed and Prince, hex socket, Scrulox, Robertson, clutch-head, Pozidriv, Supadriv and Quadrex—to name a few. Some of these types differ only by the manufacturer. For example, Scrulox and Robertson screws are square-recess fasteners. And Supadriv and Pozidriv screws feature the same cross-point design. Therefore, in certain instances, the same driver can be used on different screw types. But remember, it's important to match the right size and type of screwdriver to the screwhead.

TYPES OF SCREWDRIVERS

Now let's take a close look at the 22 screwdrivers shown.

1. Torx—You may have noticed the use of a six-point, star-shaped fastener on most late-model cars and trucks. These fasteners, called Torx screws, are also found on lawn and garden equipment, appliances and televisions. The Torx driver shown is designed for use with T-20 size screws. It has a 3-in.-long chrome-vanadium steel blade and a hexagon-shaped plastic handle.

2. Insulated screwdriver—Designed for use by electricians, this fully insulated driver has a blade that is sheathed in a plastic sleeve. Only the very end of the tip is exposed. Insulated screwdrivers are intended only as a protective measure against shorting out a circuit. *Never* depend on an insulated driver to protect you from a constant flow of electricity. The driver is available in 3-, 4-, 6- and 8-in. models.

3. Cabinetmaker's—Designed for shop work, this traditional cabinetmaker's screwdriver features a turned oval beech handle, a heavy steel ferrule and a chrome-vanadium steel blade. Note that the upper portion of the blade is flattened to accept a wrench when extra torque is needed.

4. Spiral-rachet—Drive screws quickly and easily with a spiral-ratchet screwdriver. Simply push down on the spring-loaded shaft to turn the driver bit. Adjust the three-position switch to drive screws, remove screws or to lock the shaft for use as a conventional screwdriver. The 9-in.-long driver comes with three drill bits, two slotted screwdriver bits and

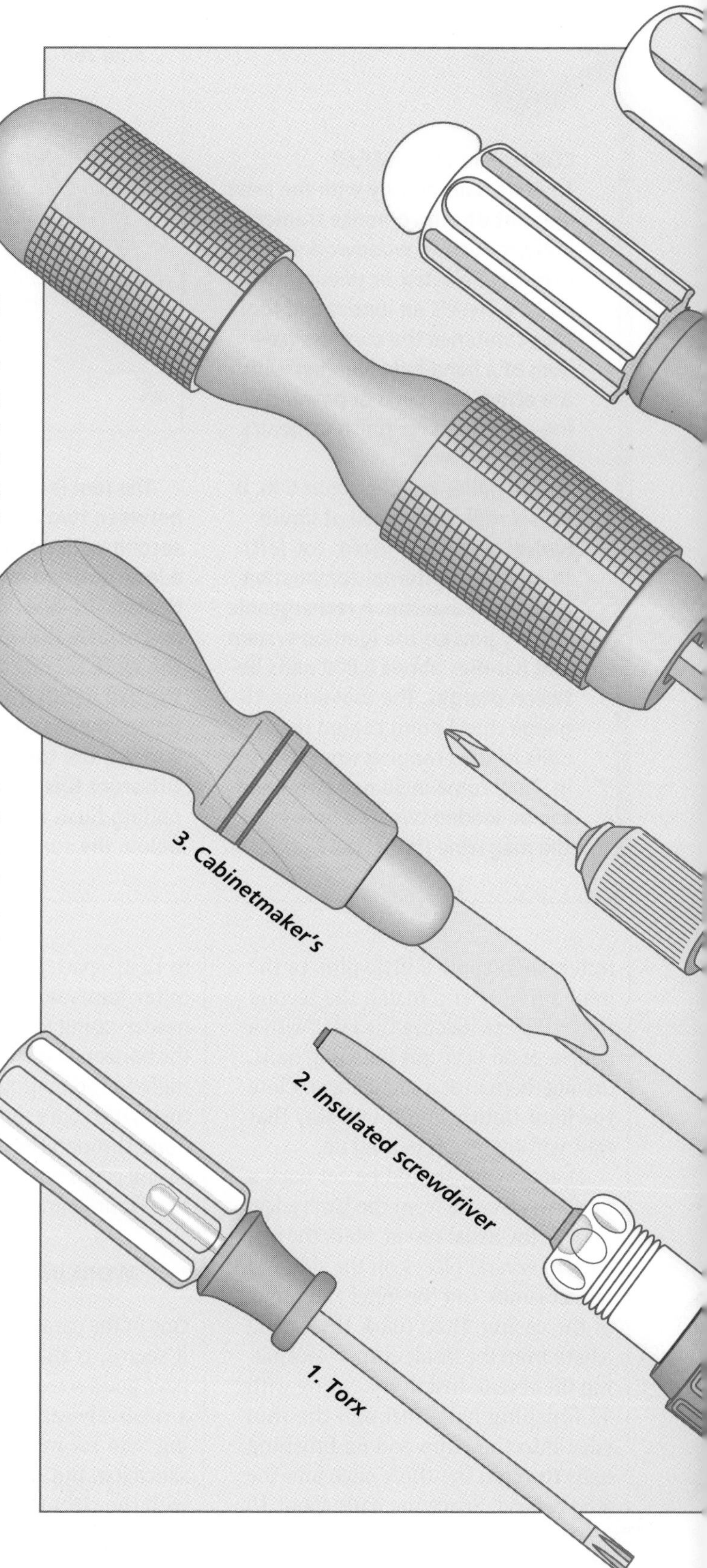

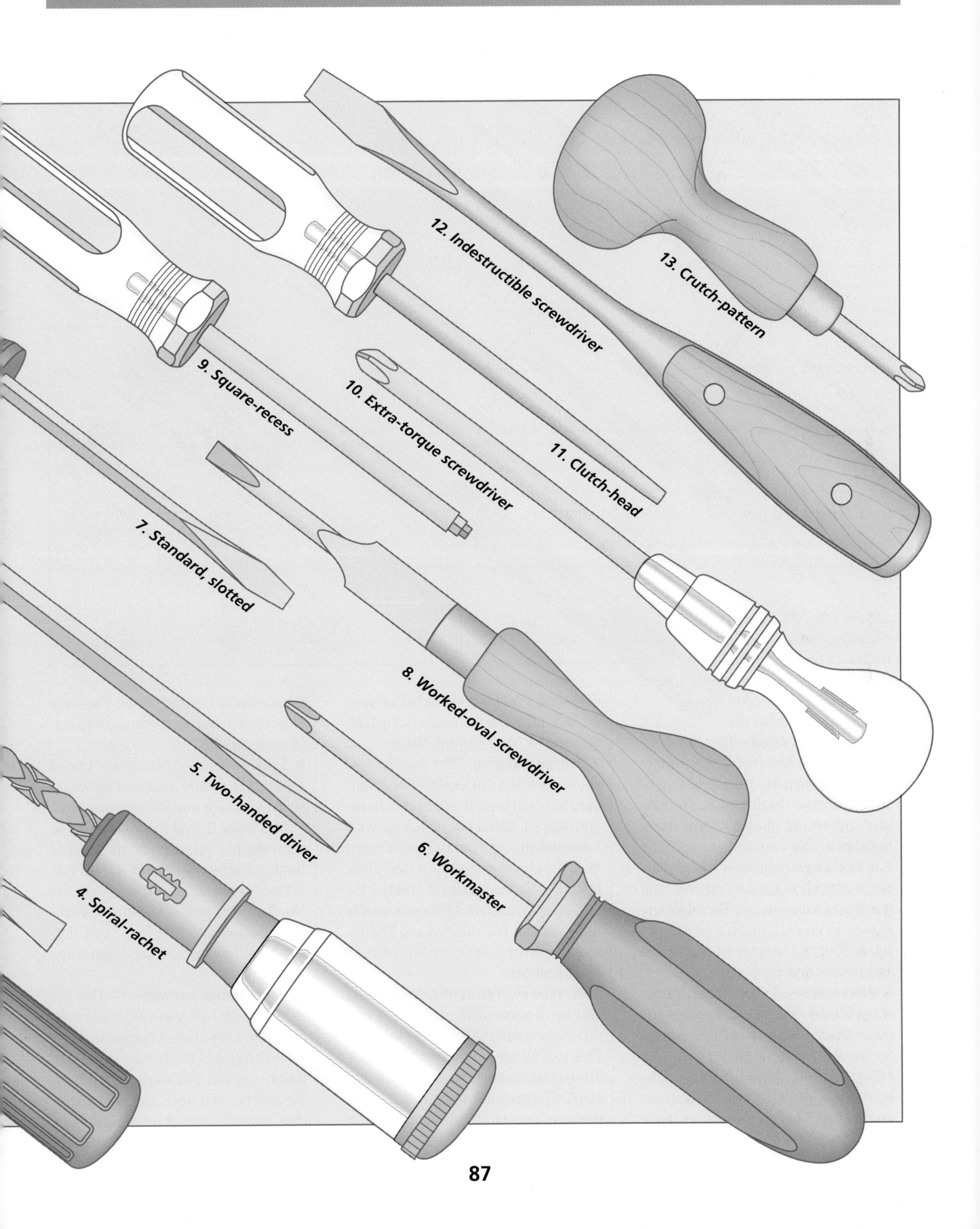
12. Indestructible screwdriver
13. Crutch-pattern
9. Square-recess
10. Extra-torque screwdriver
11. Clutch-head
7. Standard, slotted
8. Worked-oval screwdriver
5. Two-handed driver
6. Workmaster
4. Spiral-rachet

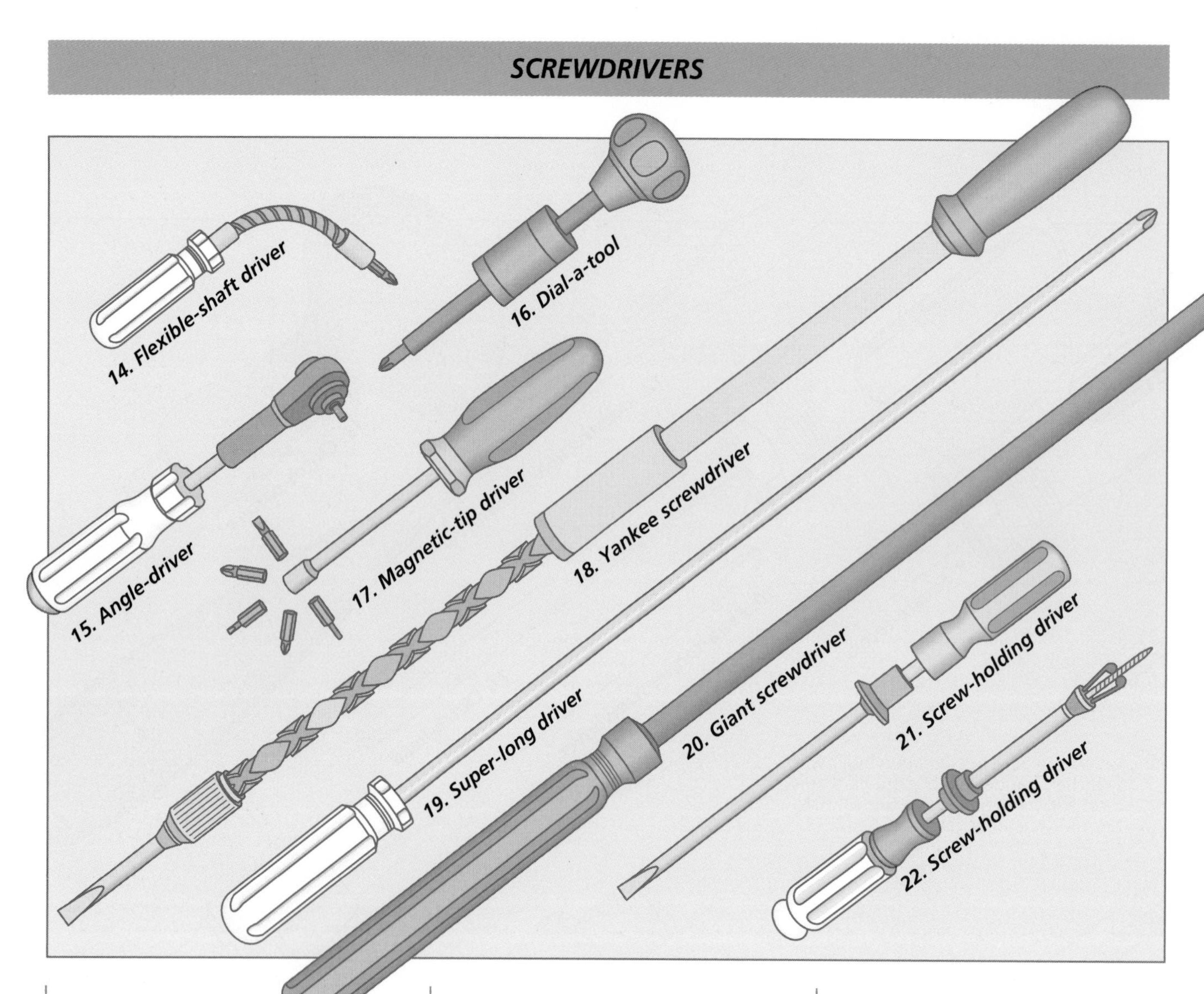

a No. 2 Phillips bit—all of which store in the handle.

5. Two-handed driver—This Swedish-made screwdriver features a unique double-grip handle that allows you to apply extremely high torque. The 6½-in.-long, round plastic handle has a nonslip, pebble-textured surface. The 6-in.-long square blade is nickel plated for protection against corrosion and it features a narrow tip. This style tip, known as an electrician's or cabinet tip, is designed to work in deep holes and narrow spaces.

6. Workmaster—This popular line of screwdrivers features tapered, triangular-shaped plastic handles designed for greater turning power with less effort. The tools have blades of high-strength boron steel with precision-ground tips. The line includes a variety of slotted, Phillips and ratchet drivers, including a versatile magnetic tip tool. Shown is a No. 1 Phillips driver.

7. Standard, slotted—The popular tool shown here is a fine example of a standard screwdriver. It features a hexagon-shaped, fluted plastic handle with a nonslip thumb rest and ball-shaped end. The chrome-vanadium steel blade is nickel plated and heat treated for durability. This style driver is available in 17 sizes for both slotted and Phillips screws. Also available are sets of 9, 18 and 21 pieces.

8. Worked-oval screwdriver—Here is another improved version of the traditional cabinetmaker's screwdriver. This tool features a wider, flatter handle to produce greater torque with less effort. The precisely milled blade has a flattened portion to accept a wrench for additional turning power. The blade is secured to the beech handle by a solid brass ferrule.

9. Square-recess—This square-tipped tool drives square-recessed fasteners such as Scrulox and Robertson screws. You're likely to find these fasteners in recreational vehicles, boats, mobile homes, hobby equipment and on furniture hardware. The driver shown fits No. 2 screws and it features a 4-in.-long blade along with a four-sided, fluted plastic handle that has a contoured thumb rest.

10. Extra-torque screwdriver—This is a British-made tool featuring the proven design of a traditional cabinetmaker's screwdriver, but the handle is made of tough acetate. The oval-shaped handle and tapered neck give a comfortable, powerful grip. A set of six drivers,

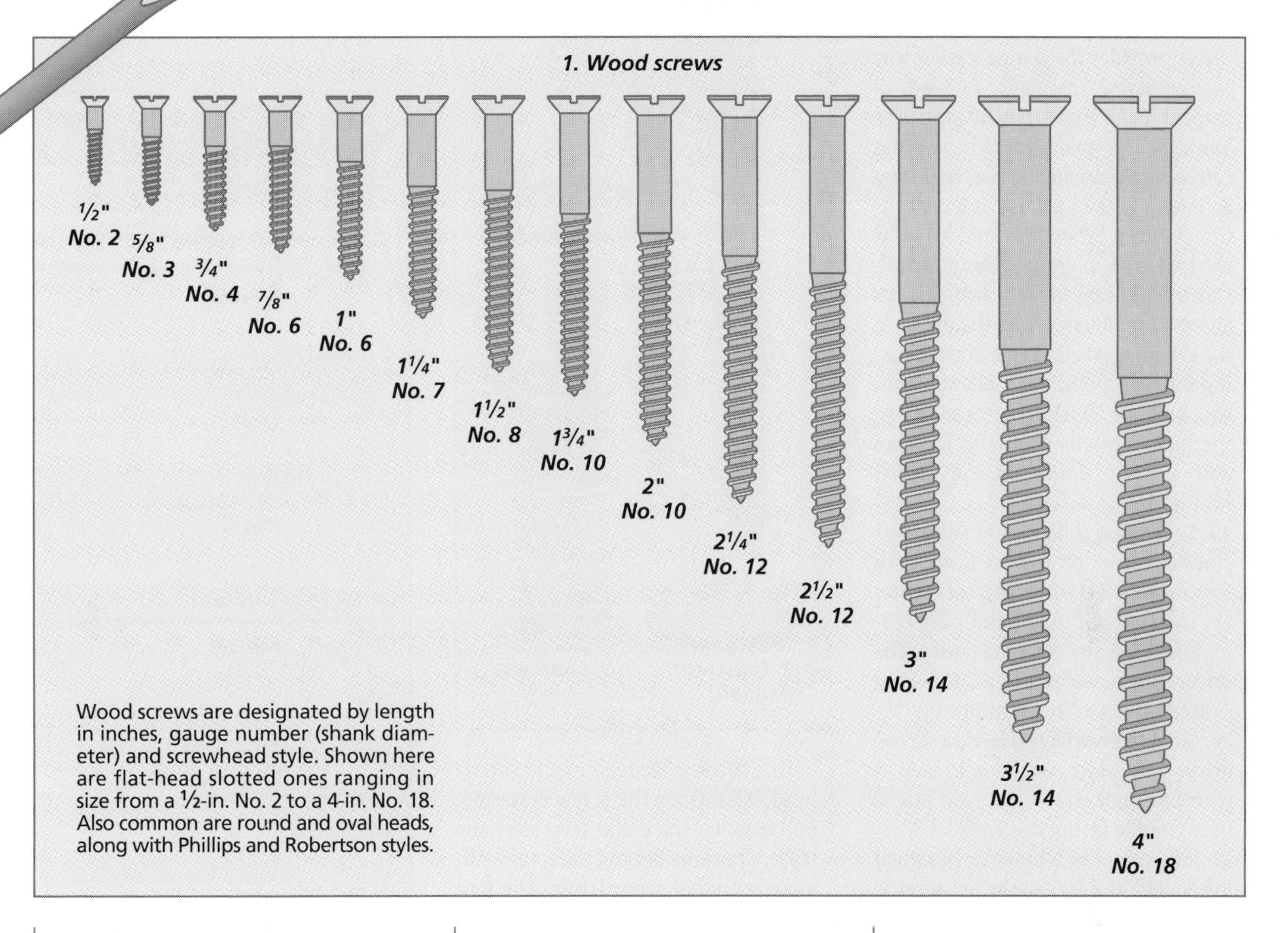

Wood screws are designated by length in inches, gauge number (shank diameter) and screwhead style. Shown here are flat-head slotted ones ranging in size from a ½-in. No. 2 to a 4-in. No. 18. Also common are round and oval heads, along with Phillips and Robertson styles.

including four slotted and two Phillips, is available.

11. Clutch-head—The clutch-head type of screw features a distinctive bow-tie shaped, recessed head. These screws are used commonly in mobile homes, cars, boats, appliances as well as electric motors. This screwdriver has a 3/16-in.-dia. tip milled to fit clutch-head screws precisely. The driver features a 4-in.-long boron steel blade and a hexagon-shaped plastic handle.

12. Indestructible screwdriver—If you're tough on tools, try this super-durable screwdriver. It features a solid steel blade that extends all the way through the handle. Two inserts of hardwood form an oval grip. A set of three slotted screwdrivers with blade lengths of 4, 6 and 8 in. is available.

13. Crutch-pattern—The large, flattened-oval handle of the crutch-pattern driver affords you the ability to deliver tremendous torque to stubborn screws—especially in tight quarters, since the tool is only 5¼ in. long. The 2⅛-in.-wide maple handle is fitted to a 1⅜-in.-long No. 2 Phillips driver. A crutch-pattern slotted screwdriver is also available.

14. Flexible-shaft driver—The ¼-in.-dia. shaft of this slotted driver bends to work on hard-to-reach screws. The 7½-in.-long tool has a hardened steel tip and a 3-in.-long fluted plastic handle. It also comes with a Phillips tip.

15. Angle-driver—Called a Skewdriver, this unique tool simplifies work in corners and at awkward angles. Its geared mechanism holds a driver bit at a 60° angle to the blade. Simply turn the handle to rotate the bit. The tool has two slotted bits and two Phillips bits that store in the hollow handle.

16. Dial-a-tool—This unique screwdriver has a barrel built into the shaft that houses six bits—three slotted, two Phillips and an awl. To select a bit, pull back on the handle, rotate the barrel to the desired bit and push the handle forward until it locks in place. The six bit profiles are printed on the barrel to make selection easy.

17. Magnetic-tip driver—If you're tired of carrying around four or five different screwdrivers in your pocket, then try this versatile five-in-one driver. The tool comes with two slotted bits, two Phillips bits and a T-15 Torx bit—all of which store conveniently in the hollow, triangular-shaped handle. The 4-in.-long aluminum shaft is fitted with a magnet that allows the bits to hold steel screws securely.

18. Yankee screwdriver—The Yankee spiral-ratchet, quick-return screwdriver provides the fastest, easiest way to drive screws manually. A favorite of carpenters for more than 40 years, the Yankee has a spring-loaded shaft that can be set for driving screws, removing screws or locked for use as a conventional driver. When it's extended fully, the tool is 25 in. long without the bit. Contracted and locked, it measures about 17 in. Always store the driver in the extended position and when releasing the lock, point the tool away from you, hold the chuck securely and allow the shaft to extend gradually. It comes with a 9⁄32-in. slotted bit and a No. 2 Phillips bit.

19. Super-long driver—You will never come up short on the job again with this mighty 24½-in.-long screwdriver. The round, fluted handle and 20-in.-long blade deliver extra power. The driver shown comes with a 20-in.-long slotted blade or No. 2 Phillips tip.

20. Giant screwdriver—Here's a screwdriver that you're not going to keep in your back pocket. In fact, you might have trouble fitting this colossal 33½-in.-long driver in a toolbox. Designed for No. 20 and larger slotted screws, the tool features a ½-in.-dia. hexagonal-shaped steel blade and a 9½-in.-long, fluted plastic handle. Also, this is the only driver here that's recommended for use as a pry bar and lever.

21. Screw-holding driver—Here's one version of a screw-holding driver. The blade is split in two halves. As you push the sliding collar forward, the blade halves become wedged in the screwhead's slot. Once the screw is started, pull back on the collar to release the blade. Continue driving the screw with a conventional screwdriver. The tool has a ¼-in.-dia. x 8-in.-long blade.

22. Screw-holding driver—Work with this clever tool to start slotted screws in tight, restricted spaces. The driver has two spring-loaded metal jaws that hold a screw securely on the tip to permit easy starting. Push the collar on the blade forward to spread open the jaws; release the collar and they close

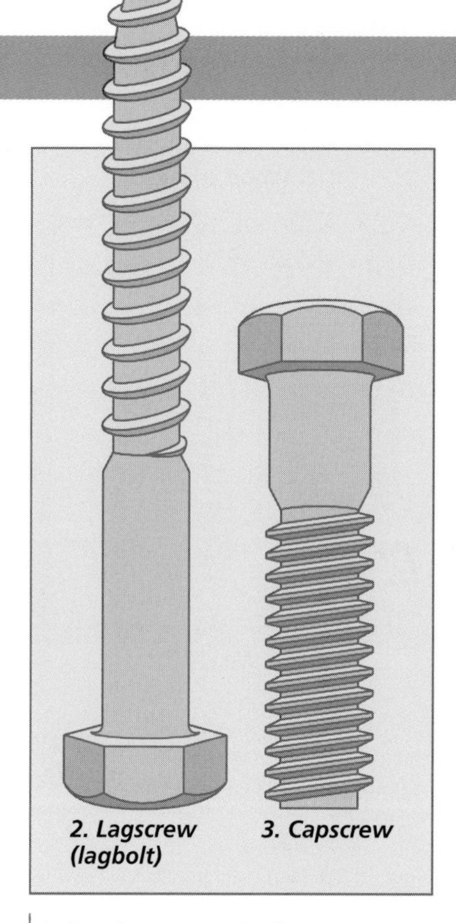
2. Lagscrew (lagbolt) *3. Capscrew*

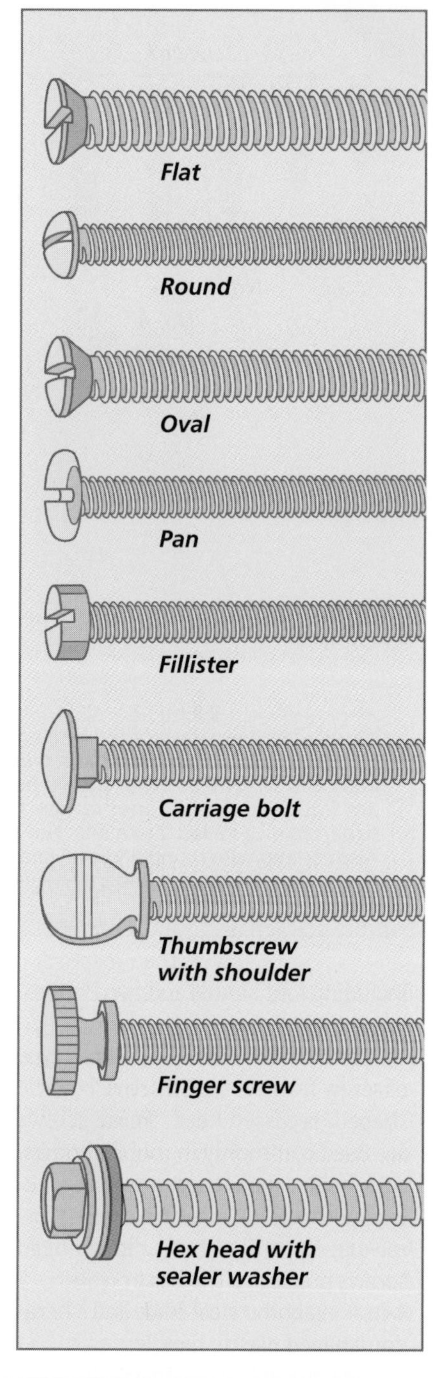

▶ **SCREWHEAD STYLES.** ***Profiles of nine common styles of screwheads are shown at right.***

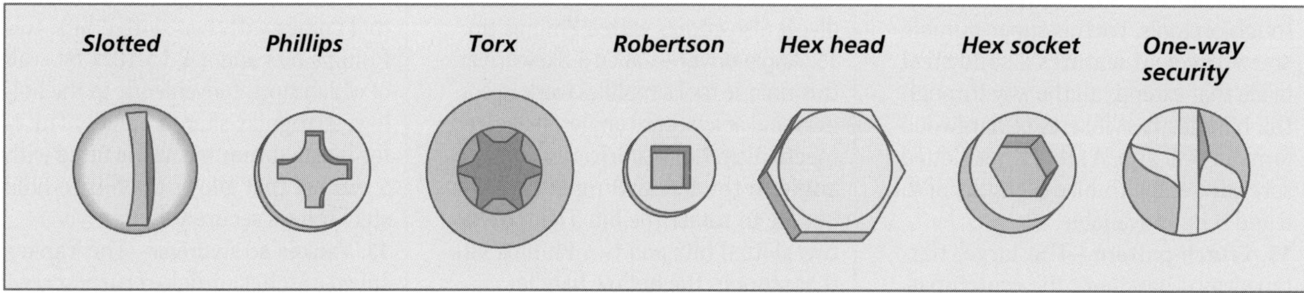

▼ **SCREW-DRIVE TYPES.** ***Shown below are the seven most common types of screw drives.***

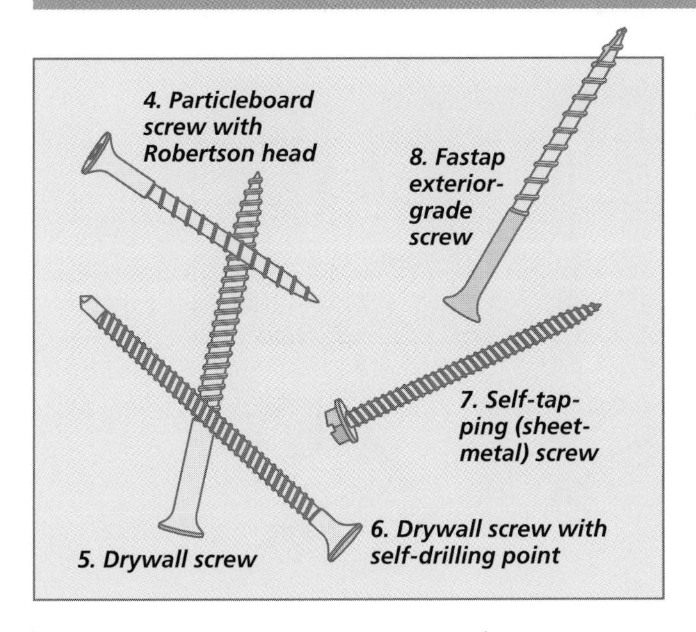

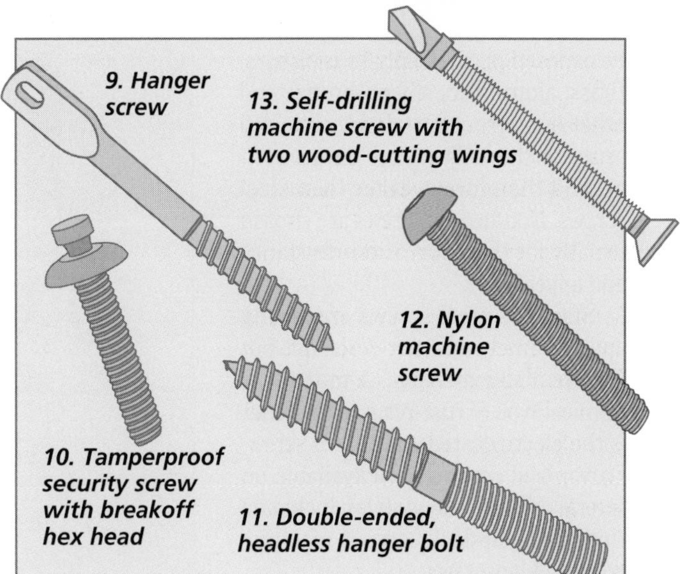

automatically. The screw-holding driver comes in 4- and 5-in. models.

PROPER SCREWDRIVER USE

The screwdriver is probably the most used and certainly the most abused of all hand tools. Screwdrivers are routinely subjected to a variety of abuses, including being used as a chisel, pry bar, punch, scraper, paint stirrer and can opener. However, the most common abuse is simply using a screwdriver that doesn't fit the screwhead. This practice abuses both the screwdriver and the screw. The results often include chewing up the screwhead and causing excessive wear on the driver tip which, in turn, promotes cam-out.

Here are a few guidelines to follow to ensure safe, effective screwdriving. *Never* use a screwdriver as a pry bar; an overstressed blade could shatter, causing an eye injury. Always match the tool's tip style *and* size to the screwhead. Keep the handle free of grease and oil to ensure a nonslip grip and don't use a screwdriver for any job other than its designed purpose.

SCREW SPECIFICS

During the third century B.C., when an inclined plane was modified into a twisting spiral to lift water for irrigation, the screw was born. Through subsequent centuries, the original screw design evolved to become a fastener of parts. Different styles were developed as screws became evermore popular.

Today, the ubiquitous screw is available in many hundreds of styles and sizes to satisfy virtually all fastening jobs. However, selecting the correct fastener from a sea of choices is sometimes a little tricky. To help you make the right choice of screw, a variety of styles are gathered here that every do-it-yourselfer should know about. Note that the styles shown include wood screws, sheet-metal screws, machine screws and a few specialty screws, too.

There are several factors to consider when selecting a screw, including the type and thickness of the material being fastened, the style of screwhead and threads, and the screw diameter and length. Also, if the fasteners are going to be exposed to moisture, be sure to use weather-resistant screws to prevent rusting.

Screws are made of various materials depending on requirements of strength, appearance and corrosion-resistance. Most screws are made of zinc-plated steel. The shiny plating is attractive and offers the screw minimum resistance to rusting should it

▼ **NUTS AND WASHERS.** ***Shown below are three common types of nuts and washers used with bolts.***

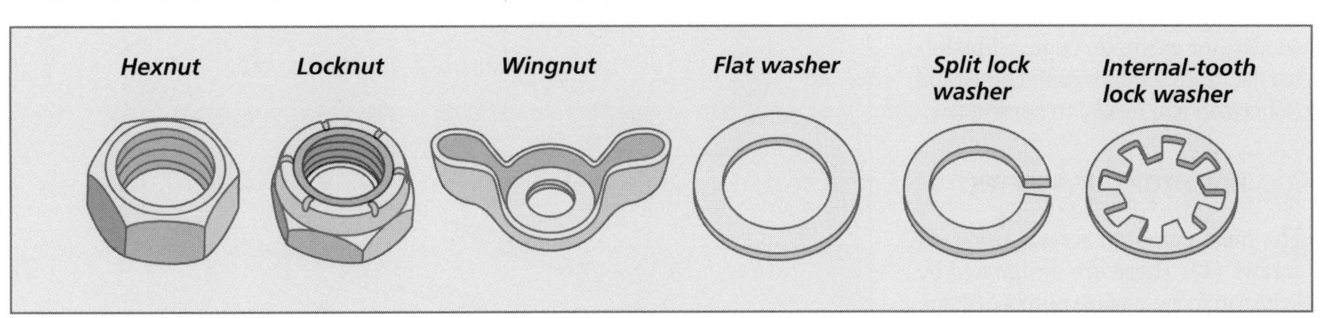

be exposed occasionally to moisture. Brass, aluminum, silicon-bronze and other nonferrous metals are also used as screw stock. These metals are softer, and therefore, weaker than steel screws. Nonferrous screws are chosen usually for their corrosion-resistance and appearance.

Stainless-steel screws are strong and extremely weather-resistant, but they're also expensive. A more economical type of rust-resistant fastener is the electroplated galvanized screw. Galvanized coatings are available on several different screw styles, including thin-shanked deck screws, machine bolts and lagscrews.

DRIVE TYPES AND HEAD STYLES

The screws used most often by do-it-yourselfers are slotted and Phillips, with either a flat or round head. But several other types and styles are worth noting. Besides slotted and Phillips, common types of screw drives include Torx, Robertson, hex head, hex socket and one-way security. And while flat and round heads are the most popular, other styles of heads include oval, pan, fillister, carriage bolt, thumbscrew with shoulder, finger screw and hex head with sealer washer.

Torx screws are found on late-model cars and trucks. Robertson screws, also called square-drive screws, are liked by cabinetmakers for their non-slip head and thin shank. Tamperproof one-way screws are driven with a standard screwdriver, but can't be removed with conventional tools. Remember, screw types and head styles are available in different combinations. Wood screws, for example, come with slotted flat heads, Phillips round heads and Robertson pan heads, to name a few.

INVENTORY OF SCREWS

The most common screws are wood screws **(1)**. These are designated by length in inches, gauge number (shank

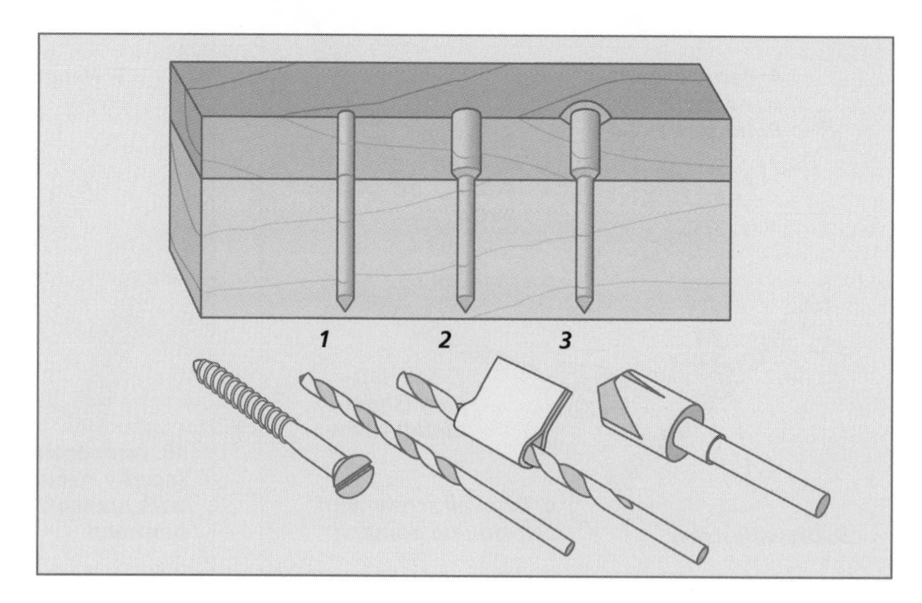

▲ **SCREW HOLES.** ***Boring screw entry holes involves three basic steps: (1) pilot hole, (2) shank clearance hole with masking tape depth gauge and (3) countersink hole for screwhead.***

► **COUNTERSINK.** ***A countersink bit (1) matches the size and shape of the screw. It replaces three bits (2) because it bores all holes in one step.***

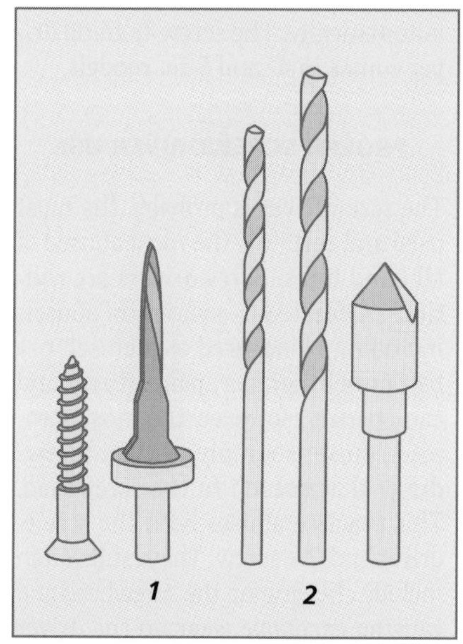

▼ **ADJUSTABLE COUNTERSINK.** ***Fixed collar on standard countersink (1) prevents the bit from counterboring. However, an adjustable countersink (2) can sink and counterbore.***

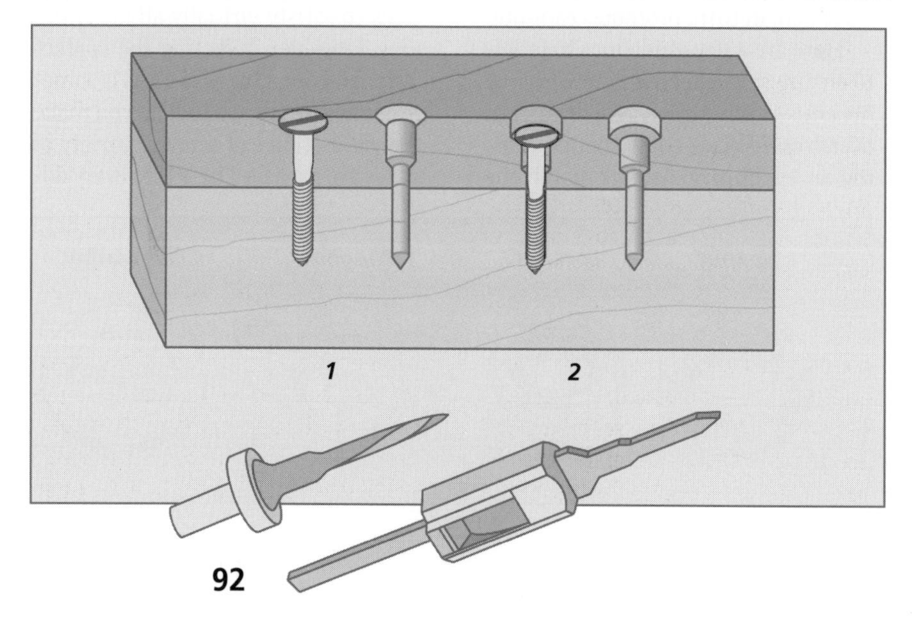

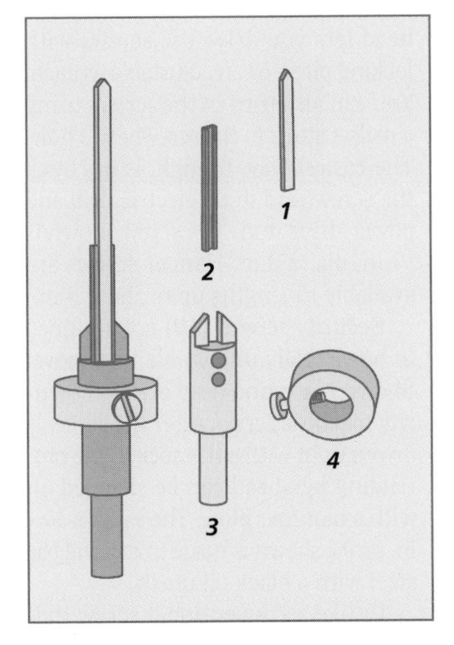

◀ **ADJUSTABLE LENGTH BIT, 1.** ***An adjustable length bit has pilot (1), shank (2) and countersink (3) bits as well as a collar (4) in one tool. The thin pilot bit can break easily.***

▼ **ADJUSTABLE LENGTH BIT, 2.** ***An adjustable length bit, however, is very versatile because it can sink (1) and counterbore (2) for same size screws of different lengths.***

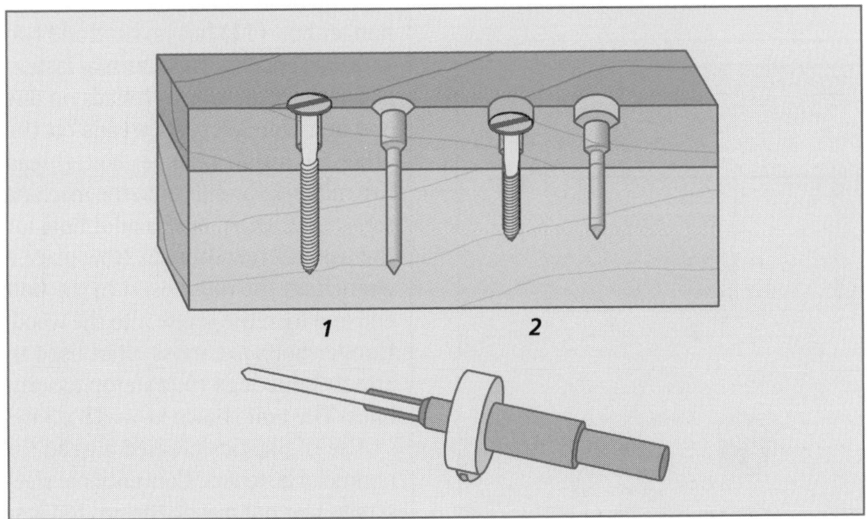

diameter) and screwhead style—for example: 1½-in. No. 8 fh (flat head) screw. Shown are 14 flat-head wood screws ranging in size from a ½-in. No. 2 to a 4-in. No. 18. The higher the gauge number, the larger the screw shank. However, each gauge number comes in several lengths. Therefore, a 1-in. No. 12 has a thicker shank than a 3-in. No. 8 screw. Wood screws are commonly available with flat, round, and oval heads in slotted, Phillips and Robertson styles. Also, screw lengths are measured from the screw tip to the part of the head that is flush with the wood. Measure a flat-head screw to the top of the head, a round-head screw to the bottom surface of the head.

Wherever possible, screw through the thinner piece and into the thicker piece. As a general rule, two-thirds of the screw's length should be driven into the thicker board. Here's the proper method of installing a wood screw. First, bore a pilot hole to a depth equal to about three-quarters of the screw length. The pilot hole must be slightly smaller in diameter than the threaded portion of the screw. Next, bore a screw-shank clearance hole through only the first, thinner board. Finally, countersink the hole and drive in the screw. If you plan to drive the screw below the surface and conceal it with a wood plug, counterbore a shallow plug hole before boring the pilot hole. These drilling steps can also be performed in a single operation using various specialized bits.

When standard wood screws are too small, move up to lagscrews **(2)**. These long, large-shank screws—also called lagbolts—provide extra holding power when joining large-dimension lumber. They have hexagonal or square heads that are driven with a socket or wrench. To transfer pressure over a larger area, use a large diameter washer. Lagscrews are usually available in diameters from ¼ to ⅝ in. and lengths from about 1 to 8 in. The hex-head type shown is ½ in. dia. x 4 in. long.

A cousin of the lagscrew is the capscrew **(3)**. Like its kin, a capscrew has a hex head and large diameter shank. However, capscrews have machine-screw threads for use in tapped holes or with individual nuts. Machine-screw fasteners are designated by the gauge, threads per inch and length in inches. This includes capscrews, machine screws, carriage bolts, machine bolts, stove bolts and threaded rod stock. For example, the capscrew shown is ½-13 x 2 in.—that is, ½ in. dia., 13 threads per inch and 2 in. long. For typical home and shop jobs, National Coarse (NC) capscrews of standard strength—indicated by a plain, smooth-surfaced head—are sufficient.

The next screws are designed for specific applications. The first **(4)** is for use in particleboard. Its thin shank and deep, wide threads give more holding power than standard wood screws. Made of heat-treated, zinc-plated steel, the screw has a Robertson-drive flat head. Shown is a 1¼-in. No. 8; 2- and 3-in. lengths are also available.

Next are two 2½-in. No. 8 drywall screws. They're used to attach gypsum wallboard to wood and metal studs.

Both screws feature a thin shank and a Phillips, self-countersinking bugle head. The difference between them is the points. One **(5)** has a sharp, needle point for use in wood and thin metal—it's excellent for general woodworking and cabinetmaking as well. The other **(6)** has a self-drilling point for driving into 20-ga. or heavier metal studs. Drywall screws are designed to be driven with an electric screwgun, but you can use a Phillips screwdriver.

Self-tapping screws **(7)**, commonly known as sheet-metal screws, tap their own threads in light-gauge metal and wood. Most have pan or round heads. The 2-in. No. 10 screw shown features a slotted hex head with a built-in washer. It can be driven with a slotted screwdriver or socket. Self-tapping screws are available in sizes from ½-in. No. 4 to 2-in. No. 14.

For your next outdoor project, try FasTap Plus exterior-grade screws **(8)**. These screws, similar in design to drywall screws, have self-countersinking bugle heads, thin shanks and sharp self-starting points. A special coating gives superior protection from moisture, salt spray and corrosive chemicals used in treated wood. The screws are available in sizes from 1⅜-in. No. 8 to 6-in. No. 10.

An unusual-looking fastener is the hanger screw **(9)**, which has wood-screw threads and a flat head with a hole through it. Hanger screws are used primarily for installing suspended ceilings. The wires that support the ceiling are attached to them. The flat head lets you drive the screws with locking pliers or an adjustable wrench. You can also turn in the screws using a nailset stuck in the screwhead's hole. The easiest way, though, is to chuck the screwhead in an electric drill and power-drive it in. The screw shown is ¼-in. dia. x 3 in. Hanger screws are available in lengths up to about 5 in.

Security screws **(10)** are designed to be virtually impossible to remove. Shown is a round head breakoff security machine screw. After the screw is driven tight with a hex socket, the protruding hex head can be snapped off with a hammer blow. The ¼-20 x 1¼-in. screw shown is made from solid bar steel with a black oil finish.

Unlike a conventional screw that has one head and a threaded shank, a hanger bolt **(11)** has no head and two threaded shanks. This unusual fastener has machine-screw threads on one end and wood-screw threads on the other. To install a hanger bolt, thread two nuts side-by-side onto the machine screw end. Then, bore a pilot hole for the wood-screw threads. Now place a wrench on the nut closest to the bolt end and turn the screw into the wood. Hanger bolts are most often used to attach table legs to tabletop assemblies. The bolt shown is 5⁄16-18 x 3 in.

Use of plastics created a need for nonmetal fasteners. Conventional steel screws tear out plastic threads too eas-

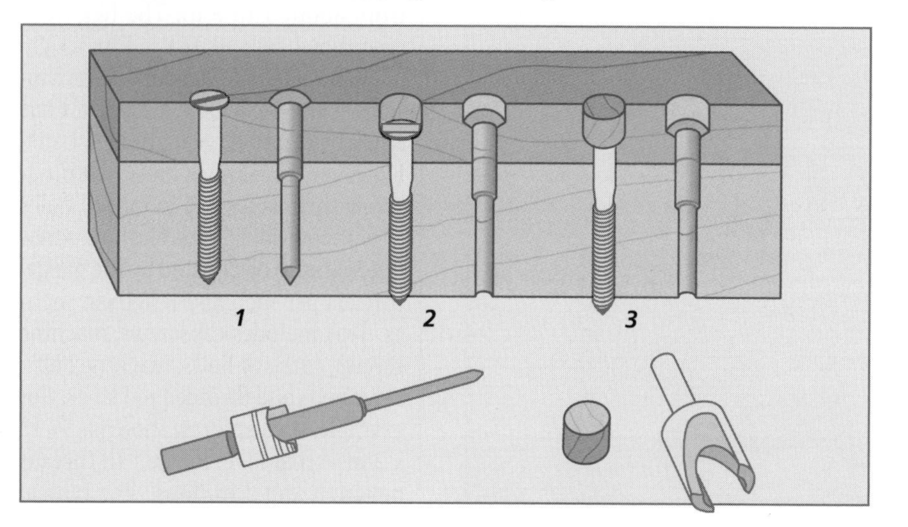

▲ **INSTALLATION METHODS, 1.** ***Screws can be installed three ways: (1) flush, (2) ⅛-in. counterbore for wood filler and (3) ¼-in. counterbore for a wood plug.***

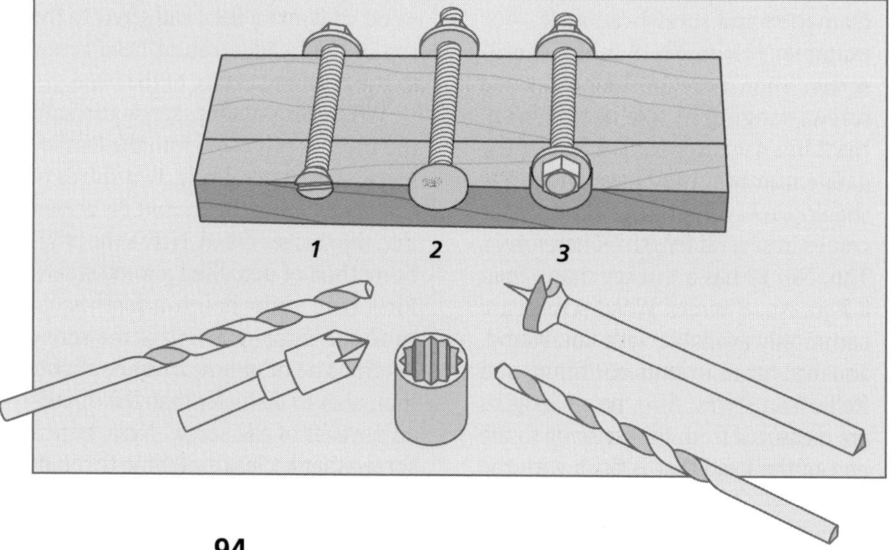

► **INSTALLATION METHODS, 2.** ***Other methods include: (1) machine screw countersunk, (2) carriage bolt with only a clearance hole and (3) bolt with wide counterbore for washer.***

CORDLESS POWER SCREWDRIVER

Here's a cordless, battery-powered screwdriver that resembles a conventional screwdriver—rather than an electric drill. Designed for easy, one-hand operation to drive and remove screws and nuts, the tool accepts any ¼-in.-dia. hex-shaped bit.

The high-torque, low-speed motor of the tool delivers 130 rpm to provide excellent control that reduces cam-out and stripped screwheads. Forward and reverse rotation of the tool is controlled by a rocker switch on the handle *(below)*. A collet lock can be engaged *(right, top)* to allow you to use the tool as a manual screwdriver to loosen stubborn screws. Once the screw has loosened slightly, disengage the collet lock and press the rocker switch to remove the screw under power *(right, bottom)*.

The tool comes with a 120-volt charging stand that can be bench- or wall-mounted and a double-ended bit for Phillips and slotted screws. The tool's nickel-cadmium batteries can be recharged for up to as many as 1,000 times.

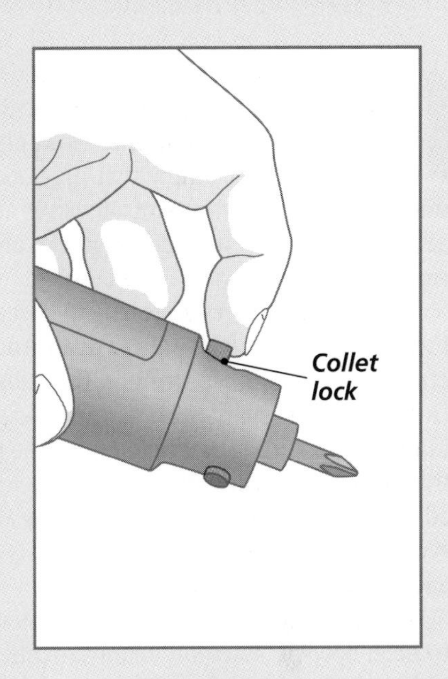

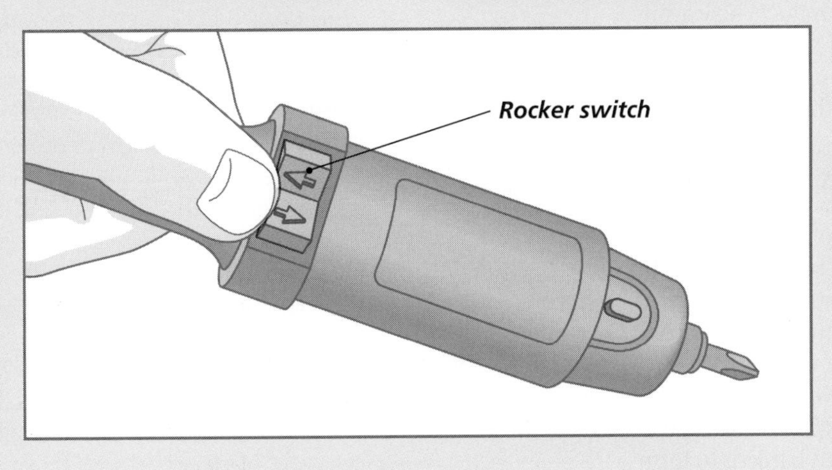

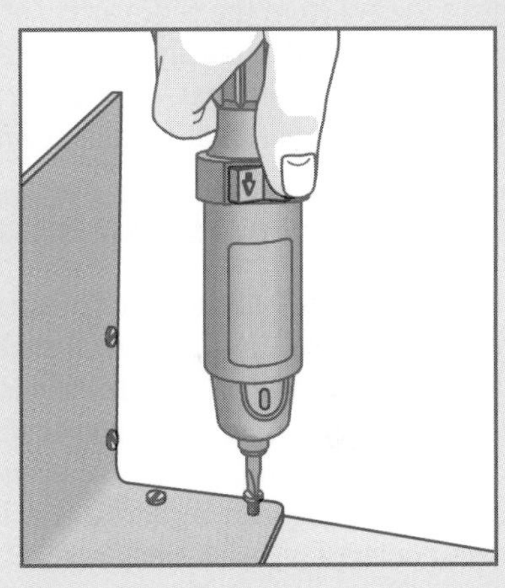

ily. Nylon screws **(12)** are used to fasten plastic parts and assemblies. Nylon is lightweight, strong and, of course, fully rustproof. The slotted, round head machine screw shown is ¼-20 x 2 in.

The last screw **(13)** features a self-drilling point that bores and reams wood and taps steel in one operation. The 2½-in.-long screw has a large, No. 3 Phillips flat head, 12 to 24 machine screw threads and two protruding cutting wings. The wings bore and ream wood, then break off as the self-drilling point taps steel. Use these screws with an electric screwgun to fasten plywood and 2-by lumber to metal that's .089 in. thick and thicker.

NUTS AND WASHERS

Nuts and washers are generally used with bolts for fastening metal parts. Machine screws, or bolts, as they're often called, fall into this category, along with carriage and stove bolts.

There are two basic shapes of nuts: square and hexagonal. A cap nut, covering the visible end of a bolt, is a hex-shape variation. A locknut, hex-shaped like the hexnut, has a nylon insert that locks onto the bolt's threads. Both a hexnut and locknut must be wrench-tightened. One exceptional-shaped nut is the wingnut. Its two flat protrusions allow for hand-turning where the nut must be loosened and tightened often.

Washers serve several purposes. A flat washer eases tightening and lock washers add an extra measure of holding power. There are three types of lock washers: split, internal-tooth and external-tooth. The external-tooth lock washer, with teeth on the outside of the hole and farthest from the bolt's shank, can withstand greatest torque.

ADHESIVES

If you're a typical woodworker, chances are that you spend very little time thinking about how glue works. Your primary concern is simply that glue *does* work. However, understanding the nature of adhesives and how they interact with wood will help guide you in always selecting the right glue for each job.

The use of adhesives dates back at least as far as the ancient Egyptians. These original glues, made from animals and vegetables, changed little through the subsequent centuries. During the first half of this century, however, the adhesive industry grew in leaps and bounds. The primary causes for this sudden, rapid growth were the development of synthetic adhesives, a growing plywood industry and the demands of World War II. The adhesive industry has continued to grow and develop steadily up to the present.

Today's adhesives are highly specialized and formulated to meet specific assembly requirements. But choosing the right adhesive from the wide variety of products now available can be a little confusing. Presented here are requisite workshop adhesives that will handle virtually all gluing jobs—a sampling of what's available on the market.

ADHESION ANSWERS

A detailed analysis of the mechanisms of adhesion would easily fill a book—in fact, several such books do exist. In practical terms, though, the situation is quite simple: Glued surfaces bond together at the points where they make contact. This may sound simple, but even a very smooth surface is quite rough on a microscopic level and, therefore, makes contact only on a small percentage of its total area. Glue fills these tiny irregularities and then hardens to form a solid connection or bridge between the glued pieces.

When glue soaks into a wood's porous surface before hardening, it creates a bond called mechanical adhesive. The strongest holding force in a glued joint, however, is known as specific adhesion. Specific adhesion works by attracting unlike electrical charges that are found in every material. The positive and negative charges in the glue are attracted to the charges in the workpiece. In practice, both mechanical and specific adhesion can and do occur at the same time.

A successful glue joint also depends on the strength of the solid bridge—the hardened glue itself. This is known as cohesive strength. The molecular action that holds the glue together is cohesion. And if that were all there was to it, choosing the best adhesive would be easy—simply pick the glue with the highest cohesive strength.

But there's more to it. Adhesive joints are subject to a variety of stresses and the highest-strength glue for one type of stress may be a poor choice for another type. Glues are strongest when the forces trying to pull them apart are perpendicular to the glue line—tensile stress—or parallel to it—shear stress. In both tensile and shear stress, the force is spread evenly over the entire glue joint.

Conversely, peel and cleavage stress create the weakest glue joint because all the force is applied along the edge of the joint. A glue that produces joints with tensile strengths

WORKSHOP ADHESIVES

	BASE MATERIAL	SHELF LIFE	INITIAL GRAB
White	Polyvinyl acetate	18 mo.	30 sec. to 2 min.
Yellow	Aliphatic resin	18 mo.	10 to 60 sec.
Liquid-hide	Animal hides	12 mo.	Slow
Hot-melt	Thermo-plastic resin	N/A	Very fast
Contact-bond	Flammable solvent	12 mo.	Tack-free 15 to 30 min.
	Nonflammable solvent		
	Water-based acrylic		Tack-free 30 to 60 min.
Instant-bond	Cyano-acrylates	9 to 12 mo.	Very fast
Resorcinol	Resorcinol resin	24 mo.	Very slow
Epoxy: Fast set / *Slow set*	Epoxy and polyamine resin	24 mo.	Slow
Plastic resin	Urea-formaldehyde resin	12 mo.	Very slow
Acrylic resin	Acrylic resin	12 mo.	Fast
Urethane acrylic resin	Urethane and acrylic resin	24 mo.	1 to 2 min.
Construction	Solvent-based	12 mo.	8 to 12 min.
	Water-based		Slow to medium

SETTING TIME	CURING TIME	STRENGTH	CLAMPING REQUIRED	MOISTURE RESISTANCE	HEAT RESISTANCE	COLOR WHEN DRY	BEST USES
30 to 60 min.	24 hr.	High	Yes	Poor	Poor	Clear	Wood and wood products
20 to 45 min.	24 hr.	High	Yes	Fair	Good	Clear to pale amber	Wood and wood products
12 to 16 hr.	16 to 24 hr.	High	Yes	Poor	Excellent	Amber	Wood and wood products
10 to 45 sec.	1 min.	Medium	No	Good	Poor	Clear, white or brown	Wood and wood products, metals, plastics and ceramics
Bonds on contact; 3 hr. open time	24 hr.	Medium	Possibly veneer or laminate bends	Good	Good	Amber	Wood veneer or plastic laminate to wood, plywood or particleboard
Bonds on contact; 5 hr. open time				Fair to good	Good to very good	Clear	
10 to 30 sec.	2 to 4 hr.	Very high	No	Fair	Fair	Clear	Wood and wood products, metals, plastics, ceramics and rubber
10 to 14 hr.; 4 hr. open time	24 hr.	Very high	Yes	Excellent (waterproof)	Good	Brown	Wood and wood products
5 to 10 min. 2 to 4 hr.	12 to 24 hr.	Very high	Yes	Good	Good	Clear, white or gray	Wood and wood products, metals, ceramics, glass and marble
12 to 14 hr.; 4 hr. open time	14 to 24 hr.	High	Yes	Very good	Good	Light tan	Wood and wood products
3 to 8 min.	5 to 20 min.	Very high	No	Good	Good	Clear or amber to tan	Wood and wood products, metals, ceramics, glass and marble
2 to 5 min.	20 min. to 2 hr.	High	No	Good	Good	Clear to pale amber	Wood and wood products, metals, ceramics, glass and marble
10 to 15 min.	24 hr.	Medium-high	Possibly light bracing	Good to very good	Fair to good	Light tan, black and others	Paneling, drywall and subfloor
20 to 30 min.			Finishing nails for paneling	Fair to good	Good	White to off-white	Paneling, subfloor and ceiling tile

greater than 1,000 psi (pounds per square inch) typically has peel strength values of 10 to 50 psi along the joint edge.

Stress to glue joints is also caused by change in temperature. Adhesives and workpieces expand and contract as the temperature rises and drops—but not necessarily at the same rate. If there's a large difference in the degree of their expansion and contraction, the joint will pull apart. Flexible adhesives are less affected by temperature change than rigid ones.

▲ **USING ADHESIVES.** ***Choose the right glue for the job. Setting time refers to how long an adhesive needs to dry before you can remove clamps. Curing time indicates the approximate period to wait before putting the glued piece into use—not when the adhesive has fully cured. Most glues continue to cure for several days before reaching full strength. For best results, always read and follow the manufacturer's instructions printed on the glue container.***

FAVORABLE FEATURES

Besides strength, there are other characteristics to consider when choosing an adhesive. A fast-setting glue, like hot-melt or cyanoacrylate, allows you to assemble small parts very quickly without fussing with clamps. A slow-setting glue, such as hide glue, allows you to work at a leisurely pace, which is necessary when building large, complex projects. A disadvantage of slow-setting glues is that the assembly must remain clamped for several hours. This can become a nuisance if you don't own a lot of clamps.

Other features to consider include heat and moisture resistance, color when dry and shrinkage. In regard to cost, most glues are relatively inexpensive and, like many items, more economical if bought in large-size containers. Two-part glues, like epoxies

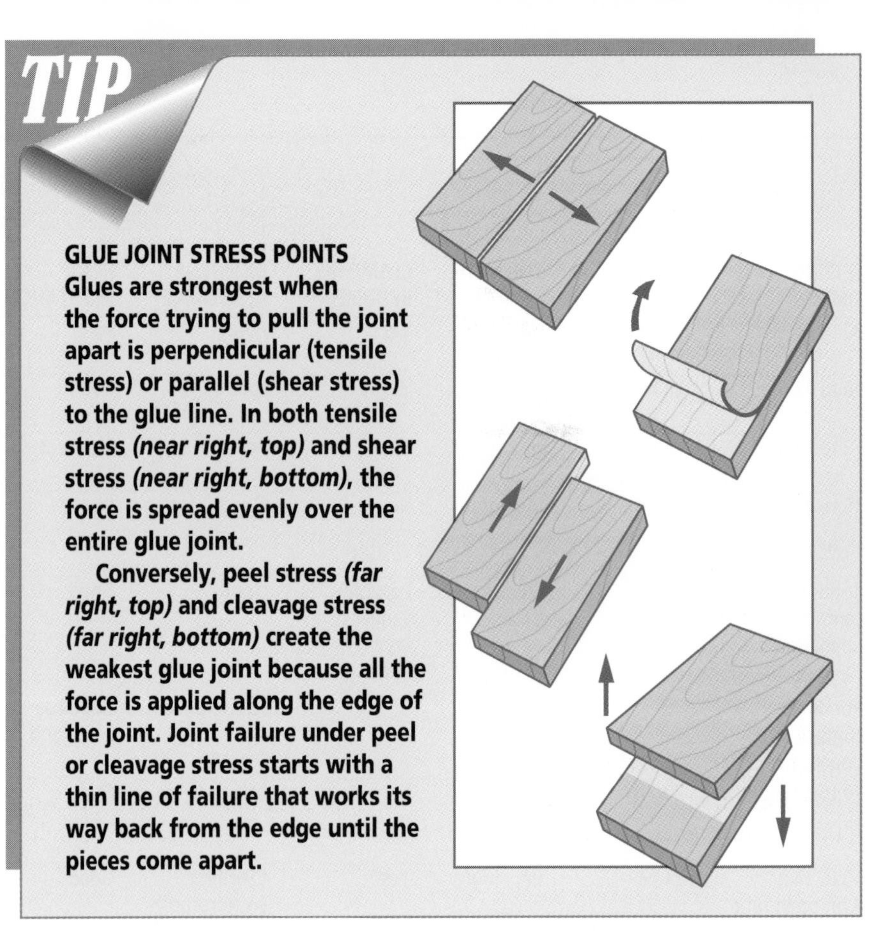

GLUE JOINT STRESS POINTS
Glues are strongest when the force trying to pull the joint apart is perpendicular (tensile stress) or parallel (shear stress) to the glue line. In both tensile stress *(near right, top)* and shear stress *(near right, bottom)*, the force is spread evenly over the entire glue joint.

Conversely, peel stress *(far right, top)* and cleavage stress *(far right, bottom)* create the weakest glue joint because all the force is applied along the edge of the joint. Joint failure under peel or cleavage stress starts with a thin line of failure that works its way back from the edge until the pieces come apart.

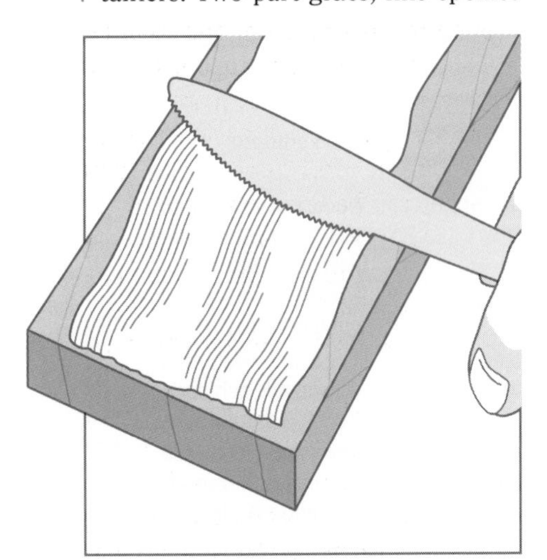

▲ GLUING SURFACES. *One of the biggest errors made by neophyte woodworkers is to apply too much glue. A small, serrated plastic knife is an excellent, uniform spreader.*

▶ GLUING EDGES. *When using woodworking glues that come in plastic bottles with spouts, apply a thin, zigzag bead of glue and rub the parts together to spread the adhesive.*

and resorcinol, are on the high end of the price scale.

Your best insurance for a successful, long-lasting glue joint is printed right on the container. Glue manufacturers provide valuable information, directions and safety precautions on each label. Be sure to read them carefully. Also, additional specifications are often available from the manufacturer.

▲ **GLUING TIGHT SPOTS.** ***A needle-nose glue injector puts glue in tight places. It can glue a chair rail, as here, or a veneer blister, for example.***

ADHESIVE SPECIFICS

Now, let's look at the most common workshop glues.

White glue—This is the most popular household glue on the market. Made of polyvinyl acetate (PVA), it's a good general-purpose glue for use on wood and wood products, as well as porous materials such as paper and leather. White glue is nontoxic, odorless, nonflammable and it sets quickly (less than 1 hour) and dries clear. It has low moisture resistance so don't use it on outdoor projects or where moisture is a problem. Specially formulated PVAs are available for use by children.

Yellow glue—Also known as carpenter's glue, this is an aliphatic resin formulated for use on all types of wood and wood products. Like PVAs, yellow glue is water-based, but it sets quicker and has better moisture resistance than white glue. Aliphatic resins have good heat resistance and aren't affected by most of the common solvents found in varnish, paint and lacquer. Yellow glue dries almost translucent and is sandable so that it won't clog abrasive paper. This is also an excellent glue for poorly heated workshops since it can be used in temperatures as low as 45°F. But remember, at lower temperatures a longer curing time is required.

Hide glue—Made from animal hides, hooves and bones, this is one of the oldest glues still in use today. It now comes in easy-to-use liquid form. For purists, hide glue is also available in solid chips that must be liquefied in a heated pot before use. Hide glue is suitable for all types of wood and wood products. Its long setting time is convenient when extra assembly time is needed. Hide glue is very strong but it has poor moisture resistance.

Hot-melt glue—Hot-melt glue comes in waxy 4-in.-long sticks for application with an electric glue gun. This is an ideal glue for hobbyists and crafts persons. It sets almost instantly and can be used on nearly all materials, including wood, metal, ceramics and cloth. Hot-melt glue comes in several

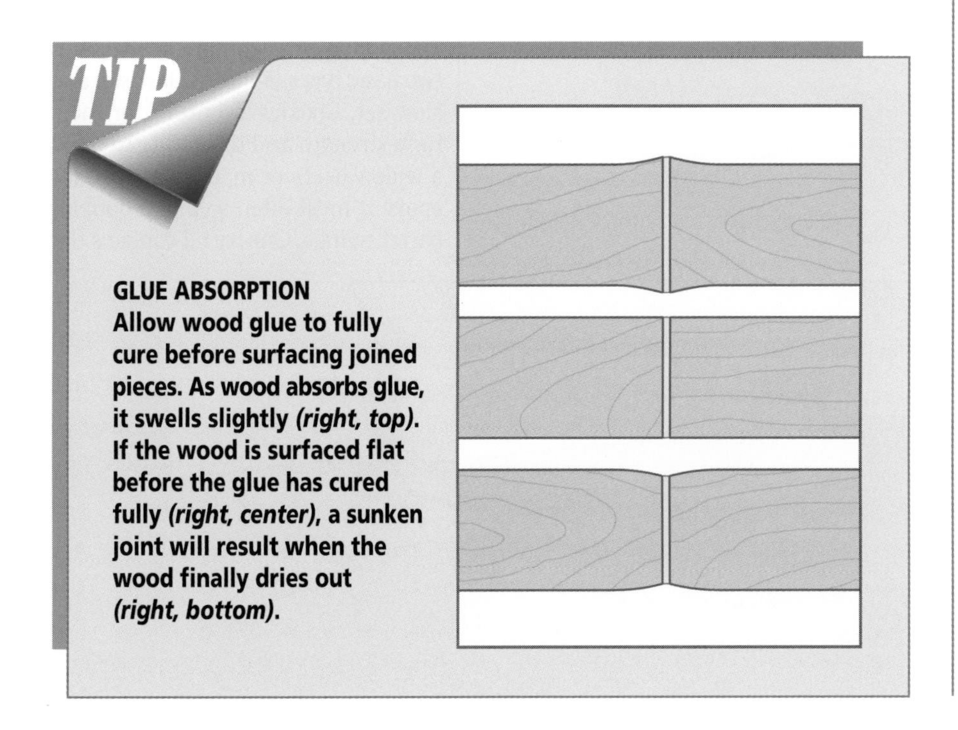

TIP

GLUE ABSORPTION

Allow wood glue to fully cure before surfacing joined pieces. As wood absorbs glue, it swells slightly *(right, top)*. If the wood is surfaced flat before the glue has cured fully *(right, center)*, a sunken joint will result when the wood finally dries out *(right, bottom)*.

formulas, including general purpose, flexible caulking for application around plumbing fixtures and a brown-color wood-tone type. When working with hot-melt glue, avoid applying it to very cold workpieces. The glue doesn't bond well to cold surfaces. *Caution:* Be careful not to touch the glue gun tip during use; it's extremely hot.

Contact cement—There are three types of contact cements available: flammable, nonflammable and water-based. All are used mostly for adhering wood veneers or plastic laminates to a particleboard or plywood core. Apply contact cement to both surfaces using a brush, roller or spray gun. Once the adhesive is tack-free, press the parts together. As implied by its name, the cement bonds on contact. Flammable solvent-based cement must be used only in well-ventilated areas and never near an open flame, pilot light or running electric motor. Its advantages are that it dries very quickly and is the cheapest of the three base types. Nonflammable solvent-based cement is the most expensive and ventilation is required during application, but it dries quickly and is safe near open flames. Water-based cement is medium-priced and extremely safe to use. It's nontoxic and nonflammable, but it has a painstakingly long drying period—often up to 1 hour. Don't use water-based cement on metal surfaces. It could cause corrosion.

Instant-bond glue—More commonly known by such trade names as Krazy Glue and Super Glue, these remarkably strong, super-quick-setting adhesives are cyanoacrylates (cyanogen and acrylic resins). They work very well on nonporous materials such as glass, metal, ceramics and many plastics. Thick, gel-type cyanoacrylates can also be used on porous surfaces such as wood and paper. One small drop is all that's necessary for most repair jobs, so use the adhesive sparingly. These glues also bond skin instantly so use them carefully. Use acetone or nail polish remover to dissolve hardened cyanoacrylate.

Resorcinol glue—This adhesive is a two-part resin that dries completely waterproof. And it's arguably the strongest wood glue available. One minor drawback is that resorcinol dries reddish-brown in color. The glue comes in two cans: a powdered catalyst in one and a liquid resin in the other. Measure the two parts in separate containers to avoid contaminating either can and mix them thoroughly on a scrap board with a putty knife. Wear eye goggles and a respirator while mixing as protection against the catalyst dust. Use resorcinol on all outdoor projects and marine applications.

Epoxy glue—Epoxies are available in two basic types: 5-minute fast-set, and slow-set. Epoxies are noted for their high strength and the ability to bond a wide variety of materials. Fast-set epoxy is most often sold in a double-barrel syringe. One barrel contains the

▲ **USING A BRUSH.** ***A brush is an ideal tool for coating large surfaces such as wallpaper with a thin, even coat of adhesive. Brushes are also handy for large woodworking jobs.***

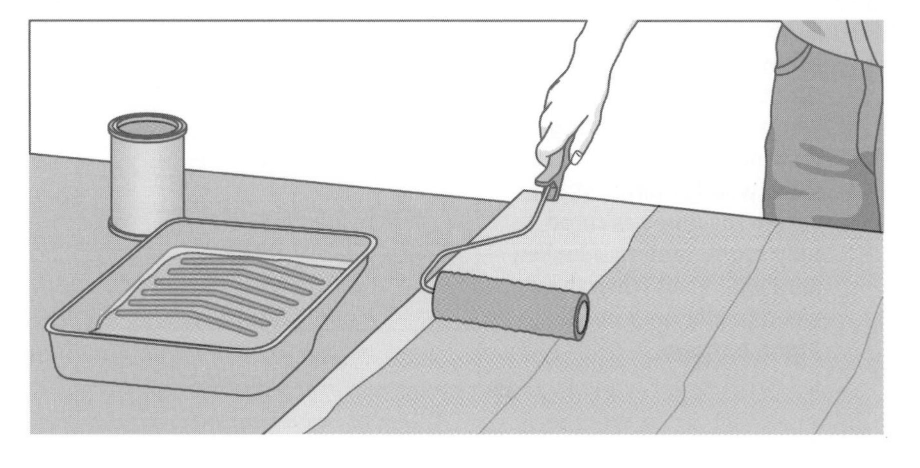

► **USING A ROLLER.** ***Use a roller to apply contact-bond adhesive to plastic laminate. Apply a thin, uniform coat of glue in overlapping passes, then even out the adhesive.***

▶ **APPLYING EPOXY.** ***The plunger on this epoxy-cement applicator forces out proper amounts of hardener and resin. Use this type of glue to join parts that can't be clamped.***

▼ **USING A NOTCHED TROWEL.** ***A notched trowel spreads adhesive for fastening ceramic tile and other material. Use a trowel with properly sized notches, as specified on the adhesive container.***

resin and the other is filled with the hardener. Push the plunger to dispense equal amounts of each ingredient. Mix the glue thoroughly before use. It sets in about 5 minutes but cures in 12 to 24 hours. Slow-set epoxy comes in two separate containers—usually squeeze bottles or cans. It can sometimes be found in syringe containers, too. Work with slow-set epoxy when you need more time before the glue sets. Mix equal amounts of resin and hardener on a scrap board with a putty knife. As with all two-part glues, mix only as much adhesive as you can use in one application. Slow-set epoxy usually sets within 2 hours, but it can take up to 4 hours depending on the temperature.

Plastic resin glue—This adhesive is a urea-formaldehyde powder that when mixed with water becomes a powerful wood glue—which is both heat and moisture resistant. Although plastic resin has a long setting time (12 to 14 hours), it's a favorite of cabinetmakers because of its long pot life (about 4 hours), high strength and nearly invisible glue line.

Acrylic resin glue—These glues are sold in two-vial blister packs that house a primer and an adhesive. You apply the primer to one surface and the adhesive to the other. When you press the surfaces together, setting action begins immediately. After about 60 seconds, you can usually let go.

Urethane acrylic resin glue—These are called anaerobics because they cure without oxygen. They're best used to glue nonporous surfaces in very tight, gapless fits. Glass to glass, metal to metal or metal to glass are the typical applications. Anaerobics don't hold as well for broken pieces from which tiny particles may be missing.

Construction glue—Construction adhesives are usually packaged in cartridges designed for application in caulking guns. They fall into two general categories: solvent-based and water-based. The solvent-based group includes neoprenes and styrene butadienes. Though more expensive, neoprenes are considered by many professional builders to be the cream of the crop. Water-based types also include acrylics and PVAs. Like other water-based glues, they set slowly but their performance is high. It's unlikely that you'll find any of these labeled by chemical category, but price is a guide. Construction adhesives secure wall paneling, drywall, subflooring and ceiling tile.

OTHER GLUE VARIETIES

Missing from the chart is an entire group of household adhesives, typically sold in quantities of a gallon or more. These glues are used for putting down carpet, resilient floor tile, ceramic tile, wall tile, acoustical ceiling tile and wood parquet flooring, among other things. While properties differ from brand to brand, performance of established brands (including those packaged by floor covering and tile makers) is uniformly high. None, except the ceramic wall-tile adhesives, are unusually strong, since great strength isn't a particular requirement. In fact, a certain resiliency in these adhesives, often labeled "cements," is beneficial.

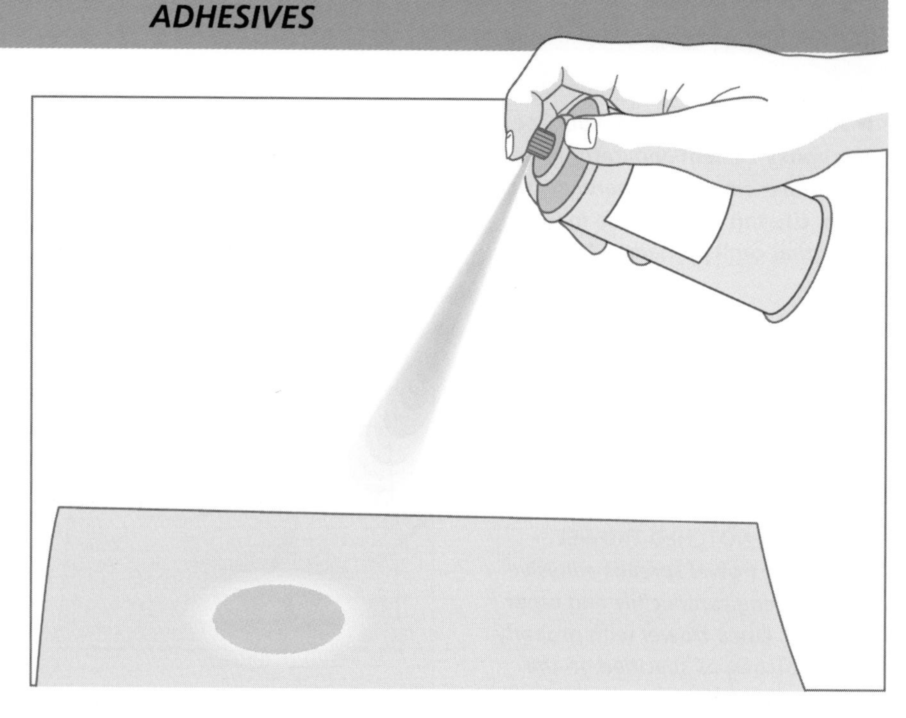

▲ **APPLYING SPRAY ADHESIVE.** ***Spray adhesive bonds paper such as a print to a backing without penetrating through to the front. Spray both surfaces and let them dry for a few minutes, then join them.***

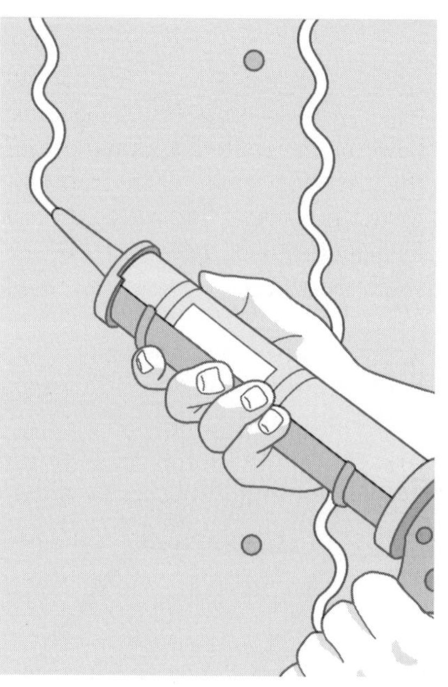

◀ **USING ADHESIVE CARTRIDGES.** ***Panel adhesive and other types of construction glues are often packaged in cartridges. Apply them with a caulking gun, laying out beads in vertical zigzags.***

WORKING WITH WOOD GLUE

For some reason, purists tend to reject white or yellow glue and opt for hide glue. The truth is that professionals in today's mills and shops use yellow glue by the ton. Old World craftsmen, were they here to make a choice, would likely do the same.

Both white and yellow glues have superb holding power. The white gives you a bit more working time than the yellow, which is important for a beginning woodworker. Once you've mastered your gluing techniques, you will want to move up to faster-setting professional glue.

Surface preparation is vital to gluing a strong joint. Many glue-joint failures result from too much dependence on the glue's holding power and not enough on surface preparation. To get a strong glue joint between two pieces of wood, the mating surfaces should be clean and an exact fit. Always test-fit parts before you apply glue.

The single biggest gluing error by neophyte woodworkers is to use too much of the stuff. In addition to making sloppy joints, excessive glue will produce a weaker joint. The correct way to use glue is to spread a thin layer on both surfaces to be joined—just enough to cover them. No matter how you spread the glue, you must keep it away from the edges if you want a tidy joint, one with little glue squeeze-out. Since end grain absorbs glue by capillary action, give it a second coat. Wait a few minutes to let the glue get tacky; this reduces sliding action. Then, press the pieces together. Except for contact cement, you should apply clamp pressure immediately after bonding two glued surfaces. To keep from marring the surfaces, use wood scraps as pads between the clamps and workpiece. Let the workpiece rest 24 hours.

Pressure applied to glued pieces will inevitably cause some squeeze-out. It may be barely visible to your eye, but it will pop into view as soon as your stain is applied. Rather than wipe off excess glue with a damp cloth before it dries, allow it to set overnight. Then, the glue can be carefully removed with

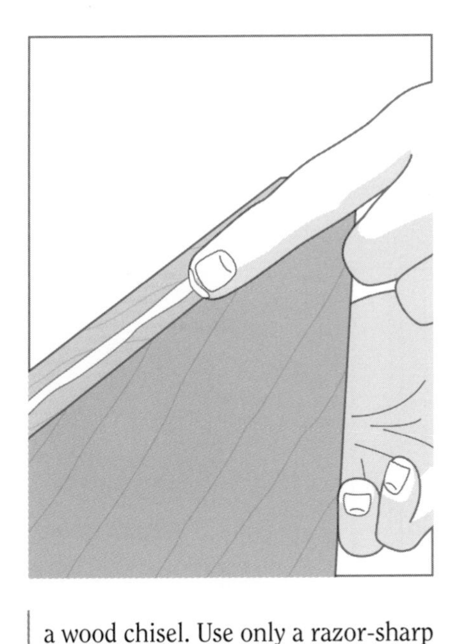

◀ **CLEANING SQUEEZE-OUT, 1.** ***To avoid excess squeeze-out on hard-to-clean inside joints, run your finger along the inside edge after spreading the glue. This will wipe off potential squeeze-out before parts are joined.***

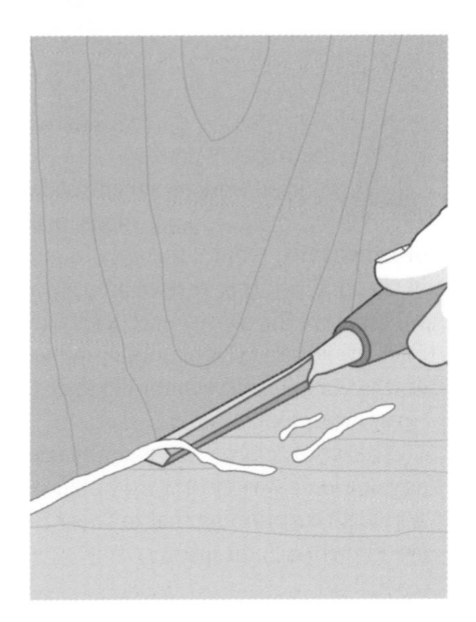

▶ **CLEANING SQUEEZE-OUT, 2.** ***Unless you plan to paint the piece, don't wipe off squeeze-out with a rag. Instead, let the glue set until it is dry, then shave it off with a sharp chisel. This leaves a clean wood surface.***

a wood chisel. Use only a razor-sharp chisel and work with the bevel edge up to avoid any chance of gouging the surface. Hold the blade edge at a slight angle to the glue line to remove the flakes of glue. Follow up with a piece of 120-grit sandpaper wrapped around a wood block. Test to see if there is any glue remaining by dampening the surface with water.

AVOIDING GLUE SPOTS

When you get glue on your hands during an assembly session, the natural reaction is to wipe it off on a rag. This, however, generally doesn't remove *all* the glue. And glue carried from fingertips to work surface is probably the biggest reason for ugly white spots on shopmade pieces. Glue left on wood acts as a sealer, which means the stain you apply won't penetrate. The resulting white spot is the mark of a novice. One trick to use to keep your hands free of glue is to keep a pile of sawdust available in a convenient spot. Every so often during a gluing session, scoop up a handful of sawdust and rub it in your hands, then discard it. The sawdust acts like a blotter and keeps your hands clean of spot-producing glue.

MAKING WOOD FILLER
Sander dust from a wood project mixed with glue makes a matching wood filler for gouges in the piece. After preparing the mix *(right, top)*, work it into the gouge with a putty knife *(right, bottom)*. Don't make the mix too wet with dark woods; this tends to make the patch too dark. Dust from a belt sander works quite well for this type of patch.

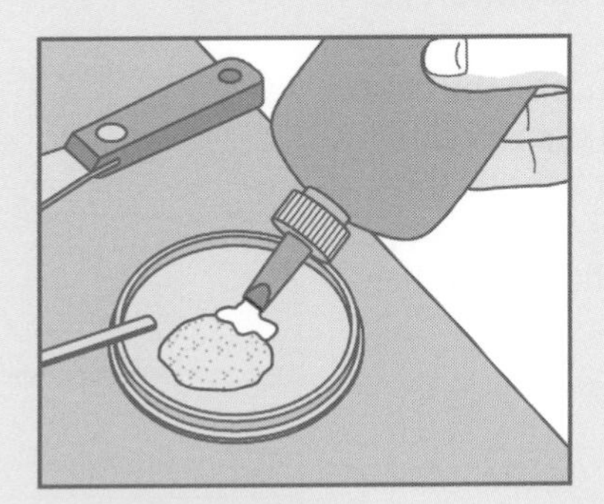

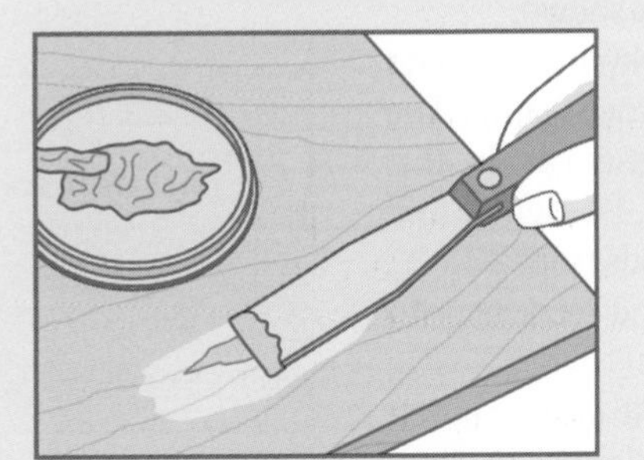

ADHESIVE SHELF LIFE

Few things are more frustrating than carefully gluing a wood joint or a broken object, only to see the glue line fail hours or days later. Why does it happen? If you used the right glue and followed the manufacturer's instructions, perhaps the glue was too old.

If you buy the right glue in small quantities for a particular job and label it with the purchase date, you'll minimize your chances of using old glue that might fail. Shelf life is conservative for adhesives listed in the chart. Most makers claim their products will last a minimum of two years. But this includes the time from factory capping to distributor shelf to you—a period of three to six months. Unfortunately, glue makers aren't required to put the production date on the container.

CLAMPS

All varieties of do-it-yourself work, whether woodworking, metalworking, model making or handicrafts, require the use of some type of clamp. When they're used properly, clamps will improve the convenience, safety and accuracy of any job. And you're unlikely to meet a woodworker who doesn't believe in the old saying that "you can never own enough clamps."

The word "clamp" is generally used to describe any of a wide variety of work-holding devices. Also, it's worth mentioning that in Great Britain, clamps are known as "cramps."

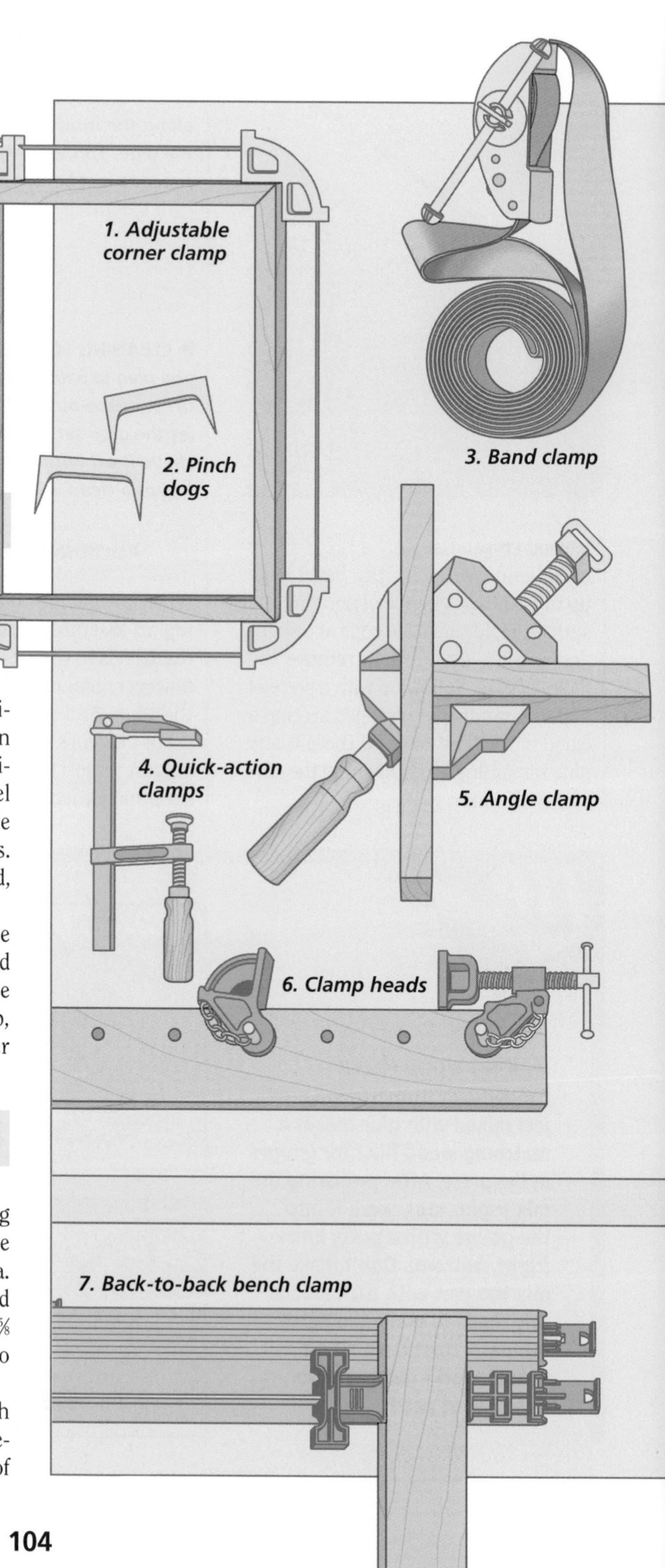

CLAMP CATEGORIES

Generally, clamps can be grouped into five basic categories: C-clamps, bar and pipe clamps, handscrews, band and web clamps, and specialty clamps. Specialty clamps are designed for assembling miter joints, picture frames and irregular-shaped workpieces.

However, the patriarch of the clamp world is the old reliable C-clamp. Versatile, easy-to-use C-clamps are available in sizes ranging from 1 to 18 in. (maximum clamping capacity). Look for C-clamps with high-quality, heat-treated steel or iron frames. Avoid cheap, bargain-variety clamps made of inferior materials that will bend and twist under stress. Check that the screw runs smoothly and that the swivel pad, while seated securely, pivots freely.

The kind of clamps you should own depends on the type of work you're doing. A basic starter group of clamps should include several C-clamps of various sizes, four 2-ft. and three 4-ft. bar or pipe clamps, two 8-in. handscrews, a web clamp, and a few 2-in. spring, or pinch, clamps. Then, add other clamps to this group as the work requires.

INVENTORY OF CLAMPS

Now, let's take a detailed look at the clamps shown.

1. Adjustable corner clamp—Tackle tough, awkward clamping jobs with this versatile adjustable band corner clamp. The clamp uses four cast aluminum corner blocks and a ⅜-in.-dia. steel band to assemble square, rectangular, triangular and round workpieces. Clamping capacity extends from 2⅝ x 2⅝ in. to 36 x 36 in. (or 12 ft. around). The band retracts onto a reel for neat storage.

2. Pinch dogs—Don't be fooled by their simple design; pinch dogs are valuable, effective clamps designed for use in edge-joining boards. Hammer pinch dogs into the butt ends of

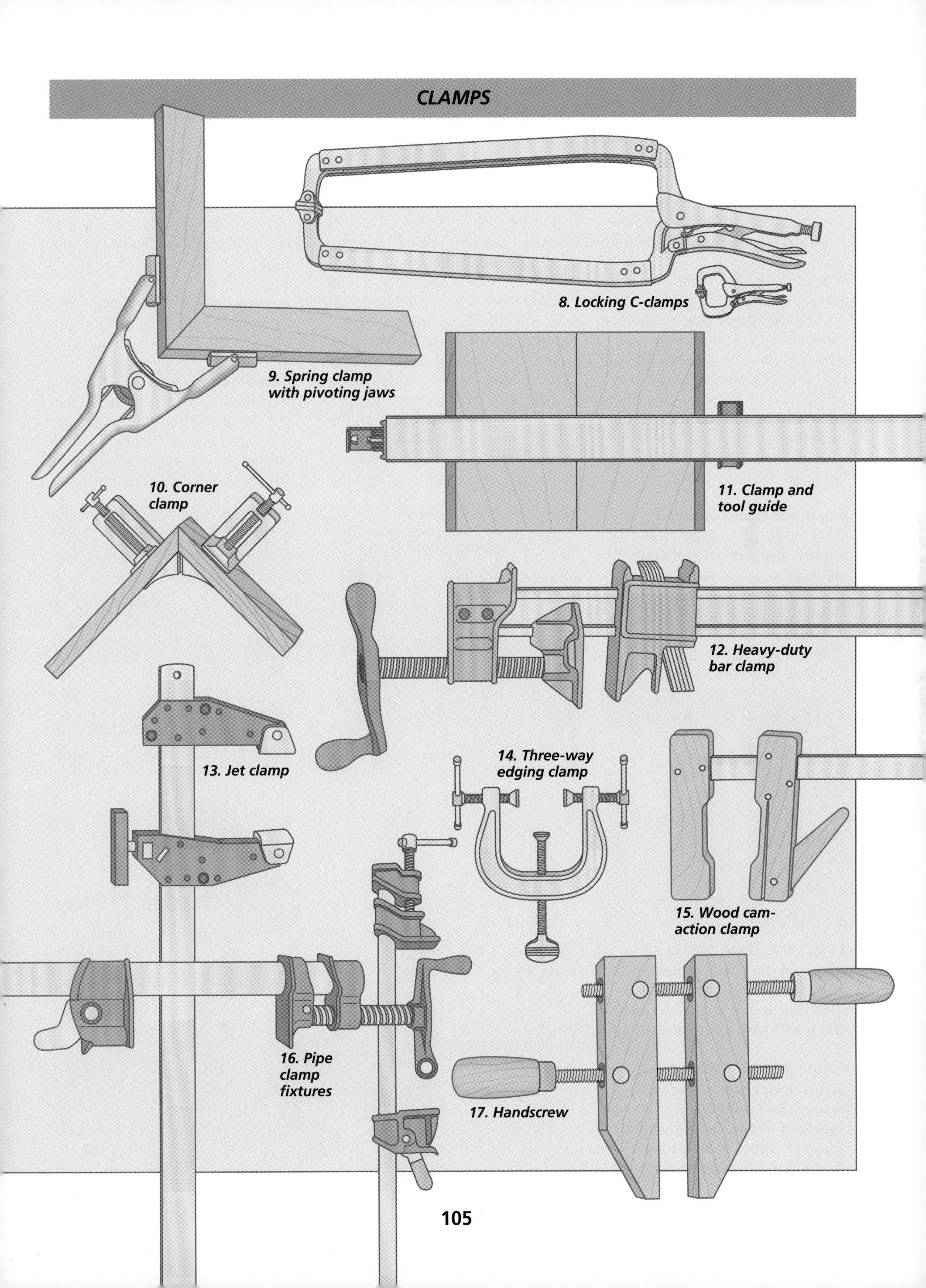
8. Locking C-clamps
9. Spring clamp with pivoting jaws
10. Corner clamp
11. Clamp and tool guide
12. Heavy-duty bar clamp
13. Jet clamp
14. Three-way edging clamp
15. Wood cam-action clamp
16. Pipe clamp fixtures
17. Handscrew

two glued-up boards straddling the joint lines. The dogs will pull the glue joint closed and prevent the boards from shifting. Pinch dogs are available in pairs in five sizes ranging from 1 to 3½ in. wide.

3. Band clamp—For clamping round, oval and odd-shaped workpieces, nothing beats the simple band clamp. This clamp features a 1½-in.-wide super-strong nylon band and steel ratchet mechanism. Simply turn the 6-in.-long handle to tighten the band. A 20-ft. clamping capacity handles oversized jobs easily.

4. Quick-action clamps—Designed for quick, easy operation, this style clamp has become a workshop favorite. The lower jaw slides easily on a zinc-plated bar and locks securely in position under the slightest pressure. The cast-iron jaws come with protective plastic pads. Quick-action clamps are available in seven sizes ranging from 5-in. capacity with a 2-in. depth to 20-in. capacity with a 5-in. depth.

5. Angle clamp—To clamp right-angle joints quickly and easily, work with this German-made tool. Assemble a variety of joints including miter, corner butt, T-joint, rabbet and dado. The plastic-coated metal jaws adjust automatically to accept pieces of varying thicknesses. Clamping capacity of the angle clamp is 1⅛ in. for T-joints and up to 1¾ in. for miters.

6. Clamp heads—Make bar clamps to virtually any length with this pair of clamping heads. The durable cast-iron heads fit onto any 1-in.-thick board. Bore a series of holes in the board to accommodate the ⅜-in.-dia. steel pins that hold the heads in position. Each head has a 1⅝-in.-wide x 1⅞-in. clamping surface.

7. Back-to-back bench clamp—The same innovative design that's employed in the clamp and tool guide is used in this bench clamp—only doubled. A bottom set of jaws locks the 3½-in.-wide clamp to a workbench, tabletop or

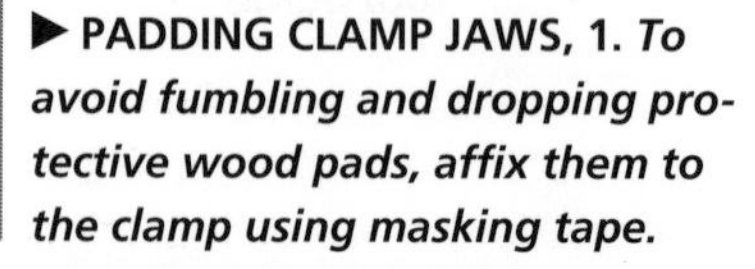

► **PADDING CLAMP JAWS, 1.** ***To avoid fumbling and dropping protective wood pads, affix them to the clamp using masking tape.***

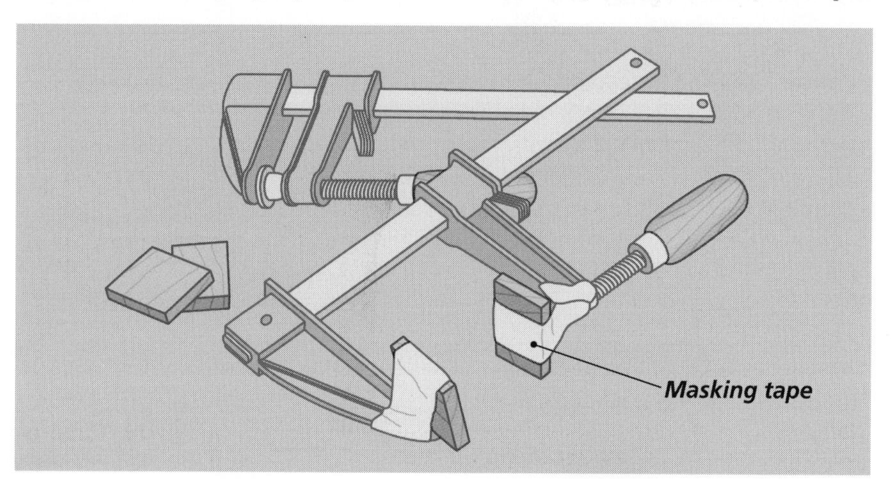

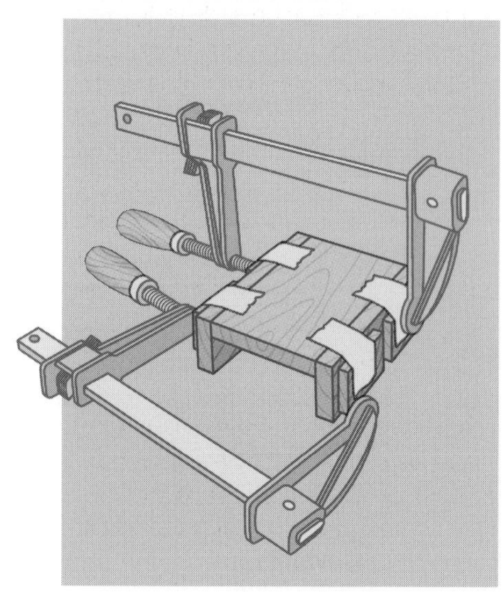

▲ **PADDING CLAMP JAWS, 2.** ***For many clamping tasks, you may prefer to tape wood scraps to the workpiece. Place pads opposite each other so that both jaws are shielded.***

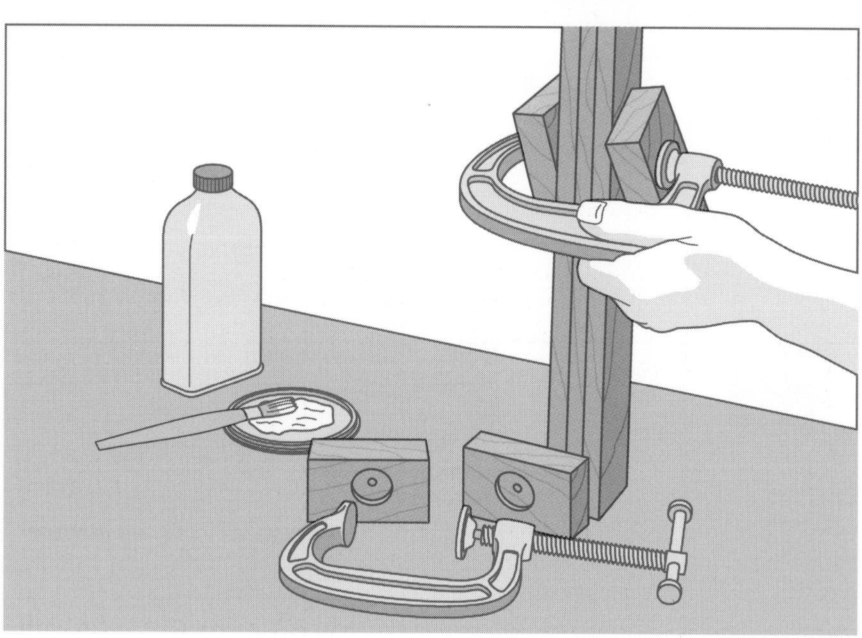

► **PADDING CLAMP JAWS, 3.** ***These clamp cushions have holes bored a bit larger than the diameter of the clamp jaws. They're handy because they don't fall out of place when the clamp is loosened slightly.***

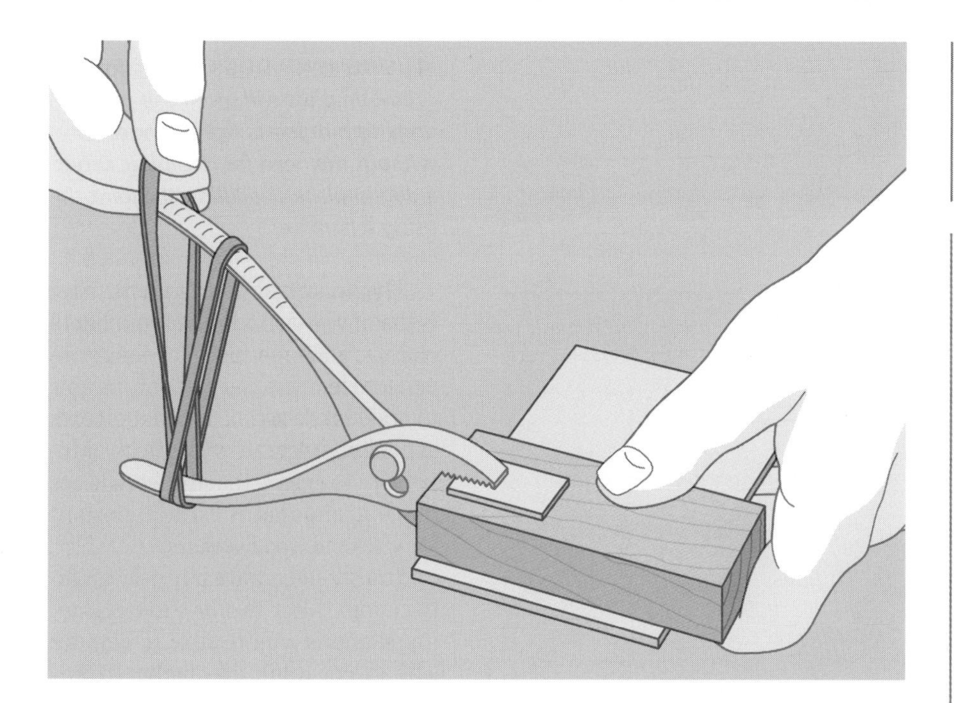

◀ **CLAMPING WITH PLIERS, 1.** ***Here's a good stunt for small-job clamping. Position slip-joint pliers with hardboard pads and slip a rubber band over the handles as shown.***

sawhorse. Then, adjust the upper jaws to grip the work. The clamp's low-profile design allows you to sand, plane, carve and rout without interference from the jaws. Two capacities are available: 18 and 36 in.

8. Locking C-clamps—From the makers of the famous locking pliers come these quick-locking C-clamps. Each clamp features a knurled adjustment knob, quick-release lever and swiveling clamp pads that protect the work's surface and permit gripping tapered pieces. Locking C-clamps are sold in 4-, 6-, 11-, 18- and 24-in. sizes.

9. Spring clamp with pivoting jaws—Each jaw of this clamp has ten tiny teeth that grip and hold angled workpieces securely. The pivoting jaws are most helpful when assembling compound miter joints, irregular-shaped moldings and other tough-to-clamp joints. Maximum capacity of the clamp is 3½ in.

10. Corner clamp—Assemble miter and other 90° corner joints accurately with this English-made corner "cramp." Its design allows you to glue and nail the pieces together while they're clamped securely at 90°. Made of cast iron with precisely machined faces, the clamp will accept workpieces up to 2-in. wide. It can be screwed to a benchtop for added stability.

11. Clamp and tool guide—This unique, innovative tool is a combination bar clamp and straightedge guide. It consists of a ½ x 2⅛-in.-wide aluminum channel that's fitted with durable plastic jaws. To lock the clamp tight, press down the cam-action lever. The low-profile design provides an obstruction-free straightedge for guiding a router or circular saw. It can also be used as an auxiliary fence on a band saw, drill press and table saw. The guide comes in 24- and 50-in. capacities.

12. Heavy-duty bar clamp—When a job calls for extreme clamping pressure, try this powerful bar clamp. Industrial-quality features include a heavy I-beam bar (7/16 x 1½ in. wide), large cast-iron jaws, ⅝-in.-dia. screw and a short-throw handle that permits two-handed tightening. It's available in four capacities ranging from 24 to 60 in.

13. Jet clamp—This bar clamp is part of an elaborate system that offers a wide variety of bars, jigs, attachments and adapters to handle practically all clamping jobs. Unlike most bar clamps, *both* jaws of the Jet clamp can be positioned anywhere along the ¼ x 1¼-in.-wide steel bar. Two jaws come with a bar in 10-, 19½-, 39- and 59-in. lengths.

14. Three-way edging clamp—Here's an indispensible tool used to apply and repair moldings, decorative trim and banding on the edge of a workpiece. The C-clamp design features a third screw that applies right-angle pressure to the edge. Adjust the two clamping screws to position the third screw for off-center pressure. Clamping capacity is 2½ in.

15. Wood cam-action clamp—Here's an excellent tool for light- to medium-duty clamping. The white beech jaws with cork pads won't mar delicate work or veneers. The lower jaw slides easily on a galvanized steel bar. To lock the clamp tight, pull the wood cam lever located on the lower jaw. The clamp is available in four capacities ranging from 7¾ to 23 in. Its jaw depth is 4 in.

16. Pipe clamp fixtures—Make long-reaching pipe clamps economically with these iron clamp fixtures. The two-part fixtures fit on standard black

▼ **CLAMPING WITH PLIERS, 2.** ***Locking pliers also work fine when the workpiece is small, as with the pair of dowels here. Tape the jaws to shield them from the work.***

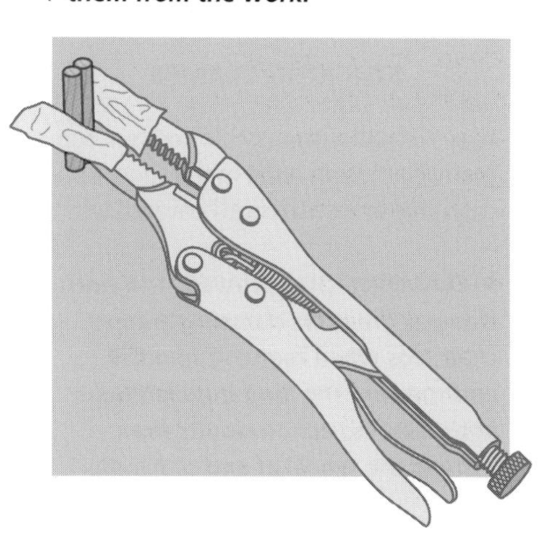

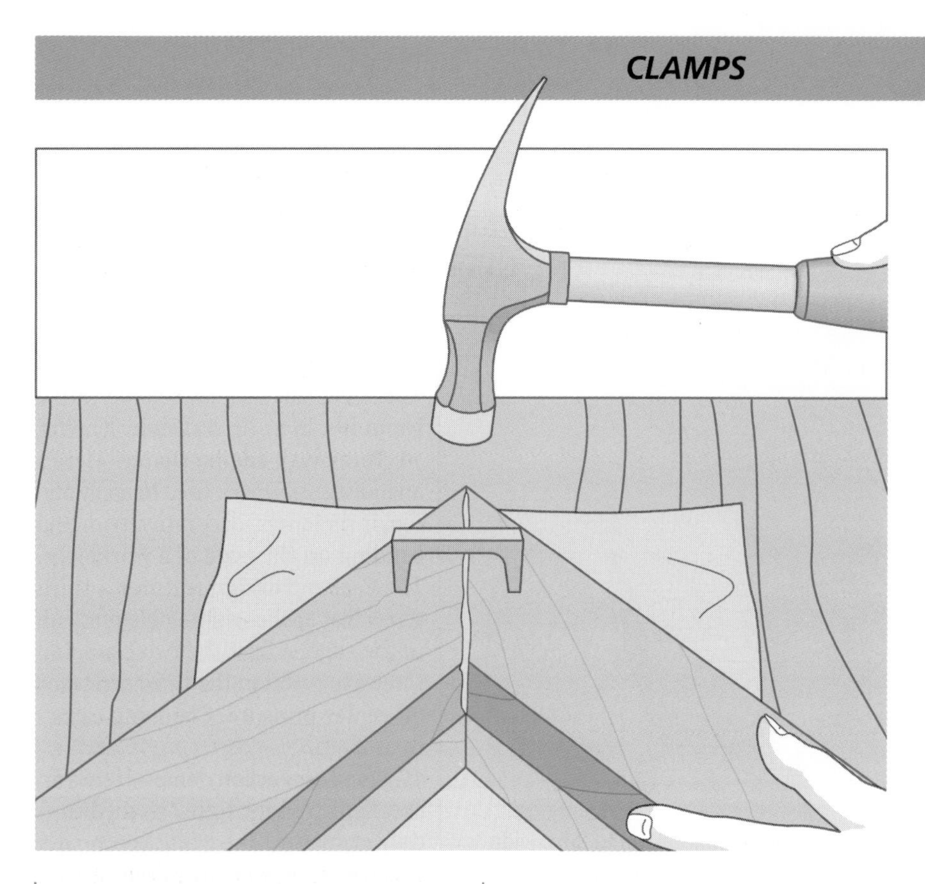

◀ **USING PINCH DOGS.** ***Professional cabinetmakers will often use pinch dogs to pull joints tightly together without the need for clamping. Drive a dog in place straddling the joint using a hammer.***

pipe that is commonly sold at hardware stores. Capacity is limited only by pipe length. Shown are clamp fixtures for ¾- and ¼-in.-dia. pipe. Fixtures for ½-in.-dia. pipe are also available.

17. Handscrew—No workshop is complete without a few of these traditional woodworking clamps. Handscrews feature solid maple jaws and dual handles that give you the ability to apply tremendous pressure. Adjust the jaws for clamping tapered and offset workpieces. They're available in six sizes ranging from a 6-in. jaw length with a 3-in. capacity to a 16-in. jaw length with a 12-in. capacity.

STOCKING CLAMPS

It is virtually impossible to have too many clamps on hand in the shop. You can have one entire wall covered with clamps and put practically all of them into service on just one do-it-yourself building project.

Buy clamps for your shop as the particular need arises. In most cases, the savings created by building a project yourself will more than offset what you might have to lay out on the various holding devices necessary for getting it done expeditiously.

The important point to remember is that if you own a limited number of clamps, each job takes far longer to perform because you will only be able to undertake a certain amount of work at one time. A healthy clamp inventory helps to ensure that the work keeps moving, and that is extra-important for weekend woodworkers.

You should always buy only quality clamps. After two or three clamping sessions, you're sure to wonder why anyone would ever bother to purchase poorly-made clamps.

A relatively inexpensive way for you to build up a supply of clamps is to start with pipe clamps. Here, you pay for the clamp fixture, then purchase black pipe to suit the length you need for the job. For example, you can have pairs of varied pipe lengths (18, 24, 36 in. and so on) for each set of clamp fixtures. Then, you merely use the clamp heads with the pipe lengths that the particular job calls for. When you buy the pipe, thread both ends to suit the

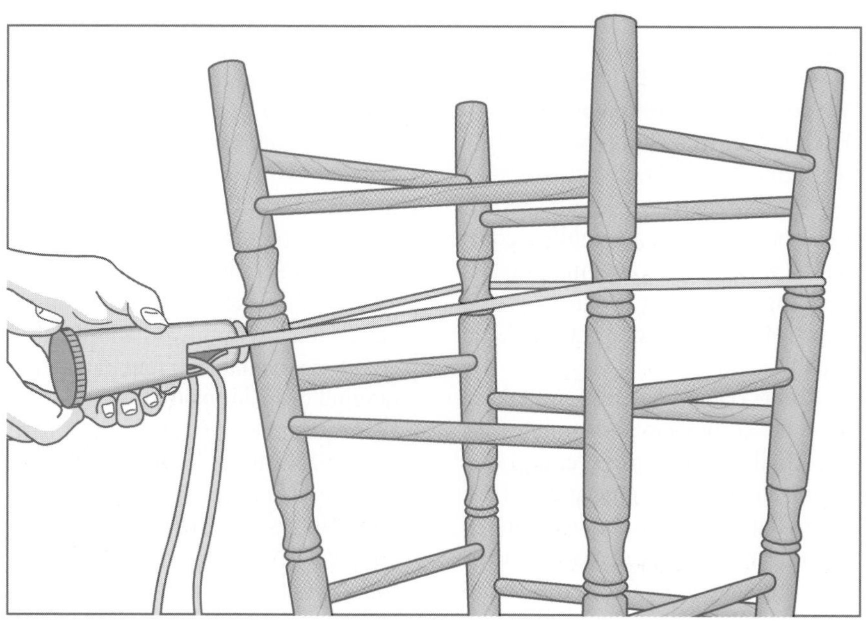

▶ **CLAMPING ODD SHAPES, 1.** ***A cinch clamp is great for clamping around chair legs when regluing spindles and the like. The loop is pulled tight and clamping action results from turning the wheel at end of handle.***

clamp fixture. Eventually, though, you should progress to bar clamps since they have greater strength and rigidity than bar clamps.

A final point here: Don't think the only clamps available are those that your hardware store has on display. Ask your dealer for a look at his catalogs. In them, you will find a surprising array of clamps for all jobs.

BASIC CLAMPING

The biggest bugaboo about setting up a clamped arrangement for a project is that you never have enough hands to handle the workpiece, clamp weight and adjustable jaws of the clamp all at the same time. That's why craftsmen create holding jigs, whenever possible, for cradling bar clamps so that the work can be set in between the jaws.

But in many instances, you must bring the clamps to the work. And if the surface being clamped will be visible on the finished project, it is imperative that you protect the workpiece from the jaws of the clamp. Failure to do so will result in a damaged work surface. To properly protect a surface, you must insert scrap pieces of wood as pads between the jaws of the clamp and the workpiece.

One way to simplify this task is to use masking tape to hold the protective pads in position while you set up and secure the clamps. You can use either one of two methods. To avoid fumbling and dropping the pads, you can temporarily attach them directly onto the jaws of the clamp. This method usually serves perfectly well for small-scale benchtop assembly projects. Or, especially for large-sized workpieces, the better method is to tape the pads onto your work. Just make certain that the pads are taped into position directly opposite to each other so that both jaws of the clamp are shielded from the workpiece.

Another option is to make yourself some hardwood cushions. Bore shallow holes in scrap blocks a little bit larger than the diameter of the jaws of your C-clamps. Then, you can simply slip the jaws into the cushions and tighten the clamp. The cushions are extremely handy to work with because they don't fall out of place when you need to loosen and adjust the clamp. In use, they stay in position until the jaws of the clamp are loosened to a greater degree than the depth of their holes.

ODD-SHAPE CLAMPING

Clamping small or awkwardly-shaped workpieces can be a particular challenge, especially if you're ill-equipped. In these instances, beginning woodworkers often have a tendency to overclamp. However, with practice—and a little ingenuity—you'll develop proficiency in efficient clamping.

One stunt for small-job clamping is to use locking pliers. Just be sure that you first tape the jaws to protect your work. Slip-joint pliers can also be used. Position the pliers using hardboard pads to shield the jaws, then slip a rubber band a few times around the handles to apply clamping pressure.

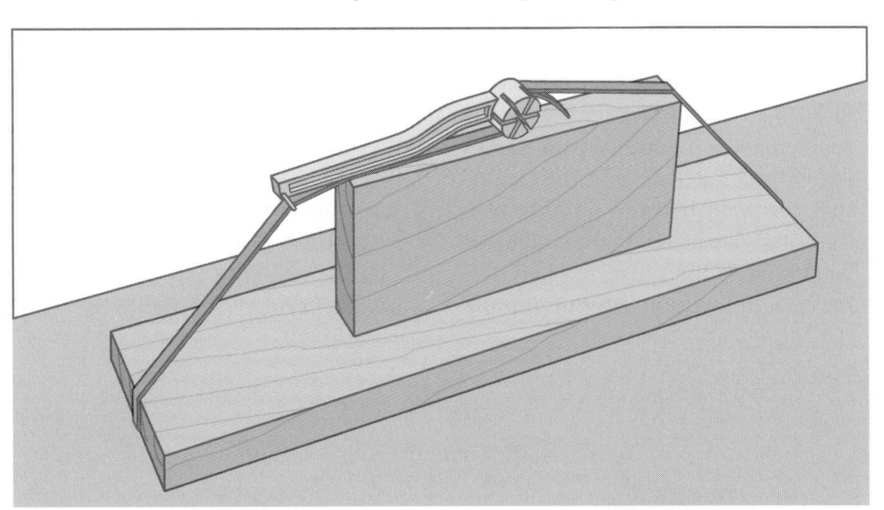

▲ **CLAMPING ODD SHAPES, 2.**
With a tensioning clamp kit, clamping is done by threading the strap ends through the tool barrel and then pushing the handle down to catch the hook under the strap.

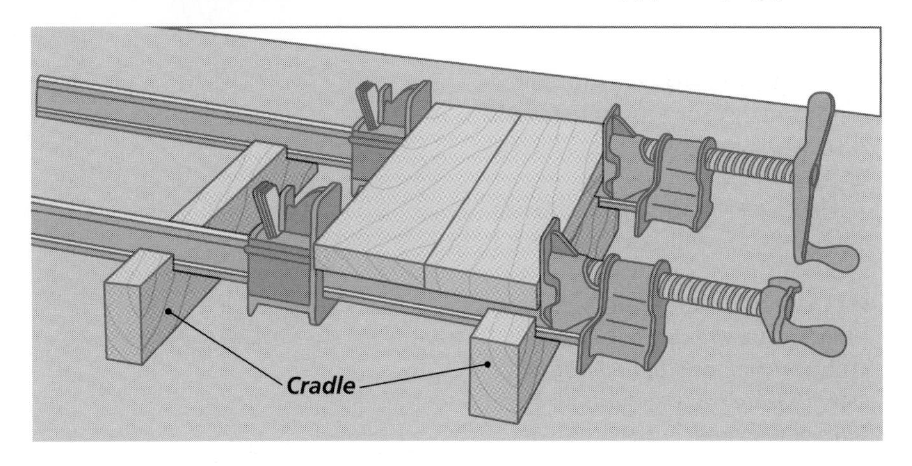

▶ **USING A BAR-CLAMP CRADLE.**
A cradle to hold bar clamps frees both hands to align the work and tighten the clamps. Notches sized to suit the clamps are cut into lengths of stock appropriate for clamping job.

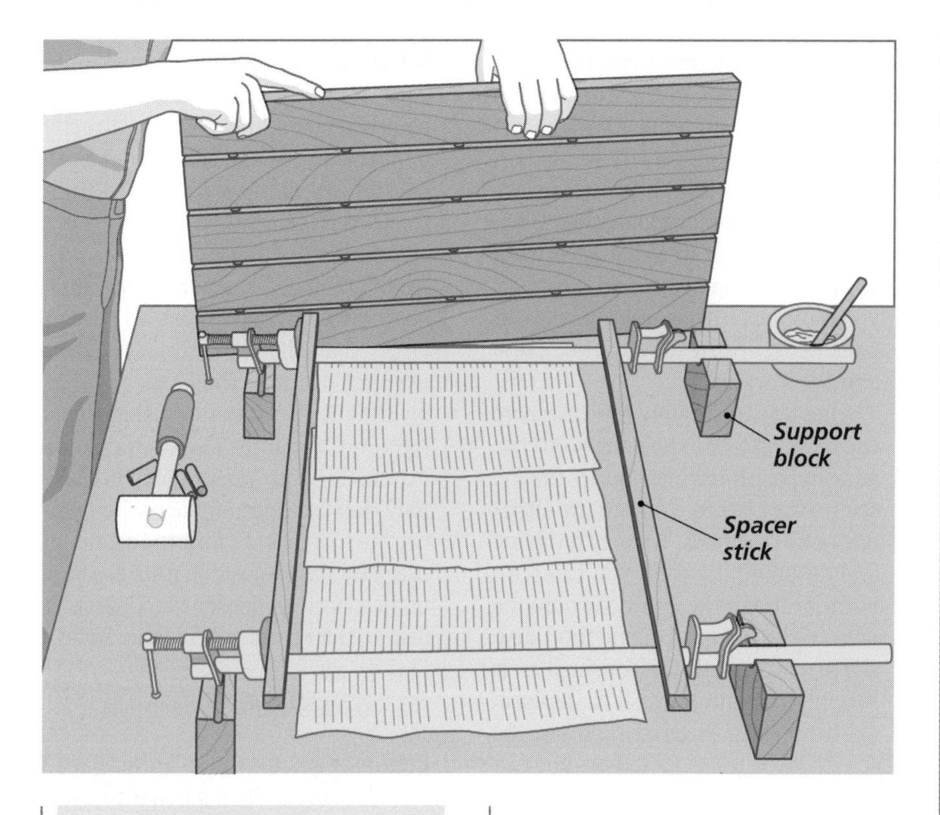

◀ CLAMPING LARGE PANELS, 1. ***Set pipe clamps on support blocks and place spacer strips of appropriate thickness on the clamps, then apply glue to the board edges.***

BAR-CLAMP CRADLE

As every woodworker knows, it can get pretty hectic when you try to hold a workpiece in position, keep bar clamps from twisting and turning, and tighten the bar clamps—all at once. Often an exercise in frustration, it's sometimes downright impossible.

Professionals, as a matter of practice, usually fashion some sort of a simple clamp-holding device so that both hands are free for the clamping task involved. Beginning woodworkers in these instances often have a tendency to overbuild, to create more jig than is needed. The exact opposite, however, is usually called for in the workshop, where the byword should always be "keep it simple."

Here's an idea for a bar-clamp cradle that fits the bill exactly. In fact, it calls for nothing more than two pieces of 2 x 3 stock cut to a length that is appropriate for the span of your clamping job and notched to fit the clamps that you want them to hold. In use, the clamps are placed in the cradle and your work is then inserted between the jaws. Note that in order to turn the clamp handles, the entire assembly must be turned on the workbench so that the handles overhang the front. At the job's conclusion, simply place the cradle in your shop scrap box.

CLAMPING BOARD PANELS

Assembling several narrow boards to make a panel is a common workshop chore, especially with wider boards increasingly difficult—and expensive—to get. For best results, proper stock preparation—surfacing and jointing—is vital. But equally important are proper clamping techniques. Often a glued panel will turn out cupped or twisted because of improper clamp placement and the failure to use proper supporting components.

These problems stem from the fact that the head jaws of pipe clamps have some play in their design. If the clamp is applied to the edge of the board so that the pressure screw in the head jaw is off-center—relative to the board

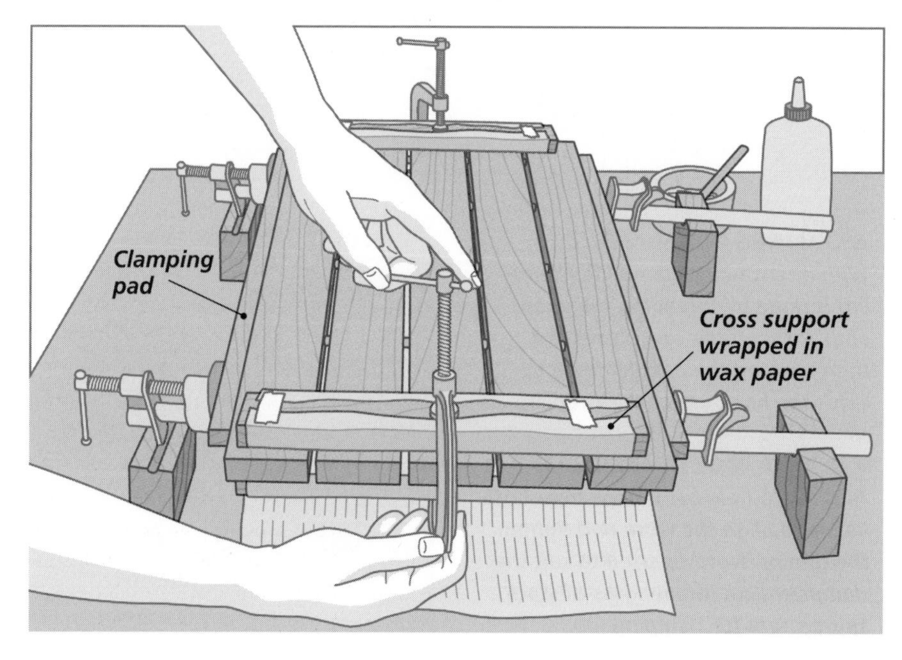

▶ CLAMPING LARGE PANELS, 2. ***Place the panel on the clamps between clamping pads and tighten slightly. Lightly clamp cross supports on both sides of each end.***

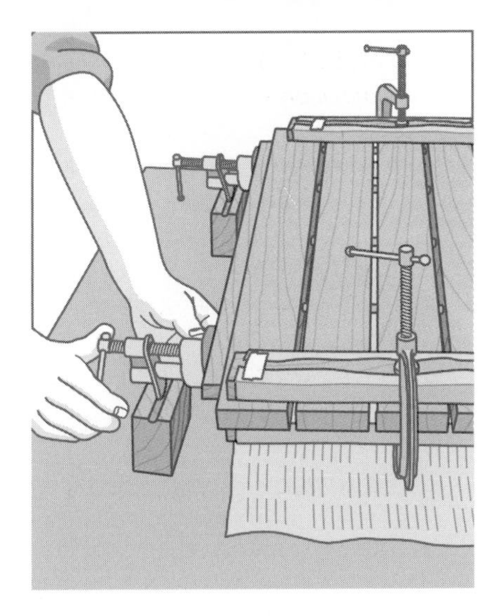

▲ **CLAMPING LARGE PANELS, 3.** ***Alternately tighten each pipe clamp to close the joints. Don't overtighten the clamps. This forces out too much glue and weakens the joints.***

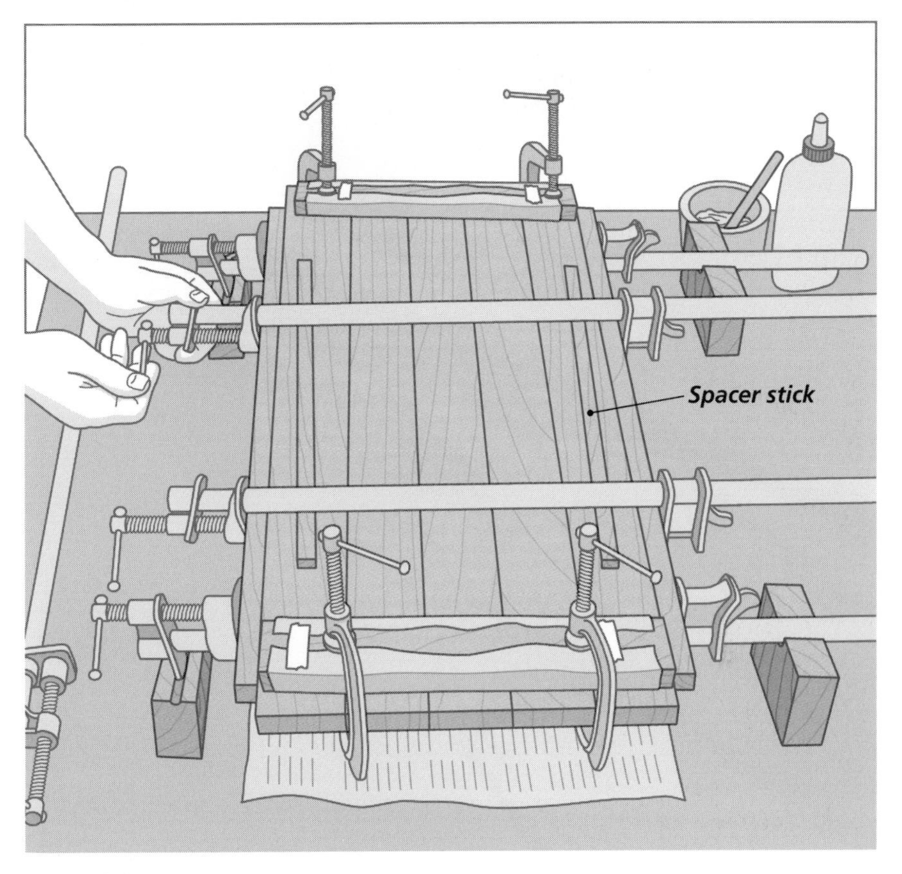

▲ **CLAMPING LARGE PANELS, 5.** ***Place spacer sticks on the panel to support extra pipe clamps and to help keep the panel flat. Tighten the clamps to same pressure as the others.***

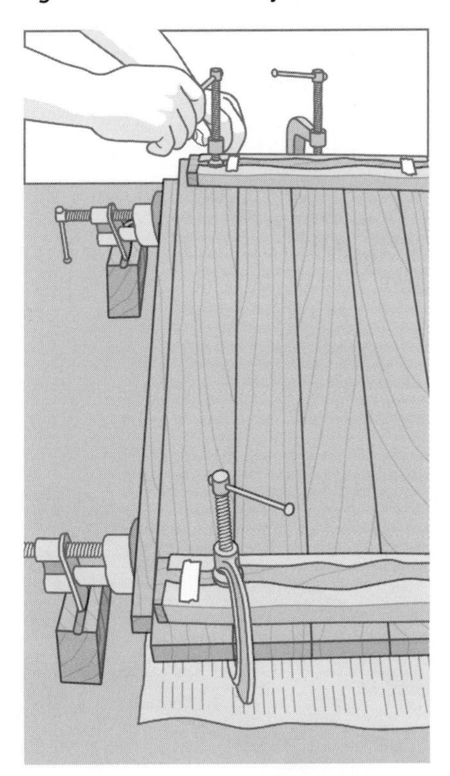

▲ **CLAMPING LARGE PANELS, 4.** ***Once the joints are closed, shift C-clamps to the ends of the cross supports and add another C-clamp at each end to bring the support tight.***

edge—the jaw tilts and tends to make the panel arch in the middle. If the clamps are applied off-center in opposite directions, the panel will twist. Pipe clamps also have a tendency to tip over because of their relatively high center of gravity. This can be annoying when you're rushing to clamp a joint tight before the glue dries.

All these difficulties can be resolved with the straightforward clamping system described here. The system uses clamp supports of 2 x 4 stock to stabilize the head jaws and pipes, clamping pads of scrap stock to guard the panel edges from clamp damage, cross supports covered with wax paper to align the ends of the boards so the panel stays flat, and thin spacer sticks that center the head jaw on the panel edge and help keep the panel flat, too.

Place two pipe clamps on support blocks and spacer sticks of suitable thickness across the clamps. Apply glue to the board edges and set the panel on the clamps between clamping pads. Note that ring direction of board ends must alternate to keep the panel from cupping. Tighten the clamps slightly.

Use C-clamps to lightly clamp cross supports on both sides of each end and alternately tighten each pipe clamp to close the joints. Do not overtighten the clamps; this weakens the joints by forcing out too much glue. Once the joints are closed, shift the C-clamps to the ends of the cross supports, and add another C-clamp at each end to bring support tight. Place spacer sticks on the panel to support extra pipe clamps and to help keep panel flat. Tighten all the clamps to the same pressure.

PORTABLE POWER TOOLS

CIRCULAR SAWS

Whether you're a homeowner about to build a new deck, or a seasoned professional with a roof full of rafters to cut, a circular saw is one tool that you can't do without. When it comes to cutting lumber, no other saw combines power, speed and accuracy in such a compact, portable package.

Like most power tools, circular saws come in a variety of styles, sizes and prices, and most manufacturers offer at least one model. The most popular saw size is 7¼ in. The dimension signifies the maximum diameter blade that the saw can handle. This size easily cuts through nominal 2-in. construction lumber—even with the blade set at 45° to the base.

The most common type features a motor axis that is parallel to the axis of rotation of the blade. The motor is linked with the blade shaft via helical gears that reduce motor speed to about 5,800 rpm. Some carpenters prefer a design where the motor axis is at a right angle to blade rotation. These saws are usually worm-gear driven, and are only offered in a professional-level price range.

FEATURE VARIATIONS

Although most circular saws are similar in appearance, depth-adjustment mechanisms typically fall into one of two categories: pivot-foot models, where blade depth is regulated by pivoting the base at a point at the saw front; and drop-foot saws, where the base moves up and down in a straight line. Pivot-foot saws force you to hold the tool differently at various blade depths, but are generally lighter, simpler tools. Drop-foot saws have the advantage of constant handle-to-base relationship regardless of depth of cut, but the sliding mechanism is sometimes prone to jamming. The handle on a drop-foot saw may be designed to favor certain types of work. If it's nearly parallel to the base, the saw is called a top-handle model and is useful when you're positioned directly over the work. However, if you're cutting large panels and likely to be behind the saw pushing it, a push-handle model with the handle angled back is more comfortable to operate.

Circular saw bases are made of thick aluminum or thinner stamped steel that's ribbed and bent up at the edges for stiffness. Although the aluminum type looks more substantial, it's doubtful that it provides any great advantage other than offering a better edge for following a cutting guide.

While all circular saws are up to the usual cutting chores, many of them display an assortment of inaccuracies that you don't expect to find. For example, few have a provision for adjusting the base edge parallel to the blade, and many show a misalignment as measured from the front and back

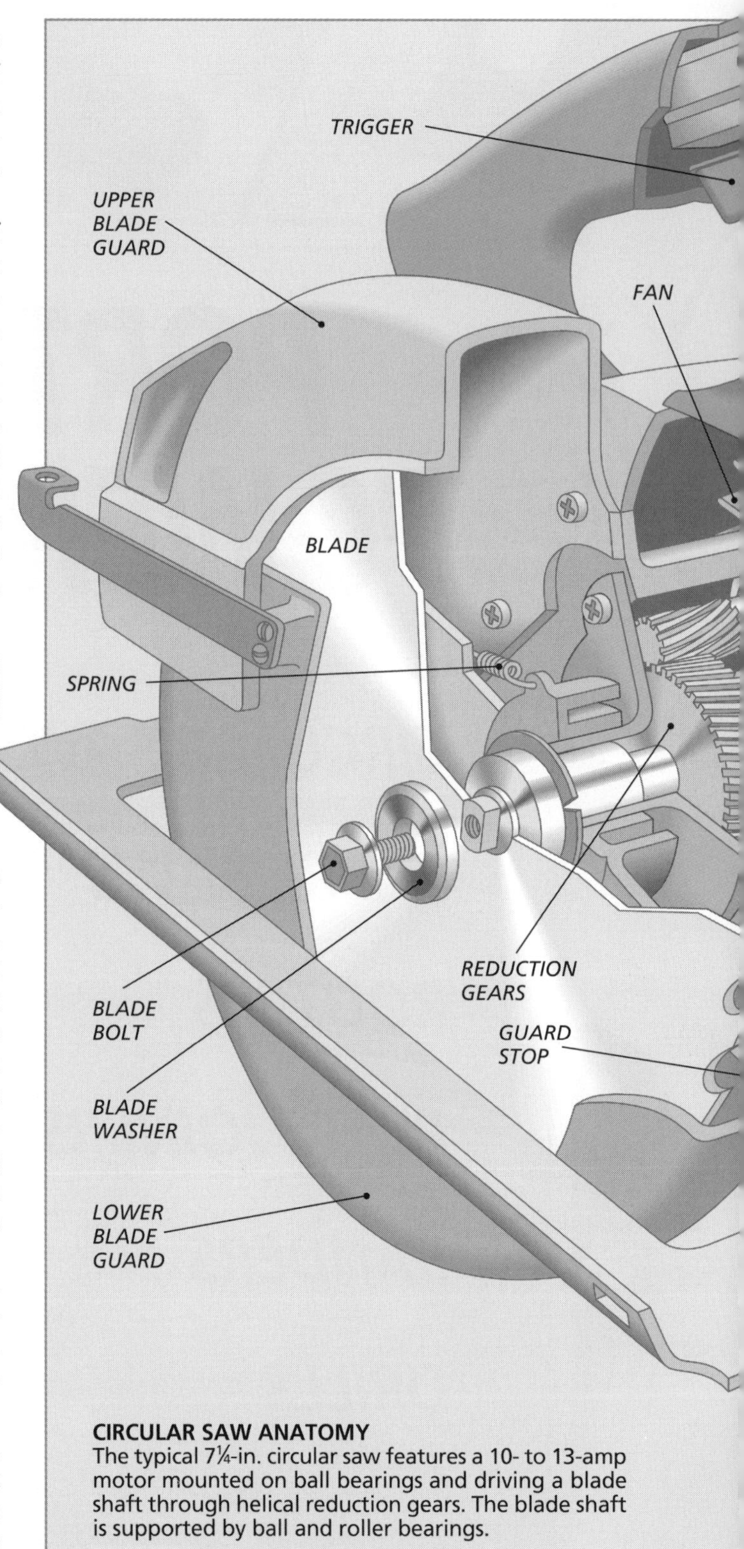

CIRCULAR SAW ANATOMY
The typical 7¼-in. circular saw features a 10- to 13-amp motor mounted on ball bearings and driving a blade shaft through helical reduction gears. The blade shaft is supported by ball and roller bearings.

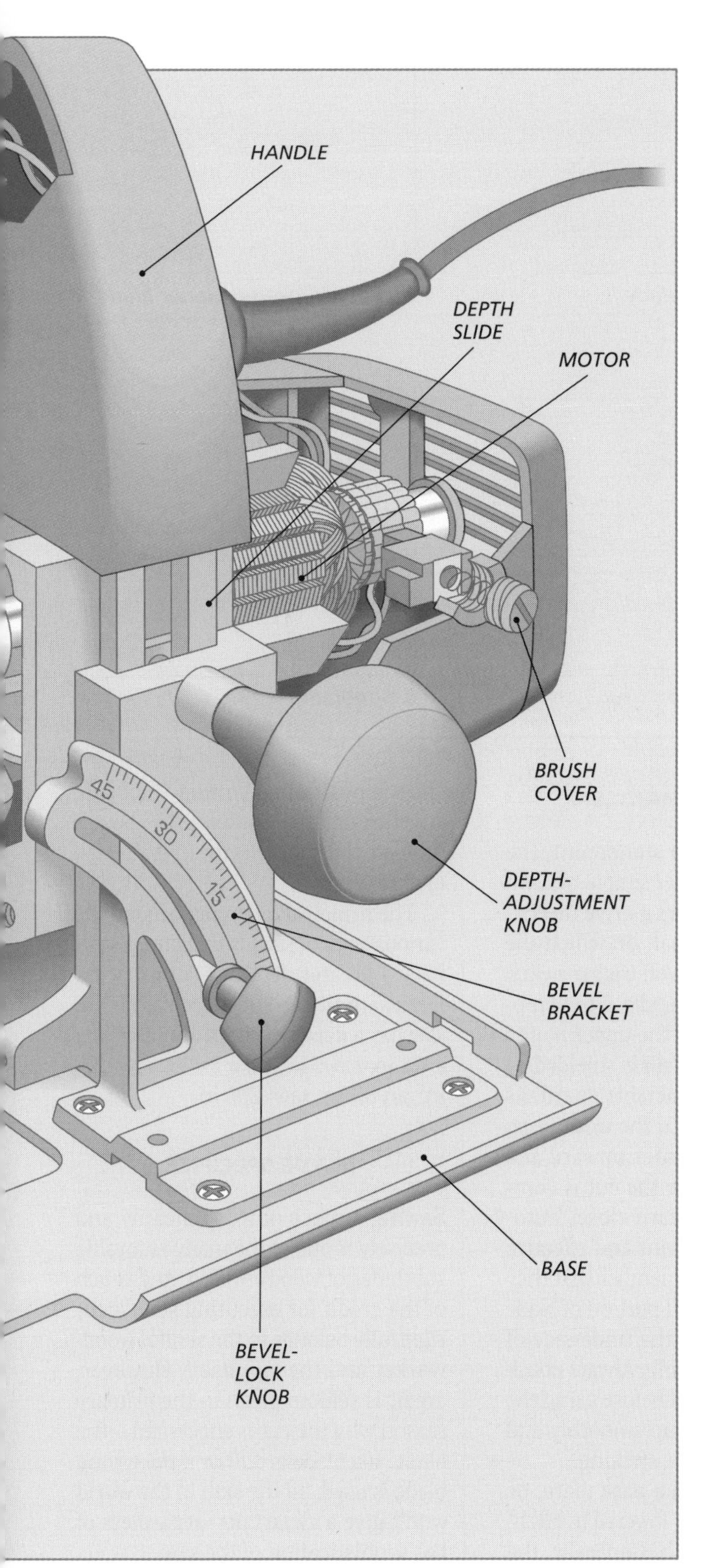

of the blade to the base edge. Also, blade shaft end play (measured as in-and-out motion at the blade bolt) can range as high as .005 in., and in most cases is reflected in detectable side-to-side play at the blade circumference. And while many saws incorporate setscrews as a stop to quickly and accurately set the base for a 90° cut, the setscrews can be loose, causing them to vibrate out of position as the saw is used.

What does all this add up to? Perhaps nothing if you're framing a house. However, if you plan to use the best possible, smoothest cutting blade that you can buy and use your saw with straightedge guides for precision work, many circular saws won't be up to the task.

MAKING YOUR CHOICE

When comparing saws, the tool specifications that should influence your buying decision the most include the horsepower, amp rating, bearings and maximum depth of cut at 90° and 45°. The safety features to look for include an electric brake that stops the blade within seconds of releasing the trigger and a slip clutch that prevents dangerous kickback and motor burnout. Should the blade become bound in a cut, the clutch will override the connection between the blade and the motor—allowing the motor armature to rotate even though the blade is stopped. Choose a saw that has a front handle or knob for additional control and a heavy-gauge, sturdy, wrap-around shoe.

In terms of cutting speed and power, it's difficult to distinguish one circular saw from the next—the blade type and

▼ CORDLESS CIRCULAR SAW. ***The typical cordless, battery-operated 6½-in. circular saw shown here features a cutting depth of 2⅛ in. at 90°.***

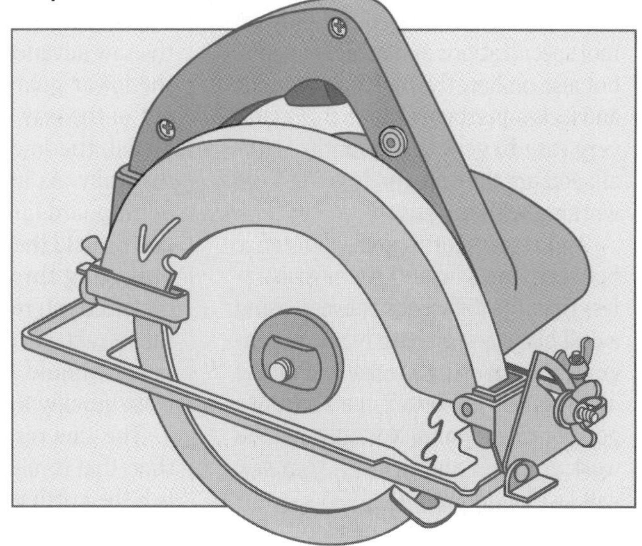

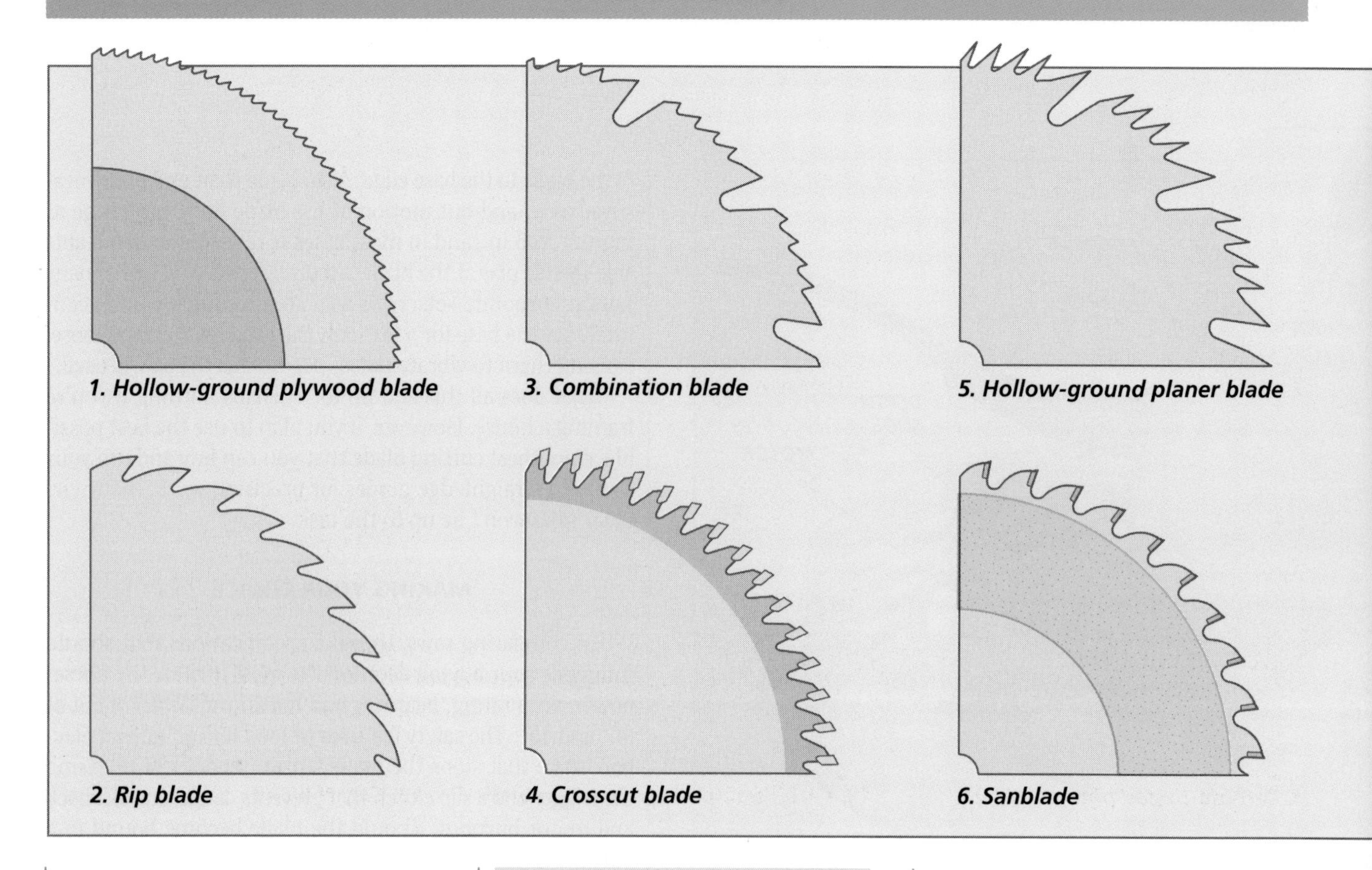
1. Hollow-ground plywood blade
2. Rip blade
3. Combination blade
4. Crosscut blade
5. Hollow-ground planer blade
6. Sanblade

its condition have a far greater effect. However, handling and balance go a long way in determining how any one saw *feels* like it's performing. The ability of the blade's lower guard to retract smoothly and effortlessly is one of the most important factors here.

Every circular saw has advantages and disadvantages, and it's worthwhile choosing the one that suits you best. Make your choice based not only on tool specifications and measurements, but also on how the tool looks, sounds and feels—personal criteria that aren't very easy to generally quantify. After all, *you* are the one who is going to be working with the saw.

And remember that the difference between one saw and the next is far less than the difference between using a dull blade and a sharp blade. In other words, choosing a make and model of saw is less important than having a good blade on hand. Not only will the work go easier and be safer, your saw will last longer, too.

SAW MECHANICS

From a pure design standpoint, the circular saw is a rather simple tool. An electric motor powers a drive mechanism that spins a shaft on which the blade is bolted. An on/off trigger switch is built into the top handle. A fixed protective guard covers the upper half of the blade. Its lower half is shielded by a spring-loaded retractable guard. As the saw advances into the workpiece, the lower guard rotates upward and out of the way. Once the cut is completed, the lower guard closes automatically. As important and effective as the guards are, remember that they don't shield the small portion of blade projecting through the underside of the piece you're cutting. Always check the retractable guard before using the saw. It should slide up smoothly and close quickly without sticking.

The saw rests on a base plate, or shoe, that is raised or lowered to establish the cutting depth. Generally, the shoe is positioned so that the blade cuts through the workpiece by about 1/8 in. Also, the shoe tilts for making bevel cuts up to 45°.

The principal difference among the various sizes of saws is that larger saws have a greater depth-of-cut capacity. For example, at 90° a typical 5½-in. saw has a depth of cut of about 1¾ in.; a 6½-in. saw: 2⅛ in.; a 7¼-in. saw: 2 7/16 in.; an 8¼-in. saw: 2 15/16 in.

BLADE SPECIFICS

Sawing a piece of wood cleanly and precisely is one of the many enjoyable subtleties of woodworking. And much of the credit for executing such a cut rightfully belongs to the skillful woodworker and the saw itself. However, credit is seldom given to the primary reason why the cut is successful—the blade. If a blade is dull or if the wrong blade is used, all the skill in the world won't give a clean cut—regardless of the sophistication of the saw.

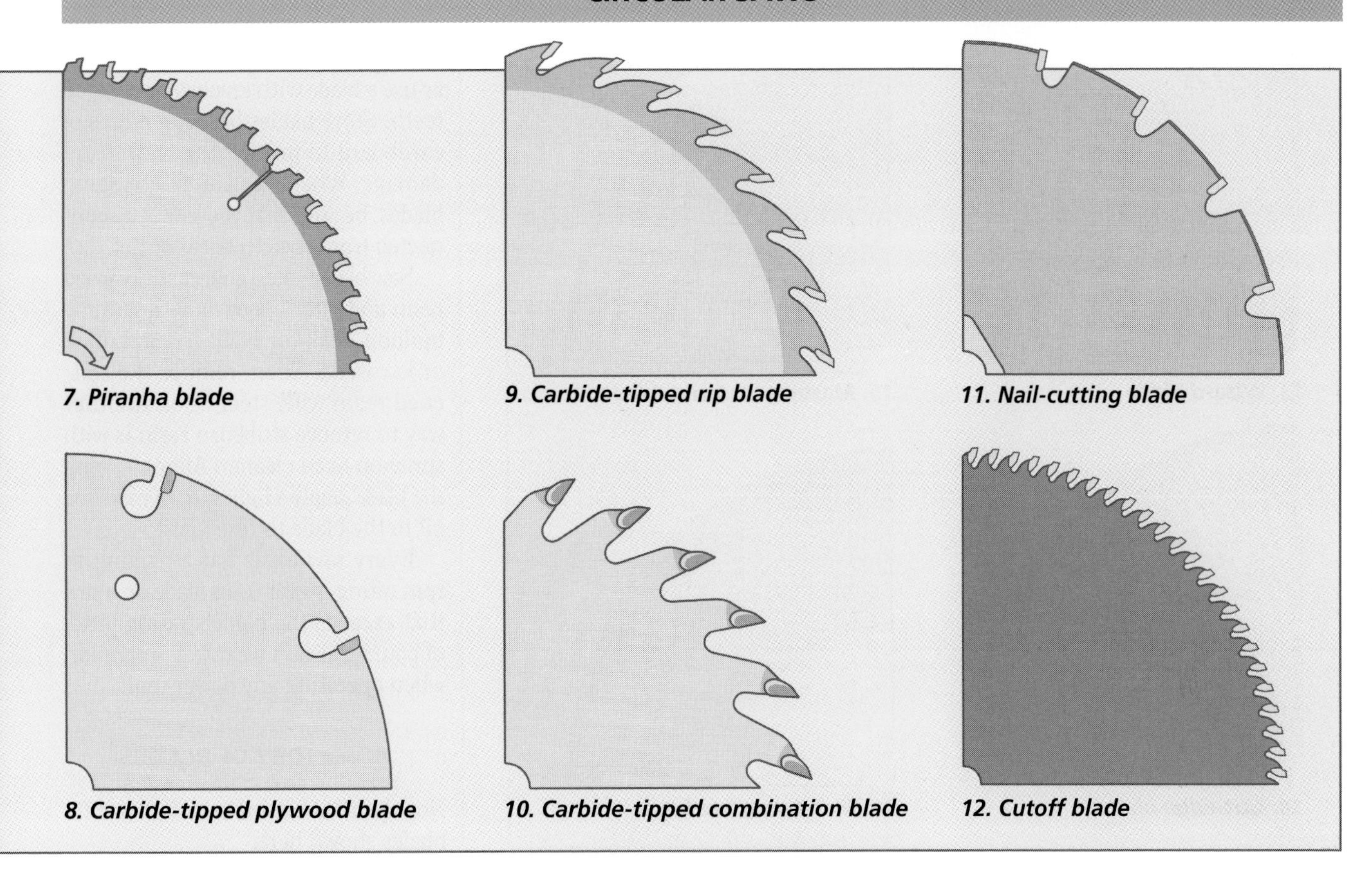
7. Piranha blade

9. Carbide-tipped rip blade

11. Nail-cutting blade

8. Carbide-tipped plywood blade

10. Carbide-tipped combination blade

12. Cutoff blade

Circular saw blades come in different styles and sizes to cut a wide variety of materials. The blades that are shown here represent a sampling of the incredible number available. Most of them also are suitable for using on power miter saws, table saws and radial arm saws.

Choosing the correct blade depends on several factors, including the kind of saw, type of cut and the material you're cutting. There are blades available for sawing nearly every imaginable material, including wood, plastic, metal, concrete, ceramic tile, cast iron, hardened steel, bricks and marble.

Another deciding factor in choosing a blade is the degree of smoothness desired. There are many blades available that will produce a super-smooth cut. However, for certain jobs an extremely smooth cut isn't especially important. In these instances, you may want to use a less expensive, faster-cutting blade that gives a slightly rougher cut.

STYLES OF BLADES

Every saw blade is designed for a specific purpose since no single blade can handle all possible cutting tasks. There are some versatile combination and general-purpose blades that can rip and crosscut. However, these blades don't perform either cut as well as a blade made specifically for ripping or crosscutting. Some of the most common blade styles include rip, crosscut, combination and plywood.

You also have a choice of blade construction: steel or steel with carbide-tipped teeth. Steel blades have teeth that are cut in the blank forming the body. The teeth are then sharpened and set, or bent, alternately to the left and right of the blade. This forms a kerf slightly wider than the body to prevent the blade from binding in the cut. Steel blades are inexpensive, and while they dull quickly, their teeth are easily resharpened right in the workshop using a file.

Carbide-tipped blades are the choice of all serious woodworkers. These long-lasting blades have teeth that are made of super-tough tungsten carbide. The teeth are brazed to a steel body and then ground sharp. A carbide-tipped blade will remain sharp many times longer than a steel blade. However, once it does become dull, a carbide-tipped blade must be sent for professional sharpening. Carbide is rated for hardness on the Rockwell scale. Most blade manufacturers use C1, C2, C3 or C4 carbide. Carbide that's rated C4 is the hardest with a rating of 94. (A diamond, for example, rates 100.) Look for blades with large, C4-grade tips. The larger the tips, the more often the blade can be resharpened. How long a carbide-tipped blade will last before it needs resharpening depends on many factors, including its quality, how often it's used and, most importantly, what type of material was cut with it. In the average home workshop, however, a good-quality, C4-grade carbide-tipped

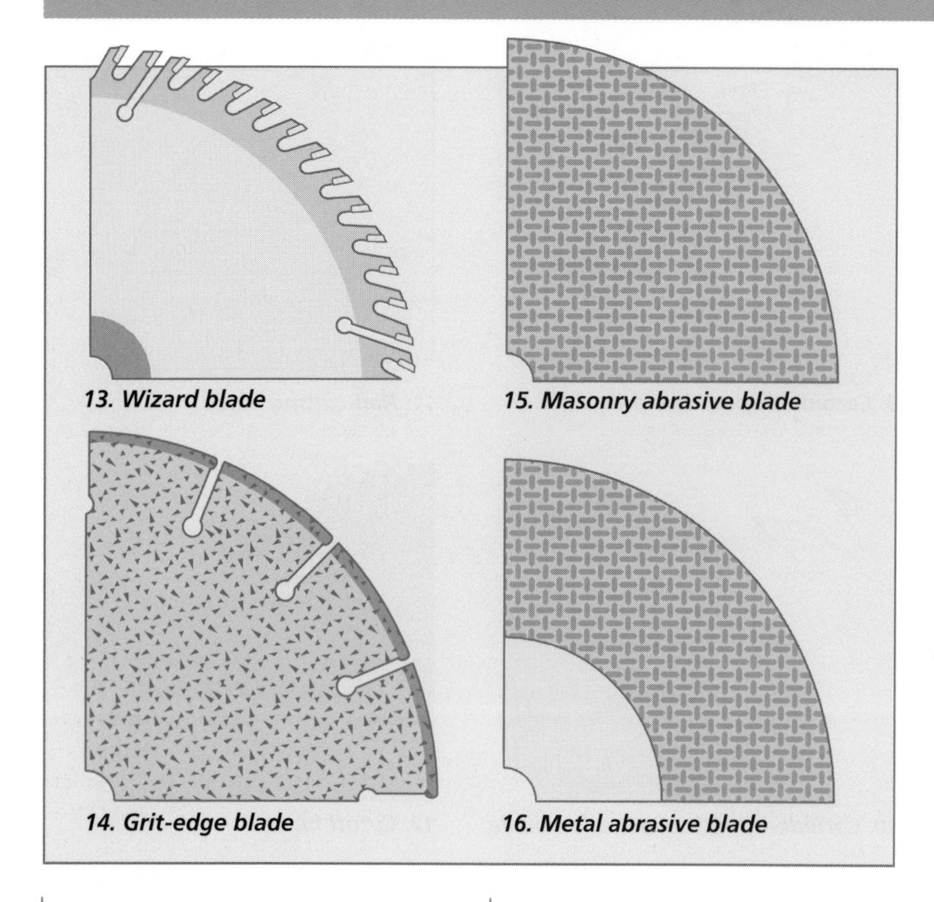
13. Wizard blade

14. Grit-edge blade

15. Masonry abrasive blade

16. Metal abrasive blade

blade might last a full year without resharpening, and have a lifetime of many years with proper care and periodic sharpening.

TELLTALE TEETH

The designed purpose of a saw blade is often revealed by its teeth. Generally, the fewer teeth that a blade has, the rougher it cuts. Conversely, use a blade with many teeth for a smooth cut.

Blade teeth come ground in four common shapes: alternate top bevel (ATB), triple-chip grind (TCG), flat-top grind (FTG), and four-tooth with raker. ATB teeth have very sharp alternating top bevels that sever wood easily and smoothly. ATB blades are often used for crosscutting and mitering.

A TCG blade is not quite as sharp as an ATB blade, but holds its cutting edges longer. Therefore, it needs to be resharpened less often. TCG teeth produce a smooth-cutting, general-purpose blade that can rip and crosscut.

For fast, aggressive sawing, use an FTG blade. This heavy-duty tooth pattern is used primarily on rip blades. Flat-top teeth cut like tiny chisels.

The four-tooth and raker blade consists of two pairs of ATB teeth and one FTG raker. The ATB teeth sever the wood and the raker cleans out the kerf. This type of tooth pattern is popular with combination blades.

Note that some blades have deep gullets between the teeth. Gullets are necessary in aggressive-cutting blades to clean away wood dust and chips. Also, some blades have narrow expansion slots cut in their edges. Expansion slots let the blade expand slightly when it heats up; otherwise, it would warp. The round hole at the end of each slot prevents stress cracks.

BLADE CARE

Saw blades are most effective—and safest—when they're sharp. Replace a blade once it has become dull and never use a blade with cracked or chipped teeth. Store blades between pieces of cardboard to protect the teeth from damage. Whenever you're changing blades, be sure that the saw is disconnected from the electrical outlet.

Saw blades often collect sticky wood resin and pitch. To remove a gummy buildup, soak the blade in turpentine or kerosene. Then, remove the softened resin with steel wool. Another way to remove stubborn resin is with spray-on oven cleaner. After cleaning the blade, apply a light coat of machine oil to the blade to resist rust.

Every saw blade has a maximum rpm rating. Never use a blade on a saw that exceeds the blade's rating. And, of course, always wear eye protection when operating any power tool.

INVENTORY OF BLADES

Now let's take a look at the specific blades shown here.

1. Hollow-ground plywood blade—With its 146 tiny teeth, this 7¼-in. blade is designed for splinter-free sawing of plywood, paneling and wood veneers. The blade is hollow ground to prevent binding. It's thickest at the toothed edge and then it tapers down slightly, for about 1⅜ in., toward the center. This allows the teeth to have no set for smooth cutting. The blade is also available in 9-in. and 10-in. sizes.

2. Rip blade—Large teeth and deep gullets allow a rip blade to cut effectively *with* the wood's grain. Use it primarily on a circular saw or table saw to rip softwoods and hardwoods. Rip blades are commonly available in sizes ranging from 6½ in. to 10 in.

3. Combination blade—For fast, semi-smooth woodcutting in any direction—rip, crosscut or miter—use a combination blade. The blade shown has 12 sets of teeth. The sets are separated by a deep gullet and each set has five teeth—one raker and four precision-filed-and-set teeth. Combination blades are popular, in part, because

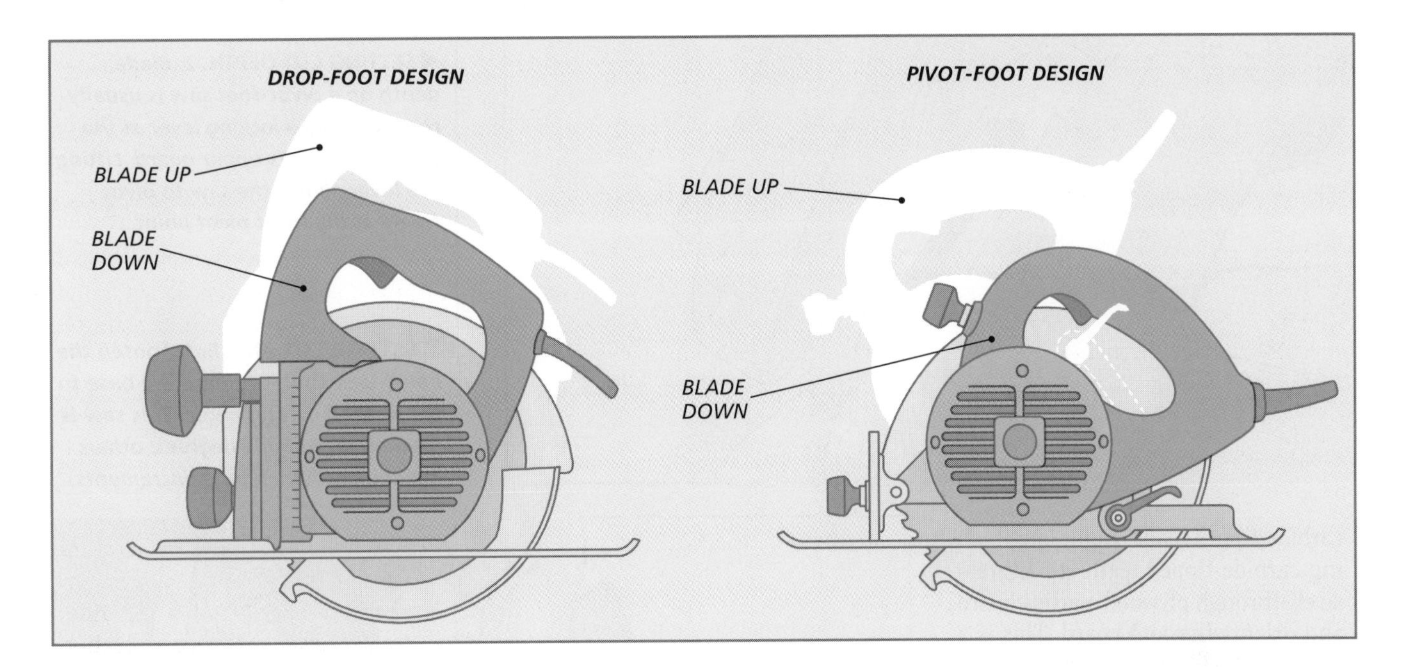

▲ **FOOT DESIGN.** ***Circular saws use a drop-foot or pivot-foot mechanism for adjusting blade projection below the base. The drop-foot's straight-line action maintains the handle-to-base relationship at all cutting depths. Pivot-foot saws must be held differently at various cutting depths.***

▼ **SETTING CUT DEPTH, 1.** ***On a drop-foot saw, adjust cutting depth by loosening the depth-adjustment knob and sliding the base up or down. Graduations indicate depth of cut in inches or centimeters.***

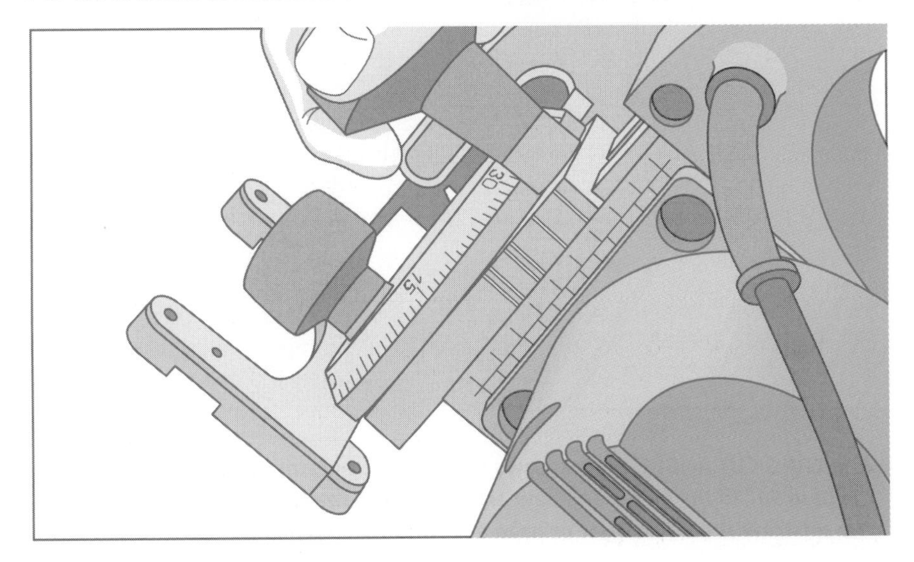

they reduce the number of times you need to change blades. They're sold in sizes from 6½ in. to 16 in.

4. Crosscut blade—This carbide-tipped blade is designed exclusively for cutting across the wood's grain. The teeth are at a lesser angle—known as the rake or hook angle—than a rip blade, contributing to smooth, clean cuts. Use this blade for crosscutting all types of wood, plywood and particleboard.

5. Hollow-ground planer blade—Here's another blade that produces super-smooth cuts. The teeth of this blade have no set. Blade clearance in the kerf is provided by the hollow-ground feature—the blade is thinner near its center than at the teeth. Use this blade for finish cuts only, especially when cutting fine hardwoods. To achieve the best results, be sure to advance the blade slowly and steadily.

6. Sanblade—Here's a unique general-purpose woodcutting blade that cuts and sands. The 10-in., 40-tooth blade shown has 80-grit aluminum-oxide abrasive bonded to both of its sides. The smooth-cutting blade also features ATB C4-grade carbide teeth for executing rip, crosscut and miter cuts. When the abrasive wears out, return the blade to the manufacturer for "re-abrasing." Other sizes range from 8 in. to 14 in.

7. Piranha blade—This general-purpose blade has ultra-sharp, curved, carbide-tipped teeth. The blade's unusual tooth design combined with the thin kerf body allows the Piranha to cut both quickly and cleanly without getting bogged down. Use it to rip, crosscut and miter all types of wood, plywood, hardboard, particleboard and plastics. It's available in various sizes from 5½ in. to 10 in.

8. Carbide-tipped plywood blade—A version of the plywood blade is this

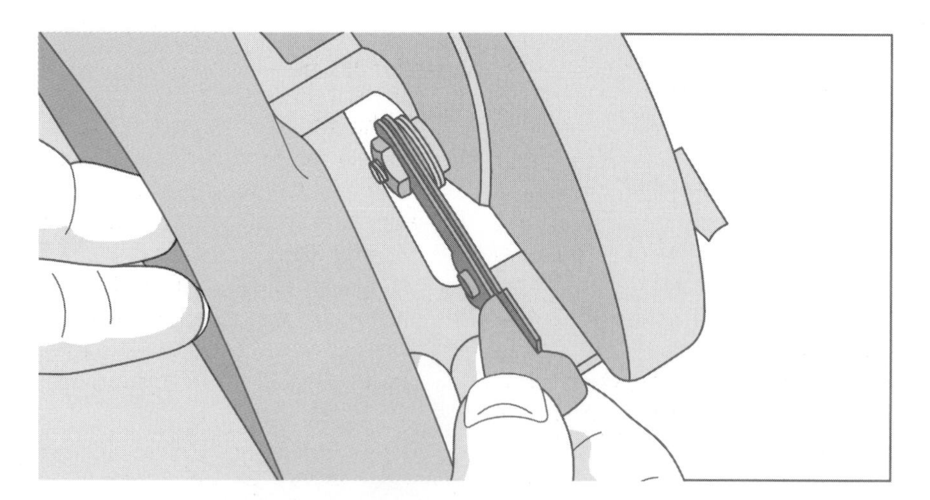

◀ **SETTING CUT DEPTH, 2.** ***Blade depth on a pivot-foot saw is usually controlled by a locking lever at the rear of the saw's upper guard. Lifting the lever allows the saw to pivot freely at the front pivot point.***

carbide-tipped blade. Eight long-lasting carbide-tipped teeth cut aggressively through plywood, particleboard and oriented-strand board. This is a good rough-cutting blade for sheathing and floor underlayment.

9. Carbide-tipped rip blade—Like a steel rip blade, this blade has large teeth and deep gullets for fast, aggressive ripping without getting bogged down in the cut. However, this blade is equipped with 30 long-wearing, FTG carbide-tipped teeth for superior cutting. It's available in a variety of diameters ranging from 8 in. to 16 in.

10. Carbide-tipped combination blade—For smooth, clean, general cutting, nothing beats a carbide-tipped combination blade. The blade shown has 24 tungsten-carbide-tipped teeth for performing rip, crosscut and miter cuts. Carbide-tipped blades come in various styles, with the number of teeth ranging from eight to 60, for cutting a wide variety of materials, including wood, composition boards, plastic and also nonferrous metals such as aluminum, brass and copper.

11. Nail-cutting blade—When it's necessary to saw through lumber or flooring that contains an occasional nail, this is the blade for the job. Its tough carbide teeth are specially ground to help resist breakage. Also, the teeth are set at a negative hook angle—they actually tilt back slightly. Shown is an 8-in., 18-tooth blade.

▼ **SETTING CUT ANGLE, 1.** ***Loosen the bevel-lock knob to rotate the base to the desired cutting angle. This saw is graduated in single degrees; others may be graduated in 5° increments.***

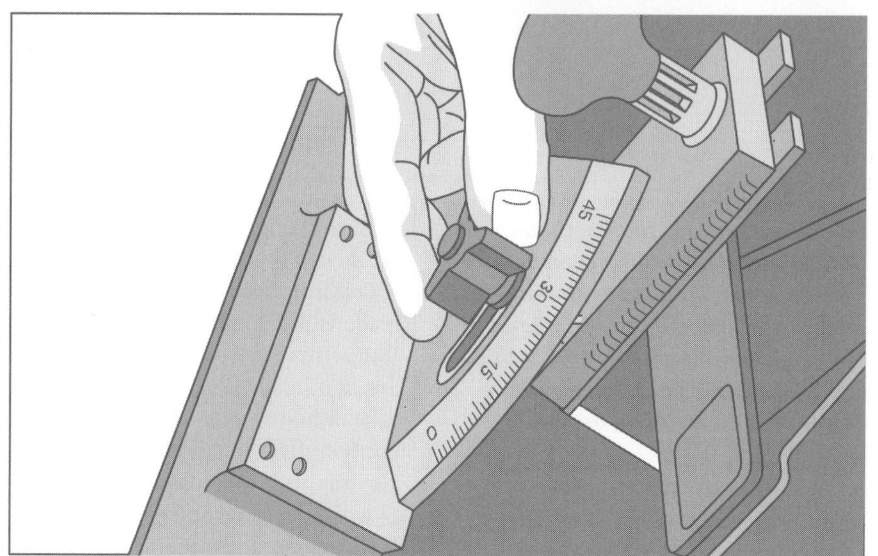

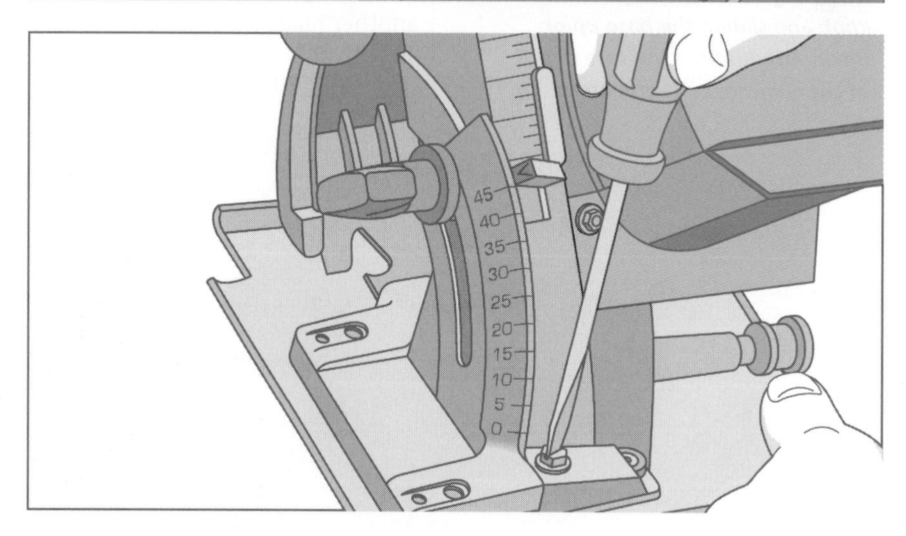

▲ **SETTING CUT ANGLE, 2.** ***Most saws have a setscrew stop for setting the base 90° to the blade. This saw also features a setscrew for 45°. The setscrew should be tight or have a locknut to keep it in position.***

12. Cutoff blade—The high-performance cutoff blade is engineered for one specific task: to give glass-smooth crosscuts consistently with virtually no splintering. Use the blade on all species of hardwoods and softwoods. The 12-in., 96-tooth blade shown features ATB C4-grade carbide teeth. The blade's body is equipped with laser-cut expansion slots and a special anti-grip coating that is self-lubricating. Blades in diameters ranging from 8 in. to 15 in. are available.

13. Wizard blade—Here is a relatively new type of saw blade that provides superior woodcutting through modified tooth design. The 10-in., 60-tooth blade shown is made specifically for use on a power miter saw. Its thin kerf design puts less strain on the motor and keeps stock loss to a minimum. The ATB teeth are ground to a razor-sharp 30° bevel instead of the standard 15°. This ensures super-smooth crosscuts with practically no splintering. There's also a versatile combination blade that can rip, crosscut and miter wood, plywood, particleboard and plastic laminate. The blade's 60 TCG teeth are ground to a clean-cutting 45° angle instead of the more usual 30° angle. Both types of blades come in sizes from 9 in. to 14 in.

14. Grit-edge blade—For cutting the tough stuff, nothing beats the grit-edge blade. Its unique cutting edge is made of thousands of tiny tungsten-carbide chips. Use the blade for sawing through sheet steel up to 16 gauge, synthetic marble, particleboard, Lexan, fiberglass, tempered hardboard and other abrasive materials. Sizes from 6½ in. to 10 in. are available.

15. Masonry abrasive blade—This is a toothless type of cutoff blade that's made of fiberglass-reinforced silicon-carbide abrasive. It comes in two different grades: one to cut hard materials such as concrete, marble, granite and glazed ceramic tile; and one to cut soft to moderately-hard materials such as concrete block, common brick, flagstone and limestone.

16. Metal abrasive blade—This blade is also a toothless cutter, but it still provides plenty of bite. It's a metal-cutting type of abrasive blade. Made of aluminum oxide, the blade is designed for cutting through virtually all varieties of ferrous and nonferrous metals, including steel, iron, aluminum, brass, copper and bronze. The blade is reinforced with fiberglass to help prevent it from shattering. Note that while this metal cutoff blade looks almost exactly like the masonry cutoff blade, the two blades are constructed of different materials for different cutting purposes and are *not* interchangeable. Sizes of the metal abrasive blade range from 6 in. to 8 in.

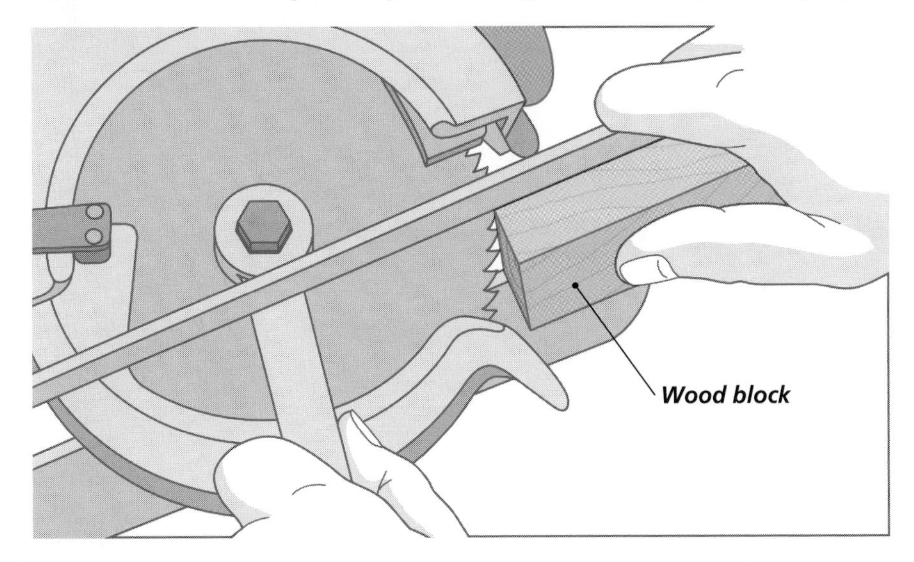

▲ **CHANGING BLADES.** ***An arbor lock makes blade changing easy. If your saw doesn't have an arbor lock, jam a wood block into the blade to keep the arbor from turning as you loosen the arbor nut.***

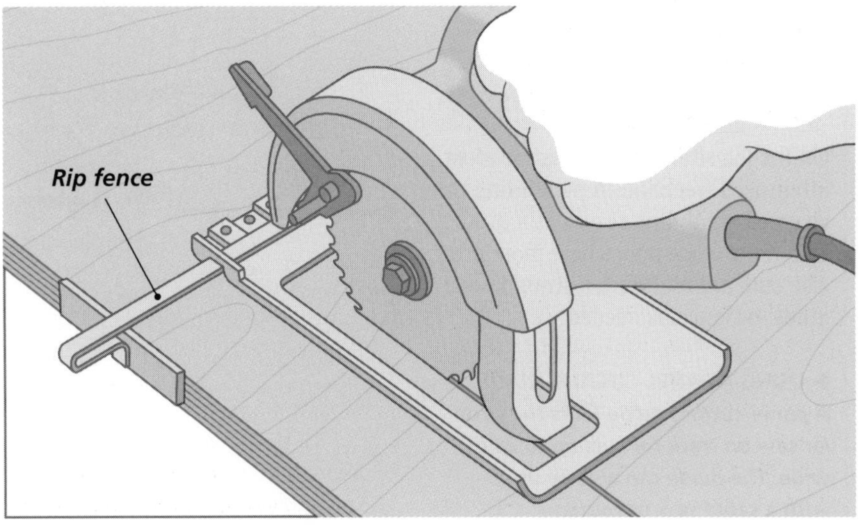

► **USING A RIP FENCE.** ***Most circular saws come equipped with an accessory rip fence. Attach the T-shaped fence to the saw's shoe for making narrow rip cuts.***

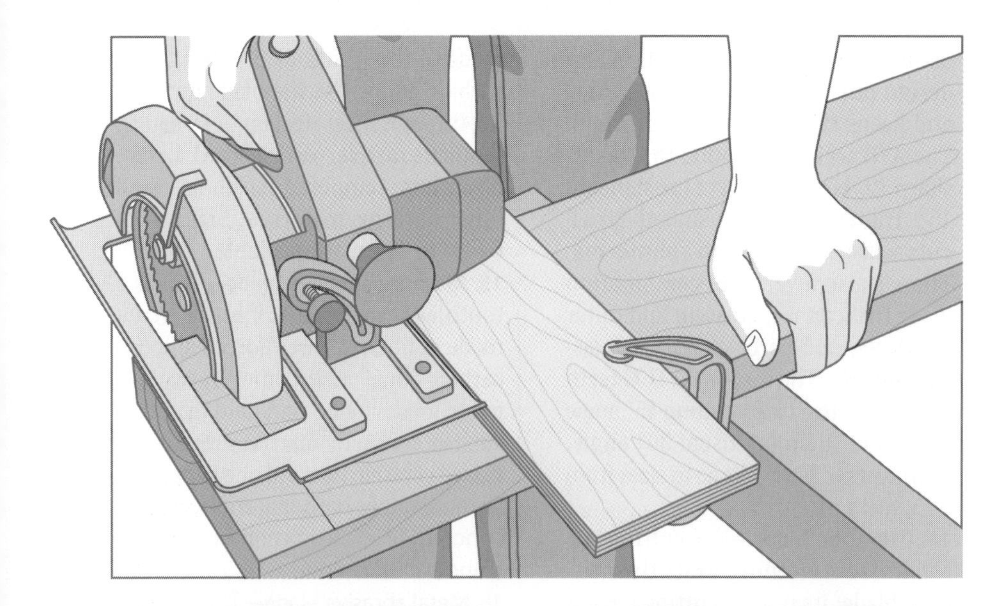

◀ **USING A STRAIGHTEDGE GUIDE, 1.** ***Measure from an inward-facing blade tooth to the edge of the saw's shoe to determine where to clamp a straightedge guide. Use this dimension to position the straightedge guide exactly parallel to the cutting line, then make the cut.***

▼ **USING A STRAIGHTEDGE GUIDE, 2.** ***An offset block—a board that's equal in width to the distance from an inward-facing blade tooth to the edge of the saw's shoe—helps position the straightedge guide quickly. Clamp the guide, then remove the offset block to make the cut.***

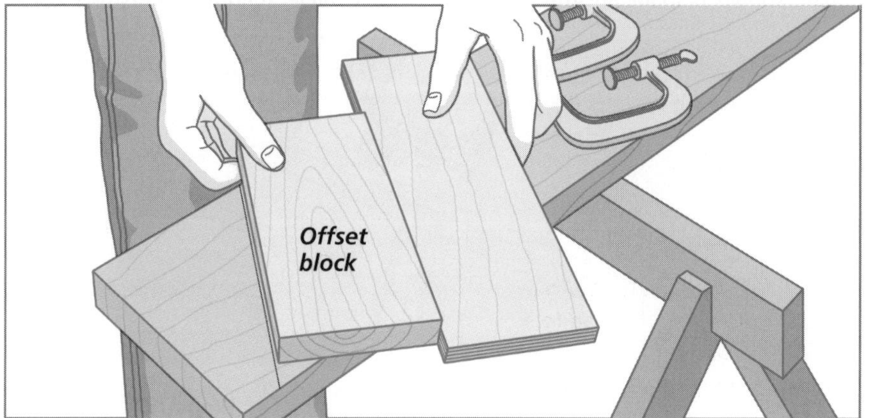

SAWING SAFETY

There are a few simple rules that you should follow to promote safe sawing. Always unplug the saw to adjust the shoe and change blades. Use a sharp blade that is the proper type for the material being cut. Make certain that the arbor nut is tight. Check the saw's retractable blade guard to ensure that it's operating properly. Protect your eyes with goggles or a face shield.

Support your work on both sides of the cut to prevent pinching the blade in the kerf. Allow the saw to reach its maximum rpm before starting the cut. Let short cutoffs fall freely to the floor. And, finally, always disconnect a power tool when you're finished.

GUIDED STRAIGHT CUTS

On the job site, a circular saw is most often used freehand. A pencil line or snapped chalk line serves as a guide. But in the workshop, where more precise cuts are required, a straightedge guide, or fence, is needed.

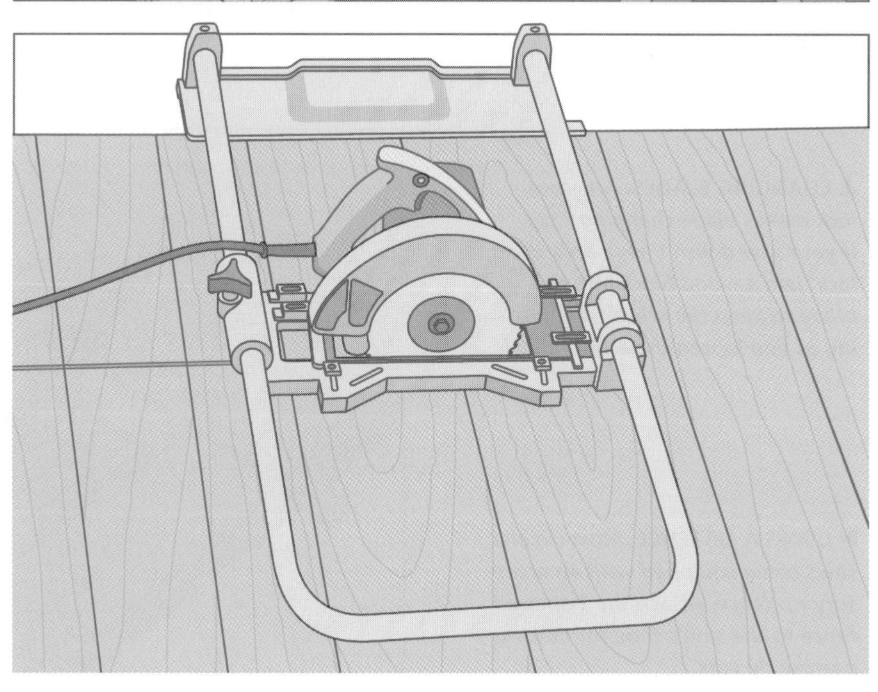

▶ **USING A PANEL-CUTTING GUIDE.** ***A panel-cutting guide locks the circular saw on track for cuts up to 24 in. wide. The guide can also be used with a sabre saw or router.***

▼ **USING A PROTRACTOR GUIDE.** ***The shopmade jig shown here allows you to cut precise miters. Adjust the guide to the desired angle and tighten the wingnuts. Use the handle to hold the guide securely against the workpiece edge while cutting.***

▼ **MAKING LONG CUTS.** ***Nail a 6-in.-wide strip of ¼-in. plywood to a piece that's at least 12 in. wide, then run the saw's shoe along the edge of the narrow strip to trim the wider piece to size. The guide is now ready for positioning and clamping. While cutting, keep the saw securely against the guide strip.***

The simplest type of guide that you can use is a straight board clamped to the workpiece parallel to the cutting line. The distance between the line and the guide must equal the distance from the saw blade's teeth to the edge of the shoe. A quick, easy way to position the guide is to use an offset block—a ½-in. plywood board equal in width to the distance from the blade to the outside edge of the shoe. Simply hold the offset block on the line of cut and butt the guide against the block; no measuring is necessary. Make the cut with the saw's shoe held firmly against the straightedge guide.

Another convenient shopmade jig, especially for making long cuts, is a self-aligning guide. To make the guide, start by nailing a 6-in.-wide x 8-ft.-long strip of ¼-in. plywood to another ¼-in. plywood piece that's about 12 in. wide x 8 ft. long. Then, trim the wider plywood panel while guiding the saw's shoe along against the edge of the 6-in.-wide piece. To use the guide, simply clamp it to the workpiece with its edge on the cutting line, then make the cut.

PROTRACTOR-GUIDED MITERS

For sawing accurate miter cuts, use a shopmade protractor guide. The easy-to-make guide adjusts for angles up to 45° left and right. It can also be set for making square (90°) crosscuts.

Build the guide using a 6-in. plastic protractor and a pointed, ¾-in.-wide x 4¾-in.-long bar of ⅛-in. aluminum as the angle indicator. Use a 21-in.-long piece of ¾-in. x 2½-in. hardwood for the support fence, a 3-in.-long piece of ½-in. x 1¼-in. hardwood as a base for the indicator, and cut a 5½-in.-long handle out of a 2 x 4. The hardwood adjustable fence that holds the protractor is ½ in. x 4½ in. x 19 in.

A 1¾-in. carriage bolt through the indicator and a 1¾-in. hex bolt through the base of the protractor, each fitted with a washer and wingnut, are used to lock the adjustable fence in position at the desired cutting angle.

Hold the guide using the handle on the support fence. Insert two ⅝-in.-long anchoring pins, cut from brads or 2d finishing nails, into the edge of the support fence to keep the guide from shifting during use. Insert the pins with their points protruding about 1/16 in. The sharp points will stick into the workpiece to anchor the guide.

The dimensions of the accessories described can be altered to suit your specific saw and work. However, never use any guide or jig that prevents the saw's safety system from functioning properly. Shopmade tools presented here are intended to *increase* the safety and accuracy of the saw.

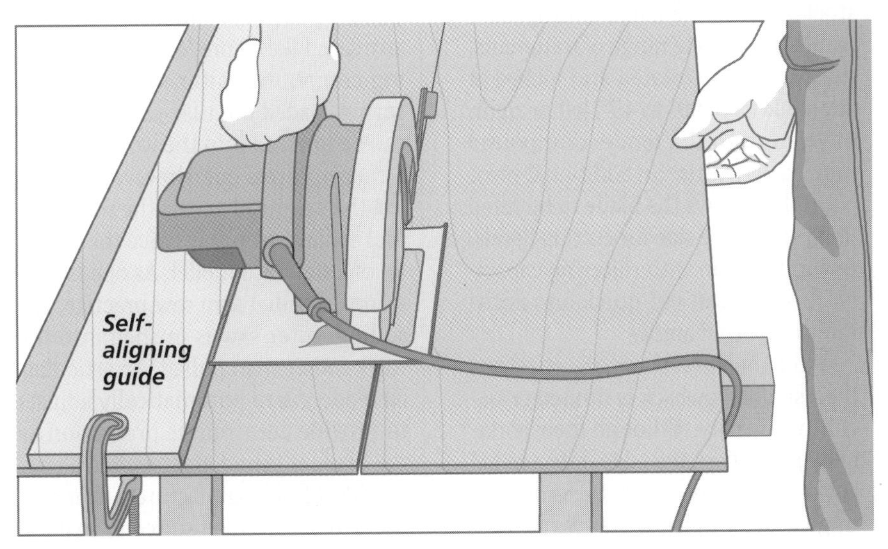

PANEL-CUTTING GUIDE

For the do-it-yourselfer who wants to add accuracy and safety to paneling and other remodeling jobs, a store-bought panel-cutting guide will come in handy. You can usually use one with a circular saw, sabre saw or router to cut sheet material such as plywood, paneling, particleboard and hardboard. The guide typically permits cuts from ½ in. to 24 in. wide and bevel cuts of up to 45°. Normal depth-of-cut capacity, however, is reduced by about 11/16 in. when using this type of guide.

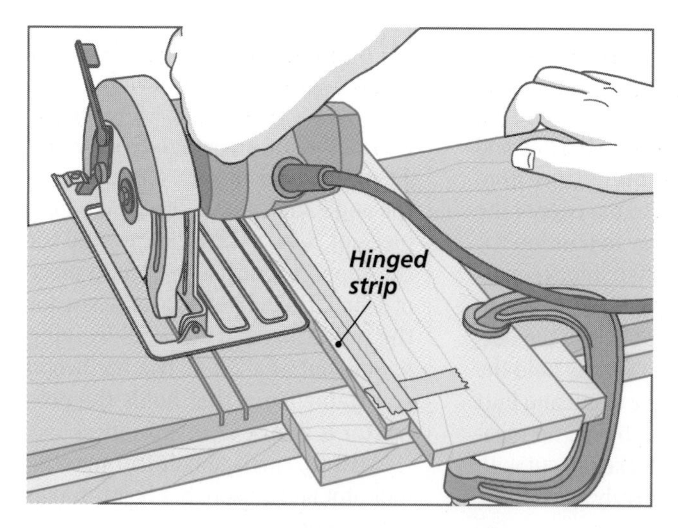

◀ **CUTTING DADOES.** ***Use ½-in. plywood for a dado-cutting guide. Tape a strip to the guide equal to the dado width minus the blade's thickness. Flip the hinged strip back and use an offset block to position the guide, then make the first cut. Flip the strip down to make the next cut. Make repeated cuts to remove waste between the kerfs.***

▼ **MAKING POCKET CUTS.** ***A tall fence is helpful in making pocket cuts. Retract the blade guard by hand and raise the rear of the saw so that the blade clears the work, then start the motor. Lower the saw slowly until it sits flat, then advance it along the fence to the corner. Reposition the fence for the remaining cuts.***

POWER MITER SAWS

It goes without saying that the cutting of wood to length accurately—and at a precise angle—is one of the most fundamental operations in woodworking. Whether your particular job entails rough carpentry, finish work or cabinets and furniture, the accuracy and speed of your crosscuts determine the quality of the finished project and the efficiency of your production. Years ago, woodworkers relied on a stiff, long backsaw and miterbox to get the job done. In its most basic form, the miterbox is a simple wooden jig for holding both the stock and the saw at a consistent angle.

Today's power miter saw has rendered the traditional miterbox all but obsolete. Some versions are little more than a heavy-duty circular saw mounted on a pivot so the saw can be swung down into the stock. The work is held against a fixed fence that supports the stock against the blade rotation. To handle a complete range of miter cuts, the saw can be rotated and locked at any angle from 90° to 45°, left or right, in relation to the fence. Compound miter saws feature an additional pivot point that allows the blade to be tilted up to 45° to one side for cutting bevels. In combination with mitering capacity, this tool can cut quick and accurate compound angles.

While both versions are effective, their single drawback is limited crosscutting capacity. Although their portability gives them the edge over a radial arm saw in many cases, the crosscutting capacity of most standard miter and compound miter saws is limited to the width of a 2 x 6 cut at 90°.

The latest version of this tool has addressed this problem by employing a sliding carriage much like a radial arm saw. Like its predecessors, the sliding compound miter saw features a spring-loaded circular-saw head that can be lowered into the work to make a chop, or press cut. However, by sliding the saw head across the work, the tool achieves roughly twice the capacity of a standard model. As opposed to standard radial arm saw practice, the sliding miter saw is pushed into the work rather than pulled. An articulated blade guard automatically adjusts to provide continuous protection as the blade is raised and lowered.

Most blade manufacturers offer synthetic blade designs suited to making the best possible cuts on a miter saw. Some miter saws come with a combination blade that has positive-hook teeth—their underside angles back to form a chisel-type cutting edge. Ideally, users should replace this blade with a negative-hook, carbide-tipped blade to eliminate lifting thrust as the blade is pushed through the stock.

EXTENSION TABLES

Miter saws are intentionally designed with small tables so that they're easily portable. But unless proper support for long work is provided, the work is difficult to hold in place, and accuracy and safety are compromised. Optional accessories for supporting stock are offered by many manufacturers, but extension tables are easy to build and feature greater stability, capacity and versatility. Note that two extension tables are required—one for each side of the saw. The tables are an exact mirror image of each other, except that one requires an angled notch on one corner to allow the blade to reach maximum mitering capacity. Secure an adhesive-backed measuring tape to the back top edges of your extension tables at the appropriate distance from the blade kerf. In conjunction with stop blocks, this gives a quick and accurate way of cutting stock to length.

MITER SAW OPERATION

Because of its relatively small base, it's best to bolt the miter saw down to a stable work surface to prevent it from tipping over or otherwise shifting. And never remove the blade guard of the miter saw or attempt to defeat its protective action.

▲ CUTTING WIDE STOCK. ***This tabletop jig handles stock up to 16 in. wide, and has tracks for cutting 45° miters, as shown, as well as 90° square cuts. Make the jig's track width to accommodate the shoe of your circular saw.***

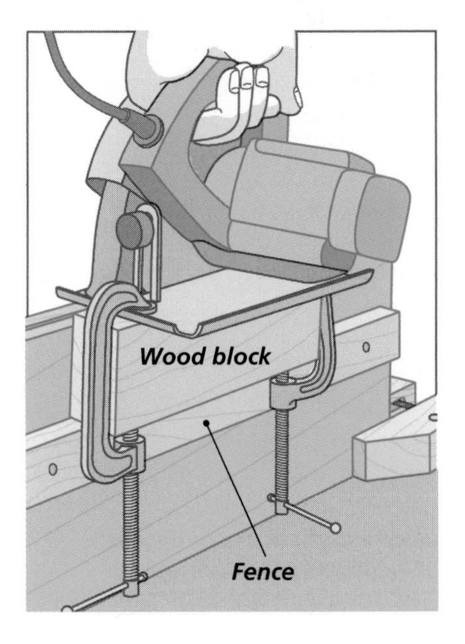

◀ CUTTING RABBETS. ***Clamp a wood block to the bottom of the saw's shoe, measuring from each end to be sure it's parallel. Tack-nail a fence to the side of your work to support the block on the saw and advance slowly while bearing down on the fence. After making the edge cuts, set your work flat and reposition the fence to make cuts to form rabbets.***

The basic operation on miter saws is the press cut. This is used for narrow stock with a cross section that falls within the periphery of the blade at its lowest position. Miter saws are available that handle stock up to 5½ in. wide in this manner.

For press cuts on a sliding compound miter saw, first push the carriage back toward the guide fence and lock it in place. Secure the workpiece, switch on the power and wait for the blade to reach full speed. Then, gently lower the saw head to make the cut. After switching off the power, allow

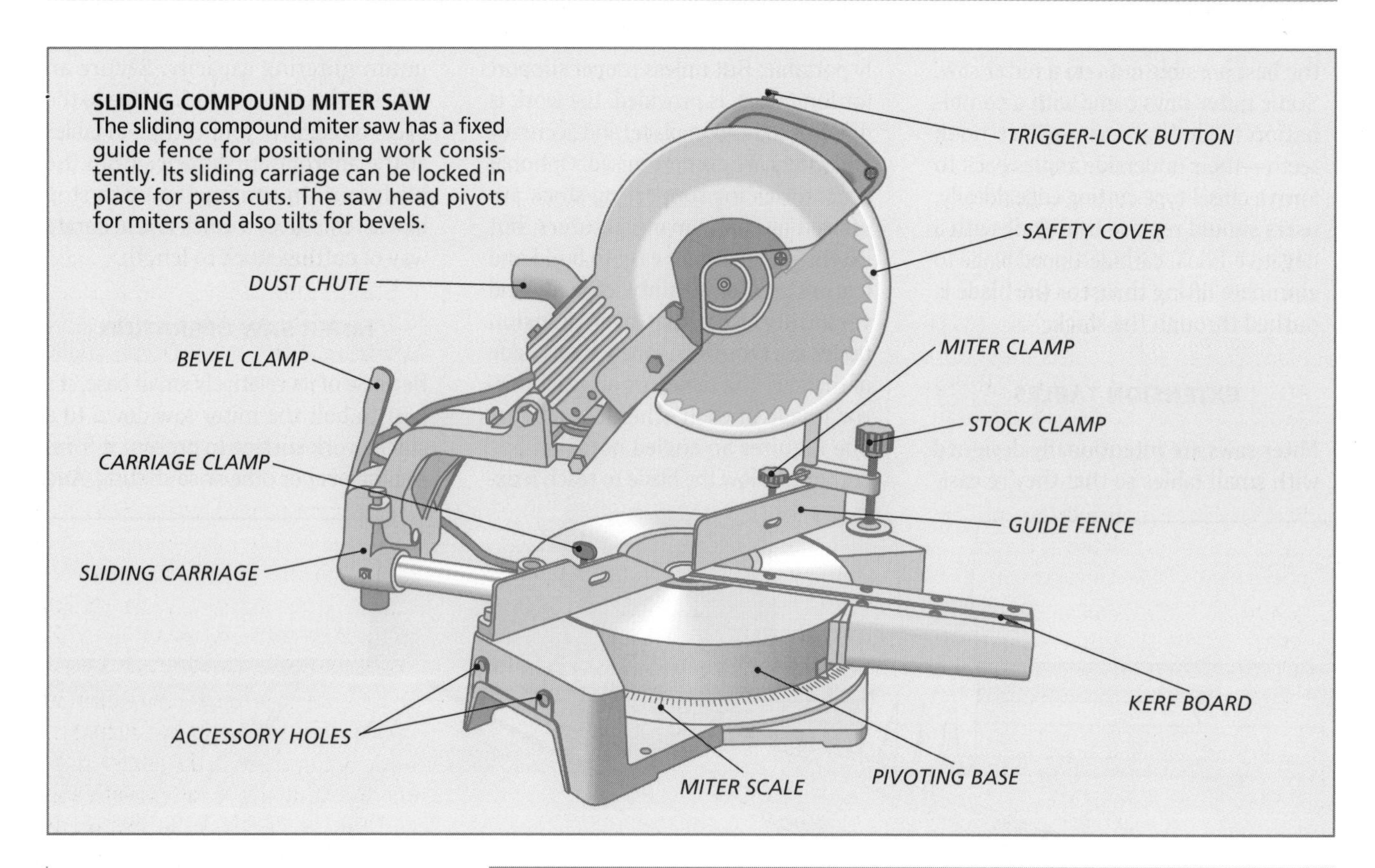

the blade to come to a complete stop before returning the head to the elevated position.

For accuracy and safety, ensure that the workpiece is held firmly against the guide fence, and that sawdust and small scraps are kept clear of the saw table and fence. While it's common to hold the stock in place with hand pressure alone, clamping it down is the best bet for an accurate cut. Always check that the miter and bevel locking knobs are tightened, and that any other adjustable components are properly secured before making a cut.

The smoothness of the cut is influenced by the rate of feed—how fast you push the saw head down—and the type of blade. A slow feed produces a finer cut than a fast feed. And a 60-tooth blade produces a smoother surface than a 24- or 48-tooth blade. You can afford coarse cuts when framing or performing rough carpentry, but molding, picture frame and furniture joints require the smoothest cuts.

▲ **MAKING PRESS CUTS.** ***On a sliding compound miter saw, the carriage is locked at the fence position. A press cut is then made by gently lowering the blade into the stock.***

When crosscutting to a cut line, it's often difficult to position the stock so the blade splits the line precisely. Many pros align the lowered blade a little to the waste side of the line with the power off. With the head raised, the saw is turned on and a light test cut is made. After raising the head, the work is shifted a bit to bring the line closer to the blade and a second cut is made. The process is repeated until the stock is accurately positioned for the final cut.

Stock that's too wide for a press cut is handled with a push, or slide, cut. Loosen the carriage lock and pull out the carriage completely. Turn on the power, lower the saw head completely and push the carriage toward the fence to finish the cut.

Stock that's wider than the saw's sliding crosscut capacity can be handled by first cutting into the wood as far as possible from one side. Then, flip over the stock, align the blade with the kerf and finish the cut from the other side. Another way to increase crosscut capacity slightly is to insert a spacer block under the work so that a wider portion of the blade makes the cut.

Repetitive cuts are best made with a stop block clamped to the saw or an extension table. Many manufacturers offer an adjustable stop for their miter saws. When setting the stop, first cut one of the pieces to exact length. Then, without shifting the work, slide the stop up against the opposite end and clamp or lock it in place.

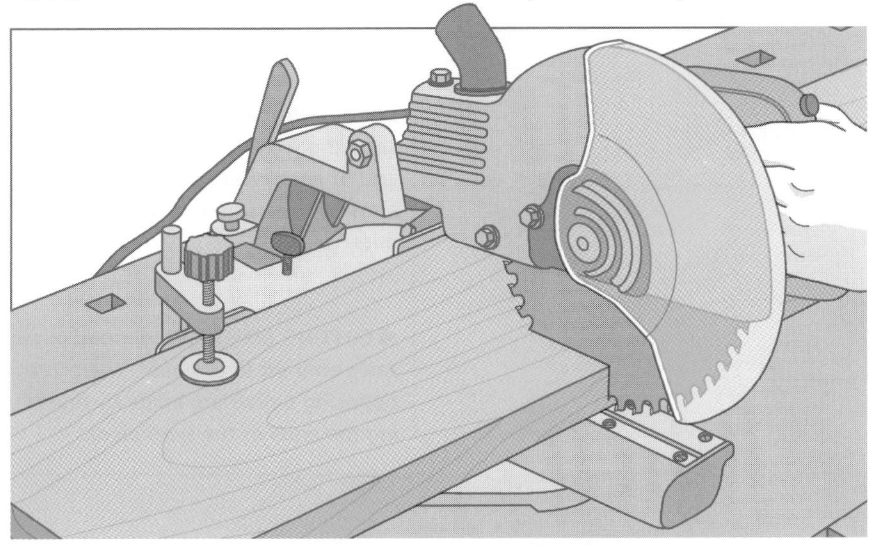

▲ **MAKING SLIDE CUTS.** ***To make a slide cut, move the carriage to its extended position. Then, start the motor and push the blade through the workpiece.***

MITERS AND BEVELS

To adjust the saw for a miter cut, simply loosen the screw that locks the pivoting base, rotate the base left or right, and align the pointer with the desired angle on the miter scale. Then, tighten the locking screw. Most saws have detents so the saw head can be quickly set at commonly used miter angles.

As with ordinary, square crosscutting, using a stop block simplifies the task of cutting repetitive miters and makes the work more accurate. While it's generally better practice to place the finished piece between the stop block and the blade, sometimes the length of the work requires placing the stop block on the waste side of the cut line. To cut rafter ends for a boxed cornice, for example, set the stop block on the waste side of the cut so that the blade is aligned with the angled rafter end line. Cut all the rafters with each end butting the block. Reposition the stop block to cut the miter that frames the underside of the cornice, flip over the rafters and make the second cuts.

To cut mitered frame members to exact length with a miter stop block, first cut a miter on one end of each frame piece. If the faces of the stock are different—as with molding—cut the first miter on the same end of all pieces. Next, rotate the saw head to the opposite side and align the edge of the

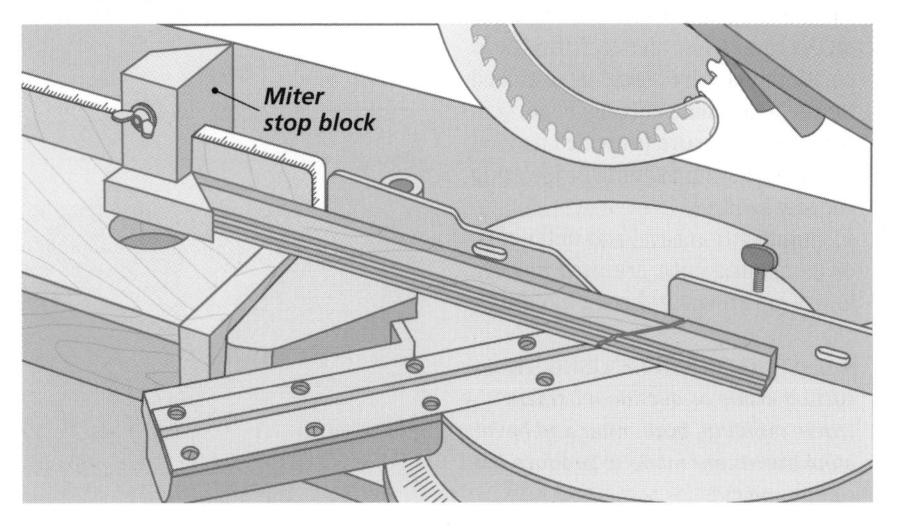

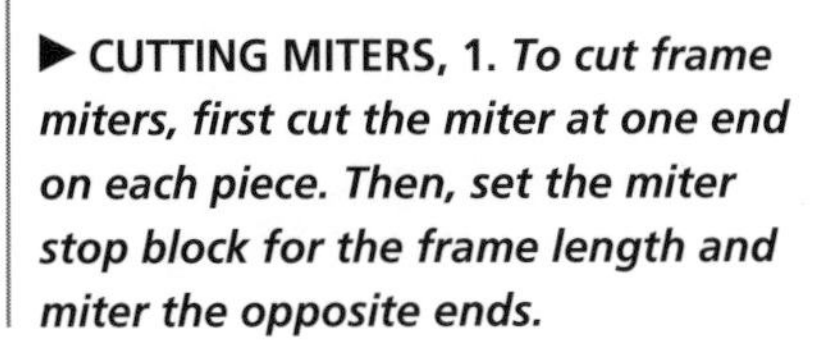

► **CUTTING MITERS, 1.** ***To cut frame miters, first cut the miter at one end on each piece. Then, set the miter stop block for the frame length and miter the opposite ends.***

miter stop block at the desired position, then make the cut. You can also set the stop block by cutting the first piece to a mark on the work and using this piece to position the stop block at the other end of the work. Or, you can cut the pieces to exact finished length and use a stop block on the waste side of the miter, positioned so the blade intersects the corner of the work. For moldings, you'll have to shift the blade angle and stop block to the opposite side to cut the opposing miters.

Angled cuts that appear on the side of the board are generally called bevels. Where miter settings can be made to the left or right, bevels can only be cut on one side of the table. To make a bevel cut, loosen the locking screw and tilt the saw head to the desired angle on the bevel scale, then lock the saw in position. Cuts are made as described for press and slide cutting, bearing in mind that pressure is applied parallel to the blade when sliding or lowering the saw head.

Combination bevel and miter cuts, or compound cuts, are used to form joints for crown and cove moldings,

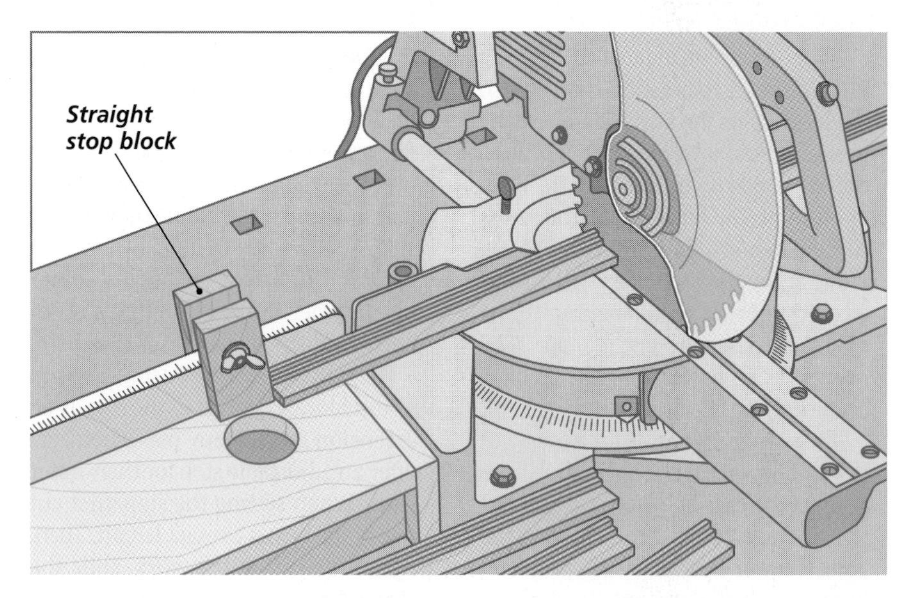

▲ **CUTTING MITERS, 2.** ***To cut miters with a straight stop block, first cut each frame piece squarely exactly to length. Then, clamp a scrap stop block to the table so the blade intersects the work corner and cut one end of each piece. Cut the opposite ends by reversing the stop block and miter angle.***

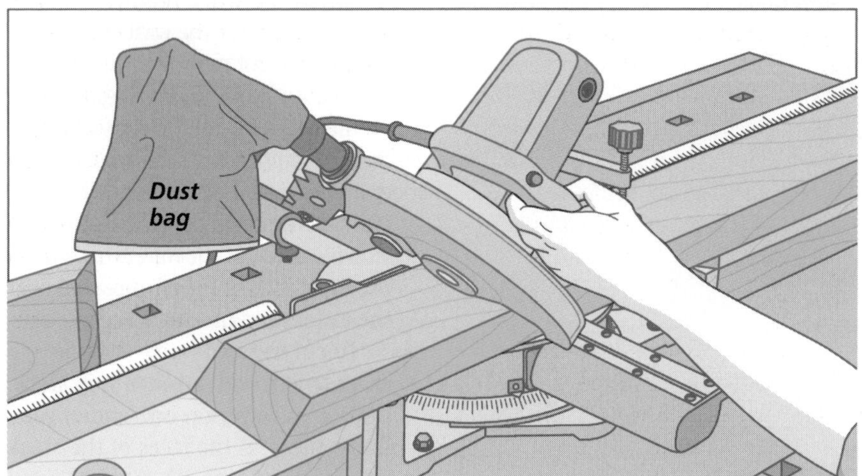

◀ **CUTTING BEVELS.** ***Compound miter saws only tilt to one side. Therefore, opposing bevels are made by reversing the ends of the workpiece.***

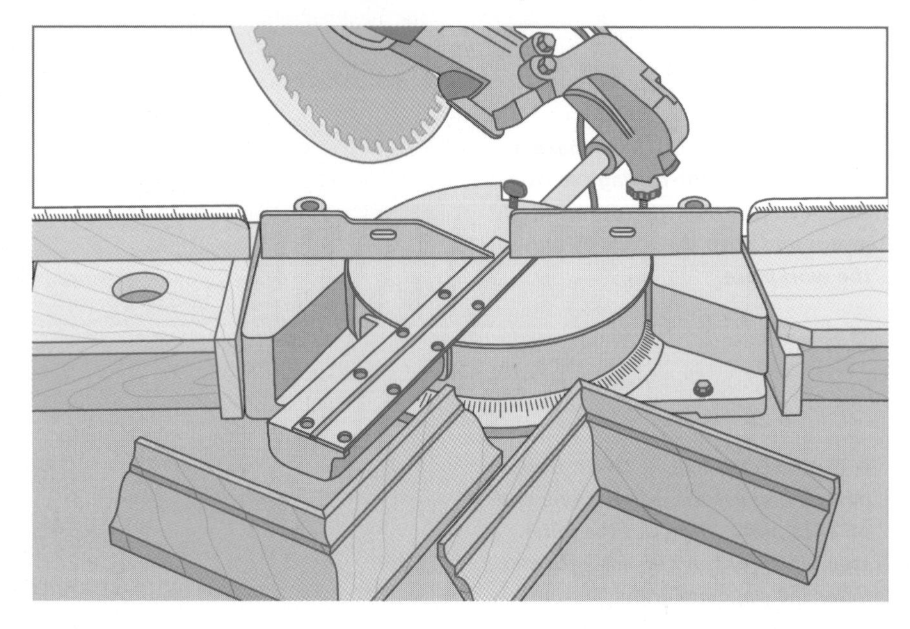

▶ **CUTTING CROWN MOLDING.** ***When cutting inside or outside miters on crown molding, both miter and bevel adjustments are made to produce the compound cut.***

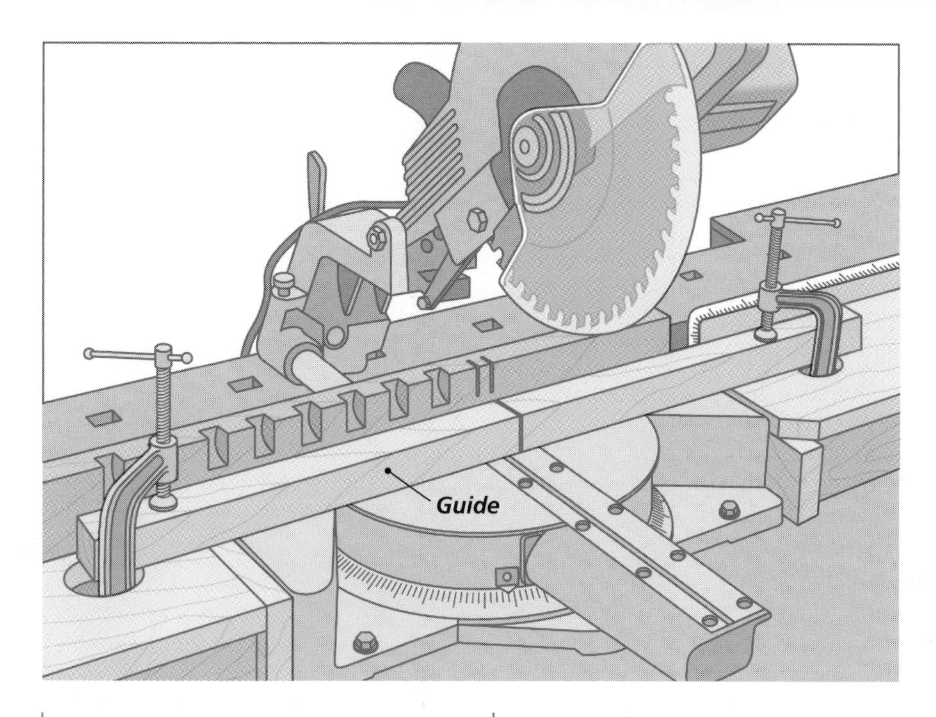

▲ **CUTTING DENTIL MOLDING.** ***To make dentil molding, position and lock the carriage so partial cut is made. A kerf in the guide strip helps in aligning the workpiece.***

and for work with slanted sides. Since the compound miter saw can be tilted for left bevels only, opposing-angle cuts require shifting the miter angle from one side to the other and alternating the edge of the work that contacts the fence.

For crown molding, the standard is a 52° ceiling angle and a 38° wall angle. To set the saw for a 45° inside corner miter, set the bevel angle at 33.9° and the miter angle at 31.6° to the right, and hold the molding's ceiling edge against the fence. The waste falls to the right of the blade. For the opposite end, pivot the miter cut to 31.6° left and hold the molding's wall edge against the fence. Most compound miter saw manuals list typical settings for inside and outside joints.

SPECIALTY CUTS

With a few simple adjustments, the sliding compound miter saw can be used to cut dentil molding, dadoes and repetitive surface designs. The latter two can only be made on saws that feature a stop adjustment that limits the cutting depth of the blade. Although a sliding compound miter saw isn't as versatile as a radial arm saw or table saw for special applications, it will handle a wide variety of work.

To make dentil molding, first lock the sliding carriage in position so that when the head is brought down, a partial cut is produced in the work held against the fence. Position the work vertically, and use a 2 x 2 guide strip clamped to the extension tables that lets the work slide across the table for each successive cut. Cut into the guide strip to make a kerf that's lined up with the blade. Then, mark the dentil positions on the work and align the marks with the kerf in the guide strip to make accurately positioned cuts. After making the two cuts that define the width of each dentil, remove the waste with successive overlapping cuts.

A dado blade must never be used on a miter saw. Instead, remove the waste with a series of overlapping cuts. To cut a dado, first adjust the saw's stopper plate to the desired depth of cut. Then, clamp a 1 x 3 spacer to the table, moving the work away from the fence so the bottom of the blade can traverse the entire length of the dado. Use a kerf cut in the spacer to align marks on the stock with the blade.

▼ **CUTTING DADOES.** ***Lock the blade's depth for partial kerf and make slide cuts to cut the dado. A spacer clamped behind the workpiece ensures uniform cutting depth.***

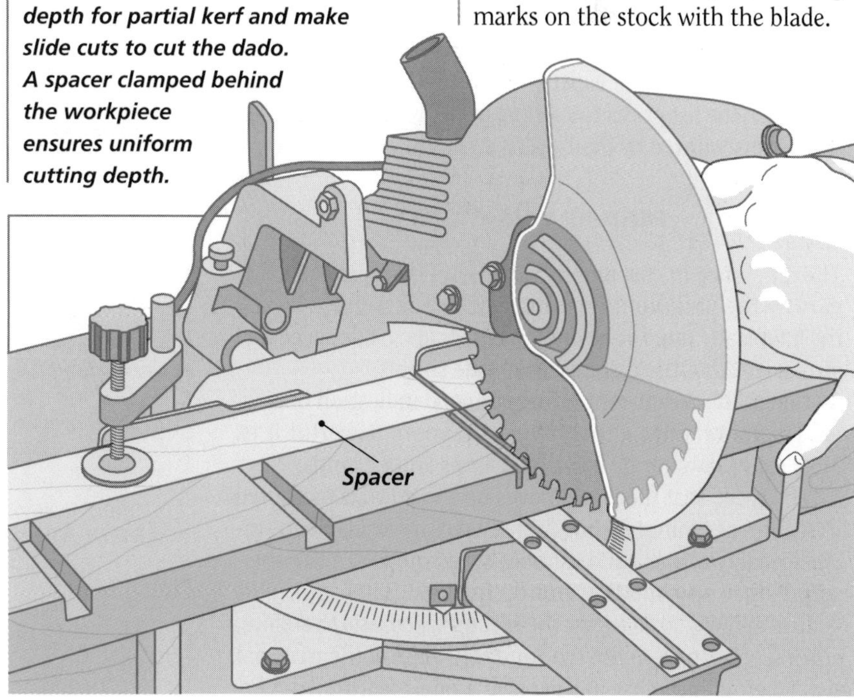

SABRE SAWS

If your biggest needs are to produce fast, straight rips in stock up to 2 in. thick, crosscut with speed and accuracy at bevel angles from 90° to 45°, or cut plywood straight and square, then go buy a circular saw. However, if you're willing to trade off some speed and accuracy for the ability to follow curved or straight lines, cut totally enclosed holes of any shape and have metal-cutting capability, you're in the market for a sabre saw.

The sabre saw's unique design and versatility have made it one of the most popular portable power tools in use today. Home do-it-yourselfers like the tool's user-friendly design and relatively safe style of cutting. And professional tradesmen find sabre saws valuable for use both in the workshop and at the job site. However, the sabre saw's most outstanding features are its ability to make curved cuts and, when fitted with the appropriate blade, cut a wide variety of materials—including wood, metal, plastic, brick, leather and ceramic tile, to name a very few.

Sabre saws, also known as jigsaws or bayonet saws, are available in many different models from a number of tool manufacturers. As with most other kinds of tools, more horsepower means greater cutting power. Most consumer-type sabre saws range from ⅙ hp to ⅝ hp, with the ⅓-hp models usually adequate for the average do-it-yourselfer.

There's a considerable variation in the cost of sabre saws, from the inexpensive, occasional-use versions to the more expensive, professional models. A good-quality sabre saw in the low-to-mid price range would usually do for most do-it-yourselfers. However, a full-featured professional sabre saw is generally worth the expense if it's used fairly often. And don't take the list prices too seriously; many of these tools are heavily discounted by mail-order and industrial suppliers.

FEATURE VARIATIONS

The difference in cost among sabre saws is accounted for in part by the variations in features offered. Sabre saws are most typically rated according to amperage, blade speed and stroke length—the distance the blade travels.

Generally, the current rating is a good indication of power. The more amps a tool draws, the more powerful it is. Most sabre saws range between 2 amps and 4½ amps.

The speed that the blade moves up and down is measured in strokes per minute (spm). Sabre saws are available in single-speed, two-speed and variable-speed models. A variable-speed sabre saw operates from 0 to about 3200 spm. This feature allows you to adjust the blade's speed, and therefore, cutting efficiency, to the type and thickness of the material that's being cut. Most inexpensive models feature trigger-

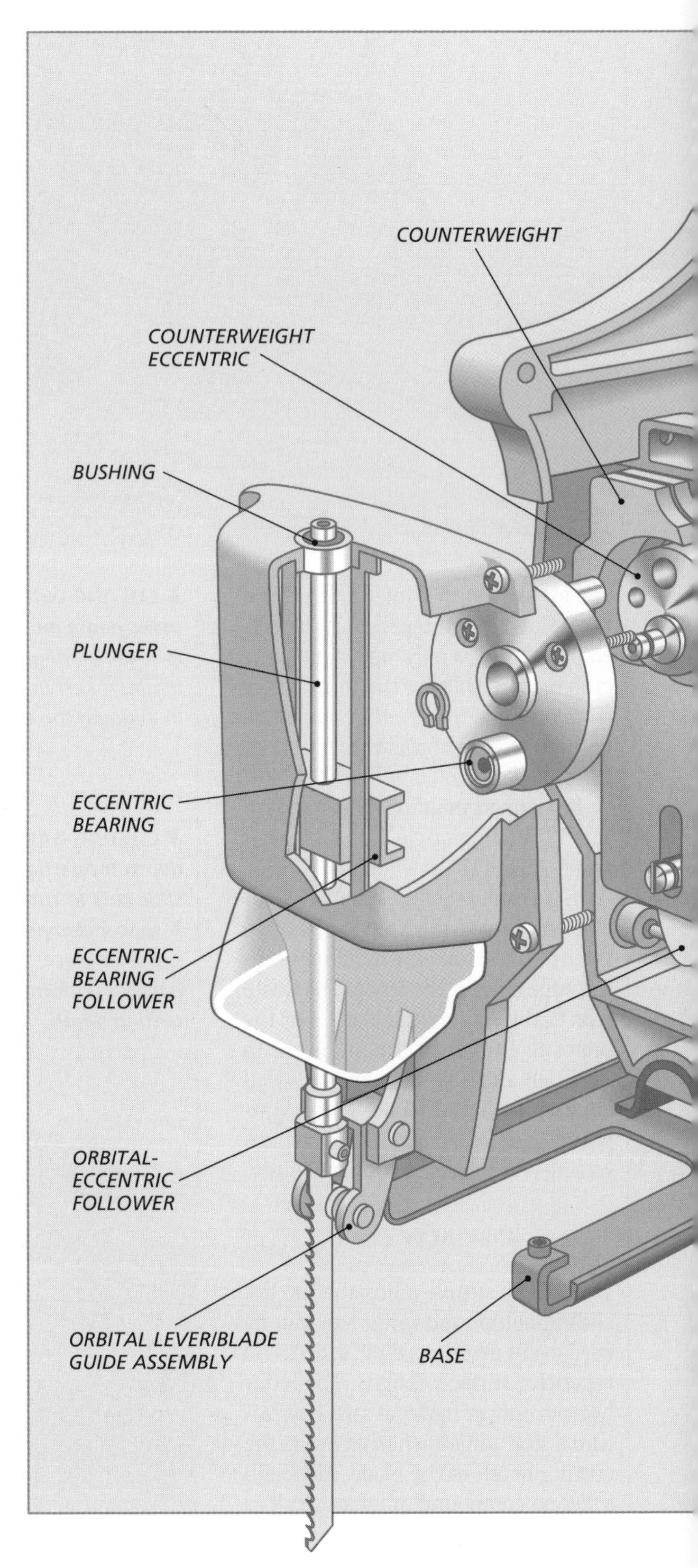

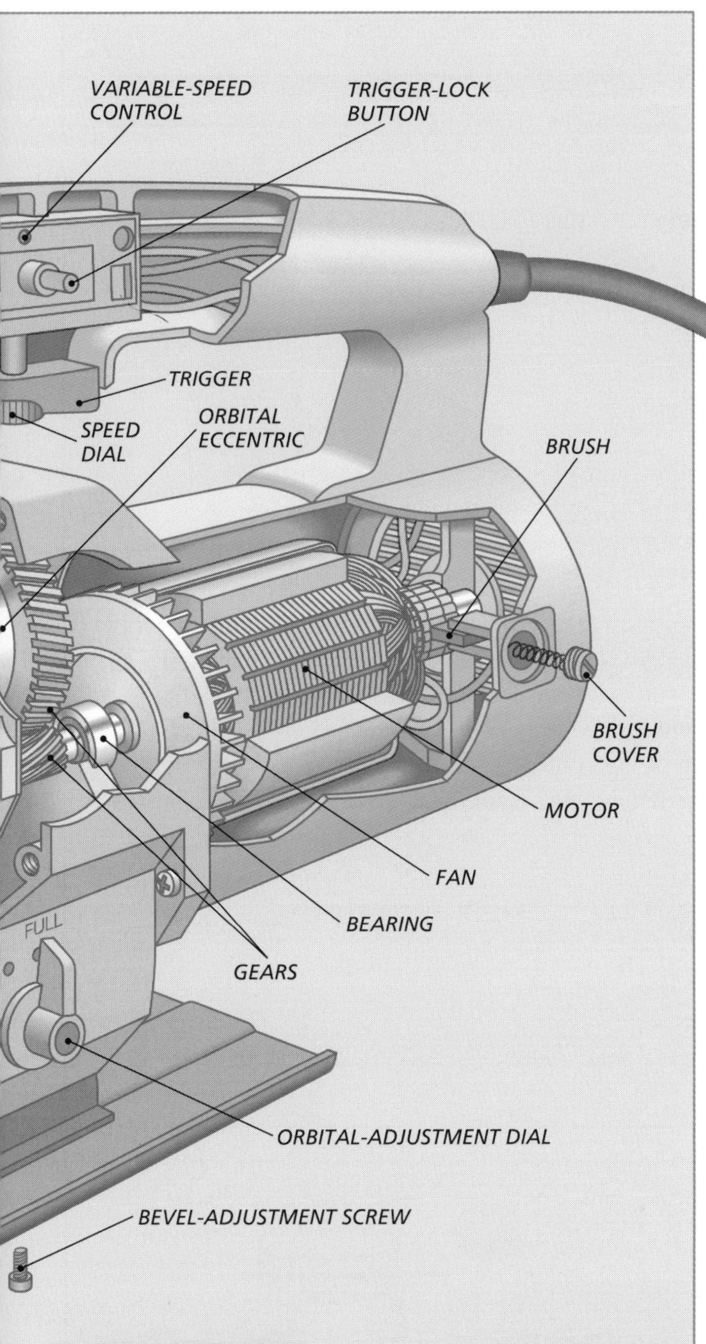

SABRE SAW ANATOMY
In orbital sawing, reciprocating action is combined with in-and-out motion of the blade roller guide. As the eccentric bearing rotates, the orbital eccentric moves in the opposite direction, controlling the follower that pivots the orbital lever/blade guide assembly. A cam linked to the orbit-control adjustment lever regulates the effect of the orbital eccentric follower on the orbital lever/blade guide.

controlled variable speed. On more expensive tools, variable speed is either trigger controlled or set by means of a separate speed dial. The professional trigger-controlled tools are equipped with a speed dial on the trigger that allows the blade speed to be set and held at a specific rate.

The blade stroke length of sabre saws ranges from ½ in. to about 1 in., depending on the particular sabre saw; a 1-in. stroke length is the most common. The longer the blade stroke, the greater the number of saw blade teeth that will be doing the actual cutting.

Most sabre saws cut with a straight up-and-down, reciprocating type of action. Other saws provide orbital-action cutting, where the blade cuts into the work at a slight angle on the upstroke and then moves away from the work on the non-cutting downstroke. Orbital action means faster cutting with less chatter, along with increased blade life since there's no friction on the downstroke. And with increased cutting speed comes the ability to more easily handle thick stock. On the negative side, however, accuracy in terms of both a square cut and the quality of the cut diminishes. Most orbital-action sabre saws feature a three- or four-position switch for selecting the desired cutting motion—from straight reciprocating through various degrees of orbital action.

Another worthwhile feature that's found on some models of sabre saws is a scrolling mechanism. This allows you to rotate the blade 360°—while cutting—to obtain superior control when working on intricate scrollwork and highly detailed shapes.

Many models of sabre saws today are available with electronic speed control that monitors the cutting load and maintains a constant speed. If you're cutting through stock that varies in thickness, it may help. Otherwise, simply setting an appropriate speed and adjusting the cut rate by feel should work fine.

Sabre saws come in two different, basic designs. The standard top-handle configuration is the most common and allows easy one-handed operation. Some pros, though, prefer the barrel-grip design—where one hand holds the motor housing and the other grips a knob mounted over the front of the tool. Although this type of arrangement offers increased control for curve cutting, choosing one or the other is really a matter of personal comfort.

Other convenient features that are worth looking for in a sabre saw include ball-bearing blade guides, a built-in sawdust blower, a large, stable base, blade wrench storage and a base insert that helps to minimize splintering. And make sure that you also check out the latest models of this tool: the new cordless sabre saws.

► **SABRE SAW BLADES.** ***Blades for sabre saws come in a wide variety of styles, shapes and sizes. Shown at right is a sampling of what's most commonly available.***

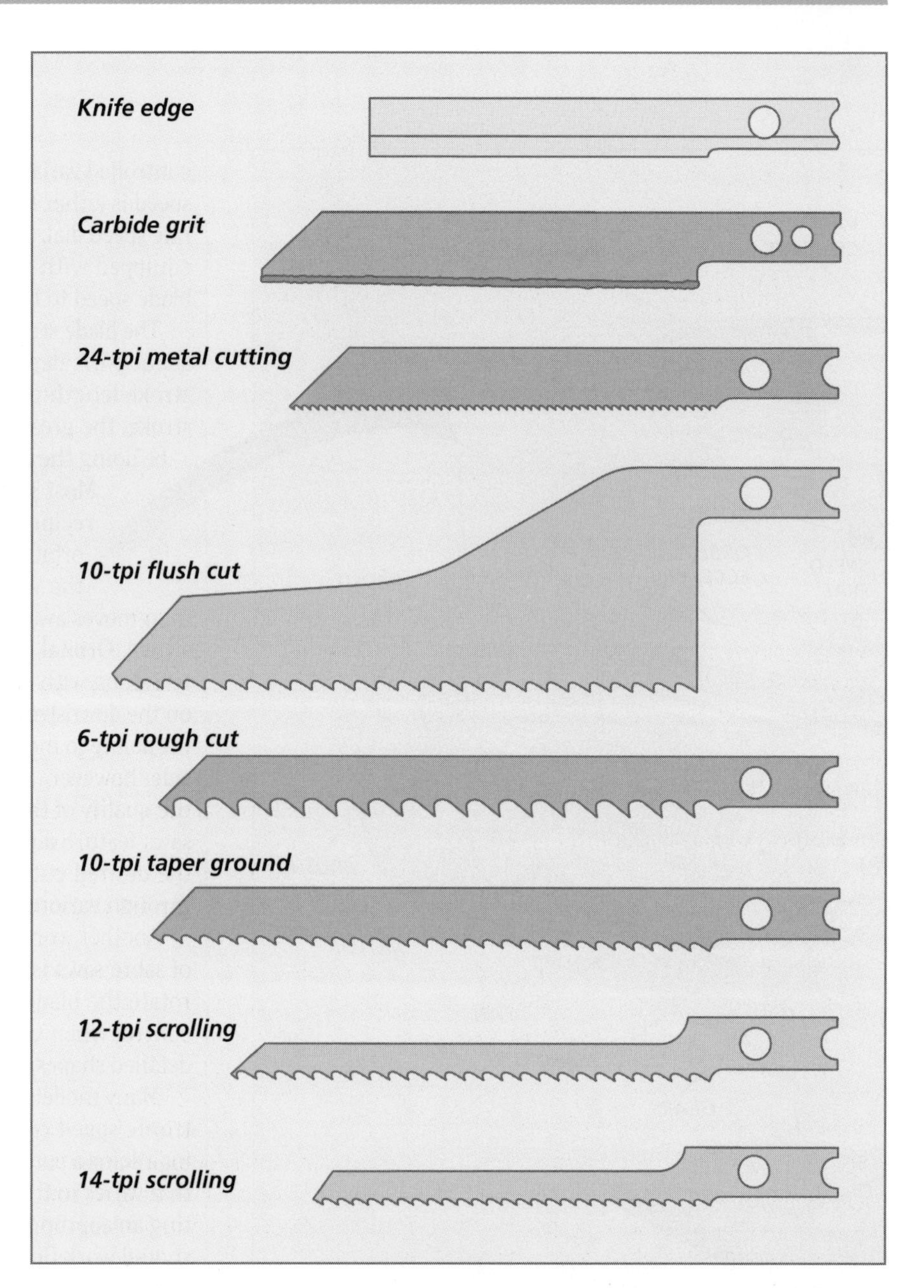

MAKING YOUR CHOICE

Because sabre saw performance is so closely related to the material being cut and the blade that's installed, the only way to really compare tools is by testing them using one type of blade on the same material. Unfortunately, there is no standard blade-holding system for sabre saws and some tools can only take one type of blade. The most common blade—a straight shank with a semi-circular notch at the top and a hole in the side—can't be installed in some models. And for some tools in which the blade can be fitted, its use is not recommended. One blade that's becoming increasingly popular features two small protrusions near the top. Offered as standard equipment with some tools, the blade doesn't fit other models.

Most sabre saws can be fitted with a T-shaped fence for sawing parallel to the edge of stock. Making the system work properly, though, depends not only on the condition of the blade and the uniformity of the material being cut, but on the precise alignment of the blade with the base. A slight misalignment will cause the blade to gradually bend, creating a twisted kerf. If the blade bends far enough, the tool will no longer track against a straightedge and the cut veers. Some sabre saws are so severely misaligned they cannot be held against a straight guide strip at all.

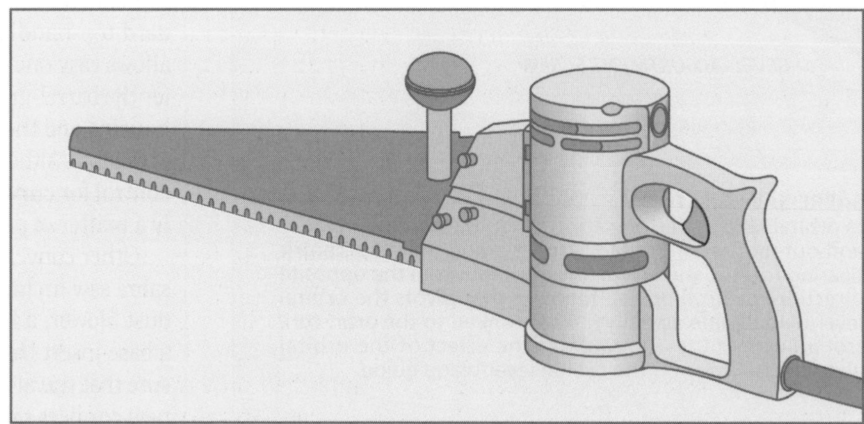

► **RECIPROCATING SAW.** ***For rough cuts and demolition work, use a reciprocating saw. Because its blade cuts in both stroke directions, there is practically no kick or pull. The extra handle over the blade makes the tool comfortable to support.***

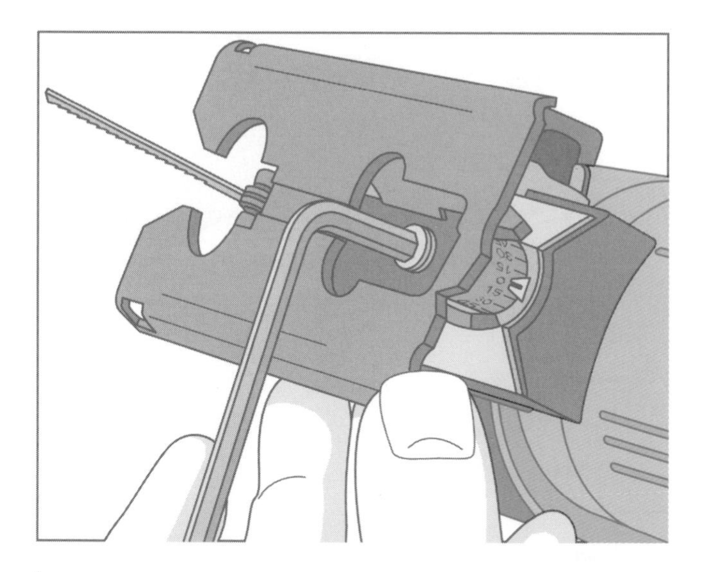

▲ SETTING CUT ANGLE. *Loosening the bevel-adjustment screw unlocks the base to adjust for bevels. This system is controlled by an Allen wrench supplied with the tool, and features notches that engage at common angles.*

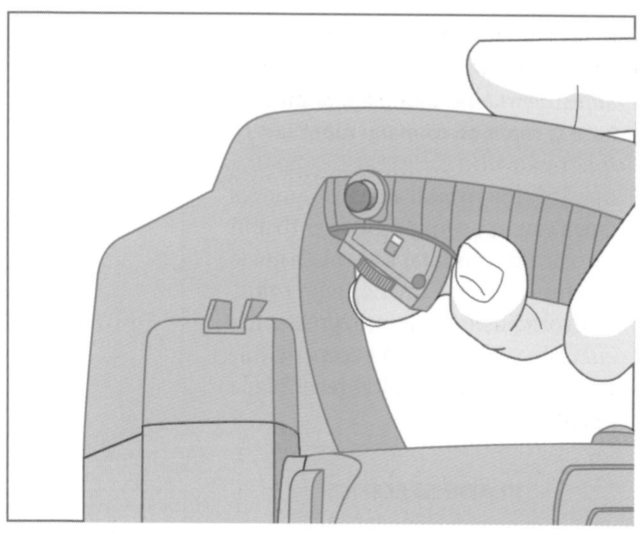

▲ SETTING BLADE SPEED. *With many sabre saws, the speed is varied at the trigger. A trigger-mounted dial on this model sets the maximum speed at which the trigger can be locked. Other saws feature a separate speed-control dial.*

THE BOTTOM LINE

A good sabre saw doesn't just cut well; it also must be both easy and comfortable to handle so you're free to concentrate on the job at hand. It should also be made with the same care and attention to detail that you'd strive for in your finest work. While some models will have a definite edge in terms of comfort and handling, others will show themselves to have more aggressive, straight-tracking performance.

Although sabre saws are used primarily for freehand cutting, guiding the tool along a straightedge or with a fence is clearly an option that manufacturers are featuring to enhance their product. And it isn't unreasonable to expect that before any extra frills are added, the blade clamp of the tool—the fixture that holds the blade in position in the saw—should be engineered so the blade will be accurately aligned with the base.

The blade clamp is a common weak link in sabre saws, so examine it closely. Be sure that the blade clamp fits on the shaft of the saw without excessive play. Any wobbling in this clamp will be transferred directly to the blade. While virtually no sabre saw will track with circular-saw accuracy, you'll find that some models are so blatantly misaligned that guided cuts would prove to be downright impossible.

In general, you're well advised to choose a sabre saw that will accept universal, straight-shank blades. Avoid getting a particular model that uses only specially shaped blades.

Other points to look for when comparing sabre saws include the cutting capacities in wood and metal, and how smoothly the shoe adjusts for cutting angles. And finally, choose a saw in which adjustments and blade changes are made with a screwdriver, rather than with a hex-key wrench. It seems that you can always find a screwdriver.

In the end, however, your decision on which sabre saw to purchase should be made according to the same criterion applied when buying other kinds of tools: Choose the sabre saw that will best handle the types of jobs you most expect to do. For example, if you plan to use your sabre saw primarily for around-the-house carpentry tasks—where you can expect lots of cuts in walls and ceilings—you will probably prefer a lightweight version to help keep your arms from tiring. But if you intend to use your sabre saw in the workshop most of the time, you're better off picking a heftier model equipped with a good-sized shoe that will afford you greater control and accuracy when cutting on the workbench or over a pair of sawhorses.

SAW MECHANICS

Regardless of the particular model you may own, all sabre saws function on the same basic set of operating principles. Simply put, a motor-driven gear assembly powers a shaft up and down. A blade clamp attached to the end of the shaft holds the blade securely.

In orbital sawing, the reciprocating action of the shaft is combined with in-and-out motion of a blade roller guide. When the blade is fully extended after its downstroke, an eccentric bearing that controls the reciprocating action is at bottom dead center and an orbital eccentric that controls the in-and-out motion is at top dead center. As the eccentric bearing moves

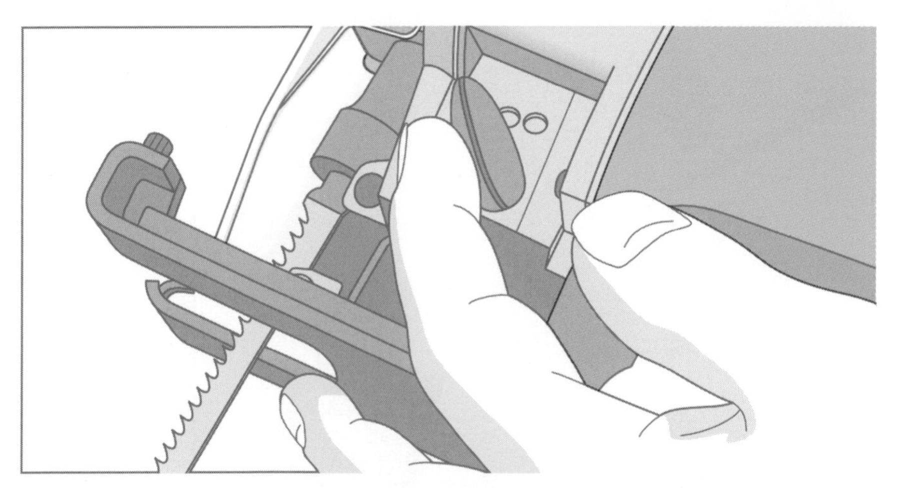

▶ **ADJUSTING ORBITAL ACTION, 1.** ***A side-mounted, four-position orbital-adjustment lever like the one shown here is common to many sabre saws.***

upward, the orbital eccentric moves downward, pushing a follower that in turn pivots an orbital lever/blade guide assembly. A cam linked to an orbit-control adjustment lever regulates the effect that the orbital eccentric follower has on the orbital lever/blade guide assembly.

BLADE SPECIFICS

Sabre saw blades are available in a wide variety of different styles, shapes and sizes for cutting virtually every material. The choice of blade to use depends on the type of material that's being cut, speed of the cut and smoothness required. The blades are listed according to their designed cutting purpose and the number of teeth per inch (tpi). As with blades for most types of tools, the more teeth a sabre saw blade has, the smoother and slower it will cut. Fewer teeth produce a rougher, faster cutting blade. The length of blades typically ranges from about 2½ in. to 4 in. Specially made blades up to 12 in. long are also available.

When cutting sharp corners and tight curves in wood, try using a narrow scrolling blade. To achieve ultra-smooth cuts, work with a taper-ground blade that features no-set teeth. Saw directly up to a perpendicular surface by using a flush-cutting blade. This type of blade is offset so that the teeth extend to the front edge of the base. Wood-cutting blades commonly range from a low of 3 tpi (very rough cut) to a high of 14 tpi (smooth cut). Metal-cutting blades range from about 14 tpi to 32 tpi.

For extra durability, try working with bi-metal saw blades. These blades feature tough, high-speed steel (HSS) teeth that are welded onto a resilient spring-steel base.

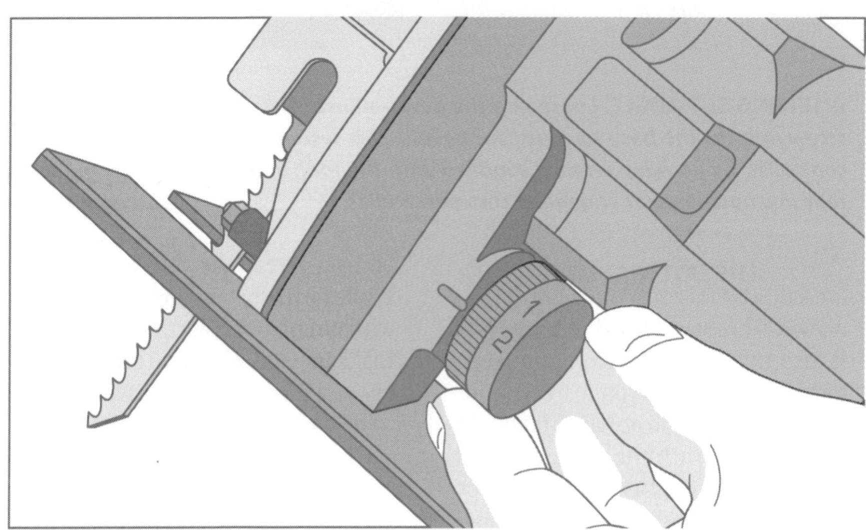

▲ **ADJUSTING ORBITAL ACTION, 2.** ***Some sabre saws feature an orbital-adjustment dial located behind the housing, as shown, or mounted in the housing.***

▼ **ADJUSTING ORBITAL ACTION, 3.** ***Here, an orbital-adjustment lever is mounted behind the housing. It pivots at the center and can be operated from either side.***

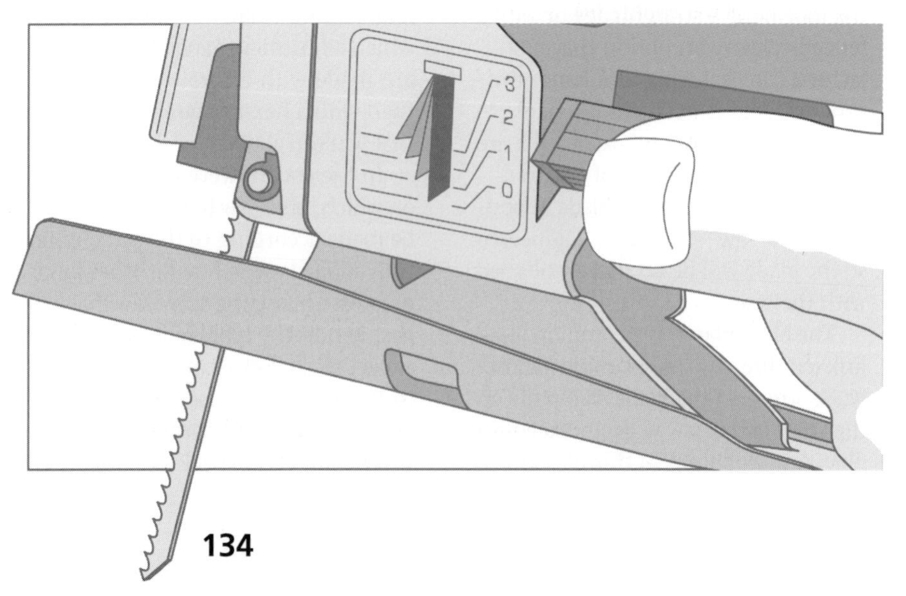

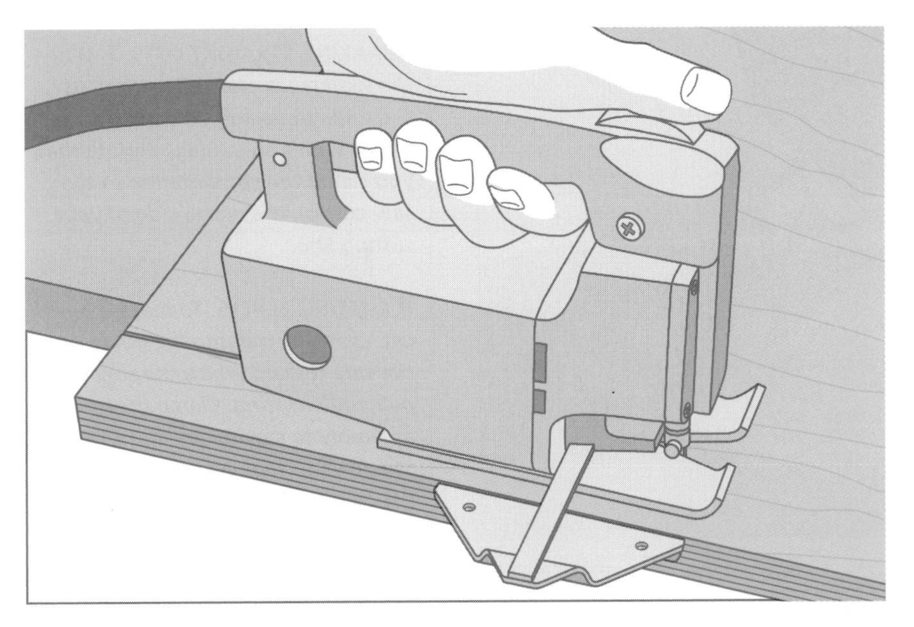

◀ **MAKING STRAIGHT CUTS, 1.** ***Make a straight cut near an edge using a rip guide, positioning it so the kerf will be on the waste side of the line being cut. This way, if the saw should veer from the work edge, it will drift into the waste area.***

▼ **MAKING STRAIGHT CUTS, 2.** ***When holes in the workpiece don't matter, tack on a wood strip with 4d finishing nails. Mark the exact location of the guide every 12 in., then pull the strip to each mark to tack it. If inadequately nailed, the strip may bow.***

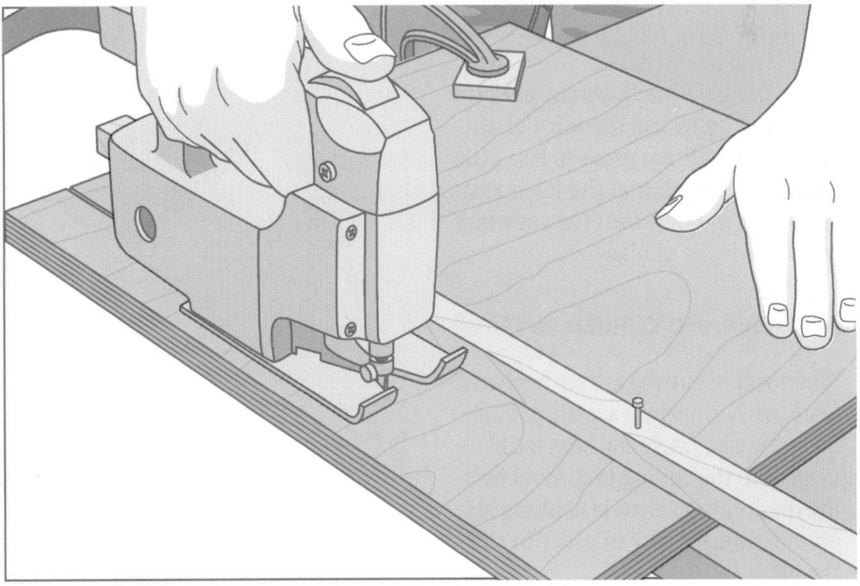

There are also a couple of toothless types of blades worth mentioning. A carbide-grit blade is available for sawing a variety of hard, abrasive materials such as ceramic tile, slate, steel, plaster, brick and fiberglass—to name a few. The blade is made up of thousands of tiny tungsten-carbide particles bonded to an alloy-steel base. One other valuable toothless blade is the knife-edge blade. Use this blade for cutting rubber, leather, cork, vinyl, cardboard and foam rubber.

Most sabre saws accept a standard ¼-in. straight-shaft blade. As already mentioned, however, some models will only accept blades that have a specially shaped shaft. While these types of tools work as well as the others, their blades often can be a little difficult to obtain. Standard straight-shaft blades are sold at virtually every hardware store, home center and lumberyard.

SAWING BASICS

A sabre saw is most often used freehand to make straight and curved cuts in wood. Freehand cuts are fine for rough work, and usually can be made with better than reasonable accuracy if you make sure that the workpiece is firmly clamped in place.

Because the sabre saw cuts on the upstroke, any splintering that results will appear on the top surface of the workpiece. Whenever possible, therefore, saw the work with its good side facing down.

When this isn't possible, there are some other methods to help reduce splintering. Use a fine-cutting, taper-ground blade on a saw that's fitted with a base insert and advance the tool slowly. Another trick is to score the cutting line with a sharp utility knife prior to sawing. Alternatively, you can apply a strip of masking tape to the workpiece and mark your cutting line along it. In addition, it's worthwhile obtaining a special reverse-tooth type of blade that cuts on the downstroke, virtually eliminating the problem of top-surface splintering altogether.

FREEHAND STRAIGHT CUTS

To help ensure that straight freehand cuts are made with the greatest degree of accuracy, work with a relatively wide blade. Support your piece as close as

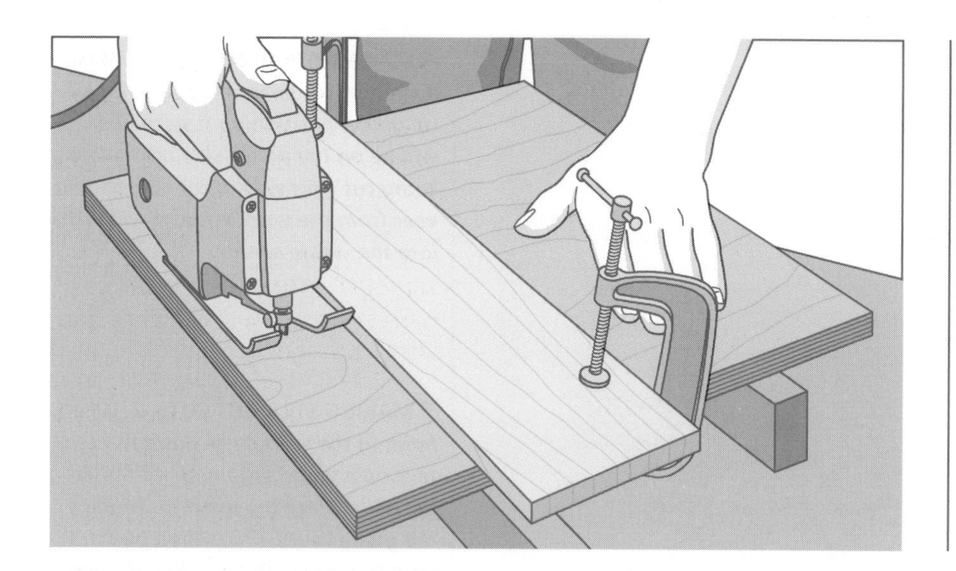

◄ **MAKING STRAIGHT CUTS, 3.** ***When the workpiece can't be marred, use C-clamps to position a wide board—which won't bow. Make certain that you clamp the straightedge so the saw cuts on the waste side of your cutting line.***

▼ **CUTTING BEVELS.** ***To make a bevel cut, clamp a straightedge guide on the side toward which the saw will pull while cutting. Clamp the entire assembly to sawhorses that the work straddles so that you can keep your hands out of the blade's path. Use a rough-cut blade and a slow feed.***

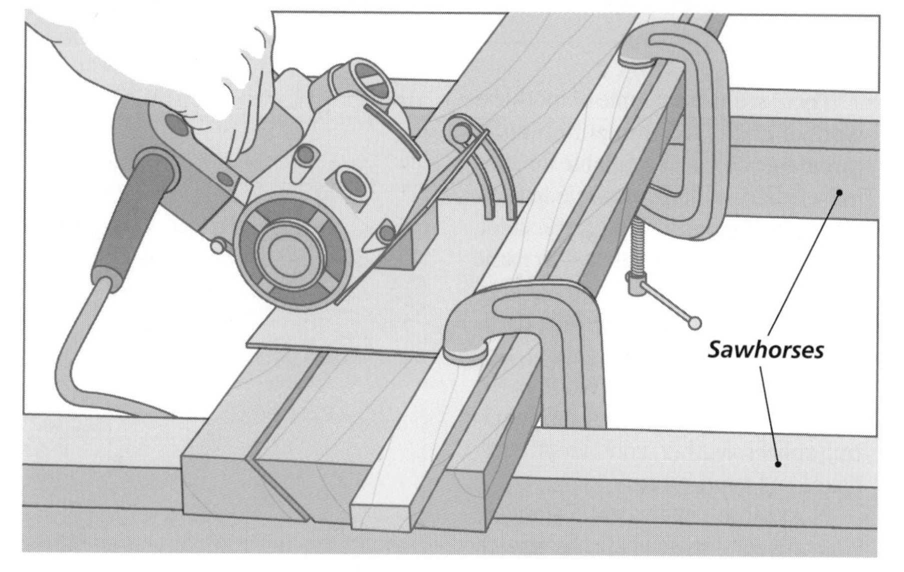

possible along each side of the cutting line with lengths of 2 x 4, making sure that there is enough clearance under it for the blade to pass.

Working with a flush-cut blade to saw right up to a perpendicular surface can sometimes prove to be a little tricky. You'll find that the job is easier to do if you first start the cut using a standard type of blade.

FREEHAND CURVED CUTS

When you're cutting curves freehand, work with a narrow scrolling blade. Steer the saw slowly and keep the blade tangent to the cutting line. Avoid making the common error of applying side pressure on the saw in order to steer the blade.

Some curves cannot be completed with a single cutting pass if there are sharp turns and angles involved. In these instances, you should make several passes, cutting out large portions of the waste first to minimize the danger of splitting the piece.

The best way of handling a sharp inside corner is to saw right into the corner, then stop the blade to back it out and bypass the corner. Continue along the cutting line and come back later to clean up the corner.

A common problem when making curved cuts is blade strain. This usually occurs when the back edge of the blade hits the side of the kerf as it rounds a corner. The result can be a twisted or broken blade, or a blade that binds in the cut and possibly mars the piece.

A blade that's too wide for the curve being cut is usually the cause of binding. The solution is to either work with a narrower blade or make a series of release cuts from the edge of the piece to the tightest portions of the curve. By removing waste up to these points, there's more room for the cutting edge to maneuver and the blade won't bind in the kerf.

When the edge of the workpiece is a short distance from the line you're cutting, you can avoid binding of the blade by veering off the cutting path to saw to the edge. Then, come back and continue the cut at a gentler angle.

MAKING INTERIOR CUTS

If there's a single job that makes owning a sabre saw a must, it is performing cutouts—a frequent need in the workshop, as well as in household carpentry. The sabre saw is especially useful for making plunge or pocket cuts in the middle of a workpiece. And once you've mastered good cutting techniques with your sabre saw, you will be able to make better cutouts faster

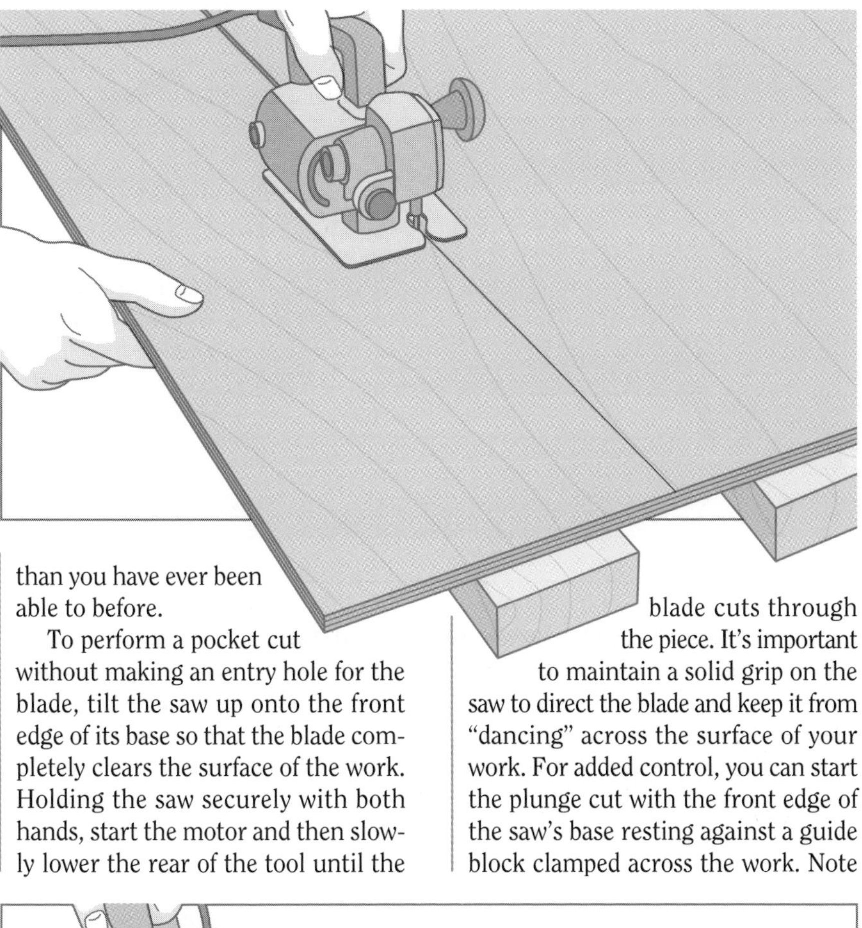

◀ **CUTTING FREEHAND, 1.** ***To ensure straight freehand cuts, use a relatively wide blade and support the workpiece close to each side of the cutting line with flat lengths of 2 x 4.***

than you have ever been able to before.

To perform a pocket cut without making an entry hole for the blade, tilt the saw up onto the front edge of its base so that the blade completely clears the surface of the work. Holding the saw securely with both hands, start the motor and then slowly lower the rear of the tool until the blade cuts through the piece. It's important to maintain a solid grip on the saw to direct the blade and keep it from "dancing" across the surface of your work. For added control, you can start the plunge cut with the front edge of the saw's base resting against a guide block clamped across the work. Note also that your piece must be properly supported on lengths of 2 x 4 or straddling sawhorses, with sufficient clearance for the blade.

Once the blade is lowered fully into the work and the base of the saw is sitting flat on the piece, proceed with making straight cuts as far as you can go. Stop the blade and back up the saw to bypass corners as necessary, then go back later to finish them. Once the bulk of your cutout has been removed, you can reverse the direction of the saw up to 180° to ease the task of clearing waste from the corners.

Sometimes the width of the cutout is too narrow to allow the blade to turn corners in the usual manner. To clean out a square corner in these instances, tack-nail a stop strip across the end of the opening at a distance equal to that from the blade to the front of the saw's base. Then, make repeated cuts as necessary up to the stop.

As an alternative, you can make an internal cutout by first boring an entry hole for the blade of the saw using a

▲ **CUTTING FREEHAND, 2.** ***Cut out sharp inside corners in stages. Saw right into the corner, then back out the blade. Come back and make the finishing cuts.***

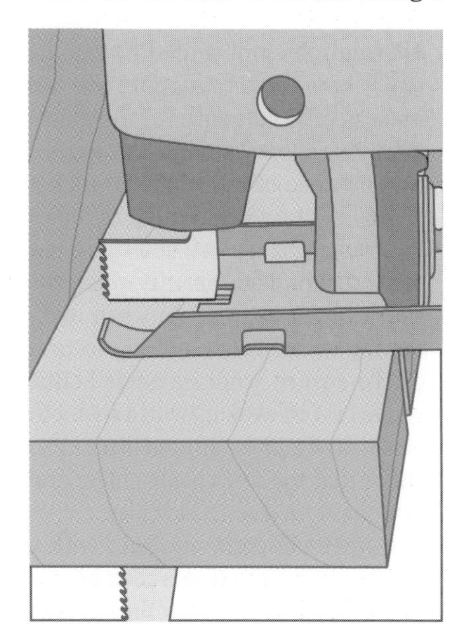

▶ **MAKING FLUSH CUTS.** ***A flush-cut blade allows the saw to cut right up to a perpendicular surface. The procedure works best if you start the cut with a standard blade.***

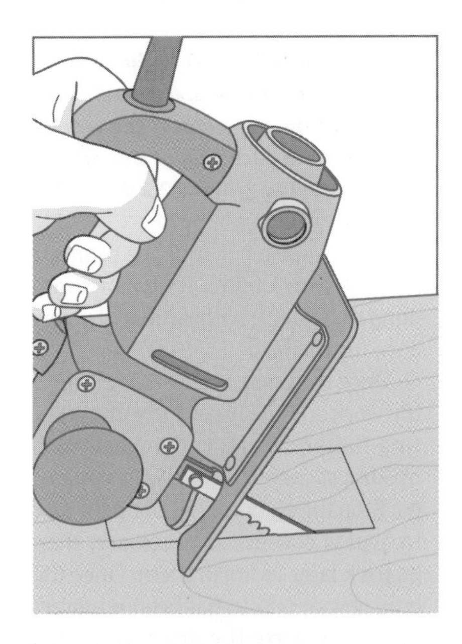

▲ **MAKING POCKET CUTS, 1.** ***To make a plunge cut in the center of a board, tilt the saw on its nose and start the motor, then slowly lower the rear end of the tool. When the base is sitting flat, proceed with the cut.***

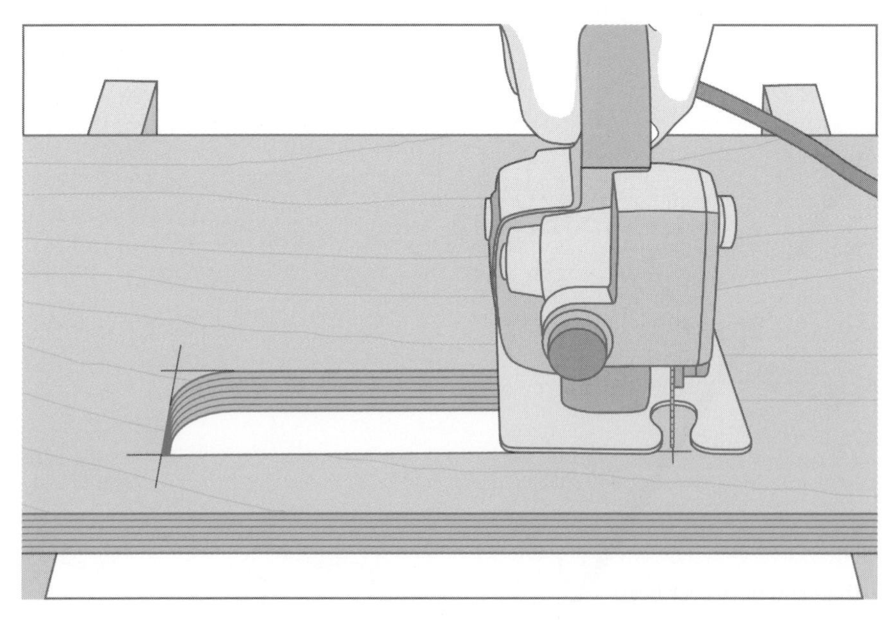

▲ **MAKING POCKET CUTS, 2.** ***When the cutout is removed, reverse the saw direction 180° and cut out the triangular corner pieces. Straddle the workpiece on sawhorses for both blade clearance and maximum support.***

▼ **CUTTING CIRCLES.** ***For best results, use a rough blade with a heavy set—which helps assure blade-turning clearance. Adjust the saw to its fastest variable-speed setting and push the saw at a slow feed rate.***

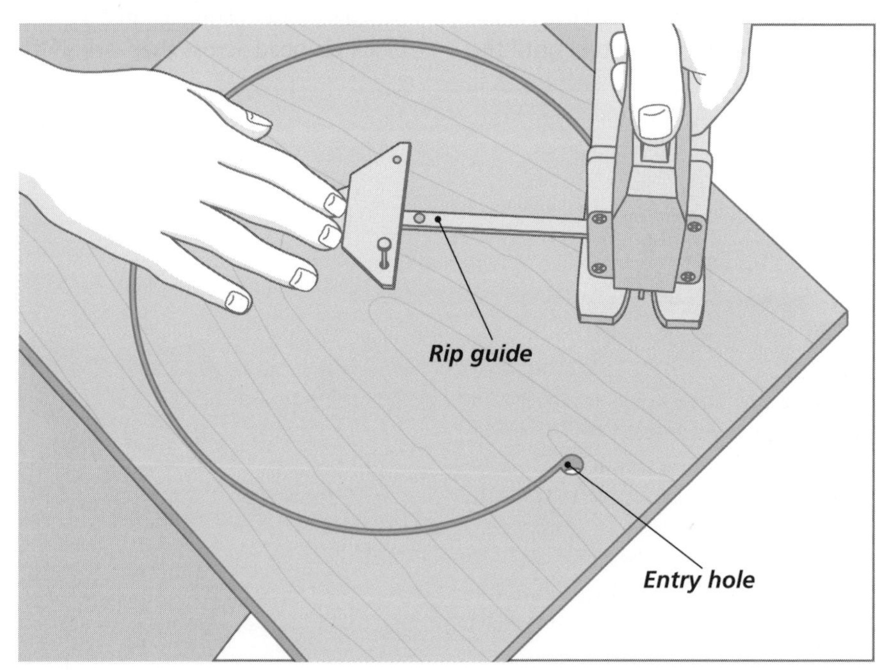

drill. A neat, quick method is to bore a hole at each corner of the cutout. This way, you eliminate altogether the need to come back and clean out the last bits from the corners.

GUIDED STRAIGHT CUTS

Although the tool is used freehand a majority of the time, a sabre saw can make precise cuts with the assistance of various jigs and straightedge guides. And because of the vibration that is caused by the reciprocating action of the blade, you are well advised to use some sort of guide against which the shoe of the saw can bear when making any straight cut requiring accuracy. To ensure accurate guided cuts, you're best off working with a set-tooth blade—not a taper-ground blade. Also check that the saw's blade holder and shaft have no side-to-side play.

Some saws come equipped with a T-shaped rip guide that is adequate for relatively short cuts near the edges of stock. If the straight line you're cutting is within the capacity of the rip guide that came with your saw, use it whenever possible. You will notice that the rip guide is designed to engage the edge of the workpiece before the blade enters the edge to help start the cut.

When making a straight cut with your rip guide, be sure that you position it so the kerf will be on the waste

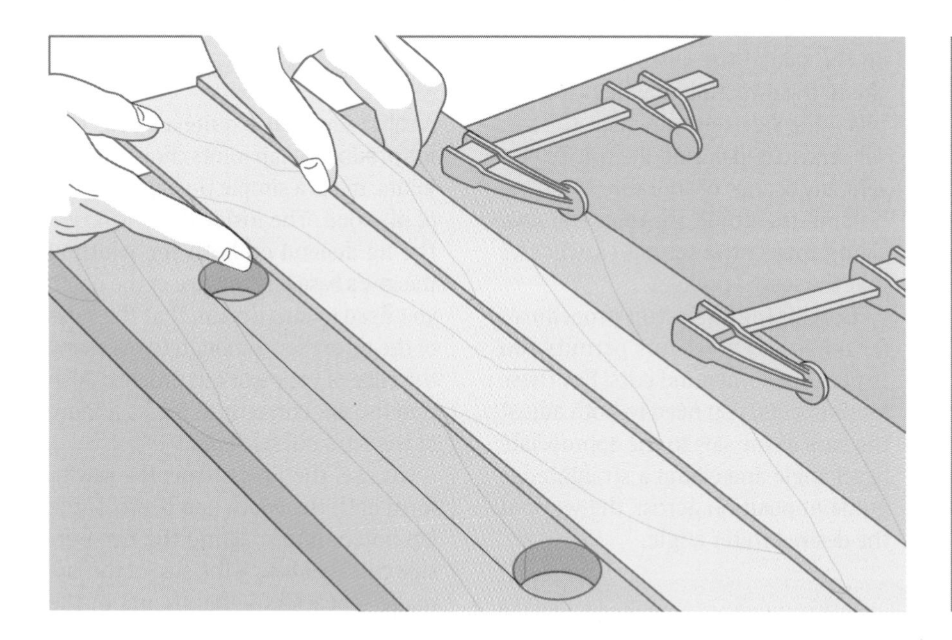

◀ **USING AN OFFSET STRAIGHTEDGE.** ***A customized cutting guide like this one requires no measuring. Simply position the edge of the guide along the cutting line. The saw blade will follow the guide's edge.***

▼ **CUTTING EDGE HALF LAPS, 1.** ***This U-shaped jig simplifies cutting edges for half-lap joints. The jig guides the saw for the two outside cuts, then interior kerfs are cut freehand.***

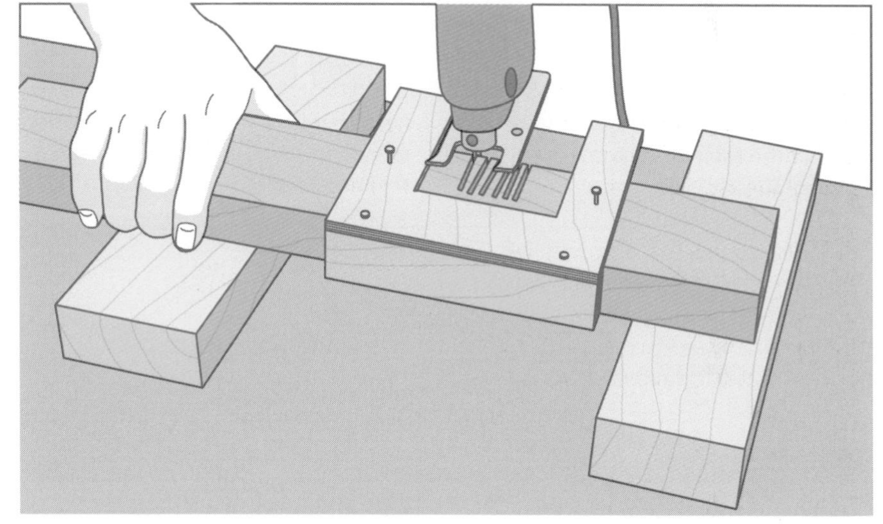

side of line being cut. This way, if the saw should wander away from the cutting line, it will drift into the waste area. It's also a good idea to hold the rip guide against the edge of the work with one hand. If you allow the saw to travel into the waste area too frequently, you may have trouble picking up and following your cutting line later—even with the guide.

A shopmade straightedge guide is easy to make and often provides a better way to ensure straight, accurate cuts. For your guide, use a straight piece of wood such as a rip of plywood. Simply clamp or tack-nail the guide securely to the work and run the saw along it.

Note that the guide should extend beyond the end of the work in order for you to align the saw at the start of the cut. Position the guide so that the kerf will be to the waste side of the cutting line and remember that the distance from the guide to the line you're cutting must equal the distance from the blade to the edge of the saw's base.

To eliminate the need to measure from the cutting line to the guide, you can make a customized cutting guide from two pieces of ¼-in. plywood or hardboard. Glue and nail a 1½-in.-wide plywood strip to another strip that's about 5 or 6 in. wide. Then, guide the saw along the edge of the narrow, top strip to trim the bottom strip to the proper width. To use the guide, simply align its edge with the cutting line on the work, clamp it firmly in place and make the cut.

For straight cuts on the interior of a panel of plywood, guide the saw by means of a tacked-on wooden strip. To eliminate any chance of the guide strip bowing, drive in a 4d finishing nail every 12 in. or so along it. Mark the guide strip's location from the cutting line in a number of places and pull the guide strip to the marks as you nail your way along the cutting line. If it is inadequately nailed, the guide strip may bow during the cut.

For guided interior cuts on smaller panels, it's best to work with a wide, straight board and clamps. Sight down the edge of the board to check it, and toss aside any board with a bow. Again, make certain that the guide board is clamped so the saw cuts on the waste side of the cutting line.

MITERS AND BEVELS

Cutting miters with a sabre saw is no different than making other types of straight-line cuts. Any wide, straight board that's clamped to the work at the desired angle can serve as a cutting guide. Just position the guide at a distance from the cutting line equal to that between the blade and the saw's shoe, ensuring the kerf will be to the waste side of the cutting line. To correctly align the saw at the start of the cut, extend the guide beyond the end of the work.

If your saw is capable of performing bevel cuts, adjust the base to the required angle and use a rough-cut blade at a slow feed rate. The straightedge guide you use must be positioned on the side of the cutting line opposite to the direction in which the saw tilts—the side toward which the saw will tend to pull during the cut. To prevent any chance of an injury to a hand holding the guide ahead of the saw, clamp your entire setup to sawhorses that the work straddles.

Combining the setup procedures for miter and bevel cuts permits you to perform compound cuts. For these kinds of cuts, you need to both adjust the base of the saw to the appropriate bevel angle and clamp a straightedge guide in position across the work at the desired miter angle.

MAKING LAP JOINTS

A sabre saw is also quite a handy tool for producing lap joints. For edge-lap joints, make a simple U-shaped jig out of plywood. The inside dimensions of the jig depend on both the width of the saw's base and the size of the notch you need to cut. Ensure that the sides of the jig are long enough to overhang the edge of your work in order to position the saw correctly at the beginning of the lap's outside cuts.

In use, the jig controls the saw to form both the width and depth of the lap notch. After making the two outside cuts that define the size of the lap, make repeated freehand cuts in the middle of the notch. These kerfs simplify the task of breaking out the waste with a chisel. Two boards cut in this manner lock together tightly and form a clean, invisible joint.

The cuts for end half-lap joints are made by attaching a plate of plywood to the saw's base. This shortens the stroke length of the blade and determines the depth of cut—which should be equal to one-half the thickness of the stock. Nail or clamp a straightedged board to the workpiece to guide the first cut and establish the shoulder of the joint. Then, make several freehand cuts through the waste area.

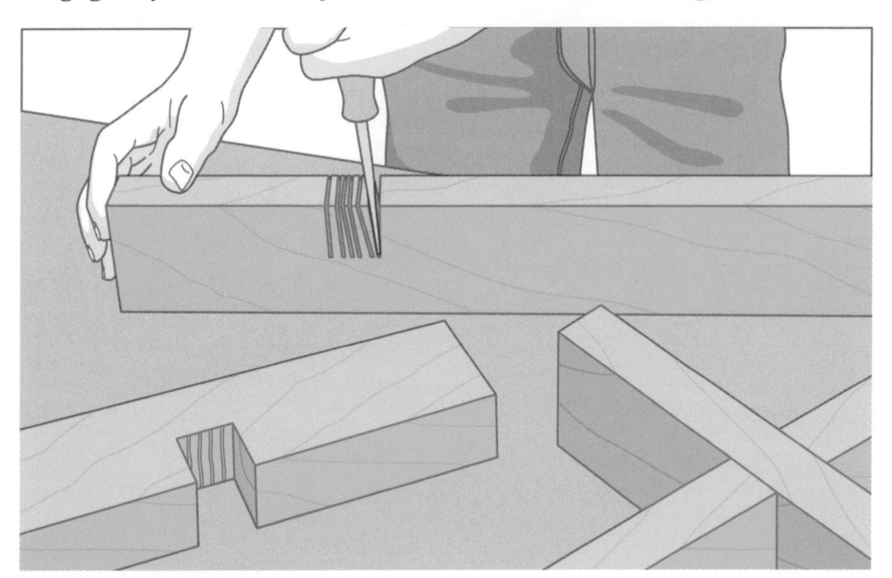

▲ **CUTTING EDGE HALF LAPS, 2.** ***Cut out the waste with a wood chisel. The two parts lock together and form a clean, invisible joint.***

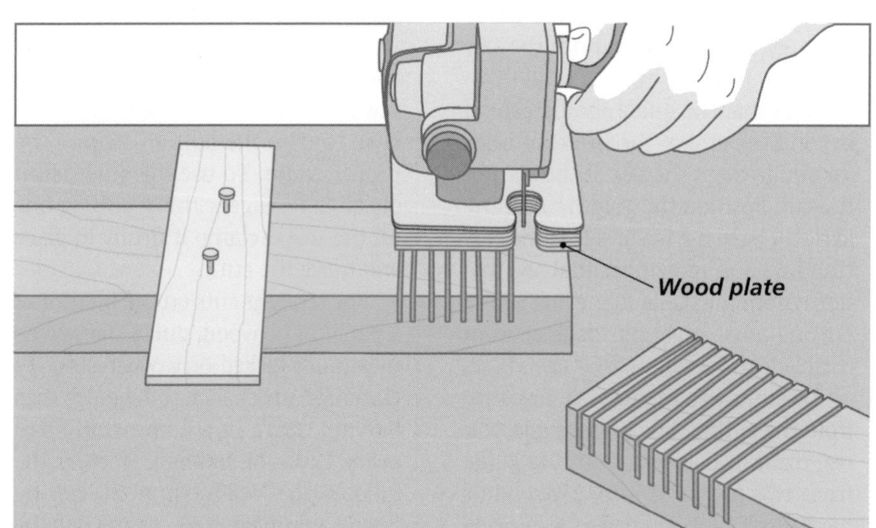

► **CUTTING END HALF LAPS, 1.** ***Cut end half-lap joints using a short blade. A wood plate under the saw's base controls the depth of cut. A nailed strip guides the first cut.***

◄ **CUTTING END HALF LAPS, 2.** ***Using a wood chisel, carefully break out the waste and scrape the joint smooth. When assembled, the half-lap pieces form a clean, strong joint.***

▼ **CUTTING SHEET METAL.** ***To obtain chatter-free cuts in sheet metal, place the work between two sheets of ¼-in. plywood or pieces of cardboard and support it on lengths of 2 x 4.***

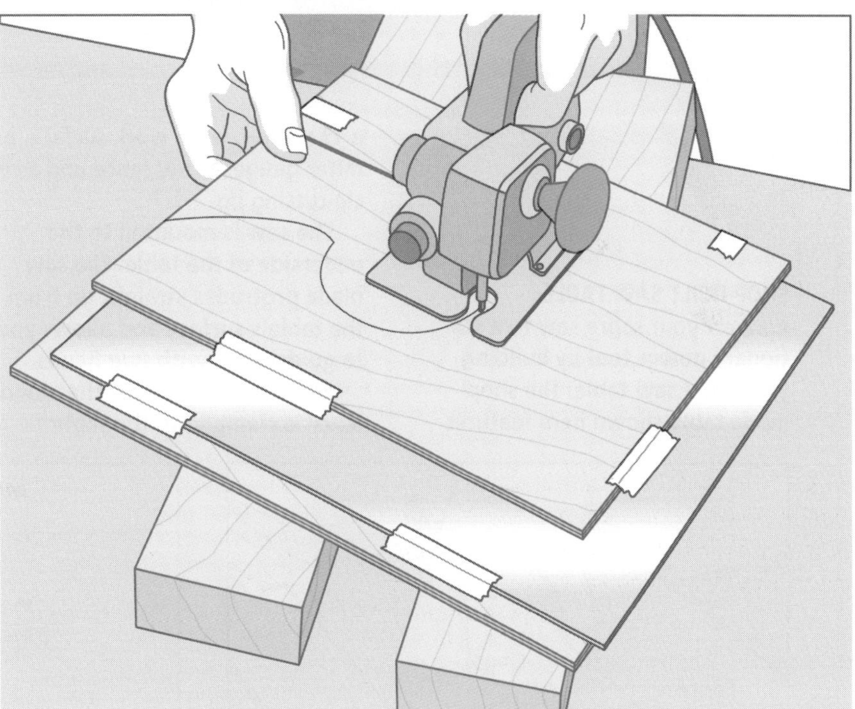

Use a chisel to break out the waste and scrape the joint smooth. When the two pieces are assembled, the end half-lap joint formed is clean and strong.

CUTTING CIRCLES

Cutting circles in stock is another job that makes owning a sabre saw a must. The rip guide that comes with many saws features a drilled pivot hole so that the guide can be tack-nailed in place and used to cut circles. For circles that exceed the capacity of commercial guides, you can easily make your own guide out of ½-in. plywood. Here are a few points that you should know about in order to be able to cut perfect circles.

First, although your initial inclination might be to work with a fine-tooth blade, the best blade to use for cutting circles is a rough-cutting type with a heavy tooth set. The reason is that this kind of blade will cut sufficient clearance for making the turn around the circumference of the circle accurately. By cutting a little to the waste side of your circle's circumference, you'll have enough stock left to sand edges smooth.

Second, you should perform the cut with the maximum number of blade strokes per inch. To achieve this, set the saw to a fast speed and work with a slow feed rate. If the cutout opening must be perfect, bore an entry hole for the blade just inside the circumference of the circle. For a cutout disc, make the entry hole along the outside of the cutout's circumference.

Finally, to cut a circle of the correct size, the distance from the blade of the saw to the pivot point of the guide must be equal to the circle's radius. Adjust the guide so that the pivot point lines up precisely with the *front* edge of the blade. Make sure that your work is adequately supported and stop the saw periodically during the cut to shift the piece; the blade should cut only the work, not what's supporting it.

DUPLICATE CUTTING

The design of the sabre saw makes it one of the most adaptive, versatile cutting tools you can have in the workshop. One task in which the saw excels is in the production of duplicate pieces.

A simple option for repeated curved cuts is to use the first piece you cut as

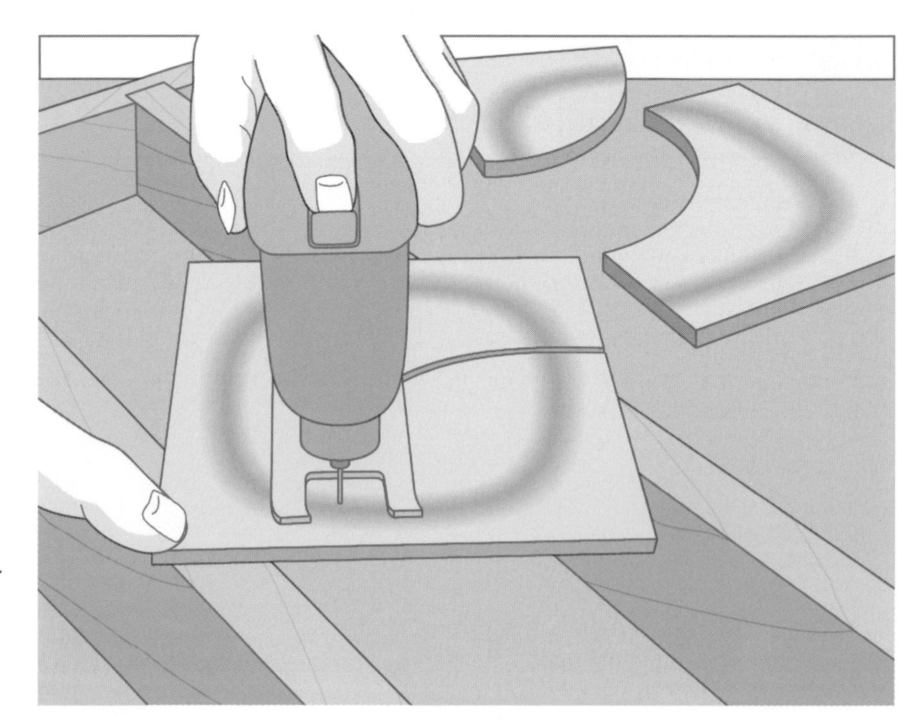

► **CUTTING CERAMIC TILES.** ***A tungsten-carbide grit blade will cut ceramic tile, slate and other very hard, abrasive materials. Apply slow, steady pressure on the saw.***

TIP

SHOP-BUILT SAW TABLE

Convert your sabre saw to a stationary power tool by building yourself a saw table. The shop-made table shown here features a 17 x 18-in.-wide work surface, a miter gauge, a saw fence and a circle-cutting jig.

The saw is mounted to the underside of the table. The saw blade protrudes straight up from the table's surface and allows you to guide work with two hands.

For accurate rip cuts, the wood fence is clamped to the table *(below, left)*. Angled as well as square crosscuts are executed with the miter gauge. The gauge slides in a 5/16-in.-deep x 3/4-in.-wide slot that's routed in the 1-in.-thick tabletop *(below, right)*.

The tabletop is formed by two layers of 1/2-in. plywood. The top layer is made of three pieces of plywood. This is necessary to form the

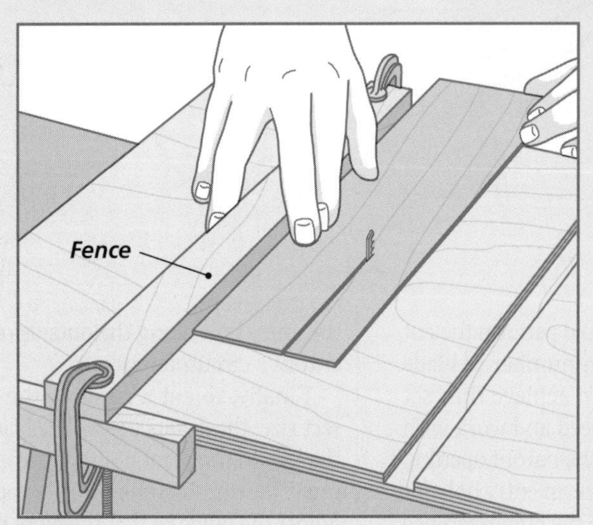

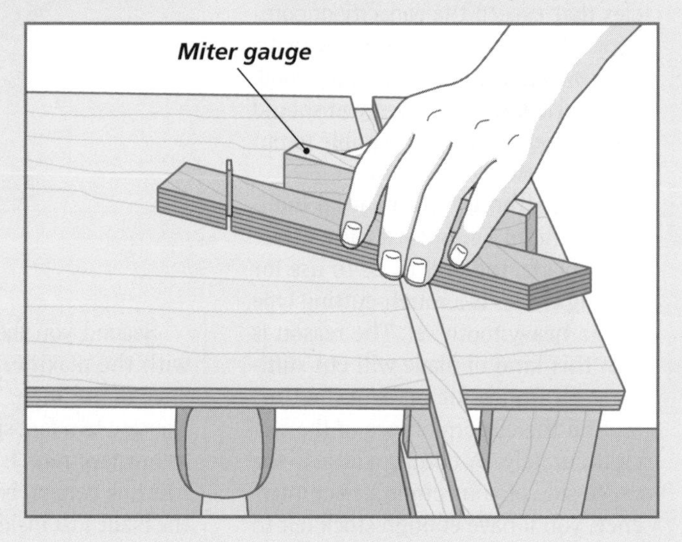

an edge guide for the other pieces. Cut the piece to be used as the guide a little longer than the others to help in aligning the saw at the beginning of your cuts. Carefully sand the edge of the guide; you'll want the base of the saw to run along it smoothly.

Set your next piece on a work surface and mark the start of the cut on its leading edge. Align the blade of the saw with the mark and butt the guide against the edge of the saw's base. After measuring the distance between the back edges of the pieces at both ends to make sure they're parallel, clamp the guide in position.

Place a small piece of masking tape on the base in line with the blade to help in keeping the saw on its cutting path. Feed the blade into the stock and proceed with the cut, keeping the portion of the saw's base with the tape flush against the guide.

Stack sawing is also an effective way of cutting duplicate pieces—provided that the stock is not too thick. Cutting multiple pieces in a single operation is both efficient and ensures that they are all exactly the same.

Using nails or clamps to hold the pieces together in preparation for cutting can be hazardous should the blade accidentally come into contact with one of them. A safer approach is to use double-sided tape to keep the pieces held together. Make sure that the ends and edges of the pieces align properly.

The limit to which you can stack saw is set by the length of the blade you can use. The blade must be longer than the combined thicknesses of the pieces you're cutting; don't attempt this technique with a blade that is too short. Proceed slowly with your cut.

CUTTING METAL

Metal cutting is done at a slower blade speed than wood cutting. When sawing thin metal, it's important that at least two teeth of the blade make contact with the edge of the work. Otherwise, the cut will be extremely rough and the teeth of the blade may be sheared off. Check the package the blade came in for instructions on the type and size of metal that it's designed to cut.

To obtain clean, chatter-free cuts in sheet metal, place the work between pieces of cardboard or ¼-in. plywood. Support the work securely on lengths of 2 x 4 and apply slow, steady pressure with the saw.

dovetail-shaped pivot-bar groove. The ½ x 1¾ x 16-in. pivot bar houses a ½-in.-long pivot point that is cut from a finishing nail and ground to a sharp point. Eight 5/16-in.-deep holes are bored in the pivot bar to house the pivot point. To cut perfect circles *(right)*, the pivot point must align exactly with the front edge of the blade's teeth.

The pivot bar slides in the groove and is held in place by a wooden handle, called a pivot-bar lock cam, that's located under the bar. The lock cam is bolted off-center to create a cam-action lever. Therefore, as the handle is turned it wedges against the bar for a secure hold.

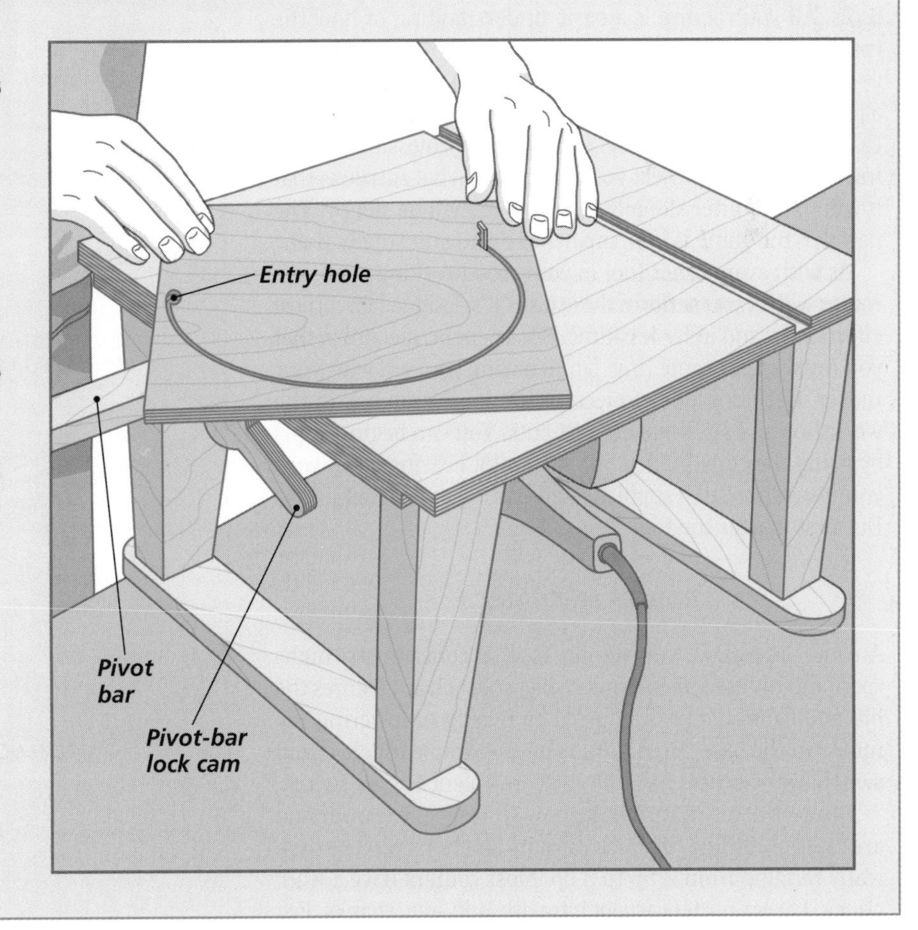

ROUTERS

Of all the portable power tools found in a typical woodworking shop, the router is arguably the most versatile. When fitted with any one of the hundred of bits available, the router's capabilities are almost endless. Some of the more common uses include cutting cabinet joints such as the dado, rabbet and mortise-and-tenon; trimming plastic laminate; shaping decorative edges; milling moldings; and carving signs and plaques.

A wide range of different router accessories and attachments are available for special jobs such as turning table legs, cutting machine threads in wood, routing precise dovetails, cutting frame-and-panel doors, and forming letters and numbers. The router can also be mounted upside down in a worktable for use as a small shaper.

Since a router can perform so many different tasks, it's often considered a sophisticated tool by the uninitiated, and as a consequence, novice woodworkers have traditionally shied away from using it. In truth, however, a router is no more difficult to operate than any other portable power tool. In fact, in some ways it's easier and safer than most power tools. All you require is a basic understanding of how the router works and a little practice.

The router is forever touted as the tool that lets you add a professional touch to your projects. But the statement isn't exactly the truth. Actually, *you* put the professional-looking touch on any project you undertake. What *is* true is that if you use a router sloppily your project will be sloppy. The name of the game is craftsmanship—and *you* supply that.

As with every other tool in your woodworking shop, the router will let you perform those tasks it's designed for almost effortlessly, and in far less time. For openers, recognize that you must spend some time familiarizing yourself with your router. Get out a pile of pieces from your scrap box in the workshop and start making test cuts. You can begin simply by using the edge-guided bits with pilot bearings and work your way up to such sophisticated cutting as dovetail joints. But first master the tool.

ROUTER MECHANICS

A router is really a very simple tool. It consists of a high-speed motor fitted into a base. A split-collet chuck secures the bit, and depth of cut is adjusted by raising or lowering the motor in the base. Most routers have a simple toggle on/off switch, while others have a more convenient trigger switch.

Routers come in various sizes with respect to power and are rated according to chuck capacity and horsepower—typically ranging from ½ hp to 3 hp. Most routers have a ¼-in. chuck. Larger routers accept bits with ½-in.-dia. shanks. For

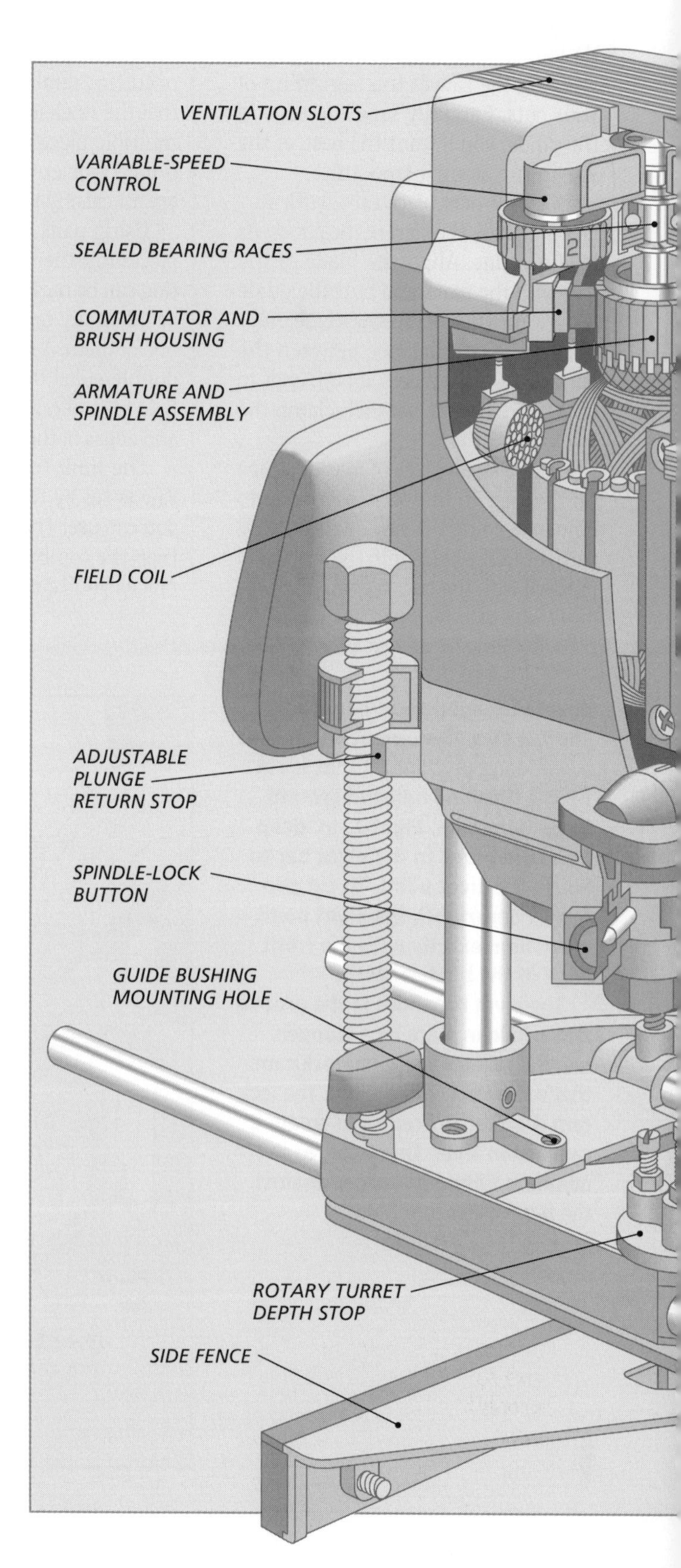

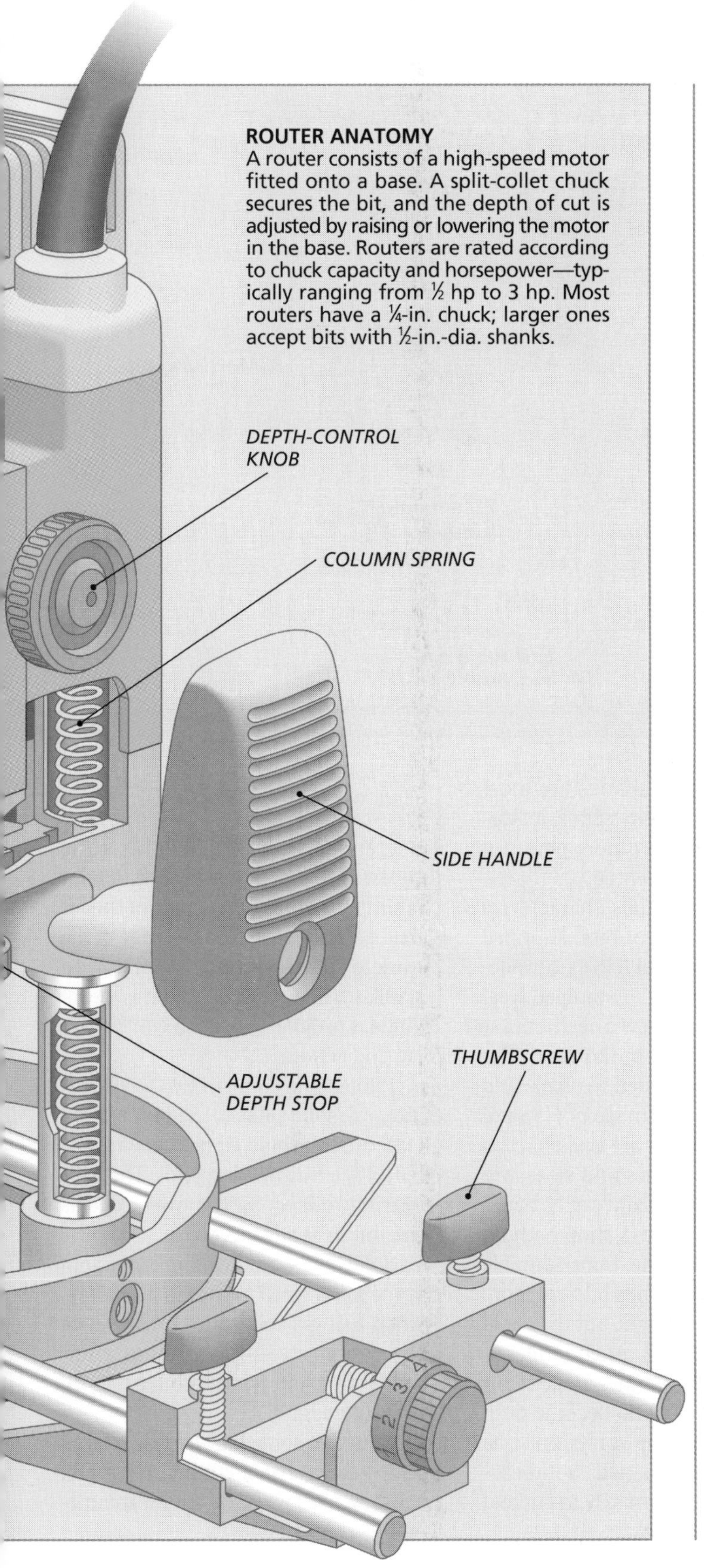

ROUTER ANATOMY
A router consists of a high-speed motor fitted onto a base. A split-collet chuck secures the bit, and the depth of cut is adjusted by raising or lowering the motor in the base. Routers are rated according to chuck capacity and horsepower—typically ranging from ½ hp to 3 hp. Most routers have a ¼-in. chuck; larger ones accept bits with ½-in.-dia. shanks.

general woodworking, a 1-hp router with a ¼-in. chuck is adequate. However, if you're using a router primarily as a shaper in a router table, then consider going for a 3-hp router with a ½-in. chuck.

A high-speed tool that operates from 20,000 rpm to 28,000 rpm, the router performs similarly to the stationary shaper, except that it is taken to the workpiece instead of the other way around. The reason for the high speed is that many shaped edges will not allow for hand sanding; they must be smooth enough to finish as soon as they are made. Therefore, if you have a router with a speed of 25,000 rpm, you'll get an impressive 50,000 blade passes per minute when you work with a two-flute bit.

Most routers come equipped with a universal motor that operates on a single-phase, 25- to 60-cycle, AC or DC circuit of the same voltage as shown on the tool's nameplate. Operate your router only at the voltage shown on the nameplate or the motor will burn out.

Nowadays, virtually all power tools are double-insulated so you don't need the old three-prong, grounding-type plug. But if your router does have a three-wire cord, be sure to use the proper adapter so that the tool is safely grounded.

Take the time to thoroughly read the manufacturer's manual that comes with your router. Quality toolmakers have the user's interest at heart; they want you to master the tool so that you can get the most out of it. If you're satisfied, the chances are your next power-tool purchase will be the same brand. In addition to operating instructions, the manual will also provide a maintenance rundown. It is in your best interest to care for the tool as suggested.

GETTING STARTED

Since the work end of the router—the bit—is always out there in space ready to do its job, even on your fingers, make it your habit from the start to keep the tool disconnected from a power source until it is ready to be used. When changing a bit, *always* unplug the tool and—in most cases—remove the base. Some routers come with two wrenches. One is used to hold the motor's shaft to keep it from turning and the other wrench loosens or tightens the chuck. Other routers have a convenient shaft-lock button. When depressed, the button keeps the shaft from turning so that only one wrench is needed to remove a bit.

Insert the desired bit into the collet until it bottoms, then back it out ¹⁄₁₆ to ⅛ in. This procedure is to protect the collet from breaking due to heat expansion. Finger-tighten the collet nuts until they're snug against the shank of the bit, then reach for the wrenches to finish up the tightening.

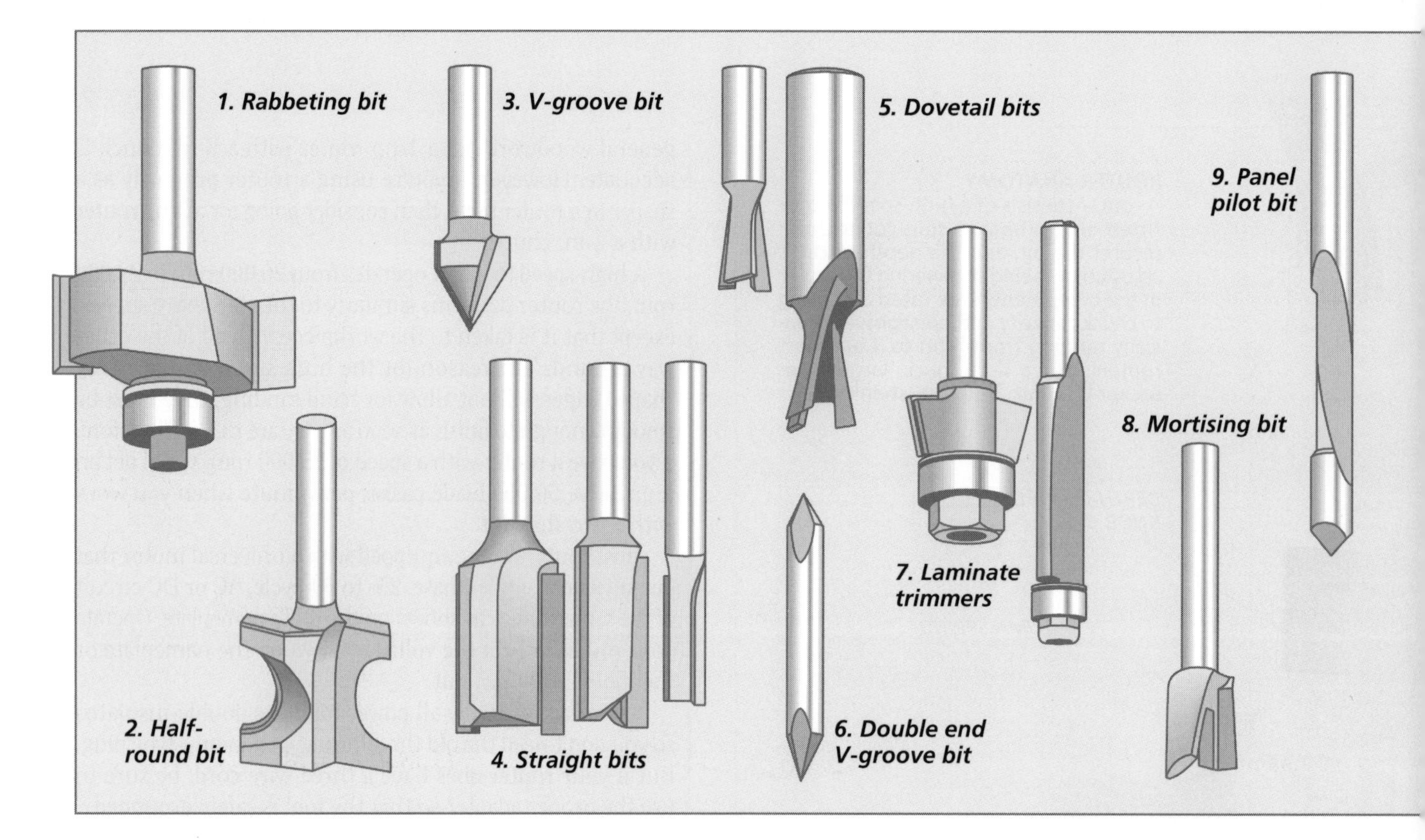

Make absolutely certain that the collet is fully tightened before supplying power to the router. Failure to correctly install a bit and tighten the collet could result in the bit hurtling off like a piece of shrapnel.

BIT SPECIFICS

There's no question that the router is a super-versatile, indispensable power tool and is standard equipment in most woodworking shops. However, without a bit, a router is pretty much like a Porsche without an engine—perhaps nice to have, but not of much useful value.

To help you get the most from your router, the following is an overview of the various bits that make the router such a versatile, must-own power tool. Router bits come in hundreds of sizes and styles for shaping, trimming and carving wood and plastics. Since the vast majority of do-it-yourselfers own a router with a ¼-in.-capacity chuck, bits with ¼-in.-dia. shanks are most common. However, bits with ½-in.-dia. shanks that fit larger, more powerful routers are also presented.

Four basic materials characterize the manufacturing of bits: stamped steel, high-speed steel (HSS), carbide-tipped or solid carbide. Stamped steel bits are relatively new and the least expensive. Made from flat steel, the bits are stamped, rolled to shape and then hardened. Bits made of HSS are popular because they are available in a wide variety of shapes and sizes, are relatively inexpensive and can be hand-sharpened right in the shop with an aluminum-oxide stone. Super-durable tungsten-carbide-tipped bits are more expensive than HSS bits, but they hold a sharp cutting edge much longer—some claim up to 20 times longer than HSS bits. Once they do become dull, however, carbide-tipped bits must be professionally sharpened. Solid carbide bits are used primarily to cut and trim plastic laminates.

BIT STYLES

Router bits are available in two basic styles: with a pilot or without. A pilot is simply a non-cutting part of the bit that rides along against the edge of the work to control the cut. When using a standard, non-piloted bit, some sort of guide is ordinarily used to control the cutting action.

Piloted bits come in two forms. An integral, solid pilot is used on piloted HSS bits. Carbide-tipped bits are fitted with a ball-bearing pilot. The ball-bearing rolls along the work edge as the router is advanced.

Solid pilots, on the other hand, spin at the same speed as the bit. Therefore, when using a solid-pilot bit, advance the router steadily—without stopping—to avoid friction burns along the work edge.

Note that some bits are designed as scaled-down shaper cutters. These bits must be used with the router mounted in a router table.

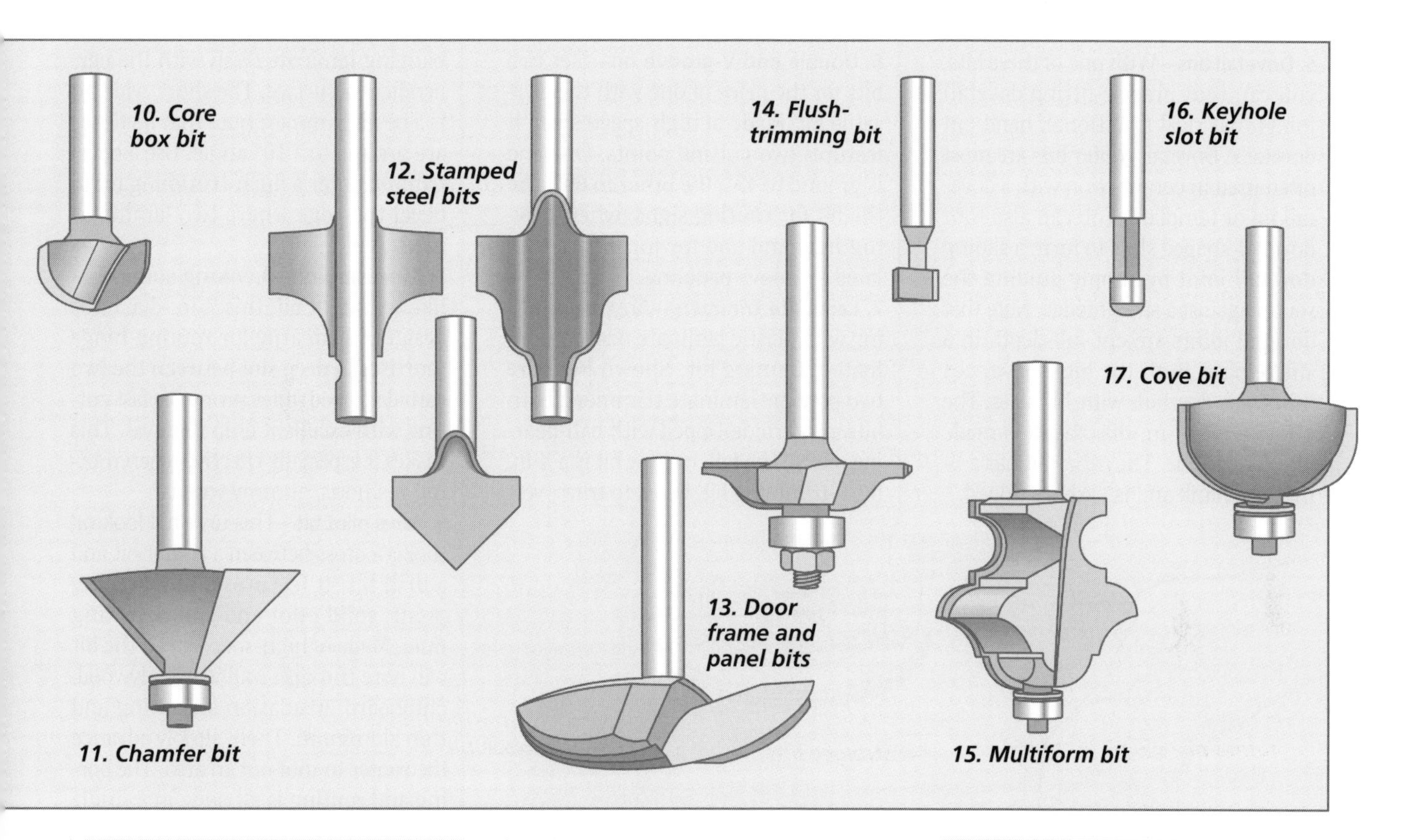

INVENTORY OF BITS

Here's a rundown on some of the specific bits commonly available for use in a router.

1. Rabbeting bit—As its name implies, this bit is designed to rout rabbets for rabbet joints. If you build boxes, bookcases, drawers or any kind of cabinet, you should have a rabbeting bit. Rout a rabbet gradually in several passes. Lower the bit slightly after each pass. The ¼-in., carbide-tipped bit shown cuts a ⅜-in.-wide rabbet. A ball-bearing pilot controls the width of the cut.

2. Half-round bit—This bit allows you to rout a half-round shape in the edge of a board in a single pass. The carbide-tipped bit has two flutes that cut a ½-in.-dia. bullnose. Use it to shape the edges of drawer sides and tabletops, and form decorative half-round molding. Rout stock thicker than ½ in. to create a half-round with bead detail. Since the bit features no pilot, use a straightedge to guide the router.

3. V-groove bit—Milled entirely from solid carbide, this bit cuts V-shaped grooves in wood and plastics. The ½-in.-wide cutting head is ground to a 90° angle. Use the bit to create decorative accents on furniture and millwork; it's also excellent for routing signs. The bit is also offered in ¼-, ⅜-, ⅝- and ¾-in. dia.

4. Straight bits—Nearly every router-bit collection starts with a few straight bits. Shown are the three most valuable sizes: ¾-, ½- and ¼-in. dia. These simple bits are used for cutting dadoes, grooves and rabbets, and for certain edge-jointing operations. Each bit has two carbide-tipped flutes for smooth, fast cutting.

▶ **ARBOR SHANK BIT KIT.** ***An economical way to start or add to a router bit collection, this set includes five carbide-tipped cutters, along with a ¼-in. ball-bearing piloted arbor that comes with a washer, two bearings and a locknut.***

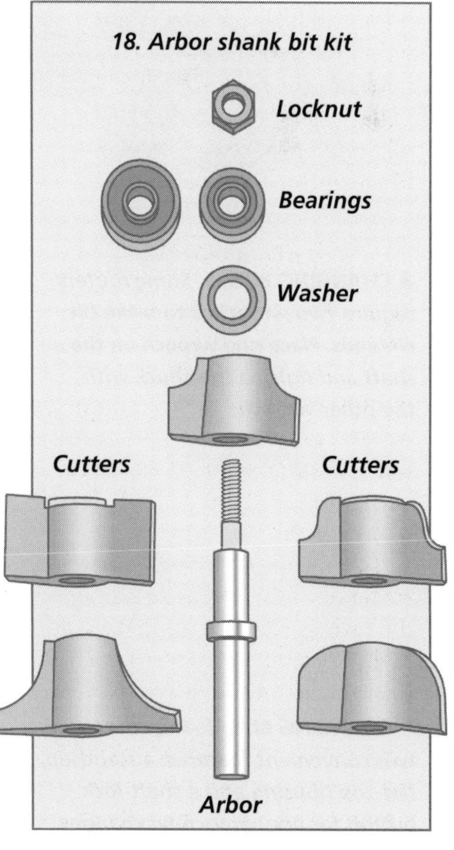

5. Dovetail bits—With one of these bits, you can rout precise-fitting dovetail joints that rival traditional, hand-cut dovetails. Dovetail router bits are most often used in conjunction with a dovetail jig or template. You can also rout dovetail-shaped slots to form a sliding dovetail joint by simply guiding the router against a straightedge. Note that dovetail joints are cut full-depth in a single pass. Both the bits shown cut ½-in.-wide dovetails with 14° sides. The bit with the ¼-in.-dia. shank is made of solid carbide. The other bit has a ½-in.-dia. shank and is carbide-tipped.

6. Double end V-groove bit—Get two bits for the price of one with this versatile bit. Made of high-speed steel, it features two cutting points. One end is ground to 45°; the other to 60°. Use the bit for routing signs, when carving freehand and for forming simulated V-groove paneling.

7. Laminate trimmers—Anyone working with plastic laminate needs a laminate-trimming bit. Shown here are two popular laminate trimmers; both bits are carbide-tipped with ball-bearing pilots. The tall, narrow bit is a ⅜-in. flush-trimming bit. Use it to trim overhanging laminate flush with the perpendicular surface. The short, wide bit is a bevel trimmer; note that its flutes are ground to a 10° angle. Use a bevel trimmer after a flush-trimming bit to bevel the edge where two laminates meet at 90°.

8. Mortising bit—Looking somewhat like a straight bit, this ½-in.-dia. bit is designed primarily for routing hinge mortises. A deep slot between the two carbide-tipped flutes promotes fast cutting with excellent chip removal. This makes it especially effective when routing resinous, gummy woods.

9. Panel pilot bit—This unusual looking tool is a cross between a router bit and a drill bit. It features a self-drilling point, solid pilot and spiral cutting flute. Made of high-speed steel, the bit will bore through wallboard, plywood, chipboard, insulation sheathing and thin aluminum. Then, simply advance the router to rout out an area. The boring and routing is all done in a single operation. Use the bit to cut door, window and vent openings.

10. Core box bit—This round-nose bit is used most to rout flutes in columns, doors and period moldings. It can also be used to carve signs. To convert it to a cove bit, attach an edge guide to the router's base so that only half of

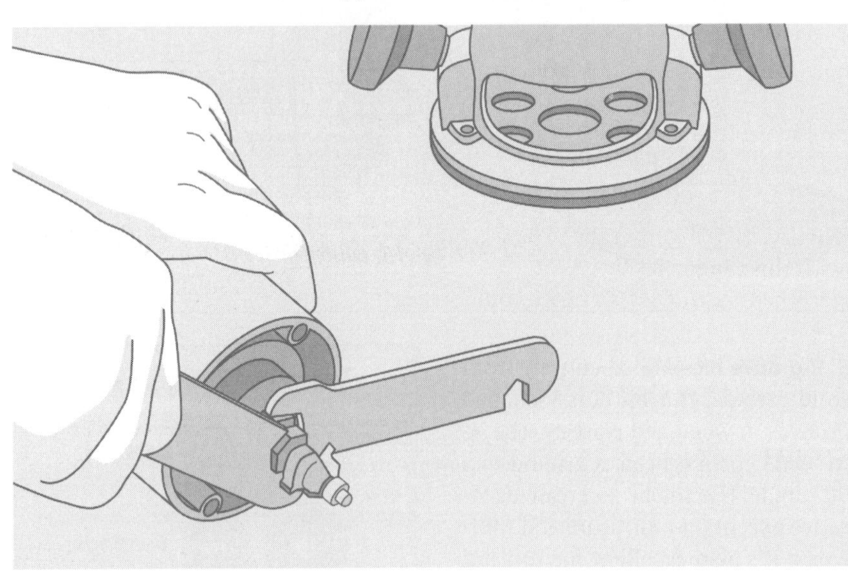

▲ **CHANGING BITS, 1.** ***Some routers require two wrenches to make bit changes. Place one wrench on the shaft and tighten the chuck with the other wrench.***

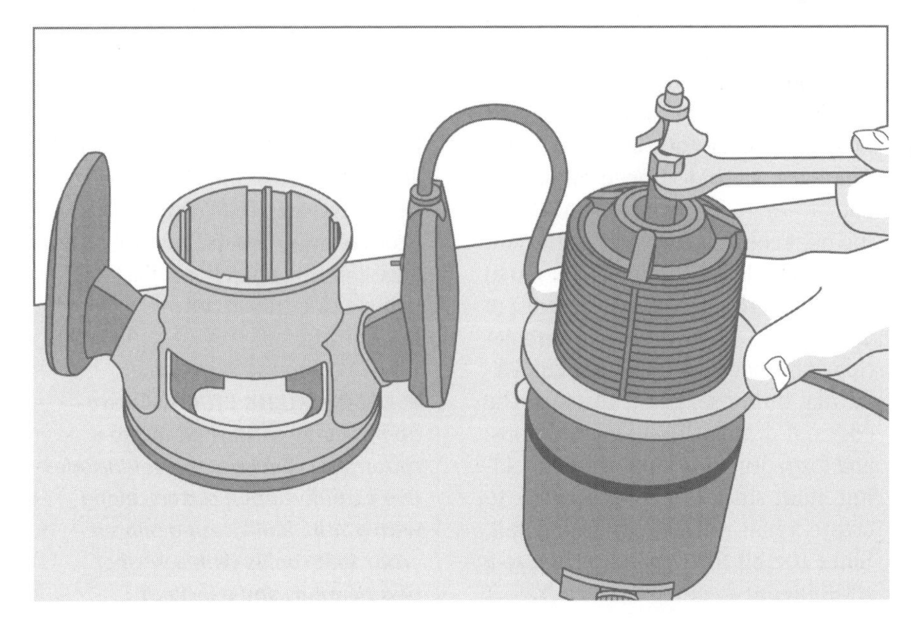

▶ **CHANGING BITS, 2.** ***This router has two convenient features: a stand-up, flat-top housing and a shaft-lock button for one-wrench bit changes.***

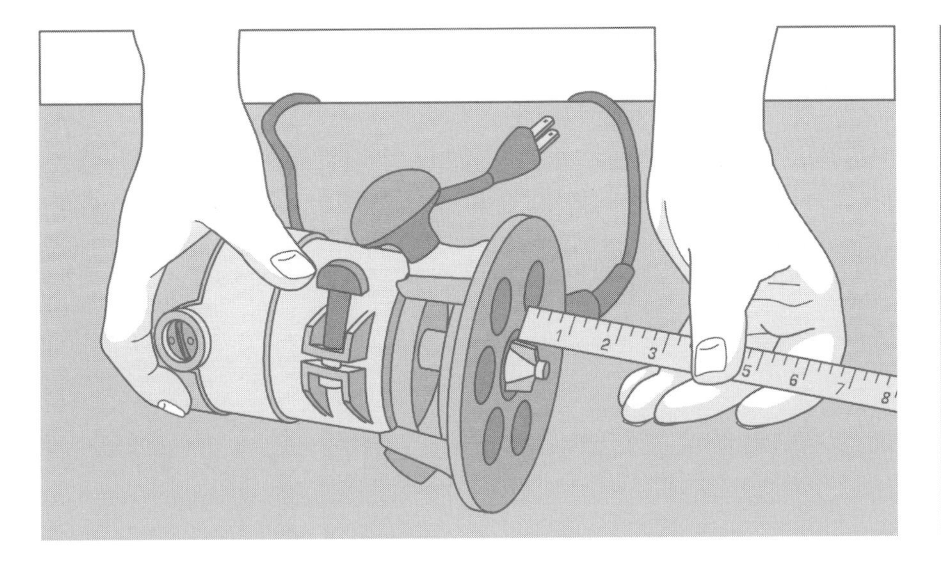

◄ **SETTING DEPTH OF CUT, 1.** ***To establish the cutter depth, you can use the scaled ring supplied on many routers, or simply check the bit with a ruler—as many professionals do.***

▼ **SETTING DEPTH OF CUT, 2.** ***Another easy method is to hold the installed cutter against the marked workpiece. Waste is marked clearly with an X to prevent miscutting.***

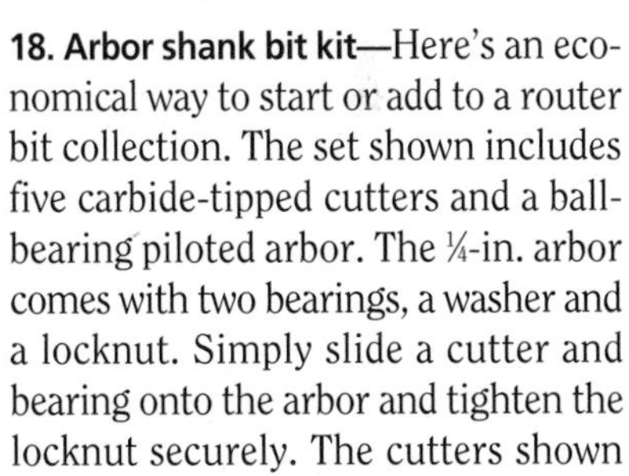

the bit's profile is exposed. The bit has a ¾-in.-wide, carbide-tipped head.

11. Chamfer bit—There are several ways to chamfer an edge, but none is quicker or more accurate than with a router. The chamfer bit shown has two large, carbide-tipped cutting edges that are ground to 45°. A ball-bearing pilot controls the bit. The chamfer size can be adjusted by raising or lowering the bit.

12. Stamped steel bits—These economical bits are available in 23 different sizes and styles, and are available individually or in 5-piece and 15-piece sets. The bits shown are beading, V-groove and Roman ogee. A major reason for the popularity of these bits is their cost: about half as much as conventional HSS bits.

13. Door frame and panel bits—Anyone with a ¼-in. router can now mill traditional frame-and-raised-panel cabinet doors easily. The bits shown are for use only with the router mounted in a router table: a cove-style raised panel cutter and a ball-bearing piloted coping and sticking cutter. Both are carbide-tipped. The coping and sticking cutters come in a pair—the one shown and one identical, but inverted cutter.

14. Flush-trimming bit—Similar to a ball-bearing piloted flush-trimming bit, this solid carbide bit trims plastic laminates flush. The bit features a solid pilot and a ⅜-in.-long cutting edge. The style of this bit allows for cuts in tighter spots than with a ball-bearing piloted bit.

15. Multiform bit—Turn your router into a production molding machine with this unique bit that's designed to produce standard moldings. In fact, with this one bit you can make 39 different moldings. Twelve of the moldings are made in a single pass. The remaining 27 molding shapes are formed with two passes over the bit. Custom-shaped moldings can also be cut. The bit features a ½-in.-dia. shank and measures 4¼ in. long. A bit for serious woodworkers, it is for use only in a router table.

16. Keyhole slot bit—Use this unique HSS bit for cutting keyhole slots in the back of picture and mirror frames, small cabinets, and other wall-hung items. Lower the bit into the work to bore a ⅜-in.-dia. entry hole and then advance the router to mill a recessed slot. The finished keyhole that results will slide over and lock onto the head of a screw or nail.

17. Cove bit—For shaping decorative edges and milling moldings, the cove bit is a standard, must-own bit. This type of bit comes in a wide variety of sizes and styles. The HSS bit shown has a solid pilot and two flutes that cut a ½-in.-rad. cove.

18. Arbor shank bit kit—Here's an economical way to start or add to a router bit collection. The set shown includes five carbide-tipped cutters and a ball-bearing piloted arbor. The ¼-in. arbor comes with two bearings, a washer and a locknut. Simply slide a cutter and bearing onto the arbor and tighten the locknut securely. The cutters shown are: ¼- and ½-in. rounding-over, cove, Roman ogee and rabbeting.

CARING FOR BITS

To obtain the best performance and longest life from your router bits, keep them sharp and clean. Hand-sharpen your high-speed bits using an aluminum-oxide sharpening stone. Send out your carbide-tipped bits to a professional sharpening service.

To ensure smooth operation, clean bits frequently of all wood resin and pitch, contact cement and caked-on wood dust. This is especially important with ball-bearing piloted bits. Soak dirty bits overnight in turpentine or kerosene. To remove contact cement, try lacquer thinner. Then, wipe the bits clean with a soft cloth and spray on a light coat of oil to deter rust.

To prevent damage to the cutting edges, store your router bits carefully—as you would a fine saw blade. An effective storage rack is a simple board with ¼-in.-dia. holes bored in it. Place a bit shank-first in each hole and store them in a dry, dust-free location.

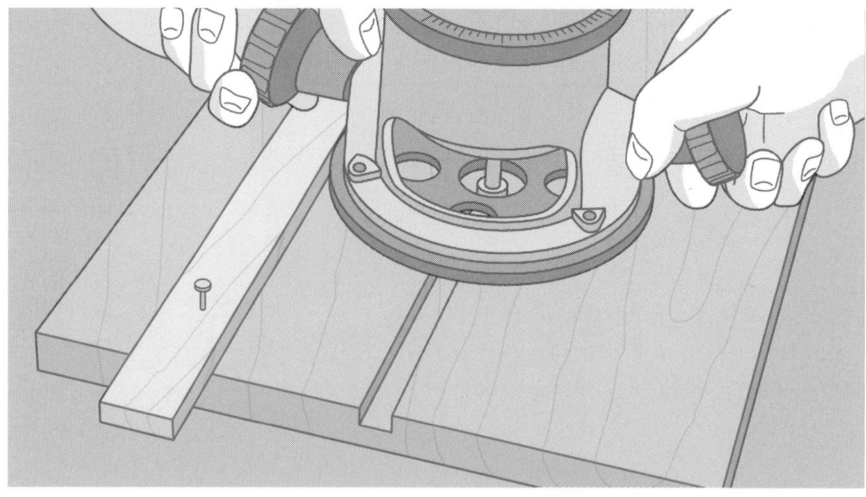

▲ **MAKING GUIDED CUTS, 1.** ***Guide the router against a straightedged board that's nailed or clamped in place to the workpiece. Allow the guide to overhang the work to support the router at the start.***

SETTING CUTTING DEPTH

The procedure for setting depth of cut can vary somewhat from one type of router to another. Therefore, you'll need to refer to the manufacturer's manual that came with your router for specific instructions.

On many routers, there's a depth-adjustment ring for setting the cutting depth of an installed bit. To set your depth of cut using the ring, place the router on a flat surface and loosen the motor unit, then slide it down until the bit barely touches the surface and retighten it. By rotating the ring until it hits the base unit, the bit is set for a depth of cut of 0 in.

Noting the position of graduations on the depth-adjustment ring in relation to the index on the base unit—usually a point or an arrow—rotate the ring to achieve the desired depth of cut. Finally, loosen the motor unit and slide it as far into the base unit as the ring permits, then retighten it.

▼ **MAKING GUIDED CUTS, 2.** ***Here, a guide bushing protrudes from the base of the router and rides against a template made of ¼-in. plywood. The bit extends below the bushing to shape the workpiece.***

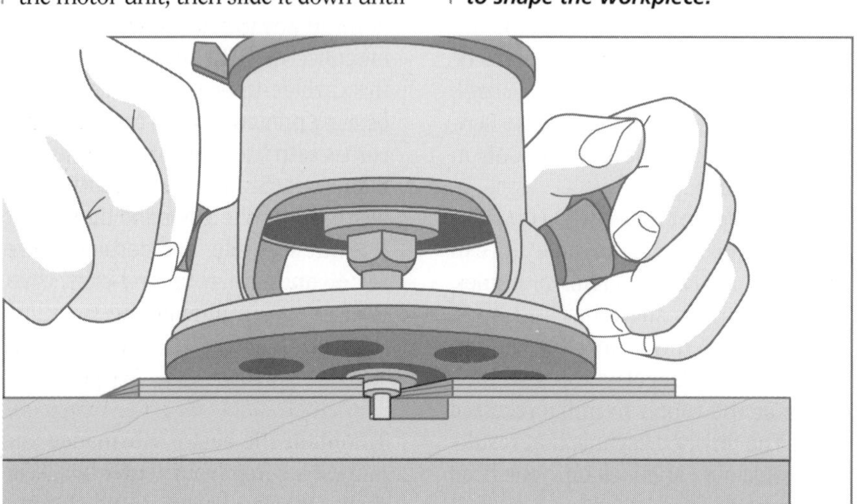

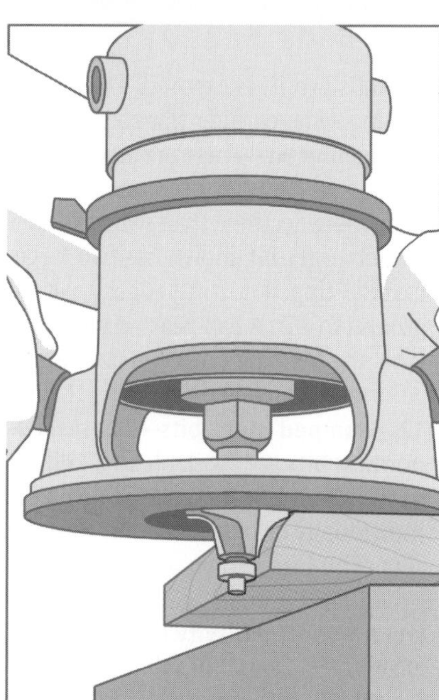

▲ **MAKING GUIDED CUTS, 3.** ***For precise control when edge shaping, use a ball-bearing piloted bit. The bearing rolls along the uncut portion of the edge to guide the cutter.***

An alternative way of setting depth of cut that is used by many professional woodworkers is to simply check the bit with a ruler. Another easy method is to hold the installed bit up against a marked workpiece and then make the necessary adjustments.

One trick to setting depth of cut makes use of the fact that certain cut-

► **MAKING GUIDED CUTS, 4.** *In this example, an edge guide accessory that's mounted on two steel rods is clamped to the base of the router. The guide rides against the edge of the work to control the cutter.*

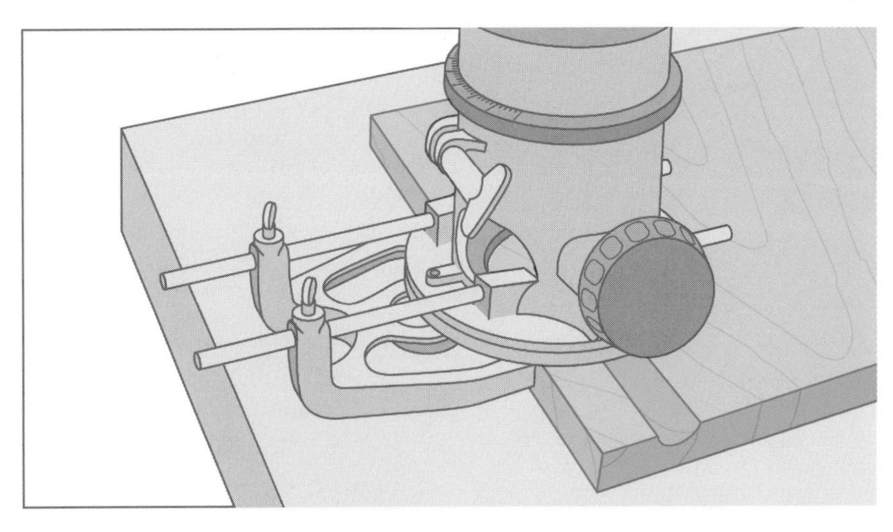

▼ **MAKING GUIDED CUTS, 5.** *With the assistance of the edge guide, it's even possible for you to rout a circle. Note that to prevent movement of the work, the workpiece is clamped from the bottom to the workbench.*

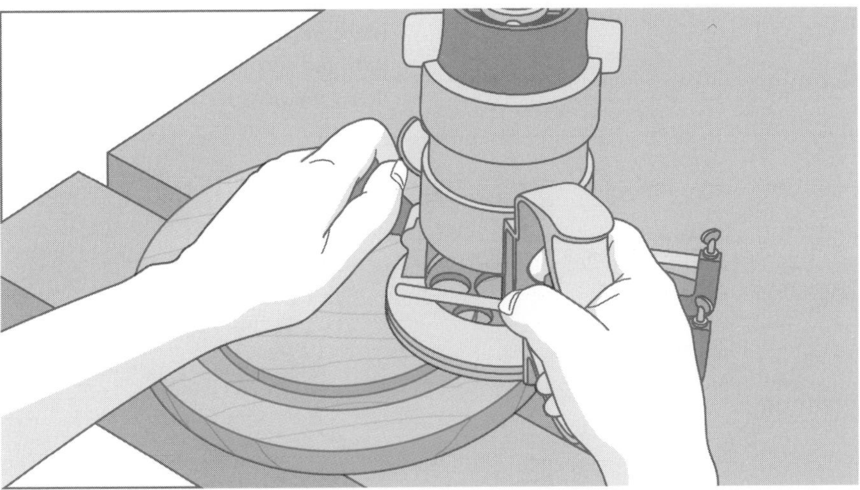

ters are used more often than others in the type of woodworking practiced by most do-it-yourselfers. These include the rabbet, straight and mortise bits. Make yourself a board with cuts plowed by these bits to depths of exactly ¼ and ⅜ in.—the usual depths for work with ¾-in.-thick boards. Then, every time you need to set a ⅜-in. rabbet bit ⅜ in. deep, for example, there's no fiddling with rulers. You can simply and quickly set the bit using your precut board.

PROBLEM PREVENTION

There are five basic ways to guide a router: (1) with a piloted bit; (2) with an edge guide; (3) freehand; (4) against an edge; and (5) with a template or jig. The methods are listed from easiest to most difficult—the order in which a beginner should tackle them.

For any operation you undertake with a router—as with all other power tools—you should always wear eye protection. Having the right bit for the job installed correctly and your work set up properly are your best assurances of achieving the routing results you want. Of the few problems that can occur when routing, most are easily avoided.

Trying to rout with a dull bit is a sure way to burn the work, and also puts undue strain on the motor. And remember that a high-speed steel bit dulls much more quickly than a carbide-tipped bit—especially when routing hardwood and particleboard. For clean, smooth cuts, use only sharp bits.

When you're using a solid-pilot bit, advance the router slowly to prevent friction burns that result from an overheated pilot. Ball-bearing pilots will very seldom burn an edge. However, be aware that they can burn the work if the bearing freezes up. Clean the bearing frequently with thinner and keep it lubricated. This is especially important when trimming plastic laminate. Contact cement and laminate shavings tend to clog and stall a bearing quite easily.

Splintering can sometimes occur when a bit exits the work edge at the end of a cut or when routing plywood. To prevent tearing the edge of a workpiece, clamp a scrap board to it. This way, any splintering will occur on the scrap board, not the workpiece.

When plywood is routed across the grain, the veneer often splinters. To avoid this, scribe both sides of the line of cut with a utility knife before beginning to rout. This allows the veneer to break off cleanly along the knife cuts without splintering.

Counterbored screwholes, missing knots and other voids in your work must be filled before routing with a piloted bit. Remember, the pilot rides along the edge. Should the pilot fall into a hole, the bit will gouge the work.

Also remember the importance of feed direction—the direction in which the router is moved around a work-

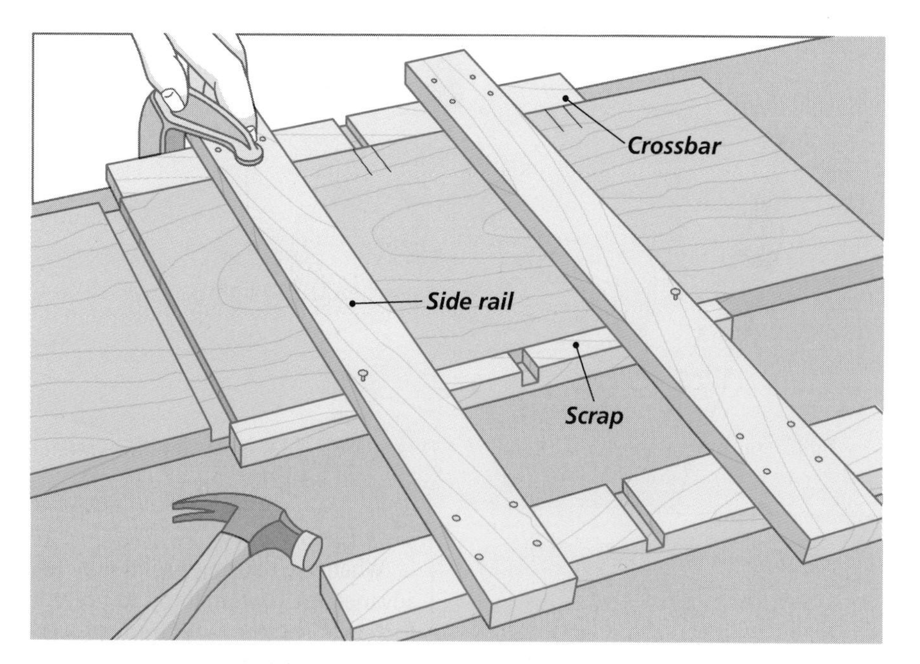

◀ **CUTTING DADOES, 1.** ***This easy-to-make jig saves setup time and ensures accurate dadoes. Mark two lines on the workpiece to show the outside edges of the dado, then align one edge of the ½-in. channel in the crossbar with one of the lines. Tack a scrap strip to the jig on the opposite side of the workpiece.***

▼ **CUTTING DADOES, 2.** ***Clamp or tack the jig and workpiece securely to the bench and make the first pass, guiding the router between the side rails. The scrap strip tacked in place prevents splintering as the bit exits the work. Reposition the jig so it's aligned with the second line of the dado to make the next pass.***

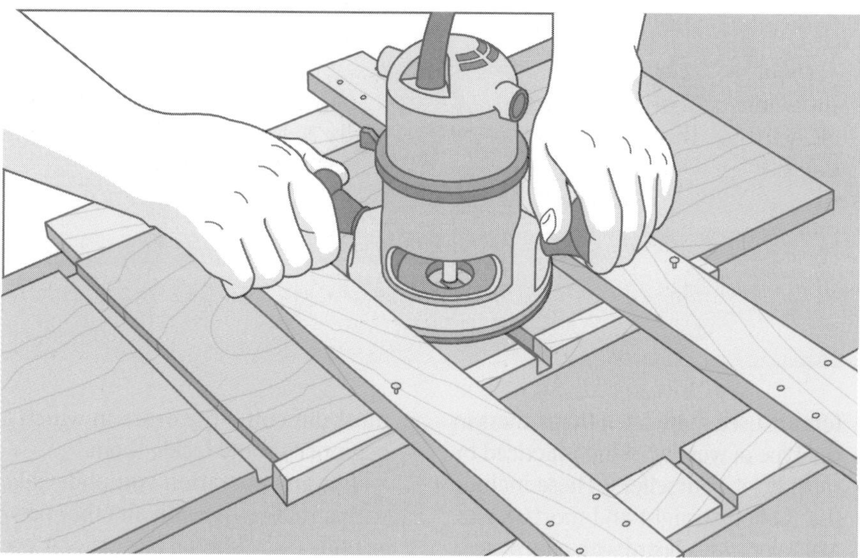

piece. The general rule is to always rout *against* the rotation of the bit, or from left to right when facing the edge of the work. Since the bit rotates clockwise, you should therefore move the router counterclockwise along an outside edge; clockwise along an inside edge. By feeding this way, the bit spins into the work and pulls the tool up against the edge. This technique is safe and effective, but it does cause splintering occasionally.

However, like most rules, there are a few exceptions. In some instances, the router can be fed in the same direction as the rotation of the bit. Routing with the bit's rotation is useful, for example, when trimming veneer, very hard, thin wood or other materials that splinter easily. Caution must be exercised, though, to keep the router from running along the edge.

Always start the router with the cutter standing away from the wood, then feed the spinning bit into the workpiece. For greatest control, position yourself to pull rather than push the router. Apply steady pressure so that the bit is constantly cutting new material. Moving too slowly risks friction burn marks on the work; advancing too quickly can cause tear out.

Proceed patiently with your work, making several small cuts rather than one or two heavy passes. As soon as a cut is completed, release the trigger to turn off power to the router. Do not put the tool down until the cutter has stopped spinning.

GUIDING WITH A PILOTED BIT

A piloted bit provides controlled cuts along the edge of a board. Almost all decorative edging is done with a piloted bit. Because the pilot rolls against the uncut portion of the work edge to control the cutter, it's important for the edge to be in perfect condition. Otherwise, the pilot will enter any void and cause an identical indent in the decorative edging.

▶ **CUTTING ARCS AND CIRCLES.** ***Rout arcs and circles with this simple shop-made jig made out of ¼-in. plywood. Traced from the router's subbase and mounted directly onto the base, the guide pivots on a nail driven through a hole in its arm.***

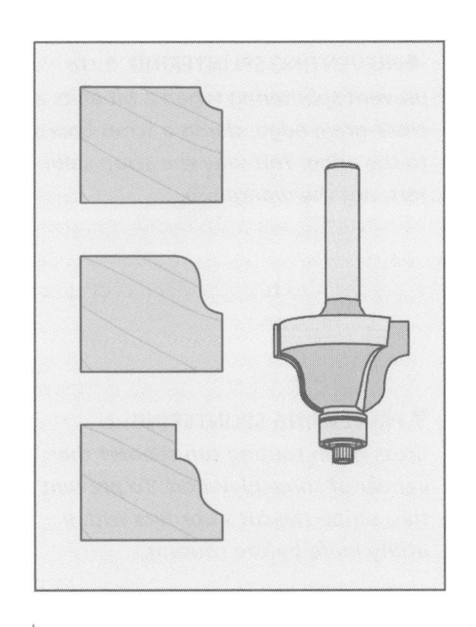

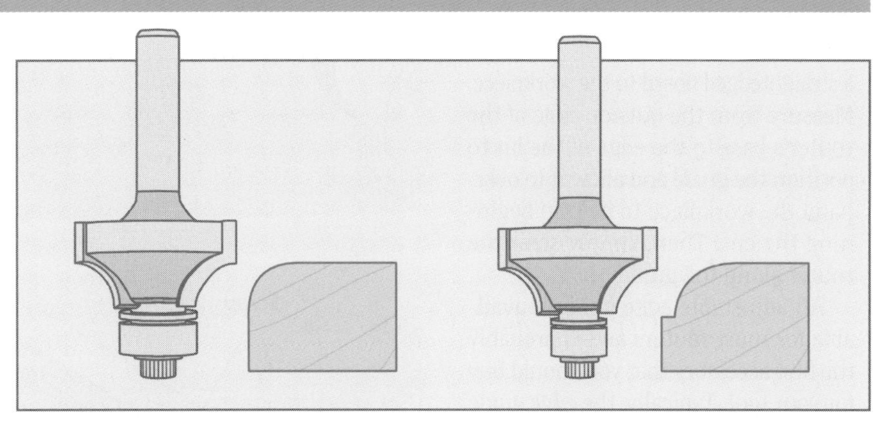

◀ **USING BALL-BEARING PILOTS, 1.** ***These three different profiles were all cut using the same ball-bearing piloted bit. Variations are made by adjusting the depth of cut.***

▲ **USING BALL-BEARING PILOTS, 2.** ***Changing pilots turns a rounding-over bit into two cutters. A larger pilot rounds over as at left; a smaller pilot gives bead cut as at right.***

The router's bit spins in a clockwise direction, so an outside edge is always routed from left to right. Feed the tool in about ¼ in. or so from the left end of the work and move it right for a couple of inches, then bring it all the way to the left and off the work. If you are routing just the one edge, keep the pilot from turning the corner or you will edge-shape the end of the work as well. If necessary, you can tack-nail a straightedge guide to the work in order to prevent this.

To finish the pass along the edge, feed the router into the work at the point you stopped and advance slowly to the right end. Alternatively, you can complete the bulk of the pass from left to right and then come back to finish off the left end. But make no mistake, as simple as this routing task will eventually be for you, in the beginning it takes practice to master.

When routing more than one edge, always rout the edges that are against the grain first. You will learn that as the bit exits end grain on the far end it is not uncommon to have some splintering. If this is your last pass, it means that the finished adjacent edge may be splintered. But by starting with the cuts that are against the grain, you can eliminate any tear out with the cuts along the grain that follow.

Remember that a constant rate of feed is needed to achieve a smooth cut. The point is to work your tool so that the router is operating at its highest possible rpm. This will vary, depending on type of material being worked, depth of cut and sharpness of the bit.

USING AN EDGE GUIDE

A straightedge guide is one of the simplest ways of guiding the router and making perfectly straight cuts. The easiest method is to tack-nail or clamp

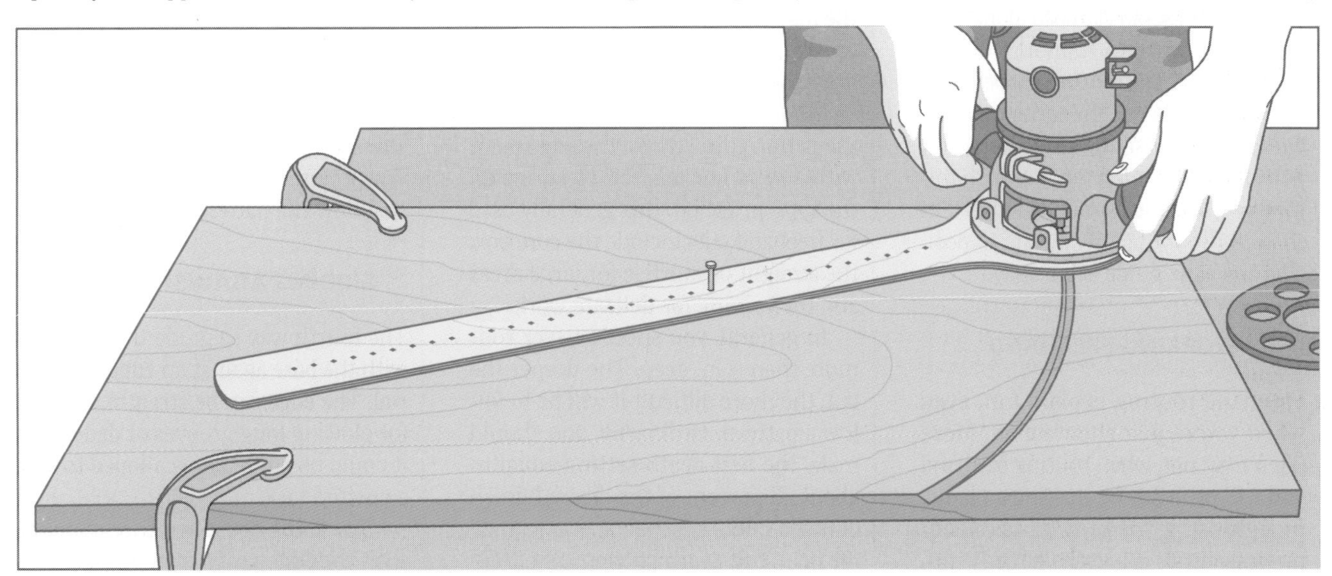

a straightedged board to the workpiece. Measure from the outside edge of the router's base to the edge of the bit to position the guide and allow it to overhang the workpiece to help in beginning the cut. Then, simply steer the router along the guide.

An adjustable edge guide is available for most routers and is probably the first accessory that you should buy for your tool. Typically, the edge guide fits onto two rods that clamp onto the router's base. Take the time to read the manufacturer's instructions for your edge guide to ensure that you install and use it correctly.

Handy for cutting along the edge of boards, the edge guide is used most for routing decorative grooves parallel to edges and for cutting grooves on long pieces. To start shaping, butt the edge guide up against the edge of the work and tilt-elevate the router to clear the cutter. Start the motor, then lower the bit into the work and advance the router slowly.

Once you have mastered the basics of using the edge guide, you owe it to yourself to try new techniques. For example, an edge guide is particularly useful when cutting blind mortises for hidden-spline miter joints. Or, you can cut a dovetail-shaped groove in an edge with the help of the edge guide and two pieces of scrap clamped along each side of the work to support the shoe of the router. The mortise shape in the mating edge is cut the same way, but with the cutter set to leave the center portion intact for the tongue. With this kind of work, it's especially important to keep the router steady and to position the edge guide accurately.

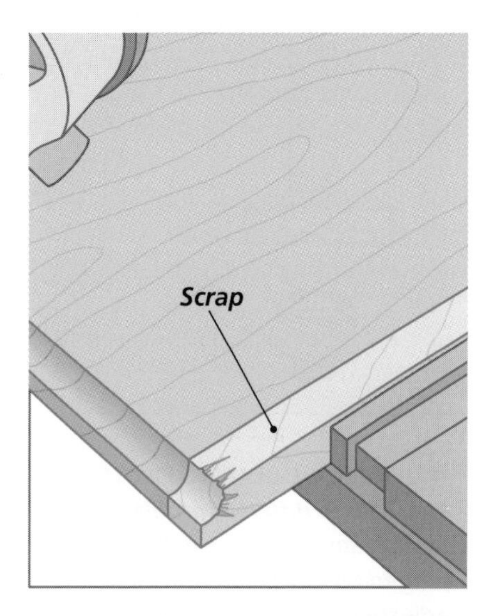

◀ **PREVENTING SPLINTERING, 1.** ***To prevent splintering when a bit exits a cross-grain edge, clamp a scrap board to the edge. This way the scrap splinters, not the workpiece.***

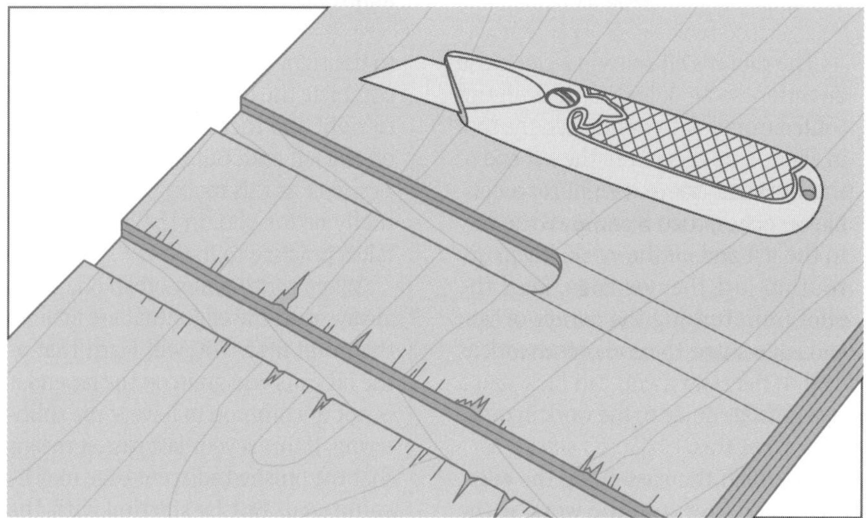

▼ **PREVENTING SPLINTERING, 2.** ***Cross-grain routing can splinter the veneer of some plywood. To prevent this, scribe the cut's borders with a utility knife before routing.***

WORKING FREEHAND

Freehand routing is plain fun, even when you're just showing off. More often than not, when routing freehand you will probably be making a plaque or sign using one of two basic techniques: cutting a pattern directly into the material; or, routing out the background, leaving a pattern that's raised from the surface.

To do freehand routing, first put the pattern directly on the workpiece with a pencil or marker. Next, install the appropriate bit. Bits generally used for freehand cuts include the core box, the straight or mortise for large areas and the veining for delicate work.

In general, you should never rout more than ¼ in. deep. The deeper the cut, the more difficult it will be to follow a pattern. Ordinarily, you should make the first depth setting equal to about 25 percent of the desired finish cut. The initial cut then acts as a guide for final, full depth cutting.

When routing freehand, work slowly from left to right and keep the cutter biting into new material. Wearing eye protection is absolutely imperative since you often need to get your face down close to the base of the router to follow the pattern with the bit.

GUIDING AGAINST AN EDGE

The fourth way to guide the router is with the base against an edge of material. The edge can be straight, such as for plowing long grooves or dadoes, or it could be curved or scalloped to suit a custom task.

Clamp the board or other material with the edge you're tracing securely

▼ **CUTTING MOLDINGS.** ***Here's a safe, easy way to rout your own decorative moldings. Shape the edge of a wide board with the router, then rip off the narrow molding.***

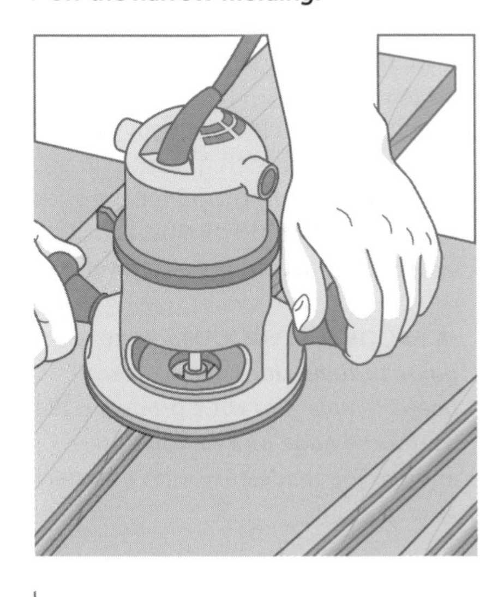

to the top surface of the work being routed. Overhang the work enough to direct the router at the start of the cut and ensure that none of your clamps will obstruct its path. Guide the router in a counterclockwise rotation—left to right, as when shaping an outside edge—and advance steadily, making sure that you keep the shoe in direct contact with the edge at all times.

A typical application of such cutting would be the plowing of dadoes to receive let-in shelves on opposite vertical panels in a bookcase. When the panels are laid out flat, they can be clamped or tack-nailed together side by side so the dadoes can be cut across them at the same time.

USING TEMPLATES AND JIGS

A wide variety of templates, jigs and other aids—both shopmade and store-bought—can significantly increase the capabilities of the router. However, since many commercial accessories for the router elevate the user into the world of advanced wood craftsmanship, some of the simpler do-it-yourself tools are not designed for their use.

Template guide bushings are locked in the subbase of the router by screws, nuts or other means, depending on the manufacturer. In place, the collar of the guide bushing projects down from the shoe of the router, riding the edge of a template or other pattern—such as for cutting a dovetail or routing a mortise for a hinge. If you are heavily into woodworking—or plan to be—you will at some point want to master the use of a guide bushing, if for no other reason than to be able to produce accurate dovetail joints quickly.

To rout a very exact, unique shape or a number of identical pieces, use a guide bushing in conjunction with a straight bit and a template cut from ¼-in. plywood or hardboard. Tack-nail or clamp the template securely to your work and direct the router so that the guide bushing rides along against the edge of the template. The bit project-

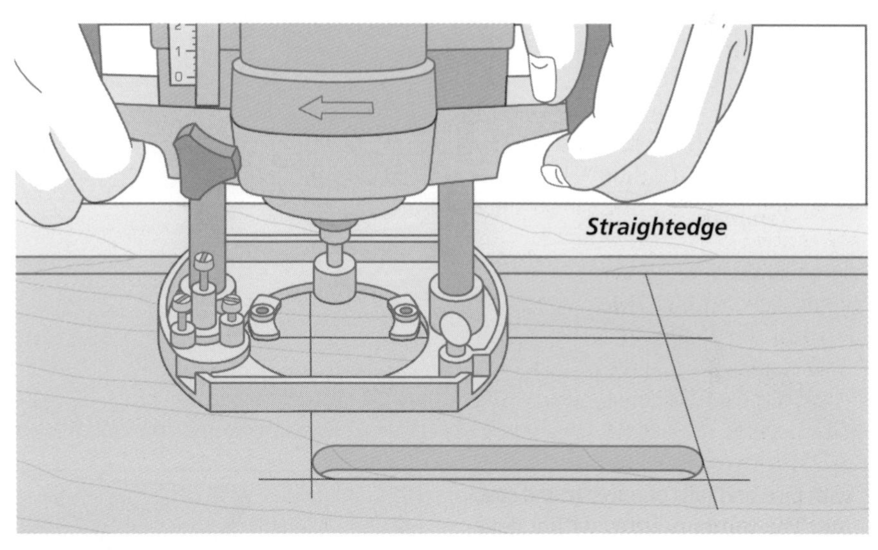

▶ **MAKING STOPPED CUTS.** ***Its spring-loaded base makes a plunge router especially useful for cutting stopped dadoes and slots. With the depth stop set, plunge the router into the work and advance it slowly along a clamped straightedge.***

▼ **CUTTING MORTISES.** ***A router is an excellent tool for cutting mortises. Attach an L-shaped wood fence to the edge guide for extra support and greatest control.***

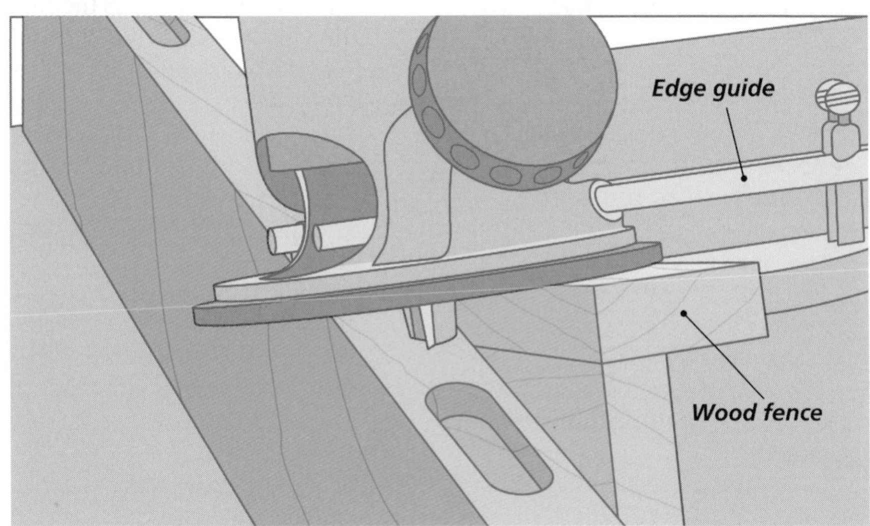

ing below the guide bushing cuts the work to match the edge of the template precisely.

GUIDED DOVETAIL CUTS

Dovetail templates are among the most popular accessories that are available for the router. These allow you to cut precise-fitting dovetail joints quickly and accurately.

The most common type of dovetail template produces half-blind joints with pins and tails of one size and spacing. The router is fitted with a dovetail bit and a guide bushing, and the pieces to be joined are clamped in the template at a right angle. The mating pins and tails are then cut in the pieces at the same time.

Some dovetail templates cut traditional, through-dovetail joints that mirror hand-cut joints—but are made with greater speed and precision. The pieces to be joined are positioned flush under adjustable fingers and clamped in the template, then the fingers are spaced as desired and locked in place. The fingers guide the router, which is fitted with a guide bushing, to cut the joint. The pins and half-pins are made with a straight cutter while following the angled guide fingers. The tails are formed by following the square-end fingers using a dovetail cutter.

DADO-CUTTING GUIDE

A router is an ideal tool for cutting dado joints. Here's an easy-to-make jig that will save set-up time and ensure accurate dadoes. The jig consists of two side rails that guide the router connected by shorter crossbars that straddle the workpiece. Cut the parts from ¾-in.-thick, straight, warp-free boards. Nail and glue the jig together, making sure that the space between the rails equals the diameter of the router's subbase.

Most dado joints are ¾ in. wide. But ¾-in. plywood or particleboard is not always ¾ in. thick—it's very often less, which results in loose, sloppy joints if the dado is cut with a ¾-in.-dia. bit. Therefore, design the jig for use with a ½-in. straight bit. This way, two passes are made to rout the exact width of

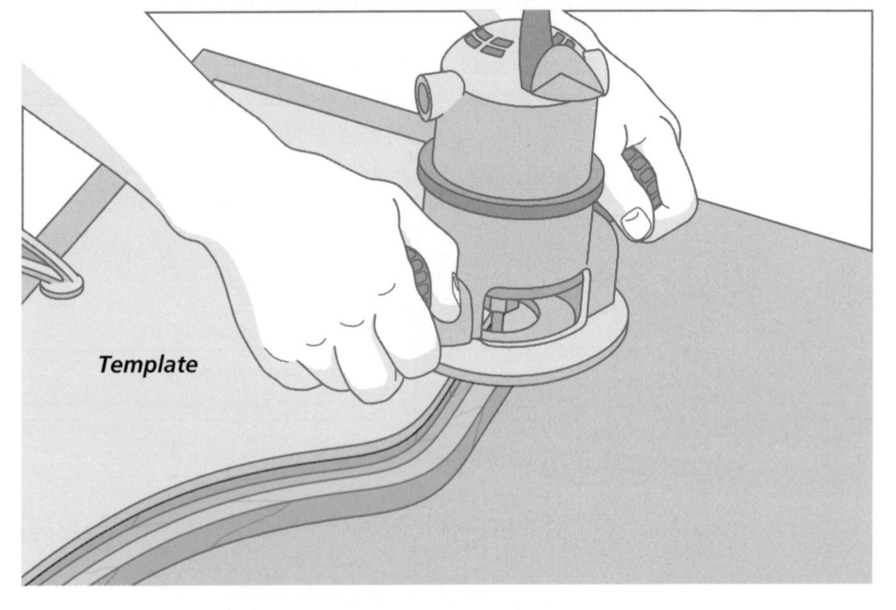

◀ **GROOVING CONTOURS.** ***Here, a guide bushing rides along a hardboard template to cut a groove in the contoured edge of a rolltop desk—another job made easy with a router.***

▼ **PLANING SURFACES.** ***This simple setup turns a router into a surface planer. The router is attached to a stiff board that spans the workpiece on two wood rails.***

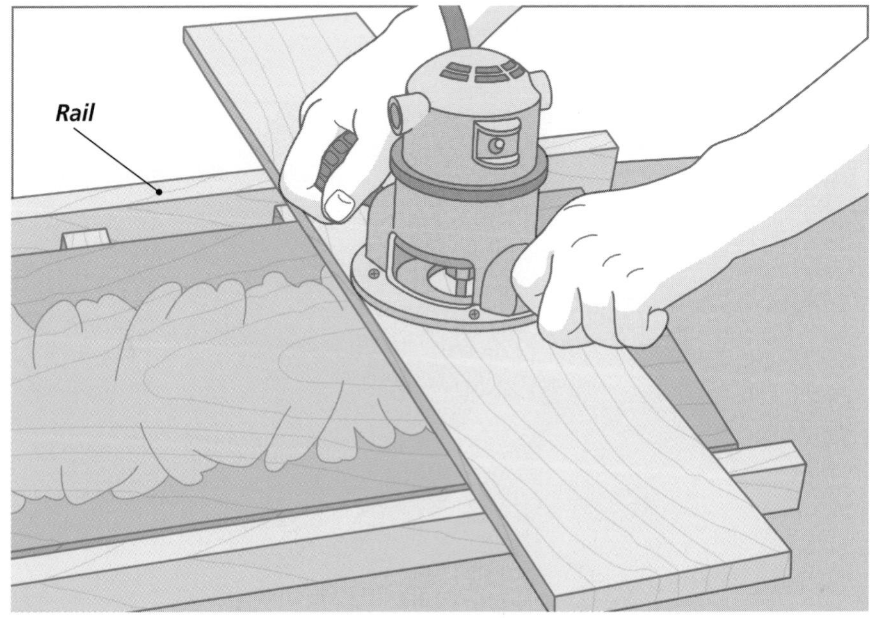

the mating piece. A scrap strip tacked to the jig at the end of the cut helps prevent splintering as the bit exits.

CIRCLE-CUTTING GUIDE

If you use a router just for straight cuts, it will still be an indispensable tool. However, to increase its versatility, there are a variety of guides you can use for cutting arcs and circles.

You can make your own simple circle-cutting guide from ¼-in. plywood or hardboard. The length of the guide is optional, but 3 ft. long is adequate for most work. Cut the circular end of the guide to match the router's subbase. Then, bore pivot holes in the arm of the guide spaced 1 in. apart.

To use the guide, remove the subbase from the router and screw the guide directly to the router's base. Use the same screws used to hold the subbase to the base. Then, measure off the desired radius of the circle or arc and drive a nail through the appropriate hole in the guide's arm. The nail acts as the pivot point.

Start the router and slowly swing the tool into the workpiece. Be certain to keep the work surface clean and free of obstructions to allow the arm to slide smoothly. The guide can be used to rout complete circles or any portion of a circle.

As with all other routing procedures, make deep cuts in several passes. Lower the bit slightly after each pass. Use the guide to make circular grooves or cut through the workpiece entirely to form a perfectly round or round-top piece.

▶ **CUTTING HALF-BLIND DOVETAILS, 1.** ***This template allows the router to cut tricky half-blind dovetail joints. The router is equipped with a guide bushing and dovetail bit.***

▼ **CUTTING HALF-BLIND DOVETAILS, 2.** ***With the template, cutting of the tails and mating sockets is simultaneous. The half-blind dovetail joint locks together tightly.***

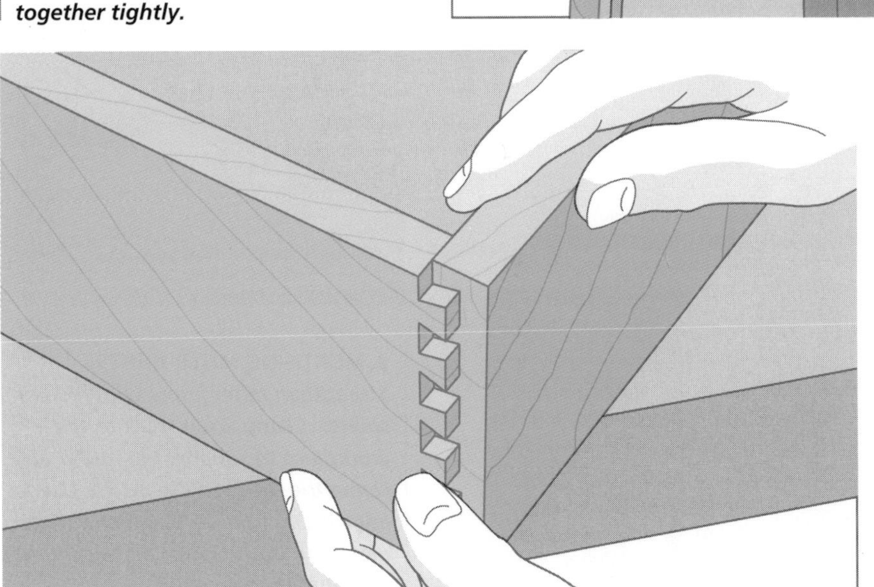

SURFACE PLANING

A router will never replace a planer, but for small surfacing jobs, here's how you can make yourself a simple planing jig. Bore a 1½-in.-dia. hole through the center of a board that's about 6 in. wide x 36 in. long. Remove the subbase from the router, install a ¾-in. straight bit and screw the router's base to the board.

Clamp the workpiece between two wooden rails, then span the rails with the router-and-board assembly. Make sure your setup lets you work in the direction that's parallel to the grain. Lower the bit gradually into the workpiece to smooth the surface and make shallow passes, cutting no more than ⅛ in. deep at one time.

PANEL-CUTTING KIT

Getting a panel-cutting kit for your router means controlled, decorative cuts no longer require painstaking figuring and preparation, nor jigs that become useless as soon as you've used them once. The kits are designed for making face cuts on cabinet doors and drawer fronts, but usually can be used for decorating any square or rectangular panel up to a certain size.

The typical kit includes four, 36-in.-long guide rails that are equipped with special clamps for aligning and attaching to the workpiece. Once the rails are secure, any set of four templates are simply snapped into the corners formed by the rails. Also usually included is a set of blank templates that you can use to make your own pattern. A radius attachment will allow you to plow arcs from 5- to 17½-in. ra. A guide bushing that rides along the rails and templates may or may not be included in the kit.

To cut a pattern, the first step is to clamp the work upside down in the rails. If your work is smaller than the rails in either dimension, the rails just extend beyond the abutting rail. Then, flip the assembly over and snap in the templates for the design you want into the four corners.

Install a grooving bit in your router and set it to the desired cutting depth. Practice with a test piece before making a run on your work. Then, simply direct the router across the work surface along the rails and the templates.

To use the radius attachment, you should clamp one of the rails to the

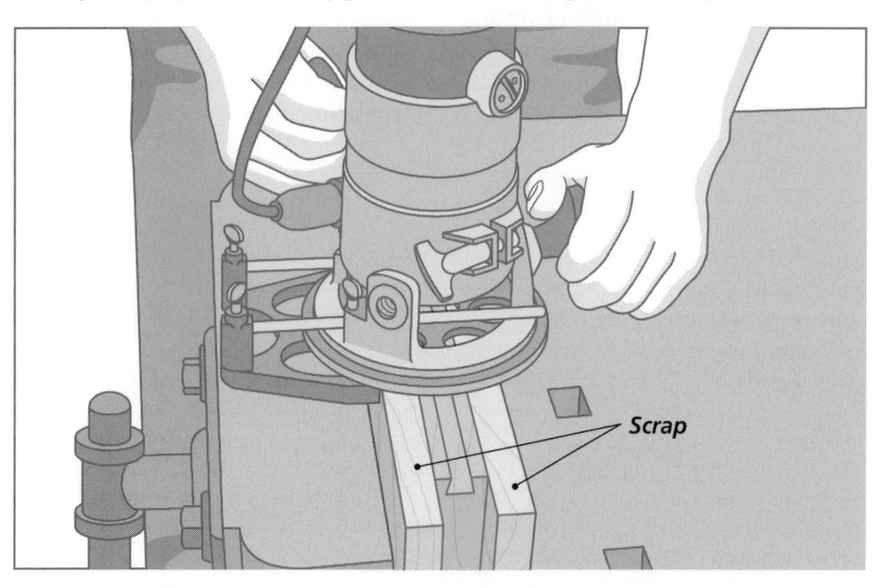

▲ **CUTTING EDGE DOVETAILS, 1.** ***Cut dovetails to join boards using an edge guide and two pieces of scrap stock clamped to support the router shoe. Locate the guide accurately.***

▼ **CUTTING EDGE DOVETAILS, 2.** ***The mortise shape in the mating edge is cut using the same technique, but the cutter is now set to leave the center portion, or tenon, intact.***

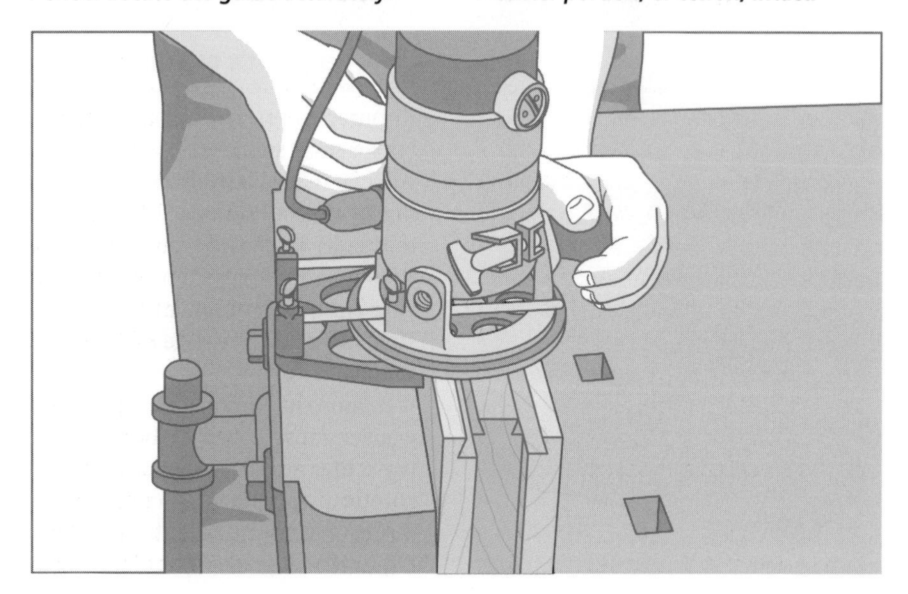

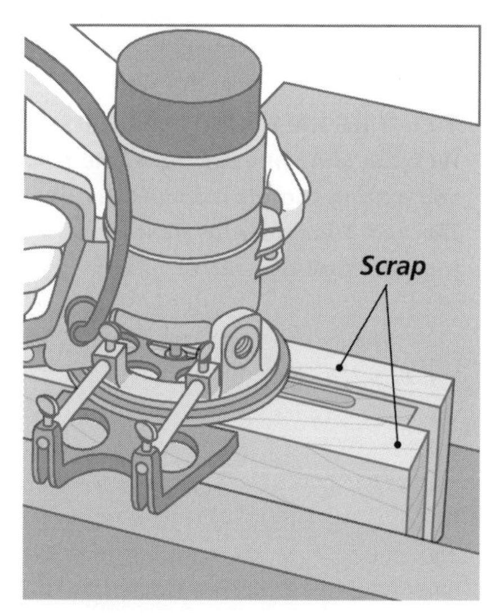

▲ **MORTISING MITER JOINTS.** ***Strengthen miter joints with hidden splines. Clamp scrap stock to the workpiece to support the router and clamp the setup to the bench. Use an edge guide to ensure accuracy. After mortising both pieces, make splines and glue them in place.***

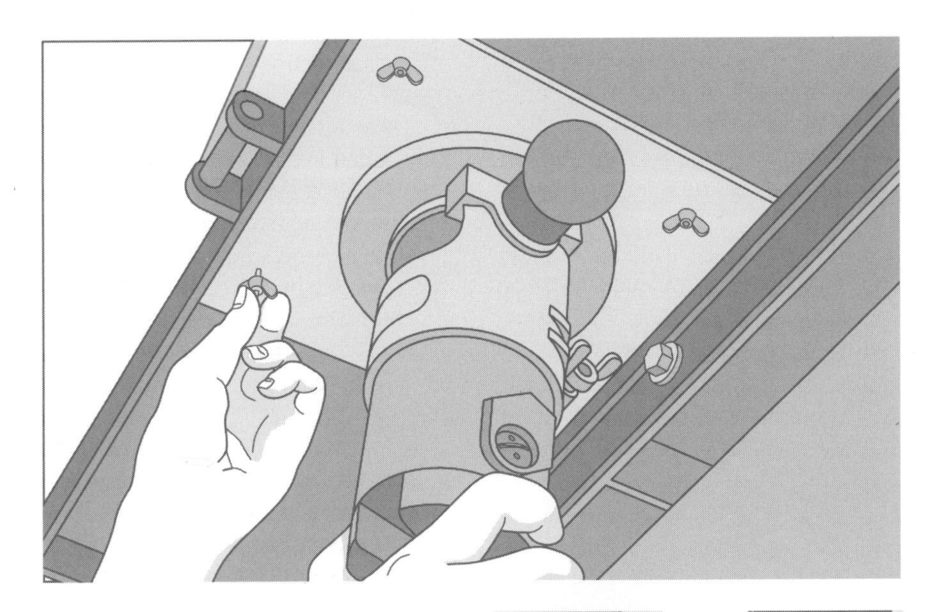

◀ USING A ROUTER TABLE, 1. ***A bolt-on router table provides a way to increase your routing capabilities by using your table saw. The router is attached to an adapter plate that is mounted to the table underside.***

▼ USING A ROUTER TABLE, 2. ***Here, the table saw's fence is used to rout a groove. Auxiliary wood fence that comes with router table is notched for partial edge routing. A pivoting guard shields the cutting action.***

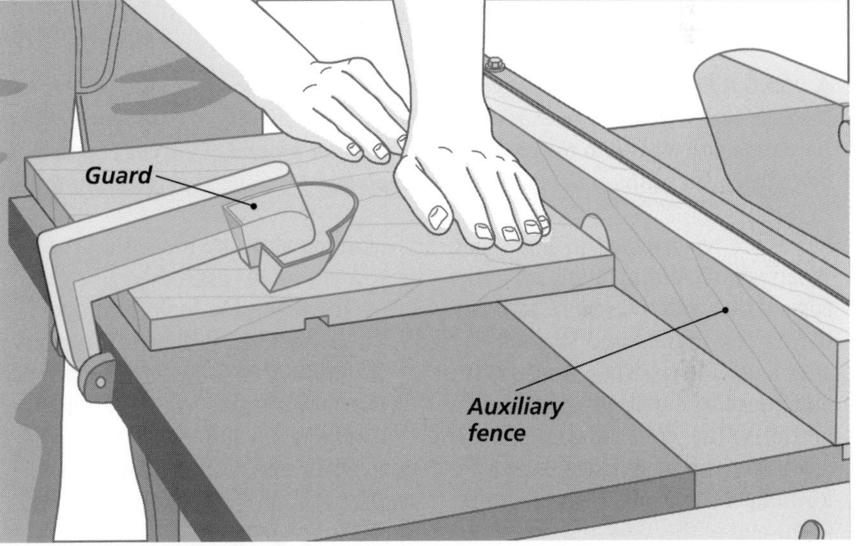

work. Then, attach the arm-mount to the router's base and fit the assembly into a pivot bracket that's mounted to the rail. The radius of the cut you want is set by adjusting the reach of the arm and securing a pivot-point lock.

PANTOGRAPH CUTTING AID

A pantograph is yet another accessory that's available for most routers. This cutting aid allows you to make relief-carved decorations, plaques and signs out of wood in set percent reductions from an original pattern.

To use the pantograph, all you have to do is clamp the router to a floating plate that holds an arm with a handled stylus at the end of it. As you move the stylus to trace over your pattern, the router is guided in one of the preset reduction ratios to reproduce the pattern on the surface of your workpiece. To check your progress, you can lift the stylus to raise the floating plate holding the router.

TABLE ROUTING

Mounting your router in a table permits you to perform stationary routing, freeing your hands to feed work into the bit and affording you much greater control over cutting operations. Safer than hand-held routing, stationary routing is also required in order to control certain types of cutters with large heads that exert considerable force against the work.

Mounted in a table, the router can be used to make moldings and raised panels much like a shaper. Many types of commercial router tables are available, usually with a guard to cover the bit and an adjustable fence for guiding stock into cuts. Customized tables are relatively easy to design and make in the shop.

One commercial type of router table makes use of your table saw. The table, typically of heavy-gauge steel, bolts to the edge of the saw table. The router is attached to an adapter plate, which then is secured under the table with wingnuts. The adapter plate will usually accommodate a sabre saw, too. With the router mounted, you can utilize the table saw's fence to make precise grooves, dadoes and rabbets.

When your router is mounted in a table, your cutting depth depends on how far the bit projects above the work surface. The width of cut is set by the amount that the bit extends beyond the fence. Most commercial tables have a split fence. For partial cuts, the two

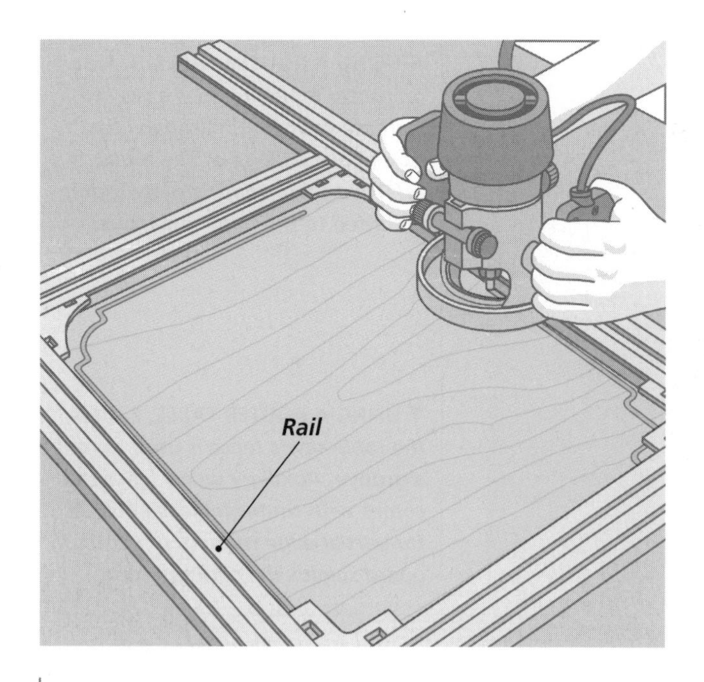

▲ **USING A PANEL KIT, 1.** ***Clamp your work upside down in the guide rails, then flip over assembly and snap templates for design you want into the corners. Run the router around periphery with bushing riding rails and templates.***

▲ **USING A PANEL KIT, 2.** ***Only one guide rail is necessary to work with the arc routing accessory. The radius of the cut you're making is set by adjusting the arm's reach and securing the pivot-point lock.***

halves are typically left in alignment. When you're routing along an entire edge of the work, however, start with the fences aligned and stop the cut after a few inches. Then, advance the outfeed fence so that it touches the cut portion of the work and complete the operation. This technique prevents the forming of a concave shape, or snipe, at the end of the work.

PIN ROUTER ASSEMBLY

In conventional hand-held and stationary use, the router can perform a wide variety of cutting operations. And you can even further add to both your router's usefulness and your woodworking skills by mounting the tool to a pin router assembly.

The assembly looks and operates somewhat like a drill press. The router is mounted in a carriage positioned over a worktable. A depth-adjusting handle raises and lowers the carriage to obtain the desired depth of cut.

The most essential part of the pin router is a ¼-in.-dia. steel guide pin that projects from the surface of the worktable. The guide pin is secured in a pin block, which is adjusted to center the guide pin directly under the bit of the router. When the edge of the workpiece is moved against the guide

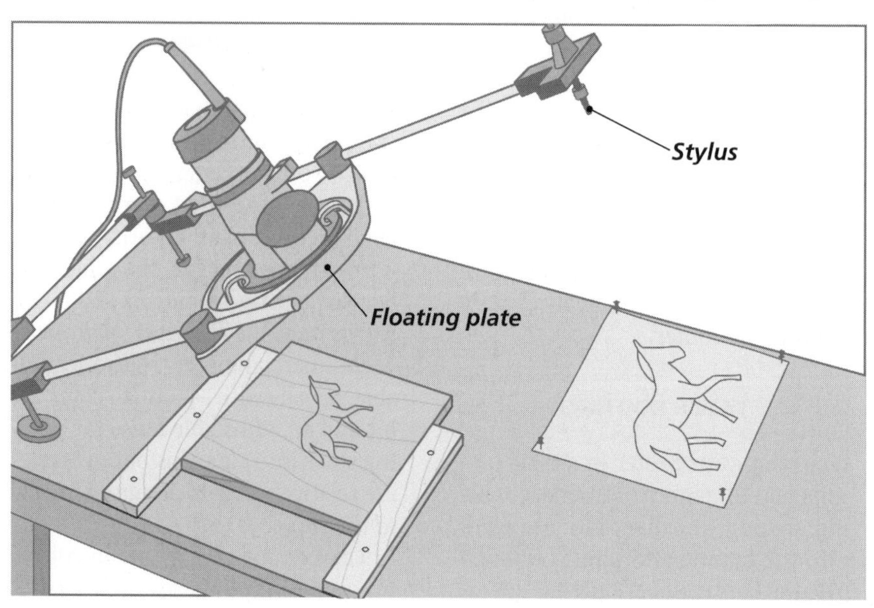

▶ **USING A PANTOGRAPH.** ***This accessory allows you to relief-carve from an original pattern. Clamped to a floating plate, the router moves in a preset reduction ratio to reproduce the pattern you trace with the stylus. The pantograph pivots up for checking progress.***

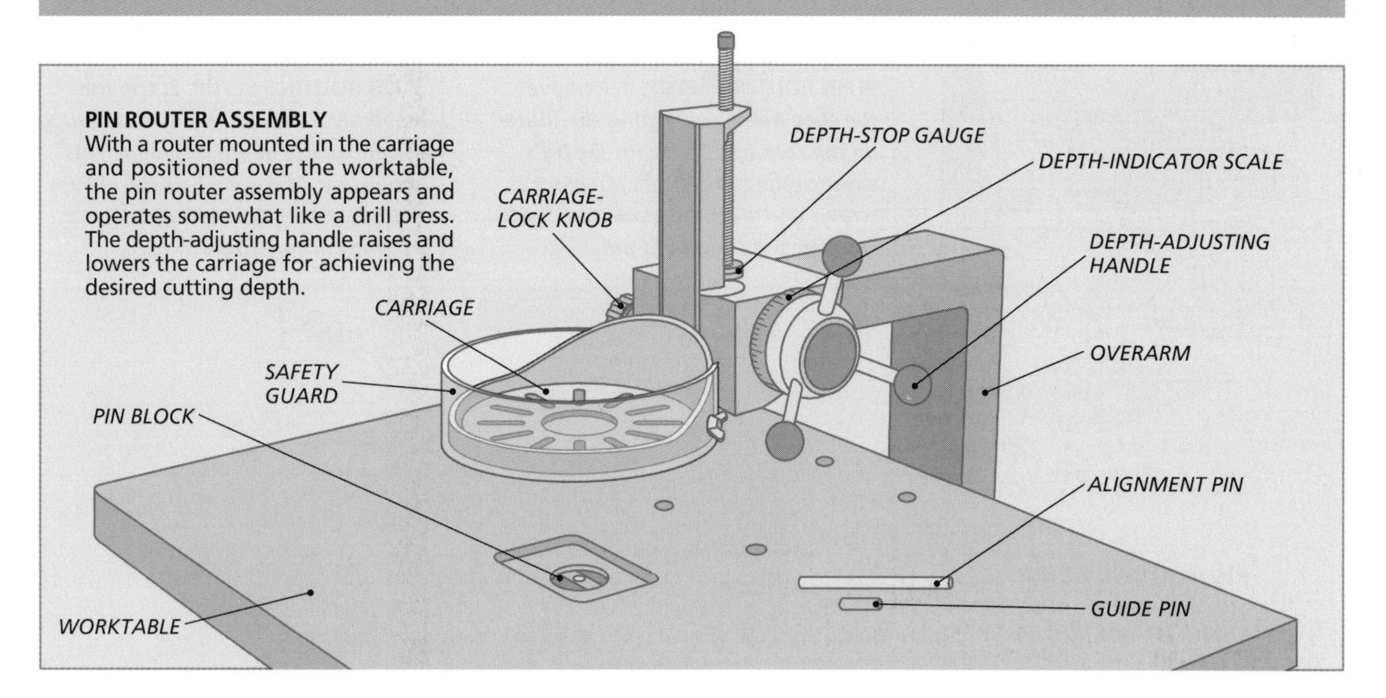

pin, the cutter shapes the edge accordingly. An advantage of pin-guided routing is that controlled, uniform shaping can be done using pilotless bits.

Also, when using cutters with 3⁄16-in.-dia. solid pilots the problem of edge burning is eliminated. This is because the larger 1⁄4-in.-dia. guide pin creates a gap between the unprotected edge of the workpiece and the spinning pilot of the bit.

TEMPLATE PIN ROUTING

Template-controlled routing is one of the most popular functions of the pin router. Templates of 1⁄4-in. hardboard serve as patterns, allowing you to make exact repetitive cuts with ease, speed and accuracy.

Cut your template to the desired shape and nail it to the underside of the workpiece. As the guide pin follows the template, the desired shape is cut into the top surface of the workpiece by the bit.

Templates also can be used for both the partial and full-edge trimming of workpieces. When you are full-edge trimming, cut the workpiece slightly larger than the template. Then, steer the template along the guide pin—which, remember, is aligned with the cutter—to trim the overhanging edge of the workpiece perfectly flush with the template.

Surface carving requires templates that have interior cutouts. First, place the template over the guide pin, corralling the pin within the cutout. Then, slowly lower the cutter into the workpiece and use freehand movement to carve out the surface of the workpiece. The trapped guide pin prevents any cutting by the bit beyond the borders of the template.

Another type of template cut is surface grooving. Surface-grooving templates are used to cut curved grooves across the surface of a workpiece. This technique employs two templates that are spaced 1⁄4 in. apart to form a channel. Pass the workpiece over the guide pin, steering the guide pin into the channel of the template. The confined guide pin will keep the workpiece on track, preventing any off-course drift from taking place.

BALL-BEARING PILOT ROUTING

When you are using router bits fitted with ball-bearing pilots, there is no need for a template, so the guide pin is removed from the worktable. After setting the router's depth of cut, simply steer the edge of the workpiece along the bit's ball-bearing pilot. The ball-bearing pilot will serve to guide the workpiece, thereby establishing a uniform cutting edge.

FENCE-GUIDED PIN ROUTING

When the guide pin is removed and a fence is clamped to the worktable, the pin router performs much like a stationary shaper. The fence guides the workpiece to produce a wide variety of straight cuts, such as rabbets, dadoes, grooves and mortises.

Full-edge jointing is possible using an offset fence. Cut the fence's receiving end wider than its feed end. The offset compensates for the amount of stock that's being removed by the cutter, thereby permitting the fence to provide full support for the workpiece along its entire length. Use a 1⁄4-in.-dia., double-flute straight cutter and don't offset the fence by more than 1⁄8 in. You should avoid attempting to remove too much stock at once or you will risk dulling the cutter and overloading the router, with possible damage to the motor as a result.

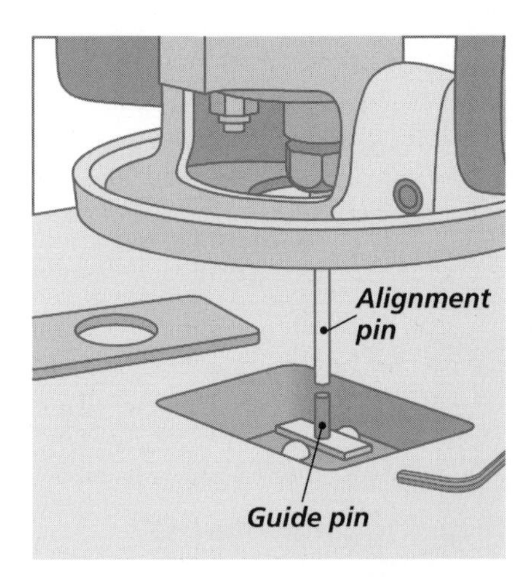

◀ PIN ROUTING SETUP, 1. ***Remove the shoe before mounting the router on the carriage. To locate the bit's exact center, loosen the pin block's screws and shift the guide pin directly under the alignment pin.***

▼ PIN ROUTING SETUP, 2. ***Use the assembly's knurled depth-stop gauge to control the depth of plunge cuts accurately. Make it a habit to always double-check your setting to avoid making cutting errors.***

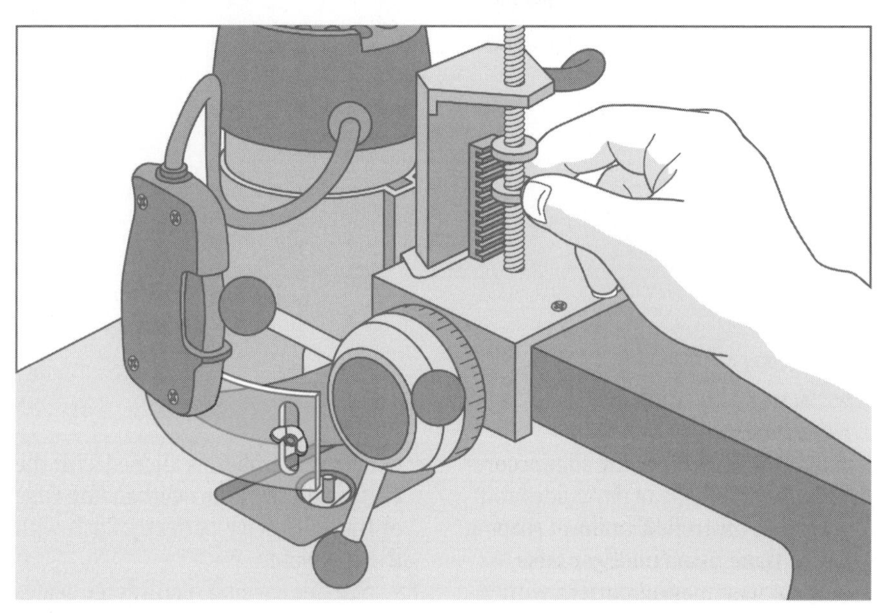

PIN ROUTING SETUP

The first step in setting up a pin router assembly is to take the subbase off the router and mount the router's base securely to the carriage support plate. Remember to always unplug the router before mounting, making adjustments and changing bits.

The next step is adjusting the guide pin to align with the router's cutter. First, chuck the alignment pin into the router. Then, lower the carriage using the depth-adjusting handle until the alignment pin is ⅛ in. above the guide pin. Tighten the carriage-lock knob to hold the carriage in this position. Now, adjust the pin block so the guide pin is directly under the alignment pin. To check for precise final alignment, remove the guide pin and lower the carriage until the alignment pin enters the guide pin hole. If necessary, readjust the pin block until you achieve perfect alignment.

PIN ROUTING PROJECTS

Here are different techniques and procedures for making three simple projects: a pediment (ornamental crown detail) using dual templates; a candy tray employing a surface-carving template; and a picture frame shaped with ball-bearing piloted cutters.

Whenever routing—regardless of technique or type of cutter—remember to always feed the work against the rotation of the bit. Also note that for clarity the illustrations on these projects do not show the safety guard in position on the pin router assembly. During actual pin routing operations, you should always set the safety guard ¼ in. above the work.

Pediment—A pair of hardboard templates are used to make the pediment. Cut one template to match the outline of the pediment's back panel. Shape the second template so that it conforms to the inside curve of the built-up molded crown.

Transfer the shapes of the templates onto two boards. Then, rough-cut the boards ¹⁄₁₆ in. larger than the templates' outlines. Now, tack-nail the templates to the underside of their respective boards. Use a ¼-in.-dia. straight bit to trim the rough-cut boards flush with the templates.

Two cutters are needed to shape the molded crown's profile. First, rout the crown's lower portion using a ⅜-in. beading cutter. Then, install a ⅜-in. cove cutter to form the concave upper portion of the crown.

The next step is to cut the molded crown from the board to match the top outline of the pediment's back panel. Then, cut the molded crown in half to form the left- and right-side crown molding. Glue and nail the pieces of the crown molding onto the pediment's back panel, allowing the top edges to overhang ¹⁄₁₆ in. Trim the pediment's top edge flush using a ¼-in.-dia. straight bit. Top off the pediment with a finial turned on a lathe.

Candy tray—Start by nailing a piece of ¼-in. hardboard to a ¾-in.-thick board of mahogany. Then, cut out and edge-sand the shape of the candy tray on both pieces simultaneously.

Now, remove the hardboard and cut out the compartments of the candy tray. Sand the interior edges of the cutouts smooth. Then, reattach the hardboard to the workpiece for use as a template.

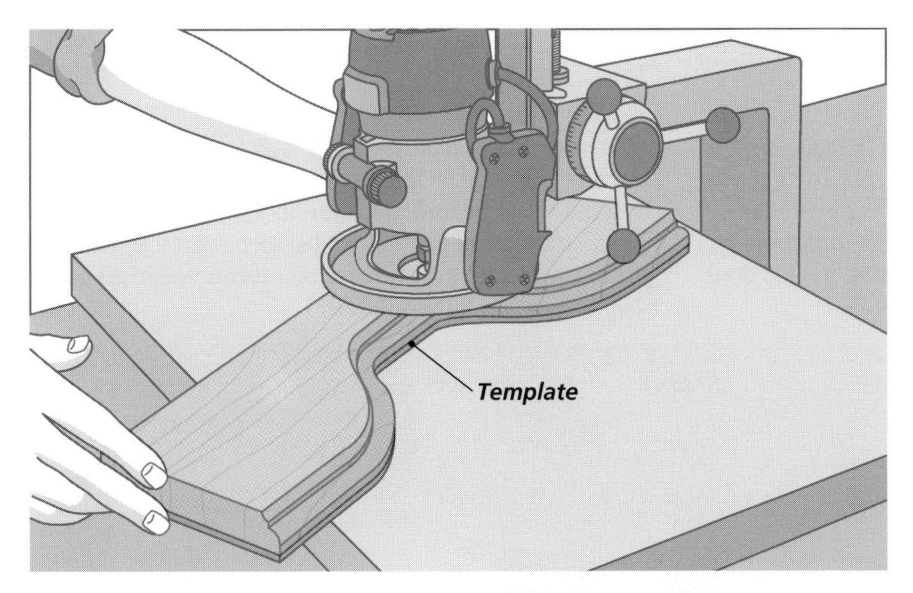

◀ **PIN ROUTING PEDIMENTS.** ***Two cutters are used to shape the molded crown of this pediment. Rout the first pass with a beading cutter. Here, the second pass is being made with a cove cutter.***

▶ **PIN ROUTING SURFACES.** ***In this example, perimeters of tray compartments are grooved by keeping the guide pin against inside edge of a template nailed to bottom of workpiece. Make final leveling passes with extremely shallow cuts.***

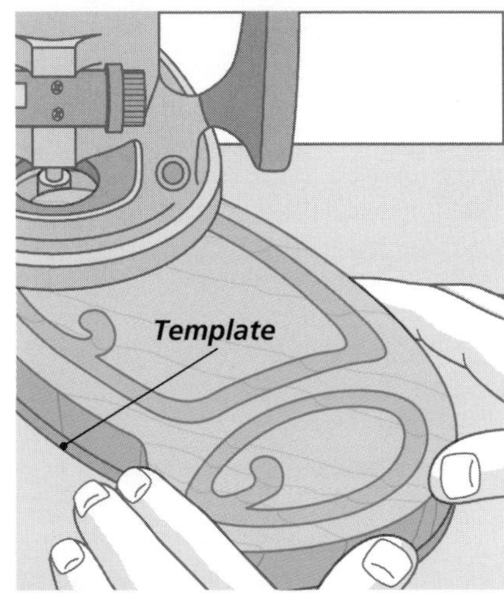

▼ **PIN ROUTING FRAMES.** ***To shape the frame's outside edge, remove the guide pin from the pin block and use a ball-bearing pilot. Here, a recess for glass is routed into the frame's back inside edge with a rabbeting bit.***

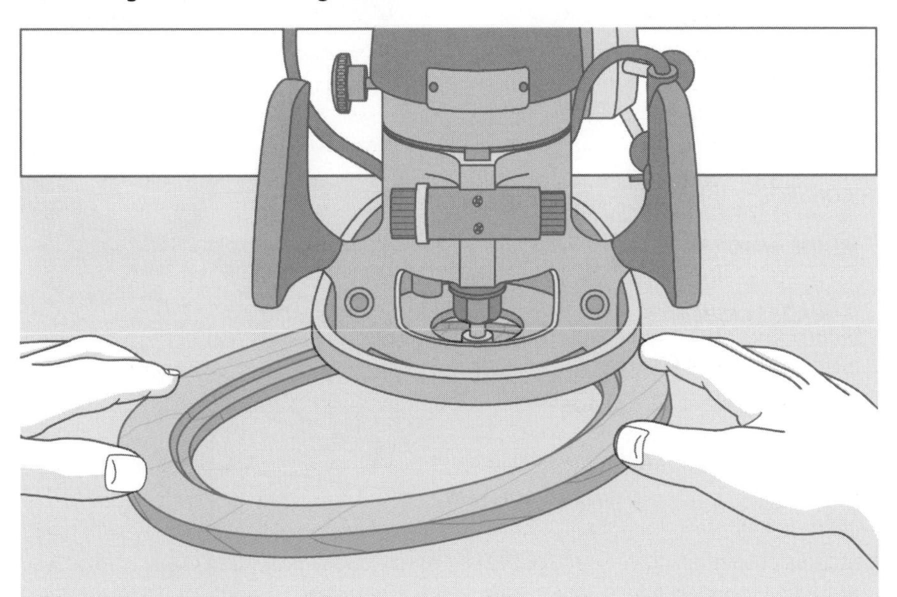

Next, install a ¾-in.-dia. core box cutter in the router for carving the compartments of the tray. Adjust the depth-stop gauge to a cutting depth of ⅛ in. Position one of the template's cutouts over the guide pin, start the router and make a plunge cut. Lock the carriage in this position using the carriage-lock knob. With the guide pin against the inside edge of the cutout, slowly move the workpiece against the rotation of the cutter to groove the perimeter of the compartment. Lower the carriage ⅛ in. on each pass until you reach ⅝ in. deep. Repeat this procedure for the other compartments.

Now, place one of the template's cutouts over the guide pin, perform a plunge cut and lock the carriage. Using a freehand movement, shift the workpiece back and forth to clear out the waste area. Continue working this way, taking deeper cuts in increments of ⅛ in. until you achieve a depth of ⅝ in. Repeat this procedure to carve out the other compartments.

Finally, ease the sharp outside corners of the candy tray. For this procedure, change to a ¼-in. rounding-over bit and reset the depth of cut.

Picture frame—An oval frame's decorative edge and rabbeted glass recess are both routed with ball-bearing piloted cutters. As is the case with all ball-bearing piloted routing, a template is not required so the guide pin is taken from the worktable.

After sawing the frame's oval shape, finish-sand the inside and the outside edges. Next, rout the decorative outside edge with a ½-in. beading cutter. Then, place the frame face down on the worktable and use a ⅜-in. rabbet cutter to route a ¼-in.-deep rabbet in the back inside edge.

PLATE JOINERS

Most woodworkers would agree that the bulk of woodworking is simply a matter of joining pieces of wood together in a neat, strong and efficient manner. And in case you haven't looked up from chopping dovetails lately, there's a new tool for getting the job done that's catching on with pros and amateurs alike.

You may have read about the tool, seen it advertised and perhaps even tried one out. The tool has been referred to as the most significant innovation in joinery since the wood screw. It's one tool that's generated such interest and demand that manufacturers are tripping over themselves to get on the bandwagon. And, there simply

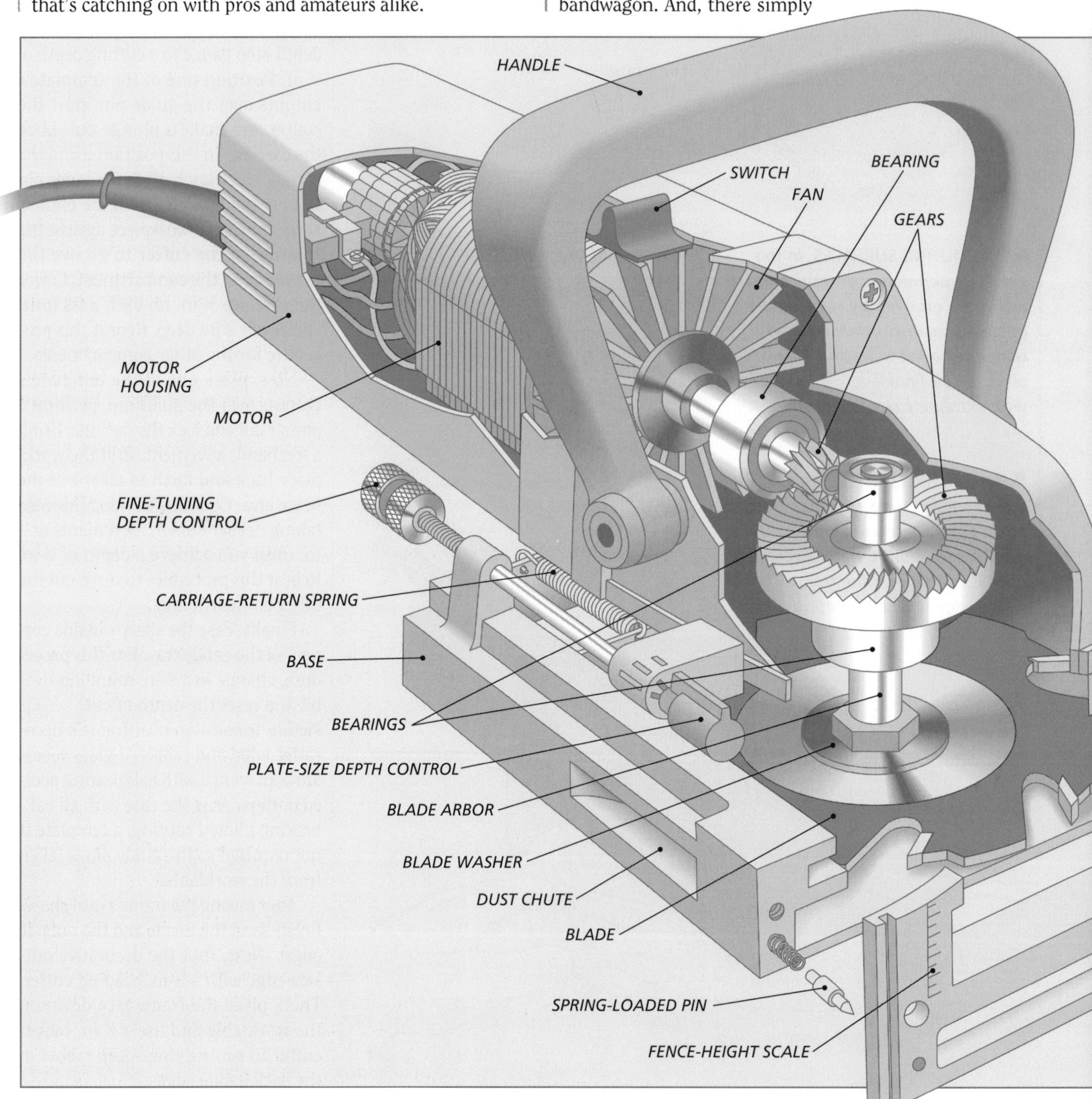

has never been a better time to bring your workshop into the 20th century—with a plate joiner.

Originally developed as a system for quickly assembling panels for case construction, plate joining has captured the imagination of woodworkers of all persuasions. In place of a traditional, full-length spline, plate joinery makes use of one or more oval-shaped plates, which are often called biscuits. The beauty of the system is that it's very fast, tolerant of minor alignment errors, relatively strong and only requires that components be prepared for simple butt joints.

The plate joiner's job is to cut aligned slots in two mating surfaces that accept the plate. It performs this task with a small, carbide-tipped blade and a system of reference surfaces and fences that allow the slots to be positioned and registered both accurately and consistently.

PLATE JOINER ANATOMY
A plate joiner cuts aligned slots for a plate in two mating surfaces using a small, carbide-tipped blade along with a system of reference surfaces and fences. Most plate joiners feature a cylindrical-shaped motor housing and a right-angle gear drive that powers the blade, and typically have a spring-loaded straight-line cutting action.

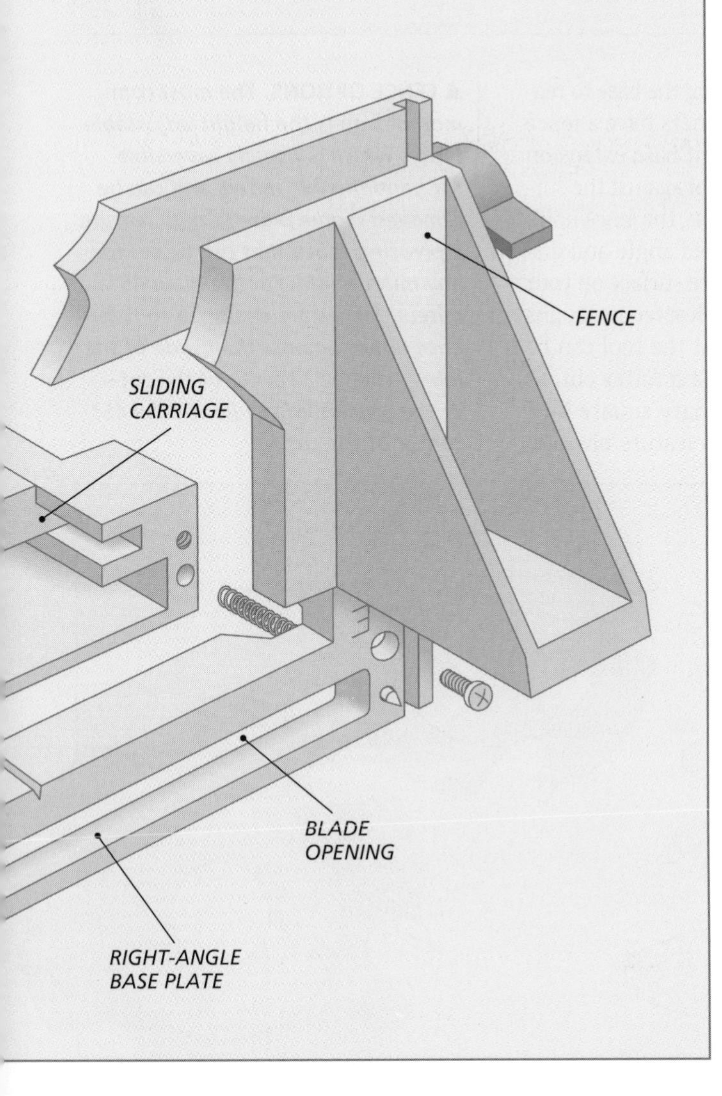

SYSTEM PRINCIPLES

The plate joiner itself is essentially a small, plunge-cutting circular saw. It's designed to quickly and accurately cut matching slots in pieces that are to be joined. Oval-shaped wooden plates are glued into the slots to join the pieces.

The plates are made of die-cut beech, with the grain oriented in a diagonal direction to resist breaking in the completed joint. The plates are compressed so that they're slightly thinner than the slot.

When the plates come in contact with water-based glue, they quickly swell, locking the joint together. This means that you can usually remove your clamps much sooner than with conventional joints so that they're free for use on the next assembly.

Unlike dowel joinery, which requires precisely aligned holes, plate joinery permits as much as 3⁄32-in. lateral alignment of the components immediately after assembly. This permits any slight misalignment of the slots to be then easily compensated for.

Although relatively new to most small workshops, plate joinery was developed in the mid-1950s by Swiss cabinetmaker Herman Steiner, who subsequently marketed a plate-joiner system throughout Europe. Low-cost plate joiners have recently made this method affordable for virtually all small shops and home woodworkers.

ABOUT THE TOOL

Several manufacturers offer different models of plate joiners. But although the tools have some design variations, their basic components are similar. All plate joiners are designed to accommodate the three standard plate sizes: small (No. 0), medium (No. 10) and large (No. 20).

Most plate joiners are equipped with a cylindrical motor housing and a right-angle gear drive that powers the blade. In fact, manufacturers generally base their plate joiners on an angle grinder in their product line. After making a few necessary modifications to handle the saw blade, all that's

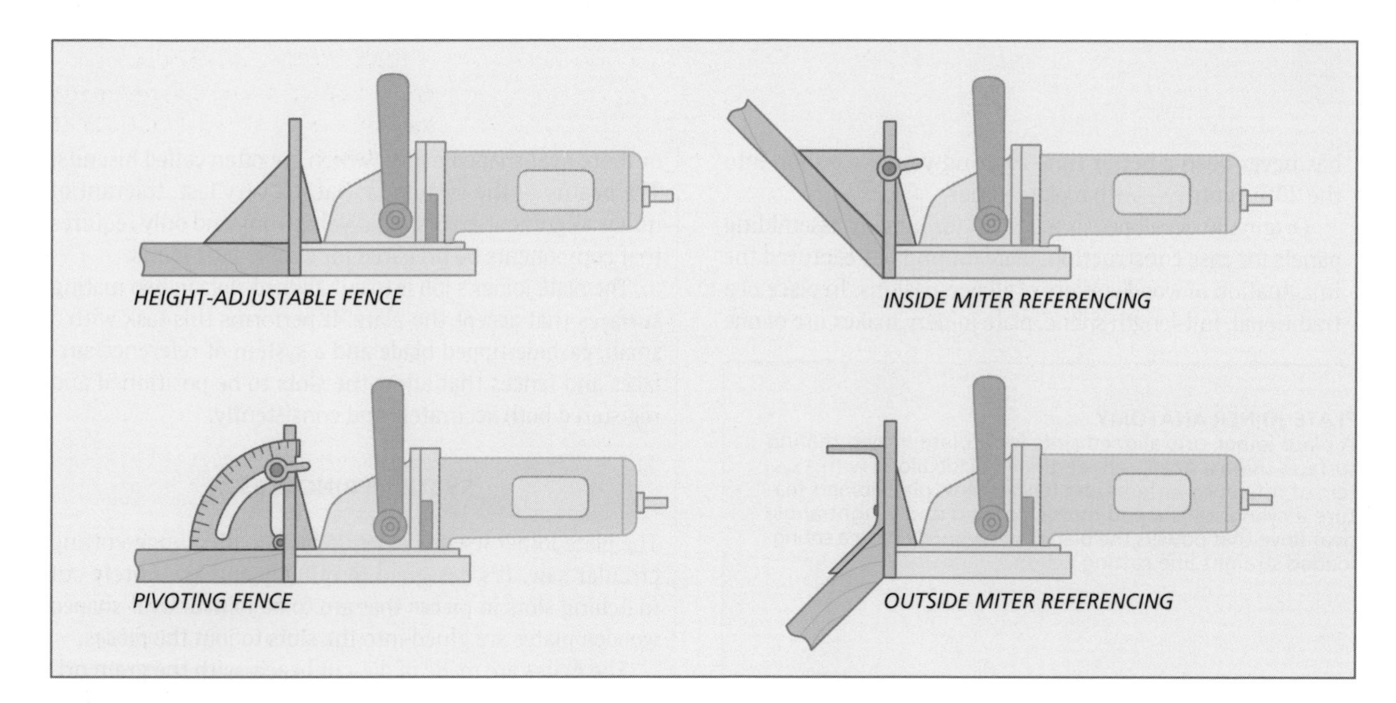

then required is a design for the blade housing and base that allows the blade to cut into the wood and subsequently retract safely inside the housing. Most plate joiners feature a spring-loaded, straight-line cutting action. Some models, however, have a spring-loaded, pivoting cutting action.

The base of a typical plate joiner not only houses the blade, but acts as a referencing surface for making a cut. Its bottom surface is parallel to the plane of the blade. When both the workpiece and the tool's base are resting on a flat surface such as your bench or tablesaw top, repetitive cuts will be positioned uniformly. The side adjacent to the tool's base—where the blade opening appears—is square to the bottom of the base and is held up against the workpiece. Because many applications, such as shelf construction, require that the tool rest on this surface, this side is extended to provide better support.

▶ **PLATES AND BLADES.** ***To handle a wider range of plate sizes, some plate joiners offer a small blade in addition to the standard size. Plate sizes vary from the large 3¼-in. version to the small 1½-in. type.***

In addition to using the base to register a slot, plate joiners have a fence mounted on the front base extension for registering the tool against the surface of the work. In use, the fence holds the tool at the desired angle and distance from a reference surface on your workpiece. The simplest fence designs are reversible so that the tool can be held securely against a miter cut, as well as handle ordinary square butt joints. Some models feature pivoting

▲ **FENCE OPTIONS.** ***The most common design is the height-adjustable fence, which is usually reversible for handling 45° miters and can be removed. Some plate joiners feature a pivoting fence that can be set for any miter angle. For handling 45° miters, fences are designed to reference either against the inside of the joint—the 135° corner of the cut—or the outside of the joint—the 45° corner of the cut.***

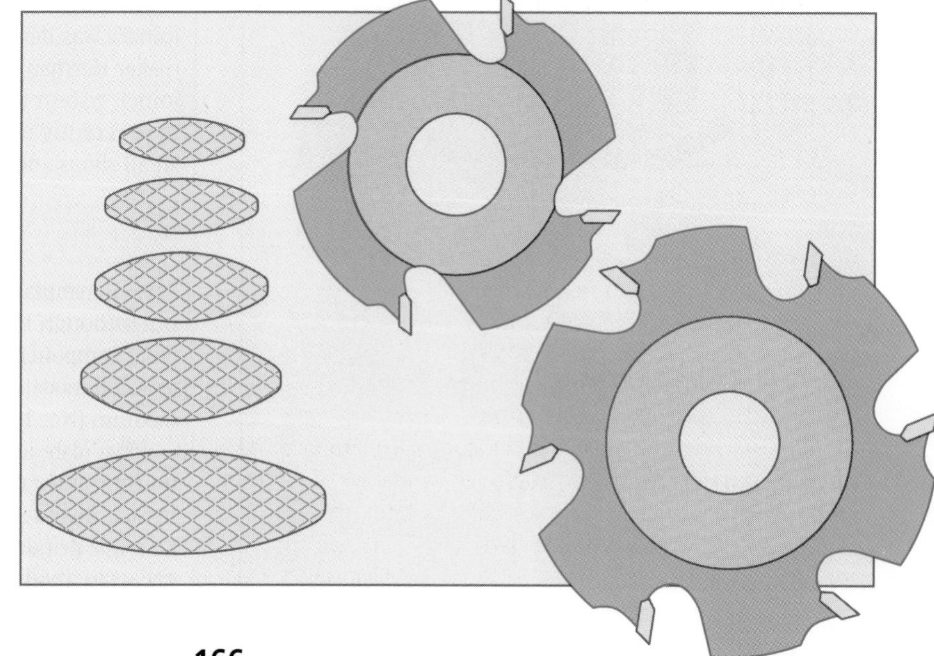

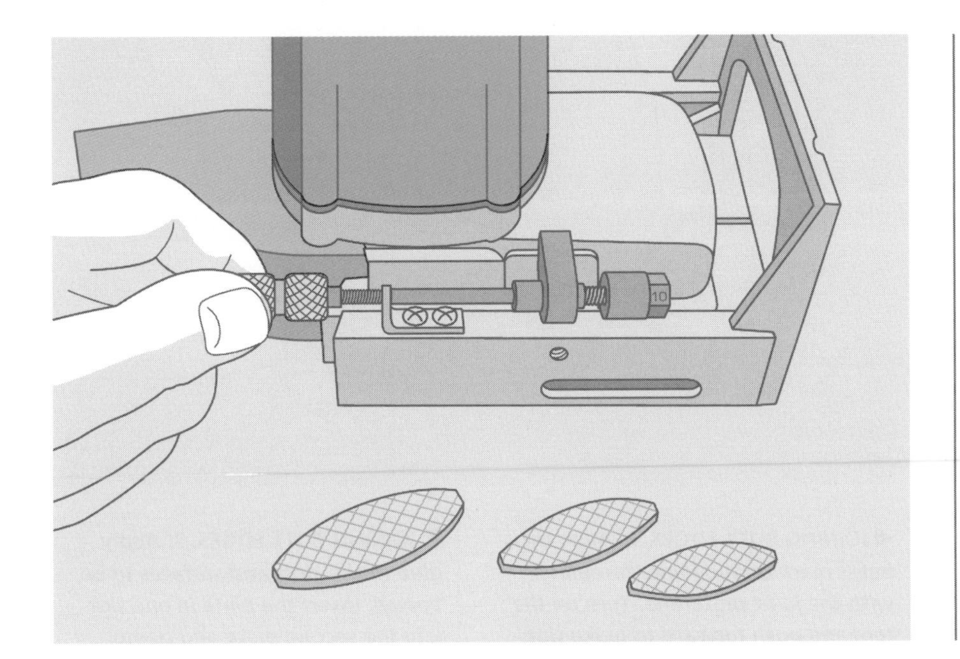

◀ **TOOL SETUP, 1.** ***Adjustable depth-of-cut stop has three positions to suit the standard plate sizes. Knurled knob permits fine-tuning.***

▼ **TOOL SETUP, 2.** ***With the fence removed, the faceplate and blade are visible. Spring-loaded pins grip the work to keep it from shifting.***

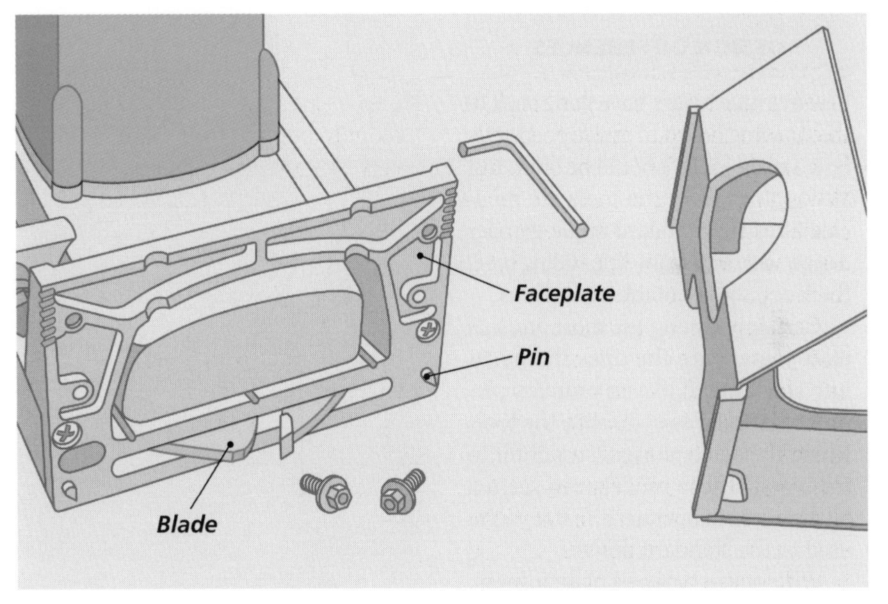

fences that can be set for any miter angle. Others have non-pivoting fences that can handle only the more common 45° and 90° operations.

For handling 45° miters, the fences for plate joiners are designed to reference either against the inside of the joint—the 135° corner of the miter cut—or the outside of the joint—the 45° corner. Because miter joints in cabinet construction are seen primarily from the outside, referencing to this side of the joint ensures that the visible faces will be aligned even if the two pieces are of different thicknesses. Some models are equipped with fences that handle both inside and outside miter referencing.

While the distance of the slot to the working face of the stock is set by referencing with the plate joiner's base or fence, positioning a slot along the joint is done by lining up an alignment mark on the tool with a slot location mark you make on the stock. To prevent the tool from shifting as the cut is executed, most models have spring-loaded steel points or spurs next to the blade opening. Others are equipped with non-marring pads, and have the entire surface around the blade opening covered by rubber.

DECIDING TO BUY

Although a plate joiner is not the most versatile tool to have on hand in the shop, there's no denying its usefulness. Designed principally to perform only one task—the joining of two workpieces—the tool does this single job extremely quickly and well, in a way that is simple, safe and forgiving of small errors.

Possibly in an effort to counter the negative impression that the plate joiner is strictly a one-dimensional tool, many manufacturers are now offering blades for wood trimming as an option. Several have gone so far as to design their plate joiners to function almost like small power saws, capable of comfortably trimming a plywood panel or cutting grooves.

With plate joiners, power isn't really an issue. Performance of these tools is more closely related to their individual features, flexibility, ease of use and quality of construction.

► **JOINING BUTT EDGES, 1.** ***The first step in making a plate joint is to align the mating pieces and mark the center of the joint on both pieces.***

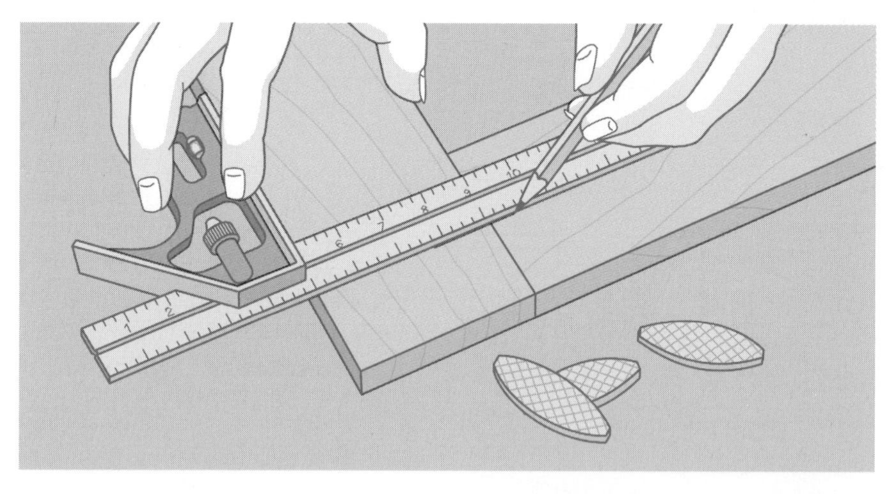

◄ **JOINING BUTT EDGES, 2.** ***Align the index mark on the joiner faceplate with the joint centerline. Turn on the tool and push forward to make slot.***

▼ **JOINING BUTT EDGES, 3.** ***Apply glue to the slots and surfaces to be butted. Insert the plate in one slot, join the second piece and clamp.***

DESIGN DIFFERENCES

Few manufacturers have gone back to the drawing board to question exactly how a plate joiner should be built. But although most of the tools are modeled after the standard angle-grinder design with a straight-line sliding base, there are some notable exceptions.

Certainly among the most unusual plate joiners are the ones that pivot into stock much like an ordinary pivot-foot circular saw—unlike the tools where the blade plunges straight into the wood. These models can seem a bit awkward to operate at first if you're used to the standard design.

With these types of plate joiners, the blade opening is not located directly in front of the motor housing, but on one side. This configuration allows the tool to be used also as a trim saw or groover. And because the blade of the tool is so close to the blade housing, you can trim close to a wall or obstruction—places that ordinary trim saws can't reach.

In keeping with the multipurpose nature of these plate joiners, the tools often have a few other unconventional features. Typically, there are auxiliary handles that—together with the motor housing—permit the tool to be held in just about any position. And the depth-adjustment control usually isn't the typical stop system that quickly locks in place for different plate sizes. Instead, there may be a simple adjustment screw and a depth scale that indicates appropriate cutting depths for the various plates—a system that may be slower, but makes sense for using the tool as a small saw or groover.

To handle 45° miters, there is usually a special 45° block that is attached to the tool's base. Unlike a typical 45° fence that's held against the work, the attachment rests on your work surface and supports the tool at 45°. For other angles, however, you'll need to make special shims.

Also, unlike typical plate joiners, the position of the blade in relation to the tool's base may be adjustable. This means that the base of the tool can act as an adjustable reference for handling stock of different thicknesses. Other makes require use of a sliding fence—a slightly less accurate mechanism for consistent kerf location.

Another departure from the angle-grinder adaptation route are the plate joiners that have the motor axis set parallel to the axis of the blade arbor and transmit power by a belt—instead of the right-angle gear system that's usually used to transfer power from the motor to the blade arbor. Some claim that this arrangement produces a quieter tool, but others dispute that there is a significant improvement in sound levels as a result.

In addition, positioning the motor vertically necessitates a new approach to how the plate joiner is held. And on the surface, these versions of the tool seem like they might be easier to handle. Plate joiners, by their very nature, are often held in varying and awkward positions. However, while the standard design may not be the best, these variants don't actually provide much of a real advantage in actual operation.

FENCE VARIATIONS

Some of the most significant differences in the handling and performance of plate joiners are attributable to the design of their fences. It's on this particular feature that manufacturers have come up with some of the most interesting twists on the conventional concept of the tool.

The majority of plate joiners come with a removable sliding fence for positioning the blade relative to the work surface. The maximum depth of fences varies; most fall somewhere within a range of from 1 in. to 2½ in. With a fence that's made for use in plate-joint positioning, sawing or grooving, the spacing range can go up to an impressive 4 in. On most tools, the fence is reversible for handling 45° miters.

While the fence configuration of plate joiners often appears similar, a closer look turns up some notable variations. On some models, for example, the right-angle front base plate isn't fixed, but pivots from 0° to 90°. Certain tools feature a pivoting faceplate that also can be adjusted for height; some even pivot both forward and backward for referencing against either face of a miter joint and have a fence that simply folds up when you don't need it.

The pivoting faceplates of tools that can't be adjusted for height are positioned to handle most standard cabinet-thickness stock; there's usually a small shim provided that attaches to the fence for handling thinner work. To make this type of system more versatile, some manufacturers include a sliding fence that fits onto the tool's

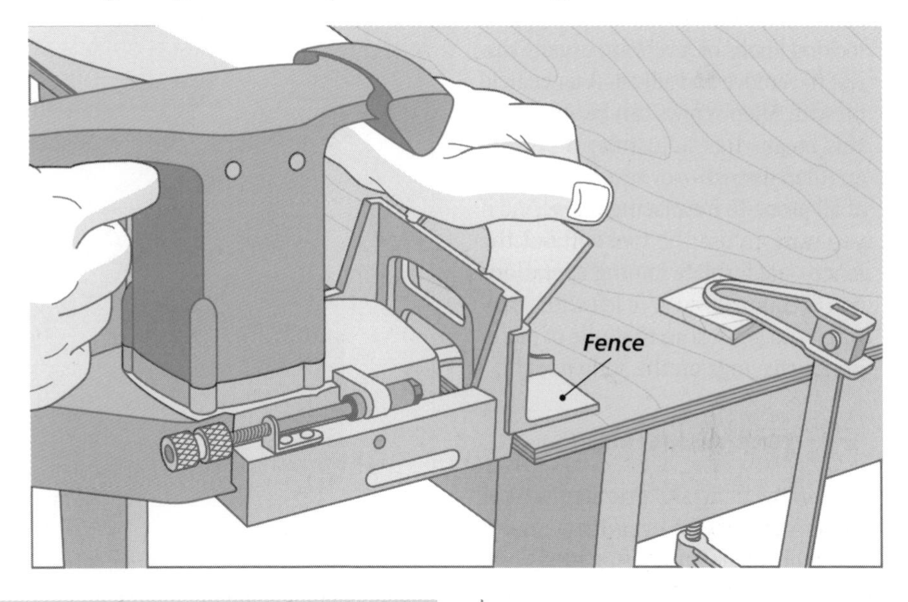

▲ **EDGE-BANDING PANELS, 1.** ***To place slot at center of thin stock such as a ¼-in. plywood panel, install the fence at correct distance from blade.***

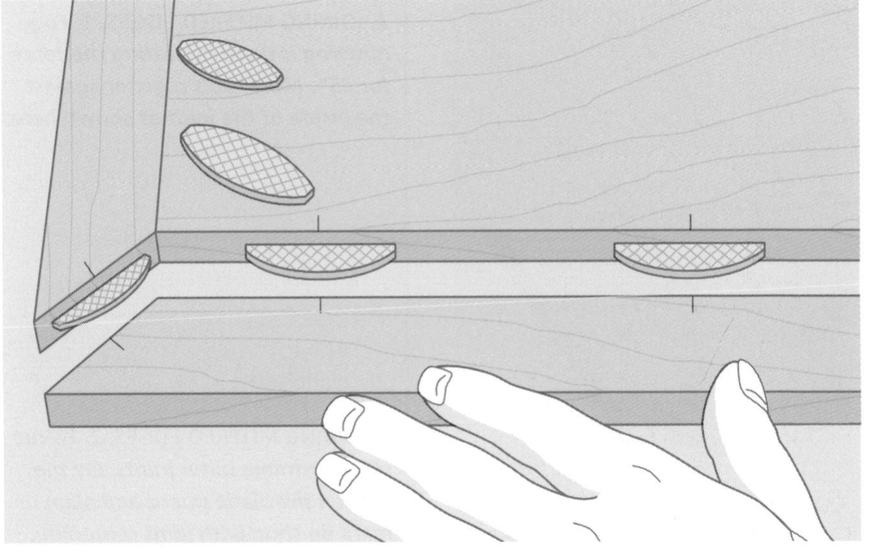

◀ **EDGE-BANDING PANELS, 2.** ***This mitered edge-banding uses two plate sizes: No. 10 for the narrow miter and No. 20 along the panel edges.***

pivoting faceplate. When the pivoting faceplate is used alone, miters are referenced against the inside surface of the joint. When the sliding fence is installed, miters are referenced against the outer surface.

Some tools provide a simple and elegant alternative to the standard type of reversible fence. With these models, the back edge of the reference surface on the fence is chamfered at 45°. This chamfered corner supports the tool against a 45° miter, while the front horizontal part of the fence handles 90° butt joints.

A quality tool has a fence that slides smoothly. Fences that have a pair of locking knobs or levers are usually easiest to remove and adjust. A fence held on with Allen screws can be annoying; this means that adjustments require an Allen wrench—or several, if you're at all prone to misplacing them. And if you want to use the tool without the fence—many plate joining operations don't require it—you're left with small screws to get lost in that pile of plate-joiner shavings on the shop floor.

TOOL ADJUSTMENTS

Ease in handling and operating a plate joiner depends on everything about the tool functioning effortlessly and smoothly. This means that not only the sliding base is flawless, but all the adjustments required in using the tool are well thought out.

There are obvious advantages, for example, in the plate joiner with a faceplate and fence that are each locked or unlocked with their own single lever. And a depth-stop knob that is separated from the fine-tuning depth adjustment helps prevent accidental altering of settings when changing from one plate size to another.

With most plate joiners, the scale for measuring the blade-to-fence spacing is graduated in ⅛-in. increments; some are graduated in increments of 1/16 in. or include a scale in millimeters. The scale indicates the distance from the fence to the top of the blade. Some pivoting-fence accessories feature no scale for gauging the blade's distance from the fence.

Although the center-of-cut indicator mark is typically cast in the tool's base, it's not always highly visible. To

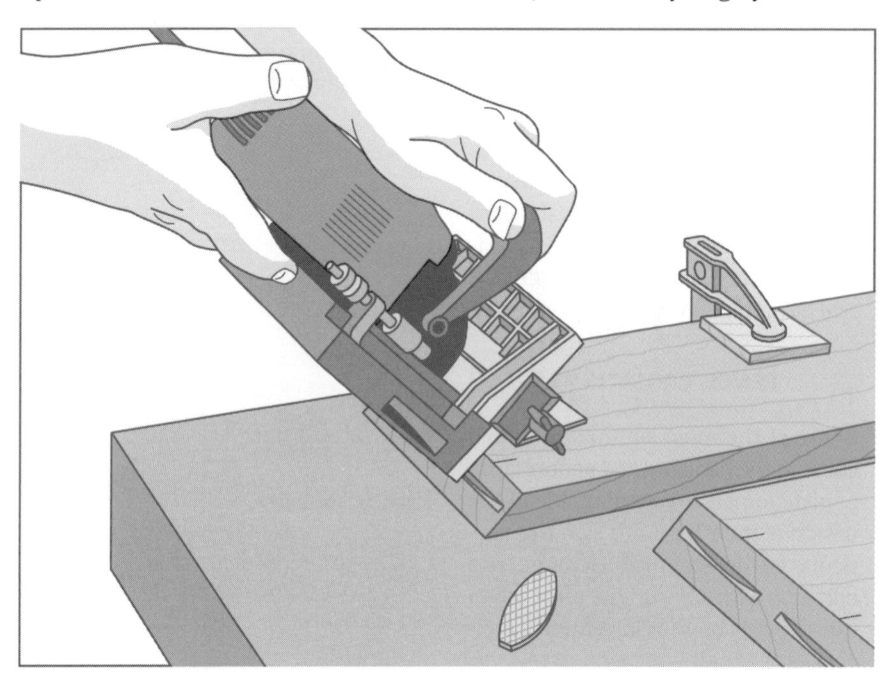

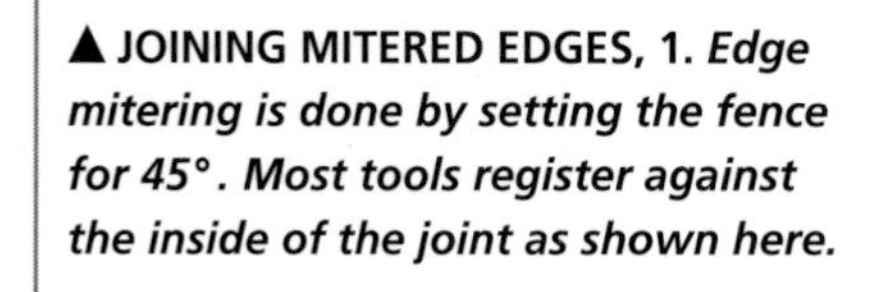

▲ **JOINING MITERED EDGES, 1.** ***Edge mitering is done by setting the fence for 45°. Most tools register against the inside of the joint as shown here.***

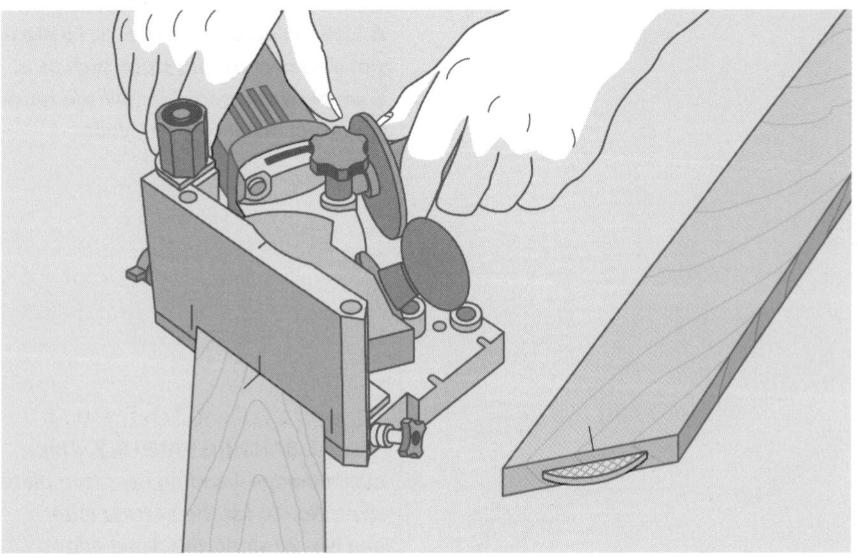

◀ **JOINING MITERED EDGES, 2.** ***To cut slots for frame miter joints, lay the tool on the blade guard and align mark on shoe with joint centerline.***

compound the problem, on some tools the plate location marks on the stock are invisible with the fence in the miter position at certain depths.

Blade changing should be a relatively simple procedure. With some plate joiners, however, it's not—too many parts to remove that complicate the job, adding to the risk of inadvertent dulling or damaging of the blade. On the better designed tools, the base is easily released and slides away to expose a spindle lock that holds the blade while a nut is loosened.

Certain models are designed with an unconventional, two-piece base that separates for blade changing. Because of this construction, however, you have to make sure that the entire base of the tool is properly supported whenever it's used as a reference surface. Otherwise, you may experience some minor misalignment across the thickness of a workpiece.

Another worthwhile feature to look for on a plate joiner is a sliding-switch control that can be used intermittently or locked on. Usually, after you've cut your stock and laid out the plate positions, you're ready to cut a number of slots in one session. In this situation, a way to lock the switch in its on position is handy so you're free to hold the tool conveniently for the job at hand. A switch that's mounted on the top of the motor housing works equally well

▲ **EDGE-TO-FACE JOINING, 1.** ***To join a shelf to the side panel of a cabinet, first clamp the shelf to the side panel at the joint location. Mark the joint centers on both pieces.***

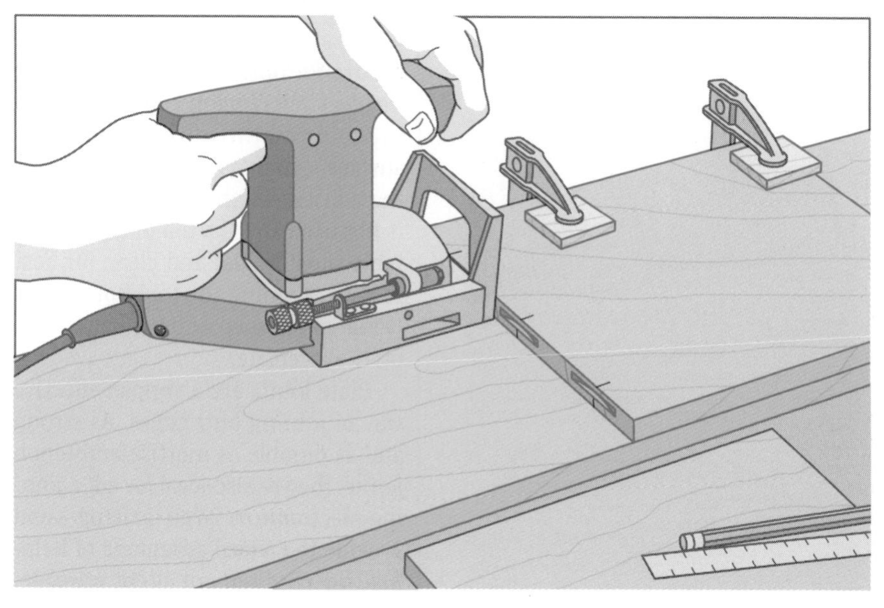

◀ **EDGE-TO-FACE JOINING, 2.** ***With the base of the tool held flat against the side panel, align the index mark with the slot centers and cut slots in the shelf edge.***

for right- or left-handed use. Lefties will have to adapt if the switch is located on the left of the motor housing—as it is on many models.

Plate joiners that have the entire area around the blade opening covered with rubber provide you with an anti-slip surface that will handle any size stock you're joining. The majority of models, though, come equipped with spring-loaded, steel locating points; check that they retract properly for sawing or grooving. A few include neither rubber padding nor steel pins near the blade opening to help keep the tool in place during a cut.

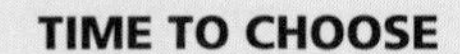

TIME TO CHOOSE

When you come right down to it, all models of plate joiners cut plate joints. With this in mind, even a tool at the lower end of the price range can look pretty good. And an inexpensive model is certain to bring plate joinery into workshops that otherwise would have gone without.

However, if your workshop notions extend to something a little more substantial, you're likely to be better off going for a heavier tool with a metal base and fence that comes with knobs for adjusting the fence instead of Allen screws. And of course, if you're going to use your plate joiner often—and your budget can withstand the cost—it's not likely that you'll be disappointed with the high-price versions of the tool.

PLATE JOINERY BASICS

The speed and effectiveness of the plate joiner are attributable to the ease at which the tool can accurately register the plate slots so that the mating pieces will be aligned properly. The basic procedure for operating the plate joiner involves referencing both the base of the tool and the work against a flat surface—such as your worktable. In these instances, the plate joiner's fence is not used and the top of your worktable must be flat and clean for best results. Aligning the tool horizontally is accomplished with the index mark on the faceplate.

Plate joints are a simple, effective way of joining butt edges. As strong and as durable as mortise-and-tenon joints, they're also ideal for edge-joining pieces into a large tabletop—and provide the added advantage of helping to straighten out slight warpage.

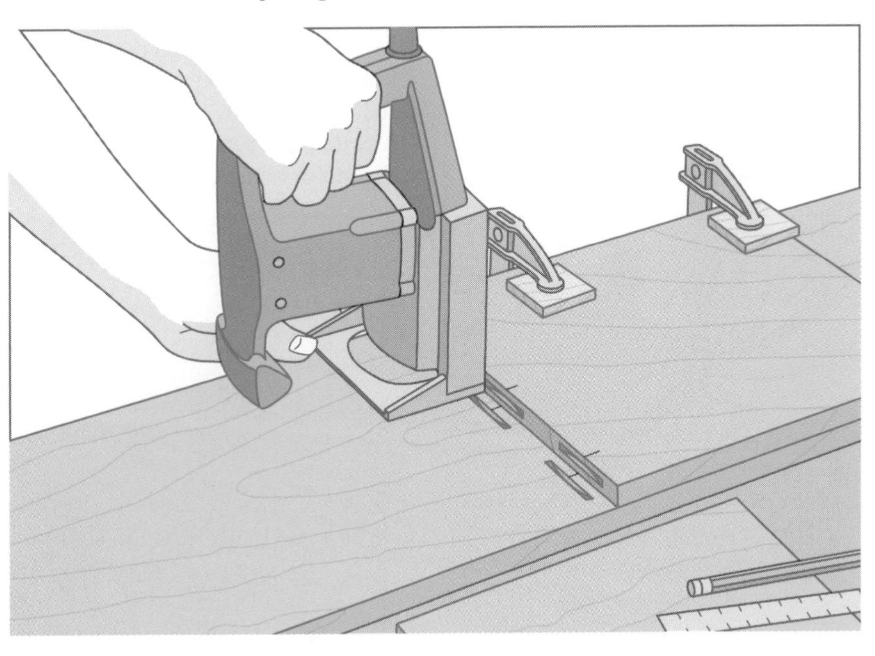

▲ **EDGE-TO-FACE JOINING, 3.** ***To cut corresponding slots in the side panel, hold the tool upright against the shelf edge and align the index mark with the slot centers.***

▼ **EDGE-TO-FACE JOINING, 4.** ***After all the slots have been made, apply glue, insert the plates and assemble the pieces. Check for accurate alignment before clamping.***

▲ **EDGE-TO-EDGE JOINING.** ***When edge-joining lumber, reference slots from the best side of the stock. Place slots 2 in. from the ends and from 4 to 8 in. in between.***

▼ **DOUBLE-PLATING JOINTS.** ***Here, two plates are being installed at the corners of a mitered frame for extra strength. A band clamp will hold the pieces until the glue sets.***

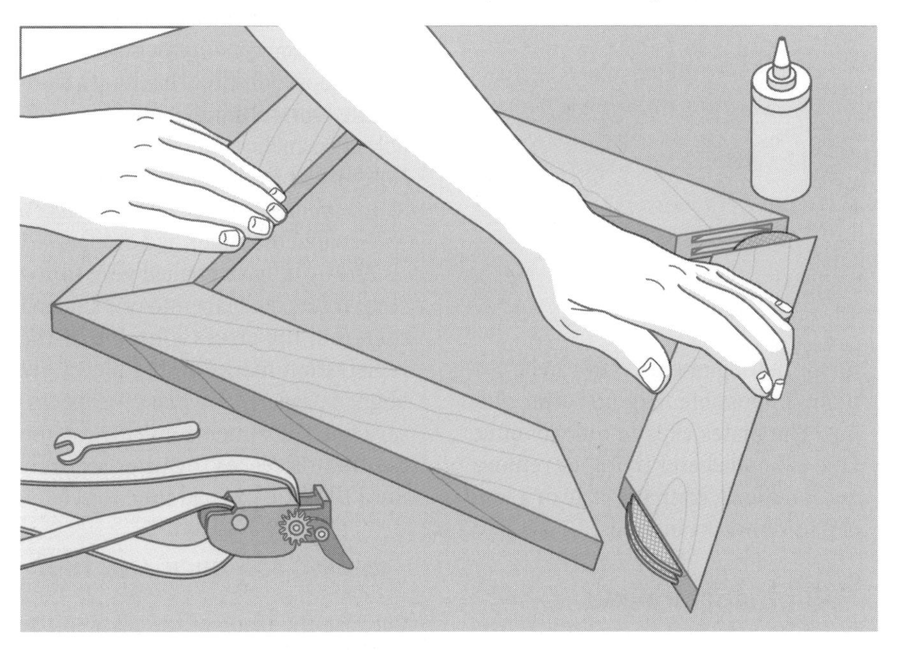

▼ **JOINING OFFSET EDGES.** ***Offset joints can be made by supporting the tool on a spacer block to locate the slot. An L-shaped piece of scrap holds the work in place.***

As well, they're a quick method of joining carcase panels together and then adding shelves to the unit.

The thickness of the stock you're using determines the size of plate that you should use for a project. For thicknesses of ¼ to ½ in., choose No. 0 plates. Select No. 10 plates for stock that's ½ to ¾ in. thick; No. 20 plates for thicker boards. For still thicker stock, you can cut parallel slots for two plates to provide added reinforcement.

Always use the largest plate permissible for the joint being made. Bear in mind that the actual slot is longer than the plate that's suited for it. This places limitations on the width of stock that can be used for both regular face frames and mitered frames. A No. 20 plate, for example, will require at least a 3-in.-wide surface for the slot to be completely contained. The small No. 0 plate needs a width of about 2¼ in. Making mitered frame joints allows for the use of slightly narrower stock since the angled joint face is longer than the stock width. Often, two size plates will be necessary in one assembly.

Set the depth of cut of your plate joiner according to the size of plate that you're going to install—slightly deeper than one-half its width is recommended. Although there aren't any hard and fast rules on the spacing of plates, the closer together you position them, the stronger your joint will be. Locating plates from 4 to 8 in. apart is usually advised. When you're not

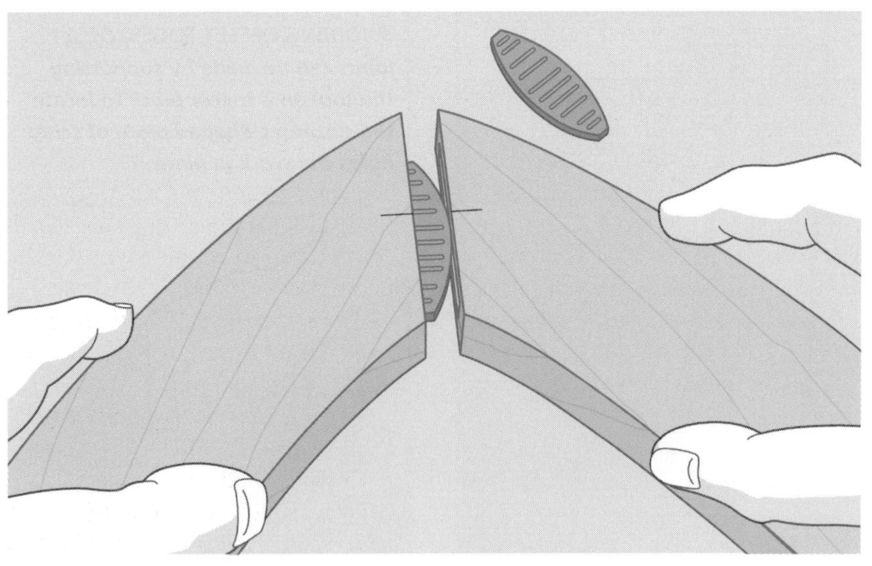

▲ SPECIAL-PLATE JOINING, 1. *These plastic plates hold components together securely with or without glue. Use this type of plate wherever clamping is impossible.*

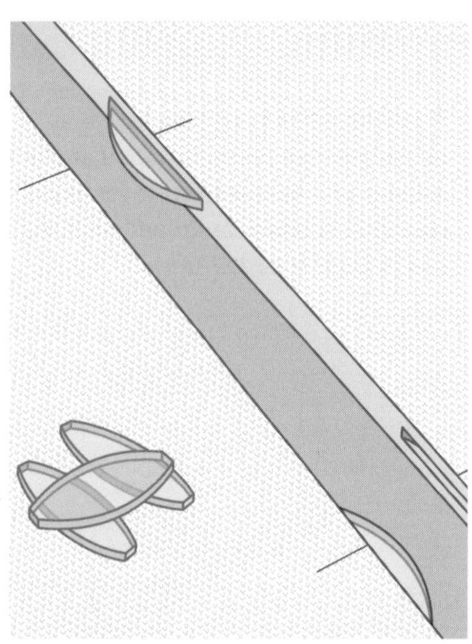

► SPECIAL-PLATE JOINING, 2. *For aligning and stabilizing solid-surfacing materials, plastic, translucent plates are available.*

working with your plates, keep them stored in sealed plastic bags in a spot that stays dry; because they soak up moisture and expand, humidity can make them swell prematurely.

While you don't have to center plate slots precisely in the edge or end of pieces, you should avoid locating them too close to the face of a board. After the stock has been sanded, a plate that is installed within ¼ in. of a surface may produce an unsightly dimple effect—often called a "biscuit pucker."

Make it your practice to dry-assemble your joints to check that they fit. Although plate joints are forgiving of minor misalignments, they can be virtually impossible to adjust after gluing. The plates expand quickly once glue is applied and trying to remove one is difficult; often the plate or a wall of its slot breaks instead.

BUTT JOINING

For the typical end-to-edge butt joint, the first step is to align the mating pieces exactly as they are to be joined and mark the center of the plate slot onto each piece. Keep in mind that while the index mark on the tool's faceplate aids in aligning a slot with the end or edge of the stock, the actual surface of the worktable registers the slot across the thickness of the stock. Therefore, when working in this manner, be sure that the worktable is flat and clean, and place the finish side of the pieces down for the best alignment.

With both the plate joiner and the work resting on the worktable, align the index mark of the plate joiner with the mark you made on the first piece. Turn on the tool's motor, then quickly advance and retract the blade to perform the cut. Repeat the procedure to cut the slot in the other piece.

Assemble the joint to test it, then apply glue to the slots. While the most direct way to apply glue is to simply squirt a little along the slot and push it in with a thin stick, this method isn't very efficient; and with fast-setting glue and many slots to fill, it can be frustrating. The best tool for this job is a specially designed glue bottle that has a narrow nozzle with holes on the sides for distributing glue evenly in the slot. However, you can improvise a simpler and cheaper substitute by using a slim-nozzle hair-coloring applicator available at cosmetic counters. Increase the hole size of the applicator's nozzle to 3⁄32 in. for the thicker glue and use a wax-coated toothpick as a stopper.

After you have applied glue to the slots, insert the plate into one slot and then join the pieces. Check that the registration marks on the pieces are aligned properly and make any necessary fine adjustments quickly. Clamp the mating pieces together securely until the glue has had time to set.

JOINING FOR THICK AND THIN

Because the blade of the plate joiner is centered 7⁄16 in. from the plane of its base, the tool registers a slot that's centered 7⁄16 in. from one face of the stock. Although this places the slot slightly off center in lumber that is ¾ or 13⁄16 in. thick, the asymmetrical slot has little ultimate effect on the integrity of the joint. Just be sure that the working face of each piece to be joined is placed down on the worktable before the cut is made. When the stock is especially thick or extra strength is required, you can simply cut two parallel slots, each 7⁄16 in. in from the stock faces.

For precisely centering the slot in thin stock or when the small size of your work prohibits using a worktable as a reference surface, use the plate joiner's adjustable fence. For a basic edge-to-edge operation such as applying a solid-wood banding around a plywood panel, first adjust the fence so the slot will be positioned appropriately across the thickness of the stock. Then, mark the slot positions on the mating pieces. Hold the fence firmly against the face of the work with the faceplate against the stock edge. Align the index mark and make the plunge cut. When you make the corresponding slots in the adjoining stock, be sure that the fence is held against the same working face to ensure good alignment of the pieces.

MITER JOINING

To make slots for plates in an edge-miter joint, set the adjustable fence in the 45° miter position and perform the cuts. Most plate joiners register the cut against the inside work surface. Models equipped with a fence that registers against the outside work surface ensure the outside of the joint will be aligned regardless of any variation in the thickness of the stock.

Plate-joined mitered frames are easier for you to assemble than dowel-joined frames because the component pieces can be shifted slightly for the best alignment. Wrap a band clamp snugly around the perimeter of the frame to hold the pieces together until the glue sets.

EDGE-TO-EDGE JOINING

Like doweling, plate joinery is an excellent way to align and strengthen glued-up panels. For good alignment of the boards, choose the best side of each one and make these sides the reference faces for all of the slots. In this way, any variation in thickness from one board to the next will be apparent only on the poorer side of the assembled panel. Locate your slots 2 in. from the ends of the boards and 4 to 8 in. apart in between.

EDGE-TO-FACE JOINING

In addition to joining stock edge to edge, the plate joiner excels at edge-to-face joints typical in shelf and cabinet construction. And because there's no traditional joinery involved, each component can be cut to its exact size for assembly.

To join the edge of a shelf to the side panel of a case, for example, first mark the location of the shelf on the side panel. Position the shelf edge flat along this mark, align the side edges of both pieces and secure the components with a clamp so that they don't shift. Then, mark the slot locations on the components.

With the fence removed, rest the base of the plate joiner on the side panel and cut the slots in the edge of the shelf. To cut the corresponding slots in the side panel, place the base of the plate joiner up against the edge of the shelf, align the centered index mark with the slot locations and perform the cuts. After all of the cuts have been made, apply glue to the slots and install the plates, then assemble the components and clamp until the glue sets.

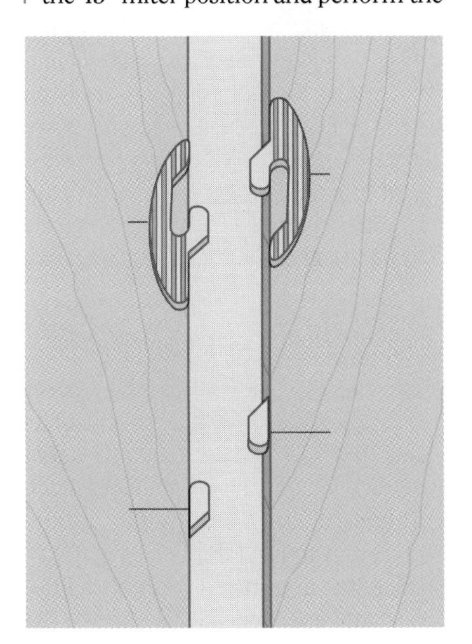

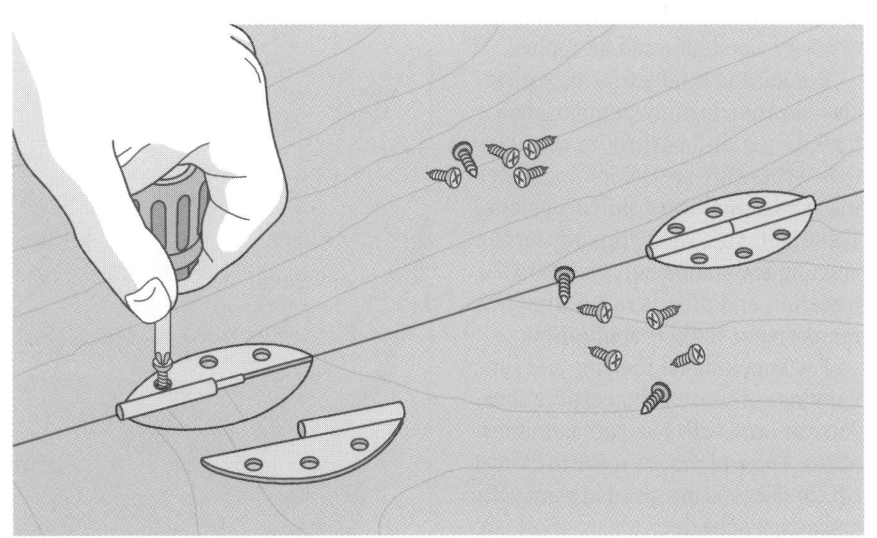

◀ **SPECIAL-PLATE JOINING, 3.** ***The fittings shown on the surface of the panels at top are for inserting into No. 20 slots—as indicated at bottom.***

▲ **SPECIAL-PLATE JOINING, 4.** ***These hinges are flush-mounted in recesses milled with a plate joiner. Their halves detach for easy installing.***

MAKING OFFSET JOINTS

Offset joints such as the leg-to-apron joint of a table are easily made by positioning a spacer block under the base of the plate joiner and resting the stock directly on the worktable. An L-shaped support block that is clamped in place behind the workpiece, for example, takes the thrust of the plunge cut and allows you to work with both hands on the tool.

SPECIALTY PLATES

Most tool manufacturers offer only the common wooden plates in the three standard sizes; some provide wooden plates in five sizes, one smaller and one bigger than standard, for use with their models. However, there are also several special-purpose products available that increase the versatility of any type of plate joiner.

For example, when it's impossible to apply clamping pressure, there's an adhesive plate that can usually solve the problem. The plate is made of plastic and features barbed cross ribs that grip the sides of the slot. Although no glue is necessary with this type of plate, ordinary wood glue can be applied.

For joining solid-surfacing materials—an increasingly popular choice for kitchen and bathroom countertops—there are special joining plates made of translucent polypropylene. These plates are used primarily for the aligning and stabilizing of joints in the material, and glue is not normally a requirement in their application.

For knock-down shelving and similar kinds of construction applications, you can work with two-part aluminum plates. These plates are made to fit into No. 20 slots and are glued in place with a two-part adhesive.

Detachable cabinet-hinge plates are made that fit into mating slots cut in doors and cabinets. Available in left- and right-handed versions, they come in brass, nickeled-steel or black finish.

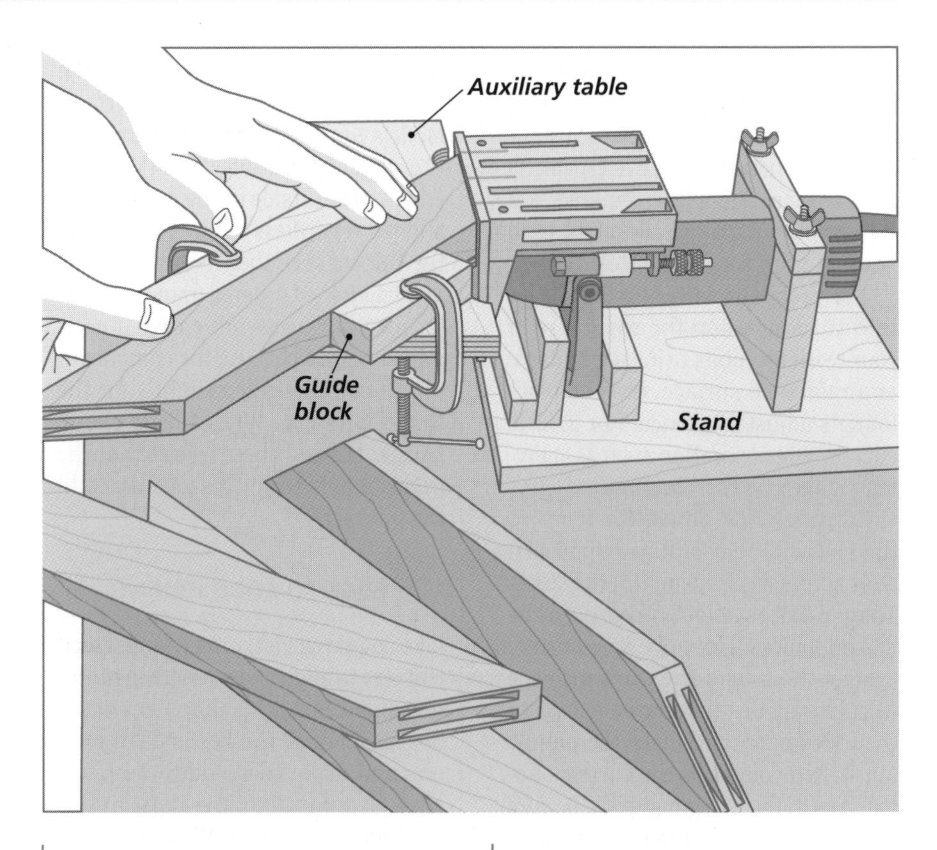

▲ **STATIONARY-TOOL JOINING, 1.** ***A bench-mounted plate joiner is ideal for working on small parts and repetitive jobs. Here, guide blocks uniformly register stock for miter joints.***

▼ **STATIONARY-TOOL JOINING, 2.** ***With this shopmade bevel platform appropriately positioned on the stand's auxiliary table, slots can be cut for miter joints of any angle.***

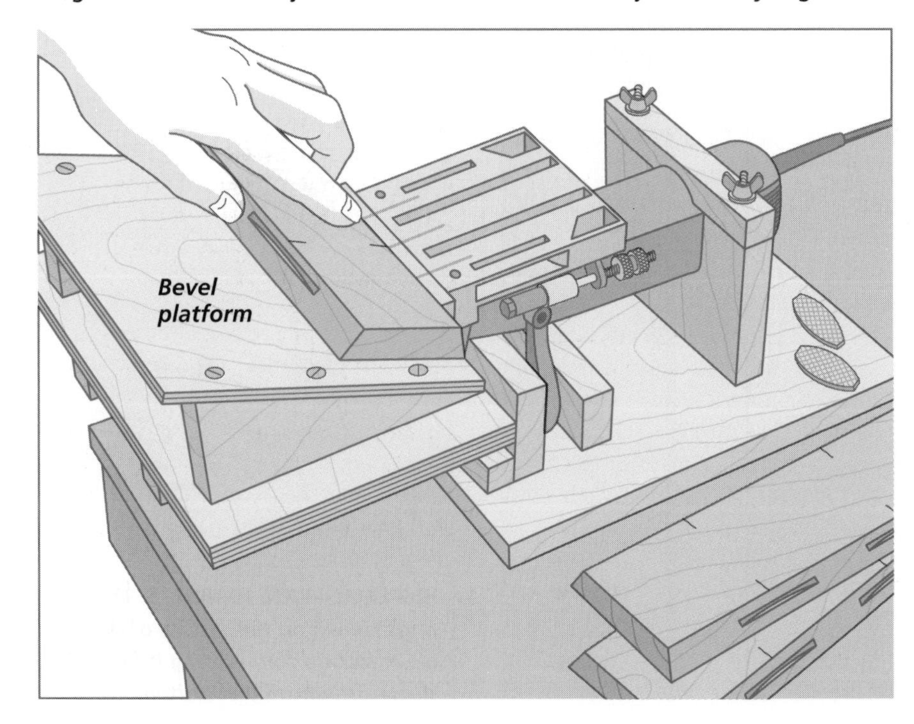

◀ **STATIONARY-TOOL JOINING, 3.** ***A bevel platform can also be used on its own with the plate joiner for bevels other than 45°. Be sure to clamp your work securely to prevent it shifting.***

▼ **STATIONARY-TOOL JOINING, 4.** ***This platform jig consistently positions both the plate joiner and the stock. A pair of projecting nail points in the base anchor the workpiece.***

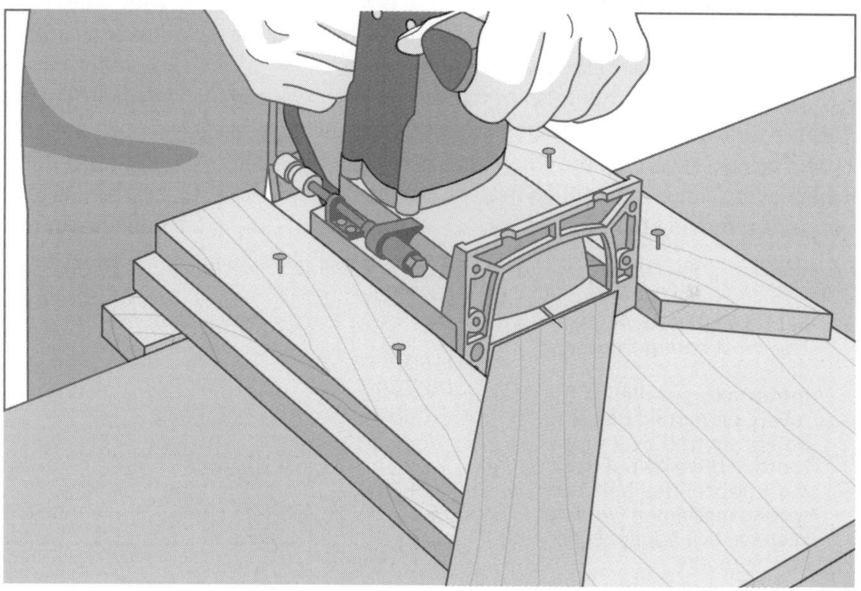

JIGS AND FIXTURES

Although the portability of the plate joiner is a desirable feature, handling small stock or performing repetitive work is better done on a stationary machine. And a shopmade stand can be easily designed and built to convert your plate joiner into a versatile stationary tool.

A basic stand for the plate joiner consists of a wooden base with support blocks that hold the tool in place upside down. Shape the rear support block to fit around the motor housing and hold the tool level. Add a small curved piece onto the front support block that fits inside the tool's handle.

To lock the plate joiner to the stand, make a crosspiece that can be tightened over the motor housing and onto the rear support block by means of two hanger bolts and wingnuts. A slide-in block with finger holes is needed to wedge the handle tightly in place on the front support block.

A simple auxiliary table can be made out of ½-in. plywood that is reinforced underneath with two cleats. To attach the table, you'll need to drill four holes for flat-head screws through the fence of the plate joiner. Note also that the table may require cutouts in order to provide clearance for the tool's fence-height adjustment controls.

When using the plate joiner in conjunction with the stand, blocks can be clamped to the table to align the stock and ensure accurate repetitive cuts. You can handle edges that are beveled to any angle with the addition of a simple bevel platform. Just construct the platform at the desired angle and use a pair of nail points protruding from the bottom to hold it firmly in position on the table.

When the plate joiner isn't in the stand, a similar type of bevel platform makes joining edge miters other than 45° easy. And holding narrow pieces is facilitated by using a platform with blocks that position the tool and the stock. Two nail points protruding from the base of the platform serve to hold the work while the cut is made.

SANDERS

There are many aspects of woodworking that are enjoyable and satisfying—even fun. Sanding wood, however, isn't usually considered by many to be one of them. Unfortunately, though, sanding is a necessary and important part of the building process.

Presented here are guidelines and shop-tested techniques for using four popular types of power sanders: the belt sander, the ¼-sheet palm sander, the ½-sheet finishing sander and the disc sander. The information provided will help to make smoothing wood less of a chore for you, enable you to achieve better results and assist you in getting the most from each tool. Besides smoothing wood, techniques for using a power sander to remove rust from metal and polish finished surfaces are also included.

Belt sanders are the most popular way to remove stock and smooth surfaces. They're designated by the size of the sanding belt they use, and techniques are shown for three common versions: 2½ x 16 in., 3 x 21 in. and 3 x 24 in.—the smaller number representing the width of the belt and the larger number equal to the belt's circumference.

The palm sander and finishing sander are both types of orbital sanders. These tools are extremely safe and easy to use. The disc sander, on the other hand, is very aggressive in its abrading action and caution must be exercised in order to prevent removing too much stock.

BELT SANDER BASICS

You've just finished gluing up boards for a tabletop. The glue is dry, and it's time to remove the clamps. And whether you've done this job a hundred times or this is your first effort, the next steps are to inspect the joints and check the panel for flatness. Don't be surprised if there's a ridge at every seam due to misaligned boards. Even the best lamination requires some surfacing before the panel is ready for final sanding and finishing.

Woodworkers have two solutions to the problem. You can either get a hand plane and shave the surface flat, or you can plug in your belt sander and wear away the imperfections. While a sharp plane—lubricated with a little elbow grease—will handle the job, many workshoppers opt for the belt sander.

Not only does the belt sander remove stock quickly and with little effort, the tool produces a uniform surface regardless of changes in grain direction. And controlling the degree of smoothness is simply a matter of installing the appropriate belt. There's no blade sharpening, and the adjustments required are minimal.

If all of this sounds too good to be true, in a way it is. The belt sander's voracious appetite makes it one of the more difficult power tools to control. If it's not handled with skill,

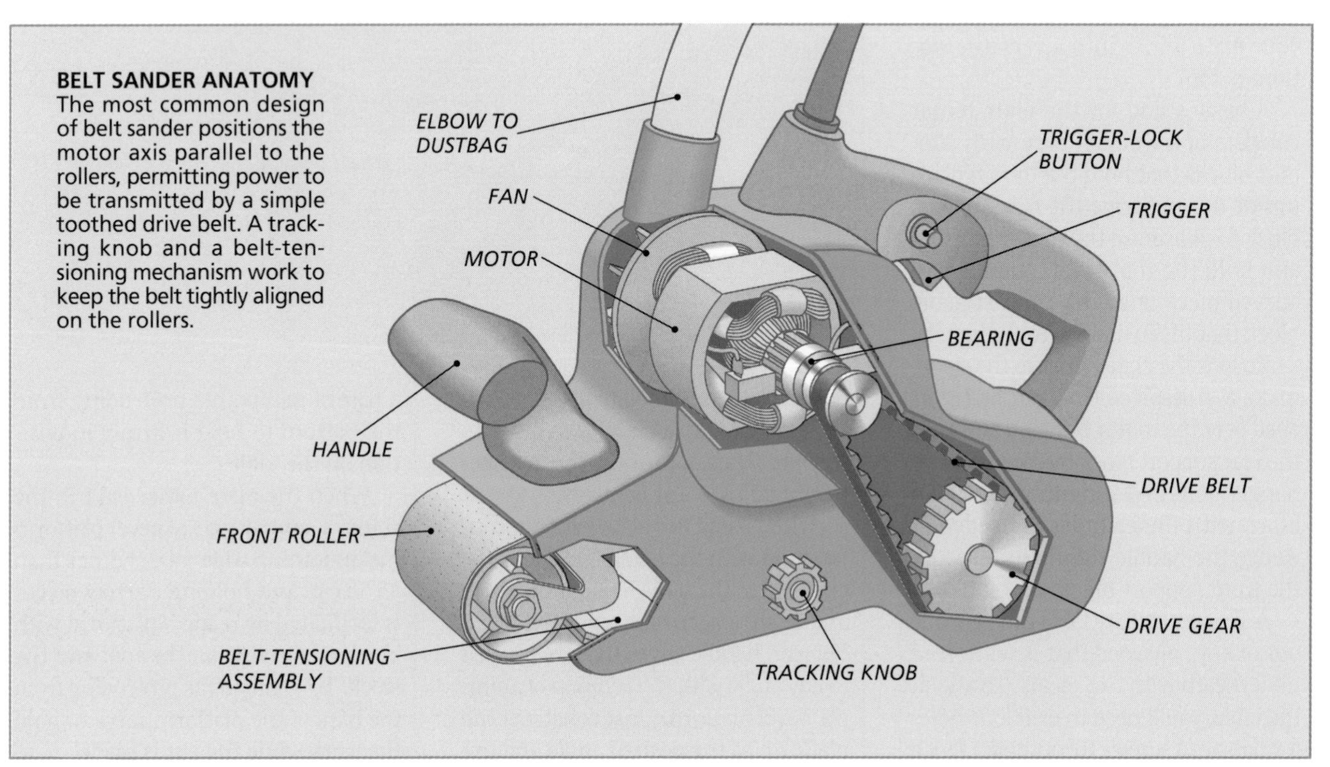

BELT SANDER ANATOMY
The most common design of belt sander positions the motor axis parallel to the rollers, permitting power to be transmitted by a simple toothed drive belt. A tracking knob and a belt-tensioning mechanism work to keep the belt tightly aligned on the rollers.

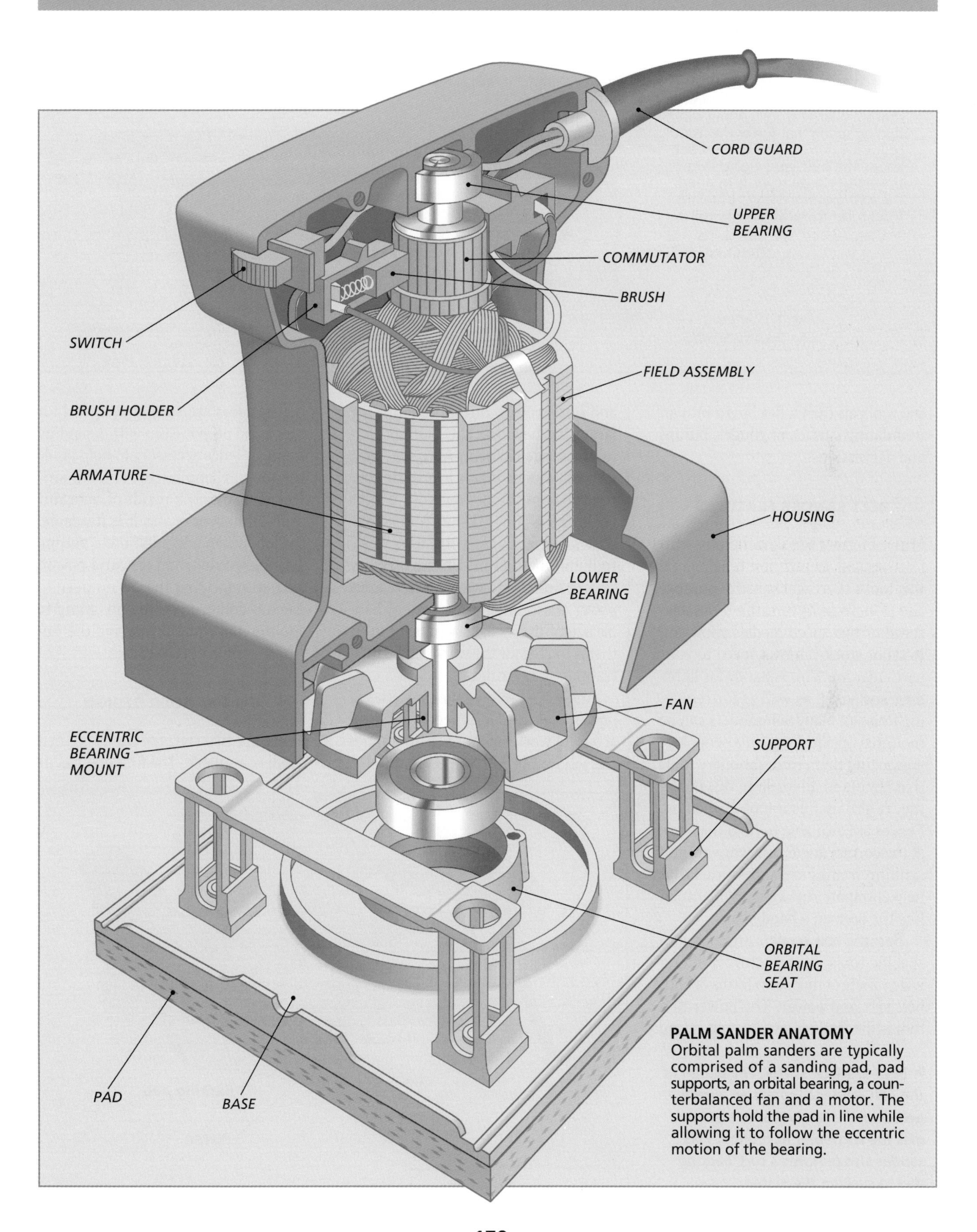

PALM SANDER ANATOMY
Orbital palm sanders are typically comprised of a sanding pad, pad supports, an orbital bearing, a counterbalanced fan and a motor. The supports hold the pad in line while allowing it to follow the eccentric motion of the bearing.

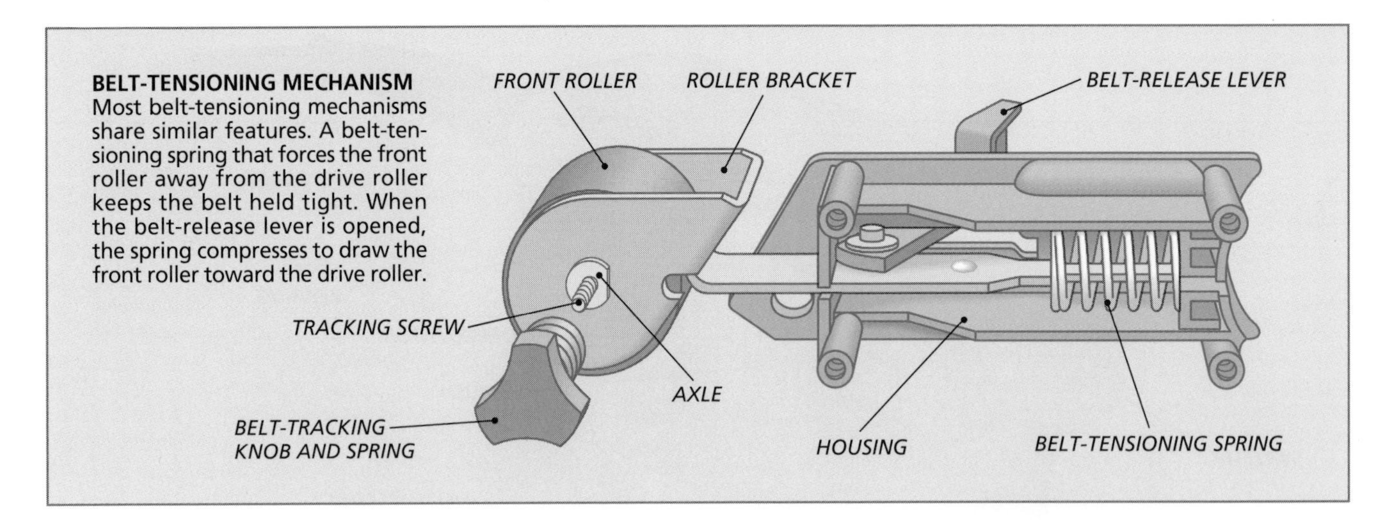

BELT-TENSIONING MECHANISM Most belt-tensioning mechanisms share similar features. A belt-tensioning spring that forces the front roller away from the drive roller keeps the belt held tight. When the belt-release lever is opened, the spring compresses to draw the front roller toward the drive roller.

the tool can turn a flat board into an undulating surface of gouges, bumps and depressions.

BELT SANDER FEATURES

Many of today's belt sanders come with features and accessories to help tame this tool's overeager sense of purpose and to increase its versatility. Variable-speed or two-speed models allow you to tailor stock-removal speed to your particular job. This is handy for light-duty surfacing, as well as for removing finishes. Many belt sanders can be mounted upside down on a benchtop, converting them into stationary tools that handle small work. In this mode, they're also useful for tool sharpening. Fences are available to hold the work at the correct angle, and wrap-around sanding frames are accessories that help eliminate surface gouging much like the base on a hand plane.

Because belt sanders are such job-specific tools, manufacturers offer a wide variety of models in terms of both belt size and power. The power of a tool is determined by the amp rating and horsepower, but in general, the larger the belt size, the more powerful the sander. When you're shopping for a belt sander, it pays to analyze your needs before you get out your checkbook. Unless you're doing a lot of large-scale sanding, it's likely that a 3 x 21-in. tool will fit the bill. Unlike circular saws or drills, for instance, where extra power doesn't mean you cannot handle a light-duty job, using a belt sander that is too big for the work can be frustrating—if not ruinous.

And where many other varieties of power tools are designed to produce accurate work far more easily than if the job had been handled manually, belt sanders are simply designed for speed and power. Even with a sanding frame or fence accessory to help guide the tool, getting a true, smooth surface is as much a result of operator skill—if not more—as it is if you did the job by hand. In addition to getting a sander of the right size and power, keep in mind that there's no need to pay top dollar if you're only going to use the tool occasionally and the finished work isn't that critical.

BELT SANDER DESIGN

There are two styles of 3 x 21-in. belt sanders available. The first one has its

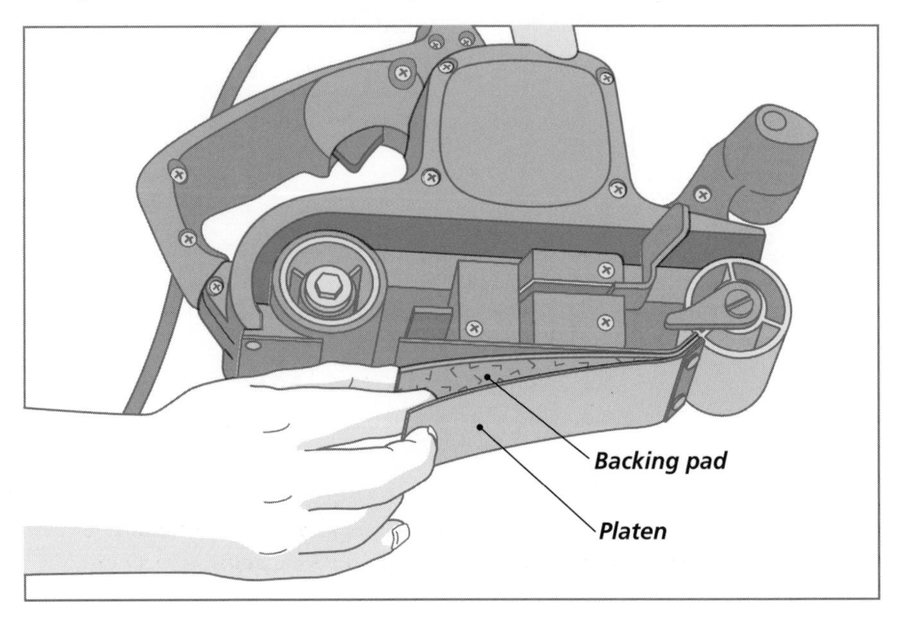

► **BELT SANDER SETUP.** ***The platen of the belt sander supports an abrasive belt over the sanding area and handles the friction of its motion. This sander also features a cork backing pad to cushion the platen.***

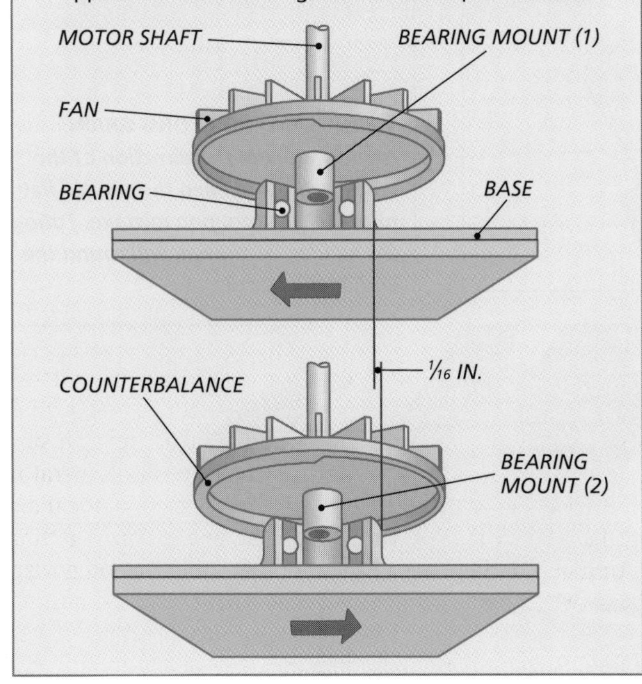

▼ **ORBITAL SANDER SETUP, 1.** ***With the swing-arm clamping system of this orbital sander, the retractable arm is first pushed out, then lifted. This opens the spring-loaded clamp for loading the paper.***

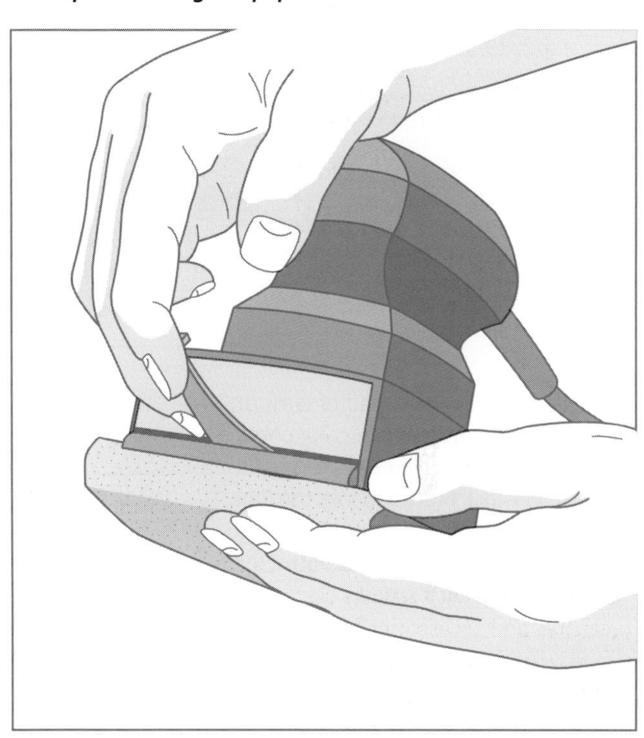

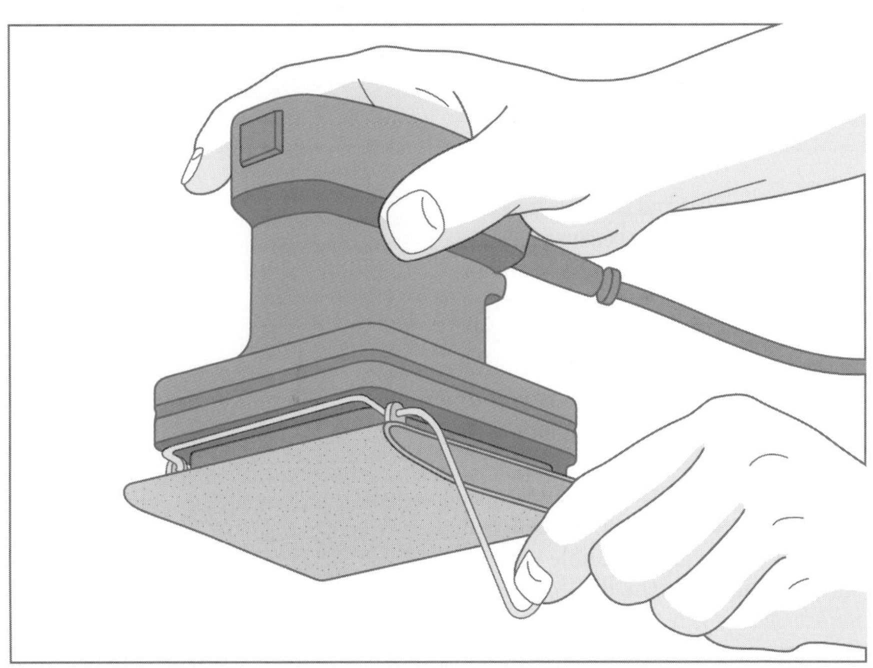

▲ **ORBITAL SANDER SETUP, 2.** ***The bent-wire clamping system of this orbital sander utilizes the spring tension of the wire to hold the paper. A lever on each side controls the clamping at each end.***

motor mounted at a right angle to the length of the tool. This transverse type is also the standard model for the larger, heavy-duty versions. In the second configuration, the motor is placed parallel to the length of the tool. Called inline belt sanders, they're more compact, easy to flip over for use on the bench and generally require less effort to handle.

In addition to a motor-and-drive system, all belt sanders have a spring-loaded belt-tensioning mechanism to keep the belt taut on the rollers—usually a metal front roller and a rubber drive roller that prevents slippage. A belt-release lever backs off belt tension for removing the belt, and a tracking knob adjusts the position of the front roller to keep the belt from shifting too far to one side; on some models, tracking of the belt is adjusted automatically. The sanding area of the belt is supported by a metal platen, which

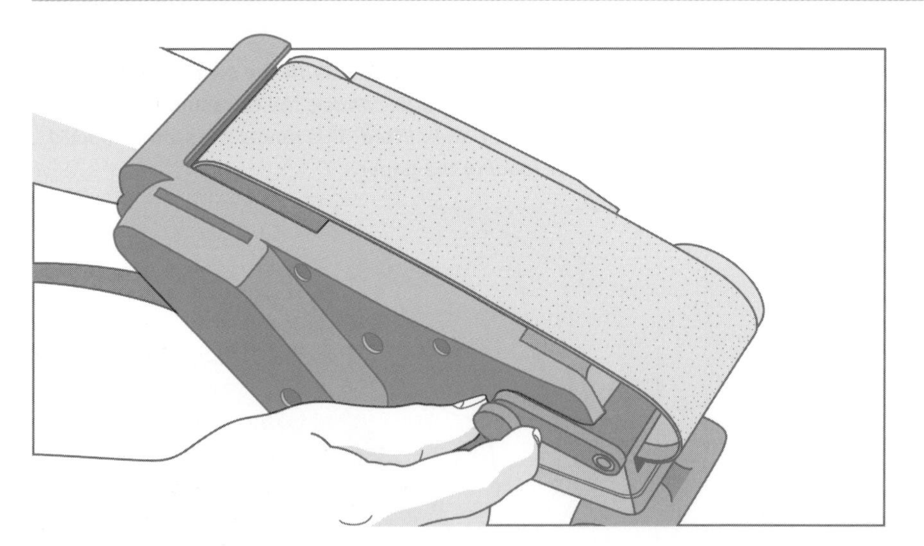

◀ **ADJUSTING BELT TRACKING.** ***Most belt sanders have a belt-tracking knob near the front roller. While the sander is running, turn the knob until the belt is centered.***

▼ **BELT SANDING ALONG GRAIN.** ***Always work in the direction of the wood grain and keep the sander flat to avoid this common mistake. Tilting the sander, as shown, will round the end of the board.***

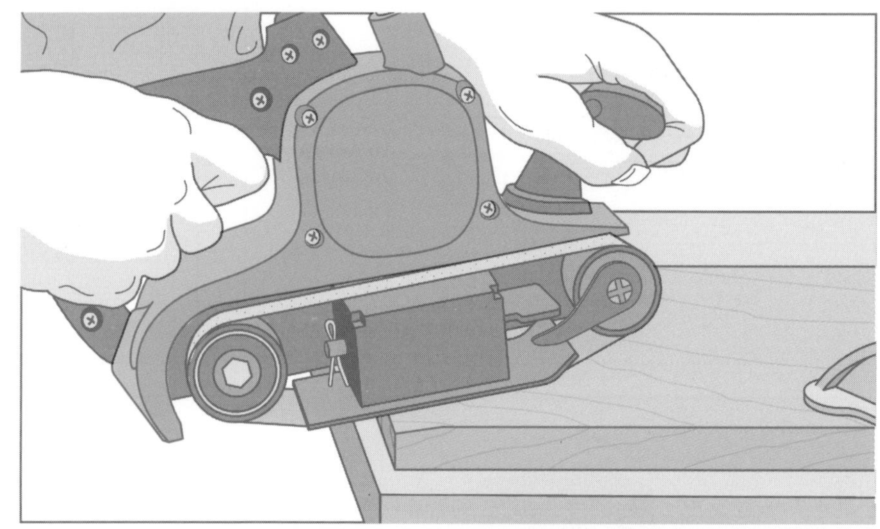

may be backed with a pad of cork or rubber. Belt sanders typically come equipped with a trigger switch, as well as a trigger-lock button to lock the tool on for continued operation. Variable-speed models also feature a control for adjusting the belt's speed.

THE BELT SANDER FOR YOU

When deciding on the belt sander to purchase, be sure to check out the features of various models. As well, you'll probably want to know how fast each tool removes material. You can get an idea of how effective the tools are by comparing their specifications—most specifically, the weight, maximum belt speed as measured in surface feet per minute (sfpm), platen area and motor size. Maximum belt speed can range from about 600 sfpm to 1600 sfpm. Amperage ratings typically vary from about 3 amps to 10 amps. All this information is supplied in tool catalogs.

All things being equal, a heavier belt sander will remove stock more quickly with less effort, and a higher speed produces the same result. Given a consistent belt width, a larger platen area will also contribute to faster sanding. However, in all cases you need a motor that's powerful enough to maintain belt speed once the tool is set on the wood. More subjectively, a comfortable, quiet, vibration-free tool with well designed handles and controls may feel more effective simply because it's easier to handle. Check the procedure for changing the belt, a simple practice that shouldn't be a troublesome task.

Other features worth looking for include a design that permits you to mount the tool upside down for use as a stationary sander, an extra-long power cord, a belt-release lever and, most importantly, a dust-collection bag. Belt sanders create an incredible volume of dust and while the dustbag won't

▶ **BELT SANDING ACROSS GRAIN.** ***Although sanding across the grain isn't ordinarily recommended, the procedure is a good way to remove stock quickly from rough lumber.***

▲ **LIGHTWEIGHT BELT SANDING.** ***Weighing only 4½ lb., this belt sander is small enough to operate with one hand. Light weight is especially important when you're shaping wood.***

▼ **CLEANING ABRASIVE BELTS.** ***Extend the life of abrasive belts by cleaning them with a rubber eraser stick. Hold the stick against the running belt to remove wood dust.***

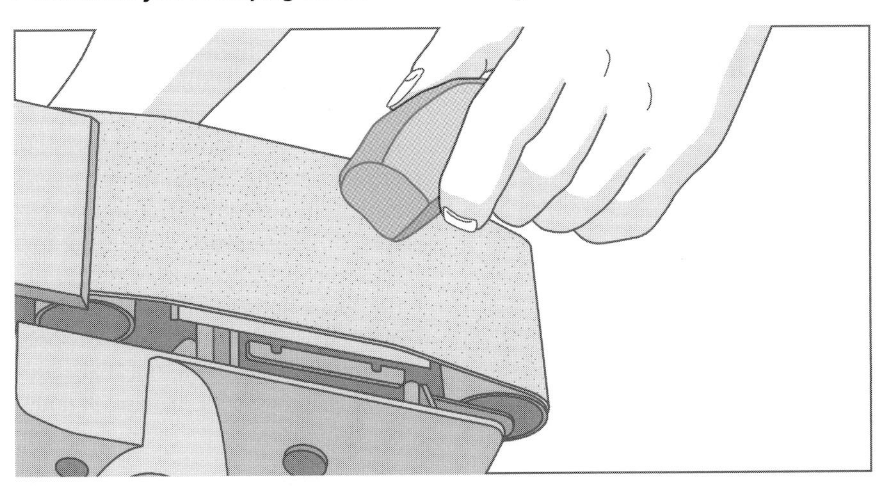

collect all of it, capturing most of it is certainly a real plus.

Note that the prices usually quoted for belt sanders are the manufacturer's suggested retail prices. In order to be competitive, most dealers and mail-order distributors sell for less, and it's worth doing a little comparison shopping on price so that you'll get the most belt sander for your money.

BELT SANDER TECHNIQUES

While the belt sander is an excellent all-purpose sander, it's also one of the most misunderstood—and consequently misused—power tools in the home workshop. When it's used properly, the belt sander can save you many hours of arm-wearying work and help you to produce projects with a truly professional finish. Many beginning woodworkers, however, have a tendency to ask the belt sander to perform sanding tasks for which it isn't designed. The tool shouldn't, for example, be used to remove great amounts of stock best handled by a block plane. Read the manufacturer's manual that comes with your tool. There are three basic reasons why: (1) to make sure that you learn how to use the tool correctly, (2) to know what maintenance is—and is not—required and (3) to learn what accessories the manufacturer offers for use with the tool.

Make certain that you keep abrasive belts of a variety of different grits on hand. Abrasive belts are commonly available ranging from 50 grit to 180 grit; the lower the number, the coarser the grit. Stock coarse 60 and 80 grits for shaping and rough sanding such as removing paint. For general home and shop carpentry, lay in a healthy supply of belts in the 100- and 120-grit range. These medium-grit belts are good for smoothing rough surfaces as well as for removing minor surface scratches and irregularities. Use finer grits for final smoothing; some of these are not available in all belt sizes so check this point before buying your tool. Most hardware stores and home centers carry abrasive belts, but it's usually more economical to purchase them by the dozen from a mail-order woodworking supply firm.

When changing abrasive belts on the belt sander, the first step is to eliminate tension—a specific procedure that varies from one model to the next. Remove the old belt and slip the new one over the rollers, making sure that the arrows on the inside surface of the belt point in the direction of travel. Restore tension, then plug in and turn on the tool to adjust the tracking of the belt. Even if your belt sander has a dust-collection bag, always wear a dust mask or respirator when using the tool to prevent the inhalation of fine wood dust. To avoid overheating of the tool, clean the air ports regularly with compressed air.

Belt sanders are not particularly difficult to operate, but they do take some practice before you become comfortable with the weight and balance of your particular tool. One of the most common mistakes is pressing down too hard during sanding. This will only clog the belt, reduce the tool's effectiveness and put undue strain on the motor. Allow the weight of the tool to provide downward pressure and use both hands for guiding.

Be sure that the workpiece you're sanding is fastened securely in place with clamps or butted against a backstop—which can simply be a board that's nailed or clamped to your workbench. Guide the tool in straight, overlapping passes in the direction of the wood's grain to prevent leaving lasting, cross-grain scratches. You can move the sander side to side across the width of the board as long as the belt remains parallel with the wood's grain. However, although sanding across the grain isn't ordinarily recommended, the technique is a good way to remove stock quickly from rough lumber.

Keep the sander flat on your work surface and moving at all times. Avoid the common mistake of tilting the tool off the end of a board, which will round the edge. Equally poor technique, however, is to stop the sander with the platen short of the edge, which will usually result in a dished, or concave, surface at the end of the board. Sanding in one spot for just a few seconds will quickly create a depression.

To sand small, awkward or irregular-shaped pieces, mount the sander on your workbench. If you're setting up the tool in a vise, avoid overtightening; too much clamping pressure will break the housing. When operating the sander in this manner, work uniformly across the abrasive belt to prevent it from wearing unevenly.

You can extend the life of your abrasive belts by cleaning them with a rubber eraser stick. Simply hold the stick up against the belt while it's running on the tool to remove clogged particles of wood dust.

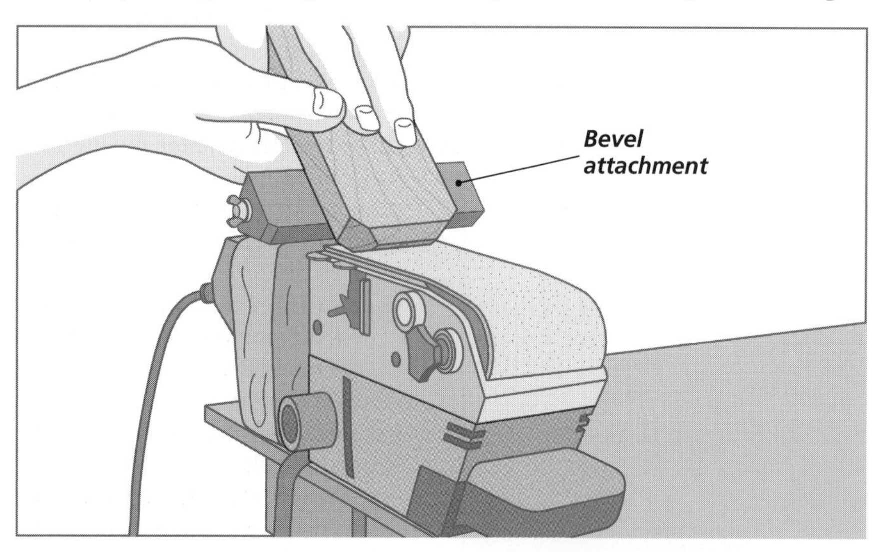

▲ **STATIONARY BELT SANDING, 1.** ***A flat-top belt sander can be clamped to your workbench for use as a stationary tool. The special attachment shown aids the sanding of bevels.***

PALM SANDER BASICS

Most home workshops are equipped with a range of power tools that not only take the fatigue out of woodworking, but also do the job with a high degree of precision. Sanding is no exception.

Orbital sanders are designed specifically for preparing finish-ready surfaces and for light sanding between coats of finish. Unlike belt and disc sanders, the tools aren't intended to remove large amounts of material. In orbital sanding, a sanding pad moves rapidly in a steady series of tiny circles, or orbits, while remaining in a relatively fixed position in relation to the tool's housing. The combination of small orbit diameter and high-speed motion provides for a tool that sands quickly, but without marring or gouging the work.

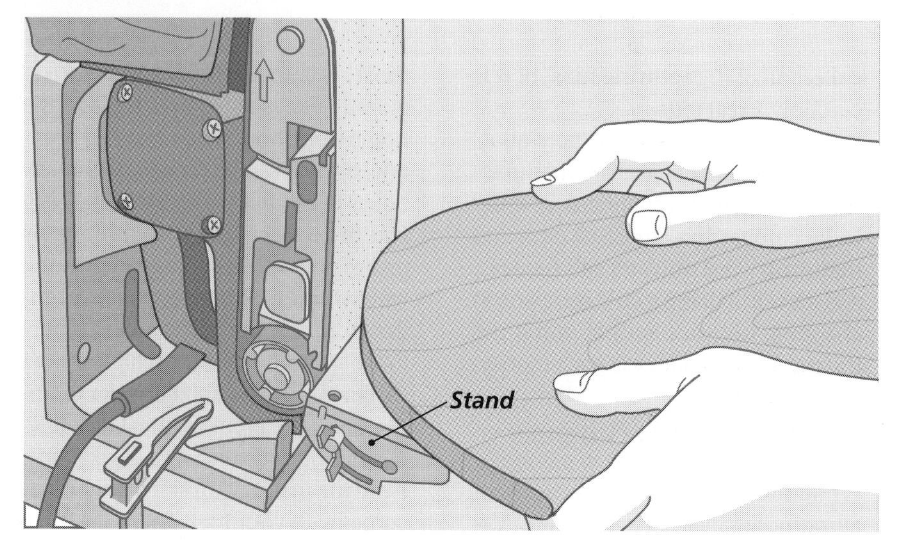

▶ **STATIONARY BELT SANDING, 2.** ***Here, the front handle of the belt sander has been removed and the tool is bolted onto a stand to convert it to a benchtop sander. The table tilts to a 45° angle.***

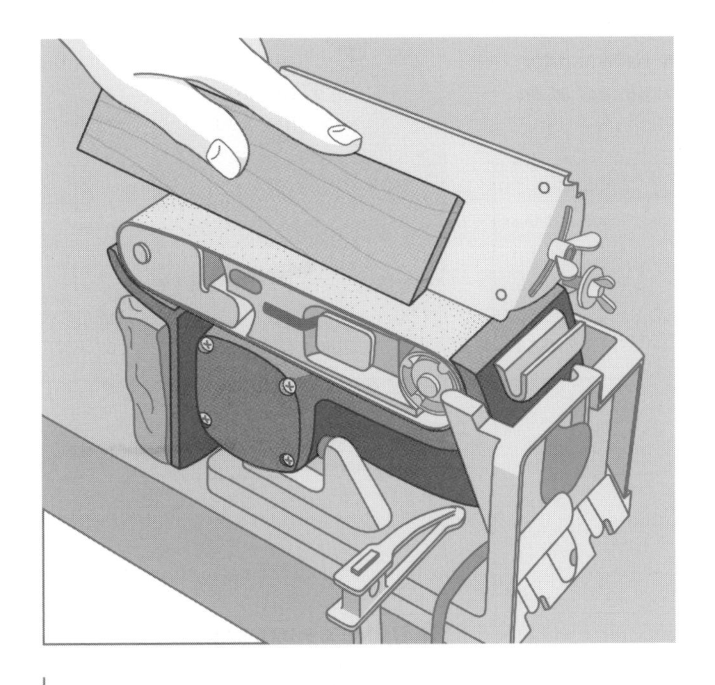

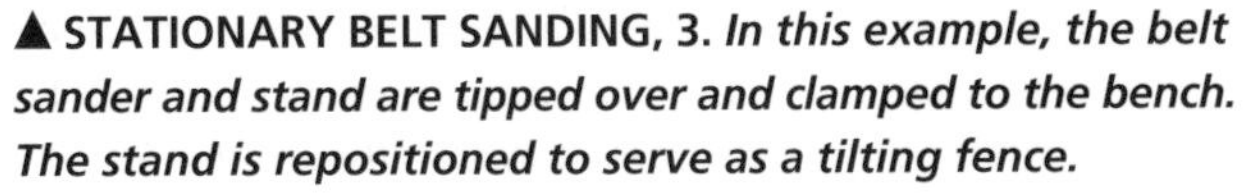

▲ STATIONARY BELT SANDING, 3. *In this example, the belt sander and stand are tipped over and clamped to the bench. The stand is repositioned to serve as a tilting fence.*

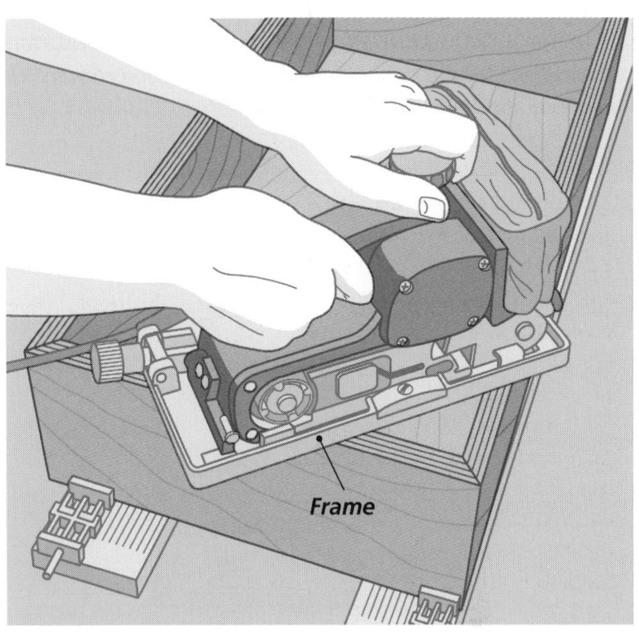

▲ USING A BELT SANDER FRAME. *A sanding frame keeps the belt sander level to prevent gouging on broad surfaces or to span two edges, as with this drawer top.*

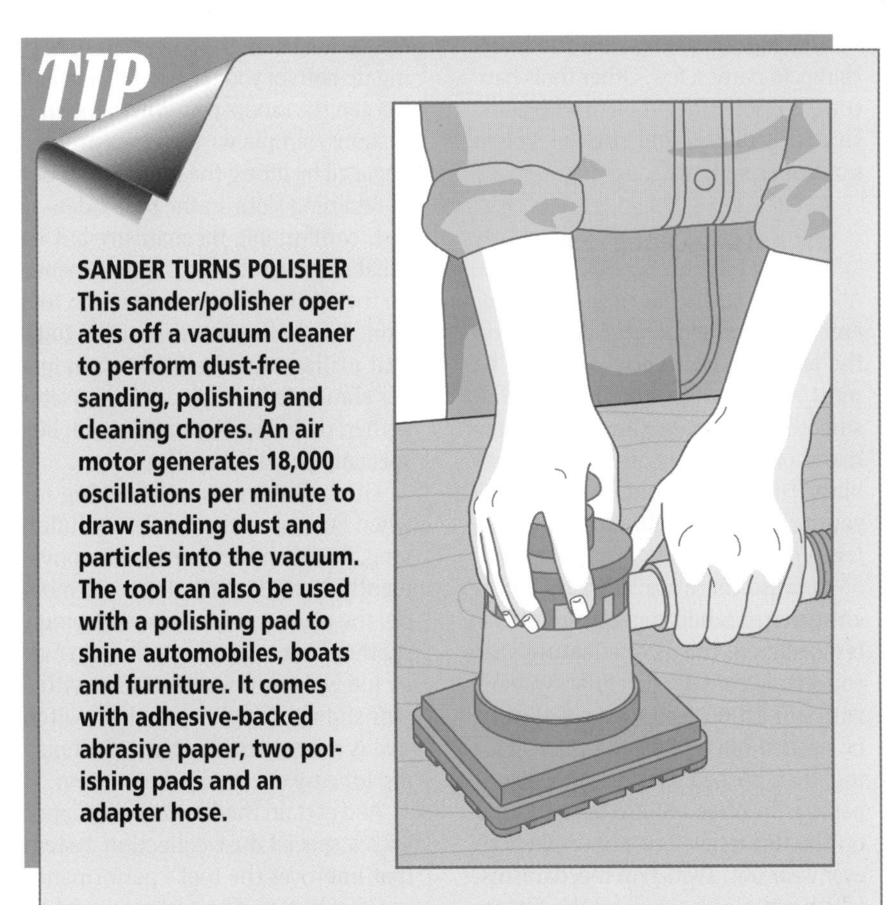

TIP

SANDER TURNS POLISHER
This sander/polisher operates off a vacuum cleaner to perform dust-free sanding, polishing and cleaning chores. An air motor generates 18,000 oscillations per minute to draw sanding dust and particles into the vacuum. The tool can also be used with a polishing pad to shine automobiles, boats and furniture. It comes with adhesive-backed abrasive paper, two polishing pads and an adapter hose.

One of the most popular types of orbital sanders available is the ¼-sheet palm sander, which accepts a ¼-sheet of standard 9 x 11-in. sandpaper. There are many different models of the tool on the market, all of which produce an equally acceptable finished surface. However, in many aspects of their performance, the tools demonstrate clear contrasts. Cutting speed varies considerably, for example, as does the level of vibration and noise. From one model to the next, there's also a wide range of contact-torque—the tendency for the tool to spin when it touches the wood. As a general rule, many of the harder-to-handle tools actually cut more quickly than the smoother-operating models.

PALM SANDER FEATURES

Palm sanders are classified according to their number of orbits per minute (opm). Most of the tools fall within a range of from 12,000 opm to 15,000 opm. Amperage ratings typically vary from about 1.2 amps to 2 amps.

▼ **USING A PALM SANDER, 1.** ***Besides smoothing flat surfaces, the palm sander is excellent for the softening of sharp edges and corners. Hold the sander at an angle of about 45°.***

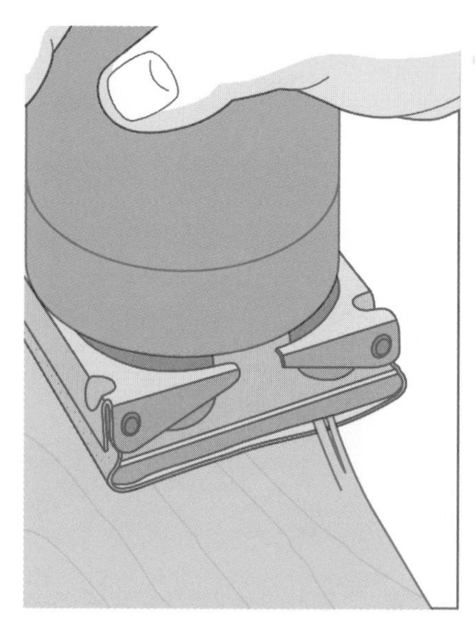

▲ **USING A PALM SANDER, 2.** ***Advancing with the open side of the sander can cause the edge of the abrasive paper to catch on splinters, as shown. Rotate the sander 90°.***

Palm sanders are typically equipped with either a rubber or felt sanding pad. It's claimed that the soft, sponge-rubber pad is superior for contoured surfaces and the harder felt is a better choice for flat surfaces. However, the performance and handling variations among the tools are probably far more significant to the general woodworker than the differences in pad material. If a sander is to be used exclusively on contours, a softer pad would seem to be a plus. However, pad thickness also plays a role. The unusually thin ⅛-in.-thick rubber pad on some models, for example, does not have the resiliency of the 5⁄16-in.-thick pad on others. Most rubber pads average about ¼ in. thick.

While the manufacturers appear to have reached a general consensus on how these tools should look and work, they haven't come to agreement on how the sandpaper should be attached. On most models, the sandpaper is held onto the tool's pad by clamps—usually a pair of spring-loaded metal jaws. But there are many variations in the clamping system: single-arm, twin-arm, swing-arm, bent-wire and lever-clamp, to name a few. Other tools have tried to resolve the problem with adhesive-backed, peel-and-stick or Velcro sandpaper systems.

THE PALM SANDER FOR YOU

Allow your particular needs and preferences to influence your decision on the palm sander to buy. You may be most interested in a tool with solid, smooth performance and all the earmarks of heavy-duty quality and reliability. Or, sheer cutting speed may be your priority, with vibration and noise levels of no concern.

Because there are so many different types of sandpaper-clamping systems offered, this is one feature that you should consider carefully. Systems with stiff-action swing arms that must be pushed out and pried up for loading, then pushed back once the sandpaper is in place tend to be very hard on the fingertips, but are unlikely to ever wear out. Twin-arm mechanisms, which can also be hard on the fingertips, at least have the advantage of freeing up both of your hands to align and tighten the sandpaper. With bent-wire systems, simple wire clamps are disengaged by lifting the looped ends out of retaining slots on the base sides—a fast, comfortable mechanism, but its reliability over the long term depends on the ability of the wire to retain tension. And remember that while tools that utilize adhesive-backed sandpaper eliminate the clamp problem altogether, they also demand that you buy specially-prepared sanding discs.

Other features worth looking for when buying a palm sander include a long, flexible power cord and a conveniently-located switch. On some models, the power cord may be annoyingly short or kinky. On others, the grip may be too wide or uncomfortable, with a stiff sliding, toggle or rocker switch that is recessed too deeply in the housing for easy one-handed operation.

And certain models come equipped with a special dust-collection system that improves the tool's performance as a fast cutter. The system works by

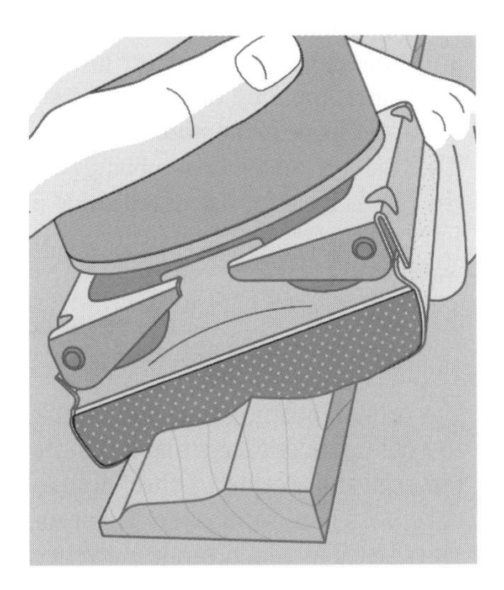

▼ **USING A FINISHING SANDER, 1.** ***The unique design of this triangular-pad sander permits working in confined spaces, such as in between louvers, where ordinary sanders can't reach.***

◀ **USING A PALM SANDER, 3.** ***For sanding contoured, irregular-shaped surfaces, install a thick, sponge-rubber pad on the sander. The soft pad contours to the shape of the work.***

▼ **USING A PALM SANDER, 4.** ***When fitted with an optional rubbing pad, the palm sander can be used to polish a finished surface with rottenstone and water or mineral oil.***

vacuuming dust up through holes in the sandpaper and the tool's pad. Each time you install a new piece of sandpaper, you must punch properly placed holes through it with a template that's supplied with the tool. Less dust collects between the sandpaper and the wood, helping to keep the sandpaper cleaner. But don't expect all the dust to go into the bag. Some remains on the wood just to keep you honest.

Finally, after weighing all the pros and cons of each tool and selecting the one that seems to suit your requirements best, you'll probably be interested in the dent it will make in your bank account. Keep in mind that the retail power tool market is very competitive. It pays to check out several distributors and catalog tool dealers to find the best price.

PALM SANDER TECHNIQUES

A vast majority of palm sanding is done with fine and very fine sandpaper, usually between 120- and 220-grit papers. However, medium-grit paper, such as 80 grit, can be used to smooth semirough surfaces and remove shallow scratches. Then, follow up with progressively finer sandpaper to achieve the desired degree of smoothness.

Another important procedure is to always brush off the sanding surface when you're switching to a finer-grit sandpaper. This will remove any of the loose abrasive grits of the previous, coarser sandpaper that could scratch the surface. You should get into the habit of employing this sweep-clean routine for all types of sanding you do—whether by power tool or by hand.

When you're working with a palm sander, apply only sufficient pressure to control the tool and guide its movement. Avoid the temptation to push down too hard on the tool in an effort to speed up the cutting action. This common error results in undue strain on the tool's motor and can produce deep, circular scratches in the work surface. If small, superficial scratches do appear in your work surface, you can remove them with a little light sanding by hand—in the direction parallel to the wood's grain—using very fine sandpaper.

Always moving a palm sander in the direction of the wood's grain isn't quite as important as with a belt sander. But the technique will create a smoother surface than sanding across the grain. And while a palm sander isn't limiting in the direction in which the tool can be moved, working so that a closed side of the sandpaper sheet leads is recommended. Advancing the tool along one of its open sides can cause the edge of the sandpaper sheet to dig into the surface or catch on splinters.

Besides smoothing flat surfaces, a palm sander is also an excellent tool for softening sharp edges and corners. Light in weight, it's relatively easy to hold and control at angles using only one hand. When you're sanding contoured, irregular-shaped surfaces, try installing a thick, sponge-rubber pad on the tool. The soft padding provides a flexible cushion of support for the sandpaper, molding itself to the contours and shape of the work. And when it's fitted with an optional rubbing pad, the tool is ideal for use in polishing a finished surface with rottenstone and water or oil.

FINISHING SANDER BASICS

The orbital finishing sander is similar to a palm sander except that it is more powerful and accepts a ½-sheet of standard 9 x 11-in. sandpaper. This provides twice as much sanding surface as a ¼-sheet palm sander. Note that some tool manufacturers also offer a ⅓-sheet finishing sander that measures about 1 in. narrower and 2 in. shorter than a typical ½-sheet model.

Finishing sanders, just like palm sanders, are rated according to orbits per minute. The typical range of these tools, though, is lower—from about 10,000 opm to 12,000 opm. The exceptions are high-speed finishing sanders that are rated as high as 20,000 opm.

Most finishing sanders are equipped with spring-loaded clamps to hold the

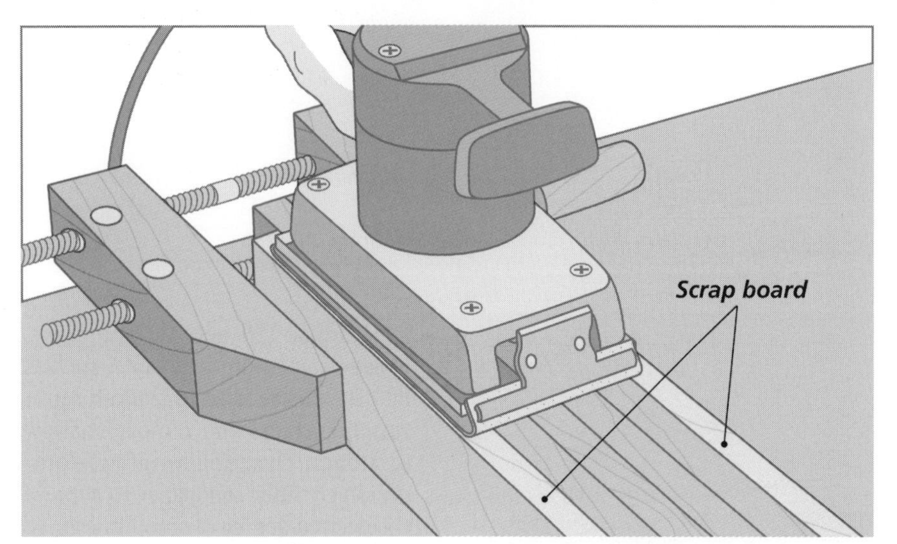

▲ **USING A FINISHING SANDER, 2.** ***Gang sanding saves time when edge sanding. Two scrap boards placed on the outside prevent rounding of the inner workpieces.***

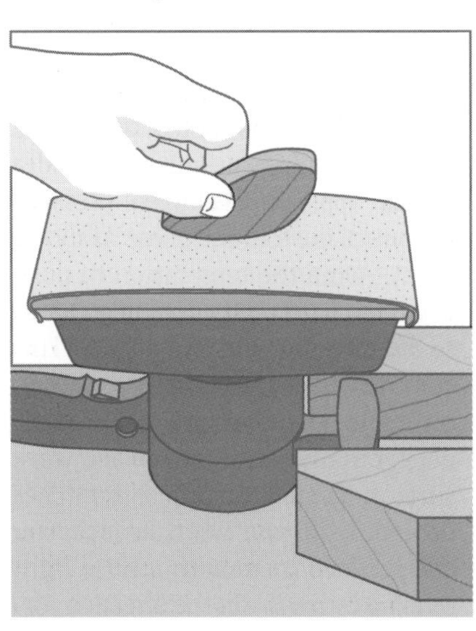

◀ **USING A FINISHING SANDER, 3.** ***To smooth small, odd-shaped pieces, clamp the sander upside down to the bench. Work over the entire abrasive pad to prevent wearing out one spot.***

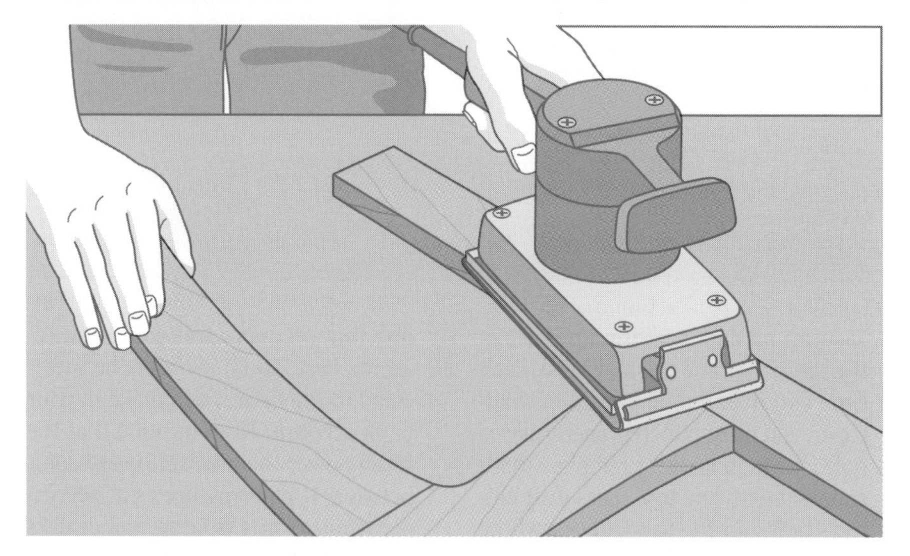

▲ **USING A FINISHING SANDER, 4.** ***The circular motion of the sander makes it ideal for sanding across right-angle joints. There's little chance of cross-grain scratches.***

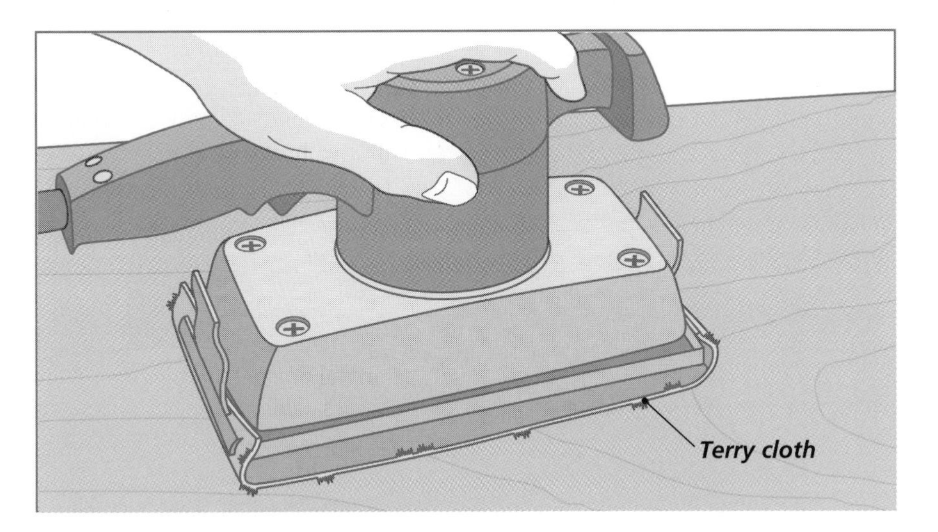

◀ **USING A FINISHING SANDER, 5.** ***Cover the sander's pad with a double layer of terry cloth and buff paste wax on furniture. Use a clean section of cloth for final buffing.***

▼ **ROUGH DISC SANDING.** ***For rough sanding such as removing paint, press down on the tool so about one-third of the disc makes contact with the surface. Keep the handle low to avoid gouging the wood.***

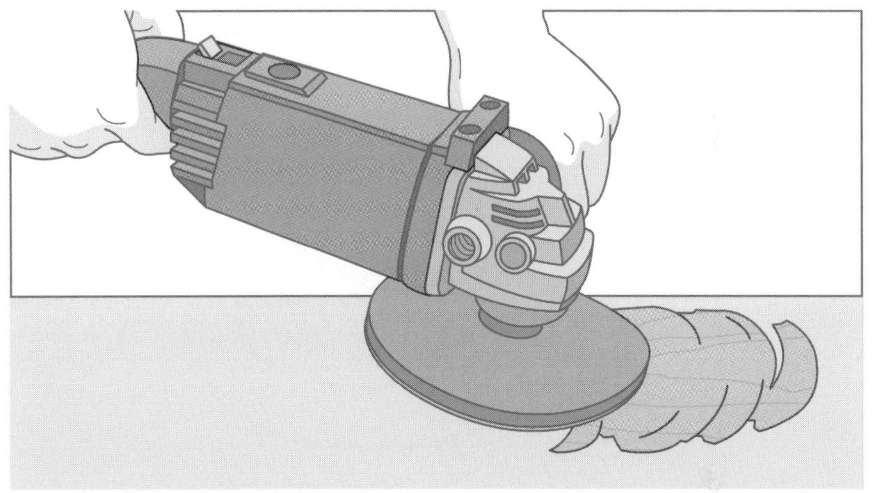

sandpaper, although there are exceptions—again like palm sanders. Many tool manufacturers also offer dustless finishing sanders that come with dust-collection bags.

FINISHING SANDER TECHNIQUES

Unlike the one-handed palm sander, two hands should be used to control a finishing sander. Again, it's important not to push down too hard on the tool. Slight pressure is all that's necessary to allow the sandpaper to do its job. Be sure to pull the abrasive paper tight on the pad when installing it; if it's loose or floppy, the tool doesn't work as effectively.

A ½-sheet finishing sander is particularly useful for smoothing large surfaces such as tabletops, plywood panels and cabinet doors. And the circular motion of the tool makes it the ideal choice for sanding across right-angled joints, since there's little likelihood of causing cross-grain scratches. However, you must be careful when sanding near edges not to let the tool's pad tip over the edge. The semi-soft pad has a tendency to round over edges and corners slightly. Also remember to thoroughly sweep the work surface clean whenever changing to finer-grit sandpaper in order to keep abrasive-grit leftovers from scratching the surface on your next pass.

You can save time when smoothing edges by ganging pieces together. Just clamp scrap boards along the outside of the assembly to prevent any rounding of the pieces between them. Clamp the sander upside down on your workbench for smoothing small, odd-shaped pieces. Move the piece around on the sandpaper to distribute wear evenly on the sheet.

A finishing sander also provides a quick, efficient way to smooth joint compound and the like that have been applied for drywall repairs. Other, less common uses for the sander include rubbing paste wax onto furniture by covering the tool's pad with a double layer of terry cloth or other soft material. Or, use the tool with 600-grit silicon-carbide abrasive paper to polish metal surfaces, applying a little mineral oil first to remove rust stains.

SPECIALTY FINISHING SANDER

While finishing sanders with conventional pads are great tools for quickly smoothing broad surfaces in preparation for finishing, they have their limitations. Where the tools fall noticeably short—literally, as well as specifically—is in their ability to handle inside corners and work in small, confined areas. These places must be smoothed with a lot of tedious sanding by hand—at least, that's the way it used to be. Now, there's a finishing sander with a unique design that solves the problem.

The most distinctive feature of this finishing sander is its triangular pad,

► **DISC SANDING EDGES.** ***Be careful when maneuvering the sander. The edge of the disc can easily slice into the work, as shown. Keep the sander moving on the surface.***

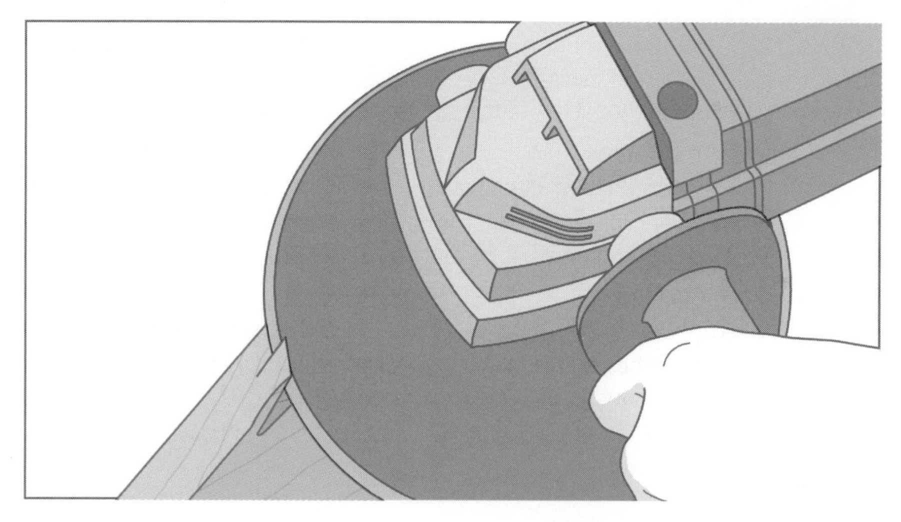

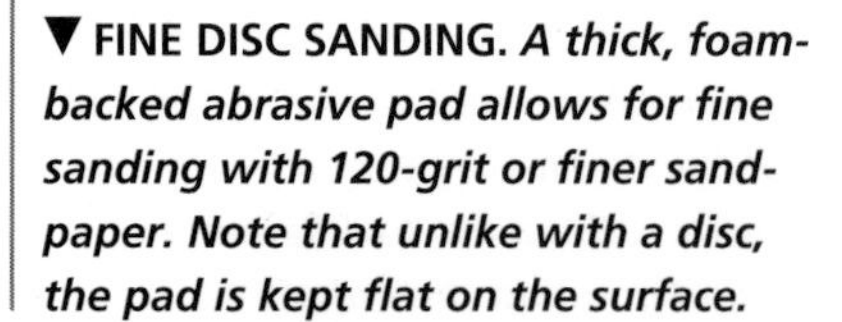

▼ **FINE DISC SANDING.** ***A thick, foam-backed abrasive pad allows for fine sanding with 120-grit or finer sandpaper. Note that unlike with a disc, the pad is kept flat on the surface.***

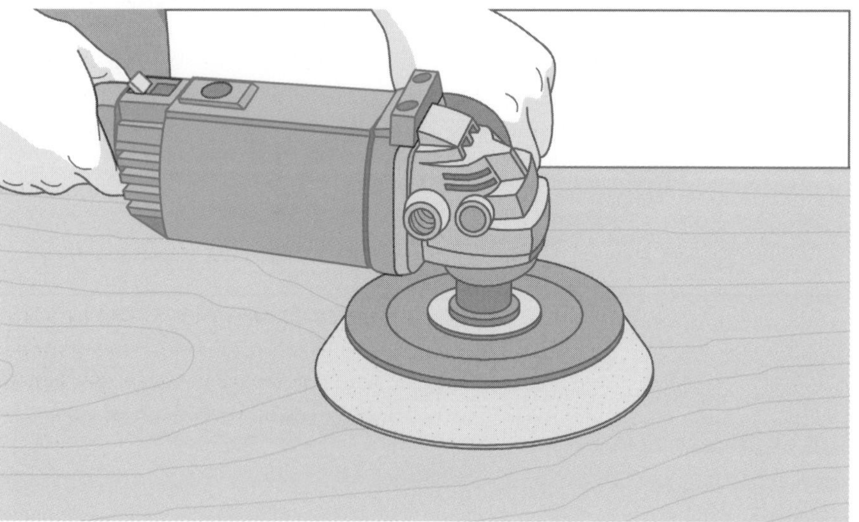

which enables the tool to reach into corners without damaging adjacent surfaces. Unlike the pad on a standard finishing sander, which orbits in small circles, the triangular-shaped pad of this tool oscillates back and forth in 2° arcs at a speed of 20,000 oscillations per minute.

The sander measures only 10½ in. in overall length, and it weighs in at just under 3 lb. The tool's light weight and narrow body make for both comfortable handling and good control. From corner to corner, the tool's triangular pad measures 3⅛ in. There's one pad for the tool that features a Velcro surface to accept Velcro-backed abrasive sheets, a system that permits you to remove and reinstall a sanding sheet many times. A plain pad is also available for use with adhesive-backed, peel-and-stick sandpaper sheets.

The tool performs exceptionally well in a wide variety of tricky situations. For instance, in the difficult task of sanding the panel of a finished frame-and-panel door down to bare wood, the sander will result in a sharply defined sanded panel surrounded by a completely unmarked finished frame. And the tool also excels in work on metal. However, note that the manufacturer recommends the use of peel-and-stick sandpaper for continuous metal sanding and other tasks where the Velcro pad may overheat.

An industrial-duty sander that is built to last, it's not a typical off-the-shelf consumer tool and is relatively expensive. The sander comes with a carrying case, wrenches and sheets of 60-, 80- and 120-grit Velcro-backed sandpaper. Optional accessories for the tool include a regular pad and peel-and-stick sandpaper, and a dust-extraction system that includes a perforated sanding pad and perforated sandpaper. While the tool is not a substitute for a regular finishing sander, it's ideal for handling the tricky sanding problems encountered in all phases of custom and production woodwork, refinishing and auto body work.

DISC SANDER BASICS

The versatile disc sander is actually two tools in one. It accepts abrasive discs for aggressive shaping and sanding of wood, or a lamb's wool bonnet for polishing finished wood and painted metal surfaces. In fact, disc sanders are commonly used in auto body repair shops and other commercial applications for grinding metal.

A disc sander consists of a powerful motor that spins a flexible rubber backing pad. The pad provides support for the sanding disc or polishing bonnet. Tools with pads of various diameters are available, but the 7-in. models are the most common. And since sanding takes greater speed than polishing, look for a two-speed tool to get the most for your money. For example, a typical 7-in. two-speed model operates at 1900 rpm and 3400 rpm.

DISC SANDER TECHNIQUES

Make no mistake; the disc sander is a rough, no-nonsense tool. When fitted with a sanding disc, the rotary action of the tool's pad results in semi-circular cross-grain scratches, and practice is needed to sand without gouging the surface. However, this same raw power makes the disc sander an excellent tool for rough work such as shaping wood, removing paint and cleaning rust from metal. When operating the tool, wear eye protection.

When using the tool with an abrasive disc, apply enouh pressure to flex about one-third of the disc flat on the work. Keep the tool moving at all times and hold it at a slight angle to the surface. The edge of the disc can easily slice into the work, so be careful in maneuvering the sander. Tilting up the tool's handle too high will cause the disc to dig in and gouge the surface. And once the work is gouged, it can be incredibly time-consuming, if not impossible, to correct the damage.

For full-face sanding tasks, fit the sander with a thick, foam-rubber abrasive pad and use 120-grit or finer sandpaper. Keep the tool moving on the surface and note that unlike a disc, the pad must be held flat against the work.

If using a lamb's wool bonnet to polish finished wood, first apply paste wax to the surface with a damp cloth. Let the wax dry for about 15 minutes, then buff it with the polisher set on low speed. Keep the bonnet moving at all times to avoid burning the wax.

For stationary sanding, remove the tool's side handle, then install a short 2 x 4 and secure it with a long bolt. Clamp the 2 x 4 in a vise to hold the tool upright. Use a foam-rubber abrasive pad for a flat sanding surface.

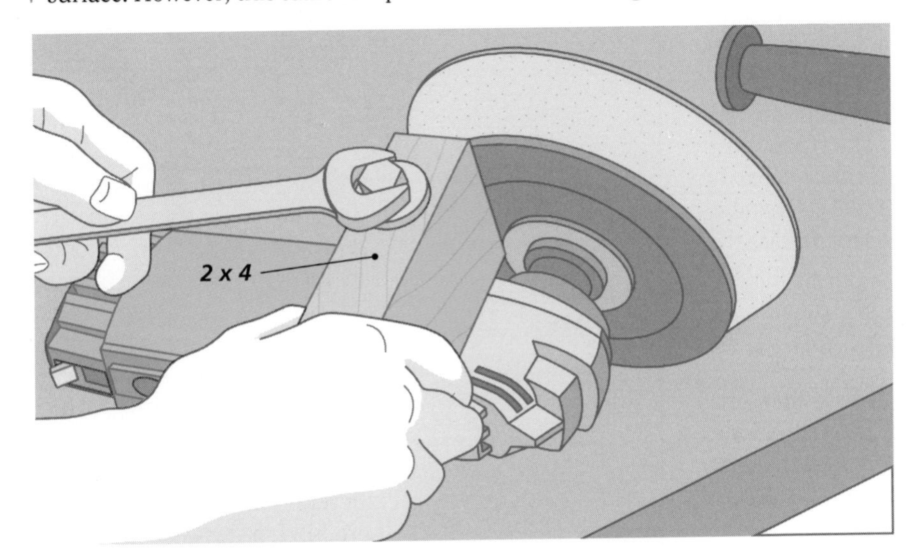

◀ **STATIONARY DISC SANDING, 1.** ***To convert the disc sander to a stationary tool, first remove the side handle and install a short block of 2 x 4. Secure the block with a long bolt.***

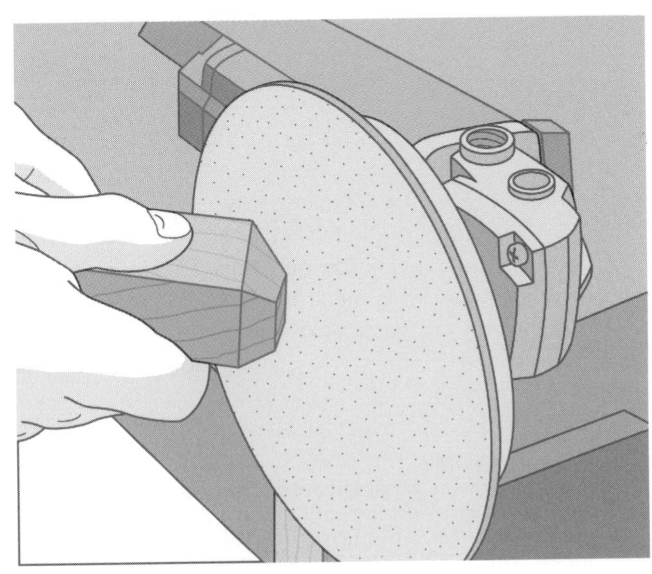

▲ **STATIONARY DISC SANDING, 2.** ***Clamp the 2 x 4 in a vise to hold the sander upright. Use a foam-backed abrasive pad to provide a flat sanding surface.***

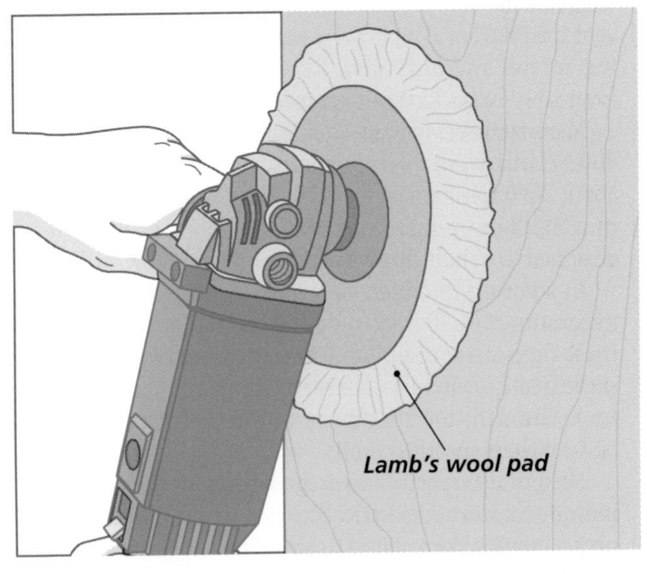

▲ **DISC SANDER POLISHING.** ***A lamb's wool bonnet is used for polishing jobs. Apply paste wax with a damp cloth and let it dry, then buff with the sander at slow speed.***

DRILLS

There are tools you might like to own but never get around to buying, and there are tools you simply can't live without. Within the latter group, there's one tool that stands out as the basic power component of every tool kit: the electric drill.

Without question, the electric drill is the most popular power tool. It's not difficult to explain why. In a world where tools are designed for specialized tasks, the drill stands out as a true jack of all trades. You'll not only use it to bore holes in materials ranging from wood to metal and concrete, but you'll drive screws and nuts, wire-brush away rust or paint, drum-sand contoured edges, stir paint and, with a small earth auger, even help out in spring bulb-planting chores.

Power drill capacity is designated by the maximum-size shank that the chuck can accommodate. The three most common sizes are ¼, ⅜ and ½ in. Although chuck capacity does provide some indication as to what the tool can handle, drill bits are available with step-down shanks to increase the capacity of the smaller tools.

FEATURE VARIATIONS

The most popular class of portable power drills is the ⅜-in., variable-speed, reversible (VSR) design. For most situations, it represents an ideal compromise in terms of power, weight and ease of handling. Variable speed provides full speed control—from 0 to maximum rpm—via finger pressure on the trigger. This permits slow-turning, low-rpm starts that prevent the bit from skipping and wandering. It also makes driving screws and nuts easy. Reverse-rotation capability is invaluable for backing out jammed bits and removing screws.

Manufacturers usually offer this tool in two versions that differ primarily in their top speeds. Higher-speed tools (0 to about 2000 rpm) are better at handling relatively small holes in wood. Lower-speed models (0 to about 1200 rpm) are designed to handle large-diameter holes and metal drilling.

In addition to chuck size, most manufacturers specify maximum capacities in wood and metal. For the most part, these figures are useful only in comparing two drills of the same make—where a consistent standard is used for each tool. You will find that many of the tools can be pushed beyond their specified limits.

Makers also specify amperage ratings for their drills that indicate maximum electrical current usage. While these figures generally correspond to actual power output, you may find that a tool of lower amperage actually outperforms a slightly higher-rated tool.

Although many models of drills feature ball bearings and needle or roller bearings, some may still exhibit side-to-side

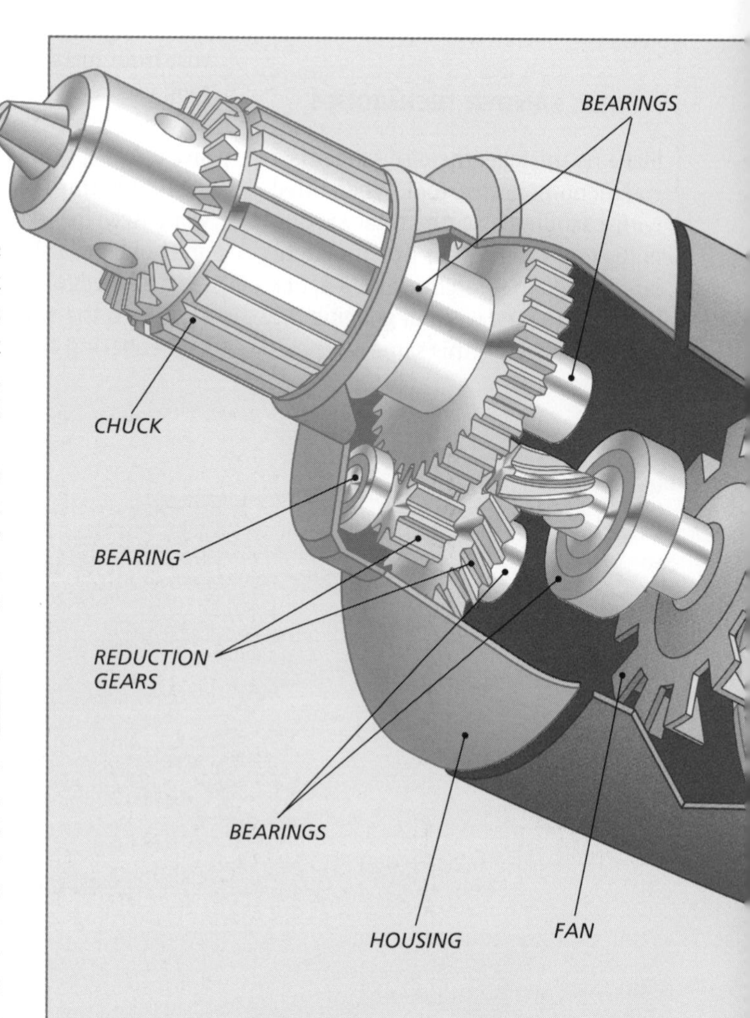

DRILL ANATOMY
The typical ⅜-in., variable-speed, reversible drill has a pistol-grip housing containing a compact, powerful motor. Trigger-controlled variable-speed switch adjusts rpm to suit material and job. On most models, trigger-lock button locks tool at maximum speed. Reduction gearing lowers motor speed and transfers torque to chuck.

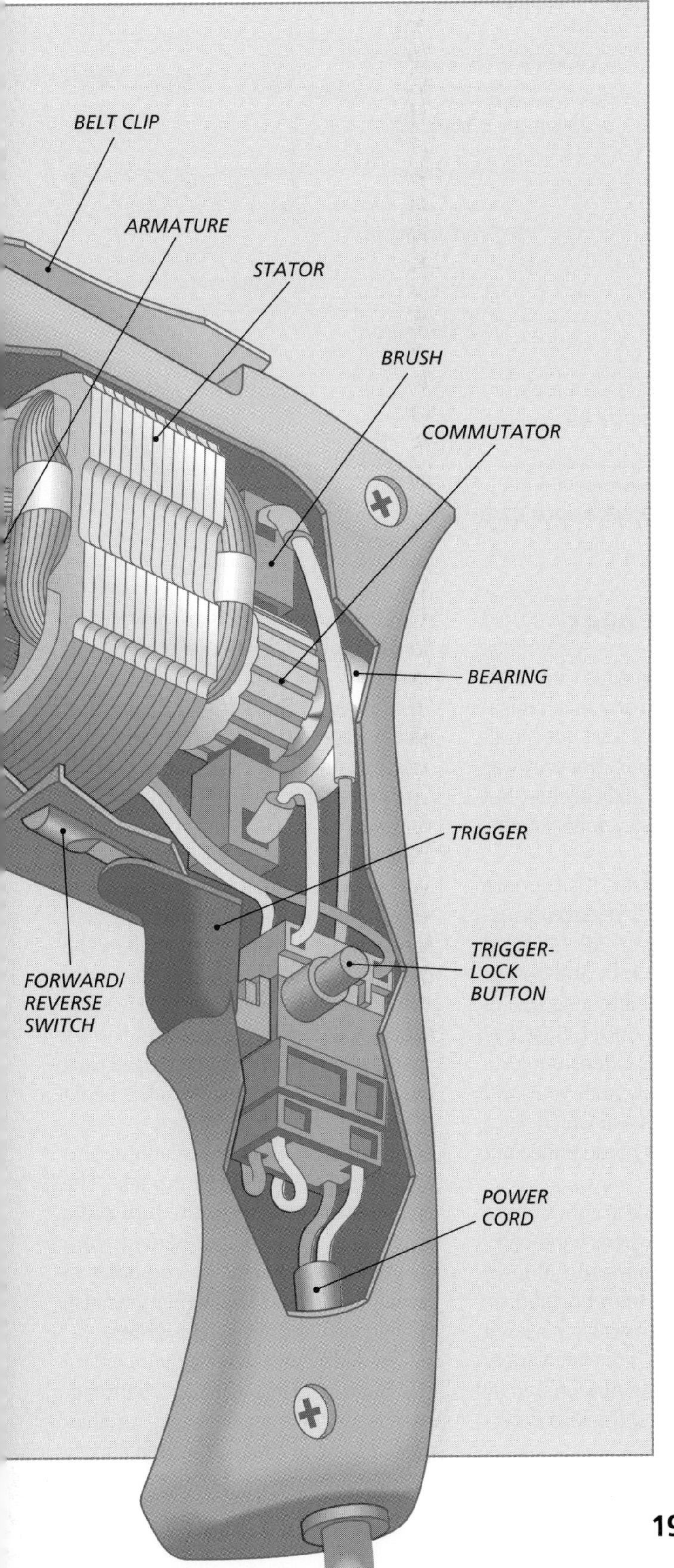

looseness, or radial play, at the chuck. Given the type of work that these tools are designed to handle, this may not be much of a problem. However, it's reasonable to wonder if a sloppy bearing isn't the result of designing a tool via an accountant's balance sheet rather than at the drawing board.

Several manufacturers offer drills that come with an auxiliary handle—an important accessory for heavy-duty hole boring. And some types come with a clip for holding the tool on a belt. Another handy feature to look for is a speed dial that permits the trigger to be locked at any point in the speed range. By eliminating the need for finger pressure on the trigger entirely, this feature is especially helpful when sanding or polishing. And many manufacturers now offer models with electronic circuits that maintain the selected speed while the tool is under load.

Another important tool feature is double-insulated construction to ensure protection of the user from electrical shock. Check the nameplate on the drill to be sure that the tool is double-insulated. Alternatively, a grounded tool, identified by a three-prong plug on the power cord, also provides electrical shock protection.

DESIGN ALTERNATIVES

Of course, the standard type of pistol-grip electric drill isn't the only way to bore holes. Like all other tools for the home workshop, there seems to be a virtually endless number of variations that ensure you'll have the right drill on hand no matter what the job.

One of the most unique-looking models of the drill features a motor and housing that are at a 55° angle to the axis of the chuck. The tool is gripped right below the chuck, where there's a large, lever-type trigger switch. While this is one of the best drills for working in confined spaces, it's also a well-balanced, comfortable tool for use in ordinary boring and screw-driving operations.

The standard solution to boring in tight spaces, however, is the right-angle drill. And if you need right-angle drilling capabilities but are unsure that you require a dedicated tool, right-angle drive attachments for conventional drills are available from most tool manufacturers. The attachments are usually geared so that reversing them end for end in the drill provides a second speed range.

When it comes to boring a hole in concrete, you may make some headway with an ordinary drill and a carbide-tipped masonry bit. However, if you really want results, use a hammer drill. This tool works like an ordinary drill, but at the flip of a switch enhances the rotating action with a pulsating, up-and-down percussion action. For real heavy-

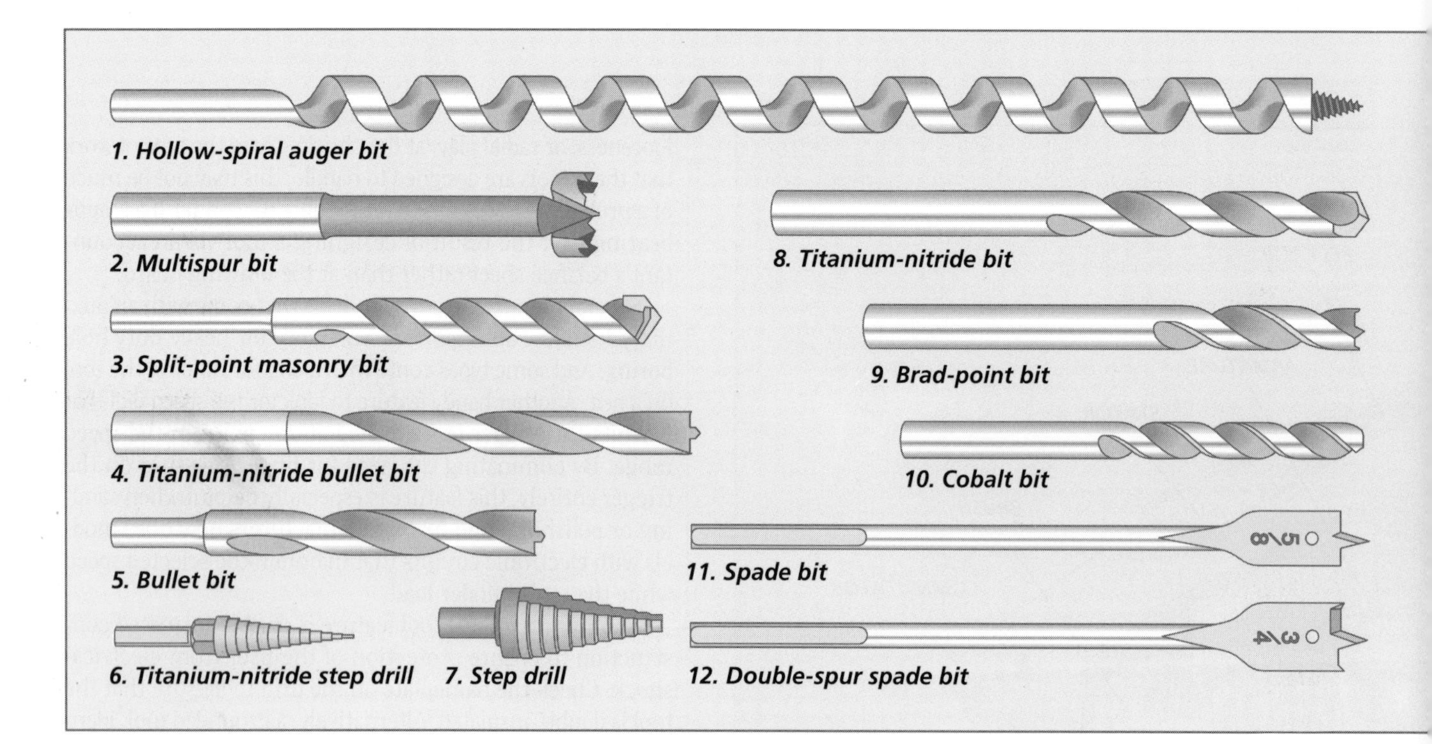
1. Hollow-spiral auger bit
2. Multispur bit
3. Split-point masonry bit
4. Titanium-nitride bullet bit
5. Bullet bit
6. Titanium-nitride step drill
7. Step drill
8. Titanium-nitride bit
9. Brad-point bit
10. Cobalt bit
11. Spade bit
12. Double-spur spade bit

duty boring, rotary hammers are available that allow for either combined rotary/percussion action or percussion action alone.

Also available are specially designed drills for boring holes in studs, joists and other construction framing where no other heavy-duty tool will fit. Unless you're a plumber or have been around the building trades for a long time, some of these monsters may look like props for a science-fiction movie. A typical two-speed model spins at either 300 or 1200 rpm and is capable of handling up to 4⅝-in.-dia. self-feeding bits at the slow speed.

And there are naturally times when all you need is a big drill—plain and simple. In these situations, you'll probably end up using a single-speed, ½-in. model that spins bits at about 500 rpm and can handle up to 3-in.-dia. holes with a self-feeding bit. On these drills, there's usually a spade-type rear handle directly in line with the chuck for transmitting force effectively. A top-mounted auxiliary handle on the tool serves to provide needed control in high-torque situations.

CORDLESS TOOLS

Not too long ago, the odds were high that anyone who had any mechanical inclination at all had at least one "cordless" drill in the toolbox. Not only was the hand drill simple and effective, but the power to drive it was, quite literally, always at hand.

These days, however, it's the rare individual who hasn't replaced muscle with electric power. All you need is an outlet to plug into and you're physically connnected to a source of constant power. No outlet close by? Enter the ubiquitous extension cord, by which you can easily carry your drill up a ladder to the roof—at which point the plug has invariably been pulled out of the outlet.

Well, there's a modern compromise between your go-anywhere, hand-operated drill and your powerful plug-in tool. For the ultimate in portability, there's the cordless, battery-powered drill. And judging by the wide variety of tool models that are now offered by major manufacturers, the idea is certainly catching on.

Most cordless drills are powered by rechargeable 1.2-volt nickel-cadmium batteries. The number of cells that are contained by the batteries determines the voltage of the tool, and higher voltage usually means more power. Drills are commonly available in 3.6, 6, 7.2, 9.6 and 12 volts. Tools with a rating below 7.2 volts are light-duty, designed for only occasional use. On these less expensive models, batteries are usually integral with the tool—when the batteries are dead, so is your drill until the tool has been recharged. Heavier-duty models with independent battery packs allow you to keep a charged pack in the tool while a spare pack is being re-energized in the charger.

Cordless drills are available as single-speed or two-speed models. The two-speed versions of the tool add a high gear for jobs that benefit from higher rpm, such as boring holes of small diameters. The higher gear also allows you to drive screws faster.

In addition to fixed-speed control through gearing, the tool manufacturers also offer an electronic variable-speed control that's activated simply

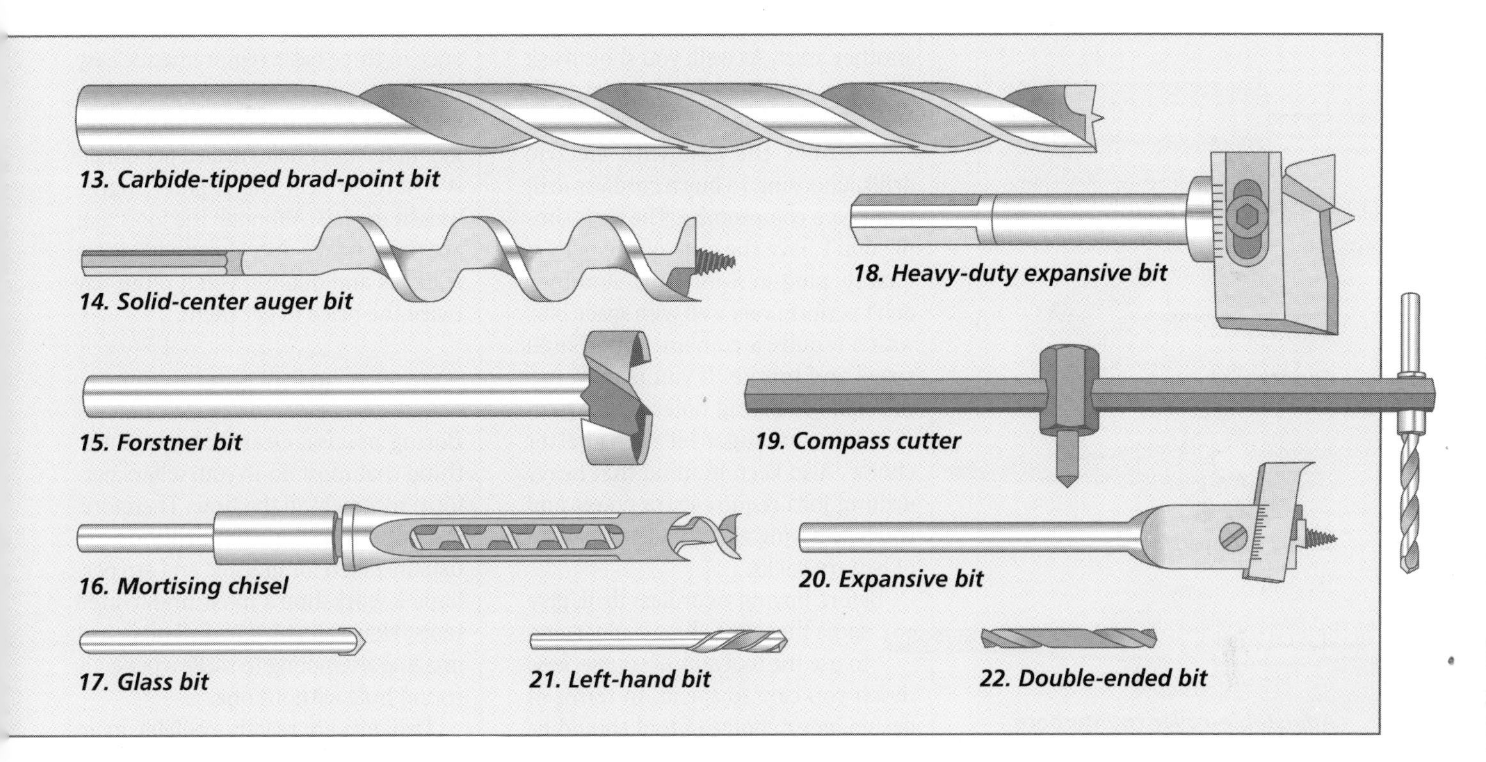

by varying pressure on the trigger. This feature is invaluable for driving screws and can also come in handy when you are using small bits.

Another popular option with cordless drills is an adjustable clutch for disengaging the tool's motor at preset torques. It's a handy feature in preventing overdriven screws, which can result when operating the tool in direct drive. However, if you're only driving a few screws at a time, you'll probably spend longer trying to find the appropriate clutch setting than it would take you to do the job in direct drive.

A reversing switch for backing out stuck bits and removing screws is standard, and most drills build in an off position on the reversing switch to deactivate the tool. Typically, the drills also have a provision for the storage of their chuck key. Some models, however, sensibly resolve this problem by featuring a keyless chuck with a pair of rings that are hand-tightened against each other to lock the bit. If the chuck becomes overtightened in use, a small release rod (stored in the tool's handle) can be used to pry it open.

CHARGER NOTES

The batteries of cordless drills tend to heat up during use. And they shouldn't be charged when they're hot. The time it takes for the batteries to cool should be added to the manufacturer's stated charge time to get a realistic idea of how long it takes to recycle the batteries. For instance, it may actually take you up to 1½ hours to recycle a recently drained battery pack using a one-hour charger.

Some tool chargers are designed to automatically wait until the batteries cool down before recharging. All fast chargers feature an automatic cutoff to avoid overcharging. After charging is complete, some models go into a trickle-charge mode to keep your batteries topped up.

SUMMING UP

When it comes to purchasing an electric drill, you can't really go wrong. There's no such thing as a failure in this group of power tools, and they all do pretty much what they're supposed to do. Even if you're a fairly active do-it-yourselfer, you're likely to be quite satisfied with any one of the ⅜-in., VSR drills on the market. Although each manufacturer's solution to the design of the tool varies, it's easy to get used to any particular model of this drill. And if you comparison shop through mail-order tool catalogs, you'll find that the price differential among models of drills isn't always quite as great as it first appears.

Electric drills are rated according to their power in amps and by their no-load speed in rpm. Amperage ratings typically vary from 2 to 6 amps. The higher the amperage rating, the more powerful is the tool. On the other hand, though, as power increases, rpm drops. So, if you're looking for power in a drill, go with one that has higher amps and lower rpm.

Before you reach for your wallet, make sure that you pick up and handle the drill. The tool should feel balanced and comfortable in *your* hand. Check that the tool's controls are both conveniently located and easy to reach. Provision for an auxiliary handle is

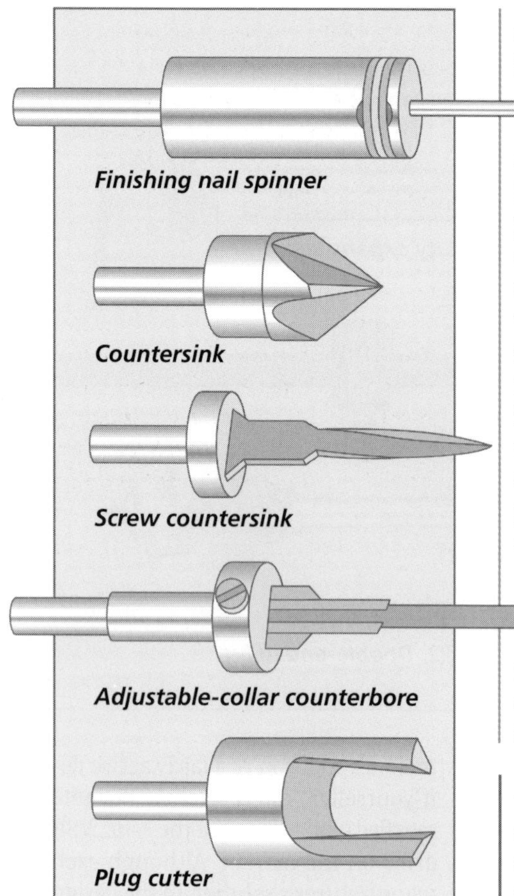

another asset. As well, you should ask if there is a full line of accessories available for use with the drill.

Unlike the case with electric drills, choosing to buy a cordless drill is always a compromise. The tools simply don't have the guts of the better-quality, plug-in ⅜-in. drills. And they don't perform very well with spade bits, which require a combination of high speed and torque. If you plan to use the tool for boring holes larger than ⅜-in. dia., an auger bit is the better choice. Also keep in mind that heavy drilling jobs require extra power and you'll be paying with frequent changes of battery packs.

Before buying a cordless drill, give some thought to how you're going to use the tool and, of course, how much you care to spend. In terms of design, your choice of tool should be the one that *you* feel achieves a balance in three basic requirements: easy handling, comfort and the power when you need it for the occasional heavy job. In terms of holes drilled per dollar, it's hard to beat the smaller, lightweight models. Although the tools that are more heavy-duty do provide extra features and quality, you'll often pay twice the price to get them.

◀ **FASTENING SPECIALTY BITS.** ***A wide range of specialty bits are available that simplify the task of boring holes for fasteners. Here are some of the most useful ones.***

BIT BASICS

Boring precise, clean holes is something that most do-it-yourselfers perform routinely all the time. Therefore, it's not surprising that drill bits are usually taken for granted and are perhaps a workshop's most underrated tools. How valuable are drill bits? Just imagine attempting to make a perfectly round hole without one.

Drill bits are readily available in an astounding number of sizes and styles for use in nearly every imaginable type of material—including wood, metals, plastics, concrete, brick, ceramic tile and glass, to name a few. Most bits are designed for use in a portable—electric or cordless—drill. Other bits are

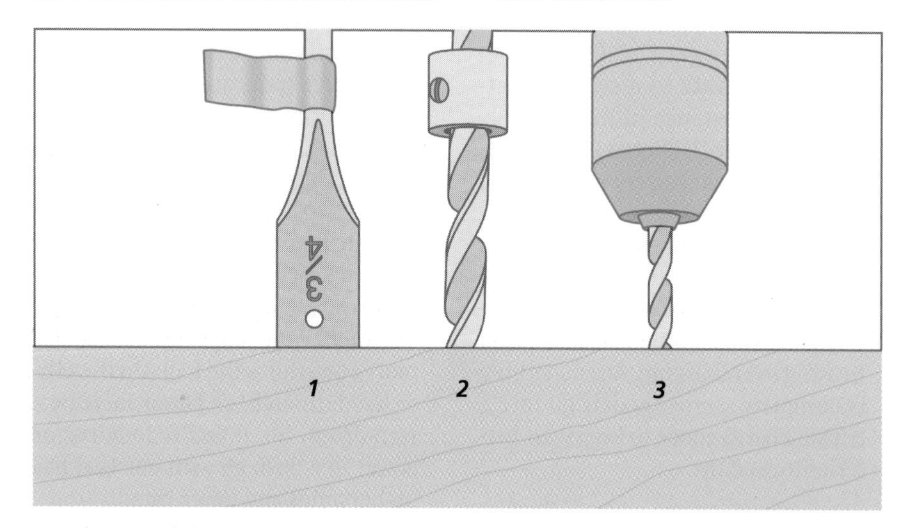

▲ **SETTING DRILLING DEPTH, 1.** ***Three ways to control drilling depth include (1) a simple masking tape flag, (2) a metal depth-stop collar and (3) an adjustable collar for drills from 1/16- to 1/4-in. dia.***

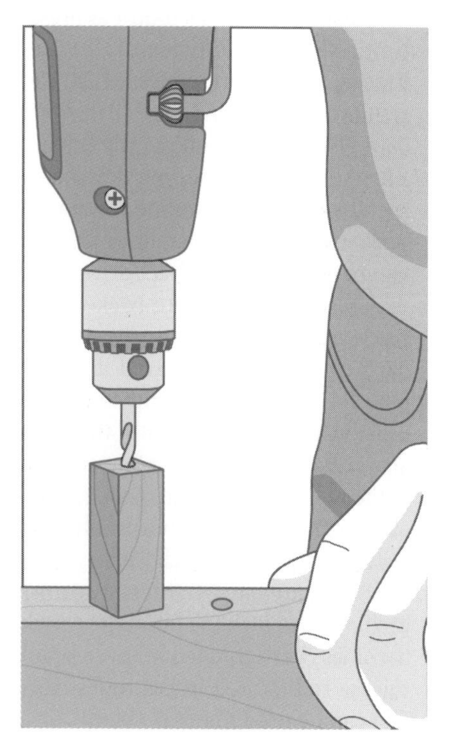

▶ **SETTING DRILLING DEPTH, 2.** ***Another way to set drilling depth is to use a wood block with a through center hole as a depth stop. Cut the block so that the bit protrudes the desired amount.***

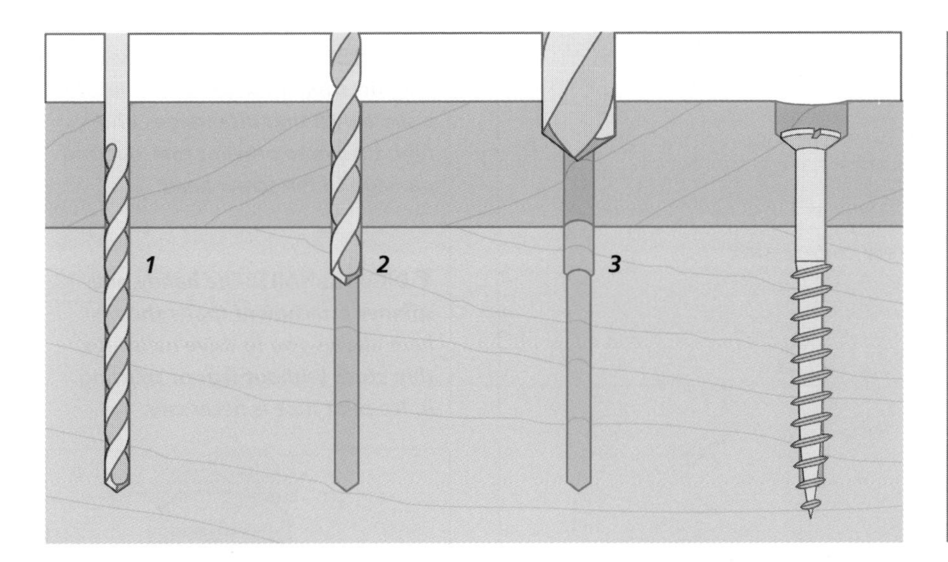

◀ **COUNTERBORING, 1.** ***Shown here is the sequence for counterboring a wood screw using twist bits: (1) bore the pilot hole, (2) bore the screw-shank clearance hole and (3) counterbore the screw head.***

▼ **COUNTERBORING, 2.** ***When counterboring for a bolt, do not bore the bolt hole first (1). Instead, first bore the large hole for the bolt head, then bore the clearance hole for the bolt shank (2).***

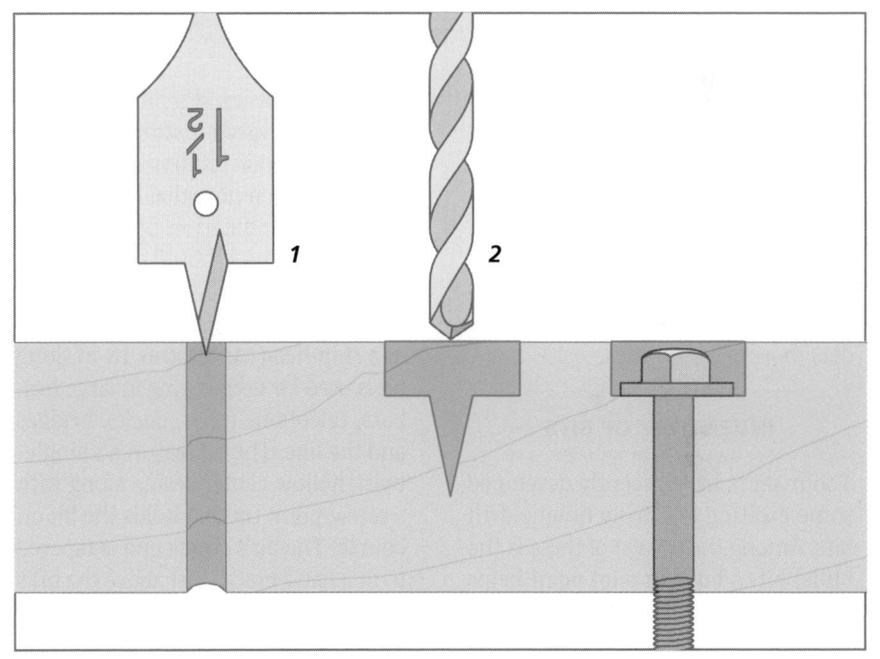

made specifically for use only in a hand brace, hand drill or drill press. Some bits can be used in more than one tool, however it's important that you never use any bit or accessory in a tool it's not designed for.

Drill bits are sized according to the diameter of the hole they bore. Most bits are classified in fractional sizes—inches or metric. But some bits use wire-gauge numbers or letter sizes. Twist drill bits are most commonly available in fractional sizes from 1⁄64-in. to ½-in. dia. Bits up to about 1-in. dia. are also available, but they're tougher to find. Wire-gauge number bits range from No. 1 (decimal equivalent: .2280 in.) to No. 80 (.0135 in.). Note that the higher the number, the smaller the diameter of the bit. Letter-size bits range from A (.2340 in.) to Z (.4130 in.). For use as a comparative reference, note that the decimal equivalent of a 1⁄64-in. bit is .0156 in.

Technically, the metal-cutting tools are called drills, while all others are known as bits. But while twist drills are designed for drilling holes in metal, they're also commonly used to bore holes in wood and plastic—especially in diameters smaller than ¼ in. Since the flutes of a twist drill don't expel wood chips very effectively, it's important to withdraw the drill frequently to prevent chips and dust from clogging the flutes. Also, keeping the hole free of chips will enhance the drill's cutting action and prevent overloading of the tool's motor, which could cause burnout.

For boring holes of large diameters in wood, there are several bits available—including spade, auger, multispur and Forstner bits. Selecting the right bit to use depends on the workpiece, the size of the hole to be made and the required quality of the work. Spade and auger bits are the economical choice for general wood boring and rough carpentry work, particularly for holes larger than ½-in. dia. where super-precision isn't necessary. These bits tend to cut a little rough, so for the best performance you should operate them at about 1500 rpm. For finer work that necessitates precise, smooth-cut holes, use a multispur or Forstner bit. These bits have shallow center points that permit boring deep, flat-bottomed holes without breaking through the backside of the workpiece.

Other types of bits are also common. A brad-point bit, for example,

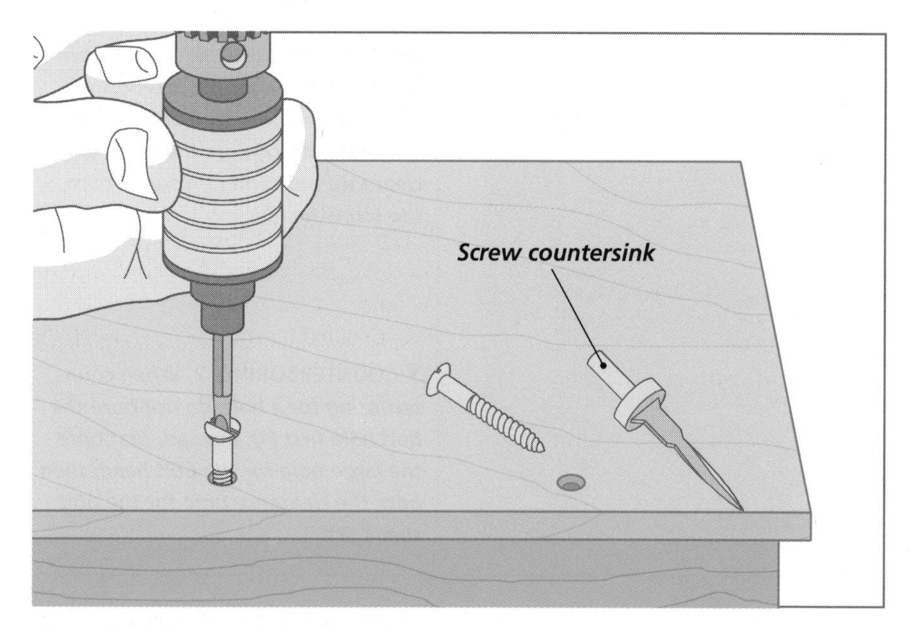

◄ **DRIVING SCREWS.** ***The screw-driving attachment in use here features a slip clutch that disengages under high torque to prevent cam-out and damage to the screw head.***

▼ **DRIVING NAILS.** ***The handy nail-spinner attachment that's shown here allows you to drive nails into thin stock without fear of splitting it. No pilot hole is necessary.***

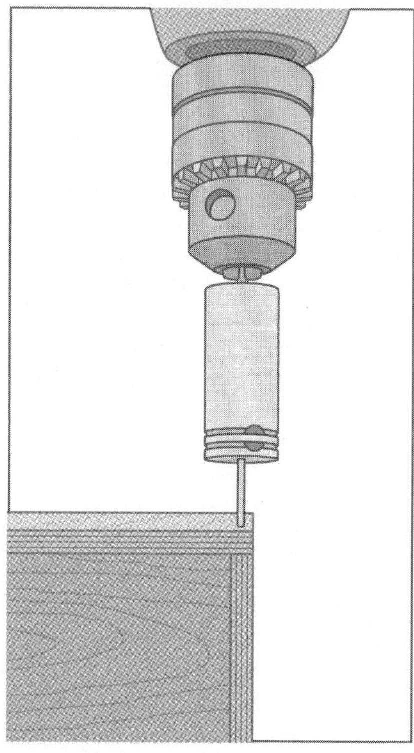

will also bore a smooth, true-diameter hole in wood. Or, for times when neatness doesn't count, there's the fast-cutting hollow-spiral bit that is most frequently used to bore holes through house framing in order to run electrical wires. This bit's great length—usually 18 in.—provides extra reach and deep-boring capabilities.

INVENTORY OF BITS

Toolmakers have recently developed some exciting and truly unique drill bits. Among the newest of these is the bullet bit. A built-in pilot point helps this bit to cut quicker and minimize walking—the tendency of the bit to wander off course.

Step drills allow you to drill several different size holes with the same bit. They're designed for drilling in thin materials, especially metals and plastics. And there are now carbide-tipped brad-point bits, improved spade bits and split-point masonry bits.

Also note that many manufacturers are now offering bits coated with titanium-nitride. These gold-colored bits boast superior performance over standard high-speed steel (HSS) bits.

Here is a collection of bits for handling virtually every possible hole-boring job. However, it's not likely that you'll need every bit shown. Instead, add bits to your toolbox as you need them and remember that price is usually a good indication of quality. In other words, you should expect to get only what you pay for.

1. Hollow-spiral auger bit—Also known as a ship-head car bit, this 18-in.-long bit is used for deep boring in large timbers, telephone poles, docks, bridges and the like. The bit features a single-twist, hollow-center design along with a screw-point tip that holds the bit on course. The bit's chuck end is tapered to fit a hand brace. Just above the bit's tapered end, the shank is hex-shaped. To use the bit in a portable electric drill, simply hacksaw off the tapered end. The bit is available in sizes ranging from ¼-in. to 1½-in. dia.

2. Multispur bit—For precise holes in fine woodwork, try a multispur bit. Designed for drill press use, it features a rim-guided cutting head that makes it easy to bore angled and overlapping holes. The cutting head has rows of sharpened teeth and a ⅛-in.-long center spur for providing smooth, nearly flat-bottomed holes. Bit sizes range from ⅜-in. to 1½-in. dia.

3. Split-point masonry bit—Until quite recently, boring a hole in concrete, cement block, brick or plaster was a slow, laborious process. However, this new bit features an aggressive cutting, split-point, carbide-steel tip that bores three times faster and lasts 10 times longer than regular types of masonry bits, according to the manufacturer. The bits come in five sizes from 3/16-in. to ½-in. dia.

4. Titanium-nitride bullet bit—Thanks to its unique design, the bullet bit easily outperforms standard twist-drill bits—especially when drilling metal. In fact, according to its manufacturer, the titanium-nitride bullet bit will drill four times faster and last 14 times longer than standard HSS bits. Bullet bits come in 29 sizes ranging from 1/16-in. to 1/2-in. dia.

5. Bullet bit—This bit performs as well as its titanium-nitride counterpart and is claimed to last seven times longer than standard HSS bits. The pilot-point tip ensures no-walk starting and an enlarged flute chamber hastens chip removal to prevent jamming. Acute-angle cutting edges translate into faster drilling and—even more important—into no binding and lockup as the bit breaks out through the backside of the workpiece. Regular bullet bits come in the same 29 sizes as the titanium-nitride versions.

6. Step drill—The No. 4 step drill shown can drill 12 different size holes from 3/16-in. to 7/8-in. dia.; a No. 1 model drills 13 different size holes from 1/8-in. to 1/2-in. dia. These HSS bits feature a sure-starting point and a single flute. The multiple-step design of the drills allows for the enlarging of the hole a little at a time. Simply stop drilling when the desired size hole is made. Designed primarily for drilling in steel, copper, brass, aluminum and other thin metals, these bits can also be used to bore holes in plastics, composition boards and thin wood. The relatively high cost of the drills is offset by the fact that you need fewer bits and by the convenience of not having to stop working to change bits so often.

7. Titanium-nitride step drill—A recently introduced version of the step drill, this bit is similar to the models just mentioned except that it has two cutting flutes and a titanium-nitride coating that helps it stay sharp up to six times longer than HSS step drills. The bit shown will drill 13 holes ranging from 1/8-in. to 1/2-in. dia. A nine-hole model will drill hole sizes from 1/4-in. to 3/4-in. dia.

8. Titanium-nitride bit—A full line of twist drills coated with titanium nitride are available. The super-hard bits have many advantages over standard HSS

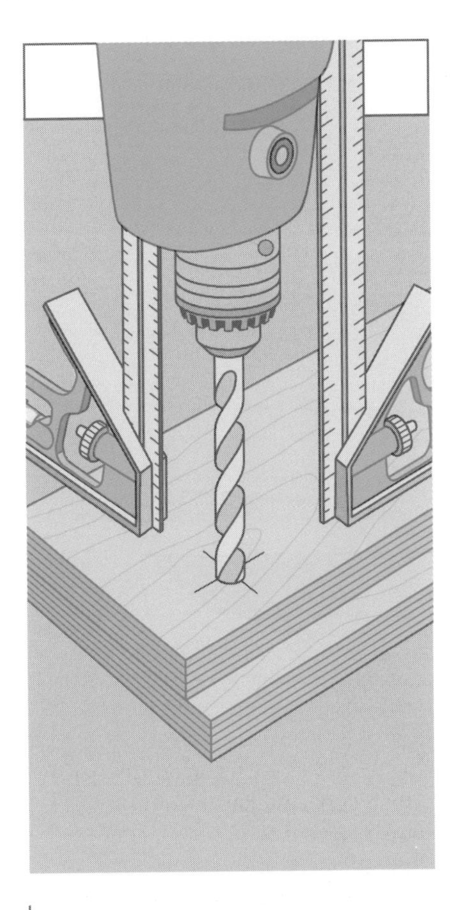

▲ BORING PERPENDICULAR HOLES, 1. ***To help you bore perpendicular holes freehand, position two set squares as shown. Align the drill bit with the blades of the squares.***

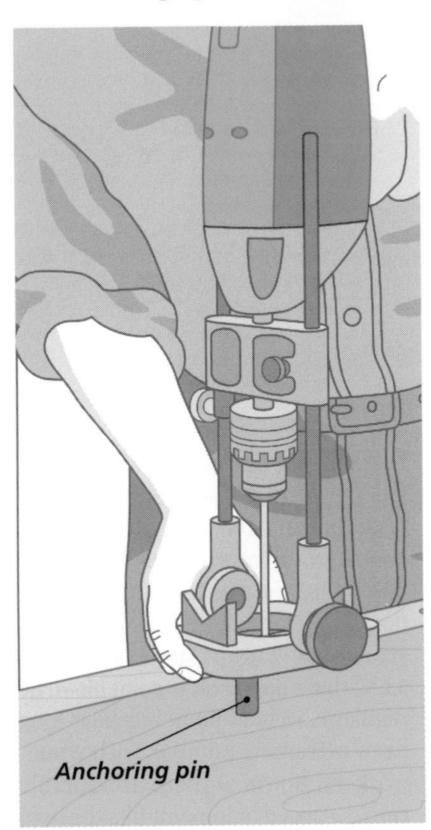

◀ BORING PERPENDICULAR HOLES, 2. ***Use a drill guide to bore perpendicular holes in narrow edges. Removable anchoring pins center the guide on the workpiece.***

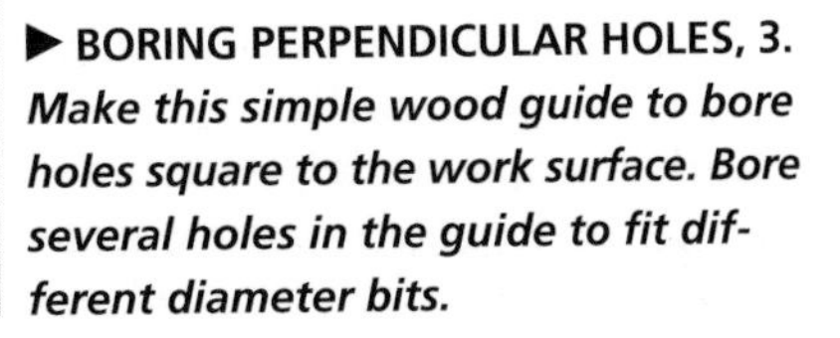

▶ BORING PERPENDICULAR HOLES, 3. ***Make this simple wood guide to bore holes square to the work surface. Bore several holes in the guide to fit different diameter bits.***

▶ **BORING ANGLED HOLES, 1.** ***When boring an angled hole freehand, make use of a sliding bevel as a guide. Adjust the square to the desired angle of the hole.***

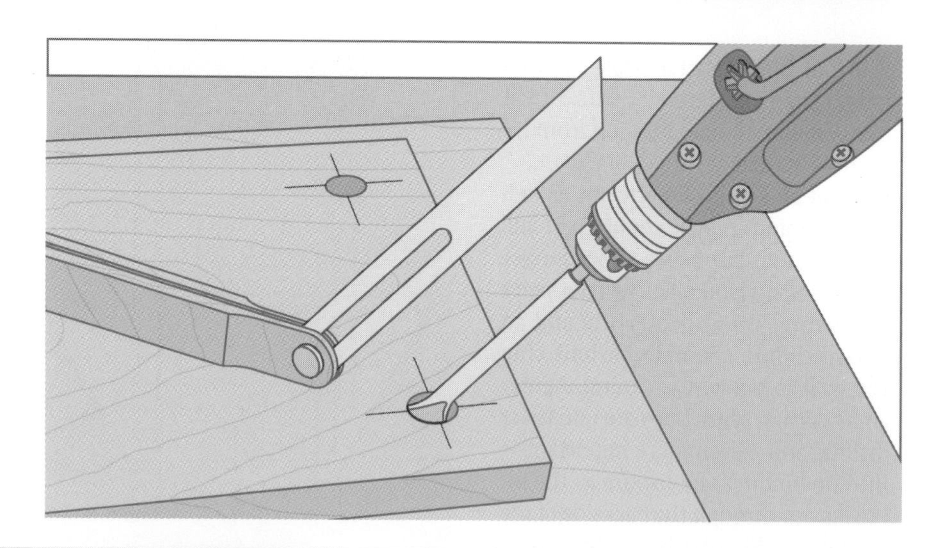

▼ **BORING ANGLED HOLES, 2.** ***Make a simple wood-block guide to bore angled holes. Align centerlines on guide with hole centers to position the bit accurately.***

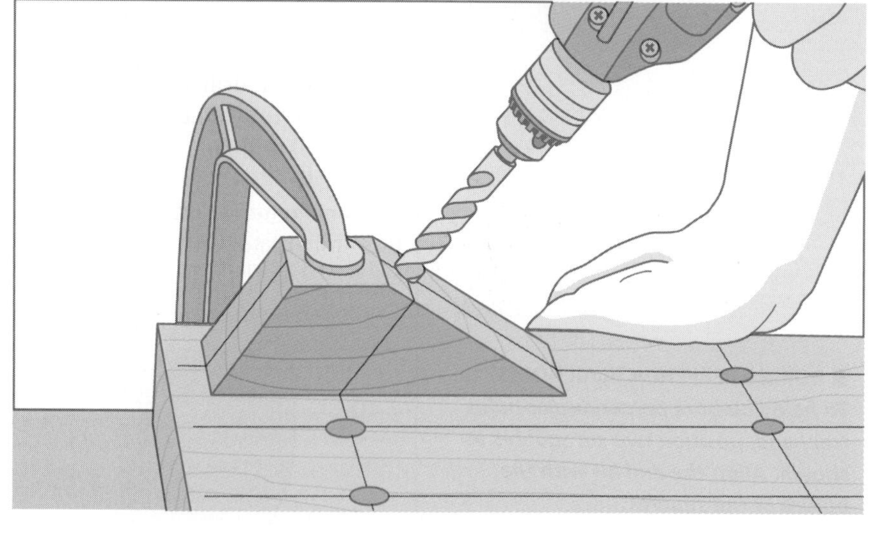

▼ **BORING ANGLED HOLES, 3.** ***The most accurate way to bore angled holes is with an adjustable guide. Here, a Forstner bit bores shallow, flat-bottomed holes.***

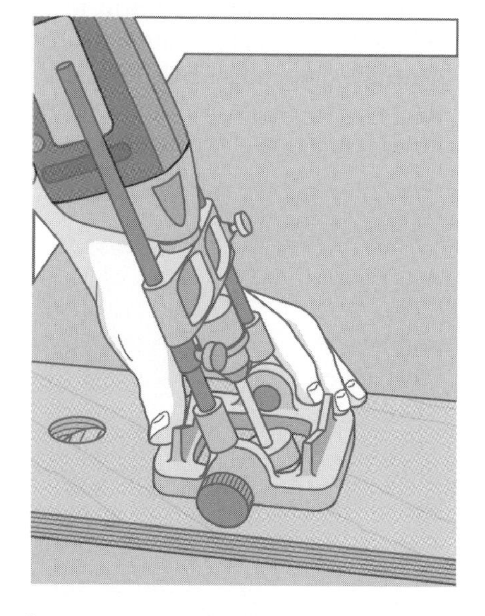

bits, especially when drilling metal. The biggest pluses are that they stay sharper longer and cut easier, enjoying up to six times the life of HSS bits. The bits also stay cooler at high speeds and require less pressure. Titanium-nitride drills aren't cheap, but can be economical for anyone who does a lot of drilling. They're available in 29 sizes from 1/16-in. to 1/2-in. dia.

9. Brad-point bit—A favorite of many woodworkers, a brad-point bit features a sharpened center point for quick, sure starts and two cutting spurs that scribe the wood for fast, smooth holes. The HSS bit also features extra-deep flutes for fast, clog-free boring. A five-piece set includes 1/4-, 5/16-, 3/8-, 7/16- and 1/2-in.-dia. bits.

10. Cobalt bit—This rather ordinary looking 3/8-in.-dia. twist drill bit is made of super-tough cobalt. It's designed specifically for drilling in extremely hard, abrasive metals such as stainless steel, chrome, armor plate and titanium. Other sizes range from 1/16-in. to 1/2-in. dia.

11. Spade bit—The 5/8-in.-dia. spade bit shown here is one of the most popular woodworking bits in use today. Spade bits are fast-cutting, inexpensive and easy to sharpen with a file. Use spade bits in a portable electric drill or drill press. They come in 17 sizes ranging from 1/4-in. to 1 1/2-in. dia.

12. Double-spur spade bit—Here's a 3/4-in.-dia. bit that is an improvement on one of the most commonly used woodworking bits. The new bit has two protruding spurs that scribe the wood for faster cutting and a sharpened, horizontal groove on each side for cleaner holes. Like the standard spade bit, the double-spur model is available in 17 sizes ranging from 1/4-in. to 1 1/2-in. dia.

13. Carbide-tipped brad-point bit—The regular HSS brad-point bits have long been extremely popular with woodworkers, but now there are durable carbide-tipped brad-point bits that will

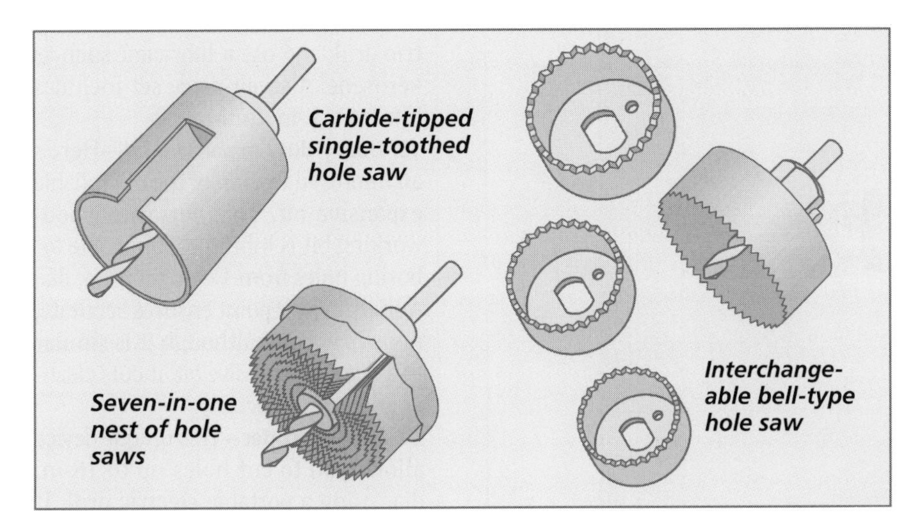

◀ **CUTTING HOLES, 1.** *Hole saws are available for cutting large holes in materials such as wood, plastic, sheet metal, ceramic tile and masonry. Shown here are three common types.*

▼ **CUTTING HOLES, 2.** *Because a hole saw doesn't cut away all the waste within the hole it makes, the tool is the quickest method of cutting large-diameter holes in most materials.*

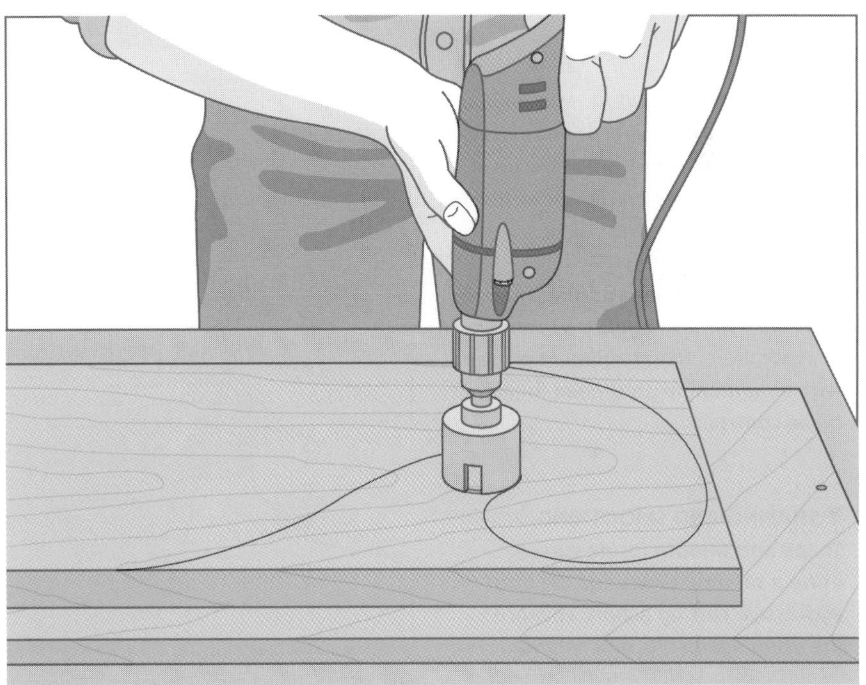

outlast HSS bits many times over. The bits have super-sharp carbide cutting edges and a center spur that eliminates walking. These are excellent bits for boring very hard, exotic woods. They're available in nine sizes from ⅛-in. to ⅝-in. dia.

14. Solid-center auger bit—This 1-in.-dia. wood-boring bit, also known as an electrician's auger bit, is designed for rapid, if not smooth, boring. It's most often used to bore holes in house framing to run electrical wires. The 9½-in.-long bit features a deep, chip-clearing, spiral flute and a quick-start screw-point tip. A sharpened cutter that is located near the bit's tip scribes the wood and speeds the boring process. The bit can be used in either a hand brace or an electric drill. For use in an electric drill, simply cut off the bit's tapered end to expose the hex-shaped shank. Other sizes of this bit range from ¼-in. to 1¼-in. dia.

15. Forstner bit—For fine woodworking and cabinetmaking, the Forstner bit is in a class by itself. However, don't allow yourself to be fooled by imported Forstner-type bits; the one that's shown here is the genuine Forstner bit, invented by Benjamin Forstner and patented in 1886. Contrary to popular belief, the bit's circular flange only guides the tool. The actual cutting is done by two horizontal, hand-sharpened edges. Use Forstner bits in a drill press to bore perfectly flat-bottomed holes, precise angular holes, overlapping holes and any fraction of a hole in the edge of the workpiece. Like most unique, quality tools, Forstner bits are not cheap. Sizes range from ¼-in. to 3-in. dia.

16. Mortising chisel—It may be hard to believe, but this ½-in.-wide woodworking bit bores square holes. Use this bit in a drill press to bore a series of overlapping holes to form a mortise to accept a matching tenon. The tool consists of a wood-boring bit housed in a hollow, square chisel. Chuck the bit in the drill press. A special yoke (not included) attaches to the drill press and clamps onto the chisel. As pressure is applied, the bit removes a vast majority of the stock and the chisel cuts the round hole square.

17. Glass bit—Believe it or not, this very simple bit permits you to drill holes through glass, china and ceramic tile. It consists of a diamond-ground piece of tungsten-carbide steel welded to a steel rod. Operate the bit at slow speed, either in a drill press or portable elec-

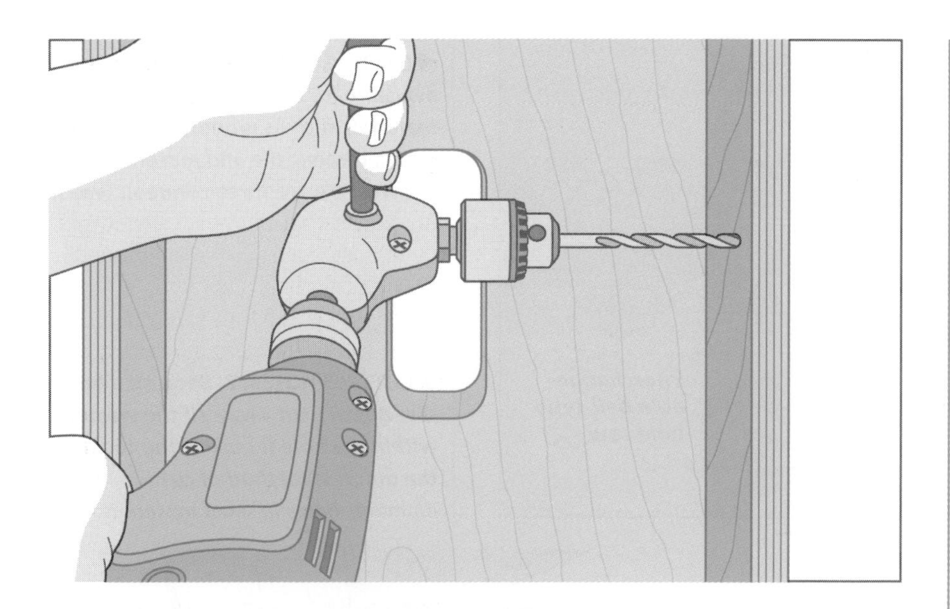

▲ **TIGHT-SPOT BORING.** ***A right-angled drive head for your drill permits working in confined areas. Since the gear ratio is 1:1, there's no change in the rpm of the drill.***

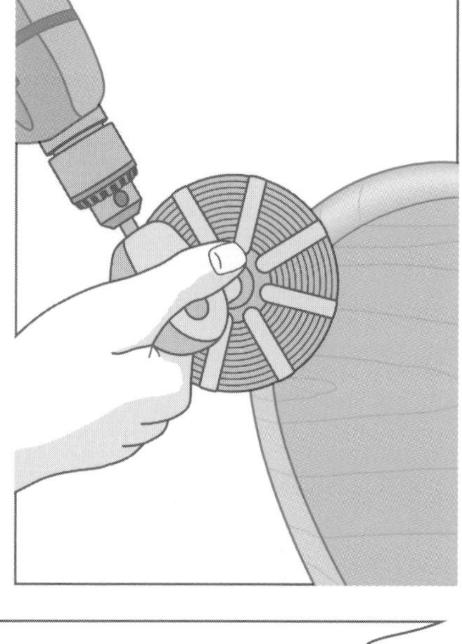

► **SHAPING AND SMOOTHING, 1.** ***Use a disc rasp for fast, aggressive removal of stock. Here, the attachment is used with a right-angle drive head for additional control.***

▼ **SHAPING AND SMOOTHING, 2.** ***Shape and smooth inside curves using a sanding drum. For the most aggressive cutting action, advance the drum against its drill rotation.***

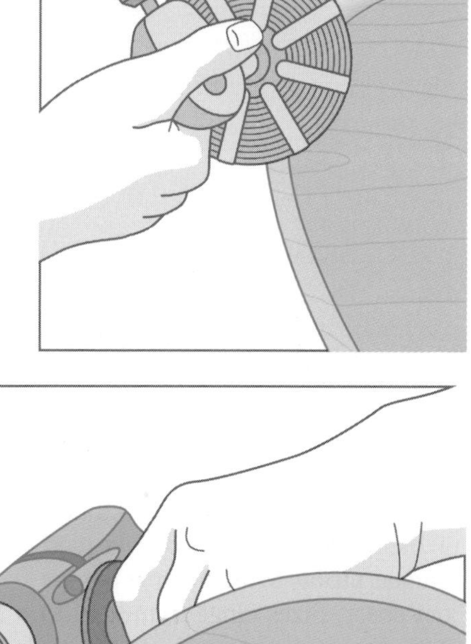

tric drill, and use a lubricant such as kerosene. A seven-piece set includes bits from ⅛-in. to ⅜-in. dia.

18. Heavy-duty expansive bit—Here's an improved version of the old reliable expansive bit. This versatile woodworking bit is infinitely adjustable for boring holes from 1⅜-in. to 3⅛-in. dia. A sharp center point ensures accurate, nonslip boring. Although it is similar to a regular expansive bit, it cuts cleaner and more precisely.

19. Compass cutter—This unique device allows you to cut holes up to 18-in. dia. using a portable electric drill. It consists of an adjustable trammel stud and a side-cutting twist drill bit. Insert the trammel stud in the center of the work and tighten the drill chuck onto the bit. Then, drill into the work and apply pressure with your free hand to the horizontal rod. It cuts rings and discs, too. The tool adjusts from 1½-in. to 18-in. dia. for use on wood, fiberglass, plastic laminate and light-gauge sheet metal.

20. Expansive bit—Here's a versatile, adjustable wood-boring bit that can bore holes from ⅞-in. to 3-in. dia. To adjust the bit, simply loosen the screw and slide the cutter to the desired position. A convenient, direct-read inch scale is stamped right on the cutter. The ⅜-in.-dia. shank can be used in a drill press, hand brace or portable electric drill.

21. Left-hand bit—Notice something odd about this ⅜-in.-dia. bit? That's right, it has left-hand spiraling flutes. This unique bit is used to extract broken bolts, screws and threaded studs. Operate the bit counterclockwise in a reversible drill. In most instances, the left-handed drilling action alone will loosen the broken piece. Otherwise, use a straight-flute screw extractor. Other bits range in size from ⅛-in. to 5/16-in. dia.

22. Double-ended bit—Designed primarily for metalworking, this bit is actually two drill bits in one. Only 2½ in. long, it's known as a screw-machine

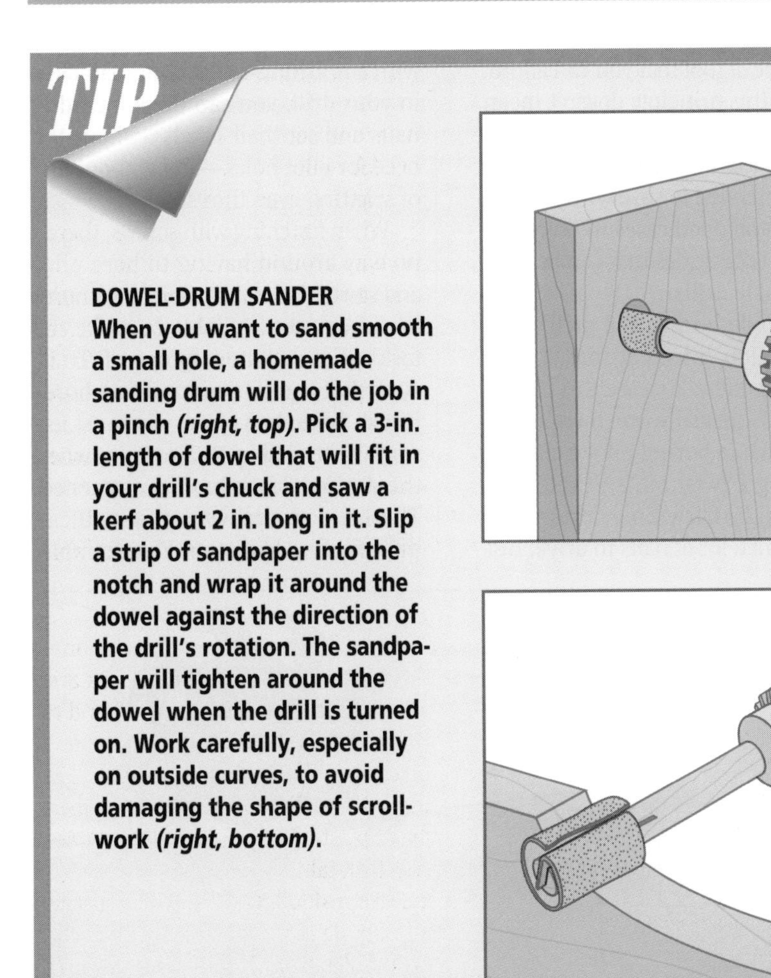

TIP

DOWEL-DRUM SANDER
When you want to sand smooth a small hole, a homemade sanding drum will do the job in a pinch *(right, top)*. Pick a 3-in. length of dowel that will fit in your drill's chuck and saw a kerf about 2 in. long in it. Slip a strip of sandpaper into the notch and wrap it around the dowel against the direction of the drill's rotation. The sandpaper will tighten around the dowel when the drill is turned on. Work carefully, especially on outside curves, to avoid damaging the shape of scrollwork *(right, bottom)*.

length bit, and is ideal for drilling thin stock such as sheet metal and aluminum. A 135° split point on each end ensures quick starts and fast cutting. Double-ended bits are available in various fractional and wire gauge sizes.

DRILLING BASICS

The basic use for a power drill is to bore holes in wood or metal. Yet, many users of drills often lack a real understanding of the fundamentals in boring holes for nails, screws and bolts. And in many instances, a lead hole is advisable when fastening with nails. The procedure is a must in hardwoods and often essential in softwoods to prevent the wood from splitting.

To choose the correct bit for boring a pilot, or lead, hole for a nail, use the storage case for your set of twist bits. Find the hole in the case that the nail enters easily, then take the bit of the next smallest diameter. By inserting the nail into the next largest hole in the case, you'll get an idea of why using a bit of a larger diameter would eliminate the nail's holding power.

Install the bit securely in the chuck of the drill. To avoid any chance of the bit drifting—that is, moving laterally—across the workpiece, use a scratch awl to punch a slight indentation at the location for the nail. Bore the pilot hole equal in depth to about two-thirds the nail's length at the same angle you plan to drive the nail. Once the pilot hole is bored, the nail can be driven without fear of splitting the wood—even when it's being set near the edge of a board.

For a screw, the procedure is much the same except that you need to use two bits: one for a pilot hole and another for a starter hole. Two different-sized holes are required for a screw in order to accommodate the different diameters of the threaded and unthreaded portions of its shank—or the screw either will be too loose or won't turn home. Using the storage case for your twist bits, find the hole that the screw enters with ease. This is the correct bit to use for boring the pilot hole. The next smallest bit is the one to use for boring the starter hole.

Working with the larger bit, bore the pilot hole through the first piece—the one you're fastening. Position the pieces and use the same bit to pinpoint the location of the hole on the second piece. Then, change to the smaller bit to bore the starter hole in the second piece. Bore the starter hole equal in depth to the screw's length if you're working with hardwood; one-half the screw's length if you're working with softwood. If you're driving a flat-head or oval-head screw, a countersink bore is also necessary to set the head of the screw flush. This step isn't required if you're working with a round-head or pan-head screw.

Note that when you're counterboring to install a bolt and nut, the procedure is different. You should first bore the larger hole for the bolt's head, then bore the smaller clearance hole for the shank of the bolt. If you bore the hole for the bolt's shank first, you'll then have difficulty centering the hole for its head.

SPECIALTY BITS FOR FASTENERS

Few experienced do-it-yourselfers are fans of the all-in-one type of tool. And beginners learn pretty quickly that you ultimately profit when you buy the best

▼ **SHAPING AND SMOOTHING, 3.** ***A rugged, flap-type sander sports strips of sandpaper around a wheel. It is useful for sanding rough scrollwork and other irregular shapes.***

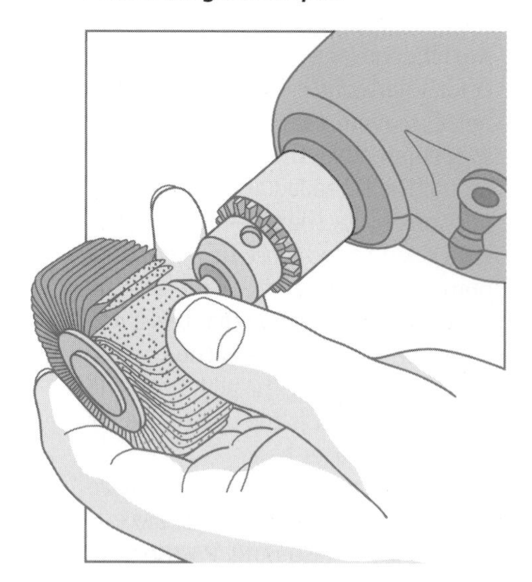

of each type of tool that you can afford. However, this principle doesn't mean you should bypass sensible—and in some instances ingenious—accessories that are intended for use with various tools. Several good cases in point are the handy accessories that can be used with portable drills.

Since hole boring is a drill's primary function, a look at some of the accessories offered to ease this particular task is especially worthwhile. For example, while boring pilot holes for nails using a twist bit isn't difficult, the job can be fairly time-consuming if you've got a lot of nails to drive. But with a finishing-nail spinner chucked in your drill, you can drive finishing nails and set their heads without the need for pilot holes—and without fear of splitting even thin stock.

When fastening with screws, there's no way around having to bore pilot and starter holes, but there are a number of devices available to make the task easier and more foolproof. To be sure that the bit you're using bores just so far and no more, you must use some sort of stop to alert you when the desired depth has been reached. There are several ways that you can improvise a drill stop. For example, you can fashion a quickie stop by slipping a tight-fitting rubber washer over the bit. Be careful, though, because this type of stop will move under pressure. Or, one of the simplest methods of all is to wrap a strip of masking tape around the bit flag-style. Again, you'll need to check that your stop doesn't shift. Alternatively, you can buy a commercial set of stop collars in diameters matching your twist bits; a hex wrench is supplied for tightening and loosening. Or, there are also adjustable depth-stop collars for use on bits from 1⁄16-in. to 1⁄4-in. dia.

Another option is a countersink bit. Available in sizes ranging from 1⁄2-in.

► **SHAPING AND SMOOTHING, 4.** ***These versions of the flap-type sander feature slashed strips, which can be used on both inside and outside curves of scrollwork.***

▼ **SHAPING AND SMOOTHING, 5.** ***The flat sanding pad in use here has a pivoting shaft that keeps the pad in full contact with the work, preventing low spots and gouges.***

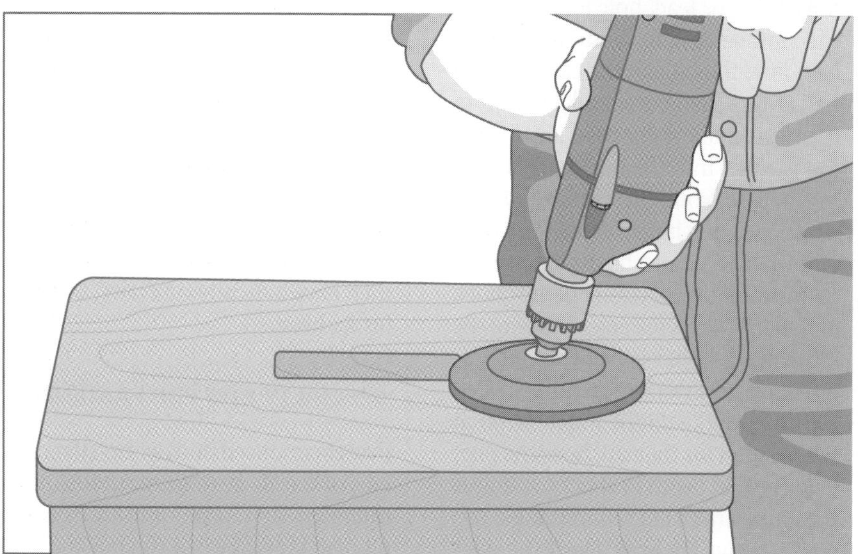

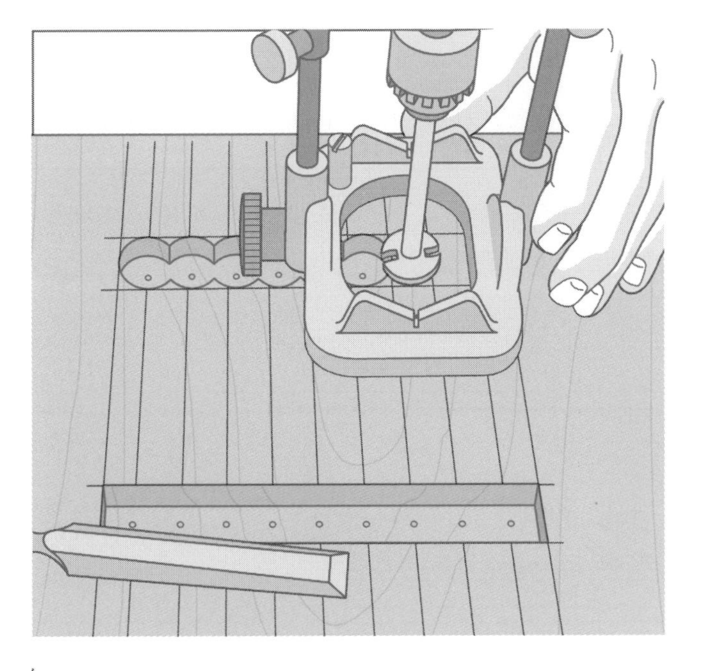

▲ **USING A DRILL GUIDE, 1.** ***To speed mortising jobs, use a drill guide to bore overlapping holes of uniform depth. Then, chisel the mortise to the finished size.***

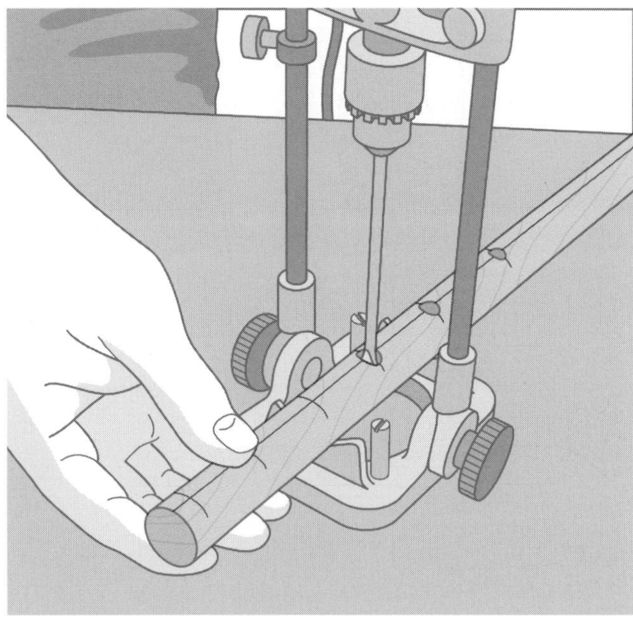

▲ **USING A DRILL GUIDE, 2.** ***The base of a drill guide features two V-shaped blocks that hold round stock securely for center-boring. Position the bit at hole centerlines.***

to ¾-in. dia., these bits drill countersink holes in wood and plastics; HSS types can also be used in metal. Some countersink bits even come with an adjustable stop collar. A combination bit, however, is the ideal solution to boring holes for screws. With this type of bit, you can bore pilot holes, starter holes and countersink or counterbore holes all at once. Combination bits are available in diameters matching screws and have an adjustable stop collar. You can purchase combination bits individually as you need them.

After boring holes for screws, you can install them quickly with a screwdriving attachment. This accessory features a slip-clutch that disengages at high torque to prevent cam-out and damage to a screwhead.

ENSURING HOLE ACCURACY

You can obtain drill-press accuracy from a portable drill by using various guides and jigs. When working freehand, make use of simple measuring and marking tools. To help bore perpendicular holes, for example, position two squares at a right angle to each other and align the bit with their blades. For angled holes, use a sliding bevel square that's set to the desired angle as a guide.

The most accurate method of boring holes is to use an adjustable-angle guide, one of the most popular accessories for the drill. The guide attaches between the drill and the chuck, and can be locked at 90° or adjusted to an angle from 45° to 90°. Additional features of the guide include a built-in depth stop, V-shaped blocks that hold round stock securely and anchoring pins for accurate centering on narrow stock. Rim-guided bits like the multispur and Forstner bits are best used in such a guide to bore angled holes, overlapping holes or any portion of a hole in the edge of stock.

Any one of the many types of doweling jigs available can also be used to bore perpendicular holes accurately. Note that some doweling jigs are self-centering while others can be adjusted for boring off-center holes.

Wood-block guides for boring perpendicular and at angles are both easy to make and use. To ensure accuracy, bore the holes in the guides using a doweling jig or drill press. Bore five different-size holes in the perpendicular guide to accept commonly used bits—typically ¼-, 5⁄16-, ⅜-, 7⁄16- and ½-in. dia. To make an angled guide, bore a perpendicular hole in the block and mark the desired angle on the side of the block with a sliding bevel square, then saw along the line. Cut the top flat for a clamping surface.

USING HOLE SAWS

A hole saw permits you to cut large holes up to 4½-in. dia. in wood, plastics and sheet metal. Three basic types of hole saws are available: the interchangeable bell-type, the nest of saws and the carbide-tipped saw. There are hole saws for cutting ceramic tile and masonry, too. To guide the hole saw and keep it cutting on course, the tool features a small-diameter center-pilot bit—usually ¼-in. dia.

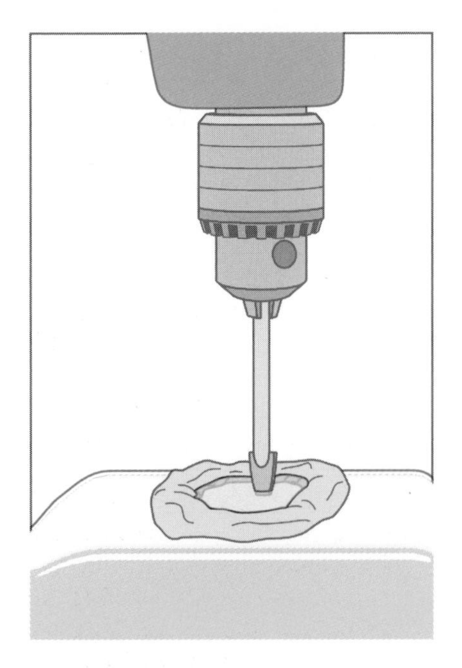

▲ **DRILLING GLASS.** ***Drill glass using a carbide-tipped bit. Make a dam out of putty or modeling clay to form a shallow reservoir for the kerosene used as lubricant.***

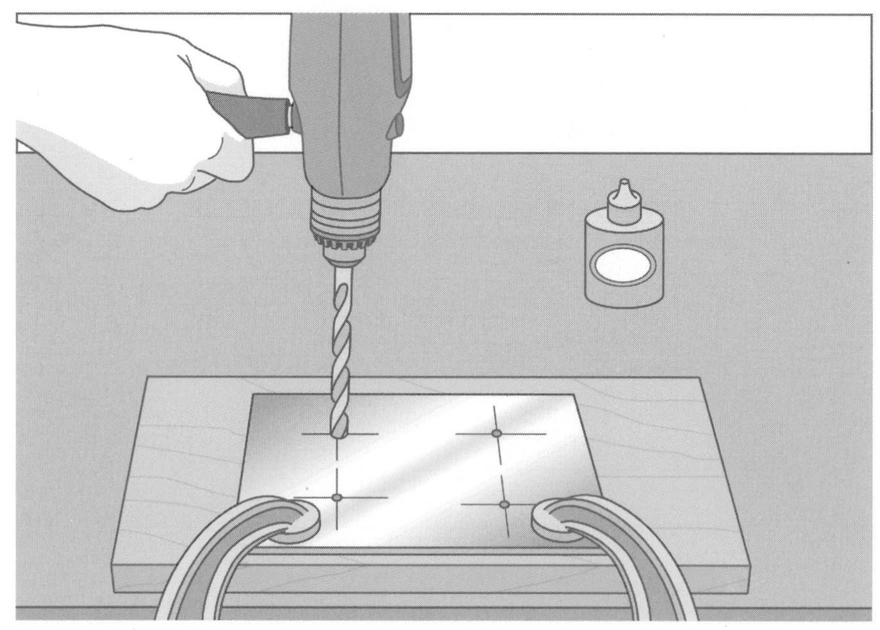

▲ **DRILLING METAL.** ***Clamp your work securely. Start by drilling small pilot holes, then drill holes of the larger, desired diameter. Auxiliary handle gives added control.***

▲ **DRILL-POLISHING, 1.** ***Remove rust, grime and paint from metal with a cup-shaped wire brush attachment. Wear eye protection to avoid injury from stray wire strands.***

The common bell-type hole saw is available in high-speed steel and with long-lasting carbide-tipped teeth that are especially effective for cutting abrasive material such as plastic, fiberglass or cast iron. A nest of saws comes with hole saws of different diameters (usually seven) and a backplate/mandrel fitting. One advantage of this type of hole saw is that you can install two saws in the backplate at the same time and cut out ring-shaped pieces in a single pass. The carbide-tipped hole saw features a rigid housing fitted with a single tooth. Said to last up to 50 times longer than conventional versions of the tool, this hole saw can cut entirely through 1½-in.-thick stock in one pass.

METAL METHODS

Drilling in metal necessitates a somewhat different approach than boring in wood. First, for the drill to start cutting without wandering across the surface, you must always strike a starting point with a center punch. Then, drill a small-diameter pilot hole and follow up with the larger drill of the desired diameter. This two-step procedure is necessary because the small dimple

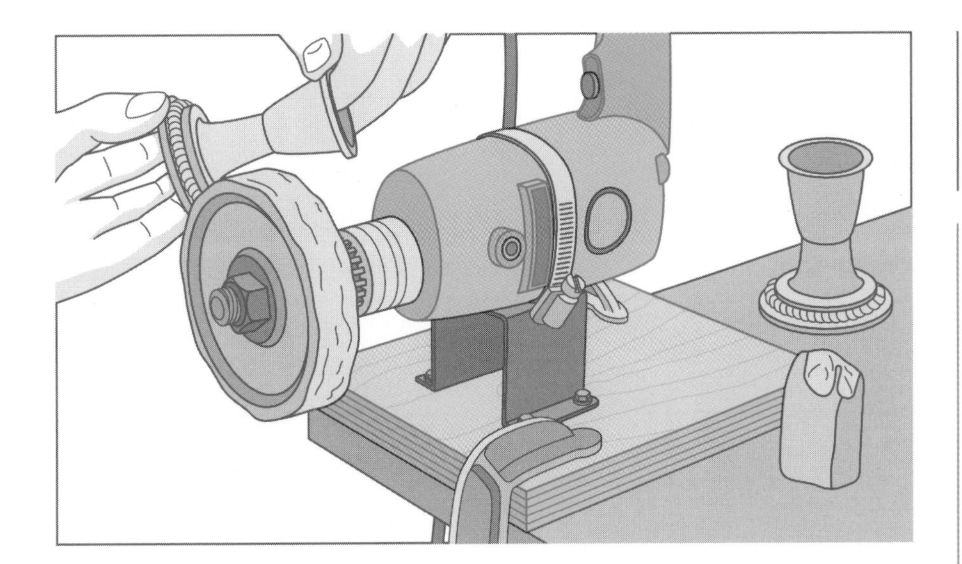

◀ **DRILL-POLISHING, 2.** ***Transform your drill into a stationary tool by using a horizontal drill stand. Here, the stand is clamped onto a workbench for buffing silver.***

created by the center punch won't keep a large-diameter drill from wandering.

When a twist drill breaks through the backside surface of a piece, it often grabs and snaps, tears the piece from its clamps or pulls the tool out of your hands. To avoid these dangerous situations, it's important to release pressure on the drill just before it exits the piece. Keep a firm, two-handed grip on the tool and apply only light pressure to complete the hole. If your drill can accommodate an auxiliary side-mounted handle, use it for additional control of the tool.

Drilling metal with a ¼-in.-dia. HSS drill takes a tool speed of about 1000 rpm. A ½-in.-dia. drill requires about 500 rpm. Cast iron, copper and brass are drilled dry—there's no need for lubrication. Steel and wrought iron, however, should be lubricated with oil. Lubricate aluminum with kerosene or turpentine. And while it's important to wear eye protection when operating any power tool, this is especially true when drilling metal.

SANDING ACCESSORIES

After drilling holes, the second task you are most likely to use a portable drill for is sanding. Accessories such as drum sanders and flap sanders that make the smoothing of scrollwork and other irregular-shaped surfaces easier have been around a while, and are valuable tools to have in the workshop. Although these accessories are simple in concept, you do need some practice with them to achieve good results. For example, a drum sander that's improperly used on an outside curve can ruin the shape of scrollwork.

TIP

DOVETAIL JIG

This tool lets you produce half-blind dovetail joints with a ¼- or ⅜-in. drill. The dovetailer consists of a self-clamping template, cutter guide, auxiliary handle with depth stop, cutter holder and drill arbor, and ½-in. dovetail bit. Straight bits are available for cutting box joints.

First, clamp the jig to the workpiece to rout the sockets. Chuck the arbor into the drill and slide the cutter holder into one of the jig's channels. Then, start the drill and push the cutter into the work *(right)*. Repeat for each channel. Next, cut the tails using the channels on the side of the jig. Since the tails are cut through the work, clamp a backup board to the workpiece to prevent splintering and to keep the cutter from hitting the jig.

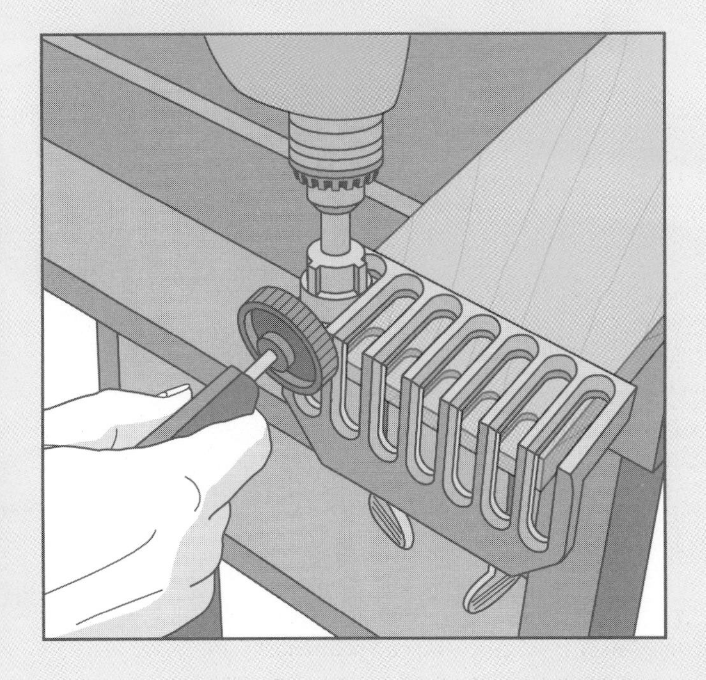

STATIONARY TOOLS

TABLE SAWS

The heart of a well-equipped woodworking shop is the table saw. And the reason is simple: The table saw is more than just another tool. It's an extremely versatile and accurate piece of equipment that can handle all the basic woodworking cuts—rip, crosscut, miter, bevel and compound angle cuts—and then some. Its large table makes it ideal for cutting both solid-wood boards and plywood panels. It accepts a wide variety of blades and attachments, too, such as a dado blade or molding cutterhead.

Special abrasive saw blades are available for cutting thin metal on a table saw. They're especially useful for crosscutting thin-wall tubing such as conduit. Use only reinforced, resin-bonded abrasive blades; non-reinforced blades may shatter.

The table saw is also unsurpassed for cutting joints such as butt, miter, spline, tenon, rabbet, dado, box, tongue-and-groove and lap. The saw's use of a rip fence and miter gauge, along with its precise blade adjustments, all contribute to making the tool highly accurate and very exact.

However, you should not be scared off by the table saw's impressive workshop sophistication. It's actually a relatively simple tool to use safely and effectively. Note that the saw's blade guard should be used whenever possible. In some of the illustrations presented here, the guard has been removed only for clarity of the work action. Also, you should wear eye goggles or a face shield when using the saw. Even with the guard in place, the blade has the tendency to throw chips and dust toward the operator.

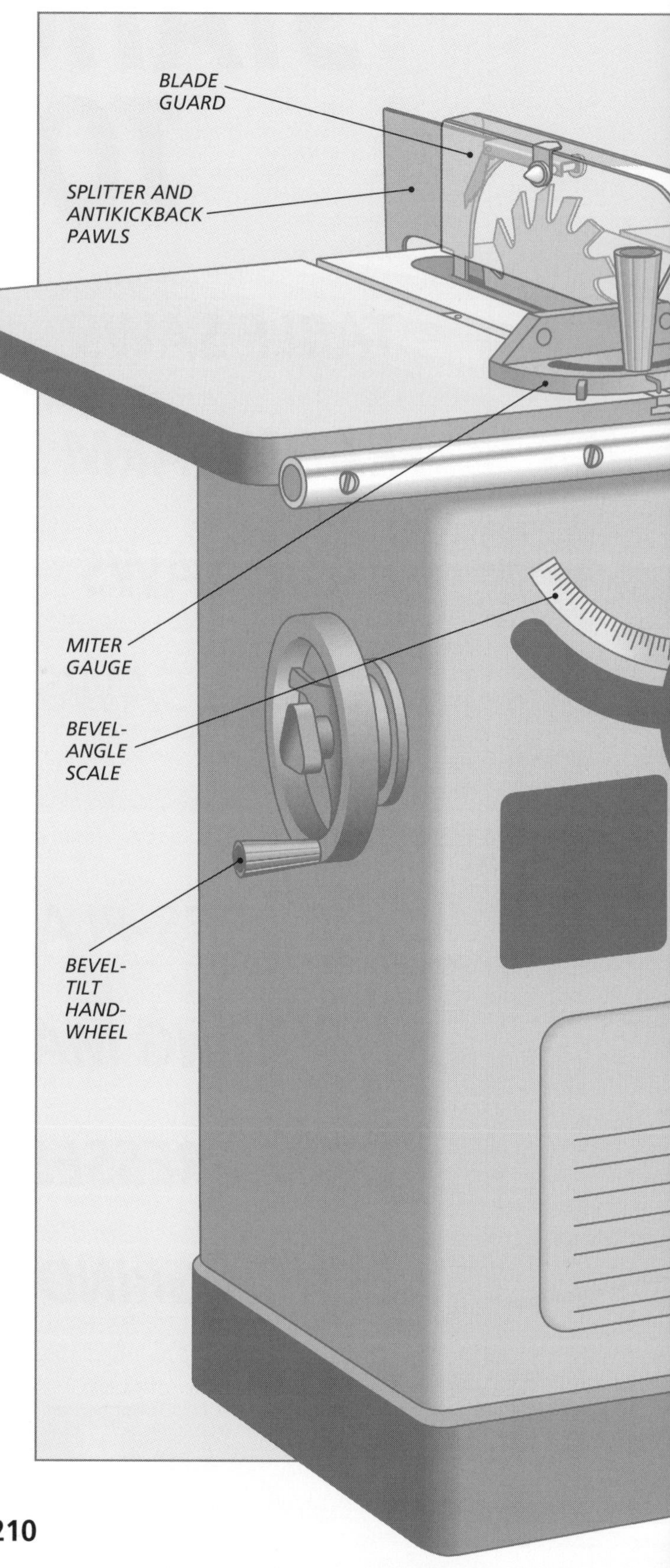

TABLE SAW MECHANICS

A typical table saw consists of a motor and arbor assembly that is housed in a base cabinet or stand. The saw blade is mounted onto the arbor, which is connected by a belt and pulley to the motor. Blade adjustments are controlled by two crank-type handwheels. One handwheel controls the blade's height above the saw table. The other one adjusts the bevel angle of the blade—from 0° to 45°.

The rip fence slides on guide bars at the front and rear of the table saw, and can be locked anywhere along the bars at the desired distance from the blade. Shallow slots that are milled into the saw's table on both sides of the blade accept an adjustable miter gauge. Use the miter gauge for making crosscuts and miters.

Table saws are designated according to the diameter of the blade used. Models are available in 8-, 9-, 10-, 12- and 14-in. sizes. The 10-in. size, however, is clearly the most popular saw for the home workshop. Standard equipment also includes a blade guard, antikickback pawls and a splitter. The pawls are designed to grab the workpiece and prevent it from being kicked back toward the operator. The splitter is a thin metal bar mounted directly behind the blade that keeps the kerf open and prevents the work from pinching the blade.

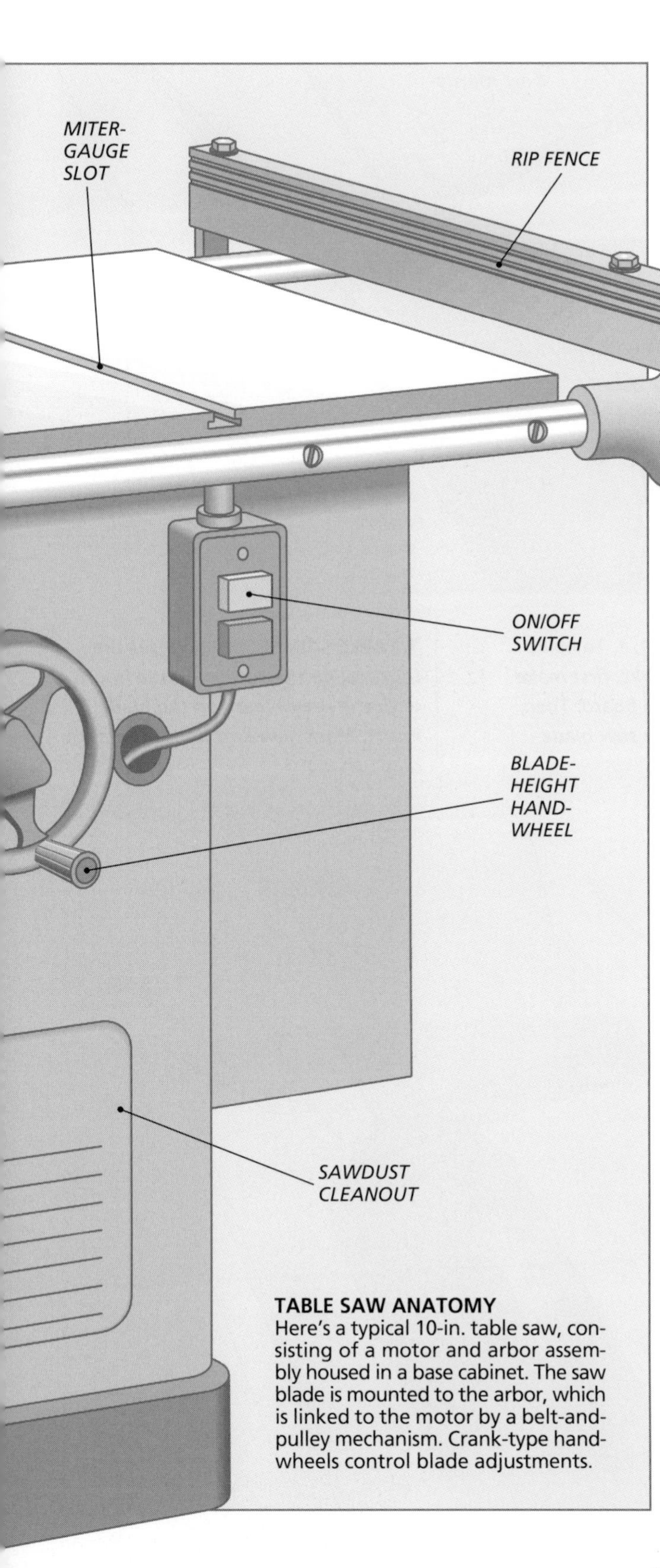

TABLE SAW ANATOMY
Here's a typical 10-in. table saw, consisting of a motor and arbor assembly housed in a base cabinet. The saw blade is mounted to the arbor, which is linked to the motor by a belt-and-pulley mechanism. Crank-type handwheels control blade adjustments.

TABLE SAW SETUP

A table saw cannot perform with precision unless all of its adjustable components are aligned properly. Frustrating problems—as well as safety hazards—can result from incorrectly set components, including excessive vibration, heightened risk of kickback, damage to the blade, burn marks on workpieces and inaccurate cuts. Errors of as little as 1/64 in. can sometimes be enough to adversely affect the quality and strength of a workpiece.

The components of the table saw that contact and guide the workpiece during cutting operations require the most attention: the table, blade, rip fence and miter gauge. At the beginning of every work session, you should check that these components are properly aligned, and make the necessary corrective adjustments.

Conduct your checks with the table saw unplugged. Start by adjusting the setscrews of the table insert to make the insert perfectly flush with the table. Then, crank the blade to its highest setting in order to check the table alignment and angle of the blade.

To check alignment of the table, hold or clamp a perfectly squared wood block against the miter gauge and butt the end of the block against a tooth at the front of the blade. Rotate the blade from front to back with one hand as you slide the miter gauge and block toward the rear of the table with the other hand. The block should stay butted against the tooth of the blade. If the block binds against the blade or a gap opens between the block and the tooth, align the table following the instructions in your owner's manual.

To check the angle of the blade, remove the table insert and butt a combination square up against the blade between two of its teeth. If the blade isn't perfectly flush with the square, use the bevel-tilt handwheel to adjust the blade as necessary to eliminate any gap.

Next, check the alignment of the rip fence by positioning it along the miter-gauge slot in the table. Eliminate any gap between the fence and the slot by adjusting the fence according to the instructions given in your owner's manual. Typically, an adjustment bolt for the fence is provided at the front of the table.

The miter gauge must be aligned with both the table and the blade. Take the gauge out of its slot and set it on the table. First, check that the gauge's head is square with the edge of its bar using a combination square. Use the adjustment handle on the gauge to correct any out-of-squareness. Then, butt the combination square against the miter gauge and check that they fit flush. To have any gap corrected, you will need to have the miter gauge professionally machined square.

To check the alignment of the miter gauge with the blade, install the gauge in its slot and butt a carpenter's square against it and across the blade between two teeth. The square should fit flush. Make any correction necessary to the gauge by loosening its adjustment handle and pivoting its head, then retighten the handle securely.

Finally, here's a quick-fix for a miter gauge with too much side-to-side play in its slot. Remove the gauge and set it edge-up on a board, then strike the edge in a staggered pattern every inch or so along it using a prick punch and ball-peen hammer. The bumps that result along the edge of the bar will provide a tighter fit in the slot. If the fit of the gauge is too tight, simply file the bumps as necessary.

TYPES OF BLADES

The key to getting a smooth, clean cut with a table saw is to select the right blade for the job. The basic types of blades include rip, crosscut, combination, plywood and hollow-ground planer. As well, however, there are a wide variety of specialty blades designed for specific cutting purposes.

Rip blades are designed with chisel-like teeth for sawing along the wood's grain—that is, ripping. The deep gullets and relatively few, large teeth of the rip blade produce a fairly rough cut and generate large particles of dust and chips. Crosscut blades, obviously, are used to cut across the wood's grain.

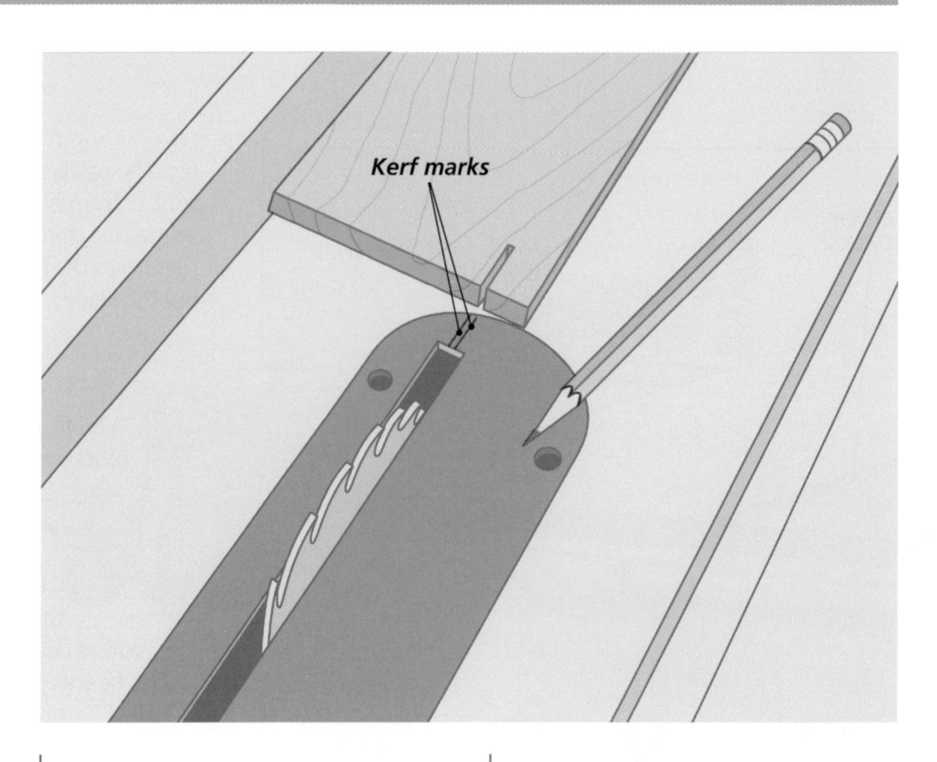

▲ **TABLE SAW SETUP, 1.** ***To make blade alignment marks, first make a short cut in a scrap board. Then, mark the kerf on the saw blade insert with a pencil.***

▼ **TABLE SAW SETUP, 2.** ***To set the fence, align the cutline on the board with the pencil mark on the blade insert. Mark new kerf lines after each blade change.***

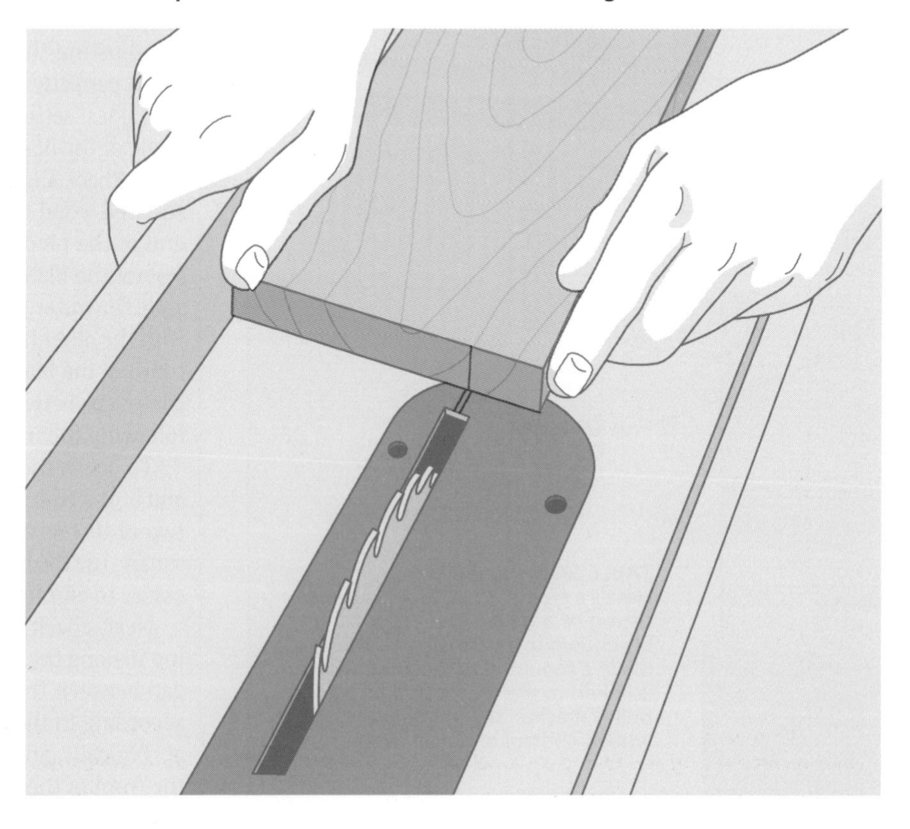

Featuring more, shallower teeth than a rip blade, the crosscut blade makes smooth cuts and creates fine particles of dust. A combination blade is a general-purpose blade that can be used for both ripping and crosscuts. Although the combination blade doesn't perform quite as well as either a rip or crosscut blade, its cutting versatility means less frequent blade changes. A hollow-ground planer blade gives an extremely smooth cut because its teeth are not set. The body of the hollow-ground planer blade tapers slightly from the teeth to the hub, providing clearance in the kerf and eliminating binding.

Variations in the standard crosscut blade include antikickback and thin-rim types. The antikickback crosscut blade features a projection between teeth that limits the aggressiveness of each cutting bite, thereby reducing the risk of kickback. The thin-rim crosscut blade produces fine finish cuts, with the narrower kerf that it makes putting less strain on the motor.

A plywood blade has a high number of small teeth that yield smooth, splinter-free cuts in plywood and wood veneers. The teeth of the plywood blade are less efficient, however, in highly abrasive manufactured panels such as particleboard. For these types of materials, a melamine blade works best. The teeth of the melamine blade are spe-

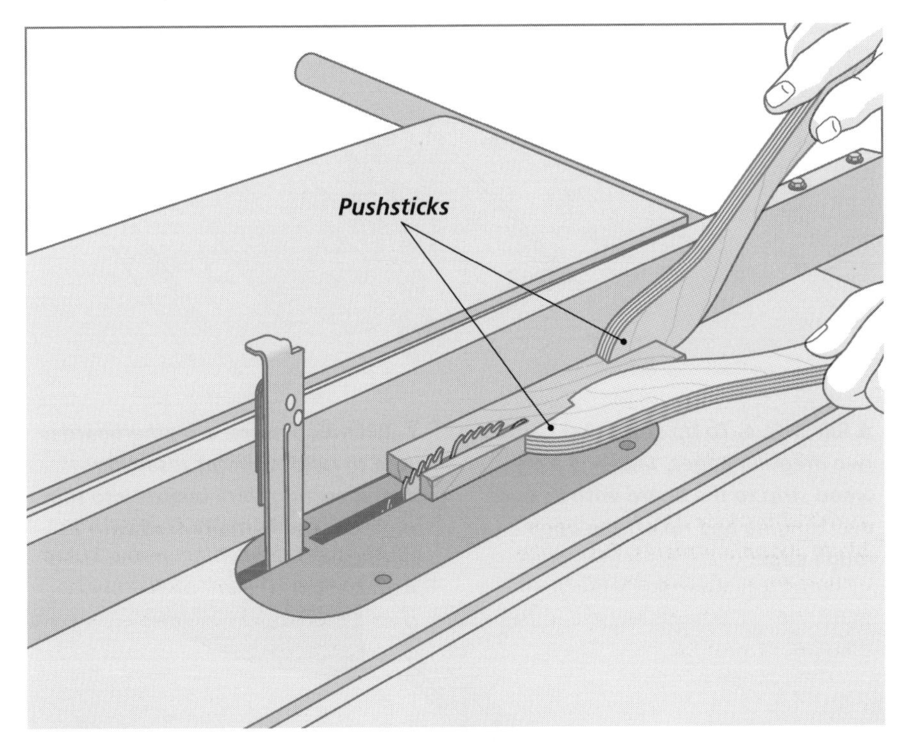

◀ **RIPPING, 1.** ***Use pushsticks when you're ripping narrow pieces. Cut pushsticks from ½-in. plywood. For some types of work, two pushsticks are needed, as shown.***

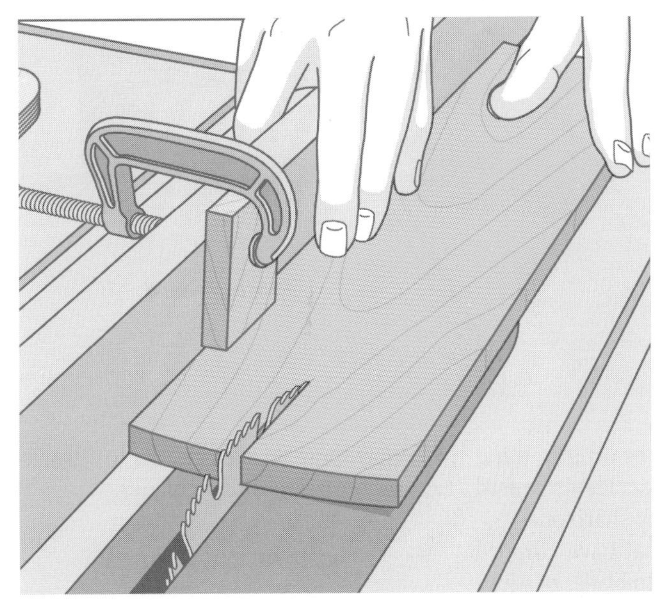

▲ **RIPPING, 2.** ***To rip a cupped board, cut it with the concave surface facing up. Clamp a wood block to the fence as shown here to keep the board from rocking.***

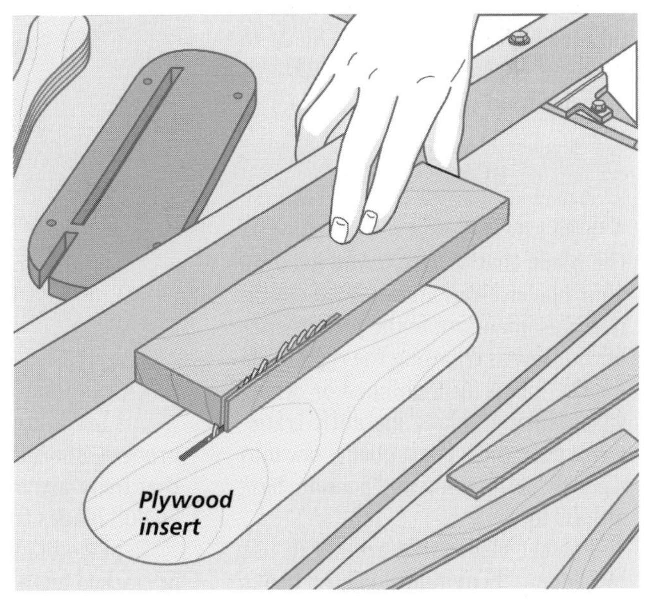

▲ **RIPPING, 3.** ***When ripping thin strips, replace the standard table insert with a plywood one. Raise the blade through the plywood to form the narrow slot.***

cially designed to cut through abrasive glues and produce chip-free cuts.

When you're looking for a smooth-cutting blade that will remain sharp longer, choose a carbide-tipped blade. Four basic tooth designs are used for carbide-tipped blades, each one having its own particular advantages and applications. The flat-top grind (FTG) type features flat-topped cutting teeth for ripping. The alternately beveled, highly sharpened cutting teeth of the alternate top bevel (ATB) type make it ideal for crosscutting. The two other designs allow for ripping and crosscutting: the triple-chip grind (TCG), which features flat-topped raker teeth alternating with teeth that have their edges ground to 45°; and the alternate top bevel with a raker (ATB/R), which has four alternately beveled teeth alternating with a flat-topped raker tooth.

By combining a two-faced sanding disc with a carbide-tipped saw blade, a Sanblade achieves fast, accurate and extremely smooth cuts with virtually no splintered edges—even in plywood and manufactured panels such as particleboard. High rpm enables the 40-grit aluminum-oxide abrasive that's bonded to both sides of the blade to sand cut edges as smooth as 120-grit abrasive used normally.

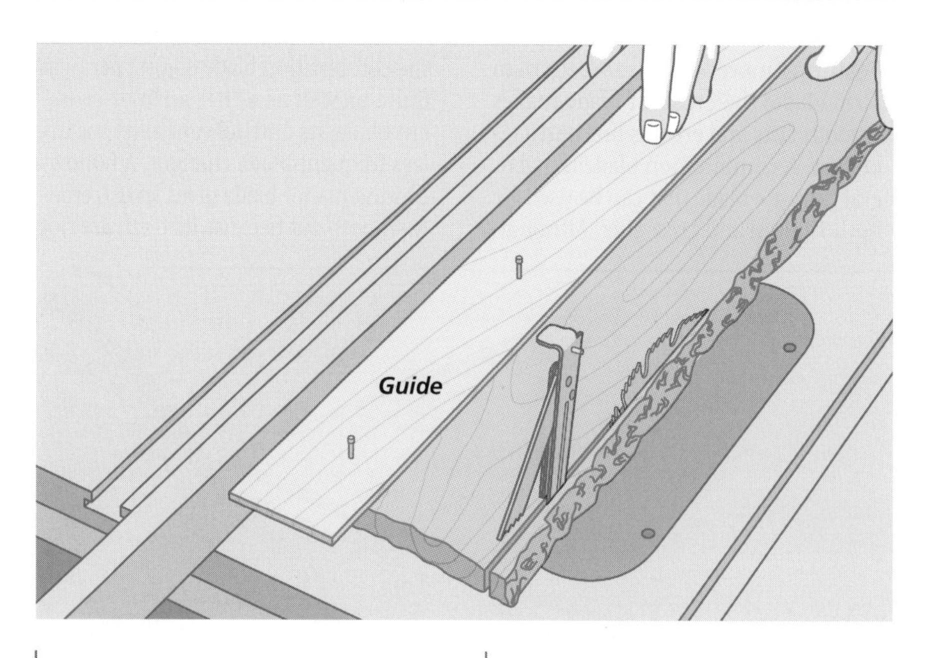

▲ **RIPPING, 4.** ***To rip stock that has two irregular edges, tack-nail a plywood strip to the board with its edge overhanging and rip off the open rough edge.***

▼ **RIPPING, 5.** ***Here, a featherboard is used to hold work for resawing—that is, cutting thick boards into thin ones. Cut the featherboard with a band saw.***

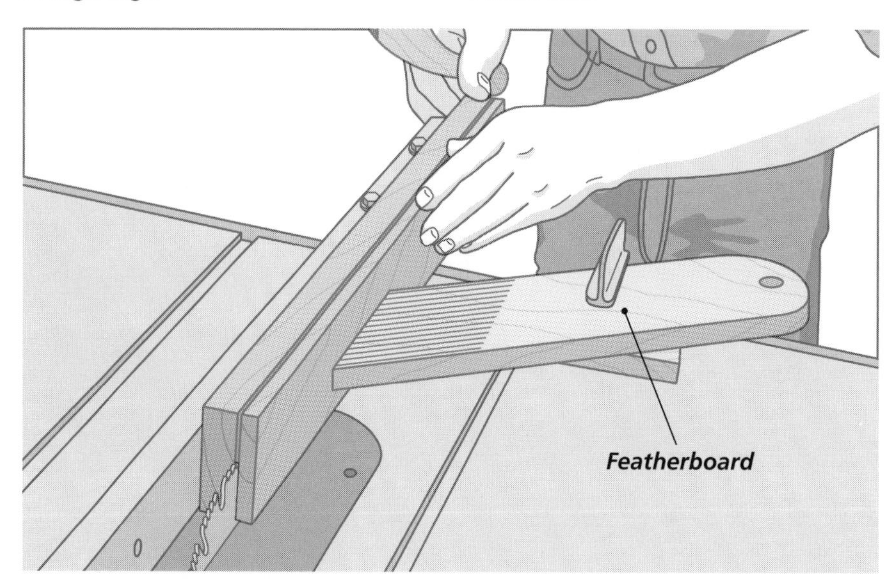

BLADE CARE

A table saw is always only as good as the blade that it turns. And keeping your blades clean and in good condition is as important to the performance of your saw as choosing the right blade for the job. A dull, chipped or otherwise damaged blade instantly transforms even the highest quality saw into a poorly performing and possibly hazardous tool.

Protect blades that are not in use by hanging them individually on hooks or setting them apart between pieces of cardboard. Avoid stacking blades loose one on top of the other—a sure way of damaging them. Keep your blades properly sharpened, bearing in mind that there are more accidents caused by dull blades than by sharp ones.

Replace blades that have chipped or cracked teeth. Clean blades of sticky resin and pitch that can interfere with their ability to cut smoothly by soaking them in turpentine or kerosene and scrubbing them with steel wool. Apply spray-on oven cleaner to dissolve stubborn deposits on blades.

CHANGING BLADES

Make certain that the power cord of the table saw is unplugged before you change the blade. To take off a blade, stand at the front of the saw's table and

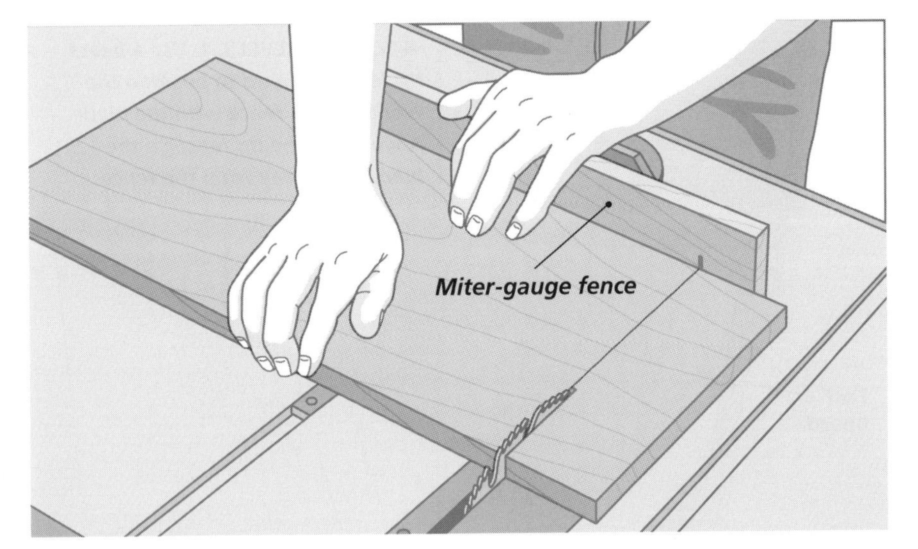

▲ CROSSCUTTING, 1. *For crosscutting a wide board, one hand holds the work against the miter-gauge fence while the other hand pushes both of them forward.*

wedge a scrap block against a tooth of the blade to keep the blade from turning. Loosen the arbor nut using the wrench supplied with the saw. Note that the arbors of table saws are usually reverse threaded, so the nut is loosened by turning clockwise rather than counterclockwise. Remove the nut by hand, making sure that it doesn't drop into the machine. Then, carefully slide the blade and washer off the arbor.

Position a new blade on the arbor with its teeth pointing toward the front of the saw—the direction of the blade's rotation. Install the washer and thread the nut onto the arbor by hand. Then,

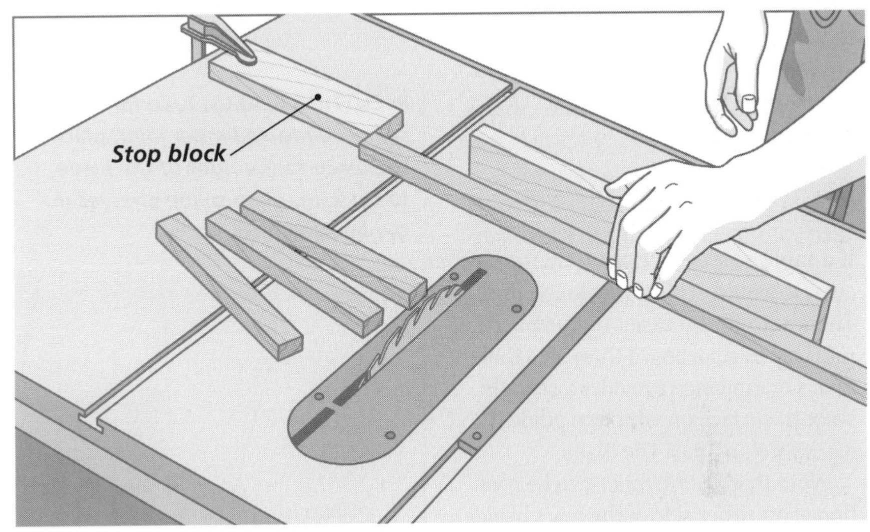

▶ CROSSCUTTING, 2. *A stop block clamped to the saw table allows for identical repetitive cuts. Butt the work against the block and advance the miter-gauge fence.*

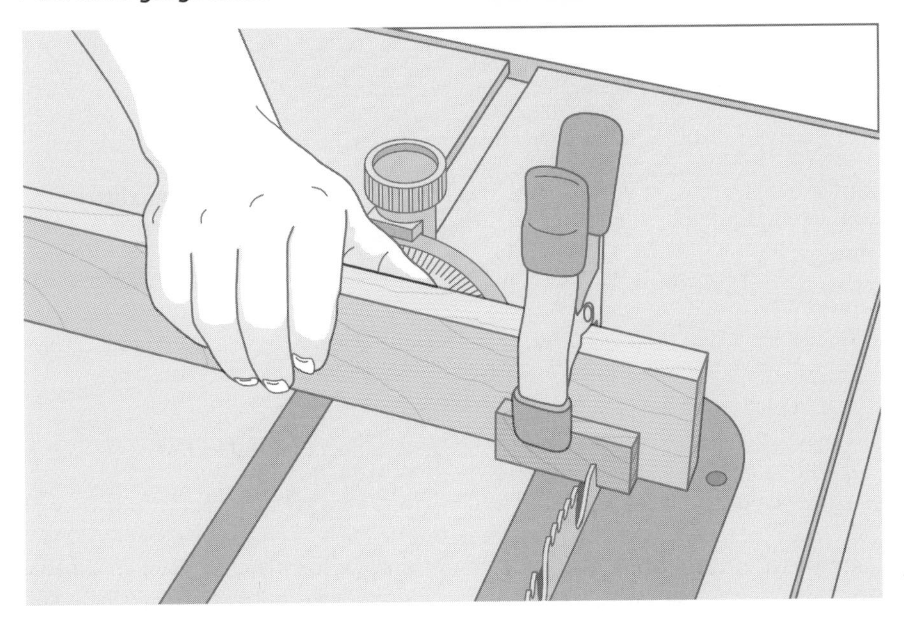

◀ CROSSCUTTING, 3. *Never take chances when crosscutting small pieces. Use a spring clamp to hold the work securely against the miter-gauge fence. Keep your fingers well out of harm's way.*

grip the blade securely using a cloth to protect your hand and finish tightening the nut with the wrench. To prevent overtightening of the nut, avoid using a scrap block as a wedge to hold the blade stationary.

BLADE ADJUSTMENTS

Adjust the angle of the blade, if necessary, before setting the blade's height, again working only with the table saw unplugged. To set the blade at the correct cutting angle, remove the table insert and crank the blade to its highest setting. Adjust a sliding bevel to the cutting angle desired, then adjust the blade's angle until the sliding bevel can be butted flush against the blade between two of its teeth.

A blade that's set too high can be a safety hazard. Set too low, the blade cannot cut properly. For most types of through-cutting operations, crank the blade until it's visible about 1/4 in. above the workpiece. The blade can be set at a specified height using a tape measure or a special gauge that's "stepped" in 1/4-in. increments. Such gauges are available commercially, or can be easily made in the shop using scraps of 1/4-in. plywood.

RIP CUTS

If a table saw were used only for rip cuts, it would still be a valuable tool. There's simply no easier or more accurate way to rip a board than on a table saw. The rip fence provides a straight, smooth surface on which to guide the work into and past the blade.

Note that the rip fence can be positioned on either side of the saw's blade, although the vast majority of rip cuts are made to the right side of the blade. Be sure that the rip fence locks securely to the guide bars and parallel to the blade. Most rip fences can be adjusted exactly parallel to the blade.

When cutting on the table saw it's extremely important to keep your fingers away from the blade at all times. Even the best blade guard can't prevent all accidents. This is especially important when making narrow rip cuts. As a general rule, always use a

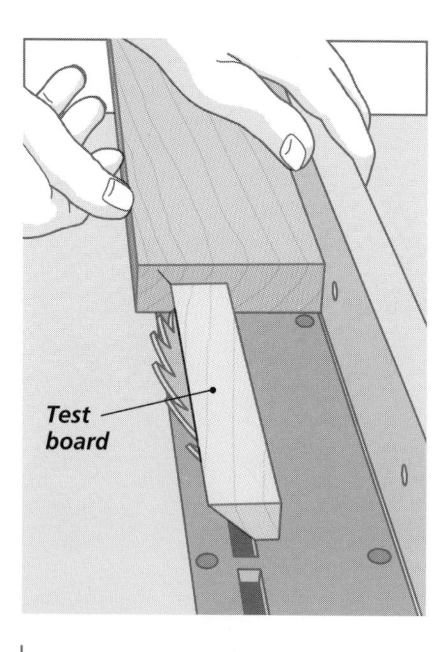

◄ **CUTTING BEVELS, 1.** ***Use a bevel rip test-cut board to position the work and rip fence with the blade. Always set the rip fence so the blade tilts away from the fence.***

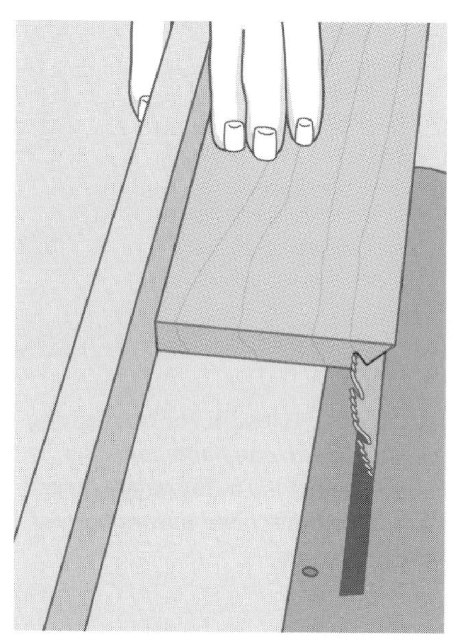

► **CUTTING BEVELS, 2.** ***To form a spline-reinforced miter joint, place the fence to the right of the blade to cut 1/2-in.-deep spline grooves in the beveled face.***

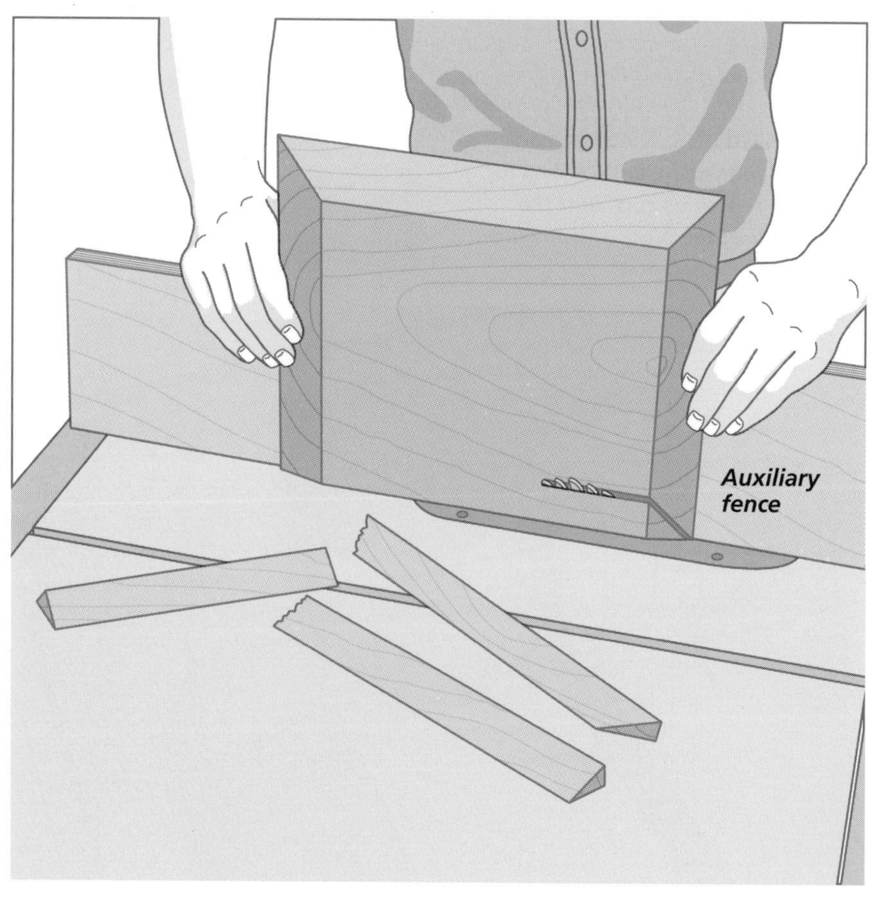

► **CUTTING BEVELS, 3.** ***Bevel cutting allows you to make raised panels. Install a tall auxiliary fence to the rip fence for support. Make the bevel crosscuts first.***

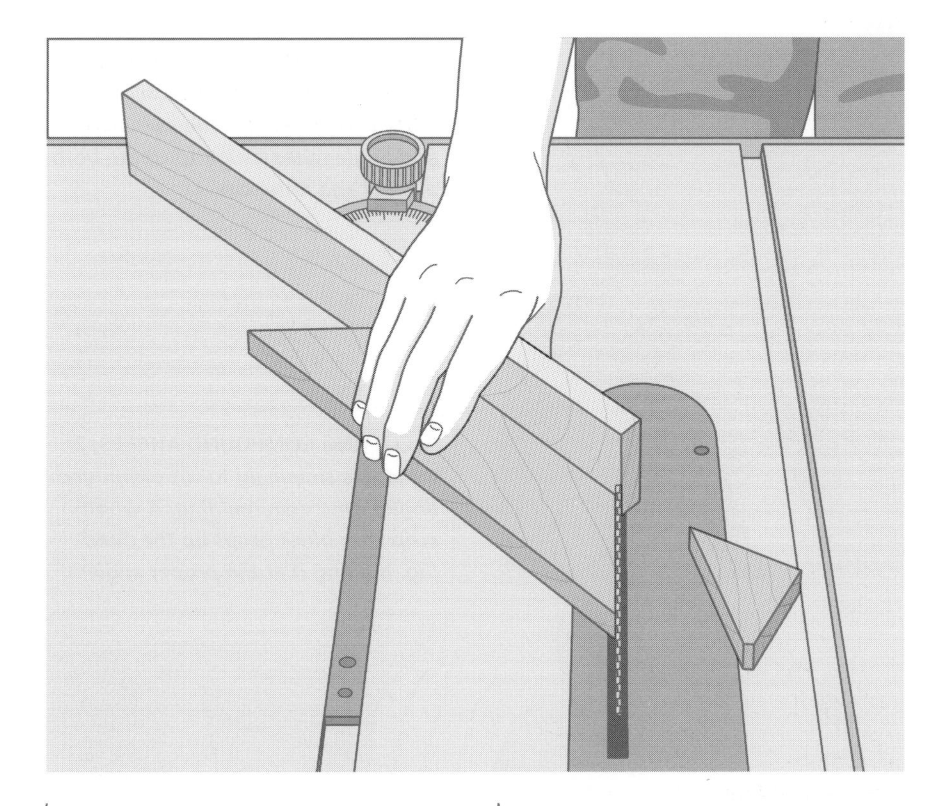

▲ **MITERING, 1.** ***Here, the miter gauge is in the open position and set back from the blade. When mitering a wide board, the miter gauge will be off the saw table.***

▼ **MITERING, 2.** ***This shop-built mitering platform jig provides an easy way to cut miters. Hold the work against the angled block and push the platform forward.***

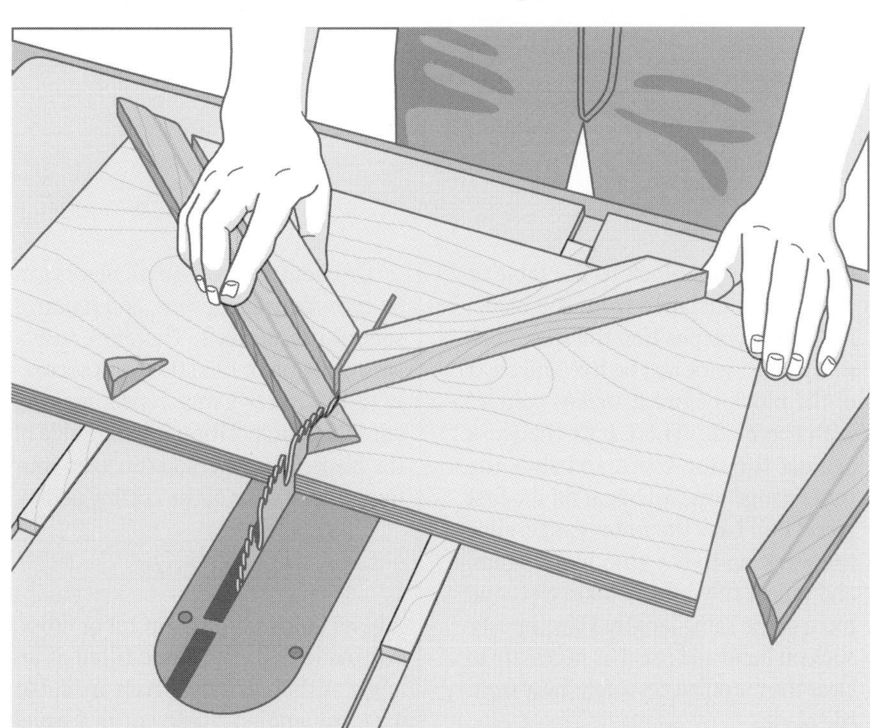

pushstick when you're ripping a board that's less than 3 in. wide. When you're ripping wider boards, it's good practice to keep a couple of fingers wrapped over the rip fence as you push the work by the blade. This will help prevent your hand from accidentally slipping into the blade.

When ripping thin strips, replace the table's insert with a shopmade one to minimize the gap around the blade. Using the table's insert as a template, cut your insert out of plywood that's the same thickness. Set the blade to its lowest setting, then position your insert in the table and place the rip fence across it to one side of the blade. Turn on the saw and slowly raise the blade to its highest setting to cut a slot in the insert.

Rip cupped stock with the concave surface facing up. To prevent the board from rocking during a cut, clamp a wood block to the rip fence above the board so that its edge is held in position on the table.

When you rip long stock, the work must be supported on the outfeed side of the table. One solution is to build an auxiliary worktable that's the same height as the saw table and position it at the outfeed side of the saw. Another solution is to make a simple T-shaped work support that's fitted with a wood or steel roller. Clamp the support to a sawhorse so that the roller is at the same height as the saw table.

Guiding a board along against the rip fence is fine as long as the board's edge is straight. But how do you make a straight rip cut on a board with two rough, irregular edges? Well, here's how. First, tack-nail a narrow rip of plywood to the board so that the plywood slightly overhangs the board's rough edge. Direct the board into the blade with the plywood guide against the rip fence. Then, remove the plywood guide, turn the board around and guide its just-cut straight edge against the fence to trim the remaining rough edge.

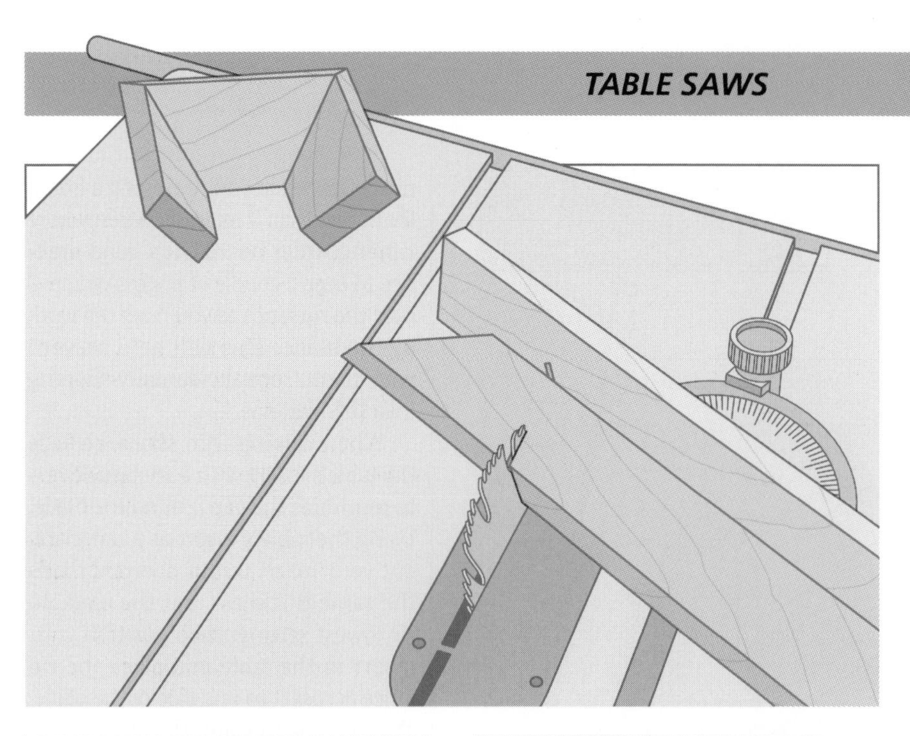

◀ **CUTTING COMPOUND ANGLES, 1.** ***Here's the setup for a typical compound angle cut. Tilt the saw blade and angle miter gauge to create both a bevel and miter cut.***

▼ **CUTTING COMPOUND ANGLES, 2.** ***Build this simple jig to cut compound angles on crown molding. A wood-strip stop block props up the molding, holding it at the proper angle.***

CROSSCUTTING

The table saw is excellent for making crosscuts—especially in short, small-dimension pieces. For this type of cutting operation, the miter gauge is used to support the work as you guide it into the blade.

The problem with a standard miter gauge, however, is that the work-bearing surface is much too small. This can be remedied by screwing an auxiliary wood fence to the miter gauge. Make the fence out of ¾-in.-thick stock about 3 in. wide and 14 in. long.

Using the auxiliary fence also makes it easy to align the cutline on a board with the saw's blade. Here's the way this is accomplished: First, raise the blade about 1 in. above the table and make a cut through the fence. Then, use the cut in the fence as a reference mark for the blade. Simply align the board's cutline with the kerf made in the fence.

Note that you should never use the miter gauge in conjunction with the rip fence. Move the rip fence well out of the way during crosscutting operations to eliminate the chance of cutoff pieces becoming jammed between the blade and the fence.

To crosscut several pieces to the same exact length, use a stop block. Clamp the stop block to the table at the desired distance from the blade. Make sure you position the stop block so that the work will be free and clear of the block before it makes contact with the blade. Then, butt the work against the stop block and slide the miter gauge forward to cut off the first piece. Pull back the miter gauge, slide the work up to the stop block again, and repeat the cut to obtain a second piece of the same length. Have a push-stick on hand and use it as necessary to clear the cutoff pieces safely away from the blade.

Crosscutting very small pieces can be extremely dangerous, and requires special precautions. Therefore, use a spring clamp to hold the work securely to the miter gauge fence, making sure that you position it to one side of the blade. This way, you can keep your fingers well clear of the cutting action.

BEVEL CUTS

A bevel cut is simply a rip cut or crosscut made with the blade tilted at an angle. Although most bevels are cut at 45°, any angled-blade cut is a bevel

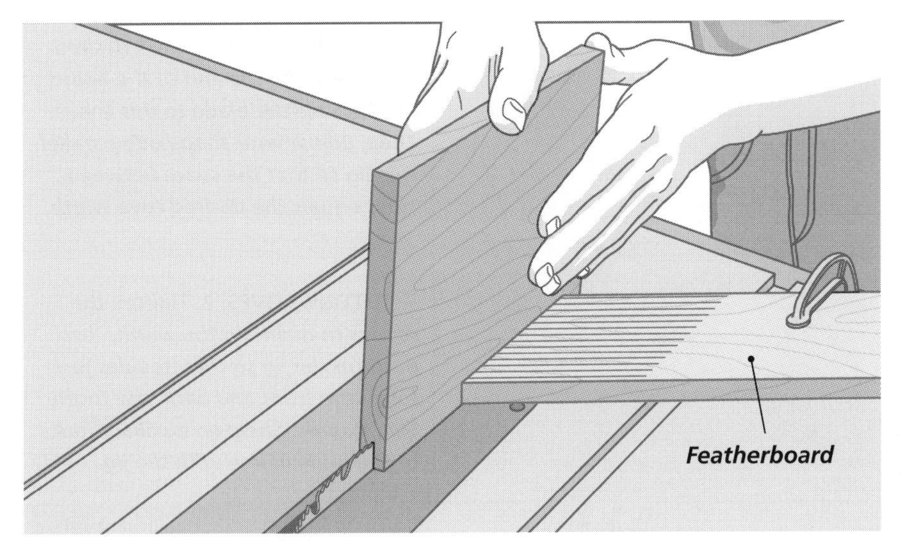

cut. Some table saws have blades that tilt to the left, but most tilt right. In either case, when making a bevel rip cut, always position the rip fence so that the blade tilts away from the fence. Otherwise, there's a risk that the workpiece could become jammed between the blade and the fence.

Positioning the rip fence for a bevel rip cut is a little tricky. However, here's a quick, accurate way to position the fence exactly. First, make a bevel rip test-cut in a scrap board that's at least 10 in. long. Next, place the test-cut board against the blade and align the cutline on the workpiece with the beveled surface of the test board. Then, lock the fence in place.

The miter gauge is utilized for making bevel crosscuts. First, make a pass over the angled blade to cut through the miter gauge's auxiliary wood fence. Then, simply align the cutline on the workpiece with the kerf in the fence.

▲ **SAWING RABBET JOINTS, 1.** ***When using a standard saw blade to cut a rabbet, make the edge cut first. Clamp a featherboard in place to press the workpiece against the fence.***

▶ **SAWING RABBET JOINTS, 2.** ***Readjust the blade height and fence position for second cut. Pass the work between the blade and fence to prevent kickback of cutoff strip.***

▼ **SAWING RABBET JOINTS, 3.** ***A standard saw blade can cut large, deep grooves. Shift the rip fence slightly after each pass to get a groove of the desired width.***

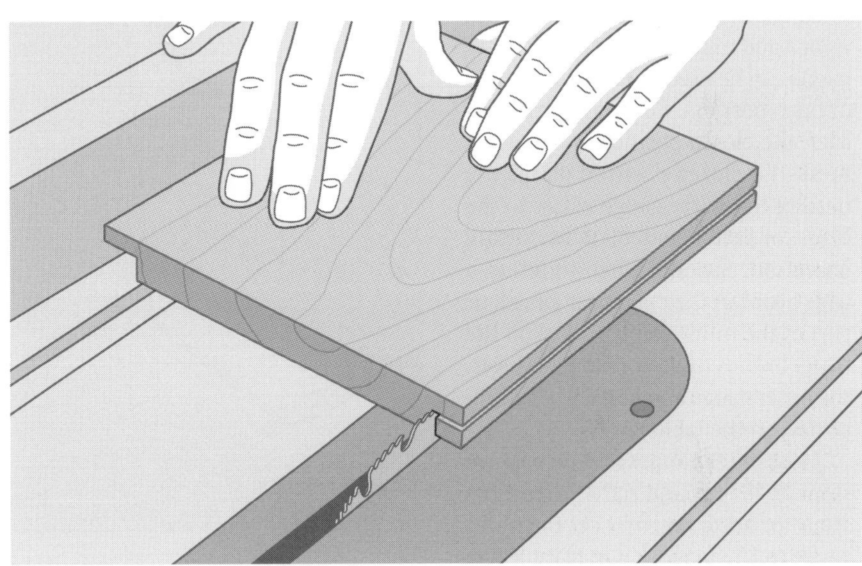

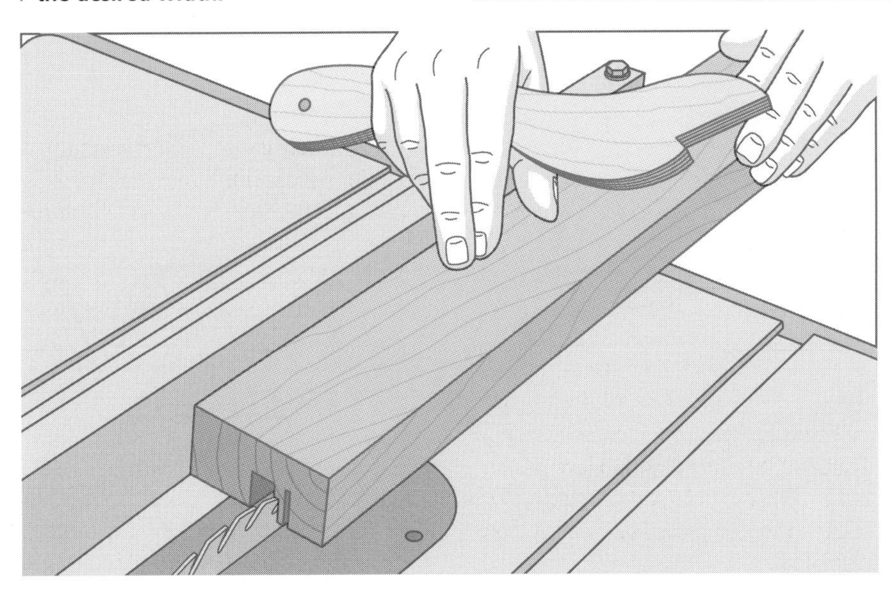

MITERING

A miter cut is simply an angled crosscut. And like bevel cuts, most miters are cut at a 45° angle, although any angled crosscut is a miter. As is the case with square crosscuts, the miter gauge is used for mitering, too.

◀ **CUTTING COVES, 1.** ***Mark desired cove depth on the end of the board and elevate the blade to this line. Then, adjust your shopmade parallel-rule jig so that the space between sides equals the desired cove width.***

▼ **CUTTING COVES, 2.** ***Tighten the screws to maintain the width, then position the jig so that its sides just touch the front and back saw tooth. Temporarily clamp an auxiliary fence to the table in line with the jig.***

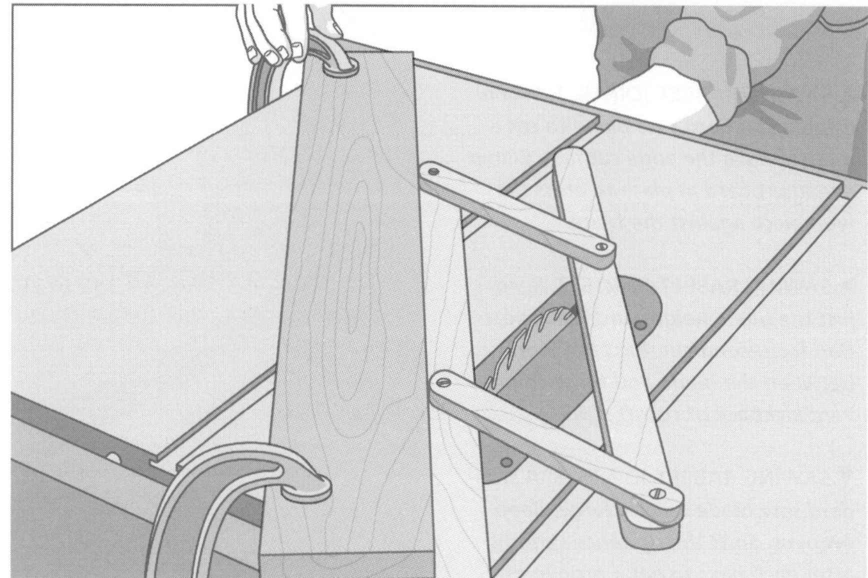

A typical miter gauge is designed to adjust up to 60° for both left- and right-hand miters. Note that the miter gauge can be used in either the closed or open position. For most jobs, however, the closed position is preferred. First, the closed position places the head of the miter gauge closer to the blade for better control of the cutting operation. Second, when mitering a wide board in the open position, all or part of the miter gauge will be off the table. In the closed position, however, the miter gauge and board will be supported on the table.

Most miter gauges feature positive stops at 45° left and right. To test the stops for accuracy, first set the miter gauge to 45° and lock it in place. Then, make a miter cut and check the angle of the cut with a miter square or combination square. If the cut isn't exactly 45°, readjust the positive stop on the miter gauge.

If you have a job that calls for a lot of mitering, such as when installing trimwork or making picture frames, a simple mitering platform jig can greatly simplify the task by providing you with a quick, accurate way of cutting

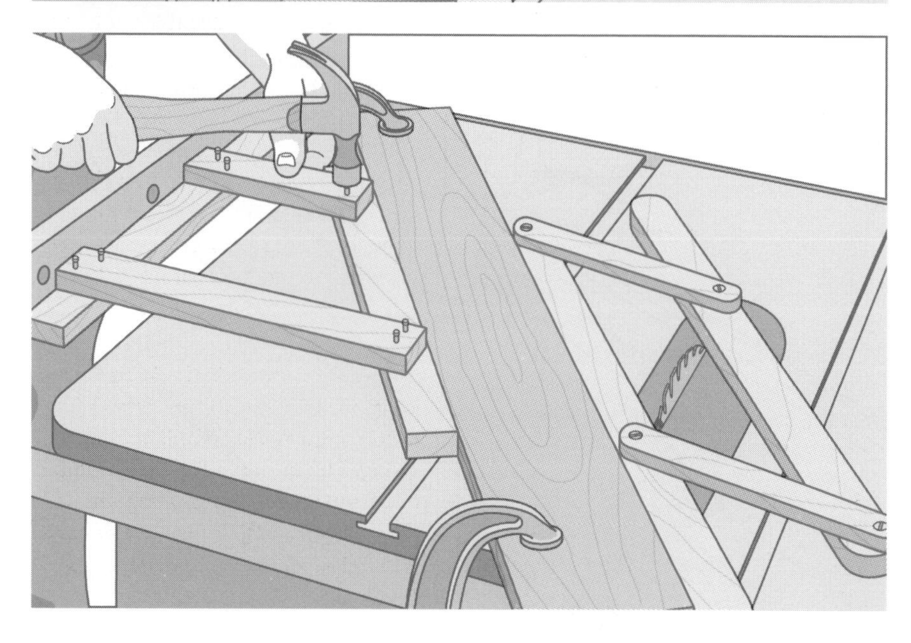

▶ **CUTTING COVES, 3.** ***Build an angle frame that fits precisely between the auxiliary and standard fence. Use the angle frame to reposition the auxiliary fence so that centerline of workpiece and blade align perfectly.***

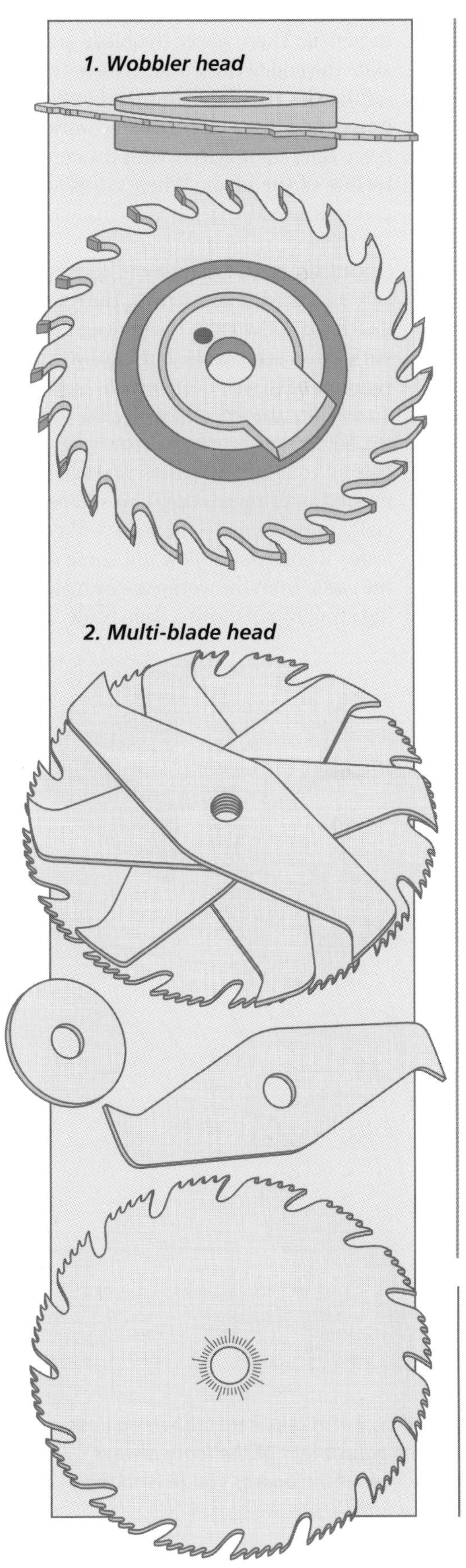

both left- and right-hand 45° miters. To make the jig, cut a 15-in.-wide x 22-in.-long platform out of ¾-in. plywood and attach two hardwood rails to its underside that ride in the miter-gauge slots. Support the work on two ¾ x 1½-in. hardwood blocks that are glued and screwed to the platform to form an exact 90° angle, their front edges set at a 45° angle to the blade. Hold the work against the appropriate block and slide the platform forward into the blade to make a cut. Apply wax to the rails as needed for smooth sliding in the miter-gauge slots.

COMPOUND ANGLE CUTS

A compound angle cut is a combination miter and bevel. The cut is made in a single pass with the blade tilted and miter gauge locked at the angles desired. Compound angle cuts are used to build boxes and pedestals with tapering sides as well as to form splayed legs for chairs and tables. Since two exact angles must be set for the cut to be dead-on accurate, make a couple of test cuts and then check the joint.

Crown and cove moldings also call for compound angle cuts because they are installed at an angle where a wall meets a ceiling. However, rather than tilting the blade, leave it set at 0° and use a shop-built jig mounted on the miter gauge to hold the molding at the proper angle. The jig consists of a ¼-in. plywood platform mitered at 45° on opposite sides that's screwed to a 1 x 3 wood fence. A ¼ x ¾-in. wood strip nailed to the leading edge of the platform so the molding is propped at the required angle serves as a stop block.

◀ **USING DADO BLADES, 1.** ***Two kinds of dado heads are common: (1) the adjustable "wobbler" blade—a single blade mounted on a wedged hub; and (2) the multi-blade set—two outside cutting blades and several inside chipper blades separated by washers.***

SAWING RABBET JOINTS

The popular rabbet joint is a strong, easy-to-make joint that joins boards at a right angle. A rabbet is simply an L-shaped cutout made in the edge or end of a board.

Usually, the depth of a rabbet equals half the thickness of the stock being rabbeted. The rabbet width must equal the total thickness of the stock being joined to the rabbet. For example, joining two ¾-in.-thick boards would take a ⅜-in.-deep x ¾-in.-wide rabbet.

There are two ways to cut rabbets on a table saw: using a standard blade, or using a dado blade. Both methods work well, but the dado-blade technique is preferred because the rabbet can be formed in a single pass. When using a standard saw blade, two passes are required to cut a rabbet.

A miter gauge is used to cut rabbets on the ends of short boards, but when working with long boards or plywood panels, utilize the rip fence. Note that when using a dado blade, an auxiliary wood fence is attached to the rip fence, concealing part of the blade.

Adjust the blade elevation and fence position for the desired size rabbet. Make a test cut in a scrap board, check the rabbet dimensions and make any further adjustments. When advancing the work over the blade, maintain pressure against the fence and down on the table. Although the blade is concealed during the cut, for safety's sake don't press down directly over it.

CUTTING COVES

Cutting coves is relatively simple to do on the table saw, allowing you to design and create a wide variety of different moldings that are not commercially available. The operation is performed by clamping an auxiliary fence to the table at an angle to the axis of the blade. As the workpiece is pushed along the fence, it contacts the blade at an oblique angle, which results in a broad, expanded kerf. This kerf can take many different shapes, all of which are elliptical, not true arcs.

The depth of the cove is controlled by the height of the blade above the table. The cove's width is controlled by the angle of the fence. A simple jig, called an adjustable parallel rule, is used to establish the angle of the fence that will produce the cove you desire. Make the jig out of 1 x 2 pine stock: two pieces 9 in. long for the ends; two pieces 22 in. long for the sides. Join the four pieces using 1-in. No. 12 panhead screws that act as pivots.

The following example explains how the jig works. Assume you want to cut a cove 1⅛ in. deep and 3¾ in. wide. First, raise the blade to a 1⅛-in. height. Next, adjust the jig so that the inside edges are 3¾ in. apart. Hold the jig in this position and then lower it over the blade so that both sides just touch a tooth. Leave the jig on the table in this position and carefully clamp the auxiliary fence to the table in line with it.

This establishes the proper angle of the fence but not the proper distance between the fence and the blade. In order to do this, you need to construct a small angle frame out of scrap stock that fits precisely between the auxiliary fence and the regular fence. Now, you're free to unclamp the auxiliary fence and shift it along the angle frame until the workpiece properly intersects the blade.

To find this point of intersection, you must first establish the centerline of the cove you want on the end of the workpiece. Draw the centerline clearly on the end grain of the workpiece in pencil. Then, lower the blade and slide the end of the workpiece over it. Adjust the auxiliary fence and angle frame until the centerline of the workpiece lines up precisely with the centerline of the blade. When satisfied, clamp the auxiliary fence securely to the table.

Cut the cove gradually in successive passes until you achieve the final depth. In softwood a ⅛-in.-deep cut per pass is acceptable, but hardwood requires passes no deeper than ¹⁄₁₆ in. To produce the smoothest possible finish, adjust the blade for extremely light cuts on your last two passes. And when making an extremely deep cove—especially in hardwood—the work will go faster if you first hollow out some of the waste from the workpiece by making straight cuts with a dado blade.

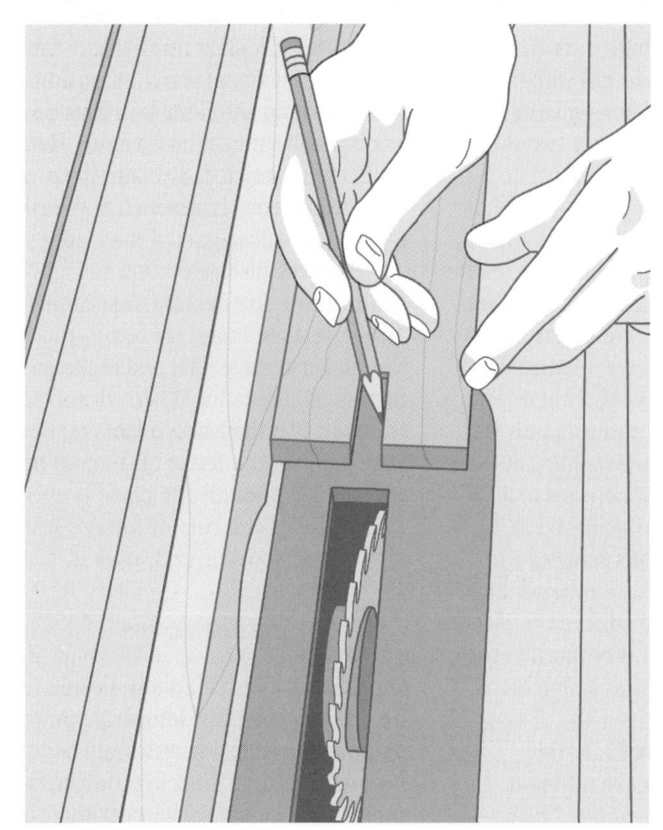

▲ **USING DADO BLADES, 2.** ***To determine exact distance from blade to fence, make test cut in scrap. Move board back and mark cut edges on table. Adjust fence for rabbet by measuring from marked lines.***

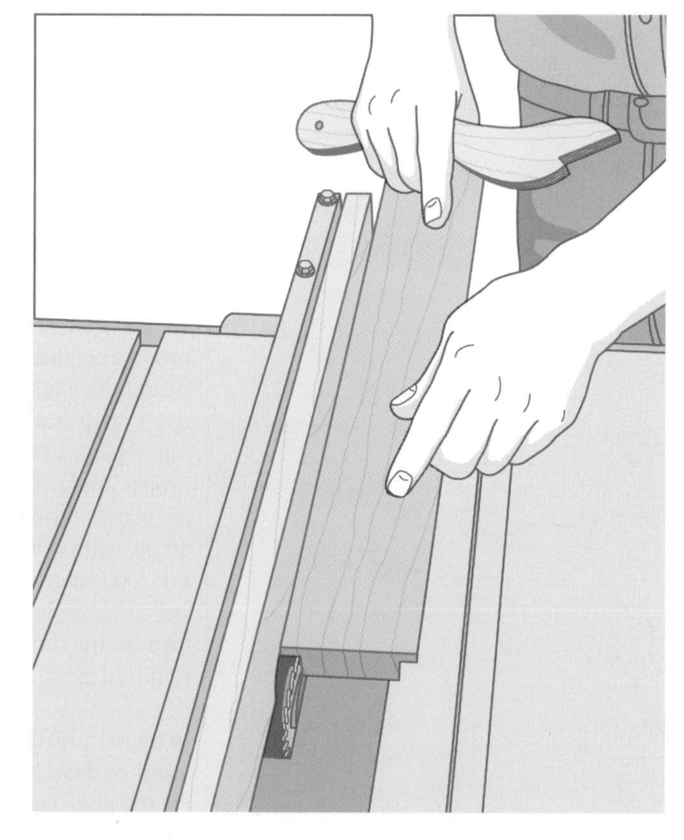

▲ **USING DADO BLADES, 3.** ***Cut duplicate rabbets against the fence because one adjustment of the fence always yields the same cut—even if the boards you're working with vary slightly in width.***

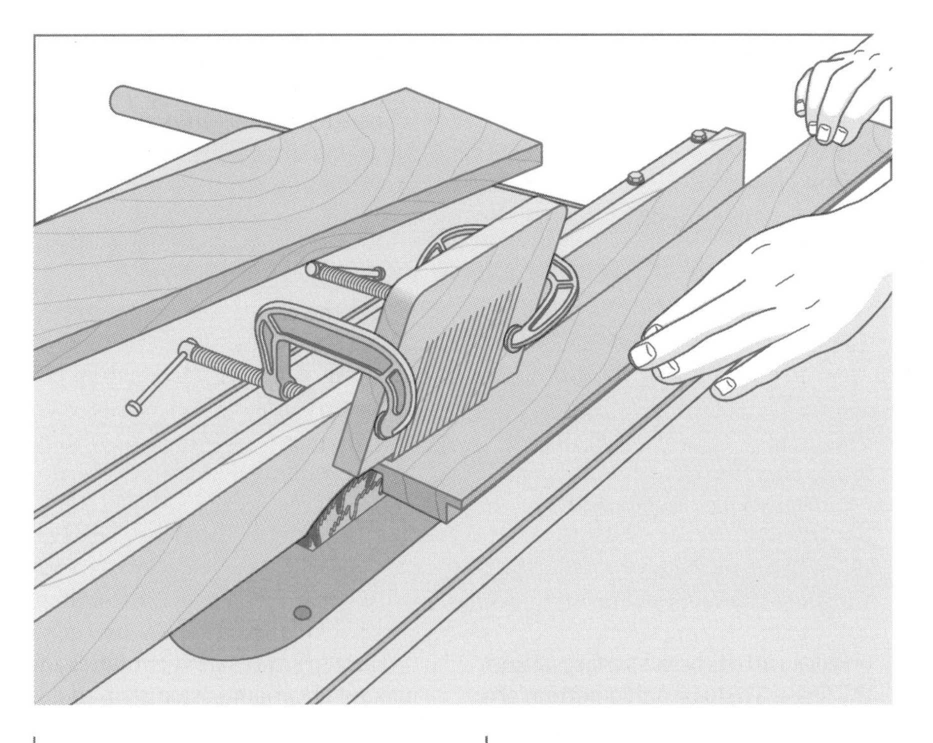

▲ **USING DADO BLADES, 4.** ***Use a featherboard hold-down when rabbeting bowed stock. This keeps the board flat against the table for consistent depth of cut.***

▼ **USING DADO BLADES, 5.** ***When a cut is made away from the fence, use an adjustable hold-down jig with the steel finger over area being cut so that the board stays flat.***

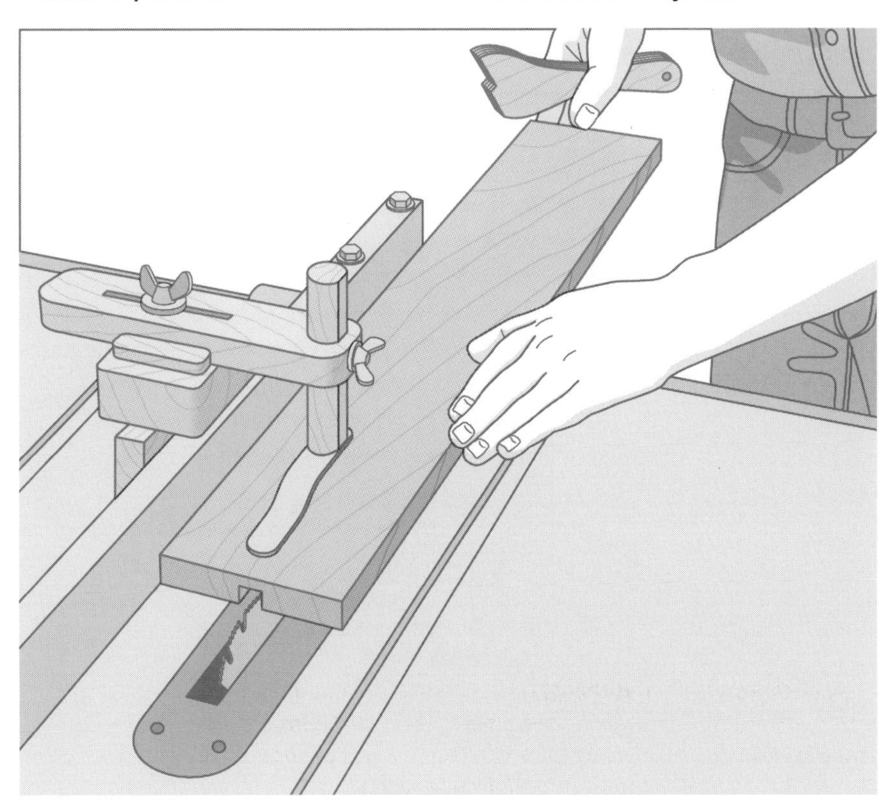

USING DADO BLADES

Common joints like rabbets, dadoes and grooves can be done with a regular blade by making repeated cuts. But to increase working speed, accuracy and efficiency, a dado blade is indispensable because it can be adjusted to different widths of cuts—typically from 3/16 to 13/16 in. Two different kinds of dado heads are commonly available: the adjustable "wobbler" blade and the more conventional multiple-blade set.

The wobbler dado head consists of a single blade mounted on a wedged hub. By turning the hub dial, you can tilt the blade slightly away from the hub's true vertical plane. Then, when mounted on the saw's arbor, the blade will rotate with a side-to-side motion, or wobble, and produce a wider cut.

The multiple-blade dado head consists of two outside cutting blades and several inside chipper blades separated by washers. The blades are installed one at a time on the saw's arbor, and the kerf width that results depends on the blade combination used. Paper or cardboard washers also can be inserted to make finer adjustments.

Each type of dado head has its own advantages. The wobbler can be adjusted on the saw's arbor for quick changes in the width of cut without removing the blade. The multiple-blade set, on the other hand, permits blades to be spaced apart for the cutting of tenons or tongues in one pass.

When you're cutting against the saw's fence using a dado blade, work with an auxiliary wood fence. Attach the auxiliary fence to the saw's fence, then slide it over the rotating blade to cut a recess in it. To establish the exact distance from the blade to the fence, make a test cut in a scrap board, then move the board back and mark the kerf on the table's insert in pencil. If the table's insert won't take marks, apply a piece of masking tape and mark it. Measure from the marked kerf lines to adjust the fence for the cut.

▶ **USING DADO BLADES, 6.** ***To cut blind rabbets, clamp stop blocks to fence. Then, butt work against the rear block, lower it into the blade and push it toward the front block.***

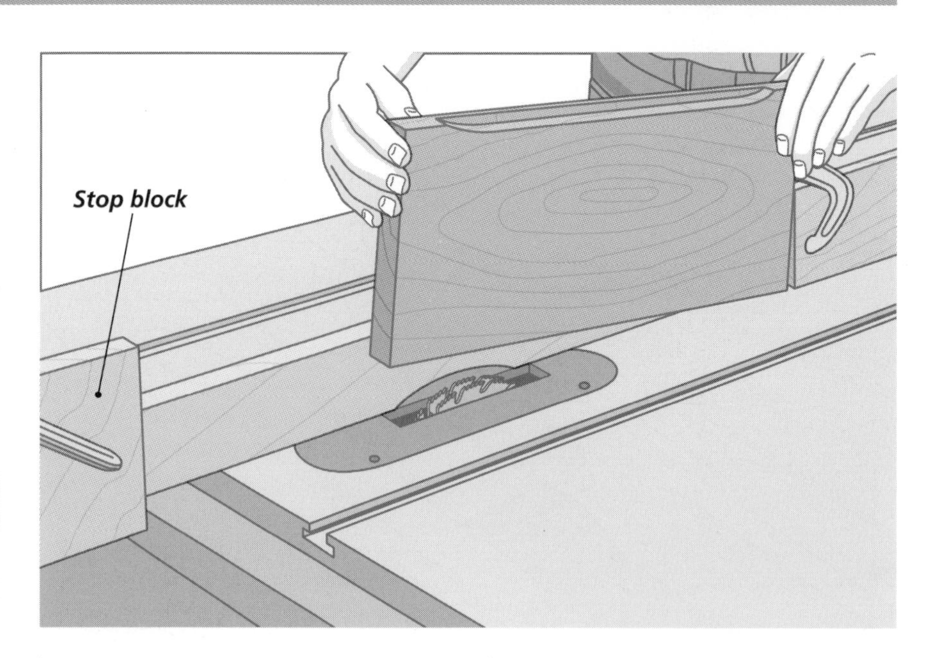

Since dado blades remove so much stock in one pass, the possibility of kickback is great. Be sure to always hold the stock firmly, feed it slowly and make deep cuts in several passes—particularly in hardwood.

USING MOLDING CUTTERHEADS

A few of the many time-saving jobs that you can perform with a molding cutterhead include milling custom and standard moldings, shaping decorative edges, cutting ornate frames and surface-planing stock. A cutterhead holds three identical blades, or knives—of which more than 30 different-shaped sets are available. Since many cuts use only a portion of the knives' profiles, a single set of knives can produce several different shapes. Additionally, sets of knives can be used in combination, sequentially one after another. Some sets of knives, though, must be used full profile in order to achieve the correct results.

To use a cutterhead on the table saw, the blade guard and table's insert must be removed. Replace the table's insert with a shopmade plywood insert that has a wider, but shorter opening. Then, attach an auxiliary wood fence to each side of the saw's fence, making sure that you cut a notch in the bottom edge of them to allow for clearance of the knives. The two auxiliary fences permit you to work on either side of the cutterhead.

There are two ways to feed work into a cutterhead: flat on the table, or on edge with its broad surface against the fence. To shape only a portion of a board's edge, feed the work flat on the table with the edge to be cut guided against the fence. This is known as an inboard cut. When shaping the entire edge of a board, pass the work between the fence and the cutterhead, guiding the uncut edge against the fence. This is called an outboard cut.

Here are two safe techniques for making small-dimension strip molding. For the first method, simply cut the desired shape onto a board that is at least 3 in. wide, then rip the strip molding from the board. The second method requires the use of a simple strip-molding jig comprised of a 2 x 4 that's rabbeted to accept the molding stock and a ¼-in. plywood base with a

▶ **USING DADO BLADES, 7.** ***Cut spline grooves in mitered ends using an improvised U-shaped tenoning jig. Center board in jig must be the same thickness as the fence.***

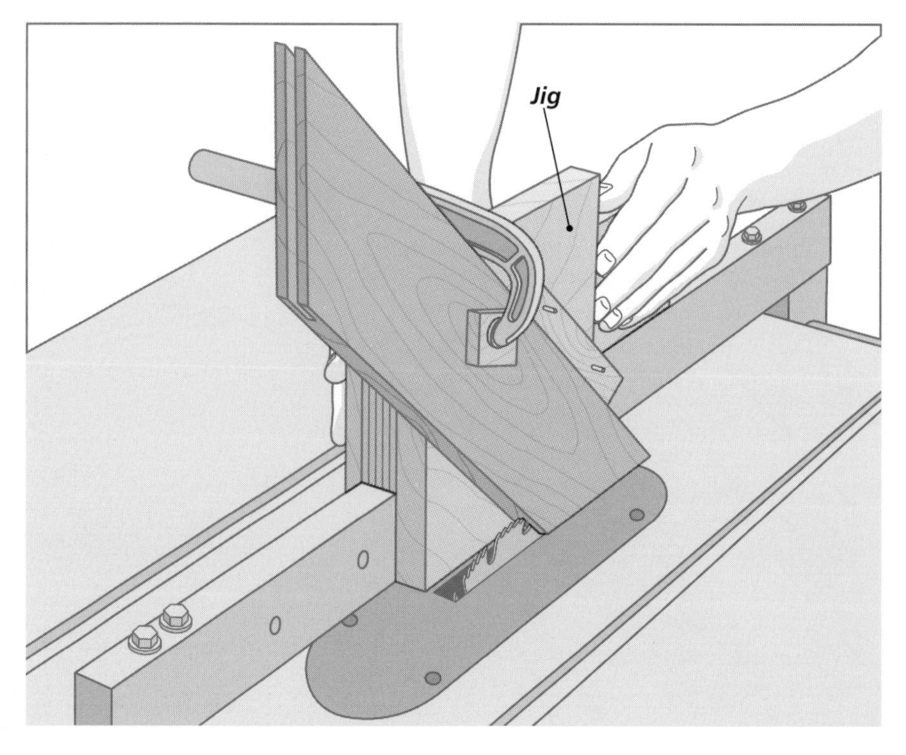

window cut out of it to allow for clearance of the cutterhead. Simply feed the molding stock into the jig and pull it through from the outfeed side. Note that the cutterhead is completely concealed by the jig.

Use the miter gauge to cross-grain shape the end of a board just as you would for crosscutting. As the knives exit the workpiece, though, splintering will surely occur. To prevent this, insert a 1/4-in.-thick wood backup strip behind the workpiece. As the cut is made, the backup strip will splinter but the workpiece will be cut cleanly.

Most cutting is made with the cutterhead set in the vertical position. However, the cutterhead can be tilted to any angle desired to produce a wide variety of shapes and profiles. But since a tilted cutterhead cuts a wider path than a vertical one, you'll need to make a new insert for the table.

Regardless of the method you use, be sure to always make your cuts in stages. Increase the depth of cut slightly with each pass until the shape that you desire is formed. This is especially important when working with hardwoods that splinter easily. Feed work slowly over the cutterhead in order to reduce the chance of splintering, chattering and kickback.

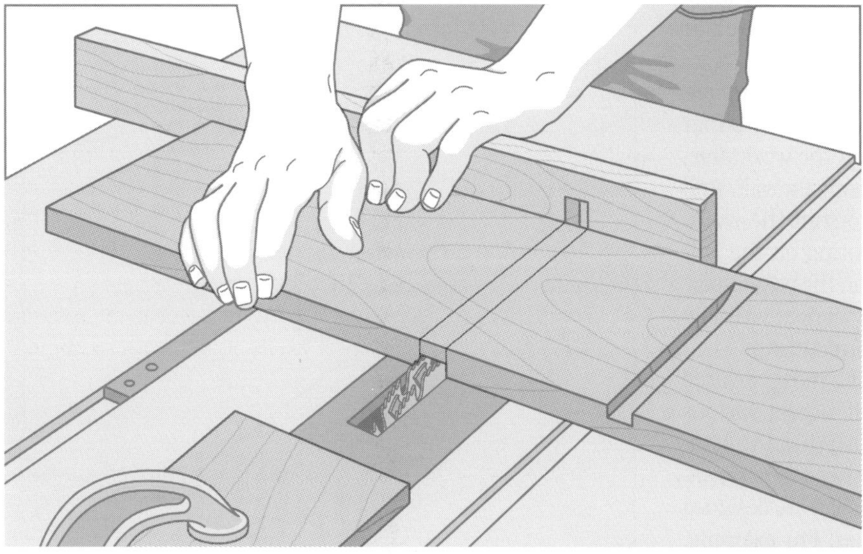

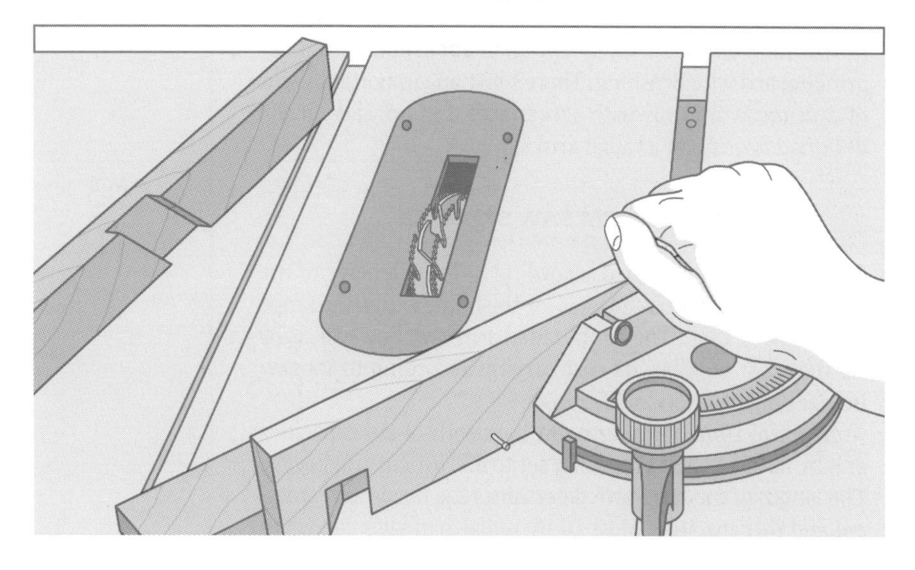

▲ **USING DADO BLADES, 8.** ***For precise cuts, make a notch in the miter-gauge fence and transfer cutlines to top of board. Align marks with notch and push board into blade.***

◀ **USING DADO BLADES, 9.** ***To make repeated stopped dadoes of consistent length, clamp a stop block to the table in front of the blade, then push stock to the block.***

▼ **USING DADO BLADES, 10.** ***When cutting angled dadoes, work tends to creep "downhill" from the blade. To prevent this, tack-nail stock to miter-gauge fence.***

RADIAL ARM SAWS

After years of promising yourself a fully-equipped woodworking shop, you've finally gotten the time and set aside the space that's required. Now, the burning question is: What stationary power tool should you purchase first? For most woodworkers, the answer comes down to a choice between a table saw or a radial arm saw. And while both tools are undeniably valuable, if a choice must be made, there are many who would put forward several reasons for recommending the radial arm saw.

First, for making crosscuts, perhaps the most common woodworking cut, the radial arm saw is the ideal tool. This is especially true when crosscutting a long board. Just imagine trying to crosscut a 2 x 12 that's 16 ft. long on a table saw. Yet, on a radial arm saw, this operation would be a simple task. And because the blade of the saw is positioned above the work, aligning the line of cut accurately with the blade is easy because it's clearly in view.

Another benefit of the radial arm saw is that it takes up relatively little space in the workshop. Since the work either remains stationary or passes laterally across the worktable, the tool can be positioned permanently against a wall. And most cuts can be made without having to shift the work. Instead, the tool itself moves, its arm pivoting on the column and its motor swiveling and rotating on the yoke—permitting the blade to be pulled through the work at virtually any angle and simplifying setups for custom cutting.

As well, the radial arm saw is arguably the most versatile woodworking tool that you can buy. It will accept various saw blades, dado blades and a molding cutterhead to handle virtually any woodworking cut you may need to perform. And on most saws, both ends of the motor's shaft are designed to accept a wide range of useful accessories. For example, with the proper accessory, you can use a radial arm saw for horizontal boring, surface planing, drum sanding, buffing, grinding and wire brushing. There's just one important point of caution: Work only with accessories that are specifically designed for use on a radial arm saw.

RADIAL ARM SAW SPECIFICS

Radial arm saws are sized according to the diameter of the saw blade that they use. Models for the home workshop range from 8 in. to 12 in. The 10-in. radial arm saw, however, is by far the most popular, its cost varying according to its particular construction and features.

A typical 10-in. radial arm saw has depth-of-cut capacities of 3 in. at 90° and 2⅛ in. when set to 45° for cutting bevels. The length of the saw's arm determines the maximum crosscut and rip capacities. Most 10-in. radial arm saws can rip to

RADIAL ARM SAW ANATOMY
Looking much like a circular saw suspended above a worktable, the radial arm saw's many pivoting and sliding parts permit the tool to cut into a workpiece from a variety of different angles and directions. Shown here is a typical 10-in. model.

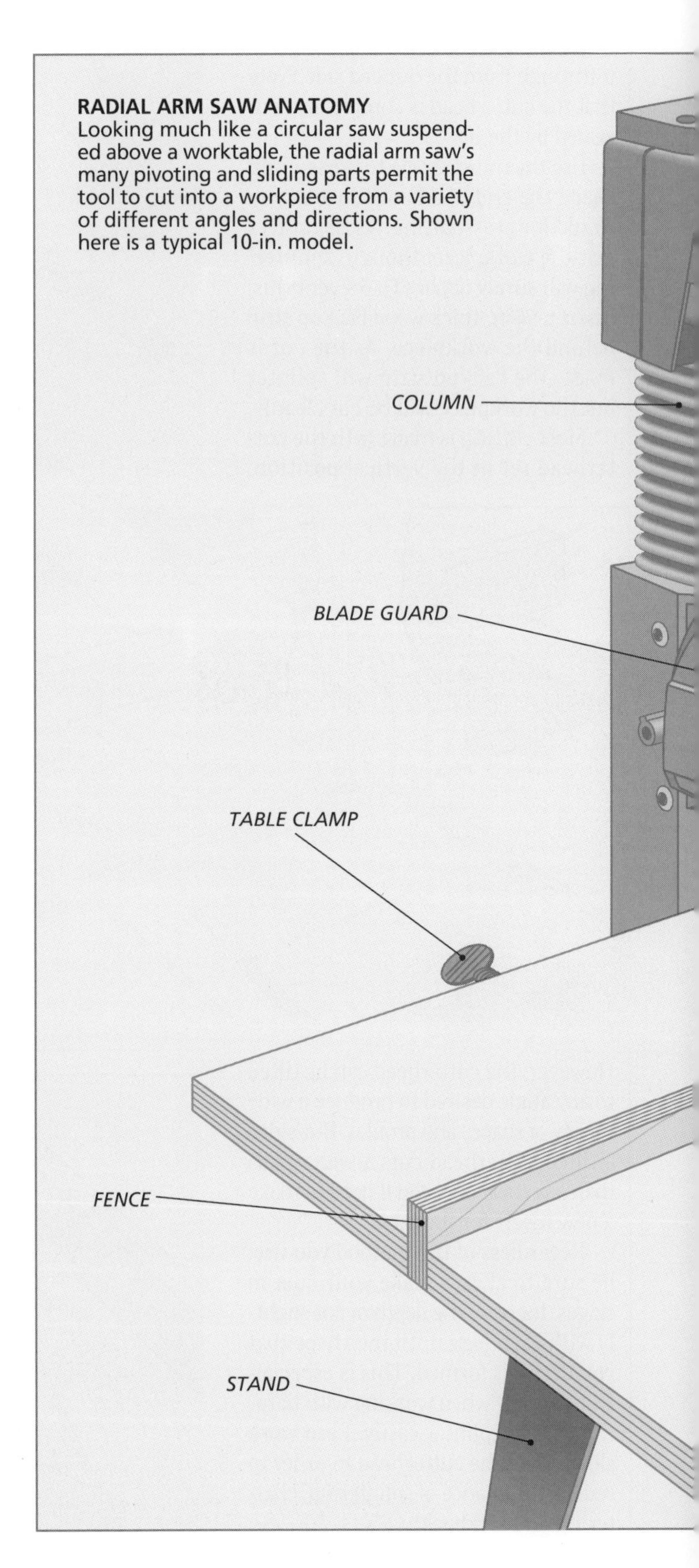

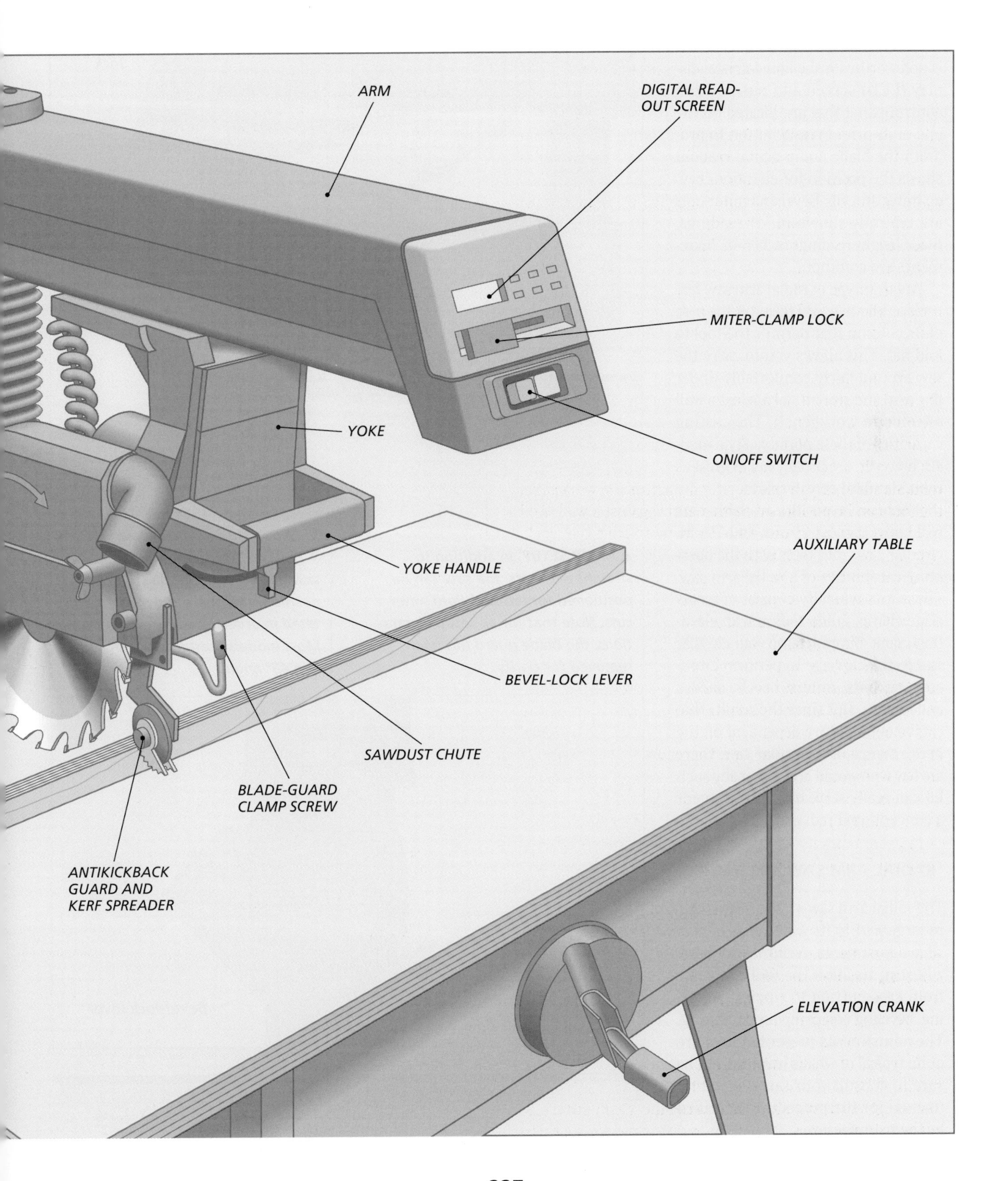
ARM
DIGITAL READ-OUT SCREEN
MITER-CLAMP LOCK
YOKE
ON/OFF SWITCH
AUXILIARY TABLE
YOKE HANDLE
BEVEL-LOCK LEVER
SAWDUST CHUTE
BLADE-GUARD CLAMP SCREW
ANTIKICKBACK GUARD AND KERF SPREADER
ELEVATION CRANK

at least 24 in., which allows you to cut to the center of a 48-in.-wide panel.

An electronic-type radial arm saw is noteworthy for the liquid-crystal display (LCD) screen and push-button control panel that are located on the end of its arm. Press a button to program the blade and a digital readout shows the position for elevation, bevel, miter and rip. Bevel and miter cuts are typically shown in ½° readings. Blade height readings of .005-in. increments are common.

Another type of radial arm saw features a unique swivel fitting at the base of its column that permits the tool to fold flat. This allows you to carry the saw around fairly comfortably under one arm and store it flat against a wall or under a workbench. The cutting capacities of these portable-style models, however, are usually not as great as their standard counterparts.

There are even kits available that will convert most 7¼-in. and 7½-in. circular saws into tools with the operating capabilities of a radial arm saw. These kits typically consist of a carriage clamp, guide rods and an elevation crank. Simply clamp your circular saw to the carriage to perform crosscuts, rip cuts, miters, bevels, dadoes and rabbets. But since the results that can be obtained are dependent on the performance of a circular saw, there are few who would argue that any such kit can really serve as a substitute for a conventional radial arm saw.

RADIAL ARM SAW MECHANICS

The radial arm saw's versatility is due in large part to its wide range of possible adjustments. A number of basic adjustments allow the tool to change from crosscutting to ripping, mitering, beveling and compound mitering. The adjustments presented here are quite typical of what's involved, but be sure to consult your saw's operating manual for the procedures specified by the manufacturer.

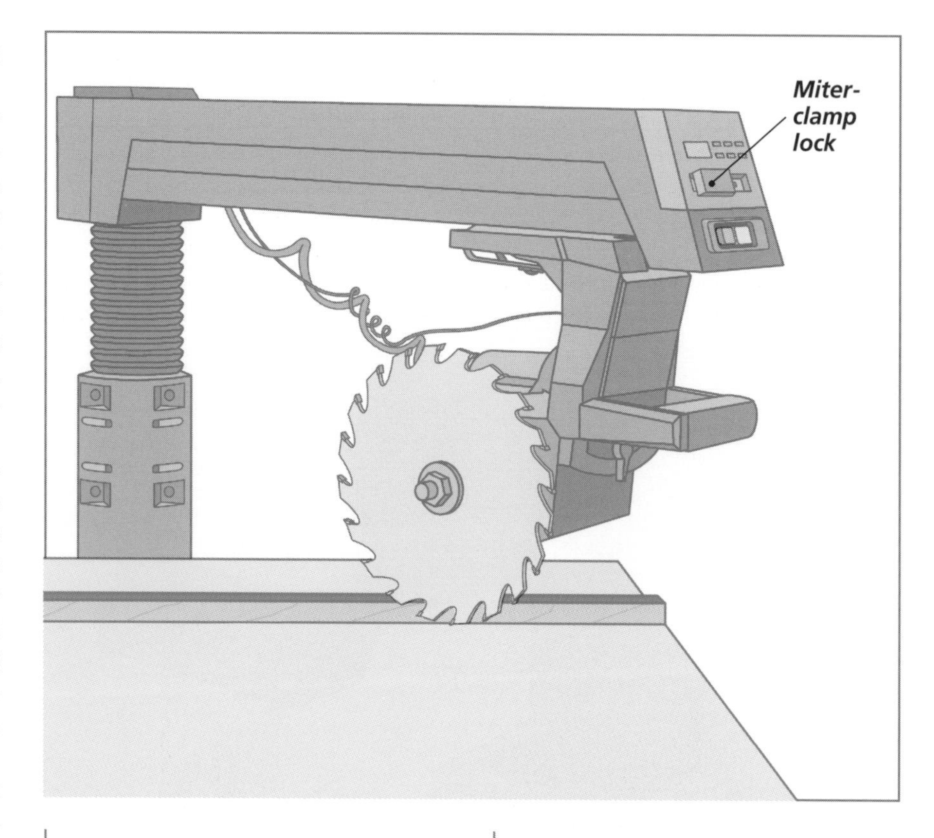

▲ **MITER SETUP.** ***In addition to straight crosscuts, the saw can be positioned for left and right miter cuts. Note that for all setup illustrations, the blade guard has been removed for clarity.***

▼ **BEVEL SETUP.** ***When the arm of the saw has been set in the crosscutting position, the blade and motor can be tilted in order to perform bevel cuts. Most models feature a positive lock at a 45° angle.***

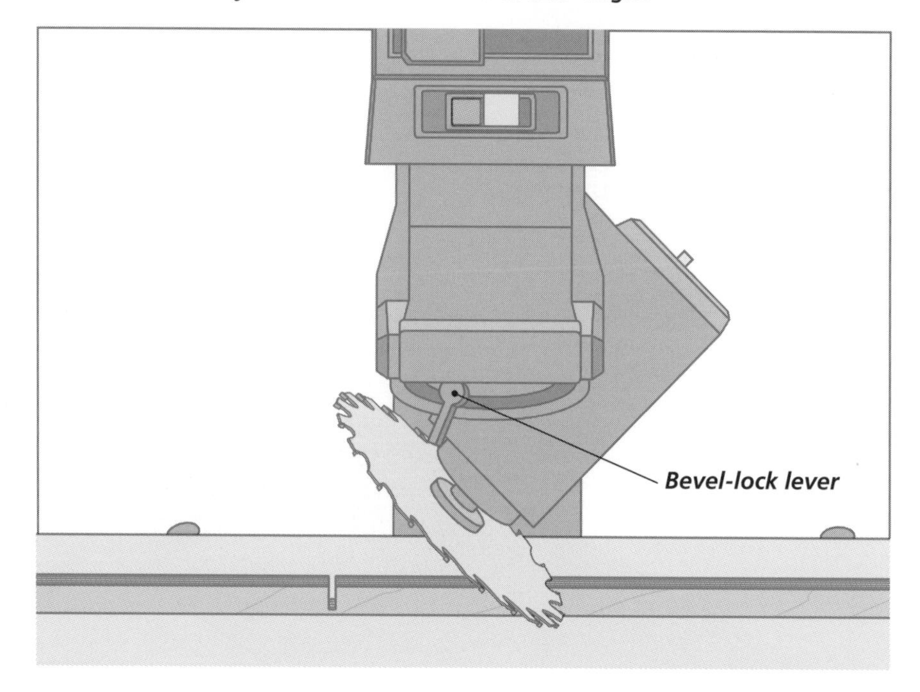

A radial arm saw consists of a yoke-mounted motor attached to a carriage. The carriage is mounted to an arm that is fastened to a column. The carriage rides back and forth on the arm, and it can be locked anywhere on the arm for operations such as ripping. An elevating crank is used to raise and lower the column to control depth of cut.

The arm pivots on the column to both the right and left for miter cuts. Be sure to raise the blade slightly above the worktable before swinging the arm to the desired angle. The motor rotates on the yoke 360° on the vertical axis, and it pivots 90° left and right on the horizontal axis. After you've made an adjustment to the saw, it's very important to lock the adjusted components in place before performing the cut.

Another important part of the radial arm saw is its worktable, which is usually made of ¾-in. or 1-in. particleboard or plywood. Often, the saw's worktable is a three-board surface that consists of a large front table and two rear boards—one narrow (about 2 in. wide) and the other somewhat wider (about 6 in. wide). The front table is fastened to the saw's base. The rear boards are usually positioned behind the fence and held securely in place by tightening the saw's table clamps.

Make the saw's fence out of hardwood or hardwood-veneer plywood. Having a three-board worktable for the saw is useful because it provides you with three different locations for positioning the fence. The fence can be placed between the front table and the first rear board, between the two rear boards or, for maximum cutting capacity, behind both rear boards. The farther back toward the column of the

▲ **RIP SETUP, 1.** ***Most rip cuts are made with the saw blade positioned between the fence and the motor, as shown here. This setup is commonly known as the in-rip position.***

▼ **RIP SETUP, 2.** ***For wider rip cuts, set up in the so-called out-rip position. Note that the blade's rotation and therefore the feed direction change between in-rip and out-rip modes.***

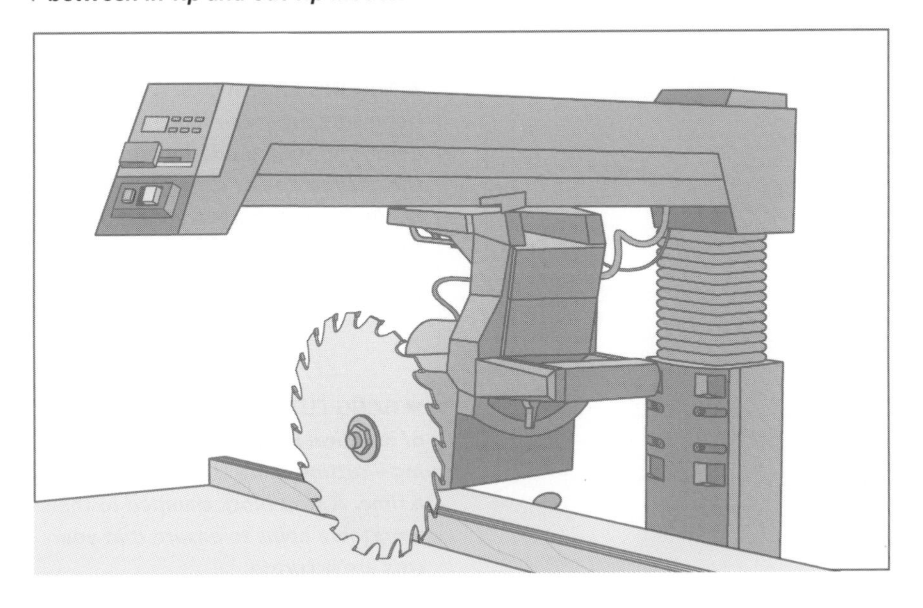

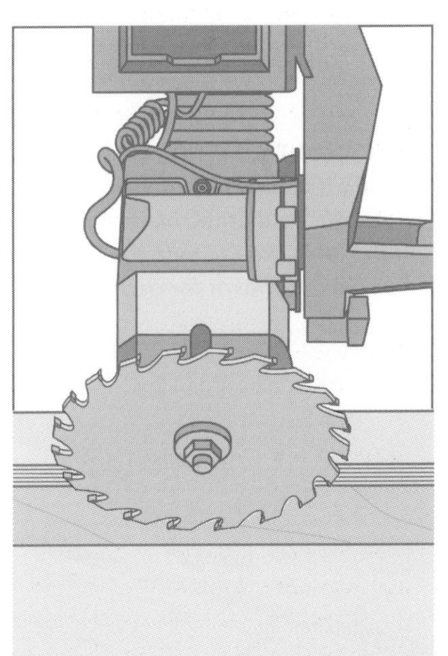

▲ **RIP SETUP, 3.** ***A radial arm saw can also handle beveled rip cuts. Position the saw in the rip mode, then pivot the motor and blade to the desired bevel angle.***

saw that you position the fence, the greater is the cutting capacity.

BLADE BASICS

Most radial arm saws come equipped with a combination saw blade that can be used for ripping, crosscutting and mitering. For best results, however, you should always use a blade that's designed specifically for the type of cut you're making. Use a rip blade for ripping and a crosscut blade for crosscutting and mitering.

High-speed steel blades are relatively inexpensive and readily available, but better cutting performance can be achieved using carbide-tipped blades. Also, some blade manufacturers offer blades designed specifically for use on a radial arm saw. These carbide-tipped blades reduce overfeeding—the tendency of the blade to feed faster than it can cut.

A significant consideration in the blade to use on a radial arm saw is the hook angle—the angle that's formed by the intersection of one line drawn from the tip of a tooth to the center of the arbor hole and one line drawn parallel to the tooth's face. The larger the hook angle of a blade, the bigger is the blade's bite. And the bigger a blade's bite, the greater is the risk of the blade running across the work when crosscutting or lifting the work when ripping. For both types of cutting, feeding the work through the blade slowly and firmly is very important. While a blade with a hook angle of 30° would be suitable for use on a table saw, the same blade used on a radial arm saw would be a potential hazard. For work on a radial arm saw, use a blade that has a hook angle of no more than 15°.

▲ **HORIZONTAL SETUP.** ***Horizontal cutting is possible by rotating the motor 90° so that the blade is parallel to the table. Again, note the blade guard is not shown for clarity.***

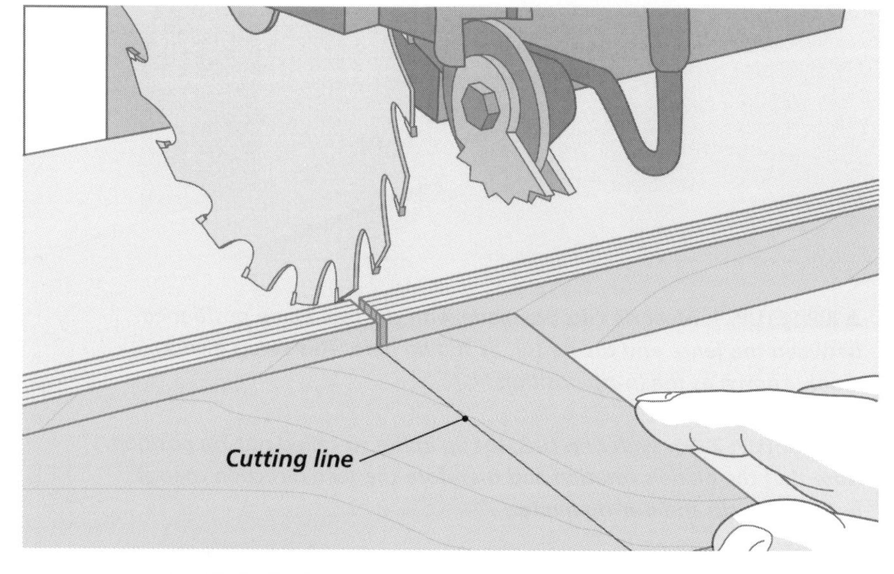

▲ **MAKING CROSSCUTS.** ***A single, clean kerf cut in the fence acts as a quick-and-easy guide for aligning the desired line of cut with the saw blade. Be sure to keep your hands clear of the blade's path.***

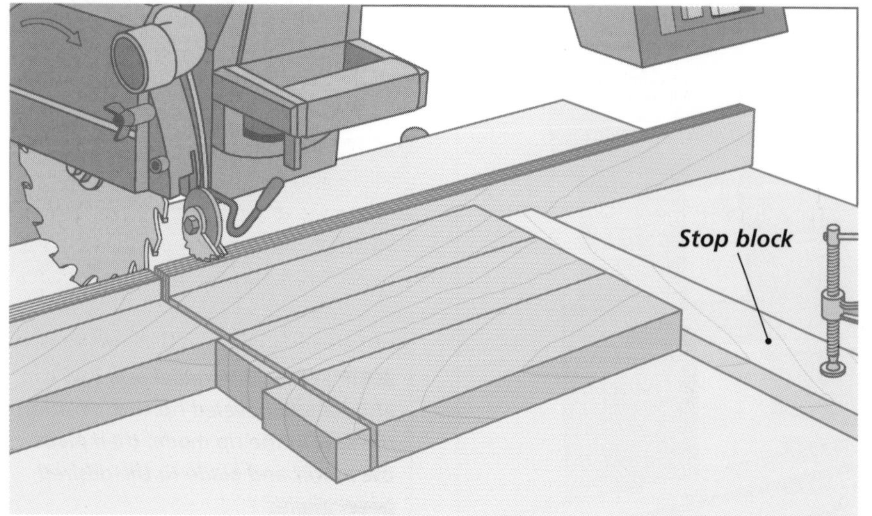

◀ **GANG CUTTING.** ***To obtain pieces of identical length, try gang sawing—cutting more than one piece at a time. A stop block clamped to the worktable helps to ensure that your cuts are accurate.***

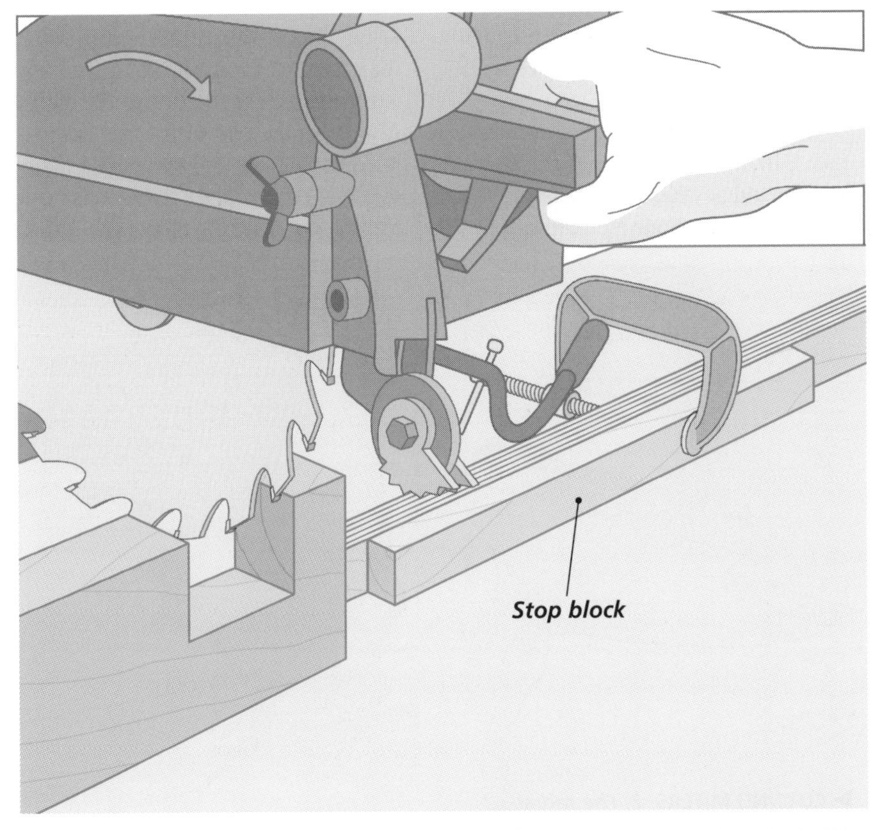

◀ **CUTTING NOTCHES.** ***To cut notches in a piece, raise the saw blade using the elevation crank. A stop block that is clamped securely to the fence serves to establish the left shoulder of the notch.***

SAWING SAFETY

A radial arm saw is a relatively easy-to-use tool. However, it's also a potentially dangerous piece of equipment. General safety precautions that apply to other stationary tools apply equally as well to the radial arm saw. Always wear safety goggles. Keep the work area around the machine clear of clutter and debris. Never interfere with the functioning of the tool's guards. Make sure that you disconnect the saw from the electrical outlet whenever changing blades or making adjustments.

There are also a number of specific precautions that will help you to ensure safe, accident-free performance of your radial arm saw. Familiarize yourself with your saw by reading your owner's manual thoroughly. If you do not have an owner's manual, request one from the saw's manufacturer.

Remember that the saw's blade is protected by a guard for good reason. Never operate the saw without having the blade guard in position. Note that in some of the illustrations presented here the blade guard is not shown in place. This was done *only* for visual clarity of the saw's action, and *not* as part of any operating procedure or cutting technique.

To help prevent kickback, use the saw's antikickback device. This device, which is attached to the front of the blade guard, consists of a steel rod with several steel fingers that are known as

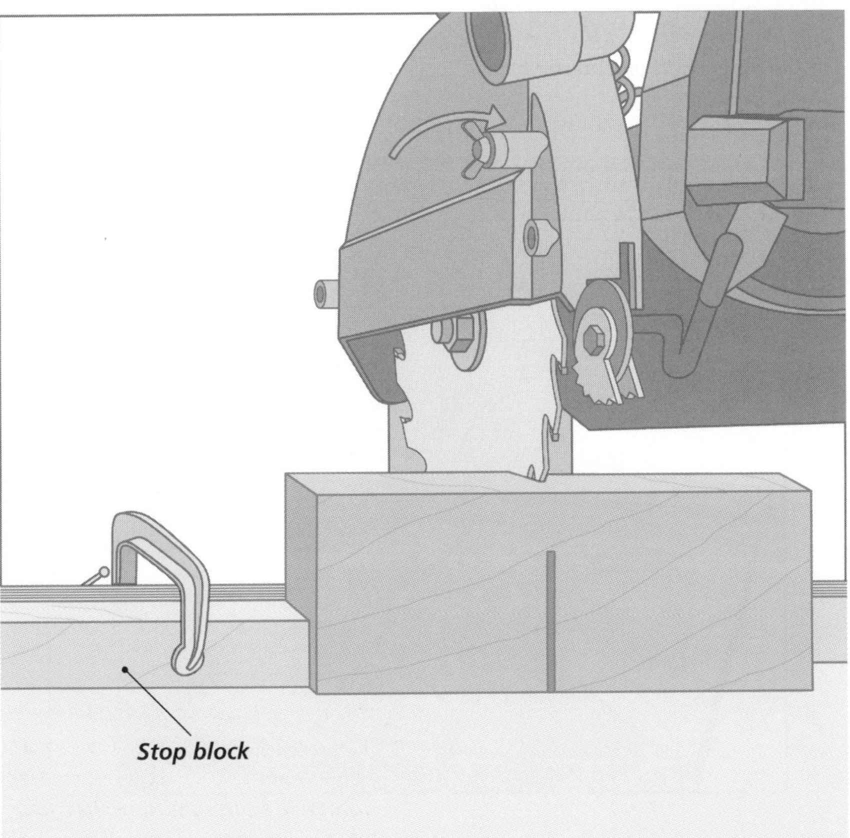

◀ **CUTTING THICK STOCK.** ***Make two passes to cut through stock that's thicker than the saw's depth-of-cut capacity. Here, a stop block is used to ensure that the two cuts will be aligned properly.***

pawls. When the blade guard is adjusted properly, the pawls drag across the top of the workpiece during the cut. If the blade happens to kick back the work, the pawls dig in and prevent the piece from moving. Some antikickback devices are also equipped with a narrow steel wheel, called a kerf spreader or splitter, that rides in the kerf and keeps it open.

When crosscutting, always maintain a firm, steady grip on the saw's handle and advance the blade slowly. Try to keep the blade from advancing faster than it can cut. When ripping, it's extremely important to feed the work against the rotation of the blade. Always make use of the saw's antikickback device and rotate the blade guard back so that its rear end is positioned just slightly above the work.

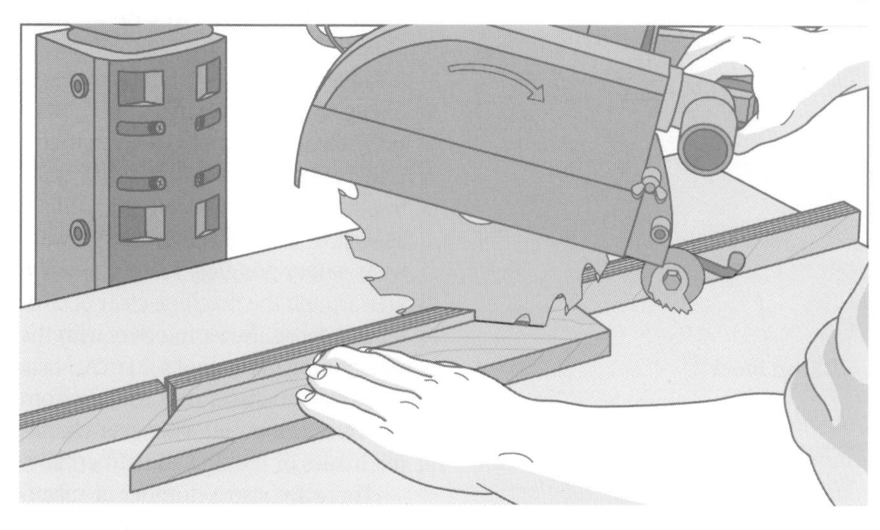

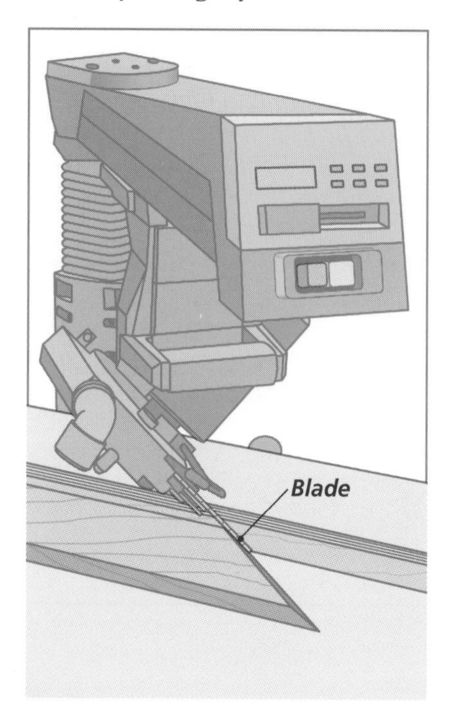

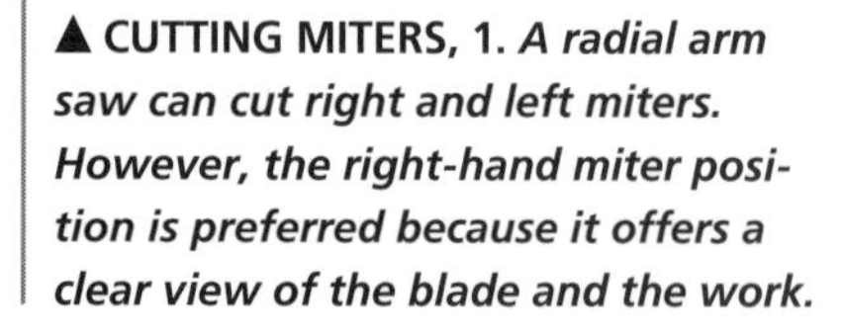

▲ **CUTTING MITERS, 1.** ***A radial arm saw can cut right and left miters. However, the right-hand miter position is preferred because it offers a clear view of the blade and the work.***

▶ **CUTTING MITERS, 2.** ***The radial arm saw excels in cutting accurate compound miters. Set the saw's arm in the miter position and the blade in the bevel mode.***

RADIAL ARM MITER GAUGE

Here's an attachment that enables you to cut precise 45°-angle left and right miters on a radial arm saw without moving the saw's arm. The radial arm miter gauge is made of sturdy aluminum with edges machined to a true 90° for producing square joints. It features a built-in C-clamp for mounting to the front edge of the saw's table. A wood cam is supplied for securing the workpiece against the edge of the guide to prevent creeping and kickback.

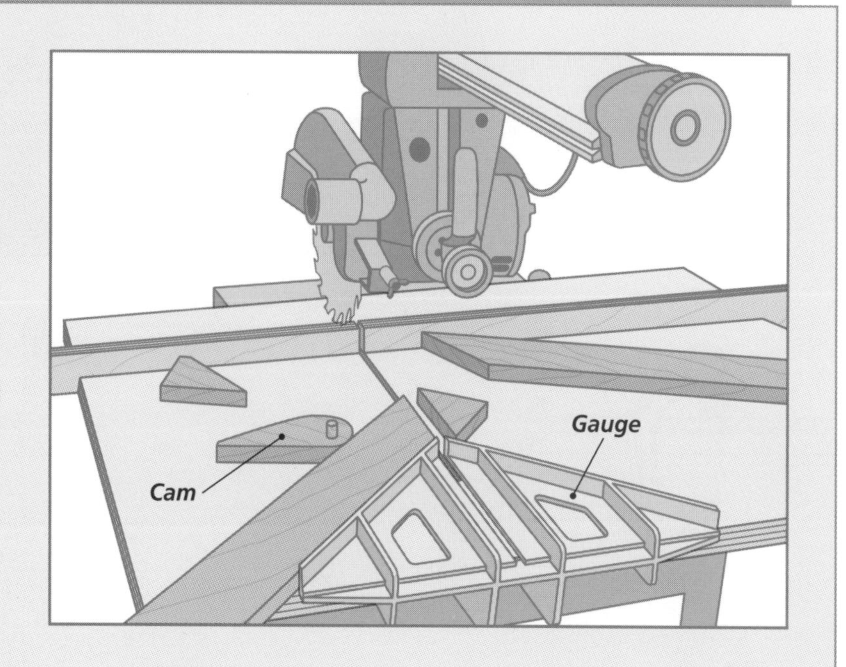

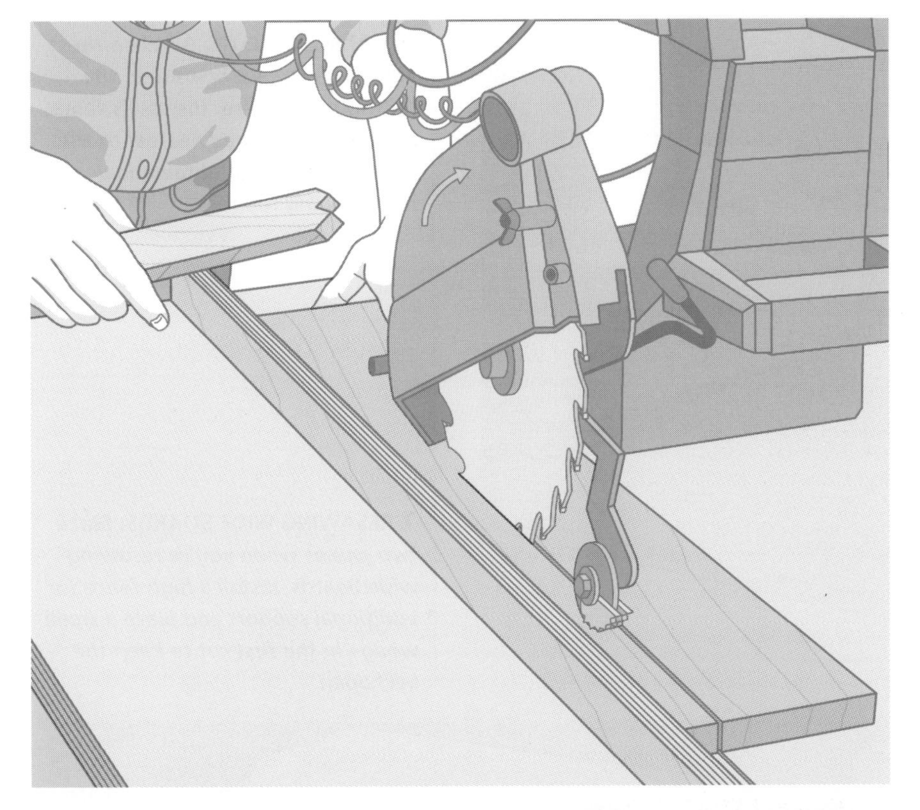

◀ **MAKING RIP CUTS, 1.** ***For narrow rip cuts, it's best to use the in-rip position. Feed the work against the blade's rotation. Note that the blade guard is tilted back to keep the work from lifting.***

This will help to keep the blade from lifting the work off the table.

SETUP FUNDAMENTALS

The versatility of the radial arm saw means that proper setup is important in order to achieve the results desired. A frequent problem is that adjustments to the saw are left too loose, causing excessive play in moving components and resulting in sloppy cuts. Without careful attention to setup, the saw will not cut with precision.

At the beginning of each project you undertake, check that the saw's table, clamps and sliding mechanisms are properly adjusted. Ideally, the table should be perfectly level relative to the arm, the clamps should lock tightly and the sliding mechanisms should operate smoothly without being either too loose or too tight.

To check the saw's table, tilt the motor until the arbor points downward with its end just above the table. Swivel the arm to position the arbor in turn over each rail nut on the sides of the table, measuring the distance between the arbor and the table at each point. If the measurements are not equal, raise the low point of the table by adjusting the rail nuts.

Test the miter clamp by positioning the arm between 0° and 45°, then lock the clamp and try to push the arm to the 0° position. To check the yoke clamp, set the yoke between positions

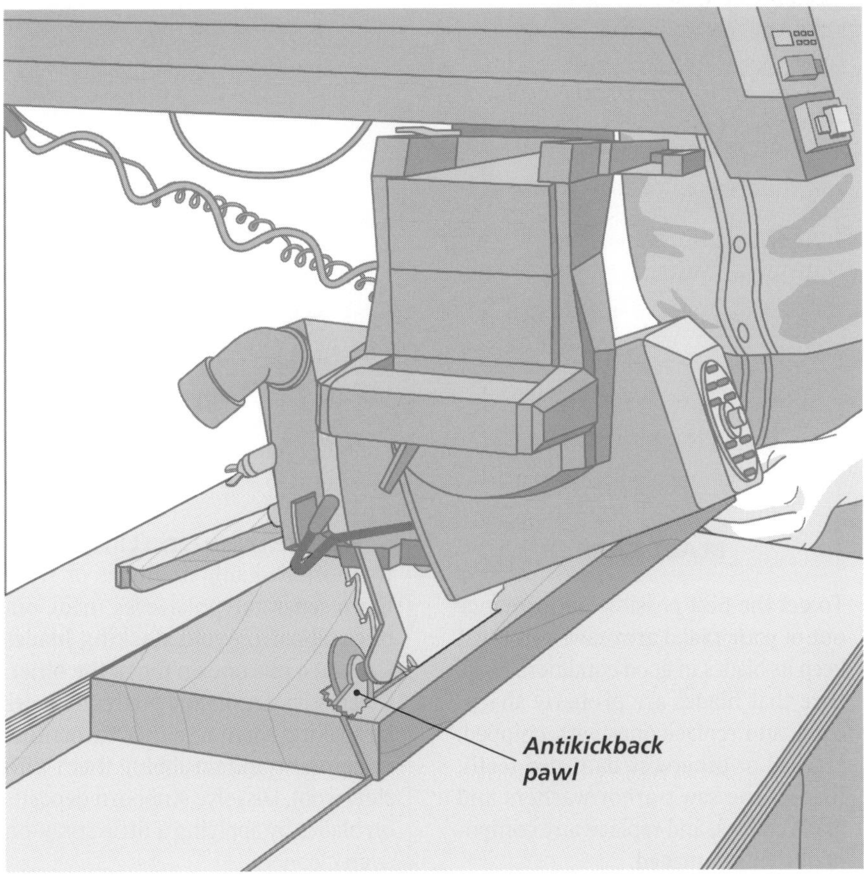

◀ **MAKING RIP CUTS, 2.** ***Here, the saw is shown cutting a rip bevel. Note the antikickback pawls resting on the stock in front of the blade. Again, always feed the work against the blade's rotation.***

◀ **MAKING RIP CUTS, 3.** ***When ripping wide panels, operate in the out-rip mode. Here, the saw's fence has been positioned nearest to the column in order to obtain maximum ripping capacity.***

▼ **RESAWING WIDE BOARDS.** ***Make two passes when you're resawing wide boards. Install a high fence for additional support and place a small wedge in the first cut to keep the kerf open.***

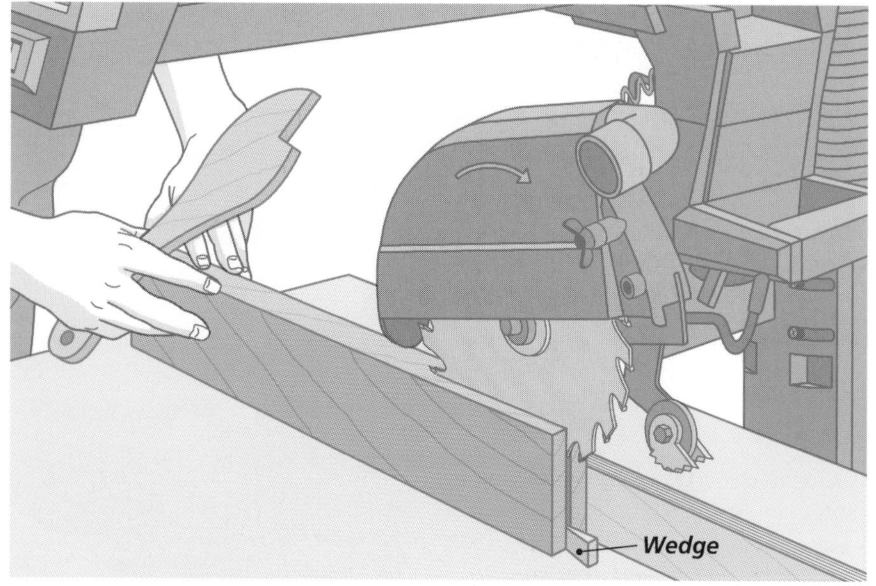

for crosscutting and ripping, then lock the clamp and try to push the motor to the crosscutting position. The bevel clamp can be tested by positioning the motor between 0° and 45°, then locking the clamp and trying to move the motor. Check the rip clamp by locking it and trying to slide the yoke along the arm. Make all adjustments necessary to correct looseness in the clamps.

Check that the saw's carriage slides smoothly along the arm and make any adjustments needed to the roller bearings. Also check that the saw's arm slides smoothly up and down without any side-to-side play or any excessive movement at the column-to-base joint. Consult your owner's manual for the adjustments to sliding mechanisms specified by the saw's manufacturer.

Make sure that the gap between the saw's table and fence is kept clear of particles and dust. Also clean off the track underneath the arm of the saw. Periodically apply a little silicone-based lubricant to the saw's moving components. And every so often you should square the saw's blade and check it for heeling—rotation that's not at the correct angle to the table.

BLADE CARE

To get the best possible performance out of your radial arm saw, you must keep its blades in good condition. Make sure that blades are properly sharpened, and replace ones with chipped, cracked or otherwise damaged teeth. Inspect the saw's arbor washers and blade collars, and replace any component that's damaged.

When saw blades aren't in use, hang them individually on hooks or store them separately in sleeves made out of cardboard. Avoid stacking blades loose in a pile one on top of the other. Clean sticky resin and pitch off blades by soaking them in either turpentine or kerosene and scrubbing them with steel wool. Dissolve stubborn deposits on blades by applying a little spray-on oven cleaner.

◀ **MORTISES AND TENONS, 1.** ***Turn the blade of the saw horizontally to cut mortises. Make a plywood support table to hold up the workpieces. The table should stand at least 3 in. high. Note that for clarity the blade guard is not shown here.***

CHANGING BLADES

Always disconnect the power cord of your radial arm saw before changing the blade. To remove a blade from the arbor, lock the saw's clamps and take off the blade guard. Loosen the arbor nut using the wrenches supplied with the saw. Place one wrench between the blade and the motor to hold the arbor steady, and use the other one to turn the nut. Note that the arbor is usually reverse threaded, so the nut is loosened by turning clockwise rather than counterclockwise. Remove the nut and the outer blade collar, then carefully slide the blade off the arbor.

Set a new blade into place on the arbor with its teeth facing in the direction of the blade's rotation. Install the blade collar and thread the nut onto the arbor by hand. Prop one wrench against the worktable to hold the arbor steady and use the other one to finish tightening the nut. Avoid overtightening the nut, and be sure to reinstall the blade guard.

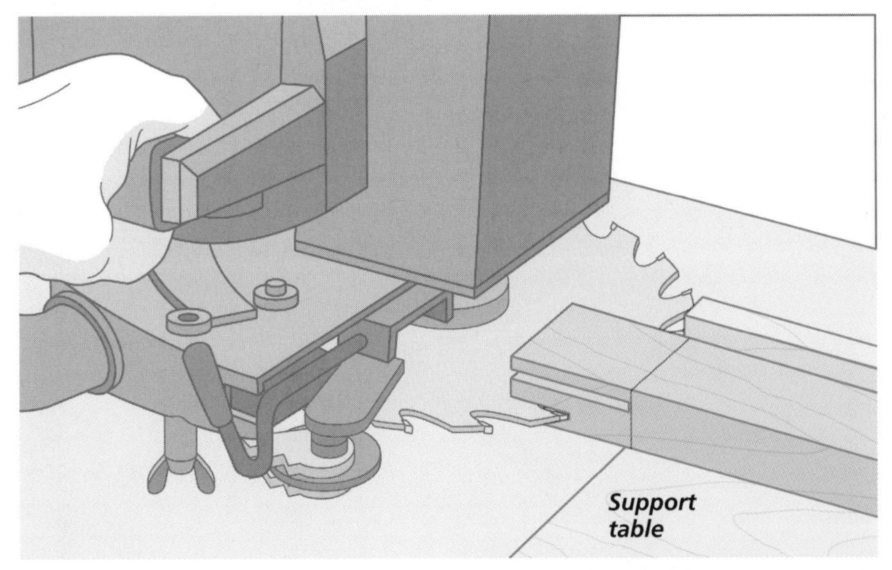

▲ **MORTISES AND TENONS, 2.** ***Matching tenons can also be cut using the plywood support table. Be sure to clamp the workpiece securely to the table and keep your free hand clear of the blade. The blade guard is again removed here for clarity.***

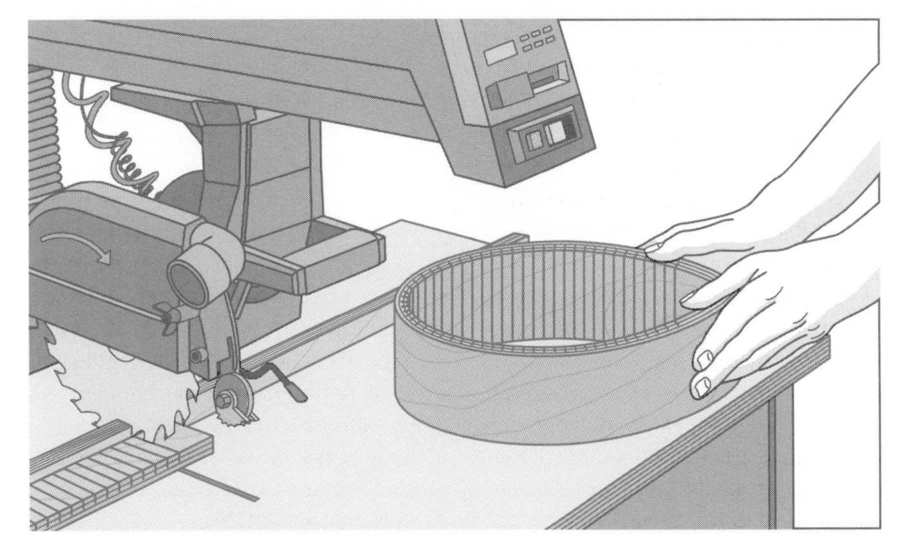

▶ **KERFING PLYWOOD.** ***The radial arm saw is ideal for kerfing plywood so that it will bend. Space the deep kerfs at intervals of about ½ in. Test the kerfs first on a scrap board.***

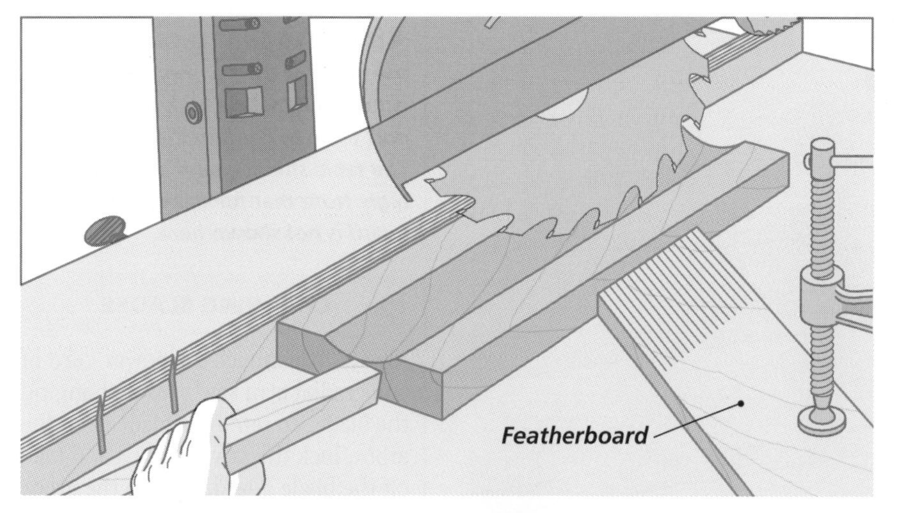

CROSSCUTTING

Straight, square crosscuts are made with the saw's arm locked in the 0° position. Hold the board against the fence with your hand well away from the line of cut. If the board is bowed, clamp it securely to the table or shim the end of it to ensure it lies flat.

For accurate repetitive cuttings of identical size, clamp a stop block to the fence at the desired distance from the blade. Then, gang the boards in position against the stop block and perform the cut across them.

▲ **CUTTING COVES.** ***To form a concave cove, pass the work under a blade that's rotated slightly on the yoke. Cut the cove gradually, lowering the blade about 1/16 in. per pass.***

► **USING A DADO BLADE, 1.** ***A dado blade allows you to cut quick, clean dadoes, grooves and rabbets. The blade adjusts—usually from 3/16 in. to 13/16 in.—for cuts of various widths.***

▼ **USING A DADO BLADE, 2.** ***To cut long grooves and rabbets with a dado blade, set the saw in the rip position. Make sure that you use antikickback pawls and a pushstick.***

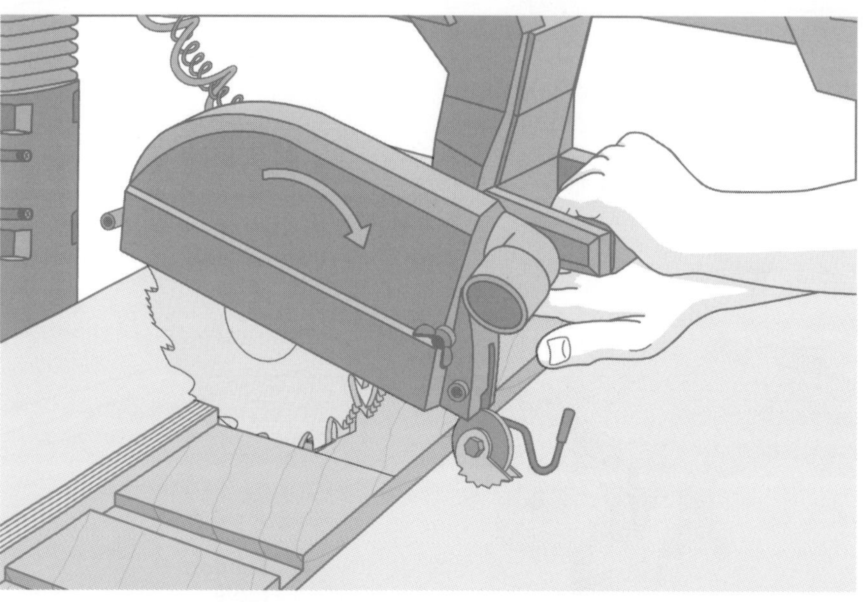

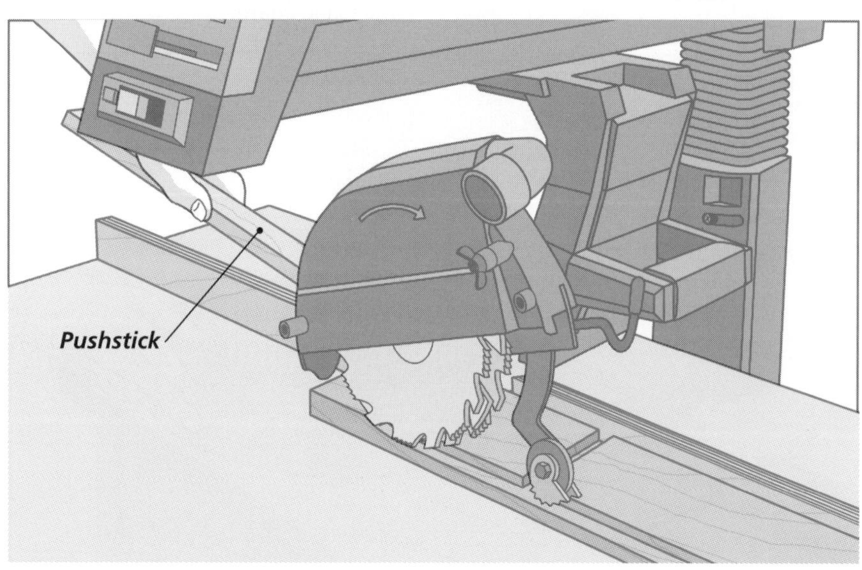

To cut bevels and chamfers, pivot the blade to the desired angle and lock it in position. Then, make a crosscut just as you would normally.

Some crosscuts—such as for mortises and tenons—are made with the blade locked in a horizontal position. In these instances, use a shopmade support table to hold the work at least 3 in. off the saw's table.

MITER CUTS

Miters are simply crosscuts that are made with the saw's arm swung to the right or left. When cutting miters on both ends of a board, it isn't always

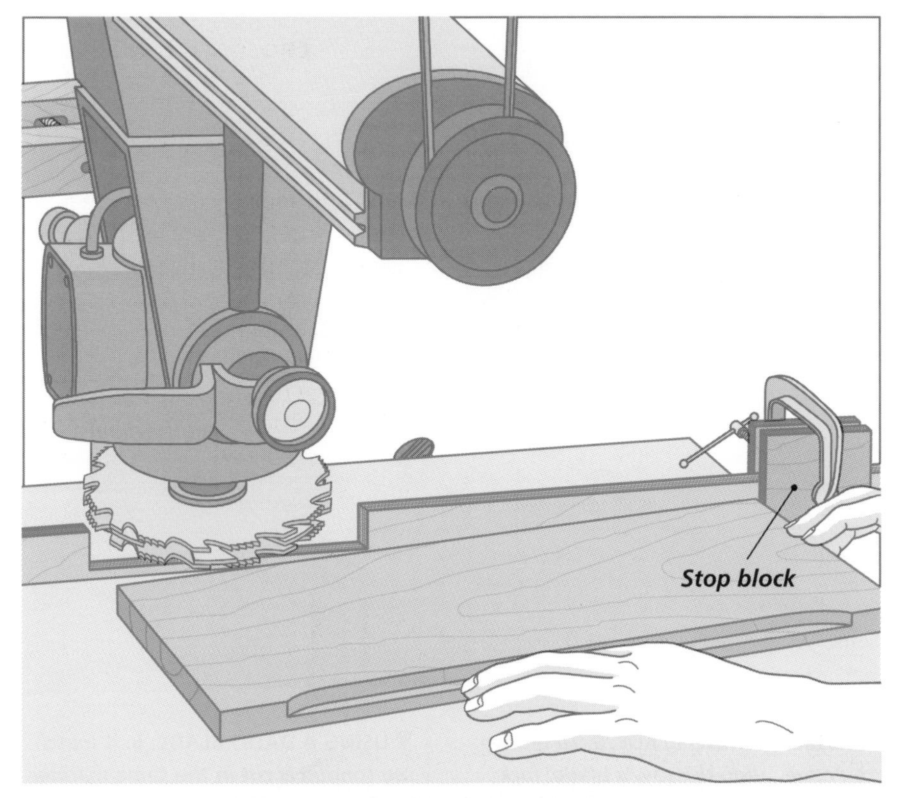

◀ **USING A DADO BLADE, 3.** ***When you're cutting stopped dadoes or blind grooves, clamp stop blocks to the fence. Butt the stock against the rear fence, then swing it into the blade. Note that for clarity the blade guard is not shown.***

▼ **USING A DADO BLADE, 4.** ***To cut a rabbet on round stock, clamp mitered guide boards against the fence and lock the yoke in place. Rotate the stock against the blade—shown here without its guard for illustration clarity.***

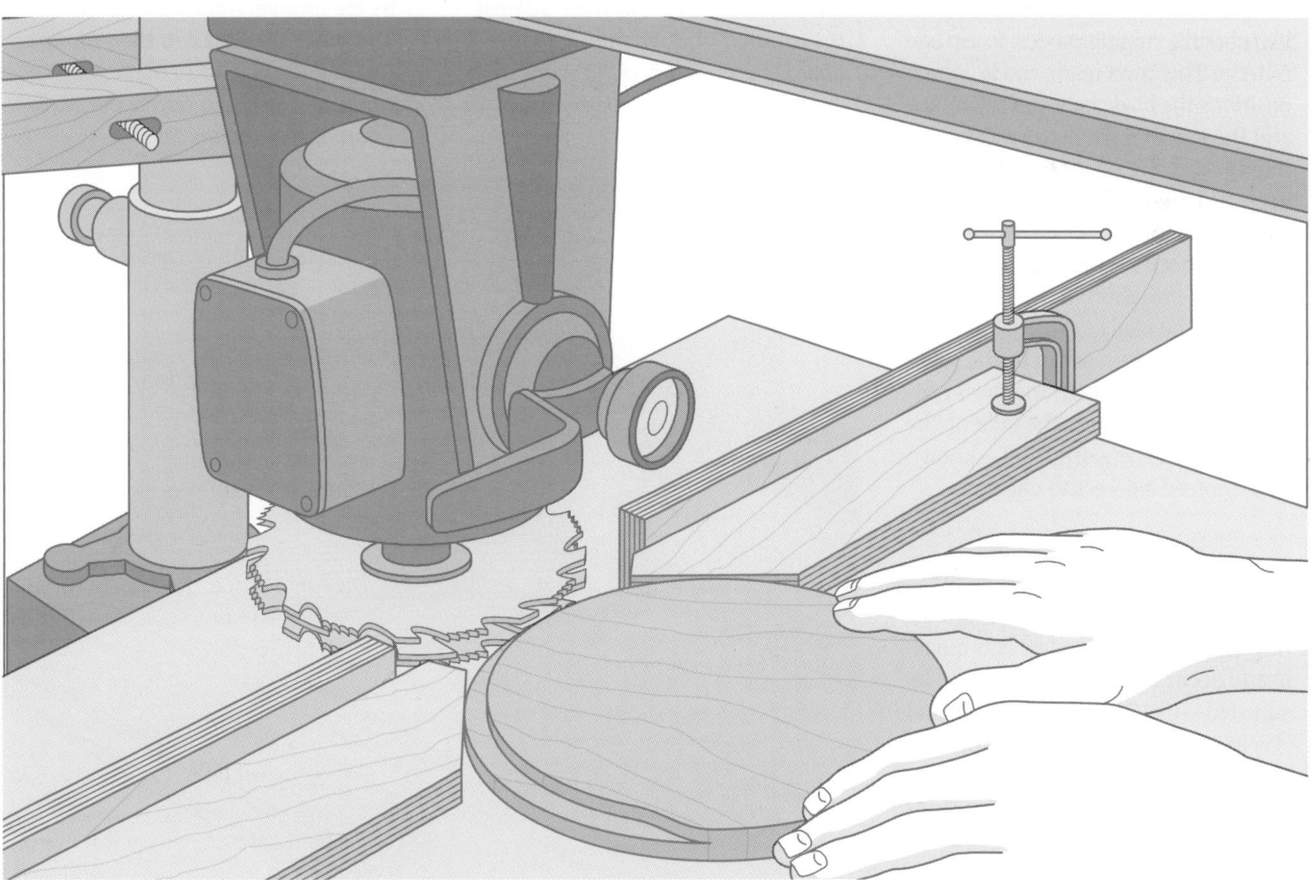

necessary to readjust the arm after the first cut is made. Often, the second miter cut can be performed by simply flipping over the board end for end. Also note that the right-hand miters are usually preferred because the saw's motor doesn't interfere with your view of the cutting operation.

To cut a tricky compound miter, simply set up the saw for a miter and bevel cut. This type of angled cut is used extensively when installing moldings and making picture frames—other projects easily accomplished with a radial arm saw.

RIP CUTS

Ripping, or cutting with the wood's grain, is done with the blade rotated so that it's positioned parallel to the fence. Then, lock the yoke on the saw's arm with the blade at the desired distance from the fence.

Note that the radial arm saw has two possible ripping modes: in-rip and out-rip. The saw's in-rip mode, which positions the blade between the motor and the fence, is the setup most commonly used. Set up for working in the saw's out-rip mode when performing wide rip cuts.

Remember to always feed the work against the rotation of the blade. Also note that the blade's direction of rotation changes from setup in the saw's in-rip mode to setup in the saw's out-rip mode. Therefore, the side of the saw you feed the work from—known as the infeed side—also changes.

USING DADO BLADES

Dado blades are indispensable for cutting dadoes, grooves and rabbets quickly and accurately. Dado blades can be adjusted—usually between 3/16 in. and 13/16 in. wide—to achieve cuts of various different widths.

Two kinds of dado heads are common: the adjustable "wobbler" blade and the more conventional multiple-

▲ **USING A DADO BLADE, 5.** ***To groove an edge, align the saw's blade, lock the yoke and feed the work against the rotation of the blade. A featherboard is used to keep the work snug against the fence. For clarity the blade guard is not shown.***

▼ **USING A DADO BLADE, 6.** ***A matching tongue is cut in the same manner as the groove. Adjust the blade height and make the first cut, then flip the board end-for-end to make the second cut. Again, for clarity the blade guard is not shown.***

blade set. The wobbler head is a single blade mounted on a wedged hub. Its width of cut is adjusted by turning a dial that tilts the blade at an angle to the hub. The multiple-blade head consists of two outside cutting blades and a number of inside chipper blades separated by washers. The width of its kerf depends on the particular blade combination used.

Each type of dado head comes with its own advantages. The wobbler head can be adjusted on the saw's arbor for quick changes in the width of cut with-

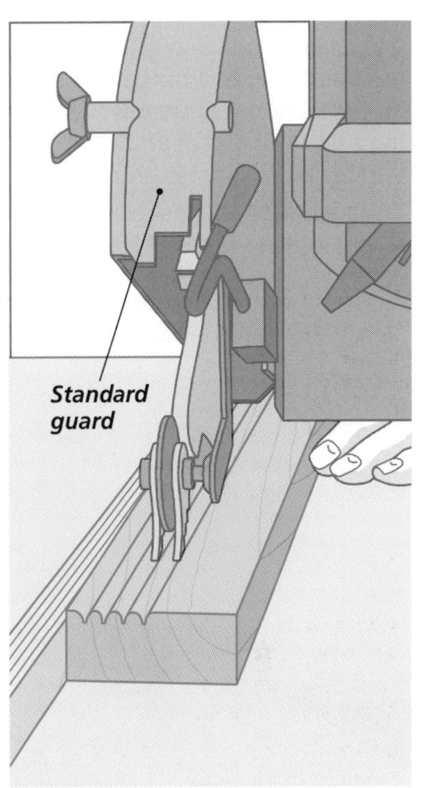

▲ MOLDING CUTTERHEAD, 2. *When using a molding cutterhead in the vertical position, install the standard blade guard. You also should make use of antikickback pawls, as shown in the example here.*

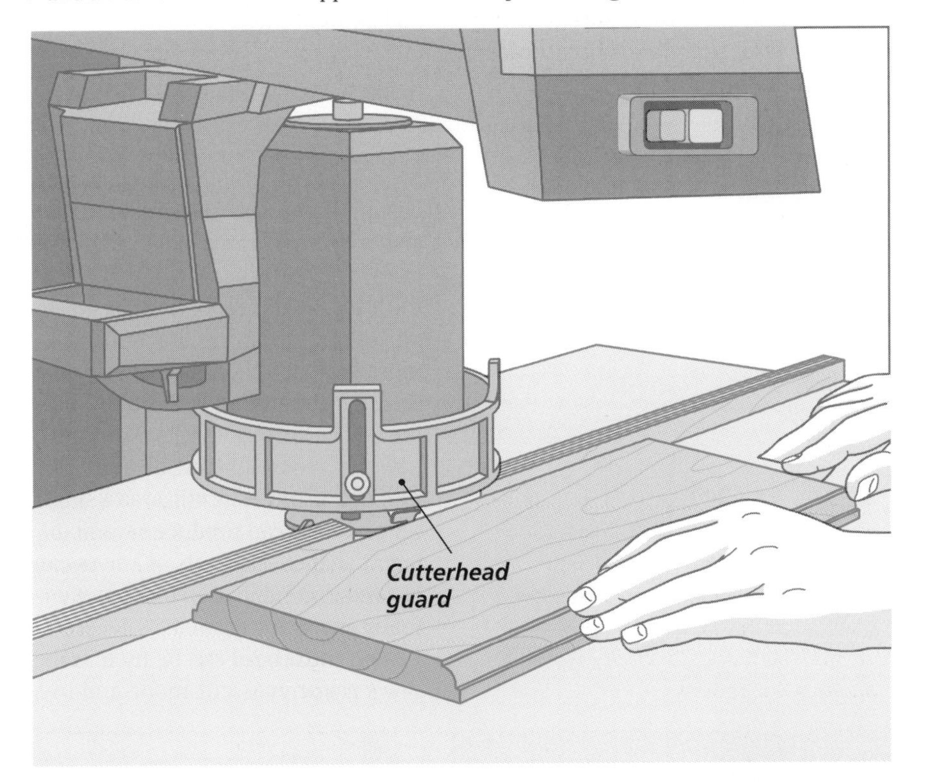

▲ MOLDING CUTTERHEAD, 1. *With its special guard in place, use the molding cutterhead to mill intricate profiles. Make certain that you feed the work against the rotation of the cutterhead—from left to right.*

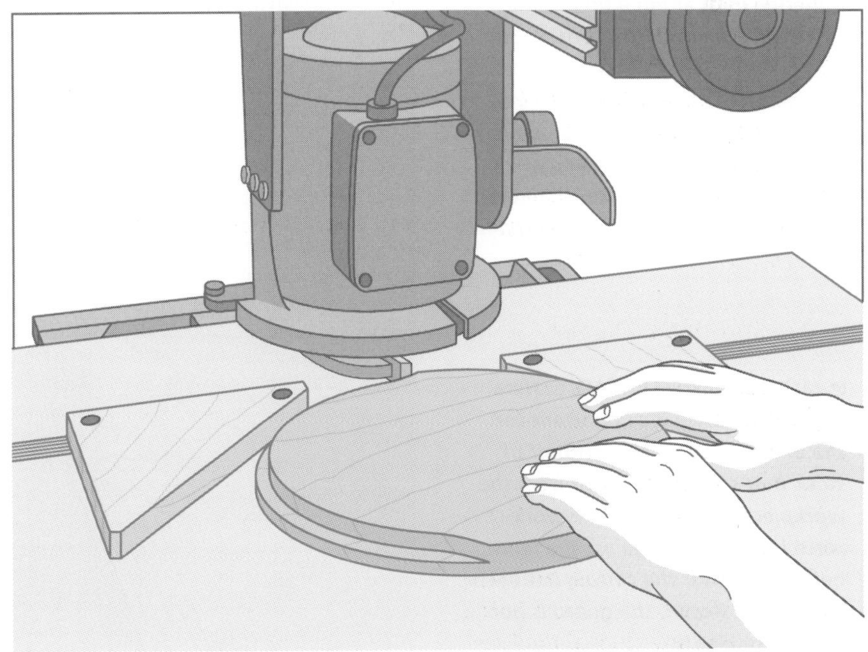

▶ MOLDING CUTTERHEAD, 3. *The simple two-part jig shown here is useful in edge-shaping circular workpieces. The triangular-shaped parts are nailed to strips that are clamped in the fence channel. For clarity the guard is not shown.*

out removing the blade. The multiple-blade head, on the other hand, permits blades to be spaced apart for the cutting of tenons or tongues in one pass.

Most cuts with dado blades are performed in several slow, shallow passes. Don't attempt to remove too much stock in a single pass. Because dado blades have a big bite, the natural tendency of the saw to self-feed the work when crosscutting is increased greatly. Therefore, be sure that you grip the yoke handle firmly and pull the carriage steadily across the work. When performing rip cuts with dado blades, once again be careful to always feed the work in the direction against the blade's rotation. Also be sure to keep both the blade guard and antikickback device in place at all times.

To cut stopped dadoes across the surface of stock, attach a clamp to the saw's arm to limit outward travel of the carriage. For stopped dadoes or blind grooves along the edge of stock, clamp stop blocks to the fence, then butt the work to the rear stop block and swing it into the blade.

USING MOLDING CUTTERHEADS

When working with a molding cutterhead, you can produce standard and custom moldings, mill ornate frames and shape decorative edges and surfaces. The cutterhead, which replaces the blade, holds a set of three blades, or knives. Sets of knives are available in more than 30 different shapes. Some sets of knives must be used full profile for the correct results. Many cuts, however, require the use of only a portion of the knives' profiles, so a single set of knives can produce several different shapes. Also, sets of knives can be used in combination to achieve virtually any shape desired.

The cutterhead can be used in the saw's rip or crosscut mode and in a

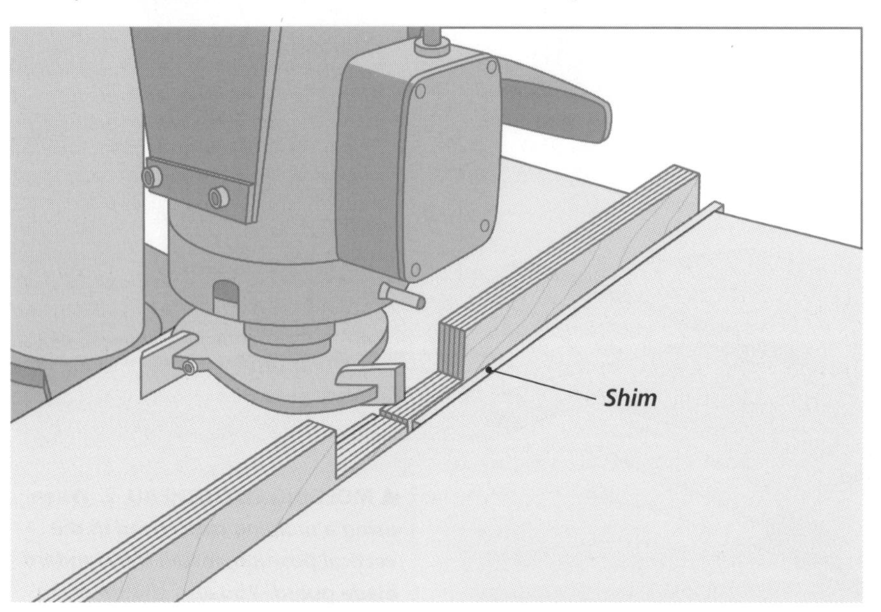

▲ **MOLDING CUTTERHEAD, 4.** ***For a full-edge joint along a board, the fence must be offset to provide support on both sides of the cutterhead. For the offset, use shims equal in thickness to the depth of cut: one in front of the infeed fence and one behind the outfeed fence. Note that the guard is not shown for clarity.***

▶ **MOLDING CUTTERHEAD, 5.** ***Here you can see why it's important for the offset to equal the amount of stock that's being removed from the workpiece. Notice how the workpiece is supported against the fence before and after the cutting has been performed. Again, the guard is not shown for clarity.***

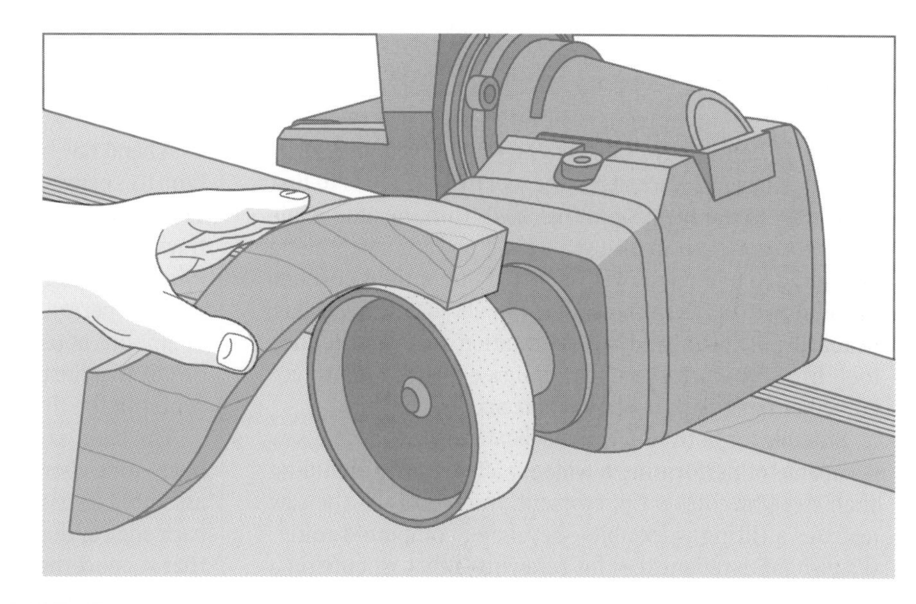

▶ **USING A SANDING DRUM.** ***Use the saw's accessory arbor—located on the right side of the motor—to attach a sanding drum. Never use such an accessory while the blade of the saw is installed.***

▼ **USING A SURFACE PLANER.** ***Here, a rotary surface planer is used to smooth the surface of boards. Set the planer accessory in the horizontal position and make shallow passes.***

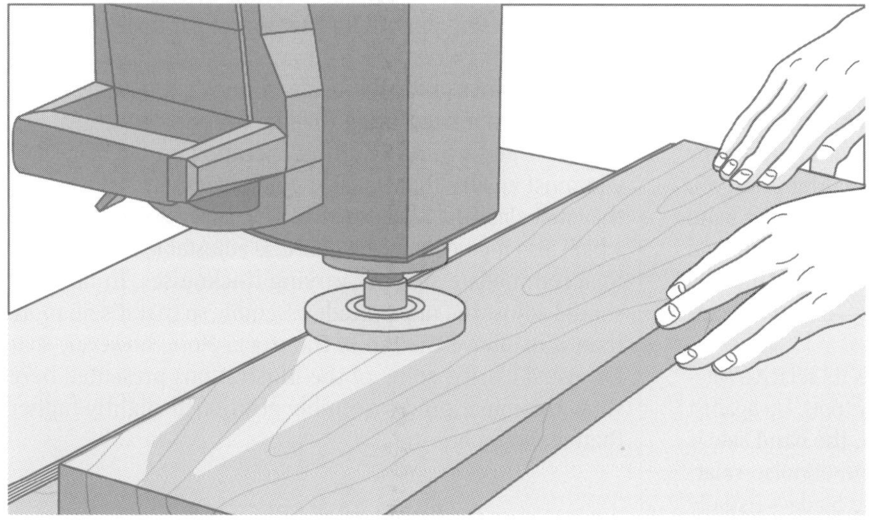

vertical or horizontal position. For top-surface cuts, position the saw's arbor horizontally so that the cutterhead rotates on a vertical plane. To perform edge-shaping cuts, position the saw's arbor vertically with the cutterhead on a horizontal plane. Be sure to use the saw's standard guard when the cutterhead and arbor are in the horizontal position. When the cutterhead and arbor are positioned vertically, install a special accessory guard.

To cross-grain shape the end of a board, position the saw's arbor horizontally as for standard crosscutting. Hold the board to the fence and pull the carriage slowly across the work. Make several shallow cuts, moving the work into the knives slightly after each pass to achieve the desired shape.

Note that it's extremely important to always feed the work against the rotation of the cutterhead. Always stop and think before feeding work into a cutterhead. If a board is mistakenly fed in the same direction as the rotating cutterhead, the knives will grab the work and shoot it out the other side.

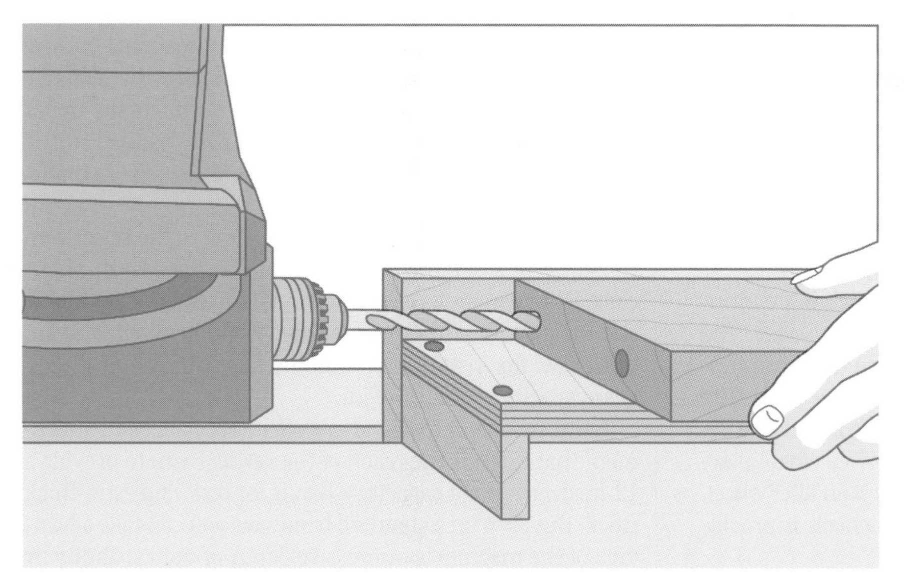

◀ **BORING HOLES.** ***A radial arm saw can also be used for horizontal boring. Mount a drill chuck on the accessory arbor and use a shopmade table to support your work.***

BAND SAWS

When woodworkers have to cut curved, irregular-shaped workpieces, the tool that they turn to first is the band saw. This saw's thin, flexible blade allows the work to be maneuvered easily and accurately along a winding line of cut as well as in and out of tight corners. The ability to perform these difficult cuts so effectively has, ironically, hurt the band saw's reputation as a versatile shop tool. In many workshops, the band saw is used *only* to cut curved or irregular-shaped workpieces.

Suitable for both rough and delicate work, the band saw is capable of performing a wide variety of cuts, including such straight cuts as rip, crosscut, miter and—if the saw features a tilting worktable—bevel and compound miter. It's also an excellent tool for resawing—that is, cutting a thick board into thinner ones. Also, when fitted with an appropriate blade, the band saw is capable of cutting various metals and plastics. Some types of band saws will even accept a sanding belt.

Not only is the band saw a versatile tool, but it's also surprisingly easy to operate. Many cuts can be made freehand by simply pivoting the work around the blade. And once you have been introduced to a few basic practices with the band saw, you'll find that through various sawing techniques and simple shopmade jigs you can expand your use of this tool to make many workshop procedures easier—including cutting curves and irregular shapes.

Yet another advantage of the band saw is its relative safeness in comparison to many other stationary tools. Up against a table saw or radial arm saw, for example, the band saw is fairly quiet, reducing the workshop problem of noise-related fatigue. Moreover, only a portion of the blade—usually about ⅛ in.—is ever exposed while the tool is in operation. And since the cutting action of the blade bears down on the work, the work is pressed against the worktable instead of back toward the operator, eliminating the risk of kickback. It's for this reason that the band saw is the preferred tool for ripping either short or narrow stock.

BAND SAW MECHANICS

The band saw is named for its saw blade, which is a continuous loop, or band, of steel with teeth along one edge. The blade rides over two wheels that are rimmed with thin rubber tires. Some benchtop band saws have three wheels. The tires provide nonslip traction to drive the blade in a clockwise, down-cutting direction. The belt-driven lower wheel powers the blade. The free-spinning upper wheel is an idler wheel. Passage for the blade as it revolves on the wheels is provided by a slot in the worktable.

A band saw has a few simple adjustments that are important to ensure accurate, trouble-free cutting operations. These basic procedures include tensioning and setting the tracking of the blade along with adjustments to the upper and lower wheels. The saw's upper, idler wheel adjusts up and down to permit installing the blade and applying the proper amount of tension. The upper wheel also can be tilted in or out to adjust the tracking so that the blade runs on the center of the tires.

The band saw is equipped with two blade guide assemblies—one above the worktable and one below. Each guide assembly consists of a ball-bearing wheel that supports the back edge of the blade along with left and right guide blocks that support the sides of the blade. The support to the back edge of the blade by the ball-bearing wheels prevents the blade from being pushed off the tires of the upper and lower wheels as the workpiece is advanced into the blade. The two side guide blocks keep the blade from twisting as the workpiece is manipulated along the line of cut.

Before performing a cutting operation on the band saw, you must ensure that the side guide blocks are adjusted so they just clear the blade's teeth. The upper guide assembly, which also includes a blade guard, is adjustable up and down to accommodate stock of varying thicknesses. In use, you should adjust the upper guide assembly so that it's no more than ¼ in. above the top of the stock. Note, however, that for visual clarity, some of the illustrations presented here show the upper guide assembly positioned slightly higher than it should be.

BAND SAW SPECIFICS

Band saws are sized according to their approximate cutting capacity as measured by their throat width—the distance from the blade to the vertical arm that supports the upper wheel. Most band saws for the home workshop fall in the 10- to 14-in. range. A typical 14-in. band saw, for example, usually has a cutting capacity of 13¾ in.

Band saws are also classified according to the maximum thickness of stock that they can handle. This depth-of-cut capacity corresponds to the distance between the worktable and the upper guard assembly when it's fully raised. A 14-in. band saw, for instance, commonly has a maximum thickness capacity of about 6¼ in.

Some models of the band saw offer a special height attachment that extends the reach of the vertical arm to provide a 12-in. depth-of-cut capacity—handy for resawing extra-thick stock. But even on a standard band saw, you can take advantage of the machine's impressive depth-of-cut capability by

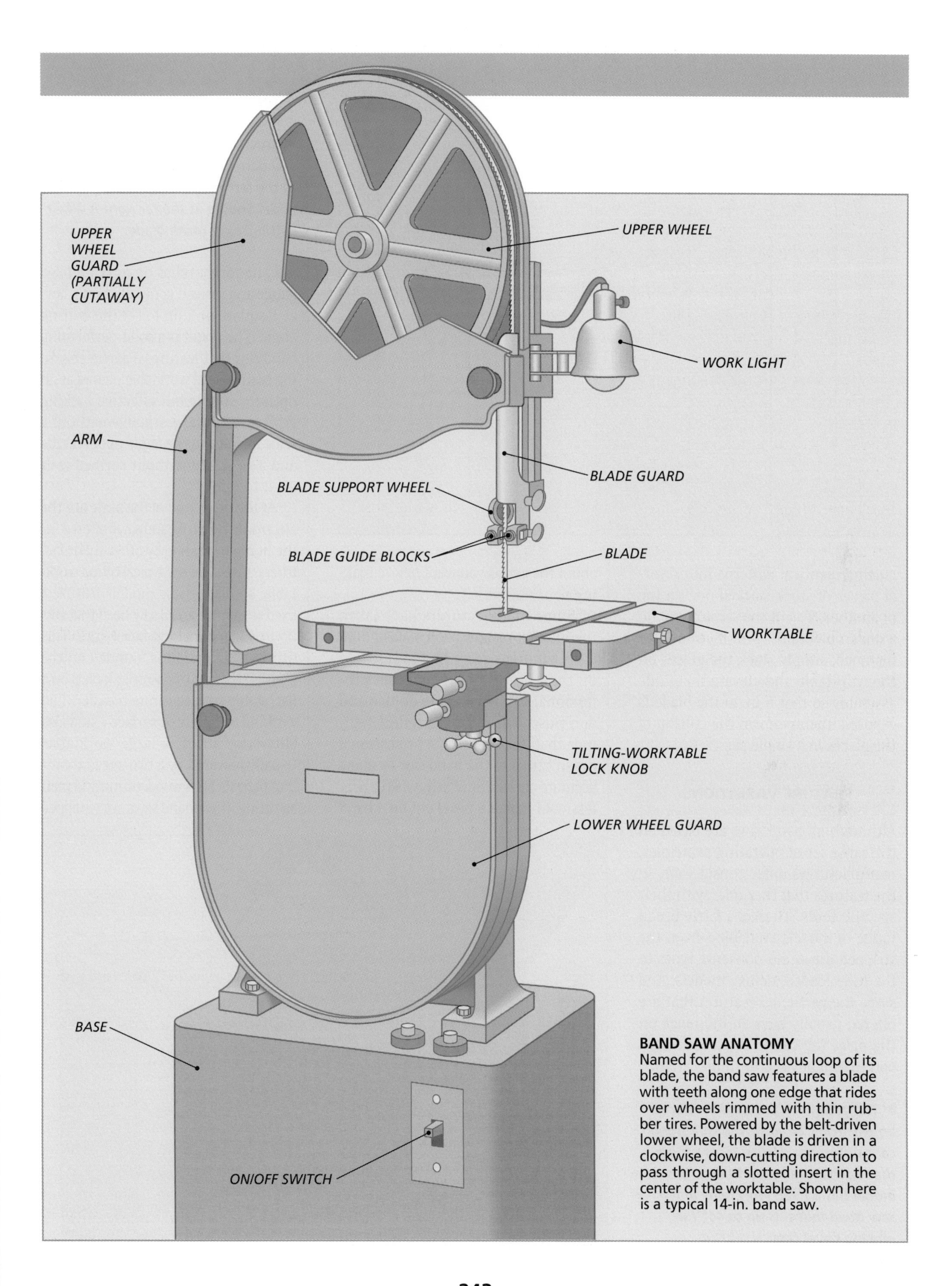

BAND SAW ANATOMY
Named for the continuous loop of its blade, the band saw features a blade with teeth along one edge that rides over wheels rimmed with thin rubber tires. Powered by the belt-driven lower wheel, the blade is driven in a clockwise, down-cutting direction to pass through a slotted insert in the center of the worktable. Shown here is a typical 14-in. band saw.

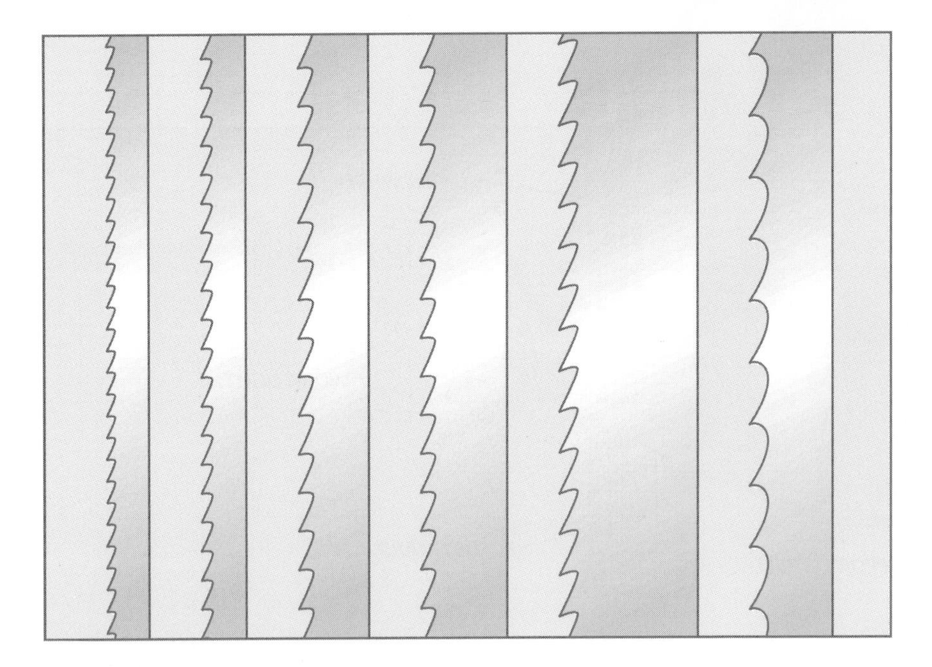

◀ **BAND SAW BLADES.** ***The group of standard-tooth woodcutting blades at the left range from ⅛ in. to ¾ in. wide. Shown at the far right is a fast-cutting, skip-tooth blade.***

cutting identical patterns into several pieces of stock stacked one on top of another. To cut the same curve on a dozen pieces of ½-in. plywood, for instance, simply stack the pieces on the worktable and elevate the guide assembly so that 6 in. of the blade is exposed, then perform the cutting of the pieces in a single pass.

FEATURE VARIATIONS

Although all band saws are based on the same set of operating principles, manufacturers differ considerably in the features that they offer with their specific tools. There's a fairly broad range of models available—from the stripped-down, no-nonsense types to the fully-loaded, deluxe models. And since the particular features that are offered usually have an influence on the price tag carried by a band saw, you're well advised to think carefully about the extras you want before making your purchase.

Some manufacturers have taken the interesting approach of designing their band saw according to research on the features of the tool that professional cabinetmakers do use and don't use. Their models reflect findings that, for instance, a professional doesn't turn to the band saw to make accurate cutoffs. Similarly, when a professional makes a bevel cut on a band saw, he rarely relies on a tool-affixed gauge and instead generally uses a bevel T-square or a jig to set the cutting angle. The result is a solid-performing band saw that features a particleboard top (with a steel worktable offered as an option), simple but effective locking devices, a tilting worktable without a scale for setting the angle of bevel cuts and a rip fence without scribed rails for it to ride in.

At the other end of the scale are the electronic types of band saws offered for the home workshop by other manufacturers. Instead of the typical tilting worktable, some of these models feature a fixed worktable and a saw head that tilts up to 45° for making bevel cuts. This tilting-head design is founded on the premise that cutting precise bevels on a flat, stable surface is much easier than working on a slanted surface—and also allows for an extra-large worktable. Usually powered by a two-speed motor that permits both woodcutting and metalcutting, these band saws are equipped

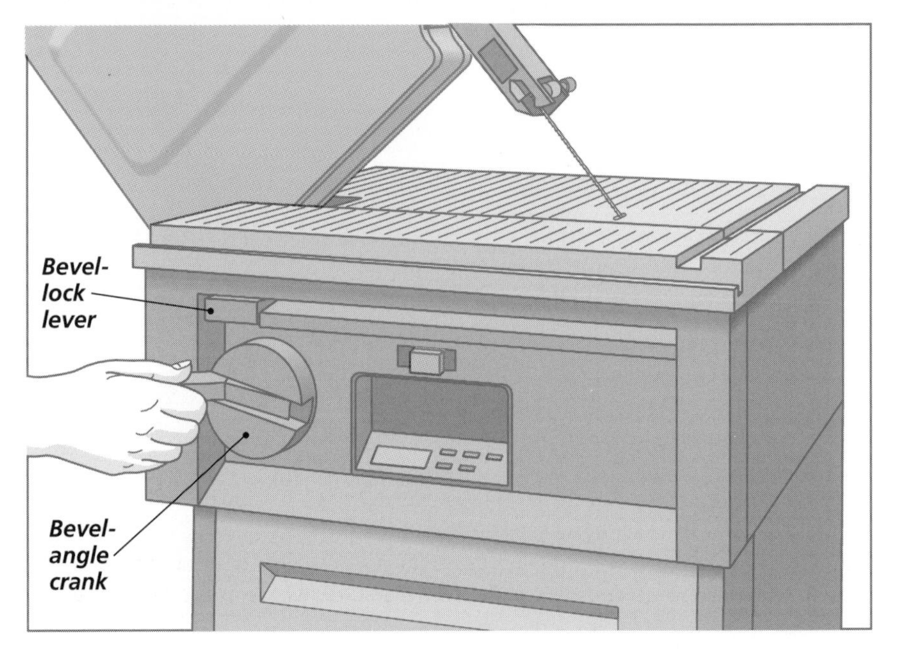

▶ **TILTING-HEAD BAND SAW.** ***Here's an electronic band saw with a significant difference. Unlike most others that have a tilting worktable, this model has a fixed worktable and a saw head that tilts up to 45° for making bevel cuts.***

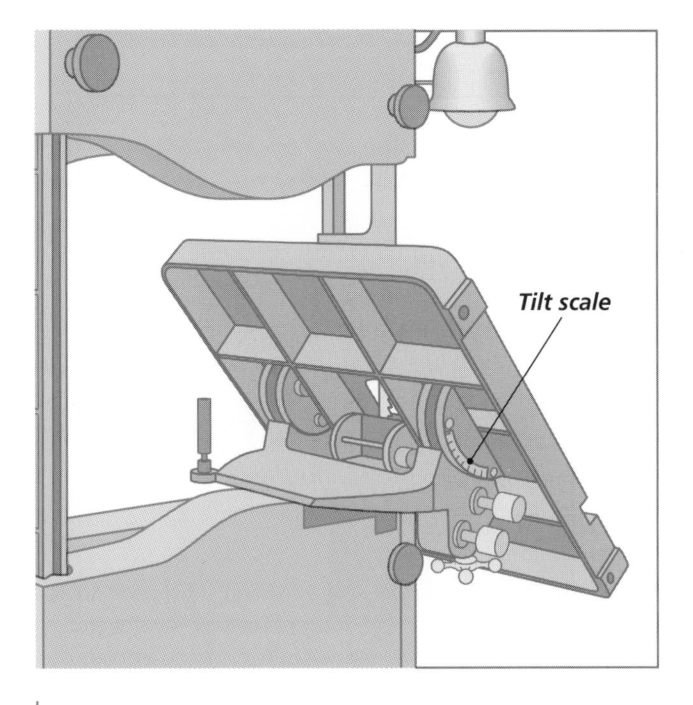

▲ **BAND SAW SETUP, 1.** ***The typical tilting worktable features high-quality, cast-iron construction. Its underside is equipped with a scale and pointer that indicates the degree of tilt.***

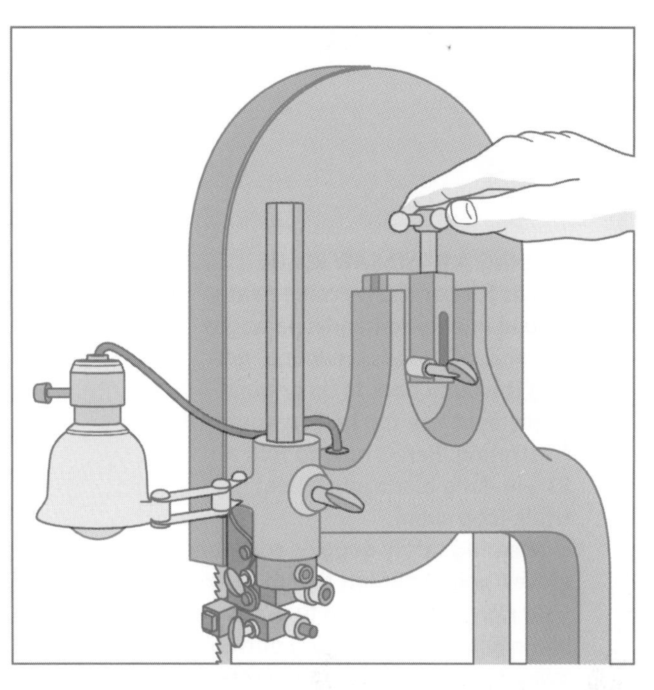

▲ **BAND SAW SETUP, 2.** ***Turning the elevating knob on the back of the saw's upper wheel guard raises and lowers the upper wheel. This procedure allows you to install a saw blade and adjust its tension.***

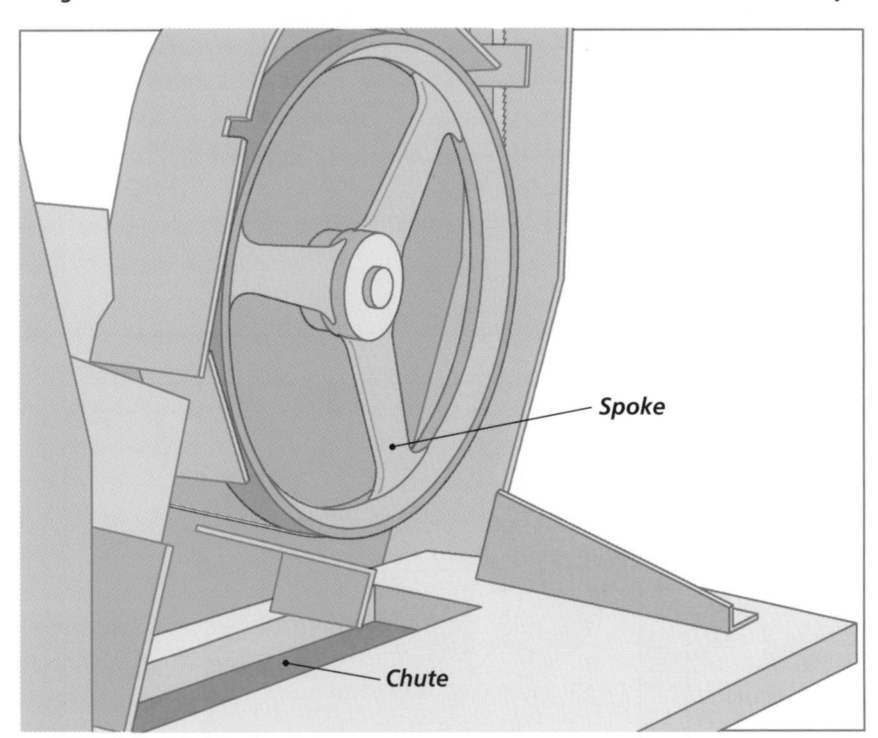

▲ **BAND SAW SETUP, 3.** ***On some saw models, the lower wheel is specially designed to collect sawdust. Tiny fins on the spokes help to direct the waste through a chute into a dustbag.***

with a liquid-crystal display (LCD) screen that provides digital readouts of blade speed, blade tension and bevel angle. They often come equipped with an abrasive belt and a platen for handy conversion into a narrow belt sander.

Benchtop band saws provide still another variation. Many of these versatile tools not only perform standard band-sawing functions, but also convert into a sander/grinder for finish-sanding workpieces and sharpening hand tools. Benchtop band saws usually come with a tilting worktable and can typically handle cuts up to 10 in. wide and 4 in. thick at 90°.

TYPES OF BLADES

Band saw blades are commonly available in widths ranging from 1⁄16 in. to 3⁄4 in. Various tooth sizes and styles are also offered. Selecting the correct blade to use depends on the type of material being cut, the thickness of the material and the type of cut.

FOLDING A BAND SAW BLADE
Blades for band saws come neatly wound in easy-to-handle packages. But once a blade is unwound, getting it wound back to its original, convenient size can be downright frustrating. Here's how to fold a 93½-in.-long blade into a neat triple-loop spool.

Wearing safety goggles and work gloves, point your left thumb up and your right thumb down to grasp the blade with its teeth facing outward, away from you *(right, top)*. Pressing firmly against the blade with your thumbs, bring your hands together slightly and pivot your right hand so the thumb points up, allowing the blade to begin to shape itself into two loops *(right, center)*.

Maintaining your grip on the blade, keep twisting it in the same direction while you now pivot your left hand in the opposite direction *(below, left)*. This will cause the blade to coil again, forming a third loop *(below, right)*. To secure the blade in this triple-loop spool, use string or plastic twist ties.

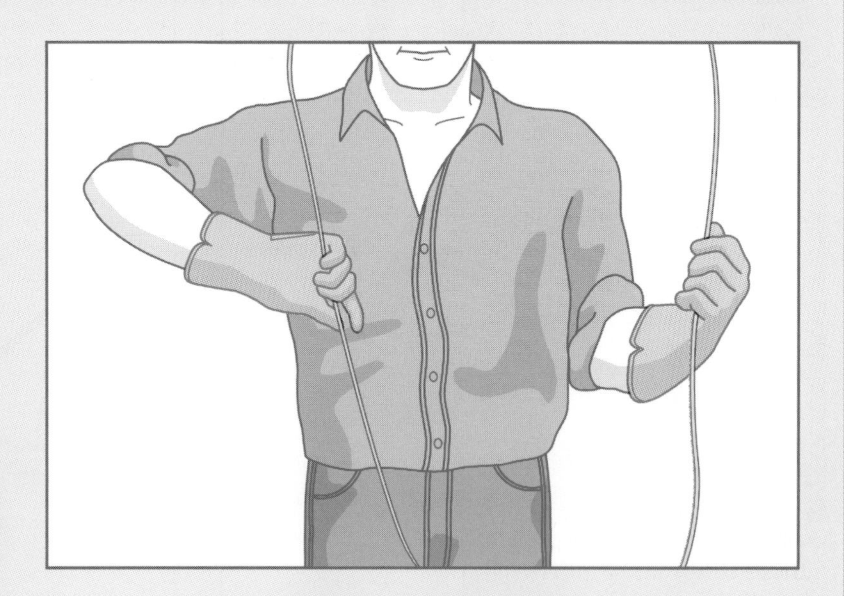

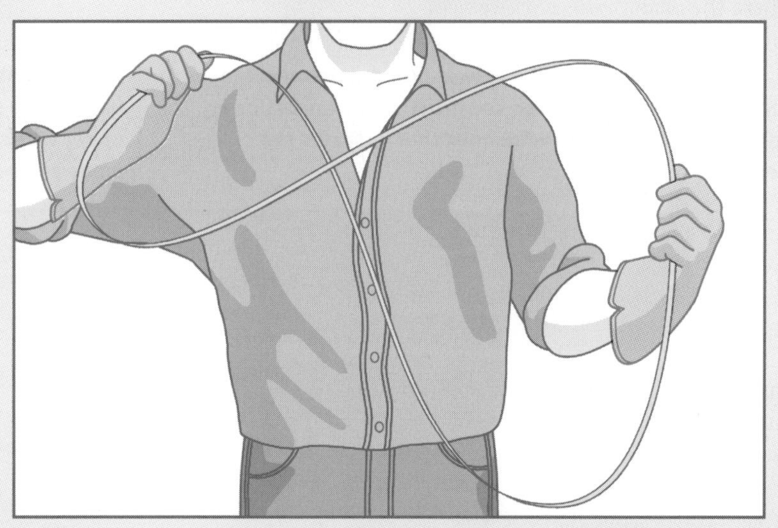

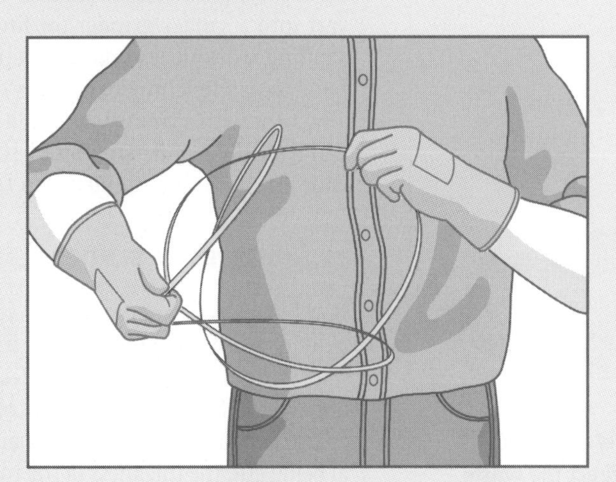

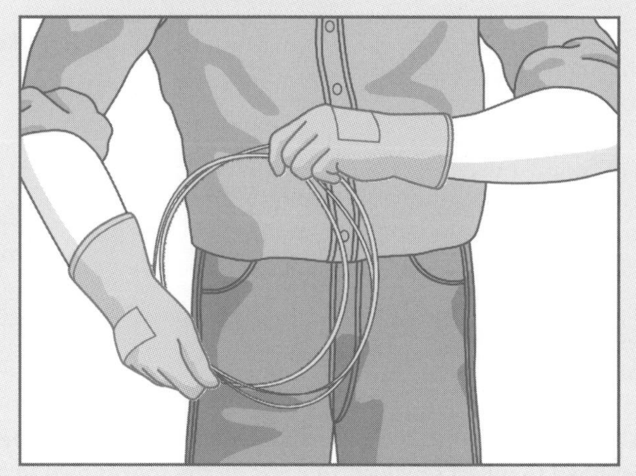

Despite the relatively narrow range of blades available for use on the band saw, choosing the right blade for the particular job at hand isn't always as straightforward as it might seem. In band sawing, there's no such thing as an all-purpose combination blade, nor any blade that's specifically designed for crosscutting or ripping. When you select a blade, you should bear in mind three factors: the blade's tooth design, its width and its set.

Band saw blades for woodcutting come in three basic tooth designs, each one having its own particular advantages. A standard blade works best for cuts straight or diagonally across the grain, making it ideal for performing intricate curves and other types of cuts where the blade's orientation in relation to the grain varies. A skip-tooth blade, so called because every second tooth is "missing," performs well when cutting long, gentle curves parallel to the grain. For ripping and resawing, use a hook-tooth blade, ideal for fast, rough, straight or curved cutting operations with the grain.

Generally, the more teeth a blade has, the smoother it will cut. To obtain smooth cuts, therefore, select a standard fine-tooth blade. For rough, fast cutting, choose a coarse-tooth blade. Coarse-tooth blades work best on soft, resinous or wet wood as well as for cutting thick stock. For extremely fast and rough cutting, try a skip-tooth blade; its large, widely-spaced teeth have deep gullets that expel wood chips and sawdust effectively.

As a rule, a wide blade is ideal for resawing. To saw curves, work with a narrow blade. The narrower the blade, the tighter a radius that it can cut. For example, a 1/16-in.-wide blade can cut a minimum radius of about 1/8 in. A 1/8-in.-wide blade cuts a 1/4-in. radius. A 1/4-in.-wide blade has a 1/2-in. radius. But a 3/8-in.-wide blade will cut a radius of only about 1½ in. A 1/2-in.-wide blade will cut a radius of 2¼ in. and a 3/4-in.-wide blade has a 3½-in. radius.

When selecting a blade, be sure to consider the tightest curve that the blade will have to turn. Don't ignore the limitations on a blade's turning ability. Trying to force a blade around a corner that's too tight will cause the blade to bind in the kerf, twist and even snap. However, because a wider blade resists deflection, using a blade that is narrower than necessary for a cut is typically not the best choice to make either. In general, you should always work with the widest blade possible for the tightest curve.

A blade's set refers to the degree to which the teeth are angled to the side, or to how much the kerf that they cut is wider than the blade—and thus to the risk of the blade binding in a cut. A light-set blade, which has minimal set, creates a narrow kerf and smooth cut, but it is also most prone to binding, restricting its ability to cut tight curves. A heavy-set blade cuts faster and is less likely to bind, but it produces a rougher cut, usually leaving behind an unsightly pattern of marks known as "washboarding."

BAND SAW BLADE SPLICER

For the owner of a band saw, a blade splicer is a must in the shop. This simple tool comes in two models: one for 1/8- and 3/16-in.-wide blades and another for blades from 1/4 to 3/4 in. wide. Use the splicer to repair broken blades or to fashion new ones economically from 100-ft. rolls of blade stock.

First, grind a 20° bevel on the mating blade ends to form a lap joint. Then, secure the blade ends in the splicer *(below)*. Align the two beveled ends of the blade, then insert silver solder into the joint and add flux to prevent the bonding surfaces from oxidizing.

Apply slow, even heat from a small-tipped propane torch until the blade turns a dull red color. Maintain this temperature for several seconds, then allow the blade to cool. The high shear strength provided by this basic silver-soldering technique forms a strong splice that usually outlasts the blade.

BAND SAW EXTENSION TABLE
An extension table is indispensable when cutting long or very large workpieces. Here's a simple 36-in.-dia. table of 1/2-in. plywood that you can make to wrap around your saw's existing worktable. It's designed to be removed easily when you don't need to use it.

The plywood table is supported by an H-shaped frame that's bolted to the saw's worktable. Cut the frame pieces from 2 x 2 stock. Next, drill and tap the edges of the saw's worktable to accept 1/4-20 machine bolts. Drill the holes to secure the two long frame pieces 1/2 in. below the top of the saw's worktable. This 1/2-in. offset accepts the extension table. Bolt the two long frame pieces to opposite edges of the worktable, using thin shims of cardboard to provide clearance for removing the extension table *(right, top)*.

Cut out the plywood tabletop, making a cutout of a suitable size to fit around the arm of the saw. Be sure that you cut a 1/2-in.-wide slot in the tabletop for the saw blade. Glue and screw the tabletop to the two long frame pieces, then attach the short frame crosspiece only with screws. Hold the frame crosspiece against the left edge of the saw's worktable and screw down through the tabletop into the crosspiece *(right, bottom)*.

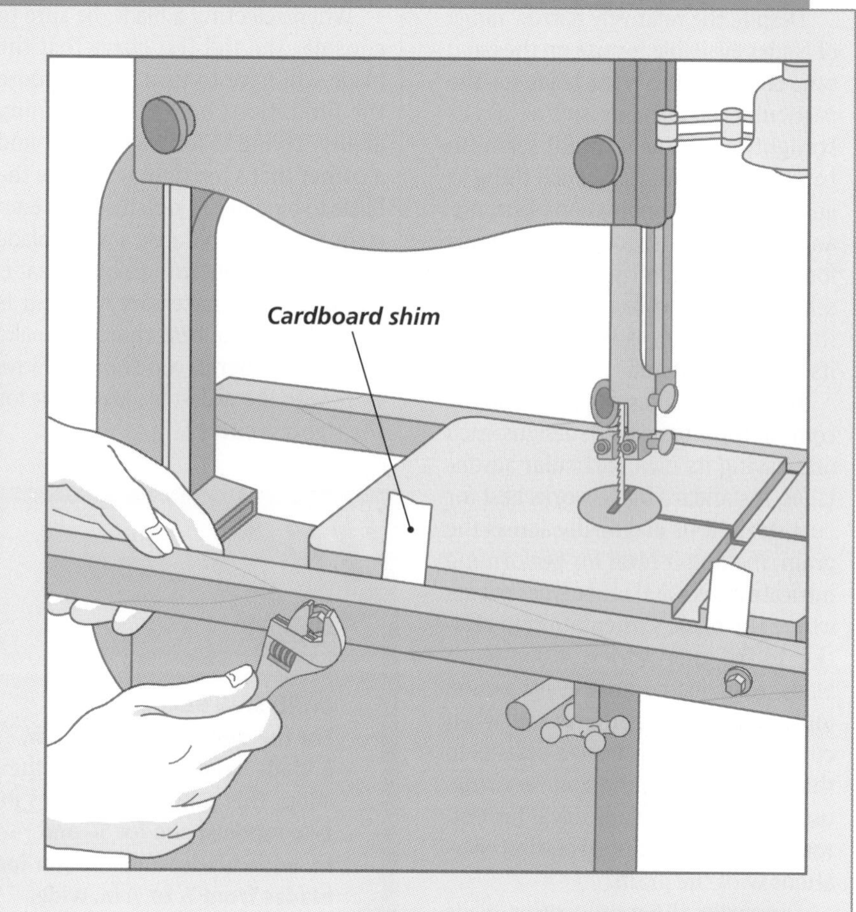

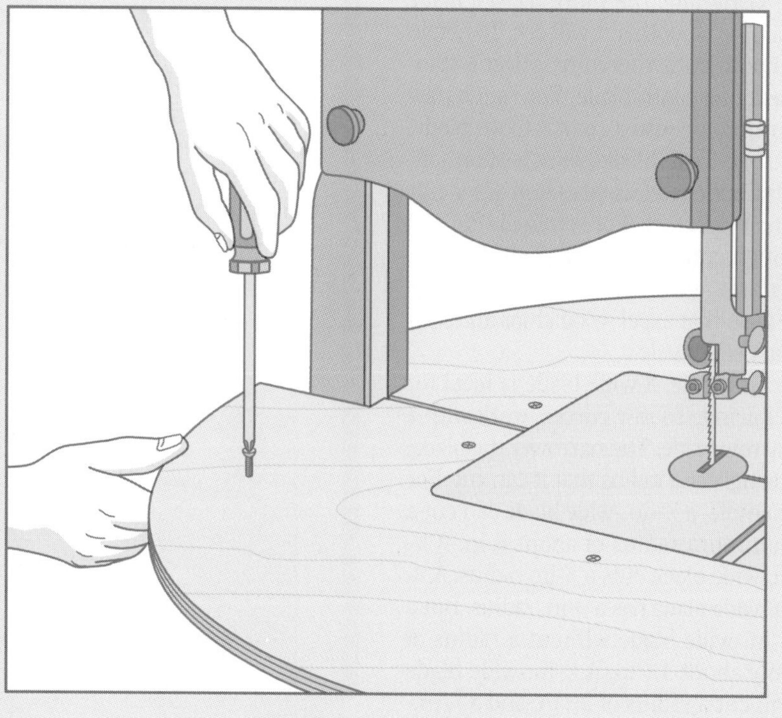

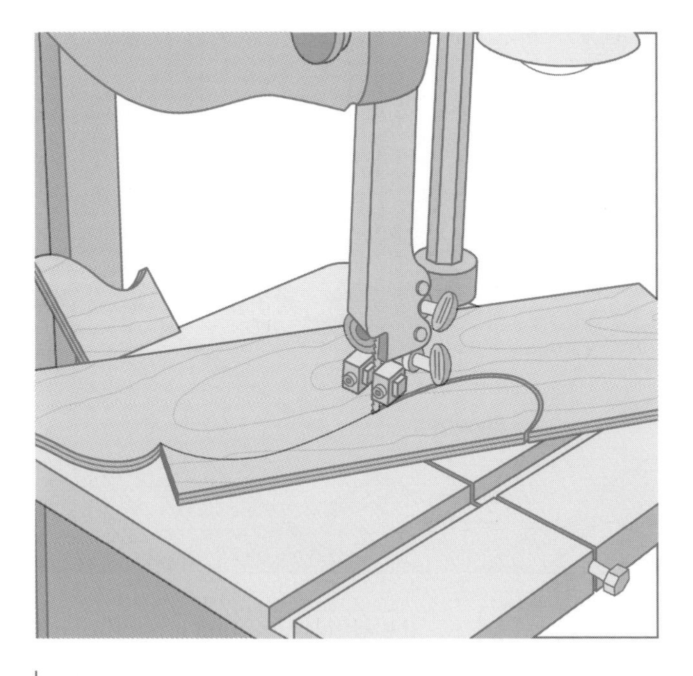

▲ CUTTING CURVES, 1. ***When two curves meet at a sharp inside corner, first cut straight into the corner. Then, make the two curved cuts to free the waste.***

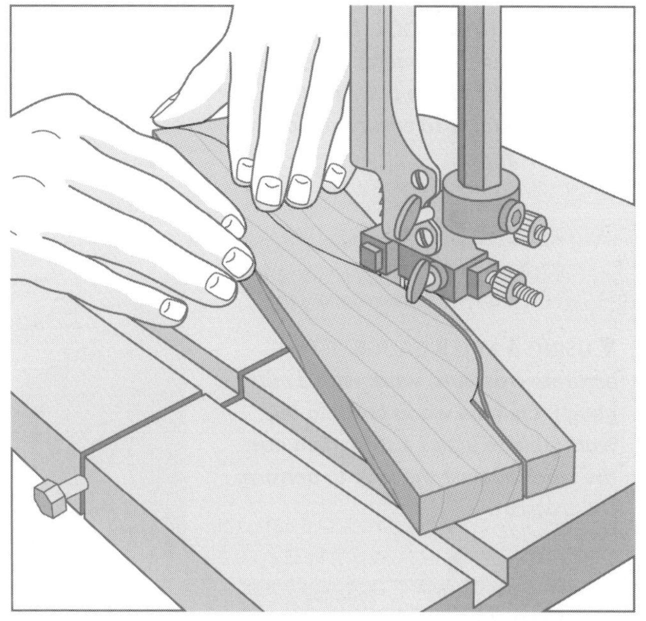

▲ CUTTING CURVES, 2. ***Saw a neat corner by first cutting straight into the corner. Then, backtrack slightly to saw around it. Come back later to finish it up.***

A band saw is an excellent metalcutting saw when equipped with the appropriate blade. But metalcutting should only be practiced on saws that are capable of operating at the necessary reduced speed. For cutting metal effectively, the saw needs to be able to operate at about 300 feet per minute (fpm) or slower. The standard speed for woodcutting is 3,000 fpm.

BLADE CARE

Keeping blades clean and in good condition is as important to the performance of your band saw as choosing the right blade for the job. Clean sticky resin and pitch off blades by soaking them in turpentine or kerosene and scrubbing them with steel wool. Blades typically have a loop length of several feet, so carefully fold them into a triple-loop spool for safe, efficient storage.

CHANGING BLADES

Make sure you disconnect the power cord of the band saw before changing the blade. To remove a blade from the saw, raise the upper guide assembly to its highest setting and lock it in place, then shift the ball-bearing wheels and guide blocks back from the blade. Next, remove the worktable's insert and take out the leveling pin, then release tension on the blade and open the wheel guards. Carefully slide the blade out of the guide assemblies and slip it off

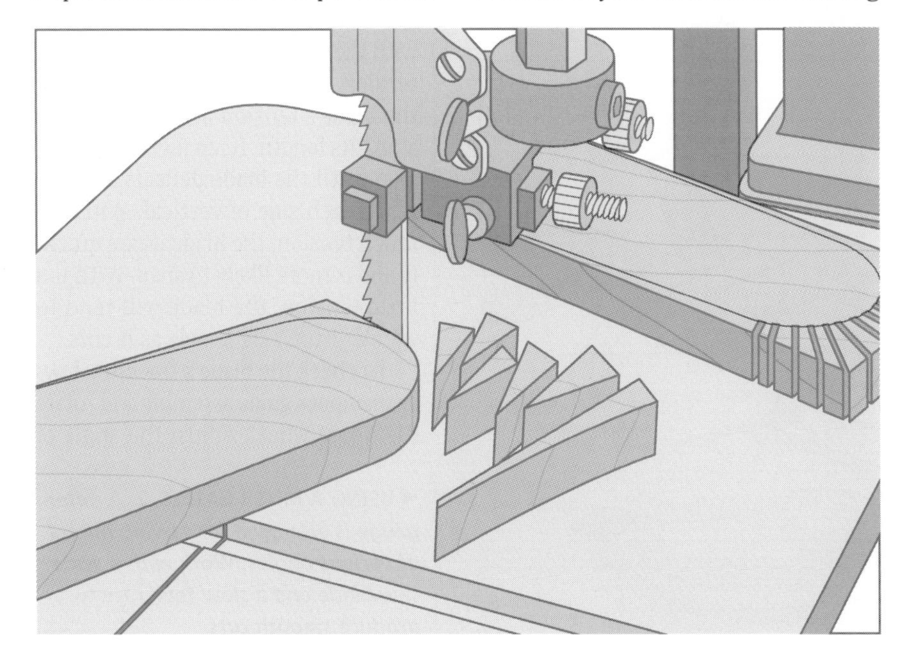

◀ CUTTING CURVES, 3. ***When using a wide blade to cut a tight curve, make a series of tangential cuts up to your cutting line. Then, cut away the waste a bit at a time.***

► **SAWING THIN STOCK.** ***To cut thin stock such as sheet metal, tape a ¼-in. plywood panel in place on the saw's worktable to ensure smooth, burr-free edges.***

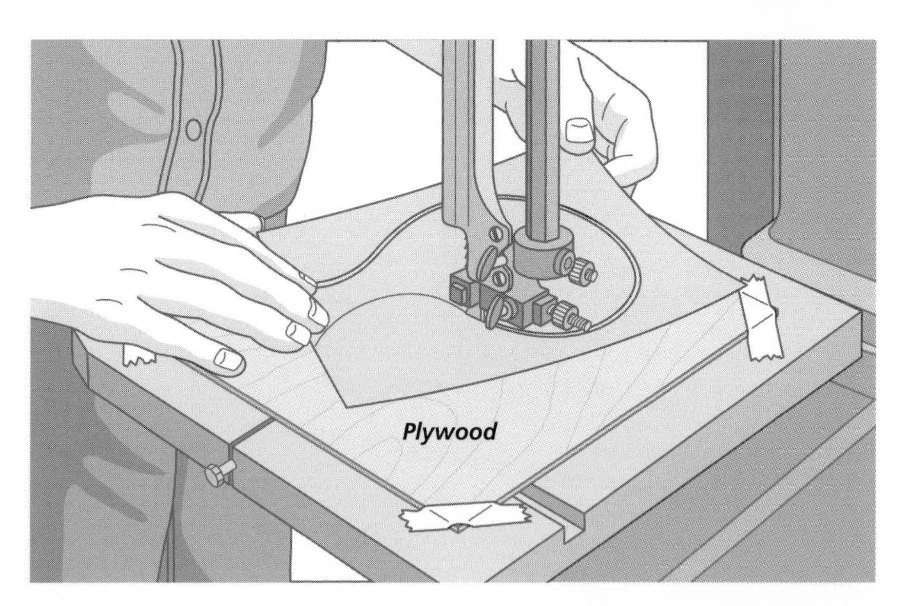

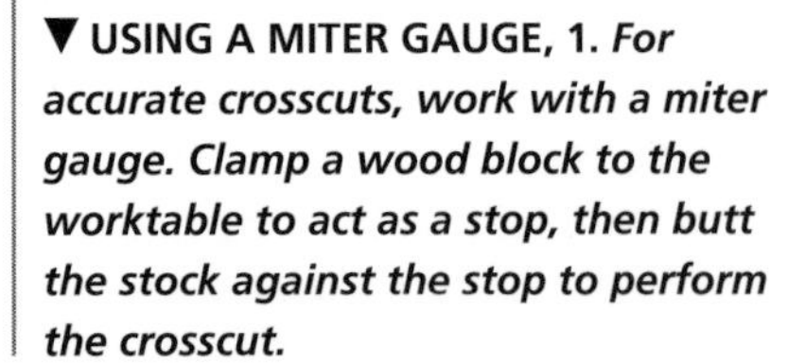

▼ **USING A MITER GAUGE, 1.** ***For accurate crosscuts, work with a miter gauge. Clamp a wood block to the worktable to act as a stop, then butt the stock against the stop to perform the crosscut.***

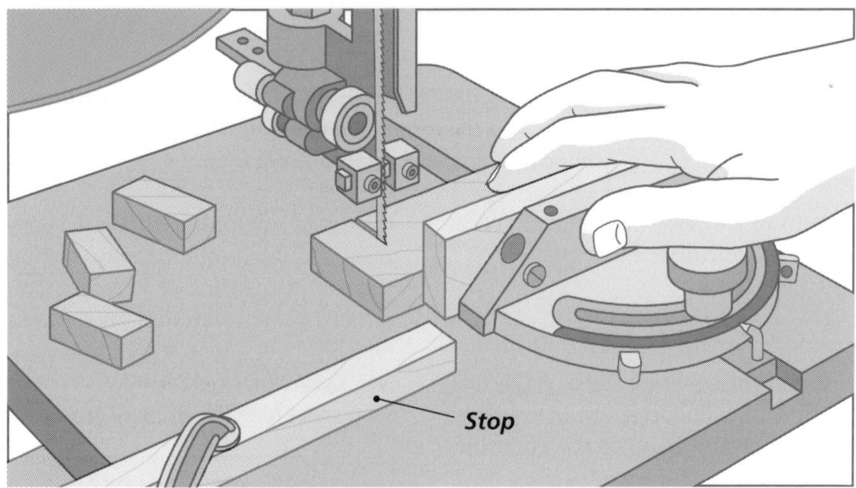

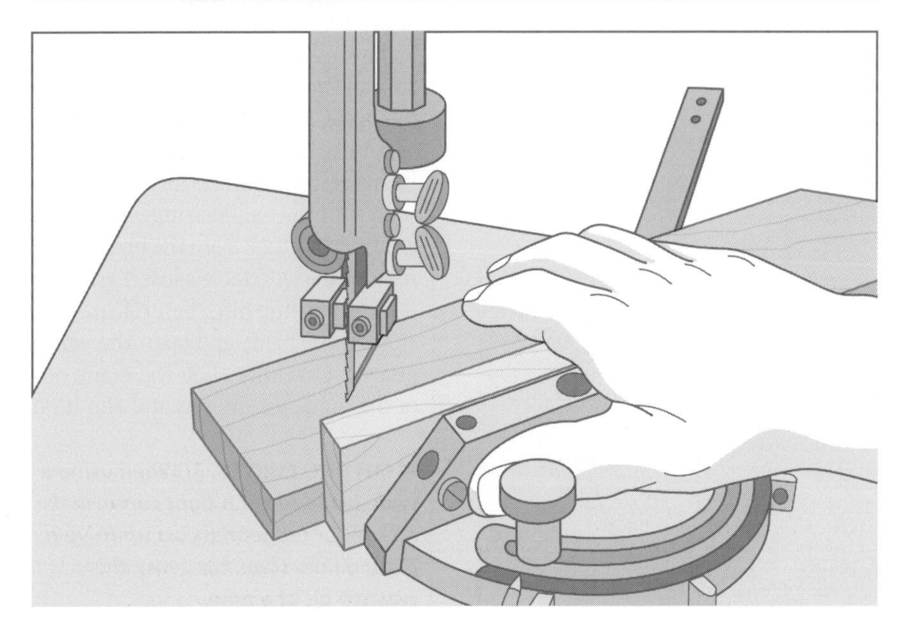

◄ **USING A MITER GAUGE, 2.** ***A miter gauge is also used for sawing miters of various angles. Work with a wide saw blade and a slow feed rate to produce smooth cuts.***

the wheels, directing it out through the slot in the worktable.

A new blade that has been folded into a triple-loop spool contains a considerable amount of potential spring, so uncoil it very carefully. Holding the blade so its teeth face you and point down, guide it in through the worktable's slot and into position, making sure that it's centered on the wheels. Then, reinstall the worktable's leveling pin and insert.

Elevate the upper wheel with one hand to increase the blade's tension and deflect the blade from side to side with the other hand to test the blade's tension. Turn the upper wheel to test the blade's tension at various points along its length. Keep increasing tension until the blade deflects about ¼ in. to each side of vertical. With too much tension, the blade wears quickly and is more likely to snap. With too little tension, the blade will tend to wander from side to side as it cuts.

To check the blade's tracking, lower the upper guide assembly and rotate the upper wheel. Adjust the angle of the upper wheel as necessary until the blade tracks directly in the center of it. Close the wheel guards, then turn on the saw to verify tracking of the blade. Once the blade is tracking properly, adjust the guide assemblies.

SAWING SAFETY

Although a band saw is a relatively safe tool to operate, general safety precautions still apply. When operating the saw, wear safety goggles and keep your hands well clear of the blade. Use push-sticks or jigs whenever cutting small or narrow stock, and don't start the cutting operation until the blade is turning at full speed.

Stand to the left side of the blade when working at the front of the saw's worktable—the side that's opposite the direction in which a snapped blade will fly. If the blade should happen to snap, turn off the saw immediately and wait until the wheels come to a complete stop before attempting to change it.

Although the blade guard shields the blade above the worktable, there is no protection from the blade right at the worktable or below it. While the saw is in operation, keep your hands out of the hole covered by the worktable's insert and don't reach under the worktable to clear away debris.

Even under ideal operating conditions the blade undergoes considerable stresses, so don't add to them with carelessness. Always feed work slowly and steadily into the blade, applying only a minimum of pressure. Use only a properly sharpened blade of a suitable tooth design, width and set for each cutting operation. Make sure the blade is correctly installed and adjusted. Avoid running the blade for long periods of time without cutting.

CUTTING CURVES FREEHAND

Most cuts performed with the band saw are done freehand—that is, without the assistance of a fence or guide. Freehand band sawing is a two-hand operation. Use one hand to push the work into the blade and the other hand to steer it along the line of cut. Make sure that your hands are always positioned well away from the path of the blade. Cup an edge of the work with the fingers of your feed hand to keep them from slipping.

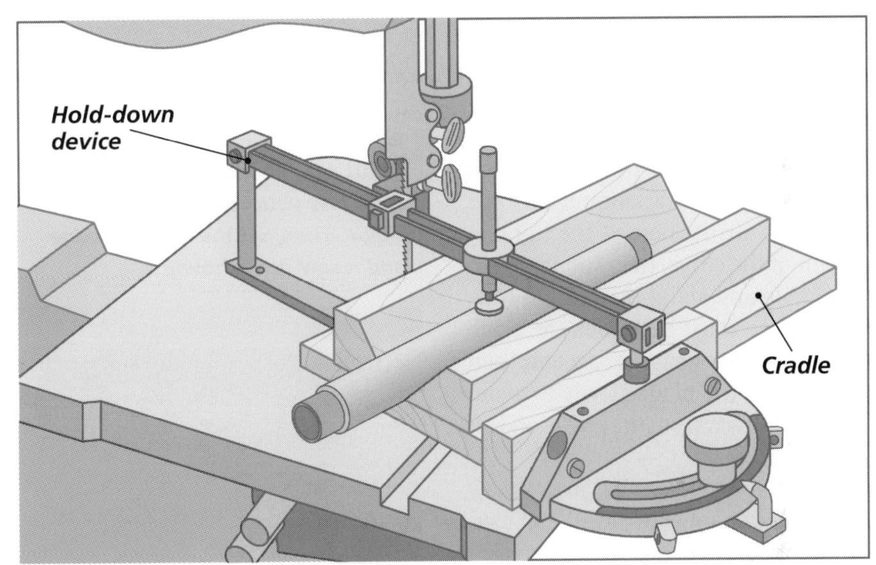

▲ **CUTTING ROUND STOCK.** ***This setup shows how to employ a shop-made V-shaped cradle and a hold-down device with a miter gauge to safely saw round stock, such as piping or tubing.***

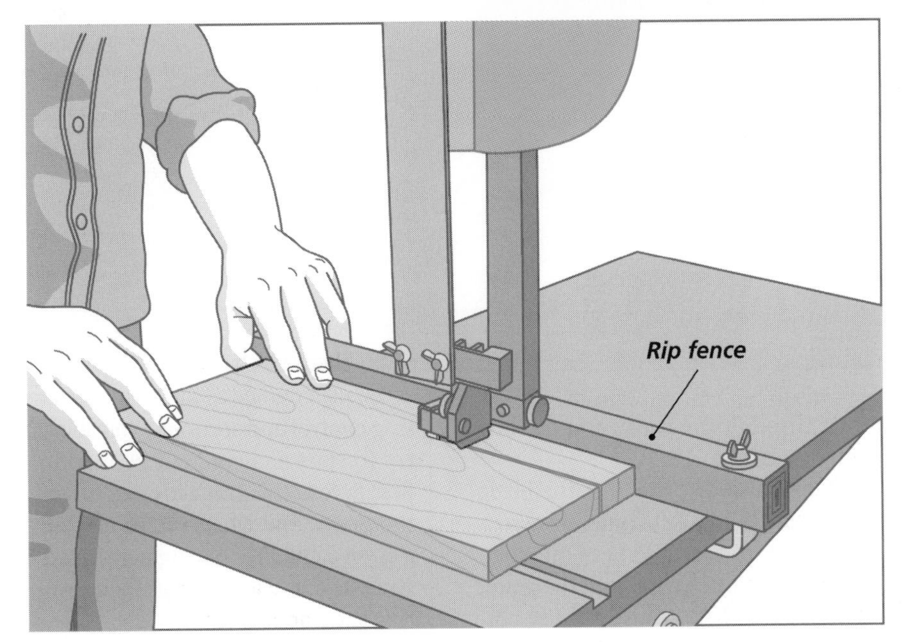

◀ **RIPPING.** ***Straight ripping is a snap with a rip fence. The simple fence shown locks positively and quickly in place on the worktable by means of two 90° studs and wingnuts.***

Before starting a curved cut, visualize the work being sawed along the cutting line. This helps to prevent the reaching of a "dead end" due to interference with the saw's arm as the work is maneuvered through the cut. Often, simply beginning the cut from the other end of the cutting line will provide enough clearance for the work. When a dead end seems inevitable, mark cutting lines on both sides of the work. Sometimes the only way that the work can be cut is to start on one side and finish on the other side.

Try to avoid having the blade get trapped in the work so that you have to backtrack to free the blade. If you can't avoid having to backtrack the blade out of a cut, begin with shorter cuts and backtrack out of them rather than starting and backtracking out of longer cuts. Or, drill a hole at the tightest point of the curve, then simply cut to the hole and along the cutting line. When you must backtrack the blade to free it, turn off the saw and then backtrack the blade slowly to avoid pulling it away from the guides and off the wheels.

When you're executing an especially intricate cut, for example, it's not usually possible to perform the operation in a single, continuous pass. But by making a series of shorter cuts, you can minimize the distance you need to backtrack the blade. And you'll also find that it's usually easier to bypass small, detailed areas and come back later after a majority of the waste has been sawed away to finish them with simple short cuts.

Or, when two curves meet to form an acute, inside corner, it's typically necessary to first perform at least one cut through the waste and directly into the corner. Then, saw along the cutting line of one curve and into the corner. Now you can simply repeat the procedure along the cutting line of the other curve to complete the cut. Many curved cuts are much easier to do if you first make a series of these release cuts through the waste and directly into the corner.

You'll also discover that the blade will easily follow a cutting line across the grain, but tend to veer off when following a cutting line with the grain. Therefore, to help ensure greatest cutting control and accuracy, you should try to start a curved cut by working first across the grain instead of with the grain. And when you're entering a curved cut after having performed a straight cut, ease up slightly on your feed rate for best results.

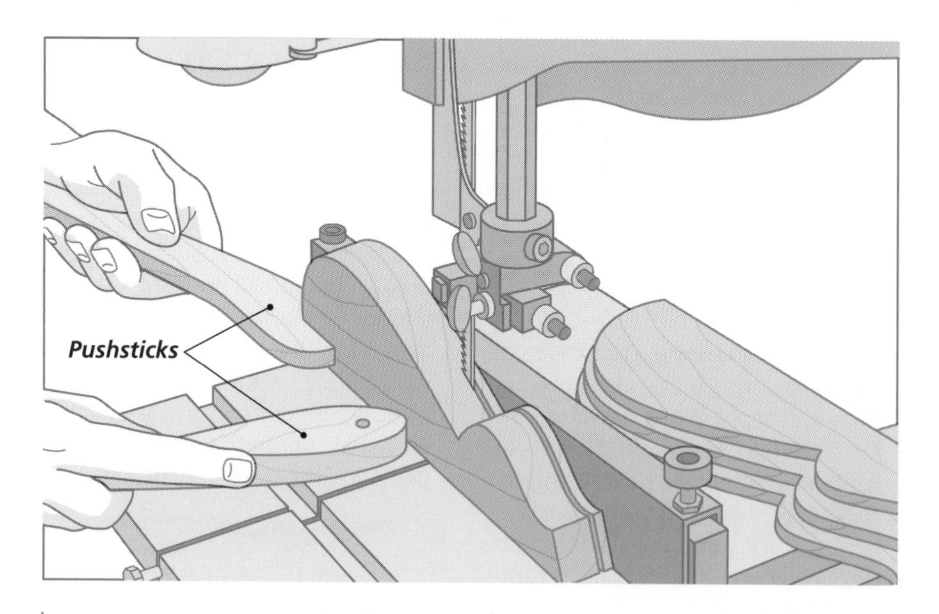

▲ **RESAWING, 1.** ***Here's an easy way to cut a number of identical parts. First, saw your stock to the desired shape. Then, set the stock on edge and resaw it, as shown.***

▼ **RESAWING, 2.** ***Clamp spring-board fences to the worktable on both sides of long stock to direct the board accurately. Note that the rear fence here is hidden by the stock.***

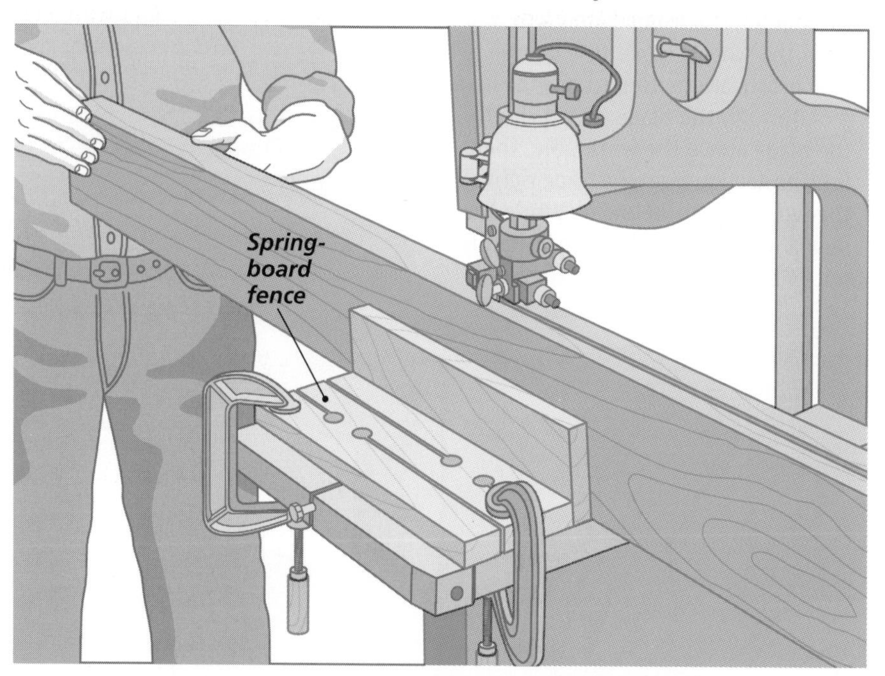

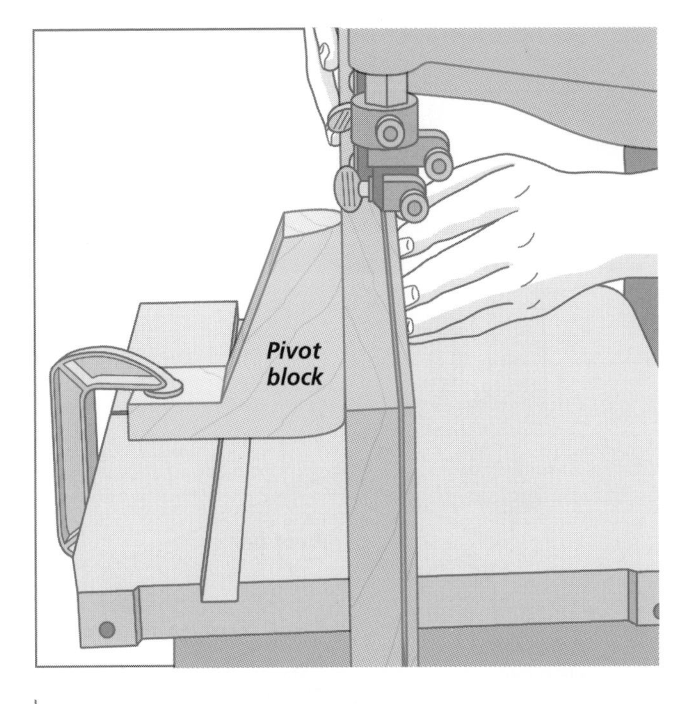

▲ RESAWING, 3. *The shopmade pivot block that's shown here allows for maximum steering in order to compensate for excessive leading of the blade. A pivot block is also useful for performing curved cuts.*

▲ RESAWING, 4. *A utility fence permits both steering and guiding. It works especially well if stock is first ripped on edges with a table saw and then the remaining waste is cut away using the band saw.*

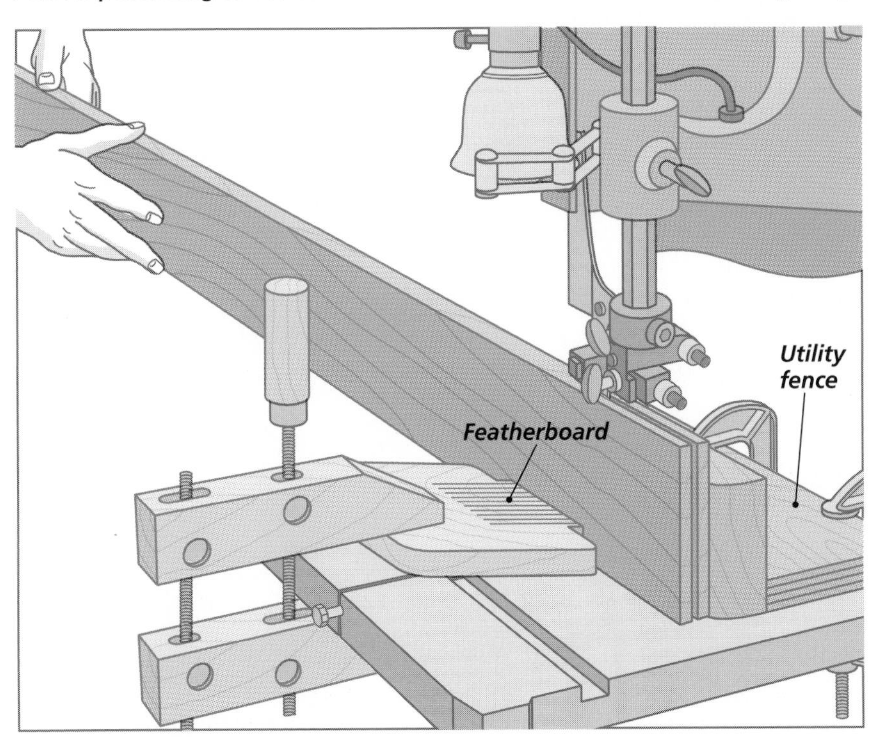

▲ RESAWING, 5. *When resawing long boards with a utility fence, clamp a featherboard to the worktable on the other side. This keeps stock against the fence when your hands can't apply lateral pressure.*

When working with thin material such as wood veneer or sheet metal, the underside of the material often splinters or forms burrs as it is cut by the blade. This is caused by the clearance space around the blade as it passes through the slot in the worktable's insert. It's this lack of support right at the blade that allows the work to splinter. To ensure smooth cuts, make an auxiliary worktable surface out of ¼-in. plywood or hardboard. Cut about halfway into the panel and then secure it to the saw's worktable with masking tape. Since the blade now has very little clearance as it passes through the panel, you can saw thin stock with virtually no splintering.

MAKING CROSSCUTS

Crosscuts are one of the most common straight cuts performed on a band saw—even though the tool's throat width limits the capacity of what can be handled. Crosscuts are possible to

BAND SAW CIRCLE JIG
Here's an adjustable circle-cutting jig for your band saw that allows you to cut perfectly round pieces up to 30 in. dia. accurately and consistently. The jig consists of a 1-in.-thick table, made from two layers of ½-in. plywood, fitted with an adjustable pivot bar *(right, top)*. A hardwood strip attached to the underside of the table fits in the saw table's miter-gauge slot. The pivot bar houses a pivot pin—a ¾-in. No. 6 screw sharpened to a fine point. The dovetail-shaped pivot bar slides in a matching slot and is locked in place by a lock-cam mechanism. Slide the pivot bar until the distance between the pivot pin and saw blade is equal to the circle's radius, then push down on the lock-cam handle to lock the pivot bar in place.

The jig has an adjustable stop cam at the end of the hardwood strip that's used to align the pivot pin precisely with the teeth of the saw blade—regardless of its width. Slide the jig forward until the blade teeth and pivot pin align, then tighten the wingnut to secure the cam.

To make a circular cut, first slide back the jig and place the workpiece on the pivot pin. Next, turn on the saw and slide the jig forward into the blade until it comes to a stop. Then, rotate the workpiece slowly a full revolution *(right, bottom)*.

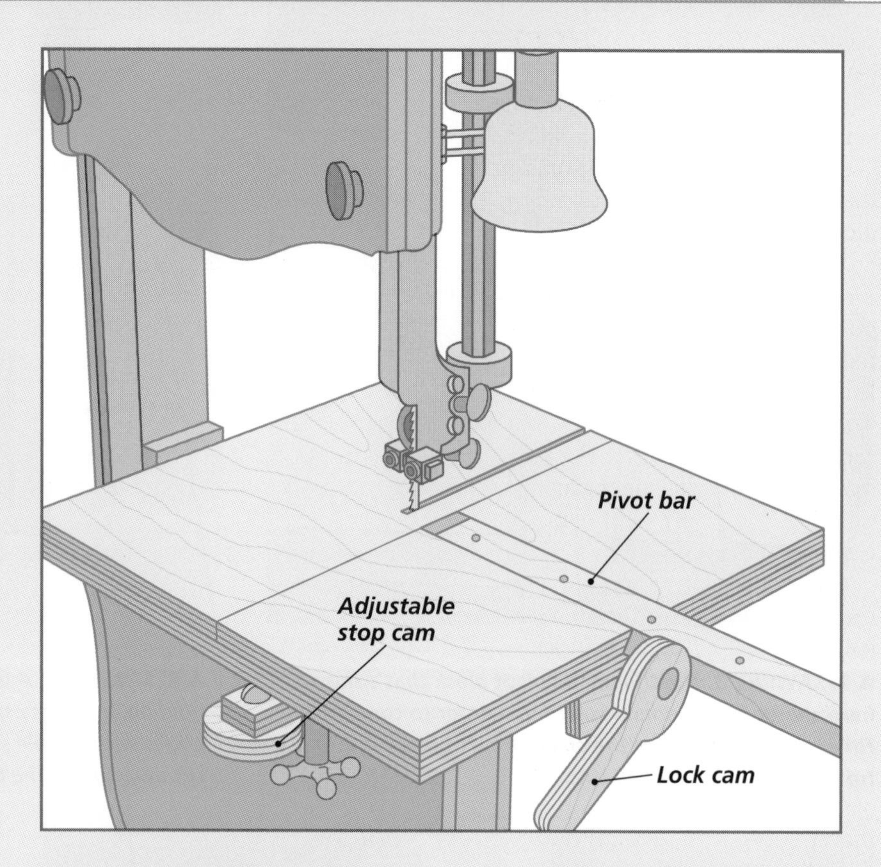

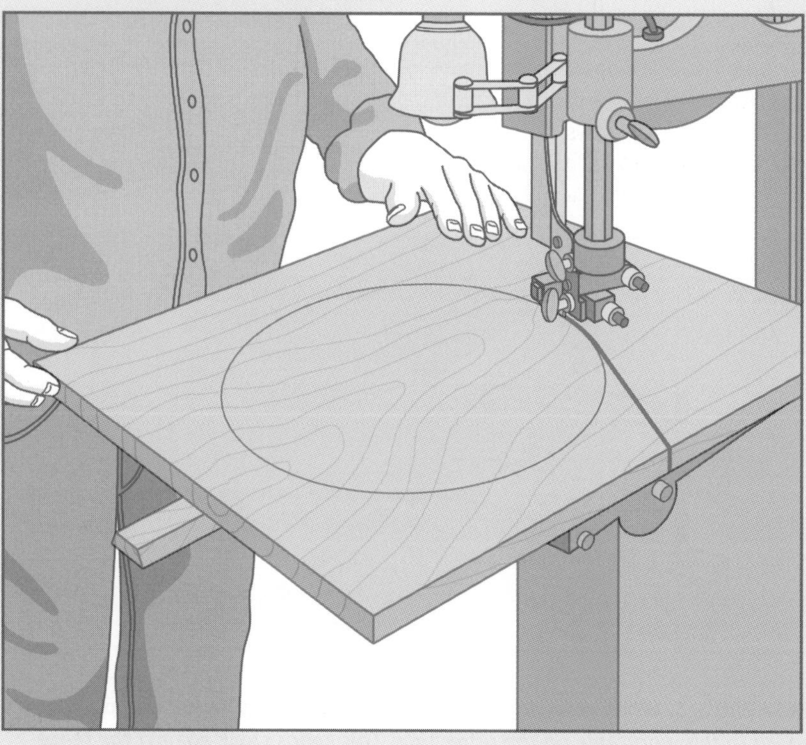

make freehand, but for really straight, accurate cuts, it's best to use a miter gauge or rip fence.

The miter gauge slides in a slot that is milled in the top of the worktable. Use a carpenter's square to ensure that the miter gauge is positioned perpendicular to the blade. Place the work flush against the miter gauge and align the cutting line with the blade. Then, push the miter gauge and the work together toward the blade with your left hand, keeping the work flat on the worktable and flush against the miter gauge with your right hand. Hook your right thumb over the miter gauge in a way that keeps your right hand well clear of the blade's path.

Follow the same procedure to use the miter gauge for performing miter cuts. Most miter gauges can be adjusted to an angle of 60° left and right. Use a sliding T-bevel to set the miter gauge at the angle desired. To ensure proper results, make a test cut first in a piece of scrap stock, then check the angle of the cut edge and make adjustments to the miter gauge as required.

Also use the miter gauge to make bevel cuts. For these operations, simply tilt the worktable to the desired angle. On most band saws, the worktable can be set up to 45° to the right and up to 10° or 15° to the left.

When using the rip fence as a guide for crosscuts, position it for the length of the cut. Then, simply butt the end of the work against the rip fence and feed it into the blade. Use both hands to feed the work steadily, keeping them well out of the way of the blade. For greatest control, straddle the rip fence with the fingers of your left hand and brace the face of the work with your right hand.

RIP CUTTING

Accurate rip cuts are possible to do with the aid of a rip fence. Much like the rip fence found on a table saw, the band saw's rip fence can be positioned anywhere on the worktable and then locked in place. If your band saw isn't equipped with a rip fence, a straight-edged board clamped securely to the worktable works just as well.

Because the blades of a band saw have a tendency to veer off a straight cutting line with the grain, making precise rip cuts requires compensating for this "lead." Although the problem is typically less pronounced with wide blades, some blade lead is virtually unavoidable. Fortunately, the lead of a particular blade is usually fairly

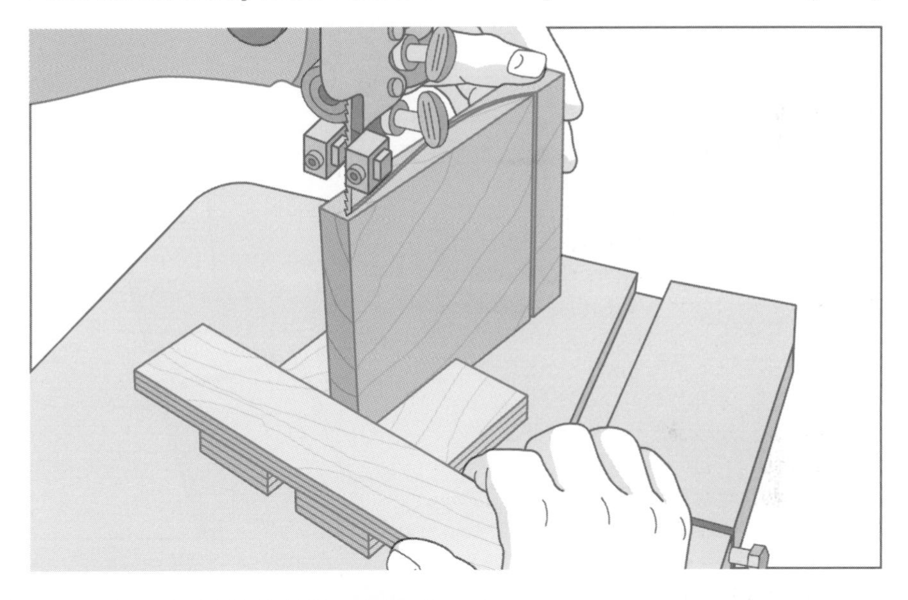

▲ **USING JIGS AND TEMPLATES, 1.** ***The simple wrap-around pushblock shown here ensures safety when executing tricky cuts. Make the block out of three pieces of ½-in. plywood.***

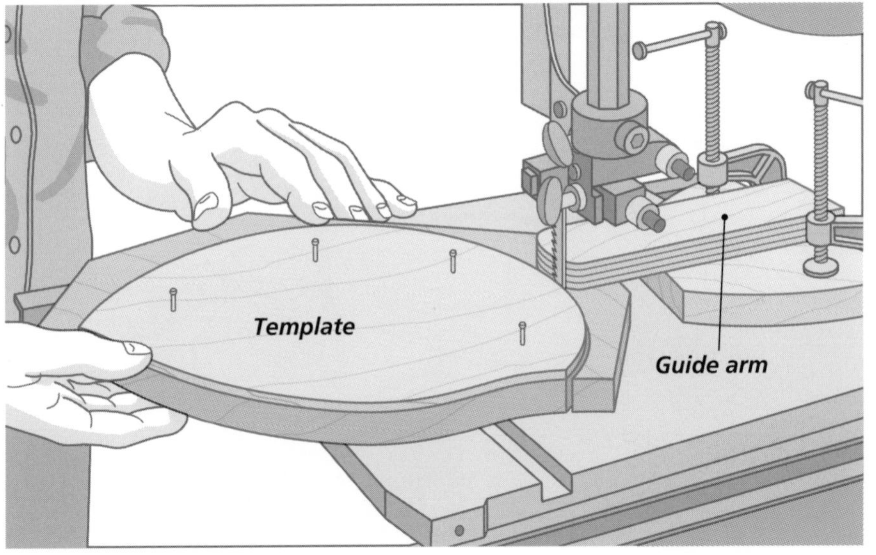

◀ **USING JIGS AND TEMPLATES, 2.** ***Try template-cutting to get large, identical pieces. Tack-nail the template onto the stock, and guide the template against a guide arm that's clamped securely to the worktable.***

constant and predictable, so it's easy to compensate for it. Simply adjust the position of the rip fence on the worktable for the blade being used.

To determine the adjustment needed for a blade, mark a cutting line on a board parallel to its edge, then cut about halfway along the cutting line freehand. To keep the blade tracking along the cutting line, you will have to angle the board slightly—the result of the blade's lead. Mark a line on the worktable along the edge of the board, then align the rip fence parallel to the marked line whenever you're using this blade. To simplify the routine of compensating for blade lead, repeat this procedure for each blade that you have on hand in your workshop.

Whenever you're making rip cuts on short or narrow work, be sure to use wood pushsticks to keep your fingers well clear of the blade. To perform angled rip cuts or compound miters, tilt the worktable to the desired angle. When cutting bevels, position the rip fence to the right of the blade so the work is downhill from the blade. This makes for a safer cutting operation, helping to prevent the work—and your hands—from accidentally sliding into the path of the blade.

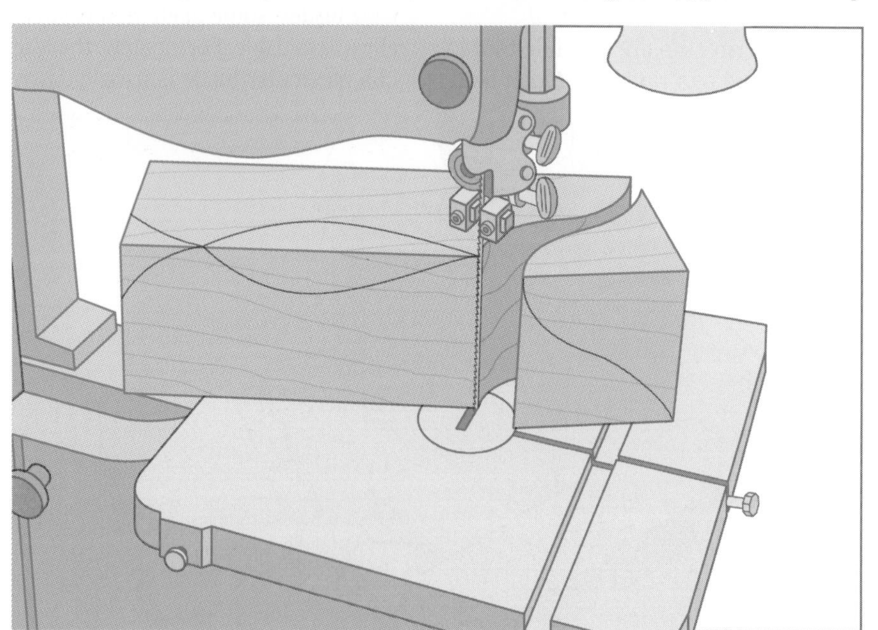

▲ **COMPOUND SAWING, 1.** ***Complex work often involves compound sawing. Mark the profiles on two adjacent surfaces of the stock, then make the first series of cuts.***

RESAWING

A band saw, by virtue of its thin blade and excellent cutting capacity, is an ideal tool for resawing—the term used for edge-ripping a board to reduce its thickness or create two usable boards out of one. The procedure can be done on a table saw if the stock is not wider than twice the depth-cutting capacity of the blade. But if the stock is wider, the operation can be performed easily on a band saw—as long as you use the right blade and a suitable guide.

For best results, use as wide a blade as possible. This is especially important when you're resawing wide stock. An appropriate blade for resawing in most instances is ½ to ¾ in. wide, with coarse teeth (three or four per in.) and good set. When such a blade is performing well, you can often resaw a board working with only an ordinary fence as a guide.

However, because of the problem of blade lead, resawing most typically

▶ **COMPOUND SAWING, 2.** ***Now, tack-nail the first cutoff parts back onto the workpiece. Rotate the work and make the next series of cuts on the adjacent face.***

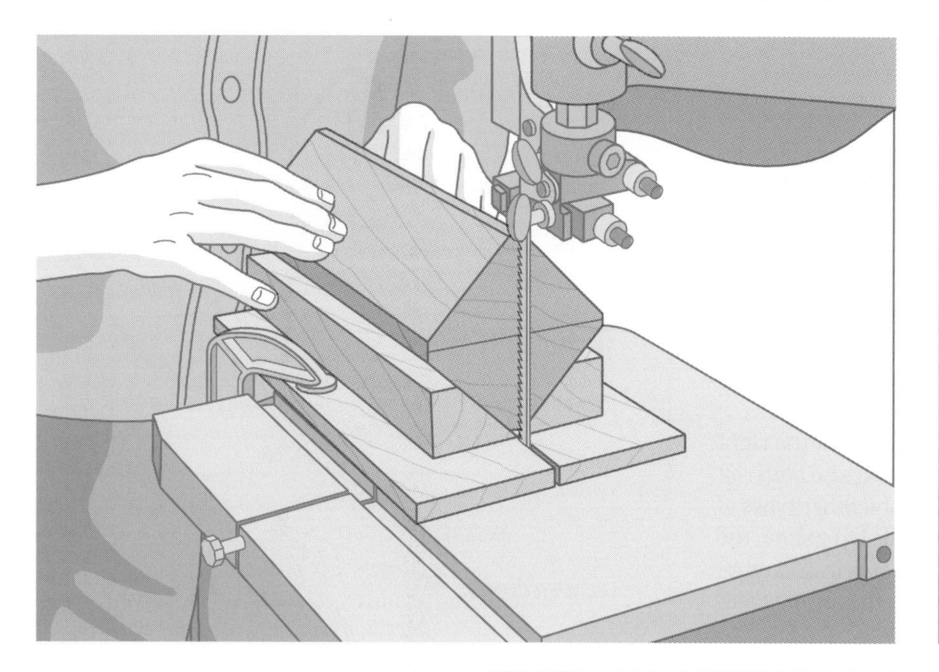

◀ **SHAPING BLANKS FOR TURNING, 1.** ***Use a V-shaped cradle to cut centering kerfs into the ends of turning blanks. Clamp the cradle securely to the saw's worktable and advance the blank into the blade.***

▼ **SHAPING BLANKS FOR TURNING, 2.** ***Tilt the saw's worktable at a 45° angle and use the rip fence to cut the corners off the blank. The octagon-shaped blank is now ready for turning on a lathe.***

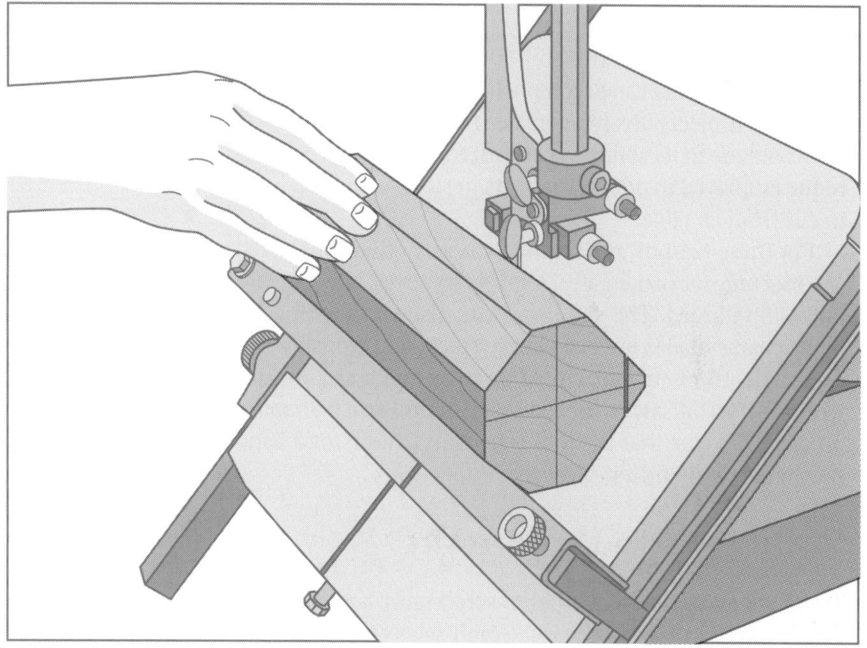

requires the use of other devices to help guide the work and keep the blade tracking along the cutting line. One of these is a simple pivot block that can be made out of a 5½-in.-long 2 x 6 set on its edge, its support end rounded into a nose and its other end cut to provide a suitable clamping surface. Clamp the pivot block to the worktable at the desired distance from the blade, then feed the work into the blade while guiding it against the pivot block. The pivot block works especially well when blade lead is excessive since it acts like a fulcrum, leaving both ends of the work free to swing in either direction.

When you're resawing a very long board and blade lead is minimal, you can be assured of cutting accuracy and safety by working with a pair of spring-board fences. Make each spring-board fence out of two pieces of ¾-in. x 4-in. stock cut to a length of 14 in. Bore ¾-in.-dia. holes through one piece 3 in. and 5 in. from each end about 1¼ in. from opposite edges, then rip a 3-in.- and 9-in.-long kerf from each end to the holes. Glue and screw the second piece to the first. Clamped into place on each side of the worktable, the two spring-board fences serve to direct the board and keep it aligned, but won't pinch the blade because of the spring action created by the holes and kerfs cut in the base pieces.

For general-purpose resawing operations, a utility fence is one of the best devices to use as a guide. To make a utility fence, cut a 7-in.-long piece of 2 x 4 and round the edges of its support face, then glue and nail it lengthwise to the edge (at the outfeed end) of a 4½-in. x 13-in. piece of ¾-in. plywood. Be sure to set the heads of the nails so that they don't interfere with the work. Because of its rigid base, the utility fence provides a stable surface to push the work against. And if the blade leads somewhat, the vertical support block of the utility fence is short enough to allow some steering of the work. When used in combination with a featherboard, the utility fence also works well for resawing very long boards.

SCROLL SAWS

The scroll saw, which is also popularly known as a jigsaw, is generally thought of as a tool that's used for freehand cutting of intricate shapes in thin stock. However, while the scroll saw can handle these particular tasks with ease, a rugged, heavy-duty type of machine will do a great deal more. Once you have mastered basic scroll-sawing techniques and discovered some of the simple jigs that you can make, you'll discover that the scroll saw is a versatile tool with great potential.

With the correct blade installed and running at the right speed, the scroll saw can cut not only wood, but also both soft and hard metals, plastics, leather, rubber and other types of non-wood materials. Relatively easy and safe to operate, the scroll saw has unfairly earned a reputation of being no more than an introductory tool for beginners to the art of woodworking with stationary machines.

The scroll saw can operate using extremely fine blades—some of them so narrow that they can virtually turn on their own radius. Because of this ability, the scroll saw is the only workshop tool that can accomplish the delicate cutting necessary for projects involving inlays. Furthermore, the scroll saw is unique in its ability to perform true piercing, the technique employed to do internal cuts in stock without a lead-in cut from an edge.

For these reasons, the scroll saw is very often considered as a tool only for handicrafts. Such perspectives, however, are not well founded. The scroll saw can also work with relatively coarse blades on fairly heavy stock, and typically features a depth-of-cut capacity of up to as much as 2 in. But while the scroll saw is capable of handling small shaping projects, it's true that the tool is no competition for a band saw in terms of cutting speed.

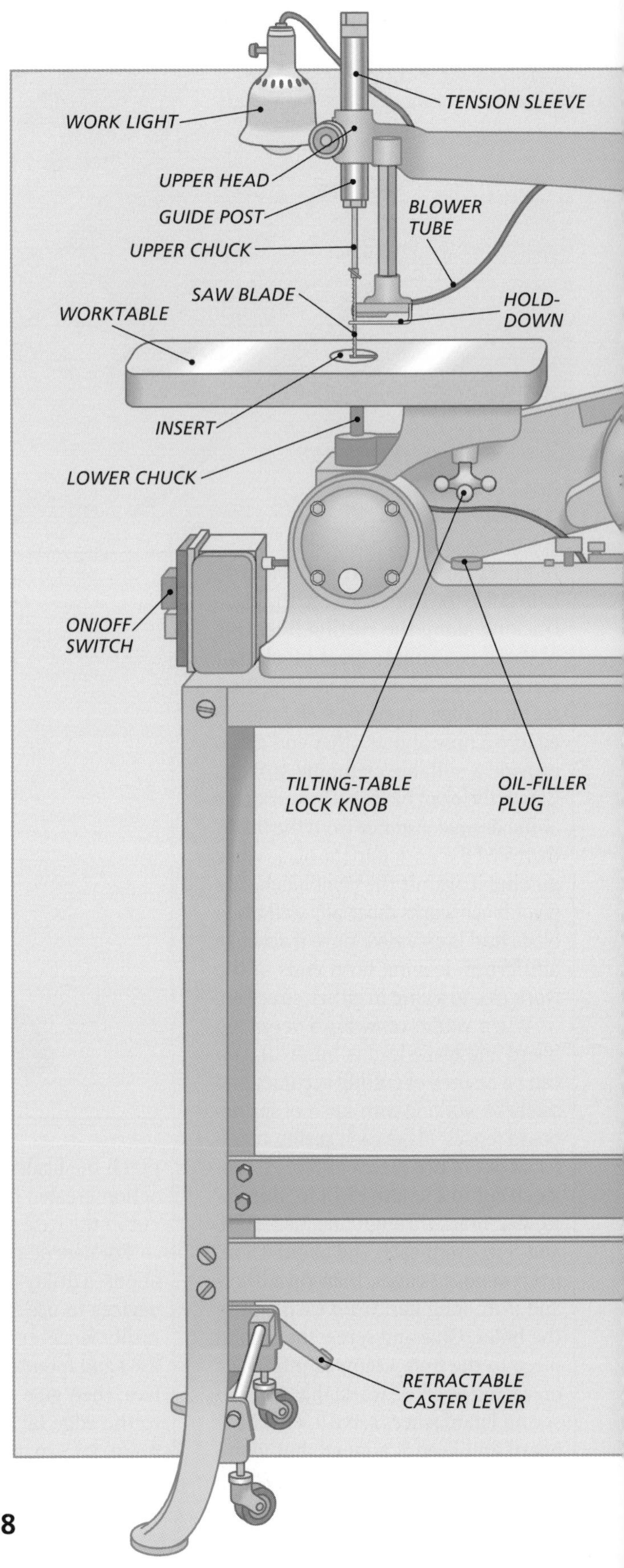

SCROLL SAW SPECIFICS

There are many different types of scroll saws, and a considerable range in size and price. Scroll saws are designated according to their throat capacity—the distance from the blade to the overarm or support for the upper structure. For instance, an 18-in. scroll saw is capable of cutting to the center of a 36-in.-dia. circle. Depth of cut for the scroll saw is calculated in terms of the maximum thickness of stock the tool can handle—which averages about 2 in.

However, many scroll saws are designed so that the overarm or support for the upper structure can either swing down or be removed. This feature eliminates the restrictions on capacity that are imposed by components above the worktable, and permits the cutting of oversized stock. When operated in this mode, the scroll saw enjoys virtually unlimited capacity through the use of a technique known as sabre sawing—whereby a short, heavy-gauge blade is employed in only the lower chuck.

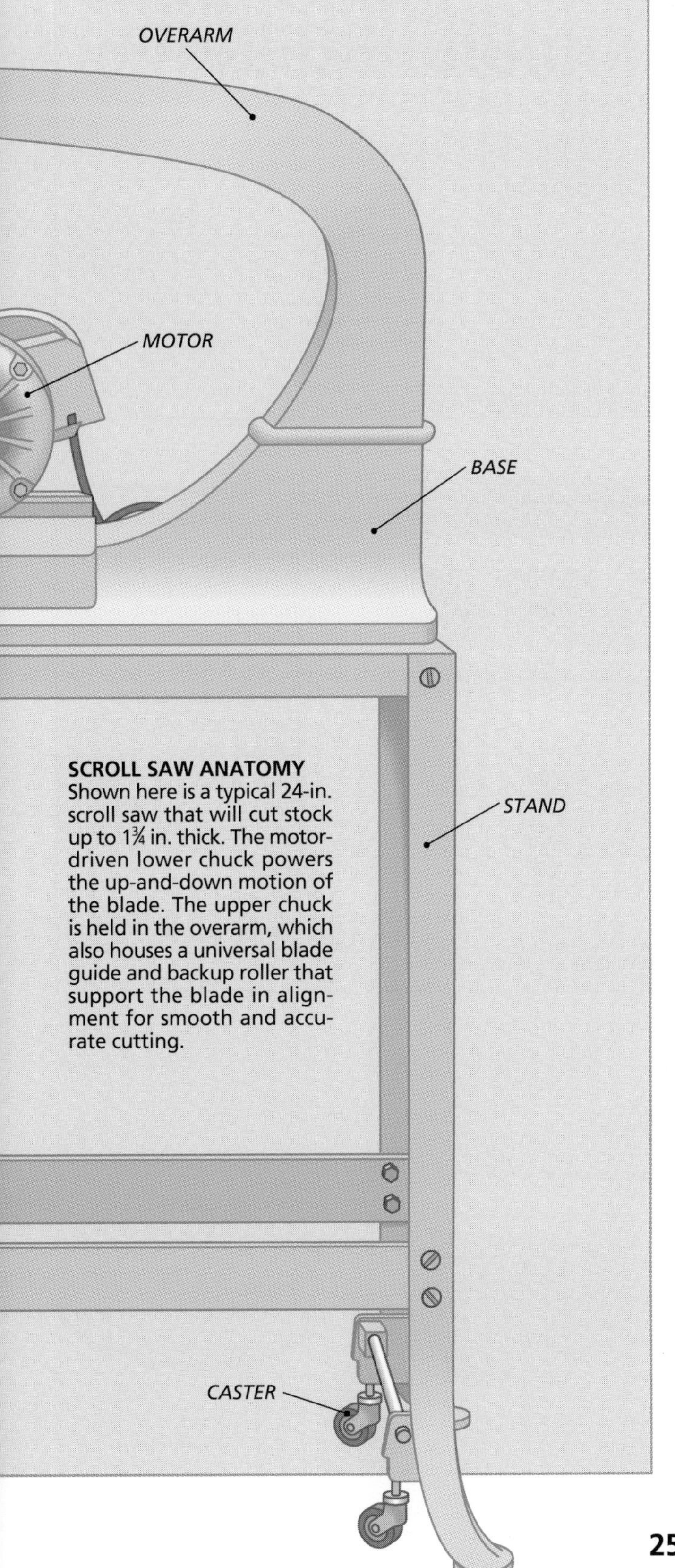

SCROLL SAW ANATOMY
Shown here is a typical 24-in. scroll saw that will cut stock up to 1¾ in. thick. The motor-driven lower chuck powers the up-and-down motion of the blade. The upper chuck is held in the overarm, which also houses a universal blade guide and backup roller that support the blade in alignment for smooth and accurate cutting.

SCROLL SAW MECHANICS

The scroll saw operates using a short, straight blade that is gripped at each end in a chuck. The overarm encases the upper chuck, and also supports a universal blade guide and backup roller that rigidly support the blade in proper alignment for smooth and accurate cutting. Typically, there's an adjustable spring hold-down that provides added accuracy and ease of operation by holding the stock firmly on the worktable—even during bevel cutting operations—and prevents the work from lifting with the upstroke of the blade.

The saw's lower casting houses a crankshaft or other mechanism that converts circular motion provided by the motor into an up-and-down motion that drives the lower blade chuck. A bearing-type crankshaft is splash-lubricated to assure smooth performance.

Scroll saws are usually available with a four-speed pulley arrangement or with a variable-speed drive. Models that have a variable-speed drive feature a control handle that is turned to set the desired cutting speed—typically from 650 to 1,700 or more cutting strokes per minute (spm).

On many scroll saws, the blade chucks can rotate 90° to permit the cutting of long stock by feeding from the side—and avoiding interference with the overarm. Quality saws feature a worktable that tilts 45° right and 15° left for routine bevel cutting. When the worktable is rotated 90°, bevels up to 45° on stock of unlimited length can be performed.

TYPES OF BLADES

Blades for the scroll saw come in a variety of widths, thicknesses and points or number of teeth per inch (tpi). The speed and smoothness of the cut as well as the minimum turning radius that can be cut relate directly to these factors. The finer the blade used, the smoother and slower the cut that can be achieved. Working with a finer blade also permits the cutting of a tighter radius. Blades range in tpi from 7 to 32. Blade thicknesses run from .008 to .028 in. and widths vary from .35 to .250 in.

Although many types and sizes of blades are available, there are only two principal blade categories: jeweler's blades and sabre blades. So-called jeweler's blades feature blank ends and are designed to be gripped in both upper and lower chucks. Sabre blades are blank on the lower end and designed to be held in only the lower chuck.

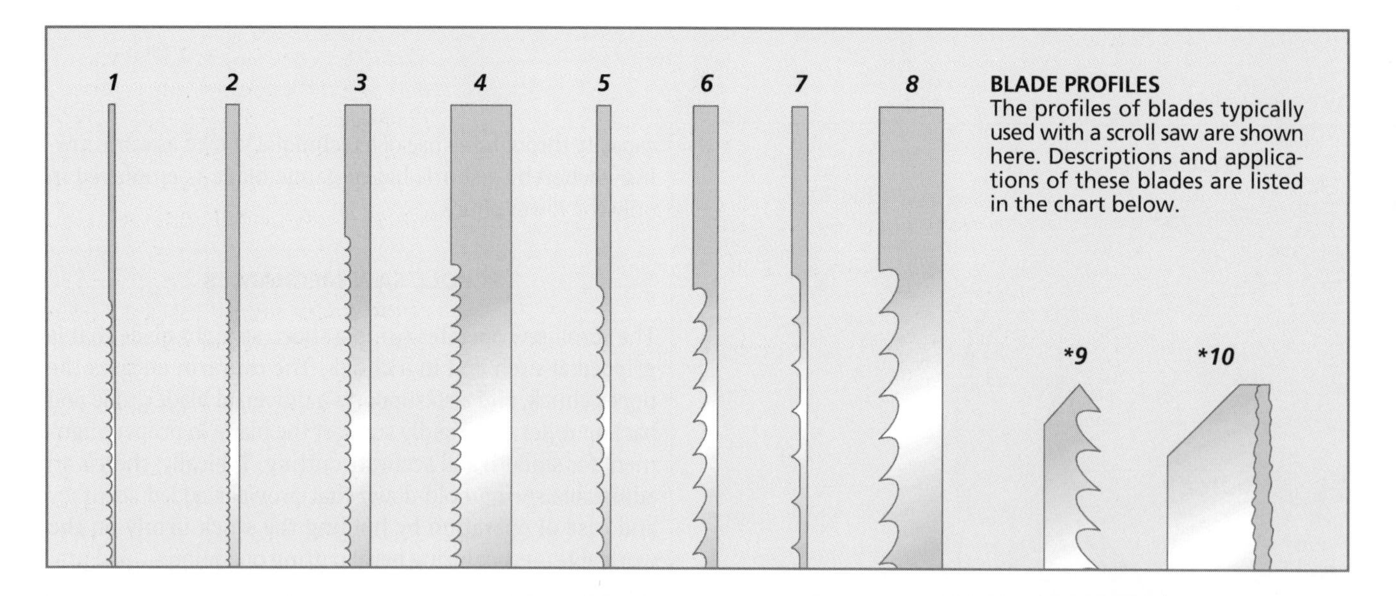

BLADE PROFILES
The profiles of blades typically used with a scroll saw are shown here. Descriptions and applications of these blades are listed in the chart below.

Sabre blades are frequently used with the saw's overarm removed or otherwise out of the way to facilitate the sawing of oversized work. They also save time by eliminating the need for blade removal and installation when pierced cuts are being made. Since the blades are supported only by an auxiliary guide directly below the saw's worktable, they are designed with a heavy cross section. Sabre blades are usually available in two sizes: .025 in. thick, .187 in. wide, 9 tpi; and .035 in. thick, .025 in. wide, 7 tpi.

There's a bit of overlap in the blade categories since some of the jeweler's blades are heavy enough to be used as sabre blades. As a general rule, turn to heavier blades as the thickness of the stock you're working with increases. Select the widest and fastest blade possible for the cutting operation you're performing. Work with a sabre blade or heavy jeweler's blade as the stock approaches a thickness equal to the saw's maximum depth-of-cut capaci-

BLADE DESCRIPTIONS AND APPLICATIONS

NO.	THICKNESS (IN.)	WIDTH (IN.)	TEETH PER IN.	MATERIALS TO BE CUT
1	.008	.035	20	Wood, plastics, hard rubber, ivory
2	.020	.070	32	Metals, asbestos
3	.020	.110	20	Wood, metals, asbestos
4	.28	.250	20	Metals, paper, felt, asbestos, mica
5	.020	.070	15	Wood, metals
6	.020	.110	10	Wood
7	.020	.070	7	Plastics
8	.028	.250	7	Wood
*9	.035	.187	7	Wood
*10	Grit edge	—	—	Problem materials

*Nos. 9 and 10 are regular sabre saw blades

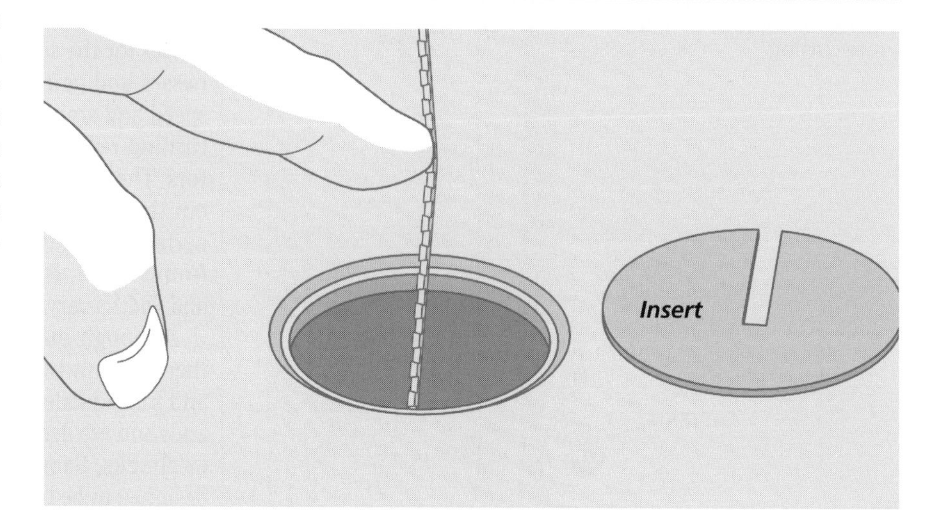

▶ **SCROLL SAW SETUP, 1.** ***A mounted blade must be tensioned so it's sufficiently rigid and straight. To do this, pull up on the blade's tension sleeve and lock it in place. The flexed blade here exhibits a lack of tension, which will cause drifting and erratic cutting.***

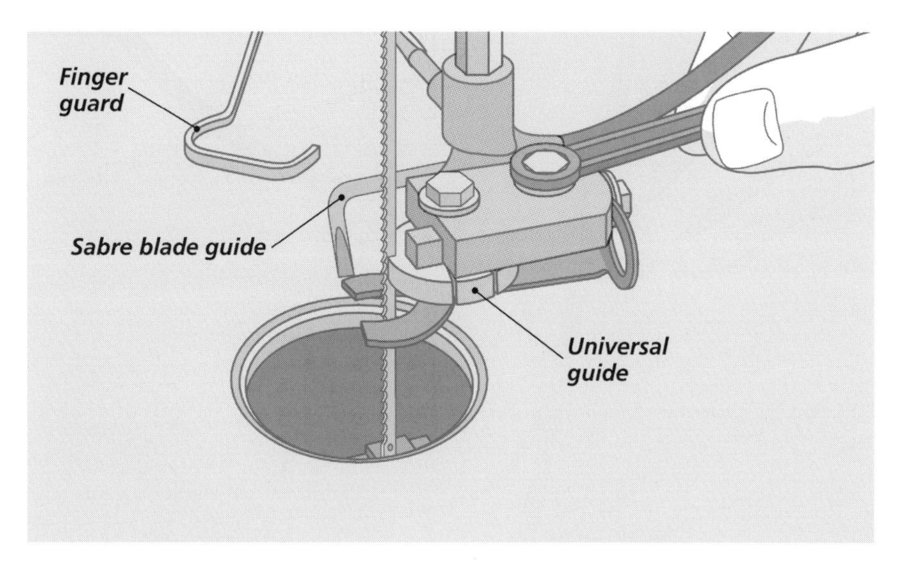

◀ **SCROLL SAW SETUP, 2.** ***Shown here is a closeup view of the blade guide assembly. A slot in the universal guide that fits around the blade has been selected and is being locked into place so the teeth just clear it.***

▶ **SCROLL SAW SETUP, 3.** ***To test the worktable for true zero, a cut was made through a scrap block, then one of the pieces flipped over and the cut edges butted together. The poor fit of pieces at right shows the table is not square to the blade.***

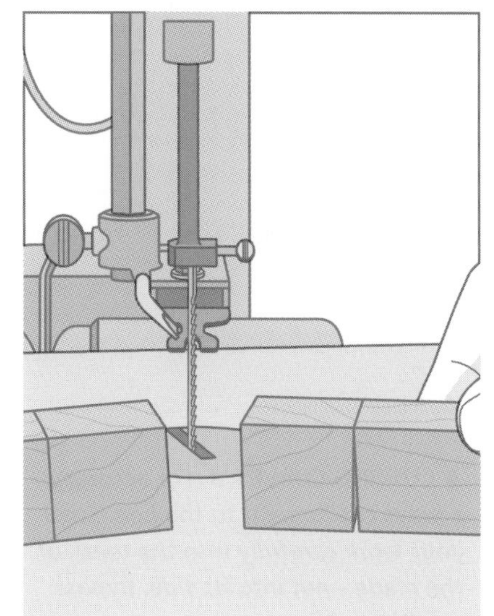

▼ **SCROLL SAW SETUP, 4.** ***Here, the saw's worktable has been removed to show the sabre blade guide in place. Note that in order to utilize this guide, the chuck housing must be rotated 90°.***

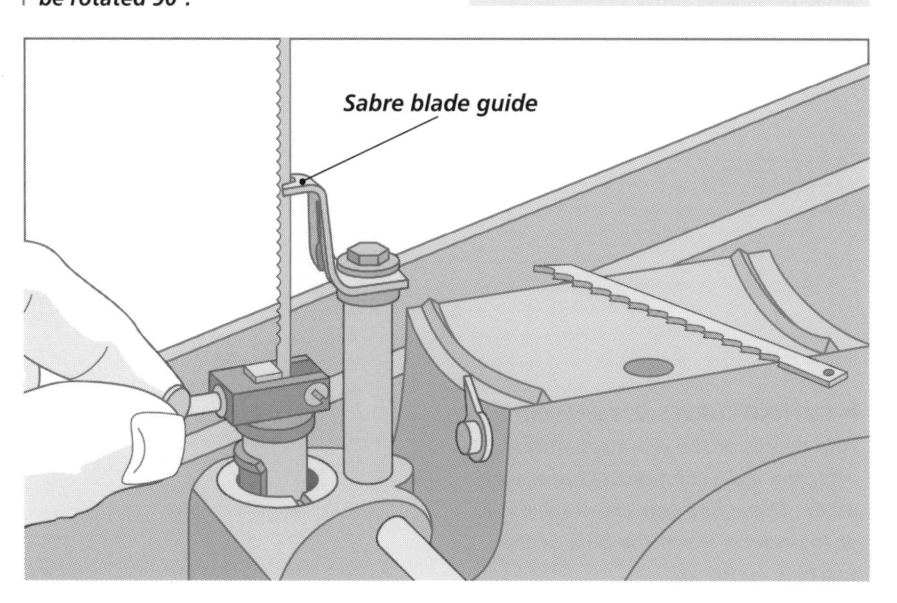

ty—and, of course, whenever the size of the stock requires the saw's overarm to be removed or otherwise out of the way.

Conventional sabre saw blades also can be used in a scroll saw. Of particular value for cutting problem materials is the grit-edge blade. Instead of conventional teeth, this blade features a cutting edge made of hundreds of super-hard tungsten-carbide particles.

As well, it's often possible to work with still-sharp sections of discarded band saw or hacksaw blades. Carefully cut off or "snap" the old blades to a length that's suitable for the scroll saw. When the width of the blades doesn't permit them to be mounted in the saw, simply grind down their ends to the chuck size.

BLADE CARE

Proper maintenance and care of your blades is as important to the performance of your scroll saw as choosing the right blade for the cutting operation at hand. No amount of scroll-sawing technique can compensate for a blade that's in poor condition.

Keep your blades sharpened, bearing in mind that there are more accidents caused by dull blades than by sharp ones. Replace blades that have chipped or cracked teeth.

Protect your blades when they are not in use by hanging them individually on hooks or setting them apart between sleeves of cardboard. Don't store blades loose in a pile.

Clean your blades of sticky resin and pitch that can interfere with their ability to perform smoothly by soaking them in turpentine or kerosene and scrubbing them with steel wool.

▼ THIN-SLICING HEAVY STOCK. ***Here's an example of the heavy yet delicate cutting that can be done with a properly functioning scroll saw. This view is of a slice that's only about 1/32 in. thick.***

Apply spray-on oven cleaner to dissolve stubborn deposits on blades.

CHANGING BLADES

While the chucks of scroll saws differ in design, they share a common purpose: to hold the saw's blade taut in position between them. Make sure that you unplug the power cord of the saw before changing or adjusting the blade. Consult the owner's manual supplied with your saw for specific information on the amount of adjustment in the chucks and the method for achieving blade alignment.

Typically, the saw is equipped with sets of chuck blocks. A setscrew on one side of a chuck allows you to position one of the blocks more or less permanently for most standard cutting. A setscrew on the other side of the chuck adjusts the second block so that the

▲ CUTTING CURVES, 1. ***For accuracy, always cut tangent to the line. Steer your work carefully into the teeth of the blade—not into its side. Bypass small details, as shown here, to cut gentle, sweeping curves first.***

► CUTTING CURVES, 2. ***Tackle intricate details of the work separately, after the main curved cuts have been made. These fine cuts are much easier to perform when the bulk of the waste is removed.***

blade is gripped securely. With some designs, the chuck has one block that is fixed in a constant position.

The important point about mounting a blade is that it must be installed so it can "jig" in a true vertical path throughout its travel during a cutting stroke. This means the blade has to be vertical when viewed from both the side and the front. When the blade's side-to-side alignment is set by the chuck blocks, front-to-back alignment can be achieved by simply mounting the blade so it abuts the back of the upper and lower chuck housings.

Here is a simple shopmade guide that helps to set a blade vertically when it's installed. To make the guide, carefully cut a straight kerf along the center of one edge of a squared block of wood—a 4-in. length of 1 x 4 will do. By situating the blade in the guide's kerf as you tighten the chucks, you can help ensure proper alignment.

Once mounted in position in the chucks, the blade must be tensioned to hold sufficiently rigid and straight. To apply tension to the blade, pull up on the tension sleeve and lock it in place. While some "armchair" craftsmen may feel otherwise, the only foolproof way to check the tension of the blade is experience. However, plucking the blade with your finger will put you on the right track. A blade that is easily deflected indicates too little tension, which will cause the blade to drift in the cut. Too much tension on fine blades will cause them to break easily.

As a general rule, apply the least amount of tension to the blade that will get the job done. Although the correct tensioning of the blade is a matter of subjective judgment, you can be easily guided by signs of poor adjustment: off-vertical movement of the blade, difficulty in following a cutting line, premature breaking of blades and cuts that are not square.

The next adjustment involves the blade guide—typically a universal type that features a disc with slots of varying widths around its rim. Select a slot that will fit around the blade and lock the guide into place. The slot should be neither too tight nor too loose, and the blade's teeth should just clear the

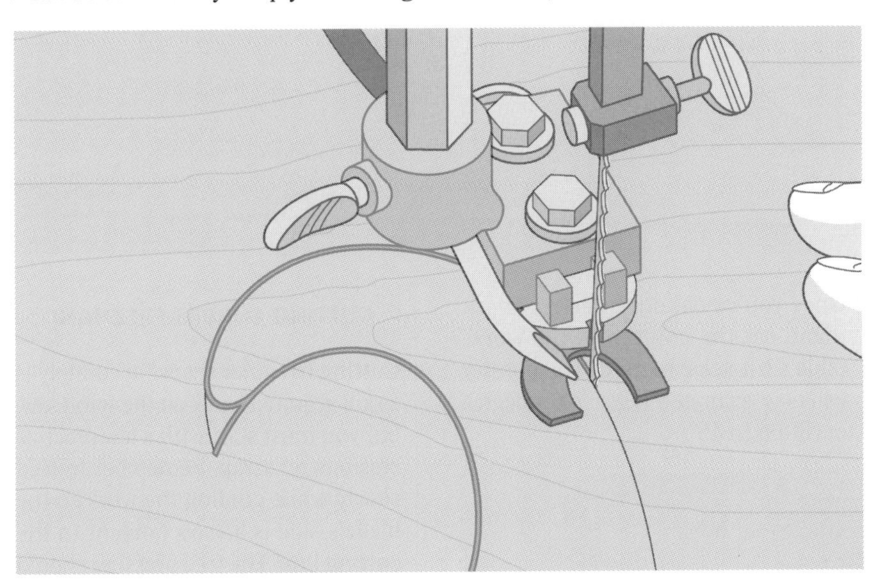

▲ **CUTTING CURVES, 3.** ***Cut right into an acute corner, then backtrack a bit and bypass it to continue the main cut. After the bulk of the waste has been removed, a short second cut is all that's needed to clean out the remaining wedge at the corner.***

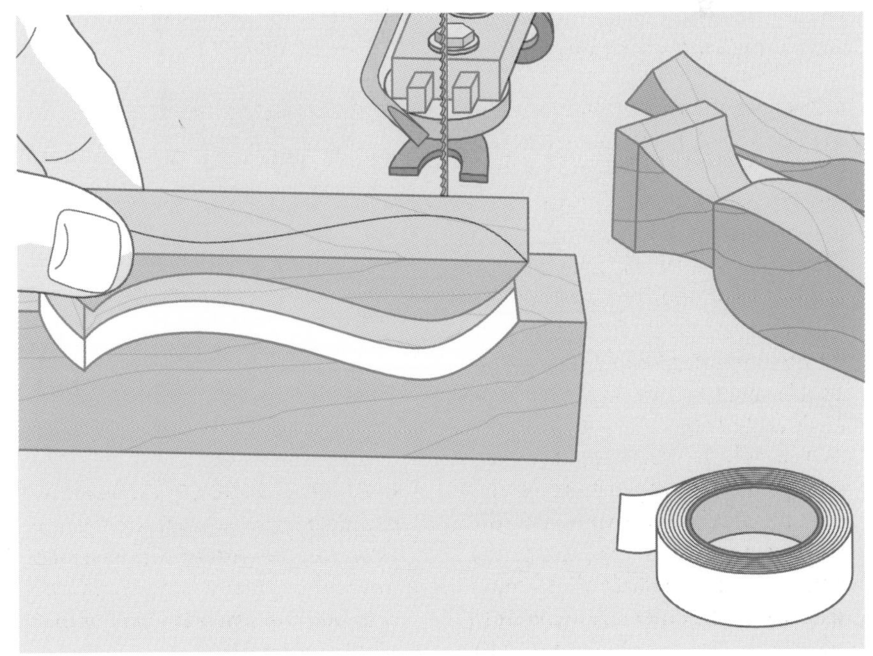

▶ **MAKING COMPOUND CUTS.** ***For compound cuts, reposition the cutoffs from the first pass back onto the workpiece and tape them securely in place. This provides a true surface on the workpiece for marking the additional cuts.***

slot, with the roller lightly touching the back of the blade.

Some blade guides are designed as a split sleeve housed in a tube. With these guides, the blade sits in the slot of the sleeve and the tube performs the job of the roller. Special blade guides are also available for use when cutting lines must be followed extremely closely. Whatever the type of blade guide, be sure that the blade can move easily and that it is not pushed forward. The purpose of the blade guide is to support the blade *during* the cut.

At the start of each project that you undertake, check the worktable for squareness in relation to the blade. Use a square to sight along the blade for the initial setup, then test-cut a scrap block. Flip one of the cut pieces upside down and butt the cut edges together. If the worktable is in true alignment, the cut edges will mate perfectly. A non-parallel joint will indicate the need for adjustment.

If an adjustment is required, make it to the worktable and not to the blade. Once you've obtained perfect alignment, set the pointer on the worktable's tilt scale to zero. The pointer will now accurately register any degree of tilt up to 45°.

▼ CUTTING INLAY STRINGS. ***Using a single blade to make intricate cuts for inlay strings would prove to be very frustrating. But two spaced blades, as shown here, can be used quite effectively to do the job. The spacer strips employed were cut from ice-cream sticks.***

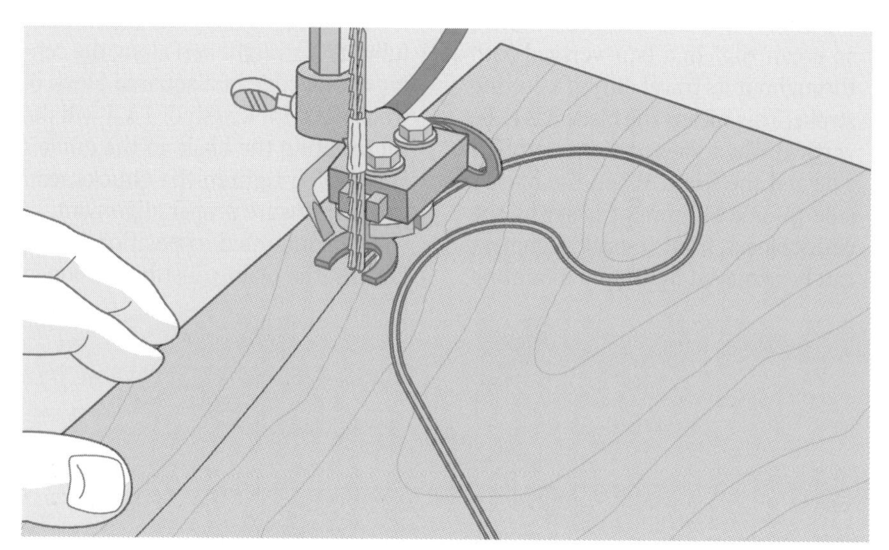

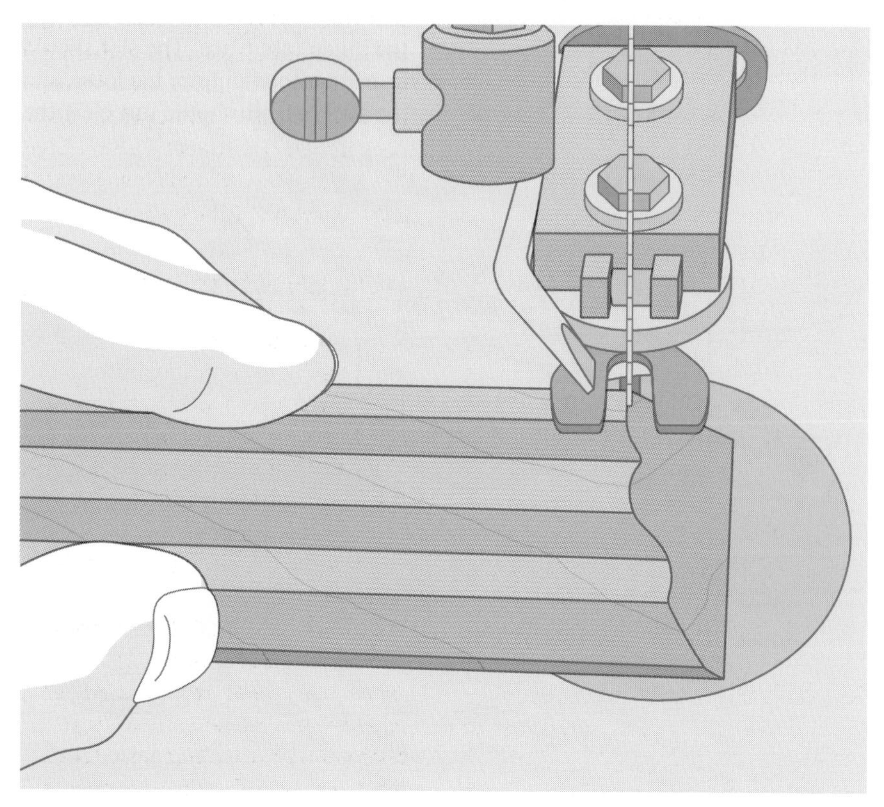

CUTTING CURVES FREEHAND

Cutting irregular shapes accurately is a skill acquired easily on the scroll saw, but you must start with a few practice sessions on scrap. Remember to feed slowly while guiding the work so the blade's side is always tangent to the cutting line. The feed pressure should always be directed forward and into

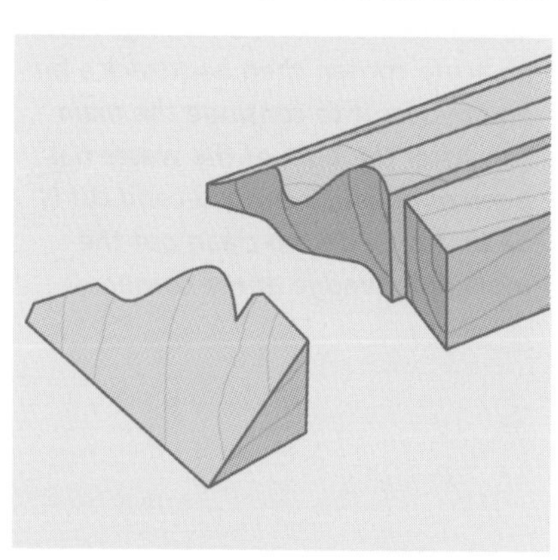

◄ CUTTING MOLDING JOINTS. ***For a coped molding joint, first make a 45° miter cut across the molding to reveal the outline. Then, follow the molding's outline with the scroll saw. Shown above is the completed cut.***

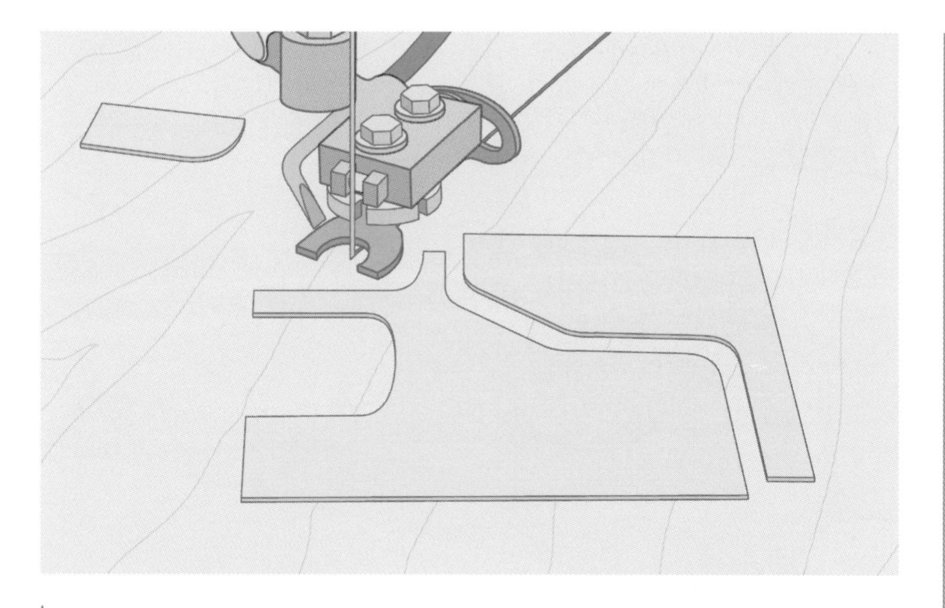

▲ **METALCUTTING.** ***A hardboard backing with a fine saw kerf that's positioned on the worktable provides zero clearance around the blade. This simple procedure is an effective way to improve cuts in very thin sheet metal.***

the blade's teeth, never into the side of the blade.

When a curved cutting line includes intricate details such as tight turns, the best results are generally achieved by making a continuous pass to cut the large, sweeping curves first, bypassing the tight spots. When the large pieces of waste have been removed, the smaller cuts can be tackled separately very easily.

When you must execute a very tight curve, keep the work advancing just fast enough so the blade is cutting into the material continuously. Don't stop advancing the work while turning it—or the blade is very likely to twist and possibly break.

Acute inside corners are rarely cut in a single, continuous pass. Instead, these cutting operations are accomplished by two passes in what is a quite simple procedure. An initial pass is made directly into the corner, then the blade is backtracked to permit rerouting it to the cutting line beyond the corner and the cut is continued. When the bulk of the waste has been cut off and removed, return to the corner to make the final cut and clean out the remaining waste.

FREEHAND STRAIGHT CUTS

Straight freehand cutting on the scroll saw is best done using a wide blade. However, when right-angled inside or outside corners are involved, such a blade will not permit you to make the turn in a small radius.

To obtain a sharp outside corner, you need only make a reverse loop off the end of the line for one side of the corner into the waste area, then lead directly into the end of the line for the other side of the corner. This cloverleaf cut leaves two straight outside edges that meet at exactly the angle desired.

For a tight inside corner, make a wide turn off one line into the waste before you reach the corner, then pick up on the other line beyond the corner to continue the pass. Return to the corner after the bulk of the waste has been removed and make two straight cuts to clean out the corner.

MAKING INTERNAL CUTS

A main feature of the scroll saw is its ability to perform internal cuts—cuts that start and end within the material—without a lead-in cut from the outside edge. For this piercing technique, the blade is inserted through a prebored hole in the waste and then tightened in the chuck. Standard cutting

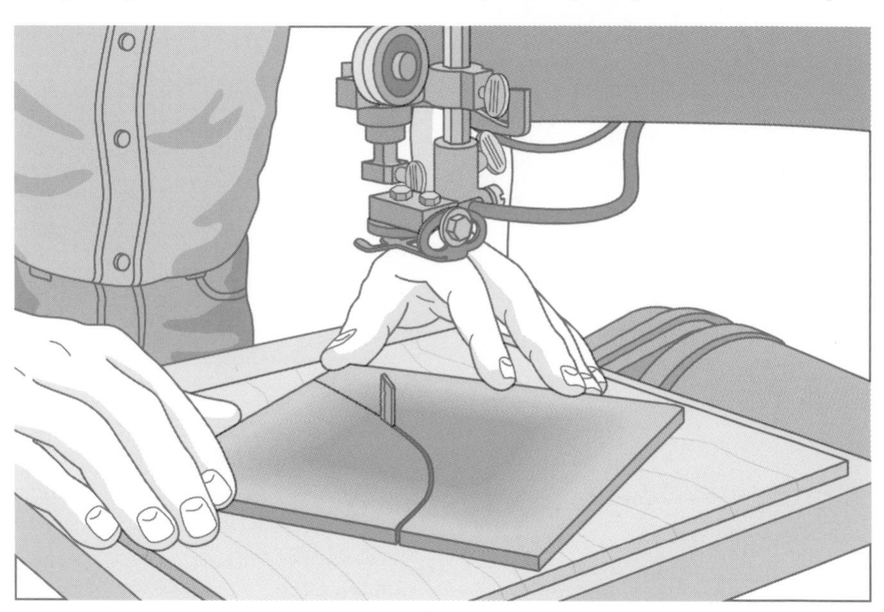

◀ **CUTTING CERAMIC.** ***Even glazed ceramic tile can be easily cut into any shape using a tungsten-carbide grit-edge sabre blade. A piece of hardboard on the worktable under the tile protects surfaces from scratches.***

procedures apply to internal cuts, but the blade must be reinstalled for each cutout being made.

Often a hole or holes can be dimensioned and positioned in the waste so that they form part of the cutout pattern, thereby eliminating some curve cutting. However, when a hole serves only to provide entry for the blade, it should be located away from the cutting line. This will enable you to see the path that the blade takes and permits steering, or tracking, the work close to the cutting line.

MAKING COPED CUTS

A coped molding joint is one in which the second piece in an inside corner is cut with a matching profile to abut the first tightly. The first step is to cut a straight 45° miter on the end of the second piece. This reveals the cross-sectional contour on the face of the molding. Then, make a straight 90° cut following the shape along the top edge of the molding.

CUTTING COMPOUND ANGLES

Compound-angle cuts can be made on the scroll saw, provided the thickness of the stock is not greater than the saw's capacity. Just be careful to preserve the waste from the preceding cut and tape it back into its original position before going on with the next cut.

Draw the outline on the first face, or plane, of your workpiece, then make the cut. When taping the waste back onto the workpiece, make certain that the tape is secure and lies perfectly flat. Note that masking tape has a tendency to catch on the worktable. Next, draw the outline on the second plane of your workpiece and make the cut. Repeat the procedure, if necessary.

ANGLE SAWING

The scroll saw provides a novel method for making raised letters, or for build-

▲ **SCROLL-CUT LETTERS, 1.** ***For the cutting technique that's shown here, the saw's worktable was adjusted to a 3½° tilt. Small-diameter entry holes for the blade were made in an inconspicuous place on the workpiece.***

▼ **SCROLL-CUT LETTERS, 2.** ***To cut the raised letters, the saw was set to cut a slightly angled bevel. A fine-tooth blade is used to provide maximum control and produce smooth edges that require no sanding.***

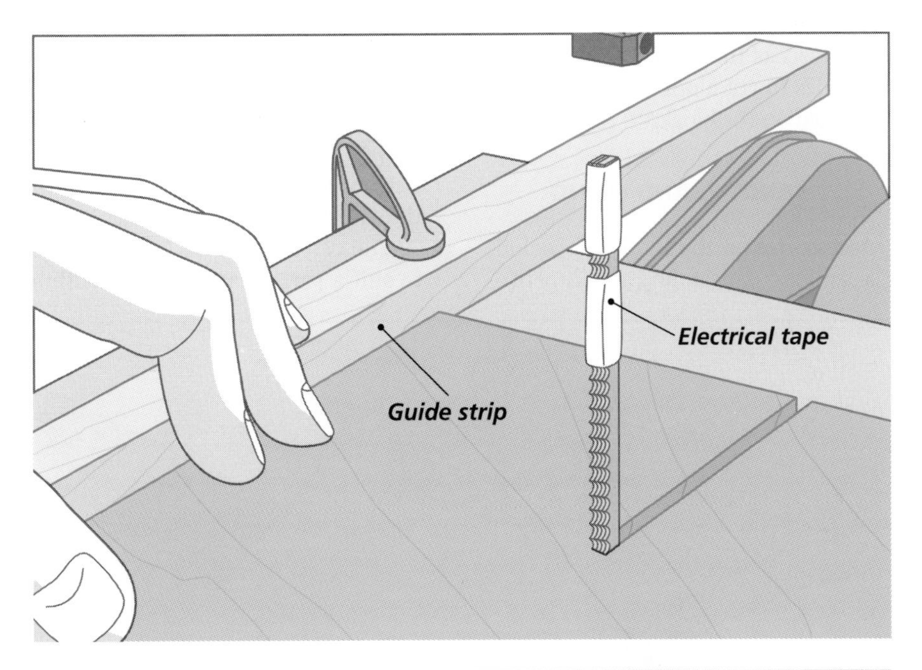

◀ **EDGE HALF-LAP JOINTS, 1.** ***Use ganged blades held in only lower chuck to cut notches in the mating pieces. Tape the blades to prevent whipping, and clamp a wood strip in place to guide the work.***

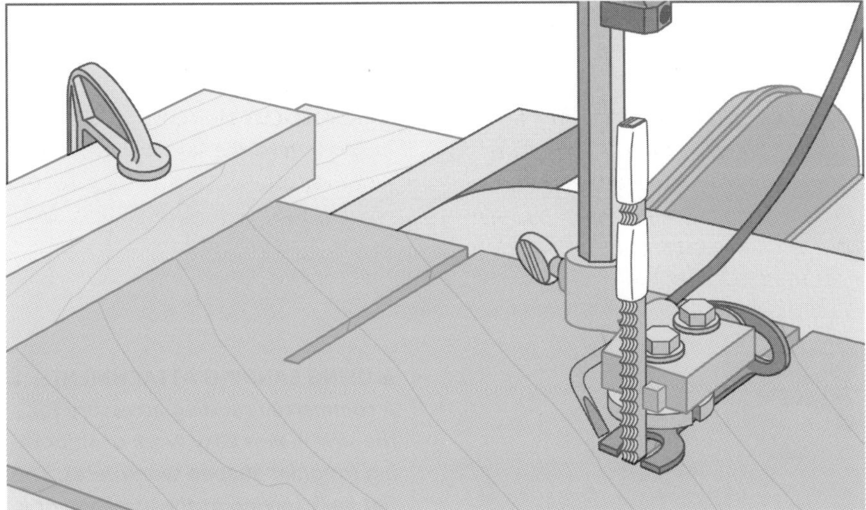

▲ **EDGE HALF-LAP JOINTS, 2.** ***When the work extends beyond the reach of the saw's worktable, simply clamp a wood block to the work so that it rides along the edge of the auxiliary angle-iron fence.***

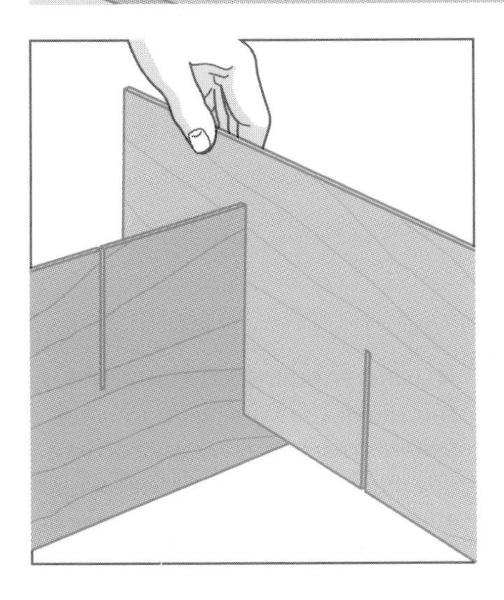

◀ **EDGE HALF-LAP JOINTS, 3.** ***With their edges notched halfway through the center, the mating pieces slide neatly together and interlock. Stock up to ¼ in. thick can be quickly and accurately joined this way.***

ing up stock for lathe turning blanks or for carved projects such as model boat hulls and the like. Simple bevel cuts are the only technique involved.

To make a raised letter, for instance, an internal bevel cut is performed with the worktable set at a slight tilt. The space left by the kerf allows the inside piece to jam tight when it is pushed up through the stock from which it was cut. The amount that the piece telescopes depends upon the width of the kerf and the degree of bevel, as well as the thickness of the stock.

In applying these variables, a good starting point for a test would be to set the worktable for a 3° bevel. Note that the stock must be kept on the same side of the blade and that if it's swung to the other side, the bevel angle will change, thus ruining the piece. In the example that's shown here, the bevel ended up being 3½°. The blade used was .020 in. thick, .070 in. wide, 32 tpi. The stock was ¾ in. thick. The resulting projection of the letters was ¼ in.

A slight departure in method would be employed in angle-sawing a model boat hull. Instead of boring one blade entry hole for each section to be cut, two holes would be bored in the stern corners. The worktable would be tilted 4° left to make the series of cuts stern-to-bow along the right side, then tilted 4° right to make the matching series of cuts stern-to-bow along the left side. Finally, cuts from hole to hole across the stern would sever the piece. By not using a single blade entry hole for each section, it would be possible to work with a coarse, 10-tpi blade (.020 in. thick, .110 in. wide) for easy cutting of 1¼-in.-thick hardwood stock. Avoiding the sharp turn at the bow would make this feasible.

CUTTING METALS

Cutting iron and steel up to ⅛ in. thick presents no problem to the scroll saw, provided an appropriate metalcutting blade is used. When cutting metals, the saw is operated at low speed. The work must be fed very slowly and never "forced" into the blade.

The open space between the blade and the regular insert of the worktable may result in burring on the underside of sheet metal and a deforming of extra-thin metal downward around the cut. To avoid this problem, cut halfway to the center of a ⅛-in.-thick hardboard panel that's the same size as the worktable. Tape the panel securely in place to the worktable, then cut the metal. The panel serves as an oversized worktable insert with no space around the blade, and the result is smooth, clean cutting.

Precise-fitting joints can be made in metal tubing when one piece of tubing abuts another at an angle. Proceed by inserting the tube to be cut into a snug hole in a block of wood. Mark the top surface of the block with an arc that's equal to the radius of the second piece of tubing. Then, wear safety goggles to cut along the cutting line marked on the block.

SANDING AND FILING

Accessories for the scroll saw include a semicircular sanding attachment—for smoothing flat and curved surfaces—plus a variety of machine files. The sander and files are held in the V-shaped jaw of the lower chuck, and both operations are performed with the saw running at low speed.

You can also make sanding blocks to suit a particular job. Start with a

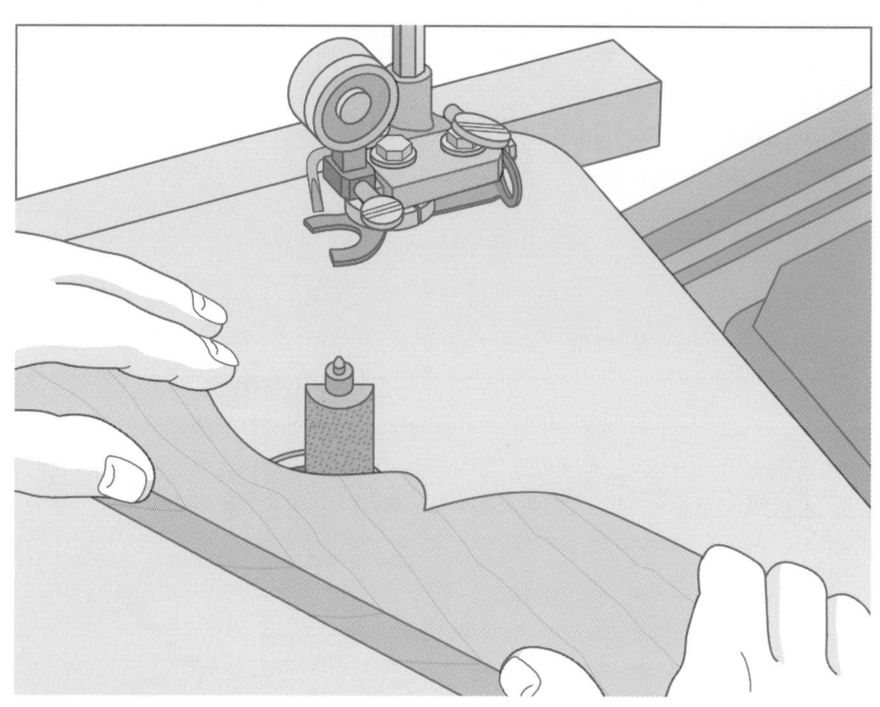

▲ **USING SANDING ATTACHMENTS, 1.** ***A commercial sanding accessory for the saw makes easy work of smoothing irregular-shaped workpieces. The flat back section of the attachment is used on outside curves.***

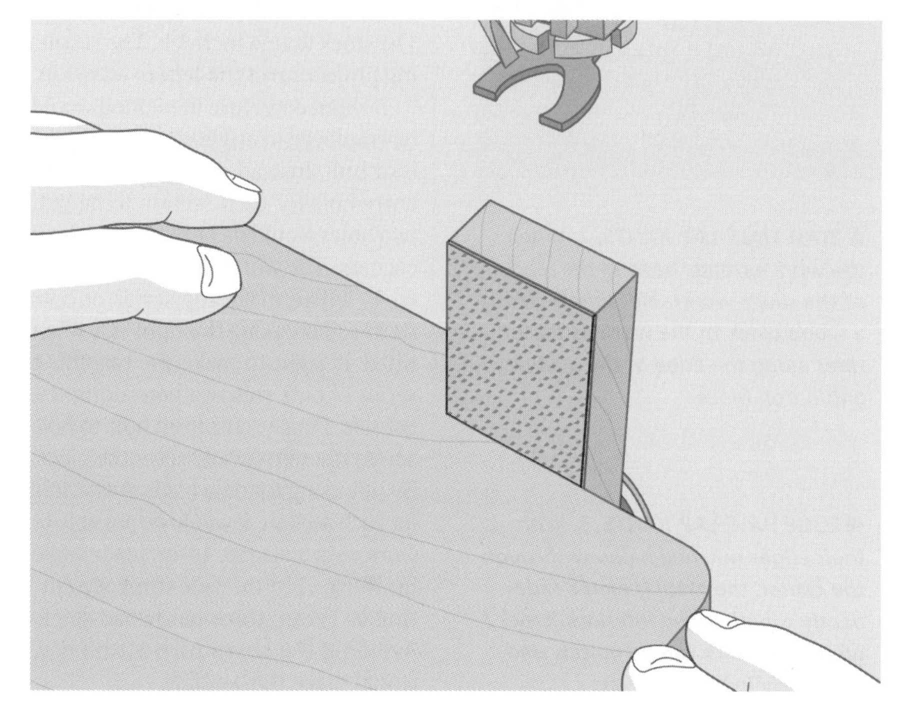

◀ **USING SANDING ATTACHMENTS, 2.** ***This shopmade sanding attachment features coarse-grit abrasive on one side and medium-grit abrasive on the other. Blocks like this can be made in a variety of shapes.***

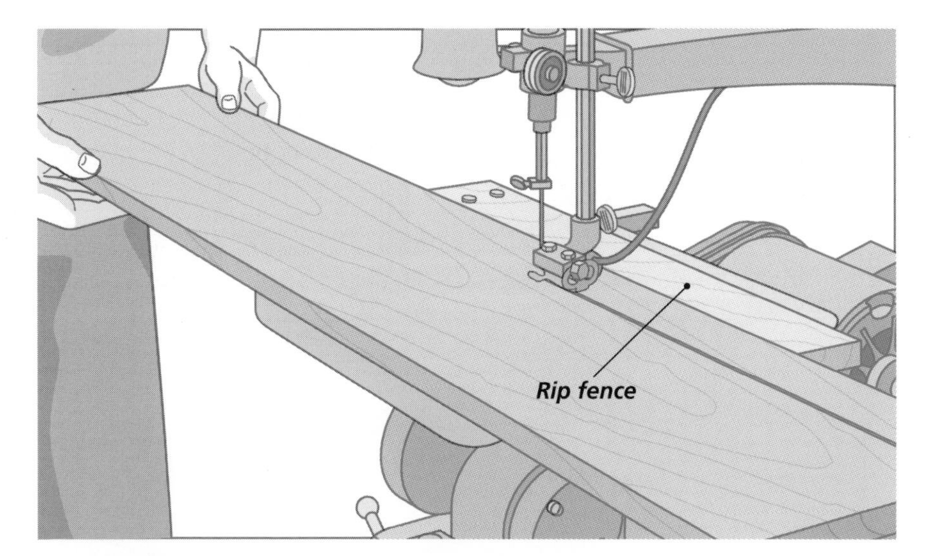

◀ **RIPPING.** ***To rip long boards, the chucks for the blade are rotated 90°. For the best cutting results, work with a coarse, wide blade and feed the workpiece slowly.***

large, flat sanding block for squaring corners and smoothing the sides of stock. Make your own sanding block from a piece of wood 3/4 x 1 3/4 x 2 1/2 in. Insert the wood-screw threads of a 1/4 x 2-in. hanger bolt into the end of the block. The hanger bolt's protruding machine-screw threads are gripped by the saw's lower chuck. Apply adhesive-backed abrasive paper to both faces of the sanding block.

RIPPING AND CROSSCUTTING

While the scroll saw is essentially a tool designed for freehand cutting of irregular shapes, it can also be used for fine ripping and crosscutting. The trick is to work with a guide. The basic guide is a rip fence. Improvise a simple fence by clamping a straight board to the worktable, or make one on which a crosscut guide can ride piggyback.

To make a fence, use 3/4 x 2 1/2 x 20-in. hardwood for the blade and 3/4 x 2 1/2 x 6 1/2-in. hardwood for the head. Bore holes for a pair of teenuts in the top of the head, then position a spacer of 1/8 x 1 1/2 x 6 1/2-in. hardboard and secure the blade to the assembly with two 1/4 x 1 1/4-in. lagscrews. You'll need two thumbscrews to screw into the bottom of the head.

An angle-iron track is attached to the left side of the worktable with two screws threaded into holes bored and tapped in the edge. The edge of the worktable is not machined square, so a shim is required below each screw to ensure that the top of the angle iron lies flush. Scratch a centerline across

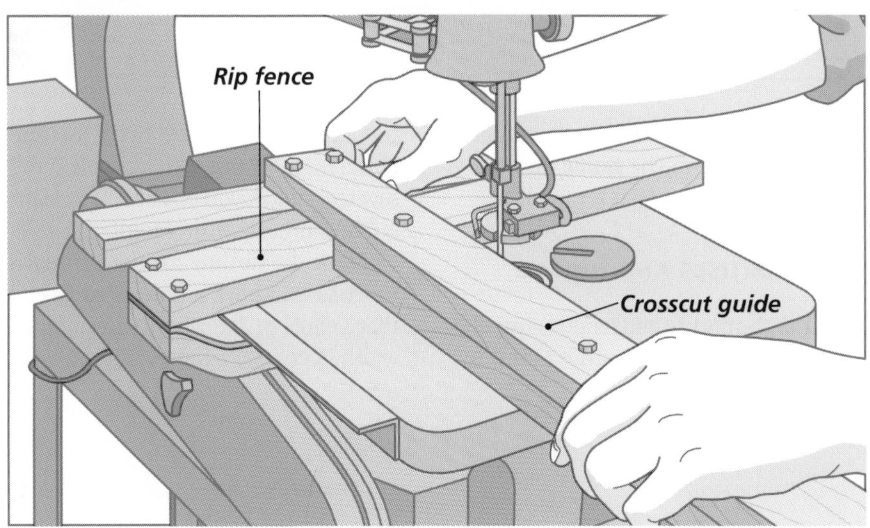

▲ **CROSSCUTTING, 1.** ***Here, a crosscut guide is shown fitting over the rip fence. The guide must ride at a precise right angle to the fence, and should be sealed with all contact edges waxed.***

◀ **CROSSCUTTING, 2.** ***When you're crosscutting workpieces flat on the saw's worktable, cutoffs are limited to a length of only 3 1/2 in.***

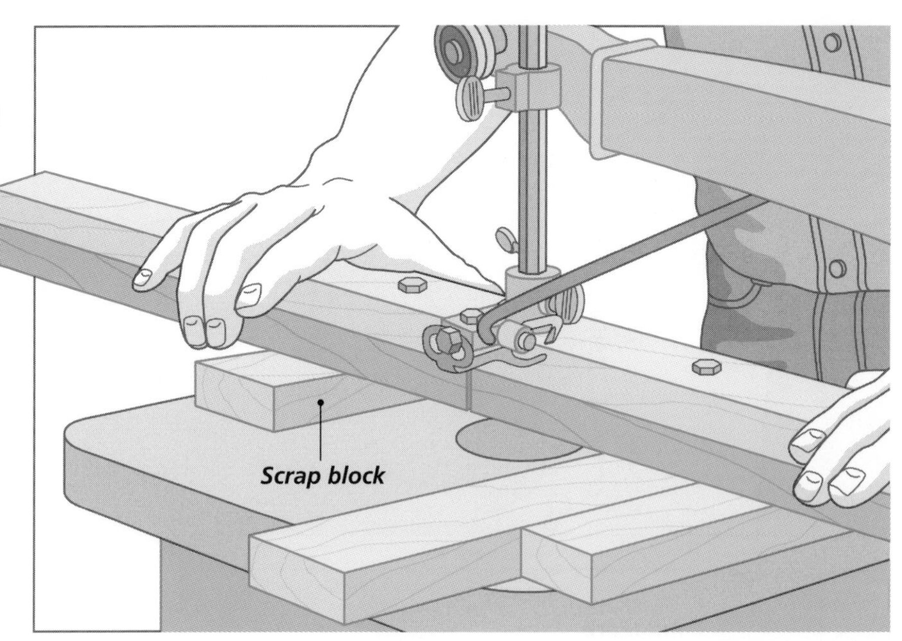

▶ **CROSSCUTTING, 3.** ***With workpieces propped up on the ledge of the crosscut guide and a scrap block, the length of cutoffs that can be done increases to 23½ in.***

the face of the angle iron in line with the blade to help to set the fence to the desired width of cut.

The crosscut guide is designed to ride over the rip fence with a snug fit. Make the guide using ¾-in.-thick hardwood: the blade 3 x 18 in., the head 2 x 15 in. and the straddle 2½ x 16½ in. Position the head 2½ in. from the end of the blade (clearance for the fence) and secure the straddle to them with four lagscrews. You'll need to cut a 1⅛-in.-wide notch in the front edge of the guide to allow for clearance of the saw blade. A nail point protruding ⅛ in. from the front edge of the guide will help keep work from slipping.

Apply a sealer coat of shellac to the wood, then sand and apply candle wax to all contact surfaces. Note that when work rides on the worktable, the crosscut cutoff is restricted to 3½ in. To increase the cutoff to 23½ in., simply rest the work on the guide and support its free end with a scrap block.

MORTISES AND TENONS

A through-mortise and tenon is usually a tricky and time-consuming joint to produce with the conventional saw and chisel method. But with a simple scroll saw technique, you can obtain a clean-cut and precise-fitting joint.

Mark the outline for the through-mortise and bore a hole at each end that's equal in diameter to the cutout's width. A coarse, 7-tooth, .250-in.-wide

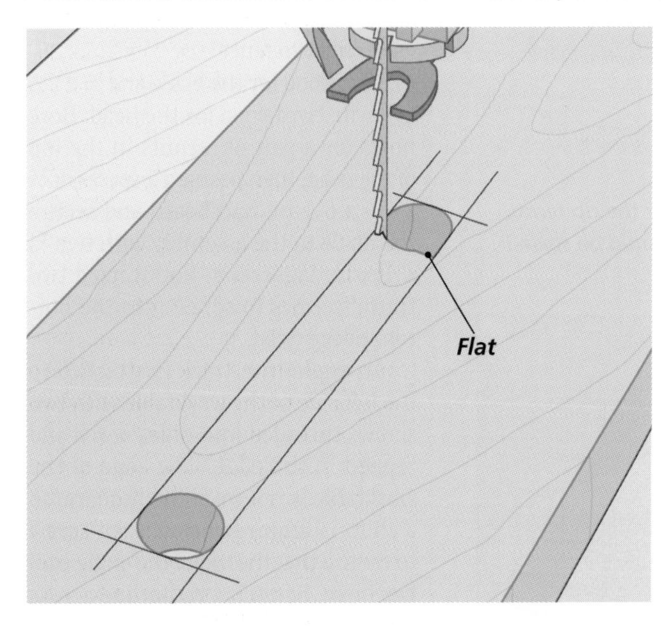

▲ **CUTTING MORTISES AND TENONS, 1.** ***Bore full-diameter holes at the ends of the mortise, then use a chisel to cut flats tangent to the cutting lines. The flats allow the blade to start precisely.***

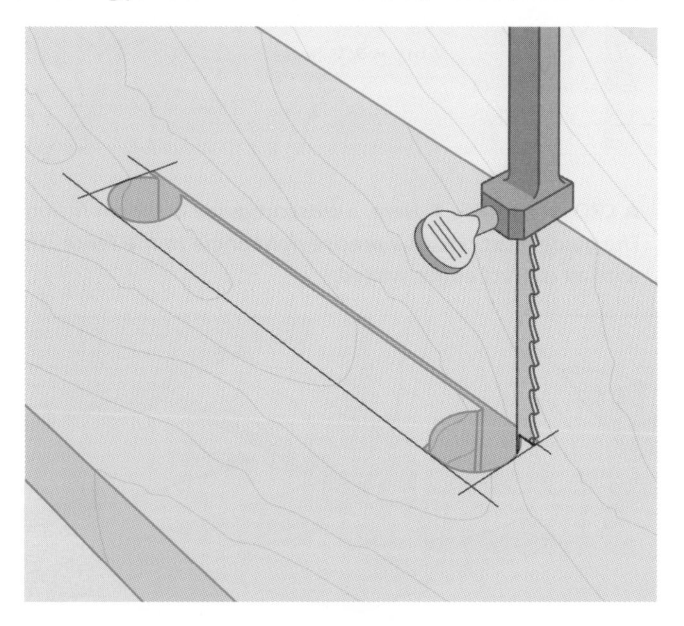

▲ **CUTTING MORTISES AND TENONS, 2.** ***After cutting to the end of the mortise, remove the blade guide and reverse the blade. Return to your start point and make a short pass to continue the cut to the corner.***

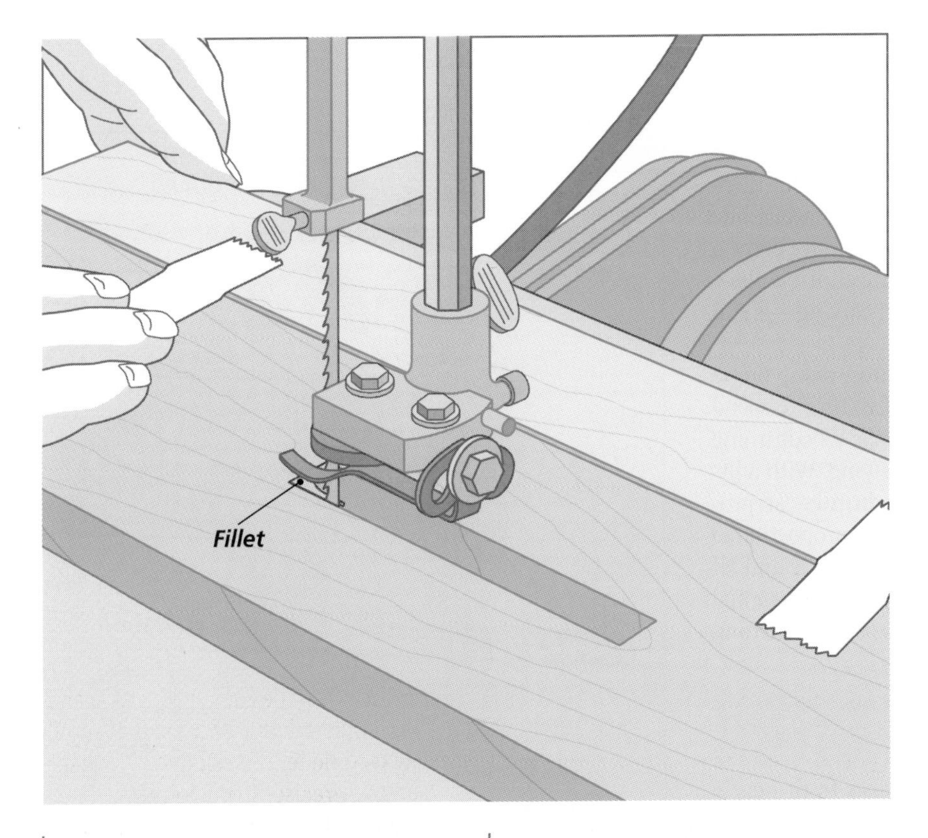

▲ **CUTTING MORTISES AND TENONS, 3.** ***Once the sides of the mortise have been cut, secure the workpiece to the rip fence with masking tape and then carefully scrape-saw the waste fillets out of the corners.***

▼ **CUTTING MORTISES AND TENONS, 4.** ***No time-consuming handwork with a hammer and chisel is necessary to make this top-quality through-mortise-and-tenon joint. The mating pieces fit together neatly.***

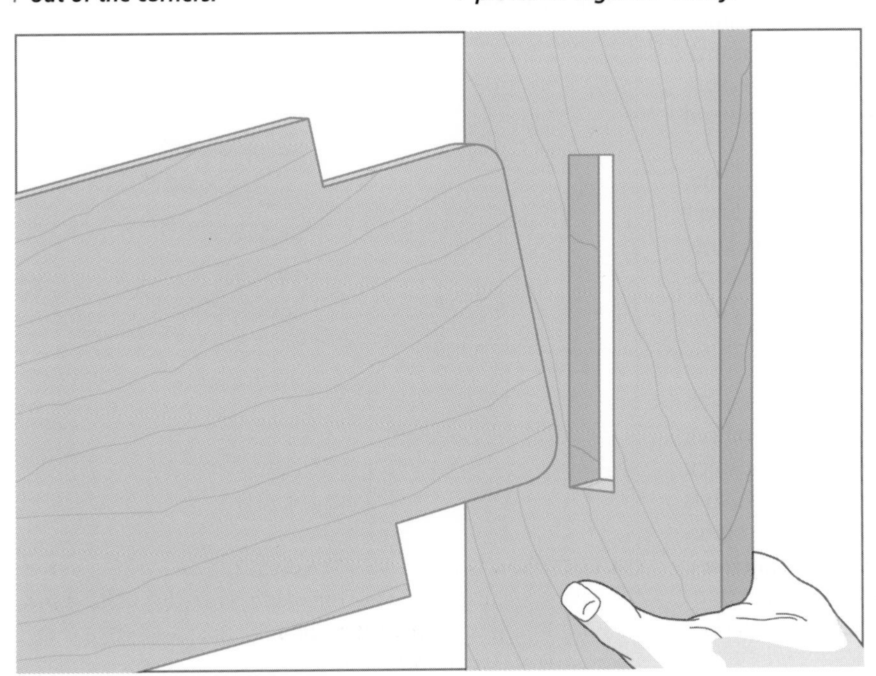

blade is recommended for this operation, so you'll need a small chisel to cut two flats tangent to the cutting lines in one of the holes in order to start cutting precisely.

Set up the rip fence and make the first cut along the length of the outline. Without moving the fence, take off the blade guide assembly and install the blade backward so the teeth face the "wrong" way. With the blade guide out of the way, pull the work back to complete the cut right into the corner of the hole you started from.

Adjust the fence for the second long cut, then make the short cut into the corner of the hole. Install the blade its normal way and attach the blade guide to complete the second long cut.

Remove the waste and you'll notice two parallel cuts with fillets in the corners. To clean out the fillets, adjust the fence so the blade's teeth abut the end of the outline and tape the work to the fence, then slide the assembly back and forth. Keep the fence against the angle-iron track to create a true and square scraping motion.

The tenon can be cut with equal ease and accuracy. Just use the crosscut guide in piggyback combination with the rip fence.

CUTTING EDGE HALF LAPS

The scroll saw can cut half-lap joints in stock up to 1⁄4 in. thick quickly and accurately. The trick is to gang up several blades so the kerf equals the stock thickness. The notches cut halfway through to the center of mating pieces slide together and interlock.

Install the blades in the lower chuck and wrap the upper ends with electrical tape. The upper chuck isn't used since it lacks the capacity to hold several blades. No blade guide can be used, nor is one needed. If the work is small, clamp a wood strip to the worktable to guide the crosscut. Otherwise, use a guide block clamped to the work so it rides the angle-iron track.

LATHES

Woodturning dates back at least to 300 B.C. when the Egyptians designed a two-man lathe for turning columns. One man supplied the power while another did the cutting. Needless to say, lathes have come a long way since then, but the basic mechanical principle—rotating stock between two points to permit carving—is still the same nearly 2,300 years later.

Today, the wood lathe is a popular item in many home workshops. For many woodworkers, a little free time to spend at the lathe is heaven. And the reason is simple: Woodturning is fun, easy to learn and instantly very satisfying. With a little practice and patience, even a novice woodturner can produce an intricately-shaped spindle, perfectly-proportioned bowl or fanciful finial—often in less than an hour and all on a single machine. However, a little experience is essential in order to acquire just the right "feel" of using the turning tools safely and properly.

LATHE SPECIFICS

Lathes are available in a wide variety of sizes to fit nearly everyone's budget and workspace. A 12-in. wood lathe is a good multipurpose model for the home workshop. Lathes are sized according to the maximum-diameter work they can turn. This dimension, known as the swing of the lathe, is determined by doubling the distance from the spindle center to the bed. For example, a lathe measuring 6 in. between the spindle and bed has a 12 in. swing.

The longest workpiece turned by a lathe is determined by the spindle length capacity. This dimension varies according to the lathe, but most 12-in. lathes, for example, measure about 39 in. between centers. Extension bed sections and longer accessory beds are available for many models.

Lathe rotation speeds vary depending on the model, too, but they generally range from 200 to 4,000 rpm. Use lower speeds for preliminary roughing cuts and for turning large diameters. Choose higher speeds for small-diameter turning and finishing operations.

LATHE MECHANICS

The lathe is a simple machine in both design and operation. The stock, or turning blank, is held between the headstock and tailstock by the centers. The headstock spindle, which is connected to the motor, houses a spur center that rotates the blank. A cup or cone center—called a dead center because it doesn't turn with the blank—is held in the tailstock spindle. Position the tailstock and toolrest anywhere along the bed to accommodate the blank.

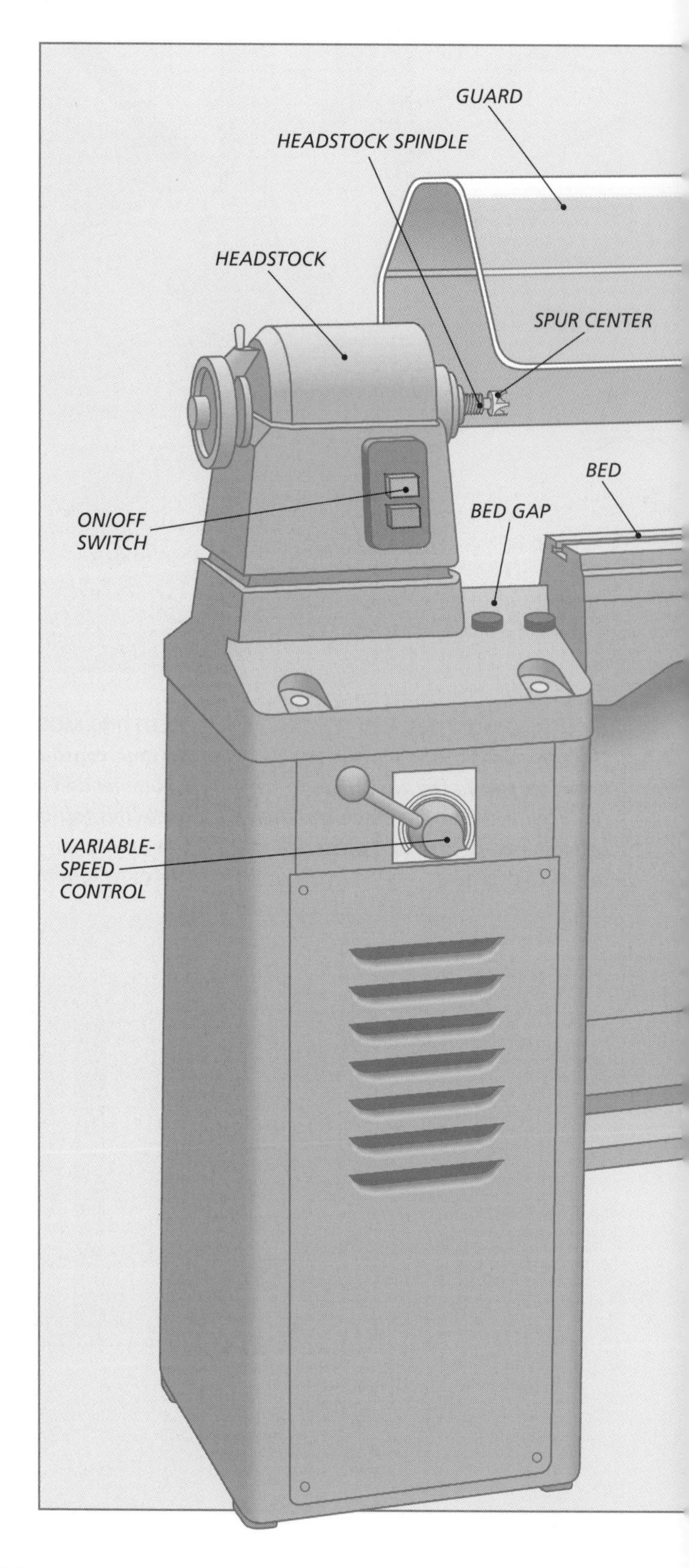

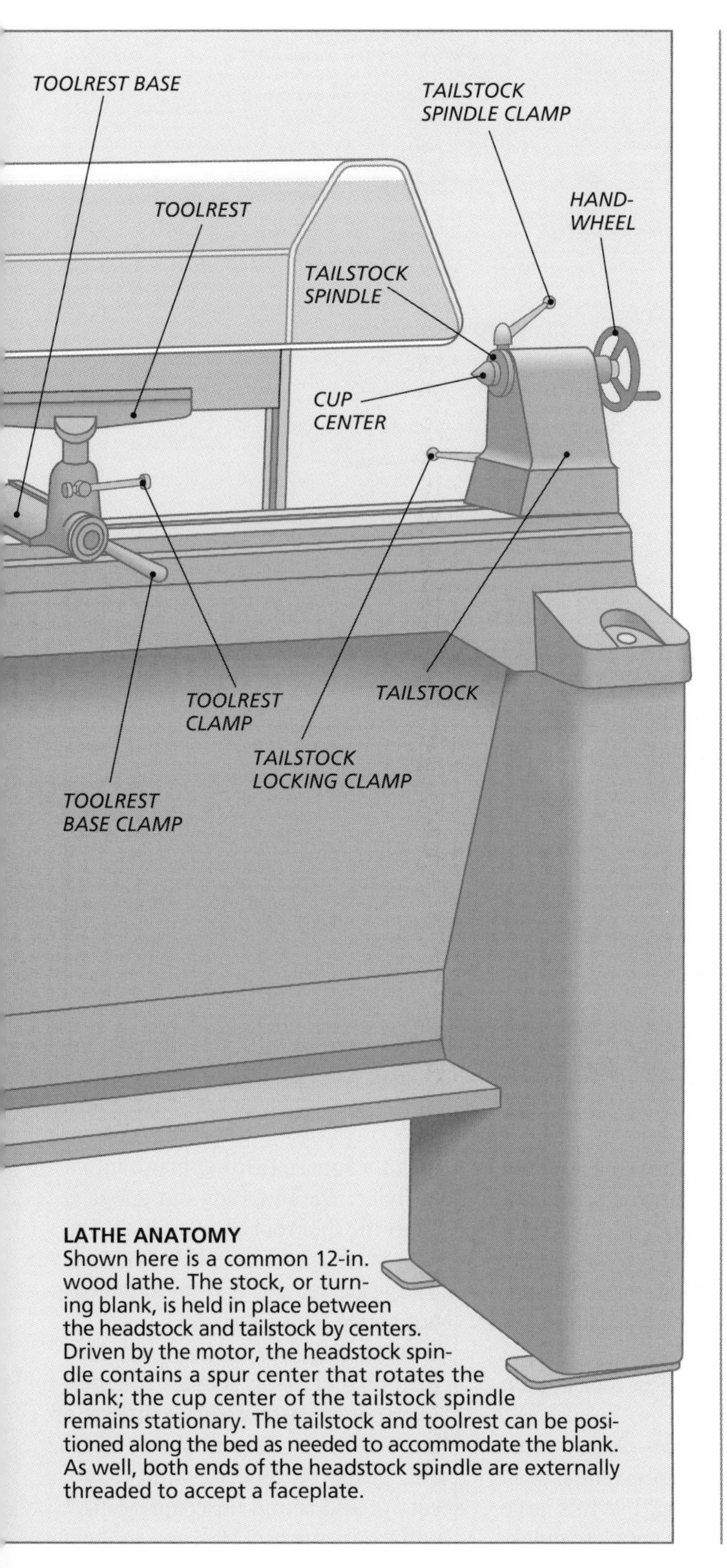

LATHE ANATOMY
Shown here is a common 12-in. wood lathe. The stock, or turning blank, is held in place between the headstock and tailstock by centers. Driven by the motor, the headstock spindle contains a spur center that rotates the blank; the cup center of the tailstock spindle remains stationary. The tailstock and toolrest can be positioned along the bed as needed to accommodate the blank. As well, both ends of the headstock spindle are externally threaded to accept a faceplate.

Woodturning between centers is known as spindle turning and is the most common lathe work. However, both ends of the headstock spindle are externally threaded to accept a faceplate. Faceplate turning is used to make bowls and dishes. Note that the bed gap at the headstock end permits turning larger-diameter blanks than is possible directly over the bed. For extra-large turnings, the faceplate is mounted on the left end of the headstock spindle—a procedure called outboard faceplate turning.

TURNING METHODS

There are two basic methods used to turn a blank: scraping and cutting. When scraping, the turning tool is held horizontally on the toolrest and fed directly into the blank to scrape away particles of wood. This is a safe, easy-to-learn technique. When cutting, the tool is held at an angle toward the top of the spinning stock so the cutting edge pierces the work and peels off shavings. The method is faster and produces a smoother finish. However, cutting also requires greater skill and more practice to master than scraping. And you must remember to never jam a cutting tool into the work since it could easily be thrown from your grasp.

TURNING TOOLS

While the lathe provides the power, the actual shaping of the wood blank is done with various turning tools. A collection of tools that every woodturner should know about are gathered together here. Some of the tools are essential to basic woodturning while others are more specialized. It's worth mentioning that while a few of the turning tools shown are sold in sets, they are usually available individually as well. All the tools shown can be purchased through the mail.

Most turning tools look pretty much the same—sharpened steel blades fitted with large hardwood handles. There are three basic types of turning tools: gouges, chisels and scrapers. The size and shape of a tool's blade determines how it's used. Most of the tools shown here are standard-strength turning tools—the most commonly used woodturning tools. Heavyweight turning tools with thick blades and oversized handles—which are known as long-and-strong tools—are available for turning very large, heavy projects. Conversely, small-scale tools are designed for shaping fine, intricate details and for turning miniature parts such as chess pieces and dollhouse furnishings.

There are no hard-and-fast rules regarding which turning tools you should own. This depends on the type of woodturning you do, the size of the lathe and, naturally, your

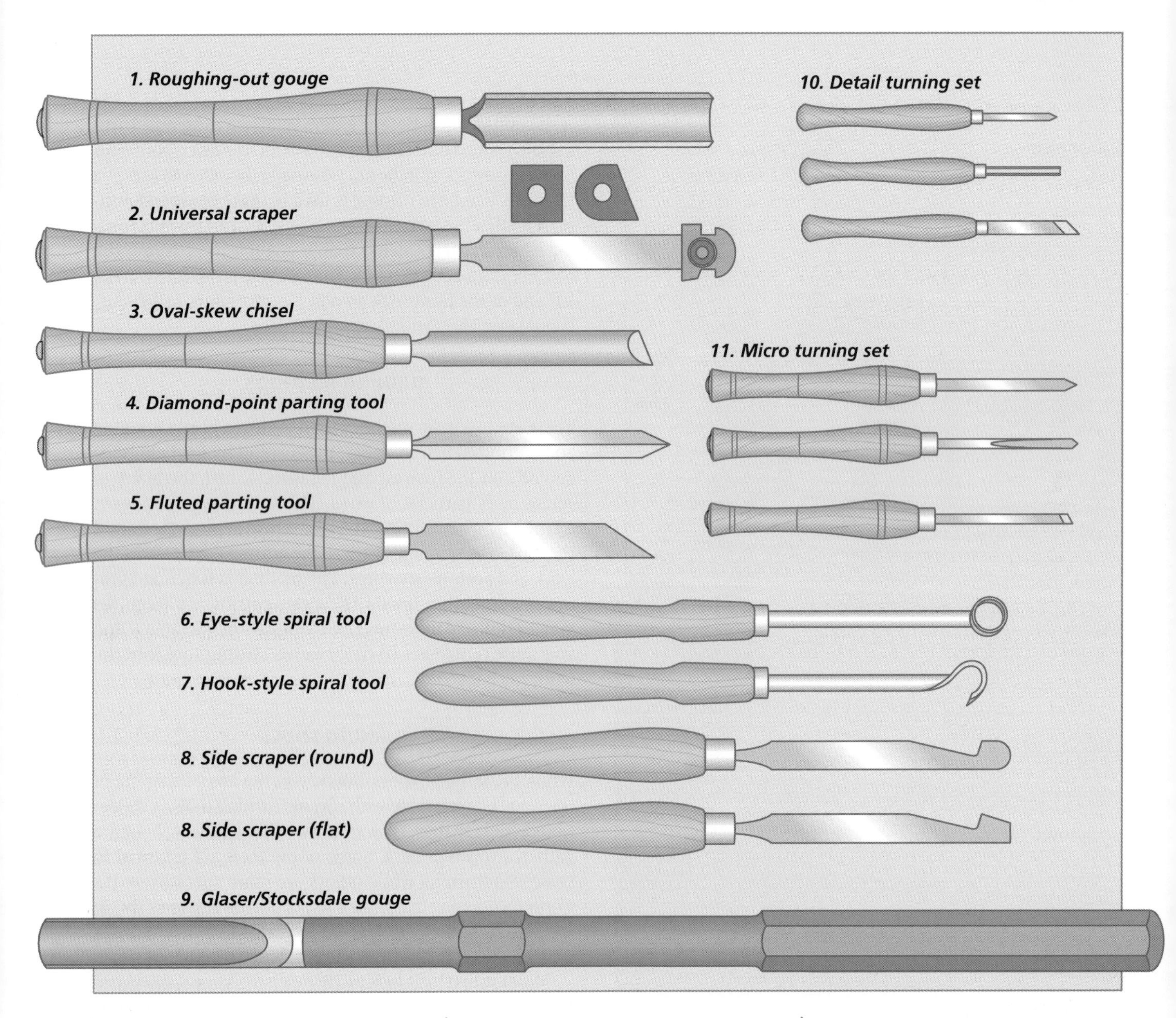

budget. For a novice woodturner, it's probably best to begin with a starter set of turning tools. Then, add tools of various sizes and styles to your collection as your skills increase.

INVENTORY OF TURNING TOOLS

Most woodturning tools are made with carbon-steel blades. However, there are newer, more expensive tools with blades of high-speed steel (HSS) that will hold a sharpened edge about six times longer than blades made of carbon steel. For most turners, carbon-steel tools suffice quite nicely. But if you turn hard, exotic woods, burls, resinous woods or laminated blanks, you should consider the advantages of working with HSS tools.

Now, let's take a close look at each of the tools shown.

1. Roughing-out gouge—Gouges come in various sizes and are essential to all levels of woodturning. Use this large 1¼-in. roughing-out gouge to quickly cut a square turning blank into a cylinder. The roughing-out gouge is often the first tool a turner uses. The 18½-in.-long tool has a HSS blade and a large ash handle. A ¾-in. roughing-out gouge is also available.

2. Universal scraper—Here's a unique turning tool that is actually five tools in one. It consists of a blade fitted to a large ash handle and three interchangeable cutters: skew/full round, square and round nose/square. The cutters are made of HSS and are held securely to the blade with a hex-socket machine bolt. A hex-key wrench is provided with the tool.

3. Oval-skew chisel—Shown here is an improved version of a common skew chisel. This skew chisel features rounded sides that allow it to slide smoothly across the toolrest without hanging up on any surface imperfections, nicks or scratches. The upper edge of the blade is ground flat to provide greater control when cutting square shoulders and ends. The tool features a 1-in.-wide HSS blade and a 12-in.-long ash handle. An oval-skew chisel with a ¾-in.-wide blade is also available.

4. Diamond-point parting tool—This British-made tool features a 7-in.-long HSS blade and 10-in.-long ash handle with brass ferrule. Use it to make parting-off (severing) cuts and diameter-sizing grooves as well as for beading work. The tool's HSS blade not only keeps an edge longer than a carbon-steel blade, it also retains its hardness at higher temperatures. This is important when there's a significant heat buildup while turning.

5. Fluted parting tool—A parting tool is used primarily to make parting-off cuts and diameter-sizing grooves. The improved parting tool shown here features a HSS blade that has a shallow flute machined along its cutting edge. The result is the forming of two sharp cutting spurs that score cross-grained fibers to ensure smooth, clean cuts. The blade is also thinner at its top edge than at the bottom fluted edge to prevent binding in the cut.

6. Eye-style spiral tool—This unusual-looking tool is used for making bowls in the traditional Swedish technique known as spiral turning. The tool's 25-mm-dia., ring-shaped cutting edge is designed primarily to shape the sides of the bowl. To use the tool, set the lathe at a slow speed and hold the blade at an acute angle to the spinning bowl. Don't force the cutting edge into the work. When used properly, the tool shears off corkscrew- or spiral-shaped wood shavings. The 16-in.-long tool has a 9½-in.-long hardwood handle.

7. Hook-style spiral tool—To complement the eye-style spiral tool, here's a hook-shaped spiral tool. The curved edge of the tool is designed for shaping the bottom of the bowl. Like its eye-style mate, the hook-style spiral tool has a carbon-steel blade that must be honed before use.

8. Side scrapers—This pair of specially-shaped tools is designed to make internal, finishing cuts on bowls, trays and similarly-shaped pieces. The two different blade profiles allow you to form round-bottom or square-bottom bowls. Both the left edge and tip of each tool are ground for use. The dual-edge tips let you undercut recesses and shape hard-to-reach areas safely. The 17-in.-long tools come with 9½-in.-long hardwood handles.

9. Glaser/Stocksdale gouge—Developed by two accomplished American woodturners, this 1-in. spindle gouge is the Rolls-Royce of turning tools. It features a 19½-in.-long black-anodized aluminum handle fitted with a 6-in.-long blade made of super-tough vanadium carbide. The blade will hold its edge eight to 12 times longer than a HSS blade. The hex-shaped handle, machined from 1-in. bar stock, provides a comfortable grip. This handsome, well-balanced tool is designed for the serious turner. A ⅝-in. bowl gouge is also available.

10. Detail turning set—These three tiny turning tools represent a set of eight 7-in.-long tools that are ideal for shaping intricate details impossible to do with standard-size tools. Work with these tools to turn miniature parts or create embellishments on larger turnings. Shown are a ⅛-in. parting tool, ⅜-in. skew and 3⁄16-in. gouge. The set also includes a ⅛-in. gouge, 9⁄64-in. round nose, 9⁄64-in. square nose, 9⁄64-in. diamond point and 9⁄64-in. beading tool.

11. Micro turning set—These three tools represent a set of five small-scale turning tools. The 10-in.-long tools feature HSS blades and ash handles with brass ferrules. These tools are slightly larger than the tools of the detail turning set, but they can be used in much the

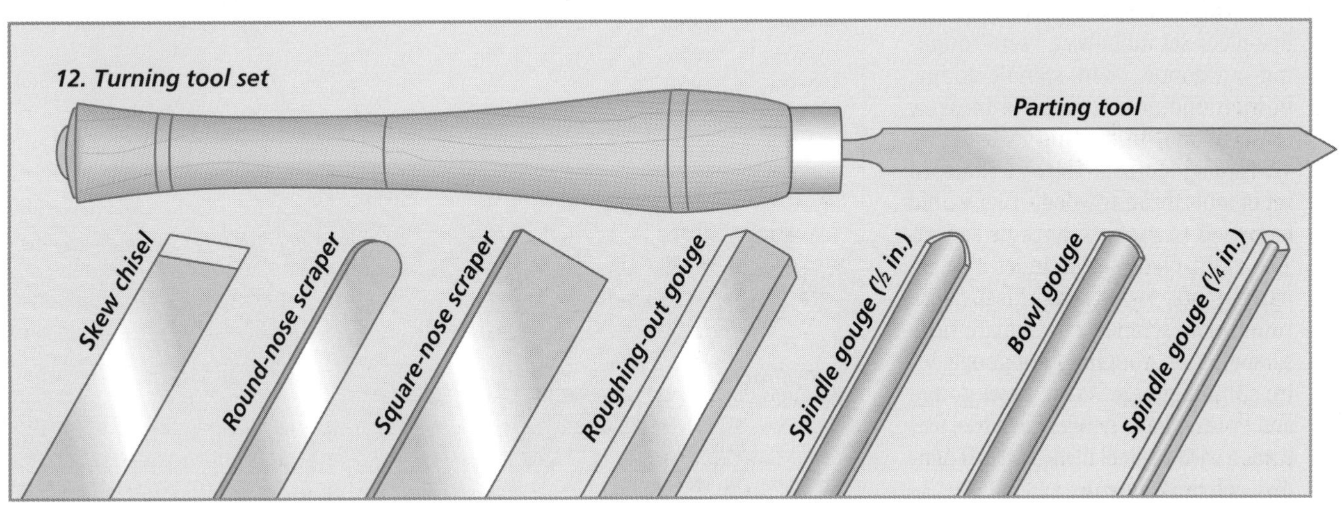

WOODTURNING SPEEDS			
DIAMETER OF WORK	ROUGH CUTTING RPM	GENERAL CUTTING RPM	FINISHING RPM
Less than 2 in.	900 to 1,300	2,400 to 2,800	3,000 to 4,000
2 to 4 in.	600 to 1,000	1,800 to 2,400	2,400 to 3,000
4 to 6 in.	600 to 800	1,200 to 1,800	1,800 to 2,400
6 to 8 in.	400 to 600	800 to 1,200	1,200 to 1,800
8 to 10 in.	300 to 400	600 to 800	900 to 1,200
Over 10 in.	200 to 300	300 to 600	600 to 900

Adjust wood-turning speeds according to the diameter of the workpiece. Use slower speeds for larger turnings.

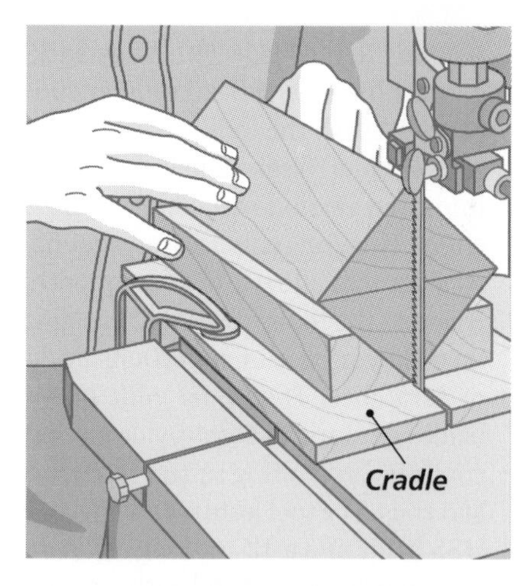

▲ **TURNING A CYLINDER, 1.** ***Locating the center on a hardwood blank is easy using a cradle jig and band saw. Shallow cross-kerfs made in the end of the blank will allow the spur center to seat firmly.***

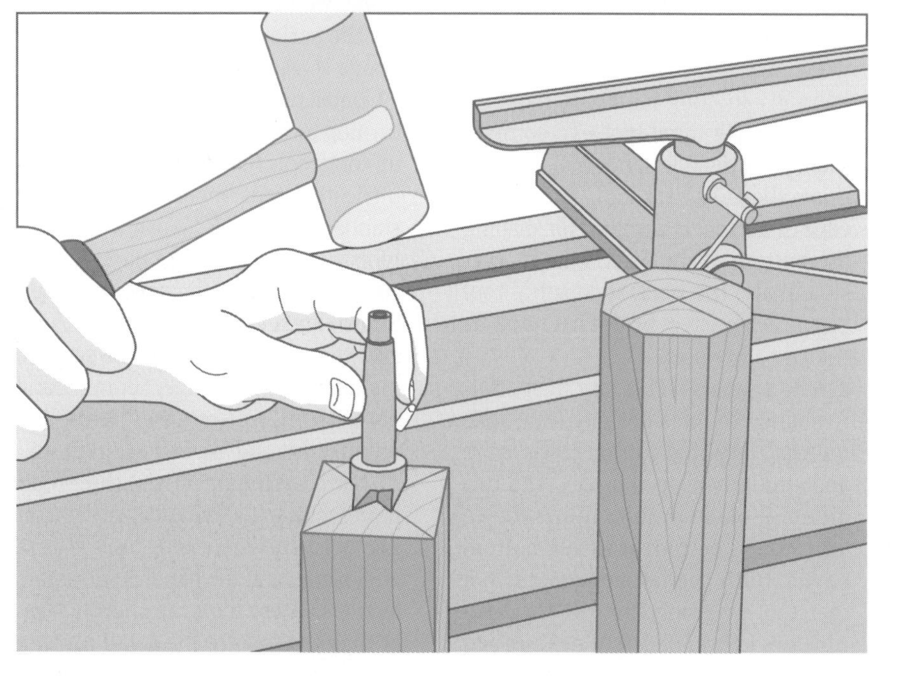

◄ **TURNING A CYLINDER, 2.** ***Drive the spur center into the end of the blank using a mallet. The reference mark on the end of the blank corresponds to the mark on the spur center to permit recentering.***

▼ **TURNING A CYLINDER, 3.** ***With the blank set in position on the headstock, clamp the tailstock in place. Then, turn the handwheel to advance the tailstock ram, driving the cup center into the blank.***

same way—to turn fine details. The five-piece set includes a 1/4-in. roughing-out gouge, 1/8-in. spindle gouge, 1/4-in. round-nose scraper, 1/4-in. skew chisel and 1/16-in. parting tool.

12. Turning tool set—Here's a standard set of tools that any woodturner would be proud to own—novice or expert. The eight-piece set includes a 1/4-in. parting tool, 3/4-in. skew chisel, 1/2-in. round-nose scraper, 1-in. square-nose scraper, 3/4-in. roughing-out gouge, 1/2-in. spindle gouge, 3/8-in. bowl gouge and 1/4-in. spindle gouge. Each tool features a carbon-steel blade and ash handle with brass ferrule.

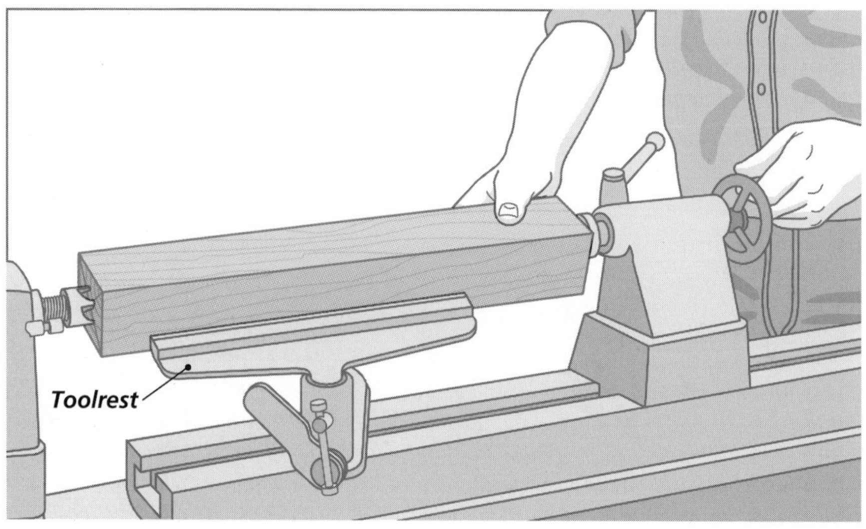

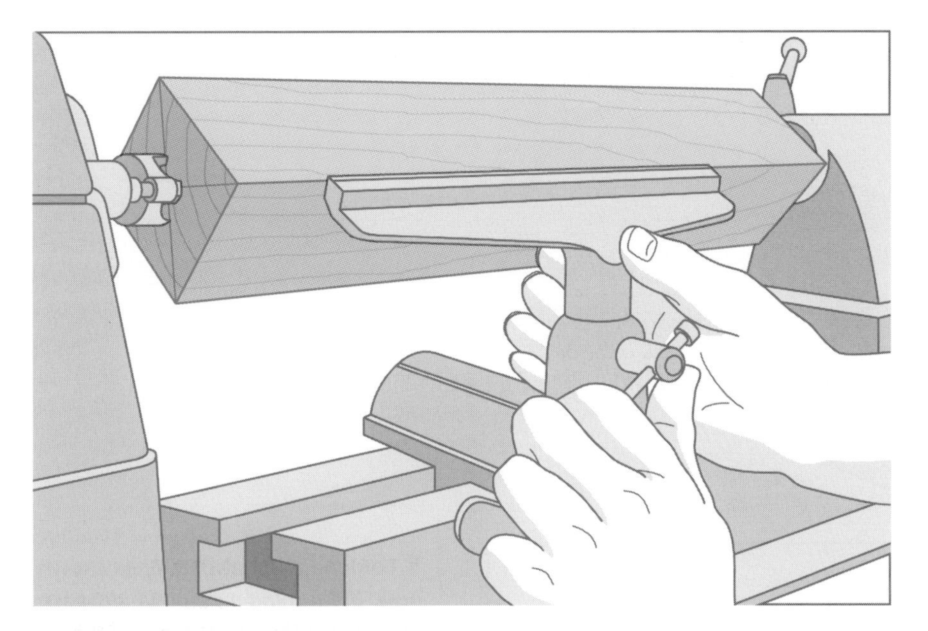

◀ **TURNING A CYLINDER, 4.** ***Adjust the position of the toolrest so it's no more than ⅛ in. away from the blank and approximately ⅛ in. above the centerline of the spindle. Clamp the toolrest securely.***

▼ **TURNING A CYLINDER, 5.** ***Using a gouge, start cutting a few inches from the end of the blank and continue toward and off the end. Repeat this procedure on the opposite side of the blank.***

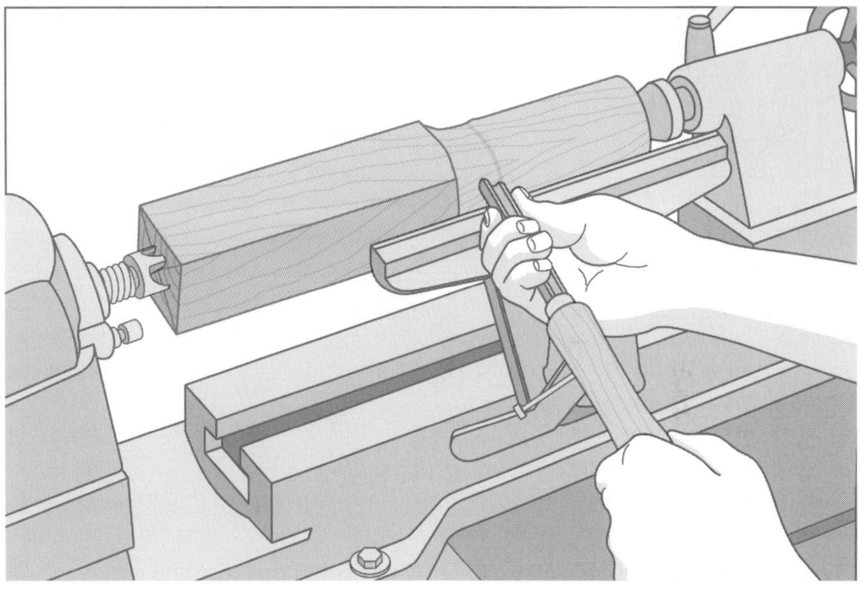

TURNING TOOL APPLICATIONS

Six woodturning tools are the ones most commonly used with the lathe: the gouge, skew, parting tool, round nose, square nose and diamond point. Few hard-and-fast rules can be made about the applications of these tools. Although each type of tool works differently, there is considerable overlap among them in what they can accomplish. This is because the results that they achieve are influenced by factors that *you* determine—such as the turning method, the feed angle and the tool's motion.

You should practice working with woodturning tools to duplicate shapes. This will help you to develop the appropriate "feel" for each tool. A quality bead, for example, can be produced using a square-nose scraper or diamond-point parting tool, even though the skew might be the tool most often recommended for the job. Surprise yourself by mastering techniques for handling tools that are *you*—a kind of work signature.

The gouge is the best tool to work with for roughing operations and when you need to remove a lot of stock. A versatile woodturning tool, the gouge can be used for scraping or cutting—and in some applications actually performs both types of actions. For faceplate turning, however, the gouge is not a suitable tool.

Having a slanted cutting edge with a double bevel, the skew is most frequently used for finish-cutting operations, forming long, sweeping curves, and cutting square shoulders, rounded beads and long tapers. In addition, the skew can be used as a scraping tool. By alternating use of the tool from one side to the other, the scraping action of its blade results in a full-V shape.

A parting tool is a scraping chisel that comes in two shapes: ground on two edges to form a V-point, or ground on a single edge to resemble a skew without beveled edges. Parting tools are used primarily for cutting diameter-sizing grooves in a cylinder. The grooves serve as depth-of-cut guides when turning a spindle.

The round nose and square nose, or flat nose, are easy-to-handle tools that are used for scraping. Beveled on only one side, the round-nose scraper is used for making concave shapes. The

▶ **TURNING A CYLINDER, 6.** ***Work with a skew to finish-cut the cylinder to size. Cut with only the center section of the blade. The tool's toe must not make contact with the blank.***

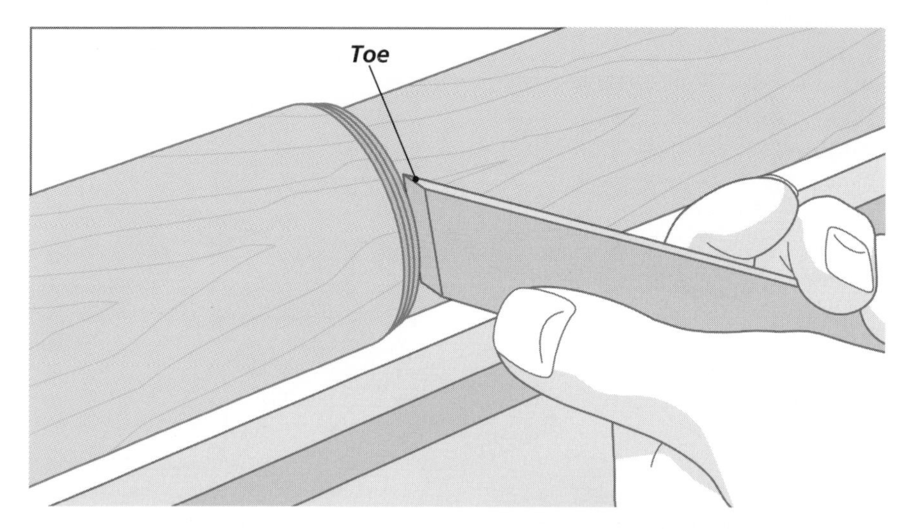

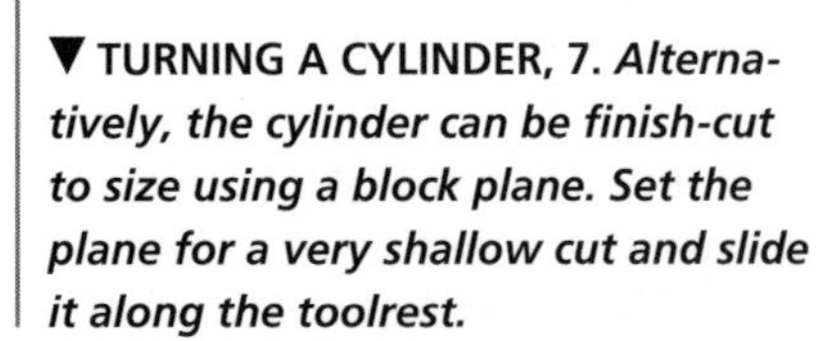
▼ **TURNING A CYLINDER, 7.** ***Alternatively, the cylinder can be finish-cut to size using a block plane. Set the plane for a very shallow cut and slide it along the toolrest.***

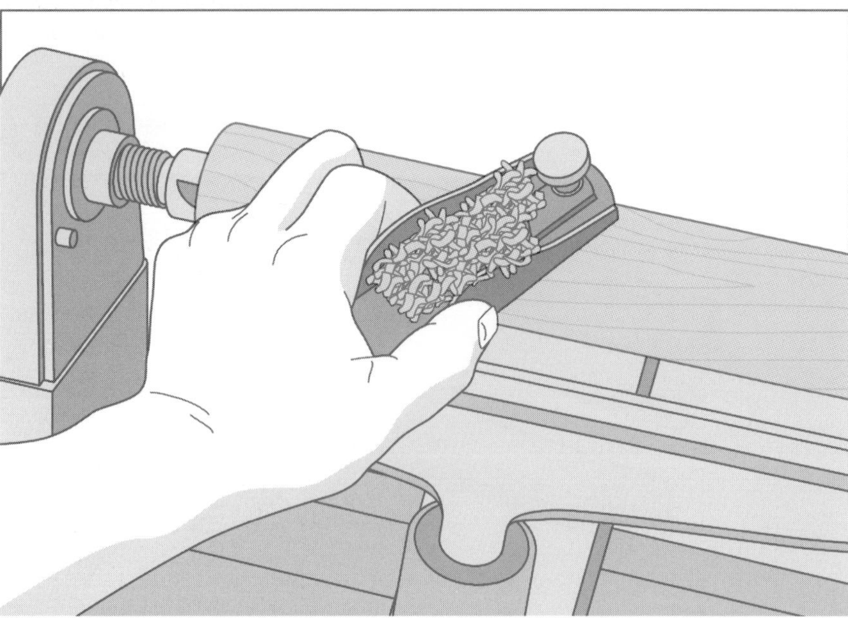

▼ **TURNING A CYLINDER, 8.** ***As shown here, the turning method you choose determines the smoothness of the surface. From left to right: scraping with a gouge, scraping with a skew and cutting with a skew.***

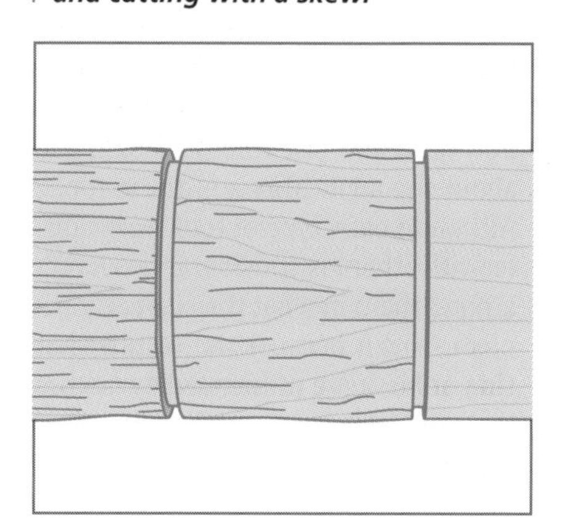

square-nose tool is used almost exclusively for scraping flat surfaces during faceplate turning.

The diamond point, which is also known as a spear point, has a pointed tip with two beveled edges. Work with this scraping tool to round off grooves and to finish the inside of corners and recesses. Producing clean lines and edges, the diamond point is most valuable in touchup applications.

WOODTURNING SAFETY

The lathe is a relatively safe stationary tool to operate, provided that you practice common sense and observe basic precautions. Never wear loose clothing or jewelry. Always wear safety goggles or a face shield. When performing sanding operations, wear a dust mask or respirator. Strictly adhere to the rules for correct handling of woodturning tools and hand position on the lathe's toolrest. Be sure to follow the guidelines on turning speeds, especially for roughing operations.

Select stock carefully and inspect it closely before undertaking a project. Avoid using wood with knots or splits. Be sure to allow laminated, or glued-up, blanks to dry thoroughly before turning. Make certain that the work is secure before you start a turning operation—and check frequently as well during the project.

Position the toolrest no more than 1/8 in. from the stock. Before turning on power to the lathe, rotate the stock by hand to be sure that it clears the toolrest. Never adjust the position of the toolrest while the lathe is running. Always remove the toolrest from the lathe's bed when sanding or finishing.

Keep your woodturning tools sharp. A dull chisel requires that you apply excessive feed pressure and doesn't contribute to quality work. Grip a tool firmly in both hands. The general rule is to hold the chisel's handle in your right hand and support its leading end with your left hand. Don't, however, close your left hand into a fist. Instead, prop the tool on the tips of your fingers and grasp the side or top of the blade with your thumb. Your index finger should rest comfortably along the ledge of the toolrest.

For many types of scraping cuts, the chisel is held at a right angle to the work and simply moved forward. When performing a cut parallel to the work, move both your hands and the chisel together, using the index finger of your left hand as a depth gauge. For many shaping cuts, the point of contact between the chisel and the toolrest serves as a pivot that is virtually maintained as your right hand provides the cutting action.

Always be sure to feed a woodturning tool slowly and steadily. Never jam the tool's blade or otherwise force it into the work. Make contact with the work cautiously, then progress a little more aggressively. Avoid the extremes of overdoing an operation and just rubbing against the stock.

Keep your woodturning tools to one side or behind you so there's no need to reach over the lathe to get them. Never use your fingers to check the work for roundness while the lathe is running—especially during roughing operations. Stop the lathe to check your progress, or rest the blade of the tool lightly against the work as it turns. The degree to which the blade vibrates is an indication of how close the work is to being round.

SPINDLE TURNING

To prepare a blank for turning between centers, first mill the stock square and cut the ends square. Next, locate and mark the center on each end of the blank with an awl. On hardwood stock, make two diagonal saw cuts on the headstock end and centerbore a small hole to help seat the spur center firmly. Make shallow cuts with a handsaw or on a band saw using a centering jig.

Then, drive the spur center securely into the end of the blank using a mallet. Now, make a mark on the end of the stock next to a clear reference point on the spur center—such as a manufacturer's logo or other distinguishing mark. This way if the blank is removed from the lathe before completion, you can reposition the spur center in its original spot.

The next step is to mount the blank between centers with the spur center

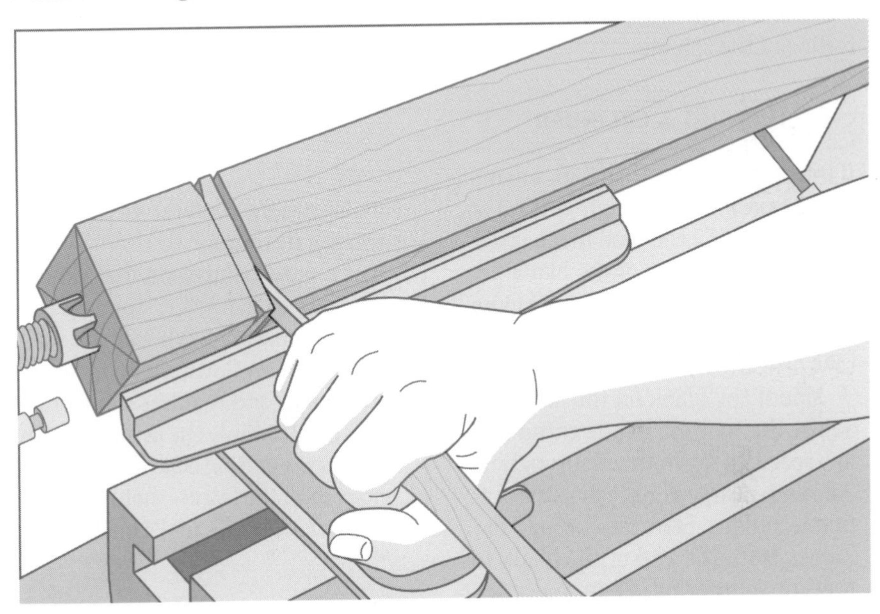

▲ **SPINDLE TURNING, 1.** ***Make small cuts on each corner of the blank's shoulder to prevent splintering of the wood. Then, use a parting tool to establish the diameter of the spindle at the shoulder.***

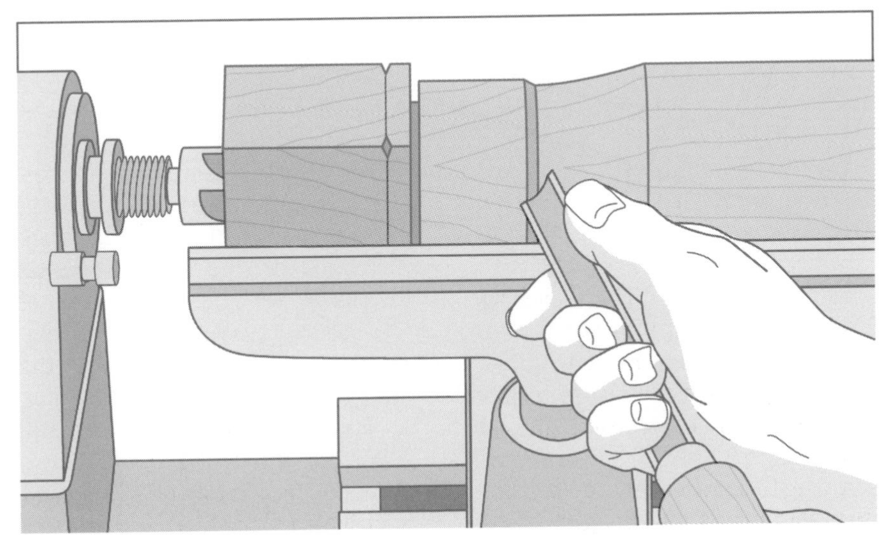

◄ **SPINDLE TURNING, 2.** ***Turn the remainder of the blank up to the shoulder into a cylinder. Note how the gouge shown in use here is rolled over to the left into the work.***

▶ **SPINDLE TURNING, 3.** ***Now, transfer diameter-sizing grooves from your full-scale pattern onto the blank. Mark grooves at distinct changes in profile.***

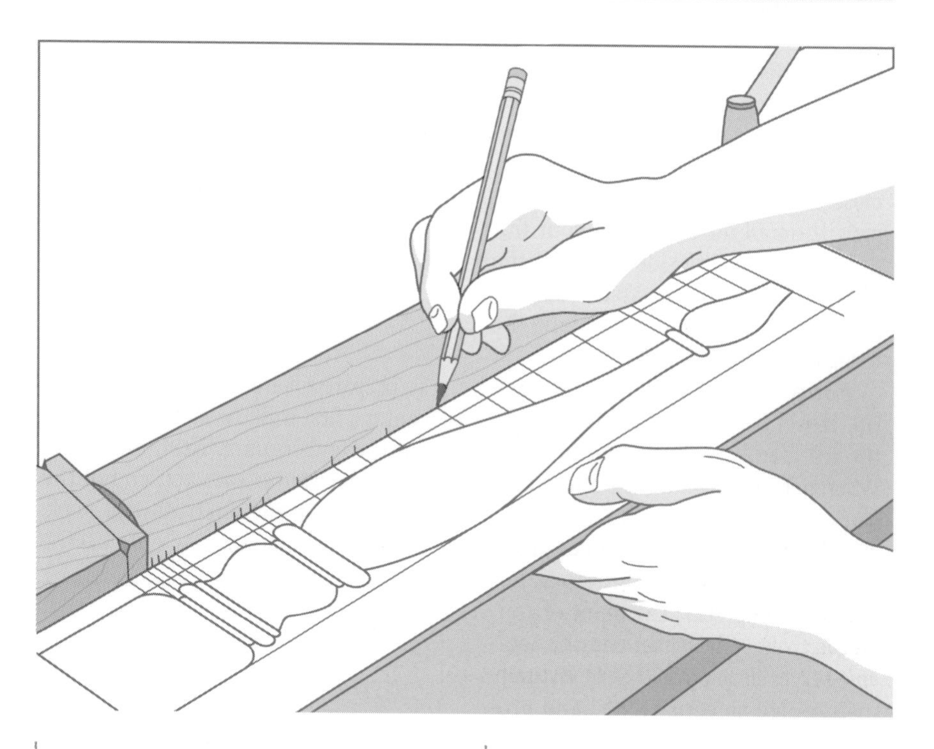

in the headstock spindle. Then, clamp the tailstock into position. Turn the handwheel to advance the tailstock spindle until the cup center seats firmly in end of the blank.

Apply oil, graphite or beeswax to the tailstock end of the work to help minimize heat buildup during turning. Finally, position the toolrest so that it's no more than ⅛ in. from the blank and about ⅛ in. above the centerline of the spindle.

TURNING A CYLINDER

If the blank is more than 3 in. square, you'll find that the rough-cutting of the cylinder is easier and much faster to do if the corners of the blank are first chamfered to form an octagon. Cut the blank's chamfers on a table saw, or using a jointer or band saw.

Mount the blank on the lathe and adjust the toolrest. While turning at low speed, perform the first roughing cuts with a large gouge using the cutting technique. Start the cutting a few inches from the end of the blank to prevent splintering. Then, move the gouge toward and off the end of the blank. Keep your index finger against the toolrest to maintain a constant depth of cut.

You should begin the second cut a few inches from the starting point of the first cut. Advance the gouge toward the end of the blank until you merge with the first cut. Repeat this procedure until you reach the middle of the blank. Then, you should start cutting close to the other end of the blank and work toward the center until the blank is rough-cut round.

Use a skew to finish-cut the cylinder to the desired diameter, stopping frequently to check the cylinder size with outside calipers. Cutting with a skew is a little tricky and requires some practice to master. Only the center section of the skew's cutting edge should make contact with the blank—not the upper point, or toe, of the tool's blade.

Set the skew flat on its side against the cylinder so that the cutting edge is pointing above and over the work. Keep the blade firmly against the toolrest, then draw the skew back slowly until the midpoint of the cutting edge is over the cylinder. Be careful not to catch the toe of the skew in the work. Raise the tool handle so that the cutting edge makes contact with the work. Now, push the skew along the cylin-

▶ **SPINDLE TURNING, 4.** ***Hold a pencil up against the revolving blank to clearly define the location of each of the diameter-sizing groove marks.***

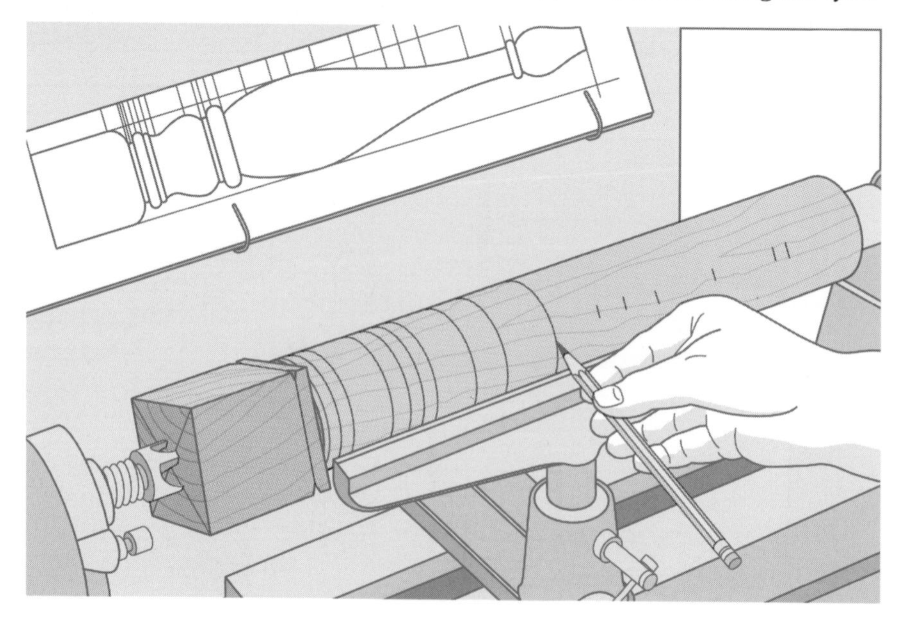

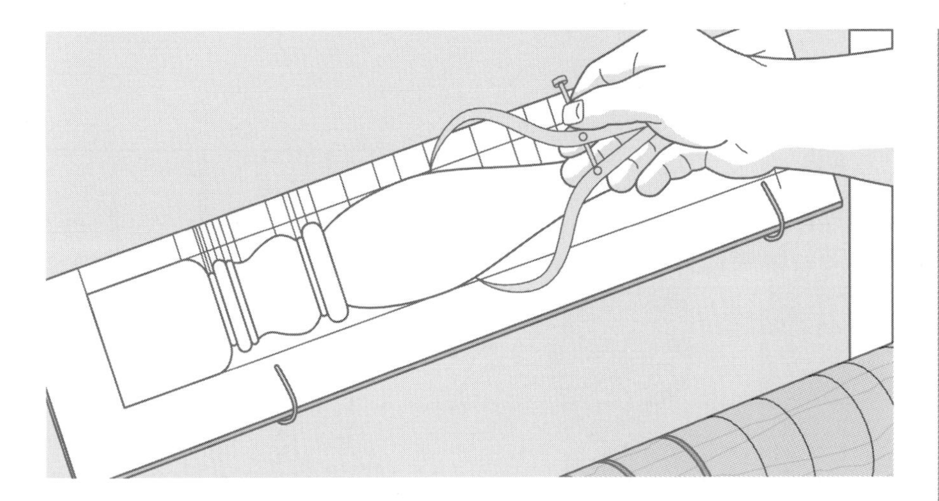

▲ **SPINDLE TURNING, 5.** ***Use your pattern to adjust outside calipers for measuring the grooves. Set the calipers about ¹⁄₁₆ in. oversize to permit finishing the blank to size.***

▼ **SPINDLE TURNING, 6.** ***Work with a parting tool to continue cutting diameter-sizing grooves. Check the grooves repeatedly with the calipers to ensure you match your pattern.***

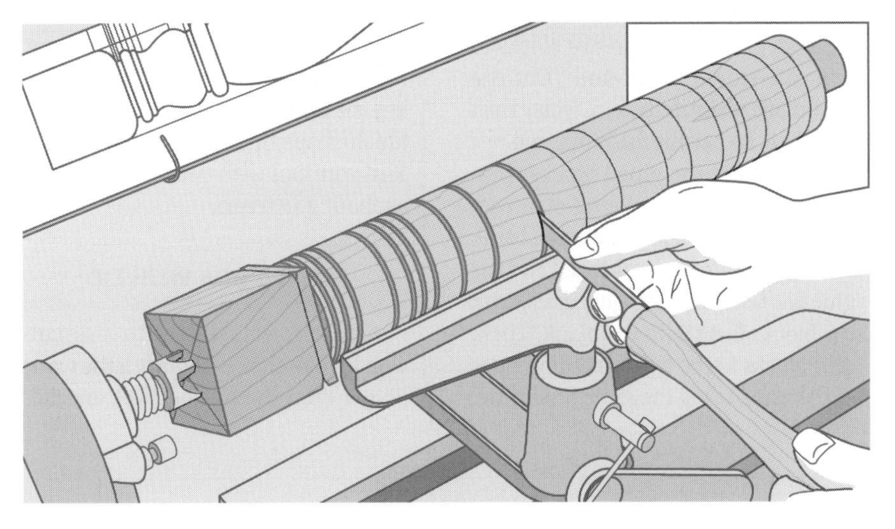

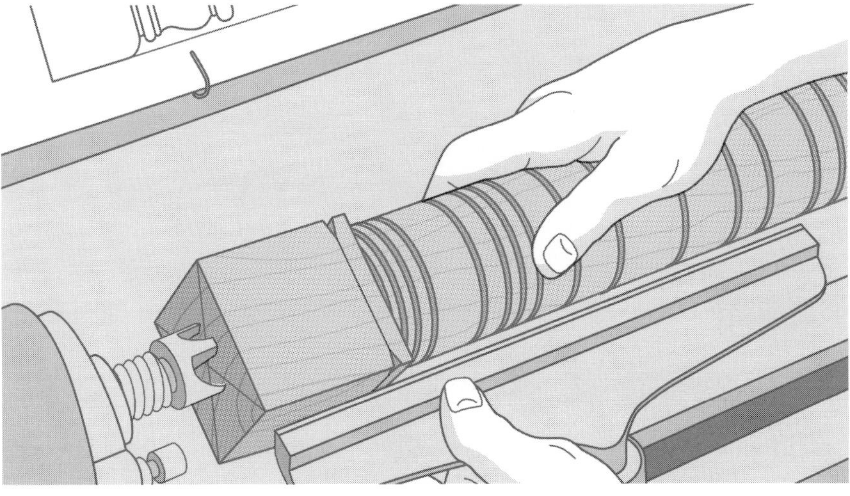

der to perform a shearing cut. Since shearing cuts are made with the tool's beveled edge set flat against the work, it's therefore essential that the bevel be ground perfectly flat.

Next, with the lathe running at high speed, finish-sand the cylinder using fine-grit abrasive paper. Be certain to remove the toolrest from the lathe's bed during sanding operations to eliminate the chance of getting your fingers caught between the toolrest and the blank.

FACEPLATE TURNING

Trays, bowls, vases and similar types of round objects are produced by faceplate turning. A faceplate is simply a flat metal disk that is screwed to the back of the turning blank and then threaded onto the headstock spindle.

Attach the faceplate to the blank using short, stout screws. When penetration of the screws interferes with the turning, glue a 1-in.-thick scrap block to the work with a sheet of paper set between them. This allows the parts to be separated easily afterward.

There are times when the diameter of the work will be too large to allow for it to be turned over the lathe's bed. In these instances, you will need to turn the work on the outboard end of the headstock spindle.

To form the turning blank for a project such as a 16-in.-dia. tray, first glue together four triangular-shaped pieces of stock. Cut each 90° segment of the blank from a board that's slightly wider than one-half of the finished diameter of the project. In the case of the tray, for example, the segments could be cut from 9¼-in.-wide boards. As well, each segment needs to be notched to form flat surfaces for C-clamps to grip.

◀ **SPINDLE TURNING, 7.** ***When you reposition the toolrest opposite the shoulder of the blank, rotate the blank by hand to make certain that there's sufficient clearance.***

▶ **SPINDLE TURNING, 8.** ***Now, round the top of the blank's shoulder with a skew. Hold the tool's blade flat on the toolrest and swing the handle slowly to the right.***

Glue and clamp the four blank segments together with plastic-resin glue.

Once the glue has dried thoroughly, rough-cut the blank to within ⅛ in. of the finished diameter on a band saw. The next step is to glue and clamp a 1 x 7½-in.-dia. wood disk permanently to the backside of the blank to serve as the tray's base. Let the assembly dry, then screw the faceplate to the base and mount the blank on the outboard end of the lathe's headstock spindle.

Next, trim the edge of the blank to obtain the desired diameter by working with a diamond-point chisel. Then, reposition the toolrest and use a gouge to rough-cut the tray's face. Make light finishing cuts with a diamond-point or round-nose tool. Any of the basic turning tools can be used for faceplate work, but with the scraping technique only. And remember to never attempt to cut across the entire diameter of the work. Cut only on the downward-rotating half of the blank.

LARGE POST BLOCKING

There are two ways that can be used to turn a very wide project in only a portion of its length. One method is to start with a blank that is slightly greater in diameter than the widest part of the finished project. Then, cut away all the waste to form the narrow section of the project. A quicker, less wasteful way is known as post blocking. This method involves the gluing-up of blocks to the blank to build up its diameter in a specific area.

First, cut the blank square and mill all four sides perfectly flat on a jointer. Next, glue and clamp two blocks to opposite sides of the blank. Cut the blocks approximately ⅛ in. wider than the blank to permit flush planing.

To prevent the glued blocks from sliding when they're being clamped, toe-nail them temporarily to the blank until the clamps are tightened and the glue has set. When the glue dries, trim the blocks flush with the blank. Then, glue blocks to the two remaining sides of the blank using the same procedure.

Next, chamfer the corners of the built-up section of the blank on a table saw, setting the blade to 45°. Mount the blank in the lathe and start turning the built-up section first. You can finish-shape the narrow neck using a Surform tool with the lathe running at about 2,000 rpm.

TURNED BOX WITH LID

For this project, start with a square wood block that is slightly wider and longer than the finished box and lid.

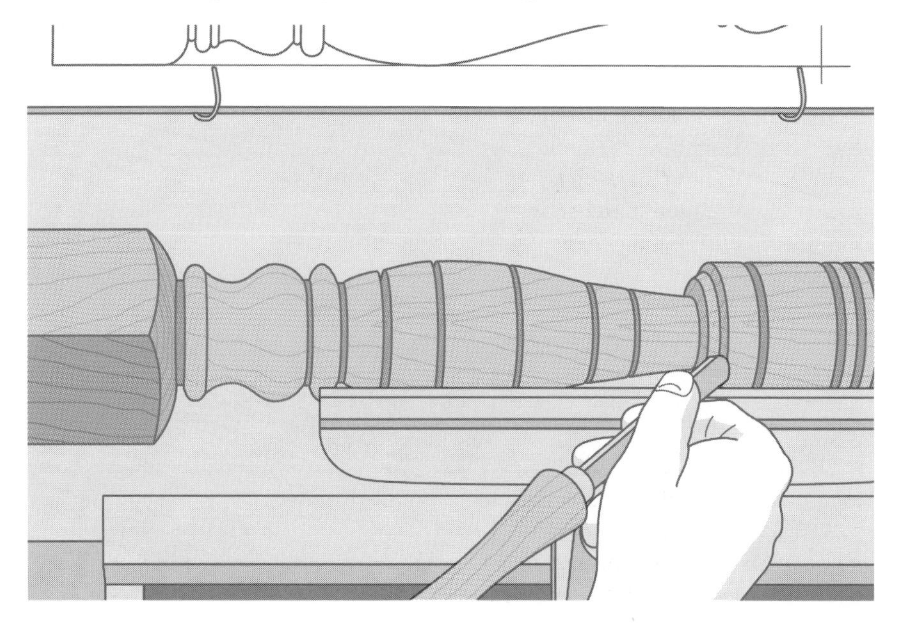

▶ **SPINDLE TURNING, 9.** ***Work with a diamond-point parting tool to remove waste quickly. Long, thin ribbons of waste material are peeled off by the tool's sharp cutting edge.***

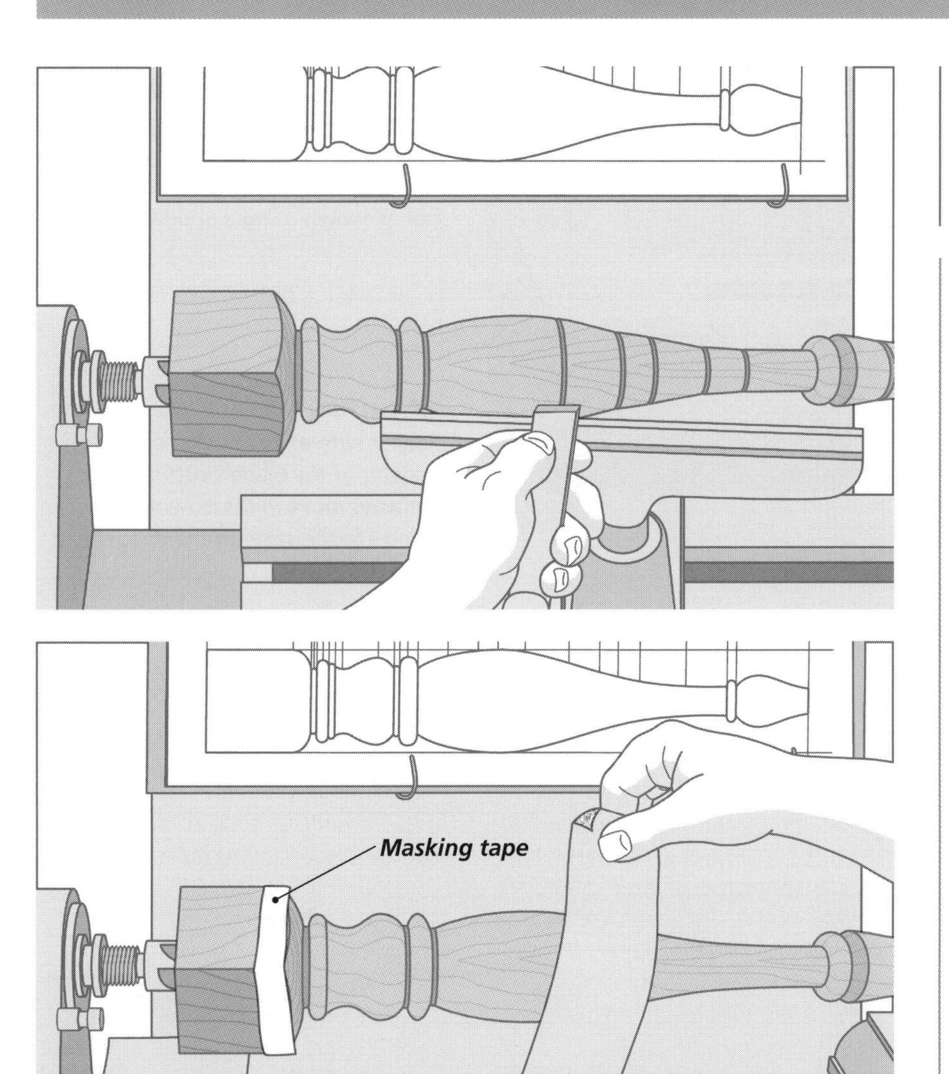

◀ **SPINDLE TURNING, 10.** ***A final leveling pass using a skew brings the spindle closer to its finished size. Move the toolrest along the spindle as necessary to continue.***

If necessary, glue up stock to obtain a turning blank of the desired size. Next, cut the lid section from the blank on a band saw. Then, trim the headstock end of the blank square and attach a 3-in.-dia. faceplate. Although the blank is faceplate mounted, use the tailstock center to stabilize the blank while you shape the exterior of the box.

After you've turned the box exterior, replace the tailstock center with a geared chuck that's fitted with a 1- to 1½-in.-dia. drill bit. Now, advance the tailstock to centerbore the end of the blank. Bore as close to the finished depth as possible.

Next, slide the tailstock out of the way and start hollowing out the interior of the box using a skew or diamond-point chisel. Finish turning the box interior with a round-nose chisel. Be certain to check the wall thickness of the box frequently with calipers.

The next step is to remove the box and mount the lid blank to the headstock with a 3-in-dia. faceplate. Turn the lid to the finished diameter and shape the underside to fit snugly in the box opening. Next, remount the

▲ **SPINDLE TURNING, 11.** ***Remove the toolrest to finish-sand the spindle. Note that a band of masking tape is wrapped around the shoulder as a safety reminder to keep hands clear.***

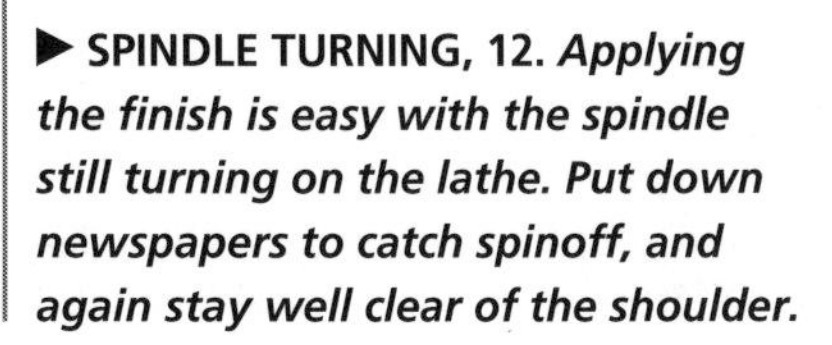

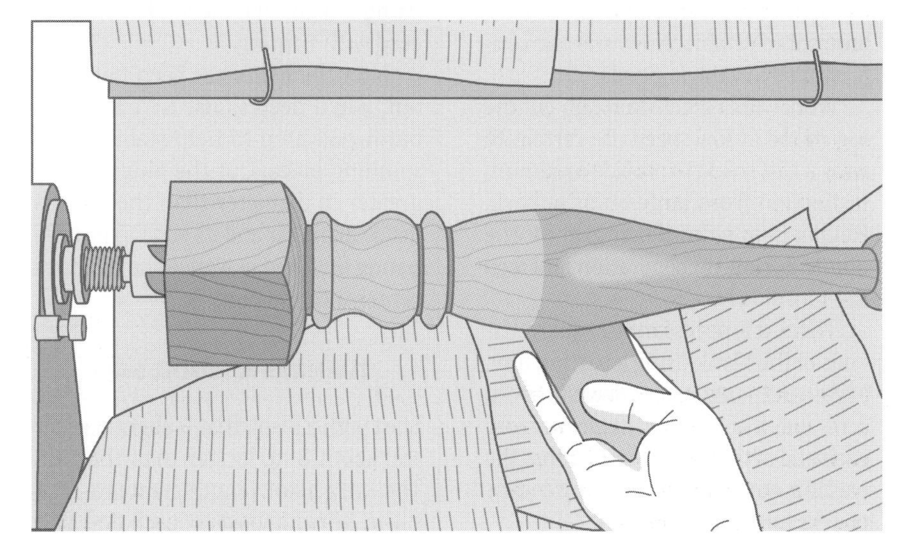

▶ **SPINDLE TURNING, 12.** ***Applying the finish is easy with the spindle still turning on the lathe. Put down newspapers to catch spinoff, and again stay well clear of the shoulder.***

◀ **CUTTING TAPERS, 1.** ***Make a long taper in a blank by first cutting diameter-sizing grooves with a parting tool. Then, remove the waste material as shown using a gouge.***

▼ **CUTTING TAPERS, 2.** ***Finish-cut the taper with a skew, using only the center of the blade's cutting edge. Always move in the downhill direction—in this case, from left to right.***

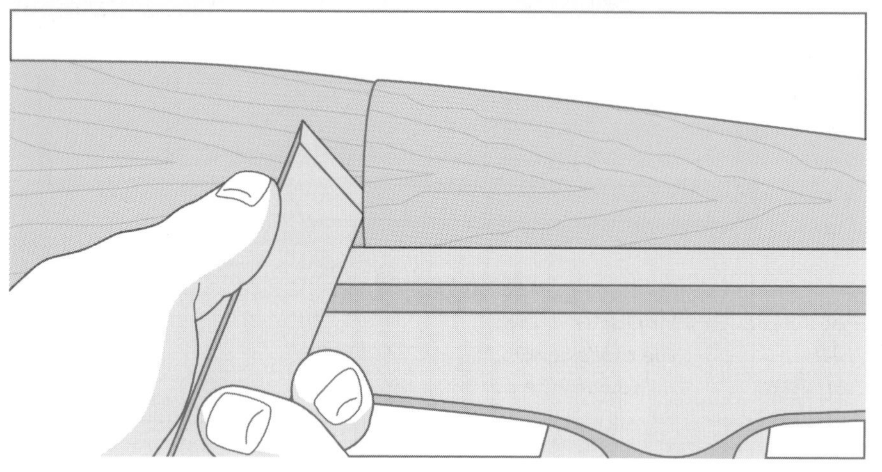

box to serve as a chuck while shaping the top of the lid. For this procedure, replace the tailstock center point with a pad insert. Be sure to position the tailstock so that the pad will hold the lid on the box.

LOG TURNING

A dry, knot-free log can make a suitable turning blank for many projects. Select a straight log that is free of long, gaping end checks, or cracks. Be sure to cut the log several inches longer than necessary to permit squaring the ends of the blank with a parting tool.

Mount the log lightly between the headstock and tailstock centers. Then, spin the log by hand. Shift the log on the centers until it spins with the least amount of wobble. Now, seat the centers firmly in the log ends.

Work with a gouge to rough-cut the log round at low speed. Be certain to wear a face shield to provide maximum protection from large chips of bark. Keep a firm palm-down grip on the gouge during this operation and feed the tool slowly.

Then, it's necessary to square the ends of the blank using a parting tool. Make a deep parting cut down to about 1 in. dia. a couple of inches in from each end of the log. Be certain that the parting cuts are clear of any minor checks in the log ends.

Now, remove the log from the lathe and cut through the remaining 1 in. on each end of the log with a handsaw. Remount the blank on the lathe using a 3-in.-dia. faceplate and proceed with turning.

After the blank has been hollowed out, you'll need to use a ¾-in.-thick hardwood plug to help stabilize the spinning piece. Cut the plug slightly greater in diameter than the blank's inside diameter and its edge to provide a snug fit. Then, advance the tailstock center into the plug.

TURNING A WOOD BALL

Start with a blank that is slightly wider and about 8 in. longer than the ball. The extra blank length creates a 1 x 1 x 4-in. turning post on each end that gives tool clearance for shaping the ball. Mark the ball diameter and two posts on adjacent sides of the blank. Using a band saw, cut along the lines on one side of the blank. Tape the cutoffs back onto the blank and saw along the lines on the adjacent side.

Mount the blank between centers and mark centerlines on all four sides using a heavy felt-tip marker. Begin turning with a gouge until the inked centerlines are barely visible. Take finishing cuts with a skew and diamond-point chisel. Next, cut partway through the posts close to the ball with a parting tool. Then, remove the blank and cut off the posts with a handsaw, then remount the ball between a cup chuck and a pad insert. Realign the ball frequently while sanding with 120-, 220- and 240-grit abrasive paper.

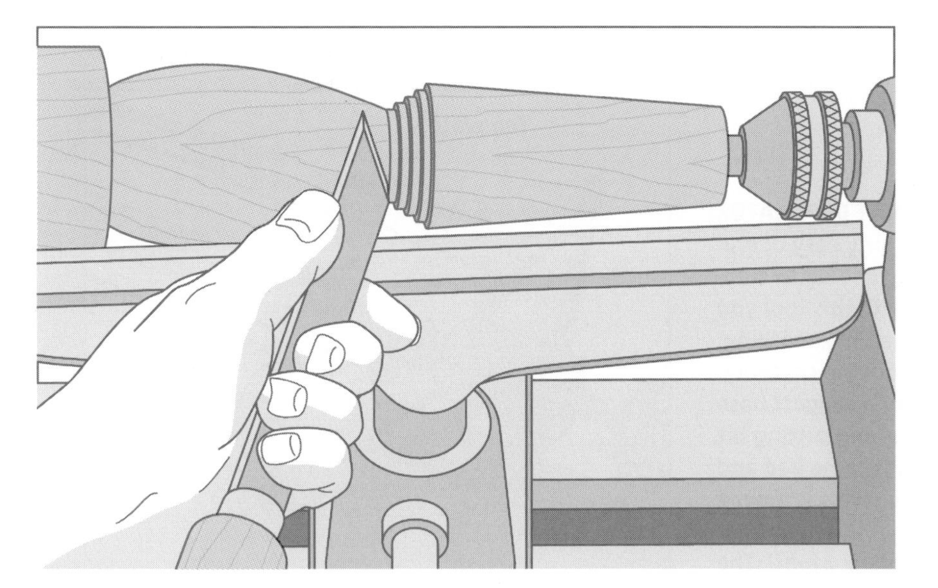

TURNING A CABRIOLE LEG

Although a Queen Anne style of cabriole leg is rough-cut on a band saw and finish-shaped by hand, the lathe is used to accurately form the circular foot and step, and even a small portion of the contoured ankle. When rounding the front of the ankle—the area just above the foot's toe—it's necessary to reposition the tailstock end off-center.

Start by tracing the profile of the finished leg on adjacent sides of the blank. Next, locate and mark the centers on each end of the blank. Then, use a compass to draw two circles on the bottom of the leg (the tailstock end): one to represent the step diameter, and a slightly larger one equal to the diameter of the foot. Use the circles as guides in turning the foot and step.

Now, draw a diagonal line toe-to-heel across the bottom of the leg. Mark the off-center location along this line about 3/16 in. inside the small (step) circle—closer to the heel of the leg, not toward the toe.

Next, cut along the profile of the leg on one side of the blank using a band saw. Tape the cutoff back onto the blank and saw along the adjacent side profile. Then, mount the leg and turn the foot and step with skew and

▲ **SHAPING CURVES, 1.** ***Shaping convex curves with a skew is similar to cutting long tapers. Always work downhill from the high point of the curve to its low point.***

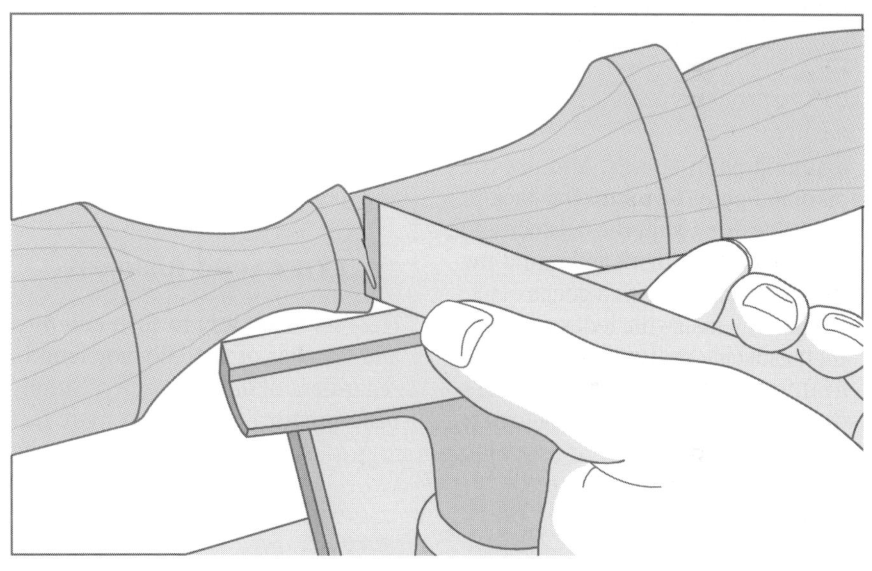

▶ **SHAPING CURVES, 2.** ***To form concave curves, move the skew into the blank and swing the tool's handle in an arc. Cut downhill toward the center of the curve.***

▼ **SHAPING CURVES, 3.** ***To square up a shoulder on the blank, work with the toe of the skew. To produce a smooth surface, take very light shavings of about 1/32 in.***

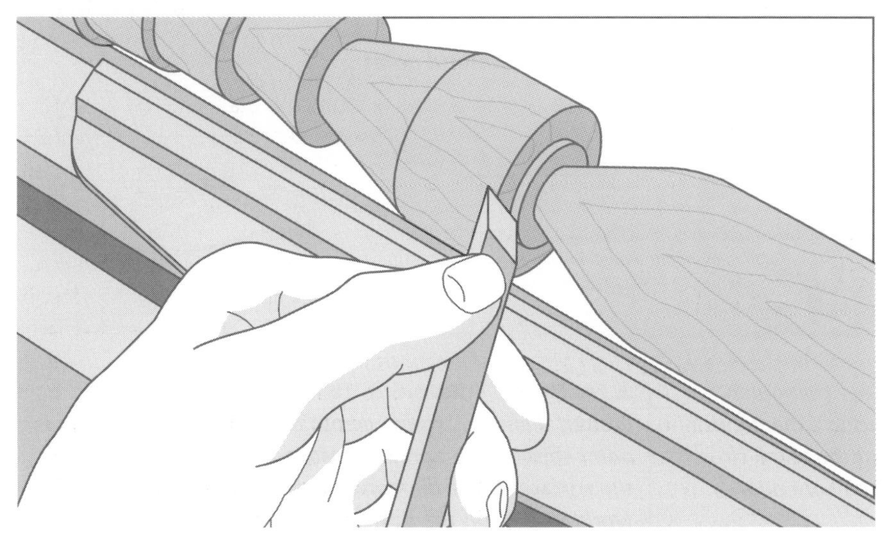

TIP

OFFSET DUPLICATOR

Turning a spindle on a lathe is a fairly easy operation. But making exact copies of the first leg to complete a set is much more difficult. With this tool you can dispense with the fuss of measuring, marking, checking and double-checking.

An offset duplicator consists of a support base and post from which a tracing stylus and cutting bit project. Two brackets attach to the lathe bed and hold the work being copied. As the stylus is moved to follow the contour of the sample, the cutter follows the same contour on the blank *(right)*. The original or sample can be either a turning or a flat, contoured template cut from a strip of hardboard.

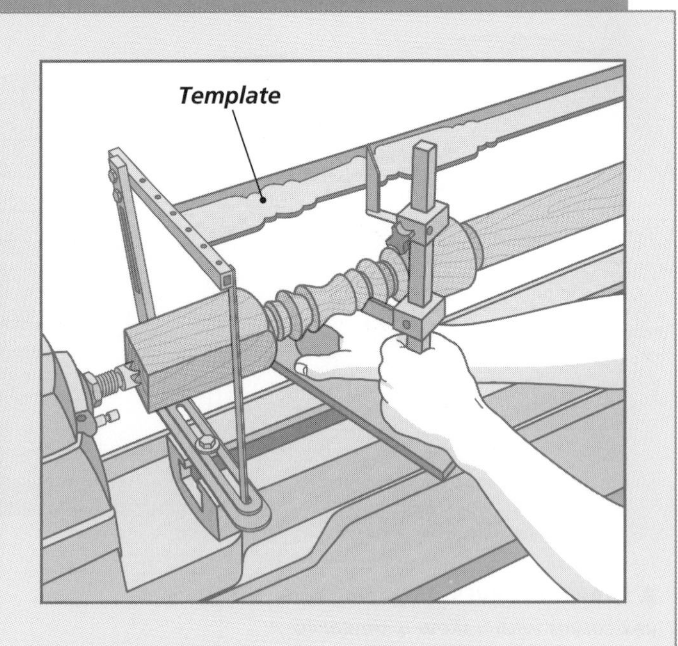

diamond-point chisels. Also use the diamond point to round the back of the ankle. Now, shift the tailstock end to the off-center mark and round the front of the ankle with a gouge.

Finally, engage the indexing pin in the headstock pulley to keep the leg from rotating. Then, shape the leg's final contour, making use of a variety of hand tools—including a rasp, file and spokeshave.

EXTRA-LONG TURNINGS

Here's an easy way to turn columns and spindles of virtually any length, regardless of lathe capacity. Simply make the turning in two or more sections that are joined by a round mortise and tenon. Be certain to locate the joint where it won't be visible, such as at a shoulder or between beads.

First, shape one section of the turning. Then, support the tailstock end with a steady rest to bore the mortise. Install a geared chuck in the tailstock and advance the drill bit into the end

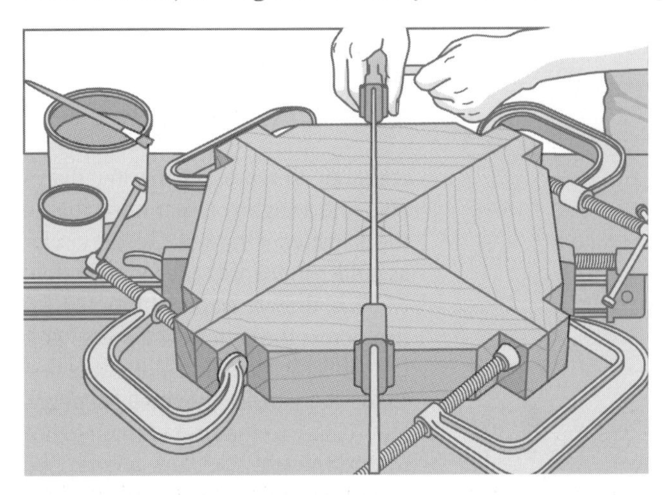

▲ FACEPLATE TURNING, 1. *Glue together four triangular-shaped segments to form the blank, producing a diamond-matched grain pattern as shown. Rough-cut the blank close to the finished diameter on a band saw, then bore pilot holes for screwing to the faceplate.*

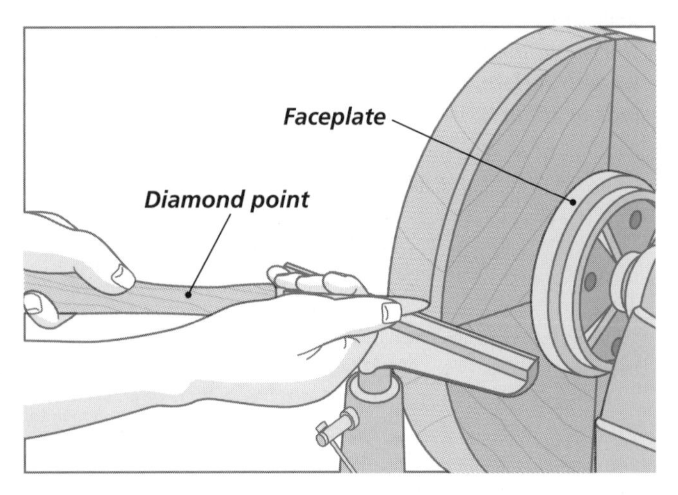

▲ FACEPLATE TURNING, 2. *To form the blank into the desired diameter, scrape across the edge with a diamond-point chisel, as shown here. Make light, finishing cuts on the surface with a diamond-point or round-nose chisel, working only on the downward-rotating half of the blank.*

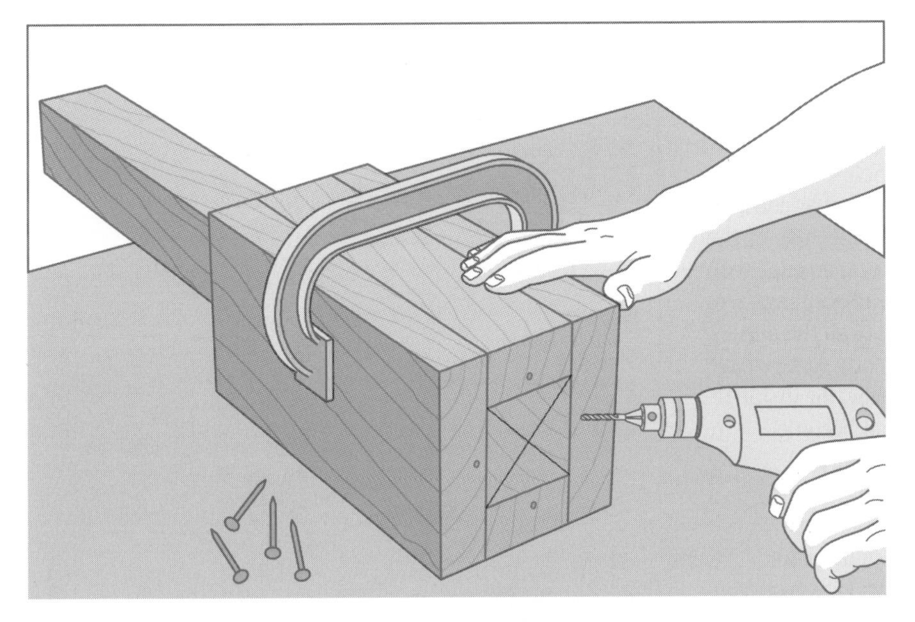

◀ **POST BLOCKING, 1.** ***Clamp blocks for the blank in position and bore pilot holes for nails. Then, apply glue and nail the blocks together temporarily to keep them from sliding while being clamped until the glue sets. Chamfer the blank's built-up corners at a 45° angle on a table saw.***

▼ **POST BLOCKING, 2.** ***Carve the blank's built-up section with a gouge. Cut diameter-sizing grooves with a parting tool, then use a gouge as shown to rough-shape the blank's long, narrow section. Finish-shape long, subtle curves with light passes of a Surform tool at 2,000 rpm.***

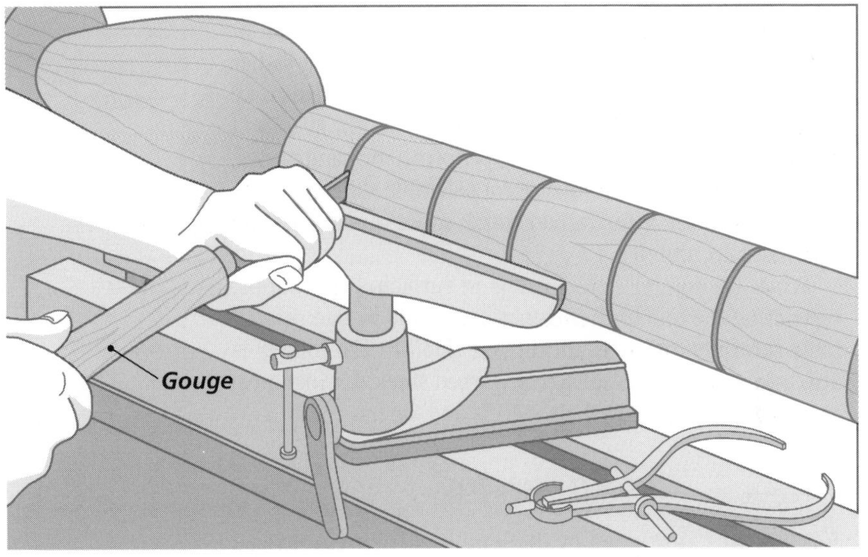

of the spinning turning. Now, shape the second section and turn a mating tenon for the mortise on the tailstock end. Use a diameter-sizing attachment on a parting tool to cut the tenon to the exact size. Then, dry assemble the turning sections, checking for a snug fit between tenon and mortise.

Turning blanks of cedar, redwood and other softwood species often begin to wobble on the lathe as the headstock and tailstock centers lose their grip in the soft end grain. The solution is to temporarily glue hardwood pads (separated by a sheet of paper for easy removal) to the blank ends.

SPLIT TURNINGS

Half or split columns and spindles are used frequently as decorative accents. The trick to making split turnings is to glue up the blank, turn the spindle on a lathe and then split it in half.

First, form the turning blank by gluing two pieces of stock together separated by a sheet of slick magazine paper. Chamfer the stock ends slightly to make it easier to pry the spindle apart with a chisel. After the glue dries, mount the blank between the headstock and tailstock and turn the spindle to the desired shape.

Now, use a chisel to carefully split the spindle in two. The paper sandwiched in the middle will allow the halves to separate easily. Be certain to scrape or sand the back of the split turnings clean before installing them.

SMALL POST BLOCKING

This technique, which is very similar to large post blocking, is used almost exclusively to make square-shouldered spindles with large-diameter midsections. To start, mill the turning blank square and joint the four sides perfectly flat. Next, glue two wood blocks to opposite sides of the blank's midsection where the large diameter of the spindle is to be turned. When the glue dries, trim the blocks flush with the blank. Then, glue and clamp blocks to the two remaining sides of the blank and let the assembly dry.

Now, mount the blank between the headstock and tailstock centers. Turn the spindle to the desired shape, working the built-up section first. If the blocks are glued on carefully, the spindle will appear to have been turned from a single piece of stock.

JOINTERS-PLANERS

A jointer may not be the first tool to purchase for your home workshop, but it is nonetheless a versatile woodworking machine that is a valuable complement to a table saw or radial arm saw. Correct use of the jointer guarantees you a straight edge on stock, an edge with the smoothness, evenness and squareness to adjacent surfaces that is required in order to ensure precision of all the dimensions of your work. Without having a perfectly square edge to position against the rip fence of a table saw, for instance, trimming stock to size introduces errors that become greatly exacerbated later on when you attempt to cut a tight-fitting joint.

The jointer is a surfacing tool used for the most part to smooth rough, irregular board edges prior to edge-gluing into panels or ripping on a saw. However, you can also use the jointer like a planer to smooth the faces of narrow boards. The machine works in principle much like an inverted hand plane, approaching the work from below rather than above with somewhat larger blades that are driven by a motor. Indeed, the task of producing smooth, even and square edges has been traditionally performed by hand planes, a painstaking process requiring considerable skill and experience that the jointer can do much more quickly, effortlessly and accurately.

While the jointer's chief use is in surfacing operations, restricting the tool to these functions would be like using a table saw only for crosscutting and ripping. The jointer is also a valuable tool in salvaging warped stock, for instance, as well as in shaping rabbets, bevels and tapers.

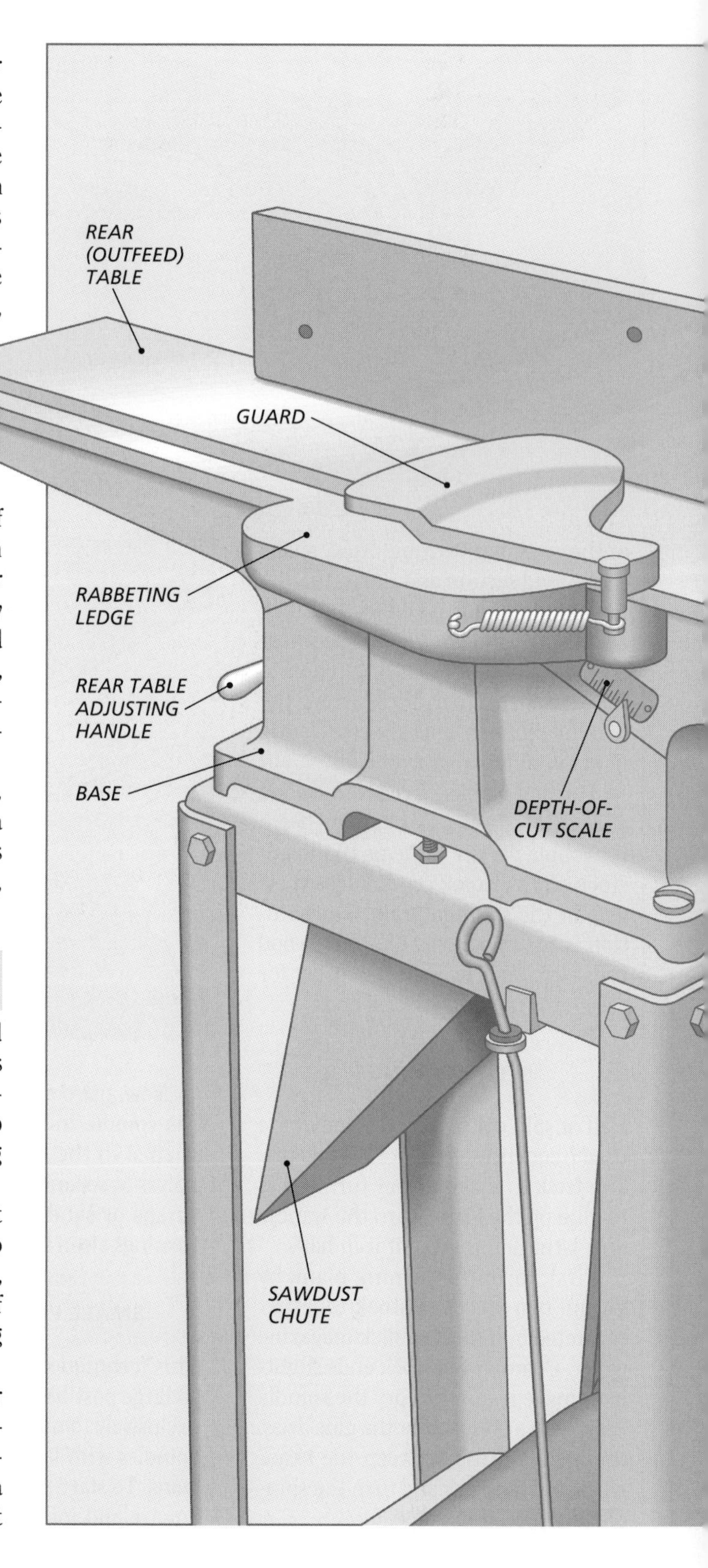

JOINTER SPECIFICS

Jointers are categorized by the length of their cutterhead knives, a measurement that influences the width of the tool's worktables and—more significantly—the machine's maximum width of cut. Common models for the home workshop range in size from 4 to 8 in., with the 6- and 8-in. types being the most popular.

Another distinguishing feature of jointers is depth-of-cut capacity, which varies from 1/8 to 1/2 in. Unless you intend to make frequent use of the rabbeting capability of the tool, however, you'll find that a model with a shallow depth of cut is adequate. Only in rare instances should a surfacing pass ever exceed a depth of 1/8 in.

When shopping for a jointer, keep in mind that a bigger machine size doesn't necessarily mean a greater depth-of-cut capability. There are both 4- and 6-in. models, for example, that have a maximum cutting depth of 1/8. Choose a jointer with worktables on both sides of the cutterhead that

JOINTER ANATOMY
Shown here is a typical 4-in. jointer. Positioned between two independently adjustable tables that are supported by the base, there is a motor-driven cutterhead that holds removable knives. An adjustable, tilting fence guides the workpiece and a retractable guard covers the cutterhead.

FENCE

FRONT (INFEED) TABLE

FRONT TABLE ADJUSTING HANDLE

TILT SCALE

FENCE CONTROL HANDLE

STAND

▲ **JOINTER SETUP, 1.** ***Check the knife alignment by clamping two steel rules to the rear table. Wedge a pencil next to the cutterhead to keep it from rotating, then adjust the knife to touch both rules.***

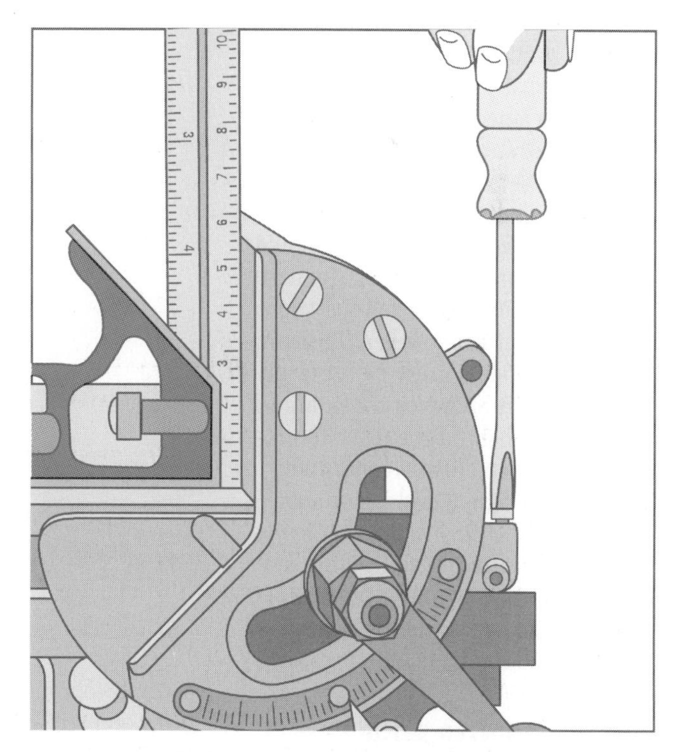

▲ **JOINTER SETUP, 2.** ***Use a square to check accuracy of the fence. If the fence is not exactly perpendicular to the table, adjust the automatic stops and indicator.***

are adjustable. And be sure the tool comes equipped with a rigid fence that can be tilted for angle cuts—and that locks securely in position.

JOINTER MECHANICS

The jointer is relatively simple in both design and operation. A base supports two worktables that are usually independently adjustable. A cylindrical-shaped, steel cutterhead positioned between the tables holds removable knives. The cutterhead is driven by a belt that's connected to the motor, and rotates at several thousand rpm.

The jointer's front, or infeed, table is adjusted for the depth of cut. The rear, or outfeed, table is for most operations positioned at the same height as the knives to support the work as it passes the cutterhead. On models with an outfeed table that is non-adjustable, the knives must be raised or lowered to the proper height.

A fence is provided with the jointer to help guide work over the cutterhead. Normally set and locked at a 90° angle, the fence on most models can be tilted forward or backward for the cutting of bevels and chamfers.

The jointer's cutterhead is shielded by a retractable guard that should always be kept in place for standard procedures. For specialized operations such as rabbeting, however, the guard on many models must be removed. Some models allow for the guard to be installed behind the fence to provide protection during rabbet cuts.

Note that the guard is not shown in some of the illustrations here *only* for visual clarity. As with other stationary tools, the jointer must never be operated unless its safety devices are installed and functioning properly.

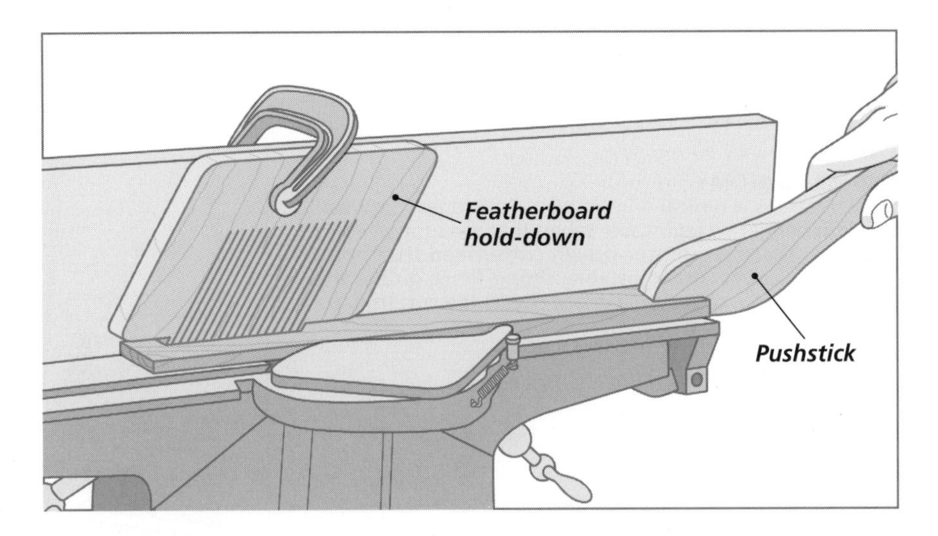

▲ **JOINTING THIN STOCK.** ***A featherboard hold-down like the one shown here is a necessity when jointing thin stock. Make certain that you clamp the hold-down directly over the cutterhead and rear table.***

▼ **JOINTING END GRAIN.** ***Joint end grain wlth slow, shallow passes. To prevent splintering of the rear edge, first make a short cut, then turn the workpiece around and make a full pass, as shown.***

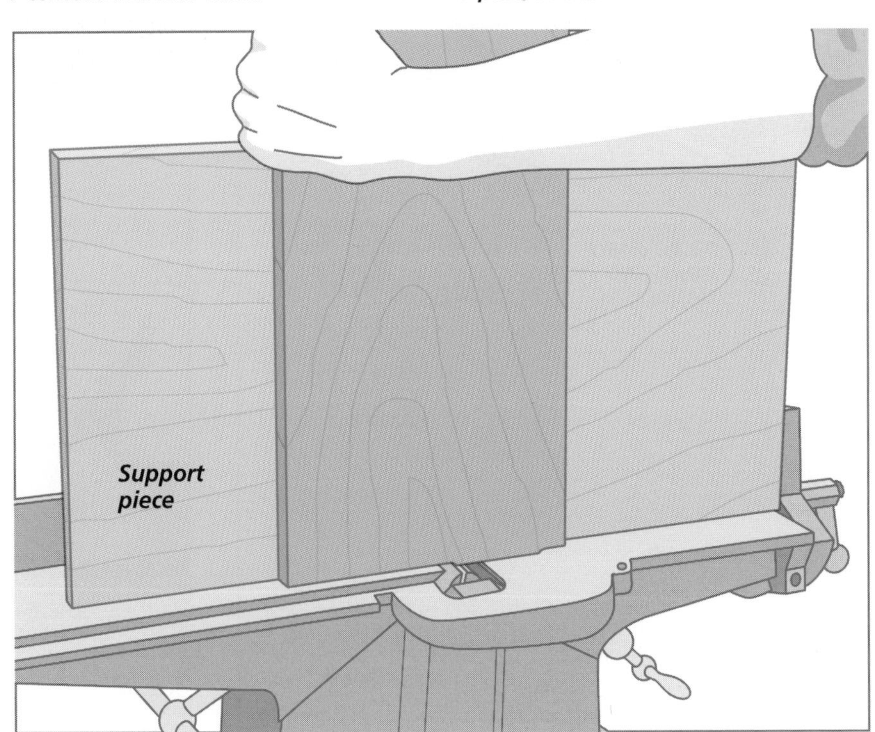

JOINTER SETUP

A jointer requires few adjustments, but these must be made carefully to obtain optimum tool performance. Achieving accurate jointing results depends especially on precise alignment of the two tables and the fence—the components responsible for guiding the work into and over the knives of the cutterhead. Before making any checks or adjustments to the jointer, however, make sure that the machine is disconnected from its electrical outlet.

Begin by checking that the knives are correctly positioned in the cutterhead. The knives must align with each

▶ **CUTTING RABBETS.** ***Cut a rabbet by passing the workpiece over the end of the cutterhead. Support the workpiece on the rabbeting ledge and position the fence to control the width of the rabbet.***

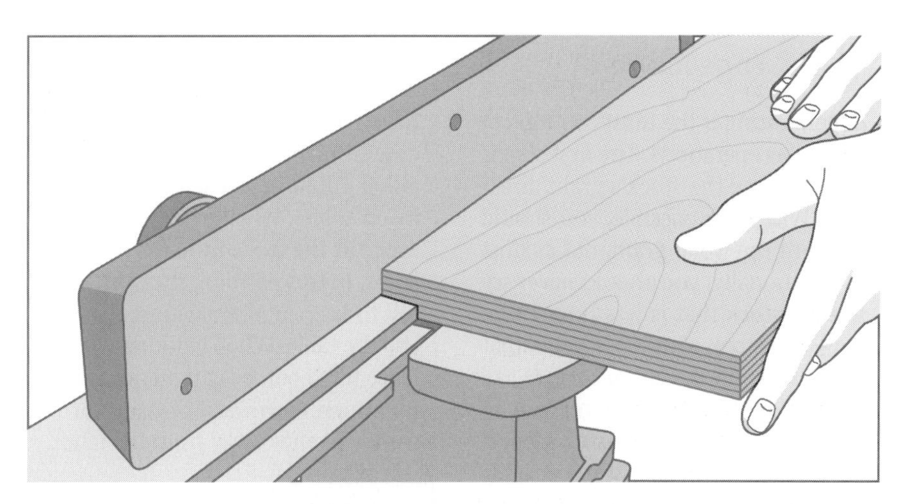

▼ **CUTTING BEVELS.** ***The safest way to cut bevels is with the fence tilted in to form a closed angle. This eases the task of keeping the workpiece in close contact with both the fence and the table.***

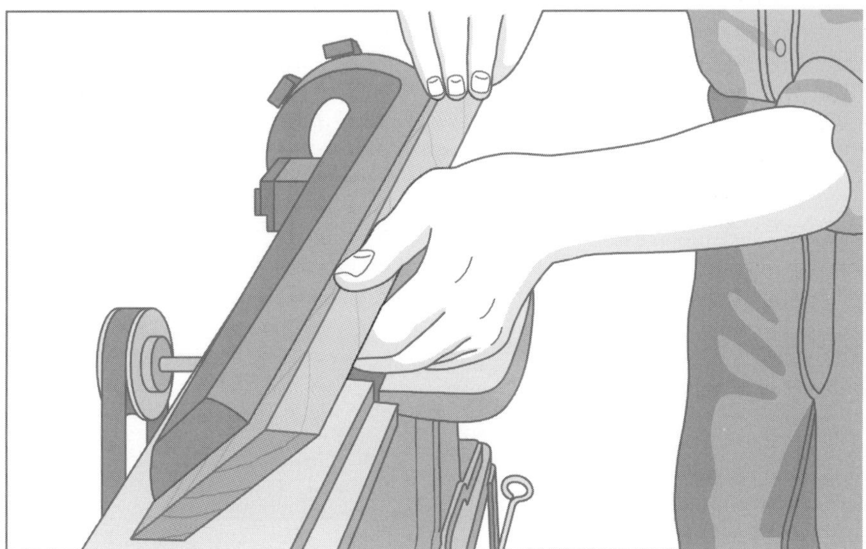

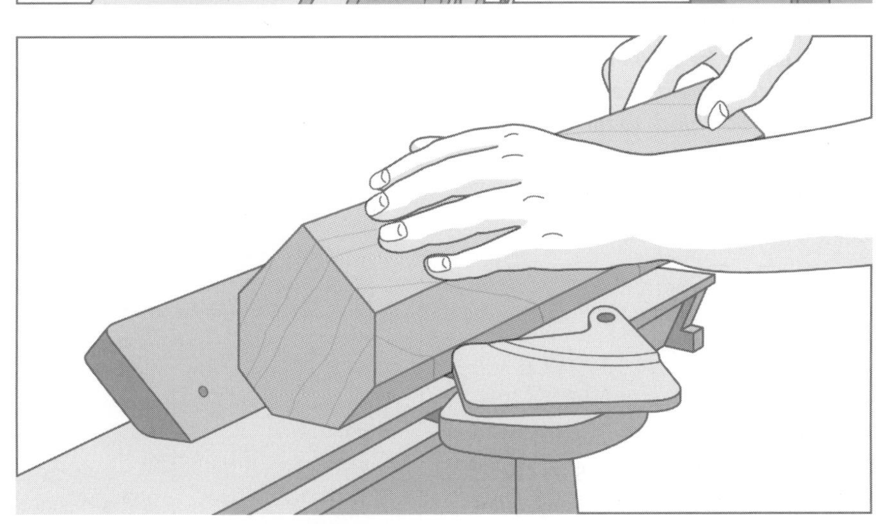

▲ **CHAMFERING.** ***Chamfering the corners of a square block is a quick and easy way to make an octagon-shaped piece. Set the fence to 45° and make the same number of passes for each corner.***

other and be level with the rear table. To check the alignment of the knives, clamp two 12-in. steel rules to a wood block that's about 1 in. narrower than the cutterhead. Install a clamp on the rabbeting ledge of the jointer to hold the guard temporarily out of the way. Next, elevate the rear table slightly above the knives and clamp the rules-and-wood-block assembly to the rear table so that the rules overhang the edge of one knife by ⅛ in. Now, lower the rear table until the rules touch the knife. If only one of the rules makes contact, then the knife isn't level with the table. Loosen the locking screw and adjust the knife so it touches both of the rules. Rotate the cutterhead and align the remaining knives to the same ⅛-in. marks on the rules.

Next, check the front table's depth-of-cut scale and indicator, or pointer, for accuracy. Set the jointer for a ⅛-in.-deep cut. Then, accurately scribe a ⅛-in. line on a test board. Make a partial cut and see if the line and cut match. If not, adjust the front table as required. Repeat the procedure until the cut is exactly ⅛ in. deep. Now, set the depth-of-cut indicator to ⅛ in.

Check the accuracy of the jointer's tilting fence using a square. When set at 0° the fence should be exactly perpendicular (90°) to the front table. Also check the fence when set at 45°. Make any adjustment to the fence and indicator that is necessary.

EDGE-JOINTING

Edge-jointing is the most common of all jointer operations. The first step is to determine the stock's grain direction. Whenever possible, you should cut with the wood grain, not against it. Additionally, you should never try to joint stock that is less then 12 in. long, nor stock with loose knots that might catch in the cutterhead.

Hold the stock firmly in place on the front table and against the fence. Advance the work slowly and steadily into the cutterhead and onto the rear table while applying pressure with your left hand. As the back end of the work approaches the cutterhead, apply pressure with your right hand.

When performing edge-jointing on extra-long stock, employ the aid of a helper or use a jig. To build a simple jig, set the jointer to the desired depth of cut and run a length of 1 x 4 halfway across the cutterhead to form an auxiliary fence. Screw short 1 x 3s to the bottom ends of the auxiliary fence to serve as extension tables, then screw through the jointer's fence into the auxiliary fence to install the jig.

Jointing end grain is a little trickier than standard edge-jointing. Be sure to feed the work more slowly and take shallower cuts to avoid the risk of kickback. To prevent the back edge of the work from splintering when the knives exit, first make a short pass into one end. Then, turn the work around and make a complete pass.

RABBETING

Rabbeting on the jointer is possible if your machine has a rabbeting ledge. The ledge extends from the front table around the end of the cutterhead. If the jointer's guard must be removed to cut rabbets, be sure to keep your hands well clear of the cutterhead.

Position the jointer fence to control the rabbet width. Adjust the depth of cut to determine the rabbet depth.

BEVELS AND CHAMFERS

Bevels and chamfers can both be executed on the jointer with the fence either tilted in (closed angle) or out (open angle). Whenever possible, however, tilt the fence in to form a closed angle. In this position, the work is easiest to keep in place against the fence and the table. When working with the fence tilted out, be careful not to exert too much downward pressure or the work will slide away from the fence.

MAKING RAISED PANELS

Raised panels can be made using any of several woodworking tools, including the jointer. First, set up for standard jointing operations: rear table level with the knives; front table adjusted for a shallow cut.

Next, clamp a wood block securely onto the rabbeting ledge to support the work at the desired angle. Make a shallow cut on all four edges of the panel. Then, lower the front table and

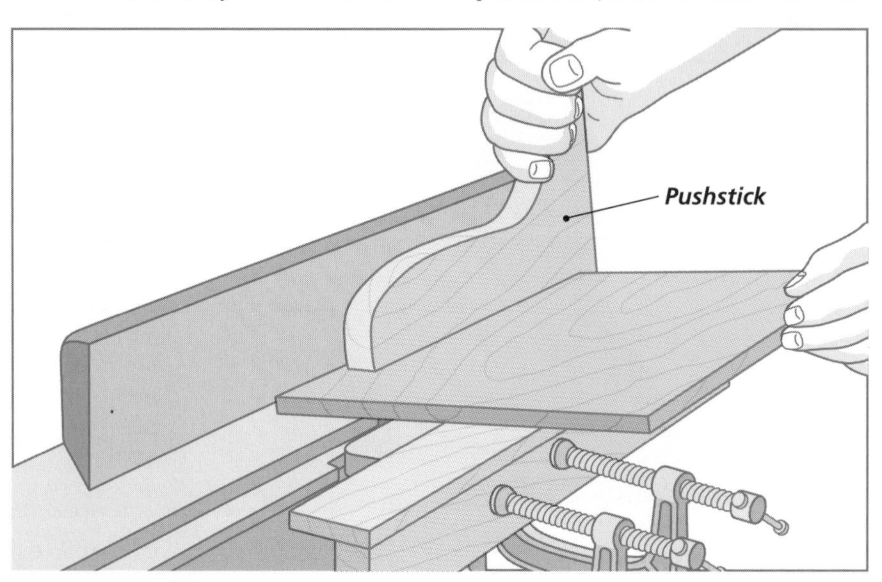

▲ **CUTTING RAISED PANELS, 1.** ***Cut raised panels for cabinet doors on the jointer with the aid of a pushstick. Clamp a wood block to the rabbeting ledge to support the workpiece at the desired angle.***

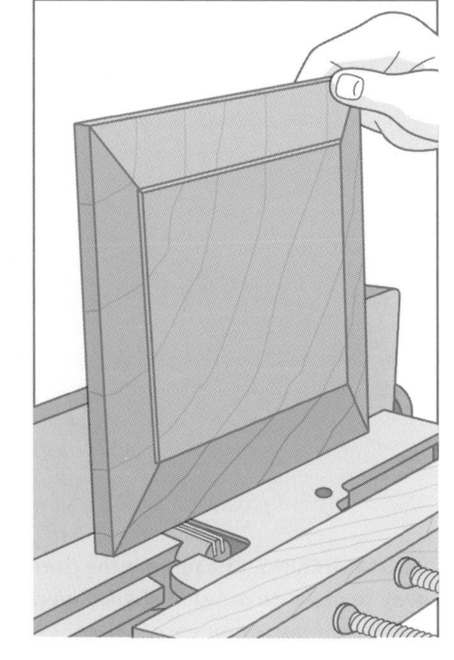

► **CUTTING RAISED PANELS, 2.** ***Cut the cross-grain bevels first; any splintering will be removed by the edge-grain bevel cuts. Then, make light, edge-finishing cuts to complete the raised panel.***

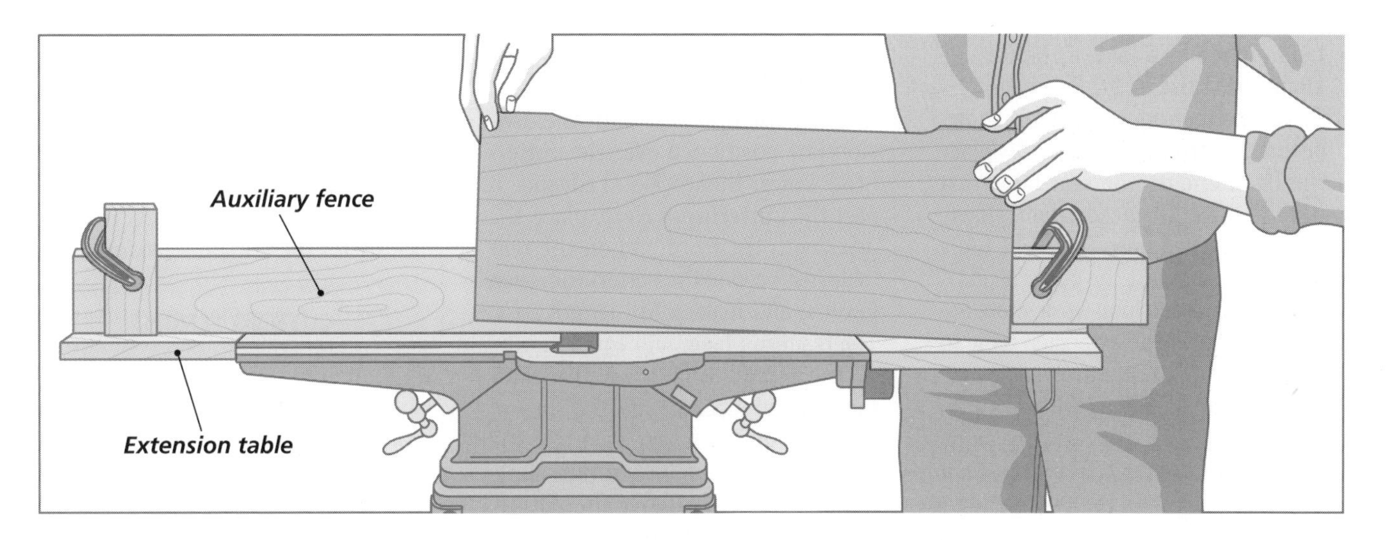

▲ **CUTTING RECESSES, 1.** ***To control the length of a recess cut, clamp start and stop blocks to the fence. Then, butt the end of the workpiece against the start block and lower it slowly onto the cutterhead.***

▼ **CUTTING RECESSES, 2.** ***Advance the workpiece slowly past the cutterhead to the stop block. Install an auxiliary fence with extension tables as shown here to provide adequate support for oversized workpieces.***

make a second pass. Keep repeating the procedure until the bevel is raised.

CUTTING RECESSES

Recesses are stopped cuts (contained within the work) that are made on the edges of a board with the fence perpendicular to the table. First, lower both the front and rear table by equal amounts below the cutterhead. Then, clamp start and stop blocks onto the fence to control the recess.

Next, butt the back end of the work against the start block and hold the front end above the cutterhead. When the board is in position, turn on the jointer and lower the work to make a short cut. Then, lift the board, turn it around and advance it in the opposite direction. Using this two-cut technique will prevent splintering of the trailing end of the work.

TAPERING

Tapering stock on a jointer is a safe, accurate operation. The most common technique employed is for the straight

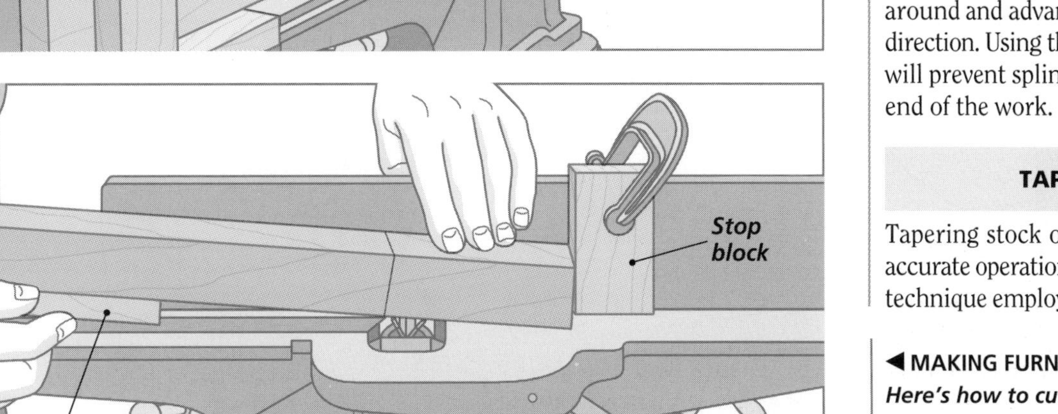

◀ **MAKING FURNITURE LEGS, 1.** ***Here's how to cut end tapers: Butt the workpiece against a stop block clamped to the fence. Then, slip a wood block under the raised leg end to maintain this angle.***

taper, whereby a taper is performed along the entire length of a board.

When tapering work that is shorter than the front table, carefully place the front end on the rear table just beyond the cutterhead. Then, slowly lower the work onto the front table and advance it past the cutterhead.

When tapering long work, there are two options: add an extension table to the jointer or use the following procedure. First, divide up the work into equal sections, each one slightly shorter than the front table. For instance, if the front table is 13 in. long, divide a 24-in.-long board in two. Then, divide the desired taper into the same number of sections. To obtain a ¼-in. taper in the example given, set the depth of cut to ⅛ in. and make two passes.

Make the first pass with the division line positioned over the cutterhead. Lower the work and advance it past the cutterhead. Next, place the work with the front end on the rear table just beyond the cutterhead, then lower it and make a full-length pass. The resulting taper will equal ¼ in.

The jointer also is the best tool for making end tapers. Mark the start of the taper on the work, then rest the work on the front table with the starting mark directly above the cutterhead. Clamp a stop block to the fence against the end of the work and hold the work at this angle to position a support block under it, then attach the support block to the work with brads. Turn on the jointer, butt the end of the work against the stop block and pull it over the cutterhead. Reposition the support block and repeat the procedure for the remaining sides.

CUTTING TENONS

Tenoning on a jointer is done with the aid of a pushblock that's assembled using only glue. Adjust the fence to set the tenon length and feed the work with the pushblock held firmly against the fence. To prevent splintering the back edge of the work, first saw a kerf to establish the tenon shoulders.

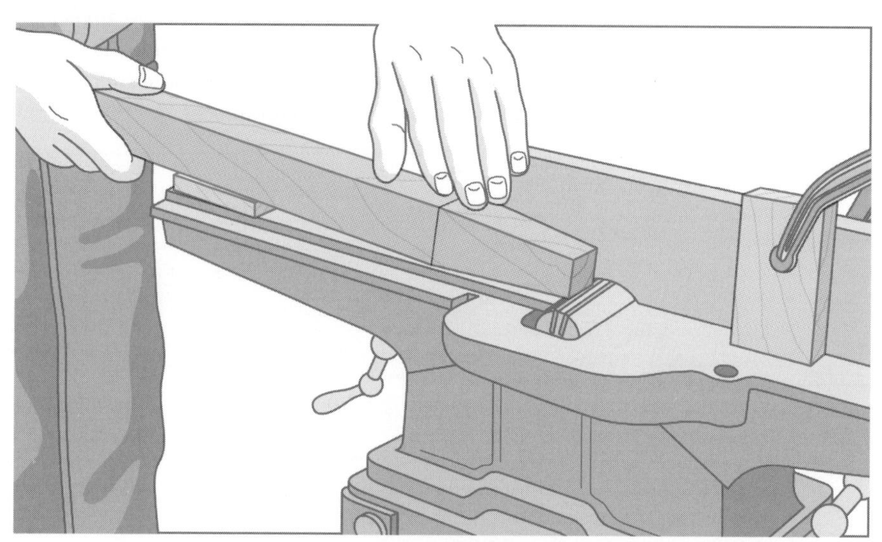

▶ **MAKING FURNITURE LEGS, 2.** ***With the block nailed to the bottom of the workpiece, stand in front of the jointer and pull the work across the cutterhead. The block's thickness determines the degree of taper.***

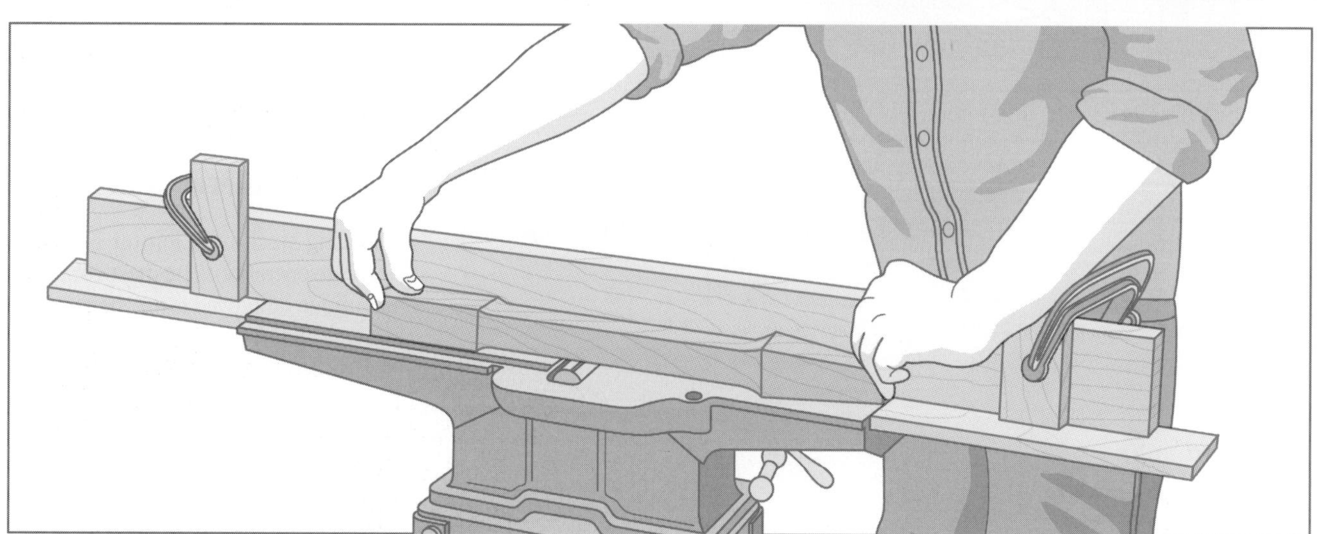

▼ **MAKING FURNITURE LEGS, 3.** ***After tapering the ends, cut recesses to form a furniture leg. Cut a short recess, then turn the leg around and feed it in the other direction in order to prevent splintering.***

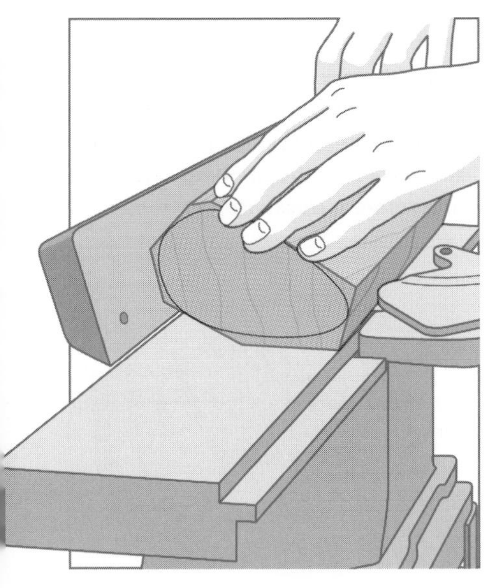

◀ **CONTOURING PIECES, 1.** ***To contour a piece into an irregular, free-form shape, make a series of shallow chamfer cuts. Keep a firm grip on the piece and rotate it slowly, decreasing depth of cut as it takes shape.***

▼ **CONTOURING PIECES, 2.** ***Finally, finish-shape the piece with the jointer adjusted for very shallow cuts. Use the fence to guide the piece in a straight line. Hand-sanding is all that's needed to complete the piece.***

Round tenons are made easily using an L-shaped jig. Clamp the jig to the rabbeting ledge of the jointer so that the work engages the knives on only the downward rotation.

TAPERING-IN-THE-ROUND

Tapering-in-the-round on the jointer with a shopmade jig that accommodates the work is a quick way to make round, tapered furniture legs. The first step is to shape the work into an octagon with the fence tilted 45°.

Next, mount the work in the jig on pins cut from 2-in. common nails. The locations of the pins determine the degree of taper, so position the back pin lower in order to form the narrower, tapered end of the leg.

Place the front end of the work on the rear table just beyond the cutterhead. Then, lower the work and make a full pass. Rotate the work slightly and repeat the procedure. After a full revolution, increase the depth of cut to further reduce the taper.

▼ **SURFACE PLANING.** ***The hold-down pushblock that's shown here is ideal for surface planing long stock. As the work advances across the cutterhead, shift your hand from the lead handle to the center one.***

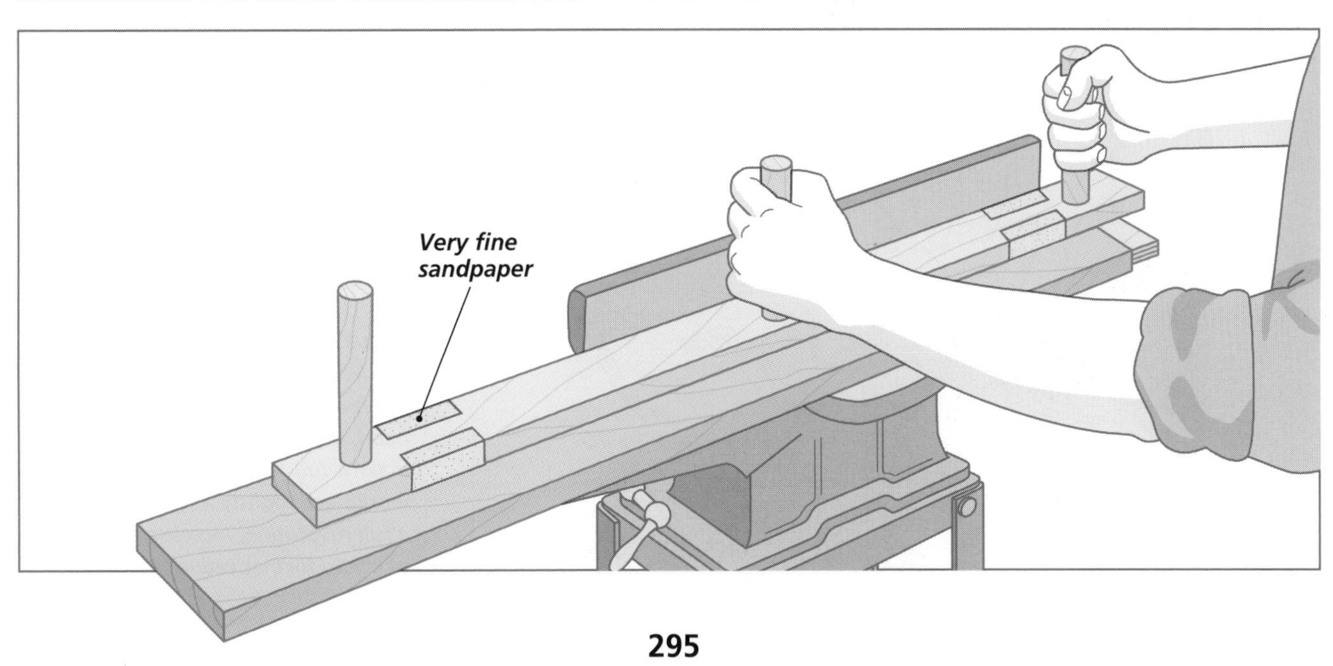

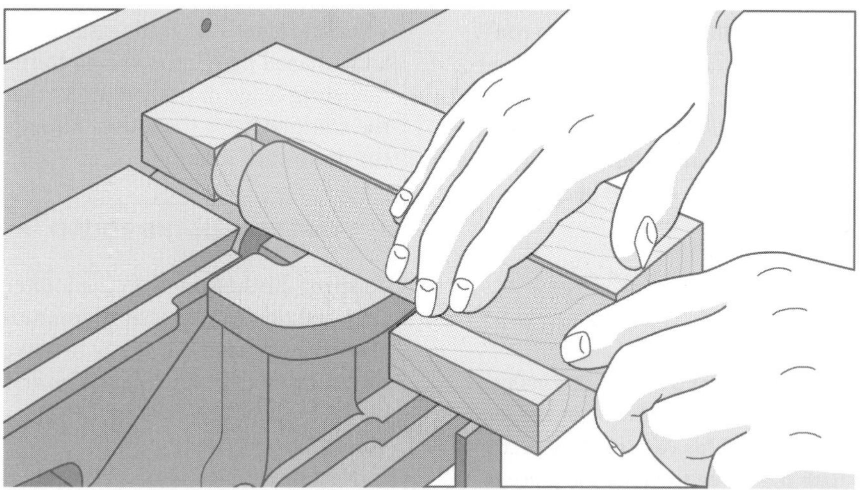

◀ **CUTTING ROUND TENONS.** ***Cutting round tenons is handled easily with the aid of an L-shaped jig. Clamp the jig to the rabbeting ledge, then push the work into the spinning knives and rotate it clockwise.***

PLANERS

While surfacing can be accomplished on a jointer, producing work of uniform thickness and with parallel surfaces is a job for a planer. The planer is ideal for smoothing rough stock, planing glued-up panels or reducing the thickness of boards uniformly—while maintaining the parallelism of opposite surfaces. The planer can also handle wider stock than a jointer, a factor in the building of large panels.

To use the planer, place the work on the infeed table and advance it to engage the feed roller. The feed roller moves the work past the cutterhead, which cuts to the depth selected. The work emerges on the outfeed table in uniform condition and with a ready-to-use surface.

Although the planer is an easy tool to operate, a couple of things must be kept in mind in order to achieve the best results. First, always feed work into the cutterhead following the direction of the wood grain. Second, while the maximum depth-of-cut capacity typically is 1/8 in., you're better off keeping to a cutting depth of 1/16 in. and performing multiple passes.

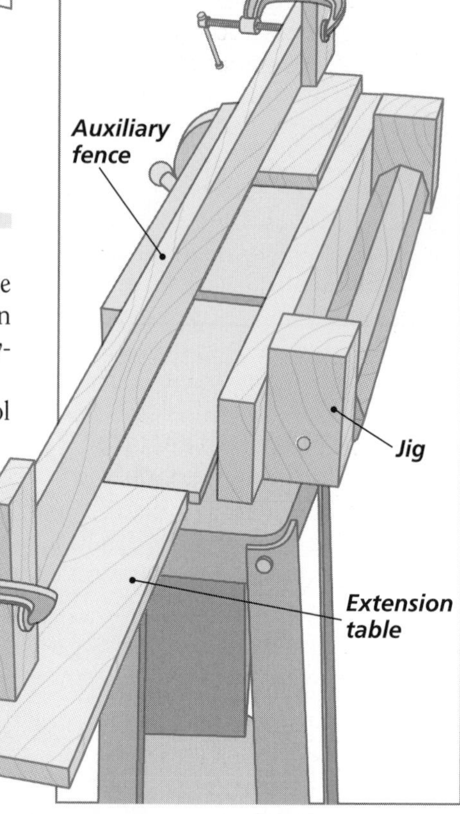

▲ **IN-THE-ROUND TAPERING, 1.** ***Here's a simple assembly for quick production of round, tapered furniture legs: a tapering-in-the-round jig, auxiliary fence and extension tables. The workpiece has been shaped into an octagon and is mounted in the jig on pins, the location of which determines the degree of taper.***

◀ **IN-THE-ROUND TAPERING, 2.** ***Set the front end of the workpiece on the rear table just beyond the cutterhead, then lower the workpiece and make a full-length pass. Rotate the workpiece slightly and repeat. After a full revolution, increase the depth of cut to further reduce the taper.***

JOINTER-PLANER

If your interests lie in fine woodworking, you might well consider buying a jointer-planer—a version of the basic planer with the logical, added function of jointer capability. This combination makes sense since planing operations often must be preceded by jointing.

If you've never used a planer, you may think it will straighten a warped or cupped board. The machine can't, though, because pressure of the feed roller flattens the board before it reaches the cutterhead. When the board is released after the cut, it simply springs back to its original shape.

However, with a jointer-planer, the jointer lets you obtain one flat surface before planing to a specific thickness. The jointer typically can handle stock up to 6½ in. wide and cut ½ in. deep. Tables that swing outboard allow you to convert from jointing to planing in seconds. The planer usually handles stock up to 8 in. wide and 4½ in. thick.

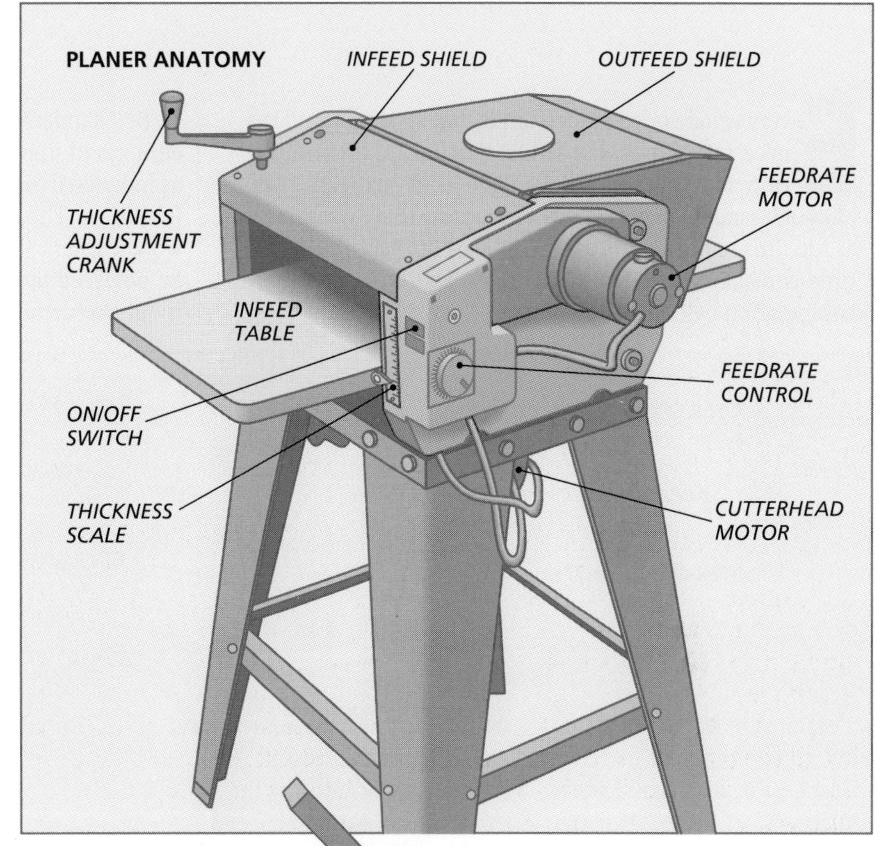

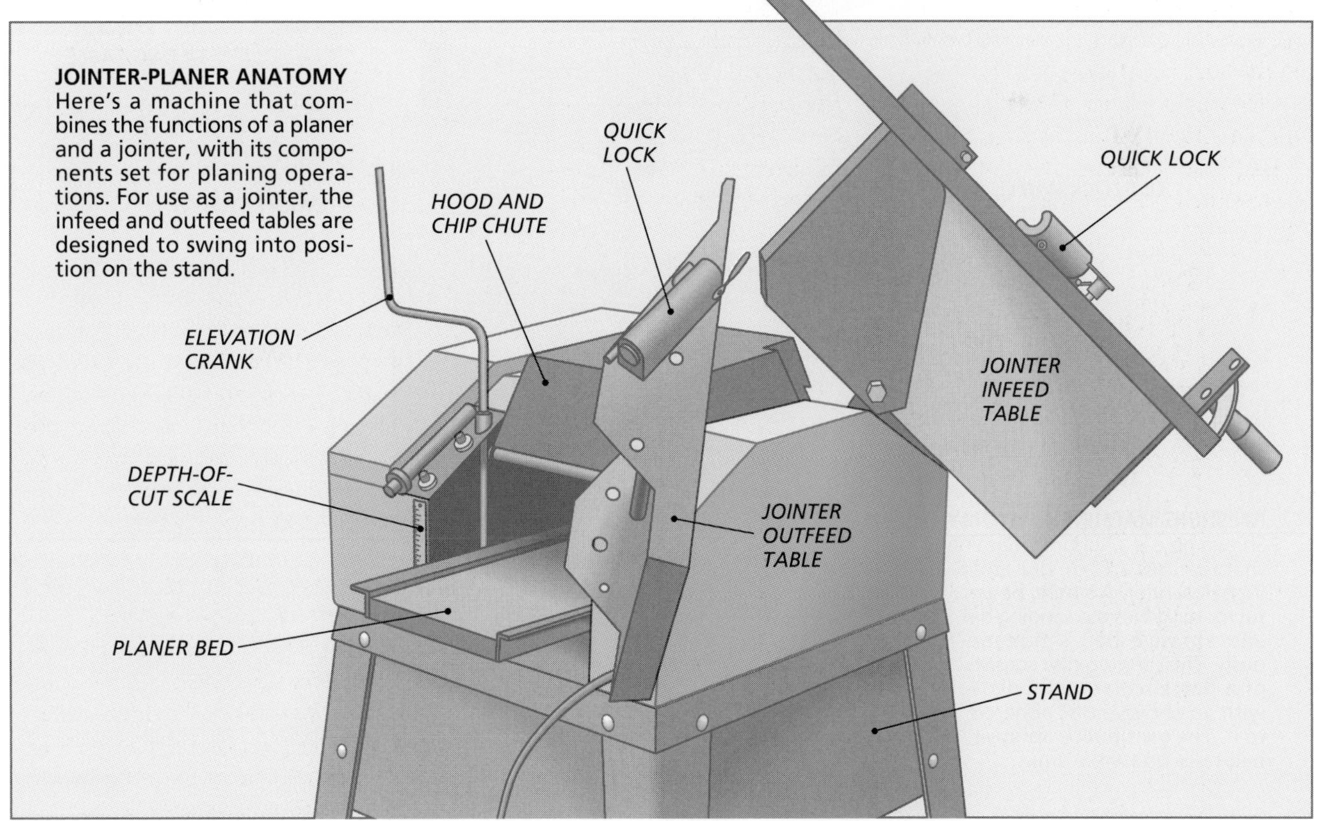

JOINTER-PLANER ANATOMY
Here's a machine that combines the functions of a planer and a jointer, with its components set for planing operations. For use as a jointer, the infeed and outfeed tables are designed to swing into position on the stand.

FINISHING MACHINES

Every woodworker understands that sanding wood is a necessary, if not glamorous, step toward the completion of virtually all woodworking projects. And although sanding may never be a procedure that's considered as fun, this requisite process can at least be made much less time-consuming and tedious with the assistance of a combination belt and disc sander.

Belt sanders and disc sanders are now standard finishing equipment in many woodworking shops. They are available as individual tools or as a single machine that provides both functions. The combination machine is often preferred by woodworkers since it allows for both types of operations to be powered by one motor on one stand. In addition, the mounting arrangement of the combination machine impos-

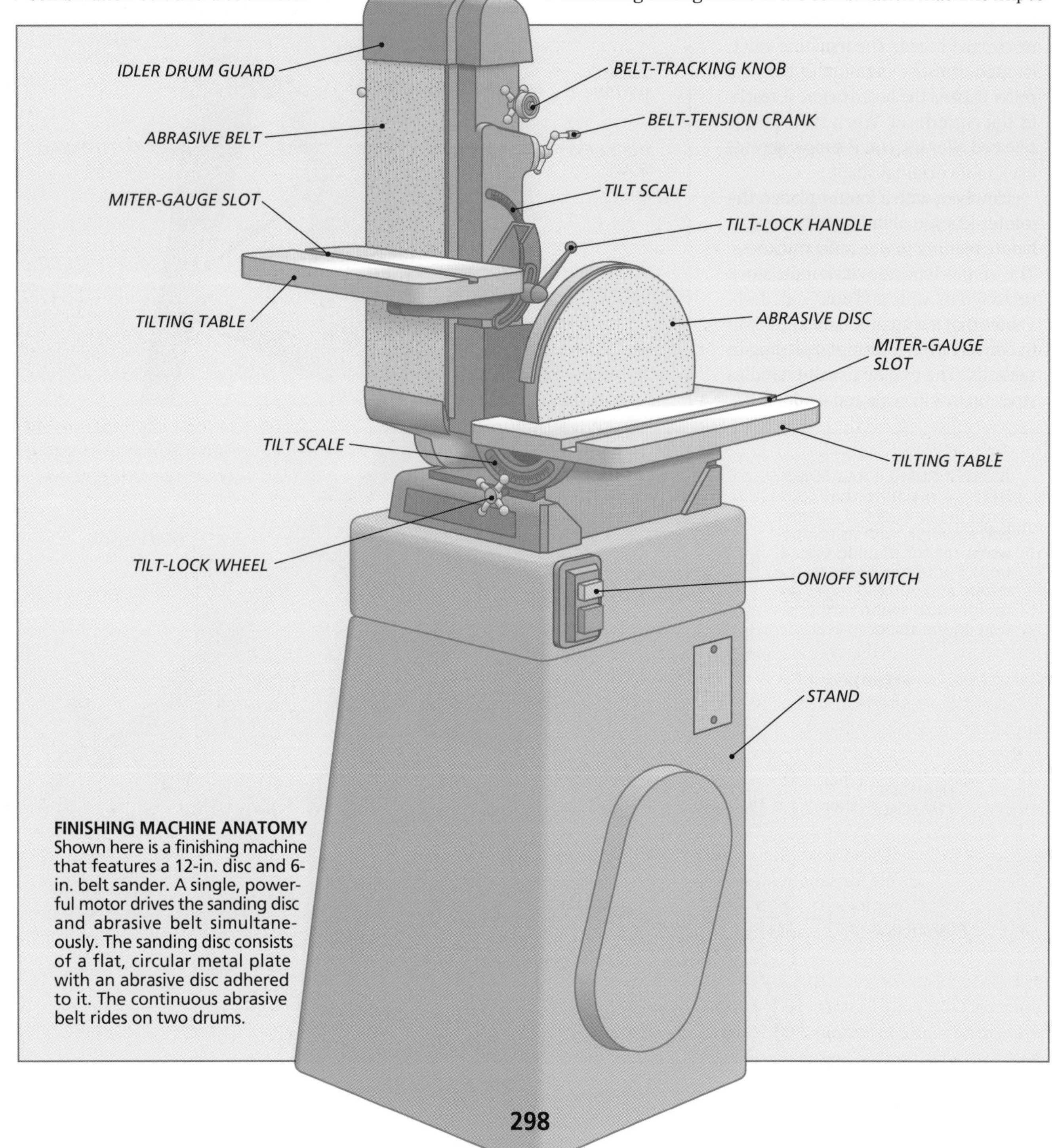

FINISHING MACHINE ANATOMY
Shown here is a finishing machine that features a 12-in. disc and 6-in. belt sander. A single, powerful motor drives the sanding disc and abrasive belt simultaneously. The sanding disc consists of a flat, circular metal plate with an abrasive disc adhered to it. The continuous abrasive belt rides on two drums.

es few limitations on functional capabilities. Virtually anything that can be performed on one of the individual tools can be accomplished on the combination machine.

Although neither the individual tools nor the combination machine are substitutes for portable power sanders, they substantially cut down on the amount of post-building finishing that most projects require. Components of projects can be sanded and prepared for final coats on an as-you-go basis before they are even assembled. As well, many sanding jobs are much easier to accomplish when you can apply the work to the tool—instead of the other way around.

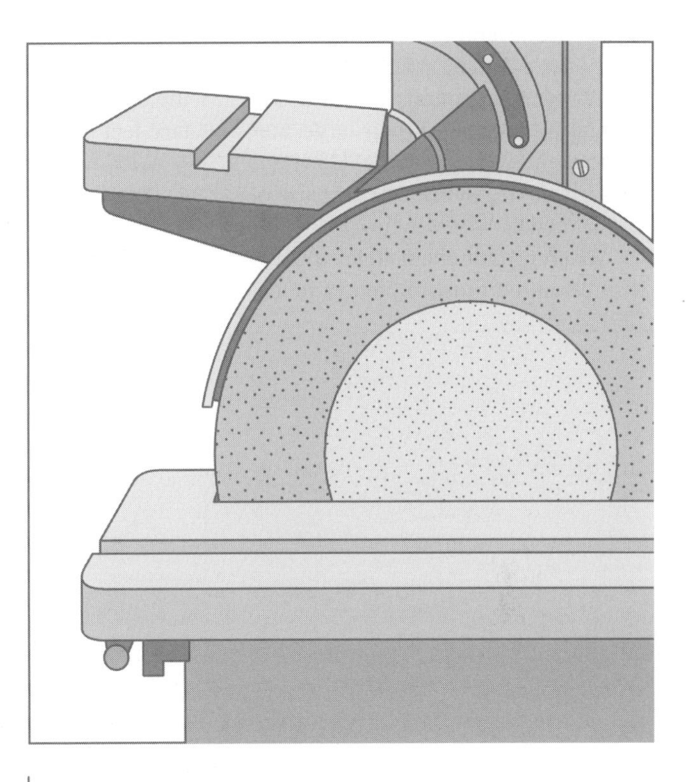

▲ **FINISHING MACHINE SETUP, 1.** ***Here's a dual-grit sanding disc that you can make simply by cutting the centers out of two discs. The disc's interior is cut from fine-grit abrasive; its outside ring is coarse grit.***

FINISHING MACHINE SPECIFICS

The combination belt and disc sander—also popularly known as a finishing machine—has a single, powerful motor that drives the sanding disc and the abrasive belt simultaneously. The sanding disc is simply a flat, circular metal plate that has an abrasive disc adhered to its surface. Disc sanders range in size from 6 in. dia. on small, benchtop models up to 12 in. dia. on stationary, floor-standing units. Miniature 4-in.-dia. modelmaker's disc sanders are also available for lightweight handicraft work. The disc sander is generally used to square, shape and finish-sand the end grain of small workpieces and for shaping outside curves.

The belt sander operates a continuous abrasive belt that rides on two drums. A flat metal backup table, called a platen, is positioned between the drums to support the belt and the workpiece. Belt sanders are designated by the width of the belt they use—typically 4 or 6 in. wide. The sander's straight-line sanding action is particularly effective for sanding the surface and edges of workpieces. For sanding inside curves, the guard is removed so that the workpiece can be applied against the end of the idler drum.

The more expensive models of finishing machines have an adjustable-angle belt sander that permits positioning the belt horizontally, vertically or at any angle in between. This allows you to lock the belt sander at the most convenient working position. Another desirable feature is a pair of tilting worktables. Typically, the tables tilt outward at a 45° angle and in toward the abrasive surface at a 20° angle. Tilting tables are invaluable for sanding precise bevels and angles. Other handy features include a miter gauge, especially for disc sanding, and a fence-like backstop for belt sanding.

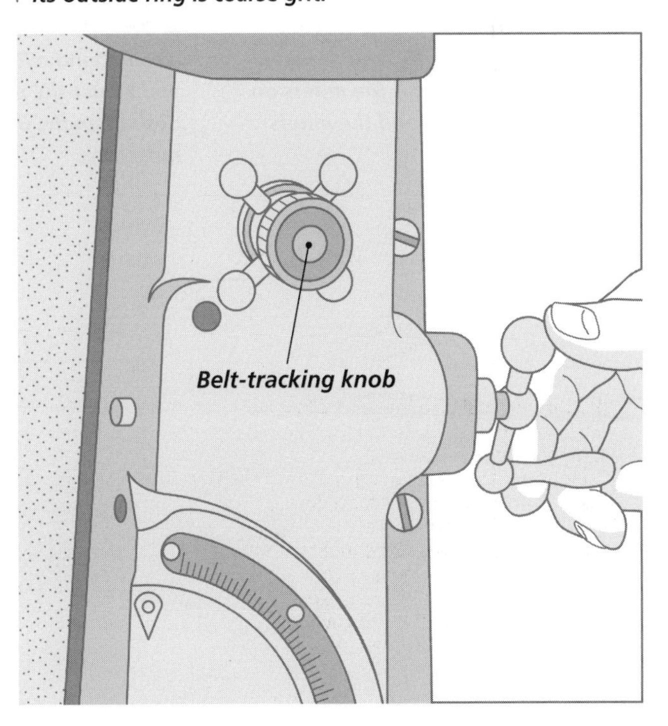

▶ **FINISHING MACHINE SETUP, 2.** ***To change the machine's abrasive belt, simply rotate the tension crank until the belt is loose enough to be slipped off the drums. Install a new belt and adjust its tracking as necessary.***

BENCHTOP FINISHING MACHINES

There are several tool manufacturers that offer a benchtop type of belt and disc sander, very often a scaled-down, miniature version of their large, stationary finishing machine. However, don't be fooled by the compact size of these models—they're no toys.

Weighing only about 40 lb., the typical benchtop finishing machine features a 6-in.-dia. disc and a 4-in.-wide belt powered simultaneously by a ⅓-hp, 4-amp motor. The sanding disc operates at 3,100 rpm and the sanding belt runs at a speed of 2,000 surface-feet per minute (sfpm).

With many of the benchtop models, the sanding belt can be positioned horizontally, vertically or at any angle between 0° and 90°. Often, there's a single tilting worktable that can be used for either disc or belt sanding operations, as well as an adjustable miter gauge for sanding square and mitered pieces accurately.

TYPES OF DISCS AND BELTS

Sanding discs and abrasive belts are commonly available in two types of coatings: garnet and aluminum oxide. Both come in a variety of grit sizes

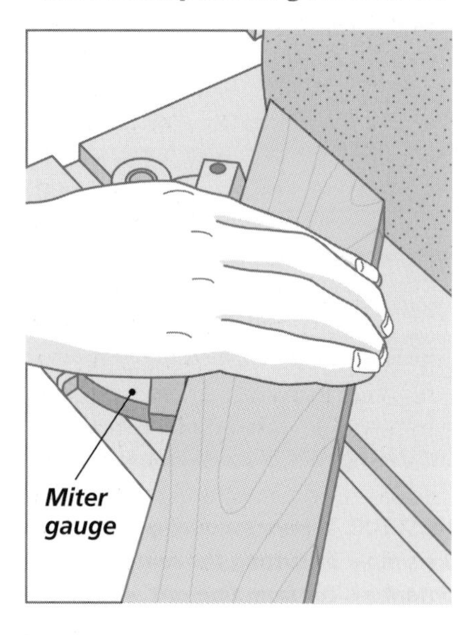

▲ **DISC SANDING MITERS, 1.** ***Work with a miter gauge to sand precise miters. First, rough-cut the miters on a saw. Then, finish-sand the miters on the disc sander.***

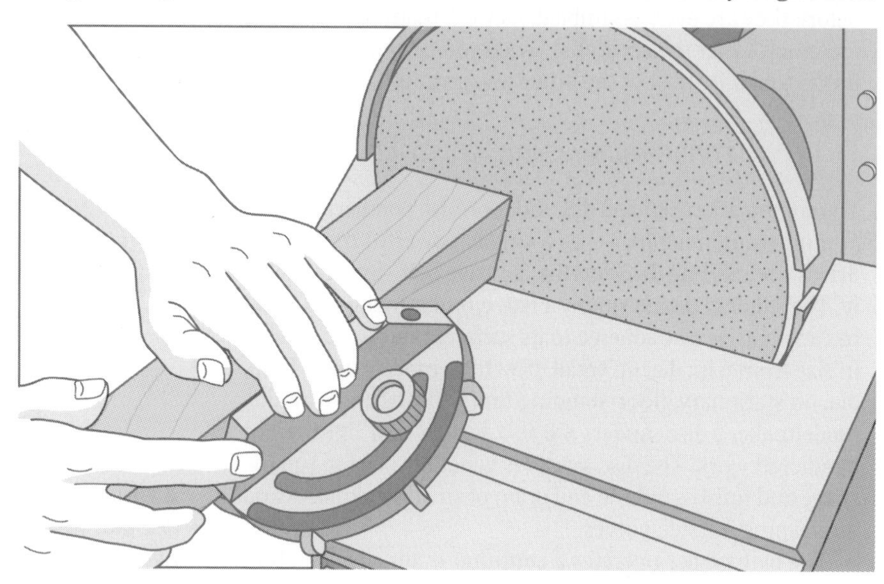

▲ **DISC SANDING MITERS, 2.** ***To sand a compound miter, tilt the table down and adjust the miter gauge to the desired angle. Be sure to precut the miter first.***

▼ **DISC SANDING CURVES.** ***Sand outside curves working freehand. Make light passes by swinging the workpiece smoothly back and forth against the disc.***

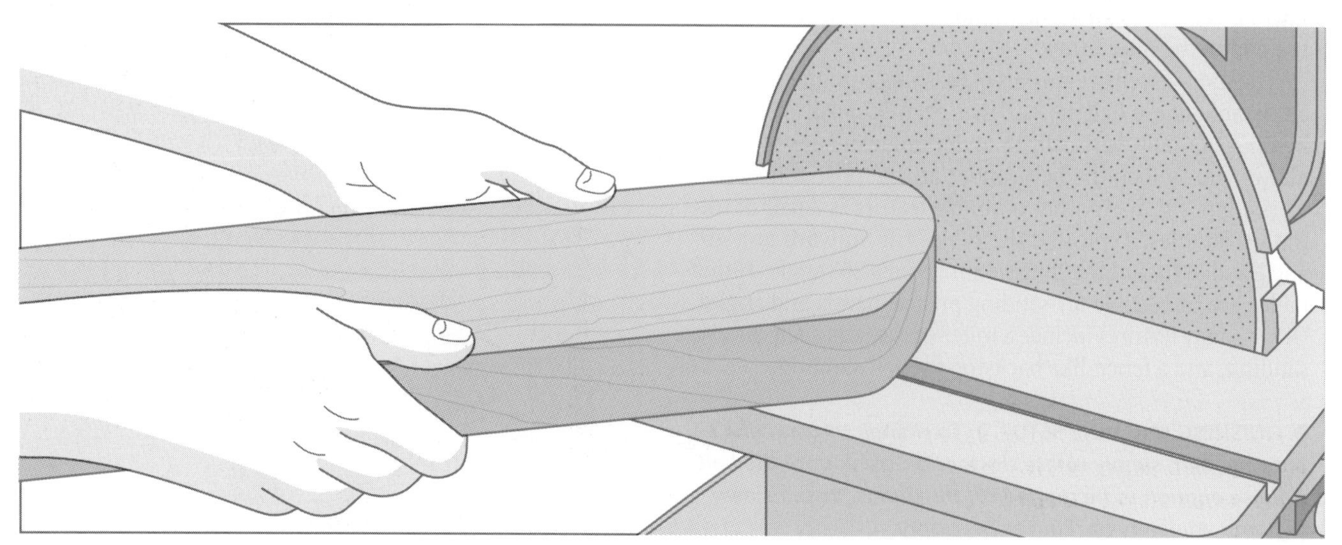

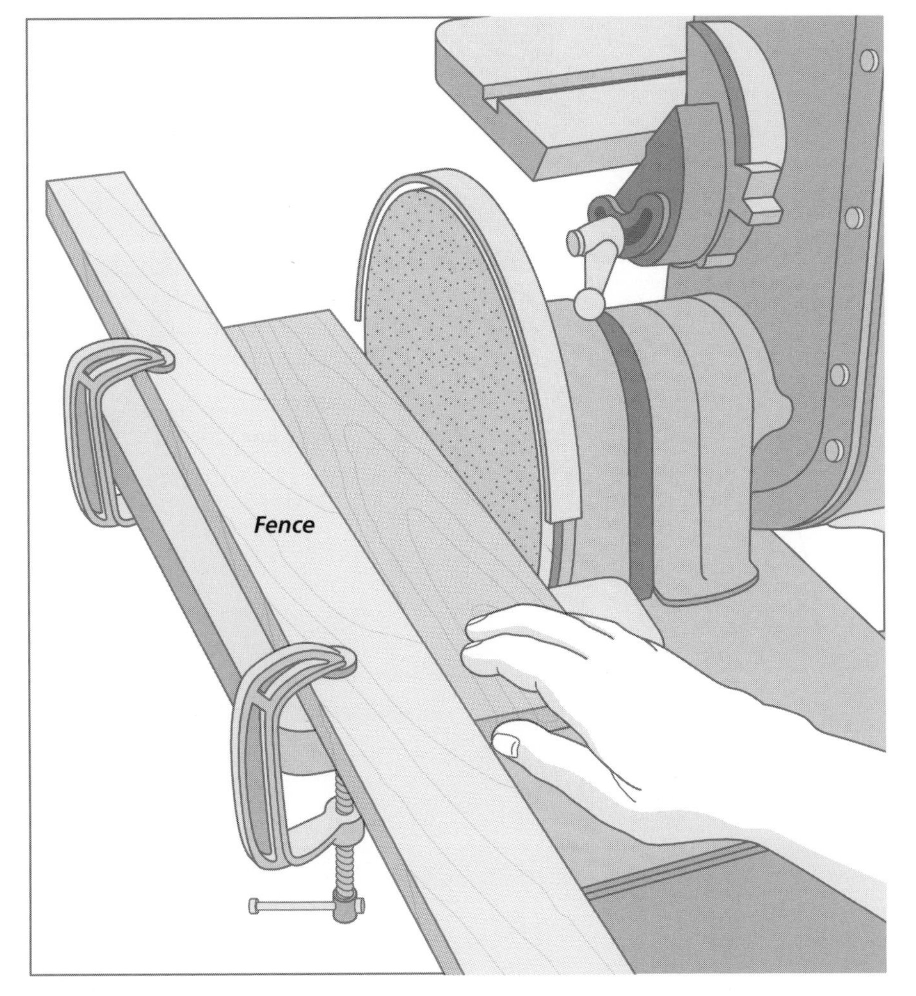

ranging from 50 to 150 grit. Use garnet-coated abrasives for sanding all species of wood. Aluminum-oxide abrasives work equally well on wood, metals and plastics.

SANDING SAFETY

However routine sanding operations may seem to be, proper safety precautions must still be followed with finishing machines—as with all tools and equipment in the workshop. Keep in mind that abrasives are cutting tools that smooth a surface by taking off material. What an abrasive can do to wood, it can also do to *you*. Keep fingers and other parts of your body well clear of the cutting action.

Sanding operations also generate a tremendous amount of dust. And no matter how the components of your finishing machine may be configured, some of the dust inevitably becomes airborne. While sanding, wear a dust mask—a respirator isn't overkill. You should also wear safety goggles, especially when there is any likelihood of holding the work against the upward-rotating portion of a sanding disc, an

▲ DISC SANDING LONG BOARDS. ***To sand long board edges, clamp a straight-edge fence to the table at a slight angle so the work clears the upward-rotating half of disc.***

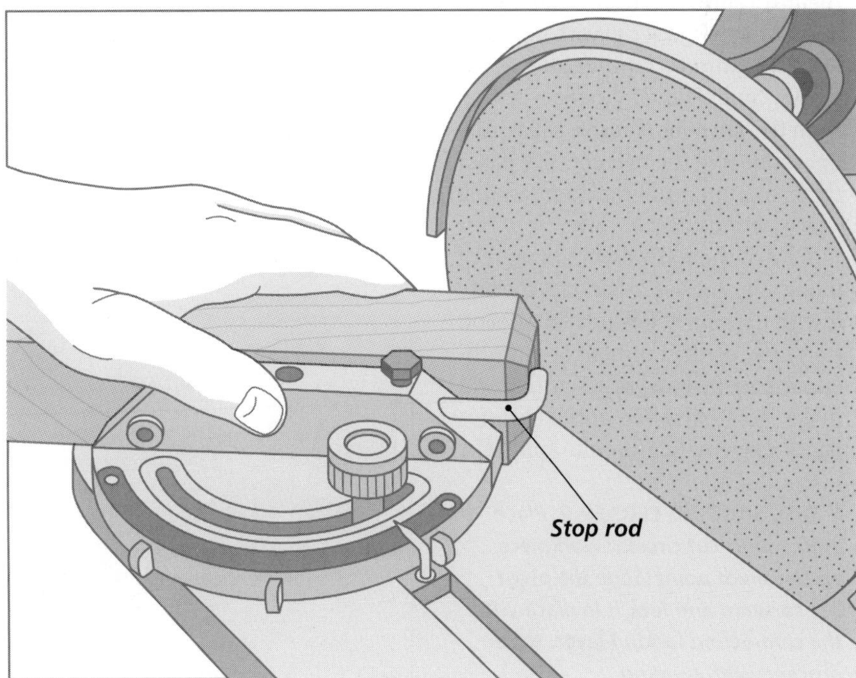

► DISC SANDING CHAMFERS. ***Form accurate, uniform chamfers on a piece easily by inserting a stop rod in the miter gauge. Adjust the rod to control the depth of cut.***

▶ **DISC SANDING CIRCLES, 1.** ***This simple pivot jig clamps onto the sander's table. The bevel-edged pivot bar fits into the dovetail-shaped groove in the plywood table and is locked by the cam-action lever.***

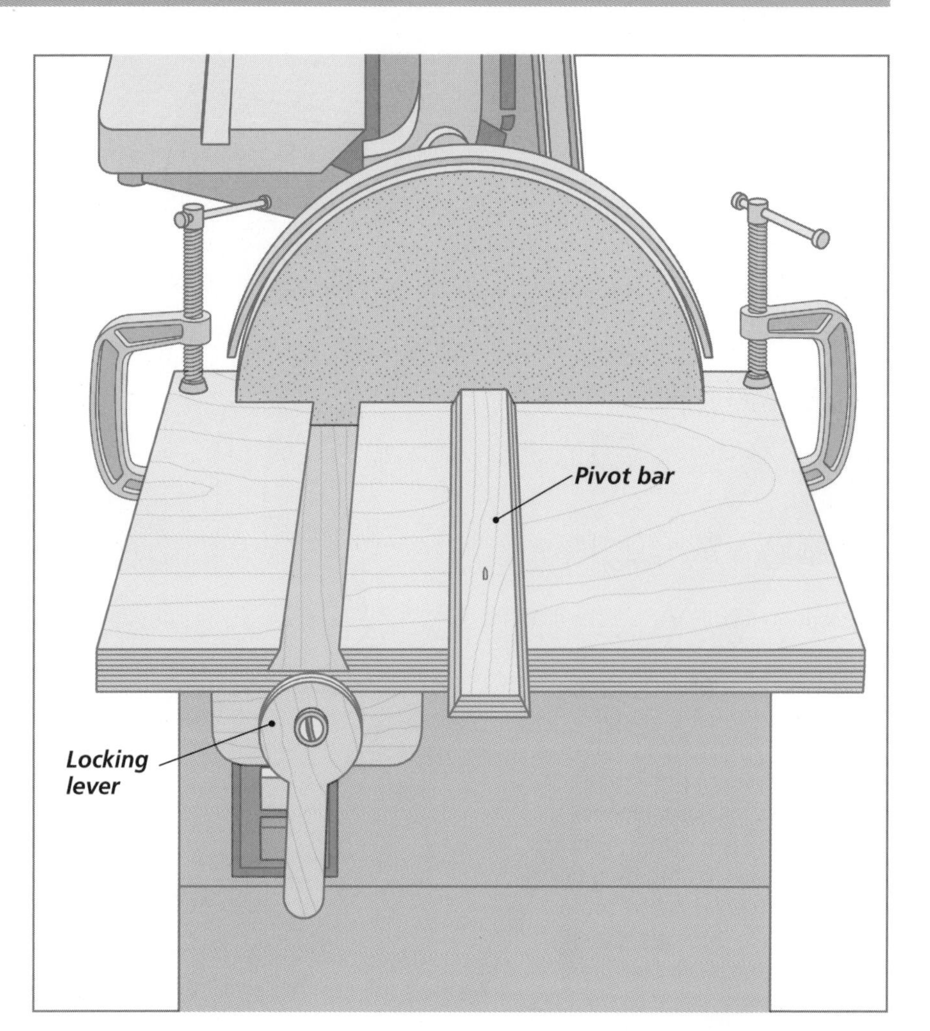

obvious instance where dust will be thrown up toward you.

Locate tables so that there is the least possible gap between their ledges and the abrasive. This gives maximum support for the work, and also helps to prevent it and your fingers from inadvertently being placed where they shouldn't be. If the work is small, don't attempt to hold it by hand. Instead, grip the work securely with a clamp or even pliers. Keep dust from accumulating around the machine to prevent its heat and friction from creating a spark-induced fire.

DISC SANDING SETUP

There are a variety of ways to mount abrasive paper onto the sanding disc. Whatever method you use, the first step is always to clean the old abrasive off the disc. If there are sticky spots on the disc, apply a solvent such as lacquer thinner and scrub with fine steel wool. Be sure to remove all foreign matter and residual glue left behind from the previous abrasive paper. Any unevenness in the new abrasive paper that's mounted will result in sanding imperfections in the work.

One of the most common ways of mounting abrasive paper onto the disc is with a specially-formulated cement. Don't use contact cement or any other permanent-bond adhesive that will make later removing of the abrasive paper extremely difficult. Apply the

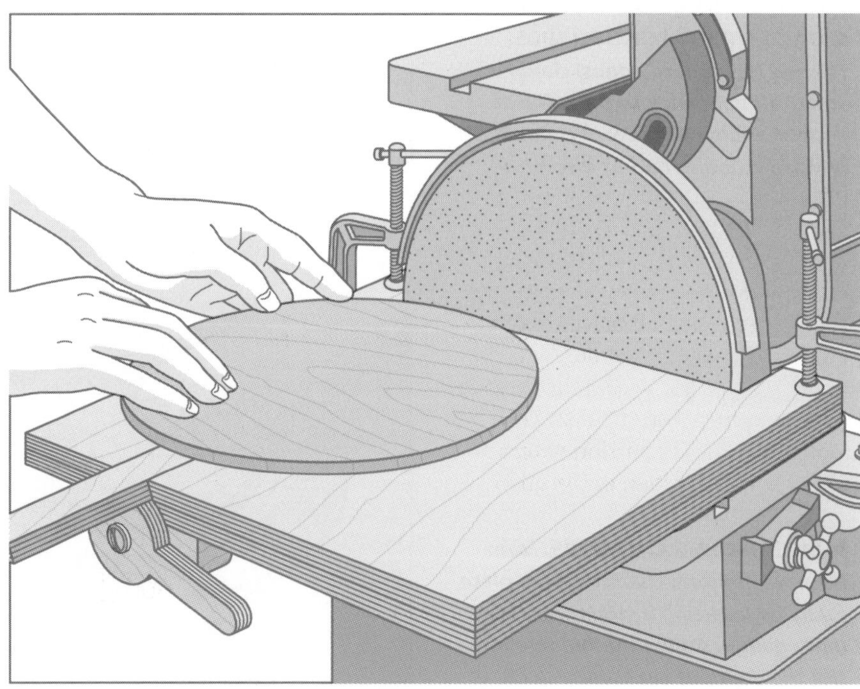

▶ **DISC SANDING CIRCLES, 2.** ***Place your rough-cut circular workpiece on the pivot point. Slide the pivot bar forward and lock it in place with the cam-action locking lever, then proceed with sanding.***

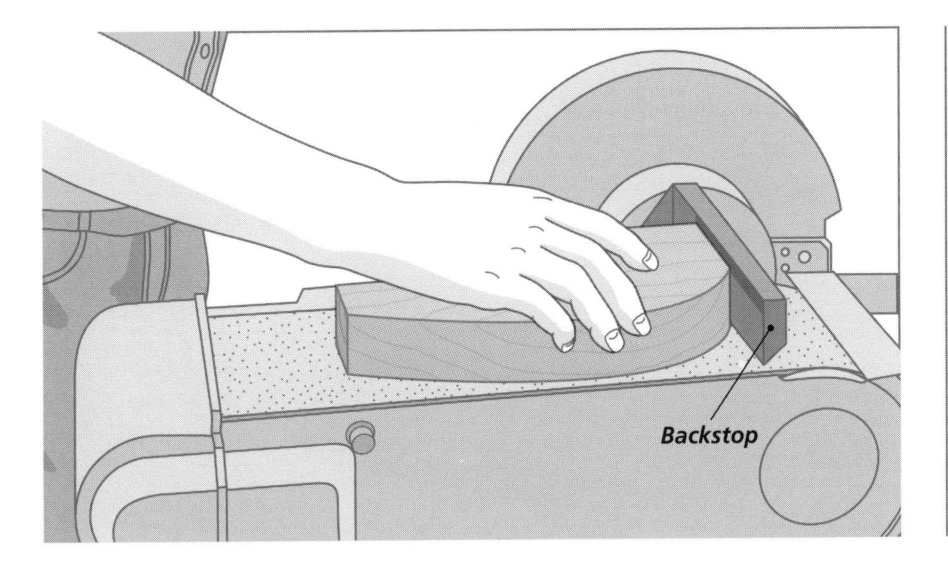

◀ **BELT SANDING SMALL PIECES.** ***Install an accessory backstop when sanding small workpieces. The backstop prevents the work from shooting off the end of the belt.***

▼ **BELT SANDING WIDE STOCK.** ***To sand a board that is wider than the belt, feed the board at a diagonal angle so that its entire surface makes contact with the belt.***

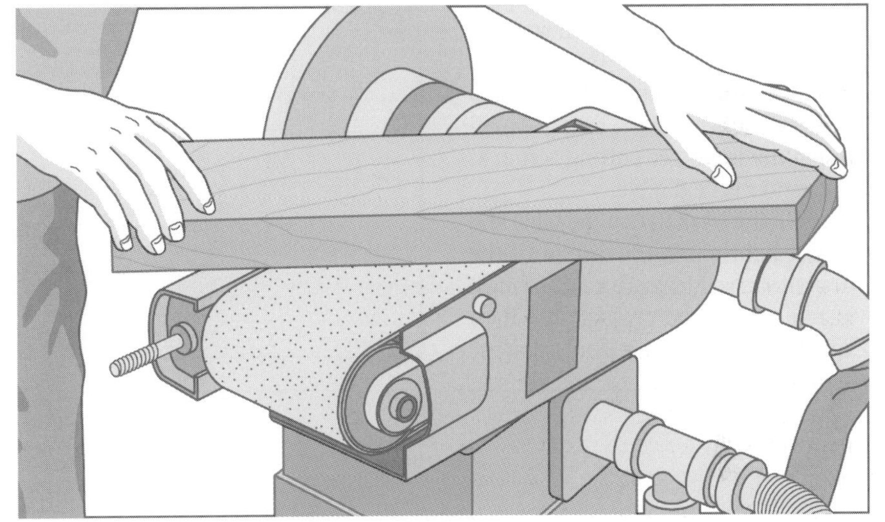

cement uniformly to both the disc and the back of the abrasive paper. Wait about five minutes before pressing the abrasive paper onto the disc.

As an alternative to working with cement, try using peel-and-stick adhesive-backed abrasive paper or the new Velcro-backed abrasive paper system. Both of these options are quick, easy-to-use and, predictably, more expensive than the cement method.

An older alternative involves the use of a shellac-like stick wrapped in a tube. The tube is peeled back and the sticky material exposed is applied evenly to the disc as it rotates. Then, the abrasive paper is pressed into place on the disc. This method works best if you hold a block of wood against the rotating disc to "warm" it.

For work that requires two grits of abrasive paper, try using a double-grit disc. Simply cut a circle out of the center of the coarser abrasive paper and cut a circle to replace it out of the finer abrasive paper. With both abrasive papers mounted on the disc, you can work on the outer portion of one grit and the inner portion of the other.

▶ **BELT SANDING CHAMFERS.** ***Use this setup to sand uniform end chamfers. Clamp a stop block to the miter-gauge fence, then hold the work to the block and press into the belt.***

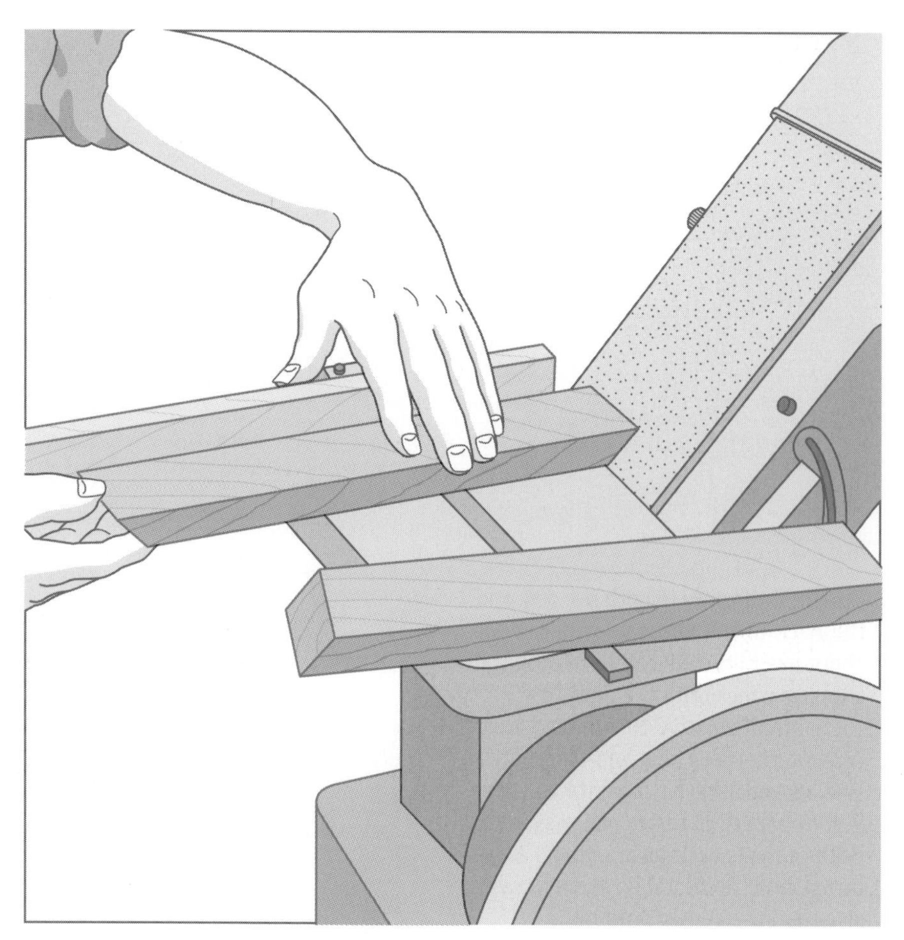

▶ **BELT SANDING MITERS.** ***To obtain better control when sanding miters, tilt the belt sander to the desired angle. This way, you can work on a table that's level.***

After you've mounted new abrasive paper onto the disc, stand back from the machine and allow it to run for a minute or two. This procedure tests whether the abrasive paper is bonded properly to the disc—and helps ensure safe disc sanding.

DISC SANDING BASICS

Disc sanding operations are for the most part done using the downward-rotating half of the disc. Therefore, the machine's true sanding capacity is only half the diameter of the disc—actually slightly less since cutting action at the center is negligible.

Hold the work flat on the table and feed it lightly into the disc until the desired shape is formed or smoothness is achieved. Avoid pressing too hard against the disc. This will only clog the

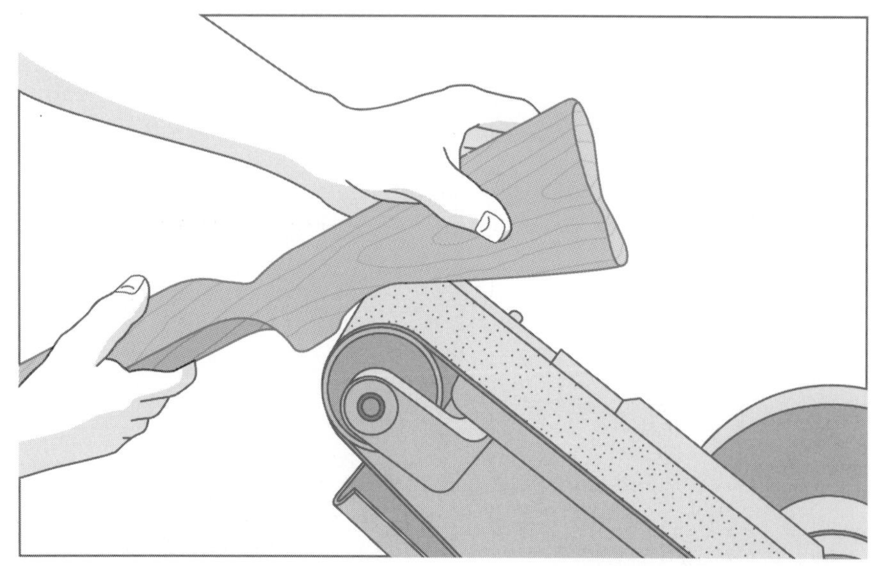

▲ **BELT SANDING CONTOURS.** ***Take off the idler drum guard to expose the end of the sander for contour sanding. Adjust the sander to a convenient working angle.***

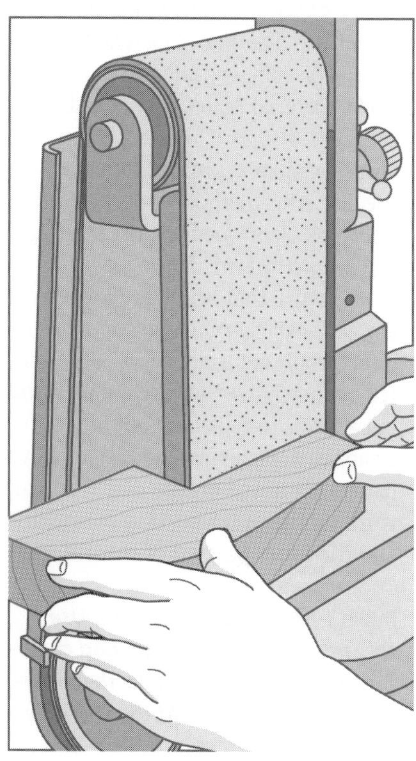

▶ **BELT SANDING CORNERS.** ***Sand square, inside corners by positioning the abrasive belt flush with edge of platen. Note that the side guard must be removed for this operation.***

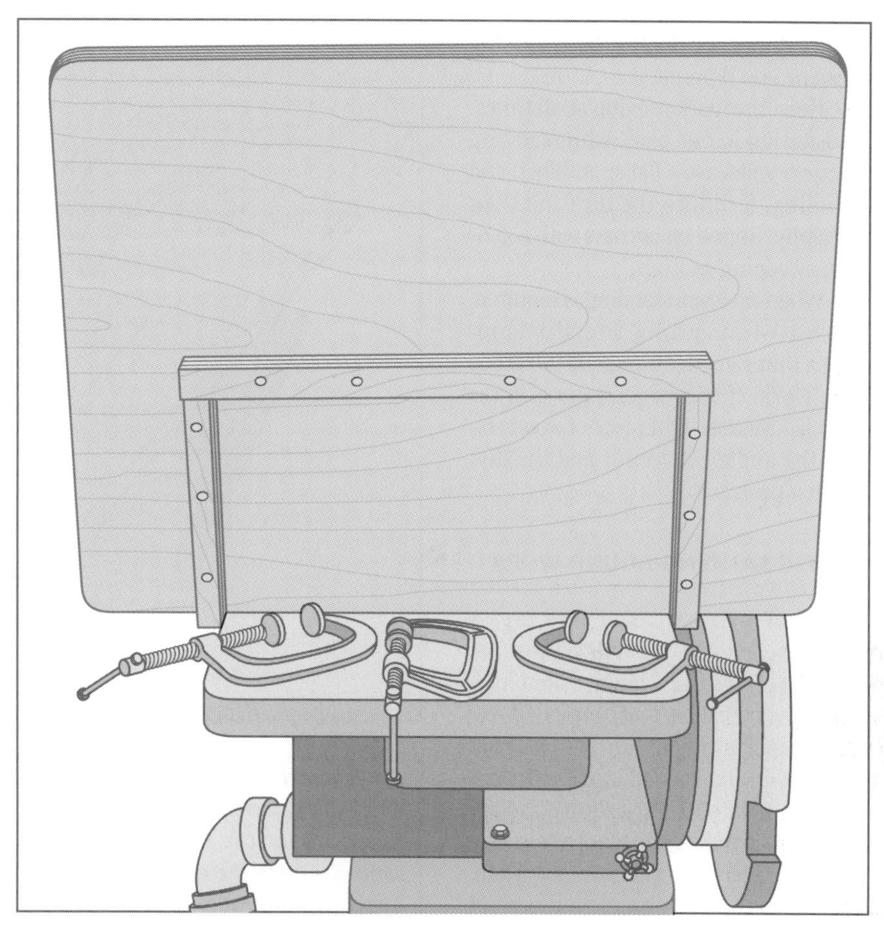

▶ **BELT SANDING LARGE PIECES, 1.** ***An auxiliary worktable handles oversized workpieces easily. Attach three cleats to the underside, then clamp the worktable in place.***

abrasive paper and cause burn marks on the work.

Since the disc rotates, this is not the machine to use for sanding with the wood grain. You can perform surface cutting by feeding the work on edge with its surface against the disc, but circular marks will be left on the work that will have to removed later by sanding with the grain.

Be extremely careful when sanding work that's longer than half the diameter of the disc. This type of operation requires that the work make contact with the upward-rotating half of the disc. Grip the work securely to keep it

▼ **BELT SANDING LARGE PIECES, 2.** ***The increased work surface provides greater stability for manipulating workpieces. Therefore, the accuracy of your work is also increased.***

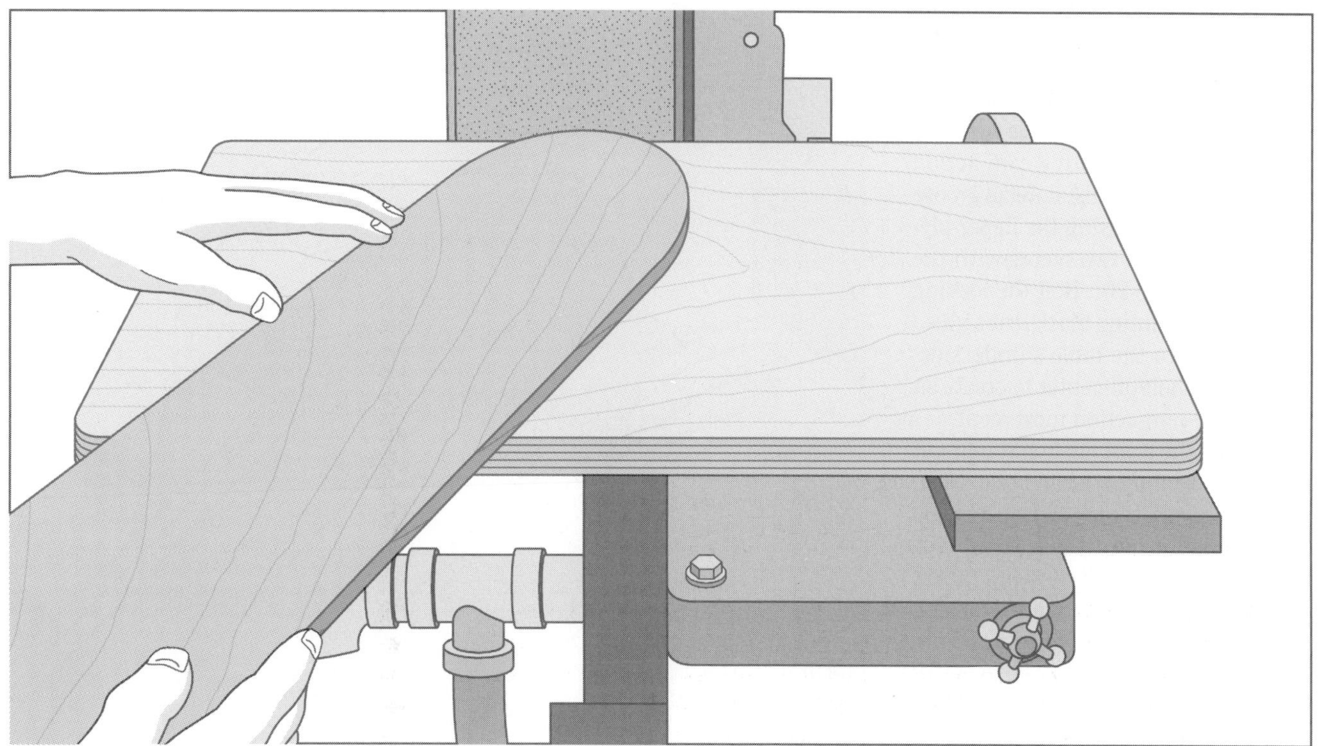

from lifting, and don't press it into the disc or you'll gouge it.

Keep the work moving at all times. Hesitating in one place while sanding a curve will leave a flat spot. When end sanding, feed into the disc and then laterally. Round off corners with a gentle, sweeping motion.

When precision sanding is required, such as when squaring an end or forming a miter, use a miter gauge to guide the work. If you haven't got a miter gauge, use a straight piece of wood and set the angle between it and the disc with a protractor.

DISC SANDING ROUND WORK

Sanding perfectly round work is easy with the aid of a shopmade pivot jig. The jig consists of a table of double ½-in. plywood panels that houses a dovetail-shaped pivot bar. Rip the pivot bar from ½-in. hardwood stock with the saw blade tilted 20°. Next, make a pivot pin by grinding the tip of a ¾-in. No. 6 flathead screw to a sharp point. Then, bore three or four holes in the pivot bar about 1 in. apart for installing the pivot pin. Countersink the holes on the underside of the pivot bar.

The adjustable pivot bar slides in a dovetail-shaped groove in the table and is locked in place with a cam-action locking lever. Form the dovetail groove in the table by cutting the upper plywood panel into two pieces with the saw blade tilted 20°. Bolt the locking lever to a mounting block that's glued and nailed to the table's underside. Locate the bolt off-center to create an eccentric, cam-action movement.

To use the pivot jig, first rough-cut the work round on a band saw. Next, mark the work center with an awl and place it on the pivot point. Then, slide the bar forward until the work makes contact with the disc. Pull the locking lever up to lock the bar in position, turn on the sander and rotate the work slowly until the entire edge is sanded. For work greater than half the diame-

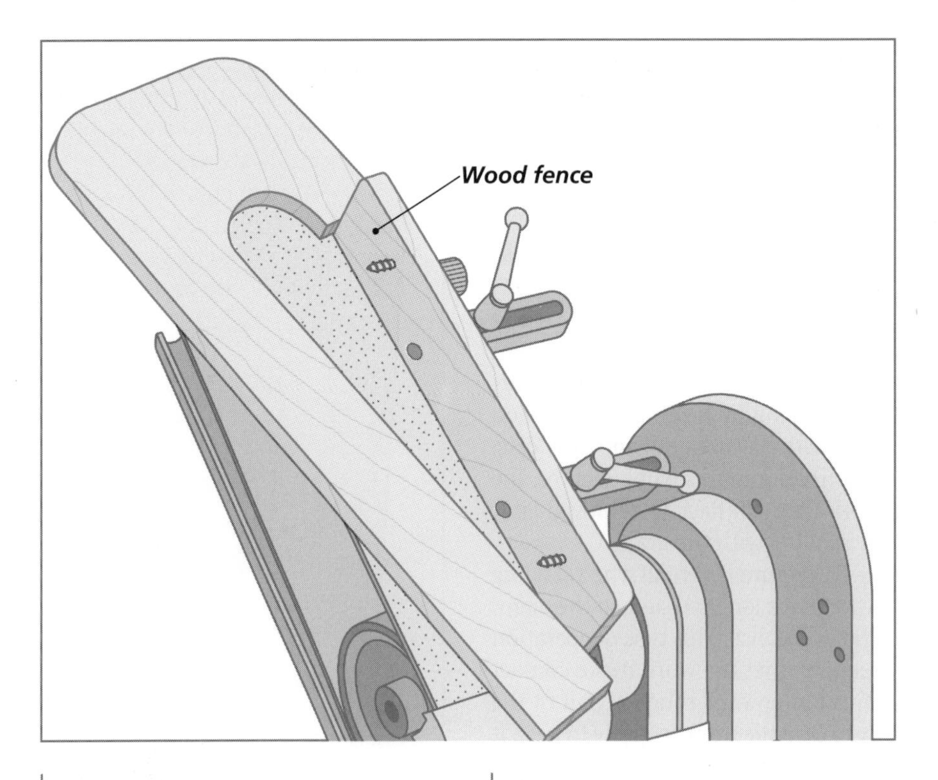

▲ **BELT SANDING CURVES, 1.** ***Make an auxiliary extension fence that wraps around the end of the belt sander. Attach the extension fence by screwing through wood fence.***

▼ **BELT SANDING CURVES, 2.** ***Keep your work flat against the extension fence to sand square, 90° edges on curved pieces. This isn't possible when sanding freehand.***

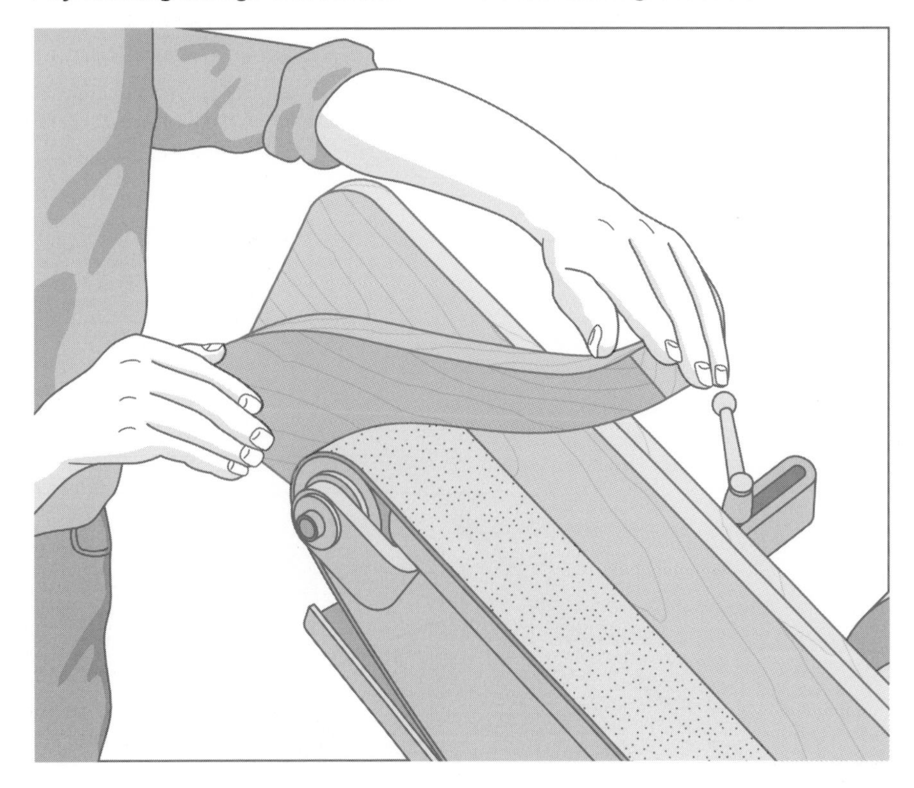

ter of the table, support the pivot bar from underneath with a scrap of 1 x 3 that runs to the floor.

BELT SANDING SETUP

The abrasive belt of the belt sander rotates on two drums: a motor-driven lower drum and an idler upper drum. Since the belt moves in a straight line, it's especially useful for sanding operations parallel to the wood grain.

The correct direction of rotation is typically marked on the back of the belt by an arrow. When looking at the drums, you'll note that they rotate in a clockwise direction, so be sure to install the belt with its arrow pointing the same way.

Lower the upper drum to reduce the distance between the two drums, then slide the belt into place. Raise the upper drum to tension the belt—but don't overdo it. Next, adjust the track-

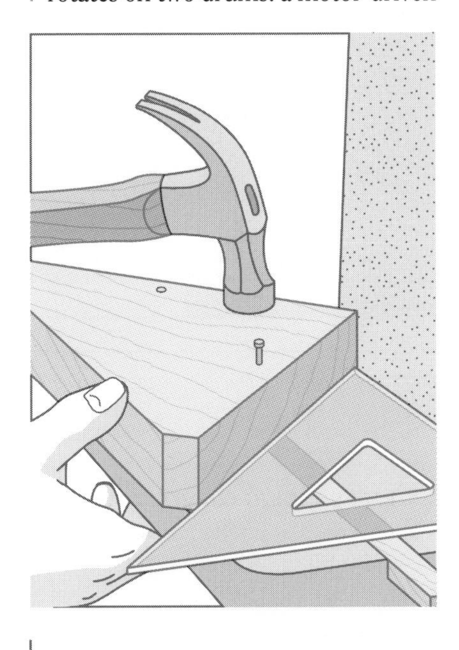

▲ **BELT SANDING MITER GUIDE, 1.** ***Make a 45° mitering guide for sanding moldings. Attach a triangular block to a hardwood strip that rides in the table's miter-gauge slot.***

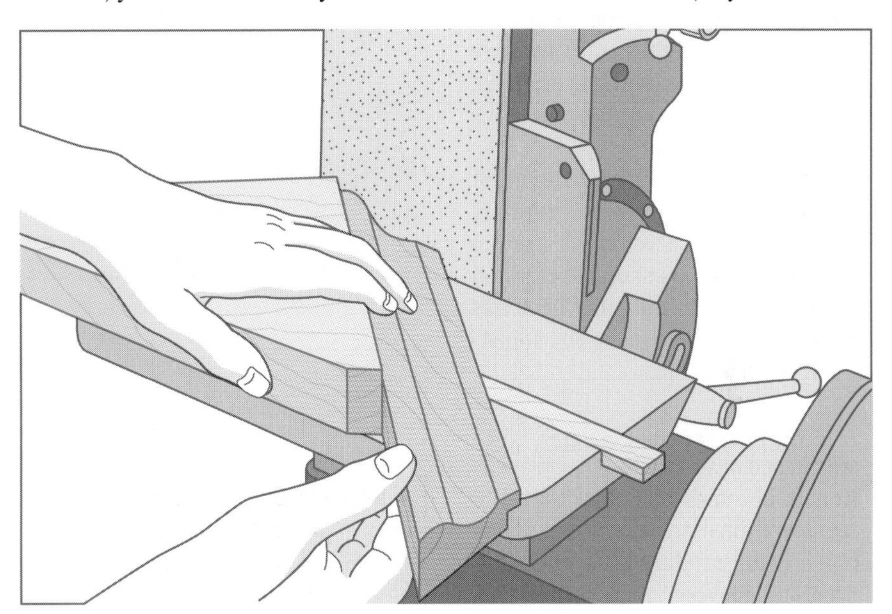

▲ **BELT SANDING MITER GUIDE, 2.** ***After miter-cutting molding slightly longer than needed, sand one end on the belt sander. The fixed angle of the mitering guide ensures accuracy.***

▼ **BELT SANDING MITER GUIDE, 3.** ***Slide the mitering guide over and sand the opposite end miter. This eliminates readjustments that are required with a standard miter gauge.***

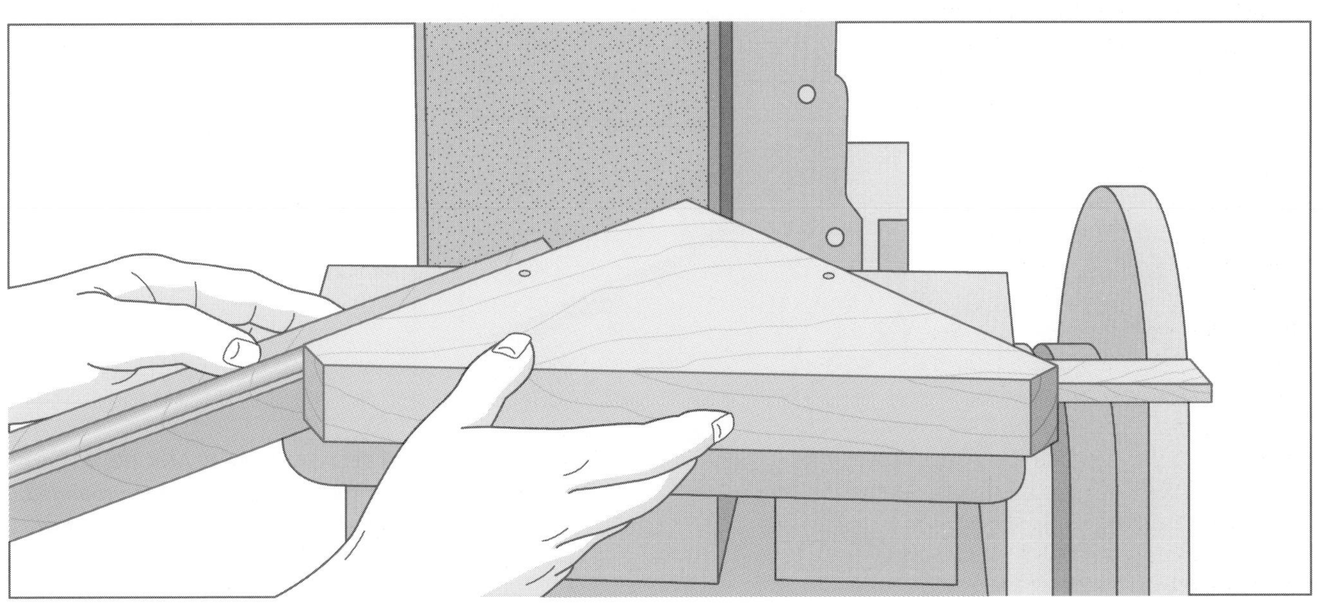

▶ **BELT SANDING BLANK JIG, 1.** ***Start with a square or octagonal, tapered blank. Nail brackets to the blank ends and clamp them to the fence. Then, remove spacer strips.***

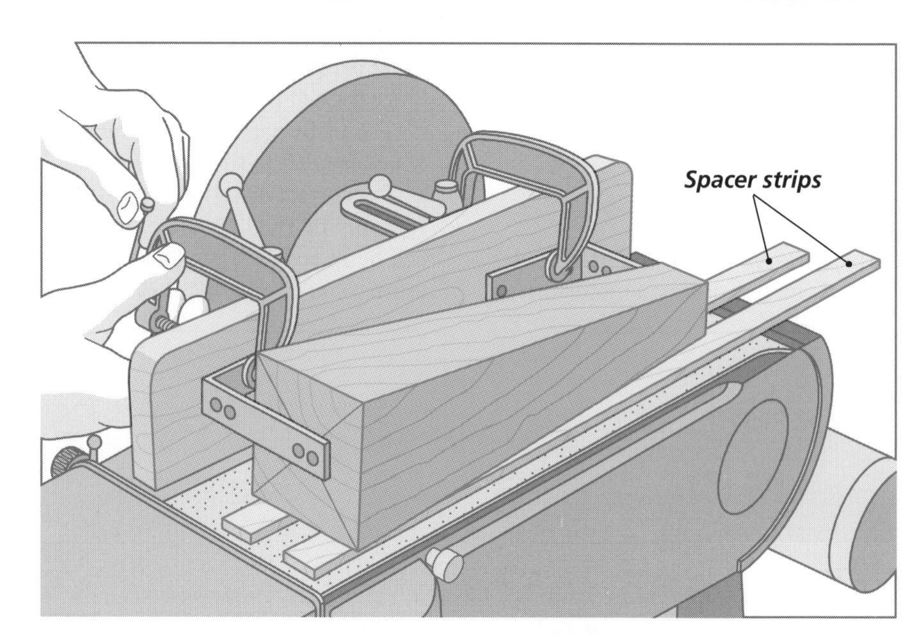

ing of the belt until it's centered on the drums and moves in a constant straight line. This is achieved by a tilt action of the upper drum. Every once in a while during sanding operations, you may need to readjust the belt's tension and tracking.

The belt sander may be set up for either vertical or horizontal sanding operations. Whichever one it's set up for, the table in its standard position must be square to the belt. Check this using a square, and make any adjustment required.

BELT SANDING BASICS

As with disc sanding, many belt sanding operations can be performed freehand. Other sanding tasks of greater precision, however, require the use of a guide to ensure accuracy.

The most common freehand operations include sanding surfaces, edges, inside and outside curves, and square, inside corners. Sand a surface with the belt in the horizontal position. Install an accessory backstop on the machine if the work is shorter than the platen. Place the work on the moving belt with

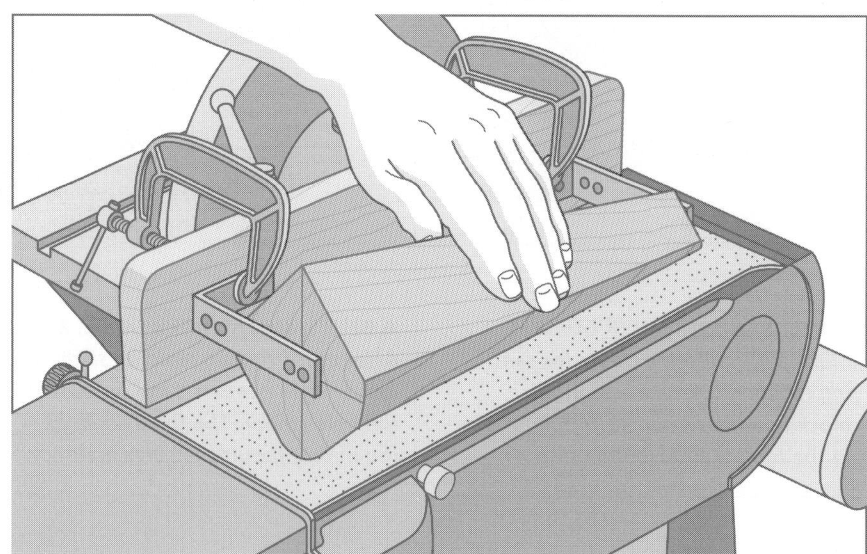

▲ **BELT SANDING BLANK JIG, 2.** ***Rock the blank back and forth steadily until enough stock has been removed to allow the corner to clear the belt. Repeat on remaining corners.***

◀ **BELT SANDING BLANK JIG, 3.** ***Once the four corners have been rounded, lower the blank slightly and repeat the sanding procedure until the blank is round.***

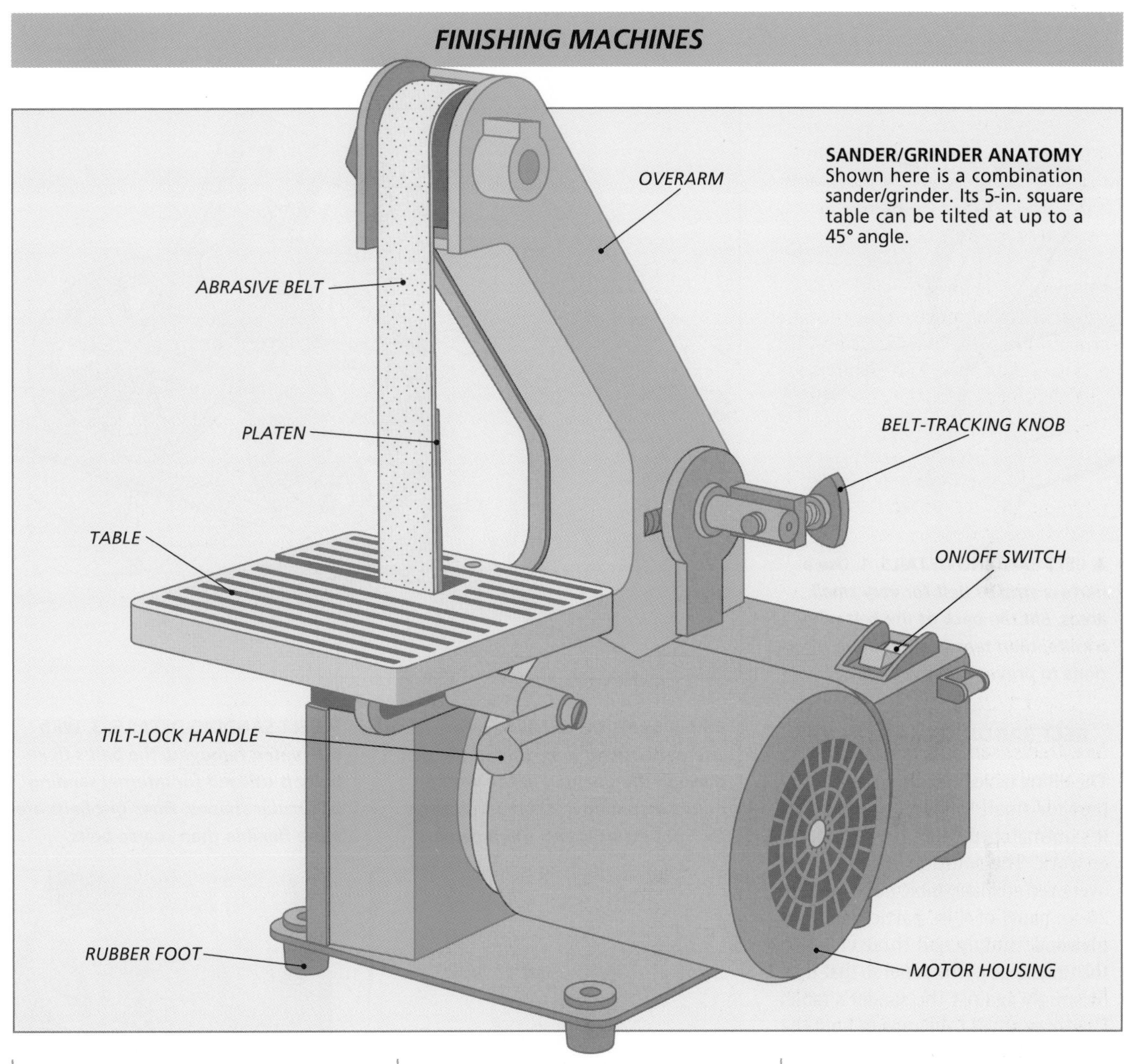

SANDER/GRINDER ANATOMY
Shown here is a combination sander/grinder. Its 5-in. square table can be tilted at up to a 45° angle.

its end against the backstop to keep it from shooting off the belt. Apply light, downward pressure until the desired degree of smoothness is achieved.

To sand a long surface, remove the idler drum guard. Grip the work firmly and feed it slowly against the belt's rotation while applying light downward pressure. When the work is wider than the belt, feed it at a slight diagonal so its entire surface makes contact with the belt. Use a fine-grit belt for this procedure to minimize the effects of cross-grain scratches.

To sand inside curves, work with the idler drum guard removed and use the exposed end of the belt. Adjust the angle of the machine and lock it at the most comfortable working position. Likewise sand irregular-shaped work freehand over the end of the belt. To sand precise, square edges on inside curves, install an auxiliary fence. Cut the auxiliary fence so it wraps around the idler drum to provide maximum support for the work with ⅛-in. clearance over the belt.

End-grain sanding is usually done with the belt set up vertically. Use a miter gauge to ensure square ends and accurate miters. However, for miters on moldings, replace the miter gauge with a shopmade mitering guide. Make the guide by nailing together two 90° triangular pieces of ¾ x 10¼ x 10¼-in. particleboard or plywood. Next, nail a 22-in.-long strip of hardwood to the pieces that's cut to fit into the table's miter-gauge slot. The guide lets you sand both right- and left-hand miters quickly and easily by simply sliding it on the table, eliminating the time-consuming and inaccurate readjustments needed with a miter gauge.

Sanding square, inside corners is possible by adjusting the belt so it rides flush with the edge of the platen. Lock the belt in the vertical position and use the table to support the work. Be sure to return the belt to its original position when you're done.

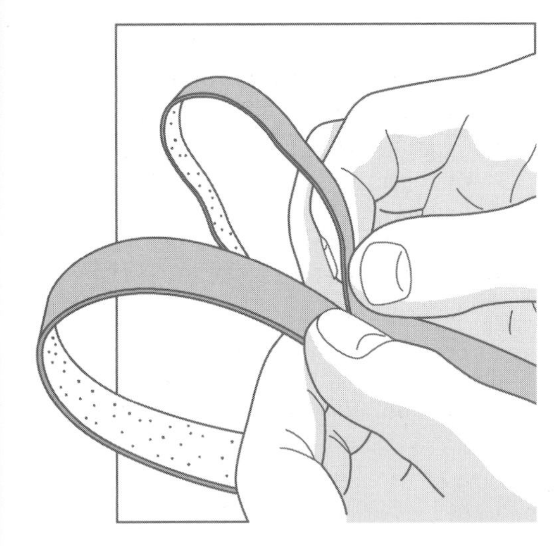

▲ **BELT SANDING DETAILS, 1.** ***Use a narrow strip of belt for very small areas. Slit the back of the belt with a knife, then tear in alternating directions to prevent unraveling.***

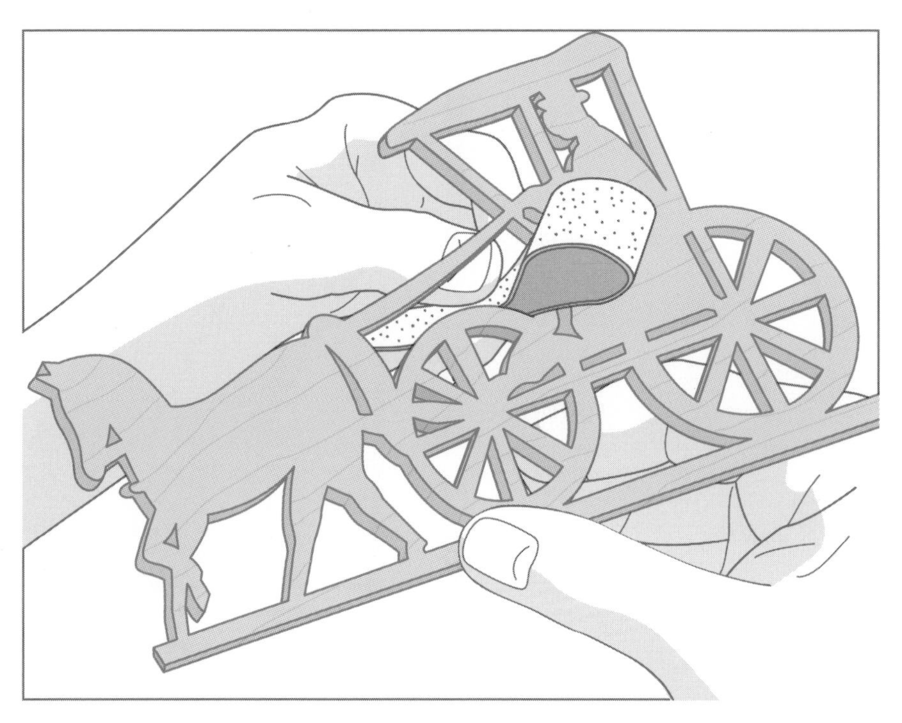

▲ **BELT SANDING DETAILS, 2.** ***For internal sanding jobs, thread the belt through the opening in the work before installing it. Use its thin edge for tight crevices and sharp corners.***

▼ **BELT SANDING DETAILS, 3.** ***With the platen removed, the belt's flexibility is utilized for internal sanding of circular shapes. Finer-grit belts are more flexible than coarse belts.***

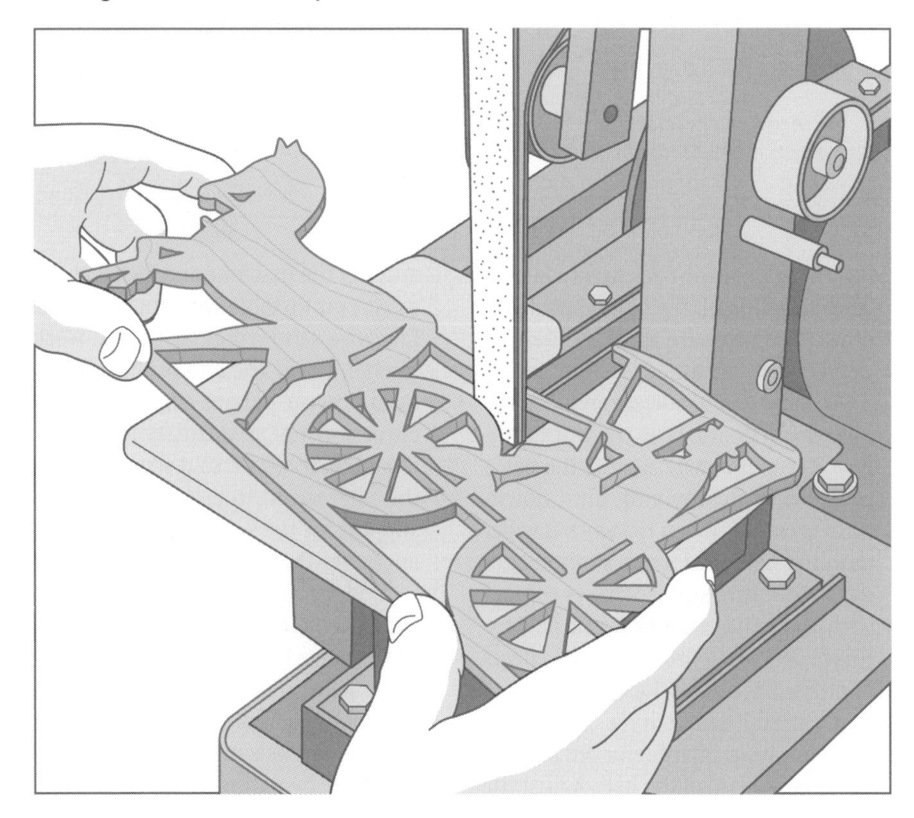

BELT SANDING LARGE WORK

The tilting table provides adequate support for small to medium work, but it's outmatched when handling larger work. The solution is to build an oversized auxiliary table out of an 18 x 24-in. panel of ¾-in. particleboard or plywood. Simply nail three cleats to the underside of the panel so that they fit snugly against the sander's table. Use three small C-clamps to hold the auxiliary table in place during use.

BELT SANDING ROUND WORK

Here's a unique, easy technique for sanding perfectly round, tapered legs. Start by cutting a square, tapered blank on a band saw or jointer. Next, nail a 4 x 4-in. L-shaped corner bracket to each end of the blank. Be certain that the nails are centered and the blank can spin freely on them. Now, with the belt in the horizontal position, clamp the brackets to the machine's fence. Place ⅛-in.-thick spacer strips underneath the blank until the clamps are tightened, then remove them before turning on the machine.

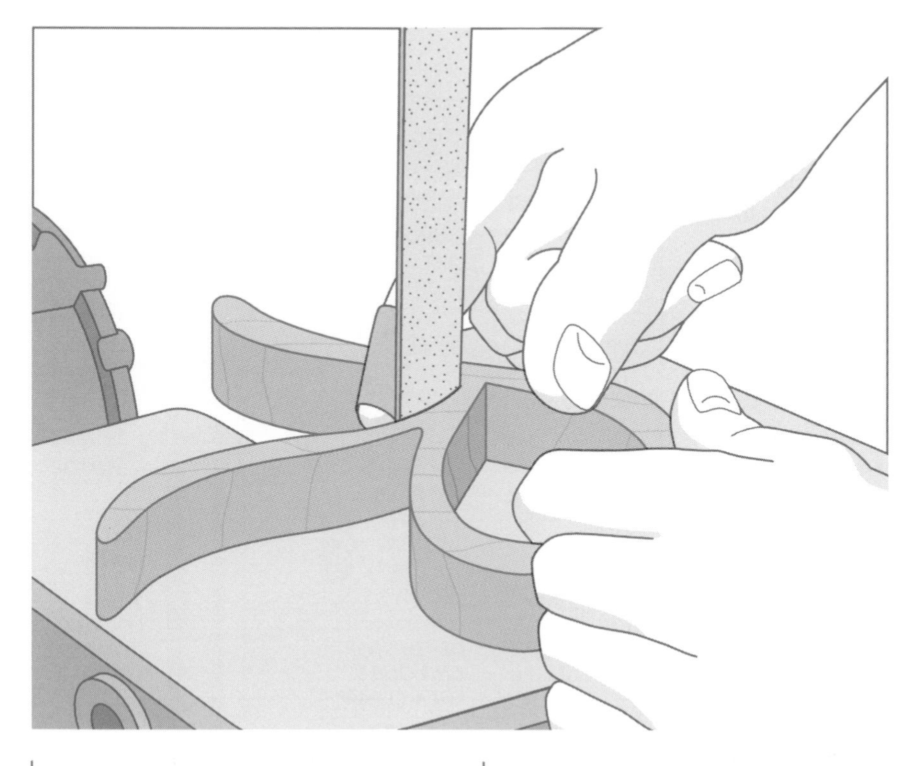

▲ **BELT SANDING DETAILS, 4.** ***Use your finger to guide the belt into tight spots. Tape or an adhesive bandage wrapped around your finger provides protection.***

▼ **BELT SANDING DETAILS, 5.** ***For sanding the most intricate details, guide the belt with a thin wood block. Make custom-shaped blocks for sanding specific contours.***

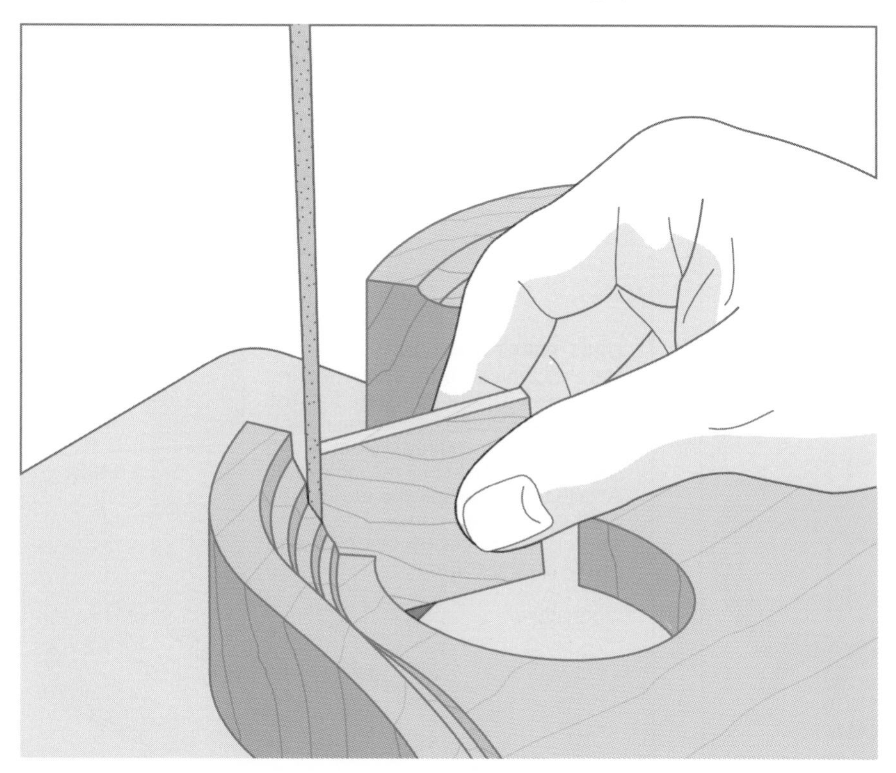

Rock the blank back and forth until enough stock has been removed from the corner to clear the moving belt. Repeat this procedure for the other three corners. Then loosen the clamps and lower the partially rounded blank slightly to repeat the entire procedure. Continue this way until the blank is completely round.

A much faster way to sand a round, tapered blank is to start with an octagonal blank instead of a square one. Also use a 50-grit abrasive belt for the initial shaping and then switch to a 100-grit belt for the final finishing.

SANDER-GRINDERS

Underrated by many, the narrow-belt sander-grinder is actually a versatile little machine that's big on performance. With the sander-grinder, you can sand, grind, sharpen, deburr, finish, contour and polish virtually any material—including wood, metal, plastics, glass and rubber.

As a sander, this machine takes over where large, broad-belt sanders—both portable and stationary—leave off. The narrower belt accurately sands intricate work quickly, thereby saving you the hours and effort it would take to sand the work by hand.

As a grinder, the machine outperforms a conventional stone grinder by cutting and sharpening faster while operating at cooler temperatures. This minimizes the risk of drawing the temper—allowing the metal to get too hot, thus weakening it—when sharpening tools or during metalworking.

The machine can easily sand and grind flat surfaces or contoured shapes of all sizes. And small surface areas can be worked with precision by simply cutting a belt into a narrow ⅛-in.-wide strip. A major feature of this machine is its ability to sand internal cuts without the need of an access cut. To perform this operation, the belt is simply threaded through the opening in the work, then remounted on its pulleys.

DRILL PRESSES

Are you getting the most out of your drill press? You're not if the drill press is being put into use only for hole-boring operations. An affordable tool, the drill press is extremely versatile, second only to the table saw and radial arm saw in importance to a home workshop.

Originally designed for metalworking, the drill press has become a valuable asset to all woodworkers—regardless of their level of skill and expertise. In addition to boring a variety of holes accurately and easily, the drill press can sand, rout, polish, saw, shape, grind, sharpen and mortise. Yet the drill press requires only a few square feet of space in the workshop. For the woodworker with limited space and a tight budget, the drill press is indeed a wise acquisition.

DRILL PRESS SPECIFICS

Drill presses are available in floor-standing and benchtop units. However, because of the additional power and capabilities that they provide, the floor-standing models are the better choice for nearly all workshops. On a floor-standing unit, the length of the column is typically from 66 to 72 in. With most benchtop models, the column is only from 36 to 44 in. long—although this limitation can be compensated for somewhat by swiveling the head of the tool so the spindle extends beyond the edge of the bench.

The rating of a drill press refers to the maximum width of work that the machine can handle, a capability that's deter-

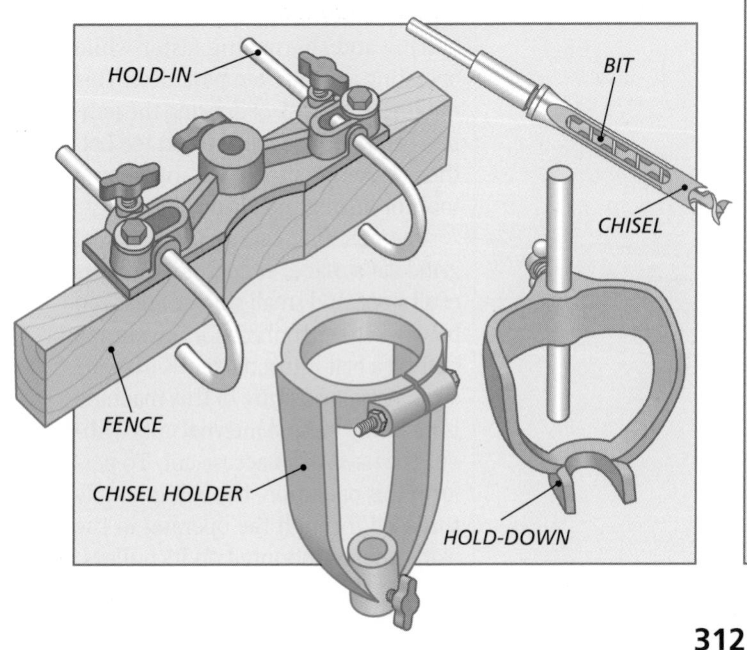

▼ **MORTISING ATTACHMENT.** ***Shown here is a typical mortising attachment. The square, hollow chisel housing the bit is held in the quill of the drill press by the chisel holder.***

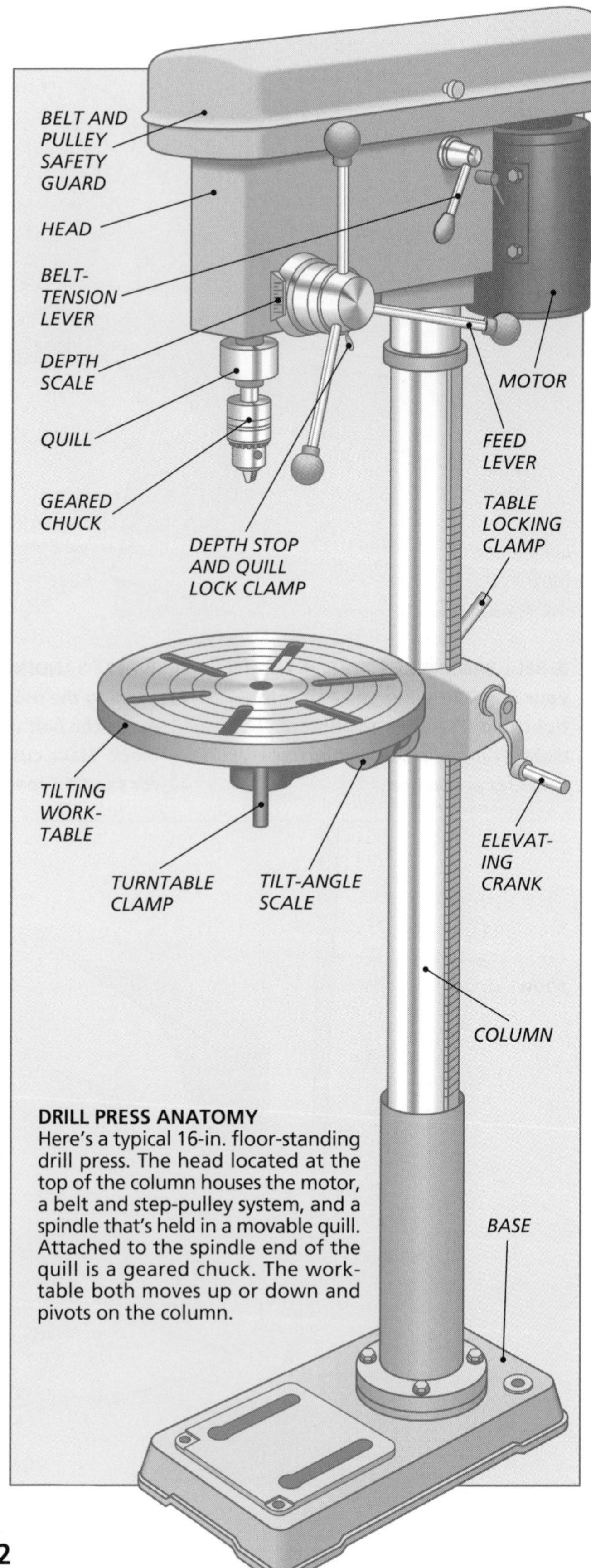

DRILL PRESS ANATOMY
Here's a typical 16-in. floor-standing drill press. The head located at the top of the column houses the motor, a belt and step-pulley system, and a spindle that's held in a movable quill. Attached to the spindle end of the quill is a geared chuck. The worktable both moves up or down and pivots on the column.

mined by the distance from the column to the center of the chuck. To calculate the size of a drill press, simply double the distance from the column to the center of the chuck. For example, a 16-in. drill press measures 8 in. from the chuck to the column. This size machine permits boring to the center of a 16-in.-wide workpiece. Most drill presses for the home workshop fall in the 11- to 16-in. range.

The drill press is powered by a motor that's usually somewhere between ¼ and ¾ hp. And the speed variability of the motor is one of the key features that distinguishes the drill press from other woodworking machines. While many stationary tools operate at a single speed that's set at the time of manufacture, the drill press can be adjusted to the speed that's appropriate to the particular job at hand. The typical ½-hp motor, for instance, provides for a spindle speed of from 400 to 4,500 rpm. Thanks to this feature, the drill press allows you to bore equally efficiently through softwoods and hardwoods of thicknesses from as little as a fraction of an inch to as much as 3 or 4 in.

Sizes of chucks for the drill press typically range from ¼ to ⅝ in., which is a measure of the maximum diameter shank that can be gripped—and not the maximum diameter that can be cut, since many bits for large holes have only ¼-in.-dia. shanks. A chuck's capacity is rated from the smallest to the largest shank that it can hold. Quality machines have chucks that start at virtually 0 in. and will grip securely the smallest of bits, while other models may not be able to grip anything that's smaller in diameter than 1/32 or 1/16 in. Power of the motor, however, is a more significant factor here since even if the chuck can hold the bit, the operation won't succeed if cutting slows or stalls.

When you're shopping for a drill press, some of the most important features to look for include a wide range of speeds, a ½-in.-dia. or greater chuck capacity, overall solid construction and a cast-iron, ribbed worktable and base. Check specifically for any side-to-side movement as the quill is lowered; there should be no play evident. Also be certain that the tool manufacturer provides service and offers a full line of accessories and replacement parts.

DRILL PRESS MECHANICS

The drill press consists of four basic components: the head, column, worktable and base. The head, which is located at the top of the column, contains the motor, a belt and step-pulley system, and a spindle that is housed in a movable sleeve called the quill. A geared chuck is attached to the end of the spindle. The quill is moved up and down with a spring-loaded feed lever and a depth stop locks the quill in place or limits its travel. The stroke or travel length of the quill varies, but most drill press models for the home workshop fall within a range of from 3 to 6 in.

The spindle speed of the drill press is usually adjusted by changing the position of V-ridged belts on pulleys. Some

▼ WOOD-BORING BITS, 1. ***Common wood-boring bits include: (1) spade, (2) spur, (3) brad-point, (4) multispur, (5) Forstner and (6) European-hinge. The cutaway sample shows through penetration by the spade and spur bits.***

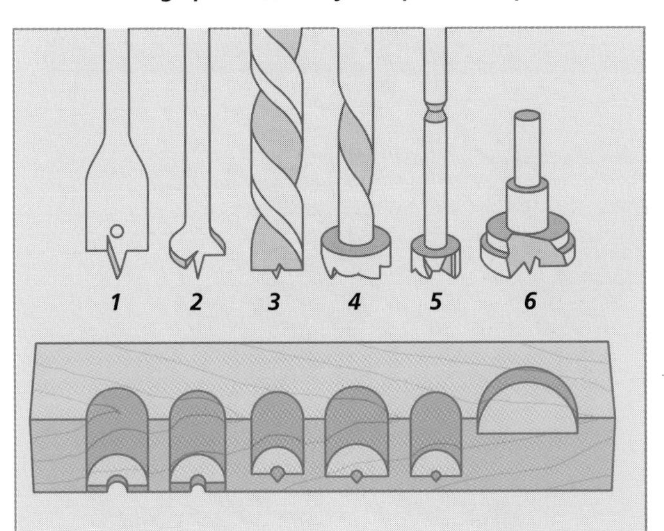

▼ WOOD-BORING BITS, 2. ***Shown in this cutaway sample are the results of: (1) three different types of screwhole bits, (2) a countersink, (3) a ½-in.-dia. x 2-in. dowel and plug cutter and (4) a ½-in.-dia. plug cutter.***

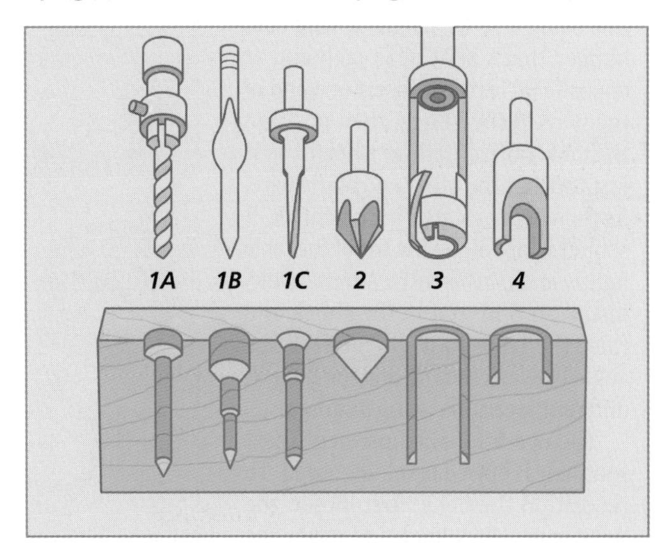

machines, however, come equipped with a speed-adjustment knob that permits infinitely variable speed settings. On a typical four-speed unit, speeds range from about 600 to 5,000 rpm. Models that have 12 or 16 speeds range from about 240 to 4,800 rpm. As a general rule, the machine should be operated at low speeds for drilling in metal, moderate to high speeds for boring in wood, and very high speeds for routing and shaping operations.

The worktable of the drill press both moves up and down on the column and pivots 360° around it. Many drill presses come with tilting tables that are invaluable for boring angled holes. Accessory tilting tables are available for some drill press models that have fixed tables, or you can easily design and build one yourself.

SETUP FUNDAMENTALS

As with all other stationary tools in the workshop, the drill press must be set up properly if the results desired are to be achieved. And while most adjustments required are operational ones that depend on the particular task at hand, the machine must be accurately set up from the start.

At the beginning of each project, check that the worktable is correctly aligned with the spindle. You can do this using a 12-in. length of wire coat hanger that's bent near each end at opposite 90° angles. Insert one end of the wire in the chuck, then position the table horizontally at a height so it just touches the other end of the wire. As the wire is rotated in the chuck, it should scrape along the top of the table lightly and consistently. Alternatively, install an 8-in. rod in the chuck and raise the table to it, then check the angle between the rod and the table at different locations using a square.

The operational adjustment most routinely required is spindle speed. To reposition the belts, first loosen the belt-tension lock knob and rotate the belt-tension lever clockwise to ease tension. Next, set the rpm desired by positioning the belts on the correct "steps" of the pulleys, working carefully to avoid pinching your fingers. Then, tension the belts by turning the belt-tension lever counterclockwise until the belt connected to the motor can be flexed with light finger pressure by the amount specified in your owner's manual—usually about 1 in. Correct tension is very important: too much resulting in excessive strain on the belt, motor shaft and spindle; too little causing the belt to slip.

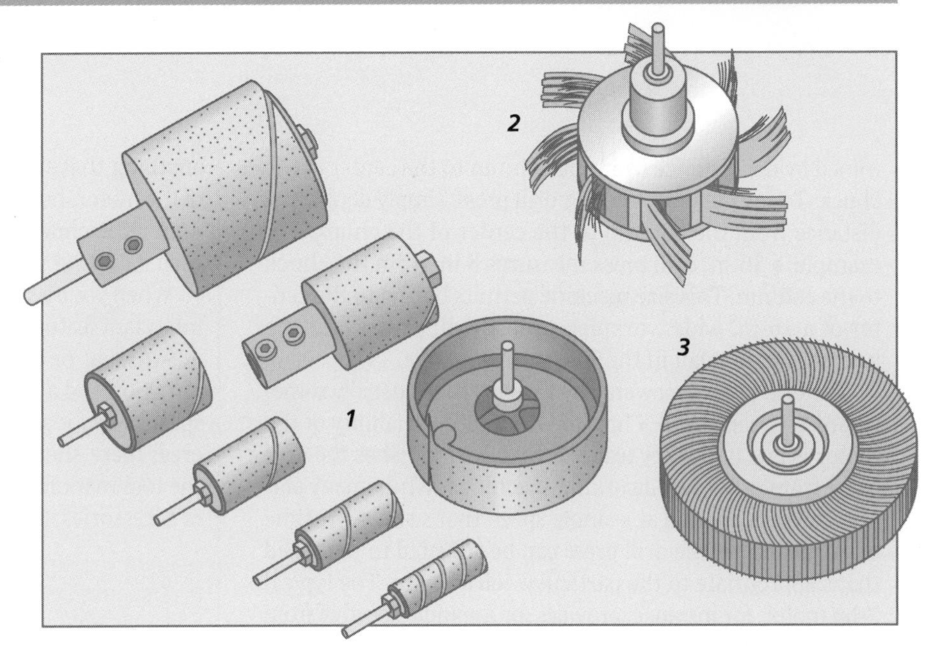

▲ **SANDING ACCESSORIES.** ***Sanding accessories for the drill press include: (1) sanding drums of various diameters, (2) a contour sander with eight brush-reinforced sanding strips and (3) a flexible abrasive wheel.***

▼ **HOLE-SAW ATTACHMENTS.** ***Shown here are attachments for cutting holes: (1) a fly cutter, (2) seven-in-one nest of saws, (3) an adjustable hole saw, (4) an interchangeable, bell-type hole saw and (5) a carbide-tipped, single-tooth hole saw.***

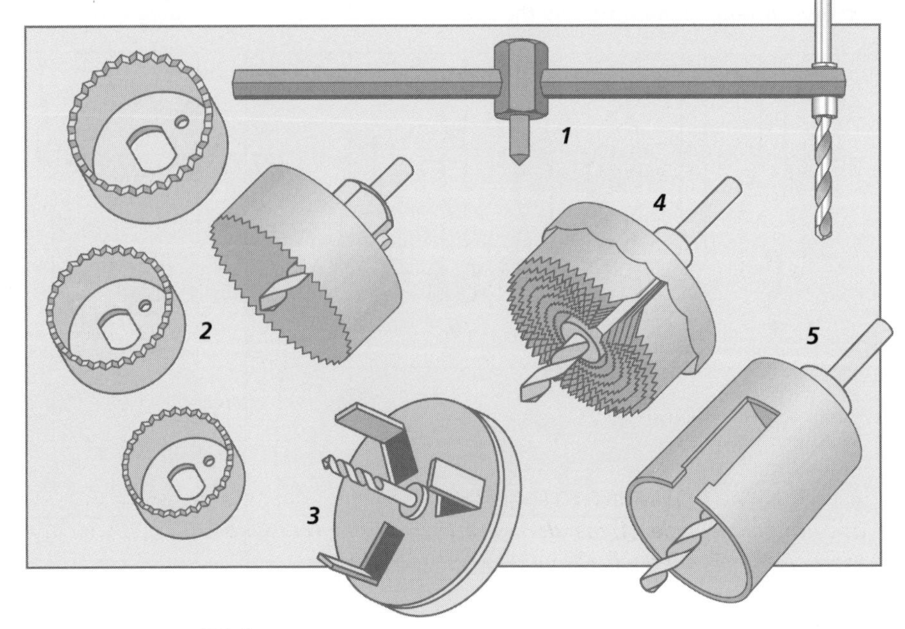

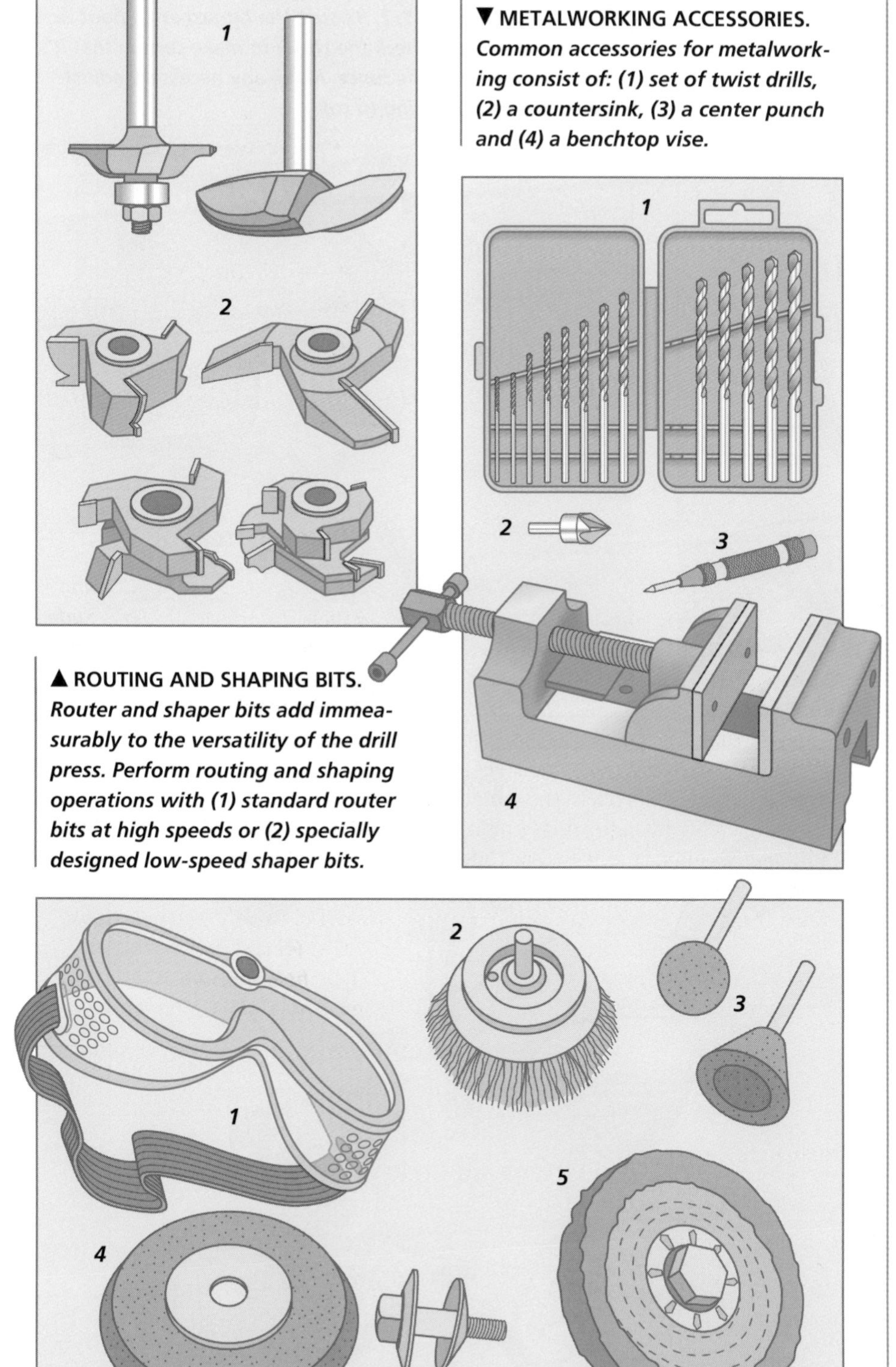

▼ **METALWORKING ACCESSORIES.** ***Common accessories for metalworking consist of: (1) set of twist drills, (2) a countersink, (3) a center punch and (4) a benchtop vise.***

▲ **ROUTING AND SHAPING BITS.** ***Router and shaper bits add immeasurably to the versatility of the drill press. Perform routing and shaping operations with (1) standard router bits at high speeds or (2) specially designed low-speed shaper bits.***

▲ **BUFFING AND GRINDING ATTACHMENTS.** ***Drill press accessories for buffing and grinding include: (1) mandatory safety goggles, (2) a wire brush, (3) grinding stones, (4) a grinding wheel and (5) a buffing wheel.***

WORK SUPPORT

Supporting work for operations on the drill press typically involves using a backup board to avoid splintering and clamps or some other type of device to prevent twisting. Both types of supporting techniques are critical to the accuracy and safety of the procedure to be done.

No matter what job you're performing, it's always wise to position a scrap block under the work. Not only will the scrap block minimize splintering of the work as the cutter exits the underside, but it will protect the worktable. When the appearance of the underside isn't important, you can rest the work directly on the table and cut through it provided the table's center hole is aligned with the spindle.

Using clamps or other devices to secure the work to the worktable guarantees that the work will not be twisted dangerously out of your hands if the cutter should grab—which often occurs at the point it breaks through the underside of the work. Safe handholding of work is possible only if the work is of an appropriately large size and the cutter is small. Long work, for example, can sometimes be positioned with one edge against the column in a way that helps counteract any twisting caused by the cutter.

In addition to doing duty as a guide, a fence can serve as a safety mechanism. The fence need be no more elaborate than a straight length of board clamped to the worktable along the work—in a position, for instance, that gauges the distance from an edge for a cut. With such a setup, any twisting caused by the cutter is absorbed by the fence—not your hands.

BITS AND DRILLS

Nowadays, the words bit and drill are used interchangeably. But to be technically accurate, bits are used for boring in wood and drills are used to drill

▼ **CUTTING MORTISES, 1.** ***Slip the chisel holder over the chuck and onto the base of the quill, and tighten the locking bolt to hold it securely. Then, secure the chisel in the holder and tighten the bit in the chuck.***

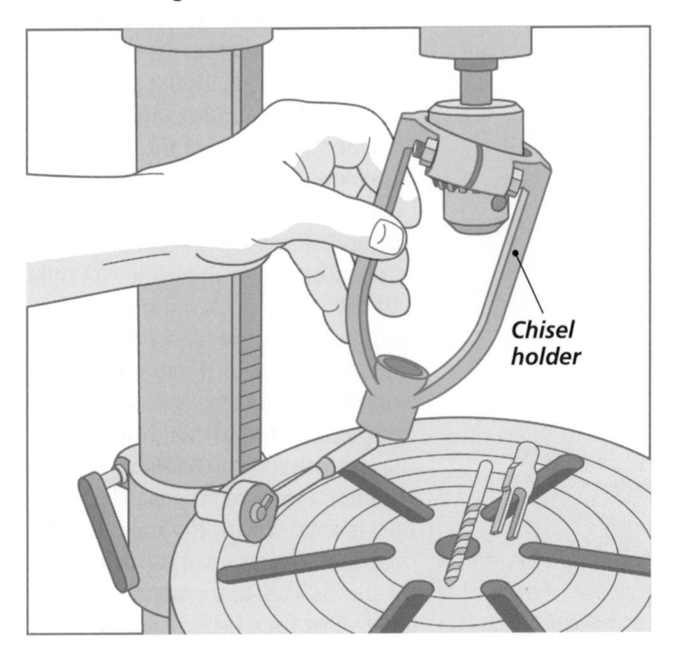

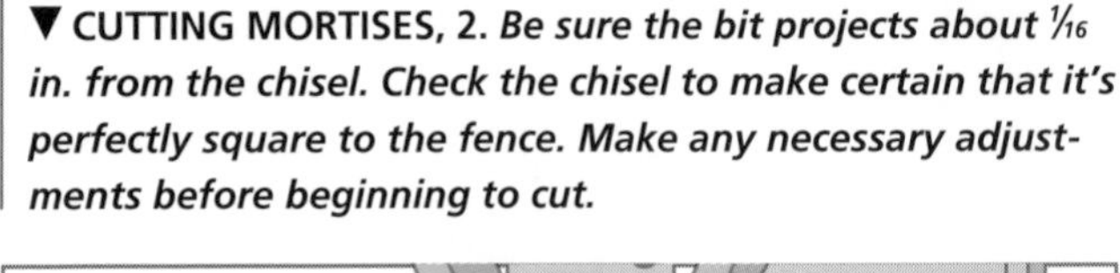

▼ **CUTTING MORTISES, 2.** ***Be sure the bit projects about 1/16 in. from the chisel. Check the chisel to make certain that it's perfectly square to the fence. Make any necessary adjustments before beginning to cut.***

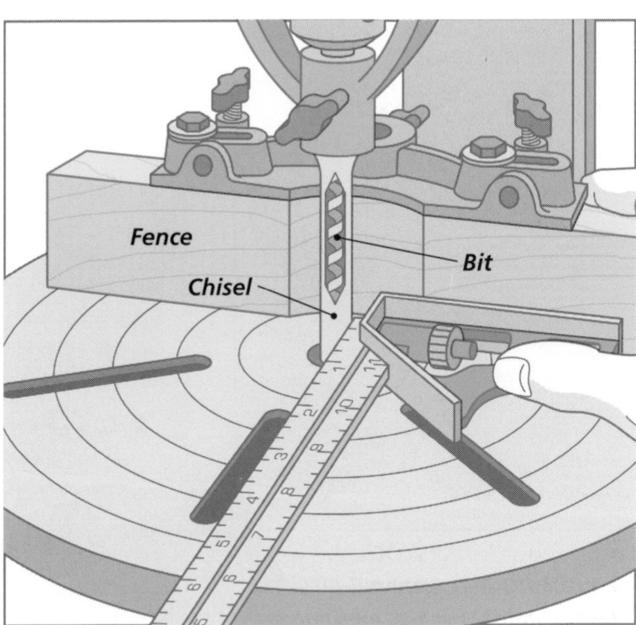

in metal. However, the common twist drill, which is designed for metalworking, is used frequently for boring in wood. In fact, for boring holes less than ¼ in. dia., there's no choice but to use twist drills.

For boring larger, flat-bottom holes up to about 2⅛ in. dia., wood bits come in several different styles—including spade, spur, brad point, multispur and Forstner. As well, special metric-sized, carbide-tipped hardware bits are available for installing European-type cabinet hinges. These clean-cutting bits produce smooth holes of exact size.

Spade bits are among the most popular hole-boring tools, largely because of their wide range of sizes and relative low cost. Their long, sharp points, slender shanks and flat blades make them especially well-suited to boring extra-large holes; quality ones feature relieved edges for even cleaner, cooler cutting. The efficiency of spade bits is greatest at speeds higher than average—the largest size, for instance, performs best at about 1,500 rpm.

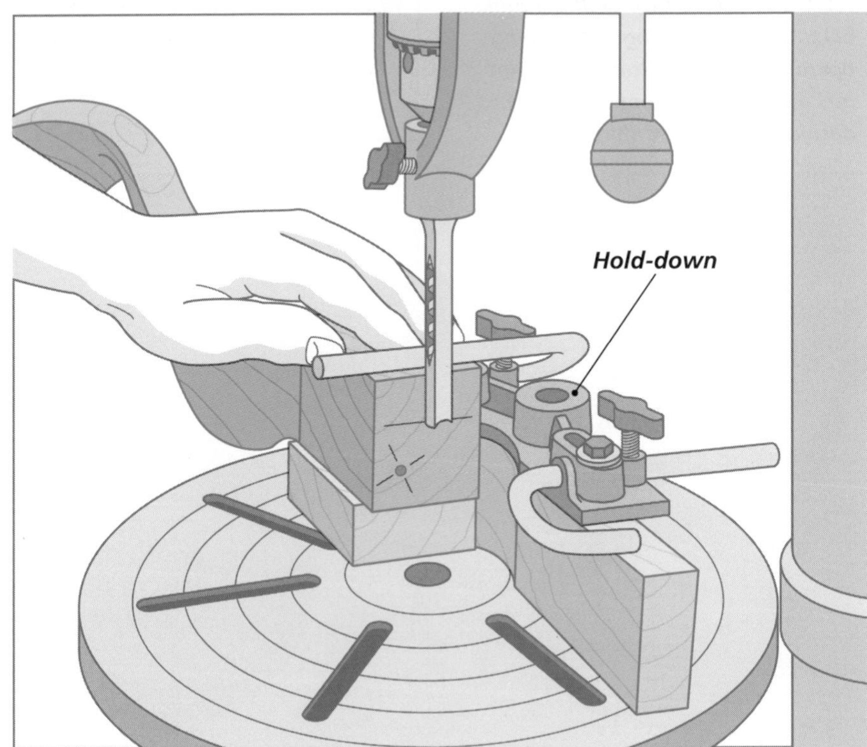

▲ **CUTTING MORTISES, 3.** ***Mark the mortise depth on the end of the workpiece, then lower the chisel to the mark and set the depth-stop mechanism. Position the fence and adjust the hold-down before cutting.***

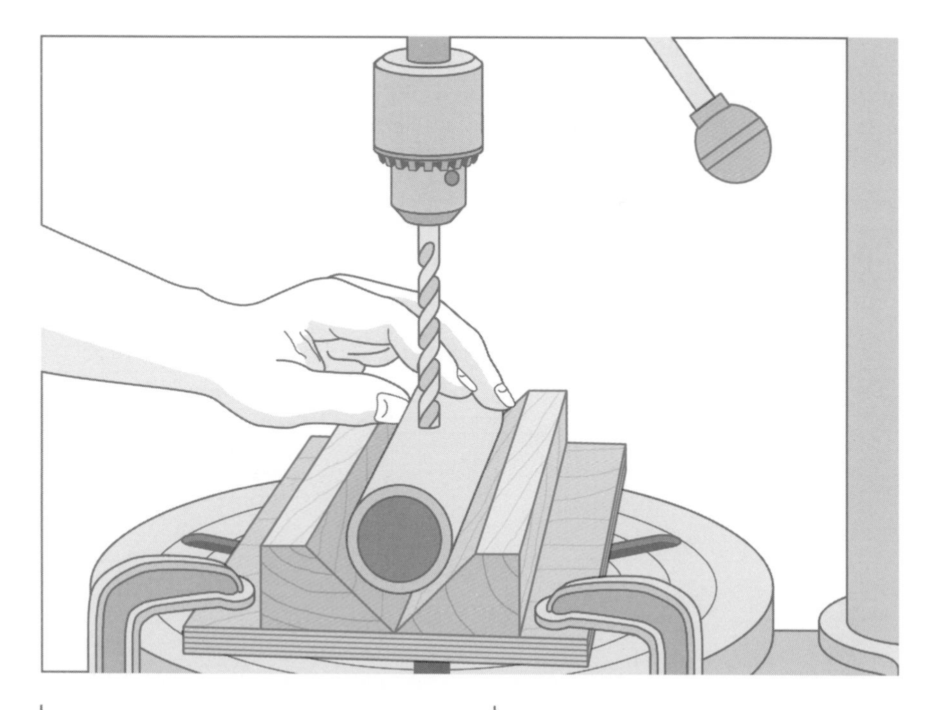

▲ **BORING ROUND STOCK, 1.** ***Build this automatic-centering V-block cradle as a holding device for boring round stock. Make the cradle from mitered 2 x 4 stock screwed to a ½-in. plywood panel.***

▼ **BORING ROUND STOCK, 2.** ***To bore into the end of round stock, simply adjust the worktable of the drill press into the vertical position with the V-block cradle clamped securely in place on it.***

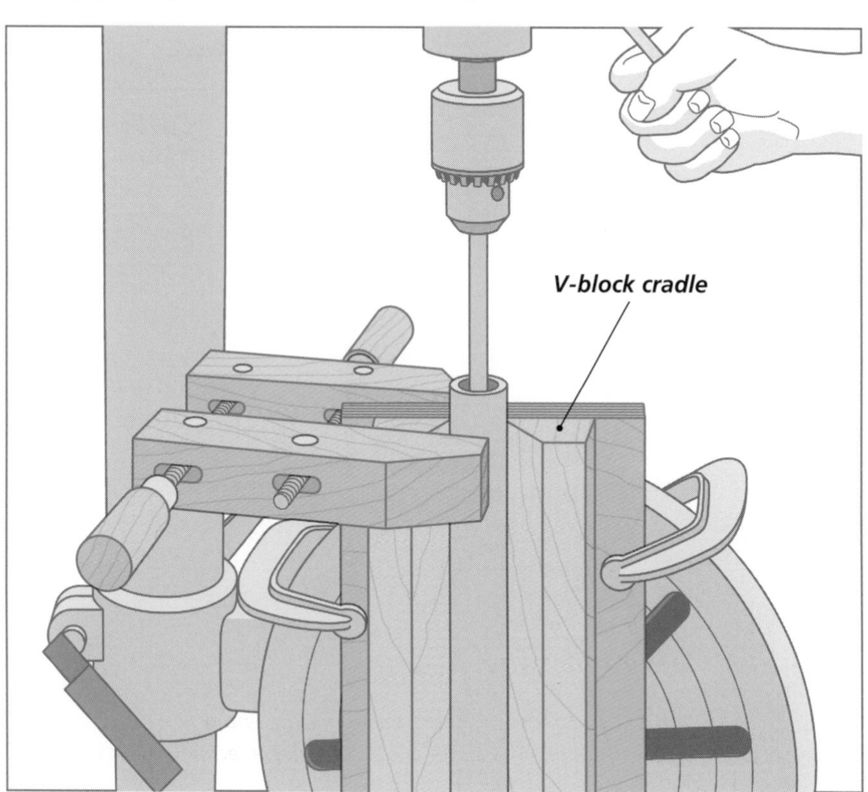

The main disadvantage of spade and spur bits is that their maximum blind-hole depth is limited because the bit's long point will penetrate right through the piece. Brad-point, multispur and Forstner bits, however, have wide cutting rims that provide unparalleled control for boring both angled holes into work and any portion of a hole in the edge of a board.

Fluted bits must be retracted frequently while they are cutting to allow waste to be cleared out of their channels. Otherwise, waste can build up in the flutes, resulting in overheating of the bit as well as inaccurate work. The objective is to always have a minimum of waste in the hole being cut.

Screw-point bits should never be used in the drill press. Since the screw is self-feeding, it attempts to take over control of the rate of penetration by the bit. Bits with points, on the other hand, allow the operator to maintain control of how fast the bit penetrates into the work.

THROUGH AND BLIND BORING

Before boring a hole through a workpiece, align the bit carefully with the center hole in the worktable. Then, clamp a backup board to the table to prevent splintering the underside of the workpiece as the bit exits.

To bore a blind hole, first mark the desired depth of the hole on the side of the workpiece. Then, lower the bit to the mark and adjust the quill depth stop to prevent the bit from cutting deeper than the desired depth.

BORING ROUND STOCK

Using some kind of holding device for round stock is virtually essential to ensure both accuracy and safety. Many different types of holding devices are available as accessories from the tool manufacturer, but here are a couple of simple devices that you can make easily in your workshop.

To bore holes accurately in round stock, make a V-block cradle. First, rip an 18-in.-long 2 x 4 on a saw with the blade tilted at a 45° angle. Then, screw the 2 x 4 pieces onto a plywood panel to form a V-shaped holder. Clamp the cradle to the worktable with the stock held in the V of the blocks. Now, bore into the side of the stock. By simply repositioning the worktable vertically, you can quickly prepare to bore into the end of the stock.

Make a second device to hold circular disks. Join two pieces of 1 x 4 in an L-shape using dowel pins. Use the device in a horizontal position to bore holes into the face of a circular disk. Reposition the worktable vertically in order to bore holes into a disk's edge.

DOWEL-PIN HOLES IN MITERS

Another useful device consists of two L-shaped blocks that make it easy to bore precisely aligned dowel-pin holes in mitered pieces. First, set the worktable in a vertical position and clamp both the first L-shaped block and the workpiece to the table. Be sure that the edge of the workpiece being bored is perpendicular to and centered under the drill bit.

Now, bore one hole for a dowel pin into each mitered end. Next, add the second L-shaped block to the table to reposition the workpiece in preparation for boring the second set of dowel-pin holes.

LONG STOCK THROUGH HOLES

There's also a way to bore a hole that's about twice as deep as the travel length of the quill. The trick is to bore in from both ends of the stock.

To ensure that the holes bored from each end meet in perfect alignment, start by boring a hole in one end of the workpiece as deep as possible. Next, bore the same size diameter hole in a plywood panel. Then, install a straight steel rod in the chuck and clamp the

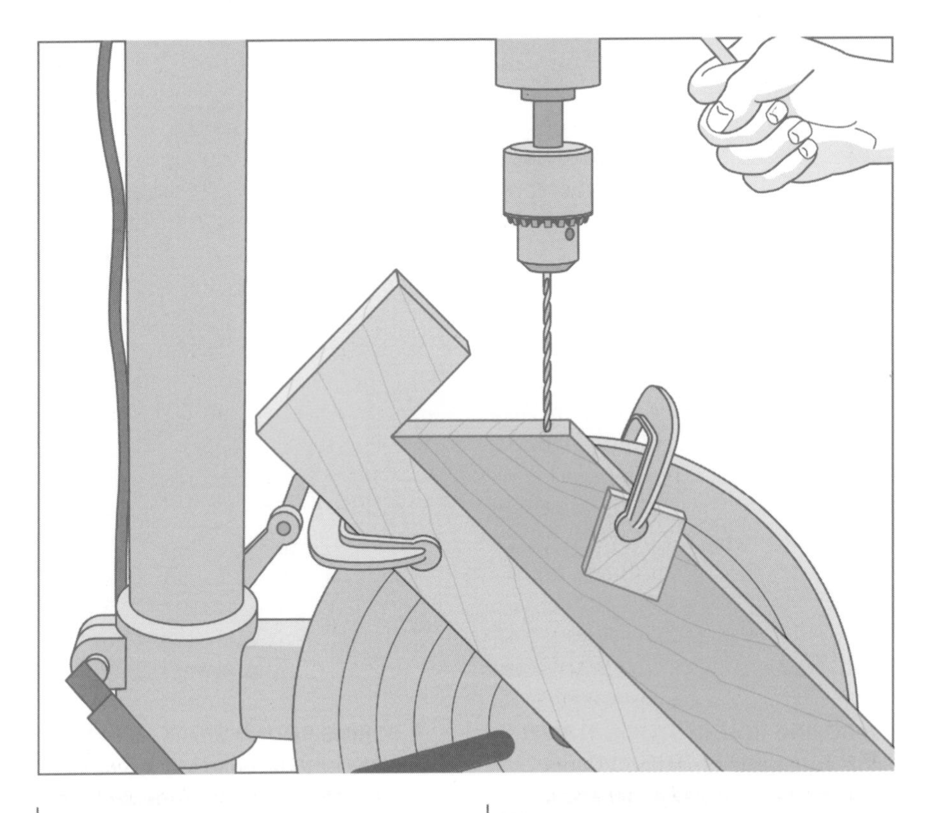

▲ **BORING DOWEL-PIN HOLES, 1.** ***Bore dowel-pin holes in mitered work with the help of L-shaped blocks. Clamp one block in place and bore the first set of holes.***

▼ **BORING DOWEL-PIN HOLES, 2.** ***Then, add a second block to reposition the workpiece for boring the second set of holes. Be sure the bit is centered on the work.***

panel in place so that the rod and hole are aligned perfectly.

Now, insert a short length of dowel into the hole in the plywood panel. Place the workpiece over the dowel and bore the second hole. To bore extra deep holes, use a bit extension or an 18-in.-long electrician's bit.

MORTISING

Cutting square and rectangular mortises is easy on a drill press using a mortising attachment. The attachment consists of a square, hollow chisel that houses a special bit, a chisel holder that clamps to the quill and a fence that guides the work. A bracket that's on the fence supports an adjustable hold-down fixture as well as two hook-shaped hold-in rods. Mortising chisels with matching bits are available commonly in four different sizes: ¼-, 5⁄16-, ⅜- and ½-in. square.

There are two important adjustments that must be performed before attempting to cut the mortise. First, adjust the bit so that its cutting spurs extend about 1⁄16 in. below the end of the chisel. This slight projection prevents the bit from striking the chisel. Second, make sure that the chisel is square to the fence to avoid an uneven, rough-cut mortise.

The next step is to mark the outline of the mortise on the workpiece. Set the spindle speed to about 1,000 rpm for hardwoods; to 2,000 rpm for softwoods. Then, adjust the depth stop and position the fence to accommodate the workpiece. Adjust the hold-down fixture and hold-in rods to secure the work firmly against both the worktable and the fence.

Now, bore a hole at each end of the marked outline to establish the length of the mortise. Apply steady, even pressure with the feed lever. Then, move the workpiece about three-quarters of the chisel width and bore an overlapping hole. Repeat this procedure until all the waste is removed.

ACCESSORY TOOLS

Accurate hole boring may be the specialty function of the drill press, but the machine can be used as well to perform a wide variety of other important shop techniques—including sanding, hole sawing, shaping, metalworking, and buffing and grinding. Since most of these operations require an acces-

▼ **BORING DEEP HOLES, 1.** ***Bore a hole into a plywood panel and use a straight rod to align the hole with the center of the chuck. Then, clamp the panel to the worktable.***

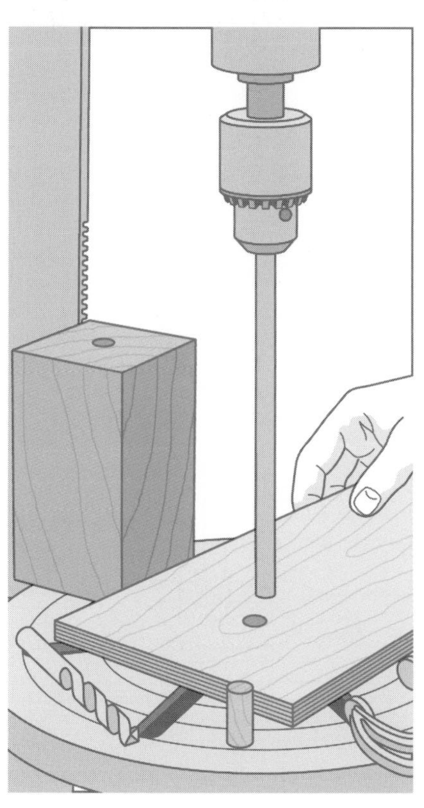

▼ **BORING DEEP HOLES, 2.** ***Insert a short section of dowel into the hole in the plywood panel. Then, place the previously bored hole in the workpiece over the dowel.***

▼ **BORING DEEP HOLES, 3.** ***Now, bore a second hole of maximum depth to meet the first. This procedure allows you to bore a hole twice as deep as the capacity of the drill press.***

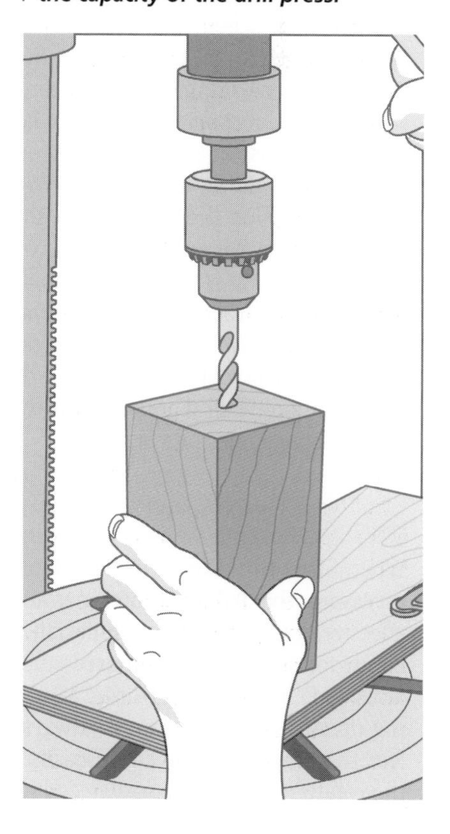

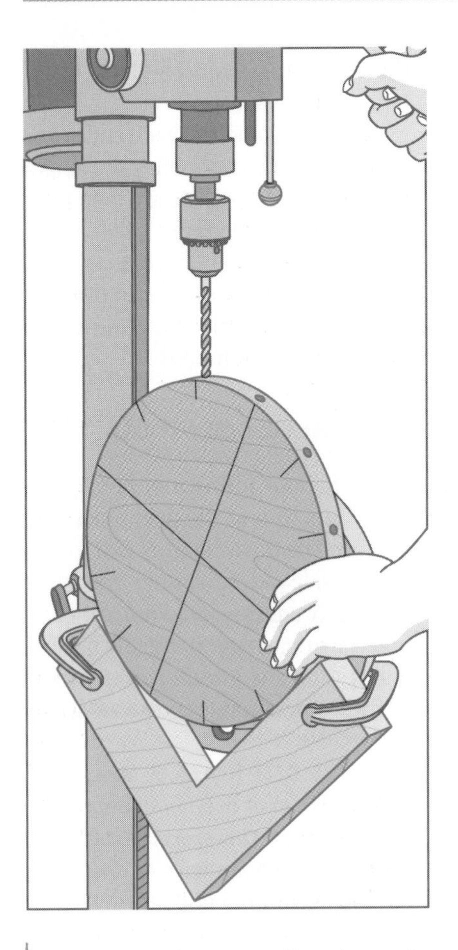

◀ **BORING INTO CIRCUMFERENCES, 1.** ***Make the right-angle holding device shown here to bore into the edge of a round workpiece. Position the worktable vertically for the boring.***

▼ **BORING INTO CIRCUMFERENCES, 2.** ***Reposition the worktable horizontally to bore into the face of the workpiece. Draw centerlines to help in the boring of evenly spaced holes.***

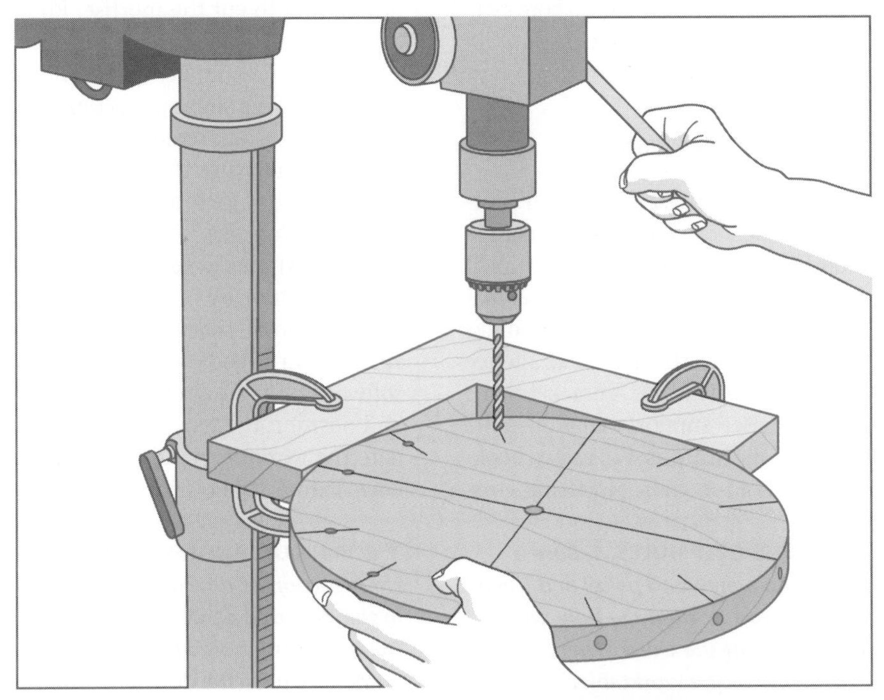

sory tool such as a sanding drum, fly cutter, wire wheel or shaper cutter, you must be certain that the tool is designed for use in a drill press.

There are additional safety considerations in using the drill press with accessory tools. Never exceed the maximum rpm rating of the accessory tool and don't use an accessory tool that is designed exclusively for the drill press in any other power tool. During all operations on the drill press, be sure to wear safety goggles or a face shield.

SANDING

When fitted with the correct sanding accessory, the drill press becomes an effective finishing machine, especially handy for smoothing contoured surfaces and curved edges. During sanding operations, be certain to always feed the work in the direction *against* the rotation of the accessory.

Sanding drums, which are commonly available in sizes ranging from ½ to 4½ in. dia., can be used for sanding both contours and straight edges. To get the most use out of the sanding drums, build yourself an auxiliary worktable out of doubled 18 x 24-in. ½-in. plywood panels, and cut dadoed slots ¾ in. wide and ⅜ in. deep in the top for a miter gauge. Equip the auxiliary table with a plywood insert that can removed, allowing a sanding drum to be lowered about 1 in. below the table's surface. To be able to utilize the entire abrasive surface of a sanding drum, construct a simple elevated plywood platform about 6 in. high. Clamp the platform to the auxiliary table and

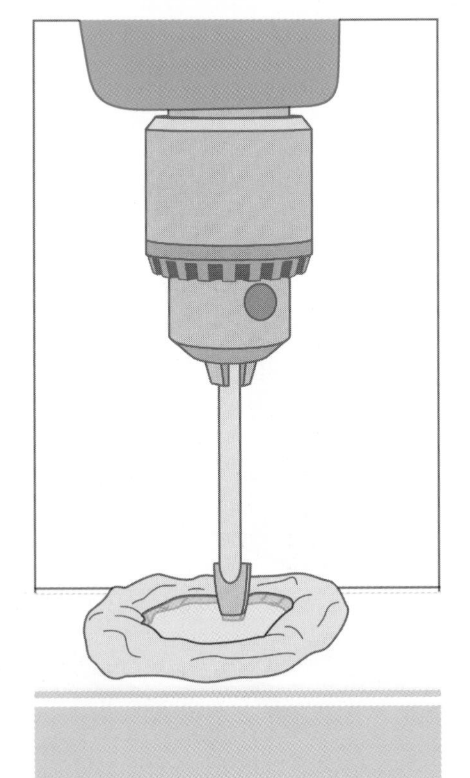

▶ **DRILLING GLASS.** ***Work with a special spear-point carbide bit to drill through glass. Make a dam out of caulking for containing a puddle of turpentine that serves as lubricant.***

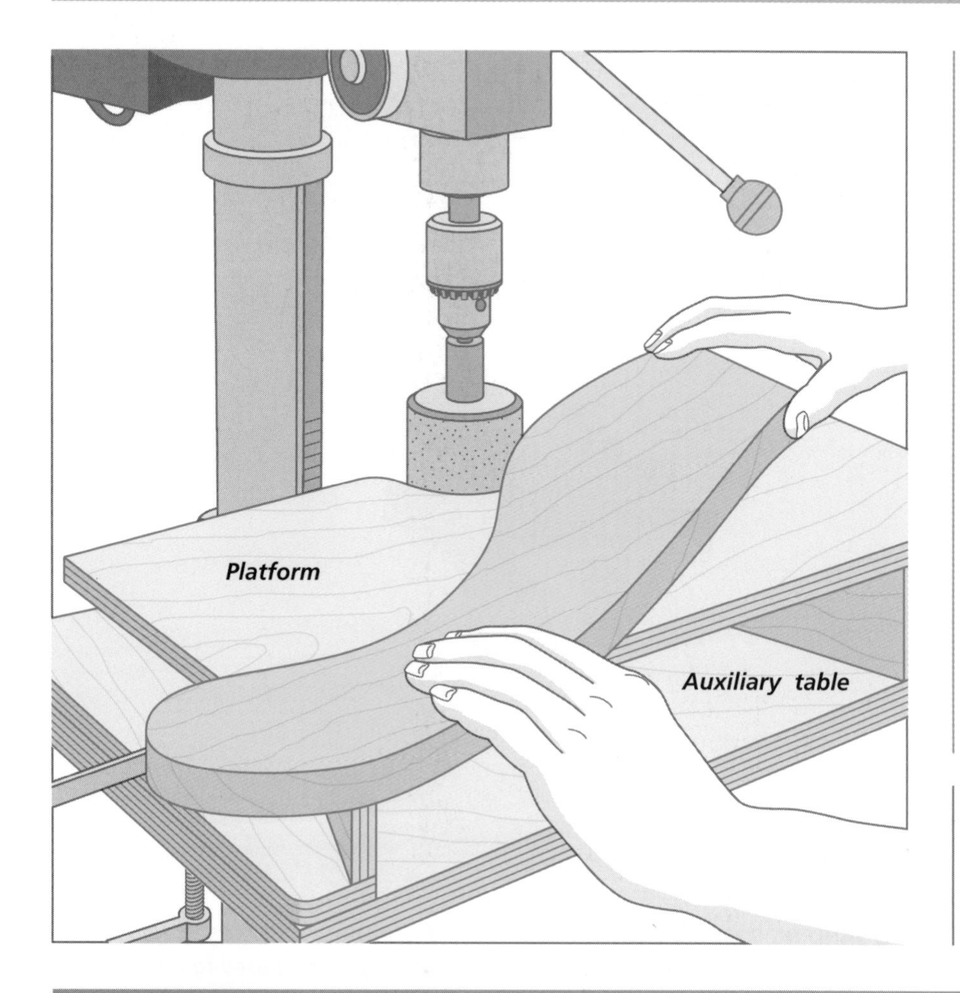

then raise or lower the sanding drum as needed to promote even, total wear of the abrasive.

When sculpting irregular-shaped workpieces, first move the worktable out of the way and work the stock freehand against the rotating drum until the desired shape is achieved. Then, replace the sanding drum with a flexible contour sander to smooth out the workpiece. This sanding accessory features abrasive strips supported by stiff brushes that conform to the workpiece. Note that the contour sander is only for finish-sanding, not for heavy removal of stock.

HOLE SAWING

To bore large diameter holes in wood, plastic and sheet metal, hole saws are available up to about 3 in. dia. For cut-

◀ **SANDING SURFACES, 1.** ***An elevated platform clamped to auxiliary worktable permits using the entire surface of a sanding drum. Feed the work against the drum's rotation.***

QUICK-GRIP DRILL PRESS CLAMP

Here's an easy-to-use clamping device that sets up quickly and swings out of the way when it's not needed. It consists of a single cast-aluminum arm that mounts on the column of the drill press. Simply swing the arm over the work, then lower and lock it to the column with the handle *(right)*.

The clamping device comes in sizes to fit drill presses ranging from 12 to 20½ in. Optional accessory kits offer add-on components that make the clamping device more versatile. These include a screw jack that increases clamping pressure, a non-marring rubber-pad cover, a straight aluminum extension bar, an offset extension and a notched hold-down for securing pipes, rods and other round stock.

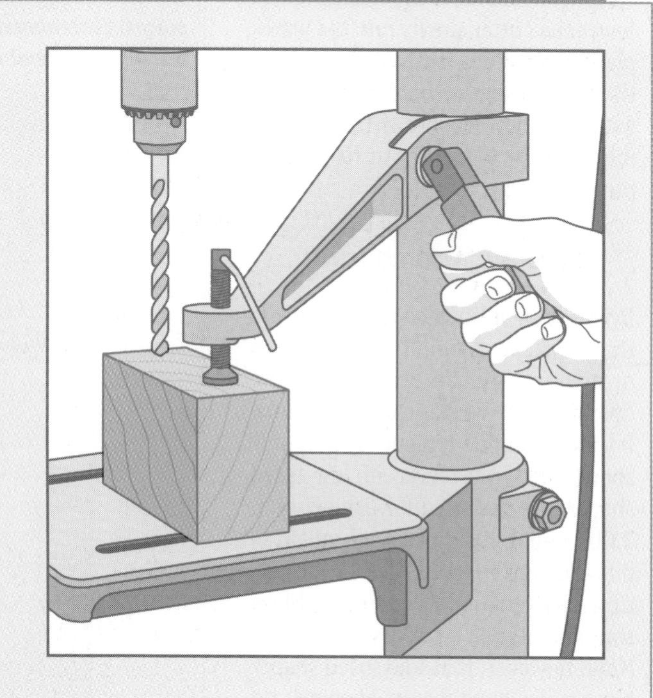

ting very large holes—up to about 8 in. dia.—use an adjustable fly cutter.

Hole saws come in several styles, but they all work in the same basic manner. Each of these tools has a pilot bit, usually ¼ in. dia., that projects from the center. The bit centers the tool and helps guide the saw through the stock. There is also a unique type of hole saw that features a single carbide-tipped cutting edge (and is claimed to last 50 times longer than conventional hole saws). No matter what particular style of hole saw you're using, it is always a good practice to back out the cutting edge frequently to clear away chips and sawdust. This will keep the tool from overheating, which can result in premature wear of the cutting edge and may cause burn marks on the work.

A fly cutter is adjustable for cutting holes of varying diameters—typically between 1¼ and 8 in. dia. Simply slide the cutter along the crossbar and then secure it by tightening the setscrew. Next, clamp the workpiece securely to the worktable, separated by a backup scrap board. Set the spindle speed of the drill press between 500 and 600 rpm. Now, turn on the machine and lower the cutter slowly into the workpiece. Don't force the tool to cut. Note that when the crossbar and cutter are rotating, they become virtually invisible. Be sure to keep your hands well out of the way.

SHAPING AND ROUTING

If you have a high-speed drill press that's capable of running at 5,000 rpm or greater, you can perform routing operations using standard router bits. If your machine's top-end speed is only about 4,000 rpm, work with low-speed shaper bits designed for use between 3,000 and 4,000 rpm. Each of these bits is equipped with at least nine cutting edges that enable you to achieve smooth cuts at a relatively slow speed. Note, however, that low-speed shaper bits are designed for use at speeds no

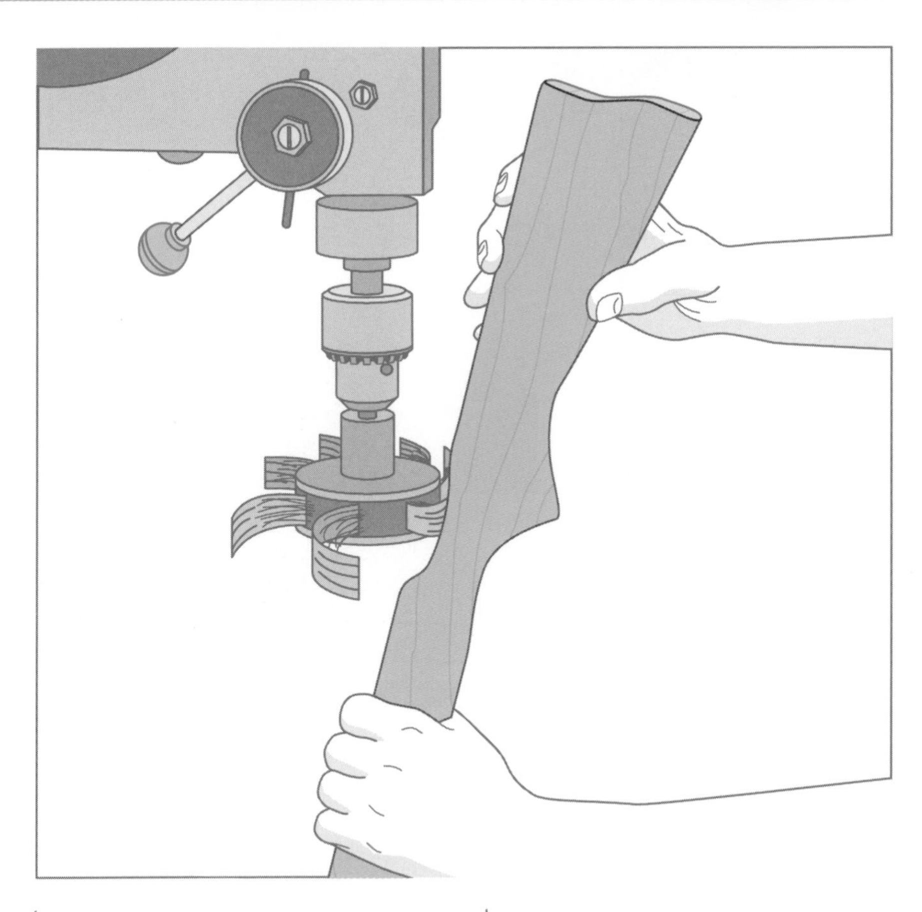

▲ **SANDING SURFACES, 2.** ***The eight abrasive strips of a contour sander conform to curved surfaces of workpieces. Each abrasive strip is reinforced with flexible brushes.***

▼ **SANDING SURFACES, 3.** ***Here, a sanding drum is used to form a concave surface on a leg that fits a round pedestal. The size of the drum must equal the pedestal diameter.***

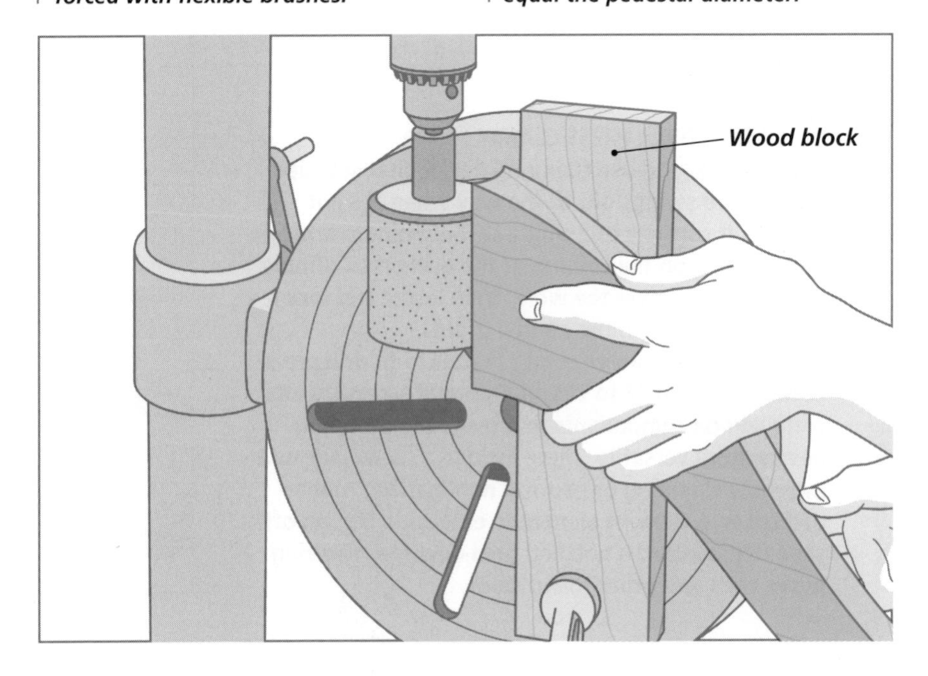

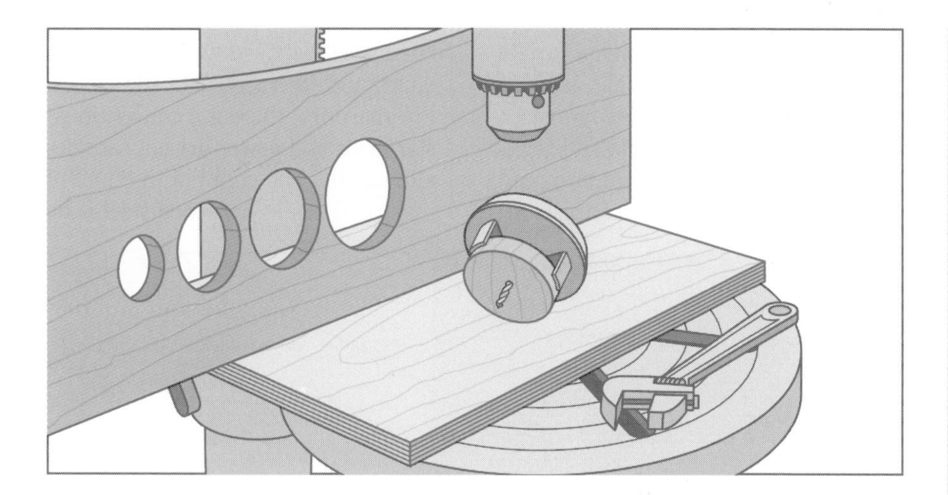

▲ **USING HOLE SAWS, 1.** ***With an adjustable hole saw, you can cut any size hole within its capacity. This one cuts holes from 1⅛ to 2½ in. dia.***

▼ **USING HOLE SAWS, 2.** ***The carbide-tipped, single-tooth hole saw has the capacity to cut through stock that's 1½ in. thick in just one pass.***

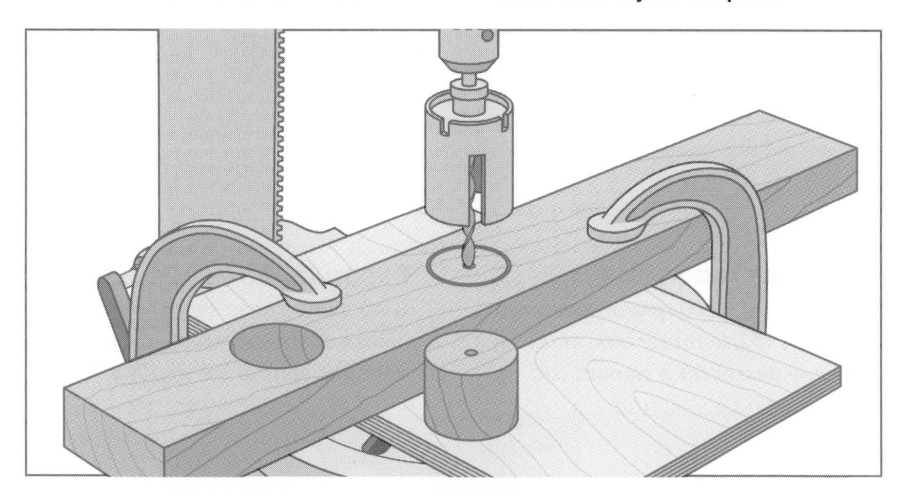

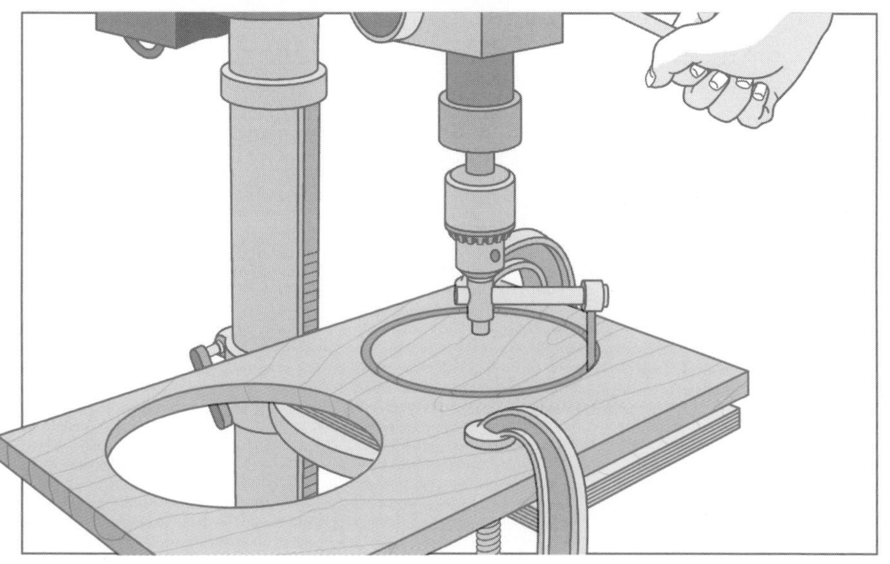

greater than 4,000 rpm, and should never be used in a router.

Regardless of whether you're using a router bit or a low-speed shaper bit, always feed the work against the rotation of the bit. And unless the bit features a ball-bearing pilot guide, install a fence to support the workpiece and control the depth of cut.

Pin routing also is possible on a drill press. Install a table insert that has a short dowel pin protruding from its center. Make sure that the dowel pin aligns perfectly with the router bit in the chuck. Next, tack-nail a ¼-in. plywood template onto the underside of the workpiece. Then, turn on the drill press and guide the edge of the template against the dowel pin. The bit will cut the workpiece as indicated by the template's shape. This technique is especially useful when producing several identical pieces.

METALWORKING

The procedures for drilling in metal are similar to those for boring in wood. However, since metal is a much harder material than wood, it's necessary to drill at slower spindle speeds and to apply less pressure on the feed lever. This will prevent overheating, which would weaken and dull the bit.

It's also very important to clamp the workpiece securely to the worktable of the drill press to prevent it from spinning with the bit. Use a drill press vise to hold small workpieces, then clamp the vise to the worktable.

When you start to drill in metal, the bit may tend to wander on the surface. Prevent this by striking a starting point with a center punch. If the mark is too small to seat a large diameter bit, drill a small diameter hole first and then drill the larger hole.

◀ **USING HOLE SAWS, 3.** ***For holes of diameters up to about 8 in., use a fly cutter. Make sure that the work is clamped securely to the worktable.***

Drilling an angled hole with a twist drill is difficult because the bit can't cut into the slanted surface. Solve this by using a two-lipped end mill to start the hole. Then, switch to a twist drill to complete the hole. If an end mill isn't available, start drilling the hole with the bit perpendicular to the workpiece. Then, tilt the workpiece to the desired angle and continue drilling.

The tendency for the workpiece to spin is strongest just as the bit breaks through the underside surface. At this point, the bit may grab and break, or it may tear the workpiece from its holdings. To prevent this, simply hold back on the feed lever slightly when the bit starts to break through.

BUFFING AND GRINDING

Cleaning, polishing, buffing and grinding a wide variety of materials are also possible on the drill press. All that you require is the proper accessory.

Wire brushes are useful for removing paint, rust and grime from metal parts. These tools are available in cup and wheel types, with either brass or steel bristles. For aggressive brushing action, use a steel wire wheel. Choose the softer, brass wire wheel for more delicate work.

Use a soft buffing wheel coated with jeweler's rouge to buff a high luster on plastics and metals. First, sand the work with lubricated wet/dry abrasive paper. Then, buff the piece on the drill press, keeping the work in constant motion to prevent scorching.

Grinding stones are available in various sizes and shapes. Use the stones for sharpening steel blades and bits, and to fabricate metal parts. Carefully inspect the grinding stone before each use. Never use a grinding stone that is fractured or damaged in any way.

DRILLING HARD MATERIALS

A new world opens up for many craftsmen when they discover ways to drill in hard material. Suddenly, a variety of new projects are possible, as more materials become available for use.

With specialized drills and techniques, it's possible to drill into hard material such as glass, porcelain, hardened steel, petrified wood, turquoise, quartz and other stone-like substances. For masonry, there are conventional star drills and power-driven, carbide-alloy drills. The common method of making holes in hardened steel is by

▲ **ROUTING AND SHAPING, 1.** ***A spindle speed of 5,000 rpm or greater is required to use router bits. Make shallow passes for a smooth cut.***

▼ **ROUTING AND SHAPING, 2.** ***When using a low-speed shaper bit, clamp a fence to the worktable to guide the work and control the depth of cut.***

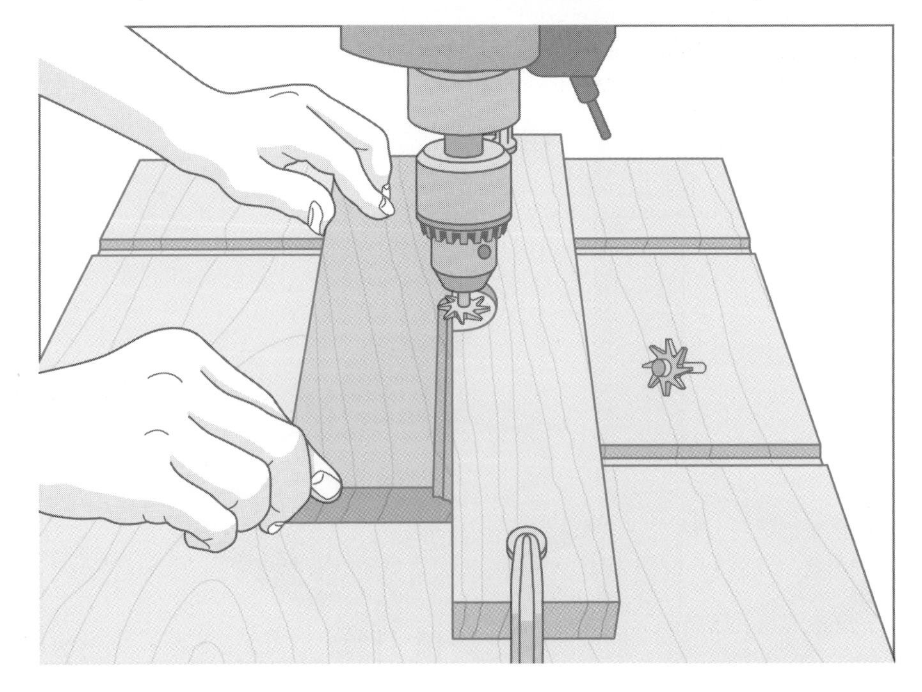

annealing, drilling with ordinary steel bits and then rehardening. For glass, stone, ceramics and hard metals, tungsten-carbide and diamond drills are the ones most often used.

ABRASIVE-GRIT DRILLING

An inexpensive method of making a hole in glass, china or similar material is to grind it through with abrasive particles on a drill press. The bit can be made from rods of aluminum, copper, brass or even a headless nail. Because of their tubular cutting ends, such bits are called core types. The desired diameter is usually milled in a lathe from a rod, then the bit is center-drilled to form a recess in which cores develop from the material being drilled.

Granular abrasive is used between the material and rotating drill—and is what does the actual cutting. The abrasive is usually aluminum-oxide or silicon-carbide grains of 80- to 120-grit size. Abrasive types include loose grains made by abrasive manufacturers, valve-grinding compound, and aluminum-oxide or silicon-carbide grains from sandpaper. Grain type and size are indicated on the paper back. Try wetting the coated surface of sandpaper with lacquer thinner and scraping grains off with a screwdriver or putty knife. Whatever the abrasive, it is usually mixed with water into a "soup."

For core-type bits, the speed of the drill press should be low or moderate. Raise the bit every 10 seconds or so to let fresh soup flow over the cutting area. When the hole is almost through, control the feed pressure carefully to prevent chipping the underside. Don't become discouraged if this method seems exasperatingly slow. Drilling rate depends on such things as hard-

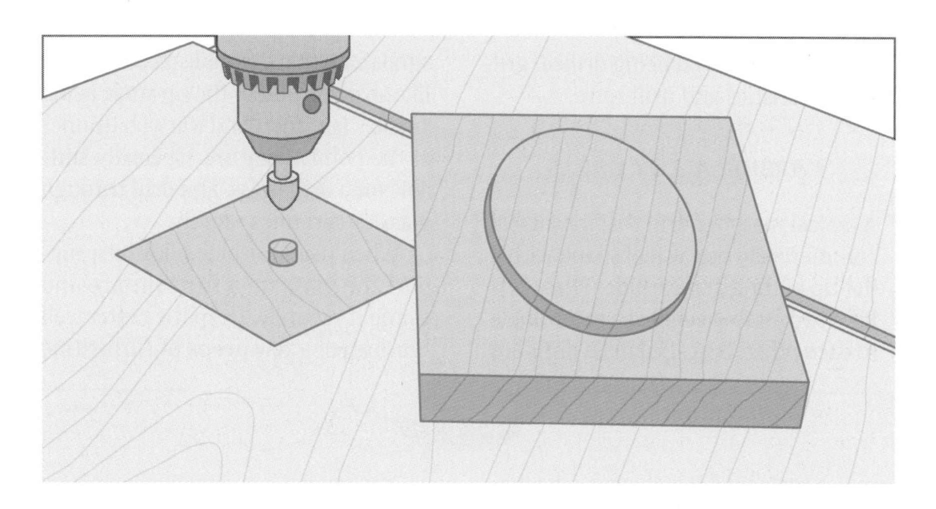

▲ **PIN ROUTING, 1.** ***A table insert with a dowel protruding from the center is used for pin routing. Nail a ¼-in. plywood template to the bottom of the workpiece.***

▼ **PIN ROUTING, 2.** ***As the edge of the template is guided along against the dowel pin, the router bit will cut the workpiece to exactly match the template's shape.***

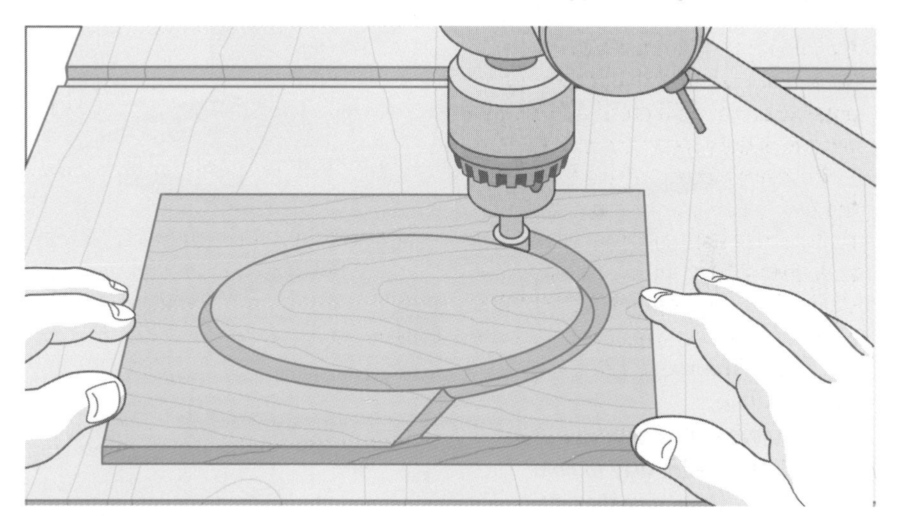

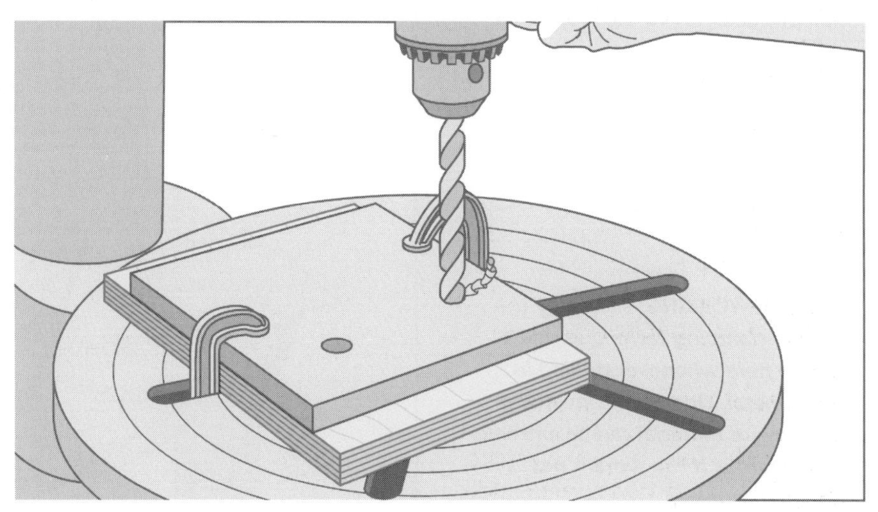

► **METALWORKING, 1.** ***Select a slow speed when drilling in metal. As the bit starts to cut through the underside surface of the work, ease up on feed pressure slightly.***

ness of the material being drilled, grit characteristics and drill rpm.

CARBIDE-ALLOY DRILLS

A typical masonry drill that's available commercially has a steel shank with a flat tip of tungsten carbide. These bits have two cutting edges at a broad angle to each other. So-called glass drills are similar, but have carbide pieces shaped like an arrowhead—the tip angle being smaller (sharper) and the web thinner at the point. They are especially suitable for a drill press, and drill through glass or ceramics rapidly.

When using carbide-alloy bits, support the glass on a firm surface and clamp it securely. Keep the cutter well lubricated; a few drops of turpentine serve as a good lubricant. Run the drill press at moderate speed, and feed the bit carefully to prevent overheating and breakage of the glass. While the bit can pass easily through the glass, there's a chance it will cause chipping around the hole as it emerges. To help prevent this, stop drilling as soon as the tip of the bit emerges (set the depth stop first) and finish drilling from the other side.

DIAMOND BITS

For drilling small, hard gemstones and the like, diamond-studded bits are recommended. A typical set of these drills includes 1-, 1¼-, 1½-, 2- and 2½-mm. sizes. These bits consist of tiny grains of diamond that are bonded to lengths of hardened-steel wire. The bits should always be used wet, with the workpiece being wholly immersed in water or a special drilling fluid.

Sometimes a dam is constructed around the workpiece to hold the fluid. This dam is formed with a caulking material or anything else that will make a water-retaining cup. The bit should project from its chuck no more than necessary to reach the desired hole depth.

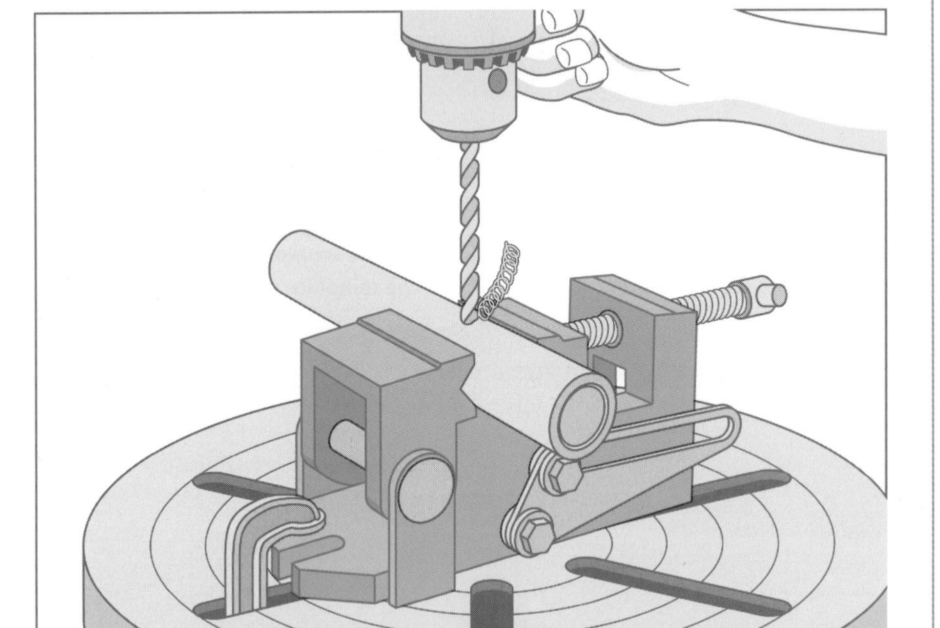

▲ **METALWORKING, 2.** ***A vise provides a safe, secure way to hold workpieces. Make sure that it's clamped securely to the worktable.***

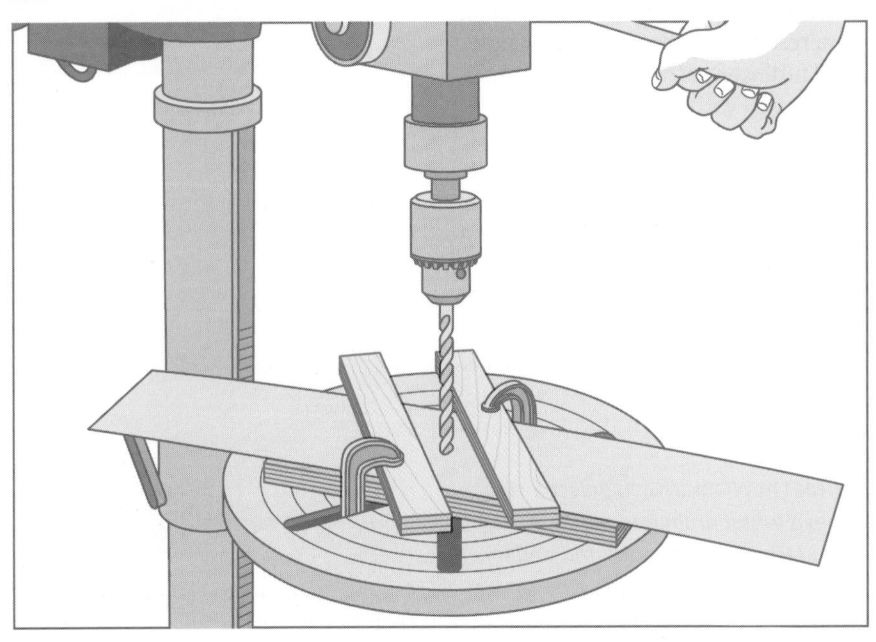

▶ **METALWORKING, 3.** ***Employ the double-clamping technique that's shown here whenever drilling in sheet metal. Operations involving this type of material can be extremely dangerous if the work is not clamped properly.***

▶ **BUFFING AND GRINDING, 1.** ***A cup-type wire brush removes rust, tarnish, paint and grime from metal surfaces easily. Grip the work firmly with both hands.***

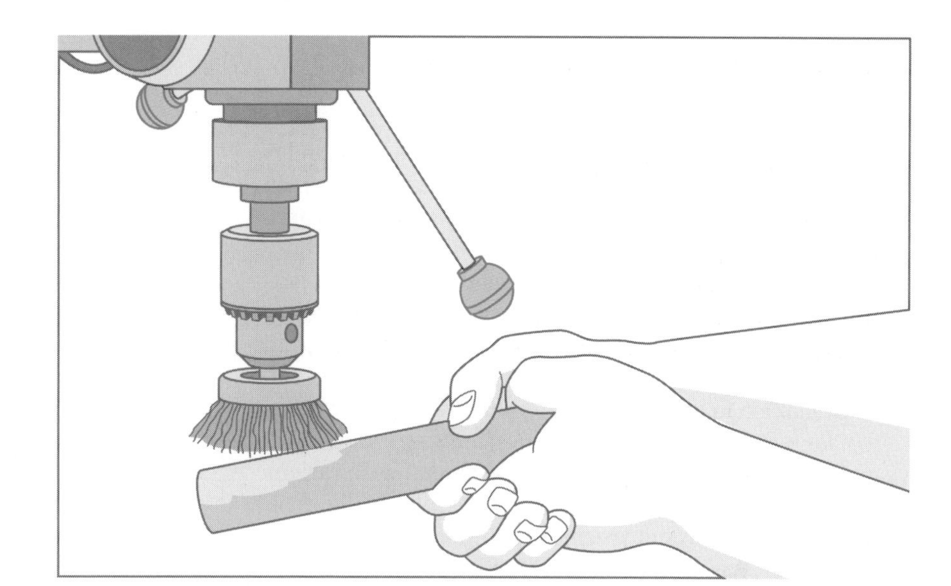

To master the technique of using diamond bits, apply pressure carefully to the workpiece until the bit "bites." The bit will then run without jumping or crawling sideways. Drilling pressure should be increased until the drill really starts cutting, as indicated by the appearance of cloudiness in the fluid. Be careful, however, not to apply too much pressure. If the drill strains or slows down, reduce pressure at once to prevent overheating and possible damage to the bit. The bit should be backed out frequently—say, every 10 seconds or less—so that fluid can refill the hole to cool the tip and clear away loosened bits of material.

Be sure the workpiece is supported firmly enough to keep it from shifting, tilting or being grabbed by the bit. For example, a small plastic box can be seated with caulking material on a piece of aluminum to form a reservoir. Secure an end of the aluminum under a metal bar that's clamped in place to the worktable. Workpieces of stone can usually be anchored to the bottom of the reservoir with caulking material, and further steadied with your fingers.

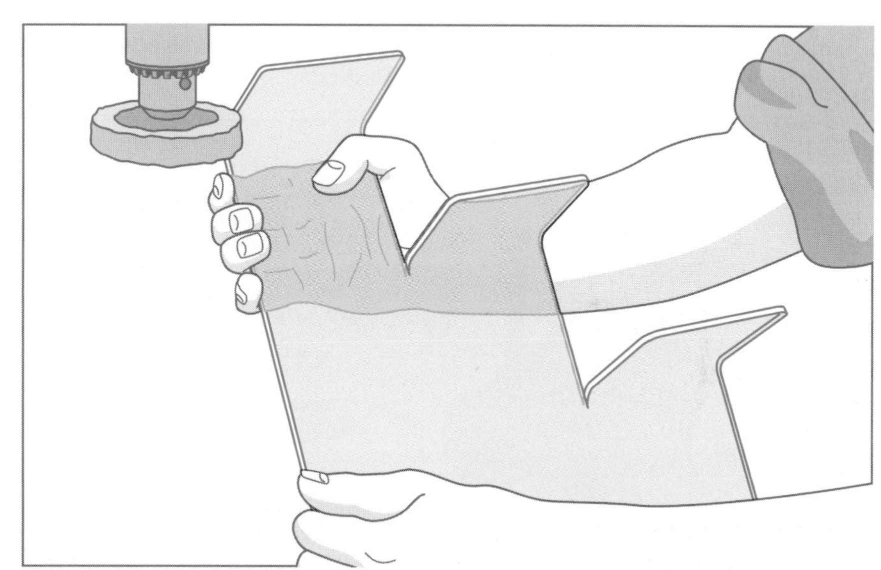

▲ **BUFFING AND GRINDING, 2.** ***Polish plastics and metals against a buffing wheel that's coated with rouge. Keep the workpiece in motion to prevent scorching of surfaces.***

◀ **BUFFING AND GRINDING, 3.** ***Sharpen router bits with a cone-shaped grinding stone. Short bolt in threaded insert holds the bit securely in a shopmade jig.***

BENCH GRINDERS

If your metalworking tools are limited to a hacksaw and a few files, you're missing out on a valuable tool: the bench grinder. Once you've had one in your workshop for a while, you'll find it indispensable in a wide variety of jobs.

Woodworkers have long recognized the grinder as a fast and efficient machine for shaping bevels prior to honing. And it's an excellent tool for putting the finished edge on cold chisels, shears, axes and other cutting tools.

In addition to keeping your tools sharp, the grinder is *the* tool for removing burrs from castings, dressing rough-sawn metal and handling general metal shaping. A wide variety of interchangeable abrasive wheels are available in different grades and types to suit specific applications.

However, this versatile tool isn't limited to ordinary grinding operations. Substitute a grinding wheel with a wire wheel, and you're ready to remove rust, scale and paint. Or switch to a buffing wheel for polishing metals and plastics.

As with any other power tool, it pays to familiarize yourself with both the principles of operation and the various accessories available so you can safely achieve the intended results. Once you know how the tool works and which wheels you should use on specific jobs, all that's necessary is a little practice to refine the techniques of grinding, shaping, cleaning and polishing.

BENCH GRINDER SPECIFICS

Compared to most other machines, a grinder is the essence of simplicity. It's basically an electrically-powered motor with a shaft on each end where wheels are mounted. Each wheel is held by a nut, with pressure distributed by washers. To keep the nuts from loosening, the thread direction of each shaft is opposite to the wheel rotation—the left shaft is left-threaded and the right shaft is right-threaded.

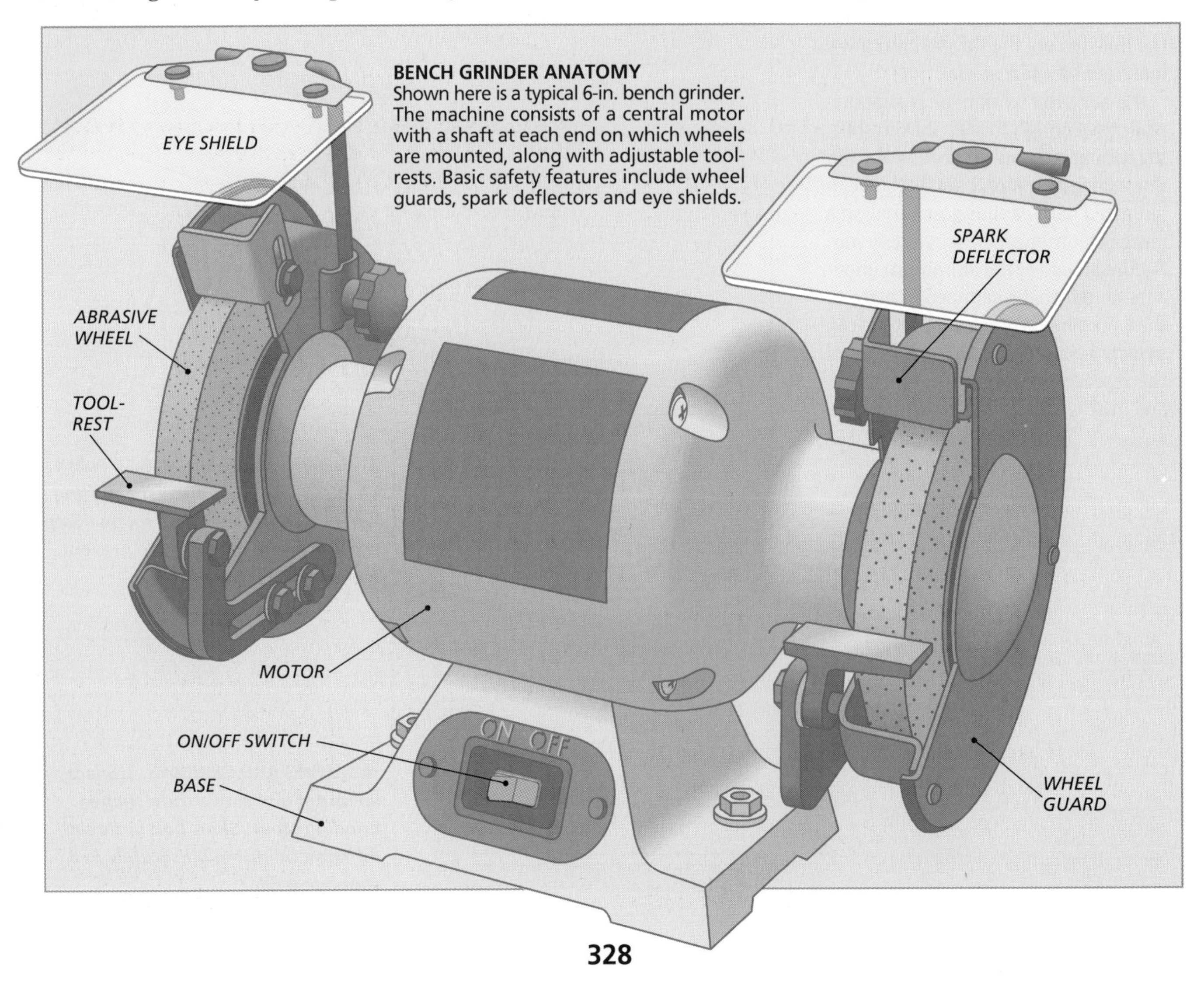

BENCH GRINDER ANATOMY
Shown here is a typical 6-in. bench grinder. The machine consists of a central motor with a shaft at each end on which wheels are mounted, along with adjustable toolrests. Basic safety features include wheel guards, spark deflectors and eye shields.

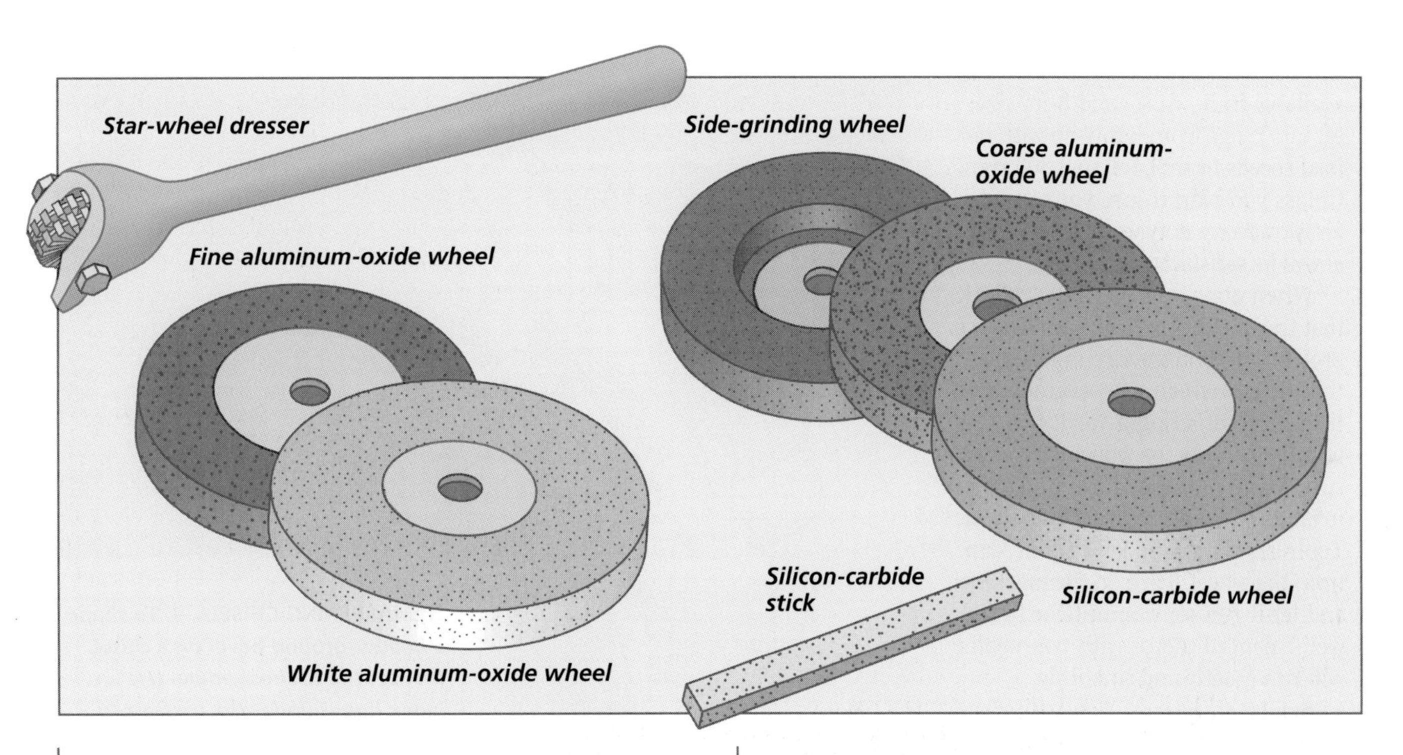

▲ **GRINDING ACCESSORIES.** *Grinding wheels are made of aluminum oxide or silicon carbide. A side-grinding wheel permits flat grinding. A star-wheel dresser and silicon-carbide stick are used to help keep wheels in shape.*

▼ **POLISHING ACCESSORIES.** *Wheels for polishing include wire wheels, fiber wheels and cloth wheels. Cloth wheels are impregnated with buffing compound before use and cleaned after they're used with a wheel rake.*

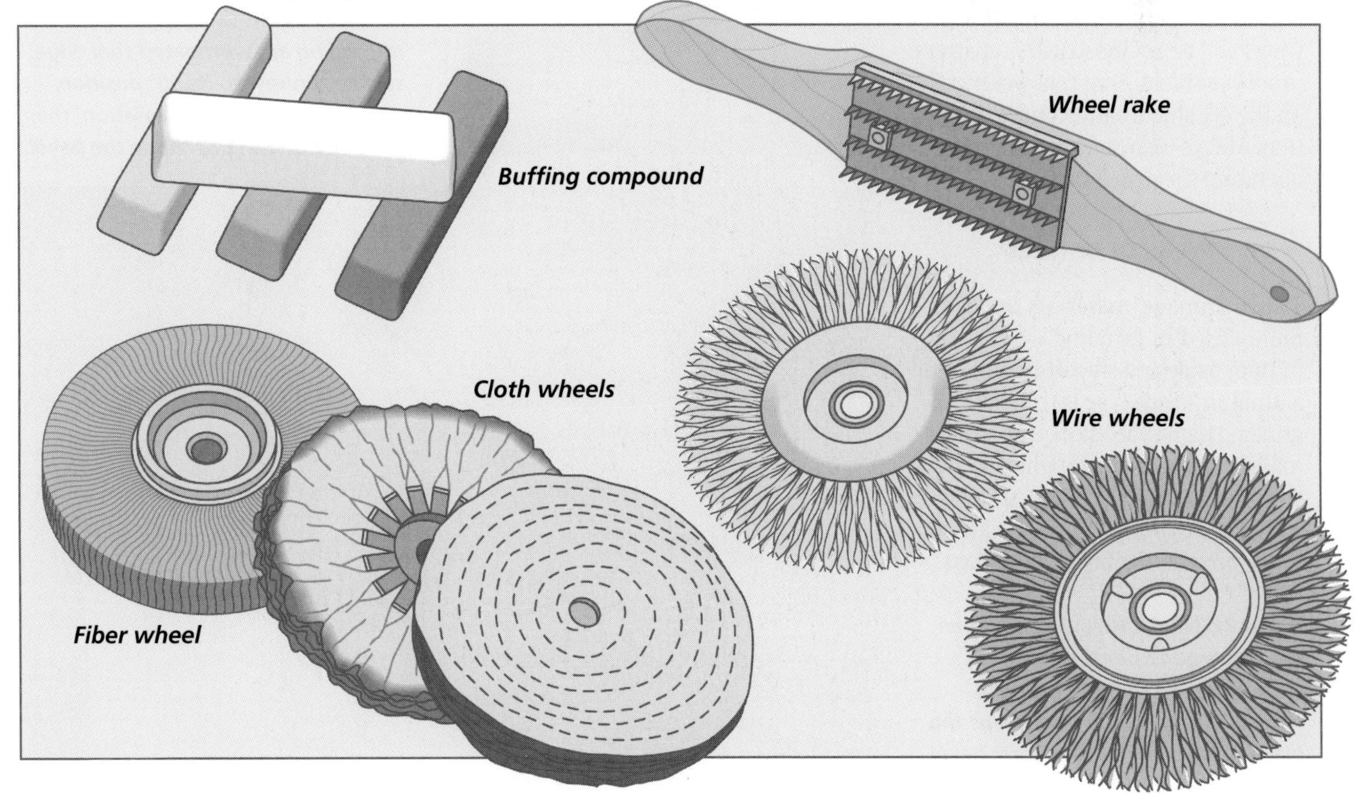

The size of the grinder is designated by the diameter of the wheel that can be used. Grinders are generally available in 5-, 6-, 7- and 8-in. sizes. Motors range from ¼ to 1 hp with no-load speeds from 3,400 to 3,800 rpm. Unless you plan to use your grinder for extra heavy-duty work, a 6-in. model will be satisfactory.

When choosing a grinder, check that the housing of the motor doesn't protrude beyond the circumference of the wheel—which will severely limit the length of straight work that can be passed across the wheel. Also make sure that the toolrests are adjustable in angle and distance from the wheel. Toolrests should be kept about ⅛ in. from the wheel. Turn on the machine and let it run for a minute or two. A well-balanced motor with true shafts will run quietly and smoothly.

Safety standards require wraparound wheel guards that cover all but a 90° segment of each wheel. The outer covers of the wheel guards are easily removed for changing wheels. On the top of the wheel guards you'll find adjustable spark deflectors and each wheel will be equipped with a shatterproof eye shield. Don't, however, rely on the eye shield alone for eye protection. Always wear safety goggles when operating the grinder.

TYPES OF WHEELS

Two manmade materials are commonly used in grinding wheels: aluminum oxide and silicon carbide. The aluminum-oxide type is the choice for grinding high-speed steel, carbon steel, malleable iron and wrought iron. The silicon-carbide type is best suited for work on cast iron, tungsten carbide, brass, bronze, aluminum and glass.

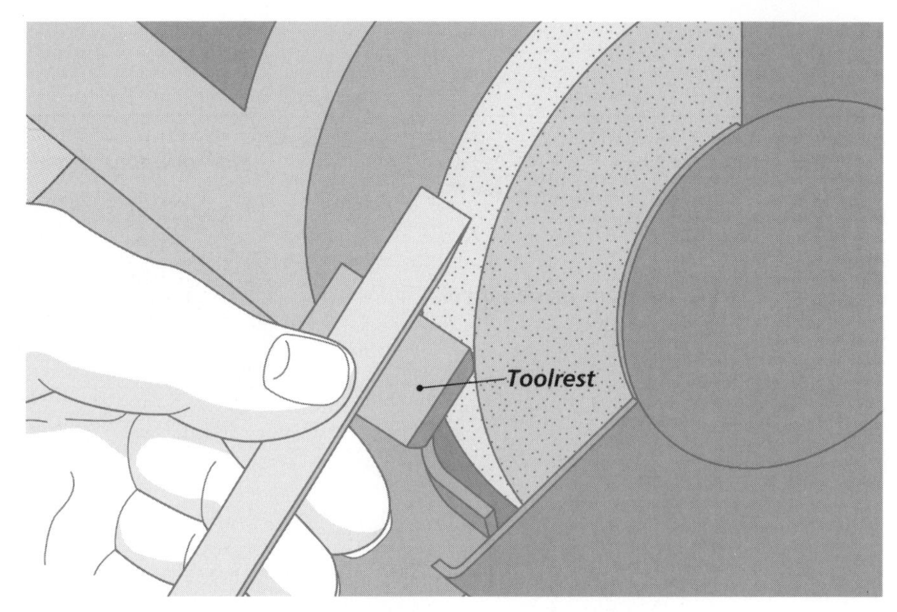

▲ **SHARPENING CHISELS, 1.** ***To shape a hollow-ground bevel on a chisel, first set the toolrest angle. Use an index finger under the toolrest to guide the chisel across the wheel.***

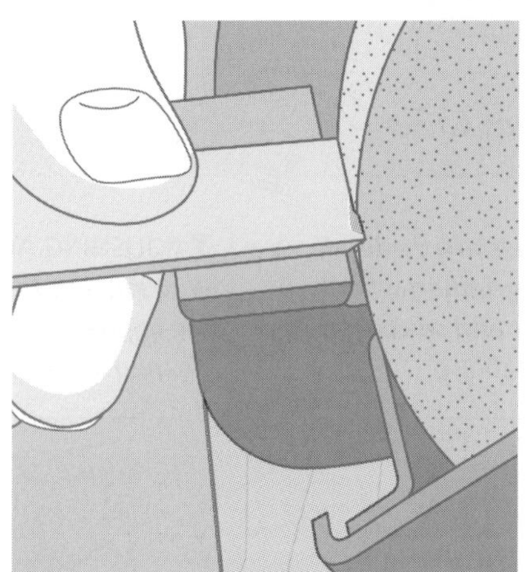

◀ **SHARPENING CHISELS, 2.** ***When regrinding an overheated tool edge, set the toolrest to its 90° position. Grind beyond the discoloration, then reset the toolrest to shape the bevel.***

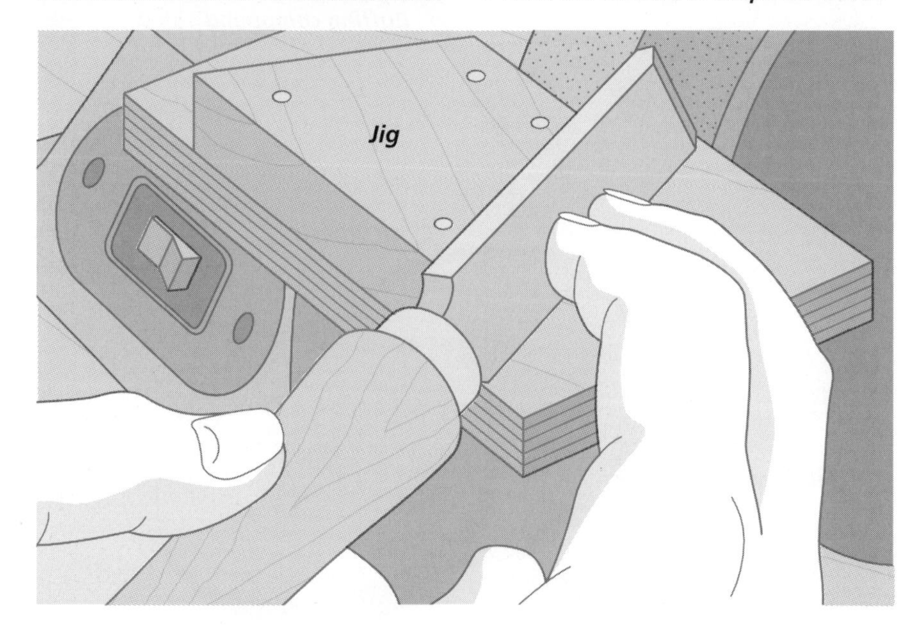

▶ **SHARPENING CHISELS, 3.** ***Sharpen the flat-ground bevel of a lathe's skew chisel on the side-grinding wheel. The jig shown here keeps the blade positioned for a uniform bevel.***

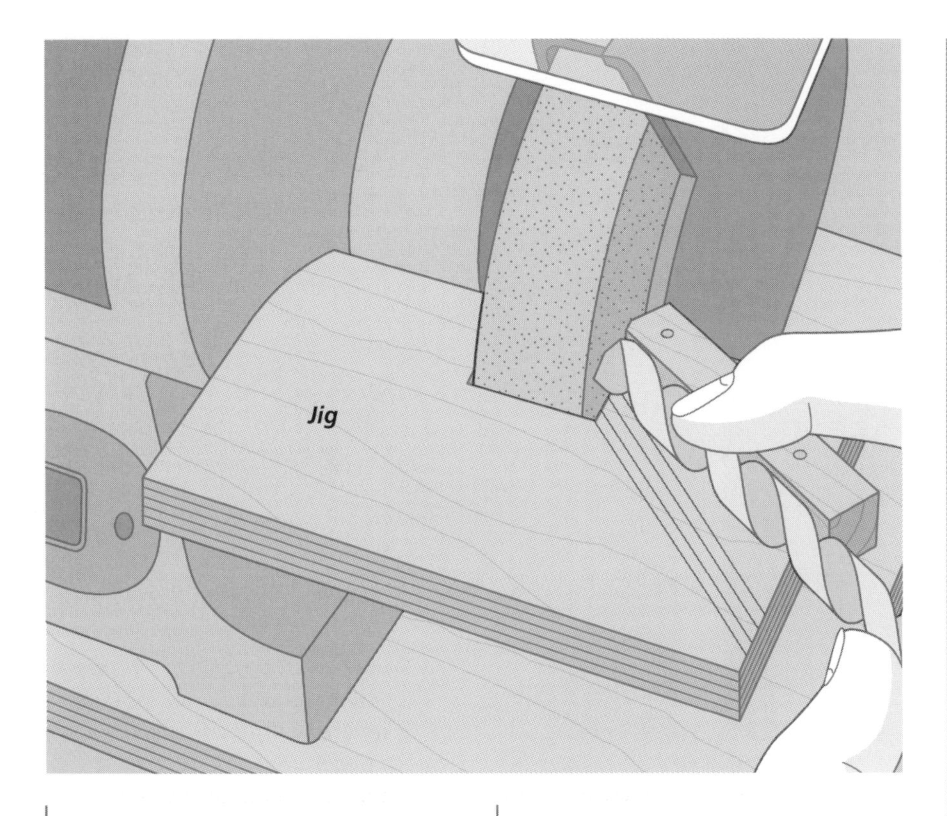

▲ **SHARPENING BITS, 1.** ***Attach a jig to the toolrest bracket to sharpen drill bits. A guide block set at a 59° angle to the side of the wheel properly aligns the bit's edge.***

▼ **SHARPENING BITS, 2.** ***Finish sharpening the bit by rotatlng it clockwise ⅙ turn while at the same time shifting it to guidelines positioned at a 47° angle to the side of the wheel.***

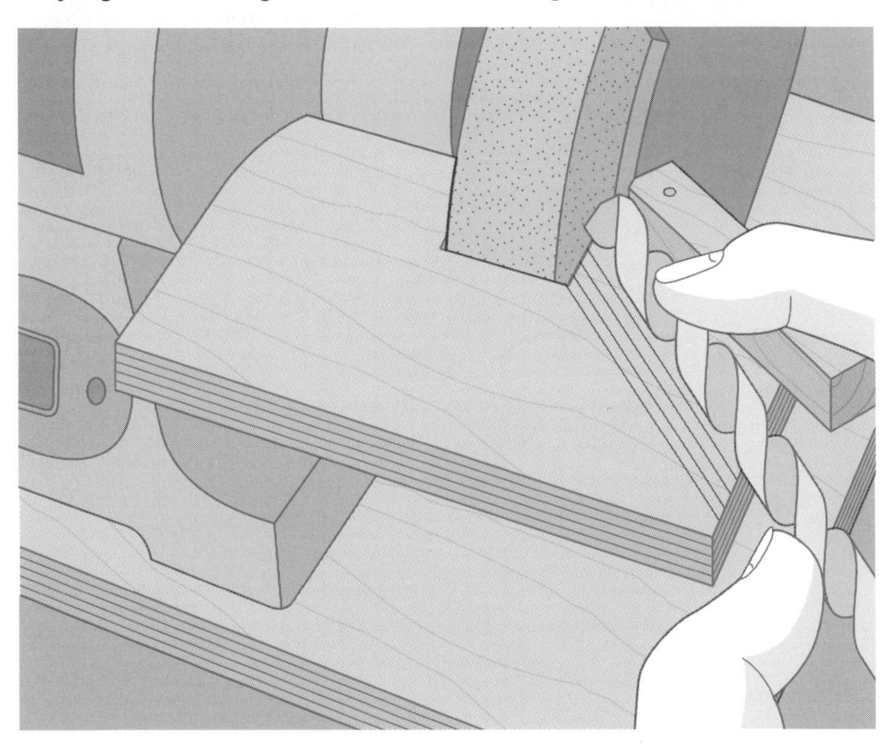

Wheels are available in grain sizes from 10 to 1,000 grit, a range that's divided into four categories: coarse, medium, fine and very fine. When you select a grain size, remember that a coarse wheel will cut faster than a fine wheel, but leaves a rougher surface.

WHEEL GRADE AND STRUCTURE

The grade of a wheel refers to the hardness or strength of the bonding agent that holds the grains together, and is indicated within a range from A to Z. Grades A to H are called soft, I to P medium and Q to Z hard.

As a rule, soft wheels are used on hard materials and hard wheels are used on soft materials. Softer wheels are especially useful for grinding cutting tools because the dulled grains readily fall away to expose fresh, sharp grains, which reduces heat buildup. A medium-grade wheel (K) is suitable for general-purpose grinding.

The structure of a wheel refers to the grain spacing or density and ranges from 1 to 15. A low number indicates dense spacing and is appropriate for hard, brittle materials. Soft metals, however, tend to clog a dense wheel and are better worked using a more open-grained wheel. Also, wide grain spacing results in a coarser finish than close spacing. Tool grinding is best done in the 5 to 8 range.

The material that holds the grains together in most wheels is a vitrified, glass-like bonding agent. Industrial wheels and cutoff wheels may have a different bonding agent.

These characteristics are encoded on the side of most wheels. In a code such as 9A 60 J8 V5, the A stands for aluminum oxide (9A here refers to one manufacturer's white aluminum-oxide wheel). Silicon carbide would be indicated by a C. The 60 refers to grain size, J indicates a medium hardness grade, and 8 stands for medium density. The V indicates vitrified bonding and 5 is a manufacturer's symbol.

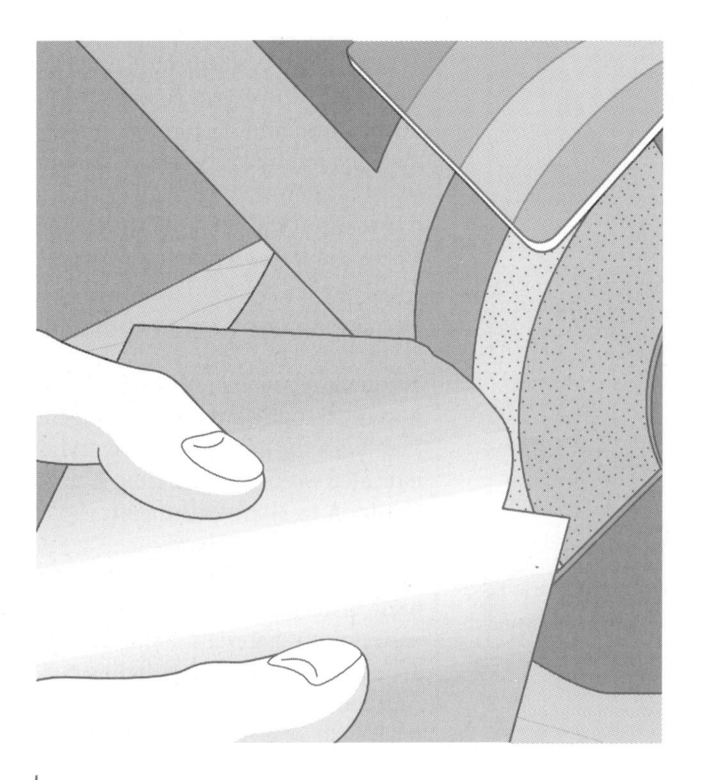

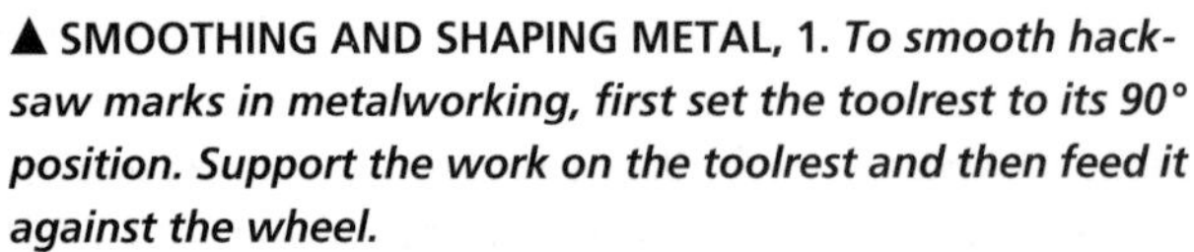

▲ **SMOOTHING AND SHAPING METAL, 1.** ***To smooth hacksaw marks in metalworking, first set the toolrest to its 90° position. Support the work on the toolrest and then feed it against the wheel.***

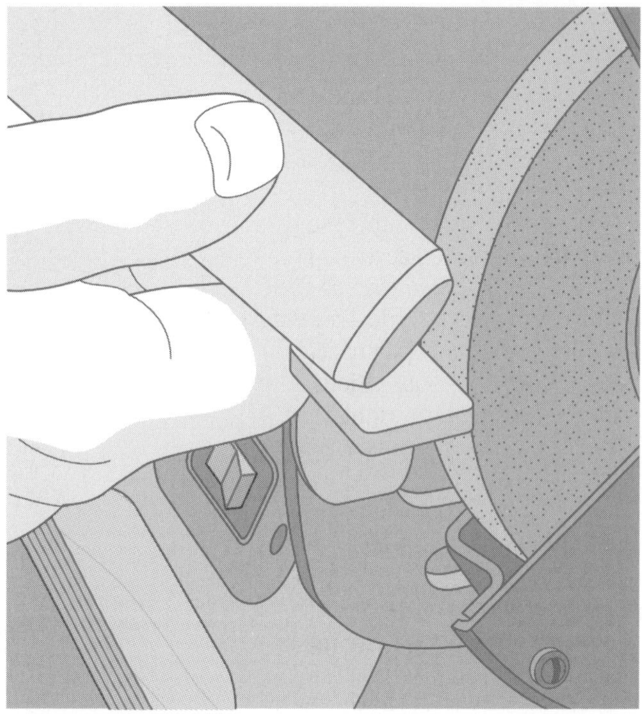

▲ **SMOOTHING AND SHAPING METAL, 2.** ***Bevel round stock by supporting it on a level toolrest and rotating the work clockwise while simultaneously moving it slowly across the face of the wheel.***

CARING FOR WHEELS

Wheel care includes using the right wheel for the job. Most grinders come equipped with two general-purpose, aluminum-oxide wheels: a 36 grit for rough work and rapid stock removal; and a 60 grit for fine work and sharpening. Add a 100-grit wheel for finish grinding and a silicon-carbide wheel for touching up carbide-tipped tools.

Side-grinding wheels permit safe use of the wheel's side whenever a flat ground surface is required. And for trouble-free sharpening of chisels and plane irons, it's worth getting a white aluminuim-oxide wheel for the fast, cool cutting it provides.

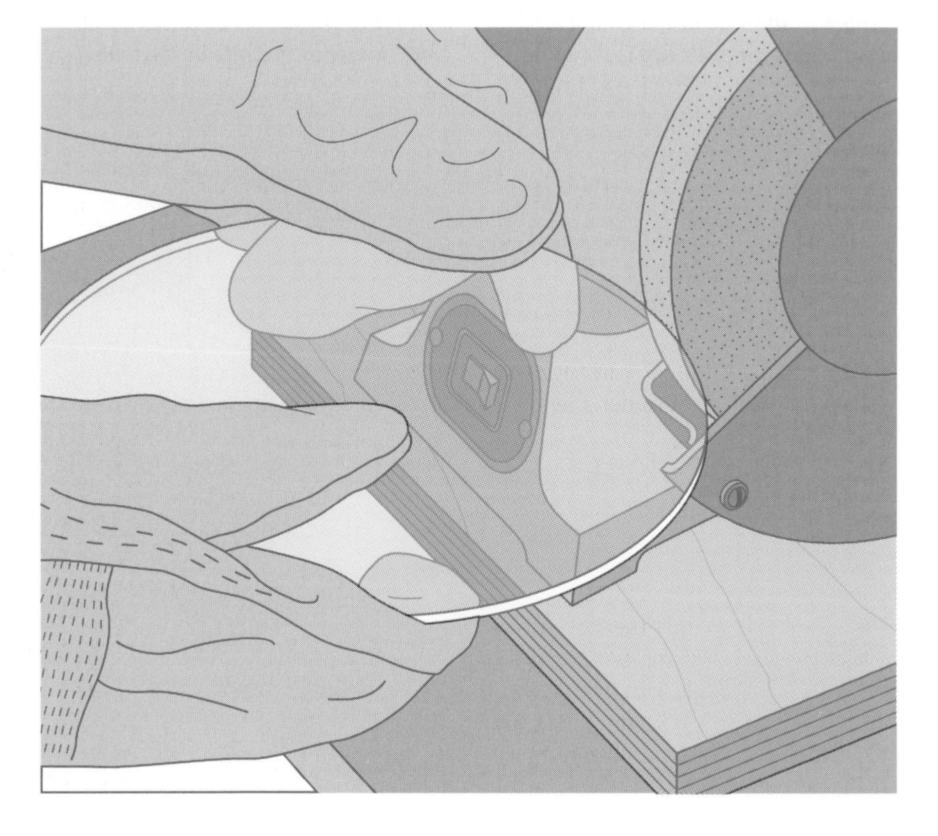

► **SMOOTHING GLASS.** ***Use a silicon-carbide wheel for smoothing glass. Remove the toolrest and guide the work freehand below the centerline of the wheel.***

When a grinding wheel is worn out of shape or becomes dull, loaded or glazed, it must be trued and dressed. Truing is performed with a star-wheel dresser, which removes material from the wheel until it runs true. Dressing is done to clean and restore the sharpness of the wheel's face and is accomplished with a silicon-carbide stick.

Always inspect a wheel for cracks before mounting it. A damaged wheel can fly apart and cause serious injury. After a visual check, lightly tap the wheel's side at four points near the circumference with a screwdriver handle. A good wheel will produce a clear, metallic ring. If the sound is dull, discard the wheel.

GRINDING TECHNIQUES

To shape the bevel on chisels and plane irons, set the toolrest so the tool contacts the wheel at the proper angle. Keeping the blade firmly on the toolrest, grind the bevel with a steady side-to-side motion and light pressure.

If a discoloration appears on the blade's edge, excessive heat has drawn the temper and the tool won't remain sharp for long. The solution is to grind away the affected area and regrind the bevel. Keep a bowl of water on hand to cool the edge as grinding proceeds.

Drill bits and lathe skew chisels are best sharpened on the side of a side-grinding wheel. Special grinding jobs like these benefit from shopmade jigs. Start with a platform of ½-in. plywood shaped to suit your grinder and cut a 1¼-in.-deep notch in it for the wheel. Secure the platform to the toolrest bracket with right-angled 1 x 4 stock.

To flat grind the bevels on a skew chisel, use a guide block with compound angles cut on each side so that the chisel will contact the side of the wheel at the correct angle—for example, a 78° bevel angle with the tool tilted 10° from vertical. Secure the guide block to the center of the platform with nails and glue.

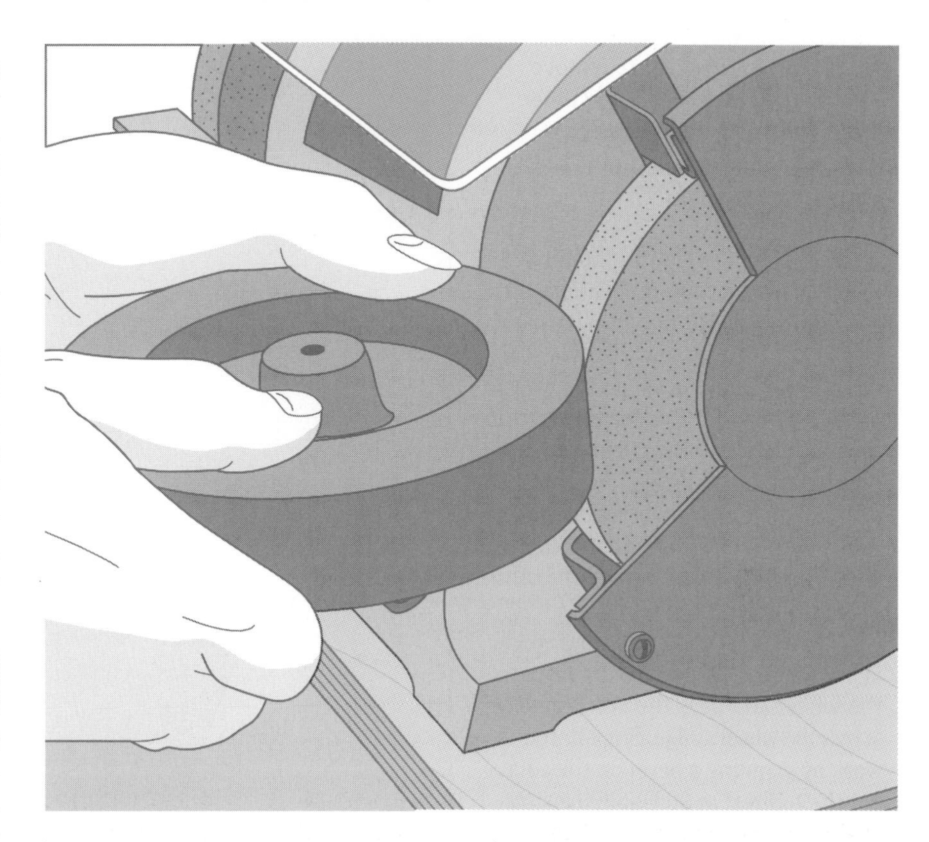

▲ **SMOOTHING CAST IRON.** ***A wheel of silicon carbide is also recommended when grinding cast iron. Avoid applying heavy pressure that may overheat and damage the wheel.***

▼ **CLEANING METAL, 1.** ***Work with a coarse wire wheel when removing rust and scaling paint. Fine wire wheels mar surfaces less and produce a satin-like finish.***

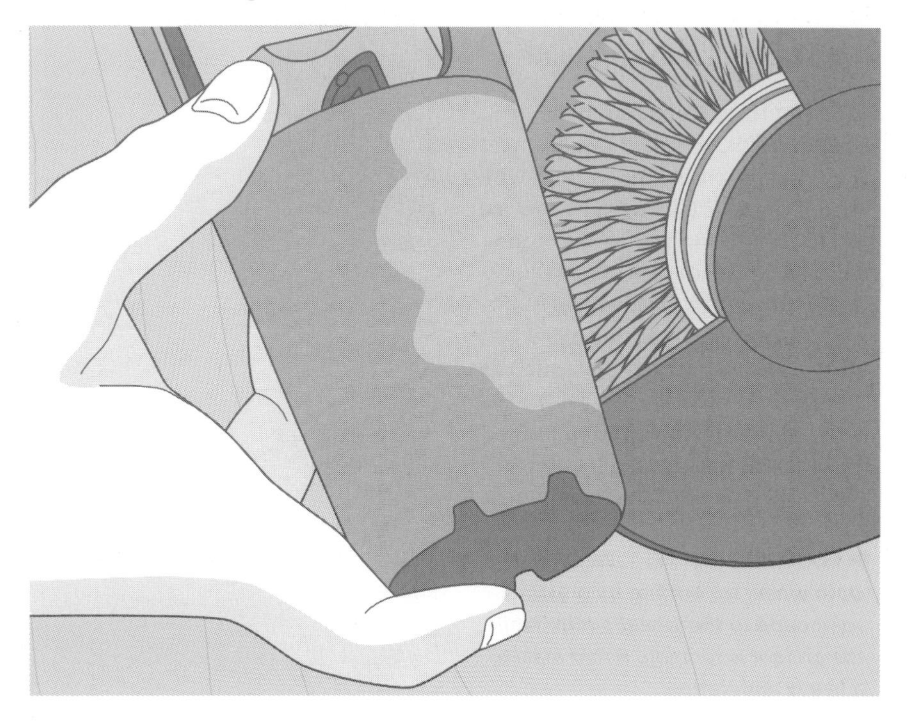

▶ **CLEANING METAL, 2.** ***To remove tarnish on garden shears and other tools, work with a fiber wheel. Always hold the tool's cutting edge away from the wheel's rotation.***

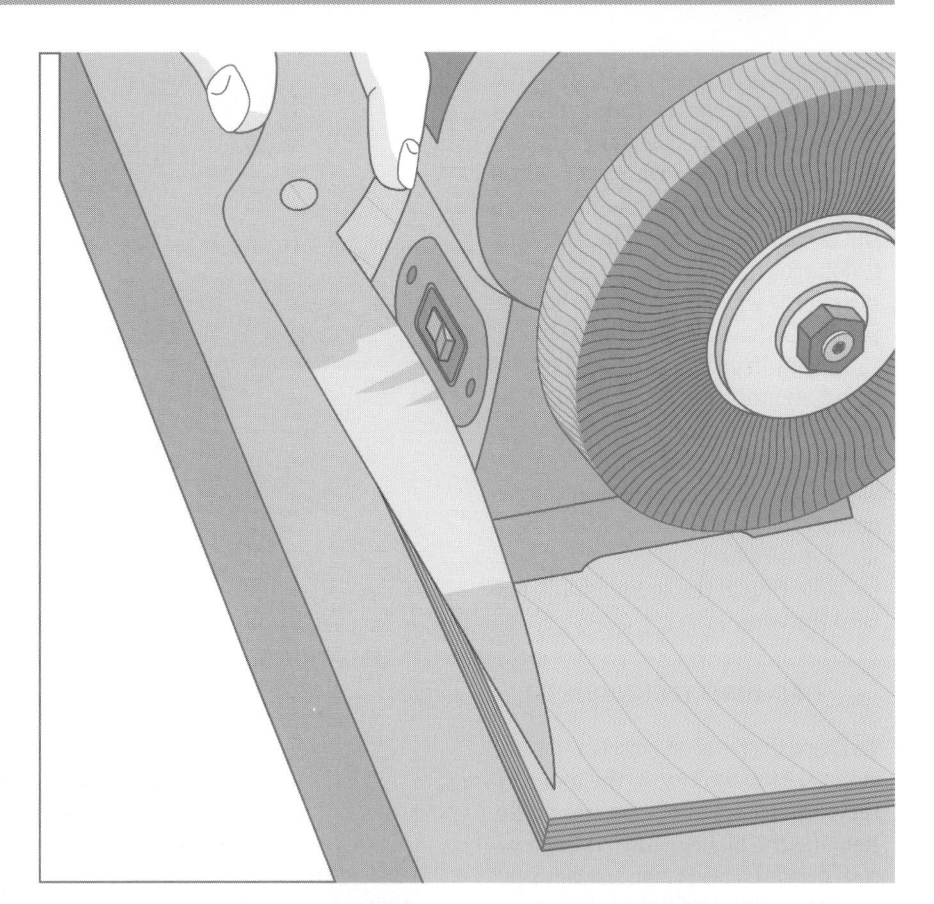

To sharpen a drill bit, attach a ½-in.-sq. guide block to the platform on the right side of the notch so it's positioned at 59° to the side of the wheel. Lay out guidelines at 47° to the wheel about ⅛ in. apart. Place the bit against the guide block so the cutting edge is horizontal. Let the edge contact the wheel, then immediately rotate the bit ⅙ of a turn while shifting it to align with the guidelines. Sharpen the other edge of the bit the same way.

When smoothing rough-sawn metal, set the toolrest at right angles to the wheel and pass the stock gently across the wheel's edge. Smooth round work by grinding a bevel on the edge. Set the toolrest at 90°, hold the stock at an angle and rotate it clockwise.

Smoothing the edges of glass is performed with a silicon-carbide wheel. Remove the toolrest and keep the work held below the center of the wheel to shape the edges freehand.

CLEANING AND POLISHING

To clean rusty, corroded metal or to remove paint, simply take off one of the grinding wheels and install a wire wheel. There are two grades of wire wheels: coarse, for heavy cleaning jobs; and fine, for delicate work that requires a satin finish. For removing light tarnish, fiber wheels are available. When cleaning edged garden tools such as shears, hold the edge away from the rotating wheel—not directed into it.

To polish metal and plastics, use a cloth wheel and buffing compound.

▶ **POLISHING METAL, 1.** ***Prepare a cloth wheel for buffing by pressing compound to the wheel's edge while the grinder is running. Avoid making a heavy application.***

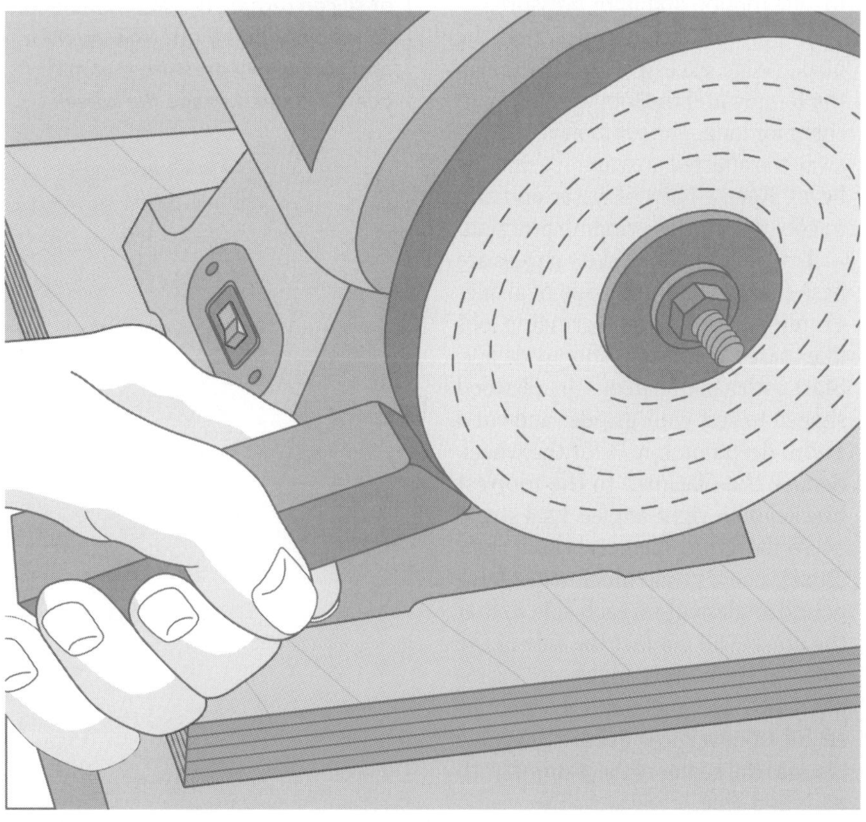

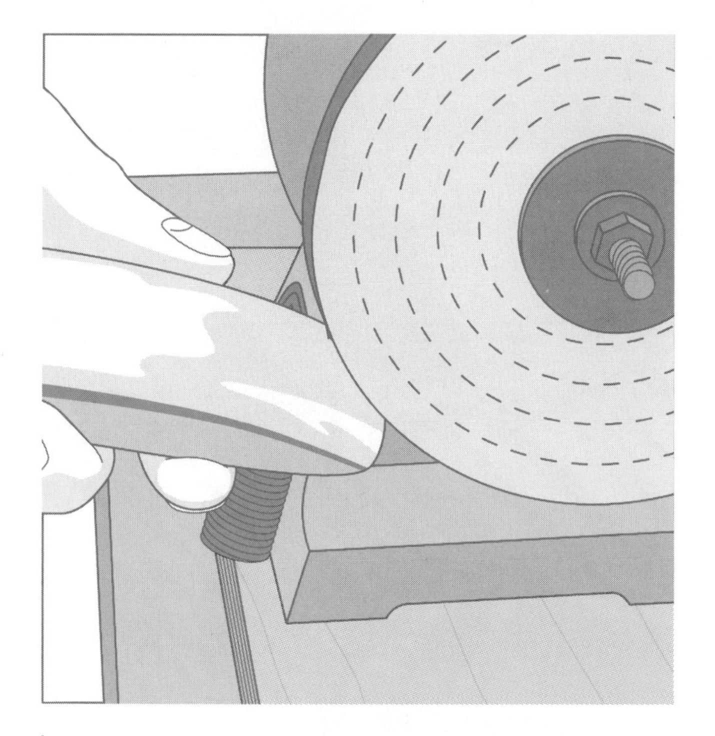

▲ **POLISHING METAL, 2.** ***Use a cloth wheel loaded with white compound—pumice—to polish chrome. Make sure you always hold the work to the lower section of wheel.***

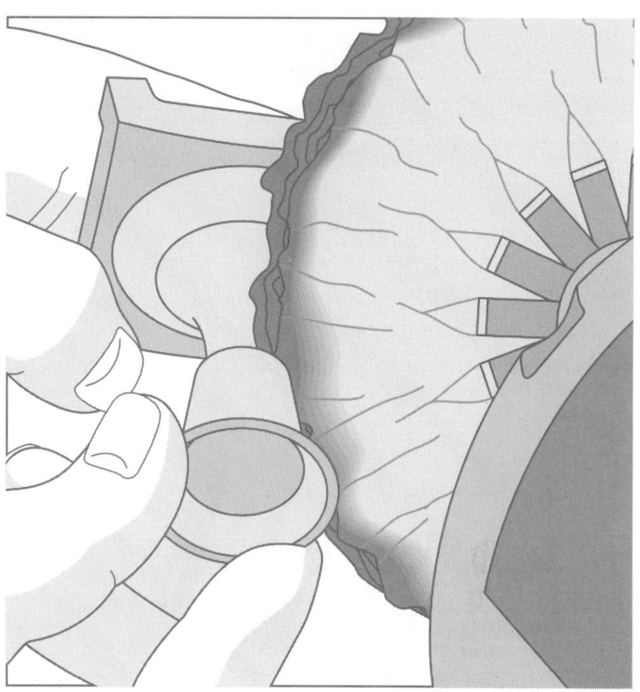

▲ **POLISHING METAL, 3.** ***Use a loose-cloth wheel for reaching into confined areas. Jeweler's rouge is an appropriate compound for polishing precious metals.***

Cloth wheels are sewn tightly or loosely, where layers of fabric are secured only at the hub. The tight-sewn wheel has a stiffer edge, but the loose-sewn wheel reaches into tight curves.

Buffing compounds are very fine abrasives and come in different grades. Jeweler's rouge, the finest grade, is for precious metals and the highest gloss. For chrome, use slightly coarser white pumice. Tripoli is medium-grade, and for the coarsest buffing, use emery.

To polish, install a buffing wheel, then turn on the grinder and hold the buffing compound against the wheel to impregnate the cloth with abrasive. Bring the work up to the lower area of the wheel and apply gentle pressure. To keep your cloth wheels in shape, have a wheel rake on hand for removing caked compound.

◀ **POLISHING METAL, 4.** ***A wheel rake is used to dress the edge of a cloth wheel. It removes caked compound and trims frayed edges flush.***

SHOP
WISDOMS

SHOP WISDOMS

Do you judge lumber by looks? Are you the type to walk up to a bin of 1 x 8 stock and pick out the two or three pieces that please the eye? If so, you are among the majority. Many people check out boards by surface appearance, grain and color—and don't care whether they're western pine, eastern hemlock or cedar. Appearance should be important in any purchasing decision on lumber. Yet, knowing how wood is graded, how different species perform, what's commonly stocked in what sizes and the way lumberyards will or won't serve you could save money—and help you to get the best wood for your project.

There are only two basic types of wood: softwood and hardwood. Easily 90 percent of all the wood sold is softwood. Cut from conifers—pine, spruce, hemlock and the like—softwood is the backbone of construction as well as most home projects, repairs and improvements. Hardwoods cut from deciduous, or leaf-dropping, trees such as oak, maple and walnut go into fine furniture and cabinetry. As more

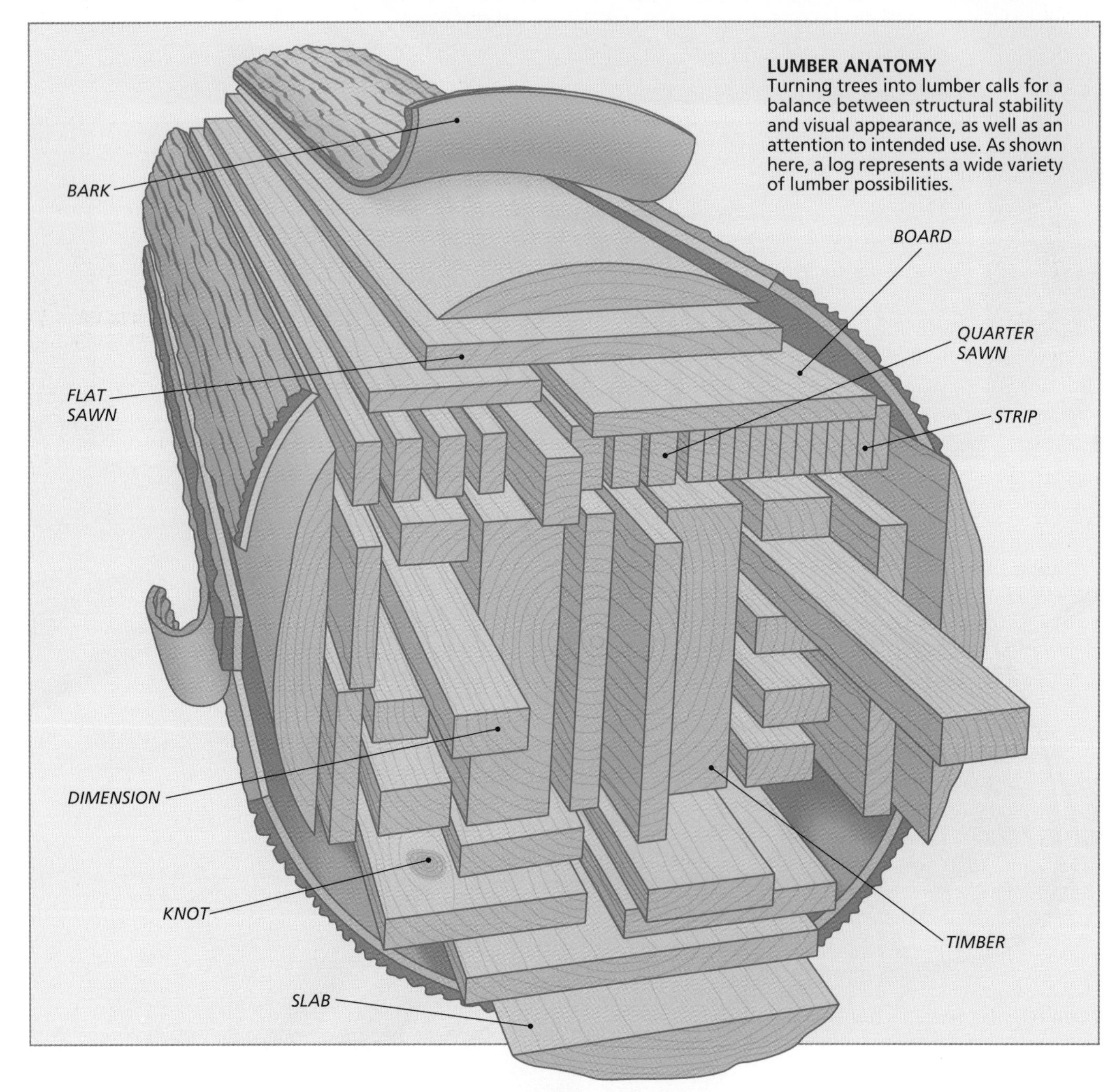

LUMBER ANATOMY
Turning trees into lumber calls for a balance between structural stability and visual appearance, as well as an attention to intended use. As shown here, a log represents a wide variety of lumber possibilities.

craftsmen take on these kinds of projects, more yards are stocking hardwoods. There are also many hardwood specialty mail-order sources.

LUMBER LANGUAGE

Lumber carries a vocabulary of its own. And a knowledge of the language involved is important to an understanding of the material and how best to work with it. For instance, the moisture content of lumber—the ratio of the weight of water it holds to the weight of oven-dry wood, expressed as a percentage—is a significant factor to consider in its use for furniture and cabinetry. Just ask anyone who has ever had a finished piece self-destruct a short time after construction because the joinery methods used didn't allow for movement of the wood.

Here's a short lumber glossary:

Green—Lumber that's freshly sawn from a log, with a moisture content above 30 percent.

Air dried—Lumber dried in a ventilated stack by exposure to normal temperature and humidity conditions, having a moisture content of 15 to 30 percent.

Kiln dried—Lumber dried in a closed chamber in a controlled environment, with a moisture content of 6 to 15 percent—ideally, 6 to 8 percent.

Rough—Lumber as it comes out of the saw, containing the marks of the saw teeth on the surface.

Dressed—Lumber that has had one or more of its surfaces run through a planer.

Worked—Lumber such as tongue-and-groove boards, grooved paneling and ogee moldings that has been shaped for specific purposes or applications.

SOFTWOOD CHARACTERISTICS

SPECIES	EASE OF WORKING	FREEDOM FROM WARPAGE	HEARTWOOD RESISTS DECAY	BENDING STRENGTH	STIFFNESS	STRENGTH AS A POST	NUMBER OF KNOTS	NUMBER OF OTHER DEFECTS
White ash	C	B	C	A	A	A	C	B
Western red cedar	A	A	A	C	C	B	C	C
Eastern red cedar	B	A	A	B	C	A	A	C
Cherry	C	A	A	A	A	A	C	*
Cypress	B	B	A	B	B	B	C	B
Douglas fir	C	B	B	A	A	A	B	B
Eastern hemlock	B	B	C	B	B	B	B	A
Western hemlock	B	B	C	B	B	B	B	B
Hickory	C	B	C	A	A	A	B	B
Western larch	C	B	B	A	A	A	A	A
Hard maple	C	B	C	A	A	A	B	B
Soft maple	C	B	C	C	C	C	C	C
Red oak	C	B	C	A	A	B	C	B
White oak	C	B	A	A	A	B	C	B
Ponderosa pine	A	A	C	C	C	C	B	B
Southern yellow pine	C	B	C	A	A	A	C	B
Northern white pine	A	A	C	C	C	C	A	B
Sugar pine	A	A	C	C	C	C	A	B
Idaho white pine	A	A	C	B	B	B	A	A
Redwood	B	A	A	B	B	A	C	C
Eastern spruce	B	A	C	B	B	B	A	B
Sitka spruce	B	A	C	B	A	B	B	B
Engelmann spruce	B	A	C	C	C	C	A	B
Walnut	B	A	A	A	A	A	C	C

A = High B = Medium C = Low * = Depends on use

Timber—A structural member measuring at least 5 in. in all directions.
Dimension—A construction member that is from 2 in. thick up to less than 5 in. thick, and 2 in. wide or more.
Board—Lumber less than 2 in. thick and 1 in. wide or more.
Strip—A board less than 6 in. wide.
Plain sawn—Lumber that is cut so the growth rings are tangent to the wide face of the board; also called flat sawn.
Quarter sawn—Lumber that is cut so the growth rings intersect the wide face of the board at greater than 45°.

DIMENSIONS AND GRADES

Actual sizes of softwood refer to the dimensions of dressed lumber. A nominal 2 x 4, for example, is very close to 2 in. thick and 4 in. wide when cut from the log. Planed smooth, the numbers come down to 1½ x 3½ in. When you plan a specific project, work with the actual dimensions of the lumber you'll be using. At this stage, it doesn't matter what the standard sizes are; you care about what you've got.

Hardwood usually is not stocked in easily identifiable sizes at lumberyards, but check the mail-order sources. If local yards stocked ½-in. boards, two buyers a year might ask for them. A standard 1-in. board, though, can be planed to satisfy many buyers needing different thicknesses.

Lumber is most typically offered in even-numbered widths and lengths; hardwood often comes in 1 ft. multiples in lengths from 4 to 16 ft. If you want a 1 x 7, the yard will rip a 1 x 8, charge you for the 1 x 8 and the cut, and give you the cutoff strip—or you can take the 1 x 8 and rip it at home.

Grade marks are stamped on most dimension lumber and many boards, although they're often missing on finished top grades. With hardwood, there is no grade mark. The two best hardwood grades, called Firsts and Seconds, are usually sold as a combined grade and designated FAS.

SOFTWOOD LUMBER* DIMENSIONS

THICKNESS (IN.)		WIDTH (IN.)	
Nominal size	*Actual size*	*Nominal size*	*Actual size*
3/8	5/16	2	1 1/2
1/2	7/16	3	2 1/2
5/8	9/16	4	3 1/2
3/4	5/8	5	4 1/2
1	3/4	6	5 1/2
1 1/4	1	7	6 1/2
1 1/2	1 1/4	8	7 1/4
1 3/4	1 3/8	10	9 1/4
2	1 1/2	12	11 1/4
2 1/2	2	Even numbers over 12	Take 3/4 off nominal
3	2 1/2		
3 1/2	3		
4	3 1/2		
Numbers 5 and over	Take 1/2 off nominal		

* Kiln- or air-dried lumber. Moisture-laden green lumber sizes are from 1/6 to 1/4 in. larger.

HARDWOOD CHARACTERISTICS

SPECIES	TYPE OF GRAIN	RESISTANCE TO SPLITTING	SUITABILITY FOR CARVING
Ash	Open	Good	Good
Beech	Closed	Fair	Fair
Birch	Closed	Fair	Good
Cherry	Closed	Fair	Excellent
Hickory	Open	Fair	Fair
Mahogany	Semi-open	Good	Excellent
Maple	Closed	Good	Good
Red oak	Open	Good	Good
White oak	Open	Good	Good
Poplar	Closed	Excellent	Excellent
Walnut	Semi-open	Good	Excellent

HARDWOOD LUMBER* DIMENSIONS

ROUGH (IN.)	NOMINAL SIZE	SURFACED TWO SIDES (IN.)
1	4/4	13/16
1 1/4	5/4	1 1/16
1 1/2	6/4	1 5/16
1 3/4	7/4	1 1/2
2	8/4	1 3/4
2 1/2	10/4	2 1/4
3	12/4	2 3/4
3 1/2	14/4	3 1/4
4	16/4	3 3/4

* Standard thicknesses. Standard lengths: 4 ft. to 16 ft. in 1 ft. multiples in various widths.

WOOD DEFECTS

Intergrown knot, also called tight or red, was a branch that grew into a trunk.

Spike knot was cut nearly parallel to the grain of the branch, weakening the board.

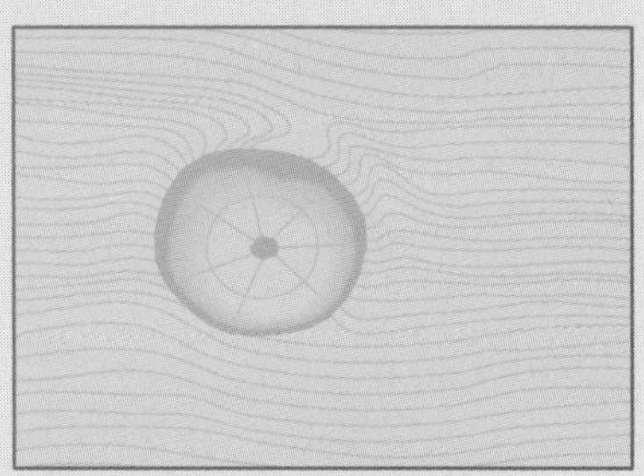
Encased knot is not firmly fixed, and was formed by an embedded branch stub.

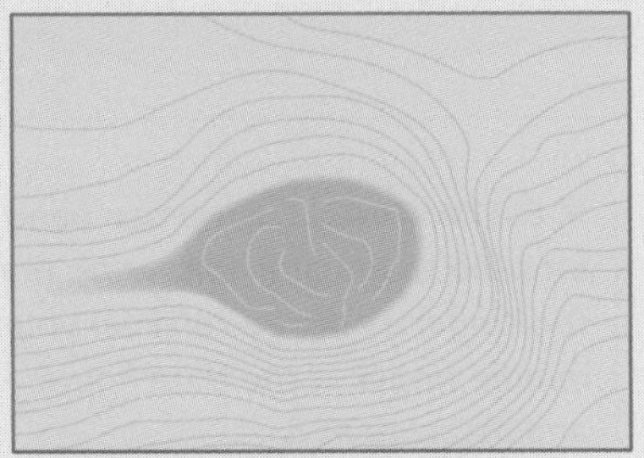
Checked knot shrank unevenly as the wood dried, creating cracks along its grain.

Unsound knot has surface damage, but it's tight and weakens a timber only slightly.

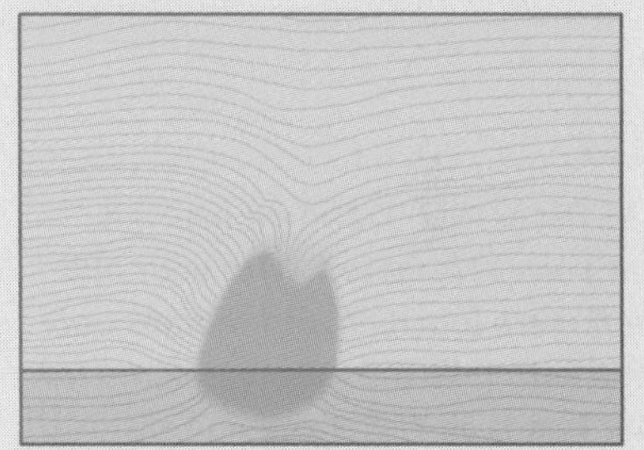
Sloughed knot was the outer section of a spike knot that separated near the edge.

Machine burn leaves a black, charred mark that usually can be sanded out.

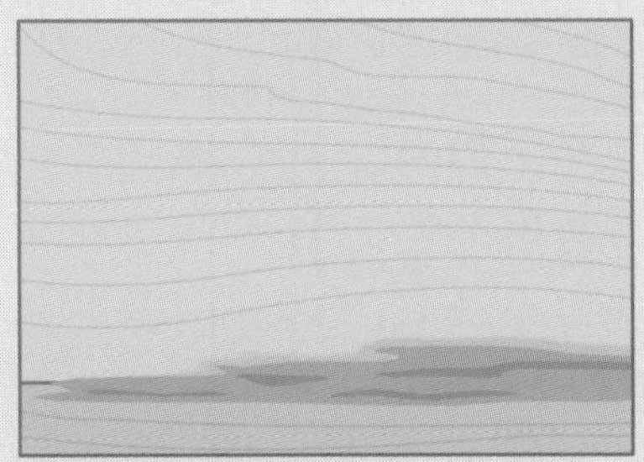
Wane is bark or missing wood along the edge of a board cut too near a log's surface.

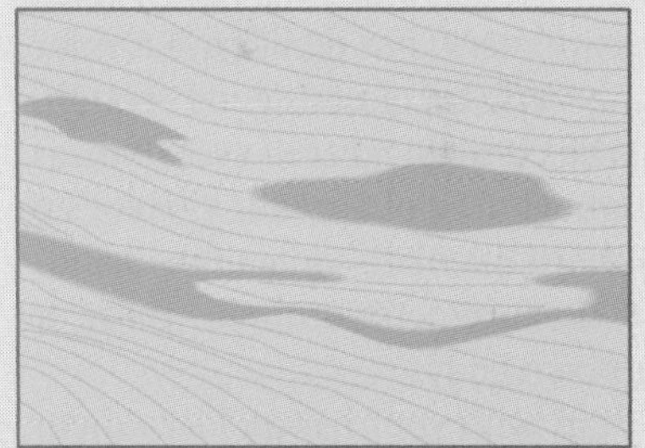
Peck, found mostly in cedar and cypress, are pockets of dry rot in a living tree.

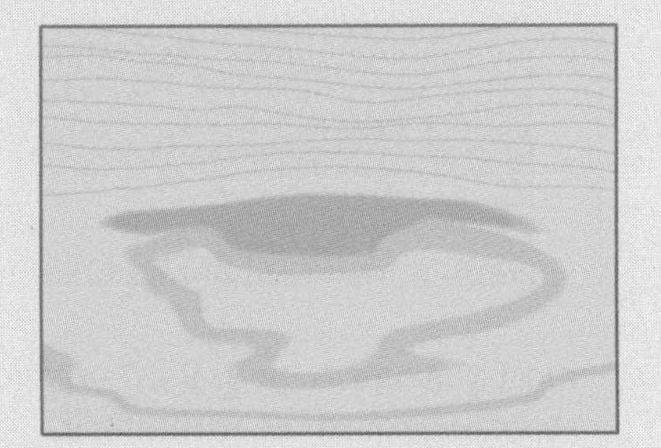
Pitch pocket is a seam or streak that holds or once held solid or liquid resin.

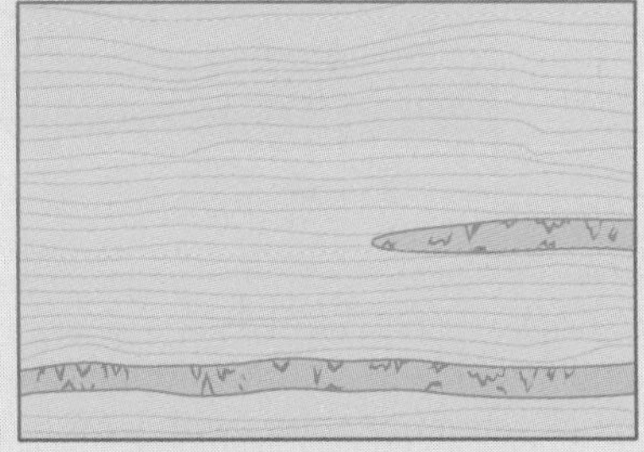
Grub holes bored by insects while the tree was alive weaken and mar a finished board.

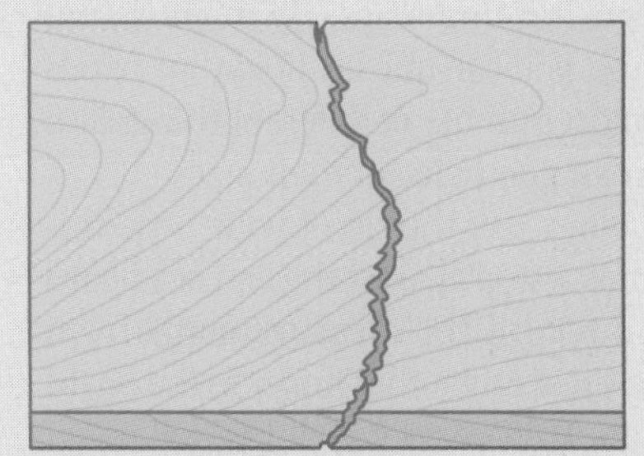
Compressed wood is on the low side of a leaning softwood tree, and can be brittle.

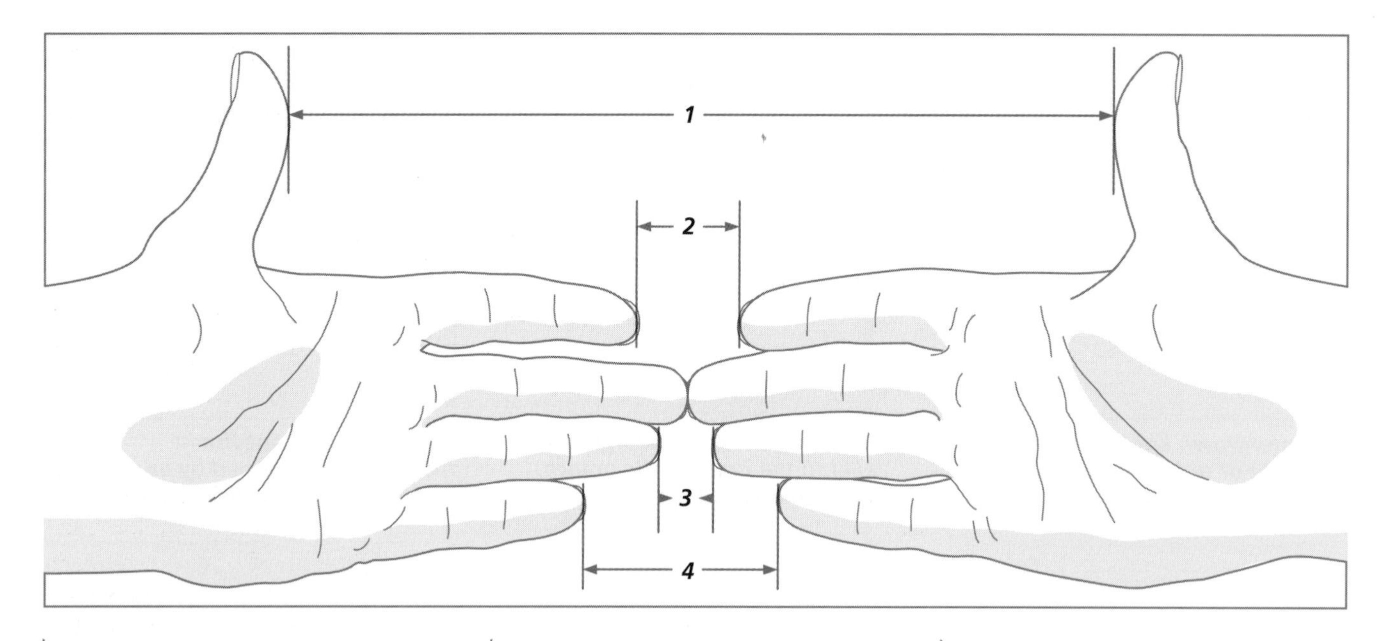

▲ **ESTIMATING, 1.** ***Shown here are four basic references: With your middle fingers touching and thumbs outstretched, take the measurements for your hands at 1, 2, 3 and 4.***

▼ **ESTIMATING, 2.** ***Three other references can be obtained easily by simply butting your little finger against an edge and taking the measurements at 5, 6 and 7.***

▼ **ESTIMATING, 3.** ***Form one hand into the shape of a gun, using the forefinger as the barrel. Fold your middle finger at the third knuckle and measure at 8.***

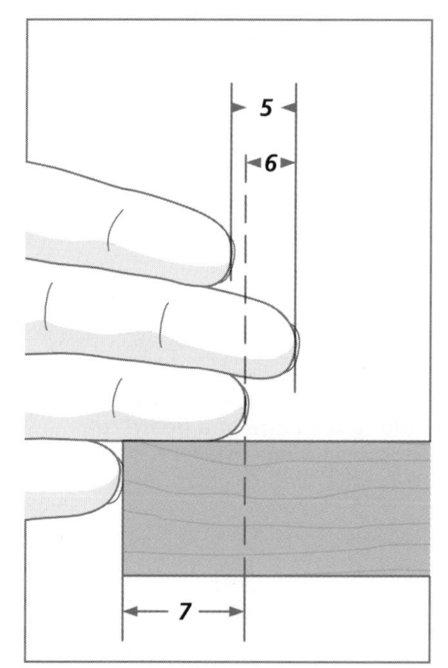

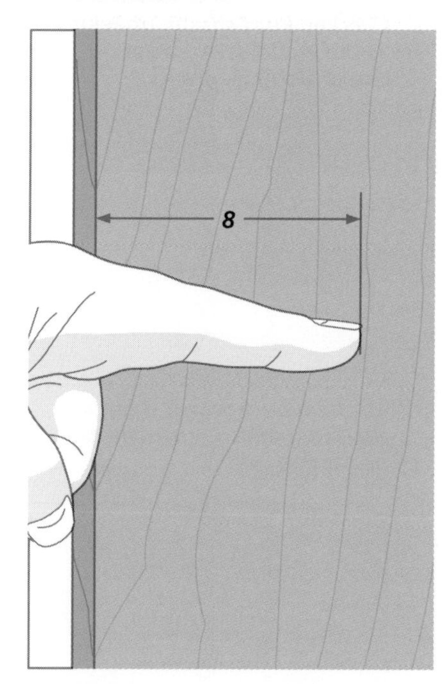

YOU'RE THE RULER

What do you do when you need a quick measurement, but don't have a ruler handy? What if close is good enough, but the consequences of eyeball measurement are not appealing? Here's a solution: calculate some of the handiest measurements around—those of your own body.

Start with your hands. Place them on a ruler with your palms up, thumbs stretched and middle fingers touching. Note the dimensions between all opposing fingertips. By memorizing these, you can quickly hold your hands up to a number of different things and have a good idea of their sizes.

Now, use the tip of your little finger as a stop against the end of a board and record the measurements from the tip of each other finger to the board edge. This works equally as well if you place your hand flat. Simply catch the nail of your little finger below the edge of what you're measuring. And using your middle finger at the third and second knuckle as a stop, you have two quick reference points with your outstretched forefinger.

Of course, dimensions on "biophysical rulers" vary depending on the individual. So, experiment—find those most valuable to you. With practice, you can be accurate within 1/16 in.

And you don't have to be measuring anything to use these techniques. They also work well as guides for repeating a measurement. For example, if you

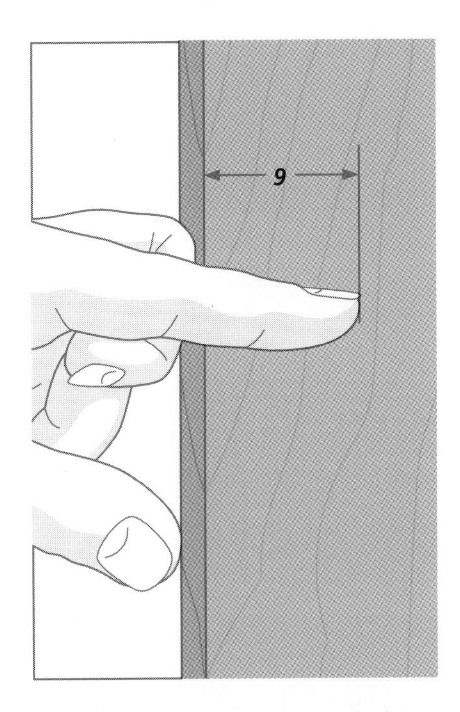

▲ **ESTIMATING, 4.** ***With your hand still formed into the shape of a gun, now fold your middle finger at the second knuckle and take the measurement at 9.***

are face-nailing something where the holes will be filled but the putty will show, space the nails evenly using your fingers as gauges.

Your palm provides valuable small measurements, such as those obtained from the creases between finger joints. Larger measurements are available, too. The length of your outstretched arm from armpit or tip of your nose to middle fingertip is useful, as is the distance between your middle fingertips when both arms are outstretched.

Get other horizontal measurements by holding one or both elbows out to the side with your hands on your waist. When both elbows are spread, you can approximate the width of such things as doorways and save the headache of trying to move something big through too small an opening.

For vertical measurements, try the distance between the floor and the tip of your nose—and remember to make an adjustment when you change shoes. The same principle applies to working with the distance between the floor and your belt buckle or chin.

Even diameters can be judged with your personal ruler. A difference in tubing sizes is known by which knuckle the tubing jams on when slid over a finger. Large outside diameters can be found by the combination of thumb and finger that most nearly encircle them. For larger diameters, both hands together give you a ballpark figure.

Your hands also give close approximations of common angles. Make a triangle with your thumbs and forefingers, then fold your middle fingers as stops against an edge. The line intersecting the tips of your forefingers and second knuckles of your middle fingers is at a 90° angle to the edge. The angle between the edge and each forefinger is 60°.

Of course, some of these measurements and angles might turn out to be things that you'd never use. But unlike your tape measure and protractor, they will always be with you.

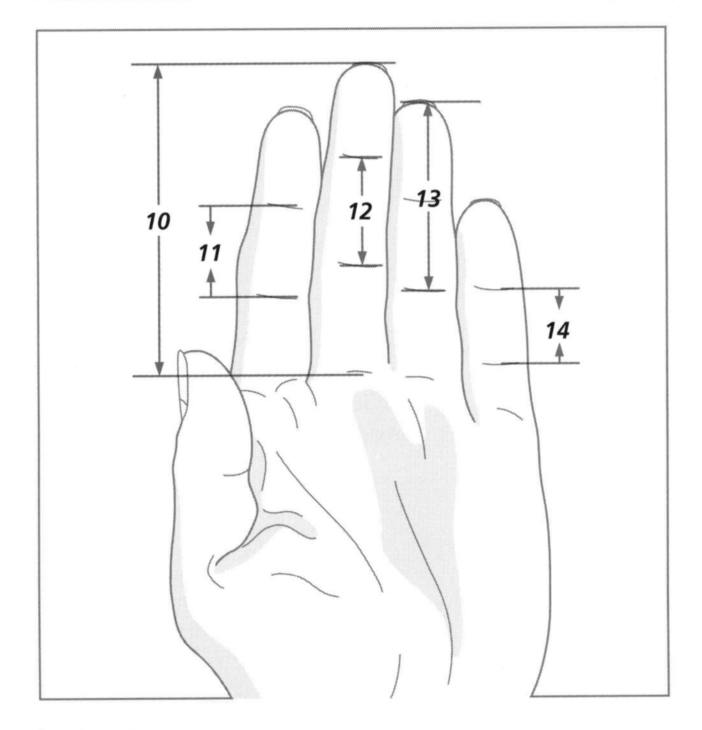

▲ **ESTIMATING, 5.** ***You've got at least five dimensions available by simply placing your hand down flat with the palm facing up. Measure at 10, 11, 12, 13 and 14.***

▲ **ESTIMATING, 6.** ***By placing your fingers together as shown here, you have a protractor reference with quick estimates for 60° angles and perpendicular lines.***

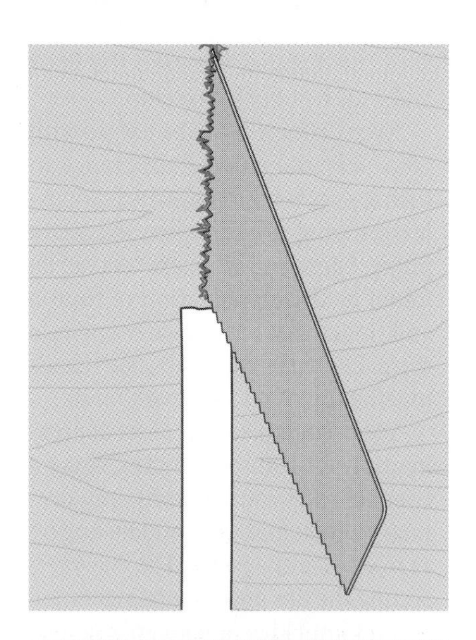

◀ **SPLINTER-FREE CUTTING, 1.** ***A backup board that's clamped tightly to the bottom of the work provides the best results. When this setup isn't possible, use masking tape.***

▶ **SPLINTER-FREE CUTTING, 2.** ***Masking tape pressed securely against the backside of the cut produces less splintering, as revealed when the tape is pulled off.***

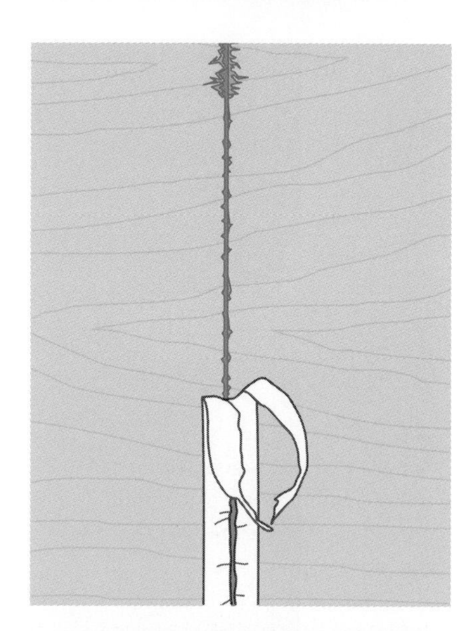

▼ **SPLINTER-FREE CUTTING, 3.** ***To prevent the splintering and tearing of crossgrain when cutting dadoes, first score along the outside edges using a utility knife.***

SPLINTERED CUTS

When sawing plywood, how can you avoid splintering the underside?

Using a backup board is best, but it must be clamped tightly. When clamps aren't available, apply masking tape along the back of the line of cut.

MISCUT MORTISE

You mistakenly chisel the mortise for a hinge in the wrong place.

Measure correctly and cut the mortise, then position the hinge. Cut a wood patch—known as a Dutchman—to fill the excess, then secure it with a

▼ **CORRECTING MISCUT MORTISES, 1.** ***Start by marking the correct measurement for the hinge. Then, score carefully along the marked lines.***

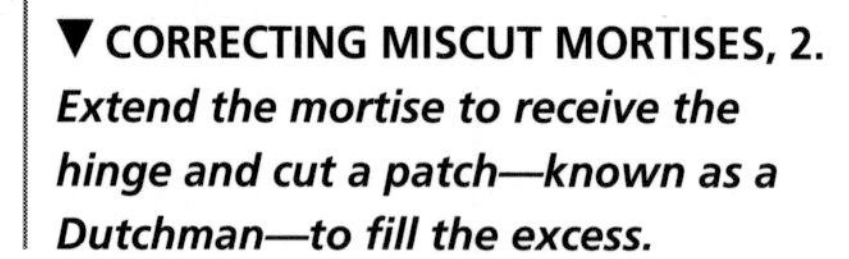

▼ **CORRECTING MISCUT MORTISES, 2.** ***Extend the mortise to receive the hinge and cut a patch—known as a Dutchman—to fill the excess.***

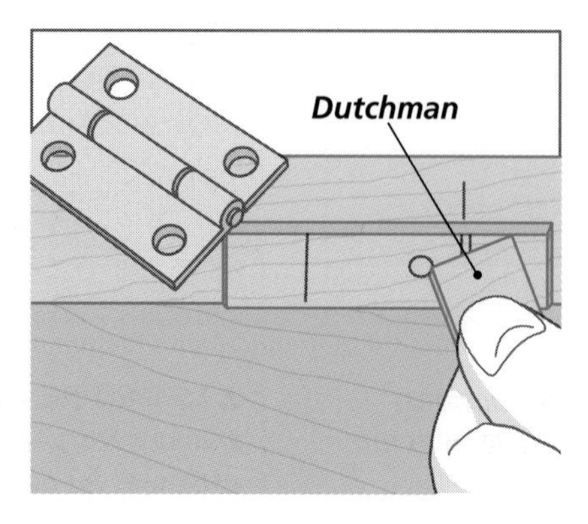

▼ **CORRECTING MISCUT MORTISES, 3.** ***Check the Dutchman for proper fit, then secure it with glue and brads before installing the hinge.***

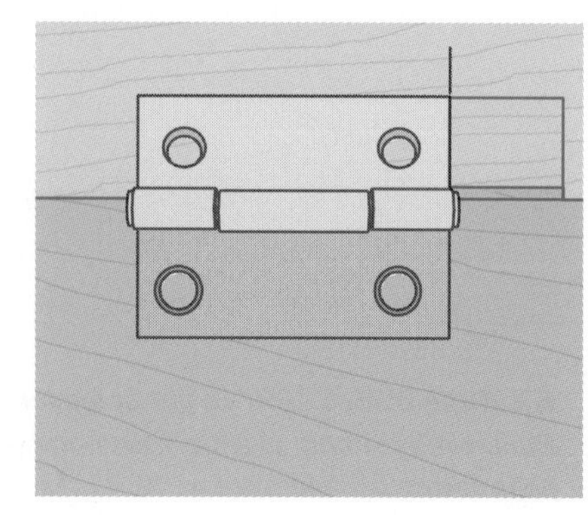

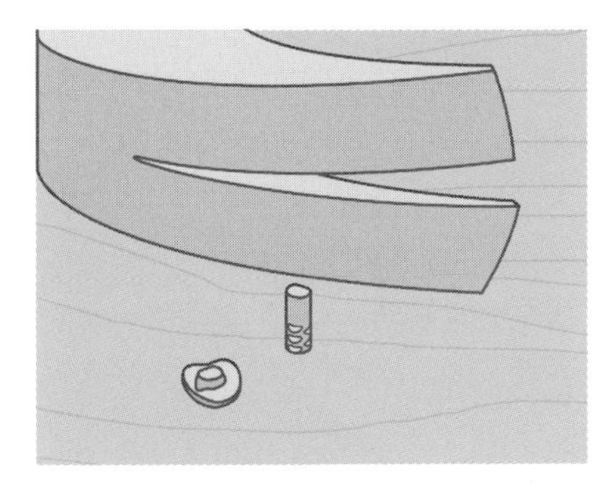

▲ LOST NAILHEAD, 1. ***Here's a problem that virtually everyone encounters sooner or later: a nailhead breaks off or becomes mangled as the nail is pulled out.***

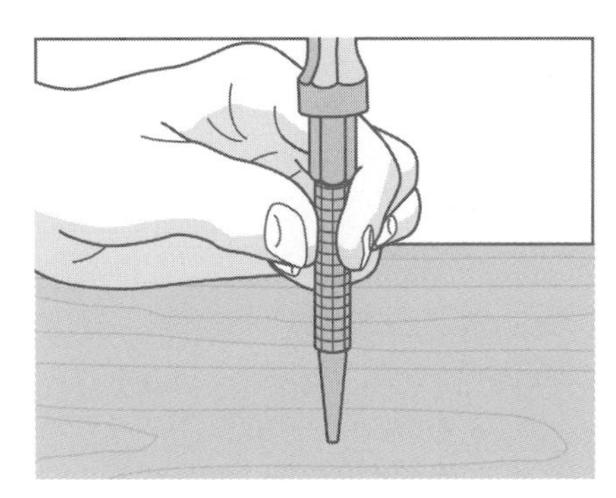

▲ LOST NAILHEAD, 2. ***One solution is simply to straighten the protruding shank of the nail and then drive it well below the surface using a nailset and a hammer.***

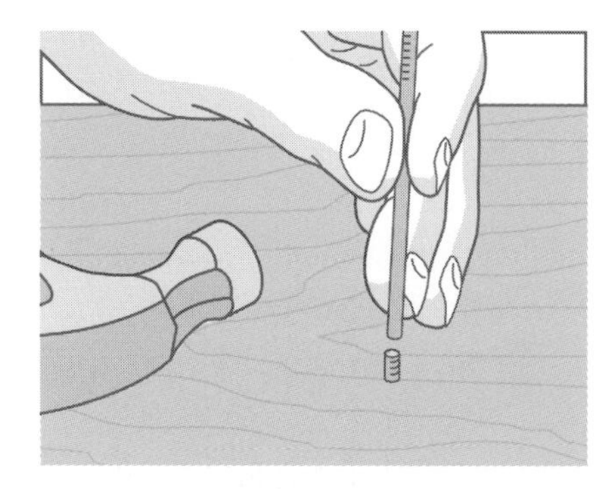

▲ LOST NAILHEAD, 3. ***If the nail must be removed, cut or file off the tip of a nail that's the same size and use it to drive the embedded nail right through to the other side.***

▼ REPAIRING SPLIT ENDS, 1. ***If the end of a board splits as you drive a nail, leave the nail as a wedge to hold the split open.***

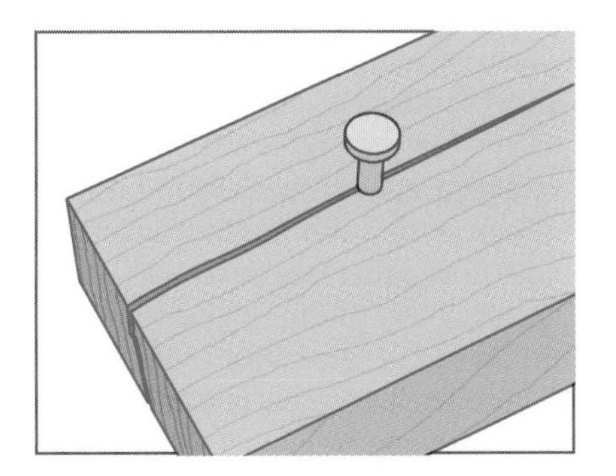

little glue and brads set below the surface; bore lead holes for the brads in hardwood. After the glue dries, fill the joints and nail holes, then sand the surface smooth.

LOST NAILHEAD

A nailhead breaks off or becomes mangled as you pull it out.

There are several solutions. Set the shank below the surface with a nailset and fill the hole, or drive it through the other side using the filed tip of a nail the same diameter. When the nail shank juts above the surface, use locking pliers to grip and rock it—like the action of a hammer's claws—until you can pull it free. A specialty tool called a nail outener works the same way.

END SPLITS

As you drive in a nail, the end of the board splits.

Force a thin line of glue into the crack, then remove the nail. When the glue sets, bore a hole slightly smaller than the nail shank and renail. Predrill holes for all fastening near edges.

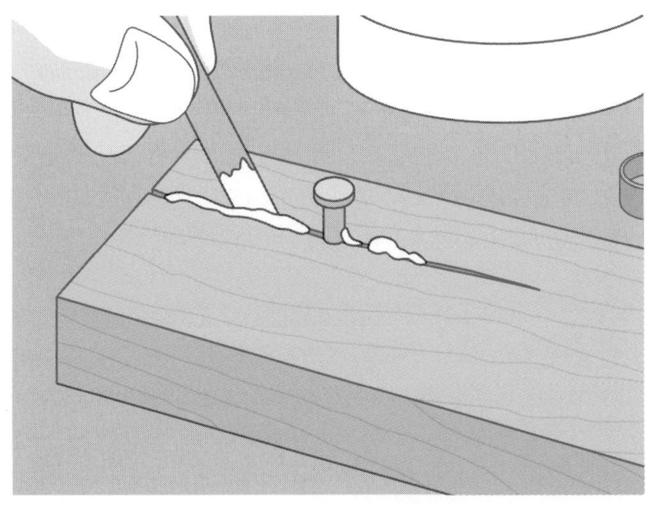

▲ REPAIRING SPLIT ENDS, 2. ***Apply glue to the surfaces along the split and work it into the opening with a thin strip of metal.***

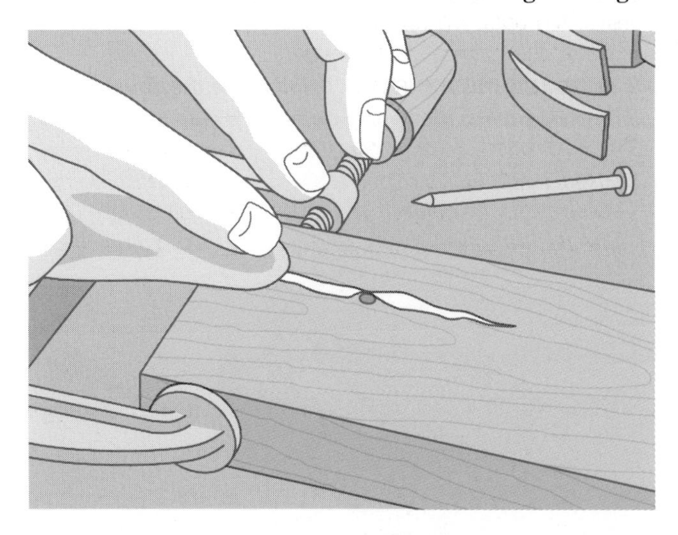

▲ REPAIRING SPLIT ENDS, 3. ***Extract the nail and clamp the end, then wipe off excess glue. After the glue dries, bore a pilot hole for the nail.***

▲ **BLIND-NAILING JOINERY, 1.** ***First, make sure that the two pieces form a tight-fitting joint. Plane and sand surfaces as necessary.***

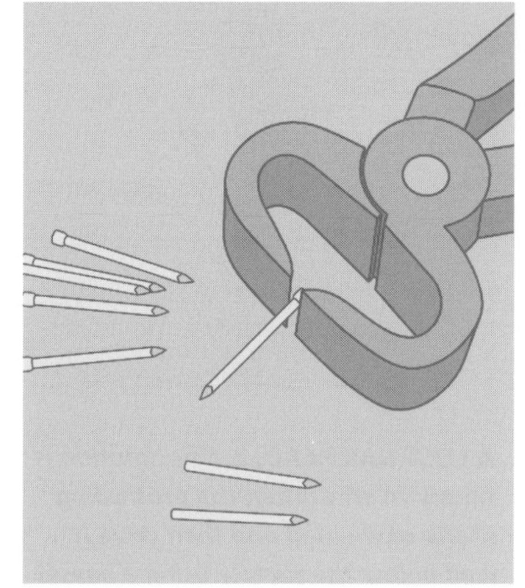

▲ **BLIND-NAILING JOINERY, 2.** ***Snip the heads off the nails before you begin hammering the nails into the edges of the pieces.***

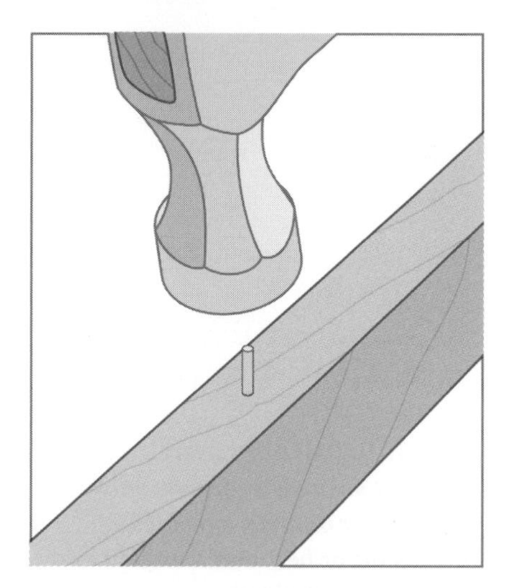

▲ **BLIND-NAILING JOINERY, 3.** ***Drive the nails partially into one piece, using the mating piece to check how high they protrude.***

BLIND NAILING

How do you join two lengths of wood without having the nailheads show?

Try a technique called blind nailing—when combined with glue, a fast, easy way of making remarkably strong wood joints. The technique is handy for a number of jobs: making finished, L-shaped edge trim, producing a wide variety of moldings and edge-joining boards to create wide panels.

First, make sure that the two pieces form a tight-fitting joint, planing or sanding edges where necessary. Next, mark nail positions on the larger piece, then cut the heads off nails with end-cut nippers or cutting pliers and drive the nails in part way—enough that they won't protrude through the second piece. Grind sharp points onto the end of the nails with a stone grinding wheel that's mounted in an electric drill or a drill press.

Apply glue to the pieces along the joint, then clamp the larger piece to your workbench with the nails facing away from the edge. Position the second piece against the nails and gradually press the pieces together uniformly with C-clamps. Place newspaper under the assembly to absorb glue squeezed out. When the glue dries, the assembly is ready to be sanded, planed or routed—without there being a risk of hitting nailheads.

▼ **BLIND-NAILING JOINERY, 4.** ***Grind or file the driven nails into sharp points, then apply carpenter's glue to the pieces.***

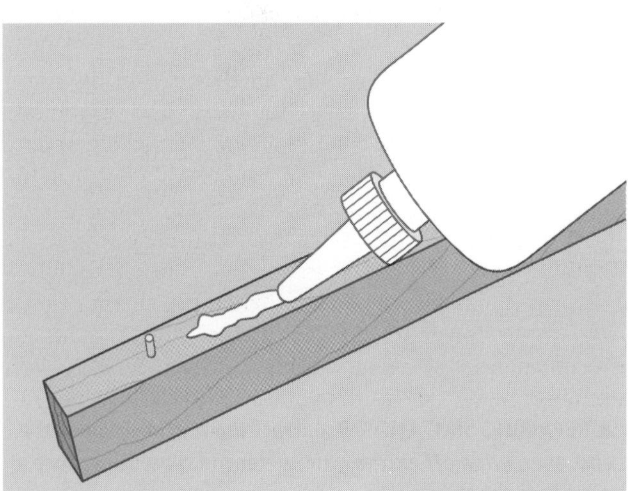

▼ **BLIND-NAILING JOINERY, 5.** ***Tighten C-clamps gradually to draw the pieces together and wipe off excess glue.***

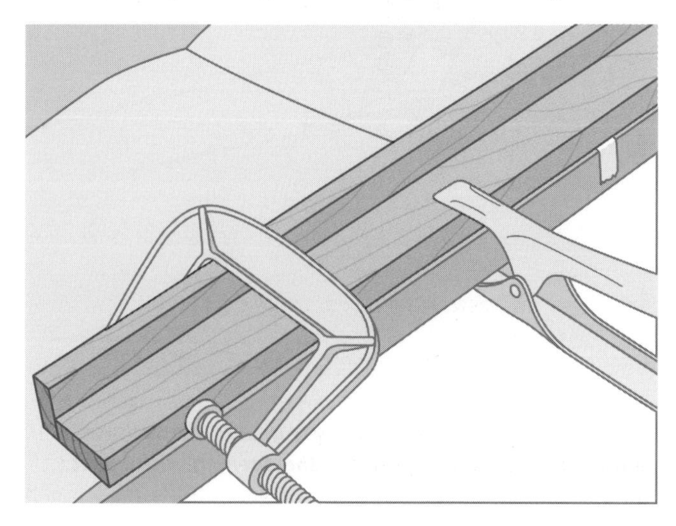

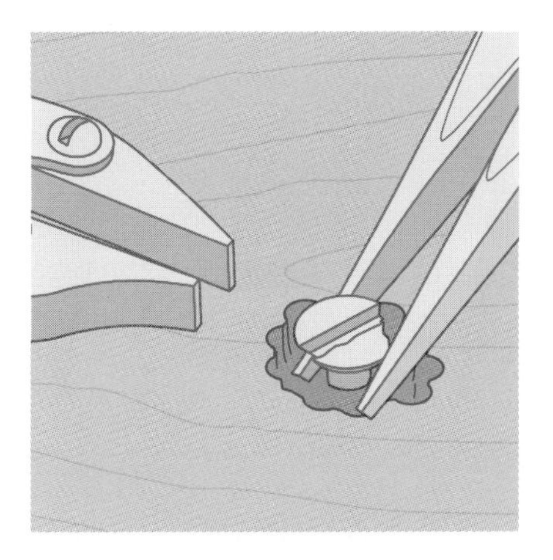

▲ **REMOVING EMBEDDED SCREWS, 1.** ***When damage to the surface isn't a problem, bore holes around the screw and use pliers to twist it out.***

▲ **REMOVING EMBEDDED SCREWS, 2.** ***To avoid damaging the surface, drill a hole into the screw. Start drilling at an angle if the surface is uneven.***

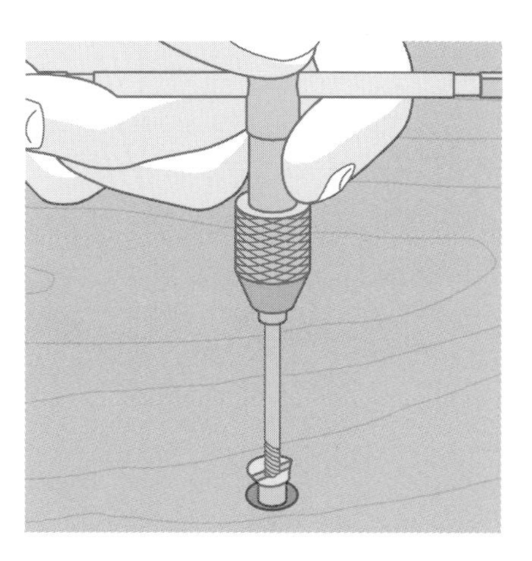

▲ **REMOVING EMBEDDED SCREWS, 3.** ***Next, insert a screw-extractor that's set in a tap wrench into the hole in the screw and twist it out.***

▼ **RESTORING BOLT THREADS, 1.** ***Here's a very frustrating problem that's all too common: a bolt with crushed threads, preventing a nut from being threaded or backed off it.***

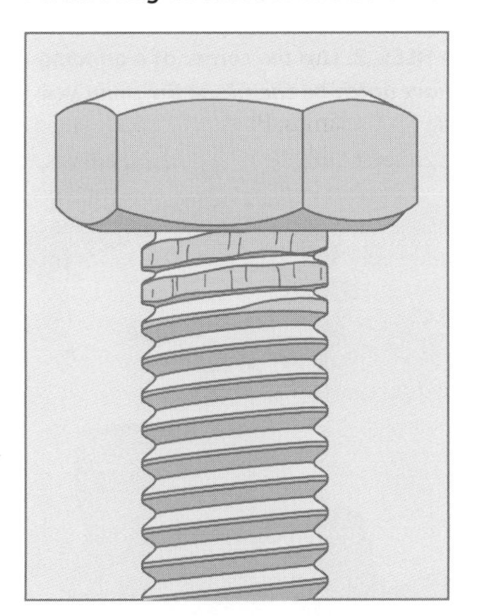

▼ **RESTORING BOLT THREADS, 2.** ***The solution is a thread restorer. Slip the tool onto the bolt at good threads and tighten the claws, then rotate the tool to recut the damaged threads.***

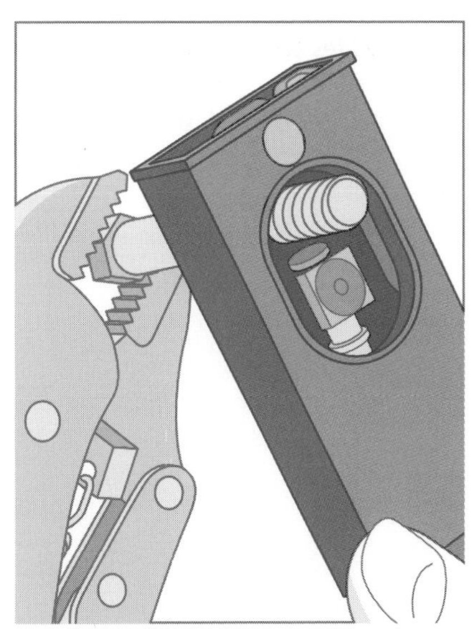

EMBEDDED SCREW

When you back out a screw, its head breaks off.

When damage to the surface isn't a problem, use a ⅛-in. bit to bore holes all the way around the screw shank; softwood can simply be punctured with a finishing nail. A little digging may be needed to get needle-nose or locking pliers around the shank. Gripping the shank with the pliers, twist and pull. If the surface can't be marred, drill a hole in the shank center about ⅓ its diameter, then carefully work the shank out using a screw extractor of a suitable size that's fitted into a socket or tap wrench.

CRUSHED THREADS

A nut won't thread or back off because the bolt's threads are crushed.

A hand-operated thread restorer is the easy solution to this problem. The tool slips over the bolt at a point where good threads remain, then its claws are tightened until its cutter is in a groove. As the tool is rotated over the damaged threads, the cutter restores them to let the nut pass.

LIMITED SPACE

How can you tighten a nut when even a right-angle wrench won't fit into the space available?

This can be a tough one. If the job doesn't require the nut to be tightened to the maximum, chances are you can reach it by hand to finger-tighten it. If the nut must be secure, you can try holding it with an adjustable grip or needle-nose pliers while you turn the bolt or machine screw with the appropriate tool. When this doesn't work, use a specialty tool called a starwheel ratchet drive. Only 9⁄16 in. high, the tool allows you to tighten the nut while keeping your hand on the wheel at all times, the ratchet eliminating the need to remove and reposition it.

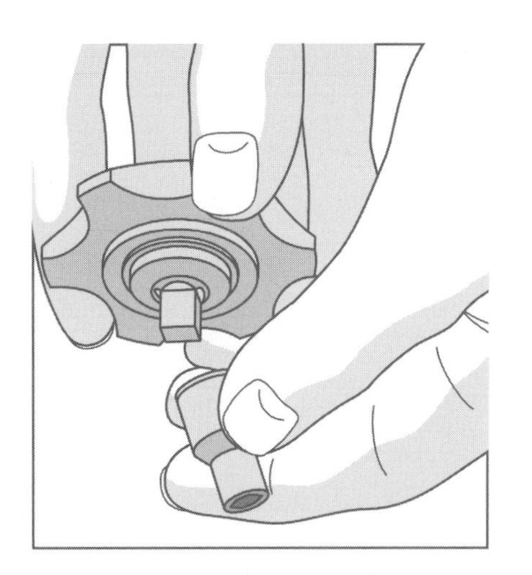

◀ **TIGHTENING TOUGH SPOTS, 1.** ***When you can't reach a nut with even a right-angle wrench and finger-tightening won't do, use a star-wheel ratchet drive.***

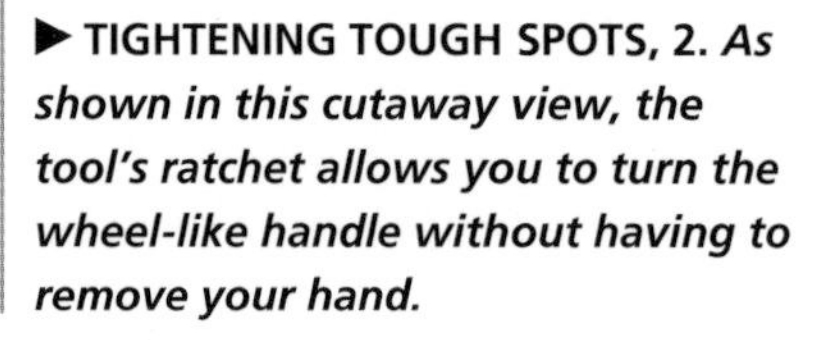

▶ **TIGHTENING TOUGH SPOTS, 2.** ***As shown in this cutaway view, the tool's ratchet allows you to turn the wheel-like handle without having to remove your hand.***

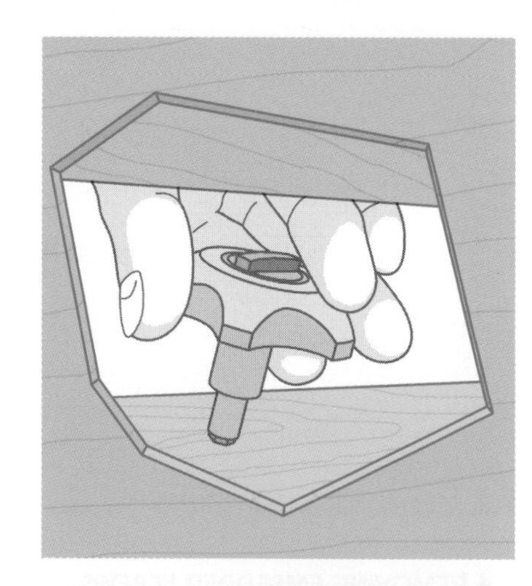

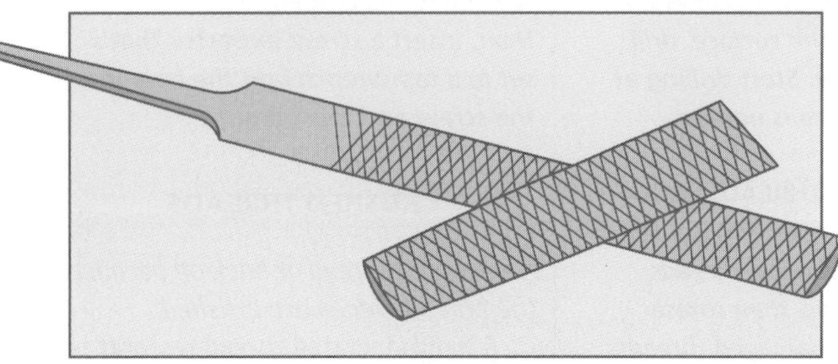

▲ **SALVAGING HAND FILES, 1.** ***Small sections of old files are handy for special applications such as power filing on a sabre saw or cutting heavy metal.***

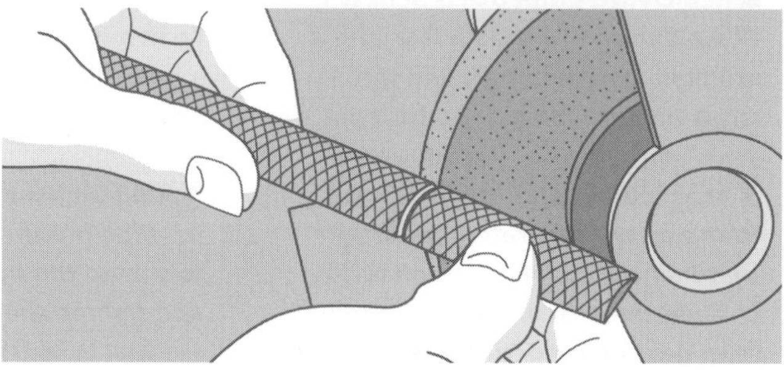

▲ **SALVAGING HAND FILES, 2.** ***Use the corner of a grinding wheel to form a shallow notch on the file at the point you want it to be severed.***

BREAKING FILES SAFELY

A section of an old file would be useful to mount in a scroll saw for power filing or heavy metal cutting.

Simply striking a file sharply with a hammer may cause the file to break erratically. And because files are brittle, there is always the danger that bits of shattered metal could fly about and cause injury. Therefore, first form a shallow notch at the point you want the file to sever using the corner of a grinding wheel. This creates a line of weakness in the metal, facilitating a clean break. Next, grip the file securely in a vise, ensuring that the notch is aligned with the top of the jaws. Wrap and tape a piece of cloth around the exposed section of the file to catch particles. Finally, wear safety goggles to strike the wrapped section of the file sharply with a ball-peen hammer.

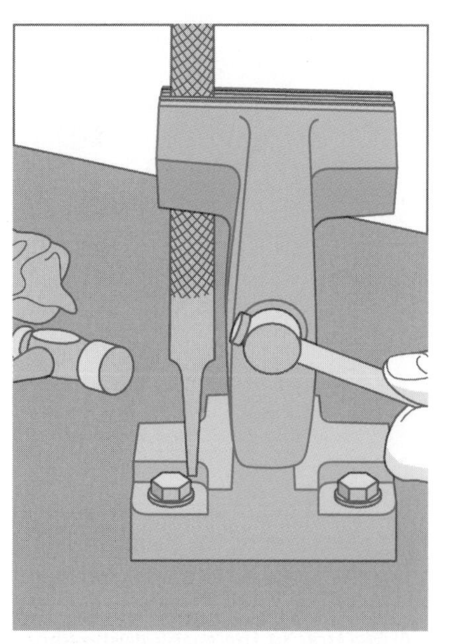

▲ **SALVAGING HAND FILES, 3.** ***Then, grip the file firmly in a vise with the notch aligned along the top surface of the jaws.***

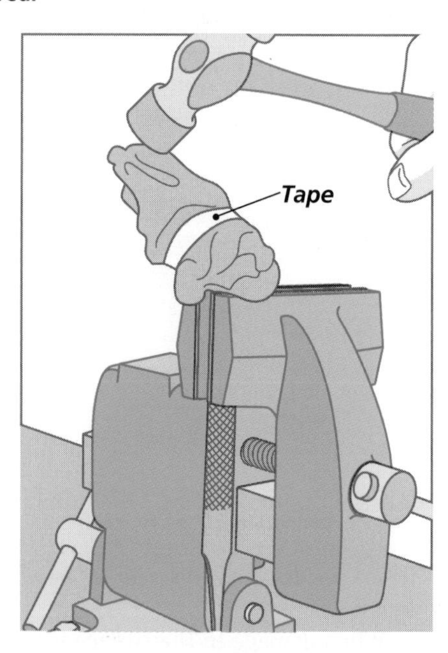

▲ **SALVAGING HAND FILES, 4.** ***Wrap cloth around the file to catch fragments, then strike it sharply with a ball-peen hammer.***

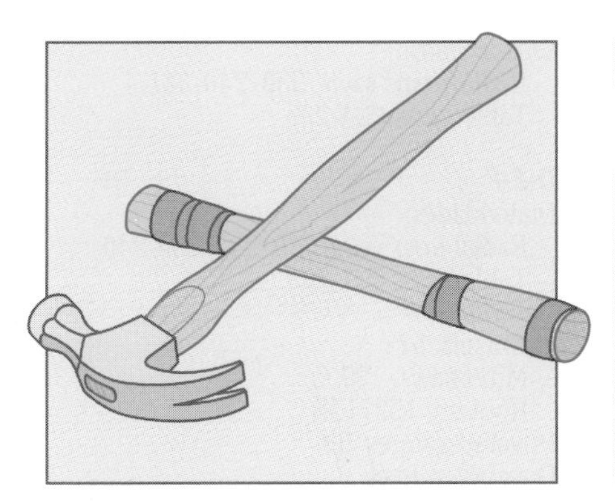

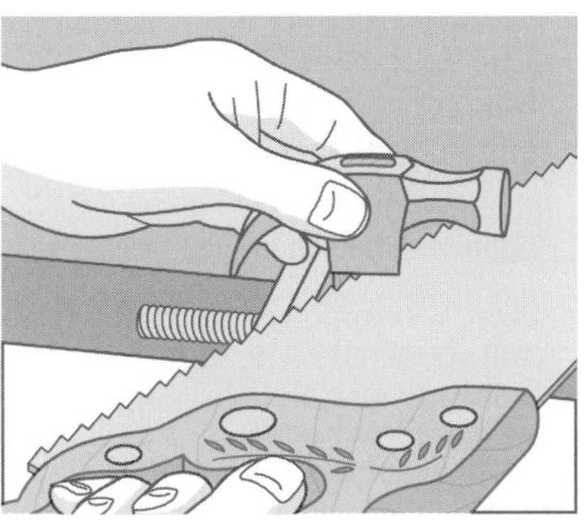

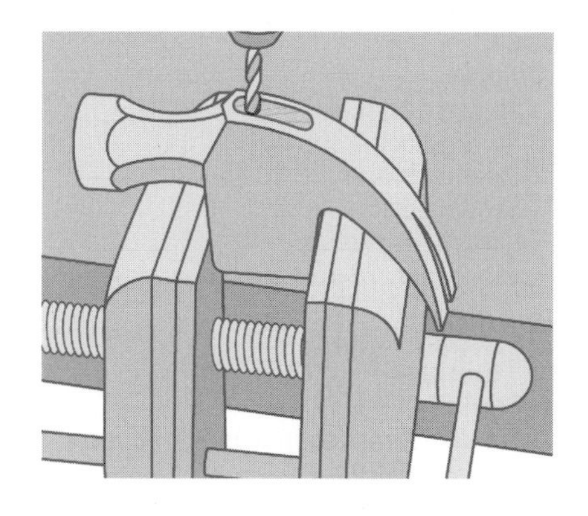

▲ **REPLACING HAMMER HANDLES, 1.** ***A damaged hammer can be salvaged if the head is still in good condition. Replacement handles are typically available at hardware stores.***

▲ **REPLACING HAMMER HANDLES, 2.** ***Clamp the hammer in a vise and cut off the old handle as close as possible to the bottom of the head using a crosscut or dovetail saw.***

▲ **REPLACING HAMMER HANDLES, 3.** ***Bore holes into the piece of handle that is left in the head's eye, then punch it out with a sharp, narrow chisel and a hammer.***

SALVAGING HAMMERS

While working with your hammer, the handle breaks.

If the head of the hammer remains perfectly usable, you may temporarily wrap the damaged part of the handle securely with electrical tape. As soon as possible, though, replace the handle following the procedure shown here. Don't bother to replace the handle if the striking face of the head is nicked, worn or otherwise damaged.

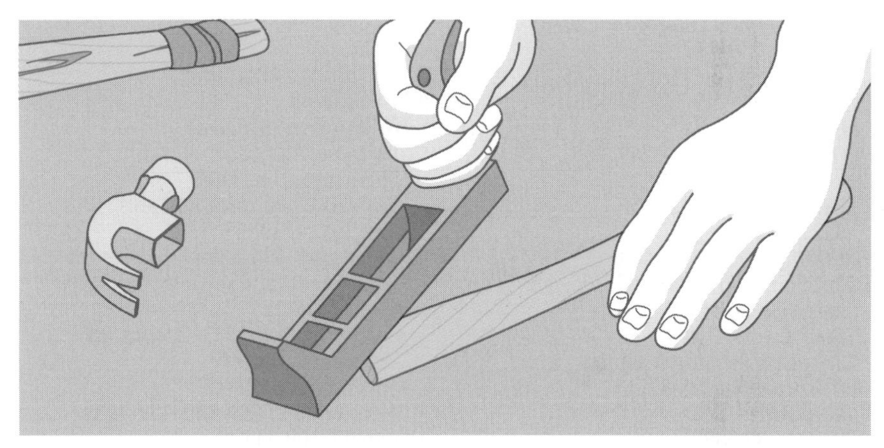

▲ **REPLACING HAMMER HANDLES, 4.** ***Customize the replacement handle to fit the head. Here, a Surform rasp is being used to plane both sides of the handle's neck.***

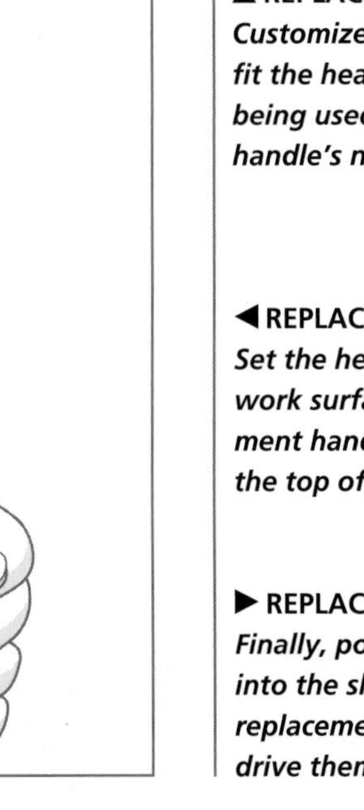

◀ **REPLACING HAMMER HANDLES, 5.** ***Set the head upside down on a solid work surface and tap the replacement handle into place, flush with the top of the head.***

▶ **REPLACING HAMMER HANDLES, 6.** ***Finally, position wedges properly into the slit at the neck of the replacement handle and be sure to drive them home completely.***

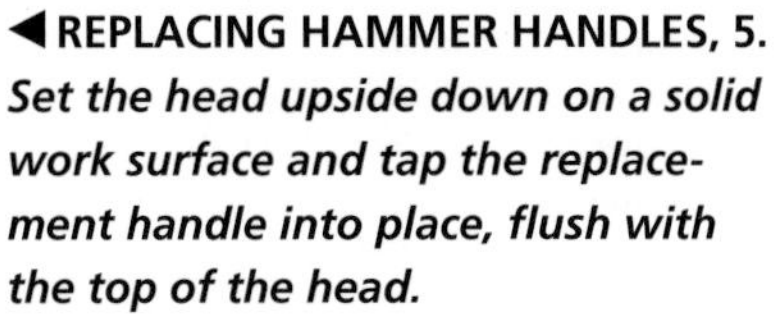

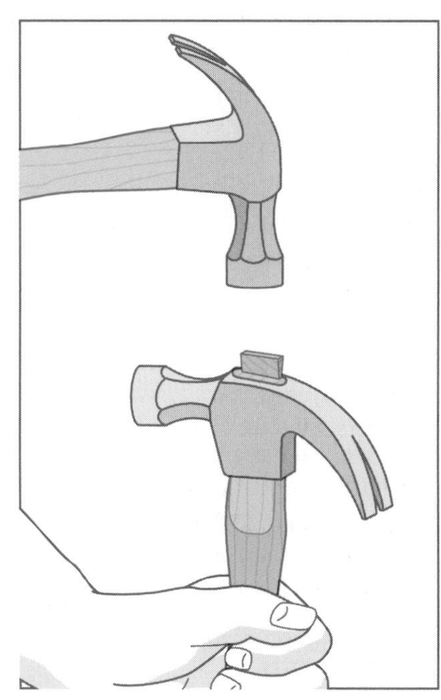

INDEX

ACKNOWLEDGMENTS

The staff of *Popular Mechanics* Encyclopedia of Tools & Techniques thanks:

Jean-Pierre Bourgeois, Neil David (Cabot Safety Corp., Southbridge, Mass.), Sara Grynspan, Tim Hazen, Garet Markvoort, Michael Mouland, The National Hardwood Lumber Association, Tout Degau, Tamiko Watanabe.